The New York Times
Twentieth Century in Review

POLITICAL CENSORSHIP

Other Titles in
The New York Times 20th Century in Review

The Balkans
The Cold War
The Gay Rights Movement

Forthcoming

The Rise of the Global Economy
The Vietnam War

The New York Times
Twentieth Century in Review

POLITICAL CENSORSHIP

Editor
Robert Justin Goldstein

Introduction by Floyd Abrams

Series Editor
David Morrow

FD

FITZROY DEARBORN PUBLISHERS
CHICAGO ◆ LONDON

For information write to:

FITZROY DEARBORN PUBLISHERS
919 North Michigan Avenue, Suite 760
Chicago IL 60611
USA

or

FITZROY DEARBORN PUBLISHERS
310 Regent Street
London W1B 3AX
England

British Library and Library of Congress Cataloging in Publication Data are available.

ISBN 1-57958-320-2

First published in the USA and UK 2001

Typeset by Print Means Inc., New York, New York

Printed by Edwards Brothers, Ann Arbor, Michigan

Cover Design by Peter Aristedes, Chicago Advertising and Design, Chicago, Illinois

CONTENTS

Preface by Robert Justin Goldstein vii
Introduction by Floyd Abrams xiii

Part I Pre-World War I, 1900–1913 1
- Press Controversies 1
- Controversies over Stage and Screen 9

Part II The Great War, 1914–1918 29
- The Allied Nations 29
- The Central Powers 63

Part III Between the Wars, 1919–1938 71
- The United States and the Americas 71
- The Rise of European Fascist States 94
- Other Countries 133

Part IV World War II, 1939–1945 147
- The Allied Nations 147
- The Axis Powers, Its Sympathizers, and Its Conquered Countries 170

Part V The Coming of the Cold War, 1945–1964 187
- Western Nations and Allies 187
- Communist Countries 200
- Latin America 234
- Africa and Asia 246

Part VI The Vietnam War Era, 1965–1974 263
- Developments in the United States and Vietnam 263
- American Allies 276
- Communist Countries 292
- Latin America 296
- Africa and Asia 304

Part VII The Decline and Fall of Communist Regimes, 1975–1999 317
- The United States and Western Europe 317
- The Soviet Union and Eastern Europe 384
- Latin America 424
- The Middle East 445
- Africa 478
- Asia and Australia 502

Subject Index 551
Byline Index 563

PREFACE

This volume attempts to present a representative collection of New York Times articles published between 1900 and 1999 relevant to what will be defined below as "political censorship." Censorship, without the "political" and defined in its broadest sense simply as the deliberate withholding of information, is undoubtedly both as old and as universal as mankind. Every father and mother talking to a child, every wife and husband relating to each other, every friend conversing with another friend and every government interacting with its population at one time or another decides not to pass on information known or opinions held—often on a routine basis. Such withholding may be intentional or unconscious, and it may occur for the widest variety of reasons, ranging, for example, from a genuine desire to spare the recipient needless emotional pain to a calculated design to manipulate feelings and/or power.

Needless to say, no newspaper, even one which, like The New York Times, seeks to be a reasonably comprehensive "newspaper of record," even attempts to cover all censorship included in such a wide-ranging definition, nor could it succeed if it tried, since, blessedly, we have not yet achieved the state foreseen in George Orwell's *1984*, in which all conversations and activities, even those conducted in private dwellings, can be monitored. Nonetheless, the scope of what The Times has covered during the twentieth century that might be broadly construed as censorship is still so vast that it could be the subject of many books. This volume makes no attempt to reproduce even a representative sampling of everything relevant to censorship published by The Times during that 100-year period, but instead focuses on what is herein termed "political censorship."

The use of the modifying term "political" is meant to imply at least three limitations on the general term "censorship." First, to be considered for inclusion in this collection, an article must concern censorship imposed directly by government authorities or, in a few cases, concern "pre-emptive" censorship by private individuals to ward off a clearly perceived threat of government intervention (for example, articles about United States movie censorship reprinted here include those from December 28, 1919, and April 12, 1921, on attempts by state legislatures to impose movie censorship, while an article from April 6, 1921, reports on movie officials promising to produce a "clean sweep" of "salacious" materials in films if government authorities would abandon their own attempts to censor the cinema.) No attempt is made herein to cover censorship in the clearly private sphere, such as attempts by private businesses to eliminate union literature from their workplace or the withholding of information about sex from children by parents.

Secondly, the overwhelming focus of this collection of articles is on attempts by governments to censor materials that are themselves focused on what would normally be termed the "political," that is on discussions of the nature of governmental policies and personnel. As suggested by the examples given above, this principle has been breached occasionally by the inclusion of articles dealing with moral censorship, especially for the pre-1930 period, to give readers a small glimpse of this subject. This focus on political material has been imposed because the scope of this collection needed to be kept within reasonable limits; because this book seeks to encompass the entire world, and generally The Times has covered political censorship on a world-wide basis but moral censorship primarily with regard to the United States; and because threats to the political as opposed to the moral order have generally been viewed as far more threatening by twentieth-century governments and have generally provoked a far greater and consistent response, reflecting the fact that the two types of censorship can be substantially differentiated.

Thirdly, the "political" modification of "censorship" is intended to focus the selection of articles on issues involving various forms of mass media, including newspapers, films, theater, television and the visual arts, which can at least theoretically be consumed by a very large public and therefore are especially likely to have potential political significance and arouse official concern. Put in the negative, no attempt has been made to include articles on subjects such as attempts by government to prevent people from speaking at meetings, teachers from teaching specific material to their classes or parents from criticizing the government to their children. This is simply an attempt to place some reasonable boundaries on what this book seeks to accomplish. Without such limits, this book would have to be retitled to indicate its concern was freedom of speech rather than political censorship.

While the three limitations listed above considerably reduced the potential universe of Times articles to be selected for this volume, the problem of finding and then selecting among the still very large remaining universe of articles remained. Theoretically, the best way of doing this would be to thoroughly read every issue of The Times published during the twentieth century, but absent that sound but not very practical approach, the task was accomplished with the use of the three indexing sources: 1) the well-known printed index of The New York Times, which covers the entire period, although, especially for censorship, in a rather unsatisfactory manner; 2) the less well known Lexis-Nexis electronic database, which is available only by subscription (usually through libraries or educational institutions) and covers only the post-1969 period, but which can be searched using keywords (citations only are available for 1969–1980; thereafter full text is available); and 3) the new and almost completely unknown Chadwyck-Healey electronic database, "Historical Index to the New York Times," available only by subscription or purchase and, as of early 2001, covering only 1863–1922 (minus 1906–1912), which allows for keyword searching but returns only citations; this database is expected to cover the entire run of The New York Times in the near future. The Lexis-Nexis and Chadwyck-Healey indexes are far easier to use and, through keyword searching, allow far more comprehensive access to articles than does the printed *New York Times Index,* but at the time of the compilation of this book they did not cover 1906–1912 or 1923–1969 and therefore only the *Index* was available for those years.

Very, very few other newspapers are indexed at all for the pre-1970 period, so the *Index* has been a great gift down the years to academic and other researchers, but using it is rife with difficulties. In the case of censorship, the problem is at its most basic: for virtually all of the twentieth century, the *Index* did not include a separate censorship entry, but only a cross-reference to other general entries, usually without even specific dates or articles (i.e. the *Index* typically says "see Books, Cinema, Magazines, Newspapers, Theater" and so forth; for the period of the two world wars, users were also referred to "War News."). Because these referenced general entries are often vast and typically include relatively few articles relevant to censorship, it was often impossible to check them in a more than cursory manner, especially since for most of the century the specific article entries listed within them usually did not give much of a hint as to whether the articles were brief accounts or in-depth reports. The only cross-referenced categories with high concentrations of articles specifically relevant to censorship—and therefore the only categories that it was possible to systematically check—were "War News" and "Newspapers" (or sometimes "News and Newspapers," another frustration in using the *Index* being that the names of categories frequently changed from year to year). Moreover, although within the newspapers category the concentration of censorship-related articles in subheadings for other countries was reasonably high, the subheading for the United States included vast numbers of non-related articles, which usually precluded a systematic scouring. Consequently, for the 1906–1912 and 1923–1969 periods when the *Index* was the only source available, articles on the United States and on mass media other than newspapers are probably underrepresented—although not absent—for purely practical reasons.

Within the definitional and practical-logistical boundaries spelled out above, the criteria used to select articles for this collection were primarily: 1) to select articles that focused on political censorship and were representative of all articles relevant to that subject published in The Times; 2) to select articles that provided substantial depth and context for their specific discussions of censorship; 3) to provide insofar as possible coverage of the entire world, thus neither focusing on nor neglecting the United States; and 4) to include a healthy selection of articles dealing with a wide variety of mass media—not only the printed press but also movies, plays, caricatures and the visual arts, which, as will be pointed out below, have usually been of equal concern to censors as newspapers and books, although the latter have attracted the overwhelming bulk of scholarship on censorship.

Sometimes these four principles conflicted with each other. For example, few articles from the pre-1920 period provided much context for their information on censorship, yet excluding all such articles would not accurately represent how The Times covered censorship during that period. Before World War I, The Times's coverage of censorship—and especially foreign censorship—was often limited to short articles with very little context. During World War I, articles on the United States became considerably more detailed while foreign coverage remained very limited. Only after World War I did Times coverage of foreign censorship regularly include in-depth articles, and thereafter the articles steadily increased in both quality and quantity, especially during the last few decades of the century. This is reflected in a slowly increasing average number of articles per year reprinted herein; thus, almost 35 percent of the articles in the book are taken from the last 20 years (i.e., 20 percent) of the entire period.

Because only a chronological organization of the articles would easily allow readers to trace changes in The Times's treatment of censorship over time, the articles are organized into seven chronological divisions, with subdivisions within each of these periods based upon geopolitical subdivisions of the world (except for the pre-World War I section, where there were not enough articles to make such subdivisions very meaningful and which instead is divided into censorship of the printed press and censorship of film and stage). Readers who are primarily interested in particular countries or geographical regions will find the index to the book a helpful complement to the table of contents, as will those especially interested in the censorship of particular media.

Although the articles in this book will speak for themselves, readers may find it helpful to have highlighted a few major themes which are reflected and repeated in this collection, with a few articles cited as representing each of these themes. A first theme is simply that political censorship has been extremely widespread during the twentieth century and that many, many regimes have clearly devoted immense amounts of time and resources to implementing such censorship; in short, governments have been enormously concerned about what information people have and about what they think, and have regarded the public possession of "bad" information and thoughts as a real threat. Thus, an article from August 17, 1958, notes that the Russian office that censored all reports by foreign correspondents at that time appeared to operate in shifts on a 24-hour schedule and was staffed by censors literate in English, French, German and Italian; a report from Poland published on October 26, 1982, suggests that every potentially political sensitive film was discussed at length by officials up to the level of deputy ministers; and a September 6, 1987, report from the African state of Cameroon noted that before publication every proposed page of every newspaper was examined by four different levels of bureaucrats and that no page could be printed and distributed without the censors' stamp. Numerous articles from the cold war period make clear that many American allies in the so-called free world, including Taiwan, South Korea, South Vietnam, Indonesia, the Philippines and France, frequently resorted to political censorship, as did the United States on a few occasions, perhaps most notoriously in the Pentagon Papers case reported in the July 1, 1971, articles on the Supreme Court ruling striking down the government's attempted censorship.

Many of the articles, such as the report on film censorship in Poland, make clear that the authorities were just as, if not more, concerned about the impact of non-written materials, such as plays, films and cartoons, as with that of newspapers and books, apparently because they were perceived as having more impact than print and also because frequently the most feared elements of the population were the poor, who were often illiterate and thus immune to the written word but were still potentially subject to subversive influences from non-written forms of mass media. A July 29, 1991, article from China reported that the authorities there had even forbidden the manufacture and sale of spiritually "unhealthy" T-shirts, such as those bearing slogans like "I'm fed up! Leave me alone!" According to the article, within a month of the initiation of the crackdown, over 1,000 offensive shirts had been confiscated along with the printing equipment for 20 designs. The official *Beijing Daily* suggested that more appropriate T-shirt slogans would run along the lines of, "I must train myself for the construction of the motherland."

A second major theme that emerges is that most, if not all, censorship regulations were inherently vague, and, at least partly as a result, they often resulted in absurd and sometimes inconsistent decision-making. Since it is virtually impossible to spell out in detail all possible forms of expression and ideas that might offend or threaten the authorities, censorship laws and regulations that were published (often they were not) necessarily tended to be so vague as to be meaningless in any precise sense—thereby likely provoking uncertainty, fear and self-censorship in those who faced sanctions for violating such provisions. Such vagueness was pervasive in both moral and political censorship. Thus, one of the very earliest articles in this compilation, on theater censorship in Washington, D.C., published on July 7, 1901, reported that under a new regulation theaters were barred from presenting "anything whatsoever" that "in any manner is offensive to common decency," while one of the most recent selections, a report from Turkey published on July 19, 1999, notes that recent press prosecutions in that country have charged offenders with "publishing written propaganda aimed at undermining Turkish unity" and with "insulting state institutions."

Such vague regulations inevitably produced bizarre, absurd and contradictory results. Thus, an April 9, 1915, dispatch from London reports on the fining of a newspaper for publishing information that had been approved by the censors and published without hindrance in another newspaper; an October 19, 1930, article from Spain noted that an article that referred to the internationally renowned philosopher Miguel Unamuno as "illustrious" had that term deleted because the censor declared "he's not illustrious to me, and that is enough"; and authorities quoted in a May 20, 1984, article on a press crackdown in Pakistan justified their policy on the grounds that "there was excessive reporting likely to create political confusion." An October 2, 1954, report on censorship in Russia noted that the same story might be cleared by the censors one day and rejected the next; a May 5, 1985, dispatch from South Africa reported that newspaper editors there spent more time with their lawyers trying to understand the implications of more than 100 laws restricting the press than they did at home with their spouses; and an October 17, 1993, article from China notes that the authorities there banned and unbanned twice within a short period the widely acclaimed (at least outside China) film "Farewell My Concubine."

A third major theme is that although political censorship unquestionably has been at least temporarily effective in silencing many newspapers and other expressive forms and in jailing many journalists and creative artists, the targets of such censorship have often resisted and evaded the censors. Although the number and variety of techniques of resistance and evasion have been limitless, one favorite method, reported on in several articles, was the printing of blank spaces where the authorities censored materials. This technique perhaps reached its logical limit in Poland in 1924, where a February 10 article reported that a Cracow newspaper published a special supplement consisting of a sheet of blank paper to protest the censorship—and that the authorities promptly seized the blank sheets and the courts subsequently upheld the confiscation on the grounds that the material had held up public authorities to ridicule "without presenting definite facts." A number of articles from World War II, such as those of March 11, 1942, and January 2, 1944, report on the widespread phenomenon of illegal underground newspapers published by anti-Nazi groups in countries under German occupation, while several articles from the 1990s report on the common use of technically illegal satellite television dishes to receive foreign broadcasts in states practicing strict censorship of domestic television (i.e., articles from China published on September 11, 1994, and from Saudi Arabia on January 23, 1996).

A fourth major theme is that censorship policy, and especially censorship policy changes, often provide a barometer of broader trends toward more or less repression in various countries—evidence that studying censorship can be extremely revealing about more general aspects of the regimes involved. This theme is illustrated in a large percentage of the articles reprinted in this volume: to give only one, unusually clear example, Times correspondent Harrison Salisbury reported on October 2, 1954, after departing the Soviet Union, that "a progressive lightening of censorship has been observed since Stalin died" a year earlier, a trend that reflected a general lessening of repression in that country. That studying censorship policy can greatly illuminate the nature of governmental policies, including its fears and hopes in general, has, of course also been true long before the twentieth century. Thus, in 1874 a French caricature journal, writing about caricature censorship in that country, declared, "One could, one day, write an exact history of the liberty which we enjoy during this era by writing a history of our caricatures." Similarly, a French legislator commented in 1880 on the French caricature censorship with the following words, which clearly apply to the deeper significance of censorship in general:

> Drawings which displease the government are always forbidden. Those which have gained official favor are displayed in the windows of all the bookstores, are sold in all the kiosks. This provides a valuable indicator for the attentive observer, curious for precise information on the tastes, preferences, sentiments, hates and intentions of those who have control and care over our destinies. In studying refused drawings and authorized drawings, we know exactly what the government fears and what it encourages, we have a clear revelation of its intimate thoughts.

Robert Justin Goldstein is professor of political science at Oakland University, Rochester, Michigan, and a research associate at the Center for Russian and East European Studies at the University of Michigan. He is the author of numerous books and articles about the history of civil liberties in western democracies, including "Political Repression in Modern America" (2nd edition, 2001); "The War for the Public Mind: Political Censorship in Nineteenth-Century Europe" (2000); and "Flag Burning and Free Speech: The Case of Texas v. Johnson" (2000).

INTRODUCTION

By Floyd Abrams

There is a terrible logic to state censorship. Joseph Goebbels understood it well. If free speech and a free press interfere with the ability of a state to act as it pleases, why not suppress the speech and stifle the press? That logic led Goebbels to instruct German publishers in 1937 that their role was "not to inform but to shake up and spur onward" and that they must be "monoform in will" even as they were permitted to be "polyform in expressing that will."

The same logic was routinely applied throughout the twentieth century by authoritarian governments far less dedicated to the brutal destruction of free expression than was Goebbels' Germany. In 1937, Brazil as well was ruled by a military government. The country was at war. Why not, then, establish a censorship regime and why not make it (as The New York Times observed) "one of the most efficient censorships ever devised in South America"? Why not censor, as Brazil did, all outgoing and incoming boat and air mail? Why not bar, as Brazil did, any newspaper from criticizing the government in power?

The logic of censorship begins with an unexceptionable notion: speech matters. People can be persuaded by it, moved by it, spurred to action by it. Twentieth century governments understood this. They understood, as Justice Oliver Wendell Holmes once observed, that "persecution for the expression of opinions" is "perfectly logical." "If you have no doubt," Holmes wrote, "of your premises or your power and want a certain result with all your heart you naturally express your wishes in law and sweep away all opposition."

Holmes, of course, was not advocating such conduct. In the same paragraph in which he articulated the logic of censorship, he denounced it, urging that "free trade in ideas" be permitted. But throughout the twentieth century, state censorship often seemed not only logical but inevitable. The form that censorship took varied, but its essence remained constant. Consider the 1925 Hungarian decree that required all crossword puzzles to be submitted to a censor prior to publication after a solution to one puzzle read "Long Live Otto." Or the 1946 ruling of an American general, acting as chief censor in occupied Japan, to delete from the English-language Nippon Times an editorial condemning "excessive acclaim" of General Douglas MacArthur. Or the Argentine satirical publication that was shut down in 1966 for referring to local military leaders as walruses. The laws in effect in Hungary, Japan and Argentina differed in significant respects. The central censorial character of each was identical.

All these examples are to be found in this volume of New York Times articles setting forth, in the revealing language used at the time, one example after another of political censorship in the twentieth century. It is a long and fascinating book that rarely shows humanity at its best. Censorship is not pleasant business, and while censors often act ridiculously, they rarely act with a light touch.

The Nazi example cited above may be a bit misleading. The censorship of that regime was not only unusually racist and murderous; it was also unusually candid. Censorship is usually masked in code words—the language of "responsibility' and "accountability", of "values" and "honor" and of "stability" and protecting "public morals." New censorial schemes are usually pronounced with regret, asserted to be temporary and declared to be consistent with principles of free expression.

Not in the German Reich, which trumpeted the New Order as offering new norms of human behavior. During the Nazi reign, the German Supreme Court acknowledged that its country did not have a "free" press as those words were used in "liberalistically governed States." The press, the Court said, was "ordered" since the regime viewed it "as a medium for the education of the national community in the spirit of National Socialism and as a means of leadership in the service of the State and nation, expecting the press not to oppose the decisions of the government but to support them and to try to bring them to concrete results."

Throughout the century, nations far more often defended their censorial conduct in more euphemistic terms. Was the new Soviet Union a despotic state? A New York Times article written in 1923 (by Walter Duranty, whose pro-Soviet sympathies later led to justified criticism of and then self-criticism by The Times) summed up the situation by acknowledging that "no opposition to the Government, either written or spoken, is allowed." Duranty went on to relate a common Soviet defense of censorship, saying, "freedom of speech in America and England are the slow outcome of a centuries long fight for personal liberty. How can you expect Russia, just emerged from the blackest tyranny, to share the attitude of Anglo-Saxons who struck the first blow against regal tyrants a thousand years ago at Runnymede?" A Russian official was then quoted as acknowledging that censorship proceeds "in the first instance from fear" and as expressing the hope that "time and the continued stability of the Soviet regime will bring us gradually into line with Western standards."

Twentieth century censorship reflected in this book varied in the degree of governmental involvement of what could be freely uttered. Not surprisingly, there are differences in kind between the censorship in totalitarian states and in democratic ones. But censorship remains the appropriate word to describe the conduct involved in both. Consider three of the articles from the first decade of the twentieth century. All are about the United States. Not one of these censorial acts was treated as a serious threat to free expression a century ago. Not one would be legally permissible today.

A 1901 dispatch reports laconically on the sentencing to jail of the managing editor and a reporter of the Chicago American for publishing an article critical "of the court's decision on an application for the forfeiture of the charter of the People's Gaslight and Coke Company." Five years later, an article describes the indictment of three St. Paul newspapers for reporting on the hanging of a criminal, notwithstanding a law that forbade "publication of details of a hanging" and permitted newspapers simply "to announce the fact of the execution." Three years after that, Spokane authorities are reported to have seized every copy of The Industrial Worker, the house organ of the International Workers of the World, for publishing an article relating the "alleged experience" of a prisoner in the county jail. "The papers," The Times reported without comment, "will be burned."

The censorship of any of these newspapers for the reasons asserted at the time would be unthinkable (as well as unconstitutional) today. More significantly, all these efforts at censorship—the first for expressing an opinion about the performance of a judge, the second for accurately reporting about governmental conduct and the third for reporting on conditions in a public facility—are rooted in the same sense of hubris: that it is for the government to determine what is best for the people to know. While this is not, by any means, the worst sort of repression, it is the worst of paternalism.

Nowhere is the effort of twentieth century states to decide what may and may not be said more comic—sometimes more lunatic—than with respect to issues of culture. One may not be shocked to read that Tolstoy's publisher was jailed for six months in 1909 for publishing one of his novels, but who would have imagined that a year earlier Parisian intellectuals would have been forced to defend their right to observe "scantily clad women" in music halls against raids by French police?

The contagious nature of censorship is also displayed. In 1908, performances of Oscar Wilde's Salome were barred in Germany. Dr. Richard Strauss objected, saying, "It is nonsense to forbid such a play! I should like to work out the idea into a musical drama." He did so and the resulting work was promptly barred in Cleveland and Chicago. The police chief of St. Louis was more worldly. The opera, he said, would be permitted "until a point where in the opinion of the 'morality squad', it gets shocking."

The boundless degree of authority to determine what might and might not be shown was startling. In New York City in 1908, police barred jokes told in dialect and permitted "acting" while barring "vaudeville." In a Mack Sennett-like comedy routine, the police watched a quartet sing and then saw "between two of the songs, the baritone [strike] the second tenor with a newspaper." "Cut that out," yells a policeman, "that's vaudeville."

How did a system of censorship work in a democratic society? It worked to bar films that were viewed as suggestive, to jail journalists who told too much truth, and ultimately to ban books. A noted example is reflected in a 1921 New York Times article under the headline "Improper Novel Costs Women $100." In its entirety, the following description was offered:

> Margaret C. Anderson and Jane Heap, publisher and editor respectively of The Little Review, at 27 West Eighth Street, each paid a fine of $50 imposed by Justices McInerney, Kernochan and Moss in Special Sessions yesterday, for publishing an improper novel in the July and August, 1920, issues of the magazine. John S. Summer, Secretary of the New York Society for the Prevention of Vice, was the complainant. The defendants were accompanied to court by several Greenwich Village artists and writers. John Quinn, counsel for the women, told the court that the alleged objectionable story, entitled 'Ulysses,' was the product of one Joyce, author, playwright and graduate of Dublin University, whose work had been praised by noted critics. "I think that this novel is unintelligible," said Justice McInerney.
>
> Mr. Quinn admitted that it was cast in a curious style, but contended that it was in similar vein to the work of an American author with which no fault was found, and he thought it was principally a matter of punctuation marks. Joyce, he said, didn't use punctuation marks in this story, probably on account of his eyesight. "There may be found more impropriety in the displays in some Fifth Avenue show windows or in a theatrical show than is contained in this novel," protested the attorney.
>
> Assistant District Attorney Joseph Forrester said that some of the chief objections had to do with a too frank expression concerning a woman's dress when the woman was in the clothes described. The court held that parts of the story seemed to be harmful to the morals of the community.

Pause for a moment on that period piece. Think what Justice McInerney would have thought if he had understood the novel by "one Joyce." Or what Joyce must have made of Justice McInerney's difficulty with his prose. Or of the defender of his book explaining away Joyce's lack of punctuation as being rooted in his poor eyesight.

It is the last line in the article, however, that is most telling. Because "parts of the story seemed to be harmful to the morals of the community," the story (and the book) was suppressed. Not for another dozen years was "Ulysses" permitted into the country.

The censors in the Joyce case were judges. In other censorship schemes throughout the world, that role was played by military officers, police and other designated officials. The tone with which they spoke was often reassuring, frequently containing denials that the process of censorship was, in fact, censorial. When George Alexander Redford, the dramatic censor in London, banned any performance of Shaw's "Mrs. Warren's Profession" in 1910, he observed that the play was "clever, but impossible" and described his own role as follows:

> I am not a censor. I never censorize over anybody. I merely used the experience I have gained from a long association with theatrical matters to administer the regulations of my office. There is no such thing as an offhand decision about interdicting a play. No play is ever prohibited without the most careful thought, and every chance is given authors to tone down their work whenever it is possible.

Redford's self-deprecating description of his own role has been unwittingly tracked by censors throughout the century. A recent study published by the World Press Freedom Committee entitled "New Code Words for Censorship" concludes that:

> The words and phrases evolve and change, but their meaning remains the same: restrictions on the news media, and thus on what the people can know. The censorship of 2000 and beyond will be more difficult than past censorship to identify, more challenging to confront and will originate from some surprising new corners. It already is coming. Not just from heavyhanded dictators, but also from sources supposedly supportive of democracy—Western linked international and intergovernmental institutions.
>
> Behind claims they are safeguarding the commonwealth these groups are grasping for power to control the news that citizens hear, see and read, through a language of benevolent-sounding hogwash that ultimately translates into old-fashioned censorship.

Whether couched in older language or new, then, the logic and the appeal of censorship remains the same. And the need to confront it remains constant.

Floyd Abrams, a First Amendment expert, is a partner in the law firm of Cahill Gordon & Reindel and is the William J. Brennan, Jr. Visiting Professor of First Amendment Law of the Columbia Graduate School of Journalism.

PART I

PRE-WORLD WAR I, 1900–1913

PRESS CONTROVERSIES

April 16, 1901

CENSORSHIP IN RUSSIA

The Rule Extends Even to Advertising Matter Printed Here for Circulation in That Country

Special to The New York Times

WASHINGTON, April 15—Consul General W. R. Holloway, at St. Petersburg, in a report to the State Department tells of the rigid censorship of all matter printed in the Russian language. This censorship extends even to advertising matter, and of this Mr. Holloway says:

"Several American exporters, desiring to reach the trade in their respective lines in Russia, ordered catalogues and other advertising matter printed in New York in the Russian language and shipped them to Russia, to be addressed and mailed by agents in Russia; but the advertising matter was refused admission because they had not complied with the Russian laws governing the censorship of the press, which requires that everything printed in the Russian language must receive the approval of the chief of the Central Committee of Foreign Censorship before it can be admitted or circulated in Russia.

"American exporters who desire to circulate advertising matter printed in the Russian language in Russia, must address a petition to his Excellency Count Alexander Mouravieff, Chief of the Central Committee of Foreign Censorship, describing the character of the publication and its purpose, to which must be attached two copies of the publication for which admission is desired, praying for permission to admit and circulate the same in Russia.

"To this petition must be attached two Russian revenue stamps of the value of 1.60 rubles, (84 cents,) preferably two of 80 kopecks (42 cents) each. This petition will be more likely to receive immediate attention if written in the Russian or French language, though the same would be translated and forwarded if sent direct to the United States Ambassador or Consul General at St. Petersburg, if accompanied by the amount necessary to purchase the revenue stamps.

"Incendiary matter has been circulated in every form in Russia; hence the authorities censor everything that is printed as rigidly as they did a century ago."

* * *

November 13, 1901

NEWSPAPER MEN IN CONTEMPT

Chicago Court Sentences Two Employes of Hearst's American to Terms in Jail

CHICAGO, Nov. 12—On a charge of contempt of court Judge Hanecy to-day sentenced Andrew M. Lawrence, managing editor of Hearst's Chicago American, to forty days in the county jail. The sentence of H. S. Canfield, who wrote the article objectionable to the court, was fixed at thirty days in jail. The cases against S. S. Carvalho, financial manager of the paper, and John C. Hammond, assistant city editor, were dismissed. Judge Hanecy declared that the cases against W. R. Hearst, majority stockholder of the paper; Homer Davenport, cartoonist; and Clare Briggs, also a cartoonist, would stand until such time as the respondents could be brought into court by the Sheriff.

Ex-Gov. Altgeld, one of counsel for the respondents, entered a formal exception to the decision. "This case, I may say," the court remarked, "is not appealable. You may file a bill of exceptions for a writ of error, however. I am willing to delay the serving of papers on Mr. Lawrence and Mr. Canfield till you have drawn your bill."

"We do not feel that we have any favors coming from this court," Mr. Altgeld answered. "We are much obliged."

A few minutes after the rendering of the decision and the imposition of the sentences as to Lawrence and Canfield Judge Dunne, upon application, issued a writ of habeas corpus as to them, returnable immediately.

The article in The American upon which the proceedings in contempt were based was a criticism of the court's decision on an application for the forfeiture of the charter of the People's Gaslight and Coke Company.

Judge Hanecy said if the matter published were allowed to go unnoticed by the court it paved the way for other attacks, and that the judiciary, if not held, in respect, would fall, with all democratic government. The article, the court declared, was not merely an attack on the court, but a bold threat to every other court. It should therefore not go unpunished.

* * *

December 3, 1901

BERLIN JOURNALISTS TRIED

Two Members of the Vorwaerts Staff Sent to Prison for Insulting Gen. von Kettler

BERLIN, Dec. 2—In the Berlin Criminal Court to-day three members of the editorial staff of Vorwaerts were placed on trial. They were charged with insulting Major Gen. von Kettler by the publication of the so-called "Hun Letters," which accused the General and his column of summary and barbarous treatment of Boxers at the time of the China expedition, and especially of shooting twenty-two Boxers at Yachiao. Gen. von Kettler maintains that these twenty-two men were shot in pursuance of the sentence of a court-martial, for the massacre of two hundred Christians.

Lieut. Stolzenberg testified that the inhabitants of the village in question were driven together in the market-place, where two Chinese Christians picked out men whom they accused of participating in the massacre. An English missionary named Lawry then examined the men accused by the two converts, and selected twenty-two as certainly being Boxers. These men were executed by Gen. von Kettler's orders.

The General told the court that these executions were necessary in order to break the reign of terror established by the Boxers throughout that whole district.

Two of the prisoners, Schmidt and John, were convicted of the charges against them and sentenced to six and seven months' imprisonment, respectively.

* * *

August 18, 1903

RUSSIAN CENSORSHIP FAILS

De Plehve's Efforts to Prevent Foreign Papers from Getting News Unavailing

London Times—New York Times
Special Cablegram

LONDON, Aug. 18—The Times's Russian correspondents ridicule the efforts of M. de Plehve, the Minister of the Interior, to prevent foreign papers from getting news of events in Russia.

The correspondents say that the mere fact that a Russian journalist finds his own press closed to all but official cooked accounts of riot and disorder invites the communication of the information to the correspondent of a foreign journal. It is a pretty safe rule to add a cipher to the figures of casualties reported officially on the occasion of labor conflicts.

* * *

October 11, 1903

RUSSIFICATION OF FINLAND

All Books Not Indexed in Library Catalogues Deemed "Forbidden"

The Helsingfors (Finland) correspondent of Das Berliner Tageblatt sends the following to his paper:

"The police authorities and censors in the Finnish cities are at present zealously engaged in looking over libraries and reading rooms. Last year the catalogues of the Helsingfors Public Library were reviewed by a censor, who designated as 'forbidden literature' all recently published books which were not indexed. He wished the books to be sent out, but decided later to leave them in the library under the condition that the public should not have access to them.

"A few days later a censor and some gendarmes entered the library and demanded the 'forbidden' books. They were told that the librarian had the key to the closet in which they were, but he was out of town.

These guardians of the peace, however, found it more convenient to close the library as well as the reading rooms for an indefinite time, opened the closets, and reviewed the entire collection again."

* * *

February 20, 1904

RUSSIA ABOLISHES CENSORSHIP ON NEWS

Correspondents of Foreign Papers to be Untrammeled

"NOT AFRAID OF THE LIGHT"

Official Says the Censorship Has Resulted in All Kinds of Slanders and Misrepresentations

ST. PETERSBURG, Feb. 19—The Russian Government to-day abolished the censorship upon all news and other telegrams going abroad.

The lifting of the embargo, which has existed for generations upon the free transmission of news from the Russian Empire, came as a direct result of the consideration of the subject by the Czar himself, and in some respects this abolition is regarded here as the most important act since the emancipation of the serfs.

Under a régime allowing perfect freedom to the foreign press it is believed that Russia will soon cease to be constantly subject to underground attack, and that she will see herself through honest spectacles.

"For years," said a prominent official to The Associated Press to-day, "our country has been the victim of every imaginable slander and misrepresentation because it was known that telegrams addressed to foreign news sources went through the hands of the Russian censor. Any story no matter how baseless or exaggerated, that was sent surreptitiously across the border, was greedily accepted abroad, especially by the Russophobes, as true because the Government would not put its official stamp upon it.

"Regular anti-Russian news factories have been in operation in Berlin, Vienna and elsewhere, and these have spread the most absurd and preposterous libels supplied by the enemies of Russia. Every act of the Government has been twisted and distorted. Insignificant student affairs or workmen's riots, such as would not attract general attention elsewhere, have been magnified into great movements of popular discontent until certain portions of the world have been led to believe that Russia was perpetually on the eve of a great revolution.

"Some English newspapers especially have conducted systematic campaigns against us. Moreover, the fact that dispatches were censored has often been interpreted as semi-official authorization, when perhaps they in no sense represented the views of the Government.

"Hereafter, the correspondents of foreign newspapers will be untrammeled. We expect to see Russia presented in her true light. The opening of the floodgates may result in the evilly disposed stirring up as much as possible at first, but we feel confident that in the end truth will prevail. We are not afraid to have the light turned on. We are proud of our country, and we are entitled to faithful and honest presentation of our current history."

Foreign telegrams, until recently, were subject to censorship at the Ministry of Foreign Affairs, but, since the death last Autumn of M. Gretch, who was at one time connected with the Russian Embassy at Washington, the censorship has been temporarily under the Ministry of the Interior, where the permanent censorship bureau of plays, books, and newspapers in Russia is located.

News telegrams addressed to foreign sources originating in the most distant parts of the empire, Vladivostok, for example, were formerly telegraphed to St. Petersburg to be passed on.

M. de Plehve, Minister of the Interior, and Count Lamsdorff, the Foreign Minister, both joined in the recommendation that the censorship be abolished.

The internal censorship is to be retained, but foreign dispatches are to be entirely free. Inasmuch as a state of war exists, telegrams from the theatre of hostilities will be subject to the same kind of military censorship enforced in all countries under similar circumstances.

* * *

March 15, 1904

ORDERS TO RUSSIAN PRESS

All News as to the Army and Fleet Must Go Through Censor's Hands

London Times—New York Times
Special Cablegram
Copyright, 1904. The New York Times

LONDON, March 15—The Times's Russian correspondents say the Russian press has received a number of circulars indicating the course to be observed in regard to the war news.

The first, dated Feb. 9, ordered editors to refrain from publishing accounts of demonstrations evoked by the complications in the Far East without special permission.

The second, dated Feb. 16, read:

"His Majesty the Emperor is graciously pleased to command that all articles and news relating to the activity of the army and fleet destined to appear in periodical publications shall be previously submitted to the judgment of competent military persons."

The Novoe Vremya has obeyed the Government's injunction to refrain from publishing attacks on Great Britain in so far as it has been careful to make a distinction between the British Government and the British press. But the distinction is gradually being effaced, and the St. Petersburg organ is slipping back into its old position of open hostility to Great Britain.

One reason for the Novoe Vremya's energetic anti-British campaign is that it is difficult to arouse national enthusiasm for a conflict with vague and distant foes. Great Britain happens to be the ally of Russia's enemy, and to arouse Russian patriotism in an acute form it would seem a promising expedient to play upon the existing dislike of England.

* * *

June 10, 1904

COMIC PAPER SEIZED

Boston Police Find Illegality in Publication's Use of the Flag

Special to The New York Times

BOSTON, Mass., June 9—During the present week the police have stopped the sale in this city of copies of the edition of June 4 of Judge, a comic publication. There was printed across a likeness of the American flag the word "Judge."

The police declare it is a clear violation of the law governing the misuse of the National or State flags.

The police of each division visited all the periodical stores and news stands and gave orders to stop the sale of the publication with the warning that prosecutions would follow if the orders were not heeded.

* * *

August 23, 1904

GERMAN ARMY SENSITIVE

Author of Franco-Prussian Reminiscences Is Fined

BERLIN, Aug. 22—The danger of publishing reflections on army officers, even after an interval of three decades, is shown in the prosecution of Ludwig Fischer, the author of a book of reminiscences of the Franco-Prussian war, in which allusions other than flattering are made to Captain, now General, Nicolai.

Fischer testified that he did not know Nicolai was alive but at the same time he introduced witnesses to substantiate the allusions made in his book. Nevertheless, he was convicted and fined.

* * *

June 24, 1905

DAMPER ON RUSSIAN JOY

The Czar Didn't Mean That He Would Grant a Constitution

ST. PETERSBURG, June 23—The official interpretation of the Emperor's speech to the delegation of the Zemstvoists and Mayors at Peterhof on June 19 is given in the following circular sent by the Ministry of the Interior to all the newspapers:

"The words pronounced by the Emperor in the course of the reception of the members of the Zemstvos and municipalities have been incorrectly interpreted by a portion of the periodical press, and several newspapers have gone so far as to deduce therefrom the arbitrary conclusion that the Emperor's words implied an extension of the imperial rescript of March 3 to the Minister of the Interior in the sense of a convocation of representatives of the people based on the existing constitutions of the countries of Western Europe, whereas it was clearly shown by the Emperor's words that the conditions of such a convocation were to be based on an order of things responding to Russian autocratic principles, and his Majesty's words contain absolutely not the least indication of the possibility of modifying the fundamental laws of the empire.

"Consequently the Central Administration of Press Affairs, by order of the Minister of the Interior, informs all publications appearing without censorship that the Emperor's words can be published only in the form in which they were reported in the Official Messenger without additions or abbreviations, and in order to prevent distortion of the significance of the imperial words it is found necessary to prohibit the publication in the press of any kind of deduction or interpretation which does not accord with the direct and clear meaning of the Emperor's utterances."

The Minister of the Interior has prohibited the publication of the Russ for a month. The paper was suspended upon the recommendation of Assistant Minister of the Interior Trepoff. Latterly the Russ, which enjoys an immense circulation, has been the Government's most severe critic, waging unceasingly a war against the bureaucracy and printing exposure after exposure.

* * *

July 21, 1905

ST. PETERSBURG, Friday, July 21—The Government has made good its threat and has suspended the Slovo for a month for open defiance this morning of the strict order prohibiting publication of the proceedings of the Zemstvo Congress at Moscow.

The Government, taking the ground that agitation pending the promulgation of the Emperor's reform project would be injurious, some time ago issued a general order against the printing of reports of illegal meetings and reiterated this order in the case of the Zemstvo Congress.

Two other newspapers, the Viedomosti of Moscow and the Novosti of this city, which have been very daring in tone lately, have received the first of the three warnings leading to final suspension. Street sales of the Novosti, which tried to organize concerted defiance by all the newspapers in the publication of the proceedings of the Zemstvo Congress, have been suspended indefinitely.

* * *

March 3, 1906

ST. PAUL PAPERS INDICTED

Must Answer Under Old Law for Printing Details of a Hanging

Special to The New York Times

ST. PAUL, March 2—The Grand Jury this evening returned indictments against the three St. Paul daily newspapers, The Pioneer Press, The Dispatch, and The News, for reporting the recent hanging of William Williams. The John Day Smith law forbids publication of details of a hanging. The newspapers are permitted simply to announce the fact of the execution.

The papers are indicted as corporations, will answer tomorrow, and probably will be fined. The cases will be taken to the Supreme Court for a test. The statute has been in force nearly ten years, but this is the first time the newspapers have been dealt with for violating it.

* * *

March 16, 1906

RUSSIAN JOURNALISTS TO DIE FOR REFORM

To Be Shot for Printing Subversive Articles

London Times—New York Times
Special Cable. Copyright, 1906.

ST. PETERSBURG, March 15—Three journalists in Chita have been sentenced to be shot under Gen. Rennenkampff's orders merely for publishing subversive articles.

According to the Slovo, over 200 persons were executed last month by sentences of courts-martial in the Baltic Provinces alone. This does not include numerous executions without trial of any sort.

* * *

June 20, 1906

EIGHT NEWSPAPERS SEIZED

St. Petersburg Authorities Suppress Comment and News

ST. PETERSBURG, June 19—The massacre of Jews at Bialystok has shocked the country and added to the general excitement, and the revelations which the commission of the Lower House of Parliament sent to investigate the outbreak at Bialystok are expected to make will only add fuel to the flames.

The Golos, a new paper edited by M. Ulianoff, a member of the Lower House of Parliament, containing an account of the horrors and charging the authorities of Bialystok with deliberately preparing the riot, was confiscated when it appeared this morning. Seven other St. Petersburg newspapers were also confiscated, two for their vigorous comment on the attitude of the authorities at Bialystok and the others for long descriptive stories of the outrages from correspondents.

A curious incident is related at Minsk, where Gov. Kurloff, whose trial for inciting the November excesses was urged by Delegate Arakantseff in the Lower House of Parliament, was to-day thanked by a delegation of Jews for measures instituted by him to prevent an outbreak.

* * *

July 21, 1906

RIOT IN ST. PETERSBURG; PAPERS ARE SUPPRESSED

Large Crowd Stones Mounted Police and Cavalry

DUMA LEADERS CRESTFALLEN

And Court Circles Are Jubilant Over the False Step Made by the Constitutional Democrats

ST. PETERSBURG, July 20—The Misla and three other newspapers of this city were confiscated to-day. The members of the editorial staff of the Misla were arrested.

The police forbade the newspapers to publish the text of the address of the lower house of Parliament to the country.

The resentment occasioned by the suppression of newspapers and the closing of their printing establishments led to disorders this evening. A large crowd stoned the mounted police in the vicinity of the Stosnossensky Prospect, and some stones also were thrown at a small detachment of cavalry. Other parties of cavalry soon arrived from all directions. The attitude of the crowd was menacing, and the cavalry twice fired volleys of blank cartridges before the mob dispersed.

The demonstration occurred when the police appeared to seal the printing establishment of the Misla in the Stosnossensky Prospect, which is in the heart of St. Petersburg. There are several foot bridges, impassable for horses, across the Catherine Canal, near the offices of the Misla, and over these the demonstrators escaped.

So far as is known there were no casualties. At a late hour to-night knots of people, after the police patrols had passed, were singing the "Marseillaise."

As M. Solomka, the chief editor of the Misla, is a Member of Parliament, M. Mouromtseff and Prince Shakoffskol, respectively President and Secretary of the lower house, communicated with the Prefect of Police to-day and demanded and received assurances that M. Solomka should not be arrested.

No further action regarding the address to the people was taken by the Lower House of Parliament to-day. The Constitutional Democratic members appear to be heartily sick of the whole episode and anxious to drop the subject if the Government is so minded, and there is a disposition to shelve the address by indefinite postponement of the question of the manner of its publication. Prof. Milukoff and other leaders of the Constitutional Democratic Party to-day carefully pointed out that the document was not technically an appeal directed to the people, but might be considered as an "explanation" addressed to nobody in particular, and from this point of view harmless.

There is no question but that the fiasco has enormously shaken the prestige of the Constitutional Democrats, and the leaders of that party are crestfallen over having been induced to play with edged tools. Prof. Milukoff, M. Struve, and others admitted frankly to-day that one effect would be to postpone to the dim future the advent of, a Constitutional Democratic Ministry, as the vote on the adoption of the address showed that the party was actually in the minority in the House and too weak to control the situation when faced by the combined opposition of the Right and Left.

Prof. Milukoff told The Associated Press to-night that he believed there was no longer any reason to apprehend the dissolution of Parliament, as the Government would rather seek to profit by its dissensions. Peterhof circles are reported to be jubilant over the discomfiture of the Constitutional Democrats.

The Strana this morning printed a report that an imperial ukase ordering the dissolution of Parliament had already been signed. In the afternoon it was reported that an extraordinary council was sitting at Peterhof, with Gen. Count Ignatieff, the noted reactionary; M. Pobiedonostzeff, ex-Procurator General of the Holy Synod; Gen. Trepoff, M. Stichinsky, Minister of Agriculture, and others in attendance, discussing the advisability of the immediate dissolution of Parliament.

The feeling of general alarm was increased this morning by the news that all night long Guard regiments had been marching into the city from the Guards' camp at Krasnoye-Selo.

* * *

August 8, 1907

ALGER'S BOY BOOKS BARRED

Worcester Public Library Puts Author In Mark Twain, Class

Special to The New York Times

WORCESTER, Mass., Aug. 7—The works of Horatio Alger, Jr., the noted writer of books for boys, have been barred from the shelves of the Worcester Public Library. Alger is now in the same class as Mark Twain. Robert W. Chambers, Walt Whitman, and many other well-known producers of literature, some of whose works have been barred from free public libraries in Worcester County towns and cities.

At the library the reason given for barring Alger's books, which have been on the shelves for years, is that they are not truthful. It made no difference to the library authorities that they were works of fiction. Furthermore, the authorities have discovered that Alger's books are too sensational.

The boys are protesting vigorously at the edict.

* * *

March 24, 1908

ROUT OUT ANARCHY, SAYS THE PRESIDENT

Calls Upon Department of Justice to Prosecute Criminally Anarchistic Editors

ACTS IN PATERSON CASE

Publication Advocates Measures Worse Than Murder, He Says—Will Ask Congress to Act

Special to The News York Times

PATERSON, N. J., March 23—Mayor Andrew McBride received to-day a letter from Private Secretary Loeb inclosing a communication from President Roosevelt showing that the President was directly responsible for the temporary order issued by Postmaster General Meyer excluding the Anarchistic weekly, La Questiono Sociale, from the United States mails. A hearing will be granted the publishers of the paper at Washington on Wednesday next, when the order will be either dismissed or made permanent.

President Roosevelt's, communication was in reply to a letter sent to him by Mayor McBride containing the translation of an article which appeared in La Questione Sociale, and asking the President to relieve Paterson of the stigma of being called the headquarters of Anarchy in this country by issuing an order to exclude the newspaper from the mails.

The President's communication was as follows:

To the Department of Justice:

By my direction the Postmaster General is to exclude La Questione Sociale of Paterson, N. J., from the mails, and it will not be admitted to the mails unless by order of the court, or unless you advise me that it must be admitted. Please see if it is not possible to prosecute criminally under any section of the law that is available, the men that are interested in the sending out of this anarchistic and murderous publication. They are, of course, the enemies of mankind, and every effort should be made to hold them accountable for an offense far more infamous than that of an ordinary murder.

This matter has been brought to my attention by the Mayor of the City of Paterson. I wish every effort made to get at the criminals under the Federal law. It may be found impossible to do this. I shall also, through the Secretary of State, call the attention of the Governor of New Jersey to the circumstances, so that he may proceed under the State law, his attention being further drawn to the fact that the newspaper is circulated in other States. After you have concluded your investigation I wish a report from you to serve as a basis for recommendations by me for action by Congress.

The newspaper article in question advocates murder by dynamite. It specifically advocates the murder of enlisted men of the United States Army and officers of the police force, and the burning of the houses of private citizens. The preaching of murder and arson is certainly as immoral as the circulation of obscene and lascivious literature, and if the practice is not already forbidden by the law it should be forbidden. The immigration law now prohibits the entry to the United States of any person who entertains or advocates the views expressed in this newspaper article. It is, of course, inexcusable to permit those already here to promulgate such views.

Those who write, publish, and circulate such articles stand on the level with those who use the mails for distributing poisons for the purpose of murder, and convictions have been obtained when the mails have been used for the distribution of poisons. No law should require the Postmaster General to become an accessory to murder by circulating literature of this kind.

THEODORE ROOSEVELT

The order of the Postmaster General was received to-day by Postmaster George W. Pollitt. The order simply bars the use of the mails to La Questione Sociale. The publication has a circulation of 2,300.

At the headquarters of La Questione Sociale, Ludovico Caminita, the editor, said: "The newspapers of this city published an article of La Questione Sociale, but they translated it worse than it was. But we do not care for the city's stand, and will continue to publish our paper and to use our right of free press and free speech."

The article in question advocated the burning of houses, armory, and police station and the arming of all Anarchists when called upon to fight the police and army. It was published on Feb. 1.

* * *

June 9, 1908

INDIAN PRESS MUZZLED

Viceregal Council Also Provides Stern Measures Against Bomb Outrages

SIMLA, June 8—The Viceregal Council, after strong speeches by Lord Minto, Viceroy of India, and other members of the Council, emphasizing the urgency of dealing with seditious outbreaks, to-day adopted two emergency measures. The first is known as the Explosives bill, which provides stern measures against bomb outrages and conspiracies; the second, the Press bill, empowers the suspension and confiscation of newspapers inciting to criminal acts.

Lord Minto was careful to explain that both of these bills should be regarded as exceptional measures to meet an exceptional situation. He added that if they were found not to be strong enough, still severer measures would be adopted.

* * *

April 29, 1909

RUSSIA CENSORS BOOKS

Restrictions on Bindings Abandoned, but Not on Reading Matter

ST. PETERSBURG, April 28—The recent announcement of the United States Post Office Department that Russia had removed the prohibition against sending bound books from other countries into Russia by mail, seems to have led to a misunderstanding in America, it apparently being supposed that the Russian Government had withdrawn its censorship over books. This, however, is not so. The customs department regulation, under which book covers were liable to duty has been abolished, and bound books are now allowed to enter as unbound, but the censorship over printing matter still persists.

* * *

May 23, 1909

SEDITION IN EGYPT

Revival of Press Law Putting Curb on Egyptian "Feeling"

CAIRO, May 8—The demonstrations of the Nationalists against the revival of the Press law have become more loudmouthed, and sedition is openly preached both in the streets by certain leaders and in the press.

The Press law will be made applicable to both foreign and native papers. The Powers are certain to give their consent to the new law, for none has any great interest in obstructing Great Britain's work in Egypt. But this was not always so, especially in the case of France when the Bosphore Egyptien developed into the most scurrilous and seditious of foreign journals in Egypt. Things came to such a pass that on Feb. 29, 1884, the Government issued a decree suppressing the Bosphore Egyptien in virtue of the rights conferred by the Press law of Nov. 26, 1881.

The proprietors took not the slightest notice, and for more than a year grew more violent than ever in their criticisms. At last they overcame the patience of Nubar, then Premier, by publishing in Arabic and French a fictitious proclamation from the Mahdi inciting the natives to rebellion. Upon this the French Consulate authorities were informed that the police would close the offices of the journal. They were requested to send a representative to be present in accordance with capitulation custom. The French Consul General demurred at this, declaring that he would send an official to resist not to aid the police.

Nevertheless, the premises of the Bosphore Egyptien were seized by the Egyptian police on April 8, 1885. Then ensued one of those scenes which, called into being by the Capitulations, really seem to more fittingly belong to the "opera bouffe" stage. France protested at the step taken. An international inquiry ensued. It was found that the house where the

Bosphore Egyptien was printed was inhabited by foreigners of various nationalities. Although the Egyptian Government had advised the French authorities, it had, according to the Capitulations, committed an international error.

So that Egypt became the offender instead of the offended party, as it undoubtedly was. There was no arguing the point. As luck would have it Great Britain had need of France's concurrence at that moment in certain Egyptian questions, and so Nubar Pasha had to make an apology to the French authorities, and had to permit the Bosphore Egyptien to reopen its offices. On her side France undertook to control the tone of the journal and to adhere to a law giving the Government effective control over the foreign press.

It is on account of the obstruction caused by the Capitulations, as typified in the Bosphore Egyptian incident, that the Press law of 1881 became an absolute dead letter in Egypt. The Anglo-French Accord of 1904 has, however, cleared the way, and the Egyptian Government will have complete power to punish the excesses of the local press, foreign as well as vernacular.

* * *

May 26, 1909

TOLSTOY'S PUBLISHER JAILED

Court Refuses to Permit Prosecution of the Author Himself

ST. PETERSBURG, May 25—Nicolai Selden has been sentenced to six months imprisonment for publishing Tolstoy's "Thou Shalt Not Kill" and other political pamphlets.

Count Tolstoy wrote to the court declaring that Selden was a passive offender, and inviting his own prosecution, but the Magistrates refused to permit it.

* * *

July 24, 1909

MADRID, via Badajos, on the Portuguese Frontier, July 23—The Spanish authorities are exercising a rigorous censorship over the publication of news regarding the war between the Spaniards and the Kabyle tribesmen on the Riff coast of Morocco. Nothing except official dispatches is allowed to be printed, and communication by telephone to the provincial newspapers has been stopped. The Government considers these measures justified on the ground of military necessity, and because of the anti-patriotic campaign being conducted by the Liberal and Republican press. The entire edition of El Pals was confiscated to-day, and all the Republican clubs were closed.

The persons arrested yesterday in connection with the demonstrations against the departure of the troops will be charged with sedition and tried by military court-martial. The outside world should understand, however, the Government officials declare, that the Liberals and Republicans are exploiting the unpopularity of the war for political purposes, and they are suspected by the authorities of inciting the Reservists, who were forced in many cases to leave their families without support, to resistance.

In response to a telegram from a group of Liberal and Republican Deputies, demanding the convocation of Parliament, Premier Maura replied that, without desiring to ignore Parliament, he considered the demand based on a false conception of the situation, as events in Africa in no wise modified the policy of the Government. The Government to-day announced the opening of subscriptions throughout the country for the benefit of families of Reservists sents to Melilia.

* * *

September 15, 1909

PAPERS THREATEN TO STRIKE

Madrid Liberal Organs to Appeal to King Against Censorship

MADRID, Sept. 14—The Liberal newspapers of Madrid have published a protest against the continuance of the Government censorship, and they threaten to strike unless this restriction is removed.

The Minister of the Interior defends the censorship on the ground of public welfare. The editors have decided to appeal to King Alfonso.

Señor Rios, a Republican Deputy from Barcelona, said today that 120 schools in Barcelona were closed and would not be reopened without the approval of the Mayor and the parish priests. He declared also that there were more than 3,000 persons in, custody at Barcelona charged with participation in the recent rioting in that city.

* * *

December 12, 1909

SPOKANE AUTHORITIES SEIZE PAPER

SPOKANE, Wash., Dec. 11—Charging that it was a libelous publication, the city authorities seized every copy of The Industrial Worker, the organ of the Industrial Workers of the World, as it came off the press to-day. The papers will be burned. The leading article is by Elizabeth Gurley Flynn, a young woman convicted of conspiracy, in which she relates her alleged experience in the county jail.

* * *

July 9, 1910

PAPER FINED FOR CONTEMPT

Manager Jailed and Others Fined for Publishing Murder Confession

Special to The New York Times

SALT LAKE, Utah, July 8—The Herald Republican Publishing Company, George Hale, General Manager; A. J. Brown, managing editor; Paul Armstrong, acting city editor, and C. R. Williams, reporter, were found guilty of contempt of the District Court by Judge T. D. Lewis to-day.

Fines of $200 on two counts were inflicted against the company. Manager Hale was sentenced to thirty days in jail and the other employes were fined $10 each.

The offense was the publication of a confession made by Harry Thorne, a murderer, since convicted, at the time of the trial of James Riley, Thorne's partner, also since convicted. The court had great difficulty in obtaining a jury and declared this difficulty was attributable to the repeated publication of the confession. The court had warned the newspapers.

The newspaper company will carry the matter to the Supreme Court on habeas corpus, and a stay of one week was granted for this purpose.

* * *

April 5, 1914

PURITANISM IN GERMANY

Eminent Men Protest Against a Proposed Drastic New Law

Special Cable to The New York Times

BERLIN, April 4—German intellectuals are at loggerheads over the projected new law to safeguard the morals of youth by banning everything suggestive of the nude or sexual from shop windows, store counters, and billboards.

Agitation for the law sprang from recent bold exhibitions of corsets, lingerie, and other feminine finery in Berlin, which are now prohibited.

The law is drawn up so drastically that it threatens grave injustice to art dealers and publishers, who may henceforth be debarred from exhibiting any painting, book, engraving, or print which deals with the human form divine unless that form be clad.

The Goethe League, which is under the management of the poet and dramatist, Dr. Ludwig Fulda, has held an active and vigorous meeting of protest in Berlin, with a view of amending the proposed "purity" law. The league holds that if the law be placed in the Penal Code as now framed artistic Germany will have forced upon it the same sort of wild, irresponsible police censorship as was contemplated by the notorious Lex Heinze at the beginning of the century.

Dr. Fulda's protest is supported by men like Prof Ostwald, Prof. Max Liebermann, Prof. von Liszt, Prof. Haeckel, Gerhart Hauptmann, Max Osborn, Walter Bloom, and a host of others distinguished in art, science, and letters.

They admit that the object of the new law is unassailable, but declare that a clearer form of interpreting and enforcing it must be found.

CONTROVERSIES OVER STAGE AND SCREEN

January 21, 1900

THE IMPERIAL GERMAN CENSOR

In an essay just published in Berlin on the theatre censorship in Prussia some interesting statements are made about the views held by the Emperor William as to the so-called modern realistic stage literature. Herr von Richthofen, formerly Police President of Berlin, prohibited the performance of Hermann Sudermann's drama "Sodom's End," and issued the decree only three days before the first performance was to take place. The manager of the theatre, in despair, hurried to him to hear his reasons, and asked the Police President to point out the passages which he found immoral, so that they might be altered or left out. Richthofen briefly answered: "The whole tendency of modern literature does not suit us."

Herr Oskar Blumenthal, the manager, replied that it was not for the censorship to suppress a whole literary movement, and he appealed to the Minister of the Interior. Minister Herrfurth answered that he could interfere only in cases of gross abuse of official power, but finally, at the urgent request of Sudermann and Blumenthal, he promised to take matters into consideration on condition that three high officials should attend the rehearsal and give their opinion. This was done, the three decided in favor of the author, and the prohibition was withdrawn.

The Police President had, however, most influential friends, who knew how to inform the Emperor of the matter. A few days after the first performance the Minister saw his Majesty, who turned the conversation to the matter. Herrfurth explained why he had disavowed the Police President. He had read the drama carefully from beginning to end, and on each doubtful scene he had asked himself whether he would hesitate to witness it in company with his wife. The Emperor replied, "You would have done better to ask yourself whether you could see the piece in company of your daughter."

At this unexpected objection the Minister ventured to show that from this point of view some of the greatest masterpieces of classical literature—by ancient Greek poets, by Shakespeare, Goethe, and others—would have been prohibited. Unfortunately, it has not become known whether the Emperor by this weighty argument was brought around to the Minister's views.

* * *

July 7, 1901

A THEATRICAL CENSORSHIP

Police to Decide What Sort of Shows May Be Seen in Washington

Special to The New York Times

WASHINGTON, July 6—The Commissioners of the District of Columbia have adopted regulations designed to prohibit theatrical performances which are offensive to decency. Authority to do so was given them by Congress just before its adjournment last March. The police are the censors, and are to decide what shows are immoral, though, of course, the final decision rests with the courts.

The regulations are of wide scope. They provide for the arrest of any person who takes part in an improper performance, "whether as an actor, performer, director, manager, exhibitor, lecturer, or employe," or who conducts "a proprietor, agent, director, manager, or employe," the building in which such performance takes place.

The punishment is a fine not exceeding $40 for each offense. The theatrical license is to be revoked if an improper performance is given in any theatre, and the proprietor of the theatre will not be allowed to take out another license for a year either for his original theatre or a new one.

Indecency is not defined in the regulations. The prohibition is against any sort of indecency, whether conveyed by speech, gesture, music, or in any other way, and to make sure that everything is included the Commissioners have added a prohibition against any performance "wherein anything whatsoever shall appear or be in any wise represented, or exhibited which in any manner is offensive to common decency."

There is also a provision which a zealous police officer might interpret as prohibiting burlesque or comic opera costumes, for it prohibits actors from "exhibiting themselves in a manner offensive to common decency."

* * *

March 8, 1908

TIRED OF PLAY CENSOR

Barrie, Pinero, and Others Denounce the British Institution

Special Correspondence The New York Times

LONDON, Feb. 20—It was a very representative deputation which waited upon Mr. Herbert Gladstone at the Home Office this week to petition for the abolition of the office of dramatic censor. As J. M. Barrie, who introduced the deputation, aid, it represented every movement for the better that there had been in the English drama for fifty years.

Whether dead or alive, great or humble, added Mr. Barrie, Englishmen of letters had been united as an almost solid body in passionate protest for nearly two hundred years against the humiliation of the censorship—a statement which nobody considered humorous, but which, on the contrary, evoked enthusiastic "Hear, Hears."

There was a chorus of approval also when A. W. Pinero had spoken. He said the British drama could not possibly hold its true rank among the arts so long as the dramatist was subjected to the menace and the insult implied in the present state of things. Both the vigor and the health of the drama were seriously impaired—by the continuance of an office which, even if it did no harm in the past, had in our day become a humiliating anachronism. It was time that the British nation should be free from the stigma of appearing to be the only part of the English-speaking world which was incapable of keeping its stage clean and wholesome save under the guardianship of an irresponsible official.

Sir William S. Gilbert had a suggestion to make. He thought the office of the Censor should have the status of a court of first instance, from which there should be an appeal to arbitrators, of whom there should be three, one to be appointed by the author, one by the Lord Chamberlain, and the third either by the first two or by the Lord Chancellor. Fees of ten guineas each should be payable to the arbitrators, and that would form a guarantee that the machinery would not be set in motion except on an important matter. These fees should be payable by order of the court either by the appellant or the respondent.

Mr. Gladstone gave a non-committal reply, and the deputation withdrew to be snapshotted by representatives of the press, which, as Mr. Gladstone had intimated would undoubtedly arrogate to itself the office of public censor in case the Lord Chamberlain abandoned the ungrateful task.

* * *

April 12, 1908

PARIS RESENTS BAN ON LIVING PICTURES

Many Defenders of the Music Hall Shows the Police Are Trying to Suppress

RUSE TO BEAT CENSORSHIP

Managers Dismiss Audiences and Then Invite Them to Return as Guests to Witness the Feature Acts

By Marconi Transatlantic Wireless Telegraph to The New York Times

PARIS, April 11, (by telegraph to Clifden, Ireland; thence by wireless.)—As a result of a spirited protest by Senator Béranger, the author of the first offenders' law and the head of the French Society for the Prevention of Vice, the Paris police raided a number of music halls this week where for the past three months the feature of the programmes has been the display of scantily clad women.

Ever since the censorship over Paris theatres was abolished such exhibitions have become bolder, until within the last fortnight the proprietors of music halls carried their daring to the extreme. Foreigners visiting Paris have been startled, and their consternation has been echoed by prominent Parisians. Finally the scandal reached the ears of M. Béranger, who wrote a stinging letter to the Public Prosecutor calling for the intervention of the police. The reply was prompt and decisive. Aside from those raided certain managers received warnings to mend their ways.

Old-timers say that this drastic reform movement which is sweeping over Paris will not last. Meanwhile, it is already condemned by certain Frenchmen, some of them well known in literary and artistic circles. They say that police intervention is entirely uncalled for. Anatole France of the French Academy, for example, publicly insists that the absolute nude is far less immoral than tights.

"There are certain matters of personal taste," said this eminent author, "with which the legislator has nothing to do. Such delicate matters should be left to the average sentiment of the crowd. There is no such thing as absolute morality. Public taste is the sole arbitrator of such exhibitions, which really offend no one. By what right can a legislator find them obscene? Such intervention is purely Calvanistic. Paris is not Geneva."

Collette Willy, the fair danseuse, who often appears in public in scanty attire, expresses an opinion similar in all respects to that of Anatole France. Other authors and artistes are expressing themselves in the same vein.

The police, however, are showing a determination to render such public exhibitions impossible, but alert managers have already discovered a ruse by which they can retain the outlawed numbers on their programmes without falling under the ban of the law. These features are reserved for the close of the performance. Just before they are scheduled to appear, the entire audience is dismissed. A private invitation is then issued to every person present to return as a guest of the management. In this way the spectacle ceases to become a public entertainment. The police have determined to make test cases of some of these pseudo private performances, and, doubtless, before the end of the week the courts, will be called upon to act.

* * *

September 27, 1908

CONTROL OF THE THEATRE IN GERMANY

Owing to the Complex Rules as to Religious Subjects and the Deference Due to Royalty the Berlin Censor Has His Hands Full

Germany is the land of regulations, and the red tape industry flourishes on no other soil' to so great an extent. Things which in America just happen are in Germany made subservient to the order which is the nation's first law. Everything is reduced to a system; the streams run obediently between walled banks, the houses never dare raise their heads higher than the fifth story, the railroads are owned and controlled by the Government, the trains carry a fixed quota of passengers, and the stranger within the gates soon recognizes the fact that there is a law controlling a man's rising up and sitting down. It is scarcely surprising to find this general scheme of control extending into the realm of art.

To present this subject of German theatre censorship to American readers is by no means an easy task, its difficulty lying in finding English equivalents for certain phases of German municipal life, which have absolutely no equivalent in our own civic institutions, and consequently none in our language. A Government official with the title of Regierungsrat (Government Counselor) fills the office of censor, and forms one of the staff of the Theatrical Department of the Polizei Prasidium, (Police Presidency.)

This is a term easily misunderstood on account of the use of the word "police." While the police system of the city comes under its control, this is only a small branch of its wide-spreading jurisdiction, which corresponds very nearly to that of our State Governments, and the Chief of this department, the Polizei Präsident (or President of Police) is a man of high social and official standing, occupying relatively the same position as one of our State Governors. The whole department is under the control of the Minister of the Interior.

It would be better to state here that what follows applies particularly to Berlin conditions, as elsewhere in Germany the work of the censor extends over a circuit including several cities. As not infrequently 6,000,000 judicial acts come up for settlement annually in the City of Berlin alone. It is necessary that a special department be provided for disposing of such business.

All-Embracing Censorship

The Theatrical Division deals directly with all questions of theatrical life in its various ramifications. It is the office of

Hermann Possart—Censor

the censor to pass judgment upon all productions in theatres, opera houses, vaudeville, concert halls, circuses—the control extending even to the cinematographs, which are found in such profusion about the city.

He must approve of all buildings to be used for any of the above purposes, must grant licenses, and see that all precautions against fire are strictly enforced and, to a certain extent, control the workings of the various theatrical agencies. The censor regards all material submitted to him from the threefold viewpoint of its political, religious, and moral aspects.

It is easily understood that in a monarchy the censorship of political questions must, of necessity, be a vigilant one, especially when the reigning monarch or any member of his family is drawn upon to furnish material. In fact, this point is so carefully controlled in Germany that no ruling member of the Hohenzollern house, either living or dead, may be presented upon the stage without the direct consent of the Emperor. This is always given, however, when the characterization is of a proper and dignified manner. The episode of "Der Tote Löwe" ("The Dead Lion") is still fresh in the public mind. Although the setting was Spanish, "the dead lion" was unmistakably Bismarck, and all the incidents pointed so undeniably to the unpleasantness between the Iron Chancellor and Emperor William that the play was not passed by the censors. Later, the decision of the censors was reversed by the higher court of appeals, to which the case was carried, but it was never produced in Berlin, as no manager would take the risk of producing a play of so personal a nature and one singularly lacking in the dramatic element.

The strict censorship of religious plays Berlin is undoubtedly influenced by the well-known aversion of the Empress to anything which deals lightly or irreverently with religious subjects. It is on record that she left the Royal Theatre one evening—where she, together with the young Prince, had gone to see the play of "King Laurens"—because her sense of propriety had been offended by the introduction of some religious episode. Paul Heyse's "Mary Magdala," which Minnie Maddern Fiske played in America, is an interesting example of the difficulty of the religious play in getting through the "needle eye" of the censor.

The records show as the reasons for the prohibition of the drama the facts that "Scriptural passages were literally quoted"—"dramatic use was made of the Passion of Christ"—"the incident of the Crucifixion was introduced in direct connection with Mary Magdala, a fallen woman"—and further offense was given by the "featuring" of the attitude of Mary Magdala toward the Roman centurion, who promises that the life of the Christ will be spared if she yield to the centurion's demands.

When a religious play is under discussion the censors are required to consult with the Minister of the Interior and the Minister of Education. In our republican land it is popularly believed that the Kaiser autocratically chops off the heads of all literary offenders, but such is by no means the case. If he objects to any work, literary or musical, that is put on in Berlin, he can make it known to the censors, and if they, or the author, choose to alter or withdraw the work, well and good. But such a step would simply be done out of courtesy and deference to the wishes of the Emperor, and in no way brought about by royal coercion or compulsion. When an author or a theatrical manager is not satisfied with the decision of the censor he has the privilege of legal redress, and can, in the last instance, carry the question up to the Oberver-waltungsgericht, or the Supreme Court of Justice for the Administration of Municipal Affairs.

Prohibiting Wilde's "Salome"

This was done in the case of Oscar Wilde's "Salome" when the first attempt was made to present it in Berlin as a drama. The censors saw fit to prohibit it, but this decision was overruled by the higher court. While the suit was pending the manager took advantage of the privilege, usually obtainable, of giving what is called a "private performance." This may only take place before an audience of strictly invited guests, the list of which has previously been submitted to the Polizei Präsidium. In the audience, on this occasion, was Dr. Richard Strauss, upon whom the play made so tremendous an impression that he said to one of his friends: "It is nonsense to forbid such a play! I should like to work out the idea into a musical drama." This impression resulted in the opera of "Salome," which is shaking the foundations of the musical world at present.

Strauss also had his bad quarter of an hour with the censors, in this case a royal one, and it was not until a year after the first performance of this epoch-making work in Dresden that it was heard in Berlin at the Royal Opera House. The decision rested solely with the German Emperor, as the two royal theatres do not come under the province of the regular censorship. It is taken for granted that the person in whom the Emperor reposes sufficient confidence to make him General Intendant of the royal theatres will have sufficient discernment and judgment to produce on these two stages nothing that will be offensive to his royal master.

It is generally believed that the royal acquiescence in the "Salome" affair was gained not so much by his reconciliation to the material handled in the text, but on account of the financial profit to be derived.

The Royal Opera House is notoriously not self-supporting, and as in addition to the annual sum of $500,000 which he gives to its support, all deficits must be supplied out of the Emperor's private income, he could not well afford to disdain so money-making a scheme as "Salome."

The moral aspects of any work of art are apt to be judged much more leniently in Germany than in England and America. Certain phases of life and morals which would be an offense to good taste if presented upon our English-speaking stages, are taken here as quite a matter of course. "The play's, the thing"—its outline, rather than its content, is the chief consideration, and if it satisfies as a work of art, the crassest exposition of moral situations is quite calmly accepted.

On certain days in the year, the censorship even extends to the music which may be performed on the legitimate concert stage. Good Friday and Busstag (Day of Repentance) are the most solemnly recognized holy days in the entire Church calendar, and at such times all theatres are closed, (the only days in the year,) and in the concert halls nothing but religious music may be permitted upon the programmes. It is then that the oratorio comes into its own, led by the first, last, and greatest favorite—the noble "St. Matthew's Passion" of Bach.

Two kinds of concessions are granted by the censors: one for "higher art," including opera, operetta, and the drama; the other for vaudeville performances. Houses like the Wintergarten, Metropole, and Apollo, Berlin's three largest variétés, are obliged to take out both concessions, is they frequently include farces or short plays in their répertoire. When only one concession has been secured, nothing in any way trespassing upon the province of the other may be given.

Every vaudeville specialty is closely scrutinized by the censors; acrobats and jugglers have to be passed upon for fear something might be introduced which would endanger the life of the public.

A regulation made by the old Emperor William I., which is still in force, is that no Prussian uniform may be copied accurately on the stage. The inaccuracy may consist of only a slight change in the shape, size, or position of a button, and is always so trifling as to escape the notice of the casual observer. Take for example the very clever comedy of "Hussar Fever," which has been drawing enthusiastic audiences in Berlin the entire season. The stage picture flashes with light and color lent it by the gayly uniformed officers, but only the initiated realize that some trifling accessory in every uniform has been altered to meet this requirement.

In Germany the theatre is taken most seriously and is looked upon as an educational factor, quite as important as the church, State or school. Shakespeare is the German Bible, and it is a well-known fact that more Shakespearean plays are presented annually in Germany than on the English-speaking stages. In Berlin alone there are eleven theatres where Shakespeare dominates the repertoire, and were the Bard of Avon to walk through the streets of the Prussian capital, anxiously scanning the posters, he would have no cause to feel himself "A Stranger in the City," as he is reported to have done several seasons ago in New York. One is practically safe in stating that there is not a single night during the real season, which lasts ten months of the year, when Shakespeare may not be heard on at least one of the Berlin stages.

There is a strong Ibsen cult, but that it is, as yet, confined to literary epicures, and has not penetrated the rank and file, is shown by a chance remark overheard by the writer one evening. The occasion was a holiday performance, and two men of the respectable working classes had been attracted by the lurid title, to indulge in tickets for Ibsen's "Ghosts." Having spent their money, they determined to get their worth of it, but as they left the theatre at the close of the performance one of them gave vent to his feelings with: "Na diesmal sind wir ordentlich 'ringefallen!" ("Well, that's the time we got left!")

Much is done in Germany for the protectors of both managers and actors. Any one wishing to secure a theatre license must be able to prove himself financially, artistically, and morally reliable for such an undertaking. He must have at his disposal a stipulated sum of money—either in the shape of a private fortune or as a guarantee from some reliable financial source, this sum to be regulated by the running expenses of the theatre under his charge. An amount covering the salaries of all persons in any way connected with the theatre, for at least a term of two months, must be deposited for the protection of this personnel in case of the bankruptcy or inability on the part of the manager to carry on the undertaking and fulfill the conditions of his contracts. To be able to judge of the artistic qualifications of any director, the censors need only consult with the presidents of the Bühnenverein, (Society of Theatre Directors,) or the Bühnengenossenschaft, (Society of Actors,) on whose lists every competent director is registered.

This Genossenschaft is an institution which was founded for the benefit of actors and actresses. They have at their disposal many millions which are used as insurance and pensions for the invalids or those who have outlived their sphere of artistic usefulness. The membership fees are merely nominal, as the funds of the society come from endowments and from benefit performances, which occur annually in every theatre in Germany, and the proceeds of which go directly into the coffers of the Genossenschaft for disbursement.

The path of the censor is not strewn with roses, and it takes a man of peculiar tact, and finesse, as well as one whose artistic and literary valuation of the work in hand inspires confidence in the entire theatrical fraternity, be it authors, actors, or managers. The office is at the disposal of the Minister of the Interior, who six years ago appointed as censor Dr. Hermann Possart, a man whose ability is unquestioned. He was reared in an art atmosphere, and although he has not followed the example of his illustrious father, Ernest von Possart, in choosing the stage as a profession, his entire life has nevertheless been a sort of preparatory school for the exacting post he is now filling. In 1904–5 Dr. Possart was sent over by the German Government to investigate American methods, and in his report to the Ministry upon his return, he found much to compliment in the management of theatrical affairs in America. He was particularly impressed by the harmoniousness of our stage settings and the lavish splendor with which our big spectacular plays are presented, and was emphatic in his praise of the efficient work done by our fire brigades, and the general perfection of our technical details.

His report was remarkably free from that Chauvinism so utterly disastrous to any just estimate of prevailing conditions in a foreign country, and he found that the theatrical life of America, like every other phase of our civilization, can give and take ideas from the older art centre of Germany.

* * *

December 20, 1908

UNDRAPED FORM CONDEMNED

Managers and Women Sent to Prison for Displays in Paris

Special Cable to The New York Times

PARIS, Dec. 19—The problem of the display of the undraped female form in the theatre seems interminable, but two cases have been settled once for all this week in the Paris courts. These are the cases of the Little Palace and the Folies Pigalle, which were first tried last July. At that time the court decided there was a difference between an obscene and an artistic display, so it condemned the manager of the Little Palace to three months in prison and two of the women to fifteen days in prison. The display at the Folies Pigalle, having been adjudged artistic, the manager and the women were acquitted. The manager of the Little Palace appealed the first case, and the Minister of Justice appealed the second.

Not only does the higher court sustain the decision about the Little Palace, but it adds a month to the prison term of the manager and doubles the time of the two women. It reverses the decision about the Folies Pigalle and gives the manager three months in prison and each of the women concerned fifteen days.

* * *

December 28, 1908

POLICE PERMIT ONLY TAME VAUDEVILLE

Sharp Eye Kept on Every Sunday Amusement and Everything Censored

EVEN DIALECT IS BARRED

Moving-Picture Shows Recruit "Educational Lecturers" to Keep the Police at Rest

New York got strictly revised vaudeville yesterday. In all of the big houses the plain clothes men of the precinct watched events while the managers watched them out of one eye. Neither the managers nor their patrons seemed to like the dilution that was served.

"It was the poorest lot of stuff that New York has seen in a long time," said one of them: "that is to say, there was too much sameness."

The managers had tried to keep within the law. There were many musical acts—numbers of them in succession. There were monologues where on weekdays there had been sketches. And then there were "educational lectures."

There were ample reminders during the day that the police had some definite ideas regarding what should and what should not constitute Sunday performances. There was the case of Cliff Gordon over at the American, one of the houses controlled by William Morris. Gordon usually delivers a political speech in costume. Yesterday afternoon he gave the speech without costume, but in dialect. Acting Captain Maher of the West Thirty-seventh Street Station ordered his arrest on the ground that he was impersonating a German.

"It's the first time I ever heard that a man could impersonate himself," said Gordon to Detective Cleary, with a broad German accent, which he stoutly maintained through all of yesterday was his own personal property, of which he could not rid himself. But he and the Sunday Superintendent of the theatre, John Pinklor, went to the station house. They were promptly provided with bondsmen.

"You see," said Gordon later. "I was saying a few things about the police when they arrested me. I told the audience that this town was really run by Hughes as Mayor, and that if Ireland should be free we wouldn't have any police force here, because all the Irishmen would return to Ireland, and we could give Sunday shows without being pinched."

A Voyage of Discovery

Gordon repeated his performance last night in the same German dialect, adding something about his station house experiences.

"Columbus said to Queen Isabelle," said he, " 'give me a few schooners and I'll discover America.' Well, give a man in this country a few schooners and he'll discover a station house. I discovered a station house this afternoon, utterly alone and unaided by schooners."

Then there was the case of the Faust brothers in a Fourteenth Street Theatre. They were giving a musical turn. According to the management of the house, one of the brothers limps naturally. As they started to leave the stage this brother limped. The audience laughed. The police said "vaudeville" and arrested them, with the manager of the house.

The opinion of Corporation Counsel Pendleton had stated that the only moving pictures entitled to a Sunday view were those illustrating a lecture of an instructive or educational value. So where moving pictures were shown, whether in vaudeville houses or five-cent moving picture shows, there was always a "lecturer." This was the way it was done at Hammerstein's Victoria:

Upon a screen was thrown the title, "Travels in Northern Europe." Then a moving picture showing a railway track with scenery on either side appeared on the screen, giving the impression of a journey from an unusual angle. The "lecturer" stepped down left, centre. As the track first appeared he announced: "Railroad track."

Then he was silent for several minutes. Meanwhile the film had spun along. The track was still in view.

"More railroad track," said the lecturer. The audience, thoroughly appreciating the situation, laughed and applauded.

The film traveled faster. The land of the journey was now in the region of snows. The reindeer appeared at the side of the track.

"Reindeer," announced the educational lecturer.

Suddenly the reindeer lowered their heads and seemed to be eating Iceland moss or snow or something.

"Luncheon on snow," said the lecturer. Then the film darkened.

"Pennsylvania Tunnel," said the lecturer.

Dull Along the Bowery

For the first time in years the Bowery was partially dark. The management of the London, Windsor, and Miner Theatres decided that they could not comply with the law and give the sort of shows that would please their patrons. So they remained closed. The People's and Grand Street Theatres gave concerts.

In Delancey Street a little five-cent place showed a moving picture of the life of Christ with a lecture. The police of the East Fifth Street Station found a little place at 15 East Third Street in which there were 381 persons, while the license permitted only 299. They arrested the manager, Max Markowitz, of 12 Second Avenue. The assistant manager dismissed eighty-two of the patrons and went on with the moving picture show with his "lecturer."

In the Thalta Theatre Bernard Young and his wife were arrested for appearing in a sketch in costume. These were the only arrests for an appearance in costume.

The police of the Tenderloin went to Keith & Proctor's Fifth Avenue and told them that they could not give a vaudeville show, as that was prohibited.

"We are not going to give a vaudeville show," said the management: "you had better wait and see our show."

They waited. Lucy Weston forgot all about costumes and sang what the management afterward called a "school girlish kind of a song." They didn't arrest her. Then there was a band that played. They didn't arrest that. Then there were monologues and an educational feature. This was a lecture on Arizona with pictures. The girl who dives in a bathing suit didn't dive, and the Gibson girls didn't come out, and the imitators didn't imitate.

The managers of the leading vaudeville houses seemed to think that the matter of the Sunday show would work itself out ultimately.

"There was only one house in the city," said one of them, "that gave a good show. They hit the people hard because their last week's bill happened to have in it many acts that by a slight modification could be made to come within the law. The other shows clearly dissatisfied the audiences. I do not think that people will want to pay for such shows on another Sunday."

Percy G. Williams, business manager of the United Booking Offices of America, which makes the bookings for most of the vaudeville houses in the city, said that he did not intend to apply for injunctions.

"Arrests will be made from time to time," said he, "and decisions will be made that will clarify things. We shall obey the law in every particular."

At the Grand Opera House, Eighth Avenue and Twenty-third Street, Capt. Kane of the old West Twentieth Street Station watched the show with four of his men. One performer spoke with an accent. The Captain and his men went behind the scenes and questioned the actor.

A Genuine Article

"I was satisfied," said Capt. Kane later, "that the man is a foreigner and speaks with an accent naturally."

In the Murray Hill a quartet sang. Between two of the songs the baritone struck the second tenor with a newspaper.

"Cut that out," said the police at the rear of the house, "that's vaudeville, if it isn't acting."

So they eliminated the quartet.

The moving-picture men of the five-cent places whose licenses had been revoked by the Mayor were happy. To be sure, they were compelled to have a "lecturer," and their pictures had to be illustrations of an instructive or educational lecture.

But they were glad to be able to operate on any terms whatever. The injunctions, which had been served on the Police Department the previous night and orders sent out by Commissioner Bingham that they were not to be interfered with had made it possible for them to be open.

However, the lecture matter was a trifle inconvenient. An usher with an extensive vocabulary of patois could not be expected to know much about Arabian pottery or the interior of China. But they did their best, and the audience enjoyed it. There were some arrests among them, however, not because of the revoked licenses, but because of alleged violations of the Sunday laws.

In the place of Max Ellenpuch, 899 Eighth Avenue, the police arrested the proprietor, saying that there was no "lecturer" and that the pictures represented robberies and kidnappings. The proprietor found some one to sign a $500 bond. And then the programme was changed and a lecturer recruited.

* * *

February 21, 1909

CENSORING THE STAGE AT HOME AND ABROAD

By A VETERAN DIPLOMAT

Where in the Old World the censorship of the stage is vested in the hands of the Government, and more especially of royalty, here in America it is exercised by the people. Sometimes the latter become rather lax in performance of their duties in connection therewith.

But, when reminded of their obligations, as they were a fortnight or three weeks ago, by Archbishop Farley, whose remarks from the pulpit of St. Patrick's Cathedral were indorsed by divines of every denomination, they do not hesitate to act. Indeed, one of the most interesting things to a foreigner has been the manifestation which they have just given of their power, in compelling the syndicate controlling some 95 per cent of the theatres of the United States, to blacklist, on the score of impropriety, certain objectionable plays that have recently been presented to the public in New York.

The syndicate in question is alleged to dominate the American stage, and has been subjected to no end of abuse in connection with its alleged tyranny. But it is the people that control the syndicate, and when public sentiment condemns a play as subversive of morality, the syndicate has no alternative but to defer to the views of its patrons and masters, that is to say, the people.

Thanks to the community of language enjoyed by Great Britain and the United States, something very much akin to brotherhood exists with regard to literature and the drama of the two countries. Successful plays, like successful books are as a rule produced almost simultaneously on both sides of the ocean.

No footlight favorites hailing from the land of the Stars and Stripes consider that their laurels have attained the necessary richness of volume and hue until they have several London seasons to their record; while in the same way all the leading English actors and actresses find it conducive to their reputation, and more especially to the welfare of their exchequer, to undertake at least two, and sometimes a still greater number of American tours.

Owing to this the nature and extent of the censorship exercised by the British Crown over the stage in the United Kingdom is tolerably familiar to people here, the more so as much has been printed in the American press about the matter.

Comparatively little, however, is known of the conditions of the censorship of the drama on the Continent of Europe. The relations between the authorities and the stage are of an entirely different character, and the control much more arbitrary. This is due to a variety of considerations.

In the first place, the opera in each of the Continental capitals, and likewise a number of leading theatres, receive large annual subventions, which in monarchical countries, come from the purse of the sovereign, while in France they are derived from the national exchequer. Without these subsidies the management would not find it possible to make both ends meet, and being in consequence dependent thereon, are obliged to comply with the wishes and directions of their paymasters.

Then, too, the authority of the executive and of the officers of the Government is more complete, more despotic, and people accustomed thereto from their birth submit in a manner that would revolt the sense of freedom of the American citizen, or even of the Briton.

Thus, an order from the Minister of the Interior, or from the Prefect of Police, addressed to a manager, is obeyed at once and without any idea of resistance or of appeal to the courts for those injunctions which are always invoked here in America against any public officer who attempts to fulfill his duty.

Yet another consideration is the extraordinary interest which the members of the reigning houses of the Continent manifest in everything connected with the stage. Some of them have distinguished themselves as playwrights, others as impresarios. A few of them have even sought applause of the public from before the footlights, while a very large number of them have taken their wives from the stage, and have thus through the influence of the companionship of their morganatic consorts, become imbued with theatrical ideas, tastes, and even prejudices. Under the circumstances, it is not astonishing that the relations between the throne and the stage are exceedingly close.

Of course the ideas of the authorities, and especially those of the sovereign are not always in accord with public sentiment, and this renders the control of the stage by Crown and Government unpopular. In fact, the censorship has been dubbed in France, Germany, Austria, and Italy, with the nickname of "Anastasie," not by way of compliment, but with an object quite the reverse.

Anastasie is understood to have been a lady who in ancient times was renowned for the contrariness and obtuseness of her character, and it is because these characteristics of hers are according to public sentiment, so conspicuous in state and royal supervision and control of the drama, that her name has been applied to the censorship. Some assert, however, that the sobriquet originates with Emperor Anastasius I. of Byzantium, who incurred the animosity of his subjects by abolishing those shows in the circus at Constantinople in which wild beasts were pitted against unfortunate slaves and captives.

Neither in ancient nor yet in modern times has the public been disposed to take a friendly view of those who interfered with its pastimes, no matter how moral or high principled the motives that prompt the intervention. Hence, Anastasie when used in connection with the stage on the Continent of Europe is meant to imply reproach and contempt.

The character and the extent of the sway of Anastasie is regulated not by any law, but purely by the taste and even by the caprice of those in authority. Thus, during the reign of the late King Leopold, who toward the close of his life developed a piety and a prudery to which he had been a stranger in his earlier years, the censorship of the drama in Belgium was extremely strict.

To-day, however, the license of the Belgian stage is unbridled, except in one particular. No play ridiculing any foreign ruler or holding him up to obloquy is tolerated for fear of international complications. But there is no objection to any fun being poked at Leopold II. himself.

At Liège, in the Flora Theatre, a play entitled "Les Fetards," (which may be roughly translated as "The Profligates,") was run recently for a number of weeks without any interference by the police, although the King was the central figure in the piece, and all the most questionable episodes of his life were represented in a way calculated to hold him up to the contumely of respectable people.

Some time later the popular Belgian comedian Crommelynck appeared in a somewhat similar play at the Scaia Theatre at Brussels, made up as the King so as to represent a most amazing likeness, with long nose, long white beard, slightly lame walk, and the peculiar stoop of the shoulders—in fact, the very image of the King.

Leopold is the only European sovereign now living to have been thus portrayed and ridiculed on the stage, and that, too, by his own people. According to some, his failure to exercise the authority which he possesses to put a stop to this unusual form of lese majesté is because he assumes that it is far more politic, from a dynastic point of view, to permit his lieges to thus give vent to their feelings, than to attempt to bottle them up and thus provoke an explosion.

Others ascribe his attitude to more cynical indifference, the result of the demoralization produced by questionable associations with women of this character of the notorious Baroness Vaughan, and the equally objectionable lady who used to go by the name of the "Queen of the Congo."

In Germany, as in Belgium, the character of the stage today reflects the morality of the ruler rather than that of the people. Emperor William's private life is as blameless as that of Leopold is the reverse. His principles on the score of morality are of the strictest, and he has in consequence thereof set his face sternly against all plays calculated to offend his own sense of propriety, or, in his opinion, to injuriously affect the public morality. His subjects, indeed, blame him for excessive Puritanism in availing himself of his power to prevent the public representation of a number of Sudermann's most powerful plays.

He insists that the stage should constitute an important factor in the raising of the tone, of the character, and morality of the public, instead of being used to develop low tastes and promote depravity. Looking upon himself in a way as responsible for the result of the lesson taught by the drama, he takes

Krieghofe

his self-imposed obligations as its censor very seriously to heart—so much so, that he is led thereby not merely to direct play-wrights what to emphasize and what to eliminate, but even to personally supervise and direct the rehearsals, and to actually school actors and actresses as to the manner in which they should play their parts.

The Opera at Berlin, and a number of theatres in that city, as well as other theatres at Breslau, Hanover, Wiesbaden, &c., all draw such large subsidies from his civil list, as to convert them into royal houses, and of course he is even still more particular about the plays produced there than at the non-subventioned theatres. Indeed, one frequently hears of his having traveled all the way from Berlin to Wiesbaden to direct a dress rehearsal.

This excites no amazement or amusement among those even of his subjects who grumble at his prudery. For they realize that he is prompted by the best of motives, namely, a consideration for their own welfare, and for that of their children. Here in America paternalism on the part of the Executive has not yet reached such lengths, and one is tempted to speculate upon the comments that would be created in New York by an announcement that President Roosevelt had come up from Washington to supervise the dress rehearsal, and to revise, in the interests of propriety, the production, say, of "Salome," or of "Thals."

Everything in this connection is relative. Queen Wilhelmina's piety and regard for the morals of the Dutch led her to prevent the production at Amsterdam some time ago of a translation of Emile Augier's exquisite play, "Gabrielle," on the score of its alleged impropriety, although it had obtained at Paris the "Monthyon" prize "for virtue" from the Academy of France.

At Rome during the last administration of Crispi, a play was prohibited from further representation, the management being subjected thereby to a heavy loss, solely because it had given offense to the Premier's wife, Dona Lina Crispi, a lady of more than questionable antecedents. Her action in the matter precipitated a Cabinet crisis. For just before Dona Lina swept out of her box with indigestion and disgust expressed upon her features, Queen Margherita, who was likewise present, in another box, had been laughing heartily, and applauding vigorously.

Queen Margherita, who is the best-natured woman in the world, and who throughout her life has been immune from every breath of scandal—the truest of wives and most devoted of mothers—could not but take exception to the behavior of Mme. Crispi, and complained of the affront to King Humbert. Dona Lina, however, insisted that the play was shocking to her notions of propriety, and caused her husband to intimate to the King that unless he had the monarch's sanction to prohibit its further performance, he would resign office, carrying along with him the entire Cabinet.

For an entire day Humbert hesitated, and then, prompted by political and dynastic considerations, gave way to the Premier, thus ending the Cabinet crisis, while Queen Margherita added one more item to the long list of causes of profound aversion which she entertained for the woman who was more responsible than any one else for Crispi's final downfall and sad death namely, Dona Lina.

In Paris, Victor Hugo's "Hernani" and other masterpieces of the dramatic art were prohibited throughout the eighteen years reign of the third Napoleon, while since his downfall the government of the Republic has at one time or another barred the production of "Thermidor" by Sardou, of "Germinal" by Zola, of "La Fille Eliza" by de Concourt, and a play the name of which I forget, but which dealt with the life of the most famous French actress of the nineteenth century, namely, Desciee, and represented her as falling in love with Baron de Renzis, who was at the time an aide de camp of the late King Victor Emmanuel, and who died as Italian Ambassador at the Court of St. James.

The family of the Baron took exception to the role in which he figured in the play, declaring that it was calculated to bring discredit on his memory, and the play was at once stopped, by order of the French Government. Indeed, the powers of the Minister of the Interior and of the Prefect of Police are very extensive in this respect, and also unquestioned, and in recent years have been successfully invoked, not only to bar the production of plays giving offense to important people at home and abroad, but even to prevent the appearance before the foot-lights of men and woman, bearers of historic names, and whose object in seeking the applause of the public was to win a "succes a scandale," and to thus extort money from their family.

One of the strictest censors of the drama in Europe, and at the same time one of its most enthusiastic patrons, is the present Sultan. Until the coup d'etat of last Autumn at Stamboul, he maintained two private companies, one operatic and the other purely dramatic. He was extremely averse to anything being represented on the stage that ridiculed religion, or that offended his sense of what was due to considerations of morality and of respect for those in authority.

A whole list of famous operas were either barred altogether, or else modified in such a fashion as to cause their creators to turn in their graves. The oddest feature, however, of these theatrical and operatic performances, at the Yildiz Kiosque, was that resulting from his prohibition to permit children to figure in the theatrical performances at night.

Thus, I recall on one occasion a performance of the opera "Norma," to which he had invited some foreign guests. When the time came for the pathetic scene where the two young children rush in and kneel before Norma, who bends down and strokes their heads and kisses them, our gravity was tried to the utmost by the appearance in their stead of two strapping, heavily mustached members of the Imperial bodyguard, booted, spurred, and "coiffed" with the tarboosh. It was indescribably funny to any one who had seen the opera performed elsewhere.

But the Sultan failed to perceive anything humorous about the situation, and showed that he was much moved by the pathos of the scene. His objection to children on the stage is, according to his own account, attributable to the conviction, shared by good old Commodore Gerry here in New York, that young people ought to be in bed at night time, and that the excitement of a theatrical performance and the glare of the foot-lights are calculated to injure their nervous system.

While many Princes and Princesses of the blood have appeared upon the stage as amateurs, some of them indeed being extremely fond of this form of diversion, there is one alone who may be said to have graduated from the dramatic profession to a European throne, namely, Prince Florestan of Monaco, the grandfather of the present ruler of the Rouge et Noir principality.

Florestan up to the time when his elder brother, Honore V., succeeded somewhat unexpectedly to the crown of Monaco through the death of a distant relative, was earning his living as a very fourth rate actor, at the Porte St. Martin Theatre, at Paris, and it was during that period of his life, when leading a hand-to-mouth existence, that he considered himself as favored by fortune in securing the hand of Caroline Gibert, only daughter of a small charcutier, or pork butcher, in one of the poorer quarters of the French capital. This matrimonial alliance assured him at least of food every day which he had often until then lacked.

When his elder brother Honore became reigning Prince of Monaco, Florestan Grimaldi abandoned the stage, and was accorded an annuity, which enabled him to live with his wife and children in comfort, and in due course he became sovereign of Monaco in his brother's stead. It is said that Florestan was exceedingly majestic and impressive as a monarch. He had the bearing, indeed, of the ruler of a mighty empire, rather than of the tiniest state in Europe. He owed that to his training as an actor of the Porte St. Martin.

If Grand Duke Constantine Constantinowitch had his way I sometimes think that he would have been glad to abandon his status as a Prince of the reigning house of Russia for the stage. For he is never so happy as when organizing and taking an actual part in some dramatic performance. According to the cable dispatches of last Wednesday, he had made his appearance the evening before at the Imperial Court Theatre of the Czar's palace of Tsarskoe Sëlo as the hero in Schiller's "Bride of Messina," which he had translated for the purpose from the German.

Some five years ago he produced, also at the Court Theatre of Tsarskoe Selo, his own translation of "Hamlet," with himself in the title role. So enthusiastic was his devotion to the study of Shakespeare's works, many of which he has translated into Russian, that in 1907 he was overtaken by the strange fate that seems to dog the footsteps of those who give themselves up to the study and portrayal of Hamlet. His mind became temporarily affected, and for a time he was convinced that he was not a Prince of Russia, but the Prince of Denmark.

Matters reached such a pass that the Emperor was obliged to appoint Grand Duke Demetrius Constantinovitch to assume the guardianship of his brother's interests and family. But by dint of complete rest and the best of medical attention, and above all, thanks to the devoted nursing of his admirable wife, he has completely recovered, and has now apparently abandoned Shakespeare for Schiller.

Let me add that the reigning Prince of Montenegro has translated into Slavio many of the works of Shakespeare, who has received a similar tribute from the late King Oscar, who translated them into Swedish, and from King Luis, grandfather of the present King of Portugal, to whom his subjects are indebted for a Portuguese version of the principal masterpieces of England's "Immortal Bard."

In Portugal, it may be added, by way of conclusion, there lives in the utmost retirement, a former American actress, a native of Boston, who became the morganatic wife of the late King Ferdinand of Portugal, and is now his widow under the name of Countess Edla.

The reigning Duke of Saxe-Meiningen (whose eldest son and heir has as consort Princess Charlotte of Prussia, sister of the Kaiser) has been married morganatically for nearly forty years to a once famous actress, Helen Franz, now Baroness Heldburg. It is mainly owing to her influence that for a quarter of a century the Duke devoted himself to the organization of the company of actors and actresses of his court theatre at Meiningen into the most perfect dramatic troupe of the age. He spared no money, time, or labor, and, guided by his actress-wife, undertook all the duties of an impresario.

Saxe-Meiningen is one of those tiny German sovereignties that invite ridicule by reason of their size, and that have furnished so fertile a theme to the satire of Thackeray and of Offenbach. But the name of this particular Duchy is celebrated throughout the civilized world, especially in the world of culture and of art, for its court theatre company. Of late years the Duke has been compelled by advancing years and infirmities to live almost entirely abroad, chiefly in Italy.

The memory, however, of the splendid company which he brought into existence still endures, to the honor and glory of little Saxe-Meiningen. Still another ruler of a petty German state to wed an actress has been Prince Henry XIV. of Reuss. It turned out to be a very happy union, and the death of Mme. von Saalburg, as she was styled, and which occurred some eighteen months ago, was such a shock to the old Prince that his reason gave way, and it became necessary to invest his son with the regency in his stead.

As to the mere Princes of the blood who have taken their wives from the stage—in morganatic marriage of course—their number is legion, and among the most notable cases has been that of Duke Louis of Bavaria, the eldest brother of the late Empress of Austria, of the widowed ex-Queen of Naples, and of that saintly Duchess d'Alencon who perished in the Charity Bazaar fire.

Duke Louis married, first, one actress of the name of Henrietta Mendel, and after her death another footlight favorite of the name of Antonie Barth. Tiring of her recently, he announced his intention of obtaining an annulment of the union, and of wedding a third and much younger actress but was fortunately dissuaded therefrom by his relatives, who pointed out to him that being in the neighborhood of eighty, he might be reasonably expected by his family to have sown his wild oats, and to have attained the years of discretion.

In fact, it is no exaggeration to state that there is hardly a sovereign house in Europe that has not to its record instances of matrimonial alliances between its members and dramatic and lyric artistes, and under the circumstances it is impossible to deny that there are many ties of relationship in Europe between the stage and the throne.

* * *

June 20, 1909

PROBLEM OF STAGE CENSORSHIP

The question of what should or should not be permitted on the stage is a kind of moral sea serpent, bobbing up serenely once in so often to promote strife or add to the gayety of nations, as the case may be. By a happy chance just now when the most tenacious of us can pretend to no further interest in the tariff discussion, when the muck-rakers have ceased from tolling, and society is at rest, there arises this old problem which forever burns and is never consumed. And in what lively fashion it comes to the front this time, with President Taft leaving the theatre in Washington and Mayor Hibbard of Boston establishing the first and only genuine censorship of the stage in America.

There are those who say the President was not actuated by moral considerations in leaving his box before a certain play was over, and there are others who say he was. This is a vexed question, but the matter of Boston's Mayor is no such thing. He is very emphatic in his statement that a few plays which have run successfully all Winter in New York may not be given in the neighborhood of the gilded dome unless the shears are first piled with vigor.

"I am determined that the shows put on in Boston shall be clean," says Mayor Hibbard.

Not only in Washington and Boston is there indignation over some of this Winter's New York productions. Here at home there has been lively discussion as to what shall be done to keep within the bounds of decency, only we are not so sure where the line should be drawn. At the National Conference of Church Clubs, recently held here, Bishop Greer went on record as declaring that it was high time for the Church to enter, the lists and "cut this canker from the modern stage."

"I am not criticising the theatre as such, but I am condemning those indecent, immodest, and suggestive plays now on the stage," said the Bishop, and he seemed very sure that the Church could and would do much. So here we have both the Church and State interested in theatrical affairs.

When Mr. Winthrop Ames, Director of The New Theatre, and therefore to be referred to as the exponent of the higher life of the stage, was asked what he thought of a censorship of plays in this country, he replied that he was not sure it would not be a good thing.

"But," he said, "the question of what shall or shall not be said and done on the stage is not to be settled by any onc man, and most certainly not by one man merely because he holds a municipal office, and who does not therefore necessarily possess any special artistic or literary judgment.

"In forbidding the production of a play one would have to be very sure that the evil intention was in the mind of the playwright and not of the reader. For this reason several men would have to pass judgment, lest, through some quirk in the mind of one of them, an intelligent and sincere piece of work might be lost to the world. Nothing that is really salacious ever lives, no matter with how much genius it is written. The plays of The Restoration are dead because they were put together for a salacious purpose. Shakespeare's plays contain many situations and lines intolerable to modern taste, but live forever because there was no evil intention. This is the eternal distinction that has to be borne in mind.

"It seems to me that in the case of plays written with honest intent we should drop the classification 'decent' and 'indecent' and adopt rather Mr. Shaw's division of 'pleasant' and 'unpleasant.' " Nobody wants anything indecent on the stage, but through reckless use the word has come to be applied where unpleasant is really what is meant. It is time to draw a distinction and to impress that distinction firmly on the public mind."

It has been pointed out in regard to the adaptations of French farces given over here that they were originally produced in theatres to which young girls are not supposed to go. Mr. Ames was hardly disposed to fancy that this distinction would work over here.

Winthrop Ames

"Isn't it a splendid tribute to the American stage that mothers have so freely consented to their daughters going to theatres without inquiry as to which theatre it might be? I don't think we will ever have the distinction that exists in Paris, where young women never step inside certain theatres."

Thus speak the dignitaries. Realizing that there are two sides to every question, the seeker after truth discussed the matter with the "young person" herself, as embodied in a bright stenographer, at whose door, there always waits a long line of youths with theatre tickets in their pockets.

"Yes," she said, "I've seen the plays talked about, and what's more I've heard all the girls in the office discussing them. The conclusions they drew seemed pretty amazing to me. They didn't seem to see much that was shocking in those French adaptations. They seemed ready to laugh at vice without taking in how lowering it is to do such a thing. I call that pretty bad, don't you? And they are all the pink of propriety and were horrified at that poor thing in The Easiest Way. They hadn't a word of pity for her, while they roared over the disreputable little creatures who took to vice just for the fun of the thing. Queer point of view, isn't it?"

"So it seems to me the stage had better get busy and educate the public somehow or else plays that give girls, without their realizing it, the idea that vice is all right when it's a joke, should be stopped."

* * *

October 7, 1910

FIGHTING THE DRAMATIC CENSOR IN LONDON

From London comes the news that eighteen dramatists have signed a letter and sent it to the papers there urging that steps be taken to make it possible to appeal from the decision of the Dramatic Censor. That makes it apparent that the fight of the British playwrights against the censor, which has been waged furiously for years, is by no means to be given up, in spite of the setback the playwrights received last Fall.

The action of the eighteen who now come to the fore has been caused by the censorial ban placed on Laurence Housman's play dealing with King George IV. and Queen Caroline. This ban, according to those signing the letter favoring curtailment of the censor's powers, shows "the imperative advisability that the judgment of the Lord Chamberlain, in his capacity as censor of plays, be made subject to appeal."

It may be pointed out that this war has been conducted with such bitterness that many of its attacks have been leveled not only at the existence of the office of censor, but at, the censor personally. His name is George Alexander Redford and he has borne these onslaughts with calm.

One interesting point about the censorship dispute is that the majority of the London managers are opposed to the elimination of the censorship. In his relation with the drama, Censor Redford deals directly with these managers, practically ignoring the authors. This is one of the things that especially galls the latter.

George Bernard Shaw has time and again said biting things about the censorship in general and Mr. George Alexander Redford in particular, several of the Shavian dramas having failed to please that captious official. One of these—"Mrs. Warren's Profession"—Mr. Redford shelved, so far as London was concerned, with the sculpted words: "Clever but impossible."

Last year Shaw again fell afoul of Mr. Redford when the latter vetoed Shaw's play about "Blanco Posnet." At that time the Irish dramatist, with sardonic gravity, suggested that he himself should be named censor of plays.

The manifesto in The London Times followed Mr. Redford's action regarding two plays by two young British dramatists. These were "Waste," by Granville Barker, and "The Breaking Point," by Edward Garnett. Of them Mr. Redford said:

"Very, very clever, but impossible."

He suggested that they publish the plays in book form, in order that the British public might judge whether or not they were suitable for production on the stage. In vain the young playwrights besieged him with entreaties and angry stormings. He would not budge an inch. Thereupon Garnett published "The Breaking Point" in book form, calling attention in his preface to the cruel treatment his work had received when submitted to the despot Redford. Barker managed to get his play produced privately by the Incorporated Stage Society, in order that he might find out what people thought of it. Censor Redford must have grinned at the verdict on "Waste." At least two London papers said that the play showed the advisability of having a censor on the job to keep such plays from production.

The office of censor came into definite existence during the premiership of Sir Robert Walpole, who was in power under George I. and George II.; before that time there was something resembling it under Queen Anne. Its primary object, it is said, was to give the Government a chance to forbid the production of Fielding's plays. For many years the censor's powers were vague, and often used for political ends, but they were made really definite in 1843, and since that time he has been very much to the fore in the history of Great Britain's drama.

A curious thing about the censorship is that it exercises no jurisdiction over plays written previous to the Walpole régime. These may be produced to-day with impunity, no matter what their character may be. Another anomaly is that no Biblical characters are allowed to have speaking parts in a play, but plays like "Everyman," in which God Almighty appears but says nothing, are allowed.

In all, there are thirty-two rules which dramatists must bear in mind if they wish to see their plays on the stage in Great Britain.

As for Mr. Redford, about whom the opposition to the censorship has raged with such fury, someone described him as "the mildest mannered man that ever scuttled a play." He has been connected with play censorship since 1873, and gets a salary of $2,000 a year. Besides that, he charges $10.30 for looking over each play submitted to him. Whenever anyone produces a play without his permission he levies a fine of $200.

In spite of his having worked in a bank, the remark of one of his enemies that he should have remained there is not necessarily true. That his leanings toward matters literary and his capacity for judging what's what in the drama may be far more respectable than Shaw and others would have us suppose, is evidenced by the fact that he is the son of a man who gave up medicine for a literary career. This man—George Redford was his name—not only won distinction as a critic on The London Times and Daily News, but counted, among his personal friends, Browning, George Eliot, Trollop, Leighton, George Henry Lewes, and Wilkie Collins.

The present censor met many of the literary lights of the day in his father's home before he ever undertook to pass judgment on plays. Before occupying his present office, he also served an apprenticeship under E. F. S. Pigott, Examiner of Plays. It was when the latter died in 1800 that Mr. Redford became a full-fledged censor.

It is not only new works, by British dramatists that have failed of late to win Mr. Redford's approval. A few years ago there was a storm of protest when he suddenly cast a hostile eye on Gilbert & Sullivan's "The Mikado," which had been playing triumphantly for a matter of twenty years all over England, the United States, and several countries on the Continent of Europe. Investigation showed that Censor Radford was not entirely to blame in this instance. The unexpected ban on "The Mikado" was, as it turned out, inspired by "somebody higher up," at whose back the censor was obliged to act even at variance with his own judgment. There were "reasons of state" mixed up on it reason connected with the British-Japanese entente. Be that as it may, Redford soon found W. S. Gilbert lined up against him in the ranks of those wishing to see his job abolished.

Then, too, several foreign plays, by dramatists of high international repute, were adjudged by the censor unfit for production on a British stage. Among these were Ibsen's "Ghosts," Maeterlinck's "Monua Vanna," and Brieux's "Maternité."

On the occasion of one of the most bitter attacks against him, Mr. Redford had a few things to say about himself and his ticklish position.

"There's no such thing as pleasing everybody," he declared. "Some persons don't seem to realize that there cannot be one sort of play acted at all the theatres, nor do they seem to realize that I do not write the plays myself, but merely read them. Most of the time nothing more is necessary. Sometimes I find a scene or a bit of dialogue, or even one speech, which I know would be offensive on the stage. In that case I communicate with the manager who has submitted the play and suggest that some changes be made and the play sent me for a second examination.

"I am not a censor. I never censorize over anybody. I merely use the experience I have gained from a long association with theatrical matters to administer the regulations of my office. There is no such thing as an offhand decision about interdicting a play. No play is ever prohibited without the most careful thought, and every chance is given to authors to tone down their work whenever it is possible."

* * *

December 1, 1910

CLEVELAND BARS "SALOME"

Mayor Will Not Let Mary Garden Appear—St. Louis Lenient

CLEVELAND, Nov. 30—Mary Garden will not be allowed to appear in "Salome" here. Mayor Baehr so announced to-day when the manager of the theatre at which the grand opera star is booked to appear soon asked him if he would interfere with the performance of the Strauss opera.

The Mayor said he would do as Chicago has done.

Special to The New York Times

ST. LOUIS, Mo., Nov. 30—Chief Young of the St. Louis Police Department, will allow the presentation of "Salome," objectionable to Chicago and St. Paul, until a point where in the opinion of the "morality squad," it gets shocking. If it grates on their finer sensibilities they will stop the performance.

While Young has taken into consideration the action of Chief Steward of Chicago, he has decided that St. Louis must judge for itself. It cannot judge without seeing the performance, and since only one performance will be given, it looks like St. Louis will see the opera and Mary Garden unmolested, for never in the history of the "morality squad" have they shut down on a questionable performance.

Many leaders in St. Louis society are opposed to the presentation, however, and want St. Louis to follow in the wake of Chicago.

Special to The New York Times

DETROIT, Mich., Nov. 30—"Salome" will not live, nor any of those average modern weird things in the musical line, but as long as criticism is directed toward the production people will want to see it," said Mme. Bernice Pasquale of the Metropolitan Opera forces here to-day.

"I am really not competent to comment intelligently on the banishment of Miss Mary Garden's Salome by the Chicago authorities. Although having several opportunities to witness 'Salome,' I have never taken the trouble to view the production. After reading about it I decided it, was too gruesome for me to see and hear. There is no soft, delicate music in 'Salome,' and therefore it could not possibly appeal to me."

* * *

May 14, 1911

CENSORS DESTROYED EVIL PICTURE FILMS

National Board Weeded Out 2,000,000 Feet of Objectionable Motion Scenes

IMPROVEMENT IN THE SHOWS

Manufacturers Working in Co-operation with Censors and Paying Part of Their Expenses

In the two years that the National Board of Censorship of Moving Pictures has been in existence it has, according to its annual report, passed upon 5,200 subjects and has caused the destruction, as unfit for public display, of 2,000,000 feet of objectionable films, which represent a value of $200,000. As each of the pictures is on the average duplicated seventy-five times and each copy would be seen by thousands of people, the board feels it has justified its existence.

In this belief it is confirmed by testimony from the authorities of many widely dispersed cities. Only Topeka, Kan., declares the influence for good of the board is not evident, while inquiries dispatched to such places as St. Louis,

Atlanta, Ga.; Portland, Ore.; Detroit, and Washington have resulted in reports of evident improvement.

The board considers it important to note that it is working with the moving picture men, and a large part of its expenses are paid by them. It has found that the manufacturers value the censorship, because of its restraining influence on the less responsible members of the trade, and believe it to be to their commercial advantage to present as high a standard as the condition of the public mind and the resources of the motion picture art allow.

The policy of the board is thus set forth in the report:

The drama of all ages has dealt with real life and its serious moral problems, and the Board of Censorship recognizes that moving pictures are essentially a form of drama. But the Censoring Committee insists that there shall be no sensationalism and no representation of crime except with the object of conveying a moral lesson. "Crime for crime's sake" is condemned. Certain socially forbidden themes are, of course, proscribed, and any leaning toward oversensationalism is discouraged.

Much that the adult receives and can healthfully digest simply goes over the heads of children, and if children are defended from the calculated immoral lesson and from excessive scenes of horror and violence, and from a too large proportion of any kind of violence, much, at least, has been accomplished. In any case the child is subject both to his parents and to the local laws which, in many cases, exclude unaccompanied children from motion-picture shows.

It is, however, pointed out that though the Board does scrutinize 99 per cent, of the moving pictures on the market, it can not, particular classes. The trade has a few films known as, "special releases" with which the board has no concern. Two of these were pictures of prize fights, another was the film showing Roosevelt in Africa. These circulate in theatres, as well as the ordinary moving picture shows, and the report declares that even the prize fights were not particularly objectionable, except insofar as any fight picture must be so.

In conclusion the Censorship Board declares that there is a certain amount or indefinite criticism of its work heard from time to time. Yet it has always courted publicity, it says, and gives full information of its methods and aims.

* * *

December 17, 1911

THE ENGLISH STAGE HAS A NEW CENSOR

Appointment of C. H. E. Brookfield Regarded with General Apprehension

VIEWS VERY CONSERVATIVE

Though He is Himself an Actor and Playwright, Mr. Brookfield Opposes Modern Tendencies

LONDON, Dec. 9—The theatrical, managerial, and playwright world of London views with apprehension the appointment of Charles H. E. Brookfield as a joint examiner of plays with G. A. Redford for the Lord Chamberlain's office. The appointment will go into effect on Jan. 1 next. In the meantime votes of protest are being registered nightly at the London theatres.

Mr. Brookfield, although an actor, author, and playwright himself, has most conservative, not to say pessimistic, views of the English stage. His opinions are on record in an article he recently wrote for the National Review, and it is from this point of view that he is now being judged as a censor of plays.

In this article he referred to the age of the Robertson comedies, the early plays of Pinero, and the English versions of Sardou as the golden age of our drama. That was enough to make students of the drama open their eyes in wonder. Even more startling, however, was it to hear him declare that during the last twenty years "I cannot see that our stage has produced anything new of which we are entitled to be artistically proud."

The modern playwright who endeavors to present problems of real life on the stage he regarded as a "type of misguided dramatist," and while expressing the view that the influence of the stage did not count for much, he wrote, "If a young person could be harmed by seeing a play, it would more probably be by a sombre dissertation on the right of a wife to desert a degenerate husband—or one of the many kindred topics so dear to the New Dramatist—than by the frivolous burlesque on ill-assorted marriages such as one finds in the old French vaudevilles."

Born in 1857, the son of Prebendary W. H. Brookfield and brother of a former M. P. for Rye, Mr. Brookfield made his first appearance on the stage in 1879, and until he retired, in 1898, he was associated with the Bancrofts, the Kendals, and with Sir H. Tree. He played in almost everything, from farce to Shakespeare.

Mr. Brookfield has been spoken of as one of the wittiest men in London, and he has written a book of short stories, a volume of reminiscences, and, with his wife, "Mrs. Brookfield and Her Circle," dealing with the life of his mother.

A few years ago it was stated that he was in an advanced stage of consumption, but the disease has been arrested.

Last year the Lord Chamberlain appointed an Advisory Board to assist the censor. It is composed of Earl Spencer, (the Lord Chamberlain;) Sir Edward Carson, Sir Squire Bancroft, Sir John Hare, Prof. W. Raleigh, S. O. Buckmaster, K. C., M. P., and Col. Sir D. Dawson, (Controller of the Lord Chamberlain's Department.) In addition to a salary the censor is further remunerated by a fee of two guineas on every play over two acts, and of one guinea on every play of less.

* * *

January 17, 1912

POLICE TO RUN DOWN ALL ILLEGAL FILMS

Mean Also to Find Out Who Is Displaying Them to Selected Gatherings

RESULT OF THE HARLEM RAID

Ownership of the Questionable Pictures Not Yet Discovered—Hall Didn't Have a Theatre License

As the result of a raid made on Monday night by detectives attached to the staff of inspector Dennis Sweeney of the Sixth Inspection District a searching investigation will be instituted by the police to discover the identity of persons engaged in the manufacture and production of indecent moving picture films.

This industry, which has sprung into existence within a few months, furnishes amusement at so-called "stags" and smokers given by private clubs or individuals to which admission is by "invitation." The invitation usually carries with it a "check room" coupon which costs the holder of the ticket a dollar.

For several months it has been known to the police that moving-picture shows of a questionable nature were being given, but evidence sufficient to justify an application for a bench warrant was not forthcoming. Owing to the fact that the tickets, or "invitations," which entitled the bearer to admission to these entertainments, were limited to a selected list, the police were powerless to get the needed evidence.

On Monday night, however, two detectives attached to Inspector Sweeney's office were sauntering along West 116th Street when they were accosted by a shabbily dressed man, who asked them if they wanted to see "something rich."

"What is it?" queried one of the sleuths.

"A ripe moving-picture show—something good—hot stuff," was the response.

Two Willing Sleuths

The detectives expressed their willingness to witness "hot stuff" of any description, and were directed to the Lenox Casino, at Lenox Avenue and 116th Street, a dance hall. They immediately notified Inspector Sweeney of their discovery, and the latter, accompanied by three, other detectives, joined them a short distance away from the hall where the exhibition was to take place.

Fearing discovery, the Inspector, who is well known throughout the district, remained behind and sent the five detectives ahead to see if they could gain admission. Arriving at the hall, two of the detectives ascended the stairs. At the top they were challenged by a dapper youth, who inquired in confidential tones whether they were supplied with "invitations."

"I had two—one for myself and the other for my friend." replied the foremost sleuth, "but, unfortunately, I left them in my other clothes."

"Wait a minute," directed the door-keeper, as he disappeared inside, Presently he reappeared at the door and beckoned to the detectives.

"Two dollars, please," he remarked in a businesslike tone. The detectives complied with his demand and were admitted.

Seated within the dance hall they found a crowd of fully a thousand men, among whom, they alleged, they recognized prominent local politicians. On the stage, or platform, had been hung a large white screen upon which the pictures were to be thrown. At the rear of the hall a small elevated platform was erected upon which was mounted an ordinary moving-picture machine. Toward this platform the detectives were unobtrusively elbowing their way, when a man in the crowd recognized them and yelled:

"The cops are here! The place is raided!"

The Operator Escaped

The operator, who had been waiting to unwind the first film, hopped off his perch and mingled in the crowd. There was a general rush for the door, which stopped when it was discovered that the exit was locked. Inspector Sweeney and his remaining sleuths had ascended the stairs and bolted the door from the outside.

When it became evident that there was no one present willing to respond to the repeated demands for the "manager" made by the two detectives who had gained admission, the door was thrown open, and by order of Inspector Sweeney the films and slides were examined. According to the police they were found to portray a wide variety of questionable poses, and the machine and films were confiscated.

As the police were preparing to remove them a man, said to have been a former Alderman, came forward and declared that they had no right to remove private property without a warrant.

"Does this paraphernalia belong to you?" demanded Inspector Sweeney. The man replied in the negative.

"The owner can claim it now or call later at the property room at Police Headquarters," was the inspector's ultimatum. "We would be glad to know who he is." When there was no response to the challenge the crowd was permitted to depart, with the exception of the door tender, who was detained and questioned. He told Inspector Sweeney that he had been employed "for the night by the Lenox Amusement Company," which he said was giving the show. He denied having any knowledge of the identity of his employers, and was permitted to go after explaining that he had been engaged by a stranger he met in a saloon.

Not Properly Licensed

At the Police Headquarters License Bureau yesterday afternoon it was learned that the Lenox Casino management had obtained no theatre license, and at the City Hall License Bureau it was ascertained that no "general show license" or moving picture permit had been issued. The confiscated machine bears the usual individual identification number, but the police said that no permit for its operation had been issued by the Department of Gas and Electricity as required by law.

No certificate as to seating capacity had been issued to the Lenox Casino by the Department of Buildings, which is demanded when a building is used for theatre purposes, nor had the Fire Department passed on the place as a show house. The only license held by the management is for a dance ball for which the requirements are not so rigid.

At the offices of the National Board of Censorship, an unofficial body which passes on the morality of moving picture films, Walter Story, the general secretary, was much interested when informed of the raid by a Times reporter. He said it had been known for some time to his organization that there existed a secret traffic in indecent films, but expressed the conviction that none of the large film producers was concerned in the business.

"We have reason to believe," he said, "that pictures have been produced by irresponsible persons which are violations of criminal statutes in any States, where they are exhibited, and are to be classed with the indecent postal card, but we can find no record of a definite instance where such a picture has strayed into a regular theatre or showhouse. Pictures of this kind are produced before persons who are expecting a questionable production."

How the Censors Work

Mr. Story explained that the National Board of Censors works in co-operation with various manufacturers of films, and is thus enabled to pass upon all films before they go forth to the various moving-picture theatres. The producing companies, he explained, are scattered throughout the country, while all the manufacturing is done in this city except in the case of foreign concerns. The Censoring Committee, which consists for the most part of settlement workers and teachers, meets on certain mornings and afternoons at appointed places and usually reviews twelve films at each session.

The big manufacturers, he said, had too much at stake to venture to produce indecent films: No photo-play was manufactured unless of sufficient merit to justify the reproduction of from fifty to one hundred and fifty copies, which sell for an average price of $100 each. Ten cents a foot, said Mr. Storey, was the trade price, and 1,000 feet was considered the trade unit for a film.

"This new development looks to me," continued Mr. Story, "like the work of men who have rented a studio with stage settings somewhere and can produce scenes with interior settings much cheaper than can the big manufacturers who are forced by competition to produce original and interesting scenes. Some time ago we heard that such films were being shown privately in this city, and we communicated with the Secretary of the Parkhurst Society, which instituted an investigation, but nothing came of it."

Deputy Police Commissioner Dillon, who has supervision of the Police License Bureau, expressed his approval of the raid made by Inspector Sweeney, and said that a determined effort would be made to trace the source of the films and to prosecute the offenders.

* * *

December 22, 1912

ASK KING TO END PLAY CENSORSHIP

Authors and Managers Declare Development of English Drama Is Hampered

PHILLPOTTS CASE IS CITED

Critics Find Less to Condemn in His "The Secret Woman" Than in "Dear Old Charlie," by the Censor

By Marconi Transatlantic Wireless Telegraph to
The New York Times

LONDON, Feb. 24—The Daily Chronicle, which is conducting a vigorous campaign against the play censorship, shows some of its absurdities by using the deadly parallel and comparing the critics opinions of "Dear Old Charlie," the work of the new censor, Charles Brookfield, and Eden Philipotts's "The Secret Woman," which the censor barred, but which was given at a private performance.

For instance The Times's review of "Dear Old Charlie" refers to its "cynical and shameless immorality," whereas of "The Secret Woman" it says: "Nobody who goes to see the play in the hope of finding prurience or blasphemy will be repaid for his trouble."

The Morning Leader, speaking of "Dear Old Charlie," says: "The whole array of gibes at marital blindness was conscientiously retailed with all the old gusto."

Of "The Secret Woman" the same paper says: "So far as search after indecencies is concerned, the afternoon was wasted."

Half a dozen other papers express similar opinions, and The Daily Chronicle declares this ample proof that the censor had no excuse for annihilating Mr. Philipotts's work.

The anti-censorites, getting no redress at the hands of Parliament, have drawn up a petition to the King which is supported by many authors, theatrical managers, and representatives of the artistic world. The petition declares that the natural development of the British drama is being hampered and checked by methods and principles which, had they existed in the days of Queen Elizabeth, would have deprived the English-speaking world of some of the chief glories of its literature, namely "Hamlet" and most of the historical plays of Shakespeare. It is further declared that the Lord Chamberlain's department has largely extended the bounds prescribed by statute for the exercise of the power of refusing to grant licenses to plays, and has prohibited some plays and forced authors to make changes in others, for reasons that are purely arbitrary and unwarranted. The petition ends:

"In view of the danger that these conditions may hinder the growth of a great serious National drama, and of the grave injury that such a hindrance would do to the development of thought and of art, your petitioners most humbly pray that your Most Excellent Majesty will be pleased to take this petition into your most gracious consideration and take such steps in the premises as to your Majesty, in your great wisdom, shall seem meet."

* * *

January 1, 1913

FOLKS FILM BILL VETOED BY MAYOR

Censorship of Moving-Picture Shows Not Needed, He Tells Aldermen

A BLOW AT FREE SPEECH

The Public Will Reject Immoral Films—Tammany's Ruse to Defeat Measure Succeeds

Mayor Gaynor yesterday vetoed the Folks ordinance for the regulation of moving picture shows in New York City. The ordinance, at the behest of the Tammany members of the board, included a clause for censorship, and it was because of this clause that the Mayor vetoed the entire measure. When the bill came before the Board of Aldermen two weeks ago Frank Dowling, the Tammany leader, made a vigorous fight for the inclusion of a censorship clause, and the Fusion members, after a fight, agreed to an amendment. It was understood then that the Mayor would veto the entire ordinance on the ground that he had no right to veto any amendment attached thereto, but the Fusion members thought that Section 40 of the Charter gave the Mayor the right to veto any clause.

There was a public hearing and the Mayor indicated that he would veto the entire ordinance. In a message to the Board yesterday, saying that he vetoed the ordinance, the Mayor said:

"The truth is that the good, moral people who go to these moving picture shows, and very often bring their children with them, would not tolerate the exhibition of obscene or immoral pictures there. A place in which such pictures were exhibited would soon be without sufficient patrons to support it. At all events, the criminal law is ample to prevent the exhibition of such pictures.

Hears of No Immoral Pictures

"I have asked these people who are crying out against the moving picture shows to give me an instance of an obscene or immoral picture being shown in them, so that the exhibitor may be prosecuted, but they have been unable to do so. What they insist on is to have the pictures examined in advance, and allowed or prohibited. That is what they are still doing in Russia with pictures and with reading matter generally. Do they really want us to recur to that system?

"Perhaps I should say I understand that comparatively few of your honorable body are in favor of the censorship. Many of you voted for the whole ordinance in the belief that the Mayor had the right to veto the censorship provisions and let the rest of the ordinance stand. But I find that the Mayor may not do that. The censorship provisions are not independent of the rest of the ordinance, but interdependent and so connected therewith that the whole ordinance must stand or fall as a whole.

"I am constrained to do this because of the provisions therein creating a censorship. It is provided that the Board of Education shall appoint one or more censors to examine all motion pictures in advance and determine whether they shall be exhibited or not.

"It has hitherto been the understanding in this country that no censorship can be established by law to decide in advance what may or may not be lawfully printed or published. Ours is a government of free speech and a free press. That is the cornerstone of free government. The phrase "the press" includes all methods of expression by writing, or pictures. In past ages there were censorships to decide what might be published, or even believed.

The Victims of Censorship

"Every Christian denomination has at one time or another been subjected to such censorship. The few were very anxious not to give freedom of speech, or of the press. They thought the many were not fit for it. They, therefore, set themselves up as censors and guardians over the bulk of their fellow-men. The centre of thought was then among the few, and they were very anxious to keep it there. But in the course of time, in spite of all opposition, the centre of thought began to pass from the few to the many, where it is to-day. It was then that censorships, and all interference with freedom of speech, of the press, and of opinion began to give way by degrees, until in the end all of them, at all events with us, were abolished. And that is now substantially true under all free governments throughout the world."

The Mayor said he hoped the board would pass the other ordinance, which has been before it for a long time and which does not contain any censorship provision.

* * *

December 20, 1913

FILM SHOW RAIDED AT PARK THEATRE

Warrants for Samuel H. London, the Producer, and Others Are Not Served

RESERVES SCATTER CROWD

Deputy Commissioner Newburger Says the "White Slave" Pictures Are Vicious

Sergt. Edward J. Quinn and a half dozen Central Office detectives from Deputy Police Commissioner Newpurger's staff made a raid upon the Park Theatre, at Columbus Circle, last night, closed the house, and ordered the discontinuance of the moving picture exhibition which has been taking place there for the past two weeks. The detectives had a warrant for the arrest of Samuel H. London, the former special investigator for the United States Government, by whom the films were manufactured, and under whose direction they have been produced. No arrests were made.

The films are entitled "The Inside of the White Slave Traffic," and, according to the programme, they are the product of the "Social Research Film Corporation." Large placards in the lobby of the theatre proclaim that "this is the only moving picture dealing with the white slave topic indorsed by the Sociological Fund of The Medical Review of Reviews."

Since the night of the first public exhibition of the films, the question as to their fitness for public display has excited much controversy. Police Inspector Dwyer and Detective Hague visited the theatre last Monday and sat through the five-reel show. As the result of their investigations a summons was served later upon Alfred P. Hamburg, manager of the theatre, by Detective Hague, who charged that the pictures were of a character likely to impair the morals of young girls. The announcement of this action on the part of the police caused the intervention of a number of persons who defended the pictures as educational.

With Mrs. Oliver H. P. Belmont, Mrs. Carrie Chapman Catt, Mrs. Inez Milholland Boissevain, Dr. William J. Robinson, Miss Beuel, associate editor of Harper's Magazine, and Dr. Ira S. Wile of the Board of Education and editor of The Medical Review of Reviews, Magistrate Ten Eyck, then sitting in the West Side Police Court, attended an afternoon exhibition of the pictures last Tuesday. He dismissed the summons against the manager after a hearing at which most of the above-named men and women, with the exception of Mrs. Belmont, who did not take the stand, testified to the moral and educational value of the performance.

Deputy Police Commissioner Newburger thereupon determined to personally investigate the complaints which continued to flow into Police Headquarters against the pictures. As the result of his investigation he laid a number of affidavits and communications before Magistrate Murphy yesterday afternoon at Mr. Murphy's home, Forty-seventh Street and Madison Avenue, with the result that a warrant was issued for the arrest of Mr. London on the charge of violating Section 1,140A of the Penal Code. This section relates to the production of an indecent public exhibition. It is understood that Magistrate Murphy also issued other warrants for the arrest of the managers of the theatre and those in charge of the production.

Sergeant Quinn and the detectives visited the theatre last night just as the second nightly exhibition of the films was ended, about 9:30 o'clock. They ordered further sale of tickets at the box office discontinued and dispersed the crowd in the lobby. They had to call on policemen outside for help. Still the crowd kept coming until 500 persons were clamoring for seats or waved small green tickets previously purchased for the 9:30 performance.

News of what was taking place had spread along Broadway north and south for blocks, and soon a large but orderly crowd of several thousand persons gathered in front of the theatre. The West Forty-seventh Street reserves were sent for, and the crowd gradually melted away.

The films which caused the trouble deal with the story of the activities of "White Slavers," their plots against immigrant girls and the manner in which they seek out their victims in large cities. The films purport to prove that there exists an underworld organization of international scope for the purpose of carrying on a traffic in women. Automobile abductions, drugged drinks, and other sensational features figure in the production. The story which runs through the films is portrayed by professional moving picture actors, but many of the scenes are staged from life.

Deputy Commissioner Newburger said yesterday afternoon:

"The pictures are vicious and are intended to cater to morbid imaginations. I think that in the previous case Magistrate Ten Eyck may have been a little overawed by Mrs. Belmont and her friends. This time we have acted after careful investigation and I am prepared to put an end to this production and others of its kind in this city."

Frederick H. Robinson of the Sociological Fund of the Medical Review of Reviews said late last night that he understood that Samuel H. London, the producer of the films, would surrender himself this morning to Magistrate Murphy at the hearing on his case, which is set for 10 o'clock in Chief Magistrate McAdoo's office, at 300 Mulberry Street.

Abraham Gruber has been retained by Mr. London, and will represent him in the court proceedings this morning. One of the managers of the Park Theatre announced that William Travers Jerome has been retained to represent the management.

PART II

THE GREAT WAR, 1914–1918

THE ALLIED NATIONS

August 7, 1914

FRENCH AIR HEROES CAN WIN $200,000

Michelin Offers Prizes—Family of an Aviator Killed to Get the Award

PRESS CENSORSHIP SEVERE

Papers Crippled and Correspondents Impeded—Volunteers' Offer Not Accepted

Special Cable to The New York Times

PARIS, Aug. 6—André Michelin, one of the best-known supporters of aviation in this country, has offered $200,000 in prizes for heroic deeds of French aviators without distinction of rank. The first prize is $20,000.

The awards will be made by a committee consisting of officials appointed by President Poincaré, who will include members of the Aero Club and the Aeronautic League. Senator Raymond will be President of the committee. If an aviator hero is killed his family will receive the award.

A proclamation issued by the Minister of War forbids the publication of news relative to war events, the mobilization, movements, embarcation and transport of troops, the composition of the armies, &c., which has not been communicated by the Press Bureau of the Ministry of War.

Communiqués will be issued three times a day.

All special editions are forbidden, as are also announcements cried or placarded in the streets.

Directors of newspapers must transmit to the official Press Bureau final proofs as soon as the last pages are made up.

A newspaper will expose itself to immediate confiscation if its proofs contain any military news which has not been communicated by the Press Bureau.

This measure cripples the Paris press and impedes foreign correspondents, for the transmission of news is undoubtedly regarded as equivalent to publication here.

* * *

August 17, 1914

CENSORSHIP BOOMS CABLE BUSINESS

Ban on Code Messages Clogs the Lines with Long Communications

THERE IS NO DELAY HERE

But Strict Censorship in France and England Holds Up Messages In Europe

The companies whose cables run to Europe reported yesterday that all lines, with the exception of those to Germany and Austria-Hungary, were working well and that they had so much business on hand that it was necessary to keep a large force of operators at work day and night. One of the companies posted on the glass of its receiving window a notice which said that it was blocked by the flood of messages submitted to it. All delays in receiving and to a certain extent in transmitting messages, it was said were due to the strict censorship enforced at the French and British terminals of the companies.

At the offices of the Western Union, Commercial Cable, and French cable companies it was said that the big increase in business was due largely to the fact that code messages were prohibited practically to all points in Great Britain, France, and the countries allied with them, which meant that whereas before the war by the use of codes a business house could send a message in ten or a dozen words, it took now from twenty to fifty words to convey the same information.

At the Western Union office a statement explaining the difficulties now confronting the cable companies was issued. The last two paragraphs said:

Notwithstanding that owing to the abnormal situation abroad all cable routes are more or less congested, we are able with our eight transatlantic cables to dispose of our traffic with reasonable promptness, delays incident to censorship excepted. Beyond London the service is slow but fairly reliable except to Germany, Austria, and Hungary, and the situation doubtless will continue to improve, especially to European and other countries which can be reached by cable routes out of London.

Through every available channel we are endeavoring to secure further modifications of the existing restrictions, and while code language in cablegrams will undoubtedly be barred until the European war is over, we are hopeful that the writing of the name of the sender in full as the signature of each message, and perhaps some of the other requirements and restrictions, will shortly be waived.

The Commercial Cable Company issued a notice to the public also, in which it pointed out that as a military censorship had been instituted in all of its foreign terminals, cable messages were accepted at the sender's risk only. In general, all cable message must be fully addressed, but in messages to firms, if the full name of the firm is given, the house number and street name may be omitted. Unless the firm's name conveys its business, the character of the business should be added, as, for example, "ship owners."

All messages to Switzerland and Turkey must be in French, but cable messages to other countries may be in either English or French. Trade terms, trademarks, and commercial marks are not admitted. Messages in German are not accepted.

"Taking everything into consideration," said an official of one of the companies, "we are doing as well as could be expected. There is, of course, and will continue to be, delay on the other side due to the censorship, but we hope to minimize even this delay soon."

The wireless situation has not changed in the last week. The Government's censorship, notwithstanding the vigorous protest of the German-American Chamber of Commerce and other German organizations, remains in force, and no messages of an unneutral nature are received or transmitted at any of the stations.

The German-American Chamber of Commerce telegraphed to Secretary of State Bryan yesterday denying a statement attributed to Colville Barclay, the British Charge d'Affaires in Washington, that the Goldschmidt station at Tuckerton, N. J., which is a German system, was opened since the war started. The Chamber informed Mr. Bryan that the station was opened officially on June 18 by the exchange of messages between President Wilson and the German Emperor.

* * *

August 23, 1914

BRITISH PRESS HITS AT THE CENSORSHIP

"Unreasonable" and "Inexcusable" Are Phrases Applied to Work of News Bureau

QUESTIONERS ARE REBUFFED

Refuse to Let English Papers Publish Some News, Even When Given Out Elsewhere

LONDON, Aug. 12—Some English newspaper men are beginning to grow very skeptical about the optimistic reports which the authorities have spread broadcast regarding the thoroughness and completeness of the preparations Great Britain has made for the greatest war in her history.

The reason for this skepticism is that, in such matters as have come directly within the cognizance of these British Journalists, there have been evidences of bungling on an almost incredible scale; and the inference drawn is naturally that there must be equal remissness or inefficiency in other directions.

These criticisms, it is necessary to stage, are directed almost entirely at departments of the War Office.

In one matter which permits of open discussion at this stage—the press censorship, and particularly the Press Bureau, which was founded both to serve as a medium of communication between the Admiralty and the War Office and the public, and thereby to serve the newspapers and public with reliable news—an unfortunate beginning has been made.

The first item of news issued by the Press Bureau gave rise to a misapprehension. It stated in a paragraph referring generally to operations in Belgium that German troops were intrenching along the line of the River Aisne. There being no River Aisne in any available Belgium maps here, it was questioned whether the River Aisne in the French Andennes was not the river in reference. Representatives of various newspapers were dispatched in hot haste to the War Office and the Press Bureau. At both all information was refused.

"But you see how important it is that the press should know whether this official communication is intended to refer to the French river Aisne or whether there is some smaller stream, not shown on any of the maps, in the neighborhood of Liege," one correspondent urged.

"We have nothing to say beyond what is contained in the official communiqué," was the reply at the War Office.

"Is the Press Bureau designed to give the public information or is it designed to befog the newspapers?" was another question put to the Press Bureau official when all efforts to obtain some elucidation of the Aisne riddle had been refused. Eventually it was ascertained that the official who had drawn up this particular communiqué had gone home and was not to be disturbed, and that nobody else at the Press Bureau knew anything about the matter.

The Daily News, in an editorial article, says:

"Most people know by now that the censor is at work and very active in this country. No patriotic person will complain of that so long as the censor does his work in a rational way, for the importance of preventing useful hints reaching the enemy is obvious. The censor becomes a subject of complaint when he becomes unreasonable, and there is an instance which shows how the thing should not be done.

"A week ago a Belgian paper published a piece of news of particular interest to Englishmen. On Sunday the French papers printed the same information with greater detail. It was not a private message, but a communication issued to the whole French press by the French War Office.

"Now this piece of news the censor over here forbids the English press to publish, although, as we have said, it concerns the English people more than any other people.

"For this action of the British censor there is no sort of excuse or justification. If the French War Office thinks the publication of the information can do no harm, how can our censor imagine it will do harm? In any case, if harm there could be it has been done already by the mere publication in France, and the repetition here cannot conceivably hurt.

"This is the most singular but far from being the only instance of utterly misplaced suppression, and it is not compensated by the laxity which allows the publication of the wildest and most palpable of fictions. Deception is of course a recognized military device, but these extravagances cannot deceive the enemy, they can only corrupt the mind of the British public. We criticise the censorship with reluctance, because in its present form it has only just commenced its work; but these blunders must be indicated if they are to be avoided in the future."

* * *

September 25, 1914

FORBIDS WAR NEWS FROM BATTLE FRONT

British Tighten Censorship But Will Continue Fuller Official Reports

Special Cable to The New York Times

LONDON, Friday, Sept. 25—In compliance with new regulations issued by the War Office. The Daily Chronicle's military correspondent preludes his articles dealing with the operations in France with the following notice.

"The following statement and surmises that arise from it are based entirely upon British, French, and German official statements and upon statements made in the public press which have passed the censor, and not upon any source of information whatever."

The London papers this morning contain outside the official communications no dispatches from abroad referring to the operations within the last five or six days, or in any way indicative of the character of the operations in progress.

The Times's military correspondent confines himself to a discussion of the need of training officers, pointing out that in one month of fighting England has lost about 1,100 officers killed, wounded, or missing. This is nearly two officers out of every five. All, the testimony shows that the Germans have suffered equally in regard to officers.

* * *

September 27, 1914

PARIS STOPS NEWS SOURCES

Censorship More Strict—British Soldiers, Driving Autos, Kept in Dark

Special Cable to The New York Times

PARIS, Sept. 26—The French press maintains strict reserve concerning the great battle of the Aisne, confining their remarks to brief elucidations of the official bulletin without adding any comment or making deductions therefrom about the probable aim or result of the strategy on either side.

Apart from the patriotic reasons for the silence, it should be said that M. Klotz, head of the Press Bureau, issued a notice yesterday, reminding the press that references to the movements of troops, or comment thereon, were strictly forbidden, and that the rule would be rigidly enforced.

The Temps tonight appeared nearly an hour late with significant gaps in the column devoted to the military situation, although the article as printed seems but little more communicative than the official statement.

A story is current about one of the best-known English correspondents in Paris which gives some idea of the attitude of the military authorities toward the newspapers. The correspondent asked an English Major for a pass to enter the zone of operations, promising to submit to him before transmission any information that he might obtain. The Major replied:

"Not only do I refuse a pass, but if you are found in my district after six hours you will be shot."

The indignant correspondent protested that his friendship was sufficiently close to guarantee his discretion, patriotism, and trustworthiness. The officer replied:

"It is not a question of patriotism or friendship. I have orders to allow no press men here. Secondly, I decline to waste in reading your dispatches the time which belongs to my country. I am quite in earnest, unless you go you will be shot."

The correspondent went.

* * *

October 1, 1914

CLEMENCEAU'S RUSE WINS

Evades Suspension Order by Changing His Newspaper's Name

TOULOUSE, (via Bordeaux.) Sept. 30—Georges Clemenceau, the former Premier, has evaded the suspension order against his newspaper, L'Homme Libre, by changing the name to L'Homme Enchainé (The Man in Chains). The paper was published as usual today.

The article which resulted yesterday in an order of suspension for eight days is a mild appeal for the preferential treatment of German Alsatian prisoners.

* * *

October 9, 1914

RUSSIA AS LIBERTY'S HOME

London Times Says Press Is Less Trammeled Than in England

LONDON, Oct. 8—In a comparison of the censorship as it is being applied in England and Russia, The Times's military correspondent says:

"We are able to discuss the campaign in the West with far less freedom than our Russian contemporaries. Free Russia, the last home of the liberty of the press, has become positively enviable to us in England. Russian reports are far more full than ours, and Russian comment is far more untrammeled and therefore more illuminating.

"We shall have a good deal to say about the English censorship when the liberty of the press is restored, but no one doubts that in the present critical phase of operations in the West Gen. Joffre is really justified in exercising dictatorship in news and comment. It is normal for all dictators to be distrustful of their closest friends, and we have no cause to complain if our dictators treat us after the manner of their kind."

* * *

November 17, 1914

BUSY CENSOR SLASHES EVEN LORD'S PRAYER

Paris Writer's Attempt at Ridicule Results in Amusing Literary Hash

Special Cable to The New York Times

PARIS, Nov. 16—As threats and entreaties have proved equally vain against the censorship, the Temps tonight attacks it with ridicule, which is regarded as the deadliest weapon in the Parisian armory.

Pierre Mille, one of the best-known contributors, writes a column article, beginning:

"Regarding the origin of the convulsion which is shaking Europe, together with the least known diplomatic secrets and the most concealed strategic projects, I am going to make some most important revelations."

Before he can reveal anything here, however, the censor intervenes with a four-line cut. He continues:

"It will be remembered that Napoleon once cried before the Pyramids—" (Here is another slash.)

The writer goes on:

"But we do not need the support of history or the remembrance of the victories won by Jeanne d'Arc at (name excised) or at Valmy by (another obliteration.) One fact I will add" (Here follows a ten-line cut.)

He continues:

"His undaunted attitude at" (This time ten lines more disappear.)

The article proceeds:

"She cried in a trembling voice: 'O, daughter, cruel'—(the woman's speech is all excised save the words "The devourers fight among themselves," although the passage appears to be taken from nothing more modern or harmful than a famous tragedy.)

The writer makes a last effort:

"The adversary's position was now very serious. Throwing himself upon his knees, he cried: 'Our Father, which art—' (Even of the Lord's prayer the censor allows only this beginning and the final "amen.")

The Temps says in a postscript:

"We regret the slashing which the censor finds it necessary to inflict, but despite it our contributor asserts that the article can still be understood."

* * *

November 21, 1914

CANADA BARS GERMAN PAPERS

Now a Crime to Sell or Possess Some New York Publications

Special to The New York Times

OTTAWA, Nov. 20—The Canadian Government has, by order in Council, decided to prohibit the entry into Canada of four German publications from New York—the Staats-Zeitung, The Truth About Germany, The Vital Issue, and The Vaterland.

More anti-British publications will be added to the list. It is now a criminal offense to sell the publications mentioned or to have them in one's possession.

* * *

December 4, 1914

CENSOR ASSAILED BY BRITISH PRESS

Ban on News of the Audacious Disaster Arouses Resentment and Protest

ANGERED BY GERMAN GIBES

Suppression in Britain of Details Known to All the World Called an Insult to the Nation

Special Cable to The New York Times

LONDON, Dec. 4—The Morning Post publishes an editorial renewing its attack upon the British press censorship with particular reference to the secrecy enjoined on the British press regarding "a certain naval mishap, now nearly a month old," particulars of which have appeared in American and other papers.

"We should like to speak plainly on this subject," says The Post, "yet the Tower may await us if we do. The British press is, in fact, forbidden to mention a mishap to the British navy of which the press of the whole world is speaking. The German press have for some time been in full possession of the facts which they gathered from America and are gloating over them, not so much because they relate to a material loss, but because their suppression in England seems to them to offer evidence that the British nation is in state of panic and is not to be trusted with the truth.

"Thus, for example, the Kolnisch Zeitung says: 'The English Government dared not communicate this serious loss, to the nation because it feared universal excitement. A very low estimate is thus placed by its own Government on the nerves and character of the English people which gives one cause to think.' We are bound to say that for once we agree with a German newspaper. It does give one cause to think.

"There is involved a mishap of considerable material dimensions, no doubt, but nothing to cause anything more than a national sigh of regret, and it is treated by the Government as if it were some appalling catastrophe so dark that merely to read about it would throw the nation into a state of frenzy. It is ridiculous, but it is also humiliating. We say plainly that it is an insult, not only to the British press, but to the British nation."

The Morning Post attributes the blame for the concealment to Mr. Churchill, and again demands that control of the Admiralty be left in the hands of experts.

The Daily Telegraph in an editorial on the same subject, says:

"A misfortune not, happily, involving loss of life is said to have occurred some weeks ago, and complaint has been made that the public has been kept in ignorance. It is reported that full accounts have appeared in American newspapers, and that the news had even been published in the German press. Are we sure that the enemy does not know, not merely something of the incident but everything? We must be convinced on this matter before we can criticize the withholding of any particular item of news."

The Times says editorially:

"The Government have received and still enjoy the full confidence of the nation irrespective of party, but they are not requiting adequately the trust reposed in them. On Tuesday we drew attention to the fact that a piece of news with which the whole world outside these islands is acquainted was still being concealed.

"At first there were excellent reasons for concealing it, but these reasons no longer obtain. Members of any club which receives American newspapers may read it and even see the pictures of the disaster. The entire German press has known of it for many days and we have numerous German newspapers in our possession in which it is discussed with exaggerated exultation.

"We have no sympathy whatever with efforts made in other quarters to base a general attack on the Admiralty policy upon this isolated incident. We believe that in all essential matters the Royal Navy is in skilled and competent hands. We are, however, very much concerned about the taunts now being leveled at the British Government by the press of Germany and America. It is being said, and we are unable to answer the charge, that our Government are afraid to trust the British public and will not tell them the truth.

"The Government have placed the press of this country in an exceedingly difficult position. We receive hundreds of letters asking us whether there is any foundation for various stories which more often than not are fables. Up to a certain point we were always able in reply to rely upon the assurance of the Government that they would deal with the country frankly. At present we cannot take this reply and the results are deplorable, as a decision originally necessary has been foolishly maintained far too long. Why not say so candidly and let us all drop this unwelcome topic?"

* * *

February 21, 1915

HOW OUR MOVING PICTURE PLAYS ARE CENSORED

Plenty of Changes Must Often Be Made Before Films Are Ready For Audiences

B-R-R-R-R-R! B-r-r-r-r-r!

"He's running that film too fast! I can't make head nor tail of it!"

"Oh, let it go; we've a big programme to see today."

"Well, turn on that fan and let's have a little air in here!"

B-r-r-r-r-r! B-r-r-r-r-r!

The scene is in the projection room of one of the large film distribution houses in New York City. It is a small room, without adequate ventilation and only such light as is afforded by the screen on which a moving picture is being thrown.

In that dark row or two of seats, as far away from the screen as space will permit, are seated an Assistant Secretary of the National Board of Censorship and several of his volunteer committee. Also, scribbling notes on each film as well as possible in the darkened room, are the critics.

The occasional cutting and slashing done by the National Board of Censors is only part of the scrutiny undergone by the films. The censors look only to the morals of the photoplays. If a film does not transgress in the way of stabbing, kidnapping, drugging, and other scenes that are tabooed, it gets the indorsement of the board and goes out upon its career.

But the critics do not spare it so easily. These employes of various trade and theatrical publications, as well as daily and weekly newspapers, have a somewhat broader function than the members of the Board of Censorship. Their business is to watch each film and pass upon its merits, exactly as a theatrical critic passes upon a new play, the greatest difference being that, whereas a theatrical critic sees but one play in an evening, the moving-picture critic sees anywhere from ten to twenty five photoplays in a single day.

One gets an idea of the immense number of films manufactured each week by visiting these supply houses, most of which have headquarters in New York. Each supply house represents a large group of subsidiary companies, scattered throughout the entire country and often in foreign lands. One independent supply house shows very close to fifty new films each week, another about thirty. Besides these there is the entire licensed group and innumerable feature companies.

The pictures are usually taken several weeks in advance of their release dates, except where the subject matter is timely, when the films are released as soon as possible.

While it wants a constant supply of new pictures, the public at the same time is becoming more difficult to please. Where once a train moving through attractive mountain scenery served to delight the eye of an observer, he now demands plot stories of decided worth. Moving-picture manufacturers are alert to get the best material for pictures. The literature of the world is being ransacked for available stories for the screen.

Competent criticism is welcomed by the producers. Some of the supply houses employ their own critics to pass upon the new films and pounce upon bits of mistaken humor or scenes of down-right vulgarity.

Moving pictures are made under the spur of competitive excitement. A scenario, or plot script, is accepted by a busy director. He hastily marshals together his company of performers. One scene is taken in a drawing room, the next on a busy street, another in a downtown office building, a fourth perhaps on a mountainside. Fitted together and shown in a short space of time, many imperfections are bound to appear. The story moves smoothly in certain places and flounders badly in others.

This is where the critic finds his opportunity.

The first tendency of a new hand at this work is to be too critical. "Why should this particular picture be exhibited at all? It teaches no moral and leaves no lesson in the mind of the observer."

"Well," comes the prompt rejoinder, "why is the average best-selling novel printed? Why is the average musical comedy produced? We cannot criticise moving pictures because they are not always educational. They have their place as simple entertainment."

Perhaps half a dozen reels will be shown, and the new member begins to wonder if there is any reason for censoring the films at all. Then there will suddenly pop into view a series of scenes that are decidedly "off the key."

In passing upon the merits of a film story the critic is usually limited as to space. He notes principally the construction, plot development, story value, continuity, and the like. There is always, of course, primarily the quality of the photography. Is it sharp and clear, or is it out of focus and hazy? Is it full of "ghosts," as occasional white, vaporish spots are called? Is it streaked with "static rays"? The latter imperfections indicate that the picture was taken under unfavorable light conditions, and detract materially from the value of the film. Clear, smooth photography is a delight to the eye, and often renders highly pleasing a film story with a plot that is merely ordinary. But where the story is of exceptional excellence the observer will often forgive faults in the photography.

The work of the director is extremely important in the making of a film. He has immediate control over the performers, oversees the work of the photographer, times the scenes, and sees that the parts dovetail together properly.

Considering the scope of the undertaking and the hurry of the work, it is not surprising that many laugh-provoking slips occur.

Gun play in moving pictures is always a source of amusement to discerning observers. In the old days the mere sight of a revolver was presumed to be a successful sensation, without reference to the manner in which it was handled. Actors were allowed to go through the most extraordinary antics with weapons. There was one picture which stands out with unforgettable distinctness, in which six excited individuals held cocked revolvers against the figure of a prisoner. After a dramatic interval the hero came dashing upon the scene and solemnly pointed another gun at the poor fellow.

In another picture, an Indian girl and her pony were supposed to drink from the waters of a poisoned spring. The pony died rather deliberately, being none too well trained. Then, just as the film was coming to a gloomy close, the pony raised its head and gave a rather humorous look in the direction of the camera. The effect of this upon the audience may be imagined.

This looseness of handling is less in evidence than before. More attention is being paid to small details, and today many films are exhibited which are practically free from minor faults.

* * *

March 30, 1915

ITALY PUTS BAN ON NEWS

Absolute Censorship on All Things Military to Start Thursday

ROME, March 28, (via Paris, March 29.)—A rigid censorship upon the publication of military news from March 31 to July 30 has been established by a royal decree issued in accordance with a decision reached by the Council of Ministers at its session, Saturday. The publication is prohibited of information regarding the formation, movements, or assignments of units of the army, navy, and aerial forces, or even of soldiers and sailors.

The prohibition includes arrangements made for the transport of naval and military forces, the sanitary condition of troops or sailors as well as details regarding armament provided on all works of defense. Even scientific discussions of military questions come under the ban, as well as criticisms of the army or navy.

* * *

April 9, 1915

FINED FOR GIVING NEWS

British Censor Passes It in One Paper, but Punishes Another

Special Cable to The New York Times

LONDON, Friday, April 9—Charles Dyson, a local reporter, was fined $25 at Portland Police Court yesterday for supplying news to the press calculated to be of use to Germany, and Edward Newman, editor of The Southern Times, was fined $50 for publishing a report of a similar nature.

Mr. Newman, while acknowledging that the publication was indiscreet, showed that a London evening paper had published the same news in a more definite form, which apparently had been passed by the censor. An Admiralty witness, pressed by the defense, was unable to give a reason for his opinion that the news was likely to help the enemy.

The Daily News, commenting on the case, complains of "discrimination by the censor between journal and journal and the extension of censorship to matters which ought to be entirely outside its ken."

An instance illustrating both these offenses, it says, occurred this week. Monday's evening papers were allowed to mention that a full page appeal to the American people had appeared in the American press, but they were not allowed to mention the subject of the appeal. Next day, however, a morning paper was allowed to tell us that the appeal was against the export of munitions of war.

"Doubtless," continues the writer, "one of the censor's assistants suppressed what another tolerated, but what is the state of mind of these gentry when any of them can think fit to prevent the English people knowing that an agitation is in progress in America against the export of munitions of war?"

* * *

May 25, 1915

ITALY'S CENSORS SEVERE

Permit Only Official Bulletins of the War to be Printed

ITALIAN FRONTIER, May 28, (via Chiasso to Paris, May 29)—Italy thus far has been more rigorous than any other country at war concerning provisions for the newspapers obtaining news of the progress of the war. No permission has been given to journalists to proceed to the front, and a strict prohibition, carrying with it severe penalties in case of infringement, has been issued against any message regarding the military operation being sent to correspondents aside from the official communications, which must be used textually without either additions or deletions. These bulletins must not be quoted in part.

The telephone service has been suppressed, and letters and telegrams are being strictly censored. The only means the correspondents have for communicating with points outside the kingdom is to travel to the frontier and file the dispatches.

* * *

June 7, 1915

RUSSIAN CENSOR ACTIVE

Berlin Hears He Has Put Many Newspapers Out of Business

BERLIN, May 25—The strictness of the Russian censor is indicated in a dispatch from Copenhagen, which gives statistics for the year 1914, showing how many Russian newspapers and how many issues were suppressed, temporarily or permanently.

The figures show that the censor proceeded against and prevented the publication of 465 issues of periodical papers and 230 non-periodicals. In 96 cases of periodicals the prohibition was only temporary, and in 24 cases of non-periodicals.

As a result of the activities of the censor in proceeding with considerable regularity against periodicals that persisted in printing undesirable material, 44 newspapers went out of business during the war.

* * *

June 13, 1915

BRITISH CENSORS' TASK ENORMOUS

How Wire and Postal Messages Are Watched Told in Memorandum to Parliament

400 IN CABLE BRANCH ALONE

From 30,000 to 50,000 Telegrams Handled Daily—Five Tons of Mail Censored Weekly

Copies of the memorandum on the British Censorship, which was presented to both Houses of Parliament by command of King George, have reached this country. The pamphlet explains the system of censorship employed by Great Britain as well as the methods of the Official Press Bureau. The censorship, the Government informs Parliament, is one of several instruments designed to prevent information of military value reaching the enemy. Pains are being taken to do this with as little interference as possible with the transmission of correspondence or the publication of news.

"In the course of the present war," the memorandum says, "it has become apparent that in censorship there lay to hand a weapon the full value of which was not perhaps anticipated prior to the war and which can be used to restrict commercial and financial transactions intended for the benefit of enemy Governments or persons residing in enemy countries."

Under the existing system the censorship is divided into two main departments, the censorship of private and commercial communications, under the Army Council, and the Press Bureau. The latter department came suddenly into existence last August and for a time the censors worked without rules, simply acting on the general instructions issued by the War Office and the Admiralty. The importance of the

Bureau grew with its size and it was soon found expedient to remove to larger quarters in the Service Institute, Whitehall. About this time it was found necessary to place under the Press Bureau the censorship of press cables.

The staff of the Press Bureau consists of the Director, who is Sir Stanley Buckmaster, Solicitor General; two Assistant Directors, a Secretary, and about fifty censors. These censors are naval officers, military censors, who are senior captains attached to the General Staff, and civilians. The latter are appointed by the Director and include former employes of the Civil Service, barristers and journalists.

Day and Night Shifts

The censors inspect all press matter which comes to the Bureau and because of the press of this business have to work in day and night shifts. By Government order all press cable messages to, from or through London are diverted by the Post Office and the cable companies into the Censor's office. Messages sent into the bureau also include inland press telegrams if they, even in the slightest way, refer to the war.

To facilitate the passage of matter through the hands of the censor a tube has been put into operation between the Press Bureau and the Central Telegraph office. As soon as a message is filed it is rushed through the tube, censored and dispatched back to the telegraph or cable office, and the memorandum instances as proof of the speedy work of the censor that only six minutes is taken to make the trip and return.

"The submission of other press matter by the newspapers is voluntary," the report continues. "Those who publish without submission do so on their own responsibility and subject to the penalties provided for breach of the regulations under the Defense of the Realm act. The greater part of the press submit a large amount of matter dealing with naval and military operations, questions of foreign policy, and like matters, to the bureau. Maps, diagrams, and photographs are also commonly submitted. The voluntary nature of the censorship accounts for many complaints, which are caused by some newspapers publishing, without submission, matter which others on submission were prevented from publishing."

Up to the time of presenting the memorandum the bureau had issued 200 orders of instruction to the newspapers. These are private and are issued at the request of the Admiralty or the War Office. The bureau distributes also all official statements issued by any branch of the Government, such as casualty lists, Foreign Office dispatches, and seat of war narratives.

Objects of Cable Censorship

The objects of the cable censorship is thus summed up: To prevent assistance being given to the enemy; to prevent the spread of false reports likely to cause dissatisfaction or to interfere with naval or military success or likely to prejudice relations with foreign powers; to collect and distribute to the several Government departments information derived from the censorship that may be of use to them; to deny the use of cables to persons or firms for commercial transactions intended to benefit the enemy, and to interfere as little as possible with legitimate British or neutral trade.

The influence of the Chief Cable Censor is far-reaching, for through his service he not only controls some 120 cable and wireless stations in various parts of the empire, but he controls in the United Kingdom messages sent over the cables of private cable companies as well as those transmitted over the Government wires. It is said that from 30,000 to 50,000 telegrams pass through the censor's hands each twenty-four hours. All cables are liable to be stopped which show clear evidence, either by the text or by the known facts as to the sender or addressee, that they relate to a transaction, whether in contraband or non-contraband, to which a resident in an enemy country is one of the parties.

The cable censors—and there are about 400 of them—are, with few exceptions, retired naval and military officers, many of whom were in commercial life when the war came.

Like the cable censorship, the postal censorship is designed to exercise a supervision with the least possible interference with legitimate correspondence. All mails which have to be censored are subjected to a slight delay, but harmless letters, the memorandum points out, are not stopped, even when coming from an enemy country or addressed to a person known to be an enemy. A letter in code or "secret" writing has not a chance to get by the censor, even though it is apparent that the messages have nothing to do with the war.

Classification of Letters

The censor has found that letters come under three general classifications. There are those of prisoners of war in Great Britain and those from British prisoners in the countries at war. These are censored in the Prisoners of War Branch. The second classification is the private letters and these are from members of the British expeditionary force and from persons within the war area; letters and parcels to and from foreign countries, and press messages sent by mail and newspapers. In this branch more than a ton of mail matter is censored each week, and this does not include the parcels. The third class is the commercial correspondence with foreign countries, and this is dealt with in the Trade Branch, and amounts to nearly four tons each week.

Letters coming directly from the area of military operations are in most cases censored locally, under orders of the Field Marshal or General Officer Commanding in Chief the British forces in the field. Those that appear to have escaped the censor are sent by the Post Office to the censors in London.

The transmission of newspapers in bulk between foreign countries and publishers and news agents of note is not subject to restriction. There is no restriction on the sale of newspapers from the enemy's country in England.

"Among the critics of the postal censorship, as among those of the cable censorship," says the report, "there appear to be two opposite and irreconcilable ideals of censorship. Complaints are sometimes received from the recipients of censored letters that their letters can only have been opened out of idle curiosity. Others, again, complain that the censored letters should never have been permitted to reach them if the censorship were efficiently performed. It may, therefore, be worth recording that curiosity is usually extinguished after a short period of employment as censor, and that the censors are not instructed to assume that the mere reception of a hostile and possibly abusive letter by a British subject will undermine the loyalty of the recipient."

* * *

July 13, 1915

WILL CENSOR MAGAZINES

Four Pittsburgh Policewomen Named to Pass on Their Propriety

PITTSBURGH, July 12—Charles S. Hubbard, Director of Public Safety, issued orders late today for the establishment of a bureau of censorship to pass upon all magazines sold in Pittsburgh. Magazines transgressing the bounds of morality and propriety will be barred and newsdealers who fall to observe the police regulations will be subject to arrest.

Four policewomen were appointed by Director Hubbard to read all publications received here each month. Verse, prose, and illustrations deemed objectionable will be marked and submitted to the Director.

* * *

October 13, 1915

PARIS PAPERS DEFIANT

Protest Declares They Will No Longer Be Dictated to by Censor

PARIS, Oct. 12—The protest of the Association of Paris Newspapers against the suppression of newspapers on account of violations of orders of the censor prohibiting the publication of certain articles complains that foreign newspapers of neighboring countries, both allied and neutral, coming into France contain news held back from the Paris newspapers by the censor.

"The French press," says the protest, "is conscious of having since the beginning of the war taken up the defense of the most sacred national interests. It has not merited the daily injuries inflicted upon it, and manifest its resolution no longer to submit to the violence imposed by those who shelter the arbitrary behind authority in power."

The protest is signed by Jean Dupuy, Arthur Mayer, Stephen Pichow, ex-Foreign Minister; Henri Simond, and other notable managers of Paris papers.

* * *

October 22, 1915

CENSORS DIDN'T KNOW VERSES OF KIPLING

Did Not Recognize Browning's Lines Either, Commons Is Told

LONDON, Oct. 21—The British censor's antipathy to poetry, as evidenced recently by deletions of lines of Kipling and Browning, when quoted in dispatches from the front, was gravely considered in the House of Commons this afternoon, when Ronald McNeill, author and Unionist Member of Parliament for the St. Augustine's Division of Kent, asked Sir John A. Simon, Secretary for Home Affairs, what poets could be quoted with immunity.

Sir John explained that the difficulty lay not in a military objection to poetry, but to the censors' failure to recognize the same. The censors attention had been called to the matter, he added, with the suggestion that they cultivate the muse.

The quotation from Kipling referred to in the foregoing dispatch is cited in a recent issue of The London Daily News, received here:

"A correspondent," says The Daily News, "had the audacity to quote the not wholly unknown lines:

The tumult and the shouting dies, The captains and the kings depart.

"The revised version of the second line after submission to the censor read as follows. 'The captains . . . depart.' One might not mention kings."

* * *

July 7, 1916

ARMY HEADS EXPLAIN PRESS CENSOR VIEWS

Reveal in War Department Statement How Newspapers Have Affected Campaigns

JAPAN'S POLICY OUTLINED

Say Sherman's March to the Sea Was Due to Information Imparted by Southern Journals

Special to The New York Times

WASHINGTON, July 6—A statement of what the General Staff of the United States Army regards as the "proper relationship that should exist between the army and the press in war" was issued at the War Department today through Major Douglas MacArthur, U. S. A., the recently appointed censor of the War Department. This statement sets forth the arguments of the General Staff officers of the army in support of the bill recently introduced in Congress at the request of the General Staff to provide for a press censorship to be put into effect when needed in the event of war.

The statement deals with the influence of the press on the conduct of the war, gives numerous instances of military successes resulting from information gleaned during recent years, and explains what has been done by Japan, England, Germany, France, and Bulgaria in the present European war. The statement discusses the Crimean war, the Franco-Prussian war, the Spanish-American war, the Russo-Japanese war, and the present conflict with regard to the influence of the press on the success or failure of armies. The statement in part follows:

"1. Influence of the press on the conduct of war.

"When other means have failed and the country has decided on war, the army and navy are the only agencies of the Government by which it can obtain its desired ends. They become paramount, and every utility and influence within the country should be brought to their aid.

"The press, powerful in peace, may become more so in war. By its editorials and presentation of news it may sway the people for or against the war and thus stimulate recruiting and hearten and encourage the fighting forces in their work, or, by adverse criticism, may tend to destroy the efficiency of these agencies.

"Again by publishing news of the movements and numbers of our own troops valuable information can be conveyed to the enemy.

"Instances of military successes resulting from information gleaned from the press during past years:

"During the Crimean war the Russians gained very reliable information regarding the works in the trenches of the allied armies and the progress of the siege of Sebastopol from the English newspapers.

Southern Press Aided Sherman

"In the American civil war the Northern generals obtained exact and valuable information through the Confederate papers. After the fall of Atlanta, Jefferson Davis, speaking at Macon and Palmetto, stated that measures had been taken in Tennessee and Kentucky to cut off Sherman's supplies from the north and that having an army in his front and rear, in hostile land, he must be annihilated. These speeches, published in the Southern and reproduced in the Northern press, soon reached Sherman. Acting on this information, and in order to keep his communication free, the Federal General began his famous march through Georgia to the sea. The reports of his successful progress, which appeared in the Southern press, enabled Grant to send supplies to meet him at the coast.

"In July, 1870, Major Krause of the German staff was able by means of French newspapers to ascertain the composition and strategical disposition of all the French corps.

"When McMahon, in 1870, attempted his disastrous march to the relief of Bazaine in Metz, to the success of which secrecy was essential, his movements become known to Prussian headquarters through English and French newspapers.

"An instance, though of less importance, may be quoted from the other side. When, on the 8th of December, 1870, General Faidherbe assumed the offensive with 30,000 men of the Army of the North, he made his diversion by way of St. Quentin, having learned from the Prussian newspapers that the first German army was in Normandy.

"During the Spanish war the success of the Cuban expedition of May, 1898, was seriously menaced by the news in the American press concerning the concentration at Tampa. Every military movement was reported in the American newspapers, and the Spanish Government had, within two or three hours, complete accounts of the American preparation for war.

"As an example of the importance of excluding from the press all mention of military movements, the following may be related:

"When it became evident to our Military Information Division in 1897 that war was certain to occur between the United States and Spain, an attempt was made to discover not only the number but the garrisons of the Spanish Army in Cuba. This was an extremely difficult task because there was little, if any, direct information upon the subject, the Spanish Government having, so far as known, discontinued the practice of announcing in orders the departure of troops for the island. But the division was a subscriber of the chief Spanish newspapers, both before the war and during its progress.

"In these newspapers mention would be made now and then of an action at such and such a place in Cuba, the name of the regiment and battalion being given. By carefully compiling such mentions during a space of time extending over many months the Military Information Division was enabled to arrive at a really accurate estimate of the strength of the Spanish forces in Cuba, with their supplies of ammunition and other resources, and moreover, was enabled to state the composition of the various garrisons scattered throughout the island.

"This information naturally was of the very greatest value to our Government. It would have been of still greater value had land operations in Cuba lasted. Now, most of this information was gathered, as already said, from the newspapers, but not from formal statements of the departure of troops, giving their number, destination, and regiment or other unit, but from the most casual and, as it were, accidental mention of the regiments and actions in the island by the Madrid papers from time to time.

"These mentions were so broken in character that it perhaps never occurred to the Spanish that they could be made the solid foundation of accurate information as to the strength of Spanish garrisons in the island, but, slight and insignificant as these data were, taken item by item they were, nevertheless, made to yield a most important result, a thing that would have been impossible had the Spanish press been totally silent on the subject of the troops serving in Cuba. Subsequent events showed that these estimates were almost exactly correct.

Japan's Policy Explained

"3. Control of Press by Japan in Russo-Japanese War.

"Japan was the first nation to completely take control of the press. In the early days of her war with Russia editors of Japanese newspapers were expressly prohibited from publishing the details regarding the organization mobilization or transportation of their country's naval and military forces.

"A warning was addressed to them emphasizing the power of the press to mar plans of operations, instances being cited from the Chinese-Japanese war of 1894–1895; and an appeal was made to their patriotism to suppress any information which, however interesting to the public, might be of use to the enemy or give him the least indication of Japanese intentions or movements. How loyally the Japanese press responded to this appeal is proved by the impenetrable mystery which shrouded the movements of Admiral Togo's ships and the marches of Marshal Oyama's armies.

"The treatment of foreign newspaper correspondents by the Japanese is well expressed in a cartoon of London Punch, which pictured a Japanese officer blindfolding a correspondent and as remarking, 'Abjectly we desire to distinguish honorable newspaper man by honorable badge.' The blindfolding of the foreign correspondents caused much ill feeling against Japan and was expressed in many articles published after these correspondents returned to their countries, but Japan gained her purpose.

"4. Control of press by Bulgaria.

"In the first Balkan war Bulgaria's mobilization and concentration was kept secret even from her own people. Correspondents after the concentration orders were received thought they were not permitted to see or report anything of value. Correspondents were, however, free to leave as they pleased, and after they crossed the boundary could publish what they pleased. Many false reports of movements, &c., were sent from neutral cities by correspondents who had never been at the front.

Great Britain's System

"5. Control of press by Great Britain in present war.

"In the present European conflict all nations engaged have instituted a rigorous censorship. Great Britain's experience must be of greater interest to us as conditions there are more nearly similar to our own.

"Great Britain appears at first to have two distinct organizations dealing with censorship. First, the press bureau, from which is given out such news as the Government desires to publish, and to which articles and dispatches to London newspapers are submitted for confirmation, permission to publish without confirmation, or suppression. Second, the cable censors, who pass on all cables filed, whether private, business, or journalistic. There is in addition a censorship of mail to hostile countries.

"In addition to the main press bureau there has been established in the Foreign Office a publicity bureau for the purpose of issuing information favorable to the Allies.

"There also exists in the Admiralty a censorship of wireless. This censorship has its authority in the general act giving to the naval and military officials the legal right to take such steps as might be necessary for the defense of the realm.

"For the period preceding the declaration of war, and for several days thereafter, (until Aug. 11,) there was no official or organized press bureau. However, the proprietors and editors of the great newspapers, irrespective of class or party, all combined to take no notice of questions which the Admiralty or War Office did not want referred to. Later the cable censorship became incorporated in the press bureau, and all press telegrams were censored at the Government central telegraph office. Cablegrams from abroad were sent by pneumatic tube to the central office, and after a censor's action sent to the addressee. Telegrams and cablegrams filed at any office were sent to the central office, and after a censor's action placed on the Government's lines or delivered to the company operating the cable.

"All press representatives were registered and any bulletin given out by the press bureau was simultaneously dictated to all. None could use it till all had received it. Before the change, made about Sept. 1, 1914, much criticism had been expressed of the methods employed, particularly that some censors permitted dispatches to pass which other censors prohibited. No correspondents were allowed at the front. Daily communiques, or bulletins, were issued from army headquarters, and these have been supplemented by weekly descriptions given out as written by an "eye-witness."

"It is understood that when the Dardanelles expedition was planned that the active heads of the great papers were called to the War Office and informed that but one correspondent would be permitted with the expedition. The newspapers were to decide on this man, and he would be in honor bound to send nothing but what was passed by the censor. Mr. Ashmead Bartlett was chosen for this purpose.

"The censorship has caused much criticism and discontent in England. The Government has been interpellated in Parliament and the press, particularly the Northcliffe papers, publish violent editorial comment. At first there was much confusion, due to the inexperience of the censors and to the lack of system. This seems now to be partly remedied.

"It was claimed, not without reason, that recruiting was impeded. Later, when more accurate statements of the losses in Flanders were permitted to be published, recruiting was greatly stimulated.

What France Has Done

"6. Control of press by France in present war.

"In France, at the outbreak of the war, the Government took advantage of the parliamentary act of 1850 which specifies that the Military Government shall have the right to suppress newspapers for disobedience of instructions given concerning the publication of military information. At the call of mobilization, shortly before war was declared, the Ministry in power commenced the organization of a bureau of press censorship.

"In a session of Aug. 5 the Chamber of Deputies passed a special act describing the military censorship to be established for the duration of the present war, but generally limiting the power of the censor to military and diplomatic information, political matters being excluded.

France, as in other nations, first permitted no correspondents at the front; later certain well vouched for newspaper men have been taken on personally conducted tours. The army issues daily communiques, supplemented by periodical 'eyewitness' stories, which are carefully worded, and which, of course, contain nothing of value to the enemy.

"7. Control of press by Germany in present war.

"Germany, as in all matters of preparation, was forehanded in her laws, and it was only necessary to issue the necessary decrees or orders prohibiting the publication of military information. While guarding the publication of useful military information, she has used the press to her advantage by permitting carefully conducted tours to the front of accredited newspaper men, especially neutral correspondents, and permitting them to publish interesting human interest stories, containing nothing of value to the enemy.

"(8. Influence of Press on Success of the Army.)

"The above has been written with a view of showing the influence that the press can have on the success of armies and the steps that have been taken by foreign nations to prevent the publication of information valuable to the enemy. There are two ways in which the press has a direct influence on the success of the army.

"First—It may, by publishing names of organizations, numbers, movements, accounts of victories or defeats, furnish information to the enemy that will enable him to deduct the strength and location and intended movements of our own troops.

"Second—By criticism of the conduct of campaigns and the action of certain officers or exploiting others the people will be led to lose confidence in the army, with the result that the moral support of the people is lost. They cry for and obtain new Generals and new plans of campaign, not based on expert knowledge and thought, with a consequent lengthening of the war or even defeat.

"On the other hand, the desire of the people to know how the war is progressing and how fare their men is one that should be fulfilled. The press is their means of this information and their mouthpiece. The right correlation of these opposing interests will furnish the solution of the proper relationship between the army and the press in war. In our country, with its numerous newspapers expressing the ideas and wishes of different political parties, the numerous telegraphs, cable lines, and wireless stations furnishing means of communication within and without the country, the difficulty of proper control is very great.

"9. Willingness of the press to cooperate with the Government.

"It is known from the statements of prominent newspaper men that the responsible press associations and newspapers will meet the Government half way in this matter."

* * *

November 9, 1916

HEARST PAPERS UNDER BAN

Their Circulation in Canada Prohibited After This Week

OTTAWA, Ont., Nov. 8—The Hearst papers have been placed under the ban in Canada. These publications have been prohibited from circulation from Saturday next. The heavy penalties of the War Measures act will apply to any one having them in possession after that date. Facilities are also denied the International News Service.

An explanatory memorandum issued this afternoon says:

"The Postmaster General of Canada has issued a warrant under the provisions of the War Measures act whereby the Hearst papers have been refused the privilege of the mails in Canada, and are prohibited from circulation in Canada in any way.

"No person in Canada is to be permitted after Saturday next to be in possession of the newspapers or of any issues of them, and any person in possession of them shall be liable to a fine not exceeding $5,000 or imprisonment for any term not exceeding five years, or both fine and imprisonment."

The managers of the Hearst papers in New York and the managers of the International News Service said yesterday that they had not been advised of the action of the Canadian Government. They expressed no surprise, however, at the report and considered it a natural sequence to the action of the British Government some weeks ago, which put the ban on the International News Service in England. They were not inclined to believe that the Canadian order would injure their service seriously.

* * *

December 3, 1916

FORBIDS CRIME MOVIES

Pennsylvania Censors Condemn Thrilling Pictures on Screen

HARRISBURG, Penn., Dec. 2—Films showing safecrackers at work, tramps stealing watches, and people taking drugs are to be eliminated from moving picture theatres in Pennsylvania, according to a bulletin issued today by the State Board of Censors. A long list of film plays, some of them thrillers, with heroines tied to tracks, is forbidden.

Scores of films in series are enumerated as condemned, including about sixty on the subject of white slavery and twenty-five on Mexican scenes, whose manufacturers the censors have been unable to locate. Prize fighting films have also been put under the ban.

* * *

March 25, 1917

CENSORSHIP RULES DRAFTED FOR PRESS

Regulations for Voluntary Use In Emergency Are Target of Newspaper Criticism

ONE ESPECIALLY ATTACKED

Proposed by Lansing, It Might, if Enforced, Check Needed Publicity on National Policies

Special to The New York Times

WASHINGTON, March 24—Regulations "relative to censorship," which newspapers of the country were asked to accept and follow voluntarily, pending the enactment of a press censorship law by Congress, were announced today after a conference between representatives of the State, War, and Navy Departments and of four press associations.

The newspapers of the country were not consulted and had no opportunity to make suggestions, and this has brought criticism on the ground that the press associations, which do not reflect opinion, were accepted as the spokesmen of the great newspaper press of the United States upon which the American people must depend for interpretations in support or criticism of governmental policies.

Most of the principles laid down in the censorship regulations have been and are being observed in spirit by the newspapers, which have endeavored to follow the wishes of officials as to what to print and what not to print at this critical period. Practically all the criticism heard after the regulations were made public was directed to the sixth regulation, which reads:

It is requested that no information, reports, or rumors attributing a policy to the Government in any international situation, not authorized by the President or a member of the Cabinet, be published without first consulting the Department of State.

It was a subject of remark that this regulation was not presented by a representative of either of the military branches of the Government, but by the State Department. It was laid before the conference in behalf of Mr. Lansing. As originally presented it was extremely drastic, and created the impression that what was sought was a suppression of public opinion and proper information and comment in regard to public matters. Objection to the adoption of this regulation in that form was immediately voiced, and as a result the phraseology was changed.

Those present at the conference, which was held in the Navy Department, were Secretaries Baker and Daniels, Counselor Polk, Major MacArthur of the Army, Commander Belknap of the Navy, Mr. Harrison of the Department of State, and the representatives of the press associations.

All the regulations had been drawn at the Navy Department with the exception of the objectionable No. 6, but opportunity for their study had not been given to most of those present who saw them for the first time when the conference was begun.

Officials of the three departments represented were made aware this afternoon that the newspapers of the country would find cause for objection to several of the regulations and particularly to No. 6. It was made plain that the press associations had no right to speak for the newspaper press of the country which reflect opinion and seek to give an idea of the impression made by governmental policies.

In this connection it was brought out that the head of one of the press associations had proposed, prior to today's meeting, that hereafter the Government should forbid the publication of any matter not contained in official statements handed out by the proper authorities, and that copies of these should be furnished only to press associations and not to individual newspapers. If this proposal were adopted the people of the country would be kept from knowledge of public happenings which Government officials did not choose to make known, and as a result it is suggested there probably would be a suppression of everything that might tend to excite criticism. It is understood that the officials concerned will reject this suggestion as unworthy of adoption in a country in which a free press is guaranteed by the Constitution. This guarantee is contained in the first amendment, which provides: "congress shall make no law . . . abridging the freedom of speech or of the press."

Objections to Regulation

One of the objections to regulation No. 6 is that its observance would forbid the publication of information obtained in a trustworthy quarter in regard to a foreign policy of Government unless the Department of State gave its consent. It was pointed out today that the Department of State might undertake to put into effect a policy that would be of vital importance to the American people, such as an abandonment of the traditional avoidance of alliances with other powers, and for the purpose of preventing the possible defeat of its plan through a free expression of public opinion could forbid the newspaper which obtained this important news from publishing it.

Officials favorable to the regulation disclaimed any desire to suppress information which it was proper for the public to know. They said that there was no intention to place an embargo on the expression of editorial opinion. At the same time it was said that the object of this regulation was to prevent the publication of statements that information had been obtained on authority when it had not come from the President or a member of the Cabinet, and speculation as to governmental policy that was not based on authoritative disclosures as to what course the Government intended to follow.

The matter of press censorship is regarded here as important to the people of the country as well as to the press. A recent tendency in Washington to conduct public affairs with the utmost secrecy has emphasized the danger of the censorship question. Little guidance is afforded the press in telling of the international situation, and the old policy of informing the newspapers of what is being done as much to prevent as to further the publication of certain news is rapidly becoming a dead letter.

Text of the Regulations

This statement, embodying the text of the regulations, was given out after the conference:

"In view of the desire of the press of the country to refrain from the publication of information harmful to the public interest, and with the intention of securing the maximum publicity with the least injury thereto, the following regulations are hereby issued for its guidance, which it is earnestly requested be closely observed:

Regulation 1. No information, reports, or rumors should be published which tend to disclose the military and naval policies of the Government of the United States. (This regulation is directed against the publication of any news or comment which might reveal the strategic disposition or operation of armies or their sub-divisions or the fleet or its sub-divisions; any measures which might be adopted in consonance with the Department of State for the furtherance of American defense, and, in general, any plans for the use of the army and navy during the existence of a national emergency.)

Regulation 2. No information, reports, or rumors should be published which tend to disclose:

(a) Movements or employment of armies and their subdivisions, fleets, and their subdivision.

(b) Movements of vessels of the navy or their arrival at or departure from any port.

(c) Departures of merchant vessels should not be mentioned, and it is desired that the name of the port of arrival be omitted.

(d) Assignment or movement, whether as groups or individuals, of officers and men of the military and naval establishments.

(e) Transportation of mails, supplies, or munitions.

(f) Information of any designs, inventions, or test thereof; or of manufacture, transport, or distribution of implements of war.

(g) Concentration of military or naval supplies or location of such supplies.

(h) Activities in or about arsenals, fortifications, Army posts, naval magazines, navy yards, naval bases, and radio stations.

Regulation 3. Publication of any maps, diagrams, or photographs which in any way might seem of military or naval value.

Regulation 4. No moving pictures should be displayed which are of military or naval value.

Regulation 5. Any doubtful matter should be submitted to the authorized representatives of the department concerned, who shall give an immediate decision thereon and keep the inquiry made strictly confidential.

Regulation 6. It is requested that no information, reports, or rumors attributing a policy to the Government in any international situation, not authorized by the President or a member of the Cabinet, be published without first consulting the Department of State.

Note—The above regulations shall not be enforced in any matters officially given to the press by properly authorized officials.

* * *

April 22, 1917

OPPOSE CENSORSHIP AS NOW PROPOSED

Newspapers of the Country Generally Find Restrictions Unjustifiable

KAISERISM, ONE CRITIC SAYS

Others Point Out That the Measure Throttles the Constitutional Freedom of the Press

Special to The New York Times

SAN FRANCISCO, April 21—The San Francisco Chronicle stand on the first amendment to the Constitution of the United States is that "Congress shall make no law abridging the freedom of speech or of the press." M. H. De Young, publisher of The Chronicle, referring to the proposed censorship section of the Espionage bill now before the Senate, says:

"I am strenuously opposed to any action being taken in the present juncture which will bring down the important safeguard of our liberties—the freedom of speech and the freedom of the press—and look upon any and all efforts to do so as a step in the direction of that system of autocratic government which it is the professed purpose of those who are warring upon Germany to destroy. The United States statutes are sufficiently explicit in their provisions to prevent abuse of the privileges of the press, and if they are not adequate they may be added to and such penalties prescribed as would deter would-be violators. But the American press should not voluntarily accede to a proposition which will absolutely debar it from criticism and practically put it under bureaucratic control.

"I am convinced of the impracticability of the Russian method of excision in a country as large and populous as ours. There are nearly 250 daily newspapers and 16,000 weeklies and 3,750 magazines in the United States. If any system of official supervision were devised, to be impartial, it would be necessary to put censors in every office. The mere statement of this necessity emphasizes its impracticability and points to the only proper course to pursue, namely, to hold publishers to a strict accountability for violations for any regulation which may be prescribed."

Grave Danger of Caesarism

LOS ANGELES, April 21—The Los Angeles Times today printed an editorial on the censorship in which it said that there was grave danger to American civil and special life in the censorship as proposed in the Espionage bill, as it undertakes to place bureaucrats of the Army and Navy Departments in virtual editorial charge of American newspapers.

"The fears of Senator Lodge that the clause is unconstitutional and un-American," it said, "are well grounded. There is grave danger in enacting a censorship clause like this that the Administration is establishing a Caesarism, a Kaiserism, at home in the very era in which it is seeking to dispossess a Caesarism abroad. The incapacity of Caesarism to deal with a crisis like the present one is well exemplified in the case of Russia.

"The crisis, while grave enough, calls for no such rigorousness as is proposed in the censorship clause, as all the world is against Germany, and there is no danger of any sort of information reaching the Caesarism of Germany calculated to hurt either the Entente Powers or the United States."

"The voluntary censorship of the American press itself would be eminently sufficient. The loyalty and patriotism of the American press has never been called in question."

Violation of the Constitution

Special to The New York Times

ST. LOUIS, April 21—The Globe-Democrat, under the caption "Freedom of the Press," says:

"The Senators who are striving to remove from the Espionage bill the power it would place in the hands of officialdom are not battling for the publishers, but for fundamental American principles, whose preservation are essential to democracy itself.

"Certain provisions of the Espionage bill violate the Constitution. A censorship, to keep the enemy from learning things of value to him, would be lawful and proper, though in this particular crisis, when America is filled with German subjects, the importance of severing all communication with Germany is vastly greater than press censorship. The legislation as proposed would prevent proper criticism and keep the people from knowing what they are entitled to know."

Should Trust the Newspapers

Special to The New York Times

PITTSBURGH, April 21—The Post tomorrow will have this to say on the censorship question:

"The regulations of the Government with respect to the publication of the news of the war should be made with regard for the unanimity with which the press has acted in harmony with the ideas of precaution without censorship laws. With this Government, founded on the principle of freedom of opinion, Congress should refrain from action against the judgment of men trained in passing on the news and whose patriotism is above question. As we are at war to do away with such means of deceiving the people as are manifest in Germany, it behooves Congress to be on guard against members who have felt the smart of just criticism of the press and would be glad to make the censorship provision the vehicle for their spite.

"No newspaper wants to publish anything that would be detrimental to the Government. No intelligent or patriotic citizen wants any newspaper to publish such information; but the newspapers and the public want something left to their judgment as to what should be published, instead of leaving the whole matter to a little board. A censorship blow at the press is a blow at the public."

Cites an Error by the Censorship

Special to The New York Times

PHILADELPHIA, April 21—The Public Ledger, in an editorial on the Espionage bill, will say tomorrow:

"America will never submit to the suppression of information to which the people are plainly entitled, and the sooner the authorities at Washington understand it the better.

"On Friday afternoon the news of the arrival in this country of a distinguished representative of one of the great powers was sent to the newspapers, but the dispatch was instantly followed by notice that its publication was forbidden by the censor. But what makes this order of the censor more glaringly foolish is the fact that the coming of this particular foreign statesman had been heralded for more than a week, and the Secretary of State had gone so far as to suggest openly a public reception in his honor.

"The newspapers of the United States are prepared to join heartily with the Government in a wise discrimination as to the wisdom and permissibility of publishing news of military operations or preparations, but neither they nor the people will submit to be bound hand and foot or to be subjected to the senseless whim of unknown, irresponsible, and inexperienced officials charged with a duty for which they are unfitted."

The Record will say:

"Temporarily the Senate has laid aside the Espionage bill to take up the bill to place the army of the United States on a war footing. The laws defining and punishing treason would meanwhile be adequate to reach all, whether aliens or citizens or professional or amateur newsmen, who collect, report, or publish information of military value in order to give aid or comfort to the public enemy. Some Senators have expressed the belief that the laws against treason as they stand are sufficient. Anyhow, a law that might result in the suppression of legitimate and honestly patriotic criticism of the Government ought not to be passed until it has had the most searching consideration."

Counsels Caution in Congress

Special to The New York Times

ROCHESTER, N. Y., April 21—The Democrat and Chronicle tomorrow will say editorially:

"The best course Congress could take would be to leave the censorship clause in abeyance for the present. The matter is not one requiring headlong haste, for the reason that the newspapers are operating under a voluntary form of censorship that so far has worked well and may prove to be all that is needed. Publication of the sailings of merchant ships from our ports, for example, has been entirely suspended at the request of the Navy Department. Publication of news also of the movements of troops is being carefully edited in order to avoid embarrassing the War Department."

"Not Accustomed to Muzzles"

Special to The New York Times

HARTFORD, Conn., April 21—"The American people are not accustomed to wearing muzzles," The Courant says, discussing the Espionage bill, "and it will be a mistake if the Government uses the war crisis to try to put one on the country today. A reasonable censorship of the newspapers seems to us all right. In fact, it would apply only to the sort of newspapers that ought not to be published, anyway. Those that would try to make money by the 'enterprise' of forestalling the Government's policy or action at home or in the field, and those that would incite to rebellious conduct ought to be shut up, and laws adequate to this cleansing process would not be unwelcome to newspapers generally.

"But if a rigid, stupid, dictatorial censor should undertake to shape and regulate American thought and forbid even passing criticism the people would not stand for it. The great body of American newspapers may be relied on not to publish anything injurious to the country to which they belong, and which in large measure they represent."

Treason Statutes Held Adequate

Special to The New York Times

DENVER, April 21—Under the caption of "Reasonable Press Censorship," The Rocky Mountain News prints the following:

"If the National Administration insists upon a gag law in the name of press censorship it will be the first to suffer. If it provides a board of partisan censors, with power to prevent honest criticism of the Administration and heads of departments actively engaged in the prosecution of the war, under the Espionage law pending in Congress, the people will rebel. We state this with the experiences of Great Britain in the first months of the war to go upon.

"Control over outgoing means of communication through the mails, by cable, or wireless, or matter in the possession of spies leaving the country, is right and proper. National danger in time of war comes from these quarters, not from the newspaper. The latter, if it is worthy the name, can be of great assistance to the Government and to the nation, provided it is not hampered by extremists or faddists. It is true that there are publications which require attention from the Government because of their persistent faking and personal antagonism to those engaged with us in prosecuting the war against German autocracy; but they can be dealt with under the law of treason."

Demands Constitutional Rights

Special to The New York Times

MILWAUKEE, April 21—In an editorial on the censorship question The Sentinel will say tomorrow:

"The publication of news that may be useful to the enemy or of a character where secrecy is desirable in the public interest may properly be forbidden, and its willful publication by an American newspaper might amount to giving that aid and comfort to the enemies of the United States which the Constitution defines as treasonable. On the other hand, there must be no suppression of that Constitutional right of free speech, which in the Constitutional meaning is expression of opinion, and it goes without saying that such right must not be so abused as to circumvent the censorship of news information by smuggling in that information under the mask of comment or criticism. The distinction between news and views is essential, and involves a distinction between proper press censorship and unlawful press muzzling."

Sacredness of a Free Press

Special to The New York Times

OMAHA, April 21—The World-Herald will say tomorrow: "There is widespread objection to some features of the war censorship bill. If there is anything sacred to the average American it is a free press, and any encroachment upon it is sure to be received with aversion. It is, of course, desirable in war time to limit as far as possible the publication of any news that will 'give aid and comfort to the enemy,' and further than that the American people will not be willing to go. The people are willing to submit to any restrictions that will aid the Government in prosecuting the war, but will resent being annoyed with unnecessary restrictions."

Says Newspapers Can Be Trusted

Special to The New York Times

MEMPHIS, Tenn., April 21—The Commercial Appeal says editorially:

"The papers can be depended upon voluntarily to print no military fact that might be of military use to the enemy. There is no necessity for a censorship bill. The Government has practically now, under military regulations, set forth certain rules which the papers will honorably observe. It will be a dangerous thing for the liberty of the public and the liberty of the people to attempt in any way to curtail free expression as to Governmental policies by the American papers.

"In those States where the libel laws are severest, and where the liberty of the press is thereby curtailed, there is the least progress, the most graft, and the most political corruption. A free press in time of war, as well as in time of peace, is necessary to the well being of the Republic."

Press May Be Depended Upon

Special to The New York Times

BUFFALO, April 21—In a first page news comment The Buffalo Express this morning says:

"The Senate yesterday committed itself to a press censorship for the war, but a proviso was added that there shall be no restriction on discussions and criticisms of the Government's acts and policies. It will, at least, be much better to have the Government act under definite law than under suspension of habeas corpus, as was done in the civil war."

The Evening News says:

"The press may be depended upon to refrain from publishing news that will be inimical to the national well-being, while still continuing to show virtue her image, scorn her own features, and ineptitude and inefficiency its form and pressure. In this time we fight for ideals, and newspapers are our fortresses, and their guns will be trained upon the enemy, not upon ourselves."

"Directed at Propagandists"

Special to The New York Times

SEATTLE, April 21—In commenting on the press censorship section of the Espionage bill The Post-Intelligencer says today:

"The provision which raised most of the objection in the Senate is designed to prevent 'discussion, comment, or criticism' of the acts and policies of the Government or its representatives. It is directed as much at misguided propagandists as it is at newspapers. While a war is in progress little good can come from bushwhacking the men we have placed in positions of responsibility. While ninety-nine newspapers will be patriotic, the hundredth might consider it good business to print valuable military information or to rail at the Government."

Favors a Definite Law for All

Special to The New York Times

BALTIMORE, April 21—In an editorial on the Espionage bill The Sun says today:

"The Sun cannot agree with certain of its contemporaries which are opposing all censorship bills and arguing that a voluntary censorship will suffice. The careless publishers as well as the disloyal publishers—if, indeed, there be any of the latter—are to be reckoned with in this connection. It is better to have a law, drawn as definitely as possible, which will apply to all alike and do away with the temptation to print a piece of doubtful news in order to score a beat on a competitor than no law at all. The trouble with the censorship section is that it does not define the character of prohibited news as definitely as possible."

* * *

May 28, 1917

CENSOR CREEL GIVES OUT RULES FOR NEWSPAPERS

Would Bar Speculation About Possible Peace, or Differences of Opinion

WITH ALLIES OR NEUTRALS

Articles "Likely to Prove Offensive" Likewise Put Under the Ban

OTHER RULES OBEYED NOW

They Are Such as the Newspapers Voluntarily Adopted—Censorship Bill Likely to be Defeated

Special to The New York Times

WASHINGTON, May 27—The Committee on Public Information, of which George Creel is Chairman and whose other members are the Secretaries of State, War, and the Navy, gave out for publication tonight a set of proposed regulations for the newspapers under the title of "Preliminary Statement to the Press." The whole is described as "regulations for the periodical press of the United States during the war."

The most interesting part of the pamphlet is the portion printed under the heading "Explanation," in which occur these passages.

For the elucidation of the above section [Section I.] the following notes have been submitted by the Departments of State, War, and the Navy:

The Department of State considers it dangerous and of service to the enemy to discuss differences of opinion between the allies and difficulties with neutral countries.

The protection of information belonging to friendly countries is most important. Submarine warfare news is a case in point. England permits this Government to have full information, but as it is England's policy not to publish details this Government must support that policy.

Speculation about possible peace is another topic which may possess elements of danger as peace reports may be of enemy origin, put out to weaken the combination against Germany.

Generally speaking articles likely to prove offensive to any of the allies or to neutrals would be undesirable.

Chairman Creel has been commonly referred to as the Government censor, but he has always insisted that his purpose is to increase instead of curtail the amount of information furnished to the press for the benefit of the people in the war period.

His statement was originally submitted in confidence to the corps of Washington newspaper correspondents, with the object of obtaining their voluntary adhesion to the regulations suggested for the government of newspaper publication during the war. At a meeting of the correspondents in the Senate press gallery, at which Mr. Creel was present, it was decided that more time was essential to study the regulations and the other suggestions and explanatory matter contained in the pamphlet. Just prior to a subsequent meeting the correspondents learned that President Wilson had written a letter to Chairman Webb of the House Committee on the Judiciary urging the adoption of a press censorship section of the Administration's Espionage bill. The correspondents had obtained the understanding that if the voluntary "Regulations for the Periodical Press" were accepted by them, there would be no further effort to have a censorship statute enacted. At that time the censorship provision of the Espionage bill appeared to have been killed in Congress.

In view of the continued effort of the Administration for a drastic press censorship law, particularly after the newspaper press had demonstrated its patriotism and loyal diseretion by the suppression of news of possible benefit to the enemy the Washington correspondents decided at a meeting held in the House of Representatives press gallery last Wednesday to take no action on the request to consider and accept the suggested regulations for a voluntary censorship.

"Foreword" by Creel

The purpose of the Committee on Public Information in making public the suggested regulations for a voluntary press censorship after the Washington correspondents had declined to consider them, because the Administration was endeavoring at the same time to provide press regulations by a criminal statute, is not known although a "Foreword" signed by Creel indicates that the committee desires to let the people of the United States know exactly what it has in mind with reference to establishing a censorship for American newspapers. The foreword follows:

Belligerent countries are usually at pains to veil in secrecy all operations of censorship. Rules and regulations are issued as "private and confidential," each pamphlet is numbered, and the recipient held to strict accountability for its safe and secret keeping. The Committee on Public Information has decided against this policy and the press is at liberty to give full publicity to this communication. It is well to let people know just what it is that the committee proposes and desires, so that there may be the least possible impairment of public confidence in the printed information presented to it.

GEORGE CREEL
Chairman. Committee on Public Information.

"The only news which we wish to keep from the authorities at Berlin," says the committee—and it italicizes its words—"is the kind which would be of tangible help to them in their military operations."

It was Information of this kind that the American press has consistently refrained from printing, and it was supposed, until the Administration served notice last week that it would insist on a press censorship provision in the Spy bill, that the present voluntary attitude of the newspapers would be brought into a more definite form through arrangement with the Committee on Public Information.

The statement reviews the attitude of European Governments with respect to press restrictions during the war, and declares that the policies of the committee will be based on the assumption that "there is the hope and belief that the printed word in the United States will equally lend itself to the national, defense and that the American press will realize the obligations of patriotism as keenly as those who take the oath of service in army and navy." The committee says that the news most desired by the enemy General Staff "will not be collected from our newspapers, but will be gained by high-grade and highly placed spies."

The committee thinks that in spite of all precautions a certain amount of spy communication probably will be maintained, and it says. "The really dangerous spies are high officials or officers in high command." The problem in America, the committee thinks, is to stop the source of such information by preventing leaks and interfere with its transmission. A censorship of outgoing cables has been established, but the committee enjoins self-restraint on the newspapers in publishing news.

The committee, after speaking of the effort of European belligerents to keep news from neutral countries, says it is not the intention to exercise such a censorship against the neutral countries of South and Central America. It notes that "nearly all the European belligerents have tried to prevent the publication of news likely to offend their allies or create friction between them," but "the committee is of the opinion that the more full the inter-Ally discussion of their mutual problems the better."

The preliminary statement also strongly emphasizes the disagreement of the committee with the methods of European press bureaus to keep objectionable news from their own people, such as reports of outbreaks of epidemics in training camps. "The motive for the establishment of this internal censorship," says the committee, "is not merely fear of petty criticism, but distrust of democratic common sense." The people won't be stampeded, the committee believes, but the knowledge that such information is suppressed will permit the circulation of enemy rumors.

The internal censorship has generally tended to "create the abuse of shielding from public criticism the dishonesty or incompetency of high officials." And "there are several well-established instances where the immense power of the censor has fallen into the control of intriguing cliques." The committee comes out flatly in opposition to such methods.

Some "Explanations"

Among the explanations given of the regulations are the following:

"The Department of War points out that trains and ships transporting troops are inviting objects of attack for individual enemies or enemy sympathizers. One person armed with high explosives may cause great loss of life under such circumstances and therefore any publication in the daily press giving advance notice of the movements of troops may supply the enemy with information of the highest military value.

"There is no objection to the publication of news regarding the location of army posts, militia, or training camps, but already a number of isolated attacks have been made on sentries and small pickets, with some loss of life. While it may be safe to print the Seventh Regiment has gone to the State capital on guard duty, it is dangerous to say the Seventh Regiment is guarding a particular aqueduct or bridge.

"With regard to the prohibition concerning aircraft and experimental tests, it is pointed out that while many of the machines used in this work are of standard types, every detail of which is commonly known, others are not, and it is to preserve the secrets embodied in the latter that a general policy of silence is requested. While secrecy as to aircraft is considered necessary, publicity as to the activities of the aviation schools, the enrollment of men for this particular service, &c., is considered useful.

"The Department of the Navy urges that no accounts shall be printed of active naval operations, successes, or mishaps until after they are officially announced. Such announcement will be made as soon as accurate reports are at hand. Editors and publishers are asked to save the public from the unnecessary distress of false rumors. The Department of the Navy does not wish to hold back information, but to assure the public of correct information.

"The fact that merchant ships have arrived is news of such importance that it is desirable not to suppress it. But it is of greater importance not to publish nor even to hint at the particular port of arrival, for it may at any time be necessary to shift shipping from one port to another, and it is desirable to keep information of such shifts of base from the enemy submarines.

"Statements from survivors of merchant ships or transports which have been attacked or sunk by enemy shellfire or by submarines, or have been damaged or sunk by mines, should not be published until the statements have been referred to and passed by the committee. The judicial murder of Captain Fryatt of the Wrexham will give point to this advice. Editors will appreciate the importance of co-operating to withhold from the enemy such information as might expose the officers and men of merchant ships to the danger of cruel and outrageous reprisal."

The Regulations

The proposed regulations themselves are comprehensive. They provide for the suppression of news matter which is already being voluntarily suppressed by the newspapers. Included among the matter to be suppressed are the following:

A—GENERAL

News regarding naval and military operations, except that officially given out.

News of the train or boat schedules of traveling official missions in transit through the United States.

Threats or plots against the life of the President or other high officials, unless announced from authoritative sources. When arrests are made, this specific charge should be minimized by mere mention as "disorderly conduct."

News relating to the activity of the secret police.

News of possible or observed movements of alien labor through the territory of the United States or their arrival at, or embarkation from, any of our ports.

B—NAVAL

News relating to the naval operations, as follows:

The locality, number, or identity of warships.

Secret notices to mariners.

All information concerning the departure of merchant ships.

All information indicating the port of arrival of incoming ships.

Details as to convoys and as to the sighting of friendly or enemy ships.

Information concerning the laying of mines.

Information regarding signals, orders, or wireless messages to or from war vessels.

Information regarding operations by or against submarines.

Information relating to drydocks and to all classes of works, repairs, alterations, or construction performed in connection therewith.

C—MILITARY

News of possible or observed movements of Canadian troops through the territory of the United States or their arrival at or embarkation from any of our ports.

Information regarding the fired land defenses of the United States, their very existence, as well as the number, nature, or position of their guns should not be mentioned.

Information in regard to the train or boat movements of troops is at all times and under all circumstances dangerous during a war and should be scrupulously avoided.

Specific information regarding the duties of small detachments should be avoided as dangerous and laying them open to attack.

Information regarding the assembling of military forces at seaports from which inference might be made of any intention to embark them for service abroad.

Information regarding the aircraft and appurtenances used at Government aviation schools and tried out in experimental tests under military authority.

Section 2, on "Questionable Matter," reads as follows:

"There are many other news items which, while not so obviously dangerous as those listed in Section 1, may be dangerous. In all cases of doubt, editors are requested to seek advice of the Committee on Public Information. The following are some examples of such doubtful news:

"1. Narrative accounts of naval or military operations, including descriptions of life in training camps. While it is desirable that the public should be kept interested in these subjects, there is always a chance that a reporter, narrating facts, may unconsciously mention something which the military authorities particularly desire to keep from the enemy: all such articles should be submitted to the Committee on Public Information.

"2. Technical inventions. It is desired that the subject of possible new military inventions should be kept before the public, but great care should be exercised in publishing any definite statements as to experiments or accepted inventions.

"It is of peculiar importance that all Government experiments in war material should be veiled in absolute secrecy. This request has particular application to the search for means to combat the submarine. Therefore all articles and news stories along these lines should be submitted for vise.

"The name of every well known inventor is connected with a single kind of work and may not be mentioned without conveying to the enemy a hint as to the nature of the invention upon which he is working.

"An instance of the menace of the specific mention of the work of an inventor was afforded by the result of the publication of a newspaper story that the well-known inventor in question had discovered a U-boat killer. The story was followed the next day, quite naturally, by another story that police protection against German agents had been immediately required to, guard both the man and the works where the experiments were supposed to be conducted. That the report of the invention had been promptly denied did not lessen the peril to life and property caused by this piece of editorial inadvertance.

"3. Many sensational and disturbing rumors will be brought to the attention of newspaper men. It is to be desired that they should not be given publicity until they have been most carefully verified; for example, sporadic epidemics may break out in some of our training camps. It would be most unpatriotic to give credence to exaggerated accounts of such inevitable mishaps. Editor's are requested to submit information which they may receive on such subjects to the committee for verification. Daily reports from the chief sanitary officers will be available. And this committee will arrange to have parties of newspaper men and reputable doctors sent to camps where sickness occurs to check up these reports.

"The above list is by no means exhaustive and is intended only to indicate the type of subject matter which should be submitted for censorship."

* * *

July 10, 1917

SOCIALISTS TO TEST THE ESPIONAGE ACT

Editors of Radical Publications Would Establish Their Right to the Mails

PLAN UNITED LEGAL ATTACK

Action of Solicitor Lamar in Declaring The Masses Nonmailable Stirs its Publishers

The exclusion by the Post Office Department of several incendiary issues, among the last being the August number of Max Eastman's anarchist magazine, The Masses, is causing some radical editors to hesitate before publishing attacks on the Government. Becoming more restive every day under the restraint of the Espionage act of June 15, 1917, they now plan to make, through a committee of lawyers, a concerted legal attack upon the action taken by Solicitor Lamar in declaring "nonmailable" all publications that might be interpreted as seditious.

Inasmuch as most of these radical publications are opposed to war and persistently attack conscription, they have come into direct conflict with that section of the Espionage act, now incorporated in the Postal Laws and Regulations as Section 481½, which declares "nonmailable" all matter which is intended to interfere with the operation or success of the military or naval forces of the United States or to promote the success of its enemies, or which is intended to cause insubordination, disloyalty, mutiny or refusal of duty in the military or naval forces of the United States, or which is intended to obstruct the recruiting or enlistment service of the United States."

Solicitor Lamar has already made use of the section. Ever since the passage of the Espionage act, he has barred from the mails issues of The Appeal to Reason, The American Socialist, The International Socialist Review, The Four Lights, and The Masses. Recent issues of many other radical publications have been held up pending further inquiry into the exact nature of their contents.

The editors and publishers of these magazines are now bitter in their denunciation of the Solicitor. They assert that the Espionage act is in itself so general and so vague that it remains purely a matter of interpretation on the part of the Post Office Department as to whether or not a publication shall be declared "nonmailable."

The management of The Masses made every effort to convince Solicitor Lamar that the August issue was innocent of wrong. Merrill Rogers, business manager of The Masses, went to Washington and begged Mr. Lamar to point out just what in the issue was objectionable under provisions of the Espionage act. The Solicitor according to Mr. Rogers, refused to specify, but insisted that the entire tone and spirit of the August issue was such as to render it "unmailable." He even threatened the editors of The Masses with indictment if they endeavored to put the issue before the public in defiance of the order.

Floyd Dell, managing editor of The Masses, said yesterday that nothing had been done with the August issue thus far. No attempt will be made to put it through the mails, as such defiance of the Solicitor's injunction would make the editors liable to five years' imprisonment and a fine of $5,000. If the magazine is put on sale on the news stands the Department of Justice, it is believed, will take immediate action against the editors.

Mr. Dell insisted yesterday that there was nothing in the paper tending to interfere with the success of recruiting for the army and navy. The issue, however, contains several cartoons on the subject of conscription, one of them being the picture of a boy tied to the mouth of a cannon, with the figures of a man and woman, representing respectively, labor and democracy, chained to the gun carriage. The magazine also contained several caricatures which were likely to hold army and navy recruiting up to ridicule.

Postmaster, Thomas G. Patten said yesterday that the Post Office declares no publication "nonmailable" without first having the authority to do so from Solicitor Lamar. No policy of exclusion or suppression is pursued against a publication as a whole, but each issue is accepted or rejected by the Post Office on its own merits.

* * *

August 10, 1917

ARREST GERMAN EDITORS

St. Paul Publisher Accused of Printing Objectionable Articles

St. PAUL, Minn., Aug. 9—Dr. Fritz Bergmeier, President of the St. Paul Volkszeitung, was arrested today under the President's proclamation of April 6. The policy of the Volkszeitung has been to "cast aspersion by innuendo" on American war measures, it was charged. Bergmeier was committed to jail pending further orders from Washington.

In a statement, Dr. Bergmeier said he had tried to make all matter printed in the Volkszeitung conform to Federal regulations. Bergmeier came from Germany twelve years ago and has taken out first naturalization papers.

Reflections on General Pershing were among the objectionable articles in the Volkszeitung, it is understood. District Attorney Jacques said no trial would be held and that the editor would be held as an enemy alien until President Wilson permitted his release.

LITTLE ROCK, Ark., Aug. 9—Curtis Ackerman, editor of a German newspaper here, was arrested yesterday charged with encouraging resistance to the draft. Henry Rector, assistant United States District Attorney, said that a young man of German parentage who had been called in the first draft had informed him that Ackerman offered to give him powders which would reduce his weight so that he would be physically disqualified. Ackerman was released on $2,500 bond.

* * *

August 19, 1917

PRO-GERMAN PAPERS UNDER CLOSE WATCH

Government Investigators Looking After Anti-American Utterances in Many Quarters

SOME MAY BE SUPPRESSED

Sections of Espionage Act to be Invoked in Checking Attacks Upon This Country's Welfare

An official of the United States Government, who is now engaged in an investigation of certain anti-American and pro-German pamphlets and weekly newspapers printed in this part of the country, said yesterday that one result of the investigation has been to prove to him that not only are the persons identified with this propaganda laboring in the interests of the enemies of the United States, but that in a majority of cases they are also working to bring about in the United States such a condition of affairs as the so-called Soldiers' and Workmen's Council sought to bring about in Russia. Within the past few weeks some of these publications have assumed a pro-German attitude even more violent than before the United States declared war on Germany.

For weeks past the Post Office and Department of Justice inspection services have been keeping a close watch on the circulation of these anti-American publications, so far as the mail is concerned, and among the possibilities of the near future is the suppression of at least some of the more violent of these papers and pamphlets. The country-wide investigation now under way is being made under the authority of Section 8 of Title 1, and Sections 1, 2, and 3 of Title 12 of the Espionage act, which was signed by President Wilson on June 15 last. These sections are as follows:

Title One

Section 3. Whoever, when the United States is at war, shall willfully make or convey false reports or false statements with intent to interfere with the operation or success of the military or naval forces of the United States or to promote the success of its enemies, and whoever, when the United States is at war, shall willfully cause or attempt to cause insubordination, disloyalty, mutiny, or refusal of duty, in the military or naval forces of the United States, or who shall willfully obstruct the recruiting or enlistment service of the United States to the injury of the service of the United States, shall be punished. By a fine of not more than $10,000 or imprisonment for not more than twenty years, or both.

Title Twelve

Section 1. Every letter, writing, circular, postal card, picture, print, engraving, photograph, newspaper pamphlet, book, or other publication, matter or thing, of any kind, in violation of any of the provisions of this act, is hereby declared to be nonmailable matter and shall not be conveyed in the mails or delivered from any Post Office or by any letter carrier: Provided, that nothing in this act shall be so construed as to authorize any person other than an employe of the Dead Letter Office, duly authorized thereto, or other person upon a search warrant authorized by law, to open any letter not addressed to himself.

Sec. 2, Every letter, writing, circular, postal card, picture, print, engraving, photograph, newspaper, pamphlet, book, or other publication, matter, or thing, of any kind, containing any matter advocating or urging treason, insurrection, or forcible resistance to any law of the United States, is hereby declared to be nonmailable.

Sec. 3, Whoever shall use or attempt to use the mails or Postal Service of the United States for the transmission of any matter declared by this title to be nonmailable, shall be fined not more than $5,000 or imprisoned not more than five years, or both. Any person violating any provision of this title may be tried and punished either in the district in which the unlawful matter or publication was mailed, or to which it was carried by mail for delivery according to the direction thereon, or in which it, was caused to be delivered by mail to the person to whom it was addressed.

The principal objects sought by those responsible for the circulation in this country of these pro-German, anti-American newspapers, pamphlets, and circulars, are:

First—To stir up trouble between the United States and Great Britain by circulating statements that England brought about the present war, that England is really an enemy and not an ally of the United States and printing cartoons and drawings the purpose of which is to create in the minds of the people of the country the impression that President Wilson and other high officials of the Government are tools of the British Government, exploited for the selfish purposes of Great Britain.

Second—To spread broadcast the statement that the United States went to war in order to save the fortunes of certain rich men and of various corporations engaged in the manufacture of munitions of war, and that President Wilson willfully and knowingly uttered an untruth when he said that the United States went to war "to make the world safe for democracy."

Third—To instigate all the trouble possible between American employers of labor and their employes, and to make the laboring people believe that they are being exploited in this war in behalf of the corporations and men of great wealth.

Fourth—To embitter the Irish-American population against the United States Government and endeavor to make them believe that President Wilson favors harsh measures in the handling of the Irish problem, this part of the propaganda being in charge of certain Irishmen who long ago left Ireland to make war on England from the United States.

Fifth—To agitate in all parts of the country in favor of a peace such as Germany favors and against which President Wilson, Lloyd George, and other Entente statesmen have time and again warned the peoples of the allied nations.

Sixth—to create the impression that American newspapers, while ostensibly owned by Americans are in fact owned by Englishmen and that the policies of these papers are secretly dictated by the British Government.

A few quotations taken at random from several issues of the various anti-American publications referred to indicate the violent and seditions nature of this propaganda. These are from recent issues of a violent anti-American publication, the avowed policy of which is to create all the trouble possible between the United States and England.

The English are so entrenched in Calais that the French are wondering if they ever intend to get out—if Calais is to be another Gibraltar!

"Three million loan subscribers."—Headline. In other words, three million Americans who are interested financially in the war—not in its ending but its duration.

"Wheat crop offers little for export. Nation must economize and use substitutes to aid Allies." Headline. Surely, the nation will eat soap, shavings, grass, anything to let Englishmen get wheat, meat, and American products. If England is going to get the good things, let's move over there and enjoy American resources.

Milwaukee.—"At a meeting of the stockholders of the German-American Bank, the corporate name of the institution was changed to the American Exchange Bank. The action was taken by a unanimous vote."—News Item. Shame on the cowards!

The British Ambassador has written a letter to Senator Hale suggesting that Portland Harbor be deepened that it may be extensively used by Canadian shipping—much to the offense of Senators King and Sherman. But why should Spring-Rice have addressed. Hale and not Congress as Balfour did, while the President sat in the gallery?

Mayor Thompson won't truckle to England, and, therefore, he is a traitor. He wants to conserve American foods for Americans first and therefore be is a menace to Americans.

The following paragraphs are from the September issue of a monthly publication, which is considered by Government agents to be one of the most dangerous published in this country:

In America the month just past has been the blackest month for freemen our generation has known. With a sort of hideous apathy, the country has acquiesced in a regime of judicial tyranny, bureaucratic suppression, and industrial barbarism, which followed inevitably the first fine careless rapture of militarism.

The United States has a more extended record of atrocities to her credit than any other nation of the civilized world. The number of negroes lynched in this country since 1885 amounts to one in every four days. Some ironical god or destiny must have brought this long story of bloody public crime to its culmination in East St. Louis last month, just as we set forth on our chivalrous crusade to rid the world of "German" frightfulness.

This week's issue of a notoriously pro-German publication prints on its first page, in box form, an article signed "Robert M. La Follette," the concluding sentences of which are a plea for the election of men to Congress who will advocate the same policies as La Follette is now advocating.

"The citizen should begin to work now," says the Wisconsin Senator. "for the election of a Congressman who represents his views on the war issues. If he would preserve his liberties, his freedom of thought and speech and action he should not be intimidated by the threats of the war traders and their newspapers."

Here is one paragraph from a four-page document recently sent through the mails by a committee said to represent the Socialist-Labor Party:

What are the reasons for America's entry into the war? The principal immediate casus belli is the interference of Germany's submarine blockade with the profitable trade with the Entente Allies and the fact that this constitutes a violation of international law. But that is no explanation in itself, as Great Britain's mine-laying in the North Sea is equally a violation of international law. But in this case the violation has been submitted to, and American ships have been kept away from danger. The talk about the killing of Americans is calculated only to stir up warlike feelings in the masses who must do the fighting. If American ships had persisted in traversing the mine-sown area in the North Sea, the British would have been guilty of taking American life also.

Besides, the capitalists who want war care nothing for American lives. When did they ever let considerations of humanity interfere with their profit-making? Think of their massacre of the working class at Ludlow, Col., at Bayonne, N. J., and many other places; and the slaughter of American workers in industry, largely preventable except for considerations of profit! Yet "we" submitted to the British violations and went to war over the German ones. Why? Because "our" sympathy is on the side of the Entente Allies. And why is that? Because if the Allies do not win, and win quickly, they may not be able to pay interest on the money that J. P. Morgan and his crowd have loaned them. Besides, we cannot afford to let the industrial capitalists lose money by interference with their profitable trade. Sooner let thousands of American young men be killed in battle.

The country-wide activities of the so-called People's Council are well known. That organization is now publishing a propaganda pamphlet called "Facts." In a recent issue there appeared these verses, captioned "The War Maker":

He walked in peace in a frock of black
In the fields beneath the Dome:
But he did not know what it was to yearn
For the place we once called home;
He did not know what it was to die
And rot in the burning sun.
A thousand men in a dripping trench
All rotting one by one.

He did not wear a gilded coat.
Nor a helmet on his head
But he spoke the word that hurled us all
On the scrap heap of the dead.

When President Wilson designated the Sixty-ninth New York as the first of the New York troops to go abroad, the Irish agitators lost no time in branding it a pro-British, anti-Irish move. This week's issue of the Gaelic American prints a long article on this "outrage," in which it says:

The rumors which have been floating around for some time in relation to the Sixty-ninth, namely, that it was to be quietly smuggled out of the country and paraded through Ireland and England, for the purpose, if possible, of turning the tide of Irish Nationalism and inducing Irish youth to go and fight England's battles in Europe—those rumors seem to take concrete shape in rushing off the Sixty-ninth in this spectacular fashion for reasons that are purely political. We find it hard to believe that the War Department can be so fatuous as to think that any such paltry attempt at befooling the Irish race in America can be successful.

But Ireland's day is coming. It is at hand. The mighty blows that are staggering England and are sending her clamoring to America for help are breaking the bonds that bind Ireland. While the last vestige of her tyranny remains to fetter the upgrowth of Irish nationality, while a shred of alien English influence works banefully against Irishmen at home or abroad. England will have Irish enmity to deal with. Irish-Americans will not be cajoled or "honored" or humbugged into instrumentalities for saving England's neck here or in Flanders.

The Post Office authorities have sent tons of such stuff to Washington for inspection by the officials of the department.

"We know all about it," said Postmaster Pattern yesterday, "and Washington is being given all the evidence that comes into our possession. As to what action is to be taken is a question I am not in a position to answer."

* * *

September 15, 1917

GERMAN EDITORS HELD

Government Will Ask Indictments Against Tageblatt Officials

Special to The New York Times

PHILADELPHIA, Sept. 14—Five officials of the Philadelphia Tageblatt, the German language newspaper which, it is charged, shaded war news to favor Germany, and which is alleged to have distorted war dispatches, were held in $10,000 bail each this afternoon by United States Commissioner Long. The Commissioner said there was evidence that the newspaper was in sympathy with Germany and that contention was substantially proved by an article in the paper.

The officials who were held in bail today are: Herman Lemke, business manager; Dr. Martin Darkow, managing editor; Louis Werner, editor in chief; Peter Schaeffer, President, and Paul Vogel, Treasurer.

To prove the contentions that the newspaper favored Germany, the Commissioner cited among other things a story headed "We are Ready." Under this heading there were quotations from a German newspaper concerning preparations being made by the German fleet for action with the United States. The Commissioner said the general tenor of the story distinctly showed sympathy with Germany.

Attacks upon the policies of the United States Government, which appeared in different issues of the Philadelphia Tageblatt, were frequently indorsed by the German Consulate of this city, according to evidence brought out at the hearing. A letter signed by former Consul Dr. George Stobbe and sanctioning several editorials submitted to him was introduced.

Before the hearing was begun, United States Attorney Kane announced that the Department of Justice was in possession of proof that the prisoners had violated the Espionage act.

A speech of Senator La Follette, according to the Government translators, was wrongly interpreted by the editors of the Philadelphia Tageblatt, when they wrote headlines quoting Senator La Follette to the effect that "Bread Riots Would Soon Take Place."

The Government will ask indictments against the six men for violations of the Espionage act in publishing seditious and treasonable articles.

* * *

September 16, 1917

100 RADICAL PAPERS MAY BE SUPPRESSED

Government Is Investigating Pro-German, Anti-American Publications

SOME BARRED FROM MAILS

The American Socialist Makes Hero of La Follette—All for Peace at Any Price

More than 100 newspapers, weekly and monthly magazines are now under investigation by the Post Office authorities in Washington. The great majority of these are owned, edited and distributed by persons identified, generally in official capacities, with the Socialist, pacifist, anarchistic, and I. W. W. movements in this country. All of them favor immediate peace with Germany, as a rule on the terms which the Prussian autocracy is said to approve, and all of them are frankly and outspokenly against the Government at Washington.

These anti-American publications are published in all parts of the United States and are main cogs in a propaganda machine which has been built up by professional pacifists, anarchists, I. W. W. agitators, and radicals who term themselves Socialists. A number of these publications have already been barred from the mails, and there is reason for saying that in the near future a drastic order will go forth barring the mails to every paper and pamphlet in the country whose policy is to urge defiance of the Government and laws of the United States.

In the office of Walter L. Lamar, the Solicitor of the Post Office Department, in Washington, a reporter of The Times was permitted to inspect the great piles of papers and other printed material got out by the so-called People's Council, the radical branches of the Socialist Party, anarchistic organizations, aliens, many of the latter enemy aliens resident in the United States since the war with Germany began.

Many Are Printed Here

With his big staff of assistants Mr. Lamar is kept busy day and night going over these pro-German and in an a great many instances outright treasonable publications. Tables, bookcases, and cabinets in the office of Mr. Lamar are piled high with copies of these papers, a majority of them published in English, and practically all of the rest printed in the German or Hungarian languages. New York and Chicago are the cities in which more than 50 per cent, of them are printed.

The most widely circulated of all the publications now under investigation was, prior to its being barred from the mails, The American Socialist, published in Chicago, the editorial page of which announces that it is the official organ of the Socialist Party of the United States. This publication has been and is one of the main supports of the pro-German peace propaganda in the United States, and an effort is now being made to continue its circulation by delivering the papers by express. There is a report in Washington that the express companies may issue instructions to their agents to refuse to accept it for transportation.

In one of the latest issues of this paper circulated by express there appears a long article dealing with the program of the so-called People's Council, of which Dr. David Starr Jordan, Winter Russell, Morris Hillquit, H. Weinberger, the lawyer who represents the anarchists in New York City, and various other pacifists, and agitators are identified. As a matter of fact, there is hardly an issue of any of these anti-American publications which are not actively supporting the work of the People's Council, an organization which one of the highest officials of the United States Secret Service recently described as "among the most dangerous anti-American organizations in the United States."

Reprint of La Follette's Speeches

Senator La Follette of Wisconsin is liked by the Socialistic press and whole pages are given over to the reproduction of his speeches in Congress and elsewhere. The American Socialist, in its issue of Sept. 1, referring to La Follette's recent effort to conscript 80 per cent of what is termed the "war profits of the country," remarks that "the Socialist demand as interpreted by La Follette, Gronna and Thomas immediately rallied strong support in the Senate."

Here are a few excerpts appearing in a recent issue of The American Socialist:

The Organized Farmer figures out that the Liberty Loan was a failure because the 2,000,000 individuals who subscribed for it probably represent the 2 per cent of the population who own 60 per cent of the wealth. It shows that the 98 per cent, who own 40 per cent, of the wealth of the land were not back of the loan.

"Business as Usual," is the slogan of the exploiters. J. Ogden Armour voices it in The New York Times. Sure, don't let a little thing like war, 10,000,000 lives, and a violation of the United States Constitution bother you. The workers will have to pay the price anyhow, why worry?

Charges that the British Ambassador, Buchanan, at Petrograd, has been using his influence to restore the old Russian regime are contained in an article in Socialist Prime Minister Kerensky's paper, The Djen. It is stated that Kerensky called Buchanan on the carpet and told him to stop his efforts to restore the Czar to the throne.

As the war mania grows stronger, life becomes cheaper in the United States. "Shoot any one who refuses to leave the trains," were the orders given to a militiaman stationed at the railroad bridge at Covington, Ky. This order had hardly been put into force when a militiaman's bullet claimed its first innocent victim. This brand of murder will assert itself more and more as Prussianism tightens its grip on the nation.

All war and no play makes Jack a dead boy.

Where there is war there can be no real liberty.

One of the circulars barred some weeks ago by the Post Office Department, so far as its circulation through the mails was concerned, was the so-called "Anti-War Proclamation and War Program" of the Socialist Party of the United States. This circular, in the form of a ballot, declared among other things that the Socialist Party calls upon "the workers of all countries to refuse support to their Governments in their wars" and adds that "we particularly warn the workers against the snare and delusion of so-called defensive warfare."

Call War a Crime

"The forces of capitalism," the document adds, "which have led to the war in Europe are even more hideously transparent in the war recently provoked by the ruling class of this country. . . . Our entrance into the European war was instigated by the predatory capitalists in the United States. . . . They are also deeply interested in the continuance of the war and the success of the allied arms through their huge loans to the Governments of the allied powers and through our commercial ties. . . . It is hypocrisy to say that the war is not directed against the German people but against the Imperial Government of Germany. . . . We brand the declaration of war by our Government as a crime against the people of the United States and against the nations of the world. . . . No greater dishonor has ever been forced upon a people than that which the capitalist class is forcing upon this nation against its will."

"In harmony with these principles" the majority committee of the Socialist Party, therefore, according to the circular barred from the mails by the postal authorities, "recommend to the workers and pledge ourselves to the following course of action:

1. Continuous, active, and public opposition to the war, through demonstrations, mass petitions, and all other means within our power.

2. Unyielding opposition to all proposed legislation for military or industrial conscription. Should such conscription be forced upon the people, we pledge ourselves to continuous efforts for the repeal of such laws and to the support of all mass movements in opposition to conscription. We pledge ourselves to oppose with all our strength any attempt to raise money for payment of war expense by taxing the necessaries of life or issuing bonds which will put the burden upon future generations. We demand that the capitalist class, which is responsible for the war, pay its cost. Let those who kindled the fire furnish the fuel.

3. Vigorous resistance to all reactionary measures, such as censorship of press and mails, restriction of the rights of free speech, assemblage, and organization, or compulsory arbitration and limitation of the right to strike.

4. Consistent propaganda against military training and militaristic teaching in the public schools.

5. Extension of the campaign of education among the workers to organize them into strong, class-conscious, and closely unified political and industrial organizations, to enable them by concerted and harmonious mass action to shorten this war and to establish lasting peace.

6. Widespread educational propaganda to enlighten the masses as to the true relation between capitalism and war, and to rouse and organize them for action, not only against present war evils, but for the prevention of future wars and for the destruction of the causes of war.

It was the policy outlined above which caused such influential men as John Spargo, Charles Edward Russell, and other prominent men to withdraw from the Socialist Party.

In Chicago there is printed a paper called The Social War. Like The American Socialist, it is barred from the mails, and is now being circulated by express. It is one of the most violently anti-American publications in the country.

In a recent issue, this paper, which circulates mostly among agitators of the extreme types, such as anarchists and I. W. W.'s, stated editorially:

Told to Refuse to Obey Laws

"The strike, sabotage, and other acts and demonstrations are expressions of consciousness. He must refuse to pay his tax to existing parasites; to obey any of the reactionary laws of the State; he must refuse to recognize that national flag which symbolizes his down-trodden condition. He must throw off the sham of patriotism and pointblank decline to serve the nation. He must refuse to be the marksman and make targets of his father, mother, brother, or sister."

In New York City, a Hungarian publication, which is marked for action, so far as the mails is concerned, referring to the sending of troops to France, remarks gleefully that these reinforcements for the Anglo-French front will not be sufficient to "make up for the Russian millions who were able to overflow Prussia, Galicia, Bukovina, and the northern countries of Hungary."

A four-page paper called The Eye-Opener, printed in Chicago, is another of the hundred or more publications which is the subject of an official inquiry.

These papers and pamphlets indicate the kind of propaganda that the United States Government has to contend with at the present time. Among the other offenders the nature of which propaganda is in keeping with the general spirit of the anti-Government campaign are The Jeffersonian, published by Tom Watson in Georgia; The Bull, published in New York; The Masses, and New York anarchist publications.

* * *

September 16, 1917

INDICT GERMAN EDITORS

Government to Rush Trial of Philadelphia Tageblatt Officials

PHILADELPHIA, Sept. 15—The five men arrested in connection with the raid by the Government on the Tageblatt, a German language daily newspaper published in this city, were indicted today by the Federal Grand Jury. The men are Peter Schaefer, President; Louis Werner, Editor-in-Chief; Dr. Martin Darkow, Managing Editor; Herman Lemke, Business Manager, and Paul Vogel, Treasurer. They will be tried for conspiring to print false reports in violation of the espionage law.

There were nine additional counts in an indictment of Werner and Darkow on the charge of treason.

It is stated that the Government will push the cases against the men, and that they will be brought for trial in a short time. They are all at liberty on $10,000 bail each.

Secret Service men, translators, and Government attorneys are busily engaged in examining the great mass of printed matter and manuscript seized when the newspaper office was raided last Monday. Two wagonloads of papers were taken, and, though some of the most expert translators in this city and Washington are working day and night, the task is difficult and slow.

* * *

September 27, 1917

MAY BAR "MOTHER EARTH"

Magazine Must Show Cause Why Mails Should Not Be Closed to It

The Post Office Department has served notice on the anarchist magazine Mother Earth to show cause why it should not be barred from the mails.

Ben L. Reitman, business manager of the magazine, sent a letter to the department yesterday in which he argued against "suppression of free speech."

"A section of the American people," wrote Dr. Reitman, "whose numbers are growing daily, (whether for good or for evil,) are anxious, desirous, and determined to read radical literature, such as is contained in our magazine, Mother Earth. It is too late to change this taste for reading matter. Mother Earth, The Masses, The Jeffersonian, The Rebel, The Free Press, The International Socialist Review, and other papers that the Government is attempting to suppress have become the Bible for millions of people living in America. These magazines are not only the reading matter and literature of these citizens, but their gospel as well. They are determined to have them, and, if I know anything about history, it looks to me as though they would get them one way or another.

"I understand that these are trying times, and our Government is in no mood to temporize with radicals and theorists, and that America is in danger and needs the support and confidence of every publication and every man, woman, and child within its domain. We are anxious this should be, but, unless America, and the Post Office Department especially, respects the rights and needs of millions of her inhabitants who are feeling, thinking, struggling, and desirous of maintaining constitutional democracy in a way which may be a little different from that desired by a small group of Senators, legislators, or officials, then America will have to suffer the experience of internal disturbances such as Russia is now having."

* * *

October 15, 1917

PROTEST CLOSING OF MAILS TO CALL

Madison Square Garden is Thronged for Mass Meeting at Which Hillquit Speaks

SEE DANGER TO WORKERS

Speakers Declare Suppression of the Paper Will Extend to All Critics of Government Policy

A protest against closing the second-class mail to The New York Call was made at a Socialist mass meeting in

Madison Square Garden last night. The big auditorium was filled to its capacity, and the police estimated there were 10,000, who couldn't get within the doors.

The Call has been cited to show cause at a hearing in Washington this afternoon why it should not be deprived of the second-class mail privilege for violating the Espionage act. Morris Hillquit, Socialist candidate for Mayor, one of the speakers last night, received an ovation lasting fifteen minutes. He said that it was vain to protest, that the Post Office Department, "accuser, judge, and executioner," had made up its mind and that "The Call is definitely and irrevocably doomed."

United States Marshal McCarthy and fifteen men, Assistant District Attorneys Content and Stanton, Post Office Inspectors Shea, Doran, and Fitch, Police Inspector O'Brien, and Herman Karpeles of the American Defense Society were on guard with stenographers to watch against anything disloyal and were determined to break up the meeting if any sedition showed itself. But there was little virulence in the references to the Government, and what there was was by innuendo rather than by direct statement.

Two hundred policemen outside kept the crowd in good order, lining the people on the sidewalks on all the streets leading away from the Garden. On Fourth Avenue the crowd extended north to Thirtieth Street. An attempt was made to hold an overflow meeting in Madison Square, but the police would not allow it.

All of the speakers saw in the suppression of the Socialist newspapers the determination of the "capitalists" to crush Socialism and "the workers."

Every reference to peace was loudly cheered, and while Morris Hillquit was speaking one of the red, white and blue streams across the ceiling of the Garden broke away at one end and slowly fell. It was a white streamer and at once there went up the cry of "Peace, peace, peace." Then a moment later another streamer floated down. It was a red streamer and grasping an analogy of Socialism triumph after peace, the crowd went wild for five minutes.

In referring to the citation of the Call, Mr. Hillquit said:

"The hearing has been set for tomorrow. The execution has probably been set for Thursday or Friday. From my sad experience in many similar cases, I assert that the so-called hearing is a farce. The revocation of second-class mailing rights means that the Call will lose practically all circulation outside of New York. The measure is intended to cripple, and, if possible, to destroy the paper. I maintain that the proceeding is without any sanction in law and that it is a flagrant violation of the most fundamental constitutional rights of American citizenship."

Mr. Hillquit said that the Espionage act was aimed at willful aid to the enemy and not at suppression of free speech.

Voices Readers' Sentiments

"The New York Call," he said, "has at no time violated or counseled the violation of any provision of the Espionage act or any other law. It has at all times voiced the sentiments of its readers and followers against war and for peace, and it will continue doing so in spite of all un-American edicts of the Post Office Department."

Mr. Hillquit said that it was unfair to ask The Call to show cause why it should not be barred from the mails without naming any alleged violation of the law. He referred to the Postmaster General as a "prolific accuser, a merciless judge, and a prompt executioner." Then he reviewed the steps of the department against The Milwaukee Leader, the Hungarian Elore, the Russian Novy Mir, the German Volks-Zeitung, the Jewish Daily Forward, and said:

And the great people of the great American Republic stand silent and passive before this boldest of all attacks upon the most vital of their rights and liberties. That is the great tragedy of it.

"There is no reason to believe that the crusade of extermination will stop at the Socialist press. Emboldened by the passive acquiescence of the people, our Post Office bureaucracy may extend the ban to all publications that dare to disagree with the policies of the Administration or to criticize public officials, and if permitted to do so under the pretext of a war measure, it may continue the lawless practice in times of peace."

Mr. Hillquit then asked every Socialist to become a circulation solicitor for The Call, to make up the circulation it would lose through disbarment from the second-class mail.

"The short-sighted Washington bureaucracy expects to stamp out the Socialist movement by destroying its organs of expression," he said. "Vain and silly endeavor. The Socialist movement cannot be killed. The Socialist movement thrives and grows and wins under persecution. The tyrants of Europe have learned this lesson to their sorrow. The German Kaiser and the Russian Czar have tried it. We are 4,000,000 strong in Germany, and the only real foe of German autocracy and the only real hope of German democracy."

Then Mr. Hillquit made a plea for his election as Mayor.

Strike Blow for Socialism

"If the people want peace and justice and liberty," he said, they must vote into power the party of the people, the party of the workers, the Socialist Party. Workers of New York, let us make the beginning here and now. Let us strike the first great blow for Socialism and democracy on Nov. 6."

Mention of Mayor Mitchel's name brought a roar of "boos." There was no mention of Judge Hylan's name by any of the speakers.

S. John Block, candidate for Attorney General on the Socialist ticket last year, presided. He seemed to enjoy the hisses his every mention of Postmaster General Burleson's name brought.

"Our public officials," he said, "are working on the theory that a little knowledge, spread by The Call, is a dangerous thing. Yes, a little more knowledge on the part of our working people will be a very bad thing for our autocratic politicians."

There was prolonged applause when he said "a secret communication has been received in Washington from Mr. Nicholas Romanoff, who up to last Spring held a position of some importance in a benighted country, in which he asks this Government to arrange matters so that he can be transferred to Washington, and he offers his services to the Postoffice Department–he would be at home there."

Ludwig Lore, editor of the Volks-Zeitung, which was cited to show cause why it should not be barred from the mails, defended his course by saying that his paper was fighting German autocracy at a time when our Government officials were hobnobbing with German Emperors and Princes.

"The Volks-Zeitung was called to Washington," he said, "but the Volks-Zeitung did not go because it thought that first the Postmaster General should show cause why it should be barred. It did not go because it could not take back one word it had said in the past or promise to be better or worse in the future."

He denied that his paper had ever been pro-German, and predicted that when "the friends in Washington and the friends in Berlin shall again be shaking hands the working classes in both Germany and America will be fighting both militarism in Germany and militarism in America."

Charles W. Erwin, editor of The Call, referred to his maltreatment by "the lords of misrule," and said; "We shall continue to be uncompromising. We will not yield an inch, and we will be heard." He said The Call had gained 20,000 circulation in the last week, and asked for 40,000 increase the coming week, adding: "The best man on my circulation staff is Postmaster General Burleson."

James H. Maurer, President of the Pennsylvania State Federation of Labor, who has been active in the work of the pacifist People's Council, spoke against the "master class." When he mentioned the name of Colonel Roosevelt there was a storm of "boos," which he interrupted by saying, " 'Tain't worth it, boys; 'tain't worth it."

He referred to the statements of Colonel Roosevelt and others against seditionists. In defending the I. W. W. he said:

"I am not an I. W. W., but I say this for them—their only crime is that they are class-conscious and consistent, and fight for their convictions."

He repeated his attack on the leaders of the American Federation of Labor, accusing them of not supporting the rights of the workers during the war, and then returned to the subject of the I. W. W.

"If the Government can destroy one kind of labor union," he asked. "what is to prevent it from destroying other kinds? I tell you, if the Washington Government gets away with what it is trying, the workers of America will be the most servile class the world ever saw."

* * *

October 26, 1917

LOYAL PRESS SAFE, BURLESON ASSERTS

Postmaster General Says Only Those Who Print Sedition or Treason Need Fear

WASHINGTON, Oct. 25—The scope of the Espionage and Trading with the Enemy acts, in so far as they affect the Postal Service, and how they are to be enforced against disloyal publications are explained at length in a letter to publishers made public today by Postmaster General Burleson.

The laws were made necessary, Mr. Burleson said, by a nation-wide propaganda, intended in every possible way to interfere with the successful prosecution of the war. He added that no publisher who was at heart loyal to his country should have any apprehension of embarrassment or inconvenience from their administration.

"No one connected with the Government," said the letter, "from the President down, seeks by reason of these laws to avoid criticism, or even attack, but no publication containing matter which falls within the prohibition of the law will be permitted to circulate."

As interpreted by the Post Office Department, the acts make it unlawful for any person, firm, corporation, or association to mail, or to transport, or carry, or otherwise publish or distribute during the war any printed or other matter:

1. Advocating or urging treason, insurrection, or forcible resistance to any law of the United States.

2. Conveying false reports or false statements intended to interfere with the operation or success of the military or naval forces of the United States or to promote the success of its enemies.

3. Intended to cause insubordination, disloyalty, mutiny, or refusal of duty in the military or naval forces of the United States.

4. Intended to obstruct the recruiting or enactment service of the United States to the injury of the services of the United States.

5. The circulation or publication of which involves the violation of any of the numerous other criminal provisions of the Espionage act, but which are not of special interest to publishers.

6. Printed in a foreign language containing any news item, editorial, or other printed matter respecting the Government of the United States, or of any nation engaged in the present war, its policies, international relations, the State or conduct, of war, or any matter relating thereto, unless the publisher or distributor thereof, on or before offering the same for mailing, or in any manner distributing it to the public, has filed with the Postmaster at the place of publication a true, complete translation of the article.

7. Referred to in the preceding paragraph for which publishers have received a permit to circulate, free of restrictions named therein, but which does not bear at the head

thereof in the English language the fact that such a permit has been granted.

* * *

November 20, 1917

INDICTS THE MASSES AND 7 OF ITS STAFF

Federal Grand Jury Charges Writers and Artists of Socialist Magazine with Conspiracy

MANAGER ALSO ACCUSED

Articles and Pictures, the Jury Says, Were Calculated to Interfere with the Draft

Six men and one woman, comprising part of the business and editorial staff of The Masses, the Socialist magazine, together with The Masses Publishing Company, were indicted yesterday by the Federal Grand Jury for violation of the Espionage act. There were two indictments, one charging the corporation and C. Merrill Rogers, Jr., business manager of the magazine, with having "unlawfully, willfully, knowingly and feloniously" attempted to use the mails for the transmission of matter declared to be unmailable, and the other, charging Rogers, Max Eastman, editor of the magazine, and others named with him of having conspired, while the country was at war, to cause, or to attempt to cause, "insubordination, disloyalty, mutiny and refusal of duty in the military and naval forces of the United States."

That criminal prosecution would follow the failure of The Masses in the courts to restrain the postal authorities from closing the mails to the magazine was clearly indicated during the argument in the lower courts, and in the Circuit Court of Appeals. It was said during these arguments that if the magazine contained matter that barred it from the mails those responsible for the publication of the unmailable matter were subject to indictment.

Immediately after the Circuit Court, on Nov. 9, sustained the action of the postal authorities, Earl B. Barnes, the Government prosecutor, laid the facts before the Grand Jury.

The Masses Publishing Company, which is named in both indictments, is charged with having violated the law at divers times from July 1 to Nov. 19, 1917, by distributing in this city and throughout the United States issues of the magazine for the months of August, September, and October, which contained matter which violated the law. The names of the other defendants in the conspiracy indictment, with the titles or the articles written or pictures drawn by them with the alleged intention of breeding disloyalty and of interfering with the Government in the raising of an armed force, follow:

EASTMAN, MAX, it is charged, between June 15 and Nov. 19, 1917, wrote and caused to be published in the August issued of the magazine an article entitled "A Question."

BELL, FLOYD, accused of the same offense in relation to an article entitled "Conscientious Objectors."

REED, JOHN, accused of having written and published an article called "Knit a Straitjacket for Your Soldier Boy."

BELL, JOSEPHINE, accused of having written and caused to be published in the August issue of The Masses a poem called "A Tribute."

GLINTERKAMP, HENRY J., accused of having drawn for the October issue of the magazine a picture representing a skeleton symbolizing death, taking the measurements of a drafted soldier for his coffin.

YOUNG, ARTHUR, an artist, charged with having drawn a picture entitled "Having Their Fling," which was reproduced in the September issue of The Masses.

Rogers is accused of having, as business manager, provided for the distribution of the magazine "against the peace of the United States and their dignity and contrary to the form of the statute in such case made and provided."

The conspiracy indictment declares that the defendants "conspired together, with other persons, unknown to the jury, to violate the provisions of Section 8 of Title 1. of the act of Congress, approved July 15, 1917, entitled 'An Act to Punish Acts of Interference with Foreign Relations, the Neutrality of the Foreign Commerce of the United States, to Punish Espionage, and Better to Enforce the Criminal Laws of the United, States.' "

The illegal acts were committed, the indictment said, "when the United States was at war with the Imperial German Government," and in order "unlawfully and willfully to obstruct the recruiting and enlistment service of the United States." It is alleged that the magazine contained articles, poems, cartoons, and pictures "calculated and intended to induce persons liable to military service to refuse to submit to registration and draft for service and to induce persons available and eligible for enlistment and recruiting to fail and refuse to enlist for service therein."

The indictment of The Masses and its staff, it was said yesterday, placed all similar publications and their editors and managers in the United States in danger of Government prosecution.

In September Mr. Eastman wrote to President Wilson congratulating him for not having adopted "the entire animus of the allied war on Germany." In his letter he denied that his magazine was part of an organized propaganda to encourage resistance to the draft.

The indictments were handed to Judge Mayer, who issued bench warrants for the indicted persons. The maximum punishment for the offenses charged is a fine of $10,000 and twenty years' imprisonment.

Gilbert E. Roe, counsel for The Masses, was asked last night to express an opinion on the indictments. He replied by saying that the first he knew of the action of the Grand Jury was when he read about it in the evening papers. He said he had not seen either Mr. Eastman or Mr. Rogers during the day.

Floyd Dell was formerly the literary editor of a Chicago paper. He came to New York several years ago, and has served as managing editor and book reviewer for The Masses.

C. Merrill Rogers, Jr., is a recent graduate of Harvard, where he made no public display of sympathy with radical movements.

Arthur Young is a cartoonist, who has treated principally of political topics. His work has appeared in several prominent magazines.

* * *

February 14, 1918

TO PROSECUTE REPINGTON AND MORNING POST EDITOR FOR DEFYING CENSOR BY PUBLISHING BANNED ARTICLE

LONDON, Feb. 13—Andrew Bonar Law, Chancellor of the Exchequer, announced today in the House of Commons that action would be taken under the Defense of the Realm Act against Colonel Repington, the military correspondent of The Morning Post, for an article which appeared in The Post on Monday, dealing with the deliberations of the Versailles Council.

The article was submitted to the censor, who refused permission for publication. The article was afterward published in a different form without being submitted to the censor.

Mr. Bonar Law announced that action would also be taken against the editor of The Morning Post.

Asked if he was aware that Colonel Repington had written for three and a half years for The Times with "perfect impunity" and without action being taken against him, Mr. Bonar Law said:

"Assuming that this is criminal, every criminal lives a long time before he is convicted."

Lieut. Col. Repington resigned from The London Times on Jan. 21, after fifteen years' service as military correspondent, and joined. The Morning Post. In an interview cabled to The New York Times on Jan. 28 he said:

"I have to thank Lady Bathurst, proprietor, and Mr. H. A. Gwynne, editor, of The Morning Post, for the fact that I am no longer muzzled, and that I can now tell the British public and the American public the truth about our armies in France. They have done a public service in enabling me to tell the truth, and I may say that Mr. Gwynne risked his personal liberty in so doing. Under the Defense of the Realm Act you can lock a man up for nearly anything, and if our War Cabinet did not know that the case which I presented on Thursday (Jan. 24) was fairly stated I make no doubt that both Mr. Gwynne and myself would be in jail already."

* * *

April 28, 1918

USES AND MISUSES OF CENSORSHIP

Modern War Function Has Developed Until Many of Its Rules Serve Only to Annoy People at Home Without Concealing News from the Enemy

By FRANCIS VINTON GREENE

Caesar and Napoleon were not bothered by newspaper reporters, war correspondents, or military attaches.

When Caesar defeated the Helvetii not so very far from Belfort, the extreme right of the present line of the Allies; or when, later, after crossing the Rhine at a point within less than a hundred miles of Liége and Verdun, he gained a decisive military victory over Ariovistus and the ancient Hun—as, please God, Caesar's descendants will in due course gain a decisive victory over Wilhelm von Hohenzollern and the modern Hun—he habitually called a scribe, who at Caesar's dictation, and in language which without exaggeration or offense can be described as more concise and lucid than that of our censor inscribed with a stylus upon a papyrus roll a concise but sufficient account, of the action. This was forthwith dispatched by a caballus or mounted man across the Alps, the fertile valley of the Po, (where the Italian Army is now at bay, and from which in Caesar's time came so much of the food needed for his army as he did not capture from the storehouses of Ariovistus,) and thence over the Apennines to the great high road leading to Rome.

The distance from the Rhine bridge, near Cologne, to the Forum at Rome was more than 800 (English) miles, and the northern part of the route was infested with Teutonic spies; but if the caballus was a vigorous and alert youth with a good horse, (as was usually the case,) and if he escaped the many dangers of the road, he reached Rome in something less than a month.

It was certain, that the information thus conveyed to the Roman public could not by any possibility reach the successor of Ariovistus (who was himself a prisoner, loaded with chains, in Caesar's camp) in less than another month. News two months old was not of much value to the enemy, and even if it reached him when less stale it was very apt, as sometimes happens under our censor, to tell him nothing which he did not already know, either through the energy of his own spies or because it was a matter of such common gossip that every fool knew it.

It was much the same about nineteen centuries later, in the days of Napoleon.

Now, Napoleon wrote reports of Jena and of Leipsic marvelously clear in expression, concealing some facts and emphasizing others. He caused these to be printed in the Moniteur Official in Paris, and the Parisians eagerly sought his bulletins, which, without odious comparison, were more interesting than those with which our censor is wont to favor us on Monday mornings. But there was no quicker way to get the news to Paris than was available to Caesar Caballus, and by the time the news got back to Blücher it was stale, and told him nothing of the things he wanted to know.

Thus, while Napoleon used the political censor to accomplish his own purposes he gave no worry to the thought of the military censor; and while his writings in the Moniteur Officiel, somewhat embellished later when he redictated them to Las Casas at St. Helena, tell us nothing about censorship, they may still, like Caesar's Commentaries, be studied with profit in connection with the problems of 1918.

During our civil war the war correspondent rapidly rose to a position of first importance. He was employed by various political Generals to give glowing accounts of their personal prowess, with the idea that these histories would be powerful factors in swaying votes at political conventions to be held after the war. The news that they furnished was printed in newspapers which a few days later, owing to the camaraderie which throughout the civil war existed between "Yank" and "Johnny" on the picket line in the long interludes between battles, were exchanged for tobacco and found their way to Richmond. Commanding Generals complained, and with reason, that not only the movements of their troops, but their plans as to future movements, became known to the enemy with distressing rapidity. Stanton exercised most ruthlessly the vast powers which Congress had conferred upon him, (and some which it had not,) but the censorship idea does not seem to have occurred to him.

In the war of 1870 the war correspondent became still more a prominent factor. Bismarck quickly saw how, by coloring and distorting his dispatches, he could use him for his own purpose. The French Generals were not so quick to realize his importance and the danger of him. It was in this war that Archibald Forbes became famous. He possessed wonderful powers of description, and the vivid, if not truthful, accounts which he sent every night from the French headquarters were eagerly devoured by the London public the next morning.

In the war of 1877 the Russian General Staff fully realized the value of accurate and discreet news and the danger of communicating intelligence to the enemy. From the Russian lines at Plevna, by courier to the telegraph office on the Danube, thence by wire to London, the news of yesterday's battle was in today's morning papers. And so much of it as the Turkish Ambassador or his advisers considered important was at the Seraskier in Constantinople in a few hours, and thence went in even less time to the Turk at Plevna, so that the dispatches written on the field up to 6 o'clock of an afternoon, describing, for instance, Skobeleff's great assault on the Krishin Redoubt, were placed on Osman Pasha's field desk (two miles away) about noon on the following day.

If they contained news which ought not to have been sent, as was frequently the case with the dispatches of Archibald Forbes, they were distinctly harmful; if, on the other hand, they were written by men who, like Frank D. Millet and J. A. MacGahan, were the soul of honor, they contained nothing (even though most confidential information had been imparted to these writers in order to enable them to understand the battles they described) that would be of value to the enemy. The elaborate regulations governing war correspondents which had been drawn up by the Russian General Staff—registration, passport with photograph, brancard with "Korrespondent" in capital letters, and various other features designed to establish the status of the writer and make his identity evident in every part of the army and hold him responsible for what he wrote—did not fully meet the case.

A CHIEF CENSOR WHO NODDED. Major Gen. Sir Frederick B. Maurice, K. C. M. G. C. B. Was until Recently "Director of Military Operations" in England, and One of His Duties Was to be Interviewed. He was Transferred to Field Duty After He Gave Offense by Comparing the Movement of Foch's Reserve Army to the Belated Arrival of Bluecher at Waterloo.

There were swarms of correspondents of all nationalities—more than eighty of them at the crossing of the Danube, of whom only four, survived the snows of the Balkans and arrived at San Stefano with the advance guard eight months later; and of these four, all engaged by London newspapers, three (Frank D. Millet, J. A. MacGahan, and E. M. Grant) were Americans. There were also upward of twenty foreign officers from almost as many nations attached to General Headquarters at the opening of the campaign, but only two, one German and one American, caught sight of St. Sophia with Skobeleff's leading regiment.

The utmost courtesy was extended to these officers, and some of them received every day as a matter of routine a copy of the orders issued to corps and division commanders for the march or fighting of the following day. They were allowed to attach themselves to any division or brigade and follow it into battle in order to make their observations at close range. So far as is known, these privileges were not abused except in two cases. In consequence of misstatements, Forbes was sent away from the army before the war was one-third over and forbidden ever to return, and the relations between Russia and England became so strained as the war progressed that the British Military Attaché was invited to return to England, with a diplomatic request that no one be sent to replace him.

It was the subtle Japanese mind that in 1904 invented the modern censor. While the siege of Port Arthur was in progress all the Military Attachés, as well as the correspondents, were lodged at Government expense at a hotel in Tokio, where they were attended by several Japanese staff officers of charming address, who brought to them from hour to hour the news received at the War Office. To their urgent requests that they be allowed to go to the front and observe the progress of events with their own eyes and interpret them in their own language, most polite response was made that for the moment this was not possible.

After the fall of Port Arthur, as Okuma advanced toward Mukden, the herd of scribes was transferred under tactful chaperons to Manchuria and followed the movements of the army at an exasperatingly safe distance. A few days after a battle, when the dead had been buried and the field tidied up and the army moved some miles ahead, the foreign officers and the newspaper men were advanced to the late scene of action and there received an elaborate lecture from a thoroughly competent, highly educated, and most polite officer of the General Staff, explaining in full detail the phases of last week's battle.

It is needless to say that this was not the way in which they or their employers desired to obtain their information. But the Japanese never changed their rules—or their politeness.

In the present war the censor has come into his full glory and the Military Attaché and his newspaper colleague have been taught their place. The number of officers engaged in opening soldiers' letters and obliterating what they imagine ought not to have been written to family or friends thousands of miles away, or in reading telegraphic dispatches and holding up the cable service from three to seven days, would easily furnish all the officers necessary for several divisions of fighting troops. As the war has progressed through its second, third, and now its fourth year, common sense has gradually got the upper hand as to the dispatches from the actual fighting lines. There are more than one skilled and trained writer close up to the firing line who give us every morning adequate, intelligent, concise, but sufficient accounts of yesterday's work with machine gun and shrapnel, gas bomb and bayonet, airplane and Zeppelin. Their reports are equal to the best of Millet and MacGahan and Davis in previous wars. They do not give information to the enemy and they do give to the public at home accurate, vivid, admirable statements of fact. They are illustrated with a profusion of lithographic reproductions of the best maps, which has not been possible in previous wars.

But if news from the front is first class and regulated by sound common sense, what shall be said of the futilities which the censor and his minions practice in regard to news at the rear? These have been so ridiculed and so widely discussed and reprobated that any further reference to them here would be a useless waste of space. But of one particular thing, of such fundamental importance to the morale of the army, very little has been said. It relates to embarkation.

During our first year of war there have been four military parades in New York—the New York National Guard on their way to entrain for Spartanburg; a brigade of the Rainbow Division, New York's only colored regiment, and a considerable part of the Upton national army division. These four organizations have marched down Fifth Avenue. They have been bid godspeed on their immortal mission by large and enthusiastic crowds, and to their dying day every man of them, will remember the event with pride and satisfaction while thousands of young men who watched them from the sidewalks have hastened to voluntary enlistment in the regular army without waiting for their numbers to be reached in the draft, so that they, too, might perhaps march down the world-famous avenue and receive the applause of those who line its sidewalks for every such occasion.

Meanwhile, during this first year of war (deleted) thousands, or perhaps hundreds of thousands, of other troops, regulars, National Guards, national army, have come into Camp (deleted) near an Atlantic port, have remained there a few days and have then at some hour between midnight and sunrise entrained upon the (deleted) Railroad and proceeded to the (deleted) piers, where they have been transferred to the (deleted) ship and (deleted) ship. They have been sent below and have been told not to show themselves on deck until after dark the next night. Then about (deleted) A. M. the ship has backed out in the (deleted) River, forming part of an Atlantic port, and before the sun rises they have shipped out to sea—like a filibustering expedition bound to the Spanish Main.

Now, the censor seems to think that by these criminal precautions he has prevented the German Great General Staff from learning when, how, and in what numbers our troops are being sent abroad, which is a colossal piece of self-deception. Any German spy who has 15 cents in his pocket can go to (deleted) station on the (deleted) Railroad and buy a ticket for (deleted) station about five miles away. He can then sit down on the bench of the first station and wait till his train comes along, which when troops are being entrained is likely to be several hours hence.

In front of his bench is the siding on which all troops entrain for the nameless piers of an Atlantic port. He can count the cars as they pull out in the darkness, and he has a fairly accurate idea of how many soldiers go in an ordinary day coach. As daylight approaches and the entraining ceases he can then buy another ticket which will convey him to a station about (deleted) yards from the transports to which these soldiers have been conveyed. Then for 3 cents more he can embark on a ferryboat which almost touches the transports as it passes the unknown piers.

If his conscience is good, as is often the case with the worst of German spies, he will pay 3 cents for every trip, but there is no law or order which will prevent him from spending the next twenty-four or thirty-six hours, until he actually sees the ships back out in the murky night into the river. Then he can take the ferry to (deleted) Street on (deleted) and thence to (deleted) Ferry, where he can get on the (deleted) Island Ferry and run parallel to the ships as they start for "over there," and he can sit in the (deleted) Island Ferry house, or walk along the street in the village of (deleted) and count the ships with accuracy, even on a dark night, for the channel is such that they pass very close to the shore of that village. At the end of his two days' tour of duty he can make a full and accurate report to the master spy, giving the number, and probably the names, of the ships which have stolen away in the darkness.

He can even, if he is of a plausible and chatty turn, report the name and number of each regiment which has embarked, for these can be obtained by rubbing up against the men when there is no officer close by in the darkness, wishing them the best of luck, and asking how they left the folks out in Ohio; to which the ingenuous lad in khaki would probably reply that he is from Indiana, the 309th Infantry, but the Ohio regiment is going to entrain next.

Having received the report, the master spy will promptly send his radiogram to Berlin—just as he would if the loading had taken place in daylight and had been fully reported in the daily papers; provided, of course, that he has radio connection with Berlin, by way of Mexico or otherwise. And if he is not thus connected, then it would make no difference whether or not the whole story was printed in the papers with four-inch headlines.

If the censor had ever experienced the reactions of battle—nay, if he had ever worn a uniform and experienced a setting-up drill—he might have some notion of the psychology of this military business; how soldiers love applause; how great commanders, like Napoleon at Arcola and Skobeleff at Plevna, expose themselves to the most fearful risks in order to gain reputation for themselves and encourage their subordinates to be courageous in face of danger; while these same great men, when they happened to run by accident into the enemy's lines on a reconnaissance, have turned tail and dug their spurs into their horses' sides until they were out of danger—because nobody was looking; how the boy who has never been out of his native village in a remote State, and never would have been but for this war and conscription, since he is going to put his life to the chance, would like to have as many people as possible see him when he starts out to do his part in saving civilization—instead of "cheesing it" in the dark and getting about as much applause as a man receives when he passes through the streets on his way from the Tombs to Sing Sing.

It's all a part of the game, this marching off to the war. It goes with the uniform, with the blatant bands and blaring trumpets, with the flying colors and the tingling blood, as the lad of 22 starts out to play with Death in a great game, and hopes he will do his part in it as well as his father and his grandfather or his uncles and their fathers did their part when in their day there were things to be settled which can only be settled by blood and suffering.

Every week for many months, if the Secretary of War speaks truly, many thousands of our soldiers have sailed for France, on the greatest enterprise since the dawn of history. No one has been allowed to see them, to bid them godspeed, to wish them the best of luck, to cheer them on the journey from which so many of them will never come back. They have been sent forth like sneaks in a cheap burglary.

Is it not time that these futilities should end? Would it not be better to march the troops in full field kit from Camp Merritt to Fort Lee Ferry, cross the Hudson River in such number of ferryboats as are necessary, march through the Hollow Way where Washington and Greene fought in 1776, and through Central Park, which so many of these boys have heard of but never expected to see, to Mr. Carnegie's house at Ninetieth Street, and then down the famous avenue to the Washington Arch and through Greenwich Village to the Cunard docks, sending the Cunard steamers to Weehawken to get their freight and passengers there, and bringing the Leviathan and the other ex-German ships to the Tenth Street piers? Let the bands play as the men march on the ships, and let every siren and whistle screech as the ships move slowly down the bay.

If people think that the method of embarkation has nothing to do with the morale of an army and the winning of the war, they know less about it than they will know two years hence.

* * *

June 14, 1918

TIMES PERIODICALS HELD UP BY CENSOR

Current History Magazine and Mid-Week Pictorial Stopped at San Francisco

KEPT FROM FOREIGN MAILS

Contained War Articles and Pictures "Which Might Reach Germany," Where Perhaps They Don't Know of the War

Special to The New York Times

SAN FRANCISCO, June 13—The New York Times Current History for May and The Mid-Week Pictorial for May 23 have been withheld from the mails for Manila, China, Japan, and India, though the action is not a matter of record in the San Francisco Naval Censorship Board. Entire lack of information on the subject was professed by the naval censors, who appeared to think that the official action had been confined to the Post Office authorities.

At the San Francisco Post Office detailed information as to why the publications had been withheld from the foreign mails was refused. The statement was made that the publications fell within the Instructions of the Censor Board as received from Washington relative to the deletion of newspaper matter calculated to give military information to the enemy. It was stated that publishers immediately would be more fully advised as to the Censor Board's decision that no publication which contained anything likely to aid the enemy would be admitted to the foreign mails.

The Censor Board sees no impropriety in allowing the utmost latitude to publications circulating within the United States, but deletion of matter that may be objectionable from a military point of view will not be sufficient. The publications will not be allowed to go outside the boundaries of the United States.

The Censor Board will not enter into discussion with publishers as to whether matter is objectionable. The decision will rest with the board, acting under instructions from Washington, it was said.

From a source other than the Censor Board it was learned that The New York Times Mid-Week Pictorial was considered as coming within the inhibitions of the Washington authorities because it contained maps and illustrations of military interest. Such matter is held to be improper for foreign circulation, whether the pictures are of foreign scenes or American. They would be allowable if not circulated outside this country, but when placed in the foreign mails for distribution abroad they will be held up. Postmaster Fay declined to particularize the illustrations which had led to the stoppage of the New York editions.

According to the instructions under which the Censor Board is acting he thought all the illustrations of military scenes, camps, and general military activities, whether American or foreign, inadmissible to the foreign mails to be sent anywhere, not excepting allied nations. If limited to circulation within the United States no objection to them would be raised.

* * *

November 15, 1918

CENSORSHIP AT AN END

Creel Officially Announces It and Thanks Press of the Country

Special to The New York Times

WASHINGTON, Nov. 14—The voluntary censorship under which the American press placed itself for the period of the war has ended, according to an official announcement today and newspapers are free from now on to tell what they please concerning military and other matters without restriction. The announcement comes from the Committee on Public Information and is understood to be preliminary to the abolition of the committee as a Governmental institution.

George Creel, Chairman of the Committee on Public Information, made the announcement in this statement:

"It has been agreed that there is no further necessity for the operation of the voluntary censorship under which the press has guarded from the enemy the military policies, plans and troop movements of the United States. The agreement may be considered, as no longer binding, and the card carrying the requests of the Government is herewith canceled.

"The Secretary of War and the Secretary of the Navy, and all others concerned with the direction of America's war efforts, join in sincere acknowledgment of the debt of gratitude owing to the press of the United States for the honorable discharge of a high responsibility. Without force of law, and under no larger compulsion than their own patriotism, the overwhelming majority of newspapers have given unfaltering obedience to every desire of the Government in all matters of military secrecy carrying through successfully a tremendous experiment in honor and trust."

The retirement of Mr. Creel from the Chairmanship of the Committee on Public Information may be expected soon. It may be coincident with an order from President Wilson revoking the appointment of the committee and directing that it close up business. The new activity in which Mr. Creel will engage has not been disclosed, but it is believed that he will attend the peace conference in an official capacity, perhaps as publicity director for the American delegation.

* * *

THE CENTRAL POWERS

August 30, 1914

BERLIN PRESS CAN'T COMMENT ON WAR

News Limited to What the Government Gives Out— Two Papers Confiscated

WOMEN RUN STREET CARS

Spy Hunting Goes On Everywhere and Some Notable Captures Are Reported

Special Cable to The New York Times

AMSTERDAM, Aug. 29, (Dispatch to The London Standard)—The Berlin correspondent of a Dutch newspaper gives the following details about conditions in the German capital:

Several industrial undertakings, especially those who work for exterior firms, have been obliged to shut their works; most of the banks open at 10 o'clock and close at 2:30; the shops generally are open during daylight.

Tram lines are manned by 800 woman conductors, and women are performing the same duties in Hamburg, Munich, and Hanover. In the beginning the public was rather amused at these women, who wear the caps and coats of their husbands, but now nobody notices them.

Newspapers are under the strongest possible control. Many, including two Social-Democrat organs in Prussia, have been confiscated, and others have been prohibited publication indefinitely. Papers are permitted to publish only official reports, so one contains exactly as much and the same news as the other. Big staffs of papers like the Berliner Tageblatt and the Vossische Zeitung are unemployed.

Press comment on the war or criticism of any Government measures are forbidden under pain of court-martial and probably death at the hands of the military authorities. Thus the only editorial attacks possible are those directed against those business firms which appear to be making use of the war to raise prices and exploit the public.

* * *

February 7, 1915

AUSTRIAN PRESS IN TROUBLE

Two Czech Papers Suspended—Those in Styria Threaten to Quit

VENICE (Via London), Feb. 6—It is reported from Vienna that the commandant at Prague has suspended the publication of two Czech newspapers, the Kladensklobsor and the Stredeczky Ziondstick on a charge of publishing articles condemning the war and making disrespectful utterances regarding the Emperor.

The Union of Styrian Journalists has sent a memorial to the Austrian Minister of Justice praying for intervention in behalf of the press which is suffering under a most rigid censorship. The journalists have decided to suspend publication of newspapers in Styria unless the censorship is relaxed.

* * *

April 18, 1915

WRY DISCUSSION OF GERMAN WAR GOALS

The Censor Passes Articles That Favor Annexing Belgium and Suppresses Those in a Contrary Spirit

Although the assertion is constantly made in letters from Germany and other German utterances that the German censor allows the press of the country to present all sides of the war news to the German people, a marked inequality in the application of the censorship to various camps of German opinion is shown in recent complaints voiced in the Social Democratic central organ, the Vorwarts, and other liberal newspapers. This inequality is shown chiefly in the censor's policy toward discussions of the "war goals," particularly in the "passing" of articles directly or indirectly favoring the annexation of Belgium and the vigorous suppression of articles opposing such a course.

Thus, the Vorwarts of March 30 cites the following vigorous agitation for the annexation of Belgium from the pan-German Deutsche Tageszeitung of the day before:

How solemn and pretty were the treaties and speeches with which, at the time, the neutrality of the Kingdom of Belgium was internationally declared and "guaranteed." But this neutrality and neutralization disappeared like snow before the sun as soon as it pleased Great Britain to organize its own against the German coalition on military, political, and maritime lines. Great Britain destroyed Belgium's neutrality as early as 1906.

Belgium, as has reportedly been asserted here, is a vital question for the German future. Belgium's coasts and harbors may never again be allowed to subserve the influence of great foreign powers, directly or indirectly. If Belgium, with its fortresses, coasts, and harbors, remained under foreign influence—that is to say, under enemy influence—then that "freedom of the seas" of which the (semi-official) Norddeutsche Allgemeine Zeitung spoke the day before yesterday would remain an empty phrase and Germany would find itself permanently dependent upon the mercy of Great Britain as a naval power and a commercial power. The eager industriousness with which Germany has now for months been admonished in England to safeguard its own future by sacrificing Belgium to Great Britain would in itself be sufficient to evoke the proper realization of the situation in Germany wherever that has not yet been felt. At any moment that suits England it could, by closing the oceans to us as a dissatisfied superior, render the overseas colonies of Germany no longer German possessions. Belgium constitutes a question that is fundamental in its nature.

Against this the Vorwarts protests:

If the Government organs permit such public championing of the annexation of Belgium, it must in consequence also permit this question to be discussed from other points of view.

That the Government does not intend to permit discussion from other points of view would appear from the following military order, issued under date of March 25 by the Acting General Commander of the Seventh Army Corps at Münster to the publishers of the Dussoldorf Volkszeltung:

The article published in No. 70 of your paper of the 24th inst., under the caption "England and We," is contrary to the truth. It ascribes the blame for the aggravation of the conflict between Germany and England to the German policy.

It cannot be tolerated that under the cloak of an objective presentation of facts a point of view entirely at variance with the German patriotic sentiment should be maintained. The article also violates the prohibition against discussion of war goals by demanding the ultimate rejection of any territorial acquisition in Belgium. Finally, the intemperate invidiousness of tone of the article most deeply offends the national sentiments.

I therefore find myself obliged to suppress your paper for three days, from tomorrow, the 26th, to and including the 29th inst. The police authorities of your city have been notified of this measure.

You must publish the text of this, my order, at the head of your next published issue without any comment.

The Commanding General,
Freiherr von GAYL

Further indications of discrimination against Social Democratic newspapers by the Government authorities are cited in the case of the Zeitzer Volksboten of Weissenfels, which, in response to many demands from wounded soldiers, wished to send free copies of its paper to invalided soldiers at the local hospital. The hospital authorities, however, refused to allow the paper to be given to the soldiers, despite the fact that military authorities had previously announced that the dissemination of Social Democratic newspapers among military persons was no longer to be prevented. The hospital authorities, however, wrote to the Volksboten:

The regulations in military institutions against the dissemination of Social Democratic periodicals have not been revoked and must, in accordance with the spirit thereof, be applied in the local reserve hospitals. Request is therefore politely made to desist from sending copies of the Volksboten, especially since there is no lack of reading matter.

HOSPITAL COMMISSION:
VON SCHEFE,
DR. WUNDERWALDT,
MIELISCH

It should be noted, however, that the Social Democratic papers contrive to get many of their views as to war-goals before their public by copying a leaf from the book of their opponents and likewise discussing Germany's future policy "indirectly." Thus, for example, the Vorwärts in the same issue in which it protests against the Tageszeitung's course, publishes an editorial on its front page, headed "Against imperialism," in which it quotes articles by Professor Franz von Liszt and the German writer, Ernst Müller-Holm, to prove that imperialism and the desire for world-rule is a distinctly English conception and that by adopting it Germany would prove traitor to its own national genius and would adopt the very vice which it is seeking in the present war to destroy in England. Speaking of the recent growth of the imperialistic idea in Germany, the Vorwärts says:

Although it is generally admitted that imperialism was the last cause of the present war, the imperialistic idea is just now winning new adherents. It sweeps through the whole bourgeoisie like an intoxication even circles that have heretofore stood aloof from every policy are now throwing themselves with exultation into the arms of the imperialistic policy. Former opponents of imperialism are now discovering all kinds of good sides in this modern form of economic development, just at the very moment when this development is in fact showing most clearly its contradictions and evil. Why, even in the proletarian ranks there have arisen defenders of imperialism who plead for its acquittal or at least urge mitigating circumstances. These defenders are most dangerous when, like the adherents of modern criminal procedure, they base their pleadings on the plea that the accused "necessarily" had to act as he did.

* * *

July 1, 1915

MORE PAPERS SUPPRESSED

German Socialist Organs Suffer for Printing Peace Appeal

AMSTERDAM, July 1 (via London)—Several Socialist papers in Germany have been suppressed for reproducing the Socialist appeal for peace, which was originally published by the Berlin Vorwarts, resulting in that paper's suspension.

The papers suppressed for reprinting the article include the Königsberger Volks-Zeitung, and the Görlitzer Volks-Zeitung.

* * *

June 18, 1916

GERMAN NEWSPAPERS WIN MORE FREEDOM

Chancellor Promises to Take Up Question of Wider Discussion of War Aims and Politics

From a Staff Correspondent
Special Cable to The New York Times

BERLIN, June 16 (via The Hague, June 17)—The Chancellor has promised the press of Germany a mitigation of the political censorship and particularly a freer discussion of forbidden topics including war aims in a letter answering the German Press Association's petition regarding the censorship evils. The Chancellor admits a justification for the complaints and says:

"Censorship measures outside of the purely military realm I regard as desirable only in so far as they are useful to the highest purpose which we all serve, namely, a victorious conclusion of the war. Unlimited freedom of discussion of so-called war aims, to my regret. I cannot promise in the immediate future, but it is in line with my wishes that the censorship be enforced mildly in this field, too. I have already taken steps to have various departments of the Government reach an understanding regarding the new rules and regulations for the ameliorated censorship promised by me in so far as may be necessary in political matters."

The Chancellor concluded by requesting the press association to work out and send him practical recommendations.

The prospect of freer speech is hailed with satisfaction by the German press. The Tageblatt says:

"At last the censorship questions will be dealt with where they belong, by the chosen representatives of the German journalists, provided the authorities really consider the recommendations and do not pigeonhole them. In this case an amelioration of the present censorship methods might be achieved which would be endurable at least during the war, a scheme creating a transition period to peace conditions which from the first peace day ought to put an end to every kind of censorship."

* * *

September 26, 1916

GERMAN EDITORS ASSAIL CENSORS

Demand the Right to Express Opinions on the Conduct of the War

ENGLAND'S EXAMPLE CITED

Suppression of Free Discussion Hold to be Inimical to the Empire's Interests

From a Staff Correspondent
Special Cable to The New York Times

BERLIN, Sept. 25—One of the clearest and most interesting signs of the new spirit of the times which is gradually but unmistakably leavening the whole social and political structure of Germany in this crucial stadium of war—a spirit so liberal as almost to approximate democratic ideals—is the continued restlessness of the German press under the political censorship, the never ceasing, though always thoroughly patriotic struggle against this organ of the Government, which, like the human appendix, has long outlived its usefulness and is now only a menace to the health of the nation.

This conscious striving for real freedom of the press, for the right to express opinions freely and publicly on controversial subjects of vital interest to warring Germany, was again and more strongly than ever before reflected in yesterday's annual meeting of the National Association of the German Press, whose discussions largely centred on the gradual "dismantling of the political censorship" promised many weeks ago in the name of the Imperial Government by Vice Chancellor Helfferic . . .

Since then some slight improvement has been noted; a somewhat more liberal spirit has animated the interpolitical censorship, and particularly in the last week was the German press able to touch with greater frankness on formerly forbidden topics. But the censorship reform has not gone far enough, and still too stringent internal censorship is rightly blamed for the present political tension among parties and factions and for such inevitable evils as the clandestine circulation of anonymous pamphlets, the widespread political gossip and scandalmongering, and the countless baseless disquieting rumors about men and matters that ought to be, but cannot be, freely discussed in the press.

The Government's argument that the political censorship is necessary to preserve the so-called Burgfrieden, (party truce,) and thus maintain a united front against foes round about, has to thinking Germans been amply disproved by the English press, whose freedom has, it is thoroughly realized here, not impaired either England's will to continue the war or the effectiveness of her warfare.

The Germans, who as a whole are astonishingly objective, are at all times keen to learn even from their enemies, and the fact that the English press can and does frequently criticise, even bitterly attack, the Government and freely discuss all subjects of interest to the nation has undeniably served as an incentive and argument to the German press to work for similar privileges or rights. As a symptom of the great change which is taking place here and which, to an American observer, seems likely to hear the most promising fruit, this propaganda for the freedom of speech and of the press deserves the serious attention of Americans as of greater importance than many indecisive battles.

The presiding officer of the National Association, Chief Editor Marx of Berlin, gave a significant clue to the changing war psychology of Germans in the following plain words:

"In our resolutions we have no intention of discussing when the Chancellor should make known his war aims. We do not desire to press the Chancellor, but, on the other hand, we do not want to be suppressed. One may consider that the discussion of war aims is harmful. We all, however, are of the opinion that to forbid it is still more harmful.

"One is forced to ask if as the result of the censorship ban of the last two years that gentle spirit and harmony, that peace of God between the parties, and confidence—in fact, everything that appeared so desirable to the Government—has been achieved. Have not, rather, despite all censorship prohibitions, bitterness and discord increased, which could not be worse if the war aims from the very beginning had been free for discussion?

"In our fight for freedom to express opinion we pursue not our own interests, but those of the whole nation. The usefulness of the press is only possible with the freedom of the press. The press can, to be sure, do harm; therefore all military matters must be considered, but the harm is not so great as the resultant benefit. Can we have victories and hang out flags every day?

"In days of anxious waiting many lose courage. Then it is the business of the press to keep up public spirit, to support the anxious ones, and keep awake the firm belief in victory. This end, however, also necessitates the faith of the reader in the press and the conviction that there are free and independent men at work. The moment when officialdom takes the press in hand the press sinks to insignificance, and it is then a matter of complete indifference whether a greater number of papers or only one normal paper is published. In all our differences of opinion we all are united by one firm will to serve the fatherland, to hold out and through the press to champion the belief in ultimate victory."

The ensuing discussion resulted in the almost unanimous agreement of the German editors with these sentiments, and the following resolution was unanimously adopted:

"The delegates approve the steps taken by the Executive Committee to obtain the removal of the political censorship. We record the fact, however, that the censorship in part has been intensified.

"The association again declares that it demands in principle that the censorship of political news cease, and that differences of opinion be permitted in all cases where urgent military interests are not involved. Further, the association demands that the confiscation of newspapers be resorted to only in extreme cases, and then always with an indication of the period of confiscation."

* * *

June 29, 1917

GERMAN NEWSPAPER ASSAILS CENSORSHIP

Hanover Volkszeitung Says the Press Is Losing the Confidence of Its Readers

COPENHAGEN, June 28—The manipulation of the German press by the authorities, the employment of the vast apparatus of the War Press Bureau for filling the newspapers with special dispatches and semi-official accounts and comments on military events, the plain and fancy distortions of truth by the Admiralty Press Bureau, working in the spirit instilled by von Tirpitz, and the glaringly inaccurate announcements of brilliant crop prospects put forth regularly at and before harvest time, have repeatedly been referred to in dispatches, together with descriptions of the working of the censorship to prevent any free discussion of public problems in Germany.

It is now possible to cite the testimony of German newspapers, which, writhing under the Government cuts in their paper supply, speak their minds freely on the conditions in the profession. The Deutsche Volkszeitung of Hanover, for example, writing of the Government efforts to control and direct sentiment, says that the contents of the German papers are almost word for word the same in all the papers, as these are fed from the same source, and are not permitted by reason of the censorship restrictions to take any independent line in news or views.

"The Government's whole effort," says the paper, "is toward the creation of a standardized newspaper, and it insists upon the unchanged publication of a mass of articles and dispatches furnished."

Parenthetically it may be remarked that it is an offense punishable by martial law for an editor to omit a comma or a word from a communication issued by a news agency and designated as official.

The Volkszeitung declares that the German newspapers are losing the confidence of their readers, who are taking their information from neutral newspapers. It says that the just complaint is now frequently heard: "The papers are all alike. We are to believe only what is set before us, and what those above us do not want is not printed."

* * *

December 24, 1917

GERMANY TIGHTENS REIN ON ITS PRESS

Vorwaerts Silenced for an Attack on von Waldow and Exposure of Food Conditions

SEEN AS WARNING TO ALL

Intimation That Criticism of Internal German Affairs Must Be Curbed

AMSTERDAM, Dec. 23—The Berlin Socialist newspaper Vorwärts has been obliged by the Government to suspend publication for three days.

LONDON, Dec. 23—The suspension of the Berlin Vorwärts is considered as a warning to the entire German press that it must curb its tongue in the discussion of internal German conditions. Although the Vorwärts for a long time has been in the hands of the so-called Government-controlled Socialists, it recently printed an attack on Food Controller von Waldow and also some very daring editorials regarding internal conditions in Germany.

The official reason given for the suspension of the newspaper is that "the article denouncing the militaristic party's demands for the annexation of large sections of Russian territory is considered likely to stir up trouble." The indications are that the censors of the Central Powers have been instructed to exercise increased severity in the publication of two classes of articles: First, those that would be likely to hamper the Central Powers in their negotiations with Russia, and second, those giving a gloomy view of internal conditions which would be likely to encourage Germany's foes.

The Hungarian Premier, in an address before the Diet on Saturday, defended the censors for suppressing articles along the latter line, saying:—

"The newspapers must not give the enemy ground for supposing that anarchistic conditions prevail in Hungary. Especially now, with peace negotiations proceeding, the authorities will act with the greatest sternness in the interest of peace."

Vorwärts, in a recent article attacked the system of the German Food Controller, von Waldow, declaring that great masses of German people were not only hungry but were literally starving. It also accused the "war profiteers and millionaires" of hoarding great supplies of food.

* * *

January 8, 1918

CENSORS' ORDERS SHOW TIGHT CURB ON GERMAN PRESS

State Department Gets Copies of Many Secret Telegrams Issued by Berlin

WARNINGS ABOUT AMERICA

Our Vigorous Preparations Admitted, but Must Not Be "Overestimated"

AUSTRIAN DISCORD HIDDEN

Papers Are Instructed What to Print as Well What Is Forbidden

Special to The New York Times

WASHINGTON, Jan. 7—An exposure of German methods of dictation to and control over the press is contained in copies of secret telegrams issued to the press by the Berlin official censorship, copies of which have been obtained by the State Department and which were made public tonight.

These telegrams show not only that the German Government, through its official censorship, told the papers what they might not print, but likewise what they should print. The importance of the dispatches lies in the additional proof they offer that the German press cannot and does not reflect the attitude of the German people.

Some of the telegrams in the hands of the State Department deal with American war preparations and they indicate that, despite German newspaper statements to the contrary, the Berlin Government itself does not underestimate the ability of America to accomplish things.

One of the orders read:

Petit Parisien informs us that five American divisions, numbering 125,000 men, may be expected in France in the Autumn of 1917. It is urgently requested not to reproduce this information without some comment. We do not wish to underestimate the ability of America to accomplish things, but must not, on the other hand, overestimate.

In order to bring a division over from America 75,000 tons must make the trip twice. Therefore, from the mere fact of lack of space, the transportation of such a body of troops within certain fixed time limits is impossible. Moreover, it is impossible to train these troops properly by Autumn. These facts, which have recently been discussed in the German war news, cannot be too strongly emphasized in the discussion of this French news.

There are repeated instructions prohibiting all mention of certain strikes and other signs of internal unrest, such as the following:

The publication and discussion of the resolution, adopted in a strike meeting of the Leipsic unions and of a telegram sent to the Imperial Chancellor are not permissible.

There is no objection to the reprinting of the manifesto of the Independent Socialist Party in case it is adversely commented upon, even without irritating sharpness.

In the interest of a victorious carrying through of the war, which is endangered by every stoppage of work, expressions of the press which recommend a strike or express themselves otherwise in favor of a strike are forbidden. Utterances which are directed against strikes are indeed not subject to censorship, but it is supposed thereby that they are kept free from immoderate sharpness which could offer material for irritating the people.

Reports concerning disturbances in Königsberg, Prussia, and concerning a warning from the Commander of the First Army Corps, which followed in the Königsberg press, are not permissible.

News about excesses and unrest in Prague may not be published.

Austrian Dissent Suppressed

Hostile discussions in the Austrian Parliament, which met last Spring, were to be carefully concealed, as shown by the following orders:

The discussions of the Austrian lower chamber may, for the present, be published only in such light as they are sent out by the official correspondence bureau.

The printing and discussion of the speeches in Parliament yesterday by the Austrian Deputies, Stransky, Korvosez, and Romanzak, are forbidden.

Last Spring a large number of Russians were repatriated from Switzerland through. Germany with the definite purpose of spreading German propaganda in Russia. Concerning them, these instructions were given, the last superseding the first:

Nothing is to be published concerning the journey through Germany from Switzerland of Russian emigrants.

Instruction revised so that the reports from abroad concerning the journey through Germany of Russian emigrants may be published, but without comment.

The following were on the economic situation:

The publication is to be avoided of anything concerning the state of the clothing material business and concerning the purchase of clothing material in the occupied, districts as well as in Switzerland.

The printing and discussion of the article, "Terrible Conditions in Warsaw for Obtaining the Necessities of Life," in No. 33 of Napszod of July 12 are not permissible.

It is not desired to discuss or even to mention the German importations from abroad, especially from Holland.

Offers of food from the occupied eastern war zone may not be published. The acceptance of such advertisements is forbidden.

Wide Range of Prohibitions

Following are copies of some of the other orders, each of them in the original being headed "Confidential":

Pr. 11-7,190.

(1) Reports concerning the Chilean bark Tinto with German seamen from the crew of the cruiser Dresden may not be published.

April 5, 1917.

Pr. 11-7610.

Concerning the most recent bomb attack by a German flying machine on London nothing may be published.

Attention is drawn to the frequent ill-humor at the front often caused when it appears, from the selection of captions for the reports of the war events, that the press out of need for sensation or awkwardness does not permit the recognition of which event is the most important.

May 5, 1917.

Pr. 11-7910.

Referring to Pr. 11-7790, May 21.

Reprinting of articles of neutral or enemy papers concerning the conditions in the Russian Army is permitted.

May 29, 1917.

Pr. 11-7846.

The publications which permit to be recognized the effectiveness of geology or kindred sciences in the service of the army are not permissible in the technical as well as in the daily press.

May 25, 1917.

(Number missing.)

It is not permissible that third persons appeal to members of the army in newspapers, brochures, or pamphlets in order to call upon them to take up positions toward any political news whatsoever. It is especially requested to hinder such appeals.

The publication of letters from the field of political content is forbidden.

June 3, 1917.

Pr. 11-8179.

It is forbidden to publish anything concerning a fire in the flying station Lawica.

June 12, 1917.

Pr. 11-8190.

It is desired that the great enemy flying machine losses in the month of May, may be strongly emphasized by large headings or in some other particular manner.

June 12, 1917.

Stress on Austrian Successes

Pr. 11-8205.

Recently Reuter dispatches have entirely English reports from Russia concerning commencing dissolution, chaos, and strikes. These are worthy of notice. It is requested always to make such news as English reports, and to assume an attitude of reserve toward them and occasionally to add thereto a critical word.

The Austrians on the Isonzo front have had very good successes. It is desired continually to take notice thereof. The whole strength of Italy is fighting against Austria, while Austria is forced to use strong forces in other directions. The Austrian success is naturally pleasing to us entirely aside from the satisfaction which it must awaken if our allies accomplish successes with their carrying on of the war. It is therefore requested to discuss continually the occurrences on the Isonzo in this sense.

It is requested that positive, interpretation with great emphasis be given the declarations on the 12th of June by the Presidents of the two Alsace-Lorraine chambers as the requested answer to Ribot's speech and to avoid all discussion of this which could weaken this positive valuation.

June 14, 1917.

Pr. 11-8220.

Advertisements of undertaking establishments which seek the removal of the bodies of fallen soldiers are not to be accepted.

June 15, 1917.

Pr. 11-8256.

For the present nothing may be published concerning the explosion which took place this morning at the Friedrichstrasse Station in Berlin.

June 16, 1917.

Pr. 11-8-26.

Attention is again drawn to the order of Feb. 23, 1917, Pr. 11-6675, in accordance with which the public expression of sentiments hostile to Germany and the spreading of untrue reports concerning the war, concerning the political, financial, and economic situation of the German Empire is forbidden and transgressions are subject to punishment

The police authorities are requested to proceed energetically against the originators and carriers of such untrue and groundless rumors, which have recently made their appearance once more, and to bring about their punishment without compunction.

Pr. 11-3405.

It is again pointed out that all reports concerning technical innovations, discoveries, and capability of production, concerning production of substitute materials of all kinds (military, chemical, industrial, those for the provision of food, &c.,) are forbidden. (Compare Pr. 11-689 of March 15, 1917, and Pr. 11-1060 of Dec. 12, 1915.)

The prohibition is for the daily and for the technical press, as well as for brochures and books.

June 23, 1917.

Emphasizing U-boat War

Pr. 11-8510.

The press has often been requested to omit the sensational publication of unimportant reports or of reports capable of misinterpretation.

Urgent cause exists to point out that it can be, on the other side, often important and right to give events and reports their proper meaning through due emphasis.

For instance, recently the English theft of cipher telegrams in the case of Hofmann-Grimm was in no wise sufficiently stigmatized.

Furthermore, it appears as if the German press does not proceed forcefully enough against the plan recently practiced by our enemies, which is justified by nothing, of discounting the effectiveness of our blockade war.

It is desired that it should be clearly and distinctly put in the foreground that the enemy offensive has utterly failed on all fronts and that the Entente has no alternative but to attempt a new offensive, as the enemy's statesmen are still against peace. Another reason for haste is the continually increasing lack of tonnage. As the Entente is very dependent on the sea for its forwarding, the freight space intended for the civil population must be added to those transports.

In one of the future issues it might be mentioned that the present situation in Russia has the appearance of being caused by the Entente with the view to her (Russia's) continuing for a time—perhaps until the actual participation by the Americans. How long that will be remains to be seen. It is of consequence to set forth the opinion that a new offensive will speedily take place as amounting to a conviction.

The question about the secret agreements between Russia and her allies must not be allowed to rest. The hostile Governments try to frustrate the effect of all publications bearing upon the agreements with all the means at their disposal in order that their people may not learn the war aims and the reasons why they were egged on into the war. There is no doubt as to the existence of such secret agreements and if these are discussed as being a matter of course the people will ultimately demand of their Governments the publications of these agreements.

In referring to the Skagerrak battle, it is of the utmost importance to use the greatest energy in freeing the neutrals from the pretended English supremacy of the sea.

June 2, 1917.

Concerning a visit in the near future of the King of Bulgaria in Germany, only such news as is marked official may be published.

June 3, 1917.

FOR THE NEWS SECTION

Early this morning toward 8 a fire broke out in the aviation station at Posen while magnetos were being cleaned with benzine. With the help of the City Fire Department they succeeded in confining the fire to one hangar and put it out inside of an hour. The service will not be injured.

June 12, 1917.

Admitting America's War Zeal

While the news about America's war preparations, such as the organization and outfitting of an army 1,000,000 strong to reinforce the French-English front, is looked upon in that form as "bluff," the spreading of which may unfavorably affect the opinion of the German people, yet the fact must not be overlooked, on the other hand, that the United States, with the support of its capacity for material and industrial management, is arming itself for war with great energy and tenacity. The war preparations in America are, therefore, as was intimated in the Reichstag at the time, not at all to be made little of, but must be taken seriously without on that account being made a source of worry.

A few days ago the Austro-Hungarian press was left free to discuss the war aims. We can unreservedly indorse the war aims given out in the majority of the Austro-Hungarian press.

Of course, the fully warranted and not inconsiderable war aims which are needed for the conservation and development of the confederated monarchy as well as for a world peace can only be achieved if Austria-Hungary adheres to her understanding with the German Empire and its allies and with positive reference to her military economy and political forces announces clearly and positively her firm will to hold out and win, as is the case with the overwhelming majority of the German people. Suggestions on this point to our press are recommended.

The high command of the army has been of late drawn to an extraordinary degree into the discussion of political points, particularly those of a domestic character. At the renewed request of the high command it is, therefore, asked that it be left out of all talk on political matter, and better still not to mention it at all in connection with such things.

June 6, 1917.

Reports about pretended negotiations for a truce on the Russian front may neither be published nor discussed.

June 11, 1917.

Pr. 11-8155

Advertisements in which dog flesh is offered for sale are not allowed. Their acceptance is forbidden.

June 11, 1917.

PART III

BETWEEN THE WARS, 1919–1938

THE UNITED STATES AND THE AMERICAS

December 28, 1919

CENSORING THE MOVIE

By GABRIEL L. HESS

During the last legislative sessions held in twenty-four States legislation aimed at the censorship of motion pictures was proposed and in every instance defeated. The fact that these twenty-four bills uniformly failed of passage is evidence that the tide of public opinion everywhere is set against the censorship of motion pictures prior to their publication.

But the prior fact that such legislation was so generally attempted is evidence that in many communities there are individuals and groups of individuals who desire to control and direct film contents for reasons which while to them seem sufficient are not founded on fact and are urged because of a clear lack of knowledge of the motion picture and its most beneficial uses.

If censorship of films were a thing which affected the motion picture industry alone my purpose in arguing against it might be attributed wholly to a desire to protect that business from strangulation at the hands of politically appointed officials whose power to confiscate the product of the studios would be supreme and unreviewable. But the principle involved is of far wider application. It affects not only the film industry but the rights of every citizen of the United States. In so far as harm can be visited upon investors in the business of motion picture production the affair is chiefly one of dollars and cents. But in the control and direction of a great medium for public entertainment and education the censorship idea contains possibilities of evil which direction the fabric of our democracy.

The sole reason why the question of censorship of motion pictures is not yet settled is that people do not clearly envisage the fact that essentially the motion picture is of the same character as the press, the novel and the legitimate drama, a vehicle for the transfer of idea and emotion from one mind to others.

Champions of film censorship argue that the motion picture should be subjected to reviews or censoring prior to public exhibitions not because it is more vicious than other entertainment enterprises but because it is more popular. It reaches more people daily than any other agency, and it reaches them more surely. If censorship is sound in principle the point is well taken, but if censorship of the stage and the press is vicious and un-American the argument for censorship of the motion picture because of its popularity and wide circulation must fail. The principle of censorship as applied to the press and the spoken drama has been adjudged evil.

Growth of the Movie

Starting at first as a "chaser" for vaudeville acts or shown to an intrepid few in lofts and barns, in a score of years the motion picture has jumped to the very forefront of the amusement field, and now no special vision is required to foresee for it a future big with possibility. Therefore, if control of the press, the novel, or the stage by a handful of official censors would be destructive of art values and subversive of the public's best interests, how much more dangerous to place the future of the screen in the hands of political appointees, with no law to guide them save individual whim or bias, no power superior to their unaided judgment as to what might or might not be "safely" shown to a supposedly free people!

The motion picture has been developed on the one hand into an authentic art and on the other hand into an educational agency of splendid promise. Shall this unmatched instrument of pleasure and enlightenment be subjected to a stultifying restraint or shall it be left free to develop under existing laws along the natural lines of public taste and public sentiment? This is the vital question which the public must answer.

Public antipathy to censorship of books, newspapers, or plays is not founded on imaginary fears. The right of free speech was guaranteed by the Constitution of the United States. The youth of the motion picture and its unique mechanical features may tend to obscure the fact that fundamentally it is one with the older, more familiar forms of expressing human thought and feeling. That fact once allowed, it is obvious that the motion picture should be permitted, under existing laws, to develop along natural and unhampered lines of expansion equally with stories, books and plays.

I say "under existing laws" because advocates of official censorship are prone to forget that there are at this time by common law and statute everywhere ample legal provisions by which salaciousness or immorality may be kept from the screen as well as from the stage and the printed page.

When last Spring it was sought to pass an ordinance in New York City for the creation of a Motion Picture Board of Censors, the Committee on General Welfare of the New York Board of Aldermen, to whom the matter was referred for decision, emphasized the point most effectively.

The committee first quoted Section 1140-a of the Penal Law, which reads as follows:

"Immoral plays or exhibitions. Any person who as owner, manager, director, or agent, or in any other capacity prepares, advertises, gives, presents or participates in any obscene, indecent, immoral or impure dramas, plays, exhibition, show or entertainment, which would tend to the corruption of the morals of youth or others, and every person aiding or abetting such act, and every owner or lessee or manager of any garden, building, room, place or structure, who leaves or lets the same or permits the same to be used for the purpose of any such drama, play, exhibition, show or entertainment, knowingly, or who assents to the use of the same for any such purpose, shall be guilty of a misdemeanor."

Inimical to Democracy

And in its report the committee remarks: "The advocates of the proposed ordinance suggest an abandonment of a court proceeding and the substitution of a censorship by the Commissioner of Licenses to determine in advance what pictures may or may not be exhibited. If such legislation as this be enacted, it can be followed by the censorship of plays and the author compelled to submit his manuscript, or the censorship of the press, and the news items and editorials in our daily papers subjected to the censor's O. K. before publication be allowed. Your committee is opposed to the creation of a censorship because it regards the remedy suggested as far more inimical to our institutions than the evils sought to be corrected thereby, and recommends the filing of the ordinance."

That last sentence strikes the crux of the whole matter. No one will deny that there is room for improvement both in the content and method of motion pictures, least of all those who are making them. But do not image this is an easy task! Public opinion is neither a definite nor a constant thing. What pleases one group offends another.

The great body of motion picture "fans" is the real and natural censor of the motion picture. For legislators to try to force this process through boards of politically appointed censors would be futile. And in failing to constructively improve the screen these boards would bring into being a host of evils which, in the words of the committee quoted above, would be "far more inimical to our institutions than the evils sought to be corrected thereby."

In the early days of the film industry, when every one who could "hire a hall" was privileged to set up as an exhibitor of motion pictures, the business was overrun by men whose sole object was to make quick money while opportunity permitted. Their offerings in consequence were often of such a character as to bring discredit upon the business. At one time Mayor McClellan of New York threatened to close all the motion picture houses in the metropolis. The managers appealed to the People's Institute to aid them in this dilemma. Under the auspices of the People's Institute the National Board of Review was organized as an independent body of volunteer citizen reviewers to examine all films submitted to them by producers.

Unofficial Reviewers

In ten years the board has developed its methods and personnel until today it is known from coast to coast as representing in its decisions the better sort of public opinion more accurately than it could be represented in any other way as yet devised.

The reviewers of the board, more than a hundred in number, are well-known, well-educated, conscientious, and public-spirited men and women working without remuneration to preserve for the screen its freedom and to improve its content through constructive criticism and advice. From a host of correspondents throughout the country the board is constantly gathering data which enables it to keep in touch with popular sentiment in regard to motion pictures and to keep its reviewers constantly informed as to what the public thinks and feels about current picture play releases. By the action of the National Association of the Motion Picture Industry, in session at Rochester last August, the authority of practically all important motion picture producers in the United States is placed back of the National Board of Review in a co-operative effort to promote progress and prevent deterioration or motion pictures.

The activities of the National Board, while they are carried on in a manner similar to that adopted by legal censors, and result in changes such as might be made by legal censors, do not constitute censorship in the proper meaning of the word. The one distinctive feature of legalized censorship is that the censor's authority is derived from the police power of the State, and once given is barely subject to review or appeal. The legal censor is guided by no law save the enabling measure which grants him unrestrictive right of judgment, and is responsible to no one save himself for the character or the results of his decisions to all practical purpose. He is invested with absolute and autocratic power.

The National Board of Review does not have that absolute and autocratic power.

* * *

June 5, 1920

REVOKES THEATRE LICENSE

Commissioner Gilchrist Says Film at Harris Is Offensive

Commissioner of Licenses John F. Gilchrist yesterday revoked the license of the Harris Theatre on West Forty-second Street, controlled by Selwyn & Co., because of the exhibition of a motion picture entitled "Some Wild Oats," which he held to be offensive. Asserting that the film had been produced under the co-operation and with the indorsement of Health Commissioner Royal S. Copeland and Dr. S. Dana Hubbard. Director of the Bureau of Public Health Education Samuel Cummins, President of the Social Hygienic Films of America, announced, last night that he would seek an injunction today restraining the authorities from interfering with the performances.

The film, similar in character to others shown here since the conclusion of the war, deals with social diseases. According to Mr. Cummins, the picture has been indorsed, by Surgeon General Blue, J. H. Moyle, Assistant Secretary of the Treasury; Congressman Julius Kahn and Health Commissioner Francis Fronczak of Buffalo.

Mr. Cummins said that when the film was completed Commissioner Copeland and Dr. Hubbard were among an invited audience which saw it and made suggestions for its betterment. A few days ago, he said, Commissioner Gilchrist expressed a desire to view the picture. Dr. Hubbard attended this exhibition, at which Commissioner Gilchrist was present, and suggested to him, Cummins declared, that he offer to sell the rights to the Health Department.

"Yesterday Commissioner Gilchrist notified the Selwyns that the license would be revoked if the picture continued," said Mr. Cummins. Health Commissioner Copeland is in Europe, Dr. Hubbard could not be reached last night.

* * *

December 7, 1920

PUT BAN ON CRIME FILMS

Pennsylvania Censors Want No Glorification of Evildoers

HARRISBURG, Pa., Dec. 6—Moving picture films that glorify crime or make criminal careers or adventures fascinating or alluring will henceforth be barred in Pennsylvania, the State Board of Censors announced today.

Films in which criminals are shown as heroes of education and refinement, who live in luxury and persistently defy and outwit the authorities by their superior wit, resources and audacity, even though in the end they are caught, are seriously objectionable, the board decreed, especially where they are shown in the end to make merely perfunctory professions of reform, while reaping rich harvest and attaining great rewards in spite of their criminality.

* * *

January 5, 1921

CHICAGO FORBIDS ALL FILMS SHOWING CRIMINALS IN ACTION

CHICAGO, Jan. 4—Motion pictures portraying criminals at work have been barred in Chicago. Chief of Police Fitzmorris announced today that three weeks ago he had given orders to movie censors not to issue permits for any screen drama that showed a crime committed, even though the end of the picture might show the criminal in a prison cell.

"It will make no difference whether the criminal shown is a hero or a villain," said the chief. "Even the showing of a policeman disguised as a burglar is taboo."

The order became public when three youthful robbers, who were sentenced to the State Reformatory at Pontiac, said their crimes had been inspired by a "crook" moving picture.

* * *

February 22, 1921

IMPROPER NOVEL COSTS WOMEN $100

Greenwich Village Publisher and Her Editor Fined for Producing "Ulysses"

WOMAN'S DRESS DESCRIBED

Prosecution, on Anti-Vice Society Complaint, Said Description Was Too Frank

Margaret C. Anderson and Jane Heap, publisher and editor respectively of The Little Review, at 27 West Eighth Street, each paid a fine of $50 imposed by Justices McInerney, Kernochan and Moss in Special Sessions yesterday, for publishing an improper novel in the July and August, 1920, issues of the magazine. John S. Summer, Secretary of the New York Society for the Prevention of Vice, was the complainant. The defendants were accompanied to court by several Greenwich Village artists and writers.

John Quinn, counsel for the women, told the court that the alleged objectionable story, entitled "Ulysses," was the product of one Joyce, author, playwright and graduate of Dublin University, whose work had been praised by noted critics. "I think that this novel is unintelligible," said Justice McInerney.

Mr. Quinn admitted that it was cast in a curious style, but contended that it was in similar vein to the work of an American author with which no fault was found, and he thought it was principally a matter of punctuation marks. Joyce, he said, didn't use punctuation marks in this story, probably on account of his eyesight. "There may be found more impropriety in the displays in some Fifth Avenue show windows on in a theatrical show than is contained in this novel," protested the attorney.

Assistant District Attorney Joseph Forrester said that some of the chief objections had to do with a too frank expression concerning a woman's dress when the woman was in the clothes described. The court held that parts of the story seemed to be harmful to the morals of the community.

* * *

April 1, 1921

GOVERNOR IS FIRM ON CENSORING FILMS

Says He Sees No Way to Regulate Movies Except by Pending Bill

THEATRE OWNERS REPLY

Serve Notice of Statewide Campaign Against Measure—Censorship Considered in Connecticut

Special to The New York Times

ALBANY, March 31—Governor Miller today, in the face of increasing opposition by motion pictures interests, made clear that he is behind efforts to establish a State censorship over the movies.

Representatives of the motion picture industry have seen the Governor on the possibilities of the passage of the Lusk-Clayton bill, which would establish the censorship and on which a hearing is to be held next week.

"I have seen a good many people both pro and con," said the Governor today, "and the more I have looked into, it the more certain I am that there is a situation that requires treatment."

He was asked if he is "for an out and out censorship."

"I don't see any way to regulate it except by censorship," he replied. "That gets down to the personal equation, and every problem gets there in the last analysis. The human element is a very large part of every problem, but I really see no other effective way to do it. Of course the word 'censorship' does not have a good ring, but of course we have all sorts of censorship now. You cannot send lewd things through the mail. If you do you are liable to land in the Federal penitentiary.

"You cannot publish obscene literature. Then there is always the question 'What is obscene?' The question gets down to the personal equation, so there is nothing new or startling about censorship, but of course it is possible when you suggest censorship to indulge in great flights of oratory in behalf of liberty. Nobody intends to abridge the liberty. I am sure, of the press or of speech or of assemblage. Those three are fundamental things to be preserved. But liberty doesn't mean license, and there is such a thing as maintaining decency. The moving picture people now say they will be good, but you have heard the old story."

Theatre Owners Make Changes

While the Governor was expressing his views, Sidney S. Cohen of New York, President of the Motion Picture Theatre Owners of New York State, served notice of the initiation of a State-wide campaign to enlist the theatregoers against censorship. He charged sponsors of the measure with being job-hunters "who are aspiring to be made paid dictators and custodians of the public morals."

Mr. Cohen declared that enactment of the censorship bill would put hundreds of smaller movie theatres throughout the State out of business.

"The censorship of magazines and newspapers, vaudeville shows and road shows eventually follows the establishment of State censorship of motion pictures," he said.

"This proposition is but another evidence of a very common disease in the body politic. That disease expresses itself in what is known as 'blue law.'

"No good ever came of censorship. It is essentially iniquitous, and its result will be graft and dissatisfaction. What begins in bigotry flourishes in hypocrisy. As a matter of fact, the moving pictures can be depended on to purify themselves. The public will purify them. The people are sound. They are moral and decent, and anything that is consistently indecent will not be popular.

"We serve notice on all producers that we want clean and wholesome pictures and we do not want unclean or sensational exhibitions. We want the public to make the distinction between the producer and the theatre owner. We, the theatre owners, make no pictures—they do. We oppose censorship on the ground of true Americanism."

Increased cost to the picture going public will result from censorship, Mr. Cohen contended.

Connecticut Legislators Hear Arguments

HARTFORD, Conn., March 31—Bills requiring a censorship of moving picture films exhibited in theatres, but not affecting films used for educational, religious or scientific information, were the subject of a hearing before the Legislative Committee on the Judiciary this afternoon. Those who discussed the measures were less than half a dozen.

There were two bills, one for a censorship and the other requiring that theatre films, ordinarily displayed, should have been endorsed by the censoring board of Pennsylvania, Maryland or Massachusetts before being shown in this State.

* * *

April 6, 1921

PRODUCERS OFFER TO CLEAN UP MOVIES

"Clean Sweep From Coast to Coast" Promised if Censorship Bill Is Held Back

BRADY ASKS YEAR'S TRIAL

Mrs. Ellen O'Grady and Others Advocate the Measure in Interest of Women and Children

Special to The New York Times

ALBANY, April 5—A "clean sweep from coast to coast" of salacious motion pictures was promised the Legislature and Governor Miller today if the State would abandon legislative plans for a censorship. The promise was made by William A. Brady of New York City, who declared, at a hearing on the Lusk-Clayton bill proposing State censorship, that he represented 90 per cent of the motion picture producers in the State.

"I know there is no desire on the part of the Legislature to destroy a great industry," he said, "and for this reason we ask you to hold this measure over until next year, in order to give the industry an opportunity to demonstrate that it can handle this situation itself.

"I stand ready to go before Governor Miller and the Legislature leaders and enter into an iron-bound agreement that we will have this entire situation disposed of within a year. We will do it by pledging ourselves not to allow our pictures to be shown in theatres where objectionable pictures are being shown. We can close those theatres if necessary and if by any chance this plan should not work out I will be here next year and talk against the producers in stronger language than any one here did today."

Supporters of the Censorship bill declared the motion picture industry was responsible to a large degree for the increase in crime and juvenile delinquency and was used by opponents of good government as a means of supporting seditious propaganda.

The hearing, held before the joint Finance Committee of the Senate and Assembly, brought together a galaxy of notables, including Rex Beach, the author, and David W. Griffith, the producer. They opposed the enactment of the Censorship bill.

On the other side were Mrs. Ellen O'Grady, former New York City Deputy Police Commissioner; Alexander I. Rorke, Assistant District Attorney of New York County, and Mrs. Clarence Waterman, Chairman of the Better Motion Picture Alliance of Brooklyn, whose bringing to the attention of the Governor alleged immoral films resulted in the drafting of the Censorship bill and Governor Miller's expressed belief that the "movies" should be better regulated.

"State motion picture censorship as proposed in this measure means strangulation of the film industry," asserted Rex Beach. "It is advocated by two groups—those who are actuated by a narrow bigotry and those who believe movies are the cause of increasing crime."

Mr. Brady dwelt on the patriotic features of the films that can and have been put to use. He said that at the request of former President Wilson the motion picture industry had, without charge, sent 9,000,000 feet of film abroad to counteract German film propaganda during the war. He declared the movie has its place in church work and in educational fields. He maintained that State censorship would be impracticable and futile.

"Why," he said, "we could not film Joan of Arc because she was burned at the stake nor the life of Jesus because of the crime which closed His life on this earth. That classic of literature 'Hamlet' would be censored off the stage because it contains five murders and a suicide."

Publication of some stories in the newspapers, notably, "the sordid details of the Stillman divorce case," was worse than many stories which find expression on the screen, E. A. Moray, Chairman of the Legislative committee of the National Board of Review told the legislators.

Other opponents of the measure included Hugh Frayne, who said he was a personal representative of Samuel Gompers, head of the American Federation of Labor; Miss Mary Graves Peck of Geneva, Mayor James Canfield of Poughkeepsie, representing the State Mayor's conference, and the Rev. L. H. Caswell of the Bronx.

Proponents of the measure, led by Mrs. Waterman, contended that films of today were defiling American womanhood, increased crime and were immoral.

Mrs. O'Grady declared her experience as a Deputy New York City Police Commissioner had shown her that boys and girls were often led astray by the so-called sex plays.

Clergymen and representatives of various church organizations and civic bodies joined in the appeal for censorship.

It is believed, inasmuch as Governor Miller has come out strongly for censorship, that the Legislature will pass the bill within a day or two and send it to the Governor for his approval.

* * *

April 12, 1921

MOVIE CENSORSHIP BILL PASSES SENATE

Bitter Debate Precedes Favorable Action by a Vote of 30 to 18

ALL DEMOCRATS OPPOSED

Eight Republicans Joined Them in Negative Vote—Measure Attacked as Un-American

Special to The New York Times

ALBANY, April 11—After a heated debate lasting three hours, the Senate early this morning passed the Lusk-Clayton Moving Picture Censorship bill by a vote of 30 to 18.

The affirmative votes were all Republican. All the Democrats in attendance, Edmund Seidel, the Socialist Senator from the Bronx, and eight Republicans voted against the bill. The Republicans who joined the opposition were: Duggan and Meyer, New York; Karle, Queens; Katlin, Kings; Fearon, Onondaga; Robinson, Herkimer; Whitley, Monroe, and Wiswall, Albany.

The Senate took up the bill under a closure rule limiting debate to half an hour each for the proponents and opponents of the measure. Senator Walker, leader of the Democratic minority, made a vigorous attack on the rule itself, declaring that steam roller tactics were particularly objectionable where bills which could not be regarded as party measures were involved.

Senate Leader Lusk, sponsor for the bill, opened the debate with a brief explanation of its provisions. The bill gives a censorship board of three members power to refuse a license to exhibition of films which in its opinion are, "obscene, indecent, immoral, inhuman, sacrilegious or of such character that their exhibition would tend to corrupt morals or incite to crime."

"Will the word 'inhuman' in the bill prevent the presentation of a murder scene on the screen? Will it prevent, for instance, the production of a play like 'Macbeth?' " asked Senator Holland S. Duell of Westchester. "I would like to know that before I vote in the affirmative on this measure."

"If the pictured scene should go so far as to corrupt morals or incite to crime, the censorship board in its sound discretion would have power to refuse a license, always with resort to a court review for the producer," said Senator Lusk.

Senator Robinson of Herkimer wanted to find out how many deputy censors would be required to censor all the films.

Senator Lusk could not answer the question, but said there would be censorship bureaus in New York City, Buffalo and Albany.

Senator Edmund Seidel, Socialist, spoke in opposition. This brought Senator Lusk to his feet in a new defense of the bill that bears his name.

"Producers of films themselves," he said "admit there is such a problem as that which has prompted legislation. In a letter which I hold in my hand, the National Association of Moving Picture Producers urge upon the members their emphatic protest, against ten different varieties of productions now shown on the screen and ask them to refrain from producing them. That is a confession.

"But that is not all. In 1916 when legislation of the same character was before the Legislature the motion picture producers came here and with trembling voices and great emotion asked us to give them a chance to clean up their own business. They got their chance and they failed to make good, as the kind of pictures they have shown during the last four years clearly indicates.

"Now, they are coming here again this year. They are raising their voices again with a tremor in them and are displaying the same emotion in a new plea for a chance to make good. Now, what they need in my opinion is not a chance to make good, but a little assistance in making good, but in giving them that assistance we will only reflect the conscience and desire of a great majority of the decent people in this State."

Senator Boylan, of New York, in opposing the bill, urged, that if films were to be censored the same rule should be applied, and with as good reason, to books, newspapers and to stage performances.

"This bill would give to three men on a censorship board the power and impose upon them a task that would be beyond men with the wisdom of Solomon," he said. "It will be up to them, for instance, to standardize the screen kiss. How long should it last? Should it last a minute or only thirty seconds to pass muster? And should there be a distinction in the length of the censored kiss of, for instance, a mother to her son or a wife to her husband returning from the service of his country at the front, and the kiss of a wife if a traveling man returning from a long trip, or perchance, of a lawmaker returning from his legislative duties at the Capitol?"

Minority Leader James J. Walker, in closing the debate, made a bitter attack on Senator Lusk, whom he accused of violating confidences in giving to the Senate the contents of the letter sent out by the National Association of Moving Picture Producers.

"This is the most un-American bill ever introduced into this Senate," he said. "You," he added, pointing his finger at Senator Lusk, "are only a step behind the crackatoo who has written a pamphlet advocating a twentieth amendment to the United States Constitution abolishing religious liberty in this country.

"Why is this bill to be rushed and railroaded through this Senate in violation of all ethics, after solemn agreements entered into by the majority leader? There is some mystery behind this haste which I have not been able to fathom.

"The Senate leader has suggested that moving picture men came here, pleading and begging for an opportunity to clean up the films themselves. If I were willing to break confidences, I could tell you full particulars to prove that the moving picture men did this in deference to suggestions from a great big man of national and international reputation, who stepped down from his great position to make that suggestion."

Senator Walker said that tax imposed on the film industry will be paid by "the man, woman and child who has 5, 10 or 15 cents or no more to spend for a little amusement."

"This proposition is pure bunk," said the minority leader. "I don't know whether I will have to apologize for using hectic language, but it seems necessary to use strong American language to make gentlemen who are ever so much more cultured and refined than I am supposed to be understand."

The bill imposes a tax of $30 per 1,000 feet on new films and $2 on 1,000-foot films already in existence which the proposed board must pass if application is made within thirty days after the law becomes effective.

* * *

April 23, 1921

BOOK MANY ENDORSED HELD TO BE OBSCENE

Publisher of 'Love in Marriage,' Said to Have Medical Value, Will Appeal

After a physician and others had testified that a book entitled "Love in Marriage, or Married Love," had scientific and medical value, the publisher, Dr. William Jay Robinson, was fined $250 in Special Sessions yesterday on the ground that its issue and sale were violations of Section 1141 of the Penal law, which relates to the publication of obscene matter. It was announced that an appeal would be taken to the highest courts, as the book had been sold for some time in Great Britain and Canada.

George Gordon Battle, attorney for the publisher, told the court that the book was a standard volume, and had a wide circulation among medical men. Dr. Robinson said that the book was published abroad by G. P. Putnam's Sons, and that a circular sent to him by the British publishers contained endorsements of well-known writers, among whom were H. G. Wells, George Bernard Shaw, Arnold Bennett, May Sinclair, Leonard Merrick, E. Phillips Oppenheim,

Eden Phillipotts and the Rev. Dr. W. R. Inge, Dean of St. Paul's Cathedral, London.

"The signatures of these authors, and of others on the circular," said Dr. Robinson, "are guaranteed to be genuine by the publishers."

The author of the book was Dr. Marie C. Stopes, said to have obtained degrees from London and Munich universities. The case has been in court since last June. Some of the witnesses for the defense at the trial in January included Kermit Roosevelt, Dr. W. J. Exner; director of the general educational activities of the Y. M. C. A.; Professor Charles B. Fagnani of the Union Theological Seminary and Professor Maurice A. Bigelow, Dean of Teachers College at Columbia University.

The fact that Presiding Justice Clarence Edwards had dissented from the opinions of his two associates in Special Sessions, said Dr. Robinson, laid a further basis for an appeal. The opinion of Justice Edwards, in part, read: "Three hundred years ago, in the light of authoritative opinion then attained, teaching the Copernican theory of the solar system was considered immoral, and Galileo, being a good citizen as well as a good astronomer, yielded to constrained authority, surrendered in large measure the joy of genius in original investigation and sharing with his fellow beings the resultant knowledge.

"True modesty is not shocked by any necessary conversation in plainest terms concerning the most intimate matters. I do not think that the evidence before us concerning the book and the manner of its sale, as shown by the testimony of the experts for the defense, received from men learned in medical science, establishes either of the propositions urged by the prosecution. Therefore I advise the court to decide the issue by acquitting the defendant."

* * *

September 4, 1921

MAKING MOVIES BE GOOD

State's New Censors Want to Be Fair, They Say, Even on Bathing Girls

How does a motion picture censor feel when he reviews a film, undertaking to pass judgment upon it for 10,000,000 residents of the State, who have been accustomed to select their own entertainment?

"That is a hard question," replied ex-Senator George H. Cobb, Chairman of the new Motion Picture Commission. "I would say that he feels pretty anxious about it, judging from my short experience. Some people appear to believe that the commission's first object is to abuse everybody else. But I can assure you that we are trying to do just the opposite thing, and there must be exceptionally good grounds before we cut a picture."

"What are the principles of censorship?"

"So far I haven't been able to find any," answered Mr. Cobb. "We are judging each picture upon its merits. I do not believe that there can be any broad generalizations as to what is objectionable."

He was reminded that in some States censors have frowned upon all pictures showing the commission of a crime.

"I believe that the censor would have to be governed a good deal by the kind of crime," he said, "and many other factors leading up to and following the deed. I am certain every one will agree that we should not have pictures which tend to corrupt the young by making crime attractive. That would be opposed to common sense and ordinary standards of decency."

"Does that mean that a picture may have a lot of gun play in it and a few hold-ups without being objectionable?"

"Suppose you judge that for yourself," said the censor, and led the way to the miniature theatre where a picture was about to be shown. It was a Western film, with a real bad villain and plenty of action, laid in a community where hard customers abound. Certainly that town needed cleaning up. And presently a young newspaper editor arrived. He got his sheet going and undertook the cleaning process. Things went along merrily, with the chief villain and all the minor villains in league to run the editor out. But he stuck to the job and there was something doing every minute. Then the villain's daughter began to exercise her gentle influence upon matters including the editor. So it was not long until everybody had turned over a new leaf and the editor had an assistant to tell him how he should conduct himself.

"What do you think about it?" asked Mr. Cobb.

"Looks all right to me."

Virtue Triumphant Preferred

"That is the sort of a picture in which crime is not made triumphant," said the censor. "Nobody has been injured, no lives wrecked by the working out of the plot. But there is another kind of Western picture in which evil situations are unduly brought forward. We had one the other day showing a dance hall scene with a single girl, scantly clad, among a score of men. A drunken brawl began and one of the men attacked the girl, tearing off a part of her clothing. That scene came out. Its elimination did not affect the continuity of the play, and its showing would have served no good purpose. It merely set an example which might be harmful, certainly one which could not be helpful to young minds."

The censor's reference to the continuity of this picture brought up a question which has long troubled the motion picture producers. They have contended that the elimination of many scenes serves to destroy the dramatic unity of a photoplay.

"We endeavor to help and never to hinder," said Mr. Cobb. "I do not believe that the commission has deleted a single scene which took anything away from a picture. In making a cut we consider not alone the scene affected, but its bearing upon the whole picture."

"Suppose that a certain scene might be considered offensive if taken by itself, but the whole plot depended upon that one episode. How would you rule in such a case?"

"Another knotty question," answered the censor. "But I think, off-hand, that the scene would have to be extremely disagreeable for us to take it out, if it really meant upsetting the whole play. These questions cannot be answered in a general way. My observation leads me to believe that every picture has a certain well-defined tone, and it is necessary to get the spirit of a picture before one can exercise judgment upon it in whole or part."

"What about the vampire pictures?"

"So far we haven't had any," replied the censor, smilingly.

"Do you find the majority of pictures good or bad?"

"Most of them are all right," was the answer. "We have only encountered a few where deletions seemed to be desirable. And we have met with a spirit of co-operation from the producers which promises to make our task much easier.

"This isn't an easy job, you know," continued the State's chief censor. "I have been going to the movies for a great many years. They are fine entertainment. It certainly would be a mistake to take anything away from them which might add to the pleasure of the people. The job calls for common sense more than anything else."

"Have you had a picture which could not be passed?"

"Yes; just one. The producers withdrew it when they got our views. It was an artist model story, and there was entirely too much modeling in it. That is the kind of a picture which could just as well not be made. Surely there is enough dramatic material in real life to spare us from erotic creations which are wholly fictitious."

It seemed a bit strange to find a censor talking of dramatic material and the preservation of a story, when the popular conception has visualized him as an autocrat armed with long shears, ready to fall upon the motion picture industry and literally cut its film to death.

"How about the censoring of captions?"

"There have been only a few which appeared to need changing," said Senator Cobb. "In such cases we are making suggestions, but have not set up any hard and fast rules. We believe that things of that kind can be worked out by co-operation with the producers. Usually it means only slight changes."

A Case in Point

So far only one strenuous objection has been made to a cut ordered by the commission. This came from the Pathé organization, following the elimination of some Texas bathing beauties in one of the news films. The scenes were news in the sense that they showed a group of girls competing for a medal offered the most beautiful. The close-ups of these girls were deemed by the commission to be a bit too close.

The Pathé organization plans to open a court fight against the commission, predicated on this incident. The constitutionality of its ruling will be challenged as preventing the public from seeing a current event reproduced on the screen. This is said to be the second known elimination from a news reel, the first having been ordered in Pennsylvania, but on a second showing the commission there passed the scene which had been called objectionable.

Major George Chandler, commander of the State Constabulary, has put in a request that pictures be censored which might have a tendency to ridicule the police, prosecuting officials or other officers of the law.

It was pointed out to Mr. Cobb that there are dishonest policemen and officials, perhaps in as great a ratio as in other walks of life, and he was asked it he believed officials should be immune from motion picture treatment any more than a banker or some other man.

"I do not think that we should show special privileges to any class," answered Mr. Cobb, "but it is not desirable to hold up officers of the law in an unjust light or in a way which might encourage law-breakers. Let me say, once more, that no rule can be set up for matters of this kind."

He was reminded that one of the most amusing comic situations known to the films was the burlesqued policeman, the sort who chase comedy heroes and fall down coal holes to be bitten by dogs. Mr. Cobb smiled. "Yes, I have had many a laugh from those pictures," he said, "I don't know that anybody ever objected to them, for I think that we all realize they are merely a burlesque, just a pleasant fiction, and not intended to harm or degrade officers of the law."

Mrs. Hosmer's Work

Mrs. Eli T. Hosmer of Buffalo is the woman member of the commission. Before taking up her official duties she had considerable experience as a voluntary censor in her home city. Her presence on the board means that a woman's views will play a large part in the determination of what pictures New Yorkers shall see.

"Isn't it true that the public has exercised its own censorship of motion pictures," Mrs. Hosmer was asked, "deciding by a kind of mass psychology what it liked best?"

"I don't think so," said Mrs. Hosmer after a moment's consideration, "for there are so many kinds of pictures. If the public liked one sort much better than another it would seem that that would have become the fashion. But I do believe that the more thinking people are demanding better pictures all the time, and that this will encourage the making of such pictures."

"Have you found your work here any more trying than when you were censoring pictures at home?"

Mrs. Hosmer is the thoughtful sort of woman. If she had been a man she might have been called judicial. She turned over this question in her mind for several moments before answering. Then she said:

"No, it is not much different, but I feel the responsibility more. The commission is trying to be just, down to the smallest detail. We go further than that, and want to be charitable. It is not a question of deciding what we like for ourselves, but of trying to decide what might be harmful to a great many people. We thoroughly understand that this is a public question, a very big public question, in my opinion. We are trying to see it for the benefit of the public, and not in any narrow or controversial spirit."

"How do you like the work?"

"It is very, very interesting—vital, I might say." We review the ideas of a great many people and every new picture is likely to present something we have not considered before. I always feel that we must be fair to the last degree and endeavor to understand the producers and spectators' viewpoints.

"Do you believe that there has been improvement or retrogression in the kind of films shown since you first began censoring them?"

Again Mrs. Hosmer considered. "W-e-l-l," she said, "I don't know that there has been very much change either way. Certainly they have grown more complicated, and to include a greater variety of situations. Almost every relation of society has been brought into them and that has made the subject more complex to judge. I believe that the instructive and travel pictures are much improved, and it seems to me that these will find a greater field as time goes on."

The new commission has been working long hours since it took office and organization work is yet under way. Films are piling up daily for review and a staff of examiners will be appointed to scrutinize these offerings. Where a film seems doubtful the matter will be referred to one of the commission, and the producer may ask review by the full commission. Up to the moment the industry is still biding its time to get better acquainted with the censors and find out just what may be expected.

The elimination of the bathing girls caused something of a stir, and producers have been asking each other if this ruling meant that all bathers would be eliminated from the screen in New York and, if that was true, would the girl in the short dress be the next to go? Mr. Cobb was asked if the lure of the beaches had been officially blacklisted.

"By no means," he answered, "we haven't any objection to bathing girls in general. It is not our purpose to bar beauty from the screen. But these particular girls were—well—a bit too much—oh, you understand."

* * *

January 17, 1922

CENSORS PROHIBIT ONLY FIVE FILMS

State Moving Picture Commission Issues Licenses for 1,330 in Five Months

ASKS FOR MORE INSPECTORS

Board Declares Most Producers and Exhibitors Seek to Avoid Objectionable Pictures

Special to The New York Times

ALBANY, Jan. 16—Out of a total of 1,335 films inspected by the Motion Picture Commission prior to Jan. 1, only five were so objectionable that the commission found it necessary to prohibit their exhibition in this State. In its first annual report presented to the Legislature at tonight a session, the commission has a great deal of praise and some censure for film producers.

Among the recommendations made by the commission is one for an amendment to the motion picture censorship law, giving the commissioners power to refuse the granting of a license or permit for films which contain unpatriotic or seditious features or matter.

Another suggestion, made with some hesitancy and not as a formal recommendation, deplores the absence of any power in the commission to "prevent people whose only claim to notoriety or distinction is their connection with some scandal or crime from producing pictures," unless the subject-matter of the picture or the manner in which it is advertised should in itself be objectionable.

The commission asks for a larger appropriation than it received last year, and suggests that it should be authorized to employ a force of paid inspectors to visit the 1,700 motion picture theatres in this State to determine whether unlicensed or prohibited films are being displayed. The commission suggests that experiments made in other States with daily reports from producers and theatre managers or with volunteer inspectors have not brought the desired results.

"Without proper inspection the commission will not only become ineffective, but the commission will be subject to more or less ridicule," the report says.

The commission says that "comparatively few of the films presented violate the standards fixed by the statute." Only one decision, the report says, has been taken into court for review by a film producer. This was where a picture had been condemned in its entirety. In that instance the commission was sustained by the unanimous vote of the Appellate Division in the First Department.

"We have found," the report says, "that the main violations during the first two or three months arose from ignorance of the law and the requirements of the commission. There has been a desire, we are satisfied, on the part of the producers as a class, and particularly the exhibitors, to cooperate with the commission in its work.

"In this connection it might be stated that since the organization of the commission there has been a material improvement in the films presented for examination and license. The leaders in the industry are coming to realize that merit in pictures brings its reward the same as in other fields of endeavor. It has been demonstrated to the satisfaction of the producer that clean and wholesome pictures are the ones that bring the largest financial return, and while there are a few producers who evidently desire to cater to the lower instincts of the human race, and present unclean, immoral and salacious films, yet we are glad to report that this number is in the great minority. The class of producers last referred to fails to recognize the responsibility which they owe society and are only actuated by greed.

"We regret very much that many of the producers of films seem to deem it necessary or wise to incorporate in films in such a marked degree the vices of the human race, and also to depict violations of law in the commission of various crimes.

The commission endeavors to enforce the law concerning films of this character and to discourage their exhibition.

Labels appended to the report show that the commission has issued permits for 6,194 pictures already on exhibition when it began work on Aug. 1, without examination. Licenses were issued for 1,330 films, of which 1,170 went through without deletions of any kind. The number of eliminations ordered by the commission were 745 from 160 films, and of these 477 involved scenes and 268 Titles.

Indecency was the ground for eliminating scenes or titles in 85 cases, and 61 deletions were ordered because the matter concerned was either immoral or tending to corrupt morals. In five instances the matter deleted was of a sacrilegious character, in 35 it depicted inhumane actions, and in 54 cases the commission ordered scenes or titles cut out as tending to incite crime.

The films from which deletions were made are classified in the report as follows; Dramas, 81; comedies, 43; comedy drama, 30; serials 7; news films, 4; educational films, 3, and cartoons, 2.

During the last five months of 1921 the commission took in for licenses or permits a total of $157,817. The expenditure of the commission, for the same period, according to the report, was $36,687.

* * *

May 21, 1922

NO PREACHERS ON MOVIE JURIES

Barred from Panel of Joint Committee Opposed to Political Censorship

The final details of the voluntary jury system, designed to obviate a political censorship of the stage by eliminating indecent plays, have just been completed. The panel of 300 persons from which the juries are to be drawn is being rapidly formed from lists of names submitted by the respective organizations of dramatists, managers, actors and vice crusaders. The tentative lists include 400 names and among them there is not one clergyman. With New York City the centre of production, the voluntary jury is expected to serve as barrier for the whole country against the salacious play.

Members of the clergy are technically ineligible to membership on the panel, according to Owen Davis, Chairman of the Joint Committee Opposed to Political Censorship of the Theatre, who explained that they came under that provision of the program which bars any person having "official or financial connection with the theatre or with any reform movement."

The elimination of the clergy from the voluntary jury system has been one of the most delicate questions faced by the originators of the plan. Even now they do not like to have it said that the clergy have been ruled out. It is suggested that if a man of the type of Wendell Phillips were proposed as a prospective venireman his name might be acceptable to the various factions of the Joint Committee who must pass on the names submitted. But frankly there will not be the slightest chance for a minister of the sensational or radical type.

The names so far submitted as prospective members of the panel are about evenly divided among men and women. The selection of the names from the tentative lists began last Thursday. This work will be continued at a meeting to be held within a few days by the Joint Committee at the American Dramatists' Society, 148 West Forty-fifth Street. As each name is approved by all the different elements on the Joint Committee the consent of the person so chosen will be sought. This process of selection is expected to continue for three or four weeks longer. By the middle of June or the first of July the system will be completely organized and ready to function when the new theatrical season opens towards the close of Summer.

Program of Joint Committee

The complete program as drawn up by the Joint Committee is here presented for the first time:

1. A panel of about 300 persons shall be chosen. Nominations for membership on this panel shall be submitted by the organizations on the Joint Committee representing the theatre; by the organizations representing the better public shows movement; by the Drama League, and by the city administration. Each of these groups may nominate from 125 to 150 candidates. The panel is to represent nothing but good citizenship, and no person on the panel shall have any official or financial connection with the theatre or with any reform movement. The final appointment for service on the panel shall be made by the Joint Committee itself.

2. When any complaints are received by city officials which are deemed sufficiently important to demand investigation, the city officials may call for a jury of twelve, to be selected from the panel above described. The representatives of the theatre on the one side and the representatives of the public on the other are to have two peremptory challenges in the selection of the jury. These challenges are to be exercised before notices of jury service are sent to members on the panel. Verdicts may be reached by a vote of nine to three members of a jury.

3. Immediately upon its appointment, arrangements are to be made for the viewing of the play in question by the jury. After viewing the play, the jury shall consider the play from two points of view:

A. Are there any portions of the play under consideration objectionable from the point of view of public morals? If so, the manager shall have one week in which to adjust the play in accordance with the report of the jury, and the jury shall then review the play. If, after reviewing it, the play is still, in the opinion of the jury, objectionable, the play shall be closed immediately, in compliance with the provisions of Section 5 of this program.

B. Is the play as a whole objectionable from the point of view of public morals? If so, the play shall be closed immediately, in compliance with the provisions of Section 5 of this program.

4. There is to be no argument before the jury, each case standing on its own merits. The findings of the jury shall be absolutely final, and shall take effect immediately.

5. It is understood that the dramatists, the theatre owners, the producing managers, and the actors shall include in their mutual and respective contracts and agreements a provision that the verdicts of the jury shall in all cases be complied with.

This outline of the jury system has been supplemented with an agreement among all the members of the Joint Committee that when a play is on trial, the author, translator or manager may be called before the jury and permitted to explain the things to which exception may be taken. The jury then may reconsider what action to take, if any.

The selection of the jury will be left to the City Administration. It is probable that this duty will devolve upon either the Chief Magistrate or the Commissioner of Licenses of the City of New York.

In explanation of the origin and purposes of the voluntary play jury scheme, Eric Schuler, Secretary and Treasurer of the Authors' League of America, Inc., who has acted as spokesman for the Joint Committe, had this to say:

"Censorship has been discussed at many meetings of the Authors' League, and has been consistently opposed by that organization." The objection is not, be it understood, against the suppression of obviously indecent material, but against official interference with the right of any individual to express himself, subject, of course, to such restraints as society in general may impose upon him.

"Mr. George Creel put the case very clearly at one time. He pointed out that every individual living in an organized society is subject to social restraints, but that the restraint is applied after the individual has broken a law and not when somebody thinks he is going to. In other words, we insist that a serious author or artist shall have the right to express himself in any way he sees fit and to present his work to the public. If the public condemns his method of expression he must submit to the verdict of society, and this verdict the members of the Author's League are willing to abide by.

"An eminently practical plan has been developed by our dramatic group for the purpose of putting these ideas into practice. The comparatively large number of frankly salacious plays which have appeared within the last year or so created a situation which would inevitably have resulted in the establishment of an official censorship—that is, political censorship—for the stage, similar to that now in effect in the motion-picture field.

"Every one, including even representatives of anti-vice societies, disapproves of the actual results of such a censorship, and it was for the purpose of evolving a better plan that, at the suggestion of the Authors' League and the Actors' Equity Association, the Joint Committee Opposed to Political Censorship was formed.

The Joint Committee consists of representatives from the Authors' League, the Actors' Equity Association, the Producing Managers' Association, the American Dramatists, the Better Public Shows Movement and the Drama League.

"The meetings of the committee have been marked by complete unanimity of opinion as to the existence of a condition in the theatre which calls for correction, and a further unanimity of opinion that political censorship would not be a practical remedy.

"All the delegates who have attended the meetings have consistently upheld the right of the author to discuss any subject whatever, in a play or other work of art, so long as the discussion be serious in its point of view; and they have all gone on record as opposed to any plan which would result in the suppression of an honest and serious play on any subject whatever. It has been the purpose of the committee to devise ways and means for eliminating frivolous plays of a purely indecent and salacious character.

"The plan finally adopted was first suggested in rough outline by Winthrop Ames of the Managers' Association. Mr. Ames suggested the establishment of a jury, somewhat along the lines of the Sheriffs' Jury, whose duty it would be to view plays against which complaints have been brought, and to decide whether or not these complaints were justified.

The fundamental idea contained in Mr. Ames' suggestion has remained unchanged. Its most important phase is that juries shall be called to pass upon a play after, and only after, a sufficient number of complaints have been received from members of the theatregoing public to warrant an investigation. The jury will not initiate proceedings at any time, but will act only when there is reason to believe that the penal statutes regarding obscene plays or publications have been infringed. The jury will not be concerned with complaints based on a divergence of opinion on religious, political historical or similar subjects."

The suggestion that the code of morality established for the drama in New York City may not meet with the approval of other sections of the country where the peculiar views of those people may decide the morality or immorality of a dramatic production is answered by the advocates of the voluntary jury system with the explanation that the panel of 300 men and women will include representatives from every part of the United States the same as would any equal number of New York citizens selected at random.

The Joint Committee Opposed to the Political Censorship of the Theatre includes the following organizations and their representatives: Authors' League of America, Inc., Jesse Lynch Williams, President, George Creel, Leroy Scott; The Actors' Equity Association, John Emerson, President Frank Gilmore, Secretary, Florence Reed; the American Dramatists Society, Owen Davis, President, Channing Pollock, Eugene Buck, Edward Childs Carpenter; The Producing Managers' Association, Gilbert Miller, J. P. Bickerton, Jr., John Golden, George Tyler, Arthur Hopkins; Better Public Shows Movement, John S. Summer, head of the Society for the Prevention of Commercialized Vice; Mrs. H. J. Glover of the Welfare Board of the Protestant Episcopal Church, Walter G. Boyle of the Y. M. C. A., and Edward J. McGuire, and the Drama

League, Mrs. Carolyn Coffin, S. M. Tucker, and Cranston Brenton.

* * *

May 21, 1922

VIRTUE MADE IN PENNSYLVANIA

By BENJAMIN DE CASSERES

The Pennsylvania Board of Film Censors would walk a thousand miles to smoke out a "Camille."

It was from this same musnud of moralists that the edict was issued last year that no picture could be shown that portrayed a mother making a layette for her unborn child. In Pennsylvania children are not born in the usual way, but are bootlegged over the roofs by storks or moonshined into the world through a cabbage leaf.

It was the same Sanhedran of Sages who ordered the title "It is a boy" cut out of "The Four Horsemen of the Apocalypse." If it had read "It is a Republican" it would have passed—in Pennsylvania.

Anyhow, "Camille" arrived in Pennsylvania on the celluloid. It was not called "Camille." It was called "The Red Peacock." The story was the story of "Camille" done in Germany. It was originally called "Poor Violette." Pola Negri was the star who coughed her way into eternity in the fifth reel in the way the younger Dumas had arranged it some years back. The names of the characters were changed, but the play is essentially the same that millions of people have seen and read.

As soon as the Pennsylvania board saw the picture they put their ivories together and ordered the following changes in "Camille," alias "The Red Peacock." I here reproduce verbatim the order. It is my most precious literary possession. As a bit of Americana I believe it is unique.

REEL 1—(a) Eliminate subtitle, "Gaston du Pont, her satellite," and substitute "Gaston du Pont, her fiancé."

REEL 3—(a) Eliminate subtitle, "Count Girgy sees an opportunity," and substitute "Count Girgy sees an opportunity to vary his hectic life with an act of humanity."

(b) Eliminate subtitle, "Violette, you may remain as maid in this house if you wish to," and substitute "Violette, my house is lonely. Let me do an unselfish act—be my ward and enjoy the comforts of my home as a sister would."

(c) Eliminate views of Girgy embracing and kissing Violette after bringing her wrap to her and all views of Girgy kissing and embracing Violette in any other reel throughout the picture.

REEL 4—(a) Eliminate subtitle, "Alfred, I love you. Take me away from this," and substitute "Alfred, I love you. I was happy as Girgy's ward until you returned. Take me away."

(b) Eliminate views of Alfred shaking his head to express "No."

(c) Insert after Alfred has fallen at Violette's feet with his head in her lap and she is fondling and kissing him, subtitle, "Come to me, Violette; we will be married at once and say nothing about it."

REEL 5—(a) Insert a subtitle after "I love Alfred—he is all I have in the world. I cannot let him go," when Violette sinks in chair and Claire goes out of the room, to this affect, "Realizing that for his own reasons Alfred had not told his father of his marriage, Violette loyally kept the secret."

(b) Insert a subtitle during the views showing Violette leaving her home and before she goes to Gaston du Pont, to this effect: "With a courageous determination to find some means of honestly earning money to aid Alfred."

(c) Eliminate subtitle, "I am here, ill in body and soul. Take me away, anywhere," and substitute "I am here, ill in body and soul. You offered to help me. Are you good friend enough to take me, unselfishly, where I can learn to dance so that I may earn money?"

(d) Eliminate subtitle. "My dear Alfred: Forgive me, I am leaving you. My illness will become a greater and greater burden on you, and our financial troubles are growing each day. You have your future to consider. Violette," and substitute "My dear Alfred: Forgive me. I am leaving you for a time that I may earn money to overcome our financial troubles, which are growing each day. I love you and hope for the future. Violette."

(e) Eliminate all views in this and other reels following of Gaston du Pont embracing and kissing or making love to Violette.

(f) Eliminate subtitle, "We will go South and there will soon be roses in your cheeks," and substitute "You may trust me. We will go South and there will soon be roses in your cheeks. You shall learn to dance there."

REEL 6—(a) Eliminate all views of Gaston du Pont making love to Violette, kissing or embracing her.

(b) Eliminate subtitle, "You'd better not dance this evening—your cough," and substitute, "You'd better rest this evening—your cough."

(c) Eliminate the word "you" from subtitle, "It was my money you loved, not me—you—"

(d) Eliminate subtitle, "Now I know you for what you are—and I'm through with you," and substitute "I'm through with you forever."

A careful analysis of this remarkable document will disclose to the future excavators and archaeologists of the ruins of American liberty the wheels in the mental processes of those who gave to the world the Great Pennsylvania Idea. Rare pickings for a future Tain or Gibbon.

It may be noted (Reel 1, a) that no Camille is entitled to a satellite within a radius of 300 miles of Harrisburg. She may have a fiancé. The fiancé must not be a satellite—but a satellite may become a fiancé. So the Home is conserved.

Count Girgy (Reel 3, a) cannot just see an opportunity. He must see an opportunity that involves an act of humanity. There can be no objection to this, as it follows the philosophy of McGuffey's Reader.

Violette and Girgy (Reel 3, c) are not allowed to embrace or kiss throughout the picture. That these changes practically destroy the picture is of no moment. Girgy and Violette, although in love with one another, are not married; therefore all contact is null and void. This is based on an old Pennsylvania tradition that one may only kiss his wife or his dead aunt.

Alfred (Reel 4, b) also loves Violette. But, as you observe, he is not permitted to shake his head "no." This is abstruse. I believe it may be explained that since the advent of prohibition "no" has become an obsolete word. It remained for the Pennsylvania Board of Film Censors to make it official.

The board marries our Camille in the fourth reel. When the time comes they will marry Hamlet and Ophelia in the second reel. They may allow Faust and Marguerite to trot along as far as the third reel before the matchmakers at Harrisburg perform the ceremony—without Papa Goethe's consent, of course. It was fortunate for Shakespeare that he got Othello and Desdemona spliced. In Pennsylvania a man may smother his wife, but not his mistress.

When I showed the above sketch of our New Freedom to Howard Dietz, the poet laureate of the Goldwyn Pictures Corporation, he wrote the following and mailed it to Harrisburg:

The Standards Of The Board

"That the theme or story of a picture is adapted from a publication, whether classical or not; or that portions of a picture follow paintings or other illustrations is not sufficient reason for the approval of a picture or portions of a picture."—Excerpt from Standards of the Pennsylvania State Board of Censors of Motion Pictures.

It doesn't always follow that if Venus or Apollo
Or the nudes of Zuloaga are translated to the screen
That the censors so omniscient will consider thatsufficient
Ground for passing on the picture as quite fitting to be seen.

Just because a Rembrandt etching is considered more
than fetching,
Still the version in the movie might not meet with he accord
Of the Pennsylvania censors, those infallible dispensers
Of morality—according to the Standards of the Board.

In this age of smut and slander, where a play is prone
to pander
To the basest and the vilest and the cheapest that's in man
There must be the chosen mortals who have passed
through Virtue's portals
And have stood out from the others as the molders of
the clan.

So this censorship committee shall prescribe to each
Penn city
Just the proper set of morals that the pictures hall afford.
They are trained in all that's flirty—they know vice—they
know what's dirty.
And they know by heart the rules they call the Standards of
the Board.

It is a curious etymological fact that Board is Wood and Wood is Board. If the Great Pennsylvania Idea spreads to the public press and the theatres, the only blameless literature in the country will be your income tax blank and your apartment lease.

* * *

July 7, 1922

CAN CENSOR NEWS FILMS

State Supreme Court Upholds Motion Picture Commission

ALBANY, N. Y., July 6—The State Motion Picture Commission has the right to pass judgment on news reels of current events, according to a decision handed down tonight by the Appellate Division of the Supreme Court. The question was brought to the court by the Pathe Film Exchange for the purpose of determining the right of the Motion Picture Commission to censor and license news films as other films are inspected. All judges of the court concurred in the decision.

The incident that brought out the controversy was the showing of a girl in scanty beach attire on the Atlantic City bathing beach. The commission insisted the picture was immoral and should be deleted. The decision tonight upholds their contention.

* * *

July 26, 1922

MOVIE CENSORSHIP PROVES IT HAS TEETH; THREE FIRMS IN COURT FOR IGNORING ORDERS

Three motion picture corporations that ignored the censorship rules of the State Motion Picture Commission pleaded guilty yesterday before Justices Freschi, Healy and Voorhees, in Special Sessions. It was the first time the State Commission has resorted to the courts to convince the film interests that they must obey the law, and Justice Freschi, who presided, made it plain to representatives of many motion picture companies present that the lightness of the penalties imposed should not be taken as an indication for the future.

A fine of $250 was imposed on the Arrow Exchange of 729 Seventh Avenue for releasing a picture entitled "Stay Down East," without having made certain eliminations ordered by the commission.

The Elk Photo Plays Corporation of 729 Seventh Avenue was fined $100 for exhibiting the "Hula Hula Dance" on March 30 last at the Star Theatre, 960 Southern Boulevard, the Bronx, in which eliminations had been ordered.

Sentence was suspended in two complaints against the Associated First National Picture Corporation of the same address. Representatives of the corporation admitted that certain eliminations ordered by the commission were not made when "The Rosary" was exhibited at the Cameo Theatre, in West Forty-second Street, in March last. The second charge was based on the display of "Smilin' Through" at the Strand Theatre in April without a license. A representative of the corporation explained that the failure to obtain duplicate licenses for the picture was due to the negligence of an employe who had been discharged.

* * *

September 17, 1922

PUBLISHER NOW SUES SUMNER FOR $10,000

Thomas Seltzer, Acquitted in Case Where He Was Arrested, Asks Heavy Damages

CLERK TO BRING ACTION

Censor Says Campaign Against Novels Regarded as Indecent Will Be Pushed

Suit for damage of $10,000 has been started against John S. Sumner, Secretary for the Society for the Suppression of Vice, by Jonah J. Goldstein of 366 Broadway on behalf of Thomas Seltzer, the publisher, on the ground of false arrest and injury to his business involved in the unsuccessful prosecution of three books. "Woman in Love," "A Young Girl's Diary" and "Casanova's Homecoming." A similar suit will be filed this week on behalf of the employe who was arrested with Mr. Seltzer and exonerated in the Magistrate's Court.

Other efforts will be made to follow up the defeat of the Society for the Suppression of Vice in the Magistrate's Court and to start a general reaction against censorship. The anti-censorship organization, of which George Creel is at the head, is planning a campaign to aid in defeating motion-picture censorship legislation in Massachusetts, where a referendum will be held at the November election, when the public will vote whether they want their films censored or uncensored. This Massachusetts election is one of the key points of the censorship struggle and will be the scene of a fierce campaign this Fall between those who want censorship and those who don't.

Other suits against Mr. Sumner and the Society for the Suppression of Vice have been threatened by publishers, who have adopted the plan of bringing a civil action every time that the Vice Society fails in its criminal action. The Court of Appeals has held that, if the Society initiates a prosecution and fails to get a conviction, it becomes a question for a jury to decide whether the prosecution was based on reasonable grounds or was unjustifiable. One verdict of $2,500 has been recovered against the society and upheld by the Court of Appeals because of a prosecution which failed.

Play Jury Is Yet Untested

The only recent triumph for censorship has been the agreement of the Vice Society, the License Commissioner and representatives of playwrights, actors and producers, to submit plays to censorship under the voluntary play-jury system. No case has yet come up for trial by a play-jury and whether the system will work or not is doubtful.

The fact that there has been no complaint and no trial as yet is taken by Secretary Sumner of the Vice Society, as proof of the efficacy of the voluntary censorship plan.

"At this time last year, there had already been a number of complaints against new productions," said Mr. Sumner. "So far this year there have been no complaints. The run of theatrical offerings this year has apparently been cleaner than for several years past, and it seems quite probable that they are better, because the playwrights and producers looked forward to the play-jury system and did not wish to run the risk of such trials.

"As to the threats which have been made from time to time to smother me and the society with damage suits, we pay no attention whatever to them," said Mr. Sumner. "We will continue to ask for prosecutions in all cases where we believe that it appears plainly that the law has been violated.

"The society has so far this year obtained thirteen convictions, two this week, of magazine publishers because of obscene matter. A large number of convictions has been obtained for selling or possessing indecent material. We have not this year obtained any convictions for the publication of indecent books, but we did last year. Although some publishers succeed in winning the cases against them, the chance of being convicted and the fact that others have been convicted is the chief deterrent against a flood of still more vicious books than we have today."

Fish-Net Woman in Many Shops

Another prosecution in which the society failed was the prosecution of the vendor of photographs of a woman costumed only in a fish net, which appears today on the windows of scores of shops in New York. The fish-net picture today exceeds the vogue once obtained by "September Morn," after Anthony Comstock had unsuccessfully prosecuted it. The fish-net figure was held by three Justices in Special Sessions to come under the classification of art. Though this particular picture has survived prosecution, Mr. Sumner said that milder art had been successfully prosecuted before and since. One setback, according to him, does not set a precedent for the policy of the society, because later prosecutions before different Judges or juries might result in conviction.

This curiosity of the law which makes the same picture, book or paragraph a crime before one Judge or jury and something artistic or harmless before another was also commented on by Jonah J. Goldstein, lawyer for several who have been prosecuted by the society.

Lawyer Points Out Difficulties

"The trouble with all such cases," said Mr. Goldstein, "is that the same thing may be a crime at one trial and an innocent thing at the next. It may be a crime with a Judge who professes one religion and not with a Judge who professes another. A lawyer cannot advise his clients whether publishing a certain thing is a crime or a lawful act. He can only say, 'That depends entirely what Judge happens to be on the bench at the time.' There is no other kind of act about which this is true. In any other case, if you know the facts, you know whether it is a crime of not. The facts may be undisputed in a trial of this kind and generally are, but still no one knows whether there has been a crime until the verdict is rendered."

In arguing this in a brief to the Court of Appeals, Mr. Goldstein quoted the maxim. "Where the law is uncertain there is no law."

"Wherever we neglect the requirement," he continued, "that every crime must be predicated upon some actual sense perceivable and proved material injury, or the imminent danger of such, determined to be imminent by the known laws of the physical universe, and, therefore, accurately definable and so defined in the statute—we say, whenever we abandon these requirements, we are condemning men on mere metaphysical speculations about unrealized psychologic tendencies, or, according to the personal ethical sentimentalizing, whim, caprice, malice, &c., on the part of those charged with the execution of the law, and thus the Judge arrogates to himself the role of the legislator, and under such enactments convictions are never secured according to the uniform express authority of any statute, and all such convictions inflict punishment for mere constructive injuries and are an unconstitutional deprivation of liberty and property because not due process of law.' "

* * *

January 19, 1924

CENSORS SAY FILMS OFTEN GLORIFY VICE

Virtue, Sobriety and the Law Are Made Unattractive, State Board Tells Gov. Smith

386 FILMS CUT IN YEAR

Board Dropped or Rearranged 2,881 Scenes and Titles—Changes in Law Suggested

Special to The New York Times

ALBANY, N. Y., Jan. 18—Declaring that vice is glorified and virtue, sobriety and observance of the law made unattractive in many films, the New York State Motion Picture Censorship Commission tonight submitted its annual report to Governor Smith.

The report asserts that the "motion pictures can be made a wonderful force with the education of our people, and under proper regulations will accomplish great good."

Pointing out that the penal law regulating legitimate theatrical performances cannot be applied to motion pictures, the report says that "undoubtedly the greatest evil is the exhibition of pictures showing the method of committing crime and escaping punishment." It continues:

"Others are intended to appeal to sex instincts. It has been said that the motion picture gives a false idea of life. People living in immoral relations are shown to be surrounded with luxuries which girls and boys who have to work for a living cannot afford. In this manner the life of the American people is misrepresented. Vice is glorified and virtue, sobriety and observance of the law are made unattractive.

Difficulties in Regulation

"The claim is often made that the law concerning the regulation of theatrical performances is adequate to punish those who produce and exhibit objectionable motion pictures. It has, however, been clearly proven that the motion picture cannot be regulated through the same agencies as the ordinary theatres. The universal demand for regulation all over the world is a sufficient answer to this argument.

"If it were possible to prevent the exhibition of objectionable films through the agencies which exist without a general statute, some locality in the country would have been able to do so. Again, the ordinary processes of the law are so slow that before a picture could be suppressed it would have a long run, and much notoriety and great harm would result."

The commission found it necessary to make 2,881 eliminations in 586 films, dropping or rearranging 2,260 scenes and eliminating 621 titles. Twenty-nine scenes or titles were regarded as sacrilegious and 26 as obscene. In 382 instances the commission decided that a scene tended to incite to crime, while 238 scenes were rated as inhuman.

The report points out that the total receipts collected by the commission during the three years of its existence were $476,233.06. The total amount expended by the State to maintain the commission for the same period was $200,288.28, leaving a net profit for the State of $275,944.78.

Found Immoral Foreign Pictures

"During the year there seems to have been a great influx of foreign pictures," the report said. "There is no agency which has any jurisdiction over them except our commission, and many of them contain indecent, immoral and sometimes sacrilegious matter. In fact, in some of them, assaults have been made upon religious sects. The majority of the producers and exhibitors, we are satisfied, have sought to co-operate with the commission and its work, and the violations detected have been comparatively few when it is taken into consideration that there are about 1,700 theatres in the State and that daily exhibitions are given in them.

"Many objectionable films are made and sent abroad for exhibition," the commission declares. "Foreigners, by reason of films of this character being shown, are given a false impression as to our country and its institutions. Frequent complaints have been made to this commission concerning abuses of this character. Poland, through its officials, claims that it was necessary for that country to enact a censorship law for the reason that the American films are very attractive to their people and had a tendency to incite them to crime. An agitation was started in Mexico to prevent the exhibition of our films due to the fact that the Mexican is always represented as a bandit or outlaw.

"These facts are not presented with the idea of indicting the industry as a whole for these abuses, but the fact that they should be remedied still remains. The majority of the producers, we are satisfied, are appreciative of their responsibility to the public, but in an industry of this character, which attracts such a variety of people, it is not strange that persons of questionable character should attempt to commercialize crime and vice.

"Another evil which has crept upon the screen is the dissemination of propaganda which is inimical to our institutions. The Department of Justice at Washington has taken cognizance of this fact, and is vigilant in watching particularly the foreign films which teach lessons which are destructive of the fundamentals of our Government. We have no power to prevent their manufacture without our borders but should prevent their exhibition within.

"The favorite argument that the regulation of the motion picture is destructive of the liberties of people and tends to restrict art has long since, in this State particularly, been proven to be without foundation. Only those portions of films which clearly violate the law are deleted. No State or country would have ever passed laws regulating the motion picture industry unless, as conceded by all reputable producers, abuses had crept into the industry and a necessity existed for their being remedied."

The board asked the amendment of existing laws so that the commission could impose in cases of willful violation an adequate penalty. Removal of the present uncertainty regarding the definition of educational, charitable or religious films was asked.

No mention is made of cases involving motion picture actors or actresses, but the commission suggests that power be given it to prevent exhibition of pictures in which "criminals or persons recognized to be of a debased character appear."

* * *

March 30, 1930

GETS 20-YEAR TERM IN VENEZUELA JAIL

Unnamed Man Admits Sending Uncomplimentary Clippings to High Official

CENSORSHIP RULES STRICT

News Reflecting on Government Barred From Entering or Leaving Country

Special Correspondence, The New York Times

CURACAO, March 17—Twenty years' imprisonment, after a confession said to have been obtained by third degree methods of the Venezuelan police, was the punishment inflicted on an unnamed individual, said to be a Colombian, for alleged violation of the censorship regulations designed to prevent any news relating to Venezuela entering the country from the world outside.

It was reported from Maracaibo that for some time past Vincenzio Perez Soto, president of the State of Zulia, had been receiving through the mail anonymous letters containing clippings from the newspapers of neighboring countries, which were not exactly complimentary to the present government. Many of these clippings came from Colombia where large numbers of political exiles are known to be waiting the passing of General Juan Vicente Gomez in order to return in safety to their homes.

The newspaper articles sent to President Perez Soto were largely criticisms of himself, General Gomez, Juan Batista Perez, president of the republic, and other henchmen of Gomez, who is still the real head of the government. It appears that the clippings were sent to President Perez Soto in order to let him know what people really think when they have a chance to express an opinion, which, of course, is not possible in Venezuela.

Peon Mailed Letter

A strict watch was kept in the Maracaibo postoffice in order to discover the sender. A man, armed with one of the envelopes of the anonymous letters, was stationed behind each letter drop to scrutinize every letter dropped through the slot. Other officials disguised as loafers and peddlers were stationed in the lobby of the building.

Finally one of the watchers caught a letter in an envelope similar to those in which the anonymous communications had been sent. He signaled to his aides outside, who at once pounced upon the person who had posted the letter. He was an apparently harmless peon, who asserted that he had been paid to mail the letter by a man generally supposed to be from Colombia and employed in a fairly important capacity by one of the oil companies.

This individual was promptly arrested and, apparently without further inquiry, was forced to confess his guilt. He implicated others, who were held several days and released with a warning not to talk of their experiences while under arrest. The man from whom the alleged confession was obtained was sentenced to spend twenty years in prison.

Lately all newspapers from neighboring countries have been confiscated and for a long time other foreign newspapers have been strictly censored and all reference to conditions in Venezuela cut out before delivery is made to the addressees.

Censor Was Conscientious

Some time ago a foreign newspaper correspondent had an experience with the cable censor in Caracas which illustrates the quality of the censorship. He had interviewed a high official of the government who had managed to talk long and say little. The story had been approved before it was filed at the cable office. A few days later the correspondent was informed that it had been held up by the censor.

When he asked the censor, who was particularly proud of his knowledge of English, why his story had not been passed, he was told rather indignantly:

"Because you insult the great Liberator. What you mean throwing stones at the grand Liberator Bolivar?"

"I throw stones at Bolivar?" the correspondent asked in surprise. "That is impossible; I am a great admirer of General Bolivar. Let me see the dispatch."

The dispatch was produced and the correspondent noted that he had written that the interview was held "within a stone's throw of a statue of General Simon Bolivar."

"There, see that!" the censor exclaimed, triumphantly. Then, in a voice of righteous indignation, he demanded: "What you mean by throw stones at Bolivar?"

* * *

March 28, 1931

CUBAN COURT VOIDS BAN ON NEWSPAPER

Says President Machado Acted Contrary to Constitution in Closing El Mundo

FREEDOM OF PRESS UPHELD

Executive Had Ordered Nine Offices Closed, Acting on Authority of Law of 1870

Special Cable to The New York Times

HAVANA, March 27—The Supreme Court of Cuba, in a decision today concurred in unanimously by the thirteen magistrates, held that President Machado's action in closing the morning newspaper El Mundo on Jan. 9 of this year was unconstitutional. In the case of the appeal made by El Pais an unfavorable decision was handed down because of the technical legal defects in the presentation of the case.

In its appeal El Mundo contended that the closing order was a violation of Article XXV of the Cuban Constitution, which guarantees freedom of the press, arguing that the preservation of this right was a basic principle of democratic government. Article XXV of the Constitution is one of the provisions which neither the President nor Congress might suspend, it was argued.

The case was handled by Dr. Mario Lazo.

The Cuban Constitution closely resembles that of the United States. Today's decision created a sensation in newspaper circles, as it has the effect of establishing for the first time since the republic was established freedom of the Cuban press.

* * *

June 2, 1931

'PRESS GAG' BARRED BY SUPREME COURT; MINNESOTA LAW HIT

Hughes in Majority Opinion in 5-to-4 Decision Holds Act Is Unconstitutional

14TH AMENDMENT IS CITED

Worse Evils Are Held Likely to Arise Than Possible Abuse of Liberty

SAFEGUARD IN LIBEL ACTION

Dissenting Opinion by Butler Says Restriction on States is Without Precedent

Special to The New York Times

WASHINGTON, June 1—The principle of the freedom of the press was upheld by the Supreme Court today when in a five-to-four decision handed down by Chief Justice Hughes the Minnesota "press gag" law was declared unconstitutional.

Chief Justice Hughes asserted that the Minnesota statute infringes the liberty of the press guaranteed by the Fourteenth Amendment, and imposes an unreasonable restraint upon publication. Joining in the majority opinion were Justice Holmes, Brandeis, Stone and Roberts. Justice Butler wrote the dissenting opinion, supported by Justices Van Deventer, McReynolds and Sutherland.

Chief Justice Hughes said the Minnesota law amounted to censorship, and that due protection from libelous or false articles were afforded by the libel laws. But Justice Butler contended that the majority decision gives the press a freedom not recognized heretofore, and construes the word "liberty" in the due process clause of the Fourteenth Amendment "to put upon the States a Federal restriction that is without precedent."

Public Officials Attached

J.M. Near, publisher of the Saturday Press at Minneapolis, took the case to the Supreme Court. The State law provides for the abatement, as a public nuisance, of a "malicious, scandalous and defamatory newspaper, magazine or other periodical." The law was enacted by the Legislature in 1925. It was sustained by the District Court and the Minnesota Supreme Court, which upon Near's appeal was reversed in today's decision here.

In 1927, Floyd B. Olson, then County Attorney of Hennepin County, which includes Minneapolis, brought action for an injunction against the Saturday Press. It was alleged that the newspaper had published scandalous and defamatory articles regarding Mayor George E. Leach, Chief of Police Frank W. Brunskill, the Minneapolis Tribune, the Minneapolis Journal, Charles G. Davis, a special law enforcement officer, the members of the County Grand Jury, Mr. Olson, and the Jewish race.

"Without attempting to summarize the contents of the voluminous exhibits attached to the complaint," Chief Justice Hughes declared, "we deem it sufficient to say that the articles charged in substance that a Jewish gangster was in control of gambling, bootlegging and racketeering in Minneapolis, and that law enforcing officers and agencies were not energetically performing their duties.

"Most of the charges were directed against the Chief of Police; he was charged with gross neglect of duty, illicit relations with gangsters, and with participation in graft. The County Attorney was charged with knowing the existing conditions and with failure to take adequate measures to remedy them. The Mayor was accused of inefficiency and dereliction. One member of the grand jury was stated to be in sympathy with the gangsters.

"A special grand jury and a special prosecutor were demanded to deal with the situation in general and, in particular, to investigate an attempt to assassinate one Guilford, one of the original defendants, who, it appears from the articles, was shot by gangsters after the first issue of the periodical had been published. There is no question but what the articles made serious accusations against the public officers named, and others in connection with the prevalence of crimes and the failure to expose and punish them."

Transcends Local Interest

As to the Minnesota law, Chief Justice Hughes said:

"This statute, for the suppression as a public nuisance of a newspaper or periodical, is unusual, if not unique, and raises questions of grave importance transcending the local interests involved in the particular action. It is no longer open to doubt that the liberty of the press, and of speech, is within the liberty safeguarded by the due-process clause of the Fourteenth Amendment from invasion by State action. It was found impossible to conclude that this essential personal liberty of the citizen was left unprotected by the general guaranty of fundamental rights of person and property.

"If we cut through mere details of procedure, the operation and effect of the statute in substance is that public authorities may bring the owner or publisher of a newspaper or periodical before a judge upon a charge of conducting a business of publishing scandalous and defamatory matter—in particular, that the matter consists of charges against public officers of official dereliction—and unless the owner or publisher is able and disposed to bring competent evidence to satisfy the judge that the charges are true and are published with good motives and for justifiable ends, his newspaper or periodical is suppressed and further publication is made punishable as a contempt. This is of the essence of censorship.

150 Years of Experience

"The fact that for approximately 150 years there has been almost an entire absence of attempts to impose previous restraints upon publications relating to the malfeasance of public officers is significant of the deep-seated conviction that such restraints would violate constitutional right.

"Public officers, whose character and conduct remain open to debate and free discussion in the press, find their remedies for false accusations in action under libel laws, providing for redress and punishment, and not in proceedings to restrain the publication of newspapers and periodicals.

"The general principle that the constitutional guaranty of the liberty of the press gives immunity from previous restraints has been approved in many decisions under the provisions of State Constitutions.

"The importance of this immunity has not lessened. While reckless assaults upon public men, and efforts to bring obloquy upon those who are endeavoring to faithfully discharge official duties, exert a baleful influence and deserve the severest condemnation in public opinion it cannot be said that this abuse is greater, and it is believed to be less, than that which characterized the period in which our institutions took shape.

Need for a Courageous Press

"Meanwhile, the administration of government has become more complex, the opportunities for malfeasance and corruption have multiplied, crime has grown to most serious proportions, and the danger of its protection by unfaithful officials and of the impairment of the fundamental security of life and property by criminal alliances and official neglect, emphasize the primary need of a vigilant and courageous press, especially in great cities.

"The fact that the liberty of the press may be abused by miscreant purveyors of scandal does not make any the less necessary the immunity of the press from previous restraint in dealing with official misconduct. Subsequent punishment for such abuses as may exist is the appropriate remedy, consistent with constitutional privilege.

"The recognition of authority to impose previous restraint upon publication in order to protect the community against the circulation of charges of misconduct, and especially official misconduct, necessarily would carry with it the admission of the authority of the censor against which the constitutional barrier was erected. The preliminary freedom, by virtue of the very reason of its existence, does not depend, as the court said, on proof of truth.

More Serious Evil in Prospect

"Equally unavailing is the insistence that the statute is designed to prevent the circulation of scandal, which tends to disturb the public peace and promote assaults and commissions of crimes.

"Charges of reprehensible conduct, and in particular of official malfeasance, unquestionably create a public scandal, but the theory of the constitutional guaranty is that even a more serious public evil would be caused by authority to prevent publication. . . .

"There is nothing new in the fact that charges of reprehensible conduct may create resentment and the disposition to resort to violent means of redress, but this well-understood tendency did not alter the determination to protect the press against censorship and restraint upon publication."

For these reasons the majority held the statute to be "an infringement of the liberty of the press guaranteed by the Fourteenth Amendment."

"We should add," the opinion concluded, "that this decision rests upon the operation and effect of the statute, without regard to the question of the truth of the charges complained in the particular periodical. The fact that the public officers named in this case and those associated with charges of official dereliction may be deemed to be impeccable, cannot affect the conclusion that the statute imposes an unconstitutional restraint upon publications."

Justice Butler Dissents

Justice Butler in dissenting, said:

"The decision of the court in this case declares Minnesota and every other State powerless to retrain by injunction the business of publishing and circulating among the people malicious, scandalous and defamatory periodicals that in due course of judicial procedure have been adjudged to be a public nuisance. It gives to freedom of the press a meaning and a scope not heretofore recognized, and construes 'liberty' in the due process clause of the Fourteenth Amendment to put upon the States a Federal restriction that is without precedent.

"The record shows, and it is conceded, that defendants' regular business was the publication of malicious, scandalous and defamatory articles concerning the principal public officers, leading newspapers of the city, many private persons and the Jewish race.

"It also shows that it was their purpose at all hazards to continue to carry on the business. In every edition slanderous and defamatory matter predominates to the practical exclusion of all else. Many of the statements are so highly improbable as to compel a finding that they are false. The articles themselves show malice.

"The defendant here has no standing to assert that the statute is invalid because it might be construed so as to violate the Constitution. His right is limited solely to the inquiry whether, having regard to the points properly raised in his case, the effect of applying the statute is to deprive him of his liberty without due process of law. The court should not reverse the judgment below upon the ground that in some other case the statute may be applied in a way that is repugnant to the freedom of the press protected by the Fourteenth Amendment."

Sees a Reason for the Act

The Minnesota act, Justice Butler continued, was passed, "in the exertion of the State's power of police, and this court is by well established rule required to assume, until the contrary is clearly made to appear, that there exists in Minnesota a state of affairs that justifies this measure for the preservation of the peace and good order of the State. The publications themselves show the need and propriety of the legislation."

It is of the greatest importance, Justice Butler added, that the States "shall be untrammeled and free to employ all just and appropriate measure to prevent abuses of the liberty of the press."

"The Minnesota statute," he asserted, "does not operate as a previous restraint upon publication within a proper meaning of that phrase. It does not authorize administrative control in advance, such as was formerly exercised by the licensers and censors, but prescribes a remedy to be enforced by a suit in equity.

"The business and publications unquestionably constitute an abuse of the right of free press. The statute denounced the things done as a nuisance on the ground as stated by the State Supreme Court, that they threaten morals, peace and good order. There is no question of the power of the State to denounce such transgressions."

Justice Butler said it was well known that existing libel laws were inadequate to suppress evils such as had been shown in this case.

"The doctrine," he said, "that measures such as the one before us are invalid because they operate as previous restraints to infringe freedom of press exposes the peace and good order of every community and the business and private affairs of every individual to the constraint and protracted false and malicious assaults of any insolvent publisher who may have purpose and sufficient capacity to contrive and put into effect a scheme or program for oppression, blackmail or extortion."

Delay in Chain Store Tax Case

Washington, June 1 (AP)—The Supreme Court today agreed to entertain a petition for a rehearing on its decision upholding the Indiana tax on chain stores. As a result, no further action can be taken in the case until October when the court returns from its Summer recess. It will decide then whether a rehearing is to be granted.

A stay in the issuance of the court's mandate sustaining the tax was asked and received today by counsel for the estate of Lafayette A. Jackson of Indianapolis, who brought the suit originally. Mr. Jackson was killed by robbers after the court rendered its 5-to-4 decision.

Review of the case of James W. Merkie, owner of the British vessel, Francis T., seized by the Coast Guard and charged with violating the tariff act off the Jersey coast, was refused.

The court consented to review a case brought by the United States, the Interstate Commerce Commission and the Hoboken Manufacturers' Railroad to enforce an order of the commission granting the railroad an increase in the division of rates on silk transported from pacific Coast ports to Hoboken, N.J. The shipments were brought from the coast by the Baltimore & Ohio and other railroads on through rates. The Hoboken Manufacturers' Railroad made the deliveries, and contended it was not receiving its fair share in the division of the rates.

The court refused to review the case in which the General Talking Picture Corporation and De Forest Phonofilms, Inc., charged the Stanley Company of America with patent infringement.

A review was refused in the case of the Niagara Falls Gas and Electric Light Company, the city of Niagara Falls and other contesting the validity of the State law under which the New York Public Service Commission prohibited the gas company from making a service charge on consumers for the installation and use of apparatus.

* * *

July 30, 1931

URIBURU TIGHTENS CURB ON THE PRESS

Argentine Papers Warned They Can Appear Only if News Does Not "Molest" Regime

PENAL EXILE FOR VIOLATION

Socialist Press Committee Refuses to Resume Publishing—Alvear and Others Leave Argentina

Special Cable to The New York Times

MONTEVIDEO, July 29—Although Provisional President Uriburu of Argentina has officially lifted the closure ban from the two Socialist dailies in Buenos Aires, La Vanguardia and Socialista Independente, the Prefect of Police has notified their editors that the papers can appear only provided they publish nothing that can "molest" the provisional government.

The Prefect also has informed the three former Congressmen, who as the party's press committee have charge of publishing La Vanguardia, that in case any "molesting" news is published the paper will be definitely closed and they will be sent to the penal colony at Ushuaia. They have refused to renew publication until the Minister of the Interior defines what is molesting news from General Uriburu's viewpoint.

The press censorship has become extremely rigid and nothing of a political nature can be published without the previous approval of the Prefect of Police, under threat of closure. Rather than seek this approval some of the most important papers are making no reference to the political situation and publishing only President Uriburu's views as expressed in official statements.

Deportations Denounced

According to Nicolas Repetto, leader of the Socialist party, who has just been released from the penitentiary, where he was imprisoned for responsibility for La Vanguardia's recent editorial demanding that General Uriburu resign, the present regime of force and violence is incapable of smothering popular opinion despite the wholesale deportation of leading politicians, and General Uriburu is sowing the seeds of widespread disorder and opposition.

Señor Repetto, in an interview given to the news editor of El Ideal of Montevideo, who is now in Buenos Aires, and sent here by courier, said:

"The deportation of such men as Alvear, Pueyrredon, Tamborini, Noel, Torello and Guido might lead some to think that this wholesale exercise of violence would annihilate the force of public opinion, which is trying to restore the institutional form of government. But such a belief would be as great a political error as was the September revolution.

"The present use of violence is a mistake which would not have occurred to any man possessing a grain of common sense, and the man who has made that mistake assumes tremendous responsibility."

Señor Repetto said the Socialist party was preparing to publish a protest against the deportations.

Puts Faith in Student

Students will rescue Argentina from the tyranny of the dictatorship just as they have rescued Chile, according to Alfredo Palacios, leader of the student movement in Buenos Aires, in an interview brought here by courier.

Señor Palacios is prominent in university circles from Mexico City southward as a lecturer on international law and the social sciences. He was . . . the Socialist floor leader in Congress but was expelled from the party because he fought a duel, which the Socialists discountenance. He has since been reinstated.

"The students of the entire South American continent are engaged in a great evolutionary movement against the conservative elements which are oppressing the masses," Señor Palacios said. "The students constitute an unsurmountable barrier in the path of the enemies of liberty.

"The students of Latin America have a mission much more exalted than in Europe, where the public is guided and influenced by mature men. In our countries the public is guided and influenced by youth.

Calls Old Generation Blind

"The old generation which now pretends to rule Argentina is impermeable to the needs of our times, deaf to the clamor of the masses, blind to the destiny of our race and reverently worshiping the past. But a great spiritual wave is moving over Latin America, firing our youth to great heroic efforts, and they will save us just as they saved Chile.

"The situation in Argentina is extremely grave. General Uriburu has no right to set himself up as judge and bar an entire political party from participation in the elections, and when he does so he has no right to quote the Constitution in support of other measures, for the Constitution no longer exists.

"However, political parties cannot be wiped out by the will of one man, and we shall continue fighting for liberty and defending the rights of the people. The march of our democratic progress can be momentarily delayed, but it can never be definitely halted. Eventually we shall overthrow tyranny."

* * *

December 3, 1933

CONFERENCE PLAN FINDS EDITORS COLD

Central American Newspapers See Little Merit in the Castro Proposal

CENSORSHIP AN OBSTACLE

With So Many Journalists in Exile Meeting Would Be Ineffective Is View

By C. H. CALHOUN

Special Correspondence The New York Times

PANAMA, R. P., Nov. 29—A telegram sent by José R. Castro of El Liberal Progresista, Guatemala City daily, to directors of newspapers in other Central American countries, proposing a press conference for greater harmony and unity of action, has started a newspaper war with the battlefront extending from Mexico to Panama.

The proposed conference was intended for the discussion of problems of Central America, including free trade among the nations, industrial and commercial development, and "the means of unifying tendencies and aspirations." One great obstacle is the fact that, excepting in Costa Rica and Panama, there is no real freedom of the press between Mexico and Colombia.

There has been actual freedom of the press in Panama for a number of years and government restraints in Costa Rica are slight and indirect. On the other hand, in El Salvador and Guatemala, censorship by the government is both direct and effective. The result of this interference, which sometimes involves the imprisonment and exiling of offending journalists, has been that the best talent is usually employed in a neighboring country.

Hospitality, but Little Pay

The fact that this is a common affliction of newspaper men who exhibit any independence has made the newspapers hospitable to their foreign colleagues. Yet the majority of them would prefer to work in their own countries. It is also true that a newspaper man who has been forced into a neighboring country has to take whatever salary that he can get, and consequently the pay is far from high.

José R. Castro, who started the newspaper war from Guatemala, is a citizen of Honduras, while Eduardo Aguirre Velasquez, a Guatemalan, is employed here on the Diario de Panama. Alfonso Guillen Zelaya, another Honduran, is in exile, and Salamon de la Selva, Nicaraguan, long exiled from his own country, is on the staff of the Panama American, and edits The Latin American Digest.

The Castro plan met with practically universal disapproval, the bitterest opposition coming from El Salvador, because Guatemala has supported the non-recognition policy of the United States with reference to the government of President Martinez. El Dia of San Salvador blames the newspapers for the spirit of ill-will that exists among the Central American republics.

La Prensa of the same city says too many Central American newspaper men are in exile and that "these expatriates have been made targets for more or less virulent attacks on the part of their home papers."

Sees No Purpose in Meetings

"As a matter of principle," La Prensa concludes, "we do not favor international conferences regardless of their nature because a long and painful experience has taught us that they serve no other purpose but to permit the delegates to eat like princes and to drink champagne and speak in torrents for a few days."

Commenting on the foregoing in The Latin American Digest, Salvamon de la Selva says: "Back of all that is the fact that El Salvador has come out strongly against the Central American peace pacts of 1923, which, as interpreted by the State Department, have served as grounds for denying recognition to the present government. The other Central American republics have felt themselves constrained to follow suit.

"In no country of Central America can it be said," de la Selva continues, "that there is real freedom of the press, Costa Rica, which comes nearest to having that freedom, uses underhand methods to silence publications printing matter that those in power dislike. The Sacasa Government in Nicaragua punishes newspaper editors for voicing opinions contrary to the official mind by having their newspapers suspend publication for weeks at a time. In Honduras, El Salvador and Guatemala, the one worry that newspaper owners live in is that their columns may carry nothing that may displease the President of the republic."

* * *

June 30, 1935

SALVADOR PUTS BAN ON 3 NEWSPAPERS

Student Weekly Also Suspended—Unrest Continues but Violence is Absent

Special Correspondence, The New York Times

PANAMA—Although the "state of siege," which is a polite name for martial law, has been lifted for some time in El Salvador, reports coming here reveal that freedom of the press has not been restored.

The deportation of three newspaper men is confirmed by reports from Guatemala and Honduras. The first to feel the displeasure of the government was Mariano A. Moran, editor of Diario de Santa Ana. Then when Carlos Manuel Flores, editor of the Diario del Occidente, commented on the deportation of his colleague, he was sent out of the country.

Señor Flores is well known as a writer in Latin America, particularly for his independence when such an attitude in some countries frequently means imprisonment and deportation. He was held prisoner for two years by General Juan

Vicente Gomez, dictator of Venezuela, until the government of El Salvador procured his release.

Another journalist to feel the strong arm of the government is Joaquin Castro Canisales, editor of The Nationalist, biweekly, whose criticism of the government has been well-considered and without reference to personalities. As a matter of fact it was hinted that he was permitted to criticize the government to create the appearance of freedom of the press.

Nevertheless, his newspaper was suspended and he was hustled aboard a train bound for Tegucigalpa, Honduras, according to reports reaching here. He was one of the leaders in the movement in December, 1931, that first placed General Martinez in power, but he was reported to have refused several government posts and a diplomatic appointment.

Public Aroused

Although the press of San Salvador has said nothing about this attitude of the government, the public has become aroused and the students, whose weekly, Student Opinion, was suspended, have protested in a manifesto and by public demonstration in which more than 100 students marched through the streets of the capital with hand-kerchiefs tied over their mouths as a protest to the gagging of freedom of expression. The protest was silent and orderly, and the police did not interfere, although it is rumored that two students, Antonio Gonzalez Cabezas and Julio Fausto Fernandez, both signers of the manifesto, were arrested.

Informed travelers arriving here report that the government appears to be ready to suppress any attempt at open revolt, although it does not seem that any direct action against the government is likely. That there is unrest and discontent is certain, but it is not so violent that the government will not be able to control it.

* * *

July 20, 1935

NEWS OF ARGENTINA UNDER STRICT CURB

Decree Demands Large Cash Bond From Correspondents and Agencies

NEW CENSORSHIP SET UP

Writers Face Penalties for Dispatches That 'Discredit the Country'

By JOHN W. WHITE
Special Cable to The New York Times

BUENOS AIRES, July 19—The Interior Ministry published today a decree signed by President Agustin P. Justo putting all newspaper correspondents and news agencies under heavy cash bonds and providing for strict control of all out-going news by the Postoffice Department.

All correspondents and agencies must be registered at the Postoffice Department and deposit bonds in the Bank of the Nation before they can operate. The bond in each case will be fixed by the Postoffice Department, but it cannot be less than 5,000 pesos nor more than 50,000 pesos.

Correspondents must keep copies of all telegraphic dispatches and mailed articles in copybooks, which are to be open to constant inspection by the Postoffice Department. This sets up official censorship of news after it is sent.

Penalties Are Provided

The decree provides for the temporary or permanent closing of news agencies, the disqualification of correspondents who send "news that is false or contrary to public morals or public order or tending to disturb public opinion or which discredits the country."

Under the foregoing provision correspondents can be punished for sending news that is admittedly true if the postoffice inspectors think it is of a nature that would discredit the country abroad. Under the secret censorship that postoffice inspectors have been exercising in the cable offices for several years it has been ruled that unfavorable market news was suppressable because it might discredit the country in foreign money markets.

The decree authorizes the Postoffice Department to draw up regulations for the control of correspondents and agencies. The nature of these regulations is not indicated beyond the assertion that they will be "such measures as the Postoffice Department deems advisable."

Liable for Damages

It provides that correspondents shall be held personally responsible for damages resulting from any news they send, apart from any criminal action that may be taken against them. The cash bond is to "guarantee compliance with this decree." It must remain on deposit for three years after the correspondent ceases sending news. The copybooks containing the copies of dispatches must be preserved for three years after the date of the last dispatch.

The decree was published late this afternoon without warning. As it does not provide for the censorship of news before it is sent it puts the burden of responsibility on the correspondents instead of on the censors and permits the punishment of correspondents three years after the news is sent.

It will effectively prevent the sending of news that might affect Argentine bond prices in foreign markets and also prevent unbiased observations regarding the political or economic situation since the postoffice inspectors can act on the result of reactions abroad after the news is published.

It also applies to news sent from Buenos Aires to interior points.

The preamble of the decree says it is incumbent on the national government to exercise control over news to prevent the discrediting of the country or its institutions.

* * *

May 31, 1936

ECUADOR DICTATOR DAMS NEWS FLOW

Special Correspondence, The New York Times

PANAMA—The government of Ecuador has established censorship of foreign correspondence like that of Fascist Italy, Soviet Russia and Nazi Germany.

No foreign news can be sent from Ecuador without the prior approval of the government, according to a decree of the dictator, Federico Paez, published in Ecuadorean newspapers just received here. "Convenience" of the government and not the truth of the facts presented is to be the test applied to such news.

However, Ecuador is not alone in such censorship. Similar restrictions apply in Guatemala, Honduras, El Salvador and Nicaragua, and, to a lesser degree, in Colombia. Panama and Costa Rica are the only countries in this section of Latin America that grant freedom to the press and to foreign correspondence.

The recent Ecuadorean decree provides that all cable and radio information to be sent out of the country of a public nature and which refers to the general order must have the approval of the Sub-Secretary of Government in the capital of the republic and of the Governors and political heads in the respective capitals of provinces or cantonal headquarters as the case may be.

"The cable company may not accept messages from any correspondent or public agent without the approval referred to. A violation of this will be punished with a fine of 500 sucres for the first offense and 1,000 sucres for each repetition."

In some cases a story may be printed in the local newspapers and there may be no question of its authenticity, still foreign correspondents are not permitted to cable the facts to their newspapers. Usually it is prohibited as "inconvenient."

* * *

October 21, 1937

TIGHT CENSORSHIP IMPOSED BY BRAZIL

Bars Egress of News That the Regime Dislikes—Controls All Mail In and Out

PRESS STRICTLY CURBED

Can't Criticize Government—Political Prisoners Sent to Camps, Army Barracks

By JOHN W. WHITE

Special Cable to The New York Times

BUENOS AIRES Argentina, Oct. 20—Brazil has established as part of her new state-of-war regime one of the most efficient censorships ever devised in South America. It not only prevents the egress of any news except what the government wants to let out but also establishes close control over all business and private mail entering or leaving the country.

All outgoing boat mail is censored at Rio de Janeiro or Santos and all incoming boat mail at the ports of arrival. Air mail to and from Argentina, Uruguay and other South American republics is censored at Porto Alegre, while air mail to and from the United States and Europe is censored at Para.

Administration of the censorship is in the hands of a board of censorship in Rio de Janeiro composed of the chief of the Press Bureau, the Minister of Justice, two army officers and two navy officers. Telegraphic and mail censorship at key points throughout the country is in charge of army or navy officers.

Newspapers Strictly Censored

All the newspapers are also under strict censorship. Among other restrictions, the newspapers may not publish any statement by a politician unless it carries his signature. No statement by an army or navy officer may be published unless it has been approved by the respective ministry.

Nothing may be published about Brazil's armaments. This clause puts an end to violent editorials against Argentina as a result of her opposition to the proposed leasing of six United States destroyers to Brazil.

The newspapers may not criticize the Vargas government nor any one connected with it, nor may they criticize the existing state of war and the manner in which it is being handled.

In actual practice the censors prevent foreign correspondents from sending any news that has not been given out officially or printed in the local newspapers.

The present state of war is a strict military regime, whereas former periods of martial law retained a semblance of civilian rule Political prisoners were formerly arrested by civilian police and held for trial in the civil courts, but they are now being turned over to the army and sent to concentration camps or military barracks.

Freed Prisoners Rearrested

When the last state of war was declared at an end on the eve of the Presidential campaign, the courts released several hundred political prisoners on the ground that there was no proof they had any Communistic connections. Under the new military regime all these prisoners have been ordered rearrested and sent to concentration camps under military control.

There are three classifications of these camps. One is an agricultural colony where persons charged with being Communists but not of a dangerous nature are to be "re-educated," as explained in a government bulletin.

The second category is a concentration camp for students and other youths "who have forgotten their civic duties."

The third is concentration in army barracks for those political prisoners whom the government has classified as dangerous Communist leaders. This classification includes many well-known Brazilians who have figured prominently as politically opposed to the Vargas regime.

Many other opponents of President Getulio Vargas have taken refuge in the Argentine and other South American embassies. The Argentine and other diplomatic representatives in Rio de Janeiro are now trying to negotiate the evacuation of these political refugees under the principle, universally recognized in South America, that a political refugee who has gained a haven in a foreign embassy or legation may be escorted to the frontier under protection of the flag of the country whose diplomatic mission has sheltered him.

THE RISE OF EUROPEAN FASCIST STATES

February 10, 1924

POLISH AUTHORITIES SEIZE BLANK PAPER

That part of Poland in political opposition to the Government is reported as highly amused at what it calls the latest Don Quixote stunt of the Ministry of Justice. It appears, according to the Vienna Arbeiter-Zeitung, that during the régime of Premier Witos, who was recently replaced by Ladislas Grabski, the confiscation of certain issues of Socialist newspapers containing more or less intemperate criticism of the authorities was an almost everyday occurrence. The Cracow Naprzod was the special object of the attentions of the police, having been confiscated twenty-five times in two months.

The Cracow paper drew attention to its situation by issuing a special "jubilee supplement," to which the following reference was made in the main sheet: "In honor of the twenty-fifth confiscation since the advent of the Witos Government we are issuing with this number a special supplement dedicated to the Minister of Justice in Warsaw and to the District Attorney in Cracow."

The supplement consisted of a sheet of blank paper. Nevertheless, it was promptly confiscated by the District Attorney, whose action was upheld by the Criminal Court of Cracow on the ground that the confiscated "publication" had held the District Attorney and the Ministry of Justice up to public ridicule "without presenting definite facts."

* * *

January 1, 1925

POLICE RAID HOMES OF FASCISTI'S FOES

Seize Issues of Eleven Hostile Newspapers in Rome, Milan and Turin

NOTE WARNED OF MASSACRE

Ex-Deputy's Letter Brought Enforcement of New Decree—King to Proclaim Amnesty

By Wireless to The New York Times

ROME, Dec. 31—In pursuance of the unanimous decision reached in yesterday's Cabinet's council to adopt all measures necessary to safeguard Italy's moral and material interests, the Government gave the thumbscrews another turn today and ordered the police to search the houses of prominent Opposition leaders.

Today's issue of six newspapers in Rome, four in Milan and one in Turin were seized and the homes of the dissident Fascist leader former Deputy Alfredo Misuri, and Gino Galzubini, and the offices of the Republican Party were diligently searched by the police, though it was not disclosed with what success.

The searches were made on the strength of information received by the police that stores of arms had been secretly collected by Fascismo's enemies and also of a report which has reached the Government that a so-called "liberty loan" was being floated in France to be used to overthrow the present Government in Italy with the connivance of Opposition leaders.

The seizure of the Opposition newspapers was occasioned by the publication of a letter by Signor Misuri protesting against the search made in his home by the police. Filled with threats and accusations against the Government and abuse of the Fascisti, it was considered by the authorities to constitute incitement to revolt and all newspapers that published it were seized.

Misuri Warns of Danger

Signor Misuri's letter, after describing the search to which his house was subjected, continues:

"I publicly ask the head of the Government, who pronounced three sentences of death against me, one of which was almost carried out, what he wishes to do with me and other Opposition leaders. Perhaps, to please the extremists of his party, he wishes to leave us unarmed for the night on which we will be massacred.

"I ask the Minister of Internal Affairs whether he does not think it would be better to arrest the unpunished authors of the attacks I have suffered instead of abusing his powers by subjecting me to further persecutions.

"I ask him also whether he does not think that, instead of searching for the few weapons I possess, it is his duty to retrieve whole truckloads of arms belonging to the State which have been given to the half-grown boys, degenerates, habitual criminals, drug addicts and confirmed drunkards belonging to his party.

"Is it possible that these super-politicians do not understand that when the situation is ripe arms are quite useless and that sticks and stones are quite sufficient to get rid of a tyrant?"

Insecurity Feeling Affects Finance

Public opinion tends to the belief that such letters which, with sweeping accusations, heap abuse upon political opponents, should be kept out of the press, to avoid further embittering the feeling between the Fascisti and their enemies, thus spreading the feeling of insecurity that in turn reacts upon the Stock Exchange with disastrous results for exchange.

Since last Monday the Italian consolidated loan has fallen from 100 lire to 98, while the dollar has risen from 23.50 lire to 24.10.

Many ask, however, whether the seizure of the newspapers does not defeat its object. It is felt that the seizure of the newspapers gives the impression abroad that the Italian internal situation is only quiet in appearance because the Opposition cannot make its voice heard and therefore merely makes worse the situation it is intended to cure.

It is admitted, on the other hand, that the present Italian law regulating the activities of the press is hopelessly inadequate. It is remembered in this connection that after Matteotti's murder one Opposition newspaper pushed its impudence to the point of stating that one of his murderers had been seen carrying Matteotti's head under his arm in a basket and displaying it to his friends as a trophy, and quoted witnesses, printing their names and addresses, to prove its story.

It was, of course, pure invention, as Matteotti's body when found was complete, but the Government was quite powerless to proceed against the newspapers for printing a false story so calculated to disturb the public order.

There is a strong outcry, therefore, to scrap all present decrees on the press and substitute for them legislative measures on the lines of those existing in America and England.

Unrest among the Fascisti meanwhile, is on the increase, due partly to a starting recrudescence of ambushes against the Fascisti. Fourteen Fascisti have been killed and many wounded in thirteen ambushes in various parts of Italy since the beginning of December and the Fascisti are calling upon the Government to take steps to protect them, since they have been prohibited from defending themselves with their old persuasive methods.

A mass meeting of Fascisti took place in Florence today to urge the Government to take a more energetic attitude, and others will be held in other cities during the next few days. It is not expected, however, that the Cabinet will substantially alter its policy till the Chamber reopens on Saturday.

* * *

January 21, 1925

CENSOR CROSSWORD PUZZLES IN HUNGARY TO CURB ROYALISTS

Special Cable to The New York Times

VIENNA, Oct. 20—Censorship on crossword puzzles is the latest measure to insure the stability of the Horthy Government in Hungary.

According to a decree issued by the Attorney General today, all crossword puzzles to appear in newspapers must be submitted to the censor, together with the solutions, prior to publication.

The measure has been promulgated because the other day a Legitimist newspaper published a crossword puzzle with solution: "Long Live Otto."

* * *

November 6, 1926

FASCISTI PUT BAN ON ALL OPPOSITION IN WORD OR DEED

'Subversive' Parties, Organizations and Press Must Go, With Penalties for Revival

MILITARY COURTS SET UP

Death Penalty Is Restored and Political Investigators Will Watch Plots

DUCE GETS MORE POWER

Mussolini Takes Over Seventh Portfolio to Enforce the New Drastic Measures Himself

By Wireless to The New York Times

ROME, Nov. 5—Premier Mussolini let no grass grow under his feet in redeeming in full the promise he made to the Fascisti yesterday that he would get quick action on repressive measures against the enemies of the Fascist régime. The Cabinet council over which he presided this morning approved a long series of emergency measures of extraordinary severity.

They include the death penalty for any one attempting the life of the sovereign or the head of the State, or any one guilty of treason, espionage or armed rebellion; dissolution of all parties, associations or organizations carrying on activity against the Fascist régime, with three to ten years' imprisonment for any one attempting to reconstitute such parties, associations or organizations after their dissolution, and two to five years' imprisonment for any one belonging to them, and a similar penalty for any one spreading their programs or doctrines: five to fifteen years' imprisonment for any one spreading abroad false or exaggerated news about conditions in Italy.

Trial by Military Courts

The Cabinet Council in addition decided that any one accused of any of the above crimes shall be tried by a special court presided over by a General of the army, navy, air force or Fascist militia, and composed of five officers of the Fascist militia having at least the rank of Colonels. The procedure used will be that prescribed by the wartime military penal code. All legal proceedings which already have been started against any one accused of any of the above crimes will be turned over immediately to one of these courts. This means that Deputy Zaniboni, General Capello, Miss Gibson and Gino Lucelli, who are now in prison awaiting trial for attempts on Mussolini's life, will be tried by what practically amounts to court-martial.

Nothing is said, however, in the decisions of this morning's Cabinet Council about making the death penalty retroactive, as was suggested by Deputy Turati, Secretary General of the Fascist Party, therefore they will escape capital punishment.

Finally the Cabinet Council approved of the institution of a special office for "political investigation" at the headquarters of each legion of the Fascist militia and the suppression till further notice of all opposition daily or periodical publications.

All Passports Are Annulled

Among the minor measures approved by the Cabinet are the annulment of all passports for going abroad hitherto granted to Italian subjects. Severe penalties are imposed against any one attempting to cross the frontiers without a passport, with specific instructions to the frontier troops to fire on any one caught in the act; authorization to the police to fix forced domiciles for any one who has committed or expressed the deliberate intention of committing actions tending violently to subvert the economic or social structure of the State or to endanger its safety or to hinder the action of the State, and lastly severe penalties are provided for any one illegally wearing the uniform or badges of any State association or institution, and especially Fascist uniforms or badges.

All these measures fall under three separate and distinct headings. One group is directed especially against organized political opposition to the Fascist régime, another is intended chiefly for the defense of the State and the third was approved in order to facilitate police surveillance over individuals belonging to subversive or opposition organizations.

Any Opposition Punishable

The provisions falling under the first heading render any form of opposition to the Fascist régime by either word or deed illegal and punishable with heavy terms of imprisonment. Not only are all opposition newspapers and publications suppressed and all opposition parties, associations or organizations outlawed, but it is even forbidden to make any effort to bring them to life again, even in different form or under a different name. The mere fact of joining an opposition party or organization, or of urging other people to join renders one liable to arrest, trial by court-martial and imprisonment. Any opposition to the Fascist régime in any form or shape is, therefore, illegal and heavily punishable.

Under the heading of measures for the protection of the State comes the institution of the death penalty for attempting the life of the sovereigns, the Crown Prince or the head of the Government, and for treason, espionage or rebellion. These measures are extremely severe.

The text of the bill which will be submitted to Parliament reads:

"When two or more persons agree to commit any of the above crimes they are for this fact alone to be punished with imprisonment of from five to fifteen years. Leaders and organizers are to be punished with fifteen to thirty years' imprisonment.

"Whoever publicly or by means of the press instigates the people to commit any of the above crimes, or approves of them, is to be punished for the mere fact of having instigated or approved with from five to fifteen years' imprisonment."

Penalties for Exaggerated News

Under this same heading come measures against the spreaders of false or exaggerated reports. These measures also are very serve. The text of the bill reads:

"Any citizen who spreads or communicates abroad under any form, false or exaggerated news or reports on the internal conditions of the country in such a way as to impair the credit or prestige of the State abroad or who in any shape or form indulges in activities of such a nature as to harm the national interests, is to be punished with from five to fifteen years' imprisonment and with perpetual debarment from public offices.

"If a citizen found guilty of any of the above crimes is abroad at the time sentence is passed, he loses his citizenship and all his goods are confiscated. The fact that he loses his citizenship does not affect the status of his sons and relations. Any gift or transfer of goods the condemned man may have made after committing the crime, or one year before it, are considered frauds against the State and these goods will be included in the confiscation. If the citizen condemned in the above conditions gives himself up to the police or is arrested the confiscation ceases and his goods are returned to him without prejudice to any rights which may in the meanwhile have been acquired by third parties."

Under the third heading, or the measures intended to facilitate police surveillance of subversive elements, come measures relating to passports, to forced domicile, &c. In addition to all these there is the institution of the special office of political investigation which will have its finger in all pies. This office will be run by the Fascist militia and will, therefore, be purely a party organization and quite independent of the police and magistrature. It will probably derive its strength chiefly from this very fact, which will give it far greater freedom of action.

All these measures, it is specifically stated in the bill, will come into force when, after their approval by Parliament, they will appear in the official Gazette and will cease five years from that date.

Chamber to Meet Tuesday

The Chamber of Deputies has been convoked for an extraordinary sitting on Tuesday, but no date has yet been set for the reconvocation of the Senate, whose approval also is necessary before the bill can become law.

Considerable changes in the present Cabinet were decided upon at the afternoon sitting of the Cabinet council. Premier Mussolini will take over the Ministry of Internal Affairs, which makes him the direct chief of all the Italian police forces and will enable him personally to supervise the application of the measures approved in the morning sitting. Signor Federzoni, the present Minister of Internal Affairs, takes over the Ministry of Colonies. In this respect the Cabinet as now amended resembles Mussolini's first Cabinet, in which the Duce was the Minister of both Foreign and Internal Affairs, and Federzoni was Minister of the Colonies. Signor Discalea, the present Minister of Colonies, probably will be appointed an Ambassador. Signor Teruzzi, the present Under Secretary of Internal Affairs, has been named Governor of Cyrenaica.

Mussolini now holds six portfolios out of the total of thirteen. He is in addition Premier, President of the Council of Ministers, Commander-in-Chief of the Fascist Militia and Duce of the Fascist Party.

* * *

November 8, 1926

PILSUDSKI CLAMPS MUZZLE ON PRESS

Dictator's Decree Penalizes the Printing of Anything His Government Dislikes

COURT TRIALS ELIMINATED

Polish Socialists Protest as Civil Officials Get Power to Impose Fines and Jail Terms

Special Cable to The New York Times

WARSAW, Nov. 7—As though foreshadowing stirring events to come within the Polish Government, Marshal Pilsudski, through his President, tonight issued a decree gagging the press in a manner equaled only in Russia and Italy, and virtually smashing another constitutional provision.

Imprisonment is provided for three specific offenses, Government officials themselves being empowered to impose fines or jail sentences without the aid of courts or juries. The decree goes into effect tomorrow.

The offenses listed are as follows:

1. The circulation of printed news concerning the State or a Minister of the State which would cause a public demonstration. The fact that such news is plainly branded only as a rumor does not minimize the offense. The governing authorities of a large city or of a province are authorized to impose a fine as high as $1,000 or a prison sentence of three months in such cases without a court hearing.

2. The printing or circulating in speeches or privately of news or rumors affecting members of the Government and Judges of the courts, either ridiculing or criticizing them, is punishable by a fine as high as $500 or a jail term of one month, the penalties being imposed out of court.

3. The printing by newspapers or periodicals of matter considered by Government officials to be derogatory even through error, is punishable by a fine of $300 or a month's imprisonment.

There is also a special act covering libel, taking the matter out of the hands of the judicial authorities. Those punished have recourses to the courts within seven days, but an appeal does not prevent the collection of a fine, nor the stay of a prison sentence.

The Socialist papers have already lodged a strong protest, and all papers except the Pilsudski organs are expected to join as the edict goes into effect. The Sejm has authority to accept or reject the decree, and unless it is thoroughly subdued by the Marshal's tactics before its meeting, scheduled for Saturday, it undoubtedly will reserve the action.

In their complaint the Socialists declare that the action is not only a plain abrogation of the right of free speech in the press stipulated by the Constitution, but is also the second occasion upon which the Government has deliberately flouted the basic law, the first being the failure to open the session of Sejm within the prescribed time limit.

The decree, coming at a time when the air is still full of talk over Pilsudski's alleged aim toward a monarchy, has caused a great furor in Republican circles, it being pointed out that during the recent extension of the powers of the Dictator even the Opposition papers have been unusually silent. Therefore it is argued that the abolishment of the free press is not the result of past attacks upon the Dictator and his associates, but is apparently in preparation for an impending radical move on his part.

Upon the appearance of the decree tonight the foreign correspondents hastily called a conference for tomorrow and will ask for a strict interpretation of the ambiguously worded document.

The Germans are especially alarmed, since, according to the text, they declare that the Government will be able to construe any news, though thoroughly true, to be embarrassing to the Government and will apply the law to them summarily, which would cause bitter international feeling and resolve itself into a campaign of persecution.

There is no mention of a censorship in connection with the decree, but the confiscation, of newspapers displeasing the Government is provided for.

* * *

December 23, 1926

DRASTIC PRESS LAW COMING IN RUMANIA

New Regulations Would Punish Severely Circulation of Stories About the Rulers

By Wireless to The New York Times

BUCHAREST, Dec. 22—The Rumanian Government will in the future punish any person who by mail, telegraph or telephone sends out news offending the King, Queen or Crown Prince. The punishment is four years' imprisonment and $100 fine. Similar punishment will be meted out to newspapermen attacking the Constitutional Government or the established order of succession to the throne.

Offenders against other members of the royal family (inclusive of Carol) will get two years imprisonment and $25 fine. Those who insult members of the regency when it becomes effective will be punished with a year's imprisonment and $50 fine.

These are the high marks of the drastic bill to regulate the press, which will go before Parliament with good chances for passage after the Christmas vacation.

The bill aims chiefly to bring order to the chaotic conditions, wherein rumors, calumnies, insults, insinuations and scandalous exposures flourish unchecked. The new law would make responsible and prosecute the publications and reporters, editors and owners, collecting from each individually. The proposed bill comprises 200 paragraphs, which contain stringent regulations concerning the press, books, public meetings, radio broadcasting, posters, &c. Any press criticism of a public official body or act, which the courts (meaning the Government) find unfair, can be punished.

The Government hopes the law will end the circulation of what it terms deliberate false reports about Rumania. While the bill does not mention foreign correspondents specifically, it says regarding infractions beyond the frontier: "Those caught in Rumania and guilty of being principals or accessories will be considered as authors and prosecuted."

The Rumanian King, in his recent message from the throne, announced that a new press law "in harmony with the State's interests" would be introduced in Parliament.

* * *

February 27, 1927

'VERBOTEN' PLAGUE THREATENS REICH

Art, Literature and the Drama Are All Subjected to Control in Spread of Censorship

BUT BEER IS UNCONFINED

Meanwhile Frankly Pornographic Papers Abound Everywhere on German News Stands

By LINCOLN EYRE
Copyright 1927, by The New York Times Company
By Wireless to The New York Times

BERLIN, Feb. 26—The fine old Prussian word "verboten," which the paternal dominance of the last Kaiser made notorious throughout the world before the war, bids fair soon to recover its paramount place in Germany's official vocabulary. The German Republic is threatened today with a plague of prohibitions more deadly than could be conceived by the most zealous of American reformers.

Virtually every form of cultural manifestation, including art, literature, drama and the cinema, is being subjected to some sort of control, moral, religious or political, or a combination of all three. About the only brand of prohibition Germany is not going in for is the American variety. Kultur may be in chains, but beer is still free.

The craze for censorship runs wild through the whole country. Already a law has been passed which compels literary expression to keep within bounds arbitrarily fixed by regional bodies recruited chiefly from officials and the churches, Protestant and Catholic.

Already the Supreme Court of the German Republic has handed down a decision convicting of high treason not only the author and publisher but the compositors, printers, booksellers, salesmen and clerks concerned with the production and distribution of any book deemed seditious by the German authorities. Already motion pictures are subject to both State and national censorship, and in a few exceptional cases minors are barred from seeing them.

Some of Restrictions Listed

Here are some of the things that are now "verboten" or censoriously controlled:

Admission of youths under 18 to theatres, art and other exhibitions and amusement enterprises not previously certified as pure by boards of police censors.

Participation of girls and boys under 18 in theatrical, operatic or ballet schools and in "life classes" in art academies.

Public performance of dances like the Charleston and Black Bottom unless danced in a manner approved by the censor.

Phonograph records reproducing songs which are considered suitable for the stage but not for the home.

Employment of minors in the movies.

Revues and cabaret shows condemned as immoral in dialogue or in display of nudity, the decision to rest with a police censorship board, including church representatives.

Of the evils which it is officially proposed to suppress that falling under the last item in the foregoing list is the most flamboyant and the last to engage the reformers' attention.

As pointed out in a dispatch published in The New York Times last Sunday, this season has produced a bumper crop of immorality on the Berlin stage. Eroticism runs rampant both in theatrical productions and in the less ambitious but equally salacious shows presented in dozens of well-patronized cabarets. Yet it was only a few days ago that the Nationalist, Catholic Centre and People's Party groups in the Prussian Diet decided to open a drive against stage indecency—with the theatrical season approaching its end.

The Prussian legislators also inject the religious viewpoint into their censorship operations. They want delegates of the Protestant and Catholic Churches to have seats on the art commission of Berlin's Police Headquarters.

Law to Bar Youths Planned

Rather more important, and certainly more far reaching, is the Government measure "for the protection of minors in place of amusement," soon to be debated by the Reichstag. This bill empowers the authorities to bar German youths from "shows and exhibitions of every kind," including all theatrical entertainments, art exhibitions, lectures and dance performances.

As the Opposition press emphasizes, the result will be the creation of a preventive censorship over all these things, since the producers or theatre managers will not want to risk having their productions forbidden to minors. Moreover, the situation, will be even more complex as regards art exhibitions, which must be guided in their views as to what constitutes artistic merit by the opinion of a police official of clergyman, lest their doors be closed to a large portion of the population.

To what absurd lengths censorious activity may go was demonstrated recently at Cologne when official exception was taken to the reproduction of a classic picture of the naked Christ Child in the Koelnische Volksseitung, organ of the Catholic Centre Party.

Pornographic Periodicals Abound

This same proposed law, which is almost certain of passage through Parliament, forecasts the exclusion of minors from ballet schools—despite the fact that the ballet dancer must learn young—dramatic and operatic conservatories and art classes sketching from a nude model. It will even prohibit, save under certain conditions, performances by youthful glee clubs.

The penalty for violation of the law will be a fine or a jail sentence. This means that a host of otherwise innocent boys and girls will be brought into direct and disagreeable contact with the police, and possibly, with prison cells.

The curious aspect of Germany's determination to prevent the contamination of her young folk through literary "dirt and trash," by which is meant obscene or sensational books and dime novels, is officialdom's failure to act against the flood of frankly pornographic periodicals now inundating the country's news stands.

Government Hit for Inaction

Some of these publications, the covers of which, almost without exception, are adorned with photographs of unclad woman, purport to be organs of the "Nacktkultur" movement, aimed at promoting physical culture in the nude.

The movement itself apparently is honest, and the only steps taken against it by the authorities are to insist on the proponents of nakedness holding their sessions in remote places screened from the public gate.

The bulk of the "Nacktkultur" periodicals, however, pander to the lowest vices. Still worse are the similarly illustrated weeklies or monthlies dealing openly with sex relations. Any minor can buy this filth in any big German city. Their publication easily could be suppressed under existing municipal ordinances. Yet no action is taken.

Opponents of the Federal law censoring literature in general, from the political and religious standpoints as well as morally, hint that the reason for this official inaction is the Government's desire to have some shocking examples of the need for censorship before the eyes of the public.

Catholic-Nationalist Bargain Seen

To the mind of the German liberal the dangerous feature in the present epidemic of interdictions is the political influence it offers to the Church leaders. The growth of clerical power under the new Marx Cabinet already has become pronounced. Evidently the Catholic Centrists and Lutheran Nationalists, who between them dominate the Administration, have struck a bargain to cooperate.

The first apparent evidence of such a deal was the drafting of a new school law by Herr von Keudell, Nationalist Minister of the Interior, providing for compulsory religious instruction in State schools.

The bill gives the church organizations the right to determine textbooks and fix the number of hours assigned to religious study in the curriculum and to voice in the management of the schools in general.

According to its Democratic and Socialist antagonists, the contemplated legislation runs counter to the Republican Constitution and threatens to destroy spiritual and confessional freedom in the Fatherland. But they will scarcely be able to muster enough Reichstag votes to prevent its passage.

Trouble for Radicals Predicted

The Democrats are somewhat embarrassed by the circumstance that it was their own colleague, Herr Kuels, Hert Keudell's predecessor, who framed and forced through Parliament the "dirt and trash" law that in liberal eyes puts a muzzle on German literature and menaces the independence of thought as well as of the printed word.

With the Leipsic Supreme Court condemning what its authors contend to be a purely objective description of the Russian Bolshevist revolution as potential treason to the German Republic, radical writers here are likely to have plenty of trouble henceforth, regardless of censorship inhibition.

* * *

March 30, 1927

RIVERA EXTOLS CENSOR AS SAVING HUMANITY

Premier Says Press Control Kept Spain Out of Trouble—Discloses Himself as Teetotaler

Special Cable to The New York Times

MADRID, March 29—Only the strictest censorship of the press can save humanity from a threatening cataclysm, Premier Primode Rivera declared in defense of his proposal to tighten the censorship in Spain.

Replying to the protests of several newspapers, he said that most of the good that has been accomplished by his Administration was due to his control of the press, not only making possible the solution of the Moroccan problem but also avoiding the involvement of Spain in the disputes between the American and Mexican Governments. As to American intervention in Nicaragua, he said:

"If I had not thrown out certain articles written for the newspapers, we would be involved in all kinds of difficulties. The same is true of Mexico."

The Premier observed a similar justification of the strictest kind of censorship in the protection of the character of public officials, especially his own. One newspaper recently published an article which escaped the censor's blue pencil, stating that the Premier was a heavy drinker.

"Everybody who knows me knows that I am a total abstainer," the Premier said. "I never touch a drop of wine, liqueur or whisky. I have a number of vices and weaknesses which I never attempt to hide, but wine is not one of them."

In order to avoid similar attacks in the future, the Premier said that it would be necessary to apply an even more strict censorship. He is known to favor Mussolini's Italian system.

* * *

April 24, 1926

POLISH LAW MUZZLES NEWSBOYS WITH PRESS

Censorship Decree Covers Size of Headlines and What May Be Printed

By Wireless in The New York Times

WARSAW, April 23—Polish newsboys will no longer be allowed to make the welkin ring with excerpts from their hottest news items. President Moscicki today signed a decree which will limit shouts of newspaper vendors to giving the name and edition of the publication. It is not only illegal to call out headlines but forbidden by the new order for newspapers to have headlines of more than one column in width.

The present edict replaces one issued the 1st of January, but which the Sejm rejected. Rather than have the muzzle removed entirely from the press, Marshal Pilsudski adjourned Parliament before the new censorship law was enacted, knowing that a Presidential enactment could be issued hemming the publishers into lighter channels than the legislators would countenance.

There is no improvement in the present decree over the one issued in January and in political circles it is taken for granted that the second censorship muzzle will meet the fate of the first one, but will remain in force as long as the Sejm is not in session.

Newspapers may be confiscated with the approval of the lower courts. Each publication is required to be signed by a responsible editor and a paper will be discontinued permanently should three fines for violation of the law be imposed within one year. The owner of a paper is also subject to fine and imprisonment should his responsible editor allow an incorrect statement to appear. Papers must print in each edition such denials as the Government gives out in official communiqués.

* * *

January 29, 1928

WHEN MUSSOLINI THUNDERS "DON'T" ALL ITALY PAUSES

The People Take Care to Heed His Many Proscriptions, Which Range From Morals to Crossing the Streets

By T. R. YBARRA

ROME—One of Benito Mussolini's favorite words is "Don't!" When he came into power here more than five years ago he found the Italians doing all sorts of things he did not like, and ever since he has been busy holding up an admonishing finger and saying, "Don't do that!" Scarcely a month passes without his deciding that there is something rotten in the state of Italy, and, presto!—out comes another, "Don't!" from his "Don't!" factory, and the Italians find another commandment which they must commit to memory.

The list of Mussolini's prohibitions has assumed formidable proportions, and there is every reason for believing that it is far from having reached its full growth. Unless all signs fail, the Italian welkin is destined to ring many times more to the booming sound of a Mussolini "Don't!"

Most important, of course, among the Mussolini prohibitions is "Don't oppose me!" The Italian dictator has explicitly forbidden opposition to himself and his régime in Italy. He considers the elimination of opposition as natural and everyday a procedure as we in other countries consider the prohibition of smoking or spitting. And there can be no doubt that, in Italy, opposition has been suppressed and shows every sign of remaining suppressed for a long time. Not only is there no opposition party in politics to question the Fascist Government's doings and threaten the head of that Government with its displeasure, but criticism of Mussolini and his policies—even the ordinary criticism which, in other lands, features almost every talk over a dinner table—is conspicuous by its absence. This was brought home forcibly to an American in Rome recently when an Italian acquaintance remarked, in the most casual manner in the world:

"Do you know, I don't particularly like your President Coolidge. He is not a man who appeals to me."

"He doesn't appeal much to me, neither," remarked the American, not feeling that there was anything in the least wrong in the Italian's remark. If he felt that way about Coolidge, thought the American, why should not be say so? The conversation continued. Another Italian stood up for the President: the first one reiterated his disapproval—and it was all done as if nothing could be more natural in the world than such a discussion. But, meanwhile, the American could not help reflecting:

Mussolini's "Don't" Has Proved Effective in the Newspaper Offices.

"Suppose I should now say that I didn't like Mussolini. Suppose that one of these Italians should say that he also didn't like Mussolini. I wonder what would happen."

He did not go beyond wondering. In fact, he knew perfectly well what would happen. Of the entire list of Mussolini's "Don'ts" none is obeyed with more scrupulous attention in Italy than "Don't oppose!"

What strikes visitors to Italy in conversations with Italians also strikes them when they pick up an Italian newspaper. In the course of a few days in Rome I read several spirited attacks on President Coolidge and the American Government one, at least, in which the language used passed the bounds of politeness—because, at that time, the American plans for building new warships had just come out and many Italians disapproved of them. Side by side with such attacks in the Roman press were also quite outspoken criticisms of men and policies in other lands, particularly in France. But nowhere was there a vestige of criticism, even veiled and mild, of Mussolini or any of the acts of his Government. His "Don't!" has proved effective in the newspaper offices of Italy. Those in charge there know perfectly well what they must not print, and—well, they do not print it.

In a recent speech, echoes of which still reverberate throughout Italy, Mussolini said a lot of extremely interesting things about his attitude toward opposition and his iron determination to treat it as a thing to be absolutely obliterated from Italian life.

"The different oppositions in Italy have collapsed," he bluntly informed his hearers. "They are scattered, finished—dust! And here the problem arises: 'How can you live without an opposition? An opposition is necessary; it fits well into the frame.'

"We reject this kind of argument entirely and disdainfully. Opposition is not necessary to the working of a sound political régime. It is stupid; it is superfluous in a totalitarian régime such as the Fascist.

"Opposition is useful in easy-going times of academic discussions, like those we had before the war, when the Chamber discussed if, how and when socialism would become a reality."

Then he paid his respects to the doctrine of a free press in these words:

"Let no one hope that, after this speech, anti-Fascist papers will again be tolerated. No! In Italy there is no room for anti-Fascists."

Mussolini's opponents may be divided, into three classes: Those who are out of the country and proclaim their anti-Fascism, those who are in Italy and keep mum about it, and those who, having failed to keep mum, are in prison. Mussolini has vigorously denied stories to the effect that the last class numbers many thousands. According to him there are only 698 persons confined in the Lipari Islands (the official prison for his foes), because they have refused to heed his warning, "Don't be against Fascismo!" In addition to the small number in prison, Mussolini said that 1,541 other Italians had received warnings and that 959 had been "admonished."

"Is this a Reign of Terror, gentlemen?" exclaimed Mussolini, in his speech. "No! It is hardly one of severity. Terrorism? No, indeed! It is social hygiene, national prophylaxis; these persons are removed from circulation as a doctor removes a contagious patient from circulation."

Mussolini's "Don'ts" by no means concern themselves merely with matters of high political and international importance like anti-Fascist opposition and the freedom of the press. The eagle gaze of the Italian Premier, ranges over big and little things alike, and there is no telling when something will arouse his displeasure and move him to add another "Don't!" to his list.

Recently, for example, he fixed his eye on jazz. The cabarets of Rome, Milan and other Italian cities, with their bright lights shining until 8 o'clock in the morning or thereabouts, seemed to him not at all necessary to Italy's welfare; the notes of American jazz melodies brought no friendly twinkle to Mussolini's eyes, no sympathetic twitching to his feet. Nevertheless, Italy might have continued for a while with a normal amount of night life had it not been for the fact that a famous night club in Rome burned down and several dancing girls lost their lives in the fire.

That made Mussolini concentrate his attention in earnest on the whole subject of night clubs. And soon thereafter he fired a red-hot "Don't!" in their direction. He forbade all dancing and music playing in public resorts after midnight. Only at duly licensed clubs (strictly supervised, incidentally) can Italians now twirl pretty partners until the small hours of the morning. Moreover, these clubs have been put on their best behavior. The slightest disorder or irregularity in likely to cause revocation of the license.

As a result Italian cities have assumed a degree of nocturnal respectability surpassing anything they could show before. Rome, especially, never a particularly exuberant place, is now as calm as a cemetery after midnight; the sounds made by a stray reveler moved to burst into song on his homeward way seem scandalous in the surrounding silence.

Then Mussolini took a good look at his fellow-citizens in general and decided that they had too many decorations hanging to their clothes. There were altogether too many Italian buttonholes, he felt, displaying little bits of ribbon, which meant that the man behind the coat was a "Cavaliere" of this order or a "Commendatore" of that, and, therefore, entitled to special consideration.

"Don't!" thundered Mussolini, and he decreed that no more medals or such like decorations were to be awarded in Italy. At first he limited the prohibition to one year; after that, he ordained, the close season on medals was to come to an end and as many Italians as ever were to be allowed to stick in their buttonholes buttons or ribbons telling the world "I have a medal at home!" But a second degree extended the close season, and now Mussolini has extended it again, prohibiting the awarding of decorations until 1930. So far there are no signs of revolution in Italy.

Another step by the Italian Premier in the "Don't!" direction is causing considerable merriment tinged with apprehension. He is preparing a revised list of the Italian nobility. Having decided that far too many Italians were using noble titles, he got a committee together and directed it to make a thorough investigation of the records in order to ascertain exactly who was privileged to tack "Prince" or "Marquis" or "Count" on his name.

The appearance of this list will undoubtedly cause a tremendous stir in Italy, for gossip insists that many a "titled" Italian will fail to find his name on the list, and will have to throw away all those visiting cards with coronets and titles emblazoned upon them and purchase a complete new set with nothing but plain "Signor" as a prelude to the Italian equivalent for Bill Jones or whatever his name is.

Of course this new degree from Mussolini will not affect genuine aristocrats in Rome and elsewhere bearing titles which have been handed down in their families for centuries. There is no worry at all on the score of Mussolini's black list among members of this old aristocratic caste—among the Colonnas, here in Rome, for example, or among the scions of the houses of Massimo and Torlonia, or Rospigliosi and Ruspoli and Aldobrandini. For Italy, it must be remembered, includes among her nobility some of the oldest families in Europe. Rome, especially, is filled with their clean-cut faces and grand old palaces, and nobody, not even Mussolini, would disturb them in the enjoyment of their simon-pure nobility and right to bear titles unless, indeed, complete abolition of the Italian nobility were contemplated.

Another "Don't!"—at least in Rome—is "Don't walk on the right side of the street!" It applies to narrow, crowded thoroughfares like the famous "Corso." Policemen, stationed at the principal corners, politely admonish pedestrians to keep to the left. It is amusing to watch the ensuing arguments.

"But I want to go to a shop on this side of the street," objects a pedestrian who has just been halted.

"How far down is it?"

"About half way along the block."

"Ah, in that case you must cross the street and cross back again when you are opposite the shop."

Off goes the pedestrian, obedient but obviously huffy. Then a pretty girl starts to walk on the right-hand sidewalk.

"You must cross the street," says the policeman.

"Ah, but I want to go to a shop on this side."

"How far is it?"

"About half way down the block."

"Then you must cross the street, and—"

The pretty girl smiles her prettiest smile.

"Oh, really, now, do you mean to say that I must go all the way across to the other sidewalk, and then—"

"No, Signorina. Since the distance is so short, you may walk along this sidewalk."

Fascisti, also, are human.

Mussolini has also visited his displeasure on the old custom of starting subscription lists which flourished in Italy before his day with the same luxuriance as in other countries. At holiday time, for instance, it was the custom to circulate among the employes in Government departments lists asking for contributions to this or that deserving institution. The head of the department would put his name first, after which the other employes, feeling that they must follow the lead of the chief, signed their names.

Many lists were also circulated in small Italian towns asking for donations to all sorts of local causes—the erection of a monument to some local hero, for example—and many an inhabitant, though he did not care a straw for the hero, put down his name for a few dollars, only too often with a lurking suspicion that there was "graft" somewhere in the thing.

Mussolini has put a stop to much of this. Henceforth, he has decreed, the circulation of subscription lists is to be strictly limited, which must have caused, an enormous number of Italian sighs of relief.

He has also ordered the closing of a large number of drinking places, since he believes that there are altogether too many such places in Italy. He became convinced of this soon after he came into power and proceeded with his customary energy to remedy matters.

Dramshops which seemed superfluous failed to get a renewal of their licenses; others, where sounds of revelry were too hilarious and uncertainty of gait among patrons too frequent, were ruthlessly padlocked.

Mussolini is particularly proud of this phase of his "Don't!" campaign. Recently he discoursed at length about it.

"We had to tackle the problem of reducing the number of drinking shops in Italy," he said, "for there were 187,000 taverns in the land. Of these, we have closed 25,000, and I shall energetically pursue this course, especially as the Government is in a position to do so. It is unlikely, you see, that we shall have to tout for any more votes from saloonkeepers or their customers—as used to be the case in the liberal-democratic days—so we can afford the luxury of closing down these marts of cheap but ruinous happiness."

But he takes care to point out that he is no prohibitionist.

"I am of the opinion," he remarked recently, "that, if reasonable doses of alcohol had done much harm to the human race, by this time mankind would have ceased, or practically ceased, to exist, because it has drunk fermented liquor since prehistoric times."

* * *

March 22, 1928

RUMANIA WARS ON CORRESPONDENTS

Official Threatens to Depart All Who Send News Unfavorable to Government

ONE IS ALREADY EXPELLED

Censorship Lid Is Clamped Down Tight on All Dispatches, Vienna Hears

By Wireless to The New York Times

VIENNA, March 21—If the most useful Balkan political weather vane, the tightening of the censorship and the opening of a "reign of terror" against Bucharest correspondents, is not playing pranks tonight, the Rumanian Government is in water the temperature of which is getting uncomfortably warm.

Reminiscent of other occasions when the situation reached a critical stage in that country, the Government has not only clamped the censorship lid down tight on all dispatches which give other than its side, of the question, but has also begun an intimidation campaign against newspaper correspondents resident in Bucharest.

At noon today, according to one message which reached Vienna from a usually reliable source, the official Government press spokesman today summoned all correspondents to his office and there informed them that "much as it would regret to do so the Government will be forced to withdraw its hospitality in the case of every man who in the future sends abroad any report which presents the Government in a bad light."

Soon after this information was received by the newspaper men it became known that one Austrian, correspondent already yesterday received notice to quit the country within twenty-four hours, but as a New York Times correspondent received such a notice a few years ago. The order of deportation was withdrawn only when the Austrian Minister in Bucharest intervened and lodged a vigorous protest at the Rumanian Foreign Office.

Bratianu Denounces Maniu

While correspondents were seeking a solution from the quandary in which they find themselves in view of this deportation threat, a number of important political conferences were being held in various parts of the city. One such conference was of Deputies of the Liberal Party and other political groups which are supporting the Government at the present time.

Before this assembly, Premier Bratianu reiterated his determination not to resign and delivered a speech vehemently denouncing the national Peasant leaders as not capable of governing the country. He said:

"Dr. Maniu's accession to power is unthinkable" because the National Peasant Party has consistently and determinedly refused to acknowledge the throne law which banned Carol and placed his son Michael on the throne. Even if such were not the case Dr. Maniu has voluntarily made a pariah of himself by joining hands with political groups who seek to encompass the country's downfall."

The groups here referred to are the Socialists who united with the peasants in the recent mass meeting demonstration against the Government.

As the Deputies cheered and shouted approval Premier Bratianu concluded his speech with the announcement that he had just received information from Paris that negotiations with France for the reduction of the war debt were successful, and that instead of 1,500,000,000 gold francs previously demanded by France the figure of the country's indebtedness had been set at 595,000,000.

Prelates Will Leave Senate

The second important conference was that of the Greek Catholic Uniate prelates. Here it was decided that the prelates absent themselves from the Senate until the Government modifies the Church law, the "iniquity" of which, they say, was demonstrated Sunday when fifteen priests were bayoneted at Targulmares. The prelates demand in particular that Clauses 9 and 45 of the law be deleted because, they hold, these clauses annul the rights of the Uniates to be recognized juridically as a corporate body and endanger the financial security of the Church.

The third conference was that of National, Peasant leaders, who discussed ways by which they can prevent the Government from declaring their party's seats vacant and calling new elections to fill them as the Government is entitled by law to do when Deputies are absent from twelve consecutive meetings.

The newspaper Lupta today reported that the Government plans to replace the National Peasant absentees with adherents of General Averescu and Professor Jorga, thus assuring Premier Bratianu 100 percent, support from Parliament.

With the Uniate Church, which is very powerful in Transylvania, making common cause with the National Peasants, some of whom are also of the orthodox Greek religion, the Government's position is generally considered weak, if not shaky.

* * *

March 17, 1929

MORE RESTRICTIONS PLANNED FOR PRESS

Draft of Proposed Hungarian Law Withdrawn After a Storm of Protest

By ELISABETH DE PUENKTOESTI
Special Correspondence of The New York Times

BUDAPEST, Feb. 25—"Tant de bruit pour une omelette"—that best expresses the opinion that was formed about the draft of the new press law moved by the Hungarian Government, and which, it seems more than probable, will be withdrawn by the Premier, Count Bethlen, after hearing all parties concerned.

The draft is the work of Secretary of State Angyán, former chief of the Press Department and the confidant of the Premier. It came as a legacy from his predecessor, now Minister of Justice Zsitvay, who never for a moment identified himself with it.

In conference on the draft of the law the government was rather disagreeably surprised to hear Mr. Degré, President of the Court of Appeal, Mr. Vary, Attorney General, and Mr. Doleschall, Professor of Criminal Law, express themselves as against the draft. Professor Doleschall also expressed opposition to the press law now in force, which was introduced by the government under Premier Count Tisza in 1914, and by force of which—the Court of Assizes being suspended since the war—scores of journalists are arrested and tried and the verdict is almost always against them.

The most injurious provision of the present law is that the indicted journalist is bound to submit all his evidence within eight days from the first day of the trial. Scarcely less injurious is the paragraph which makes the publication of information contained in documents not yet issued a crime. The absurdness of this paragraph is illustrated by the fact that journalists have been tried for publishing intimations given them by police officials. The former dean of the Hungarian journalists, the late Eugen Rakosi, was, for a passage in one of his articles, sued by a frequently punished criminal.

In a conspicuous murder case a near relation of the dead person was arrested on suspicion and the examining magistrate issued an indictment. The man proved to be innocent and sued the editors of all papers which published the steps taken by the authorities, and won all suits.

In another case a journalist was tried because he published the news that a murderer was to be hanged.

The news agency, controlled by the government, published an indictment, the newspapers printed it, and all the editors went into the dock for it. Still more interesting, a certain Márffy, who threw a bomb into the building of the Democratic Club, killing some members, was sentenced to capital punishment. During his trial he falsely accused others, and a journalist, for calling him a liar in his paper, was brought to trial by the murderer, and the judges, against their better convictions, had to bring a verdict against him.

The decrees fixing the moral and material liability for damages brought a flood of damage suits against editors. In 90 per cent of the cases the editors found it better to settle out of court rather than to face an almost certain heavy fine if the actions were tried.

It even happened that Julius Szegfü, a scientist of European renown, wrote a criticism of a book written by a member of the Hungarian Academy of Science. In a pamphlet he proved the book to be devoid of scientific facts and declared it to be the work of a writer ignorant of the matter. The usual suit followed, during which the judges did not even look at the scientific proof of the critic, but gave verdict for libel and slander, arguing that the Hungarian Academy is such an august body of scientists that a book written by one of its members could not be unscientific.

As matters stand, there is hardly a journalist in Hungary who has not been tried for some offense against the press law.

The draft of the new law provides that at least two persons shall be punished for interdicted publication—the writer of the article and the editor. In addition, it specifies the liability of the publishers. It also creates a section to be headed "official publication," in which all debates in public meetings and in Parliament are to be published without the omission of a single word. The consequence of this will be that the papers may have to publish five times as much about the speech of an insignificant member of Parliament, who might be pleased to twaddle for two hours, as about a speech of Count Apponyi that may last only twenty minutes, though being of much greater consequence.

The greatest indignation, however, was roused by the paragraph which would permit a person taking offense at an article to choose between having the writer punished or getting damages for libel. Still more offending is the paragraph stating that in such cases a journalist's previous blameless character is not to be taken into consideration, and should he happen to be a member of Parliament he may not claim parliamentary immunity.

It was but natural that the conference tore the draft to pieces. Count Bethlen tried, though somewhat nervously, to defend this reactionary monster of a law, but finally declared his intention of having a new draft made, which though it will probably follow the lines of the last draft, will certainly take into consideration the obligations of the parties concerned.

* * *

April 17, 1929

SPAIN LIMITS THE PRESS

Government Bureau to Issue Matter That Must Be Printed

Special Cable to The New York Times

MADRID, April 16—Because numerous newspapers in Spain failed to give any important space to the great demonstration in favor of Premier Primo de Rivera here on Saturday, the government announced today a new measure for the control and "guidance" of the press.

Hitherto, papers have been mainly censored only as regards unfavorable comments that they chose to print, and they were allowed a certain latitude in the selection of their material. The new measures will regulate also what will be obligatory to publish.

The Premier announces that he will immediately establish a press bureau, which will issue statements on important events containing details which the government regards as necessary for public information, and that all newspapers will be required to print these in full. These articles will be free and obligatory, in accordance with the decree regulating their character and issuance.

* * *

September 15, 1929

CENSOR THE BANE OF MIDDLE EUROPE

Nations There Invoke Him to Remedy All Ills, Ignoring the Ills He Creates

RUMOR WORSE THAN FACT

Austria Now Threatens Correspondents for Reports of Civil War Perils—Association Plans Action

By G. E. R. GEDYE
Wireless to The New York Times

VIENNA, Sept. 12—The little States of Middle Europe and the Balkans may not always regulate their affairs strictly in accordance with the Decalogue, but they all seek to observe to the letter the celebrated eleventh commandment, "Thou shalt not be found out," to which they couple a twelfth, "Thou shalt not divulge matters concerning us."

Despite countless object lessons, the censorship, together with its companions, arrest and expulsion, continues to be the most popular for remedying all political sins. Yet this veneration of false doctrines has resulted again in releasing the imp of hostile propaganda to work unchecked.

In Bucharest grizzled Colonel Stoica and forty-one other officers are facing trial on the serious charge of conspiring against the State. Despite the formal ceremonial of a court martial, which has the power to sentence all forty-two to death, the general atmosphere is that of an operetta.

Maniu Followed Old Tracks

Don Quixote sits in the dock telling the story of his musical comedy conspiracy with the demeanor of a frightened and mischievous child caught by his teacher in a piece of folly which suddenly assumes the dimensions of a crime. Yet this ridiculous conjuration of last Spring did untold damage to the government because in a moment of weakness Premier Maniu allowed the officials once again to invoke the censorship, according to their custom under the Bratianu régime.

Immediately Rumania's enemies had free play. The censorship silenced the only persons ever silenced, responsible correspondents of various newspapers, while from across the hostile frontiers of Hungary streamed the wildest exaggerations. Propagandists found themselves free to indulge in fantasies unchecked by reports made on the spot.

Immediately the operetta plot assumed the appearance of a grave conspiracy, in which were involved such personages as Bratianu, Averescu and Prince Carol. Hopes for the stability of the Maniu régime were shaken for several days as a result of Dr. Maniu's failure to keep his own promises of no censorship. Protests from financial circles, alarmed at Dr. Maniu's closing of legitimate news channels, came too late to entirely prevent damage.

Rumania has many companions in this sin against publicity. Almost throughout the Balkans the man who exposes perils or injustices is prosecuted. If he is a foreigner the cry immediately resounds that he has abused "the country's hospitality," despite the fact the only hospitality he receives usually consists in his being forced to pay more for services and goods than the native inhabitants, while he is bringing a handsome revenue to the country through newspaper cable tolls.

Put Blind Faith in Censorship

The infringer upon the sacred hospitality usually is summoned to the Ministry of the Interior or to the political police for a severe warning, if not for expulsion. Thus it is hoped to blind the eyes of foreign countries to what is afoot inland.

The lesson which the war taught as to the importance of national propaganda results in a newly-arrived journalist being surrounded with a soft-meshed net of propaganda agents. If he listens to their dulcet tones and is a good boy sugar plums in the shape of occasional colorless official interviews become his lot. If he turns a deaf ear he tears asunder the enveloping net and is promptly noted as an undesirable. Strange hints to his detriment begin to trickle through unidentifiable channels to his editor.

Curious little clicks are heard when he is telephoning, and he knows the wire is being tapped, while at times of crisis his telegrams are always hopelessly delayed.

Finally, if the government in question thinks the correspondents will stand for it they are arrested. Native correspondents are imprisoned and foreign ones expelled, providing the expelling country believes the correspondents will not receive full protection from his embassy.

Some Take the Easiest Road

The result is that any correspondent not sure of the support of his legation or his newspaper follows the easiest road—avoids unpleasant facts and swallows official reassurances. His newspaper then presents a roseate but quite misleading picture.

This condition of affairs has its humorous side. There are native correspondents in the Balkan capitals for foreign newspapers who can afford to rest for years on laurels acquired by being arrested by earlier regimes which the successors detest. Your correspondent himself has had the experience of threatned expulsion from a certain country. On inquiring somewhat diffidently a few months later of an official whether things would be unpleasant for him on his return he was assured:

"Why, on no account. So-and-so now has succeeded his predecessor, and the fact that you incurred the latter's displeasure is the surest passport to our favor."

The whirligig of time brings its revenges to journalists in the Balkans with unusual rapidity.

Special restrictions laid upon correspondents in certain countries under the dictatorial system, notably Hungary, where a definite law forbids publication of anything "damaging the reputation of the nation," like that standby of the British sergeant major anxious to get a private soldier punished. "Conduct to the prejudice of good order and military discipline," covers many sins.

Anything a correspondent writes to which those holding the reins of power object may be brought within the charge. Reports of an anti-Semitic outrage, as the Heilig correspondent of the Vossische Zeitung found to his cost when he was expelled from Hungary a few months ago on account of his reports of anti-Semitism, may fall within that category.

Dentist Headed Journalist

The presidents of local associations of journalists often are quite unfitted to defend the interests of the press. When Theodor Berkes, celebrated Balkan correspondent of the Berliner Tageblatt, recently was expelled from Belgrade because his account of the Yugoslav-Bulgarian frontier troubles displeased the Yugoslav dictatorship, a worthy dentist, as president of the journalists' association, was compelled to appear for the defense.

In some other cases such presidents either consider themselves the government's lion tamer among the wild beasts of the press or are concerned to maintain their own political and financial connections unimpaired.

With surprise and regret correspondents here read on Tuesday last the apparently hasty words of the universally respected Police President of Vienna, Johann Schober, who threatens foreign correspondents with prosecution and expulsion in connection with the report of civil war perils which recently existed in Austria. Though it was the fiery Fascist and Socialist leaders, as well as the Austrian press of all shades, which put the word of civil war into the correspondents' mouths, nobody suggests touching them but individual correspondents who have broken the twelfth commandment and "spilt the beans" are threatened.

Association Prepares Reply

True friends of Austria hope she will take to heart the energetic reply which the association of the foreign press in Austria is preparing. The association points out that its members cannot be expected to ignore speeches and articles published here by Austrians, however damaging to Austria their publication abroad may prove. The association strongly resents insinuations of threats recently uttered by a part of the Vienna press—Dr. Schuerff, Minister of Trade, leads the chorus in saying that other countries would have expelled such correspondents already—and reminds Austria how much she owes to foreign correspondents in helping in her reconstruction and in building up her tourist traffic.

Vienna knows well that withdrawal of these correspondents would mean that the last relic of its former position as the centre of an empire of 53,000,000 inhabitants had disappeared, and that neighboring capitals are only too anxious to accommodate them. The correspondents chose Vienna not because they receive special help in their work here, but because at least they are left alone.

Foreigner Often the Goat

Attempts to blame their own folly on foreign correspondents who merely recorded it and indicated probable consequences do nothing, as the newspaper Stunde has wisely pointed out, to rehabilitate the countries abroad. Only strong government action at home in the direction of disarming both illegal armies can do this.

"It is always the foreigner who is to blame," wrote Heinrich Heine mockingly a century ago in a somewhat similar case. The theory of a foreign conspiracy against Little Austria, whom every one wishes well, will not wash today.

* * *

December 31, 1929

CROATS SENTENCED FOR PRESS OFFENSES

Zagreb Court Imprisons and Fines Editors and Leaders for Articles Published

Wireless to The New York Times

ZAGREB, Dec. 30—A number of cases of offenses against the press laws of the dictatorship have just been before the courts and resulted in sentences being passed on several prominent Croats.

Both the widow and daughter of the late Stephen Raditch, Croat leader, who was shot down in 1928 in the Belgrade Parliament by Government Deputy Punica Ratchitch, were tried in connection with several articles published from their pens.

The widow, Maria Raditch, was acquitted, and the daughter, Mme. Milizar Wandekar, sentenced conditionally to two months' arrest.

The editor of Raditch's old newspaper, Slobondy Dm, which was suppressed under the dictatorship, M. Ivanitch, was sentenced to six months' imprisonment and a fine of 6,000 dinars [$105] for twenty-three press offenses.

Several other political editors were also sent to prison.

Two prominent Croat politicians, Vladko Matchek, leader of the Croats in succession to Raditch, and his lieutenant, Joseph Predavetch, who were both under arrest on other charges, were also tried for press offenses. M. Matchek was discharged and M. Predavetch was sentenced to one year's imprisonment and a fine of 1,000 dinars [$17.70].

* * *

March 30, 1930

PRESS IN BALKANS LARGELY SHACKLED

Rumanian Premier Is Forced to Break His Promises of Freedom for Newspapers

AUSTRIA HAS RIGID LAW

Censorship in Hungary and Yugoslavia Makes Lot of Foreign Correspondents an Unhappy One

By G. E. R. GEDYE
Wireless to The New York Times

VIENNA, March 27—The seizure last Monday of a majority of the non-governmental great Rumanian dailies, except the official organs of the Liberal party, calls attention to the withdrawal of a portion of the recently acquired freedom of the press in that country. It is only one incident in a series of restrictions placed in the last few months on the liberty of the Rumania press to speak its mind freely which Premier Dr. Maniu promised after the fall of Bratianu, and for a long period fulfilled his promise.

The Regent, Prince Nicholas, seems to be primarily responsible for the government, despite its professions of liberality, having revived control of the press. Dr. Maniu himself is too sound a democrat, as was emphasized Wednesday in the Chamber, to desire the reinstitution of a system under which he suffered so long when it was controlled by former Premier Bratianu.

All the Balkans is proverbially a hotbed of rumors, but Bucharest is the true capital of scandaldom. The administration of the country, always a curious mixture of absolutism, gave license to individuals to talk their worst as long as they never proceeded to deeds. Strangely enough the idea of according the members of the royal family any protection from scandalous tongues in view of the impossibility of their taking such measures to protect themselves as are open to ordinary citizens, is entirely foreign to the Rumanian legal code. Even before the war newspapers were accustomed to attack with extraordinary violence any member of the royal family whom they disliked.

Measure Insisted on by Regent

This cherished privilege has been withdrawn by a bill which will become law within a few days. Its passage is insisted on by that royal speed lover, Prince Nicholas. Within the last two years there have been three violent press attacks on his motoring manners. It was alleged on each occasion that he had stopped his car because some other driver failed to clear the road quickly enough for him, got out, and after soundly rating the offender, administered corporal punishment. On the last occasion of such an attack Nicholas insisted that two journalists were responsible. They were arrested and sentenced to imprisonment.

Not content with that Nicholas, it is stated, threatened to resign the regency unless a law defending the honor of the royal family from press attacks were drafted and passed immediately. His insistence caused a Cabinet crisis, for rather than sponsor the measure, Minister of Justice Gronian resigned. Confronted with the further prospect of a constitutional crisis Dr. Maniu sacrificed his personal feelings in the matter and supported the bill. Party discipline has insured its passage through the Chamber but caused great discontent in the Peasant party, which felt obliged to pass it, for its provisions are contrary to all the party's principles.

The idea of control of the press once admitted, Dr. Maniu found himself unable to resist demands by other interested parties for special protection.

"If it was forbidden to criticize the conduct of the royal family and regency," said the banks, "why should any one be allowed to damage our credit, which is our life itself?"

The lead in this demand was taken by the biggest bank in the country, the Marmorosc Bank Company, which recently was the victim of a dangerous press attack on its credit. In its course more than 350,000 lei deposits were withdrawn in a single day. Other institutions were also affected by the run and only the solidarity of Rumania's banks, coupled with the intervention of the National Bank, averted disaster.

The culprit in this case was the Opposition press, which printed alarmist rumors concerning the political, economic and financial situation in Bessarabia. As this was calculated to affect also the national credit, Minister of Finance Madgearu associated himself with the demand of the banks.

Second Press Control Bill

A second bill for control of the press is being drafted providing the severest penalties for any one engaging in a political campaign likely to damage the public credit or affect banks and other credit institutions. The State Attorney will also in future be obliged to bring criminal action against all persons spreading false rumors likely to damage the banks.

The banks have agreed on an original penalty for malicious or faint-hearted depositors. They state that they will refuse to re-accept deposits withdrawn ostentatiously during a crisis with the object of increasing its gravity, while the rate of interest will be reduced for other depositors who had not sufficient confidence in the banks but withdrew their money in genuine panic.

The latest action against the press was Monday's confiscation of such well-known papers as the Adeverul, Cuventul and Cudrentul and even the Indépendance Roumaine, which under the Liberals was a semi-official government sheet devoted to propaganda among diplomats for foreign consumption. This action well exemplifies how easily measures against the press can recoil like a boomerang on the head of their wielders.

Last Sunday the obstreperous but largely impotent party of General Averescu held a meeting in Bucharest, at which practically everybody of importance in Rumania was denounced in order, by contrast, to whitewash some one outside it—former Prince Carol, whose return to save the country with his unique talents from the effect of the regency and subservient government was vociferously demanded. Rumanians who remember the conduct of affairs under the former Dictator General Averescu, who was placed in power by M. Bratianu as a screen for himself and was ignominiously thrown down when he dared to aspire to independence, do not attach overmuch importance to the declamations of his party. Dr. Maniu's government, however, made the mistake of giving these fulminations importance by confiscating all papers which published full accounts thereof. Immediately General Averescu's meeting from being merely boresome became a news story of some importance and was cabled to the ends of the earth.

It is easy enough to make out a good case for press restrictions in many of these young States, for undoubtedly the newspapers often abuse the privilege of fair comment. The trouble is that it seems impossible to prevent parties abusing even more seriously the weapon which such restrictive laws put in their hands, to silence just criticism by opponents with the object of deceiving the outside world into the belief that peace and harmony reign.

Restrictive Press Law in Austria

Austria has recently been inflicted with a law to restrict freedom of the press. Its most dangerous provision is a clause rendering liable to criminal prosecution "any one who spreads or prints incorrect statements calculated to damage the prospects and credit of persons about whom made."

Like all such measures, it reads reasonably enough, but it threatens every foreign correspondent in almost every message he sends, since obviously it is not always possible for him to probe to the bottom the accuracy of every statement in the newspapers affecting persons or institutions.

By politically prejudiced judges the law might also be used to suppress criticism by political opponents. Already several such actions have been entered for trial in the Vienna courts, where articles amounting at the worst to nothing more than abuse of political opponents are made the subject of proceedings.

The best example of how such a provision can be abused was provided by an action, which was subsequently withdrawn, entered by the playwright Homunculus against the well-known Austrian author, Felix Salten, because the latter in a critique of the premiere of Homunculus's play "Wunschtraum," declared it was a scandal that so poor a play should be produced by the national theatre.

But the most effective control of the Vienna press is exercised by neighboring countries, which by the threat of withdrawing postal facilities are able to exclude or minimize the importance of, to them, undesirable news, in the majority of Vienna newspapers.

Censorship in Hungary

In Hungary an invisible censorship is always at work. There the government has power to forbid the street sale of newspapers which make themselves objectionable. This was exercised in the case of the recent Hague settlement, which the newspapers were given to understand they were expected to refrain from attacking.

When the Socialist organ Nepszava disregarded the hint and produced a series of violent articles, the responsible editor, Deputy Johann Vanzak, was deprived of his party immunity and received sentences of six months and one year imprisonment for failing to name the authors of objectionable articles. Against this, forty government deputies themselves have protested, testifying to Vanzak's unblemished reputation. In the Chamber it was pointed out that there had been no fewer than twenty-one prosecutions of the Nepszava for press offenses within two months.

Drastic Action in Yugoslavia

The general tendency in the Balkans to limit severely the newly acquired liberties of the press has been evidenced also under the Yugoslav dictatorship. Apart from the internal censorship, the internationally known correspondent, Theodor Berks of the Berliner Tagblatt, has been expelled.

Another well-known foreign correspondent, after many years' residence, has decided to leave the country. He has been literally starved out, for the enforced colorlessness of the Yugoslav press, the difficulty of obtaining facts and the general feeling of constraint have resulted in such a dearth of news that he is compelled to seek a fresh field of activity.

* * *

October 19, 1930

SPAIN STILL RULES NEWS PUBLICATION

Press Laws Govern, Although Actual Censorship Is Supposedly Over

Special Correspondence, The New York Times

MADRID, Oct. 3—Three papers felt the heavy hand of the government during the first week after the termination of the press censorship and the application instead of press laws in what El Heraldo of Madrid terms "Another phase of the war between two powers."

Books rarely have been proscribed, but another one of the tomes of "protest" literature which have engrossed most of Spain's literary effort since the end of the dictatorship has been officially blacklisted during the week and the volumes already published seized. The book is, "What May Await the King," by Don Marcelino Domingo, the Socialist, who lives in a boarding house and advocates that revolution can be a conservative affair despite the fact everyone suspects that nothing could be much too extreme for him.

Fear notwithstanding, the press has contained a little salt. El Debate, the Jesuit organ made its sensational attack on the Duke of Alba, Spain's premier peer, claiming that he was an incompetent Minister of State. La Nacion, another conservative organ and the paper of the dead dictator's party, which it is suspected the government would enjoy seeing pass away since it will not permit the glories of the dictatorship, a subject somewhat distasteful to the King, to be forgotten, states, "El Debate took the words from our mouth."

The Liberal press took the stand that the Duke's advanced educational views provoked the attack, to which El Debate contested by reflecting on the Duke's democracy. It states, "The Duke of Alba has done nothing to help our grape growers, although France's tariff cut our wine business 80 per cent. When officers of the Spanish Union of Fruiters tried to visit him in Paris he refused to see them."

Amusing cases of censorship under the dictatorship are being published. One paper was fined, it comes to light, for calling the bulls of a prominent breeder "cowardly" in the report of a bullfight. Another paper sent a story to the censor for approval which referred to Don Miguel Unamuno, internationally known philosopher and a republican firebrand, as "the illustrious Señor Unamuno." The article came back with the word illustrious crossed out. A protest called forth from the censor the remark, "Well, he's not illustrious to me, and that is enough."

* * *

November 23, 1930

PRESS CENSORSHIP

Some States of Central Europe Are Quite Subtle About It

By G. E. R. GEDYE

VIENNA—As the octopus of absolutism stretches its tentacles further across the map of Europe, so does the freedom of the foreign journalist to deal frankly and fully with the affairs of the territory which his newspaper pays him to cover contract. Every intelligent newspaper reader—and what other sort would ever concern himself with foreign affairs?—knows that if the telegram and articles sent from Rome and Moscow are to have their full value for him there is much that he must read between the lines and sometimes even something which he must delete for himself. Not only must a journalist in an unconstitutional country leave many things unwritten; he must often insert some others—official explanations, statements and reasons given, in which he places little faith—in order to escape molestation for giving the facts to which these official efforts relate.

The means by which arbitrarily ruled countries, and even some democratic States, seek to control the eye and the ear of the foreign public are varied. The most harmless is the printed propaganda which, after a brief glance, can usually be relegated to the waste-basket and no damage done. In this particular, two bitterly hostile countries in Central Europe have vied with one another since the end of the war, and it would be difficult to say which deserves the palm. At the other end of the scale comes what in military language might be called "sabotage by enemy agents at the base." The system is to engage as "saboteur" a person of some position—not a national of the interested country, but of the country which it is desired to influence—at a high salary and to make him responsible for keeping his own country's press "sweet" for the employer State. Residing chiefly in the capital of his native country, he makes it his business to be on the best of terms with the powers that be of every important newspaper. He does little propaganda himself. He keeps the fact that he is employed by, let us say, Ruritania in the background, and is to all intents and purposes a jolly, well-informed citizen of, say, the United States, and of the world. He merely happens to be especially well informed about Ruritania (as, with the entire staff of the Ruritanian Legation and Foreign Office to cram him with favorable "facts," he may well be) and gradually becomes known as an expert.

Friend of Everybody—Within Limits

It is when facts, figures and arguments unfavorable to the picture which Ruritania desires to create of herself abroad are published that he earns his salary and liberal expense allowances. Over coffee and cigars he drops hints to various "Big Noises" that their correspondent is inaccurate, ill-informed, prejudiced—best of all, that he is a "secret Red." Then on the next visit to the capital of Ruritania he meets the correspondent. He gives him an excellent dinner, matchless wines and some "good advice" That correspondent's "Very Biggest Noise," it appears, does not quite like the tone of his work. The "saboteur" knows the "Biggest Noise" well and can soon explain matters. But, as between two good pals, the correspondent should really get his information from better sources, and he (the "saboteur") asks nothing better than to have the honor of arranging this Premier Blank, President Name, Home Minister N'Existe Pas and Foreign Minister Neverwuz will be delighted to tell him exactly what should be written. And it would be a pity if the correspondent failed to agree for the "saboteur" might then—well he might be compelled to talk to his dear friend the "Very Biggest Noise" in a very different strain about the correspondent, whom the "saboteur" really longs to call his very dearest friend too.

This is the point where the perfect, correspondent either picks up his hat and walks out or takes off his coat, waistcoat and collar and walks into the "saboteur"—with both fists. But, alas! few among us are perfect, or the "saboteur" would be left isolated or a semi-invalid; and according to the degree of our imperfections varies the success of the "saboteur"—and the cautious inaccuracy of our telegrams.

For the very imperfect correspondent let me say that I do not know where he could be found on the European staff of any American newspaper—"courtesies" are provided to keep him smiling about Ruritania. They vary downward in different countries, from invitations to consume sublime sandwiches (there is no need to say which country provides the them of caviar) in the company of the greatest Ruritanians at an omnium gatherum where, if he is very pushful, he may touch the finger-tips of the Greatest Ones via crumbs in the shape of written propaganda interviews for publication (no questions allowed) and tips on the stock market, down to the unmentionable thing, "cash subsidies." The higher breed of writers glorified by the title of "authors" are not immune. More than one fine-looking volume has been written since the war and has been published by some big firm, not because the general public would certainly buy it, but because a Ruritanian Foreign Office guaranteed to buy 10,000 copies when it was written and published.

Severity for the Unregenerate

These methods are for the good boys. For the bad—among whom I proudly claim to be included—there are other cures available. Exclusion from the presence of the Great, insinuations against journalistic and even personal honor circulated to tame governmental, or temporarily governmental, organs, "blacklisting" for interviews, interference with cables and telephone communications, open censorship, official threats, arrest, expulsion. At various times I have run the gamut of the experiences, with the exception of the last two.

"That'll put Gedye's nose out of joint," a colleague observed joyously after emerging from an Italian police station recently. "He's never managed to got arrested at all let alone as a front page story." I am afraid it was quite true.

To leave the safe field of Ruritania and get on to the delicate ground of the actual position in Central Europe as noticed in a recent tour, Hungary exercises a powerful censorship on its home press by the government's power to prohibit sales of newspapers in street kiosks, the principal means of distribution. On foreign journalists it exercises all the subtler methods of influencing their pens. Its hospitality is often embarrassing, and, if avoided, evidence of Hungary's skill in "base sabotage" (which it originated and perfected) used to be quickly forthcoming. I trust this is a tale of the past today.

Yugoslavia has a merciless censorship for its own press, but despite dictatorship it has proved surprisingly tolerant of criticism by visiting correspondents though it starved at least one resident Belgrade foreign newspaper man out of existence through his fear of reprisals for sending unfavorable news, and expelled Theodor Berkes, the fearless and impartial correspondent of the Berliner Tageblatt.

Rumania is the journalist's nightmare—everything promised and nothing done. Under the government of General Averescu, once a Rumanian would-be Mussolinette, I was ordered to leave the country within twenty-four hours under pain of expulsion for cabling abroad certain dictatorial ambitions of the General which had been revealed in a Rumanian newspaper. But the General later changed his mind. The Times Geneva correspondent, Clarence K. Streit, knows that M. Bratianu could enforce such an order, though the Maniu régime long ago made full reparation to each of us for its predecessor's follies.

Bulgaria Positively Garrulous

Bulgaria provided me with a real surprise. The Bulgarian Press Department and Foreign Office has the strangely un-Balkan idea that it ought to assist journalists to get at the truth not at propaganda. In two days it had arranged and carried out without any previous notice interviews with the overworked Premier Liaptcheff, his Secret Five and the Minister of the Interior, the leader of the Opposition, the leader of the Socialists, the leader of the Agrarians, although he is considered a dangerous Red, and the Foreign Secretary. When I said in amazement, "But why should you help me to see the government's worst enemies?" the press chief replied, "We know if you are worth your salt you will hear both sides anyway. We are here to save you time."

Czechoslovakia relies largely on printed propaganda. The correspondent who conscientiously waded through every word of the heavy masses of it, with which he is liable to be deluged on the least excuse, would indeed, find little time for criticizing the country's failings, so perhaps he system has its points. There is an active censorship of the home press, and a rigorous clipping system for recording every word, favorable or unfavorable, written about the country. If the Magyar never forgets a grievance, the Czech never forgets a suspicion—and such is readily aroused. He is not a real expert in the art of "base sabotage," but he has in every country a tally of reliable "letters-to-the editor" writers, one of whom may always confidently be called upon to contest anything written which seems unfavorable to Czech interests. There are other ways, too, of preventing criticism abroad. Professor Voitetch Tuka, formerly of Bratislava University and a true Slovak patriot, spent many days showing the British writer, Sir Robert Donald, the abuses of the tyrannous Czech "colonization" system in Slovakia. As Sir Robert's niece told me, their every movement was watched by assiduous Czech spies, but Tuka laughed at them. Sir Robert's book on the revision question duly appeared. Soon after Tuka was sentenced to fifteen years' penal servitude after a most unconvincing trial for espionage and treason. Foreign correspondents, as a result of this sort of terrorism find it much less easy to acquire information on the Slovak question today.

The distinguished professor, who is openly spoken of in Slovakia as a martyr lies in a convict prison among criminals in prison clothes, eating convicts' fare. When the organ of the American Slovaks published in Chicago the appeal of his unfortunate and now penniless wife for financial aid the Czechs confiscated the entire edition of the Slovak, the newspaper which Tuka used to edit, for reprinting what the American Slovaks wrote about the case. Confiscation with its accompaniment of blank pages in the reissued newspaper after censorship is one of the surest signs' of a fettered press. On the credit side, it must be recorded of the Czechs that they vie with Bulgaria in their readiness to assist the foreign press. Every governmental personage from President Masaryk and Dr. Benes, downward, is readily accessible for either interviews for publication or more discreet conversations for information only." Resident correspondents find life very pleasant if they find the Czechs pleasant, and say so. Otherwise, life soon gets full of fuss and bother.

Austria Still Unreconstructed

Austria until the last eighteen months enjoyed the dual distinction of giving foreign correspondents less trouble and of taking less trouble to help them than any other Central European or Balkan State. A lofty indifference to newspaper men, whom her permanent officials judging, perhaps, by some native products, have always looked upon as something a little lower than a waiter and a little higher than a spy, survived defeat, revolution and dismemberment. It is told of the imperial officials of the Ballhausplatz how their misplaced hauteur to a great foreign journalist resident in Vienna turned a good friend of Austria into her bitterest enemy. In the war this enmity proved more fatal to the monarchy than any other influence. As an old monarchist remarked bitterly to me of this journalist, "If any man is entitled to the inscription on his tombstone 'Here lies the man who destroyed the Hapsburg monarchy' it is he." The journalist, whose resentment had led him before the war to devote years to a systematic study of the monarchy's many failings and the many good reasons for its abolition, devoted his pen to this end and achieved it in the face of influential opposition in his own country.

Today it is a truism that the foreign correspondent in Vienna who asks for interviews with political personalities is a fool. He is put off by the understrappers of most of them with half promises. His time is wasted by the "cotton-wool", method of never giving a direct refusal, but by requests to call again and again and again. One of the few exceptions to this was the late Chancellor and Police President, Dr. Schober, who could be relied on to say "yes" or "no" straight out to a correspondent's request, and to keep his word.

Latterly, Austria has begun to lose even her negative attraction for journalists. At home an indirect censorship has been set up through wholesale confiscations of Austrian newspapers. The result was that no newspaper ventured to tell the true story of the recent crazy plans for the seizure of Vienna by a small and determined body of picked Heimwehrmen under the former imperial General Ellissen, who was openly proclaiming that within a few months the monarchy would be restored. Foreign correspondents who have dutifully kept their newspapers informed of such matters have been subjected to attacks even in government newspapers. In one case even the wife of a correspondent was attacked because her husband cabled to his German newspaper the truth about the planned cou d'etat.

This sort of indirect censorship, coupled with dark hints of a "proscription list" of "journalists considered ripe for expulsion" by the Fascists if, and when, the latter can overthrow the Constitution, makes it necessary to modify the statement that foreign correspondents are not troubled in Austria without it being possible to modify the charge that no trouble is taken to help them. If anti-democratic tendencies receive a check however, and the bureaucracy can be awakened to the realization that Metternich is dead and Austria as much in need of friends and publicity as any other small and struggling State, the naturally helpful and good natured characteristics of the race may be shown even to the American newspaper man.

* * *

March 1, 1933

HITLER SUSPENDS REICH GUARANTEES; LEFT PRESS BANNED

Emergency Decree to Combat 'Communist Terror' Voids Constitutional Safeguards

CURB ON STATES PROVIDED

Berlin to Seize the Executive Power in Any Failing to 'Restore Law and Order'

ALL RED PAPERS BARRED

Prussian Socialist Organs Also Suppressed as Aftermath of the Reichstag Blaze

By FREDERICK T. BIRCHALL
Special Cable to The New York Times

BERLIN, Feb. 28—Last night's fire, which rendered the Reichstag building untenable for at least a year, has provided the expected basis for measures of repression throughout the Reich unprecedented save in time of war or revolution.

An emergency decree signed by President von Hindenburg and published tonight suspended all constitutional articles guaranteeing private property, personal liberty, freedom of the press, secrecy of postal communications and the right to hold meetings and form associations.

The decree also authorized the government of the Reich to seize executive power in any German State, whose government failed to take "the necessary measures for the restoration of law and order."

All the Communist newspapers throughout Germany and all Socialist papers throughout Prussia were suppressed today until after the Reichstag elections next Sunday and all suspected Communist meeting places were closed. Even the issue of the Socialist Vorwärts printed early this morning was confiscated before it reached the street.

Reds and Pacifists Jailed

Some 130 known Communists and pacifists were gathered in by the police, subjected to severe questioning and detained for an indefinite period. They include five Reichstag members alleged to have been seen in or near the building shortly before the fire.

Throughout the day the police and Nazi "auxiliary police" have swarmed everywhere. Along Unter den Linden and the Wilhelmstrasse and in the neighborhood of the Reichstag the police are carrying rifles and armored cars are patrolling the whole of Berlin.

The Nazi and Nationalist newspapers in Headlines, news and editorials inveigh against the "Red terror" and issue the direst warnings against it. Chancellor Hitler himself is quoted as remarking, "Now you can see what Germany and Europe have to look for from communism."

Nothing is being left unsaid and undone to arouse a wave of popular hysteria in advance of Sunday's elections.

That this is having its effect was indicated at the University of Berlin today, where Nazi and Nationalist students insisted on the removal of all newspapers having the faintest tinge of liberalism, including the Boersen-Courier and the Tageblatt and Vossische Zeitung groups, from the university reading room, leaving only the extreme Nazi and Nationalist organs, and they had their way.

Yet it is only in such publications as the students ousted that the faintest suggestion of restraint and common sense is traceable at this juncture. Several of them in varying forms suggest that as the Socialist newspapers are being silenced it is only fair to say that the party should be absolved of the Reichstag outrage, since the German Socialists have always been respecters of public property.

Elsewhere the tendency is unchecked to make this act of violence, as one Socialist remarked bitterly, "just a bigger and better Zinovieff letter" [the publication of which played a, large part in the overthrow of the first MacDonald government in Great Britain in 1924].

In the meantime the shabby undersized Hollander who is the sole evidence of the source of the incendiarism to which the fire can be attributed, is undergoing hourly grilling at Police Headquarters. From paper in his pockets he has been identified as a stonemason from Leyden, as having been the ringleader of local disturbances there and as being ostensibly on his way to Russia.

When he appeared at the frontier a few day ago the German police, not liking his looks, turned him back, but he succeeded in getting here, nevertheless." To all inquiries he is said to reply with a silly laugh, and he is telling nothing.

Which, therefore, leaves still open such pertinent questions as why a Communist intent on serious crime should carry his Communist card and other papers rendering him easily identifiable as such in his pocket; who his confederates were and how, if they resembled him, they all succeeded in entering so well-guarded a building as the Reichstag; how they were able to carry in with them the quantities of inflammable material—now said to have included petrol—with which the fire was started in a dozen places, and how it came about that they were so patently disregarding the well-known tenet of the Moscow leaders that individual acts of terrorism are useless, the best principle being first to attain power and then to apply a real terror of wholesale proportions.

Regardless of these unanswered questions, bearing so directly upon the stupidity of the German Communists in thus playing into Nazi hands, the official versions of the outrage—which under the present conditions of suppression and reticence are the only versions obtainable—charge openly that it is the direct result of recent orders from Moscow to attempt a Bolshevist revolution at the earliest possible moment, or at least create widespread unrest throughout the Reich.

It is charged that the German Communist press has reflected this intention, hence the wholesale suspensions. And chemists are "examining the debris of the fire for traces of combustible chemicals" and are also taking fingerprints.

However, while Berlin is thus in the throes of anti-Communist hysteria, Bavaria and the rest of South Germany, quite regardless of what the Nazi organ here describes as "this flaming signal to the nation," are occupied solely with carnival merrymaking, and from the Rhineland comes the encouraging intelligence that the present carnival season has been the banner one of all time throughout that region.

* * *

January 14, 1934

140 NAZI BOMBINGS IN WEEK IN AUSTRIA

Government Report Arouses People to a Realization of Seriousness of Situation

NEWSPAPERS ARE USELESS

Print Only Official 'Hand-Outs,' Leaving Their Readers to Depend on Gossip

By G. E. R. GEDYE
Wireless to The New York Times

VIENNA, Jan. 12—The announcement in yesterday's proclamation by the government that between Jan. 1 and 8 there were 140 Nazi bomb outrages, besides hundreds of less serious political offenses, in Austria, startled the average Austrian as well as the outside world.

The Austrian dictatorship has advanced so unobtrusively toward full power and the iron hand's grip has tightened so imperceptibly within the typically Austrian velvet glove that it is hard for the casual visitor to realize that Austria today is again a police State, much as in the days of Count Metternich.

Gradually the privileges of the free press have been withdrawn until now the newspapers are useless as a source of information as to what the people are really doing or thinking. They are obliged to print government communiqués, including the headlines, as though they were the newspapers' own articles. Yesterday the editor of the official Social Democrat organ, Arbeiter Zeitung, was fined 1,000 schillings by the police commissar for having printed one such communiqué exactly as issued, including the official orders at the head describing it as a government "hand-out." It is thus forbidden to allow the public to realize they are reading the views of the government, not of the paper.

Rumors Replace Press

The usual consequences of suppression of the liberties of the press, Parliament and free speech already are fully evident. Bored readers idly turn the pages of the now worthless newspapers and drop them eagerly to discuss the latest sensational rumor which replaces reliable press information.

"Chancellor Dollfuss going Nazi." "Nazis going for Dollfuss." "Heimwehr going Nazi." "Heimwehr leaving Prince von Starhemberg and joining Dollfuss against the Nazis." "Dollfuss resigning, as his position is hopeless." "Dollfuss so firmly established he is going to make an end of both Nazis and Socialists at one swoop." "Peasantry on the verge of joining Nazi rising against Dollfuss." "Nazis completely discredited among peasantry, who regard Dollfuss as their own champion."

These and countless other rumors which have replaced authentic news are all believed in turn. Two things generally are distrusted: official communiqués and newspapers.

Unseen hand drops violent Nazi propaganda news sheets prophesying early overthrow of Chancellor Dollfuss into thousands of letter boxes. From abroad ill-printed sheets are smuggled in in which the Social Democrats, deprived simultaneously of the privilege of responsibility and of presenting their views in their legitimate organ, urge the workers to prepare to defend "in the coming civil war" the past achievements of democracy.

Informers Among Clergy

The activities of police and informers who always profit by such régimes have gone so far that the Archbishop of Gurk, after one of his clergy was obliged publicly to retract a mistaken denunciation of a local resident as a Nazi agitator to the police, had to warn the clergy to refrain from such activities under the severest penalties.

The so-called Nazi bombs are as often as not always merely explosions in cardboard containers, but their continued detonations in defiance of all government threats do not encourage general confidence in the stability of the Dollfuss dictatorship.

The impossibility of obtaining information on questions of fact perhaps makes the situation appear even more insecure than it is. The word "authoritative" is always in the mouths of government spokesmen, but in the absence of evidence of real authority opinion is equally divided as to whether Chancellor Dollfuss will continue to plough a lonely furrow, yield to the Heimwehr's insistence on unadulterated fascism coupled with destruction of the last remnants of democracy, or after all accept the Socialists' fresh offers of support to any democratic government in finally suppressing the Nazi terrorists.

* * *

March 20, 1934

GERMAN FUGITIVES TELL OF ATROCITIES AT HANDS OF NAZIS

Americans Bear Out Tales of Outrages and Cruelties in Racial "Purging"

JEWS FLEE PERSECUTION

Pour Across Borders, Fearing for Lives—Police Apathetic and Courts Powerless

ALL NEWS IS CENSORED

People Dare Not Talk to Foreign Correspondents—Phones Tapped—Spies Overrun Berlin

Wireless to The New York Times

PARIS, March 19—Americans arriving here from Germany are expressing more and more concern over the course of events in that country. Neither the full truth about them nor the implications arising therefrom are reaching the outside world, these Americans say, nor can the truth come out except gradually and by stealth, for excellent reasons.

The first and most obvious of these is an ironclad censorship, more severe than Germany has ever known except in war time. Not only are all outgoing dispatches from accredited correspondents subjected to the closest scrutiny and passed only when certain "objectionable" subjects are either untouched or treated so innocuously that Nazi susceptibilities will not be offended thereby, but the sources of all information unfavorable to Nazi interests have been dried up.

Opposition Press Suppressed

Virtually the entire Socialist as well as the Communist press is now prohibited. The Centrist and neutral press is published under the shadow of instant suppression, should it include even the smallest item objectionable to the official rulers.

Germans are forbidden to impart information to foreigners, with the result that none dares to visit, receive or communicate by telephone with the foreign news writers. Telephone communication is tapped, and even the cafés and restaurants are full of spies and eavesdroppers.

The official Wolff Telegraph Bureau is said to be now wholly in Nazi hands, and the other news agencies are not sending out anything but the most innocuous items.

Police reports have become worthless. In fact the police, where they do not ignore the Nazi outrages, actually cooperate in them under the pretext of maintaining law and order. The courts have become mere agencies for the endorsement of government strictures and are powerless to remedy oppression.

The government (meaning the National Socialist) control of all news sources and publication outlets—incidentally, it forbids even mention of the reasons for which any newspaper is suspended—has resulted in the promulgation of what even the Germans are said to regard as transparent fictions. Thus all the outrages, all the violence are now committed by "persons masquerading in Nazi uniforms" or "professing to be Nazis."

There is, of course, neither masquerading nor pretense, and the fiction, American visitors report, deceives no one in Germany. But it does maintain the spirit of Adolf Hitler's recent commands to his followers not to refrain from violence, but only to carry out orders "transmitted from above."

Goering Reigns Unrestrained

And more directly in command of the Nazi forces than Herr Hitler, who is busy with other matters, is the militant Hermann Wilhelm Goering, whom no one seems to restrain.

It is true, according to the returning travelers, that there is no more open threatening of the population desiring to shop in the department stores, even the Jewish ones. Such measures attracted too much outside attention—and foreign capital, particularly American capital, is invested in those stores. So the printed placards held up by the uniformed Nazis at the entrances have disappeared and the stores remain open, their windows unsmashed. The former procedure, however, has given way to a quieter boycott, the result of which in the long run probably will be as effective as the old way.

But if serious, responsible Americans who are coming out of Germany are to be believed—and their position in the world, as well as the opportunities for observation they have had, entitles them to credence—the violence and outrages are not diminishing there. Violence is better cloaked, and the outrages are better protected, but both are continuing, whether they are carried out in response to orders "from above" or are a manifestation that Herr Hitler's young men have really got "out of hand."

Few of these Americans are returning to Germany. Even though they may have escaped annoyance themselves, they do not like the prevailing atmosphere, and they can discern no guarantees for the future. The same may be said of other foreigners. Germany may normally be a comfortable country for the Germans, but the prospect is that under its new rulers it will have to rely on its own resources. Foreigners certainly will not be tempted to enter.

To Be a Jew Is Held a Crime

Particularly, returning Americans say, there is no longer any doubt that to be either of Jewish faith or of Jewish origin and to exist in Germany now constitutes a crime in the eyes of the ruling faction there.

The election campaigns over, the Nazis have attained the full power they craved. There is no longer any excuse for an agitation publicly fostered and privately condoned. Yet the assistant priests of Nazism, with Herr Goering in command of the police and Dr. Paul Joseph Goebbels in charge of a "propaganda" which is to restore to Germany her "place in the sun," continue to proclaim that to "the Jewish vampire" are due all the troubles from which the Reich is suffering, and therefore it is the duty of all Germans to persecute and harass them.

There is no discrimination in the matter of assessing this crime of being a Jew. Neither professional eminence, capacity in business, public service nor private virtue is being counted against it. Professors are being driven from their classrooms, music conductors from their concert halls and actors from the stage. His patriotic writings have not served to pardon even Lion Feuchtwanger, the foremost and most popular German novelist, for the crime of being a Jew. His Berlin home has been invaded in his absence by Nazi rowdies, his manuscripts removed and his motor car stolen. He has sought refuge in Switzerland.

So have others. The Riviera, Semmering, the Bernese Alps and other resorts outside Germany have become in the last few weeks refuges for most of the Jewish families from the Reich who have the means to get there. France, Belgium, Poland, Holland and Italy are receiving daily hundreds who are poorer but just as effectively self-exiled, and Germany, is losing at a stroke some of the best brains in her financial world and many of the best in commerce, medicine, the law and arts.

Stories Almost Incredible

Some of the stories of Jewish persecution brought out by Americans who are prone neither to invention nor to exaggeration would be almost incredible if coming from more imaginative sources. It is impossible to verify them or even to inquire into their truth. All that can be said about them is that they accord generally with what is known and verified as having happened in other instances. Here is one.

Small Nazi "barracks" or headquarters for storm detachment men have now been established throughout Berlin, one or more in each quarter. Seven Jews living together in the Frankfort district of the city were ordered to go to the "barracks" in their district to undergo questioning. They inquired of the police what they had better do and were advised to obey.

At the "barracks" they were confronted with leveled revolvers and compelled under threats of death to flog one another until several of them lost consciousness. Among the victims were a father and his sons.

Here is another printed in the Paris newspaper La Liberté as coming from the American wife of a German of the Jewish faith living in Munich, who is said to have just arrived with her baby at a hotel near the Champs Elysées. The newspaper at her request prints only her initials, "F. C.," because her husband is still in a German hospital and she fears the result of the publication of her story upon him. For the same reason La Liberté declines to reveal her residence.

Ignored Warnings to Leave

She told the newspaper's reporter that her husband had been in charge of an industrial enterprise financed in the Bavarian capital by American funds. Before the recent election he received anonymous letters warning him to leave Germany, but he ignored them.

Late Friday night, when the couple had gone to bed, the doorbell rang. When the wife answered, five armed Nazis entered. Crying "Death to Jews!" they attacked her husband, using bludgeons and chairs, beating him unconscious and fracturing several of his ribs. When she protested and pleaded in broken German, she was pushed aside. Why had she married "one of the Jews who had had Germany under their control for fourteen years and now have to pay for their crimes?"

This American woman, La Liberté says, produced a pair of bloodstained pajamas and a blood-clotted club which the Nazis left behind as proof of her story. She also, the newspaper says, complained to the United States Consul at Munich, who advised her departure and is now demanding an investigation of the assault.

One returning American professes personal knowledge of the case of a Czech woman and her Jewish husband who, while returning to their Berlin home after the theatre, were attacked in a street by Nazis last week. The husband, hoping to escape, jumped on a tramcar, but was dragged out and carried off. Nothing has since been heard of him.

Cases of Nazi patrols carrying out domiciliary visits who have robbed victims or permitted themselves to be bought off by presents of liquor or money are declared to be numerous.

An instance of unprovoked brutality, to part of which an American coming out of Berlin asserts he was an eyewitness, is related by him as follows:

Jews Run Nazi Gauntlet

In Alexanderplatz was a small restaurant at which it was the custom of Jewish business men of the neighborhood to meet for luncheon. They were so in the habit of going there that they formed a sort of club.

For some weeks before the election a Nazi youth selling Der Angriff, the violently anti-Semitic Nazi organ, regularly invaded the restaurant and importuned them to buy the paper. They refused at first laughingly, then angrily expelled him.

Two days after the election the boy returned at luncheon time with a platoon of Nazis and a list of the Jewish frequenters of the restaurant. The Nazis formed a double line to the restaurant door. As the boy called out a name, a stalwart Brown Shirt seized the respectable business man bearing it and propelled him toward the gauntlet. As he passed through it, every man, first on one side and then on the other, smashed him in the face and kicked him with heavy boots, until finally the last in the line knocked him into the street.

During this procedure a larger and huskier frequenter of the "club" entered by another door. The proprietor begged him to go no further, because the Nazis inside were making trouble.

"What, me?" asked the newcomer, who prided himself on his ability to take care of himself. "Me, afraid of a few Nazis?," And he went in.

"When that poor fellow reached the street finally," said the American who told this incident, "his face resembled a beefsteak. The brutes evidently were using brass knuckles. That day I began to wind up my business. I decided Germany was no place for me."

According to an American physician who has been visiting German hospitals, Jewish members of their staffs have become the special butt of Nazi attentions. A professor whose name is known the world over and who held a position on the staff of a great Berlin hospital was carried off one night by Nazis in his own car to a woodland on the outskirts of the city and there coerced into signing his resignation. He was then abandoned there, the Nazis driving off in his car and leaving him to find his way home as best he could.

50 Listed In Clinic "Purging"

Herr Hitler's own newspaper, according to this American, has listed fifty Jewish doctors and laboratory assistants in the third clinic at Berlin University as persons to be ousted. The article listing these persons closes with this passage:

"Unfortunately, the rights of officials and the long-term contracts which these businesslike Jews have managed to secure for themselves prevent a thorough cleaning up. Nevertheless, we may expect that an end will soon be put to this organized rule of an alien race."

It is now said to be far from unusual to find almost any morning in the woodland surrounding Berlin the bodies of men killed by bullets or beatings. Three such discoveries were made last week in a single morning. The police report them as "unidentified suicides." These persons merely disappear. In some proletarian quarters in Berlin, it is said, no house has escaped a domiciliary visitation and the molestation of some dweller.

The five Nazi murderers of a Communist in Bethuen, who were sentenced to death during the von Papen regime last Summer, the court going out of its way to condemn the brutality of their crime, have now been released at the instance (announced in a press clipping produced by an American) of the Chancellor himself. The sentence was commuted to life imprisonment under the von Papen administration.

The feature of all this which most impresses Americans seems to be the comparative indifference displayed by the German people as a whole. While the Nazi excuses are deplored privately by intellectual, clear-thinking persons, there is a tendency to excuse them as perpetrated from an excess of zeal and patriotic, although badly inspired, motives. It is also admitted that the National Socialist success is bringing in recruits by the thousands and outward acquiescence in the status quo without stint.

Populace Now Joins Parades

"There is an old German saying," remarked one observant American in a conversation with the writer, " 'Whose bread I eat, his song I sing.' I have noticed in these unending processions with which the Nazis are celebrating their triumph a new feature I never used to see. Behind the band and its following of brown-shirted 'storm troops' there is now a long tail of civilian flag-wavers who never used to march with them. There are street car men, porters and workers from every occupation whose unions are now under attack. They wear Nazi armlets now, and they too sing the Nazi 'Horst Wessel' song, which is almost as much in vogue in Germany as 'Giovenezza,' which all Fascist Italy sings.

"There is a matter for the rest of the world to meditate upon. Success is in the saddle, riding high in Germany now. And failure is in the cellar, crouching low—often being dragged out to take a licking. Germany has been unified all right. They are all singing a song of success, and they are being molded into a new form which, I am afraid, may be more dangerous than the old."

All of this seems from this distance to be true enough. But there is also another saying, Anglo-Saxon and equally true. It is: "The blood of martyrs is the seed of the church." And apparently there is seed being sown in Germany now, the harvest of which some day may be terrible for the Germans themselves. For, just as when the pendulum swings far to one side it returns inevitably as far to the other, so with the seventeen millions of persons of diverse interests and diverse claims now upholding a movement which has promised all things to all men. When the Nazi movement fails to meet the extravagant bills presented to it and thus disintegrates, something inimical to it will take power in Germany. And the lessons of ruthlessness and terrorism now being taught so sternly probably are being learned with a vengeance.

Republicanism, which failed in part from overgentleness toward its enemies and excess of kindness toward unaiding neutrals, is having a bitter training now, and the remnants left of communism will only be steeled to sterner reprisals, should it be their turn that comes. The pity of it is that in this class warfare it is the decent moderates of Germany who will suffer most and longest.

* * *

April 15, 1934

PRESS CENSORSHIP CONTINUES IN SPAIN

Despite Constitutional Ban on Confiscation, Suspension and Fines, They Occur

EXTREMIST JOURNALS HIT

Telegraphic News Messages Also Are Subjected to Interference

By LAWRENCE FERNSWORTH
Special Correspondence, The New York Times

BARCELONA, April 2—The position of the press in this region is still rather precarious, notwithstanding the substitution of a republic and democracy for the dictatorship with its régime of confiscations, suspensions and finings of newspapers. The dictatorship has passed, but the confiscations, suspensions and finings continue.

To be sure, the Spanish Constitution seems to prohibit such things, but for the first two and a half years of the republic there appear to have been some reservations in the law which the general public never rightly understood, but which nevertheless permitted the authorities to curb newspapers effectively. For the past half-year or so there has been in existence the new law of public order which permits a rigid system of censorship whenever a state of alarm is declared.

A few days ago a fine of 5,000 pesetas about $650, was imposed on La Veu del Vespre, the evening edition, of La Veu de Catalunya, organ of the Opposition and generally Conservative party, the Lliga Catalara, and one of the severest critics of the government party, the Esquerra. The fine was for a news notice which the government claims was inexact and of alarmist character. The newspaper counters that the notice was exact and contained nothing of an alarmist nature.

Kind of Liberty Questioned

It further complains that the fine was imposed at the precise time that it was cooperating with the police in the suppression of certain news to promote the police investigation of a particular case. Having done this, it says, at the request of the police, the news was published by its competitors, and it asks: "What are we to do? What kind of liberty is it we have? If we do not publish the news we are in an inferior position. If we publish it we expose ourselves to new penalties."

Another outstanding case was the recent imposition of a heavy fine on a Rightist paper at the textile town of Sabadell by the Leftist Mayor of the city whom the paper had criticized.

Newspapers regularly go to the censor before publication and their appearance with blank spaces to indicate censorial elisions, just as in the days of the dictatorship, is not infrequent.

The suspension of Rightist and extreme Leftist newspapers is also a current practice. Within the past few days there have been suspended the Catholic weekly, D. I. C. and Defensa Patronal, an editor of which, Dr. Freixa Romera, was sent to jail. The extremist dailies Adelante (Forward), Solidaridad and Combate, and the weekly Tierra y Liberdad (Land and Liberty), have also been the objects of confiscations and suspensions. A reporter for Adelante was sent to jail by the Emergency Tribunal because he had written that the tribunal was unduly lenient with Fascists and unduly severe with partisans of the extreme Left.

The censorship of telegraphic press messages continued at about the same tempo during the state of alarm as before, notwithstanding that it is doubly prohibited by the Spanish Constitution, both in the article outlawing censorship and in Article 32, which guarantees "the individuality of correspondence in all its forms," except in case of a judicial order.

* * *

September 23, 1934

'GRAPEVINES' IN EUROPE EVADE OFFICIAL CENSORS

Secret Police and Press Control Cannot Stop a Flow of Rumors, Gossip and 'Bootlegged' News

By SAMUEL LUBELL

For an uncomplimentary remark concerning Adolf Hitler, published in an American magazine more than two years ago, Dorothy Thompson was recently compelled to leave Germany. It did not matter that the Nazis were not in power when her article was published, nor that she had served for many years as a foreign correspondent in the Reich.

Two days later copies of The London Times were confiscated for the fourth time since July 20, and the record shows that various Russian and English correspondents have been expelled from Germany. But among European nations it is not the Reich alone which seeks to control the press and all sources of news. Viselike, this censorship clutches almost all the Continent—and yet there is news trickling downward to the millions who wish to know what is happening.

The governments, whether in Germany, Austria, Italy or Russia, have two powerful instruments of control—propaganda bureaus and secret police. National periodicals are "inspired" by government officials, and except in Russia, where newspaper columns may publish letters of complaint and "self-criticism," nothing may be printed that is not favorable to those who rule.

Then there is the constant bombardment of the public with rhetoric over the radio and from the public platform, so well illustrated by the addresses of Mussolini in Italy and of Goebbels, the Reich Minister of Propaganda. The extension of censorship over the dispatches of foreign correspondents is the problem which has now arisen in Germany and which has presented itself before in Italy, Russia and Austria.

Combating the "Grapevine"

It is the secret police, however, who chiefly combat the "grapevine"—in other words, the diffusion of unfavorable news, which is whispered on the streets, in restaurants or cafés, at work or play, and spread in secret meetings and by smuggled handbills. In the police campaign, telephone wires have been tapped, private letters opened, conversations listened to, secret presses demolished.

Evasion of this censorship goes on, however, sometimes organized and sometimes unorganized. In Russia, the Ogpu suppressed Trotsky's "underground press"; in Italy the Fascists destroyed the "chain-letter gang" that existed a few years ago. But in Germany, and particularly in Austria, forces are still active in organized spreading of news hostile to the constituted government.

In the Reich, anti-Hitler propaganda is spread furtively, for Nazi suppression is ruthless. Across the border, from neighboring Czechoslovakia, Switzerland and the Saar, Communists and Social Democrats smuggle seditious booklets disguised as advertising matter; "horoscopes" that predict Hitler's downfall; and tiny newspapers set in microscopic print which must be read with magnifying glasses. "Groups of Five" still operate a few secret printing presses; the Communist Rote Fahne occasionally appears; and the chain-letter system is in use. This material is passed from person to person in hundreds of ways—in folded newspapers, empty match containers or stuffed mail boxes.

The Police Gauntlet

Not much of it, however, escapes General Goering's secret police; though after the June purge, anti-Hitler propaganda increased considerably and now seems to be finding receptive readers.

"Boring from within" tactics have been more successful. In May a detachment of Storm Troopers were arrested for distributing Communist leaflets on Berlin streets. In the factories, Communist agitation was reflected in workers' elections last May. Far from producing the results desired by Nazi leaders, re-elections made necessary the official appointment of almost one-half of the work councils. Lutheran and Catholic Church groups are enemies of Nazification, keeping their congregations well posted, even if news is unfavorable to the National Socialists. "Reactionary" Monarchists and Junkers have been more cautious, but von Papen's Marburg address in defense of criticism was reprinted and secretly and widely circulated.

Austrian Propaganda

In Austria, strong Nazi groups in the provinces, though weakened by their unsuccessful putsch of a month ago, have spread propaganda spectacularly in radio broadcasts from the German side of the frontier. Prohibited German newspapers have been smuggled into the country and vituperative handbills and leaflets have been printed. Occasionally the printed matter is more "subtle," as in April, when 10,000 pamphlets describing how Nazis had assisted a Socialist to escape were distributed in an effort to win over the workers.

The Austrian Socialists use quieter methods, depending chiefly on news whispered from mouth to mouth in factories, coffee houses and tenements which house thousands of sympathetic families. Constant underground contact is maintained with Socialist leaders in Czechoslovakia.

Unorganized methods of spreading news in Europe vary from the circulation of foreign periodicals to intelligent individual "reading between the lines" of government-inspired information, and to gossip and rumor.

Foreign newspapers may not be sold in Moscow, and their appearance is rigidly regulated in Italy; but in Germany and Austria, where many educated citizens speak a foreign language, they are read eagerly. For those who can read only their native language, there are Czech and Swiss journals printed in German. During troubled February the Viennese crowded in front of their news stands to see the headlines and the pictures in foreign papers. Coffee houses where foreign publications could be consulted were the busiest.

In Germany, during the week after the "purge," a foreign paper could not be obtained after 10 o'clock in the morning, and when one was opened in the streets, curious groups would gather around. German and Austrian authorities have now restricted news stand sales of foreign periodicals, but their popularity is undiminished.

Reading between the lines of official publications has almost become a game under European dictatorships. A shrewd Italian business man clips government announcements and compares them from month to month, thereby often discovering striking changes in policy and their unpublished motives.

Telltale Omissions

A much simpler method is to trace events through news omissions. When a Polish Socialist, for instance, sees the white column on the front page of his party paper he knows that the censor has been at work; and since he already is acquainted with the arguments of his party editor, his imagination often supplies what is lacking. Similarly, Germans who are well grounded in politics and economics may listen to official speeches and learn much from what has not been said.

In Russia decrees are carefully scanned for the motives underlying their issuance; and through them many Russians have learned to measure Soviet progress. Although many Russians scoff at the reorganization of the OGPU as "meaningless," yet all agree that it signifies greater confidence on the part of the Bolsheviks and probably a let-down in the intensity of class war. On the other hand, a Pravda campaign assuring peasants that they will not be exploited by collective farm managers suggests trouble with the crops.

Reversing What Is Published

The most popular method of reading between the lines, however, is to accept as true, the reverse of what the government prints. The Nazi campaign against "panic buying," for instance, served only to stimulate fears of inflation and more purchases of preservable goods. In July, when all the papers denied a shortage in the potato crop, the population only stocked up more anxiously.

Gossip and rumor have been stimulated into new life. In every capital of Europe standard rumors drift about, telling of graft and corruption, of squabbles between faction leaders. How do these whispers spread from region to region within each country?

First of all, there are the mails, which, despite official tapping, are important sources of information in all countries. From abroad come letters written by Russian, Italian or German emigrants, and these, read by the neighborhood, are given more credence than official newspapers. In Italy, where family ties are numerous and close, much news circulates through domestic mails.

Each nation has its own peculiar institutions for the spread of news by gossip. Every Viennese, for instance, has two homes—the apartment in which he sleeps and the coffee house in which he talks, and where secrets are whispered. The bazaar serves a similar function in Russia, where private trade has almost completely vanished. Amid a medley of articles on sale chattering crowds mingle; and for them the popularity of the bazaar lies in its social rather than economic purposes. Here letters from abroad are read, some of them furtively smuggled into the country from an exiled friend in Siberia.

How Gossip Travels

The Russians are naturally garrulous and have a knack for passing news by word of mouth. In the railroad cars reports are eagerly exchanged on crop prices, on ration distinctions in various sections of the country—matters that are never officially published, but are known to any Russian.

In Germany cafés and "pubs" as sources of gossip are supplemented by university students, who are numerous, fond of political discussion and usually acquainted with foreign languages. In all countries foreigners, tourists and newspaper correspondents are perpetually questioned by the curious.

Criticism of the government in power travels most popularly in the form of anecdotes from citizen to citizen. Unfortunately, most of these are difficult to translate. Some are in the form of cryptic drawings, others are intimately related to national customs, laws and languages. In Russia the poor quality of manufactured articles from Soviet factories is a standard topic for humorous complaints. In Germany personalities are often taken to task. In Austria the dubious allegiance of the Heimwehr troopers provides continual inspiration for humorous comment.

* * *

December 16, 1934

GERMANS PREFER THE FOREIGN PRESS

People Resist Plea of Nazis That Only Domestic Papers Be Bought in Reich

CANVASSERS GET REBUFF

Two Storm Troopers Assert They Would Rather Read Papers From Abroad

By The Associated Press

BERLIN, Dec. 15—A Nazi drive to wean good Germans away from their foreign newspapers has bumped into stout resistance, it developed today.

Two staunch Storm Troop men—one a wine clerk, the other a Chamber of Commerce secretary—frankly told canvassers for Nazi newspapers today that they preferred newspapers from abroad to the strictly censored local organs.

These cases, it was learned, were typical of the attitude of educated Germans in general. Either they subscribe to Swiss, French or English newspapers or they frequent cafés where foreign newspapers are kept on file.

Chicago Paper Helps One

"I learn what is going on in Germany about fourteen days after things have happened," one German commented, "when I receive the Chicago Abendpost with its dispatches from Berlin."

Minister of Propaganda Paul Joseph Goebbels's tight restrictions on the German press have led to such an influx of foreign newspapers as was never seen before the establishment of the Third Reich, and the leaping circulation of Swiss and other foreign newspapers is giving Nazi authorities real concern, the Deutsche Wochensau said.

That weekly berated the men and women who buy foreign papers as "No" men (men refusing their cooperation to the régime) and as evil-minded negative characters.

"What business have these papers to be offered in metropolitan centres like Berlin or, as is happening of late, even in small towns?" it inquired. "Why should they be displayed in the Friedrichstrasse or on the Kurfuerstendamm of Berlin or the Odeonsplatz of Munich?"

The Deutsche Wochenshau found that, in addition to the "moral damage" that these foreign papers did with their "atrocity propaganda" and their reporting of alleged facts that the German press does not carry, there is an economic aspect to the problem.

"If we may believe the assertion of the foreign publishers," it said, "the sale of Swiss papers alone amounts daily to thousands of marks, which means that in the course of a year the sum swells to many hundreds of thousands.

"That these figures may well be correct was demonstrated by a test on the Kurfuerstendamm: within five minutes a certain stand there sold foreign papers for more than three marks, while during the same time only one single Berlin paper was sold for ten pfennigs."

Trade Manoeuvre Asked

The weekly suggested that this sale of foreign papers means a considerable drain of foreign exchange, and recommended that Germany in future trade agreements insist that in return for this patronage of foreign papers the countries in question take additional German exports. The Baseler Nachrichten of Basel, Switzerland, sells 18,000 copies in Germany daily.

For some weeks it seemed that one German weekly, the War Volunteers of 1914–15, might garner some of the money now spent on foreign papers. That organ, edited by former service men, dared to treat public affairs in humorous style and to criticize government measures in the rough-and-tumble manner.

In its current issue the editors even asked foreign correspondents to cite this paper as evidence that criticism was permitted in Hitlerite Germany. Thereupon it was promptly suppressed by the government.

Two Papers Reported Failing

Two more of Berlin's old and influential newspapers, the Berliner Tageblatt and the Deutsche Allgemeine Zeitung, according to reports in newspaper circles may cease publication Jan. 1.

Negotiations are said to be under way with the Muenchener Neueste Nachrichten, whereby the Munich Journal, would publish a special Berlin edition replacing the two. The Allgemeine Zeitung, seventy-three years old, is the organ of "heavy industry." The Tageblatt, sixty-three years old, was Jewish-owned until the Nazis came into power.

* * *

January 26, 1935

AUSTRIA OPENS DRIVE ON ILLEGAL PAPERS

Minimum Sentence of One Year Is Decreed—Socialists Plan Feb. 12 Demonstration

Wireless to The New York Times

VIENNA, Jan. 25—So great is the flood of illegal Communist, Socialist and Nazi newspapers and brochures in Austria since total government control of the press that the authorities announced today that the present penalties will be much increased.

A minimum of one year's imprisonment will be imposed upon any one engaged in such illegal activities. In 1934, it is said, 34,000 illegal papers and brochures were seized by the police.

Rumors that the charges of high treason against Anton Rintelen, would-be Chancellor in the Nazi putsch of last July, will be dropped were denied in official circles today. It was explained that the case is so complicated that it will probably not come to trial before Spring.

Twenty Socialists have been arrested in Vienna on suspicion of having prepared demonstrations for Feb. 12, the anniversary of last year's Socialist uprising. The underground Socialist party has issued a call to its adherents to mark the anniversary by using no electric current and attending no places of public entertainment. On the two following days also the party will endeavor to organize small demonstrations.

* * *

March 29, 1935

NAZIS WILL SUPPRESS ALL JEWISH WRITERS

Journalists and Others Who Have Kept Jobs So Far Now Slated to Go

Wireless to The New York Times

BERLIN, March 28—Following notification to all remaining Jewish publishers that they had better sell their business, as the National Socialist authorities now have expanded the "purge" to include all "non-Aryans" in the publishing business, especially journalists and other writers who have escaped suppression so far by virtue of front-line service and other merits.

This policy is in line with previous announcements made by Max Amann, head of the Reich Press Chamber and business manager of the Voelkische Beobachter. The purpose, it is understood, is to eliminate from the publishing business by Oct. 1 all "non-Aryans," all Aryans who may be related to Jews by marriage and all those who have not been able to display the proper enthusiasm for the National Socialist régime.

Their places will be taken by young Nazi journalists now being put through a rapid-fire instruction course under the auspices of the Nazi district press office.

The doomed are receiving notification stating that no Jew is to remain active in the Third Reich's press system and that, therefore, they are notified that on a fixed date they will be excluded from the Reich Press Chamber. After that date they will be subject to punishment if they continue to write for publication.

A Prussian court has just decided that Jewish lawyers are barred from appointments to represent indigent litigants or defendants at the expense of the State.

Production of the film, "Spring Parade in Hagen," has been halted because a mob began to demonstrate against its star, Francisca Gael, on the ground that she is Jewish.

On Tuesday Nazi authorities in Berlin professed ignorance of any plan to oust all non-Aryan newspaper men from the professional roster in Germany, The Associated Press reported. No flat denial that such a move was contemplated was made, however.

* * *

June 2, 1935

CENSORS IN EUROPE EXTEND THEIR SWAY

A Close View of the Men Who Wield the Blue Pencil and Their Methods

Foreign correspondents stationed in some of the countries of Europe have noted in recent weeks a tightening of censorship imposed upon their dispatches. In France, censorship on certain kinds of cable communications has evoked a protest from the Anglo-American Press Association. The censor problem is here set forth from the standpoint of the correspondent.

By WALTER DURANTY

MOSCOW—The long period of peace in Europe which followed the Franco-German War of 1870–1871 succeeded in virtually abolishing censorship, at least so far as foreign correspondents in European countries were concerned. Even imperial Russia was induced by the efforts of the late Melville Stone of The Associated Press to remove in the early years of the century the restrictions which it had formerly imposed upon press cables sent abroad, and it might fairly be said that by 1914 an American correspondent in any of the chief European capitals could report news and express opinions with almost the same freedom as at home.

The war brought a sweeping change; military censorships were immediately established by all the powers engaged, with strict control of telegraph and telephone. The reason initially given was the wish to prevent the transmission abroad of information that might be of value to the enemy. The French were particularly insistent on this point owing to a widespread belief that during the early critical stage of the War of 1870 the German High Command had learned of an important French troop movement from an indiscreet paragraph in the Temps, which had been cabled to Holland and thence to German headquarters, and were thus able to make their dispositions for the great victory of Sedan.

This story has been repeatedly denied by the Temps and I was assured by a high official of the Duexieme Bureau at French headquarters that there was not a word of truth in it. Its effects, however, persisted, and I remember at the very beginning of the war (indeed my first experience of censorship) that a long list issued by the American Embassy in Paris of American travelers in Europe with their wives and families, who had managed to reach the French capital despite the dislocation of traffic due to mobilization of the warring countries, was not merely stopped by the French censor but roused his keen suspicion.

The censor could not understand that any newspaper would spend money on cabling a list of several hundred names and did not disguise his belief that it was really a code message. My explanation that there was hardly a town in America where one or another name would not be a matter of interest completely failed to satisfy him. He tore the dispatch to pieces before my eyes with a curt warning not to attempt anything of the kind in the future.

It was not long, however, before the theory of preventing military information from reaching the enemy gave way to the general purpose of withholding or delaying any information which the authorities did not wish to have published abroad, even when its value to the enemy was nil or so indirect as to be hardly worth consideration. During the middle period of the war the chief functions of censorship seemed to be to cover up errors and prevent anything that savored of criticism.

Toward the end of the war a new principle was introduced. It was tardily realized that foreign press dispatches had not merely a negative but a positive importance—that is to say, of "propaganda" to influence public opinion abroad. This, I may say, is a principle ever-present in the minds of European censors today.

For some ten years after the war the censorship was little more than nominal in the larger cities of Europe, at least so far as foreign correspondents were concerned. They were given to understand that they would be held responsible for anything they might write, but there was little or no delay and interference with the actual transmission of their news. Soviet Russia, was, of course, a striking exception. Foreign correspondents in Moscow were informed that none of their dispatches could be telegraphed unless they had previously been countersigned by a censor. This practice has been maintained until today.

The Soviet censorship originally professed to have no purpose save to prevent the publication of untrue statements about the U. S. S. R., but this was speedily extended to include "malicious" statements and finally what the authorities termed "persistently unfair" statements, meaning any marked tendency to dwell upon the less favorable factors of

Soviet life. The present period of tension throughout Europe has led to the practical application of the same principles in almost all European countries except Britain, Holland, Switzerland and Scandinavia, with the difference that most of the censorships are disguised and covert in operation.

Of the greater European countries the most definite censorships are established in Germany and Italy (for the moment, I except Soviet Russia). While both these countries still officially maintain a pretext that a censorship on foreign telegrams does not exist, in point of fact all press cables are sent before transmission to departments of the German and Italian Foreign Offices, where they are carefully scrutinized.

The general procedure is much the same in both countries. Unwelcome matter is cut out of the cables, and if this seems difficult or undesirable, the cables are simply "delayed" until they have lost their news value, or, in some cases, are quietly but firmly allowed to "sink without trace." In both countries, however, it is possible to evade the censorship by telephoning, a practice followed by all American correspondents in the case of news messages which they think may incur censorial interference. The question of the telephone warrants a paragraph to itself.

In Germany, for instance, the censorship is "justified" by an international convention signed, I think, in 1875 or 1876, which refers in vague terms to the restrictions that a State may place upon the transmission for publication abroad of news from within its boundaries which it considers injurious to its interests. No such convention, however, has ever been enforced in peacetime with regard to international telephone messages, and the development of modern business, particularly concerning finance and transactions on the stock markets, has made it extremely difficult for any State to limit the freedom of speech via telephone save in case of war or really acute crises.

The result has been that the cable censorship becomes almost farcical, even in Soviet Russia, because a foreign correspondent can transmit by telephone, news items which the censor might stop if cabled. Against this the authorities at present can only react by warnings or reprimands; but every correspondent in any of the three countries I have mentioned, and for that matter almost everywhere on the European Continent with the exception of Holland, Switzerland and Scandinavia, knows that he will be "held responsible" for any dispatches which give umbrage to the country to which he is accredited.

The Italians have gone even further with a recent law forbidding the transmission of any news of a military character, whether true or false (this phrase is expressly inserted), until it has received the confirmation of official publication. This, of course, applies to telephone messages no less than to cables, and quite recently the Rome correspondents of two of the largest American news agencies were "severely warned and reprimanded" for sending "premature" news about the transport of Italian troops and war supplies to Africa.

In Russia, too, the transmission of unauthorized military information is a penal offense, although, to the best of my knowledge, there have been no recent instances of anything of the kind. I remember, however, that some years ago an American correspondent horrified the Soviet censor by writing a dispatch which gave detailed information about the armaments, gun calibre, crews and fighting power of the principal units in the Red Navy.

"My God, citizen," cried the censor, alarmed into an un-Bolshevist appeal to Deity, "don't you know that all information about the Red Army and Navy is strictly prohibited? And what is more," he added sternly, "I now request you immediately to give me the name of your informant in this matter or take the consequences, which I assure you will not be light."

"Why, certainly," said the correspondent blandly. "Here is the source of my information," and he produced a book published in Berlin dealing with the navies of the world, in which the Soviet section was headed, "according to figures and details supplied by the Soviet naval attaché in Berlin."

It is worthy of note that nowhere in Europe, so far as I am aware, is there any admitted censorship of mail copy, although it is more or less an open secret that in certain countries both outgoing and incoming mail is subject to investigation. Even the Bolsheviki declare that they do not censor mail copy. The reason presumably is the time element and one may roughly put into the category of mail copy messages transmitted by travelers to be cabled outside the country in which they are written. In such cases, however, the authorities reserve the right to "deal with" any such publication of undesirable information in whatever manner they think fit.

The practice of censorship in Turkey, Poland, Spain and the Balkan States, together with Austria and Hungary, is much the same as in Germany or Italy, but varies in the vigor of its application in accordance with current political conditions at home and abroad. That is to say, the tendency is everywhere toward a more careful scrutiny of foreign news dispatches as European tension grows and to their "delay" or suppression when they contain statements which the local authorities would rather not see published. Everywhere, too, censors are giving greater attention to news of actual or potential military character, although the censorships themselves are still nominally civil.

The Baltic States (including Finland), with France and Czechoslovakia, are in a class by themselves as far as censorship is concerned. While they have no group of censors employed as a regular permanent body, there is, nevertheless a fairly careful check upon foreign news messages.

In France, for instance, cable and radio companies are required to seek instructions from the proper authorities before they transmit certain types of news. I cannot say how far this is a matter of "official order," but I know of a recent case in which a news message dealing with the French fortification system on the northeast frontier was not sent. Inquiry revealed that the transmitting corporation had "felt it desirable" to submit the message in question to "certain authorities," who in turn decided that the message should be withheld. As I say, I do not know how far this is a formal order and my statement on the subject might be officially dis-

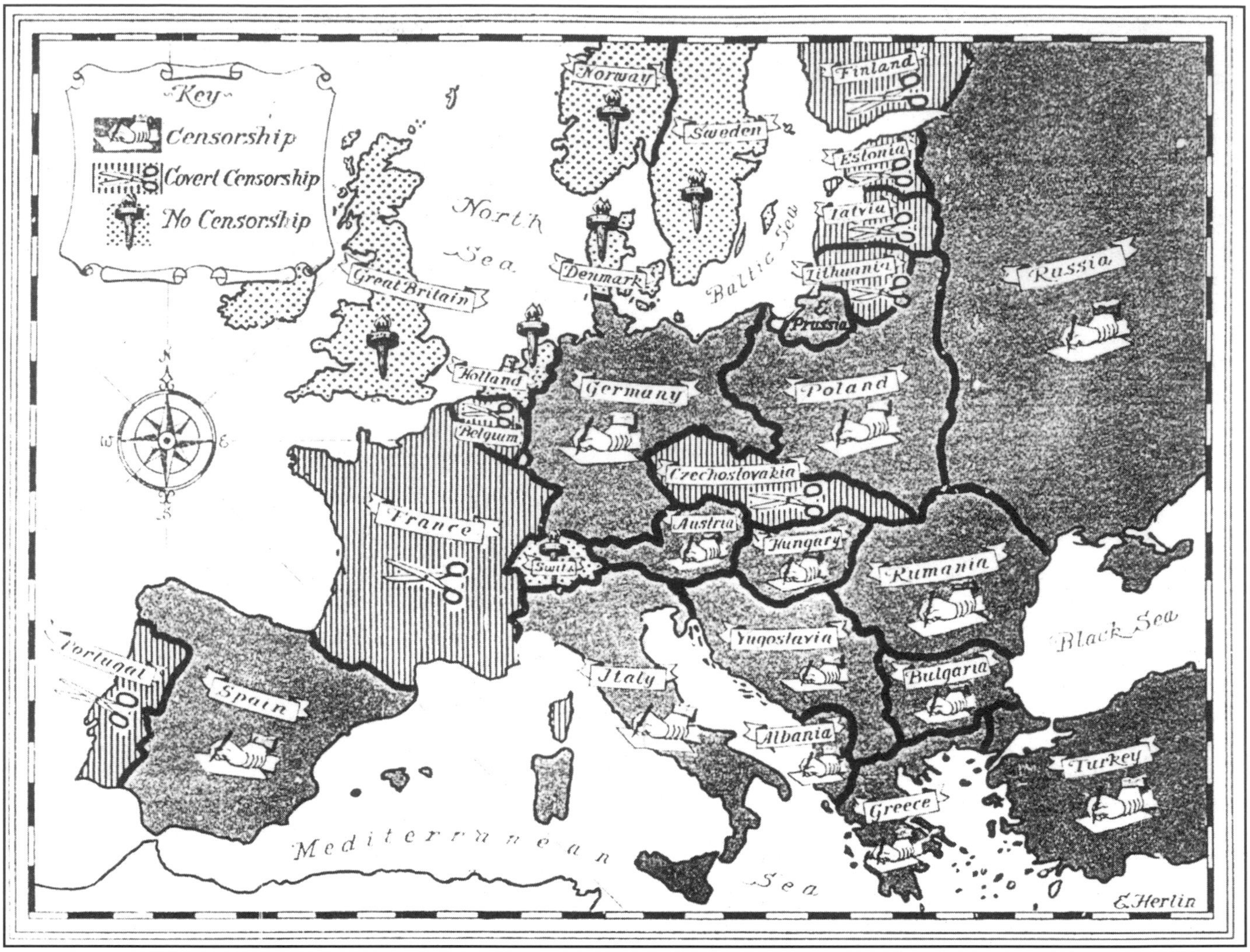

A Censorship Map of Europe—"Most of the Censorships Are Disguised and Covert in Operation."

avowed, but the facts are as I have presented them and I do not hesitate to imply that the same kind of thing might occur in any of the countries mentioned in this last category.

In all probability I have had a wider experience of censorship than any other American correspondent in Europe, because I have worked under censorships, both military and civil, during the greater part of the last twenty-one years. I find that censorships operate in two ways. I am not speaking for the moment of whether they are officially admitted to exist, as in Russia, or exist tacitly, as in Germany and elsewhere, but of how they operate in practice that is to say whether, in one case, they allow the correspondent to know what they are doing or, in the second case, they wield their blue pencils and tactics of delay and suppression without his knowledge.

Clearly all the covert censorships in present day Europe are bound to operate in the second way, because any direct contact with the correspondent would be tantamount to an admission of their formal existence. I believe, however, that the more experienced and long-established foreign reporters in Rome, Berlin and elsewhere do, nevertheless, sometimes have the opportunity of discussing "doubtful" dispatches with the censors and of modifying them in such a way as to meet censorial objections.

From practical experience I am convinced that the interests of the censorship and the correspondent alike are best served when direct contacts are possible. This was the system applied at the "press missions" established by the Allied and American Armies in the latter part of the war, and has been enforced continuously in Soviet Russia.

Under it one visualizes the censorship department as a large room where one or more officials, military or civil, according to circumstances, are constantly present to censor dispatches. If the pressure of news requires it, the officials work in shifts throughout the whole twenty-four hours, or at any rate can always be reached at their homes or elsewhere to censor copy. If news pressure is low the censorship office is open at stated hours with the general proviso that a censor can be reached somewhere in the intervals.

Correspondents either bring in their own dispatches or, as is commonly the case in Moscow, send them by a messenger with a prior understanding that the censor will call a telephone number where the correspondent is to be found in case anything in the message requires discussion. A correspondent versed in the ways of censors usually prefers to send by messenger a dispatch about whose "passing the censor" he has qualms; for should he present it himself he might awaken the censor's suspicions, which always lie close to the surface.

Such correspondents have learned to express the item or items of news, which they think the censor may wish to delete, in such a roundabout way as to have the best chance of passing. In this respect "special" correspondents, who can cable at greater length, have no small advantage over their "agency" colleagues, who are expected to state their facts in the briefest and bluntest manner. Many a time in Moscow I have heard censors accused of partiality for allowing a "special" to send a story that was expunged from agency messages, when the simple truth was that the agencies had stated the fact starkly, whereas the "special" had conveyed his information by application and suggestion instead of direct assertion.

Another useful thing to remember in dealing with censorship, especially those which are apt to prohibit so-called malicious or injurious information, is always to balance any statement of an unfavorable character by another that is favorable. Suppose, for instance, one wishes to say that the Soviet railroad system is the worst in the world. Put like that, by itself, this remark would doubtless cause the censor to reach for his blue pencil. So one writes instead, "Steel and pig iron production this week has broken all records, but railroads continue to lag far behind the program set for them, which indeed is lower than that of any other great power." Thus expressed, the message has every chance of getting by.

Generally speaking, in the open form of censorship one finds that the censors are ready to cooperate in retaining the sense and continuity of the message as a whole, even when they insist that part of it must be cut.

It is the unwritten law of all censorships that nothing may be inserted by the censor without the correspondent's knowledge and agreement, and similarly that a negative may not be cut out in such a way as completely to transform the sense of what is written. But I have been recently informed that some of the covert censorships in Europe are not sufficiently strict in respect to these points.

One of the greatest objections to any censorship is that it causes delay and of course, in the case of covert censorship, a perfectly intolerable uncertainty as to whether messages have been passed or not. Such combined conditions make the work of a reporter impossible, and the consequence is that when, as in a great part of Europe at present, the censorship is covert and one is therefore unable to learn whether a message has been passed or not, at least until the home office has had time to notify the sender, correspondents are practically forced to use the telephone or some other form of evasion about any message they think may be stopped or delayed. When censorships work openly, as in Soviet Russia now or elsewhere in wartime, it is almost always the custom to allow the correspondent to know the censor's verdict without delay.

Actually, I am inclined to question whether censorship of foreign news dispatches—for of course the control of home news and newspapers is quite another matter—really serves the purpose for which it is designed. Facts are stubborn things, as Lenin said, and an ostrich does not hide his tail-feathers by sticking his head in the sand.

Delay in the spreading of unwelcome news may sometimes, of course, be useful; at least it may enable a government or other authority to get out its own verdict of what has happened and thus lessen or soften the effect upon the public opinion of the countries to which news is being sent. Moreover, one can conceive cases where the transmission of military or other information of high moment might have grave or even disastrous consequences; but correspondents do not often have access to material of this nature, and when they do they are generally shrewd enough not to handle it through the usual channels, that is, the censorship, which would not only be sure to suppress it but might initiate awkward inquiries as to where the information had been gathered.

Such rare occasions present a real cas de conscience to the reporter concerned, because he cannot fail to know that in military matters he comes perilously close to the limits of laws against espionage, and that even in civil affairs he may be subject to expulsion from the country where he is living, or even more serious penalties.

* * *

June 23, 1935

IL DUCE STRIKES AT PRESS

But Italian Bans on Foreign Newspapers Are Neither Effective Nor Lasting

By ARNALDO CORTESI
Wireless to The New York Times

ROME, June 22—The outburst of severity on the part of the Italian Government toward the American press—which has found expression in the banning of The New York Times and the expulsion of David Darrah, Chicago Tribune correspondent—follows a number of measures of a similar nature against British journalism.

But whereas the measures against the British newspapers may have been due to the particular Italian state of mind toward the British press in general, the measures against the American papers cannot claim the same justification.

The use of strong methods in dealing with the foreign press is all the more remarkable inasmuch as it was tried early in the Fascist régime but abandoned as soon as its uselessness was realized.

The strange part of these measures, such as the one taken in The New York Times case, is that most authorities here are convinced they are powerless to change the attitude of the newspapers against which the measures are directed. The majority are willing to concede that the banning of newspapers is certain to irritate rather than placate them and will result in no financial loss for them since the number of copies sold in Italy is negligible.

These considerations, however, are not taken into account, the attitude being that the only way at the government's disposal to show disapproval when newspapers print things it does not like is to forbid them to enter Italian territory. The ban is a mere gesture, having as its only object to record the government's protest.

This is borne out by the looseness with which the ban is applied. The New York Times, for instance, was to be barred from Italy from June 12. All copies that have arrived since then, however, have been reaching the writer's office regularly, and other subscribers also have been receiving theirs as usual.

The only difference now is that no copies are on sale at news stands.

It will be interesting to see how long the ban will be maintained. In theory, the measure is to remain in force until the newspaper changes its attitude. In practice, however, such a ban is usually lifted in a fortnight or three weeks.

* * *

July 14, 1935

A MUZZLED PRESS SERVES NAZI STATE

By OTTO D. TOLISCHUS

BERLIN—One of the more caustic witticisms circulating in National Socialist Germany concerns Adolf Hitler, "Fuehrer" to all Germans and "Herr German Reich Chancellor" to the diplomatic corps, who arrived at the Pearly Gates, demanding admittance.

"Well, what good did you do in the world?" St. Peter asked.

"Why," Hitler replied, "I united the German people, abolished all unemployment and made everybody happy."

St. Peter, being a skeptic, sent an angel to investigate. The angel soon returned and reported that he had gone into the highways and byways of Germany and talked to all sorts of people, but that, sad to say, he was unable to corroborate Hitler's claims; rather the contrary.

Whereupon Hitler growled: "What did he want to go snooping around for! Why didn't he read the newspapers!"

Nobody in Germany, not even the national socialists, denies the justice of this satire on the German press, which is the point of the jest. The German newspapers, ever strong in argument and weak in information, have ceased to present a true or complete picture of their country and have, in consequence, ceased to be the main source of news for the masses. Like the Bolshevist and the Fascist press, they have lost whatever independence they formerly possessed and have been reduced to publicity organs of the government, forced in news and comment to serve the propaganda of the powers that be—to sing their praises and cover up their mistakes.x

In the words of Walther Funk, State Secretary in the Propaganda Ministry, the German press is no longer a "barrel organ out of which everybody is permitted to squeeze whatever melodies he likes, but a highly sensitive and far-sounding instrument or orchestra on which and with which only those shall play who know how, and in whose hands the Fuehrer himself has placed the conductor's baton."

To the Western world, where freedom of the press is a sacred heritage, this is a strange doctrine, sufficient in itself to pass final judgment on the German system. But this judgment is beside the point in a land which spurns it—a land which, having rejected Western liberalistic civilization in favor of a Neo-Germanic Kultur, proceeds from wholly different premises and seeks to build a new world on entirely different foundations.

Like everything else in Germany, the German press must be viewed from the perspective of the totalitarian State and the National Socialist "Weltanschauung." The first, by right of might, controls every individual and every field of activity, and tolerates any of them only in so far as they are useful to the State. The second, mystic and semi-religious, is designed to mobilize behind that State those positive spiritual forces which make up national morale, and among which the call of the blood is the most important.

Together, they envisage a Germanic Empire of power and glory, in which the individual and his personal rights are lost in the mighty onward march of the race, and which creates its own morality according to its needs.

It is a vision not without grandeur, and with a magnetic attraction for most Germans—including journalists—that is more powerful than physical force, testing the cohesion of more than one European state with German minorities. If, in practice, the totalitarian state proves to be Adolf Hitler and his aides, whose xword is its constitution and its law, and National Socialism is what they say it is, this merely enhances the mystic pull of both. At any rate, this state is not an organ of the German people, rather the German people are organs of this state, and so are all their institutions—the school, the church, the university, and the press, in the same manner as the army and the police.

In church and university, the theory is still struggling for supremacy, but in the press it is 95 per cent reality. It has not been achieved without arousing reading resistance among the German people. The effect of the National Socialist rule on the publishing business is illustrated by the following figures:

Between March, 1933, and March, 1934, according to postoffice reports, the total number of newspapers and periodicals dropped from 11,328 to 9,426, a decrease of 16.8 per cent. The periodicals suffered most, but the total number of newspapers published more than three times a week also dropped from 3,827 to 3,245. The latest count, which includes all weekly newspapers but is not strictly comparable with the postoffice count (the latter listing all trade papers), registered 2,623 newspapers toward the end of 1934, with a total paid circulation of 15,019,400. This marks a circulation drop of 1,668,145 since the Spring of 1934.

One reason for the decline of the journals was the destruction of the "Marxist" press. As against this, the National

European

Propaganda Minister Goebbels Meets the Press. Its Duty He Declares, Is "Not to Inform but to Spur Onward."

Socialist press had at first a rapid rise and filled in part the circulation vacuum. So rapid was the rise that many Nazi papers, then still in the hands of prominent National Socialist leaders, were tempted to plunge into enormous plant expansion. Soon, however, they were caught, not only by the general circulation slump but also by a perceptible drift of the reading public to the older "co-ordinated" papers—all the more painful because with it went the advertiser. As a result, many Nazi papers got into difficulties and the party had to come to their rescue.

As an illustration, the Angriff, founded by Dr. Paul Joseph Goebbels, Reich Minister of Popular Enlightenment and Propaganda, dropped from 94,000 in December, 1933, to 53,400 in December, 1934. It then merged with the Nazi Labor paper Der Deutsche, which had a circulation of 150,000, but the combined paper was 101,117 in March this year and dropped to 96,839 in April. The Essener National Zeitung, formerly General Hermann Goering's personal organ, dropped from 183,857 in January, 1934, to 135,859 this April.

Even the Voelkischer Beobachter, principal and official party paper published by Max Amann, President of the Reich Press Chamber, has a circulation of only 182,901 in Berlin and a total circulation in the Reich of 362,784. In December it had slumped to 336,527, but later gained through a promotion drive, behind which was put the combined force of the government and party machine.

When the whirlwind of the National Socialist revolution ceased tossing the German press about, it had left only two kinds of papers—the National Socialist and the "coordinated" press. Both approach, in ownership, management and personnel, the character of a State press. The first is published in the main by the National Socialist party, which is by law part of the State; the second, though for the most part still in private hands, is under such rigid State control that State ownership would make little difference.

These two kinds of newspapers constitute the "orchestra" with which the totalitarian State plays its music under the direction of Dr. Goebbels. He controls the radio and the films as well, but the press is the most important. As a revolutionary fighting weapon, the spoken word has proved superior to the written, but in the day-to-day business of government the press is indispensable.

The music for the daily press concert is written on the theory that Germany, meaning the National Socialist State, is at war against a world full of enemies—open enemies abroad and sneaking enemies at home—who must be fought on the principle that attack is the best defense. With drums and trumpets, therefore, the German press is marched into battle every day, in the approved style of war propaganda. News is carefully sifted to stiffen home morale and to avoid giving aid or comfort to the enemy. Criticism of any kind is outlawed. And he is the best man who flays the foe most and cheers his own cause loudest. The newspapers exist not for their own sake or for the sake of the public, but only for the service they render the State.

In conducting this program the attitude of the National Socialists is disarmingly frank—not unmixed with cynicism. The name of the "Propaganda Ministry" speaks volumes in itself; but beyond that Dr. Goebbels, in speeches, has scorned to dissemble his thoughts. The duty of the newspaper is, in his view, "not to inform, but to shake up and spur onward," without indulgence in that "liberal objectivity which seeks to be equally just to friend or foe, to one's own and foreign nations." On the other hand, "the right to criticize belongs to the National Socialist party alone and I deny it to all others."

In this spirit the press is instructed and supplied with material. The material comes in the main through the sole and semi-official news agency, born of the consolidation of the former Telegraphen Union and the old Wolff Agency and now known as the German News Agency. Since almost all of its news must be subjected to careful scrutiny for reasons of state, it lays no claim to speed, but since it is alone in the field neither it nor its clients can be beaten on news even if it is a day late.

Instructions are issued at a daily press conference in the Propaganda Ministry, but are supplemented with running orders which may designate even the type, the headline and the position of some individual item. Moreover, in times of stress, the orders may change constantly—to play up this, to play down that, to eliminate another thing—with the result that the German editor works always with his heart in his mouth. For a slip may cost his livelihood.x

In desperation, therefore, many editors simply go the way of least resistance, print the official or semi-official news according to instructions and renounce all creative work of their own, except perhaps to be particularly devoted to the ruling powers. But this, again, produces a deadly uniformity which not only kills the newspaper but also defeats the purposes of official propaganda. Which, in turn, may bring down on the harassed editorial heads another official thunder-bolt.

"It is asserted that the press is too uniform and dull," said Dr. Goebbels. "That is not the reader's fault; the journalist

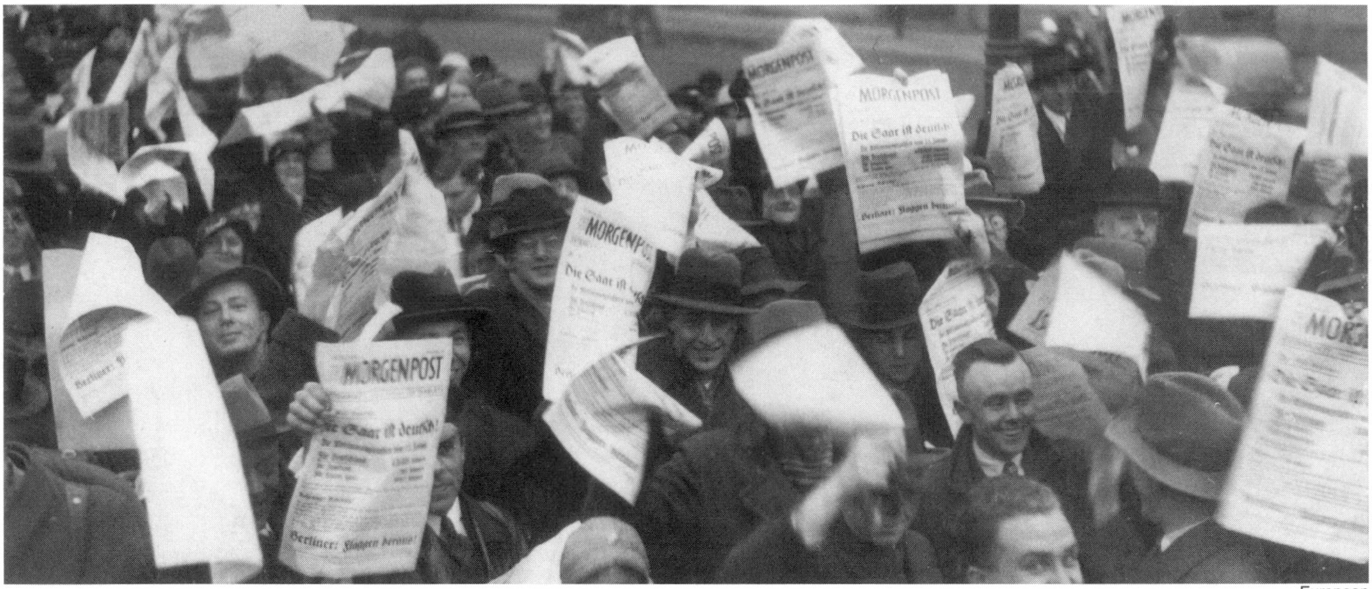

European

"Spurring Onward"—A Big Circulation Day

should be a little brighter." In fact, he went so far as to denounce the "lap dog press," called on the newspaper men to show more courage and decreed that the press should be "monoform in its will, but polyform in expressing that will."

However, any paper that stepped out of the ranks was suppressed, and Ehm Welk, editor of The Ullstein Gruene Post, who waxed mildly sarcastic over this exhortation, went to a concentration camp, while others who committed similar offenses fared only little better.

Thus the newspapers continued "uniform and dull." Papers died, circulations dropped and the public found other means of satisfying the universal craving for news that makes the whole world kin. Those who could, read foreign newspapers, some of which attained remarkable circulations in Germany. At various intervals The London Times was credited with selling 30,000 copies in Germany daily, The Paris Temps and The Manchester Guardian 35,000 each, The Baseler Nachrichten 50,000 to 60,000. But as foreign papers are constantly banned, their annual circulation in Germany is problematical. A small class is reached by illegal publications, usually Communist pamphlets disguised as innocent advertising distributed surreptitiously, or sent by mail anonymously to members of the army, the police and Nazi organizations.

Most important, however, is the "spoken newspaper"—that word-of-mouth transmission of news which seems irrepressible, even though it makes up in abundance what it lacks in accuracy. "Rumor mongering" is perhaps the most widespread crime in Germany today, which no punishment can curb. So prevalent is it that the official organ of the Reich Press Association published the following remarkable admission:

"Alongside of the printed, written and read newspaper, there has reappeared again the old oral newspaper. Beyond the visible reader of the printed paper there has formed a class of invisible readers of the unprinted newspaper. That is not the fault of the reader; the newspaper is to blame. For the newspaper is no longer a mirror of the times. It meets its epoch only by commands, not questions.

"The man who lives in this epoch and feels the many complicated problems deeply, is left without response in his many cares and needs, his joys and questions. He would like to know more, learn the connection between events, read more of the things that affect his life. But to his questions the paper has no answer. The paper does not question any more. It permits no distance, no individual judgment."

This indictment must be read in the light of the fact that the biggest domestic struggle in Germany today, namely the church conflict that is wrenching the consciences of millions, finds no echo in the press, forbidden to mention it.

But the author of this courageous indictment suggests no solution, and it may be doubted whether he knew one. For the solution that seems obvious to an American newspaper mind, namely to print more news, meets not only official handicaps, but also the opposition of the German press itself. This solution was, in fact, suggested by Dr. Hjalmar Schacht, the Reichsbank president, whose middle names are Horace Greeley.

"The influence of the newspaper," he said, "shrinks in proportion in which it expresses opinions and judgments. It should, therefore, confine itself to the reporting of facts, and at most comment on the facts." For this statement he was attacked so hotly that he beat a quick retreat.

The German press has never been a news-press, but an opinion-press, which cultivated the long leading article and looked down upon the mere "reporter." It always was the instrument of some party, cause or "Weltanschauung," and its makers were crusaders and politicians before they were newspaper men. The news-press was reproached for degrading to a business what should be a great calling for cultural and political leadership. The decisive importance of accurate information as the foundation of democratic government was

Underwood & Underwood

Searching a Suspect for Outlawed Newspapers

never recognized. Truth is always subjective, in the German mind, and words were invented, not as means of communication, but to cause action—that is, command.

Freedom of the press means different things in different countries. In Germany it always has meant freedom of propaganda. By concentrating on propaganda, the German press not only destroyed its own basic foundation, but also the foundations of the democratic State. It propagandized the German people into so many factions that they fell, like ripe fruit, into the hands of the National Socialists.

This provides, at least in German eyes, a certain justification for the destruction of press freedom. "Absolute freedom of the press never existed," says Dr. Goebbels, pointing out that German newspapers always served some party or other special interest, and that the working newspaper man had to conform to the policy of his paper. If the press is merely a propaganda organ, then, to the National Socialist mind, it is logical that the totalitarian State should monopolize it for its own purposes.

Today the German press is governed by two fundamental laws designed to make the National Socialist spirit supreme in the publishing world. The first, proclaimed on Oct. 4, 1933, and pronounced by Dr. Goebbels as "the most modern press law in the world," applies to the working journalists, called "Schiftleiter" or "writing directors." It makes the journalists semi-State officials and semi-independent of their employers in respect to their writings, for which they are answerable to the State. This, said Dr. Goebbels, is true freedom of the press, "for it is better to serve the State than an employer."

The law provides that only those shall contribute to German newspapers or political periodicals through news or pictures who are German citizens in good standing, above 21 years of age, possessing at least one year's training, and not Jewish or married to Jews as defined by the Civil Service Law. This excludes all Jews and all those with Jewish grandmothers, and under this provision hundreds of the best-known German newspaper men have been drummed out of the profession.

Those qualifying are licensed by registration in a list of the profession kept by the Reich Press Association, a State institution. Anybody who does journalistic work without being on this list is punishable by imprisonment or fine.

The second law consists of decrees issued April 24, 1935, by President Amann, of the Reich Press Chamber. These decrees proclaim the right of way for the National Socialist press, where necessary by suppression of any "coordinated" competition, and for the rest provide that even "coordinated" newspapers shall be published under strict regulations regarding ownership.

The law does not apply to the National Socialist party, which under Amann's supervision publishes most of the National Socialist newspapers, and which enjoys the further privileges of tax exemptions for its real estate, official patronage in advertising and active support and promotion of its publications by all governmental officials, including the mail men, who otherwise are threatened with dismissal.

According to talk common in Berlin, Amann first demanded 30,000,000 marks from Dr. Schacht to buy up dangerous competitors. When Dr. Schacht refused, Amann passed his decrees to eliminate "unhealthy" competition in opposition, it is said, to both Dr. Schacht and Dr. Goebbels.

These decrees, it is expected, will leave the most prominent German newspapers, like the Berliner Tageblatt, the Frankfurter Zeitung, the Koelnische Zeitung, the Deutsche Allgemeine Zeitung and the Lokal Anzeiger alive, for one reason because the Foreign Office needs them for their influence on foreign public opinion. The decrees are supposed to be directed mainly against the Catholic press and the provincial news press, the so-called "General-Anzeiger Presse," which is the most prosperous and dangerous competitor of the Nazi press.

As self-made men, the National Socialists worship success and declare it to be the measure of all things and methods. But as newspaper publishers and controllers, their success is subject to grave qualifications.

* * *

July 13, 1936

AUSTRIA CREATES STRICT PRESS CURB

Threatens to Expel Foreign Correspondents Who Send Out False Reports

ILLEGAL POLITICS BANNED

Emergency 'Law for Defense of the State' Is Similar to Decrees in Germany and Italy

By G. E. R. GEDYE
Wireless to The New York Times

VIENNA, July 12—It is perhaps something more than a coincidence that the announcement of the agreement with Nazi Germany should coincide with the proclamation by the Austrian Government of an extremely severe "law for the defense of the State" as an emergency measure, which means it does not have to be passed by the Legislative Council.

The law follows lines similar to those of measures in Germany and Italy. After providing severe penalties up to ten years for political activities of various forbidden organizations a section contains a series of threats of expulsion of foreign correspondents.

Any foreigner, it is declared, will be expelled, in addition to suffering imprisonment up to three months, for spreading "false reports calculated to cause public uneasiness or to influence foreign public opinion in a manner unfavorable to Austria without sufficient grounds for believing it to be true."

The same penalties are applicable to any one who publishes a forecast of events under similar conditions.

The same penalties are provided for a foreigner who "in any way whatever gives support to any secret news service which is carried on to the disadvantage of Austria."

It would seem that every foreign correspondent in Austria who is not prepared to run these risks of imprisonment and expulsion will be virtually confined to official sources of information, since it is impossible for the most conscientious investigator to establish the truth of every report or to guarantee every forecast on political developments.

Past experience has convinced foreign correspondents in Vienna that to apply to officials for confirmation of serious political reports is to meet with misleading answers in cases where it may suit the régime not to reveal its hand.

* * *

April 18, 1937

BALKAN RULERS TIGHTEN CENSORSHIP

Special Correspondence, The New York Times

BELGRADE—In the Balkan lands, where all governments now have openly assumed varying degrees of dictatorship, the popular strength of a government can be judged inversely by the strictness of its press censorship. It is interesting to notice, therefore, that just at present the censorship has been tightened up in every one of the Balkan countries.

In Greece it is stricter than ever before. Foreign correspondents are especially muzzled. They are not allowed to send even some things which are allowed in the local press. They are held personally responsible even for their papers' editorial articles. Not only is the local press censored but papers are forced to print articles favorable to the government.

In Bulgaria the press censorship has been greatly strengthened in recent months. No criticism of the plans for a new corporate organization of the State or of the government's foreign policy is allowed. In Yugoslavia the Stoyadinovitch government, in order to destroy the influence of the former dictator General Zhivkovitch and his henchman Yevtitch, resorted to the most democratic slogans. From Premier down, all declared themselves in favor of restoring freedom of the press. Yet local journalists say that now, after two years, the censorship is more intolerable than ever. Even the "verbal newspaper"—articles read by prominent journalists on Sunday afternoons before an audience in Belgrade—which was allowed only after close censorship, has now been banned.

Local journalists develop remarkable ingenuity in getting around the censorship. There is the classical case of the Slovene newspaper which printed a picture puzzle for children on its front page. Any child could decipher it to read "Don't go to the polls," but it passed the censor and had its effect.

* * *

May 2, 1937

GERMANY HAS REGIMENTED HER PRESS

By OTTO D. TOLISCHUS

BERLIN—The Apollo Theatre in Nuremberg witnessed a remarkable scene recently. On the stage, perched precariously on high stools, was a group of young and old men contorting their bodies and their faces in a desperate effort to imitate a musical comedy dance. It was not a graceful sight as they gingerly shook their legs while trying to preserve their balance and merely succeeded in making a spectacle of themselves. But it was fun for the bald, stocky man in front who directed them and for an audience of girls who snickered at the exhibition.

The "dancers" on the high stools were the dramatic critics of the Nuremberg newspapers. The snickering girls in the audience were members of a musical comedy show the critics had criticized. The bald, stocky man was Julius Streicher, National Socialist boss of the town, who was "educating" the critics in the new journalistic discipline, and incidentally giving an impressive demonstration of how he makes the German press dance to his tune.

Now Streicher, who as a former grade-school teacher learned the value of the drastic manner in "educating" the German people on such topics as the Jews, Christ's Nordic descent, meatless diet and nature healing, is an enfant terrible even to many National Socialists, and his latest exhibition drew a mild remonstrance from the head of the German Press Association, who objected to "unsuitable educational methods which impair the public esteem of the journalistic profession." But Streicher merely demonstrates in public what is going on behind the scenes, and his demonstration remains symbolic for the position of the German press under the National Socialist régime.

This position becomes all the more interesting, first, because of the frequent attacks by the German press on other countries, which have brought several diplomatic protests, including one from the United States against "coarse and indecent" aspersions on the American Government, American institutions and American womanhood; second, because, according to Dr. Joseph Goebbels, Minister of Popular Enlightenment and Propaganda, the German press is ruled by the most modern press laws in existence and a great campaign is under way, in the name of international peace and respect for the heads of States, to force other countries to adopt similar laws.

Whatever else the German press is, however, it is not a free press, and to say so is no longer a punishable offense in Germany. Even the German Supreme Court came to this conclusion when, in overruling a sentence by a lower court, it ruled that the German press was not a "free" press as that

From the Painting by K. Dielitz.

"The Nazi State finds its moral ideal not in the Christian saint but in the heroes of Richard Wagner's opera world"—Siegfried slaying the dragon.

term is understood in "liberalistically governed States." It is an "ordered" press—a controlled press—which, to cite the court's decision, "the National Socialist government views as a medium for the education of the national community in the spirit of National Socialism and as a means of leadership in the service of the State and nation, expecting the press not to oppose the decisions of the government but to support them and to try to bring them to concrete results."

According to Captain Wilhelm Weiss, Storm Troop group commander and head of the Reich Press Association, the German journalist now gets his instructions "directly from the State," and "the press policy of the National Socialist State is therefore merely a continuation of National Socialist State policy into the field of publicity."

Dr. Goebbels himself summarized the situation more succinctly when he said that the press was a piano for him to play on, and Walther Funk, his State secretary, used the simile of an orchestra performing under the direction of the Fuehrer's appointees.

After such authoritative declarations, it would be discourteous to doubt that the German press has ceased to represent the necessarily diversified opinions of the German people and has become an organ of the National Socialist government, expressing solely the views of that government and serving its propaganda.

Functionally there has been no great change. The German press was always an opinion press rather than a news press, and fighting for causes and ideologies was always considered a nobler journalistic enterprise than gathering impartial information on which readers could base their own judgment. Under the republican régime the German newspaper fought for many causes and many ideologies, and a discerning perusal of them gave one a fair picture of German public opinion. But in the

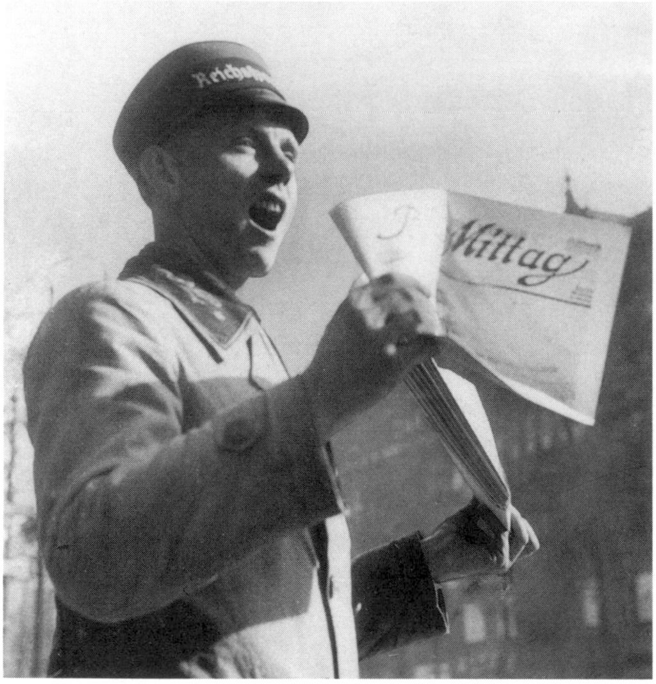

Shouting the headlines of one of Berlin's afternoon papers.

misapplied democracy of the republic all causes and all ideologies automatically turned into political parties, and the newspapers championing them just as automatically turned into party sheets, in doing which they also dug their own grave because they contributed to the political disintegration that gave the National Socialist movement its great chance.

The National Socialist State, being totalitarian, is a jealous State which tolerates no other gods besides itself. As soon as it had seized power, therefore, it also seized the German press, together with the radio, art, literature and science with the school, the stage and the pulpit, and sought to "coordinate" them all into championing only one cause, one ideology, and one party—namely, its own. In the performance of that task the German press remains as "independent" and as "free" as it likes. This side of National Socialism, "liberty of the press," reigns unrestrained, and there is no such thing as being too National Socialistic. In all essentials the German press shares the fate of the Bolshevist and the Fascist press, and woe to him who falls afoul the party line.

The actual control over the German press rests on an ideological, a legal and an administrative system, behind each of which stands the force of the State against which the individual is helpless. The ideological basis is a strange blend of social, biological and religious concepts spanning the German development from primitive tribes to a modern nation. It carries a powerful political appeal in the vision of a mighty German Reich founded on German, or more accurately Teutonic, racial unity, to hamper which is treason; and it finds its moral ideal not in the Christian saint but in the heroes of Richard Wagner's opera world. Among these heroes which represent the two sides of the German character, it has not chosen the courtly and radiant but in dependent and almost individualistic Siegfried. Rather it exalts the "grim Hagen," whose fanatical loyalty to his King-Fuehrer is more in line with what the National Socialist Fuehrer State needs, and who is therefore propagated as the hero of the German youth—although his loyalty also led Hagen into murdering Siegfried, and his "heroic" manner at King Atilla's court brought disaster upon his friends, his enemies and himself.

To understand this ideology, rooted deep in German subconsciousness, is to understand much that is otherwise inexplicable in the German scheme of things. It is to the German what the classless State is to the Russian Bolshevik, what the glory that was Rome is to the Italian Fascist and what the New Deal is to the New Dealers: it rationalizes compulsion and mobilizes that necessary support without which the system would collapse of its own weight—even though its practical application still wrenches the German conscience.

In practice, it amounts to this: Adolf Hitler issues the orders and his subordinates, the "little Hitlers," carry them out according to their lights—or prejudices.

The new legal basis for the German press has been created in five principal decrees which successively expanded the new rulers' arbitrary powers over the press and therewith furnished an instructive, example of how an authoritarian régime works. While they made the press an organ of State, they did not make it a State press, such as the Bolshevist press, nor even a straight party press. The German press still divides itself into the "official party press," which is largely owned and published by the party, and the "coordinated" press published by private enterprise under rigid supervision. The decrees are:

(1) The "Decree for the Protection of the German People," of Feb. 4, 1933, which provided for the suppression of publications likely to "endanger public security and order." In making this decree palatable, Hitler himself assured the nation that he was opposed to gagging the press and did not want to prevent "objective criticism," but that the unobjective and insulting methods of the press hostile to the new régime had forced the government to act.

(2) The "Decree for the Protection of State and People," issued Feb. 28, 1933, immediately after the Reichstag fire, which suspended the entire constitutional bill of rights, including press freedom.

(3) The decree of Sept. 22, 1933, which established the Reich Kultur Chamber and therewith introduced the "Fuehrer principle" into all German cultural activities, including the press. The Reich Kultur Chamber is a corporation under the presidency of Dr. Goebbels, who appoints the presidents and directorates of its subordinate bodies, of which the Reich Press Chamber is one. The Reich Press Chamber consists of the Reich Press Association, the compulsory organization for all working journalists, and the various publishers' organizations.

(4) The "Schriftleiter," or Journalists' Decree, of Oct. 4, 1933, which created the new discipline for the journalistic profession. It was modeled on the Fascist press law and converted the press into a "public institution," and the writing journalists into semi-State officials, "independent" of their publishers or private interests and responsible for their writings solely to the

Times Wide World and Pix.

Julius Streicher, Nazi boss of Nuremberg, makes the press of the town dance to his tune.

State. This, said Dr. Goebbels, is true freedom of the press because "it is better to serve the State than an employer." The decree obligated the working journalists to keep out of the press, among other things, everything likely "to weaken the strength of the German Reich at home or abroad, its unity, armament, kultur or economy, or to violate the religious feelings of others."

An honor court supervises the observance of this law and any journalist found guilty of violating the law can be punished by fine or imprisonment, and by expulsion from the profession.

(5) The decrees issued April 24, 1935, by Max Amann, president of the Reich Press Chamber, Hitler's top sergeant during the war, first business director of the National Socialist party, publisher of Hitler's book, "Mein Kampf," and supervisor of the entire National Socialist press. These decrees fix the conditions under which non-party publishers may continue in business and specifically provide that non-Nazi newspapers may be suppressed in favor of the party press.

The principle of the journalistic supervision is not censorship in the sense that all newspaper copy must be submitted for approval, but rather censorship at the news source combined with "personal responsibility" of the journalist and editor for what they write or print. The government's instructions are issued to the press at a daily press conference in the Propaganda Ministry.

This conference is secret and is more remarkable for what the press is ordered to suppress than for what it is ordered to print. In fact, a list of the suppression orders is far more enlightening than what appears in the press; but to reveal this list is treason for which at least one German newspaper man was sentenced to life imprisonment.

The bulk of the news is likewise supplied by more or less official sources, by the German News Bureau, which is the official agency and which also transmits any supplementary instructions issued after the press conference, and by several additional "correspondences," issued by National Socialist organizations, and one by the Foreign Office. They do not lay claim to either speed or completeness, but being official they are safe to print. Private and independent news gathering organizations are practically non-existent, except for technical topics, because private inquisitiveness is not encouraged in the Third Reich. xCriticism, even of art and drama, is forbidden, and too close an analysis of the official reports may, and sometimes does, get a newspaper xman into trouble. Even official speeches can be published only in the properly edited official text.

The main task of the German journalist is therefore "not to inform but to shake up and spur onward," to write powerful editorials and interpretations of the official news supporting everything done by the German Government, the National Socialist party, and their agents; to compose dithyrambic

Headlines of the German press (above left) reflect the will of Der Fuehrer as formulated by Joseph Goebbels, Minister of Propaganda (above). Goebbels's formula for a good press is: "Monoform in will, but polyform in expressing that will."

accounts of their activities; to whip up popular enthusiasm for them; to cover up their mistakes and shortcomings; to dispel all doubt in their omnipotent wisdom or integrity; and to squelch all their foreign and domestic enemies. He must neither express nor report independent opinions, nor seek to initiate policies, but he must have the "courage to one-sidedness" where his own government is concerned while demanding objectivity and understanding from all others. His principle must be: "Right or wrong, my country!" without attention to any modifying suffixes or prefixes of either Stephen Decatur or Germany's own honored scion, Carl Schurz. And the same rules apply to the German correspondents abroad.

Inevitably this policy has not merely suppressed German public opinion, but has also cut off the German people from all real information about the state of their affairs, and any discussion of their cares and troubles, except for the government's faits accompli and its "authoritative" interpretation of them. There is no news about the country's real political, economic and financial situation except assurances that all is well, and even the official reports are so oracular that few can understand them. There is nothing in the press about the church struggle that is shaking the German soul except praise for new governmental church decrees and attacks on alleged clerical enemies of the State. There was much in it about the German protest against Mayor La Guardia's attack on Hitler, but nothing about the American rebuke of German attacks on the United States. Nothing is said about German volunteers in Spain; all the Spanish war news come from the Franco side.

But this result is just what the government desires. Germany, it holds, is at war with a world full of enemies, struggling for her place in the sun, and the entire German people have been enlisted as soldiers in this war and must submit to military régime. "Theirs not to reason why, theirs but to do and die!"

This policy has produced a constant outcry against the "dullness and uniformity" of the German press, which threatens to impair its usefulness as a propaganda organ. The "spoken newspaper"—that is, rumors and word-of-mouth reports, sometimes of the wildest kind—is assuming a greater importance for the masses than the printed newspapers, despite prosecution of the rumor mongers, and the upper classes are getting their information more and more from the foreign press, which is attaining remarkable circulation in Germany despite constant prohibitions.

This development is so widespread that the powers that be are becoming alarmed about it and are beginning to spur the newspapers onward to be "brighter," and "more courageous," and not to turn into a "lap-dog press." But since the newspapers dare not print "brighter" and "more courageous" news, they must seek an outlet for their brightness and courage in extolling the National Socialist régime and smiting its enemies. In that, there is neither rule nor limit, and therein the newspapers are also able to carry out Dr Goebbels's formula for a good press: "Monoform in will, but polyform in expressing that will."

Whatever difference still exists among the individual German newspapers lies, therefore, not so much in control or in policy as in the tone, which also forms the principal difference between the "coordinated" and the official National Socialist press. Whereas the former "bourgeois" press continues to stand on dignity, and seeks to explain the strenuousness of the times with philosophic and historic necessities, the National Socialist press, priding itself on being a "fighting press," assumes a more heroic tone which often smacks of the barrack room. When it comes to flaying Jews, Bolsheviki, uncoordinated Germans and foreign critics it can even talk the language of the fish market, as was shown in the controversy with America.

The havoc this system has wrought among the organs of public intelligence is perhaps best illustrated by the Nazis' own figures. The number of newspapers, according to Amann's announcement at the last Nuremberg party congress, dropped from 3,250 before 1933 to 2,300 during the first quarter of 1936. The latest newspaper manual lists 2,671 newspapers, but it includes the so-called, "head sheets," which are merely different names for the same newspaper.

A comparison of total newspaper circulation is more difficult because there was no circulation check before 1933. The total as given by the newspapers themselves was 26,000,000, but it included a lot of circulation hopes. Now the newspapers must make public the number of copies printed, and Amann put the total press run of German newspapers at 19,700,000 during the first quarter of 1936. This would mark a considerable recovery from the 15,019,400 to which the press run had dropped toward the end of 1934, and this recovery is confirmed by the turnover figures of the printing business. Part of it may be due to high-pressure promotion drives under government auspices which sought to scare the people into reading newspapers lest they miss the new decrees regulating their lives and thereby incur punishment; but most of it seems to be due to compulsory circulation created by instructions to all officials and schools to read the party press.

Even that total seems meager for a nation of 68,000,000 when compared with the nearly 70,000,000 newspaper circulation of the United States and the 37,000,000 in Soviet Russia. However, while Dr. Goebbels would naturally prefer to have as large a newspaper circulation as possible, Amann's primary interest is to reserve whatever circulation there is for the National Socialist press—not, he declared, because of any financial considerations, but solely in the interest of the education of the German people. In fact, publishers so unaware of their cultural duties as to be in the publishing business for business reasons are drummed out of it.

In the pursuit of these aims, and through the dictatorial powers at his disposal, Amann has already eliminated all dangerous competition, has taken control of the famous publishing houses of Ullstein and Mosse, has smashed the two principal "bourgeois" newspaper chains of Girardet and Huck, and has cast his eyes on Alfred Hugenberg's Scherl concern and other still prosperous publishing enterprises.

Incidentally, he is also rapidly creating a National Socialist monopoly of the successful publishing business in the Third Reich and is making his own Franz Eher Publishing Company one of the biggest in the world.

Other Countries

August 3, 1919

FRENCH MOVIE CENSORSHIP

Only Those Depicting Facts or Actual Happenings Exempted

PARIS, Aug. 2—Censorship by the Ministry of Public Instruction of all motion picture films, except those representing facts or actual happenings, is provided for by a decree printed in the Journal Officiel today. The approval of the Ministry must be obtained before the pictures may be shown in public.

A committee of thirty was appointed by the Ministry to examine scenarios and films. The cost of the examination must be borne by the producers, according to a fixed scale.

The decree does not affect measures which may be taken by local authorities along the same lines in the interest of public order.

* * *

May 16, 1920

MOTION PICTURES IN JAPAN

Dr. Segeru Numata, who is in this country making an investigation of motion pictures for the Japanese Government, writes of motion-picture conditions in Japan in the current issue of The Bulletin of the Affiliated Committees for Better Films. His article in part follows.

"It is strictly prohibited by order to impair the dignity of the Imperial House of Japan or to plot a rebellion against it. It is prohibited to harm the national constitution of Japan; to raise internal disturbances; to overthrow the Government; to capture the Japanese land; to take a contemptuous attitude against Japan or foreign countries or to betray Japan. It is prohibited to disturb the social constitution of Japan; to give motion picture audiences impressions of sabotage, strikes and disturbances in connection with them, or the like, or to disturb for Japanese the love for the beautiful customs and manners of Japan. It is prohibited to present the systematic process of crimes or offenses which have a deleterious effect upon public morals. This includes obscenity, adultery (double or single), or the like; gambling, lotteries or the like; cruelty, inhumanity, atrocity or the like; instigation of abortion or the like; duel or the like, and the real conditions of demi-mondaine or the like.

"Punishment for the violation of these rules is a sentence of at least twenty days' Imprisonment or a fine of at least 20 yen.

"The Japanese Board of Censors belongs to the Police Department of every prefecture in Japan where one or two men can accept or reject any pictures they wish. This board is under the Police Department functioning under each local government. It is a part, however, of the Imperial Interior Department. It regulates, both on the administrative and judicial sides, the producer, the exhibitor, the audience and others connected with motion pictures as well as the films by inspection.

"I am now going to try to criticise the Japanese Board of Censors as I have seen them. It is a governmental establishment and so the inspection is bureaucratic and dogmatic.

Sometimes it is subject to any active and powerful political party and clan ascendency. It often, therefore, disregards social conscience and even impairs the public welfare in its social tendency or as affected by the general trend of the world. The censors are judicial officers and hold closely to the individual words or phrases of the application of the imperial law without taking in the meaning of the whole picture and its motive. We have no experts on motion pictures among the censors, nor any of the representatives, who have special knowledge or talent in our board in Japan. Our censors, therefore, have not the preparation to inspect the pictures at all. The Japanese board is not only not prepared, but the number of censors is too small. When we criticise pictures we do so from the viewpoint of the subjective or objective judgment of the individual. This judgment changes according to our humor. In order to avoid a prejudiced judgment we must have a greater number of volunteer censors representing various classes of Japan, including women, as in America. Our Board of magazines, drama and the like should be established by the people as a popular enterprise for the public welfare of Japan.

"The emphasis upon the evil influence of motion pictures in Japan no doubt has come generally from the ignorance of motion pictures of our instructors and authorities. They are insisting upon the evil side of them, but they have never utilized them for educational, scientific or spiritual purposes at all. We have now about 1,500 picture theatres in Japan proper and about sixty-five are in Tokio. They have an audience of 6,000,000 each month in Japan proper and one-tenth or 600,000 in Tokio every month. The numbers are continually growing. It is nonsense to suppress this natural tendency and social necessity at random. I do not, of course, deny the evil influence of motion pictures upon the children. The greater number of Japanese children are accustomed to go to the picture theatres. The total number in the elementary schools in 1916 was 7,454,632 in Japan proper, and one-third of the audience is children. They are crazy to see pictures."

Illustrating something of the practical application of censorship in Japan, an article in the last number of the Educational Film Magazine contains the following:

"In a Japanese picture show an actor is not permitted to beat up a policeman, or hit him in the eye with a custard pie or in any way to discomfit or discredit him and his dignity. The policeman always comes out on top or else there is no policeman in the reel.

"Mary Pickford cannot kiss anybody excepting her husband in Japanese picture houses. She might possibly be permitted to kiss her brother, but that would require deep consideration on the part of the police censors. There can be no violent struggles or knife plays in Japan.

"And now it is desired to show the young artist in his studio, the young artist whose father is a prominent banker, the young artist with bushy hair and Robert Mantell eyes who is making a Madonna portrait of the little girl of the Hull House district and who will surely marry the little maiden as soon as she has been heartbroken and they have drifted apart, only to meet on a battlefield, where he is a doughty doughboy and she a wonderfully gowned Red Cross girl, with the shells bursting all around them.

"They have gone over the top together, you know, and she wears white so that the Germans may know just where the American line is, and he wears a sport shirt and carries Old Glory in one hand while he waves a rifle in the other hand and carries a trench knife in his teeth.

"Oh, it is a terrible strain on the Japanese girls to have that man wounded. The Red Cross girl bends over his bleeding form and—she recognizes him! They start to embrace when the Japanese censor intervenes. The artist recovers and they live happily ever after in a million dollar California bungalow, where so many other movie mates have lived before them. But if the young artist should be shown in his studio, gazing soulfully at his Hull House model, the background must first be divested of all nude statues."

* * *

September 13, 1923

SOVIET STILL BARS FREEDOM OF SPEECH

Press and Public Meetings Are Under Strict Control, and No Opposition is Allowed

ALL DISPATCHES CENSORED

Foreign Correspondents Work Under Difficulties Like Those Encountered During the War

By WALTER DURANTY

Special Cable to The New York Times

LONDON, Sept. 12—Freedom of speech as the term is understood in America does not exist in Russia. Newspapers all are State-controlled and nothing may appear that does not meet the approval of the censorship. The same applies to all public speaking—indeed, even private meetings are strictly controlled.

Putting it in a nutshell, no opposition to the Government, either written or spoken, is allowed. In this respect anyway the Communists admit their "Dictatorship of the Proletariat" is a despotism, but they defend it on practical grounds.

"There are potential enemies in our midst," said Trotsky a year ago in reply to remonstrances from foreign correspondents about the harsh treatment of certain professors. "At present our position is secure enough to ignore them, but should the European situation become critical these internal enemies might be dangerous. It therefore is wiser and more merciful to expel them from Russia now than to imprison or perhaps shoot them later."

Special pleading this, it may be objected, but it exactly represents the Bolshevist viewpoint. Many Communists advance another argument.

"Freedom of speech and the press in America and England," they say "are the slow outcome of a centuries long fight for personal liberty. How can you expect Russia, just emerged from blackest tyranny, to share the attitude of Anglo-Saxons who struck the first blow against royal tyrants a thousand years ago at Runnymede? Our revolution is so recent we still may be considered in a virtual condition of war, and Western nations admit the necessity of press control when the safety of the State is at stake."

The third argument put forward is that a majority of the Russian people are in such a backward position as to fall an easy prey to any cunning speaker or writer and must therefore be protected against such in their own interest—the same reasoning, as shown in a previous dispatch, which was used to justify the Communist dictatorship.

One high Russian official put it more bluntly:

"The real truth of the matter is that the press and speech restrictions like terrorism proceed in the first instance from fear. When a régime is sure of its position and knows it is supported by a majority of the people it does not care what the minority says. When it is new or grows anxious and uncertain it tends to limit opposition or even criticism. Only time and the continued stability of the Soviet régime will bring us gradually into line with Western standards."

Censorship of News Dispatches

The question of press censorship as applied to foreign correspondents falls in a somewhat different plane. Generally speaking nothing they write meets the eyes of the Russian public—although foreign newspapers may now be received through the open mail despite the fact that officious custom men still sometimes confiscate them at the frontier. Nevertheless, censorship exists. Litvinoff told The New York Times correspondent before entering Russia two years ago there would be no censorship of foreign news except as regards military matters, which he said were taboo without special permission of the War Department. For nearly a year the Foreign Office maintained in principle at least that, although they supervised foreign news messages, there was no actual censorship. Gradually, however, a censorship did become a definite and concrete thing, with the usual characteristic faults.

In five years' experience of French censorship in civil and military affairs The Times correspondent found these results followed:

Overnervousness—Censors as relatively subordinate officials would suppress anything they were doubtful about rather than assume the responsibility or keep referring the matter to superiors.

Overzeal—Censors would grow to want everything submitted to them to be favorable to the French cause and tend to suppress criticism, however honest or harmless.

Overtenderness for Superiors—As minor officials the censors would suppress anything that might give offense to greater powers above them. Which leads up to the worst fault of the censorship as experienced in France and Russia—the inevitable tendency on the part of the censor to feel he somehow is responsible for the news passed by him, that his stamp in somehow gave it a sort of official standing. This, of course, is entirely false as the whole reason for censorship is the suppression of information that may injure the State and that alone. But the censor's personal equation becomes too strong.

One of the Moscow censors remarked naively to The Times correspondent after suppressing a dispatch, "I wouldn't mind so much if it was written from London or Paris. But the people you are attacking are friends of ours and I don't like that kind of thing to go out with a Moscow date line"—that is, with the stamp of Moscow official approval.

On the whole, however, experience with the Russian censorship is favorable enough. The censors would not only say what was suppressed before the dispatch was sent—which the French declined to do save in exceptional cases for the first three years of the war—but would listen to argument and often permit modification of the offending passage so as to maintain all or part of the news value.

News of Famous Trial Suppressed

In a trying position they are courteous and tactful and, generally speaking, there is little to complain of. Until the Butchkavitch affair. Then the element of fear came into play and the work of the foreign correspondents became virtually impossible. In a subsequent dispatch to The New York Times a brief outline of this unhappy business was given. Enough to say now that a combination of circumstances had produced a state of ferment in Soviet Government circles not far removed from panic. This was especially true of the Foreign Office, which handles the censorship, and where the consequences abroad of action the Government contemplated taking, and did in fact take perhaps were more fully realized than in the other departments.

Any accurate presentation of the facts involved an explanation of the existing ferment and the conflict of forces. For some reason the authorities declined to permit this in the slightest degree. In plain English, the fear complex dominated their usual prudence. It was not long before they realized the error, and Litvinof, on behalf of the Foreign Office, gave representative American correspondents a solemn promise that henceforth nothing should be suppressed in a news message save facts whose accuracy the writer was unable to substantiate. The promise has been kept, but the damage was done.

Favorable news from Moscow rests under suspicion, whereas unfounded reports about events in Russia broadcast by anti-Bolshevist Emigrés from Riga, Helsingfors, Reval, &c., find ready acceptance. The excuse the Soviet officials offer, that they have been so much injured in the past by malicious lies or perversions of truth, is human but won't mend matters, and the position will remain unsatisfactory until they realize that conditions in Russia now being so much better than the majority of people abroad believe, the entire absence of restrictions on foreign news would do them infinitely more good than harm.

* * *

June 15, 1924

EDITORS CONVICTED AND PAPERS CENSORED

That a special press law, such as was passed by the Senate on May 28, is hardly needed in Czechoslovakia would seem to be indicated by occasional reports of editors being convicted and newspapers censored. For instance, General Husak, former Minister of War, took the responsible editor of Rude Pravo, the Prague Communist paper, into court on a charge of libel for having named him as being involved in the gasoline scandal last Winter, with the result of the editor being sentenced to ten days in jail, or a fine of 1,000 crowns (about $30). In Brünn, two Communist editors were convicted, one of having written a semi-seditious article on the murder of Minister of Finance Rasin, and the other of having printed incitatory pieces at the time of a farm workers' strike in Austerlitz. They were sentenced to four months' close arrest and eight months in jail, respectively. For having printed a rather severe anti-clerical cartoon, the Prague Sozialdemokrat, the daily organ of the German-speaking Socialists in the capital, had a recent Sunday issue confiscated and when it came back with sharp criticism of the authorities it was confiscated again. This moved the Pravo Lidu, the Czech Social Democratic paper, to remark that "the arrogance of the Czechoslovak censors under the reactionary guidance of the Clerical Minister [of Justice] Dolansky and of the Agrarian 'Liberal' Malypetr [Minister of the Interior] is really almost incredible." Other cases of repression by local authorities are cited as affording strange contrasts to the progressive policies proclaimed in Prague.

* * *

June 27, 1926

TIGHT CENSORSHIP REPORTED IN RUSSIA

Berlin Hears New Espionage Rules Menace Correspondents With Death

"STATE SECRETS" DEFINED

Nearly All News of Political or Economic Importance is Covered by the Regulations

Censorship of reports coming out of Russia is now backed up by a revised espionage law more drastic than those in force in the belligerent countries during the World War, according to a story printed in the Berlin Information Bulletin of the Russian Social Democratic Party on June 2.

It is asserted that on May 2 new regulations were laid down by the Soviet authorities defining what in the future were to be regarded as State secrets, the unauthorized publication of which would be considered espionage and might be punished with death. In addition to information about military secrets, any stories concerning "the Treasury's holdings of foreign means of payment," or "the financial balance of the Union of Soviet Socialist Republics," may put the writer in peril of prosecution for espionage, as is also the case with "information about the plans of the Soviet Government concerning the importation and exportation of various articles and about the stock of goods for export."

Furthermore, "reports about negotiations and treaties of the U. S. S. R. with foreign States, as well as those about all measures taken by the union in the field of foreign politics or of foreign trade," are to be regarded as State secrets "in so far as these reports are not based upon official communications." Also "steps taken to combat the counter-revolution" are protected by the espionage regulations.

The writer in the Berlin emigré bulletin opines that this tightening up of the censorship in Russia is probably due to the publication abroad of reports about the Soviet Government's financial difficulties and the falling off in the exchange value of the tehervonet, despite the Treasury's efforts to hold it to par. He says the new regulation is aimed at the correspondents of foreign newspapers and also at the "under cover" men of the Social Democratic and Social Revolutionary Parties in Russia, who occasionally manage to get news across the border which does not agree with the Moscow versions of the events reported. He points out that any unofficial account of the condition of political prisoners in Russia—most of whom are Socialists and anarchists—or of unauthorized strikes, jeopardizes the author's life and makes it almost impossible to get complete reports of such matters.

The article concludes by remarking that Premier Mussolini's efforts to control foreign correspondents are mild compared with those of the Bolsheviki, and suggests that he get a copy of the new regulations and have them translated into Italian.

* * *

October 3, 1926

FRENCH CENSOR ISAIAH AND SYRIANS DUST OFF BIBLES

Verses Deleted Become Subject of Curiosity and Even Moslems Buy Testaments

The science of censorship seems still to linger in its infancy, notwithstanding the scope for its practice afforded by the great war. In Syria at the present time the French censorship over newspapers occasionally affords amusement. If the censor's sharp eye lights upon any criticism of France, the French or French rule in Syria, his blue pencil quickly deletes such portions, leaving blank, white gaps to stare at the reader and arouse in him speculation as to the missing news.

The Syrian public has become so accustomed to this practice that it judges the state of the Druse activities and of French reverses by the number of "windows" opened by the censor's blue pencil. Putting his wits together, the native reader concludes that when everything is printed in full things are going to the satisfaction of the French; but when events become unfavorable to them blank spaces are sure to let the secret out. And while it will not be known what has actually occurred to the disadvantage of the mandatory power, it is nevertheless certain that the French are meeting with reverses. Then revolutionaries and their sympathizers take courage.

Recently the Beirut censor aided the sale of Bibles and caused many a dusty volume to be brought out and read. He did it by simply cutting out a few verses from a chapter of Isaiah which the editor of Al-Ahrar had printed. Al-Ahrar is the leading Arabic daily of Syria. Its clever young Syrian decided to try a new trick on the censor. Accordingly, on May 13, 1926, in the first column of the first page of his paper he printed an editorial entitled, "Will the Censor Cut This?"

Aroused Curiosity

The editorial in Arabic began as follows: "Instead of the editorial, we are publishing the first chapter of Isaiah, so that the reader may not find any censor's windows peeking at him with their magic eyes. There is no doubt that the reader—and the censor—will sense our feelings of pain in publishing this."

Then followed the first chapter of Isaiah, word for word, from the Arable Bible. The first, second, third and fourth verses were passed. Then the censor cut out verses five, six, seven and eight. Following that white space the chapter went on from the ninth to the twentieth verses inclusive. Again the censor felt impelled to curtail the ancient prophet's language by cutting out verses twenty-one, twenty-two and twenty-three. After the second white gap, verses twenty-four, twenty-five and twenty-six were allowed to stand.

The verses deleted were:

"Why should ye be stricken any more? Ye will revolt more and more. The whole head is sick and the whole heart faint. From the sole of the foot even unto the head there is no soundness in it; but wounds and bruises and putrifying sores; they have not been closed, neither bound up, neither mollified with ointment. Your country is desolate, your cities burned with fire; your land, strangers devour it in your presence, and it is desolate, as overthrown by strangers. And the daughter of Zion is left as a lodge in a garden of cucumbers, as a besieged city."

Got Isaiah's Vision Entire

Again (verses 21–23):

"How is the faithful city become an harlot! It was full of judgment; righteousness lodged in it; but now murderers. Thy silver is become dross, thy wine mixed with water. Thy princes are rebellious and companions of thieves: every one loveth gifts and followeth after rewards: they judge not the fatherless, neither doth the cause of the widow come unto them."

Had the censor merely passed the editorial by with a smile, very few would have stopped to read through the first chapter of Isaiah. But the fact that the censor had considered it worth censoring aroused curiosity and not a person neglected to read the unexpurgated text—if he owned a Bible. Many Mohammedans who had no Bible bought or borrowed one simply for the purpose of reading those deleted verses.

Friends greeted each other with the salutation: "Have you read the first chapter of Isaiah?" That blue marking gave the revolutionaries publicity. This fact the censor observed toward evening and an order was sent out prohibiting further sales of that day's Al-Ahrar. The order came too late, for every copy had already been sold.

* * *

October 30, 1927

CHINESE CENSORS ARE A LAW UNTO THEMSELVES; THEY STOP AUTHORIZED INTERVIEWS WITH CHANG

Special Correspondence of The New York Times

PEKING, Oct. 7—The North China Government boasts of a Board of Censors so strict that the members even refuse to give their official "O. K." to press interviews authorized by the dictator, Chang Tso-lin, himself.

Two days ago Mr. Wu Ching, Vice Minister for Foreign Affairs in the Pan Fu Cabinet, summoned all the foreign correspondents to the Foreign Office. For more than an hour and a half he talked to them about the new war with Shansi, explaining Peking's stand and Shansi's perfidy.

He told the foreign correspondents they could use his name, and quote all that he said about the military and political situation.

The correspondents reminded the Vice Minister that for days the censors had been holding up all their telegrams, but with a wave of his hand Mr. Wu Ching dismissed this plaint. He had sent for the chief censor, and had arranged that there would be no more of these delays, he said.

The correspondents then reminded Mr. Wu Ching that twice within six months the censor had refused to O. K. official Peking statements. They urged that this policy was doing harm to the Northern cause.

The Vice Minister promised that veracious accounts of the campaign, and proper interviews with Peking officials, would thereafter be passed without question.

So the correspondents wrote out their dispatches and had them accepted at the cable office. They learned today that the censor had held up all but one of them, refusing to permit even the official Government explanation of the causes of the present hostilities to reach the outside world.

Some correspondents are now arranging to locate assistants at Dairen, which is Japanese controlled, and to mail their news from Peking to the cables at Dairen—thus losing only twenty-four hours.

At Tientsin the censorship is worse than it is at Peking, but the Japanese have discovered that there is no censorship at Mukden, and that the telephone lines are not watched. Japanese correspondents, therefore, telephone their news to associates at Mukden, and their messages are then telegraphed from Mukden to Dairen, and from Dairen go to Japan by cable.

The next time the Vice Minister summons foreign correspondents for an interview they will probably send a joint note of regret, saying that since the censor will not pass Mr. Wu Ching's statements they cannot spare the time for the interview.

* * *

March 11, 1928

EDITOR JAILED FOR CARTOONS OF THE TURKS

Constantinople Satires Bring Sentence of Sixteen Months To Humorist

For having published three caricatures that were deemed offensive by the Government Prosecutor of Constantinople, Yussef Sia Bey, editor of two Turkish humorous weeklies, was recently sentenced to serve sixteen months in jail and pay a fine of about $75. The Berlin Vossische Zeitung reports that the first cartoon to rouse the authorities represented an Italian sculptor, Canonica, who had been commissioned to make statues of Kemal Pasha, talking with a Turkish peasant. The peasant refers to the collection of public contributions to pay for the statues, and asks, "Shall I give still more?" The sculptor replies: "Oh, yes, give some more; I don't get all of it."

The Prosecuting Attorney asserted that this picture was a libel upon Turkish officials, as it implicated that they were grafting from the monument fund.

The editor in defense asserted that the cartoon was aimed at the idea of hiring "third-rate" imported artists to do the sculptures, instead of employing Turks. The explanation failed to convince the Court, and for this cartoon the editor was sentenced to one year in jail for insulting the Government.

The second offending caricature seemed to indicate that Persia had accepted the Turkish conditions of settling the latest boundary incident under duress. Consequently, the Prosecutor regarded it as insulting to the Shah of Persia. The defense denied intention to insult, and suggested that Turkish courts need not worry about insults to a foreign ruler. The Judge sentenced the editor to seven months and a fine of about $65.

The third disapproved cartoon was entitled "Where Our Young Girls Are Educating Themselves." It showed a Turkish girl leaving a movie theatre and looking for the gay resorts of the city in order to experience the scenes of the screen. This was held to be an immoral picture, and drew a sentence of one month and a fine of $10.

* * *

November 4, 1928

BOOK CENSORSHIP URGED FOR ENGLAND

Home Secretary Wants Authority to Ban Any Volume He Deems Indecent

HAS VERY LITTLE SUPPORT

Newspapers Fear Such Power Would Be a Step Toward Control Over All Publications

By HENRY C. CROUCH
Special Correspondence of The New York Times

LONDON, Oct. 24—Home Secretary Sir William Joynson-Hicks has suggested the establishment of a censorship of books in this country, but so far has received very little support.

His suggestion was prompted partly by the trouble that has arisen over the publication of Miss Radclyffe Hall's book, "The Well of Loneliness." This book was denounced by a London newspaper, copies of it were sent to the Home Secretary, and, at his request, Jonathan Cape, the London publisher, ceased printing the book.

A Paris publishing firm then produced the book, at an increased price, and advertised it extensively in this country. But when a consignment of copies was sent over from Paris it was detained by the customs officials at Dover.

That consignment has now been released by order of the Commissioners of Customs and Excise, so that it would appear that a Government department has negatived the action recommended by one of the leading members of the Cabinet.

In view of the fact that a director of the Paris publishing firm concerned has said that, owing to the big demand for the book, a fifth impression of it will be necessary, the Home Secretary has been in consultation with his legal advisers, and if any further action is decided upon it will probably be taken by the Public Prosecutor.

Opposition to Censorship

The powers of the Home Secretary to suppress or prohibit immoral literature are too limited for his satisfaction. If he wishes to suppress what he regards as an indecent book he must go to the courts and prosecute. It is his opinion that a censorship, on the lines presumably of the censorship of stage plays, would be a more efficient corrective.

But there is much opposition to his proposal. Some newspapers seem to fear that if the Home Secretary were invested with the greater powers he wishes he would constitute himself the sole authority to decide whether or not a book should be published. That, it is declared, would be an intolerable position, since the opinion is held that the Home Secretary, with all his earnestness of purpose, is scarcely the man to whom such important powers should be delegated. Apart from that point, these newspapers are opposed strongly to the idea of any censorship at all, apprehending apparently that it would be the first step toward the censorship of publications of all kinds. The censorship of newspapers during the war remains a very unhappy memory.

"Even if we had perfect confidence in the infallibility of the Home Secretary's taste in literature," says The Daily Telegraph, "we should still maintain that it was against the public interest to suppress every book which he found undesirable or disturbing."

Of, course, George Bernard Shaw is dead against the idea of any increased powers being given to the Home Office. He says:

"The Home Secretary can prosecute an author for an obscene libel just as he can prosecute one for a seditious libel. He can go for the author and publisher in a constitutional manner; but it is intolerable that a Government official without any form of prosecution, should be able to seize books because he does not happen to like them."

Conan Doyle for the Scheme

On the other hand, Sir Arthur Conan Doyle said that the Home Secretary's attitude seemed very reasonable.

"We do not want," he says, "to see this country in the same condition as France, which has a great quantity of pornographic literature in circulation. Personally, I hate all these sex novels. That sort of stuff is very cheap and very easy. It is very simple to make your interest out of that sort of material, and the art of writing is in avoiding it."

Ireland, also, is agitated over the question of the censorship of books, newspapers, &c. The Irish Free State Censorship of Publications bill is now before the Dail. As it stands at present, it does not satisfy a considerable body of the public, but Minister of Justice Fitzgerald-Kenney declines to accept any of the numerous amendments suggested from outside the Dail. Nevertheless, it is thought that the bill will have to be altered drastically if it is to get through Parliament.

Mr. Fitzgerald-Kenney has explained in the Dail the lines on which the Board of Censors (five in number) would administer the proposed law. A book would be condemned only when it was definitely and designedly immoral. A novel like "Vanity Fair" would not be condemned because of the conduct of Becky Sharp, nor would Shakespeare's "Othello" be denounced because of the experience of Iago. Scientific and medical works would not be banned because the words in them might appear to be indecent to the layman. The Board of Censors would not be terrorized by big names in literature. If a book or publication was deliberately indecent it would be condemned.

As regards newspapers, if the whole tone of a paper was such as to demoralize or deprave its readers it would be prohibited. It would be wrong, however, to condemn or suppress an otherwise admirable newspaper for one or two chance items or articles which were in themselves immoral. No newspaper or other publication which advocated or advertised birth control would be permitted to circulate in the Irish Free State. On that point the Government is inflexible.

* * *

September 19, 1929

CHINA ENDS CENSORSHIP

"Examiners" With Wide Powers, However, Are Created by Decree

Special Cable to The New York Times

SHANGHAI, Sept. 18—Censorship of the press has been formally abolished by order of the Nanking State Council "except in such special instances as may be considered necessary by the central authorities."

Compulsory registration of all publications is required and official examination is provided for. Rules which give the examiners power to discipline papers criticizing the government practically negative the abolition of censorship, making the mandate seem in effect merely a substitution of "examiners" for censors.

* * *

June 21, 1931

CENSORS TO PASS ON CHINESE NEWS

Regulations Apply Also to All Commercial Telegraphic or Cable Messages

SCORED BY FOREIGN PRESS

Shanghai Newspaper Warns That Move Will Create Belief That All is Not Well

By HALLETT ABEND
Social Correspondence, The New York Times

SHANGHAI, May 22—Hereafter no telegrams or cable messages may leave China for foreign lands nor be transmitted between Chinese cities unless they bear the official stamp of censors appointed by the Nanking Government or unless they are dispatched by foreign firms which are guaranteed by their consulates against sending anything in the nature of news about China which might come under the military or political ban of the censorship rulings.

The day before yesterday, for the first time in history, a Chinese Government was able to install censors in all the cable offices in the International Settlement in Shanghai, thereby clinching government control over all news leaving all of China south of the Great Wall.

Tientsin and Peiping, though excellent news centres, have long been under censorship because they are inland cities and because all messages from those points have had to pass first over land lines owned by the Chinese Government before reaching cable ends. The same applies to such news centres as Hankow and Canton. Today the only cities in China from which news can be sent without Chinese Government censorship are Dairen, Port Arthur, Mukden and Chengehun and other cities along the Japanese-owned South Manchuria Railway. This railway is paralleled by a telegraph line owned and controlled by the Japanese, and so far this line is not subject to Chinese interference. The new censorship regulations in Shanghai will also apply to all messages arriving from foreign points.

Rules Are Strict

The official regulations as announced here are as follows:

"Forwarded as well as received telegrams will be submitted to censors appointed by the Chinese Government.

"Telegrams in plain language which are found to be detrimental to China or public safety or contrary to Chinese laws will be stopped by the censors and submitted to the Ministry of Communications for consideration.

"Commercial telegrams in code handed in by Chinese well-known commercial firms must bear the seal of the firm and be signed and guaranteed by the manager of the firm. A specimen of the seal and signature must be forwarded beforehand to the telegraph office. However, in case of necessity the censors may still demand to see the code book used.

"Commercial telegrams in code handed in by other Chinese firms or persons must have a translation attached and, besides, be accompanied by the code book used.

"Commercial telegrams in code handed in by the foreign public must be sealed by the respective consulates as a guarantee. If preferred, however, a letter from the consulate vouching for the firm in question may be lodged with the telegraph office, in which case the telegrams need not be sealed. In case of necessity the censors may still demand to see the code book used.

"In case of necessity the censors may demand code books for inspection from the addressees of incoming code telegrams.

"Foreign government telegrams, whether in plain language or code, are exempted from censorship."

Press Hits at Move

The initiation of censorship here has been critically received by the foreign press of Shanghai. The American-owned Shanghai Evening Post observes editorially:

"The very existence of a censorship body, charged with the responsibility of editing incoming and outgoing information to conform to governmental ideas of favorable propaganda in every case has bred not confidence, but suspicion.

"Censorship indicates to the public mind, both here and abroad, the existence of an extremely critical situation. It is public acknowledgment that the government has become afraid to permit the free flow of information in and out of this country and breeds the suspicion that something short of the truth may be told in every piece of news or commercial information reaching the general public.

"A censorship implies, rightfully or wrongly, that facts considered harmful to the political declarations of the government are subject to editing as well as untruthful propaganda. It places the government in a position of creating a monopoly on the dissemination of information and makes necessary the calculation of the effect of completely truthful information upon a governmental policy.

"Its chief effect, we contend, will be to create suspicion that all is not well in China, rather than to allay any fears created by uncensored news reports broadcast today."

The British-owned North China Daily News says:

"Observers cannot fail to be a little uneasy. For a government anxious to establish world opinion in its favor, the censorship is a double-edged weapon. It may prevent the prompt dissemination of news and information considered to be detrimental to the government's reputation. But this process of suppressing news cannot be permanent. The mere announcement to the world that a government censorship exists immediately raises doubt in the public mind. It is only necessary to quote the example of the late regime in Spain to prove that nemesis, slow but sure, effects the due adjustments of the claims of fact.

"The policy of dragooning" the press, of insisting on the transmission of nothing but highly one-sidedly pro-governmental messages to the exclusion of all expressions of honest but contrary opinion, has never been permanently successful, the examples of Fascist Italy and Bolshevik Russia notwithstanding."

* * *

July 17, 1932

CHINESE PRESS IS TOLD TO APPLY SOFT PEDAL

News About Execution of Reds and Success of Soviet Five-Year Plan Is Prohibited

Special Correspondence, The New York Times

SHANGHAI, June 18—Chinese newspapers are forbidden hereafter to print news of the execution of Chinese Communists, and they must also refrain from publishing any news of the success of the Russian Five-Year Plan.

Secret orders to this effect have just been issued by the Publicity Department of the Central Executive Committee at Nanking. A covering letter states that "the terror in China is getting too much publicity abroad," and cites the fact that there have recently been parades and meetings of protest in the United States and in Europe because of the number of Communists and young radicals who are being executed in China every week.

Complaint is made that many articles about "the terror" which appear in the English-language press in China, and in foreign newspapers, refer to Chinese newspapers for confirmation. Therefore, the order states, the Chinese newspapers must be more discreet.

The second order states that "although Russia's Five-Year Plan is very successful, yet it is contrary to the principles of the Kuomintang."

The Chinese press is accused of publishing, "without discrimination," too much favorable news about the Five-Year Plan, which "may inspire the people and prove a hindrance in Red suppression work."

* * *

August 6, 1934

CZECHS SUPPRESS HITLERITE ACTIVITY

Police Force Increased and Radio Programs Come Under Scrutiny

NEWSPAPERS BARRED OUT

Liberal Policy, However, Extended by Government to Refugees From Germany

By R. E. KADICH
Special Correspondence, The New York Times

PRAGUE, July 19—Czechoslovakia is determined to suppress with a firm hand the activities of Hitlerites in her own territory. This policy is accounted for by the fact that the Northern and Western districts of Bohemia are inhabited almost entirely by Germans (Sudetendeutsche) among whom there are large numbers of Nationals and Nazis. Although their representation in Parliament, is relatively small, the advent of Hitlerism has undoubtedly had a heartening effect on the Bohemian-German National Socialists who boast a much older history than their party friends in Germany. The danger of the belt adjacent to Germany becoming engulfed in the movement was, therefore, a real one, and the Czechoslovak Government recently obtained from Parliament special powers to deal with an emergency, in addition to the Defense of the Republic Act which has been in force for some years.

Not only has the gendarmerie force been brought up to its full strength some 12,000 men—but 500 additional gendarmes have been enlisted to allow for the strengthening of the frontier guards, and a further increase by 300 is contemplated during the Summer months. The "dissemination" of broadcast programs from abroad, the contents of which might be contrary to public order, the unity of the republic, its Constitution or public institutions, has become an offense involving loss of the receiving license and criminal prosecution. The term "dissemination" applies to any guest or visitor of an ordinary household listening in.

The desire to bar the circulation of printed propaganda of a "subversive" nature has led to a newspaper war between Czechoslovakia and Germany, which has practically developed into a complete embargo on both sides. Even sporting, fashion and comic papers are ruled out, as it is considered undesirable to place before local readers a photographic reproduction of Hitler or the text of the "Horst-Wessel Lied," or, in Germany, news that is withheld from the public. The German Minister in Prague has protested against the prohibition of newspapers from the Reich in Czechoslovakia as being incompatible with the spirit of the trade agreement between the two countries. A similar protest has been made against the conviction by a court at Pilsen of ten Nazis—German subjects, but permanently resident in Czechoslovakia—on a charge of having attended election meetings across the border at which anti-Czech demonstrations have taken place. Such complaints are dealt with in a routine way, and relations with Germany are described as correct. German trade with Czechoslovakia—formerly the most important item in imports and exports—has, however, come almost to a standstill.

Apart from curtailing Nazi propaganda the Czechoslovak Government is pursuing a liberal policy with regard to immigration from Germany so long as the newcomers do not indulge in political activities or obtain work in preference to the local unemployed. Jews form the majority of the refugees, but there are many others who have become "undesirable" in Germany, and not a few spies and agents provocateurs.

* * *

August 12, 1934

NANKING IS TOUCHY ON TARIFF POLICY

Press Forbidden to Comment on Opposition to 'Pro-Japanese' Measure

PLAN CALLED UNPATRIOTIC

Trade Unions and Industrials Hold It Will Spell Ruin for Domestic Business

Special Correspondence, The New York Times

SHANGHAI, July 21—Any mention of public opposition to the Chinese Government's so-called "pro-Japanese tariff policy" is to be strictly censored, according to orders received here from Nanking, supplemented by a telegram of personal instructions to the censors from General Chiang Kai-shek.

The press censors of Shanghai and other cities have addressed circular letters to the editors of all newspapers warning them against publishing either news or editorial comment concerning opposition to the revised tariff, which becomes effective July 1.

General Chiang's telegram forbids all Chinese newspapers or periodicals to carry any further news or comments about the activities of business men and industrialists "in defiance of the government's tariff policy." He declares that governmental authorities will no longer tolerate the "unreasonable" attitude of the public, and that the government will ban all newspapers which may be indiscreet enough to support the stand of "ignorant merchants."

Cables Censored First

Preceding this domestic ban on news about opposition to the new tariff schedules a rigid censorship has been in effect to prevent the cabling of news of the opposition abroad.

In spite of the official muzzling or the newspapers, however, a flood of protests against the new tariff continues to reach Nanking by post and by telegraph. Literally scores of petitions urging a revision of rates are being sent to the government.

Many leading trade unions, the Shanghai General Chamber of Commerce, the Chinese Industrial Association, the Machine Dyeing and Textile Association, the Silk Printing Association, the Native Goods Manufacturers Association and many other organizations have openly joined the opposition movement. Cotton mills, paper mills, coal dealers, breweries and dealers in fish, all particularly hard hit, are also protesting vehemently.

The revised tariff is being fought not only because it threatens to cripple many native industries but also because it is declared to be an "unpatriotic measure," and a further evidence of yielding to Japan, even though Japan has taken from China the whole of Manchuria and Jehol Province—collectively an area of more than 450,000 square miles.

The Canton faction and other political opponents of Nanking and of General Chiang Kai-shek are planning to make a great issue of the "pro-Japanese tariff revision," as it is called.

This opposition puts Nanking in an embarrassing position, because for a long time the government fostered anti-Japanese propaganda and a boycott of Japanese goods.

The new tariff is so favorable to Japan that since July 1 Japanese ships are arriving in Shanghai and other Chinese ports with capacity cargoes, and most Japanese shipping lines have put additional freighters upon the runs to the China coast.

* * *

February 24, 1935

CHINESE CENSORS ASSAILED

Press and Correspondents Enter Complaints to Nanking on Harsh and Futile Regulations

Reports reaching New York from many sources in China indicate that various associations of Chinese-language newspapers and newspaper workers have finally rebelled against the rigorous censorship maintained by the Nanking Government, and that there is a fair prospect of some amelioration of conditions.

The usual way of "punishing" a newspaper in China is to deny it the use of the mails—if it is foreign-owned and published in a foreign concession area. Chinese newspapers are often denied the mails, heavily fined, closed for short periods or even suspended indefinitely. Often this action is taken arbitrarily by the military.

Dispatches Mutilated

Foreign news agencies and foreign correspondents in China suffer mutilation of both their incoming and outgoing material. Shanghai is the clearing house for most foreign news organizations operating in China, and in some cases one office may be permitted to receive a telegram from Nanking or from Peiping, while another office is not permitted to receive the same news.

Not content with deleting portions of telegrams or cables, the Shanghai censors also write in extra words. For instance, it is reported from Shanghai that telegrams from Manchuria, delivered typed, always have the words "so-called" or "puppet State" written in ink above the word "Manchukuo," and when the Emperor Kangteh is referred to the words "puppet ruler" are written in.

Lack of Uniformity

An even more irritating feature of the situation at Shanghai is that the censorship has not been uniform in all transmission offices. What the censor at one cable office may pass the censor at another may "kill" and the censor at the radio office may pass only in garbled condition.

Moreover, the censors refuse to meet newspaper men, refuse to let them know under what orders they operate, and will not divulge what classes of news are permissible and what classes are banned. A Shanghai correspondent is never permitted to know what parts, if any, of his messages have been approved for transmission.

But the whole situation has its ludicrous aspect. The Japanese have a cable of their own from Shanghai to Nagasaki, and they refuse to permit Chinese censors to enter their office. As a result, the versions of Chinese events sent out by the legion of Japanese correspondents in China cannot be touched. In many cases versions distinctly harmful to China are relayed out from Tokyo while American or European correspondents are prevented from telling the truth impartially.

* * *

December 27, 1935

REICH GETS JAPAN TO BAN CARICATURES OF STATE HEADS

Wireless to The New York Times

TOKYO, Dec. 26—As a sequel to the affair in which the Japanese Government protested in Washington against a caricature of Emperor Hirohito that appeared in the American magazine Vanity Fair, the Home Office has circularized all Japanese newspapers and magazines requesting them to refrain from publishing caricatures of chiefs of State.

According to the press, the circular originated in representations made by the German Embassy here against cartoons of Chancellor Adolf Hitler, which the embassy declared affronted the honor and pride of the German people.

Editors are discontented with the official action, which restricts the cartoonists' field, and are asserting that active politicians in the fighting arena do not have the same reason to be protected as emperors who do not mix in politics.

* * *

February 9, 1936

FREE PRESS CRY IN CHINA

By HALLETT ABEND

Special Correspondence, The New York Times

SHANGHAI—Nation-wide student demonstrations against the granting of autonomy to the northern provinces have again brought to the fore the crippling censorship under which the Chinese press labors. The students themselves are now clamoring to have the government grant real freedom to the press.

Censorship of foreign press dispatches has been reduced to a reasonable minimum. Under the new regulations governing the work of foreign correspondents, nothing in the way of ordinary news is banned, except that which pertains to the movement of government armies or items which may justly be classed as revealing "military secrets."

Foreign-language newspapers published in China, owned by persons enjoying extraterritoriality, are under no censorship of any kind, but the Chinese Government can, and sometimes does, ban certain issues from circulation by mail if undesirable, unfair or damaging news items or editorials are published.

In contrast to this freedom, Chinese news agencies and newspapers continue to suffer from strict and often unintelligent censorship.

During the present student agitation six colleges and universities where journalism is being taught have sent petitions to Nanking asking for the abolition of the censorship of the Chinese-language press. These institutions are the Central Political Training Institute at Nanking, the Peiping School of Journalism, Fuhtan University at Shanghai, Yenching University at Peiping, the Shanghai University and the Canton School of Journalism.

The petitions point out that the masses of the people cannot read the foreign-language press, and that since Chinese newspapers and magazines are so rigorously censored, Chinese patriots are perforce kept ignorant of important events vitally concerning the welfare of the nation.

In Peiping and Tientsin the censorship is now worse than ever before. Northern newspapers say that the Japanese have forced local authorities to forbid any reference to opposition to autonomy or any criticisms of the new autonomous regime.

* * *

July 5, 1936

NANKING SOFTENS CABLE CENSORSHIP

News Dispatches of Foreign Correspondents Now Free From Former Meddling

H. K. TONG PUT IN CHARGE

By HALLETT ABEND

Special Correspondence, The New York Times

SHANGHAI—After maintaining for several years one of the most inefficient and vexatious news censorships on foreign cables existing anywhere, the Chinese Government has made such sweeping changes and reforms that today, in the area directly under Nanking's control, the system of censorship has become so centralized, intelligent and effective that causes for complaint are practically non-existent.

Until a few months ago the evils of inefficient and unintelligent censorship were widespread and the responsibility for censoring news was so divided that aggrieved foreign correspondents could not determine whether military censors or Kuomintang party censors had garbled their dispatches.

In many cases dispatches were held up for so long that when they finally reached their newspapers in America and in Europe they were valueless as news.

For several years the censors not only deleted words and passages as suited individual whims, but even wrote in extra words and charged transmission for them.

Mme. Chiang Acts

During much of this period General Chiang Kai-shek was busy in remote interior provinces conducting campaigns against the Chinese Communist armies, but finally Mme. Chiang's interest was enlisted in favor of censorship reforms. When she rejoined the generalissimo in distant Szechwan province, she took the matter up with General Chiang, and the latter began an investigation.

The upshot of this investigation was that an airplane was sent from Chengtu, capital of Szechwan, to Shanghai, to take Hollington K. Tong to the generalissimo's headquarters for a conference. Mr. Tong was formerly editor and publisher of an enterprising Chinese-language newspaper in Tientsin, and had later been editor of an English-language newspaper in Shanghai.

The outcome of the Chengtu conferences was the appointment of Mr. Tong as chief censor. Orders were issued for sweeping reforms.

Today the censorship in China is no longer meddlesome, nor are news dispatches subject to delay. Under the new regulations all foreign correspondents understand fully what may and what may not be cabled abroad, and if they are in doubt Mr. Tong may be reached day or night in person or by telephone. Sub-censors are employed at all the cable and radio offices, but when they come upon doubtful passages they may not delete them upon their own responsibility, but must consult Mr. Tong by telephone.

Tong on the Phone

Under the new system correspondents are not kept in ignorance, as they were before, about changes made in their messages. Mr. Tong telephones to them at once, and discusses with them the doubtful passages. He will always listen fairly to an argument, and is often open to conviction.

Occasionally a censor at some inland city will still suppress or garble a message filed from some provincial capital, but if these instances are brought to Mr. Tong's attention he immediately transmits the facts of the case to the generalissimo's headquarters at Nanking, and prompt measures are taken to insure against a repetition of such occurrences.

The new chief censor is a returned student from the United States. He was graduated from the University of Missouri School of Journalism and later completed a postgraduate course at Columbia University in New York City.

* * *

April 18, 1937

JAPAN'S CENSORS ASPIRE TO "THOUGHT CONTROL"

Their Task It Is to Keep an Empire Free From Ideas That Might Disturb the State

By HUGH BYAS

TOKYO—A new gadget has been added to Japan's elaborate machinery for thought control. The Protective Surveillance Law provides aftercare for repentant Communists. It has been found that "thought criminals," once behind bars, are disposed to agree that Paris is worth a mass and liberty worth a timely renunciation of Marx and all his works.

The law provides that persons convicted of violating the Peace Preservation Act may be released under surveillance on giving proof that they have abjured their errors. So numerous are the penitents—or so skin-deep their heresies—that twenty-two supervisory offices under the District Appeal Courts have been opened to watch them.

In its beginning, as at its end, the machinery of thought control is operated by the police. The first turn of the wheel can be a very simple one. Two students walking across the university campus are reading a small book. A plainclothes man stops them. "Show me what you are reading." It is a student's crib, not a Communist pamphlet. If it happened to be the latter, the students would spend the night, and many more nights, answering questions in a police station.

A policeman, seated in his concrete sentry box at a street corner, motions to a shabby individual carrying a dilapidated valise. The man knows what to do. He lays his bag at the officer's feet and shows that it contains the humble plant of a shoeblack and not stolen watches.

International

Searching a suspect.

The American observer thinks one of these cases a tactless offense against human liberty; the other he regards as a legitimate exercise of police power for the protection of society. To the Japanese mind the exercise of authority is as legitimate in one case as in the other. There are offenses of thought and offenses of action. The policeman is the executive agent of society in putting down both.

"Thought surveillance" is carried out by a special secret service (Tokuko Keisatsu) and the secret service police (Koto Keisatsu). The former organization watches over "dangerous thoughts," social movements and espionage. It has a large staff and its secret expenditure is believed to amount to more than half a million yen annually. Its headquarters are in the Metropolitan Police Office in Tokyo, where it is organized in four bureaus: secret service; supervision of foreigners; labor; supervision of Koreans in Japan.

The secret service police (Koto Keisatsu) have their headquarters in the police bureau of the Home Office. They are entrusted with supervision of national and local elections, political meetings, political parties and the activities of politicians.

The "supervision of foreigners" is occasionally the subject of romantic stories. It consists simply in keeping a register of foreign residents, with their names, ages, occupations, nationality and addresses. The work is done with smoothness. On first becoming a householder in Tokyo some twenty years ago, this correspondent supplied the information required and has never been asked to repeat it. The police check up their information from time to time, but they do so through the servants, and the foreigner who stolidly attends to his own business can live for years in Japan without knowing that a department of the secret police is looking after him.

The power that drives the machinery of thought surveillance is the Peace Preservation Act. This law was strengthened in 1925 for the suppression of communism and again in 1934 when the puerile epidemic of student Marxism had subsided and when dangerous thinking was anything that clashed with the ways of militant nationalism which arose with the Manchurian adventure.

The offenses specified in the Peace Preservation Act are organization of, membership in or giving support to associations formed to revolutionize the national Constitution or to repudiate the system of private property. These were at first bracketed together in one clause and the death penalty was provided for the leaders of such organizations. The law of 1934 introduced a significant change. It separated the two offenses, maintained the death penalty for attempts to alter the Constitution, but reduced the punishment for repudiation of the private property system to a maximum of ten years' imprisonment.

These laws, plus the zeal of policemen specially deputed to smell out dangerous thoughts, produced a series of anti-Communist police raids with an imposing number of captures. But there were a thousand sprats for every red salmon in the police dragnets when the haul was examined by the courts.

From 1933 to 1936 the police arrested 59,013 persons for dangerous thoughts. After preliminary examination only 4,188 were sent for trial, though 6,056 were given the curious benefit of "suspended indictment," which means that the evidence was not strong enough to allow them to be sent before a judge. Of the 4,188 tried in court 2,144, or more than half, were given suspended sentences, which means that they were released on probation.

J. Jay Hirz.

"Thought surveillance" in action—Japanese workers, accused of being Communist, being arrested in Tokyo after a demonstration.

Thus, out of nearly 60,000 arrested, only 2,044, or less that 3½ per cent, were found to deserve punishment. If real communism be compared to an epidemic of smallpox, it appears from those records that Japan only suffered from a mild outbreak of chickenpox.

The figures, however, do not tell the whole story, for they omit the stern paternalism with which the special police suppressed student communism. Scores of thousands of the students who passed through the hands of police were not "arrested" but "detained" in police stations. Japan has no Habeas Corpus Law, but has a corresponding regulation providing that a suspected person may not be held in a police station for more than a limited time. It is notoriously evaded by such expedients as moving a suspect from one station to another or releasing him and immediately rearresting him.

Even these easy formalities are often ignored. In Tokyo alone thousands of youths, many of them of good family, were taken to police stations and kept there for several months. In theory they were being questioned; in reality, they were being given a lesson. In some cases of which this writer has knowledge the suspected youths were beaten and housed in verminous and overcrowded cells. In others they were questioned and reasoned with, not unkindly.

Punishment and supervision supplemented by extra-legal police paternalism fight "thought epidemics" after they have broken out. Subtler in its methods, which are largely unseen, is the censorship which tries to prevent dangerous thoughts from infecting Japan's people.

The visitor first encounters it when he is asked before he lands to make a list of his books. The list goes not to the customs inspectors but to an official of the Home Office. The efficiency of the examiners is not high. Words like "social" or "Soviet" fascinate them. If you should have a book called

"Social Problems in Soviet Russia," no matter who was the author, you would do well to throw it overboard.

Recently the censors have cultivated a fine olfactory sense for works that might be derogatory of Japan. References to the Emperor are fatal. The case of the Vanity Fair cartoon and more recently the cases of Fortune and the Literary Digest illustrate this side of thought surveillance. The magazine Time is a hardened offender. As those works, written in a foreign language, cannot affect the masses, the reader may draw the inference that the established order represented by the censorship is afraid of the educated people of Japan. In the writer's view, the only general inference that may safely be drawn is that the censorship is stupid.

The newspaper censorship, after being reasonably administered for many years, has been tightened up recently. Its legal basis is the Press and Publications Law. The law prohibits the publication of matter which may disturb public peace or order or affect the national defense. Interpretation is left to the officials of various departments—the army and navy, the Communications Department, the Home Office (that is, the police) and the Foreign Office. The results are to be seen in the columns of the vernacular press, which are sometimes singularly silent on matters known to every reporter in the office. The German-Japanese agreement is a case in point. Its existence was known to every newspaper office in Tokyo, but not a word appeared in print until the pact had been signed.

The censorship is often unconsciously funny. When troops leave for Manchukuo the papers announce that "the OOO unit has left for OOOOO." The public became able to guess that the Third Division had been sent to Kirin, and it was announced that in future the use of circles would be prohibited.

The photographing of scenes within a fortified zone is naturally of celestial delicacy, and recently the Nichi Nichi, in giving its readers a picture of an elephant being taken aboard ship en route to the zoo, carefully added to the caption the words: "By kind permission of the commander of the Shimonoseki fortified area." Imagination staggers at the thought of what international spies might learn from a photograph of an elephant.

A Korean paper in publishing a picture of Son, the winner of the marathon at the Berlin Olympiad, reprehensibly removed the rising sun badge which Son wore on his coat and was suppressed for an indefinite period as a lesson.

The censorship on foreign press telegrams, both incoming and outgoing, is also now exercised with a severity formerly unknown. The task has been simplified by the merger of the Dentsu and Rengo news agencies. The great bulk of the foreign news published in Japan now comes through one channel only, and that channel is closely connected with authority.

Karl Marx was long ago translated into Japanese and "Das Kapital" could be bought in the original German, in English or in Japanese at any big book store. Virtually any foreign book, desirable or undesirable, could be bought as easily. The Moscow Daily News was on sale as openly as "Lady Chatterley's Lover." The authorities were then actuated by the principle that since only a small minority could read foreign books, it was unnecessary to exclude any except the openly pornographic or revolutionary. In the last year or two, however, a characteristic change has come over the book stores.

All new books are now read by the censor before they reach the shops, and he exercises his vigilance particularly on writers who criticize Japan. The principal result to date has been to give an unsolicited boost to a few not very important books and to create abroad the impression that Japanese fear criticism. Like social climbers, they seem to feel unsure of their position and sensitive to things which thicker-skinned nations would ignore with contempt.

* * *

June 6, 1937

FREEDOM OF PRESS HAILED IN CHINA

Special Cable to The New York Times

SHANGHAI—Largely because of persistent domestic pressure, the Chinese Government has relaxed its rigid censorship of press and speech which has been enforced for the past decade. The Chinese can print or say practically anything they choose now, if their disparaging comment is directed against Japan or some other foreign power. They may not, however, make unfriendly criticism of their own government.

The Chinese are voracious readers and prolific writers and they love to talk. No action of the government could have done more to restore their confidence and self-respect than the modification in censorship. Vernacular journals are printing facts which a few months ago were only whispered, and public officials who formerly evaded all attempts at interviews are now making extremely candid speeches.

If the Chinese editors are bitter with the suppressed bile of years of enforced silence. It is not obvious in their writings. The new privilege of using the character for "Japan" instead of one meaning "a certain country," as they have in the past, in news and editorials, seems to have revived the natural dignity of race. Comment on developments in Japan now issued by the Central News Agency, the Chinese Government's subsidized press service, is moderately good, fair and accurate.

The new mode of straightforward speaking was strikingly exemplified in a recent speech which General Fu Tso-yi made to the students of Tsinghwa University in Peiping. For the past few years General Chiang Kai-shek has been the only person in China doing this kind of talking. General Fu can talk pretty much as he pleases, however, without hurting any one's feelings. He is the able young Governor of Suiyuan Province who successfully repulsed the Japanese-directed Mongol campaign against Suiyuan last Winter.

General Fu told the students gathered at the old college in Peiping to hear him that cupidity, or selfishness, on the part of individual Chinese leaders has been almost entirely responsible for China's past submission in the face of Japanese aggression.

PART IV

WORLD WAR II, 1939–1945

THE ALLIED NATIONS

September 6, 1939

PRESS RULES STIFFENED

France Sets Penalties for Using News Useful to Enemy

Special Cable to The New York Times

PARIS, Sept. 5—A new decree published today establishes most severe penalties for any infraction of the new press rule forbidding the publication of information useful to enemy powers or having an unfavorable effect on the morale of the French population.

A term of ten years in prison and a fine of 1,000 to 10,000 francs were assigned as additional punishment to the regular rules against press infractions under martial law.

* * *

September 14, 1939

ATTACK ON CENSOR MADE IN COMMONS

Lack of Information Given to Public Aids Propaganda of Reich, It Is Charged

HOARE PROMISES INQUIRY

Faulty Coordination Between Services and Ministry Gets Blame for 'Muddle'

Wireless to The New York Times

LONDON, Sept. 13—A bitter attack by the Labor Opposition on the Ministry of Information today brought assurances from Sir Samuel Hoare, head of that Ministry, that the entire question of what the British public shall know about their war was being studied and a promise that Monday night's "muddle" about publication of the news of the landing of British troops in France will not be repeated.

According to Arthur Greenwood, deputy Labor leader, there were even cases of police in the country stopping cars and confiscating any copies of papers with this information. Early yesterday morning the Ministry withdrew the ban and final editions carried all the news.

"This is not intelligent censorship." Mr. Greenwood, leading the attack, told the Commons in a speech which was only one of many tending to show that, war or no war, the Commons intends to keep its right to criticize the government. "Monday night's proceedings are an extraordinary example of stupidity and vacillation which I hope will not be repeated.

"Some people made fools of the British press and the British Broadcasting Corporation and treated the people of this country as though they were children. That kind of thing serves to bring us into ridicule abroad."

Chamberlain Notes Criticism

Earlier Prime Minister Chamberlain had taken note of criticisms of the work of the Ministry in a general statement of war and had assured the House of the government's desire to give the public the fullest possible information. At the same time he stressed the difficult job of a brand new Ministry in steering a course between the proper desire of the services to suppress news which might help the enemy and the desire of the people and press for full information. The Prime Minister asked for patience and toleration in judging the work of the Ministry.

Most Opposition criticism was the echo of much general dissatisfaction with what the government has seen fit to publish, and only the mildest sort of echo of what Fleet Street is saying, almost without exception. It was directed mainly at what was called lack of coordination between the services and the Ministry, and particularly at the lack of any imagination in dealing with what can be published.

Thus Mr. Greenwood and Sir Archibald Sinclair, Liberal Opposition leader, said that the government had been unfair both to the Air Force and the people in giving insufficient details of "the glory of the exploit" when the Air Force raided the Kiel Canal. The British people, Sir Archibald said, "having been accustomed to the high standard of work of skilled journalists, will not be satisfied with official assurance in uninformative bulletins."

"We can only win the war if our methods are vigorous, even robust or vulgar," he continued.

Mr. Greenwood also laid stress on the general dissatisfaction among foreign correspondents here, saying that many of the best of them were planning to move to a neutral capital because of lack of information and the rigors of the censorship here.

Plays Germany's Game

"Owing to these difficulties, newspapers in neutral countries, some of them most friendly to us, are relying on German sources of information, from which they obtain what is called news and plenty of it," Mr. Greenwood said. "The streams of world opinion are thus being polluted and poisoned by German propaganda through the absence of vigorous action here."

Other speakers emphasized the same point, saying British newspapers are being allowed to print only a rehash of old, uninteresting news, and that United States papers as well as those of other neutral countries were giving full information.

Sir Samuel Hoare again used the argument that the Ministry has been functioning so short a time that allowance must be made for creaks in the machinery. There had been great strain and regrettable confusion Monday night, he admitted, and promised it would not happen again—particularly visits of police to newspaper offices. Sir Samuel said there had been a bad misunderstanding between the Ministry and the War Office—it is understood that the suppression order was issued by the War Secretary, Leslie Hore-Belisha himself—but that in future a senior officer of the fighting services would be detailed to the Ministry and matters would probably go better then.

As to delays and the meagerness of official communiqués, Sir Samuel said in many cases these were due to desire of the service departments not to publish inaccurate news. With particular reference to the supposed appearance of enemy planes off the south coast last Wednesday, which caused innumerable rumors, he said that arrangements now have been made with the Air Ministry for speedier release of information on air raids.

This was the answer to a large section of British opinion, which believes that a lapse of six or ten hours between the sound of the air-raid warning and any official news about the raid is too long.

* * *

November 19, 1939

FRANCE ADOPTS STRICT RULES

A radio commentator who has a five-minute broadcast period was met by a friend the other day who said, "I listen to you and am waiting for the day when you will have fifteen minutes. Five minutes is too short."

"Not on your life," replied the veteran newsman. "Just try to find something of interest from Europe to talk about for five minutes, especially from France, where all we get is 'all quiet.' "

France, the broadcasters report, is the most bottled up as far as war news is concerned, and restrictions hang heavy on the commentators on the air from Paris.

Broadcasting in France now is maintained under a war-time code restricting the operations of radio stations, although no curb has been placed on listeners, according to information received by the Commerce Department.

Among the provisions of the now broadcasting regulations are:

"All broadcasting stations not in keeping with the needs of national interest are suppressed. The operation of broadcasting stations maintained is assured by the State or governmental services.

"Private receiving sets are left, in principle, at the disposition of their owners under the same conditions as in time of peace. Military authorities are empowered to seize any private sets which they judge of utility to suppress in the interest of national defense.

"Private broadcasting stations and broadcasting-receiving stations passing into the service of the State are requisitioned. The material of the suppressed stations is notified by the municipal authority or the public colonial authority to the qualified military or maritime authority which will cause it to be removed, kept under guard or sealed up.

"Maintenance of unauthorized stations, the establishment of fraudulent stations, the use of these stations, the communication to third parties of information received or transmitted by radio telegraph or radio telephone of interest to national defense or the security of the State, will expose the delinquents to seizure of the apparata without prejudice to the penalties applicable respectively to these facts."

* * *

December 3, 1939

CENSORSHIP IN BRITAIN ANALYZED FOR READERS

Correspondent Finds It a Military Rather Than Political Measure—Some Examples Are Offered

By RAYMOND DANIELL
Wireless to The New York Times

LONDON, Dec. 2—"Dispatches from Europe and the Far East are subject to censorship." That sentence has appeared on the first page of The New York Times almost every day since the war began. It is intended to warn readers to be on guard against dispatches that censors might have poisoned by amending or emending.

However, it should not be interpreted to mean that no honest, objective reports get out of these countries at war or near the war zones. They do.

Newly arrived visitors and letters from the United States and published comments at home indicate that suspicion of foreign news sources has outstepped the danger of contamination.

There is a newly arrived visitor in London who bursts into a correspondent's office asking for "the real inside story of the war." Then there is the friend at home who writes that it is a pity that, with all the rich, colorful story so near, so little can be written. Last but not least annoying are the knowing comments of one's colleagues who inform readers that "you can't believe a word of what those foreign correspondents send—censorship, you know."

The British Censorship

It is in the hope of straightening the record and clarifying the situation as far as this country is concerned that this article is written. The point is that the British censorship, except where it is designed to save the lives of soldiers and sailors and not the skins of politicians, is a no more serious barrier to truthful presentation of the news than the libel laws of the United States.

There has probably been more talk about less censorship in this country than anywhere else in Europe since the war broke out. That is partly because, being inexperienced at such matters, the British made a terrible botch of reconciling the necessities of war with the ideals of freedom of speech and press, and partly because the very idea implicit in the word "censorship" is as abhorrent to them as it is to most Americans.

Besides, in the early days of inactivity on all fronts, except in Poland, there was such a dearth of news that even without censorship the press would have been left in the embarrassing position of having a great "story" on its hands and no details to give its readers. Clearly a whipping boy was needed, and the visitor to Britain might have been excused if he had become confused and gathered the impression that it was censorship and the Ministry of Information with which the empire was at war. Of course, if the censors really had done their job, as many observers imagined they were, no criticism would have been heard.

More Scientific Now

However, as the war goes on, the business of censorship is becoming an almost exact science. It is being demonstrated every day that censorship need imply no suppression of news other than military and naval secrets. The proof of the pudding is in the eating; so let us see how it works.

First, there are rules that everybody understands. They are that no information about troop or ship movements may be given. The reason for this is obvious and it would be an obtuse person who quarreled with the regulations, for this is a country at war and publications about the whereabouts of troops and the sailing of ships might invite attacks.

Politics and diplomacy fall in a different category. There, generally speaking, the lid is off. If premature publication of diplomatic information might upset the applecart, the chances are that the dispatch will be held up, but the most vitriolic political attacks upon members of the government are passed without question.

One of the most important considerations of all is that no change is made in a dispatch without the writer's knowledge and approval. The correspondent has the opportunity of passing upon any suggested revisions—consenting to them or eliminating the offensive matter entirely—so that there is no chance of distortion of his meaning. The suggested changes are usually on the side of understatement, even when the discussion is one of British exploits at sea or in the air.

No Personal Matter

It should be pointed out also that the censorship here is an entirely impersonal thing—few American correspondent ever have seen the men who pass upon their dispatches. These men for the most part are drawn from military and naval circles; they have little interest in politics but a considerable knowledge of the kind of information that would be of greatest strategic value to the enemy. Just as in peacetime, dispatches are sent to the cable companies for transmission, and it is seldom in the ordinary course of events that any more is heard about them.

Nor does that imply that news must be favorable to Britain to pass without question. Recently this correspondent sent a dispatch about troubles in India. The dispatch was delayed for forty minutes and was finally released, with apologies by the censor who had delayed it. He explained that he had arbitrary orders to refer all matters dealing with India to a higher authority, but so long as the facts, though sensational, were true, there was no objection.

Then more recently there was a dispatch on how aerial mines had forced temporary interruption of traffic to the Port of London—a far from pleasant item from the viewpoint of this country. That was held up until conditions had returned to normal and then it was released with the explanation that as long as minesweepers were busy clearing the channels it would have been dangerous to publish it.

That Rumanian "Guarantee"

On the other hand, there is occasionally stupid quibbling. For instance, one night recently The Times Bureau wrote a dispatch for transmission to New York about the delivery of sixty British planes to Rumania; it was stopped by the censor because of a reference to the fact that Rumania was one of the countries that Britain had guaranteed against aggression. When a protest was made to the censor at the cable office on the ground that this was a secret that all the world knew he agreed that it was true that a guarantee had been given, but he pointed out that it was "months ago" and he had to make sure it was "still good."

There is a war in progress and there is a censorship in force in Britain. But it is a straightforward, honest rule of law with nothing sinister about it. It may prevent American readers from knowing the exact latitude and longitude where the Rawalpindi was sunk, but it does not attempt to edit correspondents' dispatches to make it appear that the victim of the German pocket battleship went to the bottom because of a boiler explosion.

Newspapers Criticize

Meanwhile, British newspapers go their merry way abusing Cabinet Ministers for imposing rationing too soon or too late, attacking the Minister of Supply for buying too much or too little and criticizing the Chancellor of the Exchequer for borrowing too little and taxing too much.

In short, it is a military rather than a political censorship that exists here.

* * *

January 11, 1940

PARIS CENSORSHIP A NEWS BLOCKADE

Negative Attitude of Officials Is Bar to Propaganda as Well as Information

REPORTERS IN QUANDARY

Some of Their Stories Sent From Conducted Tours Are 'Whiskered' at Publication

By P. J. PHILIP
Wireless to The New York Times

PARIS, Jan. 10—What is wrong with the French Information Department and censorship is that everybody who has got an official job thinks that he should do all the thinking and acting for everybody else and prevent any initiative on the part of the ordinary newspaper man.

It is as if the police force should suddenly decide that it should not only have the right to regulate the traffic but that it should control what traffic should be admitted on the streets.

The whole quarrel is between the constructive, creative civilian mind and the obstructive, negative functionary mind. It is not a quarrel of persons in any sense.

Official Outlook Hampers

The men in charge of the French censorship are courteous, charming, tolerant, intelligent and often very helpful. The men engaged in the information section under Jean Giraudoux are men of wide culture, sympathetic outlook, experience and imagination. But both the official information section and the censors are officials.

They cannot avoid putting on the official manner of thinking and acting just as soon as they get their appointments, and every one who has ever worked in a government department or watched one work knows that the first rule is to prevent anything from happening and second to avoid responsibility.

One would have imagined that the Information section would have at once convoked all the French and foreign newspaper men and fed them daily with "propaganda and news." That is what has happened in Germany and probably elsewhere. Here it is more difficult to get any information or even any propaganda out of the information section than to get a winkle out of its shell without the appropriate pin.

At the same time all or nearly all the usual channels of news are closed. One hears of a train wreck. Normally there would be a rush of newspaper men and photographers to the scene. But every newspaper man and photographer is getting the habit of staying at home instead, because he knows in advance that the police will not let him approach the scene of the accident and that the censor will not let him tell the story or publish any pictures.

Reporters Discouraged

Almost the worst crime of the censorship is, indeed, that it discourages newspaper initiative. The reporters' attitude very soon becomes:

"Why worry? What's the good?"

Sometimes the whole business becomes immensely comic. For months past the name of the town in which British headquarters are situated has been a dead secret, which, of course, everybody knew. The British even changed its name for their army purposes. Then this week a Paris evening newspaper published an account of the ceremony of the presentation of decorations by General Maurice Gustave Gamelin, the Allied Commander in Chief, to General Viscount Gort, the British commander, and dated its correspondent's story under the date line of that secret city.

Trips to the front are organized for the newspaper men to compensate for the restrictions on their professional ability to discover things for themselves. They are escorted to places and things are shown to them. They are treated with generous consideration and sometimes patience.

Stories With "Whiskers"

Then their stories are censored and sent to Paris by courier. They arrive for dispatch to America three and four days after they are written, "with whiskers on them," as one managing editor cabled to his correspondent.

What happens when an offensive begins is going to be one of the major tragedies of newspaper history if this system continues. But the official mind, even and perhaps especially when it is only temporarily official, just cannot appreciate the fact that news is not made by officials, and that even propaganda can be made only by trained newspaper men.

* * *

February 25, 1940

THE TALK OF PARIS: "ANASTASIE"

Censorship Is Considered Fair Game for the Gibes of the Controlled Press

By BERNHARD RAGNER

PARIS—Figaro shrewdly advised men to laugh at the foibles of mankind, to avoid weeping over them. Some such philosophy guides the French press in its relations with "Anastasie," the gaunt, unsightly witch who symbolizes the censorship in France today. Indeed, Anastasie has become Pleasantry No. 1 in the French Republic, and making jokes about her has developed into a minor industry which, ironically enough, exists because the censorship allows it. If she wished Anastasie could shut it down tomorrow, since she has the right of life and death over every paragraph, sentence and word published within France or telegraphed abroad.

Anastasie's real job, of course, is to prevent valuable information from getting to the enemy. Somehow jests about Anastasie herself do not fall into this category. Nor does criticism of her strange, unpredictable and (to outsiders) unaccountable antics. Here the French editor is as free as in peacetime, if he will phrase his objections with reason and moderation. Every day Anastasie is spoofed, parodied and caricatured, but she accepts it all with admirable tolerance. Seldom does she blue-pencil a good joke, blot out a witty line or "kill" a critical laugh, although aimed at herself. Unperturbed, she reads these drolleries, grins and O. K.'s publication, revealing herself as a woman of uncommon sense, on this point at least.

In consequence Anastasie is today the preferred topic for jokesmiths, cartoonists and song-writers, with Hitler as her nearest rival. Constantly satirized in rhyme and epigram, she is the unprotesting target of sarcasm, hostile barbs and spirited reproof. Once in a great while a kind word. Result: She is the most talked-of female in France today, the most debated and the most detested. She doesn't seem to mind it. Anyhow, here is her portrait, as sketched by Larousse, the French Noah Webster:

> ANASTASIE: A jocose nickname, in the world of art, literature and journalism, for the censorship. Invariably pictured as an ugly old, maid, thin, crabbed and fault-finding, she is armed with an enormous pair of scissors, which she wields in reckless, random fashion.

How Anastasie got her name nobody seems to know. Whatever her origin, she is the chief concern, the pet peeve and the main problem of the writing fraternity in France. Most newspapers stoically accept her as a necessary nuisance, abide loyally by her decisions, although protesting firmly and courteously now and then. Sometimes they win their point, and Anastasie, if convinced, reverses her decision. Indubitably she suppresses a lot of harmless information, but she can't take a chance. When in doubt about some phrase she promptly sets her scissors into action.

When Anastasie cuts a phrase, a sentence or an entire article ordinary newspapers leave the blank spaces thus created without comment, or note the fact by stating: "Twenty-six lines censored," "One paragraph deleted by the censor," etc. This practice incited one fun-loving editor to announce: "Five letters censored," leaving the reader to guess what they were.

Pugnacious and controversial organs, with a chip constantly on their shoulders, engage in vehement arguments with Anastasie. Usually this makes lively, exciting reading, valueless to the enemy, and so it is generally passed without question. Sometimes Anastasie is persuaded to change her attitude; then the editor must find some other pretext for dispute.

Still others, more philosophical in temperament, grin and bear it all with amused detachment. They good-naturedly josh the censorship, laugh at its deletions and fill in the blank space with satirical comments, pointed cartoons and spicy pleasantries. Folk proverbs and advertising slogans are twisted about to frame a witty indictment of Anastasie. Another device is to dig up an ancient speech by Prime Minister Edouard Daladier and to quote some eloquent passage eulogizing the liberty of the press. Caricatures of Anastasie are popular; so are drawings of her redoubtable scissors. René Guerin, prolific and talented cartoonist, seems to earn his living these days simply by bantering Anastasie. Every day he contrives a humorous sketch picturing Jacques Bonhomme in his ludicrous and unpleasant encounters with her.

When Le Merle (The Blackbird), a sprightly, Left-Wing, Opposition sheet, had two neighboring columns completely "bleached," the editor appropriately entitled them "Devastated Regions." One week when Le Canard Enchainé (The Chained Duck) printed an issue with more white than black, it warned readers via a "box" on its front page:

> Contrary to appearances, this number is not intended as an advertisement for La Grande Maison de Blanc.

(The house referred to is the world-famed Paris store specializing in white goods.)

Every day white spaces in the satirical press are punctuated with remarks like the following:

> In reality this news item was none of your business, anyhow.
>
> This efficient work was done by Anastasie's modern laundry.
>
> Trying to find something in this place is useless, since there is nothing here.
>
> A minute of silence, please, for this deceased article. It was the victim of Anastasie's cruel shears.

Since last August Anastasie has been on the job; she will lay down her scissors only when a victorious peace has been achieved. The press and Anastasie do not and cannot agree; their angle of vision is not the same; they start from differing premises. Occasions for friction and misunderstanding are frequent, but since divorce is impossible, they must live together as best they can.

When differences arise Anastasie and the press do negotiate and in one instance the newspapers emerged triumphant. Last August the censorship banished all crossword puzzles to prevent enemy spies from using them to communicate coded information. Immediately a protest arose from editors and readers, soldiers and civilians. Anastasie listened to reason; she offered to compromise; she would permit crossword puzzles once a foolproof plan could be devised to make them free of hidden messages. On weather reports there was no yielding; they could be used by enemy aviators; hence, they remain a State secret which it is forbidden to publish. Shipping news (except from neutral countries) is also taboo, for understandable reasons.

And yet Anastasie 1940, critics admit, is a much more reasonable and personable creature than her ancestor of twenty-six years ago. It is recalled that the suspension of newspapers, for failing to follow her advice, was a fairly frequent occurrence during the last war. To date, although the censorship creates many mystifying white spaces, there have been no suspensions of importance—except the Communist press, which exists no more. Doubtless Anastasie is more lenient, while the newspapers are more disciplined.

* * *

May 25, 1940

BARS COMMUNIST PAPERS

Australia Moves to Wipe Out the Subversive Press

Wireless to The New York Times

CANBERRA, Australia, May 24—Minister of Information Sir Henry Gullett announced to the House of Representatives today that nine Communist newspapers had been banned. The embargo on writing on certain specified subjects was removed from newspapers outside the banned list.

The government appealed to those trade unions whose press organs are controlled by Communists to terminate the Communist control as soon as possible and states that meanwhile they would be rigidly censored. The government called on all citizens to help prevent the illicit distribution of Communist propaganda which is certain to be attempted now that the Communist newspapers are banned.

Regulations were gazetted enabling trade unions to expel Communist and other subversive officials. Those expelled have the right to appeal to an arbitration court.

* * *

May 25, 1940

CUBA TO BAR PROPAGANDA

Acts to Silence Nazi and Communist Sympathizers

Wireless to The New York Times

HAVANA, May 24—The Cuban Government took first steps yesterday to suppress Nazi and communistic propaganda, after instructions to this effect had been issued by President Federico Laredo Bru.

The president called for particular attention to be given to propaganda sent by mail, published in the newspapers or broadcast over the radio. He instructed the Secretaries of Communications and the Interior strictly to enforce a decree issued during the Spanish Civil War barring propaganda by foreign sympathizers.

The Interior Department closed a radio station in Vedado, a residential section, which was said by listeners to have been broadcasting Nazi propaganda.

* * *

January 2, 1941

BRITISH CENSOR EXPLAINS

Says Aim Is Simply to Bar Useful Data From Nation's Foes

Special Cable to The New York Times

LONDON, Jan. 1—The man who watches over British cables, telephones, mails and the radio stepped before the microphones last night and told why and how he did it. He is C. J. Radcliffe, Acting Controller of the Press.

He described the censorship as "the rationing of news." Rationing is unpopular in this country where food is affected and even less popular as far as news is concerned. Mr. Radcliffe's major point was that there was no intention of hiding ugly facts from the people. He said the censorship's only aim was to bar information that might help the Nazis. He asserted that if the government permitted the announcement of town names after every bombing "it would enable the enemy to correct errors in navigation and be more accurate the next time."

* * *

January 22, 1941

BRITAIN OUTLAWS RED NEWSPAPER AND WEEKLY TO CHECK PROPAGANDA

Daily Worker Office Raided by Scotland Yard Men—The Week Also Suppressed—Government Denies Change in Policy

Special Cable to The New York Times

LONDON, Jan. 21—The British Government cracked down today on two publications that had been sniping at the British war effort from the Left. They were The Daily Worker, Communist party newspaper, and The Week, a mimeographed news letter edited by Claude Cockburn and distributed to subscribers only.

Both were suppressed and simultaneously with the order by Herbert Morrison, the Home Secretary, special police of Scotland Yard raided The Daily Worker's office and stopped publication of an edition that was just going to press. Then they searched the building and interviewed several members of the staff.

[The Daily Worker, nevertheless, appeared in mimeographed form early today with an appeal to workers to protest against the ban, according to The United Press. The single sheet foolscap issue apparently was printed secretly.]

The Home Office order suppressing the two publications explained the action was taken because "of systematic publication calculated to foment opposition to prosecution of the war to a successful issue." Under it The Daily Worker and The Week suffer the same fate as the organ of British fascism, Action, which was suppressed when Sir Oswald Mosley was arrested.

It is now an offense against the Crown to print, distribute or in any way to assist publication of the Communist newspaper or Mr. Cockburn's news letter and the police have the right to take possession of their offices.

A Home Office spokesman declared the action did not indicate a change of government policy permitting freedom of newspaper criticism of the government but was intended only to suppress openly subversive propaganda.

The decision to suppress The Daily Worker and The Week was taken only after long consideration of all the issues involved and because a warning issued to The Daily Worker when Sir John Anderson was Home Secretary had not achieved its purpose. It was decided it would be harmful to national security to postpone action further.

Two courses were before Mr. Morrison. They were to start prosecution or to suppress the publications. The official view was that the exigencies of war demanded speed and that prosecution was likely to be a lengthy process.

Mr. Morrison is accountable to Parliament for his act and it is likely that the question will be raised there about the propriety of his action, possibly by William Gallacher, the lone Communist member. It is expected Mr. Morrison will assure the House of Commons there is no objection to genuine criticism of government policy but that the systematic publication of material designed to spread discouragement and undermine morale would not be tolerated.

The Daily Worker made its debut as a Communist party newspaper Jan. 1, 1930. Last May it was made illegal outside the United Kingdom. Recently it has made many attacks on army arrangements.

Last June The Daily Worker announced that Professor J. B. S. Haldane was chairman of the editorial board.

The Week's publisher is better known as Frank Pitcairn. He is the author of several books. He was unable to get government permission last Winter to go to Finland as war correspondent of The Daily Worker.

* * *

January 13, 1942

IN THE NATION

A Summary of the Censorship Situation

By ARTHUR KROCK

WASHINGTON, Jan. 12—The American public, which has long been used to a press with freedom that Congress may not "abridge" (the word of the Bill of Rights), seems to be taking deep interest in the restrictions of information that the real perils of war have imposed. This interest is partly revealed by the fact that reader letters to correspondents and editors deal steadily and often with the matter of censorship, wherefore an occasional summary such as the following is indicated.

The situation at present is compounded of confusion, cooperation and uncertainty on the part of authorities and the press alike. The confusion can in part be traced (using White House Secretary Early's penetrating phrase) to "too much machinery." The cooperation stems from a sincere desire on both sides to have nothing published that will lend aid to the enemy. The uncertainty has its source in government's attempt to link mandatory with voluntary censorship and then determine what the rules of voluntary censorship should be.

Since the experiment is young, and every one in the United States is inured to democratic ways, it is not strange that this uncertainty should not yet have been resolved. Censor Price is working on it earnestly. And the belief continues to prevail among Washington newspaper writers that in so far as he and Mr. Early design and control the censorship pattern it will be sensible, efficient and honest.

The Abridgements

The press' ancient freedom has gone in several respects, some of which are dictated by considerations of public safety. Its foreign dispatches are being censored with that objective, and such mistakes as are being made in this editing are traceable to the youth of the system, the errors of subordinate individuals and several bites at the same cherry. Editorial comment and news expository departments have been left so far to the self-restraint and sense of responsibility of their authors—which may or may not be an enduring arrangement—, but the value of exposition necessarily has been reduced by the growing censorship of the facts on which such exposition must be based.

This censorship of these facts at the source is also a measure of public safety, and as a policy there can be no quarrel with it. Until or unless concealment is used to shield official incompetence or weakness of organization it is an essential evil of war. The enemy, for example, should not be informed of the details of the production designed to defeat him. But if all the important facts concerning it are withheld, even as a confidential, not-to-be-published guide for exposition, then it will not be possible to know whether production is being competently administered and the stream of billions is being turned into matériel at the best possible rate.

Two-Way Street

That is a problem which war has posed both for the government and for the press. Freedom in its Bill of Rights definition having vanished for the duration of the war, it remains to be seen how greatly the restrictions will affect those areas of information where censor and press may honestly and patriotically differ over what will give aid to the enemy, and those items which are annoying to officialdom, rather than of military value to the foe. Some time must pass before the degree and effect of censorship can be calculated.

Censorship is always a two-way street. From one direction comes the news that is independently gathered by the press, and the comment and exposition based on that news. From the other comes the news over which the government has control. For the first time in recent history the government is regulating the flow in both directions. The result, of course, is a greatly abridged press, and the public should do its reading with this constantly in mind.

Lately a new rule has been promulgated in Washington which could easily have the reverse effect from the excellent one intended. Unless it is changed, the press can send no representatives with the President on journeys out of Washington. It may be the rule is to apply only to trips which have rest as their objective; that point is not yet clear.

A Rumor Generator

This is an extension of the wise wartime provision that there is to be no publicity about the President's movements except that which he prescribes. His safety is concerned, and that is enough to justify the regulation. But if often representatives of the press, for the public, are not to know where the President is, the rumor-factory is sure to start operations and there will be no prompt and effective means to bomb it before it gets really going. Public morale, now the concern of so many agencies and bureaus, may be adversely affected by baseless and alarming rumors: the President has "disappeared"; he has been in that "token air raid" which may be attempted by the Axis at any time; he is "desperately ill," etc.

If the press always knows where the President is, and has its representatives near by to publish what is authorized and required, these rumors will be fewer and those that start will be still-born.

* * *

January 15, 1942

CENSORSHIP CODE ISSUED FOR PRESS

Magazine and Other Periodicals Also Covered in Plan to Keep Information From Enemy

BANS EXPLAINED IN DETAIL

Office of Byron Price Says It Is Hoped to Keep Our Publications the Freest in World

Special to The New York Times

WASHINGTON, Jan. 14—A code under which newspapers, magazines and other periodicals are requested not to publish certain classes of information which might be of aid to the enemy was announced today by the Office of Censorship headed by Byron Price.

The code is in addition to the already effective censorship over all communications between the United States and foreign countries.

Publication of most of the banned details has long been withheld by many of the periodicals under guidance of the Army, Navy and other government establishments prominent in the war emergency. In the main the censorship authorities ask for elimination of certain facts regarding munitions production, troops, ships, airplanes, fortifications, weather and the like.

The code, drafted by Mr. Price and John H. Sorrells, assistant director, will be administered by Mr. Sorrells, aided by a small board of editors and an advisory council of the publishing industry.

Text of the New Code

The text of the code as issued today is as follows:

This statement responds to the many inquiries received by the Office of Censorship, asking for an outline of newspaper and magazine practices which the government feels are desirable for the effective prosecution of the war.

It is essential that certain basic facts be understood from the beginning.

The first of these facts is that the outcome of the war is a matter of vital personal concern to the future of every American citizen. The second is that the security of our armed forces and even of our homes and our liberties will be weakened in greater or less degree by every disclosure of information which will help the enemy.

If every member of every news staff and contributing writer will keep these two facts constantly in mind, and then will follow the dictates of common sense, he will be able to answer for himself many of the questions which might otherwise trouble him. In other words, a maximum of accomplishment will be attained if editors will ask themselves with respect to any given detail, "Is this information I would like to have if I were the enemy?" And then act accordingly.

The result of such a process will hardly represent "business as usual" on the news desks of the country. On the contrary, it will mean some sacrifice of the journalistic enterprise of ordinary times. But it will not mean a news or editorial blackout. It is the hope and expectation of the Office of Censorship that the columns of American publications will remain the freest in the world, and will tell the story of our national successes and short-comings accurately and in much detail.

The highly gratifying response of the press so far proves that it understands the need for temporary sacrifice, and is prepared to make that sacrifice in the spirit of the President's recent assurance that such curtailment as may be necessary will be administered "in harmony with the best interests of our free institutions."

Below is a summary covering specific problems. This summary repeats, with some modifications, requests previously made by various agencies of the Federal Government, and it may be regarded as superseding and consolidating all of those requests.

Special attention is directed to the fact that all of the requests in the summary are modified by a proviso that the information listed may properly be published when authorized by appropriate authority. News on all of these subjects will become available from government sources; but in war, timeliness is an important factor, and the government unquestionably is in the best position to decide when disclosure is timely.

The specific information which newspapers and magazines are asked not to publish except when such information is made available officially by appropriate authority falls into the following classes:

Troops

The general character and movements of United States Army units, within or without the continental limits of the United States—their location; identity or exact composition; equipment or strength; their destination, routes and schedules; their assembly for embarkation, prospective embarkation, or actual embarkation. Any such information regarding the troops of friendly nations on American soil.

Note: The request as regards location and general character does not apply to troops in training camps in continental United States, nor to units assigned to domestic police duty.

Ships

The location, movements and identity of naval and merchant vessels of the United States in any waters, and of other nations opposing the Axis powers, in American waters; the port and time of arrival or prospective arrival of any such vessels, or the port from which they leave; the nature of cargoes of such vessels; the location of enemy naval or merchant vessels in or near American waters; the assembly, departure or arrival of transports or convoys; the existence of mine fields or other harbor defense; secret orders or other secret instructions regarding lights, buoys and other guides to navigators; the number, size, character and location of ships in construction, or advance information as to the date of launchings or commissionings; the physical set-up or technical details of shipyards.

Planes

The disposition, movements and strength of Army or Navy air units.

Fortifications

The location of forts and other fortifications; the location of coast defense emplacements or anti-aircraft guns; their nature and number; location of bomb shelters; location of camouflaged objects.

Production

Specific information about war contracts, such as the exact type of production, production schedules, dates of delivery, or progress of production; estimated supplies of strategic and critical materials available; or nation-wide "round-ups" of locally published procurement data except when such composite information is officially approved for publication.

Specific information about the location of, or other information about, sites and factories already in existence, which would aid saboteurs gained through observation by the general public, disclosing the location of sites and factories yet to be established, or the nature of their production.

Any information about new or secret military designs, or new factory designs for war production.

Weather

Weather forecasts, other than officially issued by the Weather Bureau; the routine forecasts printed by any single newspaper to cover only the State in which it is published and not more than four adjoining States, portions of which lie within a radius of 150 miles from the point of publication.

Consolidated temperature tables covering more than twenty stations, in any one newspaper.

Note: Special forecasts issued by the Weather Bureau warning of unusual conditions, or special reports issued by the Weather Bureau concerning temperature tables, or news stories warning the public of dangerous roads or streets, within 150 miles of the point of publication, are all acceptable for publication.

Weather "round-up" stories covering actual conditions throughout more than one State, except when given out by the Weather Bureau.

Photographs and Maps

Photographs conveying the information specified in this summary, unless officially approved for publication.

Detailed maps or photographs disclosing location of munition dumps, or other restricted Army or Naval areas.

Note: This has no reference to maps showing the general theatre of war, or large scale zones of action, movements of contending forces on a large scale, or maps showing the general ebb and flow of battle lines.

Note: Special care should be exercised in the publication of serial photos presumably of non-military significance, which might reveal military or other information helpful to the enemy; also care should be exercised in publishing casualty photos so as not to reveal unit identifications through collar ornaments, etc. Special attention is directed to the section of this summary covering information about damage to military objectives.

General

Casualty lists.

Note: There is no objection to publication of information about casualties from a newspaper's local field, obtained from nearest of kin, but it is requested that in such cases specific military and naval units, and exact locations, be not mentioned.

Information disclosing the new location of national archives, art treasures, and so on, which have been moved for safe-keeping.

Information about damage to military and naval objectives, including docks, railroads, or commercial airports, resulting from enemy action.

Note: The spread of rumors in such a way that they will be accepted as facts will render aid and comfort to the enemy. It is suggested that enemy claims or ship sinkings, or of other damage to our forces, be weighed carefully and the source clearly identified, if published.

Information about the transportation of munitions or other war materials, including oil tank cars and trains.

Information about the movements of the President of the United States, or of official military or diplomatic missions of the United States or of any other nation opposing the Axis powers—routes, schedules, or destination, within or without the continental limits of the United States; movements of ranking Army or Naval officers and staffs on official business; movements of other individuals or units under special orders of the Army, Navy or State Department.

Note: Advertising matter, letters to the editor, interviews with men on leave, columns, and so on, are included in the above requests, both as to text and illustration.

If information should be made available anywhere which seems to come from doubted authority, or to be in conflict with the general aims of these requests; or if special restrictions requested locally or otherwise by various authorities seem unreasonable or out of harmony with this summary, it is recommended that the question be submitted at once to the Office of Censorship.

In addition, if any newspaper, magazine or other agency or individual handling news or special articles desires clarification or advice as to what disclosures might or might not aid the enemy, the Office of Censorship will cooperate gladly. Such inquiries should be addressed to the Office of Censorship, Washington.

Should additions or modifications of this summary seem feasible and desirable from time to time, the industry will be advised.

The Office of Censorship
Byron Price, Director

* * *

March 9, 1942

PRICE LAUDS PRESS ON SELF-CENSORSHIP

Publishers and Broadcasters Cooperate Excellently 'by and Large,' Says Chief Censor

'FERVENT HOPE' IT LASTS

Otherwise 'Dark Hours May Be Ahead for Free Speech'—Fly, Others Join Radio Forum

Special to The New York Times

WASHINGTON, March 8—Commending the publishing and broadcasting industries "by and large" for "excellent" cooperation with the Office of Censorship, Byron Price, director, warned tonight that "dark hours may be ahead for free speech in the United States" if the present system of voluntary censorship proved a failure.

There naturally have been some mistakes and oversights, Mr. Price said, but he added:

"We have found no instance where any publisher or any broadcaster has shown evidence of a deliberate attempt to sabotage this experiment in self-discipline. I am encouraged to believe that no such instance will develop. I say this with fervent hope."

Mr. Price was one of five speakers, including representatives from newspaper, magazine and broadcasting fields, who discussed "Free Speech and Censorship in Wartime" on the American Forum of the Air program, carried tonight on the network of the Mutual Broadcasting System. The vital nature of the discussion was emphasized in a spirited question period following the brief talks, during which fellow-speakers fired query after query at Mr. Price, who answered some and parried others.

That flagrant and deliberate violations of the censorship code would not go unpunished was indicated in the forum period when Mr. Price said it would not be wise for any one to try "to play a game" or look for loopholes in the censorship code. One of his colleagues asked him what he would do about it, and he replied:

"We'll have to cross that bridge when we come to it—if we come to it!"

Wartime Errors Cost Lives

Introduced by Theodore Granik, who conducts the program, Mr. Price prefaced his talks with the remark that free speech to Americans means "the right to criticize, to protest and to express opinions freely."

"But it doesn't mean, and it never has meant, the right to play fast and loose with information, as distinguished from opinion," he said.

Since lives of soldiers and sailors depend on guarding against leakage of information that might aid the enemy, Mr. Price said a "timely warning" to editors and broadcasters might be in order.

This view was emphasized by James L. Fly, chairman of the Federal Communications Commission, who, speaking before Mr. Price, said that censorship was no task for amateurs, who might let "the most dangerous information" slip out.

Praising the organizational work done by Mr. Price's office, Mr. Fly said:

"The task of censorship in our wartime democracy is to ban effectively, judiciously and uniformly anything which will give aid to the enemy, and beyond that to keep the channels of information open for complete and honest news reports, fair criticism and well-rounded discussion of public issues."

Roy E. Larsen, president of Time, Inc., asserted that United States censorship still was in "the freshman class" and suggested that it pattern itself after British censorship. The British, he said, already had profited by the mistakes of the French censorship, which, in his opinion, encouraged defeatism and complacency and led to the downfall of France.

"I am hopeful that the voluntary censorship exercised by our press and the advisory censorship of Mr. Price's office will work out the proper balance between too little and too much," Mr. Larsen said. "I am confident that it will. For, if it doesn't, there is real danger that voluntary censorship will break down completely."

Raymond Gram Swing, radio commentator, declared that radio, cognizant of the great risk to the armed forces, would not want to be free from censorship. To radio, he said, censorship was not only welcome, but essential.

Marvin Asks Public View

Dwight Marvin, president of the American Society of Newspaper Editors and editor of The Troy Record, said it was highly preferable for the bounds of censorship to be established by the power of public opinion, rather than by "secret police and a star chamber." But censorship, he emphasized, must be "imposed from below, not above," and it must not attempt to go any farther than public safety demands. And as soon as the war is ended, complete freedom of the press must "snap back" automatically, because "men trained in democracy can accept no less," he declared.

Mr. Swing suggested to Mr. Price that it might be extremely helpful if the Army and Navy would let the public know just what their policy was concerning suppressing or releasing news of losses; it would be beneficial, he felt, if assurance could be given the public that such news was not being suppressed just to ease the "shock" on its morale. While this point was being discussed, one of the participants called attention to the recent incident of an important news story coming out of London before it had been released here.

Mr. Price, in reply, said that the Censorship Office did not give out news.

* * *

June 14, 1942

STATEMENTS ON PACIFIC MEET DEMAND FOR NEWS

Navy Communiques on Coral Sea and Midway Engagements Give Public Information Eagerly Awaited

VOLUNTARY CENSORSHIP ROLE

By EDWIN L. JAMES

The extended and detailed communiqués given out by the Navy Department on the Coral Sea and Midway engagements in the Pacific will naturally go a long way toward meeting what was a growing public demand for more news about what the United States is doing in the war. More than that, the public has a right to get real satisfaction out of the news because it is good news with a solid foundation. In this respect the official reports on the two Pacific battles is much better based than the mistakenly optimistic reports given out day by day when General MacArthur was fighting on Bataan Peninsula. It should have been perfectly apparent to those handling the government publicity in Washington that since we could not reinforce MacArthur, and his foes were being reinforced, we had to lose out on Bataan. It was unwisdom itself to hail United States "victories" there. But with respect to what was reported Friday it is a different story.

It is inevitable that there be some popular criticism of the official handling of war news. It has always been that way. The British made a great muddle of their information service at the start of the war. But they have gotten things on an even keel and indeed of all the combatant powers Britain seems the most frank about its losses and successes. Doubtless Washington will learn from London's experience and before long the issuance of information will be greatly improved.

Possible Unfairness

The handling of war publicity has a basic difficulty for which no one is to blame and which is inherent in the situation. While the public wants to know what happened, official quarters may have most excellent reasons for not telling. But, at the same time, it is not practicable to give public reasons why a delay in information is advisable. While the public has already become somewhat skeptical about the formal statement that information must not be given the enemy, it is often true that this consideration forms a real and valid reason for delay.

That this is true is shown by the matter of the loss of the Lexington. The carrier was not sunk in the midst of the Coral Sea engagement. She caught on fire and exploded some hours after quitting the engagement. There was a very legitimate doubt that the Japanese knew she had been sunk. Under those circumstances, as the Navy statement said, there was good reason to delay the announcement of her loss until such time as the information could not be of direct aid to the Japanese—in this case, the Navy puts it, until after the Midway business.

The communiqué on the Midway battle was issued as soon as fairly complete information was available and, admittedly, it was not easy to gather. It was not primarily a battle of ships where from vessels on one side the result could be observed on vessels of the other side. It was primarily an attack by our planes against the Japanese naval force bound eastward. Some ships, it is true, were observed to sink, but others steamed off in various degrees of damage. This meant it took the time used to try to complete the picture.

About Initial Reports

A real problem confronting the issuance of communiqués regarding sea fighting lies in this very necessity, operating many times, of delaying announcement of United States losses. There comes first an announcement of enemy losses, with no accompanying details of our losses. This is apt to give the public a distorted picture of the real results and to bring about the result that when, later on, American losses are announced the public is prone to discount the first picture it got and consequently becomes somewhat skeptical of further announcements of losses by the enemy.

Without at all casting any doubt on the wisdom of the Navy in delaying for good reasons announcements of our losses, there is room for error in that direction. In the last war there was a rule forbidding correspondents to mention United States casualties. They could kill a million Germans before breakfast any morning, but they could never kill a United States soldier. This was at a time when the American troops were attacking fixed German positions, which must entail losses. But news dispatches told only of killed Germans. The result was that when General Pershing sent over his first casualty list, running into the thousands, the American public received a real shock, which could have been avoided if the Army censorship had displayed a little better balance of judgment.

Lack of Liaison

In the last war there were many instances of a lack of liaison among the many persons exercising censorship. The American Army imposed upon certain rules issued from Washington some of the rules of French censorship, and the result was a wide variance of interpretation by censors. It was but natural that the French authorities, having to handle the psychology of a country which in 1918 had been bled white by nearly four years of warfare, took a position of great bearishness on bad news. The result on the American news, however, was that the public over here was not given a good picture of the difficulties in the way, the knowledge of which might well have been a good thing. Even to this day, how many Americans know what a serious situation confronted the Allies in July of 1918?

There is in the operation of the censorship in the United States a good deal of liaison lack right now. A censor in Washington will pass something that a Naval District Commander's office will not pass. And sometimes it is the other way round. Naturally, we have been in the war but six months and the complicated machinery of censorship takes time to work out. It is quite obvious that what is now needed is an official with complete authority to handle censorship rules and their application.

The Voluntary Censorship

There have been very few official complaints about the newspapers breaking news which the government wishes held up. The papers have shown a real desire to meet the wishes of the government, even if those wishes are sometimes difficult to ascertain with exactitude. Even though there be some people of second rank in Washington who wish to bear down on the press, their reasons relate to domestic political considerations, rather than to war news. And, to repeat, on war news the papers are playing the game.

A case in point was the loss of the Lexington. For weeks many newspapers knew of the carrier's loss, announced Friday. But they did not try to publish it. There is other naval information which many newspapers have in their possession but which is awaiting official release.

Another case relates to the visit to Washington of Premier Molotoff. It was known to scores of newspapers that the Russian statesman was in Washington, but Washington requested that nothing be said of the visit until it was announced officially and that request was rigidly observed, with one minor exception.

In other words, Washington has a press anxious to comply with any regulations which safeguard our armed forces. At the same time Washington has a real job in keeping the public satisfied that it is getting quick and reliable news of war developments. It would be useless to deny that there had been spreading a popular feeling that there was a lack of frankness in the official communiqués. Friday's statements will surely give reassurance, and the promptest possible statements in the future, with due regard for proper safeguards, will serve to keep the public reassured.

* * *

September 20, 1942

OFFICER-REPORTER PLAN GAINS GROUND IN CAPITAL

Important Officers and Civilian Chiefs Believe Only Men Who Fight a Battle Are Able to Write of It Accurately

DENY AIM TO COVER BLUNDERS

By ARTHUR KROCK

WASHINGTON, Sept. 19—In recent accounts of violent military actions the corps of reporters maintained by the independent press of the United States, Great Britain and Canada lived up to the best traditions of their dangerous craft. The eyewitness stories of the commando raid at Dieppe and of the sinking of the Yorktown included many examples of accurate, graphic reporting.

Nevertheless, there are important officers and civilian chiefs of the armed services whose belief grows firmer with every battle report that modern war requires the abolition of the independent press war correspondent and the substitution of the officer-reporter who, notably in Germany and Russia, has produced a very high grade of officially approved accounts of military action. Noting the progress of the experiment which the Navy is making in this field, a high military officer prophesied the other day that within a year the independent war correspondent will be a figure of the past.

The Navy and Marine Corps officers who sent the accounts of fighting in the Pacific actually participated in it, and good judges agree that their descriptions were clear, accurate, technically precise and yet invested with sufficient color to make them readable. Balanced against this are several facts, however. Under the officer-reporter system all newspapers must publish the same account of every action. What is reported of war will be only that which satisfies the high command as informing, but unobstructive to general strategy and current plans. The trained selective function of the civilian reporter, which produces the human interest and "feature" stories that are such an important part of the newspaper product, will be missing. No varied angle of observation or emphasis can come into such dispatches.

Marine Corps' System

In the Marine Corps, however, these disadvantages have been weighed and judged as far less important than the merits of the officer-reporter system. The Marine officer who is assigned to report action in which he participates is trained first as a soldier, and until he has acquired that status he must await training for the second part of his duty. Usually he has had a grounding of journalism at college, and sometimes in professional reporting. But he must be a soldier first.

It is the theory of this method that no one can write accurately and in proper balance of a military action unless he has participated in it and comprehends the professional factors; that such a reporter knows as a matter of professional knowledge what is censurable, and therefore his copy can be cleared more quickly and with a far lighter degree of inspection by censors. It is held that the official Marine Corps accounts proved all these points, and that the system should be extended to the Army and to the entire Navy. The Navy has been willing to try the Marine experiment without, however, dispensing with independent correspondents in the remainder of the service. The Army has not adopted the system at all. But there are powerful supporters of it in both branches, and if they are encouraged by the President and the two service secretaries they will move to impose the German-Russian officer-reporter plan throughout, to the exclusion of the independent press.

Dissatisfaction on Censorship

Both press and public in this country have been dissatisfied with conflicting rules of censorship, long delays in clearing dispatches and other military regulations for covering the news of the war. This is quite apart from the argument over whether it was necessary, for security's sake, to withhold such facts as the sinking of the Yorktown for three months and nine days and the battleship damages at Pearl Harbor for what is already more than nine months. The dissatisfaction is directed at the delay policy on dispatches, giving details of the general results of military actions which have already been announced in official communiqués.

The advocates of the officer-reporter system agree that the protests are well-based, but they employ them as support for their plan because, they say, the matters complained of would be eliminated by confining news of military action to official channels. They further assert that, if the independent war correspondent is abolished and officer-correspondents substituted, delays in reporting news will grow less under the influence of such a corps. The high commands, they say, will be much more inclined to accept the view of an official reporter that a fact may safely be dispatched than that of an independent correspondent who may not unfairly be suspected of having his judgment influenced by his calling and the interest of his employer in getting a steady flow of news.

The press, of course, is expected to oppose total adoption of the Marine Corps system, but those who endorse it and want to make it exclusive are not certain whether a majority of the newspaper-reading public will object if and when it is thus established, reasons are openly given and results are available for inspection. They think it possible, however, that a barrage of attack from the press would arouse the public to view the innovation as a military gazette plan, designed to cover up error, incompetence and defeat and as a heavy thrust at the freedom of the press.

Freedom of Press Issue

That is why its advocates have not come into the open. But they do not lack any faith in their idea because they have not yet been authorized to support in public its extension throughout the armed services. And they deny any inspiration to set up a military gazette as a shield of blunders or to abridge the freedom of the press. Civilian reporters, they point out, are already subject to the orders of commanders as to their movements and to the military censors as to what they dispatch and when. The extension, they contend, is no greater invasion, and all is made necessary by the conditions of modern war. This correspondent must concede that they speak in good faith, and that those with whom he has discussed the project include civilians who have been uncompromising in demanding release of bad news and the full facts as to military mistakes.

There is another advocacy afoot in connection with war information, but this does not appear to have as many influential supporters in Washington as the officer-reporter plan. It proposes to unite the now separate bureaus of war intelligence and publicity in both the Army and the Navy. In each department intelligence and public relations would be forged into one bureau instead of operating individually as at present, with the latter adhering to the policy laid down by the intelligence section.

Story of Submarines

It is said, to illustrate the need of the change, that last January, when the Office of Naval Intelligence learned the German High Command had ordered submarines to an Atlantic rendezvous, with instructions to start American merchant sinkings to coincide with the Rio conference, for the purpose of impressing the Latin-American countries with the weakness of the United States in defense, it asked Naval Public Relations to hold up all news of the sinkings until the conference recessed and was refused. The point was that otherwise Axis diplomats at Rio would make the very use of the sinkings for which they had been ordered. That happened. But it would seem that higher authority in the department could have decided the argument promptly, leaving the bureaus in separate operation.

* * *

December 20, 1942

CENSORSHIP NOW A YEAR OLD

Its Guiding Principles Widely Accepted, but Application Stirs Controversy

By W. H. LAWRENCE

WASHINGTON, Dec. 19—Formal and centralized, but "voluntary," censorship of the American press and radio was a year old this week, and a review of its operations in that time showed the balance to be on the credit side, though there remain many irritants to a free press which can subscribe, without hesitation or reservation, to the principle that there is no story, however good, that would justify risking the life of a single Axis opponent.

The Office of Censorship, established by executive order of President Roosevelt, operates under a Code of Wartime Practices which the press and radio have accepted as a necessary wartime regulation. Headed by Byron Price, former Associated Press executive, a staff of 13,500 has been recruited in the last year to administer the press and radio code and to censor the mail and cables which flow to or from this country and foreign countries or possessions and territories of the United States. Well over 95 per cent of the censorship employes are concentrated in the postal and cable censorship divisions, which handle thousands of letters, cables and magazines a week trying to stop vital information from leaving this country, or to intercept information from abroad which would aid this country in the prosecution of the war.

A staff of around thirty handles the application of censorship to the more than 13,000 newspapers and several hundred radio stations in this country, and the administering officials say that the cooperation given them by the American information media has been splendid.

Public Kept in Dark

Censorship has kept from our enemies much information which would have helped them immeasurably in the planning of their war against United Nations' forces, but it has doubtless kept from the American people information which was available to the enemy and which would have helped the people here judge the ability and the success of the government officials who were directing Army, Navy or production strategy.

The keeping of information from the enemy is a defensive operation, but censorship also can take the offensive, as a Senate committee learned this week when Captain Ellis M. Zacharias, acting director of Naval Intelligence, said it was the censoring of communications between the United States and one of its territories which led to the breaking up of a ring which was aiding Axis agents to refuel Nazi submarines off the Atlantic Coast.

As Byron Price puts it, the basic consideration behind censorship is simply this:

"That none of us shall provide the enemy, by design or inadvertence, with information which will help him to kill Americans."

Two Versions of Code

With this general principle as the underlying philosophy the Price organization has issued two versions of its Code of Wartime Practices for the American Press, and now is preparing a third edition for release about Jan. 15. In general, this code lists the categories of subjects about which information may not be published unless it is "made available officially by appropriate authority." Included in the restricted group are such matters as troop and ship movements, ship sinkings or damage to ships, extent of air attacks, disposition or description of airplanes, production rates, general weather information, movements of the President and diplomatic or military information.

Most of the recent controversy over actual operation of censorship, aside from press complaints about that imposed by the Army and Navy at the source, has concerned the inspection of mail between the United States and its Territories and possessions, and the quarrel between some British correspondents and United States officials over the latitude allowed them in sending news, especially that critical of the Churchill government's policy.

There is a feeling on the domestic front that the restrictions on war production records and rates should be relaxed somewhat because the output of material now has reached the point where news of it would discourage, rather than encourage, the enemy. This contention is receiving consideration in the current revision of the code.

* * *

January 24, 1943

WRITERS SEE HARM BY LONDON CENSOR

Empire Correspondents Attack Ban on Their Reporting Some Matters of Opinion

SAY MISTRUST IS CREATED

Press Union Also Criticizes the Communications With the First Army in Tunisia

Wireless to The New York Times

LONDON, Jan. 23—Extension of the powers of the censors to matters of opinion as well as to questions involving national security drew criticism today from the Council of the Empire Press Union in its annual report.

It was the opinion of the council, representing correspondents in London from all parts of the British Empire, that the remedy proposed by Brendan Bracken, Minister of Information, was worse than the abuse it was designed to cure.

What the Empire correspondents regarded as legitimate expressions of opinion had been curbed since last March 26 when Mr. Bracken announced in the House of Commons his decision empowering cable censors to prohibit the cabling of dispatches "calculated to produce ill feeling between the United Nations or between them and a neutral country."

The council pointed out that the Empire correspondents, like the Americans, protested that the retention of such a rule would "undermine confidence in the war effort and create mistrust even in the actual news given out in this country." The council reported that Mr. Bracken's promise to use the power only to prevent "a distorted picture of events and conditions in Britain" had mainly been kept.

"But," said the report, "there remain three ill effects of the government's handling of this matter. In the first place, newspaper readers overseas are left in doubt about the degree to which London cables are interfered with by the censorship.

"In the second place, a good many messages are delayed, although subsequently released, while the cable censors puzzle over their new instructions and then have to refer them to a higher authority.

"Third, the public citation of a few extracts from a correspondent's dispatches unjustly placed the Empire correspondent in some disrepute."

The council criticized press communications with the First Army in Tunisia, which it said were "extremely bad," and attributed the shortcomings to "the large number of correspondents and to some extent to interlocking censorships." Radio broadcasters, it noted, had enjoyed better fortune than the press.

The introduction of the penny-a-word rate for press cables between any two terminals in the British Empire had resulted, the council reported, in an increase of press traffic from 25,000,000 words in 1938 to 92,000,000 last year. This meant an increased volume of traffic and caused delays in transmission which the council said were additional reasons for permitting Empire and foreign correspondents in London to send important announcement texts in advance of their release date despite the danger that information might fall into enemy hands in advance of publication.

* * *

February 11, 1943

NEW RULES EASE CENSORSHIP CODE

Byron Price Orders Slight Changes Affecting Press and Radio Broadcasting

QUICK APPEALS ALLOWED

Machinery for Protests is Set Up and Some Loopholes Are Plugged

Special to The New York Times

WASHINGTON, Feb. 10—Praising the voluntary cooperation of newspapers and broadcasters as "magnificent," Byron Price, Director of Censorship, presented slightly amended codes for press and radio today.

The changed regulations, he explained, increased certain restrictions as a result of war experience and lessened others, contained in the two codes, now in operation for about a year.

The newspaper code, said Nat R. Howard, in charge of that division, carried new language, informing publications that "whenever any one else, in any part of the country, makes a request which appears to be unreasonable or out of harmony with the code," an appeal could be made at once to the Office of Censorship. This meant that if government agencies, officials or others sought to suppress news concerning which there was a question the newspapers could ask Censorship to decide.

New clauses in the press code increase caution in the publication of prisoner-of-war news, secret inks, diplomatic ships, news of forest fires and some other subjects. On the contrary, the new code makes it much easier to publish news concerning contracts between agencies and war producers.

Likewise, newspapers will have more latitude in publishing information on war casualties.

To the "general" section of the code is added a request that there be no advance publication to show where the President, will broadcast from and a further plea that nothing be published about "secret war plans."

In the broadcasting field, said T. Harold Ryan, who directs the radio code, there are heavy restrictions on news about weather. But the most significant change affecting domestic broadcasting is the incorporation of new material to guide foreign language station managers in their voluntary censorship efforts.

"The Office of Censorship by direction of the President," Mr. Ryan read from the code, "is charged with the responsibility of removing from the air all those engaged in foreign language broadcasting who, in the judgment of appointed authorities in the Office of Censorship, endanger the war effort of the United Nations by their connection, direct or indirect, with the medium."

The amended codes, Mr. Price explained merely represent efforts to keep up with the progress of the war.

* * *

April 18, 1943

MILD CENSORSHIP A RULE IN BRITAIN

American Correspondents Find an Efficient System Which Gives Little Trouble

Wireless to The New York Times

LONDON, April 17—In wartime censorship is ever present, but its workings are often smoother and fairer than outsiders believe. The censorship of Great Britain is probably the most efficient, the most liberal and the least troublesome of any belligerent country—including the United States. Here the censorship is viewed as a means of keeping military information from reaching the enemy, and any time there is the least suspicion that it is being used for any other purpose there is an uproar in the press and Commons.

Partly, no doubt, misconceptions regarding the functioning of British censorship result from Americans using their own censorship as a criterion.

Ways of the Censor

An important fact to remember is that every country has its own ideas about censorship and its own methods of using it. In some countries nothing is allowed to pass except what the government approves. In others correspondents do not know what has happened to their dispatches after the censor finishes with them. American war correspondents had a dose of that variety in North Africa at the hands of their own Army officers.

Here correspondents merely send their stories to the cable office, where they are usually passed within a few minutes. If there is any military information that would be helpful to the enemy the chances are it will be cut, but the correspondent is always told what is to be taken out and can appeal to higher authority for a restoration. The important thing is that he always knows exactly what changes are ordered and can refuse to send the story at all if the emendations change the sense or distort the meaning. Nothing can be added by the censor without the correspondent's permission.

So long as no military information is given away or squabbles among the Allies aired before efforts to resolve them are exhausted, it is all right to lambaste the government, snipe at Mr. Churchill or say that the whole British people are blundering dumbbells and the censor won't ever touch it.

* * *

October 10, 1943

THE OWI PLANS TO ISSUE NEWS AS SOON AS BRITISH

Davis Seeks Cooperation in London to Have All Important Announcements Made on Simultaneous Basis

AND THUS TO SILENCE CRITICS

By EDWIN L. JAMES

Elmer Davis, head of the Office of War Information, has let it be known that an effort is under way to reach an agreement with London on the announcements of important war news. Thus an end may be put to the system, or lack of it, whereby too large a proportion of revelations have come from British sources and, consequently, relatively fewer from United States sources. Not only is it good news that the head of the OWI has openly recognized a situation which has caused no little criticism of American authorities, but his action is a timely one. Within twenty-four hours after he announced the new project on Thursday, London sources on Friday revealed that the American Secretary of the Treasury had presented to the United States Congress plans for a $10,000,000,000 United Nations bank to aid in post-war reconstruction and development. Within a very few hours after the London publication by the Financial News, the Washington authorities issued the full plan. And to make the matter pointed, it was stated that the news was being divulged on Friday afternoon because the Financial News had revealed the project that day in London. That is progress.

If two people as able as Elmer Davis and Brenden Bracken, British Minister of Information, put their heads together they ought to be able to get something done. Nobody made a bigger mess of censorship than did the British in the first year of the war. When the Athenia was sunk a British censor killed a "take" of the story which contained nothing but the official communiqué. There was no efficient organization; incompetent people were in charge of censorship and, indeed, it is only in the past year that the British censorship has been working smoothly. It is apparent that the British have learned in their longer war experience more about the value of war publicity than our Washington authorities have learned in a shorter time.

Censorship and Publicity

It may at once be argued that there is here a confusion of war information with censorship; that they are two different matters. But it also can be held that they both have to do with the situation. And that point of view can be substantiated all along the line. That is true because the rules concerning military matters control both the OWI and the censorship. And, further than that, the censorship rules control information other than that issued by the OWI as well as they affect basically what the OWI issues. For example, the story of Pearl Harbor was known in newspaper offices ten months before it was released officially.

Take the recent speech of Prime Minister Churchill, which has been the basis of so many comparisons between what the British let be known and what Washington lets be known. There was not only the factor of Mr. Churchill's giving news which had been secret but there was the factor that much of it had been kept secret because of censorship rules.

Therefore, if Elmer Davis and Brenden Bracken have a conference, Byron Price, head of our censorship, ought to go along. Not that either Mr. Davis or Mr. Price is primarily responsible for what has been regarded as a paucity of official United States information, but together they should be able to make a very good joint report on what could be done about it.

It's Better This Time

Those who can recall the stupidity of the American censorship in the last war can realize that things have improved a lot and will not take too seriously the difficulties of today. In the last war there was a rule against mentioning American casualties. Perhaps those in high places responsible for this rule intended to keep from the Germans information which would have helped them. But, in effect, verdant censorship officials in the field interpreted it as meaning that correspondents could never mention that an American had been hurt. They could kill a million Germans before breakfast, but even when the Americans were attacking fixed German positions in the Argonne the correspondents could never hint that a German bullet had found its mark. Thus the tremendous shock to the country when General Pershing came along with his casualty lists. Certainly it is being done better this time.

One day in 1918 a colonel, head of a Corps G-2 unit, gave a correspondent a document taken from the body of a German major. It recounted that a group of prisoners from the First Division had been questioned all night and the Germans failed to get one iota of useful information from them. The major had added that the Americans were to be congratulated for having such soldiers. The American censor killed the story on the ground that it was giving information to the enemy. "Hell," answered the correspondents, "the enemy wrote it." "True enough," replied the censor, "but you must not let the enemy know how much we know about what he knows." That wouldn't happen in this war.

Anent Naval Publicity

Some people in the Navy Department—not all—are worried about naval publicity, or rather the lack of information about the Navy from scenes of action. A high official of the department recently asked some newspaper editors how it was that when MacArthur did something it hit the front pages the next morning, whereas with naval news it was different. He was told there was an explanation—a story delayed for four weeks was a month old.

There is something which both Mr. Davis and Mr. Price could work on. Now, it is perfectly true that after there has been an announcement of a naval engagement in the Pacific by Washington or by Tokyo it is wise for nothing to come from the ships until they have gotten away from the scene of action. Let's accept that. After accepting it one is entitled to ask why the dispatches have to go to Pearl Harbor and then be mailed to Washington for release when someone thinks fit. The net result is that correspondents' dispatches from warships reach newspapers from three to seven weeks after the fact, when, generally speaking, they are so much out of date that they hit Page 17 or the spike.

There is distinctly room for improvement here. It has now gotten so that it is a matter of doubt whether it is worth while sending correspondents with naval task forces. Newspapers decline invitations to add to their naval correspondents. They do this because the returns are so meager. If the Navy would help the newspapers the newspapers would gladly double the number of correspondents with the Navy.

Progress Is Expected

If the head people in Washington, including Admiral King, as well as General Marshall, get imbued with the idea that in this people's war they can get better results by taking the people into their confidence so far as may be safely done—and that means further than has been done so far—Mr. Davis and Mr. Price will have the roads open to them to meet most of the criticism which has been heard recently.

If, in addition, there can be worked out between Washington and London some common measures to meet the need of military security in military and naval activities in which both the British and Americans are engaged, there ought to be a great improvement in the joint handling of war news by the two capitals. As Mr. Davis said: "If there is really a valid matter of security involved, the standard should be the same in each country and for all officials of however great rank."

On the record General Eisenhower and General MacArthur have shown the keenest realization of the wisdom of letting the people know what is going on. Admittedly, the Navy has greater difficulties with the security factor. But the whole business comes down to a consideration of whether the security factor has not been exaggerated by some high officials. Evidently Mr. Churchill thought so.

* * *

November 10, 1943

DIARY LEADS TO ARREST

Marine Engineer Held in Jersey for Having Uncensored Matter

Special to The New York Times

NEWARK, N. J., Nov. 9—William M. Emory, 42 years old, a marine engineer, was lodged in the Hudson County Jail this afternoon in default of $2,500 bail after his arraignment before United States Commissioner William J. Bartholomew on a charge of bringing into the country and disseminating written matter before it had been censored.

Emory, who said he lived when ashore at the Courtland Hotel, New York, was arrested Sunday morning in a Hoboken tavern while reading aloud excerpts from his diary, which recounted among other things his experiences during the American landing at Salerno. Agents of the Federal Bureau of Investigation questioned him this afternoon but declined to comment on the case.

The prisoner was in a state of high nervous tension when arrested, according to the police, and was treated by an interne from St. Mary's Hospital. His condition was attributed to his experiences on merchant ships in the Mediterranean.

* * *

February 2, 1944

QUIRKS OF CENSORS PUZZLE TO WRITERS

Correspondents in the Field Astonished When Home Press Reveals Guarded Secrets

By FRANK L. KLUCKHOHN
By Wireless to The New York Times

ALLIED HEADQUARTERS IN AUSTRALIA, Feb. 1—The question of censorship in the war theatres remains a subject of key importance—as it has been since the war started—to the American people, who are anxious for accurate news.

American war correspondents in the field during various operations recently were astonished by printed disclosures at home blueprinting not only with words but maps future moves about which the men on the spot have maintained oral as well as written silence; for there is no man in the world more security-minded than a correspondent about to risk his life with a landing, whether it be in Sicily, Europe or the Pacific area. Correspondents in some theatres—principally the European—after agreeing to security censorship, have been amazed to have censors tell them bluntly, "This is being halted for political reasons."

Phrases in the general censorship rules, such as that nothing causing discord among the Allies can be printed, may lead to withholding news capable of damaging politicians at home but not aiding the enemy, except perhaps in spurious publicity campaigns. Sometimes such rules have been so employed by field commanders.

Stories Not Always Official

But there is not one news writer in the field who would write a word that would cost the life of one American fighting man. Starting on expeditions in which they know they share the risks, correspondents have been amazed to see home magazines and newspapers forecasting exactly what is going to be done and giving the enemy a chance to get set.

One example of this—although it was not the primary cause of the heavy loss of life, as it turned out—was an accurate prediction of the Navy's move into the Gilbert Islands. Sometimes, fortunately, these predictions are inaccurate, so the enemy cannot be sure they are absolutely correct.

Some serious critics believe that one reason for disappointment in the Italian campaign was that the American landing at Salerno was so well "telegraphed" that the enemy was set to meet it.

But the mere assumption that because a news article passes military censorship it has the stamp of official approval is incorrect. For example, in this theatre Gen. Douglas MacArthur confines censorship to what he regards as primary military security. Anyone can write anything he wishes to about political matters and about military matters where security in not involved. The reports may not accord with official desires, to say nothing of having official endorsement. Anyone here, for instance, is free to do any speculating he likes about General MacArthur's position vis-a-vis home policy.

Condition Alter Regulations

The views this correspondent, or any correspondent, expresses on General MacArthur's political stands are his own deductions and are not official and this will continue to remain true.

As far as military matters are concerned, this correspondent today passed a news report through censorship that Rabaul, a key Japanese base, was not neutralized. Several months ago General MacArthur said it was neutralized, but he was speaking of a temporary situation at the time. On the other hand, if this correspondent wrote an article predicting this theatre's next move, his story would be halted.

As far as this theatre is concerned, censorship, it is believed, will continue to be held to a minimum, and what leaves here through censorship does not necessarily have the stamp of official approval.

If personal observation based on experience in several theatres—Britain, North Africa and two Pacific areas—is worth while, it may be said that there is reflected a tendency on the part of the Office of War Information in Washington to issue requests or orders that can easily be interpreted to permit cutting off not only legitimate but vital criticism while paying little attention to vital security.

Security is the only type of censorship to which the war correspondents have knowingly agreed. Similarly various news services sometimes have taken advantage of certain broad orders to protect themselves from criticism. Such criticism often can be more freely expressed by commentators at home.

Correspondents covering current actions, however, have been amazed by the "spilling" of prospective moves in home publications. In the long run this will lead to tightening the censorship rules, which, with many faults, have permitted a large measure of truth to reach American people.

* * *

June 13, 1944

INVASION GAVE CENSORS RECORD 'BLUE PENCIL' JOB

By Wireless to The New York Times

LONDON, June 12—During the first five days of the invasion Allied censors at Supreme Headquarters, Allied Expeditionary Force, had the biggest "blue pencil job in the world." They had to handle more than 2,500,000 words of copy sent in by Allied war correspondents.

In addition, the censors had to scrutinize over 25,000 photographs for publication. Considerably more than 106,000 feet of battle film were run through official projectors before going to news reels during the same period.

* * *

February 4, 1945

CENSORSHIP IS WORKING TIGHTLY ON CONFERENCE

As Usual, Reports on Big-Three Parley Pour in From Abroad but There Is Nothing Available Here

SAME GAG ON PRELIMINARIES

By EDWIN L. JAMES

It is an understandable theory that when the Big Three—President Roosevelt, Prime Minister Churchill and Marshal Stalin—meet, their movements should be kept secret for the sake of the safety of the three leaders. No one is going to quarrel with that theory—as a theory. But it never works out that way. Someone always leaks; some country's censorship falls down. Most often it has been the British censorship. Sometimes, of course, the news comes from enemy sources.

The record of the United States censorship is clear; the news of these meetings never comes from American sources. And there is ample evidence that this time again it is not going to be the fault of the Washington censors if any news gets out about the Big Three meeting, which, it is reported from foreign sources, has begun or is about to take place.

However, there does seem room to ask whether our censorship, Mr. Price's branch, the naval branch and the army branch, do not carry things a little bit too far. This is written in respect to the preliminaries which, according to reports from London, Paris, Rome and elsewhere, have been going on with respect to the alleged meeting of the Big Three. During most of the past week Jonathan Daniels, as White House spokesman, and the State Department were unable to confirm that Harry Hopkins had been consulting in London, in Paris and in Rome with leaders in those capitals on pending international problems at the very time when the newspapers were carrying reports from those capitals telling in detail that Mr. Hopkins was around and telling what he was doing. That's just a little bit bathetic.

And Mr. Stettinius' Trip

Then there was the trip of Mr. Stettinius, undertaken, according to foreign advices, as a part of the Big Three plans. Indeed, the Secretary of State had said he was going with the President, and with a strict ban on any mention of the President's movements Mr. Grew began signing himself Acting Secretary of State, a title devolving upon him only in the absence of the Secretary on sick leave or on a voyage—and there was no record that Mr. Stettinius was not well.

Yet it was from Rome that the news came that the American Secretary of State was there in various conferences. And it is not to be forgotten the Americans run the censorship in Italy.

And as this is written there are reports from London, Paris, Berlin and Tokyo about the meetings of the Big Three. Practically none of them agree, so obviously some of them are wrong. But, so far as Allied sources are concerned, the remarkable thing is that their censorship allows these reports to be spread while our voluntary censorship bars any mention. Newspapers here are free to publish what they get from abroad but they can add nothing. And probably that is just as well.

News of the Conferences

That brings us to the really important issue. When the meeting is over and the blackout lifted, how about the news of what took place? It is a matter of record that the most news about any of the Allied meetings has come from Mr. Churchill's speeches in the House of Commons. It is now being alleged that Mr. Churchill does not tell all—for example, about the Teheran meeting. But it nevertheless remains true that he tells more than anyone else involved. To bring it right home, let us say that President Roosevelt has consistently abstained from informing the American people of what he did in their name at these famous meetings. If the world had had to depend on what the Washington leader revealed of what went on at Teheran it would not know as much as it has learned from other sources.

This is not the fault of Byron Price, head of our censorship, for he is not supposed to provide news. Nor is it the fault of Elmer Davis, head of the Office of War Information, for President Roosevelt does not take him along to the meetings. It is nothing more or less than the policy of the President. And why it is proper for Mr. Churchill to tell his story while out of place for Mr. Roosevelt to tell his is something not at all clear.

Short-Changing the Public

At his press conferences the President, in an affable manner, succeeds in telling very little news on international matters. It is almost fair to say that he regards these meetings as mental contests with the White House correspondents. But it is not a matter of pleasing or displeasing the correspondents; they are representing not themselves primarily, but the American public.

And Mr. Stettinius wrote a seven-page article for The Readers' Digest analyzing the Dumbarton Oaks agreements and making a plea on behalf of those agreements. The newspapers of the land, which, taken together, still have more circulation than The Readers' Digest, would have asked nothing better than to have put before the public the argument of the Secretary of State for international cooperation—but he writes it for one magazine. It is true that the State Department handed out officially copies of The Readers' Digest article as an official release, carefully timed to the magazine's release date. But this did not work very well.

Then Mr. Hopkins, the President's adviser and confidant, who never gives a Washington press interview, pictures many of the Government's plans in an article for The American Magazine—and not the first one.

This is a bizarre way for United States Government officials to make known their opinions on public matters. And Ed Stettinius doesn't need the money.

Breaking the News

So now, when the Big Three meeting is over, we shall see again. The conferees are considering matters of immense importance involving the duties and responsibilities of their peoples. Indeed, the whole issue of the foreign relations of the United States is tied up in the meeting, wherever and whenever it takes place. Is the American public going to get the news of what happens from Mr. Roosevelt or from other sources? Of course, there will be a joint official communiqué. In all likelihood it will tell as little as most such statements tell. But will there be a break from the practices of the past and will we get real explanations from American sources, or will we have to wait again until Mr. Churchill finds it timely to make a report to the Commons? It is a good bet that Marshal Stalin will not be explaining much in detail.

It isn't that Mr. Churchill does a bad job. He is, by and large, a good reporter. He used to work for newspapers. But the question is simply whether we should have to depend on the British Prime Minister, who may or may not see a given problem in the same light as his conferees.

It is not only on conferences that Mr. Churchill performs; he is the leading announcer of Allied plans on many other world matters.

And so we come back to the question whether the new conference will be marked by a favorable development toward Washington's taking more into its confidence the people of a country where public opinion is presumed to be supreme.

* * *

February 11, 1945

THE CENSOR DEFENDS THE CENSORSHIP

Byron Price Replies to Those Who Complain That Too Much News Is Kept from the Public

By BYRON PRICE
Director of Censorship

How accurate and complete is our war news? How well is John Doe, here at home, informed about the lot and fortunes of GI Joe at the front? Is too much of the truth stopped in the name of security?

These questions recently have stirred widespread discussion. They are important questions, and there is no short and simple answer to them. The difficulty of projecting a precise impression of events through space, even between two persons in the same room, is well understood. Mankind, we are told, is destined at best to see through a glass darkly, and war sets many strange designs on the windowpane. No one will ever know what a war is like unless he is there and sees for himself; and even then he will know only a part of the story. But that is no reason why the best possible effort should not be made to give the home front as much news as security will permit.

As this discussion mounts, it is only natural that the censor should become a target for castigation. All of the old reliables—"senseless," "idiotic," "asinine," "bureaucratic," and the rest—have been resurrected and launched broadside at Censorship and all its works.

Much of this is understandable and and some of it deserved. Censorship never can be an exact science. It is an integral part of war, and no war can be fought without accidents and errors and confusions. One of the anomalies, however, is that no one has charged Censorship with being too liberal and thus helping the enemy to prolong the war. The shoe is on the other foot. At a time of belt-tightening for manpower, production and rationing, when new and more severe restrictions are elbowing travelers off the trains and pushing down the thermostat in American homes, an opposite trend is proposed in many quarters for Censorship. The longer the war lasts, the more vocal is the demand for less censorship, not more.

It takes no great amount of reflection to expose the fallacy of such thinking. Censorship's responsibility is to help protect the life of the nation, and if the war has turned out to be longer and tougher than we expected, then surely there is need for increased vigilance. Thus far the correspondents on the firing line and the newspapers and broadcasters at home have done a fabulously successful job of protecting the national security. They scarcely can afford, in the national interest or in their own interest, to relax or become careless now. It is not a time to take a chance.

It is a time for even-tempered reflection, not hysteria. It is denied by no one that Censorship, which is contrary to all American principles, is a necessary nuisance in wartime. Protests against it are natural on the part of a free press, and no one should resent them. But neither Censorship issues nor any of the other grave issues of these troubled days can be solved wisely on a basis of hasty conclusions and intemperate epithet. The problems are far too important for that.

The plain and sober truth of the matter is that in no war in history and in no country in the world has the common man been given access to such detailed and comprehensive reports of warfare as those which are placed hourly before the readers of American newspapers and the listeners beside American radios. If, upon reflection, that statement needs proof, it can be found in ample measure by laying today's newspaper alongside the newspaper of 1918, or 1864, or any other wartime you may select. For the first time in history not a few, but literally hundreds, of American correspondents have opportunity to roam the battlefields under the fire of the enemy, and even to sit in council with the higher military authorities and learn in the briefing-room of battle plans which still are in the making. In what previous war, as in this one, have thirty correspondents given up their lives to the cause of public information?

But this is not, of course, the whole of the matter. The plain fact is, also, that these reporters are not permitted by Censorship to write all they know or describe all they see. Naturally. However you may qualify it, no rational person can escape the truth of a fundamental tenet of all censorship, namely, that, once a piece of news has been published widely, it must be assumed that the enemy has been informed. Actually, in these days of widespread use of interceptible radio for press transmission the enemy doubtless reads most American dispatches from the front long before those same dispatches become available to newspaper subscribers at home. In these circumstances no responsible commanding general, with the lives of his men and the fortunes of his country resting on his judgment, can fail to be anxious eternally that the enemy be not told too much.

What it comes down to then, is a problem of degree. How much should be withheld? As this is written most of the criticism of Censorship hinges on an assumption that too much unpleasant news is kept from the American public. The issue has many angles which cannot all be embraced in moderate space. A conspicuous example, which will serve as well as another, is the storm of discussion centering about the December German breakthrough in Belgium and Luxembourg. It was charged that in that instance censors operating under General Eisenhower suppressed too much. Naturally, all of the facts about that are not yet available, but many of them are.

The charges came from various sources. No attempt will be made here to consider the pronouncements of traveling salesmen and visiting fireman who, after a day or two or a week or two in contact with the rear areas of the war in Europe, came home and began lecturing as experts in military security and censorship. Nor is it necessary to engage in debate with the editorial writers of home-town newspapers who automatically, at the first alarm, wheeled out the old artillery of abusive adjectives without taking the pains or having the means to look into the matter and ascertain the facts.

There is one group of witnesses, however, whose experience and whose magnificent record of sacrifices and service more than entitles them to a respectful hearing. They are the group of American correspondents who formally protested at General Eisenhower's headquarters in France that too much about the German military thrust was suppressed.

The core of that complaint was that the correspondents were prohibited from reporting exactly what towns were in German hands. This was information, it was argued, already possessed by the German High Command, and it was information which the American public should have in order to understand the extent and stark potentialities of the attack.

The reasoning was sound, certainly, provided the premise was correct. But on this latter point some difficulty arises. Obviously we do not know and probably never will know how much detailed information was available at German headquarters. And it must be a matter of opinion also to what degree the public in this country realized the danger and how much that realization would have been aided by the addition of certain specific place names. Certain it is that streamer headlines in the newspapers and graphic announcements over the radio reminded the nation hour by hour of the sweeping reversal of events at the fighting front. No charge was made, in fact, that the military commanders were seeking to conceal the general seriousness of the situation.

Considering that situation as a whole, no one will say that the problems wrapped up in it were easy of solution. The struggle was not a single battle. It was many battles spread over an almost chaotic scene of fanning columns, divided by hills, woods and streams. Units were isolated on both sides. Parachutists were dropped behind the lines; and it is worthy of note that one captured German paratroop officer complained in hot anger that the Nazi radio had reported the town where he descended already in German hands. The information was incorrect, and the paratroop command was virtually wiped out. In this instance, at least, a true and detailed statement of the facts would have meant fewer dead Germans.

Byron Price

The conflicting estimates of the situation retailed day by day in the German broadcasts and even in the German official communiqués furnish additional testimony that the enemy was guessing. Very often the purpose of these guesses has been to exert deliberate pressure on Allied commanders to disclose the true state of affairs. An interesting observation (proving that not all editorial writers follow a blind assumption that all censorship is wrong), appeared recently in The Corpus Christi (Texas) Caller. Remarking that the Germans at first estimated American prisoners taken in the Belgium-Luxembourg salient at 40,000 and then reduced the figure to 24,000. The Caller said: "They deliberately fish for information, mistrusting their own figures, and as long as our command refuses to take the cork under, they cannot be sure."

We had great military movements of our own to conceal from the enemy. Three days after the start of the German attack General Patton was ordered to take immediate command of a bold counter-action on the southern flank of the German indentation. This meant thinning his own lines on other fronts. It meant gathering and grouping a great mass of men and material. To the north another large attack was organizing under Marshal Montgomery. A strong argument can be made that secrecy was absolutely vital, even as to the results of the first days of the actual counter-attack, so that the enemy could not grasp the full meaning and weight of our concentrations.

Nor can we omit from a judicial review of events one other circumstance always characteristic of war. The sudden German stroke presented a new, disorganizing threat of the most frightful potentialities. At such times, military machinery does not operate like clockwork. The censors on the spot were, of course, Army officers responsible to General Eisenhower. Commanders down to the lowest officer had to make decisions quickly, desperately. In matters of security they could not have known just where they were. Their wholly natural disposition was to take no chance whatever. The equally natural disappointment of the correspondents may well have magnified itself in this atmosphere of extreme tension and uncertainty, and no one could be blamed for that.

Interesting in this situation is the fact that dispatches severely critical of Allied intelligence and preparedness, and the most unrestrained accounts of battlefield horror, continued to come out of the imperiled sector without interference from the military censors. And all of this was published and broadcast in every American community.

The central issue must, in the end, come down to a matter of opinion since many of the variables cannot be resolved. So far as the public was concerned only one attempt to survey reaction actually was made, and the results may be set down here for whatever they are worth. The Office of Public Opinion Research, a private fact-finding agency, reported that it had conducted such a canvass of popular sentiment, stating the exact complaint of the correspondents and asking whether they should have been permitted to write in greater detail. Of those questioned, 7 per cent strangely enough had no opinion, 24 per cent agreed with the correspondents and 69 per cent said the information should have been withheld if the Army felt disclosure would handicap military operations.

Such is the tangled background of what may go down in history as a celebrated controversy over censorship. What is the lesson? It would take a better man than Solomon to render an unassailable verdict, but one thing surely is clear enough: Censorship is a complex business, dealing in the most dangerous of wares, and its problems are not to be solved wisely by bombast and curbstone opinion.

* * *

May 2, 1945

COPENHAGEN WRITER AGAIN PHONES STORY

By Cable to The New York Times

STOCKHOLM, Sweden, May 1—For the first time in more than five years The New York Times correspondent in Copenhagen, Svend Carstensen, tonight telephoned a story from the Danish capital. The Nazi-imposed censorship there has been lifted. Mr. Carstensen said:

"The Danes are overjoyed at their imminent liberation, but it is not noticeable on the Copenhagen streets.

"Anxious to avoid trouble on May Day, Copenhageners have been staying indoors. The blackout is still enforced and it is pitch dark in Copenhagen tonight. All Copenhageners are glued to radios listening to broadcasts on Hitler's death.

"We expect King Christian will resume his functions and name a new Cabinet any day now. In the meantime the strictest discipline is being observed so as not to give the Germans any excuses for starting more trouble."

On April 9, 1940, Mr. Carstensen was the first to give the world the news of the German invasion of Denmark in a wireless dispatch to The New York Times. His dispatch was cleared less than an hour before the Nazis seized the radio station and was the last to be sent.

* * *

May 8, 1945

BRITAIN'S CENSORSHIP IS STILL UNRELAXED

By Wireless to The New York Times

LONDON, May 7—War correspondents' biggest headache—the censorship—has not yet been cured. A revised statement of censorship policy from London is expected to be issued Thursday, and until then every word written in this victorious capital must be passed by the censor, "for security reasons," before being transmitted across the Atlantic.

The British Government has promised in the past that censorship on non-military matter would end with the war in Europe. Military censorship will be continued until the end of the Japanese war and no news of the movement of naval or military formations will be passed for immediate publication.

SHAEF censors are still at their job as usual tonight and they are carrying on their usual routine until instructions from "high up" come through.

* * *

September 6, 1945

PARIS VIRTUALLY ENDS CENSORSHIP OF PRESS

By Wireless to The New York Times

PARIS, Sept. 5—Press censorship in France practically ended tonight although details of the Government's decision have yet to be made public. On broad lines, anyway, there is no longer any control over news or articles before publication. So far as foreign correspondents are concerned this means that they may file their dispatches at will although they agreed at a meeting this morning to continue to use the Ministry of Information's transmission facilities at Hotel Scribe, which French authorities took over from the United States Army.

Press censorship had been relaxed after Germany's capitulation and was supposed to operate thereafter only as regards military information of a nature calculated to aid Japan. French newspaper circles complained that this restriction was open to wide interpretation, so wide, indeed, as to include comment on the internal political situation.

However, these complaints had become less frequent in recent months as censorship obviously became moribund.

It had been established during the period of tension immediately preceding the outbreak of hostilities in September, 1939, and it was applied with rigor even prior to the French defeat in June, 1940. Thereafter the censors received instructions from the Germans, both in the occupied and unoccupied zones.

Although censorship before publication is abolished it remains the privilege of the French authorities to draw the attention of foreign correspondents to dispatches that they may consider "unfriendly" or "tendentious."

* * *

November 16, 1945

CENSORSHIP BUREAU COMES TO AN END

Special to The New York Times

WASHINGTON, Nov. 15—After a life of one month and four days less than four years, the war-created Bureau of Censorship went out of existence tonight. Byron Price, the director, and the remaining seventy of the staff, turned over the keys of their desks, already tagged for delivery to other Federal agencies.

At its peak the bureau employed 14,500 persons, with 800 to 900 in Washington. Besides supervising a voluntary censorship by newspapers and radio, it inspected millions of tons of mail.

Begun Dec. 19, 1941, twelve days after Pearl Harbor, actual censorship ceased Aug. 15, three days after V-J Day. Since then the bureau has been liquidating itself.

Mr. Price, former executive news editor of The Associated Press, has made no plans beyond taking a rest.

* * *

December 19, 1945

PRICE LAUDS PRESS UNDER CENSORSHIP

In Final Report, He Says It Watched Unceasingly to Keep Information From Enemy

By LEWIS WOOD

Special to The New York Times

WASHINGTON, Dec. 18—The greatest challenge to the capacity of censorship in keeping vital information from the enemy during the war came in the weeks which preceded the invasion of France, Byron Price, recent Director of Censorship, stated today in his final report to President Truman.

The Nazis, he went on, knew from "elementary observation" that the British Isles were to be the springboard of the assault, but their crucial question was where and when the strike would be made. For six months, said Mr. Price, special precautions were taken against leaks, and when at last the invasion proceeded in June, 1944, "it became evident that the enemy had been kept in the dark as to the time and place of the attack."

The "best-kept" scientific secret of the war, Mr. Price reported, was the production of the atomic bomb. In June, 1943, his office asked newspapers and radio stations not to speculate about new and secret military weapons, atom smashing and other such developments. From that date until President Truman announced Aug. 6 last the dropping of the first atomic bomb on Japan, censorship kept a constant vigil. The "two-year voluntary blackout on such news was effective," he said.

Praises Work of Editors

"The value of the self-censorship program, however," Mr. Price continued, "rested, not alone on a few spectacular achievements, such as the preservation of secrecy about the atomic bomb and invasion preparations, but on the continuous day by day restraint by editors and broadcasters. It kept an inestimable amount of information from the enemy and thereby saved the lives of countless American Allied soldiers, sailors and marines."

Throughout his 154-page report, Mr. Price praised the press and radio for forebearance under censorship, which he said he considered necessary only under the stress of war. Censorship, he maintained, should be voluntary in a free country, and he added, voluntary censorship has been fully as successful as the compulsory systems of Britain and Canada.

"Censorship of the dissemination of public information must hold unceasingly," he said, "day in and day out, to the single purpose of keeping dangerous information from the enemy. Editorial opinions and criticisms never can be brought under Government restraint and ought not to be, so long as our present form of government endures; and any censorial excursion into that realm would most certainly destroy the respect and confidence of the censored and lead to collapse of the entire structure."

Emphasizing the limits within which he felt censorship in war could properly be operated, Mr. Price said that the work was twofold—to deprive the enemy of information and to collect intelligence to use against him.

"No censorship can fail to go dangerously afield unless it holds rigidly and resolutely to these basic purposes," he commented.

Against Supressing Criticism

"There are those who believe sincerely, but without counting the ultimate cost, that the censor should operate according to a broader, totalitarian philosophy; that he should undertake to suppress criticism of the Government and conceal Governmental blunders and delinquencies; that he should make fishing expeditions into private affairs having no possible connection with the war; that he should withhold from the American people, for policy reasons, information known to be available to the enemy.

"In short, that he should commit in the name of security all of the errors which have helped often enough heretofore to discredit censorships, to divorce their procedures completely from the dictates of common sense, and in the end to weaken greatly their effectiveness.

"Unless and until the day comes when the form of our Government is to be altered materially, it will not be wise or expedient even in time of national peril to undertake thus to reduce American citizens to a state of intellectual slavery. The task of prosecuting the war would be hindered, rather than helped, by any such attempt."

The Price report, filled with facts and figures, had its graphic side, when the former director told of the secrets uncovered by intercepting enemy letters, cables, telephone messages and the like. He revealed incidentally that only one copy of these intercepts is now extent.

"The director," he stated, "felt that information taken from messages by war time censorship should not be generally available for peacetime use. With Presidential approval, all but one copy of the intercepts were destroyed. The single copy was placed in a special archives file, which would be opened only by order of the President."

In revealing some of the details of how censorship worked, Mr. Price said that the enemy was in complete ignorance of the invasion of North Africa, and that the secrecy which surrounded preparations for the Casablanca conference was "unbreached" and that even when Roosevelt and Churchill met, the enemy was still throwing out feelers. The Cairo conference was not such a well-kept secret, because of an advance story naming that city as the site.

The Axis Powers, Its Sympathizers, and Its Conquered Countries

December 24, 1939

WAR NEWS IS CUT TO REDS' PATTERN

Russian Press and Radio Give the People Only the Vaguest Idea of World Events

TALK OF 'FINNISH REVOLT'

By G. E. R. GEDYE
Wireless to The New York Times

MOSCOW, Dec. 23—For two days this week the world has stood still for the Soviet citizen. The tumult and the shouting died down to a dim murmur both in Finland and in the area of war where three great powers are locked in a death struggle, in order to force the Soviet citizen to concentrate his thoughts on Joseph Stalin's sixtieth birthday.

Soviet newspapers could spare only two out of thirty-six columns from eulogies of Stalin to world affairs; the radio distributed its time in like proportion.

To the vast majority of Soviet citizens it was right to do so. Long freed of the worrisome task of culling mental pabulum from varied sources, weighing and balancing contradictory arguments and concocting a resultant dish of personal views, each for himself. Soviet citizens are accustomed to having news rationed and prepared for consumption by master chefs according to infallible recipes, served up well seasoned with sauce of orthodox opinion.

No Questioning

News not appearing in the Soviet press and radio just has not happened for the citizen of the Soviet union. What does appear there is not susceptible of argument, still less contradiction.

It is true that there is a punning Russian story based on the meaning of the words "pravda" and "izvestia"—truth and news—which says "in 'pravda' there is no 'izvestia,' and in 'izvestia' there is no 'pravda'." But those who recall it nowadays do so in the tones in which a priest of unquestionable piety may permit himself to repeat a classic pun on some Old Testament name secure in his hearers' knowledge of his faith in the literal inspiration of the Scriptures.

Dimly but faithfully the Russians try to believe that Britain, France and the United States are in the forefront of their enemies today, where Germany stood yesterday, but here belief falters as it would not if tomorrow they were told Germany again was the spearhead of hostility. That they are not so told today most believe is due to some unexplained but deep-laid schemes of the Soviet Union's leaders to lure German fascism to destruction.

They note that while the Nazis are no longer attacked they are never praised. They clearly see an outside world of cut-throat capitalism and rival imperialisms again plunged into the internecine slaughter which Marx foretold as inherent in the capitalist system, whereby it was destined finally to destroy itself in order to yield place to the socialism of the distant future, to the idyllic communism governed by the principle, "To each according to his needs; from each according to his abilities."

Views of Citizens

They see themselves as saved from being involved in the slaughter by the earlier adoption of socialism and by the protecting genius of Stalin.

The war is here regarded as a repetition of 1914, where German exploiters seek markets and colonies from French and British exploiters who fight against yielding them; the defense of democracy as a slogan of men like Britain's Neville

Chamberlain and France's Edouard Daladier is seen by the Soviet populace as the joke of the century.

Do doubts arise as to whether by attacking Finland the Soviet Union has not followed the example of the Fascist and capitalist imperialisms? If so they are probably stifled by news that the Finnish masses have "revolted" and established a popular régime in Finland which the Soviet Union is aiding against a desperate handful of White oppressors whom it is taking curiously long to brush aside.

Russians' ideas of geography always were and remain of the vaguest.

"Nemets" (German) is derived (though it sounds strange in this era of Hitler and Goebbels) from "Nemoy," meaning dumb—in respect to the Russian language—and thus a foreigner. To Russians a foreigner was the same as a German. How, then, expect the masses of today to appreciate the significance of the formation of a "government" on the fringe of invaded Finland at Terjoki?

Some Things Not Know

Soviet citizens are ignorant of the popular sympathy for Finland in the United States and elsewhere and see only foreign capitalists eager to continue their exploitation of the Finns and to seize any opportunity to demonstrate their hatred of a Soviet Union liberated from the capitalist yoke.

Of the progress of the European War Soviet citizens have a fair idea, though French and British difficulties are slightly exaggerated and their successes minimized as the gains of the Germans are slightly exaggerated.

The end is not seen as victory for either, but the final collapse of capitalism in world revolution the first step toward which is imagined to be the present "brotherly aid to revolting Finnish workers."

* * *

January 1, 1940

REICH IS ENFORCING ITS BAN UPON NEWS

'Radio Discipline' Is Latest Slogan—Listening to Any Foreigners Punished

NEUTRAL PAPERS BARRED

Strict Domestic Censorship Is Defended as a Matter of Patriotic Policy

By GUIDO ENDERIS
Wireless to The New York Times

BERLIN, Dec. 31—London and Paris are about three hours distant from Berlin by air, but since the proclamation of a "state of war" the populace of Berlin might as well attempt to establish communication with the Martians as to try to find out what is going on in those cities.

British and French newspapers, which up to the beginning of the war found a ready sale in Berlin, promptly disappeared from the newsstands and were also barred from the mails. Telephonic communications also have fallen under the military ban, while foreign news broadcasts now may be picked up only by persons who enjoy extraterritorial privileges.

Swift and drastic punishment awaits any German caught listening in to a French, British or even a neutral broadcast. Thirteen million German owners of receiving sets are being taught "radio discipline" under the slogan, "Every time you secretly listen to a hostile foreign broadcast you are taking an enemy into your home."

Channels Are Controlled

The channels through which foreign information is now made available to Germans are definitely confined to the national press and government controlled radio. There are no avenues open for the surreptitious dissemination of foreign propaganda.

German circles, moreover, hold that the few attempts made by Allied airplanes to scatter pamphlets over German towns proved futile. They declare that the character of the propaganda was so completely innocuous and ineffective that Dr. Joseph Goebbels, the Minister of Propaganda, might safely have permitted it to be reprinted in the German press as an evidence of the superiority of his own output.

The German propaganda machine, since the outbreak of the war, muffed one or two opportunities in failing to anticipate Allied competition. One was in connection with the sinking of the Athenia, when Berlin lagged behind the reports of the news. More recently, in connection with the naval encounter off Montevideo, even home criticism charged it with the failure to present the condition of the Graf Spee in its true light and thus prepare German opinion for the inevitable sequel.

Throughout the past four months Dr. Goebbels's propaganda machine has been meeting wartime requirements—in so far as they are considered essential to the nation's defense. It keeps the German supplied, through the medium of press, radio and film, with what of domestic and foreign information is deemed to be necessary to his enlightenment.

Neutrals Now Embargoed

For a long time the Reich did not dare to flout neutrals by putting an embargo on their newspapers and up to a week ago Swiss and Hungarian papers printed in German were tolerated. They are now definitely banned. The Scandinavian and Netherland press remained temporarily unmolested as it was believed a lesser source of menace on the assumption that only a limited number of Germans were conversant with those languages. But the ban on all foreign newspapers is now being extended and an exception will be made only for strictly scientific journals.

An inquisitor who sought enlightenment on the censorship policy as now practiced was told by the official Propaganda Ministry:

"We naturally are not interested in having others unload their propaganda on our people either through newspapers or by broadcasts."

While that formula may impress a neutral observer as a bit naive, it nevertheless represents the German official attitude.

The German authorities are more concerned about foreign papers printed in German than those in other languages and the increasing demand for German Swiss papers has now led to a general ban on all Swiss papers printed in German. Thus one of the few remaining sources through which foreign information printed in German reached Germany is gradually drying up.

Diplomatic Question Raised

The position in respect to Swiss German newspapers, printed in German, is especially complicated and has led to an unexpected diplomatic step.

The Swiss Government is now seeking to obtain the privilege for Swiss-German nationals residing in Germany to obtain their home papers regularly, as Switzerland is permitting the unrestricted circulation of German newspapers and is even allowing the German colony at Zurich to issue its local newspaper there.

As a further illustration of the difficulties confronting the Swiss Government, it has now suppressed the pro-Nazi Neue Basler Zeitung of Basle. That paper's circulation within Switzerland is believed to be only about 6,000 whereas that in Germany is 72,000. Up to a few weeks ago numerous Swiss provincial German papers found a ready sale in Germany. They have now disappeared from the newsstands.

The semi-official Pester Lloyd of Budapest, Hungary, one of the most popular Continental newspapers printed in German, will still be allowed in Germany for the time being, presumably out of courtesy to the Hungarian Government.

Letters Now Opened

With the military authorities now exercising a rigorous censorship of mails, the private approach to Germany is also no longer at the disposal of foreign propagandists who might have promoted rebellion through the medium of chain letters. German methods of censoring the mails, moreover, add to the delays caused by British censorship of letters en route to Germany, and so even Americans here have been without the usual seasonal greetings from home. The usual period for the transmission of this doubly censored mail is about six weeks.

Thus foreign news sources at the disposal of the German narrow down to his own press and such foreign broadcasts as he may succeed in picking up clandestinely. But the latter practice is now stigmatized as highly unpatriotic, if not treasonable, and few will take the risk of being caught.

As a result this "radio discipline" has become a matter of loyalty and honor and the press continues to dilate on the patriotic aspect of the matter. There is no denying that the temptation is irresistible when one owns a powerful receiving set as the British and French broadcasts are being disseminated in impeccable German. Those put on the air in English by the German propaganda machine are redolent of the Oxford accent and no less cleverly edited and disguised than the foreign output.

Radio Law Enforced

But a law promulgated at the outbreak of the war imposes a severe penal sentence on any infraction of this "radio discipline" and during a single week recently no less than eight Germans were sentenced to from one to two years for listening in on foreign broadcasts and disclosing the contents to their neighbors.

In a town near Danzig a man, his wife and two other members of the family were summarily sentenced to various terms of penal servitude for violating this law. Three inquisitive individuals in other parts of the Reich fared no better.

"War calls for complete concentration of the spiritual forces of our people and to that end the disintegrating effect of the enemy's propaganda of lies must be countered by all means at the Reich's disposal," the German radio owner is told. He is reminded that anybody who lends an ear to "the clever campaign of lies that is primarily intended to undermine confidence in the Reich's leadership" is a common traitor.

The mere habit of listening in, says one newspaper, constitutes a dishonorable act and makes the offender the recipient of the enemy's agitation, in that it influences his opinions. The sentences imposed on such offenders are therefore welcomed as designed to have a salutory effect on the others.

Urges Ignoring Broadcasts

The most effective method of vitiating the disintegrating effects of foreign radio propaganda, observes one editor, is to ignore it. It takes two to make broadcasts effective, he says, a sending station and an individual listener. This warning voice argues that the mere practice of picking up foreign radio news is equivalent to receiving the enemy into one's home.

With foreign broadcasts eliminated as illegal purveyors of news for popular consumption in Germany, the only remaining source for the dissemination of news is the national press of the Reich. While a considerable volume of foreign news—carefully edited—is regularly served up to German radio fans, the preponderant volume remains the prerogative of the German newspapers.

Official and local news from London, for instance, is carried under Amsterdam date-lines. Occasionally a London correspondent of some Danish or Swedish newspaper is quoted opportunely. French news reaches German readers via Brussels or some Swiss frontier point. Such news is carefully interpreted and not infrequently a distinct editorial bias is given to it. British and French parliamentary speeches are printed only in excerpts.

News reels deal almost exclusively with domestic events and the majority of films now running are attuned to wartime demands. American films continue in favor, as do translations of American best sellers. Despite rigid censorial supervision, an assortment of wartime reading matter of foreign origin reveals a liberal attitude. Even studies and biographies of British and French statesmen found a ready demand during the shopping for the Christmas season.

Any attempt to survey the volume and nature of foreign news finally reaching the average German must take into account the circumstance that the censorial procedure in an authoritarian State of such rigid structure as National Socialist Germany is predicated on considerations wholly at variance from those actuating British or French wartime policy.

To the German reader is given a minute account of the internal difficulties confronting British and French statesmen, and the opposition parliamentary criticism in those countries is freely reproduced. The German is told that the destruction of the German Empire is the aim of the war, and that note remains the dominant factor in all foreign news that is allowed to reach the German.

* * *

February 4, 1940

NOTHING, JUST NOTHING—RED NEWS FROM FRONT

Explanation of Why the Newspapers Carry More News From Finnish Front Than From Russian

KREMLIN'S HOT COMMUNIQUES

By EDWIN L. JAMES

Newspapers are receiving a good many letters from Communists, pinkish fellow-travelers and from other readers who say they are puzzled about it, asking why so much more news is printed from the Finnish front than from the Russian front. Many of the communications are loutish in character and obviously intended as propaganda arguments, but there is a minority of complainants who appear to be honest about their inquiries.

So here is an effort to explain why more news is printed about the Finns, who are trying to save their country from being conquered, than is printed about the Russians, who are trying to crush Finland.

In the first place, and important, is the fact that the Finns permit correspondents of foreign newspapers to visit their troops on all the fronts. These correspondents are given good facilities and assistance, much as correspondents were given with the French, British and American armies in the World War. There are in the field excellent and experienced men like Webb Miller and Harold Denny. They are given chances to see what is going on and are allowed to write freely. The score or more of foreign reporters in Finland produce most of the stories about the war there.

Different With Soviet

However, the Russians permit no foreign correspondents with their armies at the front. Foreign newspapers have made repeated requests for this privilege, which has been consistently denied. Therefore there are no Webb Millers and no Harold Dennys writing from the Russian front. If they were, their articles would be published just as are the articles from the correspondents with the Finnish Army.

In the second place, the Finnish leaders supply daily at Helsinki and other spots detailed information on current operations. This material is transmitted by the correspondents and agencies and gets printed. It is presented as the official claims of the Finnish Government. There may be those who think the Finns are over-optimistic and others who may not think so. But there should be no quarrel with the proposition that it is proper newspaper practice to publish the Finnish communiqués.

On the other hand, there is not only a very strict censorship in Moscow, but the amount of official information made available for foreign correspondents there is extremely meager. The daily communiqués give next to nothing in the way of information and there is no other information to be had in Russia.

Take the matter of pictures. Camera and newsreel men are welcomed in Finland and are given large facilities. The result is pictures of Finnish operations in the newsreels sent abroad and a large number of photographs available for reproduction in newspapers. The Russians supply none or very few pictures and so there are not many Russian war pictures printed. If they were available they would be printed.

The Russian Communiques

To illustrate, here are the daily Russian communiqués of the past week, all of which have been printed in The New York Times:

Jan. 27: "Activities of scouts. Soviet aviation made reconnoitering flights."

Jan. 28: "Nothing of importance took place on the front."

Jan. 29: "During Jan. 29 nothing of importance occurred at the front. Our aircraft made reconnaissance flights and had engagements with the enemy. In air encounters over different directions of the front seven enemy planes were shot down."

New Russian Denials

However, yesterday the Russians, for the second time in the past month, gave out a longer statement from the Leningrad headquarters denying various items published from Finnish sources. In the first place, there was a denial that there had been a new Russian drive against the Mannerheim Line; there had been a clash of a few companies only, it was said. It was also denied that Finnish planes had raided Kronstadt. That was called a tale spread by "mercenary agents of enemies of the U.S.S.R." The statement declared that not only were the Finns, who had "received airplanes of most up-to-date designs from France, Sweden, the United States and Italy," unable to raid Soviet territory but were unable to protect their headquarters from Russian planes.

Yet, one such communiqué a month does not give the newspapers much material to make a showing of Russian war news. In fact, it is difficult to escape the conclusion that, so far as the Russians go, there hasn't been any news since they stopped winning.

One is asked to believe that there are 200,000 to 300,000 Russian troops along the Finnish border, in Finland at some points, who for a month have been doing nothing. If the

Moscow communiqués are right, they could not have done much. If the Soviets wish a spread in the foreign press, why not explain what the Russian troops have been doing since Christmas? Are they loafing on the job? Is it too cold for them? Do they fail to overrun Finland, as was intended, for some other reasons? What's the answer?

A Matter of News Gathering

The charges of the Reds and Pinks that the "capitalistic" press is making a big show of Finnish news as some sort of a plot has ceased to be annoying; it is fast getting funny. The American press does not prostitute its front pages. It does not fail to print news because of imaginary policies. In 1917 and 1918 this country was at war with Germany. But its newspapers printed all the news they could get from Germany. Editorially, a newspaper may not admire the attempted rape of Finland by Soviet Russia. But that would have nothing to do with printing news from Russia if the Russian Government, for reasons best known to it, did not make it all but impossible to get any news from Russia.

If Russia does not wish news from her front printed in American newspapers, that is Russia's business. But at the same time it gives a color of stupidity to the yells of Communist sympathizers in this and other countries that the prominence given to Finnish "lies" represents a "capitalistic" plot against the U.S.S.R.

If Soviet Russia will open up, the American newspapers will respond. If she will allow foreign correspondents to go up north of Leningrad to find out why there has been no news from twenty-odd Russian divisions for the past month, that explanation will be printed. That is, if the Russian censor passes it.

* * *

April 2, 1940

REICH PURGES MUSIC

Phonograph Records of British Works or Playing Disappear

Wireless to The New York Times

BERLIN, April 1—The Third Reich seems to be purging phonograph records to remove all contaminating influences inherent in British music.

All recordings of British music, as well as works of composers other than British when played or interpreted by British artists, have been removed from stock and from the catalogues.

* * *

November 6, 1940

ITALY BARS SWISS PAPERS AS BIASED IN WAR NEWS

By Telephone to The New York Times

BERNE, Switzerland, Nov. 5—The entire Swiss press, with the exception of the Neue Zuercher Zeitung and the Basler Nachrichten, has been banned from Italy on grounds that it "presented unilateral reports of the progress of the Italian campaign in Greece."

Authoritative Italian sources explained Rome objected to the "prominence given to news from anti-Italian sources, notably British." They specifically point to dispatches describing "without any foundation whatsoever" a naval battle off Corfu, as well as reports of the "pretended capture of thousands of Italian soldiers when the Greek soldiers advanced into Albania."

It is understood here that official newspaper circles have been informed this measure is temporary. It will become permanent for those papers which "do not immediately give proof of adopting a more objective attitude in their reports."

* * *

January 9, 1941

FRENCH PRINT RESUME OF ROOSEVELT'S TALK

All Mention of Aid to Britain Is Omitted in Vichy's Version

Wireless to The New York Times

VICHY, France, Jan. 8—After many hours of reflection, a summary of President Roosevelt's message to Congress has been allowed to appear in the French press.

At best it is an adulterated version with many omissions, especially as regards the prosecution of the war and aid to Great Britain. Of comment, there is none.

The transfer of the Information and Censorship Departments from Marshal Henri Philippe Pétain's office to the Department of Foreign Affairs under the direction of Pierre-Etienne Flandin continues to be marked by greater severity and all the incoherence of Pierre Laval's tenure of office. Things reached such a pitch last night that it was not permitted to cable the American newspapers what the United States Ambassador had told American correspondents on American soil. [The embassy technically is part of the United States.] Dispatches on this subject had been allowed earlier in the day, but later they were "deferred" and were not released until this morning, after the matter had been brought directly to the attention of the Foreign Minister.

* * *

February 9, 1941

VICHY CHIDES PRESS AS UNIFORMLY DULL

Editors Blame Censorship for Dearth of News in Skimpy Sheets Selling at High Price

LITTLE NOW HEARD OF U. S.

Hollywood Doings and Diet of Soldiers Are Typical Items, Often Via Berlin or Tokyo

Special Correspondence, The New York Times

VICHY, France, Jan. 16—Even the Information Section here bewails the lack of interest presented by the French press and urges that it depart from a monotonous uniformity which, it is too evident, has reached the point of utter boredom.

Moreover, newspapers are relatively expensive—50 centimes for a single sheet, increased to four pages twice a week. Even at that, the scarcity of advertising and the cost of production have compelled the Temps to raise its price to 75 centimes and the Figaro to 70.

It is difficult to see how many papers can long survive. Yet the value, even the necessity of the press is admitted on all hands.

Certainly the Information Section is well founded in its urgings, but it seems to overlook that it has a twin, the censorship, which operates with a heavy hand. There are so many things that may not be printed, or at least that must be first submitted for approval. So many official communications compulsorily must be published that the making of a newspaper tends to become an automatic routine.

The gathering of news is becoming an extinct art. Editors of talent turn to the discussion of abstract notions or to pen-pictures of the rural letter carrier going his rounds. Today the French public continues to buy newspapers because it had become a habit. But how long the habit will persist if there is no value for money is dubious.

Few deny that censorship has its place in a period of armistice, that is neither peace nor war and with an occupying power having a voice in many matters. Yet there are unbiased observers who believe that in the end the censorship may defeat its own purpose by so accustoming public opinion to a daily fare of trivialities that it may fail to respond to matters of moment.

As one French editor puts it: "The critical faculty is still alive in the popular mind, and it should be taken into account in the presentation of news."

Stress on the trivial is very apparent in the matter of news from America, for instance. Public opinion in France knows—or when it does not actually know, it senses—that the United States is playing a great part in world events today. Yet the newspapers tell mostly of doings at Hollywood, of the diet of the American soldier, of funny or freak stories.

Nor is the origin of the news given the French reader without significance. Many items, even relating to the North American Continent, come by way of Berlin and are credited to the official Nazi news bureau, D. N. B., or by way of Tokyo, and are credited to Domei, the official Japanese agency. One recent report of debates in the United States Congress was even dated "From the Swiss Frontier."

There are indications already that too rigorous application of the censorship may produce unwelcome results. The Information Section itself not many days ago warned newspapers against "a flood of tracts, stickers and even oral propaganda."

* * *

September 5, 1941

FOREIGN NEWSPAPERS BARRED FROM ITALY

Exceptions for German—Decree Shuts Out Neutral News of War

By Telephone to The New York Times

ROME, Sept. 4—The last legal access the Italians had to foreign news was closed today when the Italian Government barred all foreign newspapers from Italy.

Months ago radio listeners were forbidden under threat of heavy penalties to listen to foreign broadcasts. As a result of the radio ban the sale in Italy of newspapers from neutral countries had increased greatly. Swiss newspapers, especially Neuw Zuerchen Zeitung, sold by the thousands, not only in South Tyrol, but throughout the peninsula.

The day's decree completes what was already a partial ban, since all French-language newspapers, including those published in Switzerland, were prohibited soon after Italy's entry into the war. American newspapers have not come through since early June.

The decree provides that exceptions may be made by authorization of the Ministry of Finance and it is understood this might refer to German newspapers, which are likewise hit by the general ban.

The Osservatore Romano, the Vatican City organ, which for a time was the only paper available here that gave the daily news without an Axis propaganda slant, was efficiently gagged after a short period during which its circulation increased 500 per cent to about 150,000 copies daily.

Another decree forbids the sale of precious metals and stones as well as articles made of or containing these materials in part. The reason is stated in economic circles to be the authoritative desire to prevent the flight from the lire and extend the restrictions on investment of capital in anything but State bonds.

* * *

March 11, 1942

100 SECRET NEWSPAPERS PUBLISHED IN POLAND WITH ALLIES' AID BY AIR

By JAMES B. RESTON
Special to The New York Times

WASHINGTON, March 10—Poland may be totally occupied by the Germans, but the Poles are still printing more than 100 underground newspapers, which are passed through the ranks of the Gestapo to more than 3,000,000 Polish patriots.

Count Edward Raczynski, the Polish Foreign Minister, brought to this country scores of letter-size dailies that are printed in the forests of the Warthegau and in farms and cellars around Warsaw, Cracow and Lodz, where in 1899–1901 Joseph Pilsudski, later head of the Polish State, printed the revolutionary daily Robotnik [The Worker].

Most of the papers are printed weekly, but about fifty come out every day, and Count Raczynski told of at least one that printed two editions a day, with photographs. Among the weeklies is one comic paper, Lipa, which carries under its masthead the legend: "Wesole Pismo wychodzi w Polsche w Dniach Grozy" [A merry journal published in Poland in the days of horror].

The radio, the long-range bomber and the parachute have played an important part in the development of this vast underground press service, the purpose of which is to combat German propaganda and keep the Polish people in touch with their exiled government in London.

The Polish underground press has access through the radio to detailed news of the outside world, and when offices are raided and their machinery confiscated, airplanes and parachutes carry from Britain and Russia the needed supplies.

The Polish Government has had no trouble in getting experienced Polish newspapermen to do this work. Many have been flown back to their homeland and dropped from planes that also dropped by parachute the necessary paper, stencils, photographs, ink and small hand machines.

The names of the papers symbolize the purpose and spirit of the underground press. Among the more prominent are Jutro [Tomorrow], Walka [Fight], Latarnia [The Lantern] and Szaniec [The Trench]. Almost all carry the suggestion: "Po przecztaniu oddaj drugiemu." ["After having read the paper give it to another."]

As a precaution against discovery by the Gestapo, which the leaders of the underground press have discovered to be more alert and ruthless than the Ochrana, the Czarist secret police, which tried for years to break up the underground press during the third partition of Poland, the Poles are distributing their papers according to what they call the "rule of three." Under this system a person distributing the paper knows no more than two other persons connected with the movement, the person from whom he gets the paper and the person to whom he passes it when he has finished reading it.

The penalty for reporting, publishing, distributing or reading the underground press is death under the Nazi law. The "rule of three" is designed to protect the 3,000,000 persons who, almost every day, take this chance to get the news.

News Published Quickly

The courage of the men engaged in putting out these papers is matched only by their enterprise and the rapidity with which they are printing the news. On June 23, 1941, for example, Winston Churchill made one of his periodic reviews of the war. The following day, General Wladyslaw Sikorski, the Polish Prime Minister, delivered a special address to the Polish people. A week later the National Democrat party's official underground paper, Szaniec, came out with Volume 3, Number 14, dated Warsaw, June 16–30, carrying the texts of both speeches.

The same issue of Szaniec, described under the masthead as "a bi-monthly devoted to the Polish cause in time of slavery," told in detail of the British occupation of Syria, described the bombardment by the British of the German battleships Scharnhorst and Gneisenau, told of a British bombing raid on Kiel, Emden and Duesseldorf, discussed the possibility of a German occupation of Sweden and Switzerland, and, in an article entitled "Uncle Sam and His Nephews!" deplored the fact that the United States had invented but not exploited for war purposes the armored division, the airplane, parachute troops and the fast transmission for the tank.

Pointing out that we had let the Germans develop these inventions without doing much with them ourselves, Szaniec lamented: "You have to admit Uncle Sam has a lot of light-hearted nephews!"

Report Raids on Offices

Like good newspapermen, these reporter-editor-printers even contrive to report the raids they survive at the hands of the Gestapo. On May 27, 1941, the Biuletyn Prasowy: [Press Bulletin] contained the following item:

"The day before yesterday, May 25, four of our fellow-newspaper men (three men and one woman) were writing and setting their paper in the apartment of Mr. and Mrs. Bruehl, Lwowska Street, Warsaw. Earlier in the day, two Gestapo men hid in the Opus Laundry, from where they could observe Bruehl's apartment door.

"About midnight the Gestapo men rang the bell. One of the reporters opened the door and the Germans entered the foyer. They ordered the men to stand up with arms raised, facing the wall.

"One of the Gestapo men went to the printing room. There, Leon Waclawski, the well-known writer, editor of one of our papers for several months, took a revolver out of his sleeve and shot the German, killing him with one shot.

"The other Gestapo man in the foyer shot three times at the man standing at the wall, killed him and ran away for help. The others thus got time to leave the house.

"Leon Waclawski today joined our staff. We are proud to print today his first article. Unhappily, the printing set in Bruehl's house got lost. Yesterday, the Gestapo arrested all inhabitants of the house at Lwowska Street."

83 Died in Later Raid

All the members of the underground press, however, are not so fortunate, as the following dispatch in the July 6, 1941, issue of the Glos Polski [Poland's Voice] indicates:

On July 4, a villa on the fashionable Okrezna Street at Czermiakowi, Warsaw, was surrounded by the Gestapo and S. S. Elite Guards, armed with machine guns. The house sheltered one of our printing shops which had recently been moved from the Mokotow (another Warsaw residential district) because the editors and printers were apparently shadowed by the Gestapo.

"When knocking at the door brought no response, the Germans threw hand grenades through the windows, blasted the doors open and fired inside several times with their machine guns, killing two of our men and wounding two others, who later died in the hospital. A few days later, the owner of the villa, Michael Kruk, his wife and two sons, aged 15 and 17, as well as all tenants of two neighboring houses were arrested and subsequently shot. In all eighty-three persons lost their lives."

* * *

April 11, 1943

ANTI-AXIS PAPERS OF GREEKS SHOWN

Exhibition Here Contains the Only 2 That Have Succeeded in Reaching This Country

BOTH PRINTED IN ATHENS

One Describes Itself as Organ of 'Enslaved Victors,' Other Speaks for Youth

The only two Greek underground newspapers ever seen in the United States are part of an exhibit of Greece under the Axis that opened yesterday in City College's Lincoln Corridor. The papers were smuggled out of the country by escaping refugees and were lent to the college by the Greek Office of Information.

Both papers are printed regularly in Athens and are distributed behind the backs of the German and Italian occupational forces, as are eight other sheets. Great Greece, one of the two shown, describes itself as "The Organ of the Army of Enslaved Victors." The other, Glory, is the publication of the undercover Panhellenic United Youth.

The headline of Great Greece is: "To the traitor: a word of warning." The issue is devoted to a public letter addressed to a General Tchocakoglow, a Greek Quisling who is a member of the puppet provisional government.

"We must address you by title," it reads, "because of the misfortune that you wear the uniform of a Greek officer, a uniform which the Nazis allow only you to wear.

"General Tchocakoglow: Glory in God still exists, but it is far from Greece. But there are still Greeks in uniforms, uniforms, which unlike you, they can be proud to wear. They are fighting in distant lands to bring about the day when Greece will be free of your friends, the Fascists."

The paper reveals that on March 25, 1942, the anniversary of Greece's Independence Day, the Germans and Italians placed wreaths on the tomb of the Greek Unknown Soldier and were stoned by Athens children. "You have allowed our enemies to sully the grave of our heroes," the paper says, "but you can never convince us other than that our only hope of salvation lies in a victory of the United States and England."

Glory carries on its front page the slogan: "Unity, Courage, Faith."

The papers were translated by Cadet First Lieutenant Spero Soupios, a member of City College's Reserve Officers Training Corps.

* * *

May 16, 1943

THE FREE PRESS OF ENSLAVED EUROPE

By TANIA LONG

LONDON—The stillness of the gray dawn is shattered by a shout of "Fcucr." A volley of shots rings out, a body falls. People still asleep in the neighborhood shiver and draw their blankets closer as if they had just seen something evil in their dreams. That afternoon the German-controlled press announces the execution of H. C. for distributing news intended to incite enmity against the occupation authorities.

It is nearly three years since the Nazi Gestapo, following behind a victorious Wehrmacht, ruthlessly began to crush out the last vestiges of human liberty among the conquered peoples of Europe. Shootings, beatings, threats, as well as the more refined methods of torture, were applied with open brutality to any one attempting to defy the conquerors' "New Order." Yet despite the very worst the Germans could do, they have completely failed in one of the main objectives. They have not been able to stamp out the free press—their most dangerous opponent in any of the countries they have subjugated by military force.

Whether the Germans admit it or not, a powerful press which remains free, despite the Gestapo, exists today in all the occupied nations of Europe. This free press, in the form of roughly 1,000 underground newspapers, is the true mirror of the souls of millions of enslaved people from the Arctic regions of Norway to the sun-kissed hills of Yugoslavia and Greece. It is at the same time one of the most powerful of weapons, for it continues to give hope where otherwise despair might set in, and it provides the leadership and encouragement needed to shape the growing resistance which sweeps across the Continent.

The growth of the underground press in the past two years is one of the most remarkable phenomena of the war. Under penalty of death, in constant danger of being apprehended by the Gestapo, men and women—professionals as well as amateurs—daily risk their lives in order to provide people with the truth. Thanks to them, the voice of freedom was never stilled in darkened Europe. Although at one time it only spoke in a whisper, today its voice is heard loud and triumphant by all who dare listen.

The full story of the devotion of men and women who are carrying on the struggle for freedom under the shadow of the swastika probably cannot be told until their countries are free again. Even then it will be difficult to present a complete picture of the heroism of the unknown patriots who are part of the great underground movement. For even among those working in the same cause secrecy is essential, and no one patriot is aware of the identity of more than two members of the same group. Many will no doubt go to their death quite unknown. For the executions which are publicly announced by the Germans are the exceptions rather than the rule. Hundreds of men and women are merely quietly whisked away by the Gestapo, never to be heard of again.

Yet however many may disappear, there are always more to take their places. And when the Nazis succeed in crushing underground papers, others spring up like mushrooms after a Summer shower. The underground press has been so successful in countries like France and Poland that the Nazis themselves have resorted to printing fake underground papers in order to put across their ideas to the public, for it is a common belief among the conquered peoples that anything appearing in the German or German-controlled press is a lie, but that anything printed in the underground papers can be believed. But German attempts to get Frenchmen and Poles to accept the theories printed in these false sheets have failed.

The underground papers of some countries, like their predecessors of peace days, present a pattern of the various political convictions held by their editors, but all newspapers agree in hatred of the German tyrant. In France, as in Belgium and Poland, underground papers represent all the different shades of political thought from communism to extreme rightism.

One has only to thumb through copies of the French underground papers to get a fascinating glimpse behind the scenes of that country. France d'Abord, for instance, prints weekly "communiqués" of sabotage in various sectors. La Vie Ouvrière tells what happened to a certain Albert Clément, former editor of that paper, who had sold himself to the Nazis and turned informer. Clément, the paper says, was shot by patriots who had sworn to revenge the victims of his treachery.

La Vie Ouvrière is one of the underground newspapers which the Germans began faking in everything but reading matter. The phony La Vie Ouvrière devotes one column to vilifying the Soviet Union and another to describing the joys and comforts of working in Germany.

Another French underground newspaper, La Voix du Nord, contains the first published interview with a British bomber pilot who had come down in occupied France and was hidden by a farmer in a barn somewhere near Calais. The pilot is quoted as urging the French people to take shelter when the R. A. F. comes over. "We give you time to shelter," he said; "instead, you wave and shout. It is very moving, but don't do it, for your sake and ours."

The pilot explained that the presence of civilians often hampers the low-flying operations of the R. A. F., and urged workers to desert their jobs, because, as he told them, "we will bomb the factories in France until German slave industry is wiped out."

Counting the pamphlets which appear irregularly, there must be at least 300 underground newspapers in France, as many in Belgium and Poland, and slightly fewer in Norway, Holland, Czechoslovakia and the other countries. The circulation of the best-known newspapers in some cases exceeds the figures for peacetime. For instance, the French Combat, a serious economic paper of slightly right-wing tendency, prints an edition of 40,000 copies, but since it is estimated that each copy passes through the hands of at least ten persons, its readers can be said to number 400,000.

The business of producing and distributing these newspapers is dangerous and difficult. The usual penalty for any one caught is death. The patriot is either shot immediately without trial, made to disappear, or put on the hostage list and held for slaughter until the time is considered ripe by the Germans. Many hundreds already have given up their lives in the cause of freedom. One of the best known French editors who went to his death was Gabriel Péri. Communist Deputy and foreign editor of L'Humanité, which continued its daily publication from new secret headquarters almost immediately after the Germans entered Paris. Péri, who was kept for some time as a hostage after his arrest, sent just before his execution a moving message to his friends which was reprinted in most of the underground newspapers of France. "Let my friends," he said, "know that I have remained faithful to the ideal I have held all my life. Let my countrymen know that I die so that France may live."

The Communist L'Humanité and the Socialist organ, Le Populaire, were well-established Parisian daily newspapers before the German invasion. While all other papers either folded up or agreed to "collaborate" with the Germans, these two, following carefully prepared plans, moved their staffs and printing presses to secret hideouts and continued to appear with only occasional interruptions. When the hunt by the Gestapo grew too hot there was a quick change-over to new headquarters. The only difference between their papers today and those of the pre-war era is the size, which is smaller, and the addition of a line under the name "New war series No . . ."

A few months after the German occupation other clandestine papers began to appear. Among them are Résistance, Valmy, Pantagruel, Libération, which was edited by André Philip, now a Minister in the de Gaulle government; Le Gaulliste, and so on. Some of the smaller newspapers print only fifteen to 100 copies each, with the request "Please copy and pass on."

The editor of Valmy managed to survive through more than two years of underground work in the heart of Paris and then escaped when he was tipped off that the Gestapo was on his trail. By devious routes which André Simon (as he now calls himself) will not discuss, he came to England and joined the de Gaulle movement.

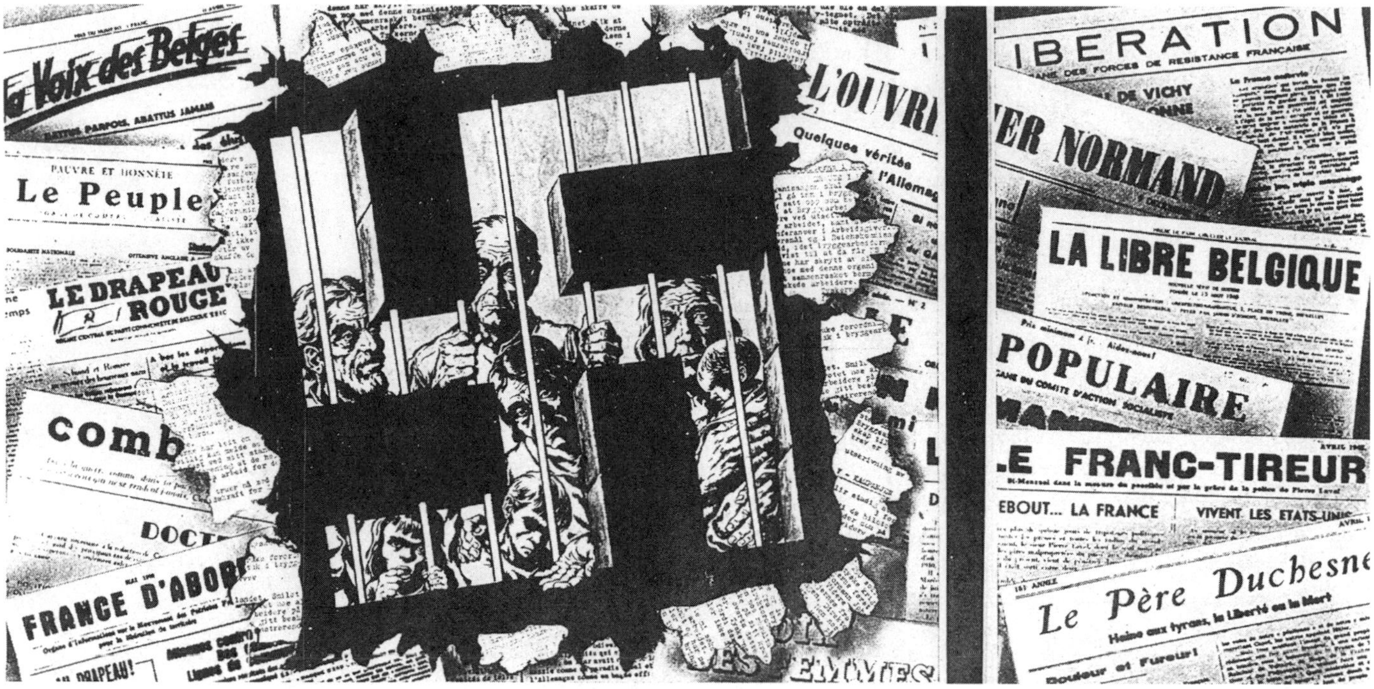

Poster decoration by Lionel S. Reiss, courtesy of the Museum of Modern Art

A month or so after the Germans entered Paris, Simon began to set the type for his first edition. The text of his single sheet called Paper was mainly an exhortation to its readers to resist the invader and to remain true to the ideals of France. He had only a child's hand printing set to work with. Because his eyes are weak he was able to set only four lines of type a night. For four months, seven nights a week, he set more type. At the end of that time he had fifty copies.

Simon had a job in the daytime in an organization which employed traveling salesmen. Two of these he enlisted to distribute his paper. Each was to choose two more trustworthy persons, and so on. Simon was not to know who these were, nor were they to be acquainted with the identity of the editor. In case one of them should be arrested by the Gestapo and forced to "talk," he would be able to give away only the names of two of his collaborators.

Simon ran out of paper for his second edition of Valmy. Stocks of paper were carefully controlled by the Germans and it would have been dangerous to walk into a shop and buy a large amount of it. But Simon knew a butcher who had more paper than he needed for what little meat there was to sell. So Simon "borrowed" enough paper to print 100 copies of Valmy.

Some months later Simon managed to get hold of a more professional printing press and work was simplified. When he ran out of ink a charwoman in a building where the Germans stored large quantities of printer's ink managed to steal it right from under the Germans' noses. Later Simon used a mimeographing machine in a business office occupied in the daytime by a young stenographer who was a distant relative. The Germans used part of the building and a German sentry stood at the entrance. The girl was known by sight to the sentry and Simon came and went freely in her company. There, in broad daylight, with German officials only a few doors away, he would mimeograph his entire edition in the space of a few hours. He always left the building empty handed in order not to arouse suspicion. The girl smuggled the papers out a few at a time.

Valmy grew in importance as the months went on and soon copies were known to have reached nearly every corner of occupied and unoccupied France, even as far away as the island of Corsica.

According to Simon, the Germans had a neat little trick to frighten the French out of reading underground papers sent by post. Hundreds of faked clandestine pamphlets or newspapers would be mailed to a list of French homes by the Germans. Immediately after the mail was delivered, and often before the victim had even had time to open the envelope containing the decoy, a Gestapo agent would enter the home and arrest the recipient for reading illegal literature. The Germans often played this trick on those whom they suspected of having underground connections, but against whom they had been unable to prove a case. Receipt of a faked pamphlet was then excuse enough to send the victim to a concentration camp.

Similar tactics are employed in Poland, where the underground press is remarkably strong and virile considering the dangers attending any illicit activities in that country. In Poland, as in Norway, owners of radio sets were ordered to turn them in to the authorities and the death sentence was imposed on most of those caught listening to broadcasts from abroad. As a result of the blackout in news, Polish underground newspapers devote more of their space to items of news from all over the world than do papers in France or Belgium, where wireless sets have not been confiscated.

From the first week of the occupation of Warsaw, brief printed news sheets began circulating from hand to hand. They provided the only remaining contact the isolated Poles had with the rest of the world. They kept hope burning in the hearts of every loyal man and woman, and did much to maintain the national pride. For every time the papers were able to publish the news of another exploit on land, at sea or in the air by Poles fighting with the Allies, the people in occupied Poland were inspired anew.

Communications between the Poles in Britain and their homeland are extremely difficult, but they do exist, and the Polish Government in London now has a semi-official newspaper appearing weekly in Poland, the "Polish Republic."

The underground press assumes a different character in every country, varying according to the needs of the people. In Belgium, where everybody disregards the German regulation and regularly listens to the radio for the Belgian news sent out over the BBC from London, the illicit newspapers print scarcely any but local news. This leaves more room for editorials. As one Belgian who escaped to London put it: "The Belgians are very well informed about world events by wireless. At 9 P. M., when it is time for the news from England, not a person is to be seen in the streets. They are all at home listening to the radio." The practice is so universal in Belgium that the German authorities are helpless. They don't have the manpower to put an effective end to it.

In this war, as in the last, Belgium is carrying on the fine tradition of the newspaper La Libre Belgique. All throughout the German occupation of Belgium in 1914–18 La Libre Belgique appeared regularly and was one of the main forces sustaining Belgian morale during those trying years. In this war again it has rallied millions of Belgians to the cause of resistance with its thoughtful and moving editorials, its scathing attacks on the invader, its powerful exposés of treachery and "collaboration."

In Norway the situation is somewhat similar to that in Poland, for the possession of radio sets was made illegal some time after the German occupation, breaking the only link the Norwegians had with their government in Britain. As in Poland, a large number of patriots defied the decree to retain their sets and every night at 7:30 o'clock they take down the news from London. Broadcasters in London always read the news at dictation speed so as to allow their Norwegian listeners to get every word down. The news and articles are then mimeographed and prepared for distribution the next morning.

Tidens Tegn, one of the oldest and most respected newspapers in Oslo, is now appearing as an underground paper, printed in some dark cellar or farmer's cottage among the hills. One which has a tremendous circulation is Det Frie Norge, the official organ of the Norwegian Government in London and a direct link between it and the people. This paper, which has the appearance of a small news magazine, appears monthly and contains photographs of the Norwegian royal family and of the Norwegian sailors and soldiers fighting abroad, advice on how to act in certain situations, commentary on domestic Norwegian politics and events, poetry, and occasionally the words and music of some patriotic song. Each copy carries the line, "This paper belongs to the Norwegian people. Pass it on."

Tortured and starving Greece, loyal Holland, Yugoslavia, Czechoslovakia, Denmark and minute Luxemburg, each of them has an underground press which is playing an increasingly important role in the Allied cause. The greatness of its influence can be measured today by the growing resistance of the conquered peoples of Europe.

* * *

December 8, 1943

'ILLEGAL' PAPER MARKS 50TH ISSUE

French Underground Organ Puts Out Special Edition—Punishments Rise

By G. H. ARCHAMBAULT
By Telephone to The New York Times

BERNE, Switzerland, Dec. 7—To celebrate the issue of its fiftieth number, the clandestine French publication Combat appeared in a large format—the size of a normal newspaper—with many photographs.

In an editorial it said: "We certainly could not let the occasion pass without proving once more to the Gestapo what the resistance movement can do." The first number of Combat was issued at the end of 1941; today it claims a circulation of 300,000.

The impotence of the Gestapo against the clandestine press is compensated for by intense activity in the matter of arrests. In the northern zone, orders come from Paris; in the southern zone, from Lyon; in either case the process is marked by secrecy and dispatch. Men, women and even children are whisked off, in many cases never to be seen again. Apparently sections are methodically combed one after the other. At present, Savoy and Isère, near the Swiss border, are receiving special attention.

Very exceptionally the Gestapo frees a prisoner. No reason is given for arrest or release. The liberated man senses that it would be as well to say nothing about his detention. Nevertheless, at least one well authenticated statement tells of cells full of dirt and vermin, where the moral hardships are even greater than the physical. The prisoner has no books, no paper or pencil, no occupation of any kind, no news and no speech with his fellows. The only break comes in the form of a quarter-hour of exercise each day.

The moral torture is described as terrible, since the prisoner can meditate only on the possibilities of execution, deportation or death from disease or Allied bombing. The ages of prisoners in this particular instance ranged from 15 years to 70. Many strangled themselves with their clothes.

Occasionally there are cases of bodily torture, but this is not the origin of all the yells issuing from the cells periodically—they are shouts of human beings realizing that in their solitude they are going mad. According to resistance circles, the French police also resort to bodily torture. Of the food issued to prisoners, the less said the better.

All signs indicate that this sort of repression will become more severe as resistance becomes more active. At the latest Cabinet meeting in Vichy under the presidency of Pierre Laval, the principal point on the agenda was the "intensification of the fight against terrorism."

It may be noted that the communiqué did not add that "the Chief of Government reported to Marshal Pétain on the business done at the meeting." There are rumors that the Chief of State has intimated to his Chief of Government that he does not particularly care to see him.

An unconfirmed report from Berlin says that Otto Abetz, resuming, after a year's absence, his functions as German representative in Paris, has had a consultation with the Marshal. But Berlin admits that "no important political developments are to be expected from this interview."

* * *

January 2, 1944

NORWEGIAN PRESS STILL FLOURISHES

Gestapo Fails to Suppress the Underground Publications—One Puts Out 100th Edition

Special to The New York Times

WASHINGTON, Jan. 1—The Norwegian Embassy in Washington has disclosed that one of Norway's best known underground newspapers, V Posten, recently celebrated the publication of its 100th edition and the beginning of its third year of existence. The paper has appeared regularly each week.

It is apparent, therefore, that the Norwegian underground press is flourishing to a degree inconceivable to those who have been fed on sanguinary tales of Nazi thoroughness in the art of suppressing the oppressed.

It is authentically reported that today's average underground circulation is almost as large as prewar averages. True, the form of the newspapers has been considerably changed. Most are mimeographed now, are much smaller, and printed on whatever bits of paper the publishers can get. But the editorial standards are as high as ever. Since each issue is produced only at grave risk to the lives of all concerned, every inch of space must be made to count.

Ridicule Is Potent Weapon

The editorial weapon is ridicule—ridicule of a type more devastating than block-buster bombs, and as corroding as mustard gas. Outlaw radio stations are doing important work too.

At the present time the Norwegian undercover newspapers of national hand-to-hand circulation include such publications as Vi Vil os et Land, Kongsposten, Norges Posten and many others.

Most of the illegal papers are mimeographed or are duplicated in some such fashion. Experiments with printed papers have been made, but it has been found that this makes the possibility of discovery by the Gestapo very much greater. Many of the papers are run by patriots working independently. Nearly all regularly contain a request to the reader to make further copies for distribution among friends.

Although hundreds of people assist in the work of production and distribution, such good care is taken to cover up tracks that it is very seldom that the Gestapo succeeds in laying hands on any of the people engaged in this work.

Substitute for Radio Sets

Through the illegal papers a spirit of solidarity is developed and inspiration is given to continue the resistance in spite of the constantly increasing pressure and terror of the Nazi overlords. The people are warned against rash and ill-considered actions, and are advised to follow the line of passive resistance and non-cooperation until the appropriate time for direct action comes.

The underground news service acquired vast importance after the confiscation of radio sets, which began in the west coastal region at the beginning of August, 1941.

Many Norwegians may yet suffer the fate of martyred heroes of the press for playing their part in the vitally, important work of maintaining the underground news service, but, the work will go on nevertheless.

* * *

January 6, 1944

ARGENTINA SETS UP CONTROL OF PRESS

Strict Regulations, Penalties Apply to Domestic Papers and Foreign Reporters

By ARNALDO CORTESI
By Cable to The New York Times

BUENOS AIRES, Jan. 5—The Argentine Government issued a decree regulating the activities of the press today. It applies not only to the Argentine press but also to foreign news agencies and correspondents.

Article I says that all publishing activities are "of public interest." By Article II, all organs of publicity edited in Argentina must be inscribed in a special register. Article IV prescribes what newspapers may not publish. It includes anything "contrary to the general interest of the nation," anything contrary to Christian morals or morality, anything that disturbs the good relations that Argentina maintains with friendly countries and any news that is totally or partly false or misleading.

Article VI says that the author of any news article or comment will be considered jointly responsible with the editor and proprietor of any organ that publishes it. Article VII provides that all editorial articles and comments must be printed under their authors' names.

Article VIII establishes that all newspapers must publish official documents and information supplied by the Under-Secretariat of Information and the Press if the Under-Secretary so requires and must, moreover, do so in the form that he establishes. According to Article IX, any organ of publicity that directly or indirectly receives subsidies or help from a foreign power must inform the Under-Secretariat of Information and the Press to obtain its approval. Article XI says that advertising on behalf of third parties "will be regulated by the Under-Secretariat of Information and the Press."

Article XII says that a special register will be instituted for journalists. According to Article XIII, no one may be inscribed in it who has committed common crimes or who pursues activities contrary to the general interest of the Argentine nation. Article XIV provides that no one not inscribed in this special register may work for any periodical or publication in any capacity.

Article XVI says that foreign news agencies and correspondents are included in the decree. They must supply signed copies of their dispatches to the Under-Secretariat of Information and the Press within four hours of filling them. They are not allowed to send any news or comment that violates Article IV.

Article XVIII prescribes penalties ranging from warnings to the closing of an offending publication and the seizure of its machinery and other equipment. Individuals will be punished by the removal of their names from the journalists' register, which will mean that they will be unable to continue to practice their profession.

* * *

April 27, 1944

PRENSA OF BUENOS AIRES IS CLOSED FOR 5 DAYS FOR OFFENDING CABINET

By Wireless to The New York Times

MONTEVIDEO, Uruguay, April 26—The Prensa, great Buenos Aires democratic daily, which ranks among the first half-dozen organs of public opinion in the world was suspended for five days today. It was perhaps the most fearless of all Argentine newspapers in opposition to the policies of the Argentine military governments that succeeded one another since the revolution of June 4, 1943.

The ostensible reason for this measure is that the Prensa published an editorial criticizing the Argentine public health authorities, charging they had introduced such stringent economies in Buenos Aires hospitals that patients were underfed and laboratory services were dangerously curtailed.

The newspaper will not be allowed to reappear after the expiration of the five days unless it publishes the full text of a two-column denial of its charges, issued by the public health authorities.

The suppression of newspapers that fall under the Government's displeasure is usually done without any ceremony by the police on instructions from the Ministry of the Interior. In the present case the Government revealed that it attached special importance to the measure against the Prensa, for it suspended this newspaper by a decree signed by President Edelmiro Farrell and countersigned by the Interior Minister, General Luis Cesar Perlinger.

At the same time the Government indicated that there was more than met the eye in the suspension by instructing all censors not to allow a single word about it to be sent abroad. This prohibition was lifted only after noon today, but foreign correspondents were allowed to cable only the bare facts.

There is little doubt that the Prensa was punished not for what it said yesterday about the public health authorities, but for its many editorials published in the last ten months criticizing all anti-democratic and anti-constitutional acts of the Argentine military Governments.

The Prensa's editorials were written with such ability that though their meaning was plain to everyone the Government never dared before today to take punitive steps.

The Government was particularly incensed by the Prensa's opposition to a decree published Dec. 31, 1943, making religious instruction obligatory in all schools. This is a subject on which the Government feels so strongly that it has taken severe measures to stamp out all criticism, punishing all newspapers and public officials who dared to breathe even a single word to indicate they did not approve.

Nevertheless, the matter was sufficiently controversial to have caused the resignation on April 17 of the Minister of Justice and Public Instruction, Dr. J. Honorio Silgueira, who wished to repeal the decree on religious instruction.

Editorial Angered Officials

Last Sunday the Prensa incurred the Government's wrath by publishing an editorial on the forbidden theme of religious instruction. It did so, however, in very cautious terms so the authorities would have no pretext for punitive measures. It limited itself to protesting against a statement made by the Federal Commissioner of National Education to the effect that all "true Argentines" favored religious instruction in the schools.

The Prensa replied that the Argentine Constitution recognized no distinction of "true Argentines" and that all citizens were "true Argentines" in the eyes of the Constitution.

Though the Prensa did not enter into a discussion of compulsory religious instruction its remarks were considered of extraordinary temerity under present conditions. The editorial gave deep offense in government circles. Many persons thought the newspaper would be closed immediately because it had never overlooked an opportunity to express its disapproval of the Argentine military governments.

The appointment yesterday of the Argentine Navy Minister, Rear Admiral Alberto Teisaire, to take over temporarily the duties of Minister of Justice and Public Instruction has done nothing to solve the Cabinet crisis. Three Ministries are still headed by acting ministers and two of them, Foreign and War, have been in this condition for almost two and a half months.

The delay in filling the vacant posts is attributed to the fact that the fight for supremacy within the Cabinet between the ultranationalist forces headed by the Interior Minister and the pro-United Nations forces headed by the War Minister, Col. Juan Perón, has not resulted in a victory for either side.

* * *

July 29, 1944

ARGENTINES LEARN FOREIGN COMMENT

Press Gives First Unmuzzled Account of Deteriorating Relationships Abroad

By ARNALDO CORTESI
By Cable to The New York Times

BUENOS AIRES, July 28—The Argentine press this morning printed ample summaries of the reactions in the United States, Great Britain and other countries to the memorandum on the Argentine situation that the State Department made public on Wednesday, as well as to the reply of Gen. Orlando Peluffo, Foreign Minister, on the same day.

This is the first time since December, 1941, that the Argentine people have been allowed to know the unvarnished truth about what newspapers abroad think of their country's foreign policy. Most of the people, therefore, are astonished by what they read. Some Argentinians are inclined to be angry and others are inclined to be sorrowful, but, in any case, the exact knowledge of what the greater part of the world is saying about Argentina cannot help contributing toward a clearer perception of the problem and perhaps toward its solution.

The Prensa dedicated a whole page to comments from Washington, New York, London, Montevideo, Santiago, Guayaquil, La Paz, Rio de Janeiro, Asunción, Bogotá, Madrid and Panama. Nación gave three columns to the same kind of material, and other papers, in proportion gave even more space.

Censorship Still in Flux

Different foreign correspondents have different stories to tell about how the Government's abolition of censorship is working. Some have had no difficulty in clearing whatever they wrote through the cable companies; others complain that some of their stories have been censored, delayed or otherwise interfered with. The same applies to the incoming service of foreign news agencies.

The trouble, as far as can be learned, resides in the fact that censors are still in operation and that all outgoing and incoming press matter passes through their hands. Not all censors interpret their instructions in the same way. In any case, the censors now certainly use a far more liberal criterion than formerly in deciding what news may be sent or received.

Nación, this morning again expresses the hope that the difficulties between the, United States and Argentina might be smoothed out. In its opinion, all efforts should now be concentrated on maintaining American solidarity intact, and this all the more necessary, it says, now that the war is approaching its end and all American States are about to be called upon to cooperate in the restoration of Europe

Prensa Retains Hope

Prensa again dedicates its main editorial to the freedom of the press and says that of all the errors committed by former President Ramón Castillo, the muzzling of the press in December, 1941, was the gravest and most regrettable. He was completely out of touch with what Argentines were thinking, Prensa says, and so at the Rio de Janeiro conference his delegates assumed an attitude from whose unfortunate consequences Argentina is still suffering.

Prensa believes that many of the misunderstandings that at present conspire against American solidarity will disappear step by step as the Argentine press recovers its right to express its opinions freely. In this connection, Prensa mentions that the state of siege of that suspended constitutional guarantees is still in force.

The Nationalist organ Cabildo derives what comfort it can from the statement it attributes to an unnamed "authorized official of the United States Government" to the effect that commercial transactions will continue unofficially between the United States and Argentina despite the official diplomatic tension.

Cabildo repeats what it said yesterday, namely, that the people, as distinguished from the Governments of the nineteen Latin-American republics, give Argentina their full sympathy and support.

Newspapers Stoned

The Nationalist organ, Federal, developed the thesis that Argentina was isolated only in a diplomatic or juridical sense because "the recall of a few ambassadors does not mean that Argentina is isolated from the rest of the continental community."

Yesterday's Nationalist demonstration, which proceeded in an orderly manner up to the moment when President Edelmiro Farrell addressed it, gave rise to some regrettable scenes later in the night. Groups of Nationalist, hot-heads marched up and down the main thoroughfares, improvising hostile demonstrations against the aristocratic Jockey Club and against shops and other premises with foreign names. The offices of the newspapers Prensa, Razón, Critica and Mundo were stoned.

Several shops selling second-hand clothing had their windows smashed, including an English drug store in one of the central streets.

* * *

June 1, 1945

ALL FREEDOM FOUND ENDED IN ARGENTINA

NEW CURBS IMPOSED

Wholesale Arrests Made and Press Is Silenced Under War 'Security'

JAILS OF COUNTRY FULL

Correspondent Says Conditions Are Worse Than Any He Saw in Fascist Italy

By ARNALDO CORTESI
By Wireless to The New York Times

BUENOS AIRES, May 30 (Delayed)—The Argentine Government had no sooner declared war on Germany and Japan and signed the final acts of the Mexico City conference than it deprived the Argentine people of what small remains of freedom they still possessed.

Under the pretext that in wartime anyone who did not approve of the Government was a traitor to his country, the Government embarked on a campaign of intimidation by wholesale arrests of prominent citizens and severe measures against any newspaper that dared to raise its voice in protest. At the same time political censorship was re-established in the vain hope that news of what was going on could be kept from the outside world.

Only last night censorship mangled one of this correspondent's dispatches dealing with the statement about Argentina, made by United States Secretary of State Edward R. Stettinius Jr. in San Francisco, and with a speech delivered to the American community by United States Ambassador Spruille Braden.

Dispatch Cut Sharply

Of five sections into which the dispatch was divided, the first was suppressed entirely, the second was edited by the censor to disguise the fact that the first was missing, the third was edited to delete thirty-three words containing the whole point of the story, and the fifth was forwarded intact. The only section that was sent as written was one containing Foreign Minister Cesar Ameghino's plea that the Argentine Government had been unjustly criticized abroad because it had been misunderstood.

Since experience has shown that there is no hope of getting the truth past Argentine censors, this dispatch is being sent by channels other than the normal ones.

Censorship was re-established by a decree dated April 28 which appeared on the Bulletin of Posts and Telegraphs on May 2. One of its articles reads:

"All telegrams are accepted at the sender's risk and are subject to retentions, delays and total or partial suppression without notice to the interested parties."

This decree, which is ostensibly a wartime measure, applied to news that is not even distantly connected with the war, despite the fact that Argentina in Mexico City undertook to guarantee free access to news.

Army Rules Parts of City

For some time correspondents were unaware that their dispatches had died in the censorship offices. Moreover, the world has been so interested in other things since the collapse of Germany that many details of the Argentine situation so far have escaped notice. The time has come to say, however, that things have happened in Buenos Aires recently that exceed anything that this correspondent can remember in his seventeen years' experience in fascist Italy.

He has seen whole sections of the city occupied by the Army in full war kit; he has seen peaceful citizens searched for arms in the streets; he has seen policemen directing traffic with revolvers in their hands.

He knows that at least one innocent man was machine-gunned while entering a subway station. He knows also that reputable citizens, like the well-known lawyer, Enrique Gil, have been arrested and that others, like the prominent business man, Jacobo Saslavsky, have been spirited away while out for an after-dinner walk; that still others, like Americo Ghioldi, editor of the Socialist newspaper, the Vanguardia, have had to choose between exile and imprisonment, and that some foreigners, like the well-known Ecuadorean cartoonist, Tony Salazer, have been deported.

When it is remembered that the above names have been given only as samples and that each stands for dozens or hundreds of similar cases, one begins to have some idea of the situation. Its gravity is confirmed by the fact that all jails in the country are full to the overflowing.

Some in Jail Two Years

It is confirmed also by this correspondent's admittedly incomplete files, which show that during the month of May alone eight newspapers were closed and seven editors and other outstanding newspaper men arrested. It is no justification to say, as the Government does, that most of the prominent men arrested recover their freedom after some days or weeks in jail, since it is well known that some unfortunates have now been languishing in prison without trial for almost two years.

It is hardly necessary to point out that the above activities of the Argentine Government, and many others like them, are direct violations of the commitments that Argentina assumed when she signed the final acts of the Mexico City conference. She undertook to abide by the principles of the Atlantic Charter, to permit free access to news, to eliminate the remaining centers of Axis influence, to support democracy and to respect the rights of individuals, and foster justice and freedom.

Foreign Minister Dr. Cesar Ameghtino promises that all these commitments will be abided by and Vice President Col. Juan Peron undertakes to hold elections at some future unspecified date but meanwhile Argentine people suffer.

The stipulations about democracy cannot be considered to have been fulfilled until the stage of siege has been repealed and the Argentine people have received the opportunity to elect a government of their choice. Until this has been done it may be expected that relations between the United States and Argentina will never be cordial, however correct they may be.

This, in turn, implies many things, among the most important of which is the presumption that the United States will be in no hurry to supply machinery and other urgently needed materials and that military equipment will not be made available to the present Government or to any government that has not been freely elected by the Argentine people. If this last point were fully understood, perhaps the army's attitude toward the Farrell regime would change radically.

PART V

THE COMING OF THE COLD WAR, 1945–1964

WESTERN NATIONS AND ALLIES

September 23, 1946

65 ANTI-FRANCO PAPERS BLANKET SPAIN DESPITE RISING REPRESSION

By PAUL P. KENNEDY
Special to The New York Times

MADRID, Sept. 22—Numerous arrests within the past ten days of persons charged with printing or distributing anti-Franco literature indicate that the Government is again concerned with its apparently insoluble problem. Three of ten students recently arrested were suspected of traffic in clandestine literature. It is known, moreover, the students throughout Spain have become intensely active.

This week-end in Vallecas precinct, called "little Russia," a huge Republican flag was attached to a trolley cable, and while a crowd gathered, handfuls of Republican pamphlets were distributed before the police arrived.

This is the first wholesale drive on clandestine publications since last April, when the better-known underground papers, such as Mundo Obrero, Socialista and Democracia, were raided, their plants destroyed and their staffs arrested. Since then, all those papers have renewed publication; others that had ceased temporarily are now circulating in full force.

A survey shows that at least sixty-five underground papers are coming out more or less regularly. Chief among them are the Communist Mundo Obrero, the Socialista, the National Federation of Labor's CNT, the monarchists' Hojas Informativas, the Republican Alliance's Democracia and an organ of the Basque autonomists.

These are all coming out on a regular monthly schedule and are distributed either through the mail or by hand, despite the risk of certain imprisonment and of almost certain torture. To be caught carrying one of these papers usually brings a long sentence.

The most active centers of publication are Catalonia and the Basque country. Most important in Catalonia are the CNT and Humanidad, the organ of the Catalán separatists. There are seven clandestine papers in Catalonia, representing all the major parties. The Basque country has about that number publishing regularly, led by Euskeda, which has appeared monthly since 1945. It is a four-page paper, carrying 7,000 words.

Pamphlets Appear Frequently

In addition to the sixty-five regular papers hundreds of pamphlets and manifestoes are printed annually. The most ambitious of these is Demócrito, the organ of a union of intellectuals. Twenty-nine issues have appeared since last November. This organization also issues occasional political study booklets designed to instruct the people how to exercise their civil duties when political freedom returns.

The majority of these publications are surprisingly moderate in tone, employing the positive theme of what should be done under a new government. This is particularly true of most Catalán and Basque publications. The most fiery of them all is Guerrillero, presumably printed in Madrid as a guerrilla organ. It ceased publication last spring but appeared again with the August issue. It publishes newsy items about outstanding raids and sometimes tells about raids to come, picturing the intended victim in a line drawing, with a rope around his neck.

Franco Officials Are Gulled

The Basques have brought out the boldest and most elaborate clandestine publication thus far. It is a 124-page slick paper special magazine called Pueblo del Pais Vasco. The magazine was printed in Barcelona, where it was passed by censors obviously unaware of Basque history. It wasn't until the magazine had been well circulated that the officials realized it was loaded with cleverly edited and powerful separatist propoganda. On the masthead were the names of seven men, described as "collaborators" in the publication. They were ordinary enough Basque names, but the officials discovered that all had been executed for nationalist activities.

The magazine also presented a nostalgic poem, illustrated with a pastoral scene that actually was a Basque shrine, the burial place of Sabina Arana Goiri, founder of the Basque Nationalist party.

The poem was entitled "The Last Lyric of Aitona." Aitona is the Basque name for Arana Goiri.

The magazine also included a picture of three priests, commending them for their "educational efforts among Basque children." Government officials in the Basque country soon discovered that it was a composite picture of three priests who had been shot by Franco forces during the civil war for preaching Basque separatism.

The authorities are still investigating, unsuccessfully, the instigators of this amazing publication, which not only distributed Basque propaganda but enriched the separatists' treasury. It carried twenty-eight pages of advertising, representing 306 reputable Basque firms.

* * *

October 20, 1946

TOKYO ARTICLE ON M'ARTHUR RAISES CENSORSHIP QUESTION

Mix-Up Follows Warning in Japanese Paper Which Censor Held in Bad Taste

By LINDESAY PARROTT
Special to The New York Times

TOKYO, Oct. 19—The action of the Allied censors in first permitting publication in Jiji Shimpo and later deleting from the English language Nippon Times an editorial article condemning "excessive acclaim" of Gen. Douglas MacArthur by the Japanese has brought forward the problem of censorship in Japan.

The question of censorship of the Nippon Times article was one of how far the Japanese may be permitted to go in their discussion of occupation personalities. On its face the editorial article, which was printed in Jiji Shimpo and censored only when the translation appeared a day later in the English-language paper, was a warning to the Japanese.

The editors of Jiji Shimpo told their readers to guard against a tendency to idolize individuals and to give greater attention to the democratic system impersonally. Brig. Gen. Charles A. Willoughby, censorship chief, apparently read deeper into the article.

"Occupation authorities," he said, "must be protected against correspondents. The article was not in good taste."

Since General Willoughby differed from his own subordinates, who previously considered the editorial unobjectionable, the question of whether there actually was an attempt to disparage General MacArthur by innuendo may be considered an open one.

One conclusion that can be drawn is that after more than a year of occupation, the popularity of the Supreme Commander is stronger than ever with the Japanese—always with the exception of the small but vocal Left Wing.

Warns of Adulation

Probably few thinking Japanese go as far as some correspondents or Kazuyoshi Yamzaki, former political journalist whose popular MacArthur biography touched off the editorial warning against over-adulation which aroused the ire of General Willoughby. Letters to Yamazaki after his book reached a circulation of 800,000 called General MacArthur "a living god," "the sun coming out of the dark clouds and shining on the world" and "the reincarnation of Emperor Jimmu," the first Emperor of Japan.

Obviously to any educated person—Japanese as well as American—such epithets are ridiculous.

But the Japanese after a year of Allied occupation are able to see many definite material advantages which have accrued to them through the presence of American troops and the working out of mild American occupation policies. For these General MacArthur undoubtedly deserves thanks.

Of the material benefits of the American occupation, one is the ever present American ration can. It is scarcely possible that any Japanese today can ignore the fact that the United States, through the difficult winter, spring, and summer until the ripening of the present rice crop, imported food which probably saved hundreds of thousands of lives. To a people whose armies notoriously lived off the countries they invaded, this is surprising conduct. When, periodically, Japanese public groups, including even the National Diet, returned thanks, these went to General MacArthur personally.

A Peaceful Country

There have been no "incidents" between the Japanese and Allied troops. Individual acts of hoodlumism have been held to a minimum. Demands made on individual Japanese in behalf of the occupation have been small enough—generally confined to demands for quarters for Allied officers. At least a start has been made toward the revival of industry and export trade and the basis of a new system of government has been laid. It must be as surprising to many Japanese as it is to many Americans that—a year after the end of the war—Japan is less of a trouble spot on the international scene than such former Allied countries as Greece, Yugoslavia, Italy or China.

None of these statements is intended to detract from the personal efforts General MacArthur has made toward the reconstruction of Japan, but they simply set his personal popularity in its proper background. If the Allied commander has won personal prestige because American policies have been popular, it is also he who would have personally suffered if Japan had been permitted to lapse into misery and chaos.

* * *

January 12, 1947

OCCUPATION COST IS SECRET IN JAPAN

Censors Also Bar From Press Many Items 'Likely to Disturb Public Tranquillity'

By BURTON CRANE
Special to The New York Times

TOKYO, Jan. 11—Our occupation costs will account for about 30 per cent of Japan's ordinary budget in the fiscal year beginning in April, but the Japanese public is not being informed of that fact. The civil censorship detachment has been eliminating from the press every reference to this subject.

The tentative figure is 17,000,000,000 yen, against the present fiscal year's originally estimated 19,000,000,000, which was expanded by supplemental appropriations to 22,000,000,000.

The policy of secrecy has been misleading. The Nippon Times reported yesterday that the Finance Ministry estimated the new ordinary budget at 59,000,000,000 yen. Then it gave detailed estimates for various purposes as low as 100,000,000 yen, but added "other items, 31,700,000,000 yen" giving the public the impression that occupation costs accounted for the balance, which was more than 50 per cent of the total.

Last year the Supreme Command forbade the Japanese to use the term "occupation costs" in their budget because many items did not seem properly chargeable. "Cost of termination of the war" was substituted with Supreme Command consent, but last month the censors eliminated that phrase from the newspapers, so "other items" was substituted.

Two Other Banned Subjects

Two other subjects have been concerning our censors. One is anything indicating that Gen. Douglas MacArthur or General Headquarters has anything to do with running Japan. The other is reparations.

Under the Japanese press code, which the Occupation promulgated Sept. 18, 1945, news must be handled truthfully and uncolored. Anything likely to disturb public tranquility or criticizing the Allies or "inviting mistrust or resentment against these troops" is banned.

A survey of items censored last month in one newspaper indicated that these prohibitions were being interpreted in the broadest possible manner. The Japan Industrial Council's appraisals of the effects of the Pauley reparations plan were heavily censored. The censors cut out the statement that the proposed reduction of machine tools and ballbearings would be impossible, that curtailment of the coal tar industry would "seriously affect goods for civilian requirements," that the total removal of the cellulose industry would affect miscellaneous goods "which have been the mainstay of Japan's export industry," that shipbuilding curtailment would oust 110,000 workers from their jobs.

Other suppressed items are hard to explain within the terms of the press code. An announcement that the Japanese Government had asked the Supreme Command for civil service personnel experts and that four men had arrived for a six-month study was completely killed. Another time the censors suppressed a story revealing that twenty-six unions of 30,000 workers employed by the Occupation had presented wage demands with a threat to walk out Dec. 20.

One of the strangest deletions was in a story about a contest sponsored by the Tokyo Beauty Shop Operators Union, which staged a competition for the best permanent wave. The final sentence, "The union plans to challenge American hairdressers to a contest on the stage of the Ernie Pyle Theatre next spring" was eliminated.

Murray Message Cut

Philip Murray's New Year message for Japanese labor was butchered by the censors. Retranslated from the Japanese, it reads as follows, with the bracketed portions deleted:

"I am happy to send a message from the American CIO to Japanese labor. Laborers of the world have many things in common and all [opposed to dictatorship in the black days before the war] are seeking peace, safety and jobs. The CIO believes in world peace and depends on the collaboration of the laborers of the whole world. This collaboration has been possible through the International Federation of Labor. [I earnestly hope the day will soon come when Japanese labor will send delegates to this fighting organization of democratic labor unions. There are American CIO members in the American Occupation's labor division, and others of our members helped reform the Japanese educational system. These men praise the Japanese masses who are longing for democracy.]"

Of sixty censored stories only two or three seemed direct violations of the press code. The following by Tatsuzo Ishikawa, noted writer, was accurate but tactless: "The laws and regulations give our people freedom, but they get none because Japan has no freedom to give them."

* * *

August 24, 1947

UNDERCOVER PRESS

By SAM POPE BREWER

MADRID—Pablo put a copy of the Falange newspaper Arriba on the cafe table. He said casually, but keeping his voice low: "I'll leave that when I go out. There is a paper folded inside for you."

When I returned to thc privacy of my home I found folded inside the newspaper a single six-by-eight-inch printed sheet of Republican opinion-critical of Generalissimo Francisco Franco's regime.

The picturesque underground press, the only means by which Spaniards can express their political ideas freely these days, has lately fallen on bad times and in recent weeks has almost disappeared from circulation. A series of police raids has rounded up many editors and frightened others into inactivity.

Even possession of a single copy of an underground paper is considered proof that the possessor is part of the organization distributing it. And distribution of printed matter hostile to the Government is looked upon as "terrorism" in Spain.

The discreetly nondescript envelopes that used to turn up in the mail have become scarcer and scarcer. The new publications that friends would bring around, folded small and carefully tucked away in their clothes, no longer come.

Spain's last little voice of freely expressed opinion is being cut off in a determined effort to see that there is no single jarring note in the chorus of praise of the Franco regime and all its acts.

In growing numbers Communist and monarchist printers alike have gone to jail for putting out their underground sheets. For a while the monarchists had benefited by the fact that Generalissimo Franco hoped to make a deal with Don Juan, the pretender to the throne. Since Don Juan and his followers have refused to compromise, the monarchist sheets, too, have been raided.

Ever since Generalissimo Franco became dictator of Spain, there has been a wide range of underground newspapers—Communist, Socialist, monarchist and anarchist. Most of them appear for a few issues and then vanish, usually when an editor or a printer is apprehended.

The newspaper with the most regular circulation and longest history probably is the Communists' Mundo Obrero (Workers' World). When its staff is caught a new one pops up elsewhere. For many months Mundo Obrero has not appeared in Madrid, but an edition printed in Galicia, northwestern Spain, appears here periodically. Another raid disposed of the staff which had been putting out the monarchists' El Barrendero (The Street-cleaner), a newspaper well known for its satire.

The police, unable to identify the editors of Democrito, rounded up all they could find of the members of the Union of Free Intellectuals, who issued it. Democrito was a mimeograph sheet, named for the Greek philosopher who thought the only way to deal with the madness of mankind was to laugh at it. It was one of the more penetratingly critical underground papers, but it did not indulge in much of Democritus' laughter.

These few publications, put out in small editions and distributed with so much difficulty and danger, are the only means most Spaniards have of getting any point of view but that of the Franco Government. They provide the only way for the bulk of the voters, poor and semi-literate, to hear of underground activity on a large scale. Their news, therefore, is widely spread by word of mouth and each new issue, though relatively few people ever see it, is discussed by thousands. Many of the copies received are worn and tattered from passing through so many hands.

* * *

July 24, 1949

REDS' WALL PRESS IRKS TOKYO REGIME

70 Communists Arrested in Osaka for Story Alleging GI's Attacked Civilians

By BURTON CRANE
Special to The New York Times

TOKYO, July 23—Borrowing Allied wartime propaganda techniques, Japan's Communists are attacking both the Japanese Government and Gen. Douglas MacArthur's occupation with "wall newspapers." Seventy persons have been arrested on charges of circulating untrue rumors and thereby violating occupation directives.

Sometimes these "newspapers" are little more than handbills pasted on walls and telephone poles. Within 100 yards of this correspondent's home, for example, there are at least a dozen kinds of such posters announcing that "if heads are cut off [Japanese slang phrase for dismissal from jobs] trains will quit running," and urging, "hurry, hurry, hurry, get rid of the present Cabinet before everything goes to pot."

The "newspaper" that caused the arrests, however, went further. It was a broadside intended for posting but purporting to carry a straight news story. Published in Osaka, this story declared that Tsuruga was a "city of horror" and described attacks by GI's on Japanese civilians. The Eighth Army, incidentally, has issued a formal denial of the story.

Charging that the wall newspaper violated the press code, Osaka police have arrested fifty-five Communists and Osaka prefectural headquarters of the national rural police have seized fifteen in the suburbs. They are due to be tried before the provost court. Taizo Takeda, editor of the Osaka Communist organ Mimposha that published the story on July 18, has been missing ever since.

Last autumn this correspondent obtained temporary possession of a number of alleged Communist documents indicating that the Communist Information Bureau was aiding the Japanese Communist party by shipping in medicine that the party here sold at a considerable profit.

This story received partial confirmation today with the announcement that the national rural police had made simultaneous raids upon eleven district committee headquarters of the Communist party and arrested six Communists on suspicion that they had violated the medical law with sales of 500 bottles of medicine tablets for 500,000 yen. The bottles were labeled "Made in England."

Because pharmaceutical analysis revealed that each of the tablets contained only about 100th of the amount of the drug indicated on the label and because the party was said to have been selling the bottles at black market prices, those apprehended have been booked on charges of fraud and price control violations, as well as on the charge of breaking the medical law.

* * *

September 10, 1949

FINLAND PROSECUTES REDS

Justice Minister Takes Action Against 3 Newspapers

Special to The New York Times

HELSINKI, Finland, Sept. 9—The Minister of Justice took legal action today against Helsinki's three pro-Communist newspapers. He accused them of "gross distortion of facts during the strike," of having abused the freedom of the press and of having conducted inflammatory attacks on "Finland's legal Government."

The editors are liable to prison sentences or fines or both. The newspapers are the Communist Tyoekansan Sanomat, the Popular Democratic Vapaa Sana and the United Socialist Ny Tid, which is published in the Swedish language.

This is the first time since the war that the Finnish Government has dared to prosecute Communist newspapers.

* * *

February 6, 1951

SPAIN CENSORS 'UNCLE SAM' TO AVOID OFFENDING U. S.

Special to The New York Times

MADRID, Feb. 5—The press censorship authorities have forbidden the Spanish press to use the nickname "Tio Sam"—Uncle Sam. On the ground that this expression might offend North American sensibilities the censors have instructed newspaper editors that in all cases it must be replaced by "United States" or "North America." It is not yet known whether the ban will be extended to "Yanqui."

The ban on Uncle Sam indicates the efforts being made to improve relations between this country and the United States at a time when there are increasing signs of latent unfriendliness in the regime toward the British and French.

* * *

October 11, 1951

REVERSES TO PRESS IN AMERICAS NOTED

Argentina's Actions Top List of Restrictions on Freedom Reported at Conference

Special to The New York Times

MONTEVIDEO, Uruguay, Oct. 10—The Western Hemisphere's struggle for press freedom during the past year has "suffered" tragic reverses, it was reported today by a committee of the Inter-American Press Association holding its annual meeting here.

The committee said that the Inter-American body considered it had a perfect right to prove or disprove violations of press freedom. Representing the uncontrolled press of the American republics, the committee asserted that it was within its power to debate and judge the question it has had under consideration. It insisted that the point of interference with national sovereignty could not be raised because restrictions on press freedom involved the defense of democracy which is the common interest of all countries in the hemisphere.

A fist fight developed during the afternoon session between two Venezuelan delegates who disagreed over whether their country's government allowed press freedom.

In alphabetical order the committee's report listed conditions prevailing in Latin-American countries. Argentina topped all others in the extent of her offenses. Although it was conceded that prior censorship is not exercised in Argentina "notwithstanding the current state of internal war, dispatches of foreign correspondents are reviewed by officers of communications compaines and anything doubtful must be approved by Government authorities."

The United States, including Puerto Rico, Canada and ten Latin-American republics as well as the British possessions of Jamaica, Bermuda and Trinidad were given a clean bill of health as far as prior censorship or other government restrictions were involved.

Bolivia was charged with the temporary imprisonment of editors or publishers during political disturbances last June. Colombia was criticized for retaining prior censorship since the state of siege declared in 1949. It was noted that Cuba closed a Communist newspaper for security reasons. A brief closing of two other publications was lifted only after the general press strike in protest Oct. 30. The Guatemalan Government was criticized for having suspended press freedom for thirty days last July. The privilege of the Nicaraguan President to impose censorship at his will was disapproved.

The report intimated that Panama may have been justified in imposing strict censorship during the upheaval last May when the country's Presidency changed hands. Recent improvement in restrictive measures enforced on the press in Paraguay was noted.

Limited press freedom and occasional arrests of editors for security reasons continue in Peru, the report said. It added that virtually no press freedom exists in the Dominican Republic and that the Venezuelan Government still imposes strict censorship.

The committees report and concluding resolution that "any member publication of our association that advocates or supports press freedom restrictions must be immediately expelled" were approved by a majority vote.

Referring to the United States, the committee observed there was an "increasing practice by national, state and local officials to conduct the business of their offices in secret; to seal or impound public records; to divulge only such information as they think is good for the people to know; to extend military security into areas of news which have no bearing on the nation's security."

* * *

March 19, 1952

PRENSA'S SEIZURE CENSURED IN U. N.

In First Action by World Body, Press Group Votes 10 to 1—Soviet Lone Dissenter

Special to The New York Times

UNITED NATIONS, N. Y., March 18—A United Nations body of news experts today condemned the suppression of the Argentine newspaper La Prensa as an infringement of freedom of the press.

The 10 to 1 vote by the Subcommission on Freedom of the Press was the first official action by any United Nations body on the Prensa case.

The same subcommission members, who serve as individual experts and not as government representatives, went on to reject—by a tie vote—a recommendation asking the United Nations to condemn the violation of press liberties by the

Soviet Union, Communist China, and a number of the Iron Curtain countries of Eastern Europe.

The defeated proposal was submitted by P. H. Chang, the expert from Nationalist China. It was promptly and angrily labeled a "dirty libel" by Vasily M. Zonov, the Soviet member of the subcommission.

The subcommission's recommendation on La Prensa protested the closing of the newspaper by "Argentine police authorities" against the wishes of the publication's "lawful owners and its staff." The subcommittee referred the protest to its two parent bodies—the Human Rights Commission and the Economic and Social Council. It called on the council to consider ways to prevent similar violations of press liberties in the future.

In sponsoring the measure, Alfredo Silva-Carvallo, the Chilean member of the group, assailed the Perón Government's "police action" in shutting down the Buenos Aires paper. Señor Silva-Carvallo, who is the editor of La Union of Valparaiso, condemned the "violence, murder and terror" which, he said, took place when the paper was closed down in March, 1951, after months of harassment by Government officials.

The Chilean expert's recommendation was backed also by Carroll Binder, the United States member, who held that "nothing in recent years had disturbed United States journalists more than the suppression of La Prensa." He also deplored the restrictive measures taken by the Perón Government against sixty other Argentine newspapers.

Mr. Zonov, the Soviet expert, who cast the single dissenting vote against the Prensa resolution, refused to explain his reasons.

Mr. Chang's recommendation to condemn the suppression of news by Communist governments was defeated by a 4-to-4 vote with 4 members abstaining.

Mr. Binder, who abstained, explained that he did so because the subcommission had not fully explored the accusations of "malpractice" made in the Chinese expert's proposal, although he agreed that there was no doubt that such evils existed.

The rejected resolution was supported by Mr. Chang and the delegates from Chile, Uruguay and the Philippines. It was opposed by the experts from France, the Soviet Union, India and Egypt. Besides Mr. Binder, the representatives from Britain, Lebanon and Yugoslavia abstained.

* * *

January 3, 1953

SPANIARDS CLIP U. S. LIBRARY FILES TO GET NEWS CENSORS DENY THEM

Despite Great Interest, State Department Halves Fund for Periodicals—Madrid Press Gives Odd Views on World

By CAMILLE M. CIANFARRA
Special to The New York Times

MADRID, Jan. 2—The regular disappearance from the files of the United States Information Service Library here of articles on Spain appearing in foreign publications has forced United States officials to keep a close watch on the library's magazines and newspapers.

The Casa Americana, as the American library is called in Madrid, receives more than 550 periodicals and newspapers in addition to large numbers of pamphlets and documents issued by the United States Government. It also has 27,000 books, which are being used by a list of 26,000 regular borrowers.

On many occasions, Casa Americana employes noticed that issues of newspapers and magazines were missing or that some articles they contained had been clipped from them. What readers seem to be especially interested in taking away are articles critical of the regime of Generalissimo Francisco Franco, it was said.

A new system was adopted recently to cope with that problem. All periodicals known to contain material that is thought likely to disappear are kept in an inner room of the library and lent to readers only upon request. Newspapers are left in the regular files in the main reading room but library clerks have been instructed to keep an eye on them. Even with those measures, articles often are found missing.

Censorship Bars Criticism

Spain's official censorship of all publications including newspapers does not permit criticism of Government policies although during the past year Gabriel Arias Salgado, the Minister of Information, and Juan Aparicio, Director General of the Press, have allowed some measure of discussion—as distinct from criticism—of problems and issues of local and national interest. As a result the overwhelming majority of Spaniards are kept in the dark as to what foreign nations think of Spain when such foreign views are unfavorable to the Government.

Another reason for the popularity of the Casa Americana is the Spaniards desire to be better informed on international events through foreign publications. Spanish newspapers have limited coverage of foreign news which is supplied them by a Government-controlled agency. Spaniards say that very often editorial comment shows a lack of knowledge of international questions, while the news either is slanted or magnified out of all proportions to suit official policy.

Typical example of Spanish journalism was the manner in which Madrid newspapers presented a statement given by Premier Stalin to The New York Times. The newspaper Ya saw it as a Times maneuver "to undermine" the Eisenhower Administration. Its reasoning was that because of the statement, General Eisenhower had been faced with the "embarrassing responsibility" of either accepting or rejecting a meeting with Stalin. Another newspaper suggested Senator Joseph R. McCarthy, Jr., investigate James Reston, who obtained Stalin's replies for any possible leftist affiliations.

Library Fund Slashed

Despite the obvious interest of Spaniards in United States life and Government policy, the activities of the United States Information Service are severely limited because of budgetary restrictions. During the current fiscal year the book fund was halved to about $15,000. About half the budget was spent on periodicals.

United States circles estimated that to attain the objective of keeping the Spaniards properly informed on United States democratic ways of life, Government policy, and intellectual and technical achievements, and of promoting better understanding, at least $50,000 would be needed for the Book Fund exclusive of appropriations for other information activities. In their opinion, Washington's approach to the information program for Spain is based on the negative premise that as there is no communism in this country there is no special need for a larger fund.

* * *

May 29, 1953

3 GREEKS JAILED FOR CARTOON

Special to The New York Times

ATHENS, May 28—The Athens Court of the Second Instance today found guilty of "contempt of authority" three persons charged with having ridiculed Premier Alexander Papagos, having portrayed him in a cartoon as somnolent and incompetent. The popular afternoon newspaper, Athnaiki was the offending journal. The owner, cartoonist and typesetter got jail sentences.

* * *

April 1, 1956

PARIS EDITOR JAILED FOR ALGERIA ATTACK

By HENRY GINIGER

Special to The New York Times

PARIS, March 31—Claude Bourdet, a prominent newspaper critic of the Government's policy in Algeria, was arrested today and charged with working to demoralize the French Army.

M. Bourdet is known in France as one of the "progressists," a group whose political views closely parallel those of the Communists. He is being prosecuted for authorship of articles in the weekly newspaper France-Observateur, which he edits. He was held in Fresnes prison, outside Paris, and will be questioned Wednesday.

A progressist is usually distinguished from a progressive by the fact that the latter is liberal-minded without being identified with the Communist line.

The Government's action against M. Bourdet was said to have been provoked by his editorial this week attacking "the dirty war" in Algeria and the projected calling up of reservists to fight it. M. Bourdet used the expression "dirty war" in quotation marks. It had been used to describe the Indochina war by those, including M. Bourdet, who opposed that French military effort also.

Premier Guy Mollet has retired to the Chateau of Rambouillet, President René Coty's country home, for the Easter week-end to meditate on the calling up of perhaps 100,000 young Frenchmen for Algeria.

The figure of 100,000 has been put forward by Robert Lacoste, Minister Residing in Algiers, as the number of reinforcements he needs to pacify the country so as to permit free elections and launch an economic and social program.

"One hundred thousand young Frenchmen," M. Bourdet wrote, "are threatened with being thrown into the 'dirty war' of Algeria, with losing the best years of their lives, perhaps with being wounded, indeed killed, for a cause that few among them approve, in a kind of combat that revolts most of them."

Staff Homes Raided

M. Bourdet was arrested at his home, which was then raided, as were the homes of other members of the newspaper staff. There was no official report that anything incriminating had been found in the raids. The Minister of National Defense explained the Government's action by declaring:

"At a time when a very special effort is being asked of the nation, of its army and of its youth, the Government could not remain insensitive to the development of an increasingly harmful enterprise of demoralization.

"It is in this spirit that the Minister of National Defense and of the Armed Forces [Maurice Bourgès-Maunoury] decided on the opening of an investigation by the military judiciary."

Protesting against the arrest of its editor, France-Observateur asserted that the Government's action had been provoked by articles that favored a negotiated peace in Algeria.

* * *

July 3, 1957

PARIS SCORED ON PRESS

Harassments Termed Severe by International Body

Special to The New York Times

GENEVA, July 2—Systematic harassment of the French and Algerian press by the French Government during the last six months has been more severe than in any country of the free world, the International Press Institute said today in Zurich.

The editor of the institutes' monthly bulletin, William Rutherford, said that recent abuses of the press had weakened democratic principles in France and had provided ammunition for communism.

The institutes' tabulation of measures taken by the French Government against newspapers and newsmen from January to June of this year shows thirty-two specific instances of suppression or seizure of newspapers and periodical publications, and four arrests or indictments of newsmen.

In all cases the Government's action was prompted by articles or editorials concerning French policy in Algeria.

* * *

May 26, 1958

PARIS CENSORING ALL NEWS MEDIA

Aim Is to Bar Disorder, but Nation Appears Calm—Algiers Radio Jammed

By HENRY GINIGER
Special to The New York Times

PARIS, May 25—The Government reacted today to the insurrection in Corsica by imposing stricter censorship on all newspapers and other media dispensing information in France.

The move was made primarily to prevent incitement to disorder that might further threaten the beleaguered republican regime. A wide survey showed the country was calm, with virtually no incidents to mar the Whitsunday holiday atmosphere.

"Preventive," or prior, censorship was established in all newspaper, news agency and radio offices, and affects all news, of whatever origin. Previous efforts at censorship concerned only news coming from Algeria. It was of self-imposed variety, with the Government cracking down afterward on those printing news it judged dangerous.

Albert Gazier, Minister of Information, said the Government wished to prevent diffusion of all appeals challenging the Government's authority or calling for violence, demonstrations or the formation of committees of public safety of the type established in Algeria.

Official censors will be stationed in the offices of all news media. They will act to halt publication of objectionable news under general orders of a coordinating committee composed of three civil servants. Policy will vary somewhat with events, it was said.

There were no indications that any hindrance would be placed on news sent out of France for publication abroad.

Events in Corsica

Newspapers were told not to give approval to yesterday's events in Corsica or to indicate any solidarity between Algeria and Corsica. Reports yesterday indicated that the Corsican uprising had been in large part led by persons coming from Algeria. The role of paratroopers who spearheaded the attack on Government buildings is to be minimized so as not to encourage a "spirit of emulation" by other paratroopers stationed in France.

The Government also started jamming broadcasts by the Algiers radio, which is in the hands of the dissident movement. The radio, which is heard especially well in southern France and Corsica, has been broadcasting appeals for solidarity in favor of Gen. Charles de Gaulle as well as mysterious coded messages that could conceivably be signals for action.

One thing the Government was powerless to halt was the wild flurry of rumors spread in Paris, Algiers and Tunis, perhaps intentionally as part of a war of nerves between Gaullist and anti-Gaullist forces.

Marseilles Reinforced

At least three major southern French cities, Marseilles, Toulouse and Perpignan, were thus reported at one time or another to have risen against governmental authority and to have come under control of committees of public safety favorable to Algiers and General de Gaulle. No informed person in any of the three points was aware of such occurrences or of anything else but the holiday quiet.

Reinforcements of 250 special security troops, under authority of the Ministry of Interior, were flown to Marseilles, where the Prefect, René Hass-Picard, and Mayor Gaston Defferre issued appeals for calm last night. There is a large Corsican colony in Marseilles and along the adjoining Mediterranean coast. Observers in the region reported complete calm.

* * *

January 6, 1960

FRENCH BAN PAPERS FOR ALGERIA REPORT

Special to The New York Times

PARIS, Jan. 5—The Government seized copies of four newspapers today in France and Algeria because they published commentaries on the International Red Cross Committee's recent report on conditions in French prison camps in Algeria.

The Red Cross report was critical of signs of continued torture and brutality in the prison camps but found that conditions generally had improved since the camps were last visited by the international organization in December of 1958.

The Communist-line newspaper Liberation was seized in Paris but later reappeared with the offending front-page article removed. Two Communist party dailies, Le Patriote de Nice et du Sud-Est of Nice and Le Petit Varois of Toulon, also were seized.

Copies of yesterday's edition of Le Monde, which published the most comprehensive analysis of the Red Cross report, were seized upon their arrival today in Algiers.

The Communist newspapers stressed the negative aspects of the report. Le Monde's summary gave equal emphasis to both its positive and negative findings.

However, any French newspaper, even one as respected as Le Monde, almost invariably is seized in Algeria if it touches unfavorably on the delicate subject of internment camps.

The League for the Rights of Man issued a statement this morning calling on the Government to use the Red Cross report to re-establish "elementary conditions of humanity" in the camps.

* * *

December 17, 1960

TALK OF MADRID: THE GRAPEVINE FLOURISHES, TO CENSOR'S CHAGRIN

Franco Regime Fails to Muffle Even a Lone Shout of 'Traitor!' Despite Stringent Control of News

By BENJAMIN WELLES
Special to The New York Times

MADRID, Dec. 16—A Falangist youth shouted "traitor!" at Generalissimo Francisco Franco during a recent solemn mass at the Valley of the Fallen shrine near here. His cry has become a favorite topic of conversation in this censor-ridden city.

The general was said to have paled slightly, but to have retained his composure. The youth, a 22-year-old member of the Falangist party's Youth Front, was on leave from military service at the time of the incident.

He has told the police that his entire unit of the youth corps had planned to shout, but that his comrades had lost their nerve at the last minute.

Jar to Idealists

There is reason to think that most of the young, idealistic Falangists left in Spain today feel General Franco has betrayed their dreams of sweeping economic-social reforms. The Falangists feel he has favored Opus Dei, a well-financed, promonarchist secular group of Roman Catholics.

Twenty-five years ago the Falangists aped the Nazis and Fascists, but the trappings of these movements have long since been cast aside. Now, as the "angry young men" of Spain, the new Falangists are burning with zeal for reforms that never come. Their bitterness, unavailing while General Franco rules and ignores them, may one day take a sharp Left-wing line when he is gone.

If normal police measures here are any guide, José Urdiales, the young man who shouted "traitor!", may have passed several difficult hours during his interrogation. But he is said to be a policeman's son and it appears he will not go before the usual army court on the usual charges of "rebellion" and face the standard death sentence usually commuted to life imprisonment.

It means he will be let off with six to twelve years in which to meditate the impropriety of his act.

A typical Spanish reaction came from a chauffeur who had parked during the ceremony a half-mile away from the shrine. When his employers returned to their car he already knew of the incident.

"So what?" he said. "It means nothing except that the censors will now grab all foreign newspapers for the next three days."

The automatic reaction of Spanish censors to any untoward incident is to ban the news in the national press and send policemen scurrying to the planes, boats and trains to seize foreign papers as they arrive.

The periodic disappearance of foreign news from the kiosks tips off the news that General Franco has once again been attacked by one or another of his "enemies."

Government censorship, the authority for which dates back to a 1937 decree, fails to stem the rapid dissemination of anti-regime news throughout Spain. In fact, it guarantees the diffusion of such news in the most distorted and pernicious form.

The censorship machinery has now become a vast monopoly, headed by Gabriel Arias Salgado, Minister of Information and Tourism.

The censors ban without appeal anything that they suspect might invoke the wrath of the Franco regime.

Texts may be approved one day and banned the next; certain texts may be authorized for newspapers but not for magazines; manuscripts may be neither passed nor rejected but shelved—without explanation.

Such erratic methods last week provoked a public protest by 227 of Spain's leading authors, poets, playwrights, critics, journalists and other intellectuals.

A New Boldness

Five years ago such temerity would have been unheard of in this muzzled land; but heavy losses in canceled contracts have given the intellectuals the courage of desperation.

News of the protest has, of course, been banned by the censors. But it has been dispersed by word of mouth and in clandestine copies.

No one here believes that the protest of Spain's top intellectuals will have the slightest effect either on Señor Arias Salgado or on his Cabinet colleague, Jesus Rubio, Minister of National Education. The protest was addressed to them both.

Both are devoted supporters of General Franco and the general has no intention of permitting free criticism of himself in Spain.

* * *

February 18, 1961

SEIZURES AROUSE THE PARIS PRESS

Papers of Right and Left Protest the Suppressing of Whole Editions

By ROBERT C. DOTY
Special to The New York Times

PARIS, Feb. 17—The French press, with unusual unanimity, published today a protest against what was termed the multiplying governmental attacks on press freedom.

From the Right—Le Parisien Liberé and L'Aurore—to the extreme Left—the Communist L'Humanité—French morning and afternoon newspapers printed accounts of resolutions on press freedom voted by the two principal press federations. These are the National Federation of the French Press and the Confederation of the French Press.

The joint resolution, addressed to Minister of Information Louis Terrenoire, focused on the question of seizures of whole editions of newspapers deemed to contain tendentious material.

Restrictions Are Urged

Declaring they were "profoundly stirred" by the seizures, the two federations asked the Minister to obtain legislation that would restrict the Government's arbitrary powers.

They asked that the freedom of expression guaranteed by the Constitution be respected in Algeria, where most of the seizures have taken place in defense of the army now fighting in the seventh year of a campaign against the Moslem rebellion.

The federations demanded that seizures be limited to ten copies of an edition rather than the entire press run, as has been the practice in the past. They also urged speedy court action by the Government either to justify a seizure or to determine a lack of justification and therefore to provide for in demnification.

* * *

June 10, 1961

LEFTIST WRITERS JAILED IN FRANCE

20 Are Arrested—Rightist Paper Is Suppressed

By ROBERT C. DOTY
Special to The New York Times

PARIS, June 9—A score of Left-Wing journalists were arrested and an extreme Right-Wing paper was suppressed today under President de Gaulle's special emergency powers.

At dawn the police visited the homes or offices of about twenty intellectuals identified with various Left-Wing—Communist and non-Communist—weeklies and news letters, carried out searches of the premises and made arrests without specific charges.

Among those seized were Paul Ricoeur, Sorbonne professor and member of the editorial committee of the review Esprit and of the patronage committee of another review, Verité-Liberté; Pierre Vidal-Naquet, professor at Caen and member of the Verité-Liberté committee, and Georges Gosselin, former member of the staff of Minister of Justice Edmond Michelet and now editor of a bulletin on North African affairs.

The journal suppressed out right was Nouveaux Jours, a violently Right-Wing, anti-regime publication.

The influential newspaper Le Monde pointed out that neither the offices nor the editorial staff of Nouveaux Jours had been troubled by police visits.

Citing the difference of treatment of the Left-Wingers, suffering personal arrest, and the Right-Wing journal, suppressed but without action against its publishers or editors, Le Monde said:

"Apart from the fact that this pretended 'equilibrium' is insane in its principle, it shows itself to be, once more, derisory in its application."

These and other recent actions of the Government, notably a decree authorizing a purge of the armed forces and the police, were taken under Article XVI of the Constitution, invoked by President de Gaulle to give himself virtually dictatorial powers during the army mutiny in Algeria in April.

The French Press Federation complained today that its earlier protest against the definitive shutdown of the three major newspapers of Algiers had gone unanswered.

The one Algiers newspaper not closed down by Government order after the April mutiny—Le Journal d'Alger—and five others in other parts of Algeria announced a strike for tomorrow in protest against the arbitrary closing of the three other Algiers dailies.

In a gesture of partial appeasement the Government authorized the appearance in Algiers of a new paper, La Dépêche d'Alger, published by the owner of one of the suppressed papers, La Dépêche Quotidienne.

* * *

May 20, 1962

SPANISH TURN EAR TO MOSCOW RADIO

Strike Censorship Thwarted by Red Bloc Broadcasts

By BENJAMIN WELLES
Special to The New York Times

MADRID, May 19—The Spanish public, frustrated by censorship, is turning to Moscow and other Communist radio broadcasts for reports on the five-week-old strikes that have disrupted mining and industry throughout north Spain.

For reasons that baffle even some Cabinet officials, Gabriel Arias Salgado, Minister of Information and Tourism, is refusing to permit Spanish newspapers, periodicals, radio or television to report the walkouts. The strikes have involved more than 70,000 key workers and miners and have affected industry across the nation.

Señor Salgado has complete power to censor every word and photograph publicly distributed in Spain, except the Catholic Action magazine Ecclesia, which last week openly backed the strikers.

His censors are so zealous in their pursuit of potential Communist influences that even photographs of society debutantes must be approved before appearing in the Sunday newspapers.

Ironically, Señor Salgado's refusal to allow even objective and accurate reporting about the strikes to reach the Spanish public through Spanish sources is now driving the public here to Communist sources for news.

Every night for at least five hours, a battery of radios in Communist capitals, including Moscow and Prague, pours forth accurate and up-to-the-minute news about the strikes in Asturias and in the Basque country.

These broadcasts are in Spanish and also in the Basque and Catalan languages. The British Broadcasting Corporation, French, Belgian and other non-Communist European radio outlets have also been furnishing the Spanish public with news unobtainable in their own newspapers.

The censorship system in Spain has been under fire for many years, but never have Cabinet officials, bankers, economists, diplomats and ordinary citizens voiced their criticism so openly. Some are delighted that the strikes have occurred.

"The strikes are the best thing that has happened in years," said one highly regarded Spanish labor expert.

This is the view of a man who is neither Communist, anarchist, Socialist nor anti-regime monarchist. It is a view shared by many men who are specialists in labor problems, are in their early forties and are politically loyal to Generalissimo Francisco Franco.

These men want a better break for Spain's 10,000,000 workers before Communist or revolutionary influences openly take up the struggle.

In recent days they have analyzed the strike situation and are citing the following key weaknesses in Spanish legislation or public administration that they say must be rectified:

The 1958 Collective Bargaining Law has no provision for independent arbitration when workers, management and the Government-appointed Syndical officials reach a deadlock. Wage claims are shuffled from one ministry to another until the workers' patience gives out, as at present.

Strikes have been illegal since 1938, but the law is now obviously unenforcible. General Franco has shown his reluctance to jail 70,000 peaceful strikers because of world opinion and becauses the Roman Catholic Church and other Spanish groups are openly backing the strikers' claims.

At least four Government agencies—the Ministries of Labor, Industry and Interior, plus the Flanage's Syndical Organization—share responsibility for labor problems. But none has clear authority. Their coordination, moreover, has been unsuccessful.

General Franco dislikes handling complex problems until they clearly threaten national tranquillity. His recent visitors say he is personally sympathetic to more pay for the miners and workers, but is still leaving details to his mutually hostile subordinates.

The capricious state censorship has kept the nation in the dark both before and since the strikes erupted.

Two years ago, Señor Salgado allowed relatively free reporting of the First Syndical Congress, although some Cabinet ministers protested that public criticism of their departments by delegates should not be published.

Since then censorship has been firm. After the strikes began around April 13, Señor Salgado permitted the newspapers to publish only a report May 5 announcing a state of emergency—for reasons never explained—in the strike-bound provinces of Asturias, Guipuzcoa and Vizcaya.

In the following days a few newspapers, published dark warnings about "foreign agitators," but with neither substantiation nor details.

Then the controlled press began running a series of articles from a reporter of the semi-official news agency Cifra, describing how Asturias was the province with the "greatest commercial activity in the first quarter of the year" and how it led all other Spanish provinces in television sets per capita.

* * *

April 29, 1963

SPANISH PRESS CURBS INDICATED IN DELAYS AND OMISSIONS IN NEWS

Text of Khrushchev-Franco Exchange Is Printed More Than a Week Late

By PAUL HOFMANN
Special to The New York Times

MADRID, April 28—Spain's national newspapers caused new speculation about the regime's press policy by printing only today the text of messages exchanged more than a week ago by Premier Khrushchev and Generalissimo Francisco Franco.

The exchange, the first on record between the Soviet and the Spanish chiefs, concerned Julian Garcia Grimau, the Communist leader who was executed here last Saturday. He was executed on charges of having committed crimes during the Spanish Civil War of 1936 to 1939 and for recent subversive activities despite pleas for mercy by Premier Khrushchev, other Communists and non-Communists.

The Grimau case marked what is considered a turning point in the Spanish regime's press relations. For the first time since last summer, the Government resorted to frequent bans of foreign newspapers here because of their reports or comments on Mr. Grimau's trial and death.

Several Papers Barred

Thursday's International Edition of The New York Times, which carried a report on a press conference in Paris by Mr. Grimau's widow, was banned as well as several issues of Le Monde of Paris and other European dailies.

Foreign newspapers had been freely available here since last summer when the regime inaugurated what it described as a liberalization of its press censorship. The Spanish press was allowed to print more domestic news and to show less restraint in editorial comment on controversial questions than previously.

Officials asserted that press censorship had been almost abolished and had been replaced by an experimental system of "consultation" between newspaper editors and state authorities.

Manuel Fraga Iribarne, a maverick member of the Falange movement, who became Minister of Information and Tourism in a vast Cabinet shuffle July 11, was seen as a champion of more freedom for the Spanish press. He announced a new press law that would lay down the rights and responsibilities of Spanish newspapermen.

This law had originally been scheduled to go to the Cortes, or Consultative Assembly, in December. However, the draft had not been published and Spanish newspapermen believe the Government is having second thoughts.

The regime appeared to favor an unshackled press when it allowed newspapers to give ample coverage to a mine strike in Asturias in the north last summer. However, recent labor conflicts were reported skimpily, belatedly or not at all by the national newspapers.

A speech by a monarchist leader on Spain's constitutional future early this month was suppressed by state censorship. Government officials were reported to have interfered lately even with the letters-to-the-editors column of a Madrid newspaper.

Incident Not Reported

In March, when students at Madrid University heckled Mr. Fraga Iribarne during an address on state censorship, the incident was not reported in the press.

A series of political trials during the last few weeks involving Communists and non-Communists were not reported in Spanish newspapers except for short official announcements indicating the range of prison terms, but not naming defendants or giving details of their cases.

On inquiry, a high official said censorship had not prevented coverage of thc trials, but that newspaper editors and reporters had not found them newsworthy.

* * *

March 10, 1964

HIGH COURT CURBS PUBLIC OFFICIALS IN LIBEL ACTIONS

It Rules for New York Times and 4 Negro Ministers in Alabama Suit on Ad

DECISION IS UNANIMOUS

Says Malice Must Be Shown—Opinion Likely to Aid Press Freedom in South

By ANTHONY LEWIS
Special to The New York Times

WASHINGTON, March 9—The Supreme Court held today that a public official cannot recover libel damages for criticism of his official performance unless he proves that the statement was made with deliberate malice.

This constitutional landmark for freedom of the press and speech came in a decision throwing out a $500,000 Alabama libel judgment against The New York Times and four Negro ministers.

The Justices were unanimous in reversing the libel award. The Court's opinion, by Justice William J. Brennan Jr., was joined by Chief Justice Earl Warren and Justices Tom C. Clark, John Marshall Harlan, Potter Stewart and Byron R. White.

Justices Hugo L. Black and Arthur J. Goldberg, in separate opinions, said the Court should have gone further and established an absolute privilege for criticism of officials, even for malicious statements. Justice William O. Douglas joined these opinions.

Related to Race Issue

The case could have an immediate impact on press coverage of race relations in the South.

Including today's case, which is subject to possible further action, The Times faces a total of $5 million in libel suits in Alabama. The Columbia Broadcasting System is being sued there for $1.5 million.

The Times argued that the purpose and effect of these suits was to discourage coverage of the racial situation. That view was supported by friend-of-the-court briefs by The Chicago Tribune, The Washington Post and the American Civil Liberties Union.

The Court did not, of course, limit its discussion to the racial context. It said that freedom to comment on official conduct, protected by the free-speech and free-press clauses of the First Amendment, would be endangered by unlimited libel awards.

Fears 'Pall of Timidity'

"Whether or not a newspaper can survive a succession of such judgments," Justice Brennan said, "the pall of fear and timidity imposed upon those who would give voice to public criticism is an atmosphere in which the First Amendment freedoms cannot survive."

Even false statements about public officials are given protection by the decision. Justice Brennan said it would put too great a burden on free speech to make a person sued for libel prove the truth of every statement.

Nor is the decision limited to newspapers or other media of communication. It bars libel or slander suits against anyone for comment on official conduct as long as they are not malicious.

The Court made no distinction between editorial and advertising matter in protection from libel suits. The fact that an alleged libel appeared in a paid advertisement, Justice Brennan said, is "as immaterial as the fact that newspapers and books are sold."

This case did arise from an advertisement—one published in The Times on March 29, 1960.

Sought to Raise funds

The full-page ad, entitled "Heed Their Rising Voices," sought to raise funds for the defense of Dr. Martin Luther King Jr., the Negro leader and for other civil rights causes. It attacked conditions in many parts of the South in strong terms.

No Southern official was named in the ad. Nevertheless four present and former city officials of Montgomery, Ala., and the Governor at the time, John P. Patterson, claimed they had been defamed.

Mr. Patterson sued for $1 million and the other officials each sued for $500,000. In addition to these five suits, which total $3 million, there are pending other libel suits that seek a total of $2 million. These are not related to the ad.

Those suing over the ad cited two paragraphs.

One of the paragraphs mentioned Montgomery. It said that leaders of a Negro college student protest there had been expelled, the campus ringed with police and the college dining hall padlocked to starve the students "into submission."

The second said that "southern violators" had bombed Mr. King's home and, among other things, arrested him seven times.

The first suit tried was one brought by L.B. Sullivan, a Montgomery city commissioner with general charge of the police there. He said that the public would connect the alleged illegal activity described in the advertisement with him and so he would be injured.

Given All He Asked

Mr. Sullivan did not try to prove any financial loss. Under Alabama law there was no limit on the amount the State Court jury could award as either compensatory or punitive damages. This jury gave Mr. Sullivan all he had asked, $500,000.

The Times was a joint defendant in the case along with four Alabama Negro ministers—Ralph D. Abernathy, Fred L. Shuttlesworth, S.S. Scay Sr., and J. E. Lowery.

Their names had appeared as signers of the ad, although they said that this had been done without their permission. The four ministers were jointly liable with The Times for the $500,000 judgment. Since they had few assets, The Times would have had to pay most of the award if it had been sustained.

The Alabama courts upheld the judgment. They found the ad "libelous per se" because they held it tended to injure Mr. Sullivan's reputation and was therefore presumptively malicious.

The one defense left was absolute truth. And The Times could not argue this because it had conceded certain errors in the ad. For example, the college dining hall had never been padlocked, and Dr. King had been arrested four times, not seven.

Herbert Wechsler of New York, who argued the case for The Times, made two alternative contentions. He said that the first Amendment barred all libel suits for comment on official conduct—the view taken in the concurring opinions today—or at least ruled out so loose a test of libel as Alabama had applied.

Former Attorney General William P. Rogers and Samuel R. Pierce Jr. of New York argued the case for the ministers. M. Roland Nachman Jr. of Montgomery represented Mr. Sullivan.

Justice Brennan followed the second branch of Mr. Wechsler's argument. He started with the premise of a profound national commitment to the principle that debate on public issues should be uninhibited, robust and wide-open, and that it may well include vehement, caustic and, sometimes unpleasantly sharp attacks on government and public officials."

He traced the history of the hated Sedition Act of 1798, which punished "false, scandalous and malicious" statements about Federal officials. History, Justice Brennan said has produced common agreement that the act was unconstitutional.

The opinion noted that today's case was "the first time" that an ordinary civil libel action had been found by the Supreme Court to conflict with the First Amendment.

Just Justice Brennan said that the effect of this suit was as repressive as a criminal statute such as the Sedition Act. He noted in passing that the maximum fine for criminal libel in Alabama is only $500.

From the history of the First Amendment Justice Brennan drew the rule that "neither factual error nor defamatory content suffices to remove the constitutional shield from criticism of official conduct."

He held that the Constitution "prohibits a public official from recovering damages for a defamatory falsehood relating to his official conduct unless he proves the statement was made with actual malice that is, with knowledge that it was false or with reckless disregard of whether it was false or not."

Alabama libel standards were much too loose to meet that test. Justice Brennan concluded, and this judgment must be reserved.

He sent the case back to the Alabama courts for further proceedings consistent with today's opinion.

But he observed that Mr. Sullivan might seek a new trial at which he might try to prove "actual malice" by The Times and the ministers. Justice Brennan therefore went on to discuss the sufficiency of the evidence in this case to meet the test.

At most, he concluded, The Times may have shown "negligency" in failing to discover the misstatements in the ad, not the "recklessness" constitutionally "required for finding of actual malice."

As for the ministers, he said there was no showing that they knew of any errors in the ad if they had authorized it at all.

Finally, Justice Brennan said that the evidence was "constitutionally defective in another respect"—it could not support the contention that the ad concerned Mr. Sullivan at all.

If Mr. Sullivan could take these vague words as a reference to him, the opinion said, then any criticism of government in general could be met by individual officials' libel suits.

The latter part of Justice Brennan's opinion, some legal observers thought, was designed to answer one point in Justice Black's concurrence. This was that, because of hostility over the racial issue, a Montgomery jury would have returned a verdict for Mr. Sullivan no matter what rules it was told to apply.

Justice Black said the Court's rules were "stopgap measure." He called for "granting the press an absolute immunity for criticism of the way public officials do their public duty."

Justice Goldberg, taking the same approach in his concurring opinion, said that the right to speak out about public affairs "should not depend upon a probing by the jury of the motivation of the citizen or press."

The Brennan opinion does leave it open to Mr. Sullivan to seek a new trial. But the Court made it plain, lawyers here noted, that it would upset any jury verdict for him based on the kind of evidence produced in the first trial.

One other case arising out of the same advertisement has been tried in Montgomery, and the jury also returned the full $500,000 demanded. That case is pending on a motion for a new trial and along with the others has been awaiting today's decision.

The other libel suits faced by The Times in Alabama arise from a series of articles on conditions in Birmingham. Officials there have sued for $2 million. The writer of the articles—Harrison E. Salisbury—has been charged with 42 counts of criminal libel.

Lawyers Are Listed

Other lawyers on the brief for The Times in the Supreme Court were former Attorney General Herbert Brownell, Thomas F. Daly, Lewis M. Loeb, T. Eric Embry, Marvin E. Frankel, Ronald S. Diana and Doris Wechsler.

On the brief for the four ministers were L.H. Wachtel, Charles S. Conley, Benjamin Spiegel, Raymond S. Harrison, Harry H. Wachetel, Joseph B. Russell, David N. Brainin, Stephen J. Jelin, Clarence B. Jones, David G. Lubell and Charles B. Markham.

In addition to Mr. Nachman, Robert E. Steiner 3d and Sam Rise Baker were on the brief for Mr. Sullivan. Calvin Whitesell was of counsel.

The Chicago Tribune's brief as a friend of the court was signed by Howard Ellis, Keith Master and Don H. Reuben.

On the Washington Post brief were Mr. Rogers who argued the case for the ministers, plus Gerald W. Siegel. Stanley Godofsky, Leslie Srager and David W. Bernstein.

Edward S. Greenbaum and Harriet F. Pilpel signed the A.C.L.U. brief. Of counsel were Melvin L. Wulf, Nanette Dembitz and Nancy F. Wechsler.

Attorneys who participated in the libel action in Alabama courts included:

Rod McLeod of Birmingham, for The Times; and Richard Watts, V.Z. Crawford and Solomon S. Scay Jr., for the ministers.

* * *

COMMUNIST COUNTRIES

September 10, 1945

A FULLY FREE PRESS LACKING IN EUROPE

Russia Leads in Retention of Strict Controls Four Months After German Surrender

By C. L. SULZBERGER
By Wireless to The New York Times

LONDON, Sept. 9—Although definite progress has been made toward the relaxation of censorships in Europe during the four months since the German surrender, full freedom of the press as it is understood in the United States still is a long way off in many huge areas. This applies both to the dispatches of foreign correspondents and to the publication of local newspapers.

In the Soviet Union, which, after all, represents almost a sixth of the earth's surface, it is reliably reported that so far there has been absolutely no change in the strict supervision of foreign correspondents' dispatches, which was strongly tightened in 1939.

Despite some international discussions on the subject, including a visit to Moscow last spring of a special "free press committee," the situation has not changed there either for local papers or foreign reporters, whose numbers remain strictly limited. The Russian authorities contend that freedom of the press as they conceive it exists internally, but their conceptions are hardly the same as ours.

Army Rules in Middle East

In the Middle East, despite Washington's emphatic proclamations about press freedom, which have been implemented in other foreign areas, it is perhaps paradoxical that the only military censorship which continues is that of the United States Army. All American reporters' dispatches pass through this, and in the past this particular branch of American military censorship has earned a remarkable reputation for stupidity.

In Eastern Europe, the censorship and transmission systems as well as the permission for reporters to circulate freely is somewhat scrambled, depending on local conditions.

As far as can be ascertained at present, the only free areas for foreign reporters are Greece and Bulgaria. In the former a British censorship still passes on dispatches of purely military interest, such as Army troops dispositions.

In Greece, the local press not only is free but, thanks to the loose Greek libel law is unlicensed. In Bulgaria there is no local press censorship, but so far there is no opposition press because of prevailing political conditions.

In Turkey, censorship of foreign correspondents continues despite talks with British and American personalities on the subject, but it now is more tolerant of criticism and of discussion of internal affairs than in the past.

A superficial relaxation of local press censorship has been introduced, but the accent is on the adjective. Although the Turkish Constitution forbids press censorship, newspapers printing material that is unfavorably regarded can be suspended without right of appeal.

In Spain it is officially contended that there no longer is any censorship of foreign reporters' stories. However, dispatches can be and frequently are delayed or cancelled under what is cited as a 1932 international convention barring material inimical to the State.

In Portugal, the local press is carefully censored, and while foreign correspondents' copy is not disturbed they complain that because of the "personal responsibility" system, whereby they may be expelled, they feel pretty nervous.

This is the principal bad news side of the picture. But one must realize that definite improvement in the freedom of news has occurred during recent weeks, even in some of the areas mentioned above.

In England, no censorship now exists. In France, foreign correspondents dispatches are transmitted without scrutiny. In Italy, the last censorship stamp—and that was purely routine—to appear on foreign reporters' copy was affixed Friday.

In occupied Germany, American and British censorship has ended for foreign correspondents. The Soviet authorities do not censor dispatches of reporters who visit the Red Army area and then return to Berlin to file. Reporters can circulate freely in the Russian zone of Berlin, but getting into the hinterland is not as easy, and it is very difficult to file from the Soviet area.

* * *

October 11, 1945

LANE URGING POLES TO END CENSORSHIP

Russia Said to Dominate There, as in Balkans, in Control of Foreign Dispatches

By C. L. SULZBERGER
By Wireless to The New York Times

LONDON, Oct. 10—The American Ambassador to Poland, Arthur Bliss Lane, is understood to be seeking to persuade the Warsaw Government to abandon the idea of "factual" censorship of foreign correspondents' messages.

According to reports here, the Polish Government contends that it does not wish to censor opinion but only "facts." But Mr. Lane is thought to be pointing out that the American concept of a free press means no censorship at all.

As far as can be learned here, no decision has yet been taken. However, because of miserable transmission conditions in Poland, local censorship is still largely a matter of principle. Dispatches must be sent via Moscow, where they pass through the rigid Russian censorship, and at any rate they frequently take many days to reach their destination.

Typical of Eastern Europe

This situation is typical of the censorship situation in large parts of eastern Europe, where, despite assurances to the most interested countries, Great Britain and the United States, foreign correspondents do not work under anything like the free-press conditions of the western world. In both Rumania and Bulgaria, whose fate figured so importantly in the recent failure of the Foreign Ministers' conference, censorship in one form or another remains difficult.

In Sofia there is an open censorship that, it is understood, is "easy" on dispatches. However, stories are then sent to the Allied Control Commission, where they are translated and recensored by Russian representatives. This process often results in considerable delays in transmission and sometimes the commission does not appear to be satisfied with the work of the Bulgarian censors.

In Rumania, it is understood from correspondents who have just returned, the censorship muddle is extremely confusing and difficult. All dispatches must be censored by both the Rumanians and the Russians. Russian censors do not work after 4 P. M., and all dispatches involving criticism must be referred by them to higher authorities for approval. The Russian censor reads neither English nor French.

It is said that the Rumanian censors usually have only minor objections to most dispatches, but the submission to the Russian censor and the necessity of translation usually result in a delay of at least one day. Anything ticklish, which is likely to be broadly interpreted, is submitted by the Russian censor to General Vinogradoff for his opinion. Sometimes American or British correspondents have had to call the heads of their respective military missions to pry dispatches loose.

* * *

November 17, 1945

CUT U.S. STORIES FED TO BELGRADE

Press Reprints Accounts of Fair Elections but Omits Qualifying Clauses

By SAM POPE BREWER
By Wireless to The New York Times

BELGRADE, Yugoslavia, Nov. 15 (Delayed)—The well-censored Belgrade press has been reprinting excerpts from dispatches sent by foreign correspondents that twist the sense of the original copy to imply that American observers believe that the Yugoslav elections give full and free expression to the people's will. Extracts from this correspondent's dispatches in particular are appearing here in a form that completely falsifies their intent.

The excerpts printed are correct, but only those that suit the Government appear.

For example, when I said that there were no sign of intimidation of voters but that this was unnecessary since in the circumstances there was little likelihood of serious opposition, the local press printed the statement without the qualification following the "but."

In case there is any misunderstanding of what previous election dispatches meant to say, the situation is as follows:

This election was probably the fairest Yugoslavia had seen, as far as the actual machinery of voting went. Some voters say it was possible to tell in which box they dropped the ball representing their vote; others say it was impossible.

Charges Unsubstantiated

I have been unable to learn of a single case of mistreatment of anybody for voting against the Government or failing to vote at all. Some voters have complained that when they arrived to vote toward the end of election day they were told that they had already voted. Some say that groups of soldiers voted in more than one place, but I have been unable to find anyone who observed a repetition except one man who was decidedly shaky about his story.

However, and this is what the Belgrade press will not reprint if it follows past procedure, intimidation at the polls was unnecessary because most opposition voters did not dare to vote against the Government. Right or not, they believed that if they voted against the Government it would be known and reprisals would be taken against them. One man with whom I talked yesterday said, "I'm ashamed to admit it, but I voted for them." When asked why, he said, "It was too dangerous to vote against."

All questions of pre-election intimidation and general terrorism are out of date, however, on an international basis. The United States and British Governments having failed to protest conditions before the voting, they can hardly fall back on those now as excuses for not recognizing the result.

Promises Not Performed

The only live question now is the conduct of this Government after the elections. Marshal Tito and his supporters made promises of democratic freedoms in the negotiations leading to the agreement with former Premier Ivan Subasitch last year. Those promises have not been fulfilled. There is still a good chance of a reasonable understanding if the Yugoslav Government, taking stock of the situation, recalls those promises and makes an effort to live up to them.

If the Government continued to ignore its engagements it would be a cause for complaint, but no foreign observer has found cause for complaint in the elections. It was in the terrorization that preceded the elections that Anglo-Saxons found much cause for complaint, but that also is a point that local censorship is unlikely to pass for publication here.

* * *

April 14, 1946

THE BLACKOUT OF NEWS IN EASTERN EUROPE

If We Are to Understand Each Other, Says an Observer, Dispatches Must Move Freely

By MARK ETHRIDGE

Publisher, The Courier-Journal (Louisville)

One of the great, tragic feats in this deeply troubled world is the inability of peoples, as distinguished from governments, to communicate directly with each other. There are, indeed, the common languages of the arts and sciences. Peoples do speak to each other through music, the theatre and certain forms of literature, but, between the United States and eastern Europe, which so desperately ought to know and understand each other, the communication ends exactly at the point where it is most needed at the moment: on the political level.

The easiest means of communication between peoples is, of course, the press of their countries. Unfortunately, in the present world tension the press is unable to perform the vital function which might greatly help the cause of peace. Worse, the use to which the press is being put, particularly in eastern Europe, tends to increase rather than to diminish the tensions and to distort the American position and the feeling of the American people. The brief short-wave broadcasts which we beam to that part of the world and the mimeographed bulletins in the reading rooms of American chancelleries may give some few people an idea of what we have really said and what we really mean, but they do not in any respect serve the purpose which could be served by a full and free interchange of news between press associations and newspapers of the two hemispheres.

As Edwin L. James, managing editor of The New York Times, pointed out in a recent article, the primary difficulty is the difference in approach, in the United States and in Russia, to what the function of the press should be. Since the Russian pattern, with variations, obtains in almost all eastern European countries, with the exception of Greece, it is that pattern with which we must compare ours to understand the difficulties.

No matter how much newspaper men in America may argue among themselves over the meaning of freedom of the press as guaranteed in the Bill of Rights, there are fundamental concepts upon which they agree. Certainly there is overwhelming agreement upon the idea that freedom of the press is not a right of publishers but of the people: an essential right asserted over the objection of Alexander Hamilton and others because the people considered it necessary to the preservation of the kind of government they wanted. It is significant at the moment that one of Hamilton's arguments was that the people's political representatives at Washington could keep them well informed about what was going on. It was the very mistrust of having the politicians tell them what they should know that stimulated inclusion of the press guarantee.

American papers have been shaped, on the whole, to that idea. The American press is not the creature or the organ of government, and it is so sensitive to government restrictions of any kind that it waged war on NRA proposals touching newspapers and even during the period of World War II operated under a code of censorship that was voluntary.

Nor are American newspapers the organs of parties. Some of them have been, and some of them have had long and continuing allegiance to organized political parties, but no major American newspaper that I know of is now financed by a party or a politician. They are on the whole the organs and voices of individuals, who exercise not only the guarantee of a free press, but frequently strain the laws of libel in dealing with public officials. Nobody gets shot or hauled up before a government tribunal for saying a Cabinet officer is a crook or the President is a liar. That fierce individualism which makes the business man repeat over and over clichés about free enterprise has its reflection in the American press.

The Russian press as it now exists grew out of and operates under a totally different concept, a concept as different as our ideologies, if that is possible. As Mr. James pointed out in his piece, the press in Russia is an instrument of government, making no pretense to the printing of news as such. Its function, as the Russian, Kuzmichev, said, is "in educating the great mass of workers, in organizing them under the exclusive direction of the party for clearly defined tasks." Information, he said, "is the means of class struggle, not a mirror to reflect events objectively." The news services are state-owned and heavily censored, so that what the reader gets about what his own government is doing has been strained through a fine netting of ideology.

There are, of course, no opposition papers in Russia, but in those parts of eastern Europe where they do exist, or where there are papers that call themselves neutral, the rigid control of news sources is implemented by indirect methods of restriction on newsprint, which is generally a government monopoly, refusal of trade-union workers to publish or distribute opposition papers, suspension of newspapers by government decree, and arrest of editors and their assistants on harrying charges or without charges.

Beyond any direct or indirect methods, however, there is a restraint on the press which is generally quite as effective as censorship or decrees. That is the fear of editors that they will overstep restrictions imposed upon their discussion—a fear which causes most of the newspapers inclined to print news or criticism unfavorable to one of the Big Three to kill the news or the editorial. The hope that liberal editors of eastern Europe nurtured through the war—that they might again, after more than a decade of dictatorships and Nazi censors, say what they thought—has turned to ashes. They have found that "liberation" has brought tyrannies no less effective than those they knew under the Nazis.

Nowhere in eastern Europe are there newspapers in the sense in which the American reader understands them. Almost all of them are party organs and most of them are merely propaganda sheets, carrying very little domestic news

When the Russians move in—Headquarters of the Soviet administration in Dresden, Germany.

and less foreign news—with that generally slanted. In Bulgaria, for instance (and it is true in other countries) an individual cannot establish a newspaper; nor can a political party be recognized as a "juridical personality" unless it has a party organ. The two go hand in hand; consequently the reader, in an effort to get at the truth, must pay his money for a great many newspapers and make up his mind about what is the truth.

Between the censorship of incoming material and the requirement that a newspaper must be the organ of a party, there is little chance for the reader to get objective news of any sort. On the contrary, what he has been getting in eastern Europe recently has been heavily slanted against the Western powers.

Censorship restrictions on our correspondents in occupied countries have been lifted somewhat in recent months. But our primary concern in trying to arrive at an understanding with the Russians, the Rumanians, the Bulgarians and the Yugoslavs is not what we get out of those countries, which is, of course, important, and generally well done by American correspondents, but what is not allowed to go in. The people of eastern Europe get an entirely distorted picture of America and American foreign policy because their newspapers cannot give them any other kind.

Since the Churchill incident is freshest in our minds, it may be used to illustrate the point.

Almost all American newspapers printed Pravda's and Stalin's blast at Churchill. Some of them even printed Stalin's speech in full. But what the Russians know about Churchill's speech is by reflection; they have not been able to read it. It is not necessary to defend Churchill's Fulton (Mo.) speech to say that it has been given to the Russians through their own propaganda agency rather than from his pen.

The Rumanian people have no more idea of what he said than the Russians have. A Reuter dispatch from Bucharest said that Rumanian censors (who operate under the Allied Control Commission, which is actually Russian control in that country) prohibited publication of reports of Churchill's speech except for a four-line reference to his support of an extension to fifty years of the British-Soviet alliance.

Brooks Atkinson reported from Moscow, during the London meeting of the U.N., that every newspaper in Moscow handled the story of the Vishinsky-Bevin debate in exactly the same way—four columns for Vishinsky, one-third of a column for Bevin. We in America know what Churchill said, what Stalin said, what Vishinsky said and Bevin said, but the 250 millions and more peoples in eastern Europe have a completely one-sided picture of the argument between Britain and Russia.

Nor has America come out any better in the deal. When we recognized the Tito Government, the document of recognition contained in addition some unkind words about Tito's methods. That was eliminated from all Yugoslav papers. Only by radio, or by a mimeographed reproduction of the American note that was put on the bulletin board at the American Embassy and distributed to 3,500 Serbs and Croats who asked for it, was American policy toward that country made clear at all. An employe of the American Ministry, of Yugoslav descent, was hauled up before the police in connection with the distribution. The people of Yugoslavia generally still do not know, and will never find out from their controlled press, that we are not too fond of Tito's methods of repression.

The same thing happened in Rumania. When we wrote a note to Rumania setting out our willingness to receive a political representative, the recognition was coupled with a statement of the conditions under which we did so. The stipulations were connected with freedom of the press, freedom of assembly, free elections and other matters which honored our Yalta pledge. Yet, unless the Rumanian people have found it out by short-wave radio or by some other means, all they know is that, regardless and heedless of our Yalta pledge, we have recognized a Government that has been oppressive and repressive of all their civil rights. The blackout could certainly give rise to the feeling in Rumania that America has reneged upon all her promises, particularly upon the Atlantic Charter.

In Yugoslavia the Russian press pattern has reached its full-flowering. Article I of the Yugoslav press law has a grandiloquent preamble which says, "No one can be prevented from freely expressing his views through the press," but on the tail end of the sentence there is this phrase, "except in cases foreseen by this law." The Yugoslav press dictator had a long foresight; twenty-seven subsequent articles outline the restrictions under which any newspaper could be seized and the editor tried for treason.

The editor of Demokratija, an opposition paper, apparently took the first article of the press law seriously. His edition of Nov. 7, 1945, on the eve of the election, was confiscated "for spreading false and alarming news that threatened the Government and the national interest." He protested by open letter. The courts upheld the Government. On Nov. 14 the printers' union refused to print the paper any more because of "its calumnies . . . and for insolently attacking our United Syndicates." (Printers' strikes in the Balkans to prevent publication of criticism of Communist-dominated Governments are not a rarity: I witnessed one in Bulgarin and knew of others.

That part of the Yugoslav press which is free to operate concentrates upon attacking the American press, playing up American labor troubles without any explanation of what they are about, and printing stories and articles critical of American foreign policy. Freedom of the press in this country is brushed off in Borba, for instance, in this way: "Only the wealthy own newspapers in America and only capitalists enjoy freedom of the press."

American correspondents intent upon doing a conscientious job of reporting Yugoslavia to us hardly enjoy their freedom to move around and read the distorted news about and attacks upon their own country.

Communist Yugoslavia in eastern Europe, fascist Spain and dictator-ridden Portugal in western Europe are not far apart in their control of fractious editors, in their distortion of news or in their attempts to discredit democracy. (Portugal's press was recently forbidden by censors to carry Stalin's conciliatory statement.)

The situation is somewhat better in Rumania, although two or three months after the Groza Government came in all independent and so-called "historic party" press had been suppressed, including a 105-year-old Transylvania newspaper that had survived the tyranny of the Austro-Hungarian Empire, the Nazis and the Rumanian dictators. Under the Moscow agreement, the Rumanian Government was to allow freedom of the press as well as freedom of political assembly. I understand there has been some improvement, but newsprint is still a Government monopoly dependent upon Russia's supply. When I was in Bucharest, newspaper men told me that the Communist organ had received a supply beyond what it could use and financed itself by selling to other newspapers on the black market. Editors were being arrested when I was in Bucharest.

Rumania's neighbor, Bulgaria, benefited from a protest made by the American Government. We protested elections called for August of last year on the ground that there was no freedom from fear and that the opposition had no press and no sanction for political activity. The Government allowed three opposition papers to come into being. Two of them are quite vigorous. One of them, the organ of Nicola Petkov, leader of the Agrarian party, was vicious and slashing in its opposition. When Lulchev, leader of the Socialists, undertook to be equally vigorous recently, his paper was suspended for ten days and he was put in jail. The organ of the Democrats was struck by the printers while I was in Sofia because of an editorial it proposed to carry. The Bulgarians have a strong sense of individualism and appreciate the fact that they can, at least, read opposition editorials even if they do not get too much news.

The Hungarian, Czech and Austrian papers may be classed as a good deal freer than but quite as nervous as papers in their neighboring countries. In fact, President Karl Renner only recently urged the Austrian papers to speak out, with this reassurance, "I assume that the occupying powers will not make difficulties for our press when things are discussed openly on which it is now silent."

An illustration of the nervousness of the Hungarian press, where suspensions occurred in two cases recently and others threatened, may be found in what happened to a sentence in President Truman's report on Potsdam in August of last year. At one place he said, "It was reaffirmed in the Berlin declarations on Rumania, Bulgaria and Hungary that these nations are not to be spheres of influence of any one power."

Nothing could have been more interesting or important to Hungarians. Some of them heard it on the radio from London, but the news agency which monitored the complete speech was ordered to suppress that paragraph and include it only in a confidential bulletin. After the entire speech had been released through official channels, a number of Hungarian papers picked it up and published the speech without deletion. There was no idea that the prohibition was sponsored by outside political forces; it arose out of the Hungarian Government's nervousness over offending Russia as the occupying country.

Mark Ethridge with the Russian member of the Allied Control Commission in Rumania.

In Czechoslovakia, where the papers are party or "state-wide organization" organs, they can and do attack local situations and conditions, but they are expected to stay within "decent limits" and not abuse their freedom, conditions to which they subscribe to the point of innocuity. There may be noted, however, a cautious spreading of the wings.

Greece enjoys the freest press in southeastern Europe, according to all reports. The Government has consistently permitted the Communists to publish their papers, although immediately after the civil war there was a certain amount of smashing of presses and other trouble. The editor of the leading Communist paper was one of the accredited Greek correspondents at San Francisco and the Greek Government facilitated his trip. His viewpoint was freely presented. Official news organs, as well as the radio, as is common in all Balkan countries, present only the Government point of view.

Not even in Greece, however, is there any free press in the sense that we know it. Whether there is any "iron curtain" in that part of the world or not, there is certainly a blackout of honest news from America that should be a matter of serious concern to us. Peoples that we so recently helped to liberate get a caricature of us, not a picture. It is generally the caricature of a rich, fat-cat fighting the battle of the capitalist, imperialistic world.

Naturally, the question arises: What to do about the situation. There are several things that suggest themselves.

Under the Yalta declaration, the United States Government can continue to insist, as it has insisted in Bulgaria and Rumania, that a condition precedent to recognition of the Government of a conquered or satellite country is that no election even relatively free can be held unless freedom is granted the opposition to have a press. It will be most difficult for the Bulgarian Government, for instance, to revoke the measure of freedom which it has given the opposition without endangering the Government itself or admitting its completely totalitarian character. The occupied countries want peace treaties and they want occupation troops removed. If we insist that the Governments of these countries shall also give the opposition freedom in their press, we can greatly help, as we have already helped in small measure.

It is utopian to hope that the United Nations will be able to adopt at any time in the near future an international code setting up standards for the press similar to those outlined, for instance, under the International Labor Organization, but the difficulty of achieving that goal should not make us despair of doing something about the world-wide exchange of information. Mr. Stettinius has demonstrated an interest in proposals looking toward that freer exchange.

The State Department can, it seems to me, become more exercised about the situation than it is. It has a good many diplomatic weapons to achieve a quid pro quo basis for the freedom of movement of correspondents, for the exchange of news, particularly official texts, etc., magazines, books and movies. It is not a question of propaganda; it is a question of recognizing that the peoples of the world can never achieve a lasting peace upon the basis of suppression of facts, distortion and plain lying by their Governments.

The recent report by Lewellyn White and Robert D. Lee of the Commission on Freedom of the Press points the way to practical measures which can be taken by the State Department through diplomatic channels. In the meantime, radio is perhaps the most effective outlet America has. To my mind, The Associated Press directors have made a most serious and short-sighted mistake in denying AP news to the Government for short-wave broadcasting. The policy is actually harmful to American interests. It is certainly a fact to which I can testify that the peoples of Rumania and Bulgaria with whom I talked trust American news above all other news because they feel that we have less selfish interest territorially and politically than any other power. They do not regard our news broadcasts as propaganda; most of them believe them more than they do the distorted, slanted news of their own Governments.

The publishers of the United States who control the Associated Press actually have in their hands a vital instrument in making not only our foreign policy but our domestic policies understood. They do great damage as long as they refuse to allow the State Department to broadcast AP news; as long as they refuse even to consider an arrangement that would meet their objections. The directors of The Associated Press are short-sighted beyond words if they think that without the help of the American Government they can get their news behind the curtain; if they think that without stimulating the desire for American news through the medium of radio they can persuade the Governments that control their press to print more—and truer—American news.

* * *

July 23, 1946

WRITER UNCURBED BY 'IRON CURTAIN' FINDS POLES AVOID SOVIET RIGIDITY

By W. H. LAWRENCE

By Wireless to The New York Times

BERLIN, July 22—I have just come back from behind "the iron curtain" and for me it was neither a barrier nor a screen.

After three weeks inside Poland I found, frankly, that conditions from a political and economic point of view were much better than I had expected.

I was free to go where I would and see whom I would—both friends and foes of the present Government. There was no censorship of anything I wrote and, unlike other correspondents who have been there, I encountered no hostility from Government quarters, which knew that the views I held were not the same as theirs.

Every facility for which I asked I obtained and I held interviews with all top governmental political figures. I thought they talked frankly with me on many subjects on which their opinions will not win friends for them in America.

The best example was the frank admission of nearly all Left-Wing leaders that the November Parliamentary elections will not in any sense be free, as the Western democracies understand that word. They will be more like the Soviet elections, with the Government attempting to control the result in advance through a single slate.

If Deputy Premier Stanislaw Mikolajczyk holds out, and it is apparent that he is going to try, then there will be a campaign of abuse and calumny, accompanied by Trojan horse tactics inside the Polish Peasant party designed to divide and conquer. If that fails, there is still the fact that the Government controls the vote-counting machinery, just as Tom Pendergast used to in Kansas City.

Having been in Moscow for sixteen months, fifteen days and four hours during the war, and having just come from the United States, I was able to apply two tests to Poland. The system the Poles have is not nearly so bad as the Russians' nor nearly so good as the United States'.

Poland's Independence Hobbled

It is a well-known fact that the principal leaders of the present regime were picked by Moscow and are loyal to it. This has the effect of reducing considerably Poland's genuine independence, especially in the fields of foreign, military and foreign trade affairs. Poland is vital to the Red Army at present as the communications route to Germany and equally as a bulwark against Germany, or any other western European power.

The biggest complaint I heard against the present Polish State, and one complaint that I agree with, is the building up of secret police machinery and the introduction of other totalitarian apparatus designed to repress or destroy the opposition. But this condition is far from being as tight as it is in Russia; in fact, M. Mikolajczyk is able to receive correspondents and denounce his own Government for alleged fraud.

The Poles are complete romantics about politics, as well as many other things, and as an American I found myself besieged by Poles who wanted to tell me how bad conditions are at present and how the Americans must help to fight the Russians to restore Polish independence.

One of the ablest men at present in the Polish Government is a Jew and a Communist in a country where anti-Semitism is rife and hatred of the Russians almost pathological. He is Jacob Berman, who has the title of Under-Secretary of State in the Premier's office, but who, as an intellectual and ideological leader in the Polish Worker's party is far more important than such a title suggests.

Indigenous Regime Is Goal

M. Berman said the present regime was trying to construct a system that would not be like Moscow's nor the Western democracies. He says neither of those systems would work in Poland. Certainly, Russian regimentation would be hard to sell to the Poles, who are the ruggedest of individualists. Whether complete political freedom is yet possible in a country that has never known it and that has entirely too large a lunatic fringe, is at least open, to question. M. Berman says it is his opinion that the Polish State would stand the stresses and strains of a completely free election.

Other top leaders with whom I talked tried to convince me, in effect, that the present Government was the best Poland could hope for. Dominant in their propaganda was the fear of Russian consequences if the Government for a moment crossed its big neighbor to the East. They seemed to have little faith that Premier Stalin really meant that Poland could be a free, strong and independent democracy unless that democracy was led by men not only friendly to Moscow but subservient to it in many things.

Farmers Not Collectivized

Economically, the new Polish system, as it has developed thus far, is a long way from the Soviet system. Agricultural lands are being divided for private ownership among hundreds of thousands of persons who insist on farming in their own way and who will not be eager for any collectivization program, such as Premier Stalin forced on Russia at great expense.

Big industries have been nationalized in Poland, but it must be recorded, in fact, that the change is being accomplished in this country with less revolutionary overtones than similar reforms are being carried out in Great Britain under the Labor Government. The fact is that, after nearly six years of occupation, all Polish industry was in a disorganized state, waiting for the Government to take it over.

The real owners and managers, who might be expected to provide opposition to any State control, either had collaborated with the Germans and thus disqualified themselves from future participation in Polish life, or had refused to cooperate with the Germans and had ended up by losing their factories and probably their lives.

The church in Poland still is free religiously and a small number of Catholic schools are in operation. There are indications that there may be some crack-down on the church, especially if the hierarchy continues its anti-Government stand implicit in August Cardinal Hlond's statement about the Kielce pogrom.

The weapon that the Government has is the seizure of church property as part of the land reform, but it is a weapon the Left Wing has been hesitant to employ because it remembers what happened in Spain.

* * *

November 10, 1946

IF RUSSIA'S MILLIONS COULD READ THE NEWS!

Would Objective Reports of Foreign Reaction to Moscow's Diplomacy Make Any Difference?

IT IS ALL ANYONE'S GUESS

By EDWIN L. JAMES

Here is an idea to play with: Would it make any difference in world relations if all the millions of Russia could read the news objectively? Mr. Churchill, in his speech Friday night, mentioned that the Russian people were directed and governed by a handful of able men "who, under their renowned chief, hold all the 180,000,000 Russians and many more millions outside of Russia in their grip." Comes election time and the Russians have the privilege of voting for one list, prepared for them by the Government, which, as Mr. Churchill said, makes it easy.

And, so, we put the question as to whether it would make any difference with Russia's millions if they had the opportunity of freedom of discussion and, above all, if they were able to read factual reports of what went on in the world and, in particular, read and know about foreign reaction to Moscow's diplomacy. It is probably true that most Russians think their Government's foreign policy is 100 per cent all right. They do not get a chance to learn of anything which detracts from that impression purveyed daily by a press run for the one purpose of glorifying and justifying the Moscow Government and the Communist party.

Thus we run into a discussion of the Russian press, and, since the only way to measure it is by comparison with the press in other countries, let us take the Russian press vis-a-vis the American press.

The American Press

Let us start out by saying that most Americans do not admire the Russian press, and to be fair let us add that most voluble Russians do not admire the American press. That clears the field for a comparison.

In this country, since it has been a country, the controlling idea about newspapers is that they should give all the facts to all the citizens with the idea that the citizens, individually and collectively, will in the long run reach a good decision. Back in 1787 Thomas Jefferson wrote a letter to Edward Carrington in which he penned this:

"The basis of our government being the opinion of the people, the first object should be to keep that right. And were it left to me to decide whether we should have a government without newspapers or newspapers without a government, I should not hesitate a moment to prefer the latter."

We have the freedom of the press as the No. 1 article in our Bill of Rights. We have gone along on the theory that the value of newspapers lies not in their advocacy of this candidate or that ideology but rather in their presentation of the news as a mirror of human activity, as real current history.

With us Mr. Byrnes makes a speech and we print the text so the reader may make up his mind. Mr. Churchill makes a speech and we print it the next morning word for word so that any reader may judge. When in international meetings contesting countries have a debate we try to give both sides a fair comparable show.

The Russian Press

It is not so in Russia. In Russia the press is an instrument of government. It is run by the regime and the party for that purpose. The Russians are very frank about it. Kuzmichev in "Problems of Journalism" writes:

"All dissertations on 'objective and complete information' are liberal hypocrisy. The aim of information does not consist in commercializing news, but in educating the great masses of workers, in organizing them under the exclusive direction of the party for clearly defined tasks. This objective will not be attained by objective reporting of events. Liberty and objectivity of the press—these are fictions. Information is the means of class struggle, not a mirror to reflect events objectively."

So when Mr. Churchill makes a speech here the text goes at once to Moscow, but nothing is printed for five days, and then quotes are used along with a three-column editorial blast. It is not a matter of giving the news of Mr. Churchill's speech; it is a matter of using material from it to form the basis for a propaganda attack. Mr. Byrnes makes a speech here advocating a firmer American foreign policy. The text goes to Moscow, all right, but what was printed was that Mr. Byrnes hoped for fair elections in Greece. The Secretary did not mention Greece.

A Comparison Is Made

There is the difference as clear as day. Our system is to let the reader know the facts so that he may form an opinion. The Russian system is to make up the citizen's mind for him and then feed him such factual material as supports the ready-made opinion.

Our labor troubles do not at all appear in the Russian press as illustrating the freedom of labor unions in our country to strike, something they do not do in Russia, but they are presented as about a penult death struggle of wicked capitalism. If there is a story in Moscow papers about unemployment in the United States, nothing is said about unemployment relief, but there is a picture of uncounted thousands dying of starvation. Which proves what the Kremlin wishes it to prove.

The British in Egypt, in Greece, in India and in Java—there you have in the Moscow press evil imperialism with a denial of human rights. But Russian troops any place—and they are in lots of places—why, they are there for the protection of human rights and for the glory of democracy—Russian style. And as for Iran—the Russian press has finally got around to talking about oil, which may show some progress toward realism on that particular issue.

Just a Hypothesis

Just as it will be agreed that the Russians have a right to the kind of government they desire or stand for, just so they have a perfect right to their kind of journalism. But, nevertheless, at a time when there is so much discussion of the future of the world depending on better knowledge, one people of another, it seems fair to ask what might be the result if Russia had a press which told its people factually about what is going on in the world. Only slightly less important would be the abolition of Russian censorship so that people in other countries could know more about what the Russian people are doing, dreaming and planning.

If it be peace the peoples want, surely no case could be made for danger to peace in a better acquaintanceship of the American and Russian people. There may be other reasons, and strong ones, for the Russians not having the same sort of objective press as democracies of the other sort have, but it certainly would not be a cause of war if the two peoples could get acquainted through their press.

No one expects this to happen overnight or even soon. But at least, it is an idea. No one expects Stalin to permit an opposition press or the Communists to permit a rival list at the polls on election day. Perhaps we will have to wait some time to see that.

But still it is an idea to play with—what difference might it make if all Russians knew what other peoples thought about them and their Government and if other people could know more about what all the Russians think about them—without benefit of censorship, going and coming?

* * *

April 27, 1947

WHY RUSSIA KEEPS THE IRON CURTAIN

Censorship Is an Old Custom With Deep Roots and, Besides, the Russians Have Many Things to Hide from the World Outside

By H. E. SALISBURY

The end of the Moscow Conference means the return of censorship on all news sent from Russia. After two months of freedom, correspondents will once again write with the censor in mind.

There is nothing more debilitating, more frustrating, to a conscientious seeker of news than Russia's censorship. Many a correspondent has gone to Moscow with high hopes and determination, only to leave a year or two later, embittered and vowing never to return.

As a correspondent in Moscow in 1944—at a time when Russian press relations were much better than now—it was my opinion that the incompatibility of the Soviet and the world press was an ulcer which constantly drained poison into Russia's relations with the world, Russia, however, insists on retaining restrictions. Only two weeks ago Stalin told Harold Stassen that "it would be difficult in our country to dispense with censorship."

The roots of Russian censorship go very deep. For an American it is natural to think of Russia's history beginning with the Bolshevik Revolution in 1917—or at least to think that the Revolution swept the slate clean. Russian propaganda has labored to produce that impression. But anyone who goes to Russia quickly finds that a revolution does not divorce a country from its history. The Russians were still Russians the day after Nov. 7, 1917, and the Bolsheviks, themselves, no matter what their theories, were still Russians.

So it is important to remember that censorship is an old Russian custom—an institution at least 300 years old. And it may be even more important to know that for generations before the Soviet regime, censorship and publication were as intimately connected as Siamese twins.

The fact is that with the exception of a few brief periods late in the nineteenth century and early in the present one, Russia has never been without censorship since the introduction of the printing press.

Delving into Russian history, you find that when an obscure Czar, Feodor II, established the first college in Moscow, in 1680, he gave it two privileges. The first was the right to publish books, the second was the right of censorship over books. Incidentally, the college also was directed to supervise all foreigners entering Russian service.

Once launched, this tradition became well integrated in Russian life. Catherine II, whose reign accomplished some of Russia's greatest reforms, came to wield an iron censorship once her fears for the security of the throne were aroused by the French Revolution. Although she herself had brought more new ideas into Russia than any ruler since Peter the Great, she imposed the most severe censorship Russia had ever seen. She was chiefly worried about the import of ideas into Russia, but the export of realistic reports was disapproved with almost equal vigor.

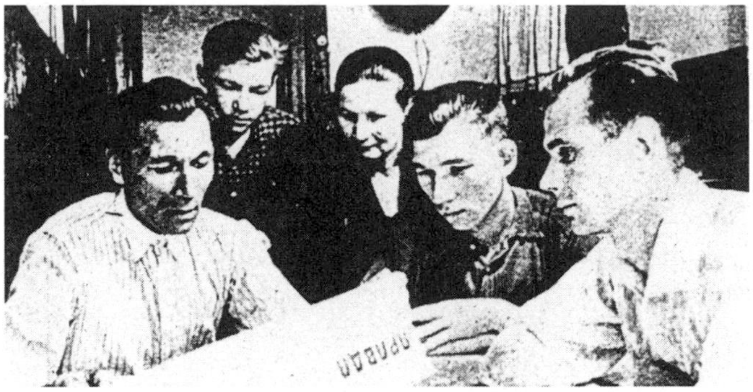

A Russian electrical worker and his family reading Pravda—the "truth."

Catherine's successors carried on the tradition. Every liberal outbreak in the West brought new suppressions in Russia. When the revolutionary whirlwind of 1848 arose, Russian censorship reached a fantastic peak.

Sir Bernard Pares, outstanding student of Russian history, described it in these words: "Newspapers were forbidden even to commend new inventions until they had been officially declared to be useful; in 1851 a commission was appointed to examine all music for the discovery of possible conspiratorial ciphers. . . . Paper came out publishing bare news without any comment. . . . Count S. Uvarov was not allowed to use the word Demos in his book on Greek antiquities, nor might he say that Roman emperors were killed only that 'they perished.' From a scientific work the censor removed the expression 'forces of nature.' Nikitenko, himself a censor, was called upon to explain what he meant by using the term 'the movement of minds.' The censor Akhmatov stopped a book on arithmetic because between the figures of a problem he saw a row of dots . . ."

The most recent edition of Baedeker on Russia was published in 1914. It warns prospective visitors to Russia against bringing into the country or taking out literature or papers of any kind. The traveler, Baedeker warns, is apt to have trouble with the frontier police. The same advice holds good today. When we set up our shuttle bombing bases in the Ukraine in 1944 one of the conditions was that no magazines, newspapers or book brought in for our troops be allowed to drift into the hands of the Russian people. Regular collections were made at Poltava of all American reading matter. The home-town newspapers, news magazines and detective stories were assembled after reading and burned.

Catherine II would have understood this Soviet ruling. It was in the Russian tradition.

When the Bolsheviks came to power they re-enacted the censorship statutes of the Czars with little change. But for the first twenty-one years or so of Soviet rule, censorship was not a major problem for correspondents in Moscow. As Walter Duranty said, they wrote as they pleased. Occasionally, a writer was punished for some flagrant abuse. One was

Moscovites—A Spring scene in the Russian capital.

expelled after he wrote a piece for a magazine which included some gross jokes about Stalin. And occasionally an unfriendly correspondent found that when he had left Russia for a breather he could not get a visa to return.

The first act of Molotov when he took over the Foreign Commissariat from Maxim Litvinov in 1939 was to announce the formal abortion of censorship. He put correspondents on their own responsibility and said that, "if dispatches published abroad were flagrantly hostile, or clearly prejudicial to the prestige of the Soviet Government, immediate expulsion of the guilty correspondents would follow." This was more a change of practice than of principle, however, and actually constituted de jure recognition of what had been de facto practice for some years.

But when war came actual censorship was reimposed and it continues, except for the interlude of the conference, to this day.

The basic purpose of the Soviet censorship, as of any censorship, is suppression—suppression of facts, theories and opinions. It raises the immediate question: What type of material is censored?

The answer is to be found in the files of any Moscow correspondent—his files of cables which have been stopped in their entirety or mutilated by censorship. Inspection will show that censors are most sensitive to dispatches dealing with Russian military affairs, foreign relations, economic conditions and political problems. They are on the alert also to halt the transmission of any report which might reflect on the dignity of the Soviet Union.

For example, precise descriptions of Soviet military equipment are blue-penciled almost automatically. One of the silliest examples of this occurred during the war, when the censorship forbade any reference in dispatches from Moscow to the Soviet eight-barreled rocket weapon, popularly called the Katuysha. The ban was continued for several years after the weapon ceased to be a military secret, since quantities of Katuyshas had been captured by the Germans. The fact that the weapon was well known abroad did not relax the censorship.

Early in 1944 new maps of the Soviet Union revealed that several of the autonomous Soviet Republics in the Caucasus had been abolished. Although thousands of the maps were printed for circulation within Russia the censorship forbade transmission of the news abroad. Yet it was obvious that there was nothing to prevent transmission of this news to foreign Governments by diplomatic code.

An equally illuminating censorship anomaly arose during the tour of the Soviet Union by Eric Johnston, then president of the United States Chamber of Commerce. Johnston, accompanied by several correspondents, was taken almost anywhere he wished to go and saw many secret military plants. Although the Russians knew that both Johnston and William L. White, who was with him, had contracted to write articles about the tour for publication after they left Russia, they refused to allow transmission from Moscow of many details concerning military plants. The censors explained that they weren't responsible for reports written outside of Russia, but they would not permit any violation of their concept of military security in stories sent from Moscow.

The fact is that the censors are likely to stop any dispatch that reflects a Soviet weakness or which might by a stretch of the imagination violate the most strait-laced concept of security. The exception to this rule is that if the Russian press itself reports a weakness or a military fact, it generally—although not always—will pass the censorship.

Thus, if Pravda attacks the machine-tool industry for mismanagement, graft and inefficiency, the correspondent can report that fact. But if he gathers his own information to indicate that the harvest of spring wheat is likely to be small because of a lag in seeding, his story will be halted.

As anyone knows, conditions in Russia are not perfect. But unless the party press has admitted an imperfection, the censorship tries to keep the world ignorant of the defect.

Russia is very sensitive to her backwardness and very proud of her accomplishments. Dispatches which reflect in any way upon the shortcomings of Soviet life are severely cut. Only in very recent days, for example, have correspondents been permitted to file stories telling the prices Russians must pay for commodities in the free markets or in the so-called government commercial stores. And any references to shortages of consumers goods or the hardships of Soviet life are frequently eliminated.

The censorship is a rather accurate weather-vane of Russian relations with the outside world. During periods of fairly good relations the censors allow the news to pass through with a minimum of cuts. When relations are troubled they scrutinize each cable with great care. News which has not been published in the Soviet press is likely to be held up for hours, even days, and finally passed only after extensive deletions.

Curiously enough, many influential Russians are aware of the irritation the censorship produces in their dealings with the West. Why, then, do they continue such a policy if they know that censorship is building anti-Russian sentiment in the West, destroying good-will and making Russia's diplomatic tasks more difficult? These men are not unintelligent, no matter how much their views may differ from ours.

Various answers have been given. Paul Winteron, wartime correspondent in Russia of the British Broadcasting Corporation and The London News-Chronicle, reached the reluctant conclusion that the Soviet Union was deliberately trying to drive foreign newsmen out of Moscow; that Russia would prefer that the world got its Soviet news from Radio Moscow and the official Tass news agency. I have known harassed Soviet officials assigned to the thankless task of handling the foreign correspondents who doubtless felt that way in their darker moments.

One of the Vice Ministers of the Soviet Foreign Office expressed a contrasting opinion. He described the Moscow correspondents as "psychopaths" and asked how, in the circumstances, Russia could give them more freedom in reporting. Another Vice Minister could see no benefit in improving the reports of correspondents. He said (the conversation occurred while the war was still in progress): "The Red Army is our best propaganda. If that isn't good enough, what difference does it make what the correspondents report?"

Others blame the censorship upon the basic incompatibility of a Communist state and a capitalist world. Still others say that Communist Russia cannot understand the standards of a free press.

Among newspaper men who have done time in Moscow, it might be noted, there is no "party line" on the censorship question. John Gibbons, an even-tempered Englishman who reports the scene for the Communist Daily Worker, fulminates against the Soviet censorship with as much enthusiasm as the most hot-tempered representative of the "western capitalist press."

When one considers the persistence of the censorship one recalls that long before the Bolsheviks seized power Russia was addicted to xenophobia—and with good reason. Few other lands have suffered so much and so long at the hands of foreign invaders. A Russian had good reason to fear foreigners and hate them. He could hardly help regarding the foreigner as an enemy who coveted his rich land and broad forests. Beneath his almost original concepts of hospitality he was apt to associate the word foreigner with "spy" or "enemy."

This was true for generations before the Revolution. The years since 1917 have not wiped out this concept—years which saw the foreign intervention in 1918–21, the long non-recognition of the Soviet regime by many western states, the possible plots of foreigners with the victims of the 1936–37 purge and, finally, what many Russians believe to be the effort of Chamberlain and Daladier to turn Hitler away from the West and toward Russia.

With this background of fear and suspicion, the censorship of western news reports to the Russian mind is merely an elementary precaution. Regarding the foreigner as a possible enemy of the state the Russian is likely to think it only natural that all reports transmitted from Moscow should be closely scrutinized.

The Russian's fear of foreigners is really rooted in the inferiority of his industry, organization and culture. Superimposed upon this fear is that which has been cultivated by his reading of Marx, Lenin and Stalin—fear of capitalist encirclement. This is a very real fear in Moscow. The Russian feels that he lives alone in a hostile world. He has friends in this world, but his enemies are more powerful.

Perhaps it is not so strange that in these circumstances the Russian is not likely to want to take any chances with a foreigner, particularly an aggressive newspaper correspondent who is constantly asking questions and popping up in places where he is likely to learn things which might help the enemy.

Since the officials who staff the Soviet press department are, after all, ordinary Russians and members of the Soviet community, it is not unnatural that they should, at least subconsciously, share the ordinary Russian prejudices and superstitions.

If you add to this the normal corollary of bureaucracy—that you can't get into trouble by doing nothing, but you are apt to get into hot water through positive action—it is not hard to understand why the Soviet censor follows a very simple rule: when in doubt don't let him say it.

All this inevitably raises the question of whether the Russians care nothing for what is published in foreign lands about their country. Have they no concern with world opinion?

The answer is that they are highly concerned. No foreign correspondents can stay long in Moscow without hearing Russians of almost every category complain about what the foreign press is saying about their country. They read in Pravda or Izvestia that antagonistic reports are printed in New York or London and ask the foreigners why Russia is so widely misunderstood. They say that the Western press is constantly "slandering" the Soviet Union.

But if you tell a Russian that half the fault—at least—lies with his own country through its failure to allow responsible journalists an opportunity to file free, uncensored explanations of what is going on, he will not understand what you are talking about. If you tell him that Soviet journalists in America are allowed to send back to Moscow any kind of report which pleases their fancy while American correspondents in Moscow are subject to the whims and vagaries of a thoroughly cowed and often ignorant bureaucracy he is likely to say that Russian journalists are "responsible" and American journalists are not.

The gap between Russian and American conceptions of the press is very wide. The Russian thinks of the press as an organ of his Government, as a didactic institution designed to educate and inform. A press which is individualistic, a press which reports events upon a canvas of its own choosing is alien to all his concepts.

One American correspondent who had a tour of duty in Moscow emerged with the firm conviction that what Russia needed was a good American publicity man. But he was quick to admit that no Soviet official would ever take the responsibility of suggesting that his country might take lessons on the publicity front from the capitalist West.

* * *

February 8, 1948

CZECHS TO TIGHTEN BARS ON CRITICISM

New Bill Would Set Prison Terms for Persons Defaming Foreign Nations, Statesmen

By ALBION ROSS
Special to The New York Times

PRAGUE, Feb. 6 (Delayed)—All citizens and residents of Czechoslovakia will be subject to punishment with about six months in prison if they violate a bill that will soon be placed before the Government to prevent the defamation of statesmen or institutions of foreign countries. The legislation, which would apply particularly to the press, was proposed in order to curb the press.

Exact details of the bill are not known. It was asked for by Vladimir Clementis, Communist Deputy Foreign Minister, before Christmas, considered by the Cabinet again after Christmas and then handed over to a commission in the Ministry of Justice for drafting. The draft is now understood to have been completed. It must come before the Cabinet and then be introduced in Parliament.

This bill is definitely unpopular here. The legislation was asked for by the Foreign Ministry, chiefly to be able to do something about Russian and Yugoslav protests. The Yugoslav Embassy has been particularly vigorous in demanding redress for anything that was considered a slur on Marshal Tito.

Public Defamation Prohibited

Prohibited under the proposed legislation would be the public defamation of a foreign nation or the representative of a foreign nation. The same protection, it is reported, is given to a foreign country's national emblems, pictures of its chief of state and the like. Some sort of evidence of animosity toward the defamed nation or person is said to be required to justify passing sentence on the offending individual. Details of the legislation are such, it was said, however, that it plainly would apply not only to the press but also to any private citizen who in public expressed contempt for or animosity toward a foreign nation or statesman in a fashion that could be considered defamatory.

The legislation as proposed would depend upon reciprocal agreements of a similar sort with other states. Its protection could not therefore be offered to countries maintaining full freedom of the press and freedom of speech. A government afforded such protection in Czechoslovakia would have to introduce similar legislation its own country, controling the discussion of matters relating to Czechoslovakia or its leaders.

This means in effect that the legislation, when and if it becomes law, will apply only to countries in the Eastern European bloc where such legislation would be acceptable.

Proposal of Newpaper Then

Another suggestion had been offered by a private committee of the Czechoslovak Newspaper Men's Association. This organization is similar to journalist organizations in totalitarian countries in one respect—membership is compulsory. Only members of this legally recognized press organization may write for periodicals. Whoever is barred from the organization cannot exercise the profession of journalist or write for any type of periodical within Czechoslovakia's frontiers.

Members may be barred from the organization and therefore from journalism if in the opinion of a properly appointed board they have been untruthful or have not carried on their work decently. The exact terminology is rather vague and open to various interpretations.

One proposal made was that criticism or ridicule of foreign statesmen and foreign countries should be controlled through such a body and the offending newspaper man should be suspended from the profession for a period of time or expelled.

The Cabinet, however, does not appear to have given this proposal serious consideration. In any case the legislation that has been prepared applies to all citizens and residents and not merely to journalists, although it is aimed specifically at the press.

As a matter of fact, the situation has become so threatening that criticism of Eastern-bloc states has disappeared from the press. Only the regular hymn of hate for the United States and American policy continues in the Communist press, together with an occasional attack on Britain, France or perhaps Greece or Spain.

* * *

February 21, 1948

RUSSIANS PLAN TO CURB NEWSDEALERS IN VIENNA

Special to The New York Times

VIENNA, Feb. 20—The Russian Commandant in Vienna's Tenth District yesterday informed a gathering of newsboys and newsdealers that they would be held responsible for the sale of newspapers containing material directed against the Soviet Union.

A Russian officer, Major Schillein, said that the United States-licensed newspaper Wiener Kurier and the British-licensed Die Veltpresse were mere propaganda vehicles intended to promote a new war.

In discussing "Speaking Frankly," the book by former Secretary of State James F. Byrnes, he added: "The Americans can carry on such propaganda in their own country but not in ours."

This was interpreted to mean that the Russians consider Eastern Austria their country.

The Austrian police prefect for the Tenth District, who attended the meeting, finally decided that the newspapers would in the future be examined daily by the police, who will decide whether they are to be released and will take the responsibility for their sale.

* * *

February 29, 1948

CZECHS BAN 27 PUBLICATIONS IN CURB ON FOREIGN PRESS; RED REGIME WIDENS PURGE

BARS BROADCASTS

'Time,' 'Life,' Organ of British Labor Party Appear on List

THOUGHT CONTROL GROWS

Premier Gottwald Calls for Uncompromising Attack on Enemies of Government

By ALBION ROSS
Special to The New York Times

PRAGUE, Feb. 28—Twenty-seven foreign publications have been banned from Czechoslovakia, it was announced today, while access to the radio has been denied to foreign broadcasters.

Among the papers and magazines banned were The Chicago Tribune, Time, Life, The London Daily Herald, central organ of the British Labor party; The London Daily Mail, and eight Paris newspapers.

At the same time thought control was being tightened throughout the country, with the press brought completely under the domination of the Ministry of Information, magazines suppressed, and editors expelled from the association of journalists.

In a speech to the organizing commission of the essentially Communist Rural Labor and Peasants Congress, which meets here tomorrow, the Communist Premier Klement Gottwald said that the purge, which has been under way throughout the country, must be deep and uncompromising. Outlining what he believed must be done in the future, he said:

"We must grub out the roots of reaction from the political parties, all legal organizations and the whole public administration so as to make it impossible in the future for such a conspiracy to be repeated."

Refers to "Conspiracy"

The "conspiracy" to which he referred was the resignation a week ago Friday of twelve Ministers who had charged that Czechoslovakia had been becoming a police state, and who had sought to force President Eduard Benes to call immediate elections on the issue. Instead the result was the selection of a new Cabinet hand-picked by M. Gottwald. This Cabinet was sworn in yesterday by President Benes.

Associated Press Radiophoto

President Eduard Benes (left) looking on as Antonin Zapotocky puts signature to document in Prague on Friday placing him in the cabinet. At right is Premier Klement Gottwald.

Rudolf Slansky, one of the founders of the Cominform [Communist Information Bureau] and secretary general of the Communist party here, will head a committee to purge all political parties of "reactionaries," it was announced today. On the committee will be Ministers from other parties who split with their party leaderships and accepted posts in M. Gottwald's new Communist-dominated regime, along with other Communists. The central action committee, it was learned, would also participate in the purge.

The Communist-controlled Ministry of the Information explained that the foreign "broadcasters had not said anything wrong in their broadcasts but they did not show a true appreciation of the situation."

Police Visit U. S. Office

Police came to the office of the United States Information Service because of the three-power protest declarations of Britain, France and the United States on Czechoslovakia that had been translated into Czech and displayed in the window. An agent of the Prague Director of Police said he had been empowered to seize the material in the window.

Copies of the Czech edition of the United States Information Service Bulletin containing the declaration were given to him. Employees of the Information Service office removed the offending edition from the bulletin board in the window, where it has been read by a considerable crowd.

Foreign broadcasts were being listened to assiduously again, during the Nazi occupation, and were widely discussed in Prague. Six domestic magazines have been banned, including Catholic, which had been widely circulated in the Catholic parishes.

Twenty-five editors and other leading journalists were expelled from the journalists' association, and this action automatically barred them from any type of journalism. In one provincial town a journalist was banned on the charge of having "cooperated with London papers," with no further explanation.

The paper of the now submissive Czech National Socialist party will change its title from Free Word to something less provocative.

Former Minister of Justice Prokop Drtina, according to an official announcement, was found early this morning lying outside his apartment window with serious head wounds. Police asserted that a note had been found in which he had expressed the intention to commit suicide. He was reported still alive in a hospital. Only official information from the police was available on the matter.

Long files of police, armed with rifles, and worker guards marched to the old town square today to be congratulated by Premier Gottwald for their work this past week. Top men of the Communist regime were there to honor the police who made a formidable show of alert power. The Premier warmly praised them, saying he had rejected completely so-called slanders concerning the mutilation of democracy in Czechoslovakia, and the police terror.

The Premier explained that the role of the police in recent days had fitted rather into his conception of democracy. He said:

"The police and the factory militia are an example of real democracy. They are ready to defend the people."

Today's police celebration and the warm congratulations extended to the police by the Communist chiefs of the state were in a sense symbolic. The celebration represented from the standpoint of official sources how mistaken the resigned Ministers were in their fear that Czechoslovakia was in danger of becoming a police state.

The great display of police might in the center of the capital during the week had dwindled away. There were only a few extra guards, around the philosophical faculty and one or two other buildings of Prague University and at a few bridges.

Premier Gottwald again announced that all import and export trade would be nationalized so that foreign customers of Czechoslovakia would deal only with the state or its agencies in the future. He also reiterated that all wholesale trade would be nationalized in the near future.

Some 80,000 persons are expected to attend the rural Congress tomorrow. This has been summoned not by the National Peasants Association, which is far from Communist or even Socialist, but by land reform committees that are under the direction of the Communist Ministry of Agriculture. However, an action committee was at work in the Peasants Association.

M. Gottwald indicated that elections would take place within the legal term of the present Parliament. This would mean about the end of May, contradicting the general expectation that the Communists wanted to put off the elections until the autumn. Evidently they now feel that elections later this spring will do them no harm.

The purge that Premier Gottwald stated today was necessary to the health of state will help fill labor battalions in the mines, excavating jobs, drainage projects and similar national undertakings. Those dismissed by action committees from newspapers, radio and many other kinds of jobs, it was learned, were receiving "blue cards" assigning them to labor battalions.

The press stresses statements made in connection with a meeting of the preparatory committee for the all-Slav Congress to meet in Prague in the autumn. Delegates to the committee meeting this past week from Russia, Yugoslavia and other Slav countries expressed enthusiasm for the events of recent days and their result.

A resolution of the committee called for a new all-Slavic hymn, and competition will be arranged for this purpose. The committee called also for work among Slav origin populations in other countries, and in particular in the Slav language press outside Eastern bloc countries.

The evident purpose of this drive is to build up sympathy for the Communist-dominated community in Russia and eastern Europe through a racial appeal to language groups elsewhere in the world, notably and obviously in North and South America, where significant groups of this type exist.

In January foreign trade with the Soviet Union had risen to 21 per cent of the total, and the total trade with the Eastern bloc was approaching the 40 per cent quota laid down under the trade program of Hubert Ripka, former Czech National Socialist Minister of Foreign Trade. The new Communist Minister of Foreign Trade, Dr. Antonin Gregor, has defined his principal tasks as "to take measures that our agreements, especially with the Soviet Union and countries with the new democracy, are consistently carried out."

Even before Minister Ripka's resignation, foreign traders from the Western countries had complained strongly that they had been unable to get deliveries of promised goods. They had expressed the beliefs that this has been because of priorities given to industries working to supply Russian and Eastern-bloc markets under the new trade agreements negotiated last year that came into force toward the end of the year.

Representatives here of United States and other Western business interests almost universally expressed the opinion that their situation would become practically intolerable as foreign trade was to be completely nationalized. Western customers, it was felt, would probably be served only after Eastern customers had been satisfied, and the present allegedly chaotic state of deliveries would get even worse.

* * *

June 1, 1949

CHINA'S REDS SCOFF AT OBJECTIVE PRESS

Maintain News Gathering Is Integrally Linked to Politics—See One Absolute Truth

By HENRY R. LIEBERMAN
Special to The New York Times

NANKING, May 30—When I called recently on a Communist official I had known in North China several years ago we talked cordially about "old times" and mutual friends as a secretary recorded our conversation in her stenographic notebook.

Asked by him about my reaction to the Communist occupation of Nanking, I replied that I was tremendously impressed by the discipline of the Communist troops but that it was difficult to find out what was happening in the world outside by depending on the Communist press here.

"Oh," he answered, "all you want is Associated Press and United Press."

"I told him I would be satisfied to read the complete news file of the Communist New China News Agency, including those stories that did not appear in the newspapers here.

Later I noted that it was a journalistic pity that the Chinese Communist revolution, one of the greatest upheavals in modern history, had been covered so indirectly and sketchily and asked for permission to visit a Communist-held village to study the party's land reform accomplishments at first hand. He replied that such a project was not possible at present and suggested that I gather my material from the past output of the New China News Agency.

Little Room for Conciliation

"It is the truth," he said. I remarked that the German philosopher Nietzsche had observed there were many kinds of truth.

"That was Nietzsche's point of view," he said.

Altogether, the conversation, the only one I have been able to hold with any Communist above the grade of minor functionary or army private, was cordial and impressed me again with the basic honesty, zeal, simplicity and devotion to China of my old Communist friend. But it was clear as never before that there was little room for conciliating our varying approaches—in this case to news gathering.

The belief in a single, absolute truth was reflected in the press re-registration notice issued on May 16 by Gen. Liu Po-cheng's Military Control Commission, which called on all Chinese magazines, news agencies and newspapers in Nanking to register so as to "safeguard the freedom of press and speech of the people and strip the freedom of speech and press of the anti-revolutionaries."

Warned on Propaganda

The publications were warned not to violate the decrees of the Military Control Commission, not to engage in propaganda against the "people's democratic movements," not to disclose "national or military secrets" and not to publish "rumors or such propaganda as to be intentionally slanderous."

Newspapers and periodicals applying for re-registration were required to submit to the control commission one year's back copies with three copies of each issue since the capture of Nanking on April 24. The data sought from the registrants included a statement of past and present editorial policies, biographies of all staff members and past and present political beliefs, political experiences and relationship with political parties and political organizations "of the publishers, shareholders, editors, correspondents and managerial staff."

Only two newspapers are now being published here—the New China Daily and the China Daily.

Addressing the Literary Arts Forum in Yenan in October, 1943, Communist Chairman Mao Tzetung noted that the prime task of Communist writers and artists was to advance the cause of the revolution. His viewpoint was echoed in an article on "Freedom of the Press" published in the New China Daily on May 24. The writer maintained that press and politics were integrally related, and added:

"Inasmuch as news is inseparable from politics, objectiveness is beyond reach. The entire process of working, from collecting information to writing, editing and publishing, is one of screening and selection. Why do you interview A and not B? Why do you write about one side instead of the other? Why do you detail one thing and brief another? Objectiveness cannot be explained. We newsworkers should work for truth but not for objectiveness."

No Ban on News Gathering

Thus far the Military Control Commission here has not banned the collection of news by foreign correspondents as the Communists have done in Peiping. Although foreign reporters are technically free to collect news, it is impossible to see responsible officials outside the Foreign Affairs Bureau, and the Nanking telegraph office says it has received instructions not to accept press telegrams.

Dispatches from Nanking must be sent by mail or courier to Shanghai, where international communication still is open.

In an article published here recently under the title "Beware of Journalistic Aggression of American Imperialism," Liu Tsun-chi, a member of the Communist press section, argued that United States news agencies and newspapers were controlled by "monopolists" and "imperialists." He asserted that generally speaking all United States foreign correspondents were "spare parts of the road-paving machine of American imperialists."

Mr. Liu, who worked for the United States Office of War Information in Chungking during the Japanese war and later in Shanghai, said the major purposes of United States news agencies abroad were to distribute and collect news "beneficial to United States imperialist interests" and to "indulge in intelligence activities in coordination with local diplomatic, military and commercial organizations.

"Occasionally they might send out some reporters who are not loyal to American imperialism," he added, "but none of such reporters could stay long in this post."

* * *

November 28, 1949

CHINA'S RED CHIEFS LIMITED IN OUTLOOK

Understanding of West Is Held Scanty and Distorted by Marxist Conceptions

By TILLMAN DURDIN
Special to The New York Times

HONG KONG, Nov. 27—If Chinese Communist leaders by now have realized the depth and extent of feeling aroused in the United States over the detention of Consul General Angus Ward, it has come as a surprise to them, observers of Chinese affairs here believe.

It is pointed out that most foreigners who have had close contact with the Communist leaders have been struck by their limited knowledge of the non-Communist world. It has been found that what they do know about such countries as the United States has been filtered through a rigid framework of Marxist concepts and often is distorted and misunderstood.

Since they have come to power on a national scale, the Chinese Communists have become more restricted than ever in their understanding and knowledge of peoples and events outside of the Communist sphere, it is believed. It is feared that their own intensive propaganda, their preconceived notions about world affairs and their self-imposed isolation from non-Communist influences are accentuating the remoteness of the Peiping leaders from the realities of the West.

The completely controlled public press in the Communist areas now makes no effort to present a daily record of world events, not even a Communist-slanted one. The columns are filled mostly with items about the domestic scene designed to promote the Communist program. News from outside China comes through the Tass News Agency and is mainly devoted to reports from the Soviet Union or its satellite nations.

A recent Chinese arrival here from Peiping, with inside knowledge of the activities of the high Communist hierarchy there, reports a special newspaper is produced for more important Peiping officials. This journal contains reports that the general public does not see but it is said even this paper would be considered pathetically inadequate as a source of objective information on world affairs by a reader of the uncensored press of the democratic nations.

The Communist leaders now are restricted further in regard to information by the absence of relations with the democratic countries. They lack the benefit of reports from representatives in non-Communist capitals and contacts with Western officials in China. The Chinese Communist propaganda machine, moreover, is believed to be a preserve of those party elements most loyal to a Moscow orientation for Chinese communism.

* * *

June 19, 1950

CZECH PRESS HEWS TO IDENTICAL LINE

Large Segment of Public Gets News Via Voice of America and B. B. C. Programs

BRITON HIGHLY POPULAR

Prague Maintains Censorship at Source by Restricting Access to Information

This is the fifth of six dispatches on Czechoslovakia by a correspondent of The New York Times who recently left that country to avoid possible arrest on false espionage charges.

By DANA ADAMS SCHMIDT
Special to The New York Times

VIENNA, June 11—It does not matter much which of Prague's eight daily newspapers you read. They all print nearly the same "news."

Their opinions on all subjects follow the same line except that they are most authoritatively expressed in Rude Pravo, central organ of the Communist party, a journal that by its large format and turgid and extravagant editorials recalls the Nazi party's Voelkischer Beobachter.

The Communist press, like the Nazi press in its time, is not primarily concerned with informing the public about what has happened; its job is to give the public the party's view of what has happened. That applies to newspapers ostensibly representing other parties as well as to the Communist party organs themselves.

A large part of the Czechoslovak public, including many nominal Communists, get around that by not reading any newspapers and diligently listening to the Voice of America and the British Broadcasting Corporation. The B. B. C.'s Bruce Lockhart has become a sort of patron saint of anti-Communist Czechoslovaks. His words are repeated reverently and in guarded tones day by day from one end of the country to the other. Many Czechoslovaks used to write him letters until a rule was made requiring persons sending letters abroad to identify themselves at postoffices.

Regular Fans Marked Down

While listening to foreign radio stations is so general that authorities have not found it feasible to forbid it, regular fans are marked down in party and police records as unreliable and those who repeat what they hear expose themselves to arrest for disseminating subversive rumors.

The same treatment was accorded customers who crowded the United States and British Information Services' libraries until the Government ordered them closed in April and May. In addition to books, magazines, phonograph records and films the Czechoslovaks found in those libraries precious newspapers that were banned from newsstands.

The newspapers from the West on public sale are The London Daily Worker and L'Humanité of Paris.

Since the public is entitled only to official propaganda, information as such is deliberately confused in the Communist mind with "intelligence." Western reporters and diplomats whose business it is to gather information are automatically suspected of espionage.

Dutch business man Johannes Louwers was convicted of economic espionage because he had asked and received from Czechoslovak associates production data such as is published in trade journals throughout the Western world. Two United States Information Service employees were held by the court to have committed espionage because they gave United States Press Attaché Joseph C. Kolarek an answer when he asked what the Czechoslovak people's reaction was to one of President Truman's speeches about the atomic bomb.

Data Held Espionage

Under a 2-year-old law for the defense of the republic, one could be convicted of espionage for gathering any information not officially published or even for correlating published information.

Application of these strictures has gradually become more intense. It was last autumn that Western correspondents with shock realized the situation, when a priest with whom they had had friendly contact was arrested. Nonetheless, even until early this year they felt able for instance, to continue to publish statements representing the Roman Catholic point of view in the church-state struggle.

There was and is no censorship on outgoing news. But since the series of trials that began in April Western correspondents and also diplomats have been restricted almost entirely to the official news agency, newspapers and each other for information.

At least three Communists who a few months ago felt sure enough of themselves to talk replied to my telephone calls during April by saying they were "terribly busy," would be for two or three weeks and would call me when they had time. They never called.

Interviews Not Granted

A trade union official whom I asked for data on the vacation and recreation program replied after lengthy consultations: "It is not possible." Of six interviews with Government officials that I requested through the Ministry of Information during the four months before my departure I received only one—at pensions headquarters. During that time Western correspondents were invited only to those press conferences and trials at which Western nations were to be attacked and insulted. The exception was United Nations Secretary-General Trygve Lie's, at which he was insulted by the Communist reporters.

Thus correspondents, like diplomats, are practically cut off from official sources. They fear to see private sources lest they compromise themselves and the sources.

That is what is technically known as censorship at the source—the same method the Nazis used until the second year of the war. Since the correspondents remaining in Prague still, in spite of everything, occasionally pick up a story that is not official they would undoubtedly feel more at ease if Czechoslovakia would follow Moscow's example by establishing direct censorship of outgoing news.

These then are the means by which Western foreigners in Czechoslovakia are being isolated from the people and the people from the Western world.

* * *

February 3, 1951

UNDERGROUND PRESS HIT

Hungary Orders All Multigraphs Reported to the Police

Special to The New York Times

VIENNA, Feb. 2—The widespread distribution of underground anti-Communist newspapers in Hungary has forced the Budapest Government to try to make the production of such sheets impossible.

A Government decree orders every organization and individual in possession of multigraphing machines to report them to the local police authorities by Feb. 15. Private persons who wish to retain possession of such machines must obtain police permission. Noncompliance with the decree is a crime punishable by one year's imprisonment.

According to information from Budapest the most widely distributed underground newspaper sheet is one that reproduces information and instructions issued by the "Free Europe" radio which has its headquarters in the United States.

* * *

April 8, 1953

SOVIET CENSORSHIP NOW LESS SEVERE

Dispatches Still Scrutinized, but Much Is Passed That Once Was Stricken Out

By HARRY SCHWARTZ

Not the least interesting Soviet development of the past week or so is the seeming loosening of Moscow's censorship over the dispatches sent out by American correspondents there. As a result, the close reader of recent Moscow dispatches is able to find clear hints and clues to the situation in the Soviet Union on topics that the censors formerly would have regarded as too sacrosanct for discussion.

The loosening up has not been general and there are still many matters that are taboo for correspondents writing in Moscow. Last week, for example, dispatches reporting the price reductions introduced on April 1 were still confined to discussing only the percentages involved and correspondents could not give the actual prices nor could they discuss the relationship of the lowered prices to typical or average earnings.

Regardless of whether Soviet censorship is relatively severe or relatively lenient at any given time, the basic fact that dispatches must pass through the censor's hands before leaving Moscow is vital to understanding them. Moscow correspondents writing their dispatches inevitably take account of the censorship and what it wishes to conceal or to publicize and thus in a sense exercise their own pre-censorship before even submitting their copy for examination. On the other hand, they are sensitive to variations in the censor's severity, and these variations themselves offer some clue to the nature of Soviet policy at any particular time.

Interpretation Permitted

Illustrative of the present less severe censorship is the circumstance that the censor permitted this newspaper's Moscow correspondent to say in a dispatch on the dismissal of Seymon D. Ignatiev because of his role in the fabrication of the "doctors' plot" that it was apparent that any new effort to instigate antagonism among nationalities in the Soviet Union, any effort to fan the flames of anti-Semitism or to stir up feelings against Jews or other minorities would be eradicated by the Government.

This statement, with its implication that before last week-end's repudiation the Soviet Government had tolerated efforts to stimulate anti-Semitism, would probably not have escaped the censor's blue pencil a week previously.

The New York Times yesterday also printed a United Press dispatch from Moscow attributing the release of the doctors "to the personal intervention of Deputy Premier Lavrenti P. Beria as soon as he took over the new combined Ministry of State Security and Internal Affairs."

In the past such attribution of a particular action to one of the highest Soviet leaders, when his name had not been specifically cited in relation to that action by the Soviet press, would not have been permitted. The censor's liberality in this case is all the more interesting because Moscow leaders know that the foreign press has been speculating that the repudiation of the "doctor's plot" is a move by Mr. Beria against those who sought to undermine his position last January.

Implied Contrasts Now Passed

An unusual amount of implied candor has been permitted the Moscow correspondents in their descriptions of the social gatherings recently between Americans and Soviet citizens in connection with the visit of a group of United States publishers to the Soviet capital. The correspondents have been allowed to report that the affability and the pleasant atmosphere at these gatherings have been most unusual since World War II and to indicate that such contacts with Soviet officials on an informal basis has hitherto been rare. The actual isolation of Americans in Moscow before these recent events is clearly implicit in all these dispatches.

That this loosening of censorship is probably linked with the current Soviet peace offensive seems likely. If so, the Soviet Government may be trying to show the Western world that it is capable of somewhat more liberal policies than those it has followed formerly, just as the repudiation of the charges against the doctors seems, in part, an effort to win a greater reputation for valuing truth than the Soviet Government may have enjoyed abroad formerly.

Soviet censorship normally in the post-war period has been most stringent regarding reporting of domestic conditions, seeking to make sure that no dispatches from Moscow give information that contradicts significantly the official propaganda line. On foreign affairs, however, a reading of dispatches that have been passed by the censor suggests that there has been somewhat greater liberality, particularly as regards permitting speculation on the possible future course of events.

* * *

October 2, 1954

RUSSIA RE-VIEWED: CENSORSHIP OF NEWS IS ERRATIC

Moscow Correspondents Regard Arrest for Taking Pictures as Routine

This is the last of fourteen articles by a correspondent of The New York Times who has just returned to this country after five years in the Soviet Union. For the first time he was able to write without the restrictions of censorship or the fear of it.

By HARRISON E. SALISBURY

The last dispatch this correspondent filed before leaving Moscow was killed in entirety by the censorship. So was the next to the last.

On the other hand, the censors did not delete a single word from any of the first six dispatches sent to The New York Times by Clifton Daniel, its new Moscow correspondent.

This illustrates one of the difficulties of generalizing about the Moscow censorship. The most important single fact about the censorship, however, is that it exists and that every line filed from Moscow must go through the censor's hands.

One day the censor is light and passes a story. The next day he kills an almost identical dispatch. Sometimes, censorship is so erratic that only differences of individual taste seem to offer an explanation.

However, in general, Moscow censorship like most of the other restrictions and handicaps on correspondents in the Soviet Union is much lighter under the new Government than it was under Stalin.

Change Is Relative

The "lightness" of handicaps on Moscow correspondents, of course, is a relative matter.

A little more than fourteen months ago the new Soviet Government in one of a series of moves to remove irritating restrictions on foreign diplomats and correspondents greatly extended the area in which travel is permitted in the Soviet Union.

Some regions remain closed—notably the Baltic states, border areas, the great Urals industrial region, a few naval bases, and virtually all the principal cities of Siberia.

However, travelers may now visit most parts of European Russia, the Ukraine and the Caucasus. Large areas of Central Asia are open and certain delimited regions of Siberia, the Soviet Far North and Far East.

It so happens that this correspondent in recent months encountered unusual attention from the Ministry of Internal Affairs.

Possibly this attention was attributable to the fact that the correspondent in recent months had done much traveling, sometimes deep into territory run by the ministry. Perhaps it has been because he has gone armed with a camera and the Interior Ministry fears a camera like the devil fears holy water.

These attentions reached a peak on a trip to Siberia. On board a plane from Novosibirsk to Yakutsk a Security Police agent jimmied the lock of my suitcase, rifled through the contents, even going so far as to slit the linen inner lining, presumably hunting for concealed documents, and he exposed some rolls of unexposed film.

This was merely by way of introduction. There is nothing unusual in the Soviet Union to find yourself, from time to time, being followed by an agent of the Soviet Secret Police or the M. V. D. Sometimes United States military attaches are honored with an escort of as many as four.

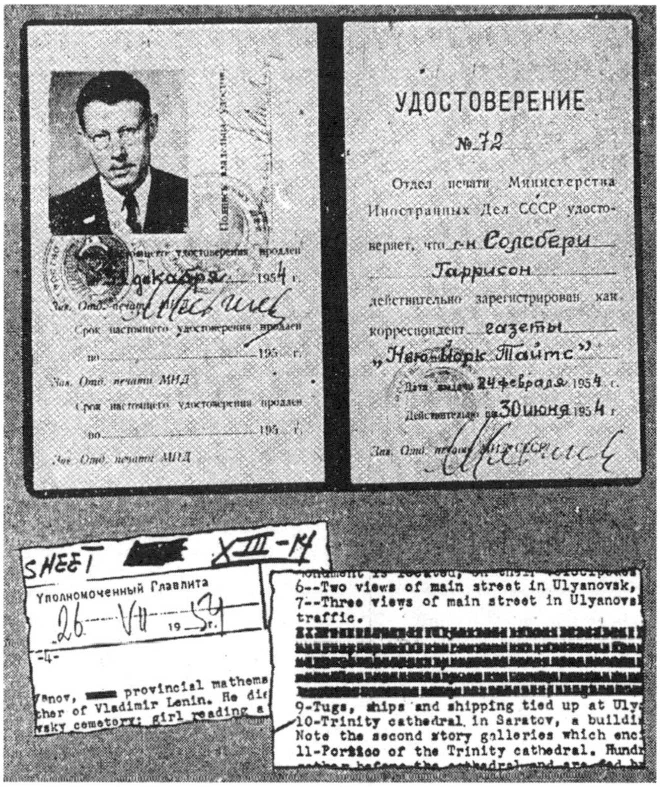

CREDENTIAL AND CENSORSHIP: Below Mr. Salisbury's press card are two examples of censorship. At left, on a corner of a sheet of picture captions, is the censor's stamp with the date—July 26, 1954—written in ink. Farther down on the caption sheet, Item 8 has been entirely eliminated. Instead of using shears, censor has X'd out lines on his own typewriter.

M. V. D. Always There

Beginning in Yakutsk and continuing throughout northern and eastern Siberia (with the exception of Chita, which is clearly an Army rather than an M. V. D. town) this correspondent was never, so far as he could determine, out of sight of an M. V. D. agent with the exception of times which he was in his hotel room.

And, at times—notably in Birobidzhan—there were at least twenty agents on the job.

It was impressive, intimidating and, sometimes, almost terrifying. Eastern Siberia is not a place in which a lone United States correspondent is likely to feel very comfortable or secure even under the best of circumstances. Surrounded by M. V. D. agents, day and night, one found it difficult to maintain a consistently objective and impassive viewpoint.

There were numerous aspects, too. The Birobidzhan hotel has no interior plumbing facilities. There is, however, an outhouse in the backyard with two compartments. By what was clearly no coincidence this correspondent never found it possible to pay a solitary visit to this homely facility.

Even as Taxi Driver

When I rode the Trans-Siberian train from Khabarovsk to Birobijan, two M. V. D. agents occupied the compartment next to mine. Even after I had gone to bed they stayed awake and on watch. An M. V. D. officer drove my cab in Khabarovsk. He didn't bother to change his uniform trousers and boots. But he collected his 100-ruble fare, just like a real taxi driver.

Two M. V. D. cars followed me to the station. Agents sat outside the Khabarovsk Hotel and openly trailed behind each time I went walking.

They were so thick around the hotel in Birobidzhan that each time I emerged on the hotel steps with camera in hand I could see them scurrying in all directions to get behind posts and fences and trees so as not to have their photograph snapped. All I had to do was raise my camera to start a small is stampede. It was funny. But it was also tragic and alarming.

A local M. V. D. official installed himself in the Birobidzhan hotel as the ostensible manager. Between keeping up his act as hotel manager and conducting all his routine M. V. D. business he was a busy man. When I walked in on him one day as two uniformed M. V. D. officers were reporting to him about a case of "speculation" on the local market he didn't even turn an eyebrow.

The custom of installing an M. V. D. officer in the local hotel as "manager" while foreign guests are in town is not confined to Birobidzhan. I first encountered it in Bukhara. As in Birobidzhan the agent was kept very busy, dividing his time between police headquarters and the hotel office. But it simplified the question of supervision.

Shadowing in Moscow (except for military personnel) is the exception rather than the rule, although many foreigners, conditioned by what they have heard about Moscow, tend to see little men following them wherever they go. Actually shadows are assigned to diplomats and correspondents usually only by way of occasional spot checks. If a correspondent should find himself constantly being shadowed it is almost a certain sign that he can expect very serious trouble from the M. V. D. That was why the amazing M. V. D. attention in Siberia was so alarming. However, no correspondent has gotten into serious trouble since Stalin's death, although several correspondents were expelled in the years between 1945 and 1953.

Ever since the assassination of the German Ambassador in Moscow, in the early days after the Revolution, a constant security guard had been assigned to the top Ambassadors in Moscow—the United States, British, French, German and Japanese. In other words, agents watched those diplomats whose assassination might provoke serious international difficulties for the Russians.

These security guards stayed so close to ambassadors that, for example, when Admiral Alan G. Kirk, former United States Ambassador once went rowing on Lake Baikal, the "boys" had to go along, too. If a United States Ambassador went to a football game, four M. V. D. men went along and sat next to him. If he went to the opera they went, too, and sat in the back of his box.

Then They Depart

The "security" was so close and so complete in recent years that the only Russians a United States Ambassador ever got to know outside of his own servants, were his "boys."

These guards, however, were withdrawn more than a year ago as one of the first of many acts of the new regime designed to eliminate minor annoyances from diplomatic life in Moscow.

However, the shadowing of foreigners on trips about the Soviet Union continues and even seems to have somewhat expanded during the summer. For example, every diplomat who travels (under the easing of travel restrictions) in his own car around the Soviet Union is closely followed by an M. V. D. escort car.

This correspondent in an automobile trip from Rostov-on-Don up through the Ukraine to Moscow was never outside the sight of an escort of four M. V. D. men in an automobile. And not infrequently two cars were assigned to him, particularly in cities such as Rostov or Kharkov or Dnepropetrovsk where it is more difficult to tail an automobile and through the Donbas industrial region where, presumably, there are more "sensitive" things from the security viewpoint.

Even a steamboat ride down the Volga warranted a four-man M. V. D. escort—two for day duty and two for night!

There were times since Stalin's death when it looked as if the censorship might have been quietly abolished without any word to the correspondents. However, each time this correspondent tested that theory by filing a dispatch on some known "forbidden" topic—such, for instance, as the secret police—he quickly found the blue-pencil wielders still on the job.

My last two dispatches that the Moscow censors killed dealt with that most touchy and forbidden topic of all—forced labor and the prison camp system. They were filed specifically with the purpose of testing the censorship, which had been extraordinarily light in previous weeks.

The easing of censorship is evidenced by the fact that no cuts had been made in Mr. Daniel's initial dispatches. In contrast to Mr. Daniel's experience, when this correspondent first arrived in Moscow in 1949 fully 50 per cent of his first fortnight's file from the Soviet capital was stopped dead by the censorship.

A progressive lightening of censorship has been observed since Stalin died.

Some very important restrictions have been eliminated. For instance, correspondents may now report retail prices of goods and describe their quality and make comparisons with United States products. This was completely banned before.

Some Data Allowed

Correspondents are allowed to write, fairly freely, about Soviet economic production, making estimates of specific figures from Soviet percentages, comparing the output with previous Russian production and with production abroad. This was banned in previous years.

Correspondents are permitted to report wages paid Russian workers. But not all wages, and comparisons and analysis of Russian wages are still stricken from most dispatches.

Correspondents are allowed, quite often, to remark on poor Russian living conditions, poor consumer goods, poor services. However, if a great deal of such material is packed into one story there are usually cuts.

Considerably more freedom is allowed in discussing and analyzing Soviet foreign policy moves, although reports of outright criticism usually are killed.

Personality material about Soviet leaders may or may not be passed. The rule seems not to be hard and fast although, in general, small human interest details are likely to be deleted.

There also is a good deal more liberty in writing about military matters—characteristics and numbers of airplanes, and so forth. However, any mention of the Ministry of Interior is cut. Almost every mention of the police, or militia as it is called in Moscow, is cut.

However, compared to former conditions there is much greater elbow room. For purposes of contrast the tabulation of censorship kills this correspondent kept while in Moscow shows that in a fairly typical month, January, 1950, fourteen dispatches out of twenty-two that were filed were killed in their entirety. Eight of these stories were direct compilations from the Soviet press, dealing with a campaign then in progress against local graft and corruption. One dealt with Soviet population estimates, one dealt with reinstitution of the death penalty, one dealt with Soviet-Chinese negotiations and one dealt with new restrictions imposed on the then resident American priest, the Rev. John Brassard.

Two years later, in 1952, censorship was somewhat lighter, but in two months seven dispatches dealing with such topics as kidnapped brides and polygamy in Central Asia were killed outright.

In 1951 out of a group of dispatches dealing with a trip to Georgia in the Caucasus, three out of twelve articles were killed entirely. These articles touched on such varied topics as Stalin's youthful career as a poet, the position of the Georgian Jews, and greetings to The New York Times on its 100th anniversary from the editor of the local Tiflis newspaper.

Area of Sensitivity

In contrast with this, only one dispatch this correspondent wrote concerning his only trip to Siberia in June was killed outright—a dispatch describing the operations of the M. V. D. However, substantial cuts were made in the stories of any materials about police, surveillance or forced labor.

Censorship is only one of the hazards and restrictions on correspondents in the Soviet Union but it is one that every reader should always bear in mind when he sees the Moscow dateline.

One of the biggest and most annoying handicaps currently encountered is being arrested for taking photographs. Since last autumn it has been theoretically possible to take pictures in the Soviet Union with full legal authority so long as the scenes, in general, were not of military or industrial objectives.

The Foreign Office even put out a circular stipulating that this was legal and proper under Soviet regulations and specifying just what could and could not be taken.

But try to make that stick in the provinces or even in Moscow. This correspondent was taken into custody within half a block of his apartment office in central Moscow a week before leaving the capital when he was snapping a simple street scene. It took fifteen minutes of argument to get free and then it probably would not have happened if the police officer on duty at the apartment had not come up and given the arresting officer the nod.

There is a policeman on the door of this building twenty-four hours a day—as at all buildings where foreigners live.

Arrest for picture-taking is so routine to Moscow correspondents that they count on an average of two or three arrests a day if they are going to be out taking pictures. One Canadian correspondent set a record by being arrested seven times in one day.

It is not always funny and it hardly ever is as light a matter as it sounds when put on paper. This correspondent has lost a substantial number of rolls of films he had to surrender to various officious individuals in Siberia and elsewhere.

Hazards Are Many

Once in a bazaar in Bukhara two native militiamen deliberately tried to arouse a crowd of natives against this correspondent in the course of arresting him for taking pictures of a local watermelon seller. At another bazaar on a remote mountain road en route to Frunze, in Kirgizhia, this correspondent was almost lodged in a local jail for no one knows how long. He was saved from this unlovely fate by a youngster whom he had been talking with on a bus who persuaded the militia to let him go by whispering that the correspondent was "an important foreign visitor." Moreover, the youngster's father was a local Communist party official.

There is no telling what you may get into trouble for if you are taking pictures. Once it was a monument beside which a colonel was standing. Apparently the colonel was regarded as a "military objective."

Another time it was an old, ruined church which happened to be across the road and up the block from a military office.

But the easiest and quickest way to the inside of a Soviet police station is to go to a local market and start snapping pictures. There are always plain-clothesmen around whose duty is to stop "speculation" and they invariably take you in hand and march you off to the station.

Then there is the question of what is formally called "access to the news." This is much simplified in the Soviet Union because there is no "access to the news" unless you consider the privilege of getting a copy of Pravda such "access."

Farewells No Problem

When this correspondent left Moscow he had no problem of farewells as he would have had in any other country. He did not know a single Russian so there was not a single goodby to be said—except to other foreigners. When a Russian in the Foreign Office press department came to his apartment to attend a cocktail party for Mr. Daniel it was the first social visit a Russian had paid me in nearly six years!

It is not surprising in this atmosphere of suppression and censorship that rumors flourish and false reports often go unchallenged. Seldom do the authorities bother to deny these reports. Although last year when rumors in Moscow that the Government was planning a new currency "reform" reached the point of runs on the banks and a swarming into stores to buy "hard goods" as a hedge against inflation Arseny V. Zverev, Minister of Finance, did issue a denial. It is interesting that Mr. Zverev's denial was believed and brought the panic to an end, whereas in the previous three or four days Communist party meetings in shops and offices had failed to have any effect on the rumor and the public acceptance of it.

Very frequently, however, rumors that are in general circulation in Moscow (as distinguished from rumors circulating in the Moscow diplomatic corps) turn out to be correct. This is only natural since substantial numbers of Russians are likely to have access to information the Government may not desire to publish. The Moscow public always finds out in advance about impending price cuts and similar Government edicts. And the Moscow public knew about the removal of Lavrenti P. Beria, former chief of the Soviet Secret Police, days before the official announcement.

Rumors Run On

This last month a typical series of rumors has been circulating in Moscow. No one can tell whether they have any basis. One report is that there was a great explosion and fire in Stalingrad in a big oil refinery there. This correspondent was recently in Stalingrad and saw no sign of this, but the report is persistent. Another report says the drought in the Ukraine was so severe that the Volga-Don canal had to be closed for a time because of the low level of water in the Don.

The only way any Moscow correspondent has of verifying such tales is to try to go out and see for himself at first hand. Requests for information to the press department of the Foreign Office seldom bear any fruit and often do not even produce the courtesy of a reply—although recently there has been some improvement.

In March, 1949, this correspondent wrote the press department and requested permission to go on a trip to see the great Stalin auto works in Moscow, a sight that is shown to virtually every delegation of visitors that comes to the Russian capital. The request was renewed annually or semi-annually.

About a fortnight ago the press department telephoned and said a trip had been arranged to the Stalin plant for the next day if the correspondent was interested in going. Needless to say he went.

In March of 1949 and at frequent intervals thereafter this correspondent requested permission to visit a collective farm in the Moscow area. Years passed. He saw many collective farms in other regions. But nothing happened to the Moscow request.

The day before he left Moscow the press department took the local correspondents out to see not only a collective farm but a state farm and a machine tractor station. Maybe it's a trend.

* * *

January 15, 1956

CZECHS ADMITTING MORE REPORTERS

Policy Toward the Western Press Has Been Changed Since Oatis Captivity

By SYDNEY GRUSON
Special to The New York Times

PRAGUE, Czechoslovakia, Jan. 14—With the Government's blessing, the long isolation between Czechoslovakia and the non-Communist press of the Western world is ending.

Four non-Communist correspondents based in Prague were joined this week by a visiting representative of The Associated Press office in Berlin. There have not been so many non-Communist Western correspondents in Prague since 1950.

Now represented here on a permanent basis are The New York Times, Time and Life magazines, Reuters and Agence France-Press.

It was in 1950 that William Oatis, Associated Press correspondent in Prague was imprisoned allegedly for spying. This was a period of extreme bitterness between Czechoslovak officials and Western reporters and the last of those who had been permanently accredited here, the representative of Agence France-Presse, left in 1953.

It was generally believed that the Czechoslovak Government's aim then was to make life so intolerable for Western reporters that none would be able to work in Prague. This policy now appears to have changed. So far as can be learned here all visa requests for Western correspondents are being granted promptly and Czechoslovak authorities here readily promise cooperation to make news gathering possible.

Freedom Is Pledged

The new correspondents here are told that they can travel freely throughout the country, see whatever they wish, except for security installations, talk with anyone and establish whatever social relations they can with ordinary citizens.

The authorities announced that Communist party and Government officials might not be as available for interviews or talks as the correspondents might wish. This has proved to be true.

Many Czechs are moreover reluctant to talk with foreigners. There is no reason for this reluctance, according to Government officials.

The newly arrived correspondent is told that the only conditions limiting his work are those that apply to any Czech. They are the sections of the penal code dealing with espionage and state secrets.

Disclosure of state secrets is punishable by death or a minimum of ten years in prison. The code spells out what constitutes a state secret. The terms are so broad that for all practical purposes anything dealing with military, economic and political affairs is a state secret unless it has been disclosed officially.

The amount of money in circulation is a specified state secret. So is any state-wide survey of income and expenditure. Negotiations and agreements between Czechoslovakia and other countries regarding foreign policy or trade are state secrets.

List A Long One

The list of state secrets specified in the code is a long one and is followed by the sentence: "All other reports and data that the Government may decide should not be made public."

[Mr. Oatis reported after he had been freed that he was accused by the Czechs of "unofficial reporting"—that is, gathering news on his own. The Czech oficials termed this "espionage." He then signed a statement to the effect that he had gathered "military information." He signed other "confessions," all of which he has since repudiated.]

There is no outgoing censorship in Czechoslovakia. Correspondents can file easily to all parts of the world without submitting their copy for reading. Presumably the correspondent must accept post-publication responsibility for his copy.

But since the first of the non-Communist reporters was permitted back in Prague, a year ago, none has been troubled for the kind of stories sent out.

* * *

August 12, 1956

CORRESPONDENTS IN CHINA GET VARIED TREATMENT

But Reports Reaching Hong Kong Say That More Freedom Is Now Allowed

By GREG MacGREGOR
Special to The New York Times

HONG KONG, Aug. 11—The invitations from Peiping asking fifteen American correspondents (later increased to eighteen) to spend a month in Communist China came as a complete surprise to the press corps here. At the time the invitations were received many American newsmen who usually make their headquarters in Hong Kong were traveling in other parts of the world.

The United States State Department rejected immediately upon receipt all applications for visas to Communist China on the ground that official approval for travel could not be granted so long as United States citizens were being held in Chinese Communist jails.

Open to All

An official list of American captives still detained in China contains the names of ten men, seven of whom are priests. Recent reports from Peiping indicate that the policy toward these prisoners is easing in most cases. Thomas Phillips, a Catholic priest recently released by the Communists, said that American prisoners no longer were being held in jails. He said they were being held in a five-room two-story house in Shanghai and were being treated well. He said he believed visiting newsmen would be allowed to visit them.

At the week-end, a report from Peiping stated that numerous requests for admission to Communist China had been received from American journalists all over the world. The Peiping Government added that any qualified American journalist who complied with formalities of application would be approved for entrance to the mainland "soon." With the exception of the eighteen invited, however, all would be required to pay their own living and traveling expenses.

Conditions Improved

From the experiences of British and French correspondents who have operated recently behind the Bamboo Curtain, it could be concluded that conditions for news coverage have been improved but still have a long way to go before they are satisfactory.

Crawford in the Newark News

"See for yourself, we've nothing to hide."

Difficulties in reaching many high-ranking Chinese Communist leaders create one major problem and language difficulties create another. While it is true that interpreters can be obtained, there is a strong suspicion held by working newspapermen that loyalty to the Government or fear reduces reliability. Interviews on any level are suspect because of the apparent fear of possible reprisals for unwise or critical comments.

Correspondents have also found that much of their news comes second hand from the information ministry after it has been broadcast to the world over the short-wave radio. They do believe, however, that unless the Chinese Communist attitude toward the foreign press is changed considerably, adequate news coverage of Communist China is a definite possibility within six months to a year after the entrance of a large group of foreign newsmen.

In describing a typical recent trip across the border from Hong Kong, one correspondent here said that he was met by a representative of the China Travel Service at the railroad station in Kowloon, on the southern tip of the mainland in the British leased Hong Kong territory, and escorted to the border.

With an English-speaking guide he visited Canton, Shanghai and Peiping. He reported that, for the most part, accommodations were good and he was treated courteously.

Later the newsman was allowed to visit Manchuria. He said he had met with almost no travel restrictions. He said that on several occasions he had lost patience with the bureaucratic demands and had written dispatches containing strong criticism. He learned later they had been passed without deletion of a single word.

* * *

February 10, 1957

RUSSIA IS RICH IN RUMORS BUT FACTS ARE HARD TO GET

Tall Tales Thrive, Nourished on Secrecy and Hidden Behind Veil of Censorship

By WILLIAM J. JORDEN
Special to The New York Times

MOSCOW, Feb. 9—When conversation palls the favorite gambit at Moscow cocktail parties is to say, "Excuse me. I have to go to collect a few rumors." Unfortunately there is more truth than fiction in that cynical remark. An appalling amount of time is taken up here trying to separate the grain of truth from the chaff of wild reports.

There are perfectly good reasons why more rumors are spread in and about the Soviet Union than in and about any other part of the world. For one thing, rumors are more likely to concern important or notorious persons or groups or countries than the insignificant. Second, it is axiomatic that rumors flourish about the unknown or little known. Finally it would seem to be human nature to spread more rumors about those we dislike or distrust or fear than about those we like or regard indifferently.

New in Soviet

One major difficulty concerns the vast difference between Western and Communist concepts of truth and the function of spreading information. It should be understood that for the Soviet Union as for all Communist states no news is "good" unless it actively promotes the interests of the state and the prevailing system. That is why every newspaper and radio station, every magazine and book is the product either of the Government or one of the organizations of the Communist party itself or officially sponsored groups like the trade unions or cooperatives. What appears in these publications or what is heard on the air is all carefully screened for content, and editors who fail to understand what is required of them can expect a stern rebuke.

A foreigner's contacts with any governmental organization—and in a Communist state there are virtually no non-governmental organizations—must be made through official channels. News reports sent abroad—like this one—pass through the hands of Soviet censors before they are transmitted. That censorship has eased considerably since the days of Stalin but it still operates, often killing rumors but just as often killing reports that would squelch rumors.

Spy Scare

Moreover, the Soviet Union is now in the midst of a "vigilance campaign" in which Russians are being told that "imperialists" are busily engaged in ferreting out all this country's secrets. One effect has been to cause Soviet citizens to think twice before they associate freely with or talk to foreigners.

Official limitations on free search for truth create an atmosphere in which the wildest kind of rumors are born and flourish. Lack of information from Moscow in turn tends to generate wilder rumors abroad.

A good example of this occurred last week when a German physician, a specialist in circulatory diseases, came here at the request of the Soviet Government to treat a member of the Government. Rumors sprang to life. Here and abroad names of several of the Soviet Union's leaders were mentioned. The rumors followed their usual course—the man named as possibly the patient became probably the patient in retelling and finally *was* the patient.

Typical Rumor

A story attributed to "intelligence sources" in a Western capital said that one member of the Presidium had been shot on orders of two others. That story, known to be false to every reporter here, was allowed to stay alive for many hours because of the reluctance of anyone in authority here to deny it and of censors to release stories on the subject. The patient has since been identified in the Western press but not in stories passed by the Soviet censor.

A favorite subject of rumors here and abroad is the position and prestige of members of the Soviet Union's leading circle, the Presidium. A vast majority of these rumors are completely false or very misleading. During the past year reports here and abroad have had almost every member of the ruling body enjoying enlarged power or on the verge of being purged. Some of these reports are written with little qualification and one might be led to think that the authors had a tape recorder under the Kremlin's conference table.

Wishful Rumors Spread

There seem to be large elements of wishful thinking in many of the rumors that circulate about the Soviet Union. The tendency is strong in some persons to hear a rumor, to find it true, to hear another similar rumor and assume it indicates a widespread trend.

Labor difficulties appear to some competent observers to be in this category. Some accounts in the West gave the impression that a massive wave of labor unrest was sweeping across the Soviet Union and threatened the functioning of Soviet industry. That does not appear be true on the basis of the best information available here.

Rumors are born in a variety of ways. Some of them come from Soviet citizens, some from foreign Communists close to leading groups here. Others start with observations of foreigners. Some may be deliberately planted.

"In the old days," a veteran of the worst era of the "cold war" and earlier said recently "rumors meant a lot more than they do now. When Stalin was around people just didn't gossip loosely. The penalties were too high. If you heard a rumor then you could be almost sure it had some basis in fact. Now people feel less afraid to talk. But the result is it's getting harder and harder to separate good rumors from bad."

Any real solution of the problem created by the prevalence of rumors about the Soviet Union would appear to depend on a drastic change in at attitude on the part of the Soviet Government itself—a change that does not now seem to be very likely. Freer access to first-hand information would be the best cure for the disease. Elimination of censorship could be another important step.

Better Understanding

It probably would mean fewer rumors in the long run. The Kremlin leaders have talked about improving understanding between themselves and the rest of the world. But there is no sign that they are willing to take the obviously fundamental steps which could lead to a better understanding though not necessarily to closer friendship. Meanwhile the rumor mill grinds on.

You can never tell, however, when the Soviet Union might decide to change its attitude. Why, I heard from a very good source only this week that. . . .

* * *

May 5, 1957

POLAND IMPOSING PRESS UNIFORMITY

Periodicals Being Reshaped to Fill Role of Unswerving Backers of Party Policy

By SYDNEY GRUSON
Special to The New York Times

WARSAW, May 4—The Polish press, which played a leading role in last year's political upheaval here, is slowly but surely being reshaped to fit the part of unquestioning supporter of the ruling Communist party's policy.

This is the way Wladyslaw Gomulka, first secretary of the United Workers (Communist) party, wants it. His objective is being achieved by the dismissal of newsmen and writers considered to be "revisionists" and by editorial changes in the papers considered to be lagging in their support of the First Secretary.

Starting with Trybuna Ludu, from which Wladyslaw Matwin was dismissed as editor in February, all the Warsaw newspapers and periodicals have been subjected to reorganization imposed openly or indirectly by M. Gomulka's aides in the Central Committee Secretariat.

Trybuna Ludu is the organ of the Central Committee. Hopes that the same orthodoxy would not be demanded of non-party newspapers have proved in vain.

Uniformity of the press is being imposed in the name of the part unity that M. Gomulka deems to be essential, if not for party survival, then for survival of the program adopted when he was restored to power last October.

Crusading Weekly Affected

Among the leaders to feel M. Gomulka's ire is Elegiusz Lasota, who gained international renown as editor of the crusading weekly Po Prostu. M. Lasota was not ousted directly. But the collegium or directing team of the newspaper, was persuaded that a change of editors was necessary and M. Lasota stepped down. He has been permitted to remain on thc collegium.

M. Gomulka has not hidden his opinion that the more liberal newspaper men and writers, whatever their merits before October, have played a destructive role since then. Premier Jozef Cyrankiewicz seems to have come to share this opinion and he is no longer counted by the Left Wing as its champion within the party Politburo.

According to M. Gomulka's views, as expressed by his aides in recent meetings with newspapermen, the press is responsible for maintaining an atmosphere of uncertainty and discontent in the country and of sharpening acknowledged divisions within the party.

The press has been charged with withholding support from M. Gomulka by refusing to write articles endorsing his position on certain important issues, as on the limited authority he would permit workers' councils to exercise. Newspapers also are criticized for having failed to pick up and develop the leads Mr. Gomulka is said to have given in his speeches.

The Communist party's right wing, usually labeled as Stalinist, has been emboldened by the anti-press campaign to the embarrassment of the national leaders. A prime example of this came in a recent Warsaw regional party meeting that dismissed the editor and deputy editor of the party's main regional paper, Trybuna Mazowiecka.

Trybuna Ludu described the meeting as "a biased and frequently brutal dispute" in which Stalinist methods dominated. A characteristic note of the discussion, Trybuna Ludu said, was: "You wanted October—well, you have it."

This attitude illustrates a major argument of the Right against M. Gomulka on the question of the press.

* * *

June 16, 1957

RED CHINA PRESS CHAFES SLIGHTLY

Editors, at Unusual Meeting, Say They Are More Free but Decry Party Curbs

By GREG MacGREGOR
Special to The New York Times

HONG KONG, June 13—Leading editors of Communist China's newspaper are much less restricted now than they were two years ago, but they are not satisfied with the conditions under which they must publish.

Following the new party line of "letting all flowers bloom together and letting diverse schools of thought contend," mainland journalists held an unusual two-day symposium last month to discuss their grievances and proposals to end them.

Reports of the editors' cautious comments reached here today.

An editor of a leading mainland daily said that political dogmatism was hampering publishers and editors alike.

Readability Held Improved

He was Chin Chung-Hua, of Hsin Wen Jih Pao, a prominent morning paper in Shanghai, who said that the new policy deserved recognition for allowing editors to make newspapers more readable, thereby increasing circulation.

But he warned of inhibitions imposed by politicians and bureaucrats.

"Our minds are still imbued with dogmatism," he said, "and we are confronted with rules and taboos as well as some pressure exerted by society. This is a contradiction we newspaper workers now face in our minds."

Mr. Chin said that since the new party line of more freedom of expression had been adopted last year, newspaper circles in Shanghai had become more alive ideologically.

"But while newspaper reporters have demonstrated greater push, they have also met greater deterrence," he complained.

Many people in the Communist Chinese Government have not paid enough attention to the new policy of accepting diverse schools of thought, he said. This, combined with the difficulty encountered by many newspaper workers in freeing themselves mentally from years of bondage under influences of dogmatism, has caused trouble, he went on.

"As a result, they have been too cautious about criticizing too much in their writings for fear of inviting interference from higher levels," he added.

Mr. Chin said that too often political leaders had ignored the press when explanations of Government activities would have been of service to the public.

Intra-Office Conflicts Cited

Interpretation of party leadership over newspaper work by some cadres has bred negative factors, he added. He said it was well known that many nonparty members worked side by side with party members in newspaper offices and that although these relations had been good in general, there had been cases of wide dissension.

Another well-known journalist, Chen Ming-teh, chief editor of Shanghai Hsin Wen Pao, complained that of the total number of 205 newspapers being published in Red China, 200 were party organs. He said that there were far too few nonparty newspapers and far too many "officials" in the newspaper business in Red China.

Mr. Chen added that units were low in efficiency and poor in quality and that many persons advocated reinstatement of "old school" journalists.

"A conference room handout can only serve as a museum piece," the editor commented.

* * *

August 17, 1958

FOCUS OF THE KREMLIN'S SECRECY OBSESSION

In Moscow's Massive Central Telegraph Office Unseen Censors Decide What News Every Foreign Correspondent in Russia May—and May Not—Report to the Outside World

By DANIEL SCHORR

Through one door—Entrance No. 10, the international communications section, of Moscow's Central Telegraph Office—enters all the news about the Soviet Union intended for dispatch to the non-Communist world by a corps of some thirty correspondents.

Not all of the 50,000 words or so a day that pour into this funnel come out the other end, to be channeled to the West. For the copy is scanned first by an unseen band, the men and/or women of *Glavit*—literally, the "Literary Bureau," actually the title of Russia's censorship.

The "bourgeois" correspondents who may, on occasion, spend half their waking hours first writing and then waiting at the *Tsentralni Telegraf* for copy that returns sometimes late, sometimes mangled, even not at all, were astonished not long ago to learn that Mikhail Menshikov, Soviet Ambassador to the United States, had said, on American television, that there was no censorship in the Soviet Union.

Not only is Russia the sole Communist-ruled country today that maintains official surveillance of outgoing news, but its censorship has reached a point of severity described by American correspondents as the most oppressive in recent years. Their comments on Mr. Menshikov's bland remark would have been picturesque; they would also have been censored.

The current toughness of *Glavit's* censors is a significant indication of Russia's relations with the world. The information these censors try to conceal—as well as the information they decide to reveal—provides clues to the thinking of the men in the Kremlin. The existence of the censorship system in itself suggests that this thinking is imbued with an obsessive sense of secrecy that stems from an ingrained fear and lack of self-confidence.

Through coded (and uncensored) communications from the United States Embassy in Moscow, the State Department has gathered examples of recent censorial arbitrariness. Some of them were disclosed in a speech by Andrew Berding, Assistant Secretary for Public Affairs:

> Correspondents were not permitted to quote an unflattering biography of Gen. Charles de Gaulle published in the Great Soviet Encyclopedia.
>
> All stories noting that the birthday of former Premier Nikolai I. Bulganin had gone publicly unnoticed this year were eliminated.
>
> In reporting the proposal for a nonaggression pact with the West made by the Warsaw Pact meeting in Moscow, correspondents were not permitted to recall that the Soviet Union had pre-war nonaggression agreements with the Baltic states (which were subsequently annexed).
>
> Remarks unfavorable to medical and health conditions in Russia were excised from reports of a Moscow news conference given by a delegation of American women physicians who had toured the U. S. S. R.

Glavit has changed somewhat since wartime days, when correspondents could meet and argue with the censors. Today, censorship is exercised impersonally and invisibly, behind closed doors.

The mechanics of censorship works this way: The correspondent submits his dispatch or broadcast script in triplicate at the cable receiving desk. A clerk registers it in her book, then takes it to the near-by censors' room. Apparently there are separate censors handling copy in English, French, German and Italian and, it would seem, they operate in shifts on a twenty-four-hour schedule.

In anything from ten minutes to two days the clerk returns to the correspondent a carbon copy of his dispatch, bearing the censor's rubber stamp. It may have been cleared without change or there may be words, lines or whole paragraphs crossed out in heavy black pencil. If the dispatch is not returned at all, it has been killed. When there is an unusual delay, the clerk will usually advise the correspondent if his story is still under consideration or if it is "dead." But "death," in this case is not always permanent; a week later the censor's instructions may have changed and the same dispatch, if resubmitted, may pass.

Cable copy is transmitted automatically when it has cleared censorship. The correspondent learns of deletions only after the dispatch is on its way to his home office. Then, he may try to send "inserts" to bridge hiatuses or he may, in disgust at the mangling cable his office to scrap the dispatch. News intended for transmission by telephone or broadcast can be sent only after the correspondent has his copy back from the censor. If in dictating he departs from the approved version, his telephone line or radio circuit may be cut. There is no explanation of deletions and no avenue of appeal—or hardly any. On rare occasions an outraged correspondent has sent a hole to the censor explaining his authority for a statement—perhaps even submitting a copy of the publication he quoted—and has had the pleasure of seeing the censor reverse himself.

The unpredictability and inconsistency of censorial action is a constant irritant. An item of information may be passed in one correspondent's copy and deleted from another's. This is partly attributable to the human factor—a change of work shift, bringing a slightly different interpretation of the rules, or a prohibition that reaches the censor after the first dispatches have moved.

Who the censors are, how they are chosen, whether men or women—these questions have been subjects of endless, and sometimes bitter, speculation among correspondents, waiting into the night as dinners get cold and faraway editors get hot. It is believed that most of the censors are men, judging from the heavy hand (literally, as well as figuratively) with which they wield the black pencil.

They appear to be well educated and academically versed in the languages they handle. But idiomatic subtleties frequently escape them, as one correspondent showed when he used this device to cast doubt on the authenticity of an announced, Soviet reduction in armed forces. He wrote: "Tell this to our soldiers, tell it to the sailors and, above all tell it to the marines!"

The censors, it is assumed, are Communist party members and of fairly high civil service rank. They appear to have quick access to high-echelon guidance, when needed. They obviously have advance information on important news breaks.

The censor is concerned, primarily, not with accuracy, but with the promotion of Soviet interests. With the greatest equanimity, the censor will approve an incorrect dispatch if it adds to Russia's prestige. For example, correspondents were permitted to file rumors that the dog in Sputnik No. 2 had been recovered alive, and a story that a rocket had been fired carrying a man—dispatches which the censors knew, or could easily prove, to be inaccurate. With equal equanimity, the censor kills many completely accurate stories if they do not reflect credit on the U. S. S. R. or if they indicate instability in the regime.

Because the rules seem to change from time to time, it is difficult to fix a pattern of what is censorable. But, over a long period, it can be concluded that the following are categories of information least likely to succeed with the censor:

1. Indications of internal unrest or discontent.
2. Suggestions of disharmony between the Soviet Union and other members of the Communist bloc.
3. Speculation on antagonisms among Soviet leaders, possible removals from power, illness or unexplained absences of the top members of the hierarchy.
4. Military information about the Soviet Union, including what is plainly visible to the observer.
5. Unflattering personal references to Soviet leaders—a rule so inflexible that it is difficult to report even that Khrushchev is *not* an habitual drunkard.

6. References to the M. V. D. (secret police) or any other organs of internal security, or their activities, such as arrests and sentences to labor camps.
7. References to censorship itself, particularly to the toughening of censorship during certain periods.

Information is normally privileged if it comes from a Soviet publication or other official source, but this is not invariably true. The censor may excise a quotation if he does not like the context in which it is used. Thus, General de Gaulle's official biography became *verboten* because the Soviet Government's attitude toward him shifted. Similarly, when Marshal Tito of Yugoslavia visited Russia in 1956, I was not permitted to recall, in connection with the dismissal of Vyacheslav M. Molotov as Foreign Minister, that he had signed the 1948 letter denouncing Tito.

Censorship extends not only to paragraphs, but to individual sentences, and even single words, and may, blatantly or subtly, alter the emphasis the correspondent is trying to give. Following are some examples of excisions from my cables and broadcasts during "normal" periods of censorship. The deletions are shown in brackets:

April 24, 1956, in a broadcast analyzing the significance of a new decree ending the absolute powers for Soviet investigative agencies:

"The latest in a series of moves to convince the public that the day of terror [the police state] and arbitrary action are ended is a decree setting up a division in the Chief Prosecutor's office as a watchdog over investigating agencies. Many of those condemned without adequate trial under Stalin and Beria are being rehabilitated [most of them posthumously]. Convictions on the basis of confessions alone have been branded as illegal, and the late Andrei Vishinsky [who practiced that kind of prosecution in some famous cases] has been denounced."

May 11, 1956, in a report on a decree permitting workers to leave their jobs:

"This is the longest stride yet taken in liberalization within the Soviet Union. It implies that a Soviet citizen, for the first time, is free [if not to choose his own job, at least] to quit a job he does not like."

These are examples of "normal" censorship—unpalatable, but understandable. There are, however phases of extraordinary censorship when the censor, usually only for a few days, simply sits on all copy pending an awaited decision, then follows a policy of maximum vigilance discouraging speculation and interpretation.

Such periods accompanied the upheaval following Khrushchev's "secret" denunciation of Stalin in his epoch-making speech at the February, 1956, party Congress, the crisis with Poland and Hungary in October–November, 1956, the Malenkov-Molotov-Kaganovich-Shepilov purge in June–July, 1957, and the later Zhukov purge.

At the outset of the de-Stalinization period, the censor seemed to have no consistent policy. One could quote denunciations of Stalin which called him "arbitrary," but not those which called him "tyrannical." One could quote a Russian worker who said, "I still think Stalin was a great man," but not quote a taxi-driver who said, "They talk about him this way now that he is dead. But if he were alive . . . ."

Khrushchev's party Congress speech denouncing Stalin, though known to hundreds of thousands in the Soviet Union and the satellites through party meetings, could not be mentioned in news dispatches for two weeks. After a text of the speech was published abroad, correspondents could confirm that there had been such an address, but still were not allowed to quote from it.

Unauthorized pro-Stalin demonstrations in his native state of Georgia led to rioting that was suppressed with scores of casualties. Moscow correspondents could neither quote reports of foreign eyewitnesses nor make any reference to the troubles.

The first three paragraphs of a dispatch I wrote on March 16, based on reports from diplomatic sources of student demonstrations in Tiflis, capital of Georgia, of machine-gun fire by police, and of the ban on previously scheduled visits to Tiflis by foreigners, were suppressed. Only the last paragraph was in part retained:

"Meanwhile, in Moscow, and reportedly many other parts of the country, there is considerable discussion of Khrushchev's speech about 'The Cult of the Individual' at a restricted session of the party Congress. Party members are being briefed at meetings [but it seems likely that the authorities will feel obliged to make a public statement soon]."

The total dispatch, as released, thus consisted of a paragraph, beginning with "Meanwhile"—a slip the censor does not usually make. He must have been under stress, too.

The next period of "maximum" censorship started with Poland's peaceful revolution against Stalinism in October, 1956, and continued through the Hungarian rebellion. We were not permitted to report the visit of Khrushchev and other Soviet leaders to Warsaw until it was officially announced in Moscow, although it had already been disclosed from Warsaw.

The censorship "freeze" reached its peak when Soviet tanks moved into Budapest to crush the Hungarian rebellion. I could not report the simple fact, on Nov. 4, 1956, that no word had yet been given to the Soviet people of the attack on Budapest. On Nov. 5, United States Ambassador Charles E. Bohlen asked Khrushchev, at a reception, if he planned to reinforce Soviet forces in Hungary. Khrushchev replied pugnaciously, "We think it will not be necessary, but if it is, we will send in more and more and more." The part of the sentence beginning with "but" was deleted from my broadcast script.

Here are typical deletions in one paragraph of a broadcast on Nov. 9:

"The Russians have been given few details of what is happening in Hungary [but they have learned from long experience how to read between the lines]. And what they have read has made a profound impression. They are eager for more information than has been given them. [At the Lenin Library, the other night, several hundred young persons walked out on a lecturer who declined to answer their questions about Hungary and Poland.]"

A tough period of censorship came again in July, 1957, when Khrushchev fended off an attempt to unseat him and purged his opponents—Malenkov, Molotov, Kaganovich and Shepilov. The first solid indication of what was afoot came on July 3, when Pravda printed an ominous editorial saying the party would not tolerate "any anti-party groups." The censor permitted direct quotations from Pravda, but no interpretation of their significance.

Word of the decision circulated through Moscow during the afternoon, but the censor would not permit correspondents to file it. One news agency arranged to have it telephoned out by a tourist from his hotel room. Other correspondents had to wait until 1 A. M. on July 4 for an official announcement that would lift the censorship boom—only to be beaten by Moscow Radio, which had broadcast the news abroad two hours earlier.

Thereafter, the censors bore down hard on stories attempting to interpret the events. No reference could be made to the vote against Khrushchev in the Presidium that precipitated the purge. No mention could be made of the role of Marshal Zhukov, whose support of Khrushchev in the party Central Committee turned the tide in his favor. Nor could the reaction of the average Russians be reflected. Here is how the censor handled my script of July 4:

"Newspapers today report that the big shake-up is getting unanimous approval at party meetings throughout the country. [As to the average Russian, who learned about it from his paper this morning, the reaction is shock and amazement that revered old Bolsheviks like Molotov are suddenly out, accused of fighting the party they so long served.] What the future of the ousted leaders is, it is hard to say . . . [Khrushchev, with his new Presidium, appears to have cleaned out the heritage of Stalin; the old guard is gone.] The post-Stalin policies move ahead with the brakes off."

Another "freeze" came during the purge of Marshal Zhukov last October. A two-line newspaper item, as he returned from a trip to Yugoslavia, said he had been dropped as Defense Minister. For two days it was impossible for us to report anything else. Not until a week later was the Central Committee resolution condemning Zhukov and stripping him of his party positions announced.

Why the Soviet Union, which vaunts its power and its indifference to "bourgeois slander," persists in maintaining a censorship that its weaker satellites and Red China forego has never been adequately explained. It is far from foolproof protection against the seepage of such "secrets" or embarrassing information as may become known to Westerners, which, as the Soviet Government well knows, are carried abroad by travelers or transmitted by embassies.

The persistence of censorship can only be explained in terms of ingrained suspicion, the durability of bureaucratic controls and the relative immunity of Russia's internal security apparatus to new currents of thought.

Censorship at the Central Telegraph Office is really only the final stage of the process. It starts at the top of the Communist hierarchy, which is disposed not to reveal anything unless there is a good propaganda reason for doing so. It continues with the average Russian, who has learned from prison sentences under Stalin for "rumor-mongering" that it is not safe to disclose or discuss anything—especially with a foreigner—until it has been officially announced. As Charles E. Bohlen, former United States Ambassador to Moscow, once put it, "Russia is hard to understand not because it is a mystery, but because it is a secret."

The sense of secrecy is all-pervasive. When I asked a Soviet scientist why sputnik launchings were not announced in advance, he said, "Because it would make an unfavorable impression if the launching failed. There is time enough to announce it when the sputnik is in orbit."

In the Soviet Union, fact has no objective meaning—only propaganda has. And the national inferiority complex is such that motives in reporting are always suspect. In a society based on controls, unhampered observation and free reporting create a sense of uneasiness.

Essentially, censorship springs from fear and distrust. The fear is heightened, of course, when there is something specific to hide—such as a wave of arrests in the Baltic states or the pro-Stalin rioting in Georgia. But, because the motives for censorship are basically irrational, there always is something to hide. For the Soviet Union considers it necessary to project an image of monolithic unity and steady progress. It feels it cannot afford to have a university student quoted as saying that young people felt uneasy about the suppression of the Hungarian rebellion. It feels that a visit by Khrushchev to Red China must be kept secret until it is known that the mission is accomplished—for basically the same reason that a sputnik cannot be announced until it is in orbit.

Some day this may change. Some day Soviet leaders may come to understand that censorship itself creates the impression of disarray that they are so anxious to avoid. But, until then, there will be many more frustrating, fretful nights for Western correspondents at the Tsentralni Telegraf.

Daniel Schorr, a staff member of CBS News, served as Moscow correspondent from September, 1956, to December, 1957, when he returned on assignment to this country. The Russians have failed to renew his visa.

* * *

January 9, 1961

PRESS IN POLAND WALKS THIN LINE

Interest of Reader Is on One Side, but Censor Is on the Other

By ARTHUR J. OLSEN
Special to The New York Times

CRACOW, Poland, Jan. 8—The Polish press, which produces the liveliest journalism in the Soviet bloc, has launched the celebration of its 300th birthday here.

In a house still standing on a square known as the Small Market, Jan Aleksander Gorczyn turned out the first Polish newspaper Jan. 3, 1661.

The tercentenary was marked by the unveiling of a memorial plaque in the wall of the Szeber House where the paper Merkuriuscz Polski was begun. This was the first of a series of anniversary ceremonies and exhibitions. The emphasis will be less on M. Gorczyn than on the achievements of the "democratic press" in Poland since it was revived in 1944.

Journalism in Poland has been assigned a mission—to "constructively contribute" to the building of socialism in Poland.

Press Mirrors Moods

Although back issues of the newspapers are an inadequate source of information on the last sixteen years of Polish history, the press has been a useful mirror of the moods of the regime.

During the Stalinist era of the early Nineteen Fifties, men and ideas marked for suppression were scourged in harsh polemics.

In the reform period of 1956, many Polish journalists tried to adopt the Western concept of independent observation of public affairs. Most of them are now paying for it in obscure jobs.

The Government censor demands a "constructive" attitude toward the regime, but he permits a broader range of opinion than any other shepherd of the written word in the Communist world.

This leaves an indistinct line of propriety that one crosses at his peril.

An Uncertain Life

The recent experiences of the weekly Polityka, the country's most pungent journal of opinion, illustrates the uncertain life of a Polish journalist.

At the moment, Polityka's editor is Mieczeslaw Rakowski, a rising young member of the Communist party, who has been able to make orthodoxy interesting.

As an editor, M. Rakowski has been an innovator with a fresh and occasionally brash touch. In this spirit last year he employed Jerzy Andrzejewski to write a weekly "diary."

M. Andrzejewski, one of Poland's best-known post-war novelists, had fallen in official esteem after turning in his party card in the wake of the 1956 reform.

In one "diary" entry last October M. Andrzejewski criticized capital punishment, likening its advocates to persons with a thirst for blood. This stirred the wrath of the powerful Public Prosecutor's office, which had just begun to demand the death penalty for such crimes as embezzling.

The novelist no longer writes for Polityka. M. Rakowski was suspended, reinstated, dismissed and—a few days after he had published a virulent attack on the United States in a trade-union paper—returned to the editor's chair M. Rakowski's ups and downs became a high level party affair.

HAD WEEKLY COLUMN: Jerzy Andrzejewski, Polish novelist. He had "diary" published in Polityka, a Polish journal of opinion.

No Trouble for Some

No such difficulties arise for Poland's senior newspaper, Trybuna Ludu, and its companion monthly magazine, Novy Drogi. These journals are the authorized voice of the Central Committee of the Polish United Workers (Communist) party.

Trybuna Ludu has correspondents in Washington, London, Paris, Bonn, Moscow, Peiping and other capitals.

Their reports, supplemented by the file of the official Polish press agency, give a broad if spotty coverage of world news. With a little help from abroad, a reader can get a fair idea of what is happening in the world from Trybuna Ludu's eight pages.

* * *

March 24, 1961

MOSCOW RELAXES NEWS CENSORSHIP

Gives Up Curb on Outgoing Dispatches, but Reporter Is Still Accountable

By OSGOOD CARUTHERS
Special to The New York Times

MOSCOW, March 23—The Soviet Union abolished today its prior censorship on outgoing news dispatches.

Correspondents were warned that they would be held fully responsible for the transmission of reports that the authorities considered incorrect or in the field of rumor.

Government controls over the sources of news, of incoming news and of all Soviet communications media continue in full force.

There was no indication that restrictions on domestic travel by foreigners would be lifted. However, Mikhail A. Kharlamov, press chief of the Foreign Ministry, said these were a matter for discussion between governments.

The action affects reporters and news broadcasters of the non-Communist press radio and television. Foreign Communist newsmen, although subject to their own form of administrative and party discipline, had not been the objects of direct censorship.

The controls, which had been in force, with two brief interruptions, from the time of the Bolshevik Revolution in 1917—in fact, there has been censorship in Russia since the early eighteenth century—partly inspired the term Iron Curtain. Their abolition was interpreted here as an indication of the Soviet Union's increasing self-confidence and its gains in prestige through the world.

Indeed, the halting of the arbitrary controls itself could be counted upon to improve the international standing of Premier Khrushchev's rule.

The announcement of the abolition, made at a news conference called by Mr. Kharlamov, followed a fortnight of widespread rumors that such a move was contemplated.

Mr. Kharlamov said that nothing had been worked out on the relaxation of controls over photographs going abroad, but that it would be considered. The authorities have not adhered too rigidly to the rule and have generally tended to look the other way when undeveloped film was carried by persons leaving the country.

Mr. Kharlamov would not discuss the broad, and indeed dramatic, political implications of the Kremlin's decision.

Term 'Censorship' Avoided

No news of the censorship action was reported to the Soviet public. Only the English-language transmission of the official Soviet press agency, Tass, which is for foreign consumption, carried a brief notice.

Soviet authorities have always avoided the term "censorship." They followed Mr. Khrushchev's practice of asserting that foreign news dispatches were subject to "correction" to "help" foreign correspondents avoid sending false news.

Not once did Mr. Kharlamov use the word censorship during his half-hour news conference before the 100-odd foreign correspondents in Moscow. He said in an opening statement merely that because of the large increase in the number of foreign correspondents—to a total of almost 150, he said—it had been decided to take measures "to facilitate communications between the correspondents and their editors at home."

"From this day forward correspondents will be able to use these facilities both at the Central Telegraph Agency in Moscow and by telephone direct from the offices, homes and hotel rooms of the correspondents," he said.

Copies Must Be Kept

The implication was that because of the growth of the foreign in press corps, the work of Glavlit, the official name of the censorship bureau, which operated unseen and unreachable behind a green door at the Central Telegraph Agency, had become so overwhelming that it was no longer possible to give good service.

Mr. Kharlamov, in warning the foreign press that "the whole responsibility for incorrect rumors will rest on the correspondents themselves," asked them to keep copies of their dispatches until the end of their stays "in case any misunderstanding on your reports may arise."

With regard to this sort of indirect censorship, which is similar to that prevailing in other Eastern European countries, Mr. Kharlamov avoided putting himself in the position of having laid down a set of taboos.

The action facilitates the mechanics of sending news from the Soviet Union. It had been required that all material be handed in at the Central Telegraph Agency. Only when the copy had been returned with Glavlit's stamp of approval—a broken arrow in the form of a lightning bolt inside a circle—could it be transmitted.

Although there were efforts to maintain the sense of sentences when cuts were made, the material often returned with paragraphs excised or with the whole article made meaningless. On more sensitive reports, there were times when the reporter would not get his copy at all or only after long delay, and then with extensive excisions.

Under Stalin, direct censorship was lifted in May, 1939, but it was reinstated that September at the outbreak of the Finnish war. At the end of World War II, Stalin again lifted censorship, for only about two weeks.

There seems to be no prospect that there will be a free flow of news into the Soviet Union in the foreseeable future. Soviet publications, films and broadcasts will remain under the watchful eye of the internal Glavlit (a contraction of the words meaning Main Literary Administration), which works under the aegis of the party hierarchy.

In recent weeks, correspondents have noticed more and more liberal treatment although it still was not possible to report suggestions of political friction between the Soviet Union and Communist China or similar political topics.

In general, the thing that most harassed foreign correspondents during the censorship was their inability to balance claims of economic and social successes with pertinent negative information.

With regard to travel, correspondents must ask permission to go beyond forty kilometers (twenty-five miles) from Moscow.

Persistent in Many Countries

Censorship in one form or another persists in many countries.

Even in Western Europe, official efforts often are made in France, West Germany and other countries to withhold, tone down or control news. This is a sort of censorship at the source, and it exists even in some sectors of Government in the United States.

In the Middle East censors from time to time use the blue pencil on outgoing news in Iraq, Jordan, Lebanon and Saudi Arabia. Israel has military censorship. Censorship is invoked at times in various African countries.

There is one-party government in many countries, and this often results in a press under the Government's thumb. This is true in Spain and Portugal as well as the United Arab Republic.

Outgoing news generally flows unhampered from Asia, except for Communist China, North Vietnam and North Korea, areas seldom opened to non-Communist newsmen.

In Latin America censorship frequently has been imposed on foreign correspondents in times of civil strife, but usually news is sent out freely.

* * *

March 24, 1961

CENSORS IN SOVIET HAD 43-YEAR SWAY

Curb on News Flow Abroad Removed Only Twice Since the Bolshevik Revolution

The Soviet Union was the only Communist country to censor news dispatches of non-Communist correspondents and it had done so throughout most of its forty-three-year history.

The elimination of this direct control over dispatches and broadcasts yesterday apparently reflects a decision that the threat of reprimand and expulsion, as employed in other Eastern European capitals, imposes adequate restraint.

Although Western newsmen in Moscow will continue to be subjected to many professional and personal restrictions, the lifting of direct censorship should permit them to send a greater variety of material in the future.

It remains to be seen to what extent the correspondents in Moscow will feel compelled to be their own censors. They will have to balance every dispatch against the possibilities of expulsion.

Hitherto the unofficial remarks even of Premier Khrushchev and other leaders were often delayed or eliminated. Man-in-the-street comment contrary to Soviet policy was never permitted. News of air crashes and other disasters and of crimes, when available normally could not be transmitted.

Soviet Sensibilities

Attempts to interpret political or economic developments on the spot almost always had difficulty passing the censors. Even items like the convening of a meeting of the Communist party's Central Committee were stopped until they had been disclosed to the Soviet people.

Many restrictions derived from Soviet sensibilities about the country's image abroad. Sometimes even shabby wooden homes and muddy roads could not be described as such. More often the trouble arose because the unseen censors were imposing regulations drawn up for Soviet publications.

In recent years the censorship was administered by an organization called Glavlit, a contraction of the Russian words for Main Literary Administration. Its operations were highly secret, but it is believed to have representatives still in the offices of major Soviet newspapers and publishing houses.

Under the pressure of a new generation of Soviet writers led by Aleksei I. Adzhubei the editor of Izvestia and Mr. Khrushchev's son-in-law, Moscow newspapers have recently been departing from the stereotyped formats of the Stalin years. It is possible that the new rules reflect a wider reorganization of Glavlit operations.

The first Soviet censorship was decreed within a fortnight of the Bolshevik seizure of power on Nov. 7, 1917. At the outset it applied only to telegraph copy, and newsmen were able to mail or telephone copy at will, with only an occasional reprimand.

Guides Were Censors

The censorship varied in degree. In the Twenties and Thirties it was not unusual for the few Western newsmen to be close friends of the censors and to have a chance to argue the case for their dispatches. Controls were lifted briefly in the summer of 1939 but reimposed at the outbreak of the Soviet-Finnish war.

During World War II the press department of the Foreign Ministry performed the censorship. Guides who led correspondents to front-line areas also checked their dispatches. Here again argument sometimes helped.

After the war, censorship was again lifted for less than a month. Stalin, like Mr. Khrushchev, followed foreign coverage of Soviet affairs and, more frankly, insisted that it was necessary to protect the nation from "slanders."

Mr. Khrushchev and his aides never acknowledged the existence of censorship. When forced to discuss it, especially on their tour of the United States, they tried to pass it off as a mere check for "accuracy" and a control on rumors.

At the Central Telegraph Agency, some articles were cleared as fast as they were written, a page at a time, some were held for hours, some for days and weeks. Some were never returned. Correspondents could send notes of complaint after their copy, but only rarely were they able to restore an excision.

The Glavlit censors also monitored telephone calls and radio broadcasts. Normally, any deviation from previously approved copy led to disconnection.

The lifting of censorship will not automatically make more news available to Westerners in Moscow. All contacts with public officials, whether in universities, hospitals, theatres, factories or the Government itself, must be channeled through special agencies. More often than not requests for information or interviews are delayed for weeks or months or never acted upon.

The situation for Soviet newsmen in the United States has been different in that they are not held responsible here for what they write.

However, the United States, in retaliation for Soviet travel restrictions, has closed off large areas to Soviet reporters. But the State Department has repeatedly—the last time in January—requested that the Soviet Union lift its restrictions or at least ease them in part. These requests have elicited no response.

* * *

May 15, 1964

NEWS FOR POLES ISN'T FOR REGIME

People Distrust Press, Seek Items Warsaw Won't Use

By PAUL UNDERWOOD
Special to The New York Times

WARSAW, May 4—Hundreds of people in Warsaw were convinced today that Aleksander Zawadzki is dead, a belief that makes clear what Poles think of what they are told about what goes on in their country.

Mr. Zawadzki is chairman of Poland's State Council and therefore nominal chief of state. He was operated on in a Warsaw hospital a couple of weeks ago for an intestinal obstruction and, according to official word, has been progressing satisfactorily.

The Polish radio reported over the weekend that a delegation of Silesian miners—Mr. Zawadzki was once a miner—had visited him in the hospital.

It was to no avail. Poles smiled significantly and insisted that they knew better, that he was really dead and that the Government did not say so for some reason of its own, possibly not to spoil the May Day holiday.

This apparent willingness to believe any report, however received, as long as it is not official could be described as almost a Polish national trait.

Control Is Traditional

It undoubtedly is partly a product of history. Poles for generations have lived mostly under occupation or dictatorial regimes that permitted the press to print only what seemed useful.

The fact that the present Communist Government controls all means of spreading information makes it also suspect. The average Pole is well aware that the Government considers as "non-news" a variety of subjects he is interested in.

Anything touching on the internal affairs of the ruling party, for example, is "non-news." It goes unmentioned in the press unless the regime decides for its own reasons that something should be said.

Any incidents indicating dissatisfaction with or opposition to the regime's policies is also "non-news." No word ever appears in print about demonstrations against living or working conditions, although they occur.

Foreign newsmen who report "non-news" developments lay themselves open to official reprimand for relying on rumors. By official definition any report is a rumor unless it appears in the controlled press.

This attitude helps to make the average Pole the more willing to accept the stories bandied around Warsaw cafes. Most of them are false; a few turn out to be true.

Rumors on Party Struggle

There are a couple of current "non-news" rumors concerning developments in the power struggle now going on inside the party in advance of its national congress.

One is that a neo-Stalinist group in the party has prepared and circulated among other party members a pamphlet taking the Chinese side in the ideological dispute that is now splitting the Communist world.

If true, this would be a thrust not only at the Russians but also at Wladyslaw Gomulka, the Polish party's First Secretary, who has publicly taken Moscow's side in the argument.

The second story is that a group on the liberal wing of the party has sent a letter around to other members criticizing the official line announced by the leadership for the coming congress. This group is reported to demand more flexible economic planning, greater decentralization and more cultural freedom.

Both these stories could be true. At least they seem logical in the given situation. But none of the Poles who insist that they are true can produce either of the documents.

* * *

June 27, 1964

CZECHS RELAX BAN ON WESTERN PAPERS

Special to The New York Times

PARIS, June 26—United States and other Western newspapers and magazines will be available in Czechoslovakia beginning Wednesday, according to an agreement reached today.

The accord was made between Viktor Lederer, a Czech postal official, and the International Circulation Managers Commission.

This will be the first display of non-Communist Western publications on newsstands in Czechoslovakia since the Communists seized the country in 1948. The agreement stipulates that the publications will be available for foreign visitors. But, as has happened elsewhere, it is expected that many of them will find their way into the hands of the citizenry.

The agreement was seen by diplomats as an important step in a loosening of East European subservience to Soviet ideological control. A similar arrangement exists with Poland and it is believed that others will soon be signed with Hungary and Rumania and that one will be concluded with Bulgaria before the end of the year.

The American publications that will go on sale in Czechoslovakia are the European editions of The New York Times, The New York Herald Tribune, Time, Newsweek, Life and Look.

A long list of British publications as well as some from France, West Germany, Italy and Austria also will be available.

* * *

Latin America

January 11, 1950

46 MORE PAPERS SHUT BY PERON COMMITTEE

Special to The New York Times

BUENOS AIRES, Jan. 10—José Visca, chairman of the joint Congressional committee investigating anti-Argentine activities, announced tonight the closing of forty-six more newspapers and periodicals on the ground that they did not properly display the fact that 1950 is "The Year of the Liberator, General San Martin."

The latest list, which brought the total publications closed for San Martin violations alone to more than fifty, included an independent daily, a German-language daily in Buenos Aires that has always taken a strong anti-Nazi line, and an Italian-language daily. The list also included the daily Tribuna, a peronista paper in Formosa, indicating nominally at least that pro-Government sheets are not spared.

Before leaving the capital for further investigations in the Province of Entre Rios, Señor Visca said tonight that the decision on reopening the papers might be deferred till May 1, when the next regular session of Congress opens.

* * *

September 17, 1952

BOGOTA EDITORS TWIT CENSOR WITH IRONY

By SAM POPE BREWER

Special to The New York Times

BOGOTA, Colombia, Sept. 16—Bogota newspapers, unable for obvious reasons to comment on the Government's new move to eliminate all controversial matter from the press, have found a means to call public attention to the situation.

They devoted their principal editorials yesterday to subjects apparently irrelevant to Colombia's present crisis.

El Diario Colombiano, which, like the Government, is Conservative but which differs with the Government on certain policies, used three columns of the page usually reserved for editorials for dissertation on the tourist attractions of St. Augustine, Fla. At the head of the article was an editorial note that said:

"For obvious reasons we welcome into these columns an article on the tourist attractions of a distant town. Tourist travel today has a vital interest. It not only stimulates the economy but broadens the view. We invite all our readers to go in search of new horizons."

The Liberal Opposition's El Tiempo did not dare at the present moment to equal the Conservative journal's irony, but it devoted its editorial space to two articles, the first on the fact that today was the anniversary of Guatemala's independence and the second, headed "Fear," discussing the use of fear as a characteristic totalitarian political instrument in the Soviet Union and Nazi Germany. No analogy was drawn to the present struggle here between the Conservative Government and the Liberal Opposition.

Even El Siglo, a newspaper owned by the titular President, Laureano Gomez, and directed by his son Alvaro, put its editorial tongue in cheek after having had two editorials stopped by the official censor. It devoted today's comment to "The Exportation of Rice" and "Pope Pius XII and Peace."

This second editorial, dealing with the Pope's statement that propaganda for peace had been abused by persons who used it as a cloak for their true motives—referring to the Communists—contained a remark by the editors that what the Pope said might well be applied to "some countries of the south," evidently referring to this one.

El Espectador Reappears

The newspaper El Espectador, which reappeared today for the first time since its plant was burned out by a mob on Sept. 6, found, like the rest of the press, that the intensified censorship, effective since Saturday night, was burdensome. It was forbidden to publish an account of the burning of its building.

Under the new rules censors are stopping not only all political commentaries but also all news about political parties. The authorities say the purpose is to prevent inflammatory articles that might lead to further violence, but the Liberals charge that the real purpose is to gag the Opposition press.

El Espectador published on Page 1 the text of a letter from the chief of censorship, Hernando de Velasco Alvarez, warning that any newspaper violating or evading censorship rules would be suspended immediately and could be indefinitely closed down.

The letter said the censors had orders to prevent the publication of anything that might cause "public unrest," including "aggressive editorials, alarming news, news and commentaries related to public order or military or police movements, criminal or administrative investigations being carried out, and any allusions to or commentaries on the events of Sept. 6."

In practice the censors are stopping all items relating to politics.

The two most important leaders of Colombia's Liberal party, now sheltered in the Venezuelan Embassy here, have decided to leave the country. Dr. Carlos Lleras Restrepo, a former Foreign Minister, has received a passport for Mexico, it was announced today. Former President Alfonso Lopez has not yet applied for a passport, but an associate said he would do so and the authorities had agreed to grant it. Dr. Lleras Restrepo is expected to go to the United States.

* * *

May 13, 1953

ARGENTINA HALTS RECEIPT OF NEWS BY THREE UNITED STATES AGENCIES

By EDWARD A. MORROW
Special to The New York Times

BUENOS AIRES, May 12—Anticipating the findings of a Congressional committee named to investigate the activities of three United States news agencies, the Ministry of Communications suspended today the agencies' communications licenses for reception of news dispatches from abroad.

The action brought to an end dissemination of world-wide news in Argentina by United States agencies and left Argentine newspapers dependent on Government services and those of Reuters, the British agency, and Agence France Presse. A third overseas agency, Ansa of Italy, has been making efforts to sign clients here.

In actual practice, today's move meant little. Ever since May 1, when President Juan D. Perón launched an attack on the United States services and called for an investigation because, he said, they had engaged in a malicious campaign against the Argentine people, few papers have continued to publish dispatches provided by these agencies.

Last Saturday The United Press was informed that its permit to transmit information to newspapers in the interior by telegraph would become ineffective on May 16.

The first agency to be shut down by today's action was The Associated Press, whose offices were visited at 3 P. M. by four representatives of the Ministry. They presented Fred Strozier, the bureau chief, with orders to close down the teletype machines bringing in news from abroad.

Today's action in suspending a license The Associated Press has held since March, 1946, was taken in accordance with a Ministerial resolution dated May 8. On that date the full membership of the Congressional investigating committee had not yet been announced.

Percy Foster, the International News director, said he had protested the action "on the ground it constitutes a prejudgement by a functionary of a matter that is exclusively in the hands of a Congressional investigating committee."

United States Ambassador Albert F. Nufer, who had been informed of the shutdowns by the news agency heads, visited the Foreign Office today but declined to disclose what representations he had made.

The Government-controlled press continued its attacks against American journalism with full force. The semi-official Democracia selected as its main target the Spanish-language American news-weekly Vision. In particular it decried the magazine's reports that President Perón was being torn between pressures of the Army and the General Confederation of Labor.

* * *

May 16, 1953

ECUADORIAN CHIEF BACKS PRESS CURB

President Says 2 Shut Papers Can Reopen if They Pledge Not to Renew 'Slander'

HIS ACTIONS ARE ATTACKED

Inter-American Press Official Draws Up Report Branding Him 'Enemy of Freedom'

By SYDNEY GRUSON
Special to The New York Times

QUITO, Ecuador, May 14—President José Maria Velasco Ibarra said today that his Government would allow the reopening of La Nacion and La Hora of Guayaquil if the owner of those newspapers, now in jail with four members of the papers' staffs, promised in a written statement that the publications would "obey the laws of Ecuador." He said that he would require a statement acknowledging that they had "slandered the Government and had attempted to provoke civil war."

The President implied that the five newspaper men, who were sentenced on May 1 to five years in jail, would be freed if those conditions were met.

In an hour-long talk, President Velasco Ibarra vigorously defended the closing of the papers and the jailing of the newspaper men.

"I am still sure it was absolutely correct for the peace of the country, for public morality and even for the dignity of the press," he said, adding: "I acted with authority but not as a dictator. The closing of La Nacion and La Hora is not the beginning of a dictatorial era."

Quick Condemnation Deplored

Before beginning to answer questions, the President said it was "lamentable" that the closing of the two papers should have been judged by the international press, "without a study of the facts."

"Not all newspaper men are infallible, any more than all governments are tyrannical" he said, "and the best way to defend the liberty of the press is to assure the honesty of the press and for the press itself to see that it has not been lacking in honor and loyalty."

Throughout the interview the President emphasized his belief that freedom of the press could not have the same meaning in Ecuador as in the United States and Europe. The people of the United States and Europe, he said, are not the same as the Indian people of Ecuador.

The two Guayaquil newspapers were closed April 28, eight days after a crowd of 3,000 persons who had been at a political meeting in support of the President marched to demonstrate in front of the building housing the two papers. There was gunfire during the demonstration and on April 24, Simon Canarte Barbero, the owner and publisher of the two papers, along with three editorial employees and the papers' business manager, were arrested on charges of possessing weapons and firing on the public.

On May 1, a legal holiday, the five were given a summary trial by the Guayaquil police chief and sentenced to the maximum term possible under an emergency World War II decree. Besides the jail sentence, each of the five was fined 10,000 sucres ($625).

The Guayaquil papers, the President said, were not closed "for upholding any principle, nor for criticizing the Government."

He charged that Señor Canarte, who strongly supported his candidacy in last year's election campaign, turned against him after he took office because the President would not go along with a plan "whereby the Government would purchase some old ships belonging to Canarte."

"Consequently he became angry and was blinded by vengeance," the President said. "All he did in his newspaper was to slander systematically, to insult people systematically and to ask the armed forces and the police to destroy the Government. If this had continued the Government could not have had a single month of tranquility for working and the Government even might have fallen."

* * *

August 22, 1953

BOGOTA PAPER SHUT IN DEFYING CENSOR

Newspaper Suspends Rather Than Yield to Order to Print Cabinet Minister's Speech

Special to The New York Times

BOGOTA, Colombia, Aug. 21—The conservative newspaper El Siglo did not appear today because the editors refused to obey an order of censorship and preferred to suspend publication.

An announcement from the State Directorate of Information and Propaganda said El Siglo would not be permitted to reappear unless it printed with due prominence last night's radio speech by Lucio Pabon Nunez, Minister of the Interior.

The dispute arose because of the exchange of accusations that had been going on between the deposed President Dr. Laureano Gomez, and the members of the new government, headed by Gen. Gustavo Rojas Pinilla.

Gomez Statement in Dispute

From his exile in New York Dr. Gomez has been making various accusations of improper conduct against the new leaders. The government slowed publication of a long manifesto by Dr. Gomez after it had been circulated here clandestinely some days. El Siglo, which is Dr. Gomez' newspaper, gave a prominent place to the text.

El Siglo had a preliminary brush with censorship because it refused to give as much display to statements by General Rojas in his conference with visiting United States newspapermen two days ago.

Last night the newspaper was ordered to print Señor Pabon's speech at least as conspicuously as had been done with the statement on Dr. Gomez. Faced with a direct order its editors decided not to publish the newspaper.

The State Directorate of Information and Propaganda issued a communiqué saying that "since press censorship exists in Colombia its function is not only to forbid but also to indicate to newspapers the form in which to conduct themselves with the state and with private persons."

It added that last night El Siglo had been told that "the speech of the Minister of Government Dr. Lucio Nunez must be published with the same typographical display than that newspaper used in publishing the texts of the message and letter of the former president, Dr Gomez, not only because it was a state document but as a rectification of charges made there [in the Goméz documents]."

It added that the editors of El Siglo, in refusing to publish the speech as indicated and, in fact, in suspending publication, had violated the press law.

The removal of censorship on outgoing press messages was formally confirmed today with the publication in the press of official announcement that all radio and cable offices had been instructed to transmit "without any sort of obstruction or censorship the dispatches of correspondents to different press organs abroad."

* * *

September 28, 1953

COLOMBIA'S CURBS ON PRESS DECRIED

Silencing of Papers by Censor's Pressure Arouses Interest Throughout Latin America

By SAM POPE BREWER
Special to The New York Times

LIMA, Peru, Sept. 27—The troubles of Colombian newspapers that may cease publication under pressure of censorship are arousing wide interest in Latin America, where it is known the same thing could happen in almost any country in certain circumstances. The battle for freedom of the press is far from having been won and the incidents in Colombia are only the latest of many proofs of that fact.

The Government of President Gustavo Rojas Pinilla established a good reputation in its first few months by apparent efforts to restore not only peace but personal liberties in Colombia. After making the gesture of ending censorship of outgoing press dispatches President Rojas Pinilla was generally expected to make good on his promise to work toward abolition of censorship inside the country. Newspapermen in most countries of South America were envious of their Colombian colleagues' prospects of being able to say whatever they thought.

El Siglo Case Caused Shock

However, the action suspending El Siglo of Bogota thirty days for publishing criticism of the whole principle of a coup such as the one that displaced its proprietor, Laureano Gomez as President of Colombia in June, came as a shock to the Latin newspaper world. The still more arbitrary action against El Colombiano of Medellin in ordering it to print the speech of a Government official added to the bad impression. El Colombiano suspended publication rather than give in to the order.

As evidence that these incidents were part of a general policy, still another newspaper, El Liberal of Popayan, Colombia, was closed ten days by the censors and announced that in protest it would suspend publication indefinitely.

The strength of feeling against these actions is shown by the fact the protest move in Bogota was led by the editors of El Tiempo, Liberal newspaper, which for years has been bitterly hostile to the Conservative El Siglo.

La Prensa, one of Lima's two leading newspapers, ridiculed the Colombian Government's pretext that the matter published was "subversive" and said "every time it is a question of silencing an organ of expression, every time it is a question of suppressing an independent tribune—today in Colombia, yesterday in Bolivia and Argentina—the same useless, specious and in the final analysis hypocritical reasons are resorted to."

Little is heard of censorship in Venezuela simply because it is so solidly entrenched.

In Ecuador the Government closed two newspapers four months, jailed their editors and also other newspapermen who protested against that arbitrary action.

In Bolivia six newspapermen are still imprisoned with the Government asserting this involves no infringement of the right of free speech because they are guilty of "subversive acts," a handy term for anything a Government dislikes.

Even Peru Isn't Immune

Even Peru, where the press suffers relatively little restrictions has had its cases. One editor was jailed last year, much to the embarrassment of the United States Embassy, for an editorial considered offensive to the United States. Another, though a native Peruvian, was arbitrarily expelled from the country for an article that displeased the authorities and then just as suddenly and without explanation was allowed to return.

In Chile the Government has been prosecuting an editor for publishing criticism made by members of Congress and angrily rejected efforts of the Inter-American Press Association to intervene.

Argentina's tight restrictions on the press show no relaxation.

Brazil, in fact, is the only country of the continent with a completely free press, one that carries a freedom of expression ordinary laws of libel would not permit in most countries.

* * *

October 8, 1954

LATIN PRESS CURBS SCORED AT PARLEY

Americas Group Reports 20% of People Under Censorship— 8 Nations Singled Out

By SAM POPE BREWER
Special to The New York Times

SAO PAULO, Brazil, Oct. 7—The battle for real freedom of the press in the Americas is still far from won, according to reports presented at the tenth annual meeting of the Inter American Press Association here.

Jules Dubois of The Chicago Tribune, chairman of the committee on press freedom, told the associations general assembly today that "an estimated 20 per cent of 162,000,000 inhabitants of Latin America are today living under perennial or periodic curtains of censorship and intimidation tantamount to censorship."

Gen. Miguel Lanz Duret of Mexico, association president, in his general report yesterday, cited eight countries in which the organization intervened during the last year in an effort to save the freedom, and even the lives, of newspaper men who had been molested for their professional activities.

Chairman Resigns

At the opening session this afternoon Mr. Dubois announced his resignation as committee chairman and recommended that a Latin American succeed him.

In his report he described the press situation in Argentina as probably the worst in the hemisphere. He also mentioned cases of difficulties over press freedom in Bolivia, Brazil, Chile, Colombia, Nicaragua and Venezuela.

The report recommended that protests against various forms of interference with press freedom be sent to Argentina, Bolivia, Colombia, Nicaragua, Venezuela, the Dominican Republic, Paraguay and Peru.

It gave a clean bill of health to the United States and the British, French and Dutch possessions in the hemisphere on the question of censorship and press freedom. In the cases of Brazil and Chile, it noted that "in contrast to what occurs in Argentina," the courts had upheld the rights of newspaper men in their clashes with authorities.

In Colombia, it said, President Gustavo Rojas Pinilla "created justified alarm among editors and publishers" with remarks in his inaugural address Aug. 7.

Under State of Siege

Colombia has been under a "state of siege" since Nov. 19, 1949, with censorship periodically relaxed and then tightened again but never removed.

President Rojas has attacked the press as irresponsible. On Sept. 24, he issued a decree on libel and slander that newspaper men fear is a gag to be applied to them at the Government's convenience. The principal objection to it is that guilt is to be decided by an official, not a jury or even a court judge.

Regarding Venezuela, the report declared that the political situation there did not justify existing censorship.

What was clear throughout the report was that despite the association's efforts and some gains, Latin America still had many barriers to full freedom of expression.

The association is growing constantly in numbers and prestige. At present 390 news enterprises are members. A conclusion drawn in today's report was that in individual countries, as in the hemisphere as a whole, the importance of the organization in defense of legitimate interests of the press had become strikingly evident.

* * *

September 17, 1955

COLOMBIA REGIME WARRING ON PRESS

Criticism of President Found Virtually Halted—Official Denies Censorship Exists

By SAM POPE BREWER
Special to The New York Times

PANAMA, Sept. 12—President Gustavo Rojas Pinilla of Colombia is waging a devastating war against freedom of speech.

It appeared to this correspondent, who recently visited Colombia, that the President had virtually eliminated newspaper criticism of his Administration. All radio stations are required to give free time to a Government news program and to refrain from news commentaries themselves, and television is a Government monopoly.

In addition, arbitrary and unpredictable censorship is affecting not only Colombia's press but also dispatches to the foreign press and distribution here of foreign publications. The situation is further complicated by official refusal to admit that incoming publications are censored.

The recent suppression of the newspaper El Tiempo has attracted more attention abroad than other moves, but it was only one thrust in a general campaign.

The President appears to be personally responsible for the movement that has given the authorities constantly growing control over all publications and other public utterances.

Newsprint Quotas Set

The latest important step was a decree issued Aug. 25, providing that paper for periodicals would be allotted by a governmental organization. Publications that need more than the quota offered them may buy paper in the open market, but it will cost them roughly twice as much as the Government paper, and they cannot afford that.

It is generally understood that the size of a newspaper's quota will depend on the degree of its friendliness to the Administration.

To reinforce its hand still further, the Government is preparing to publish a daily newspaper in direct competition with the privately owned press. The latest announcement was that it would appear early in November.

The publisher is to be Brig. Gen. Rafael Calderón Reyes, now chief of staff of the Army. He is to head a body known as the National Publications Enterprise, which will have the dual role of publishing the newspaper and of fixing the newsprint quotas for all publications. The general has said that the task of the paper will be to "aggrandize the armed forces."

Newspapers that are still fighting for free expression are being driven to the wall.

El Tiempo of Bogota, the Liberal Party's organ and one of South America's best-known newspapers, was arbitrarily closed by order of the President Aug. 4.

Colombia has a rigorous libel law dating from Oct. 1, 1954, under which the newspaper might have been prosecuted. There are other legal provisions for dealing with those who insult the President, and this El Tiempo was accused of having done. No legal action was taken, however, and none has been suggested.

The plant was padlocked by the police, and permission even to service the idle presses to protect them against corrosion was refused.

Retraction Was Refused

El Tiempo, like most Colombian papers, sometimes appeared to North Americans excessively strong in its criticism of political foes, but that was not the pretext found for suppressing it. El Tiempo was closed for refusing to print on its first page for thirty days an abject retraction of statements made by its managing director in a telegram to an Ecuadorian newspaper.

Under the libel law, the text dictated by the Government would have amounted to a confession of criminal guilt.

There had been a certain amount of provocation by El Tiempo. While General Rojas Pinilla was making an official visit to Ecuador, the director of El Tiempo, Roberto García Peña, had sent a telegram to the leading Quito newspaper, El Comercio, accusing the Colombian President of falsehood.

It said that the murder in July of a Liberal newspaper editor, Emilio Correa, and his son had been a political assassination and not, as the Government had said, the result of a dispute over a traffic accident.

Bogota's other Liberal newspaper, the afternoon El Espectador, has also been having its troubles. After the suppression of El Tiempo, it was announced that El Espectador would publish a morning edition.

The Government immediately issued a statement saying that El Espectador was forbidden to appear as a morning newspaper unless it fulfilled all legal requirements. Liberal sources say that the paper's directors have been unable to find out what these are.

Sunday Magazine Killed

Also hit by the Government's campaign, after eight years of successful operation, the Sunday magazine Dominical, published by El Espectador, announced Aug. 28 that it would not appear again.

It died through an official decision that it did not qualify as a newspaper and therefore had been obtaining its paper fraudulently. Fined 26,000 pesos, a little more than $10,000 at the official rate, it suspended publication.

Censorship, however, appears to be a problem for all papers, which are often called upon to suppress simple factual items. Even pro-Government publications have protested because the censorship seems to follow no code.

At various times, the Directorate of Information and Propaganda, the Colombian Intelligence Service (the security police), the General Staff, the Customs Department, the Ministry of Communications and various provincial officials have taken a hand in it. Each of them apparently works independently.

The office of Gen. Calderón Reyes issues some of the orders and at one time was controlling censorship, but the general replied to official inquiries that there was no censorship of publications.

There is an official office of censorship now with an Army officer in charge, but individual acts of censorship are carried out of which he apparently has no knowledge.

Pro-Government newspaper editors have protested that they get censorship orders on the telephone from officers, talking sometimes from restaurants or cafés, and cannot judge the authority of the man speaking to issue them.

Telegrams and cables are handled as if Colombia were at war. By a decree of July 4, telephone and telegraph communications are limited to twelve languages, in addition to which the clergy may use Latin.

Every cable, however, must be accompanied by a full and accurate translation into Spanish.

Imports of The New York Times have been delayed or stopped repeatedly, and at present the military authorities are insisting that the local distributor must be responsible for seeing that no issue of the newspaper circulated here contains anything that is uncomplimentary to Colombia. It was explained that this must not be construed as censorship, but merely as a measure to protect the good name of the country.

Sometimes importers of publications cannot discover who is responsible for halting a particular shipment.

Regime Called Fascist-Like

Dr. Eduardo Santos, former president of Colombia, said yesterday the present Colombian Government had embarked on a Fascist-like course. His statement, distributed in New York by the Inter American Press Association, was in connection with the closing of his newspaper El Tiempo.

* * *

December 29, 1955

BRAZILIAN CENSOR IS DEFIED IN PRESS

Special to The New York Times

RIO DE JANEIRO, Dec. 28—A revolt against censorship has erupted in the Brazilian press.

Within the last two days, two opposition newspapers in Rio de Janeiro and one that is pro-Government have defied censorship by printing violent denunciations of it.

As a result, almost the entire edition of the anti-Government morning paper Diario de Noticias was seized by the police today.

The influential pro-Government newspaper Correio da Manha and the opposition Tribuna da Imprensa were reprimanded for their actions by the chief censor. Part of today's edition of the strongly pro-Government afternoon paper Ultima Hora was seized and then released because the police censor had not seen proofs of certain articles.

Press censorship is legal in Brazil under the existing state of siege, but editors of even the most pro-Government newspapers have been deploring its existence in progressively stronger terms. Foreign correspondents, however, are not affected by censorship.

Editors have said that the situation in Brazil does not warrant censorship and that its enforcement is unfair and inconsistent.

* * *

September 23, 1956

ARGENTINES LOOK TO LOST LIBERTY

Debate Centers on Absence of Rights One Year After Overthrow of Peron

By EDWARD A. MORROW
Special to The New York Times

BUENOS AIRES, Sept. 18—A year has passed since the overthrow of Juan D. Perón, and yet there remains a great debate as to whether the human freedoms—of press, assembly and religion—are respected in Argentina.

A year ago there was no debate.

Restaurants, cafes, bars and even night clubs are noisy with political disputes. In front of the money exchange shops in the downtown section of this capital, sidewalk economists and financiers overflow into the streets and deter traffic as they argue the ups and downs of the Argentine peso.

Unlike a year ago they do not have to look over their shoulders and whisper their thoughts. Nevertheless the Government's promises of freedom of the press and rule by law have not been kept.

Many Government officials now believe that it was a foolish mistake to make these promises. They point out that the Allied powers in denazifying Germany found it necessary to limit such freedoms for a time to prevent the renaissance of what they were trying to destroy.

Liberals Are Critical

The sharpest criticism of the Government's policies stems from leftist and rightist groups that would use the Soviet Union or Franco's Spain as their models in their own application of the freedoms.

But there also is valid, criticism from liberal revolutionaries. Recently a well-known writer Ernesto Sabato, who was appointed by the Government to edit one of the magazines inherited from the Peronist chain, sounded a tocsin. He warned that the nation's press was becoming a "uniform gray" and that the public was becoming suspicious that the press was hiding truth of major importance.

Señor Sabato was dismissed for having published an article about the torture of prisoners by the police. The dismissal was one of the several examples of the difference between theory and practice by the revolutionary government.

However, the scandal caused by his dismissal resulted in Señor Sabato's appointment to a post with the Provisional President, Gen. Pedro Eugenie Aramburu, instead of an undetermined jail sentence. As have many other supporters of the Government Señor Sabato called for the liquidation of the subsecretariat of the press that controls newsprint allocations and the maximum publicity about all the errors committed by the police.

The revolutionary government inherited a gigantic propaganda machine from the Perón dictatorship. The shutdown of this chain would mean unemployment to thousands. The problem is similar to that which the Government is facing in trying to cut down the bureaucracy in Government—unemployment can breed dangerous dissatisfaction.

The dissolution of the press secretariat has lagged far behind schedule. It still controls newsprint allocations as it did under Señor Perón. The Opposition press asserts these allocations are being used as a discriminatory weapon against them. Nevertheless the rightist and leftist press is able to publish charges that it is living "under a totalitarian regime."

The greatest disappointment to Argentine liberals has been the behavior of the independent dailies.

For example, no newspaper has developed the history of the nation's top eighteen prisoners, who are confined on the island of Tierra del Fuego. For these prisoners there is no habeas corpus.

The Government, meanwhile, has announced that a call to elections will be issued a year from now. The outlook for the development within that time of a democratic party capable of winning a majority of the nation's votes and solving the problems that will remain is bleek.

* * *

November 3, 1956

COLOMBIA EASING PRESS CENSORING

Move Began Before Calling of Constituent Assembly—Two Papers Still Curbed

By TAD SZULC
Special to The New York Times

BOGOTA, Colombia, Nov. 2—The Colombian press, which had long been under one of the Hemisphere's tightest censorships, has been enjoying unaccustomed freedom in recent weeks. Editors hope it will become permanent.

The sudden relaxation of restrictions on the press by the dictatorial Government of Lieut. Gen. Gustavo Rojas Pinilla has been one of the most spectacular developments here in years.

It came shortly before the President called into session the National Constituent Assembly. The legislative group has been meeting here since Oct. 11.

As far as can be ascertained only two newspapers—the liberal Intermedio and the conservative La Republica, both of Bogota—are subjected to direct censorship. However the censorship is mild, according to their editors.

The two opposition dailies were told that all censorship would be lifted if they agreed to sign a commitment to refrain from publishing certain kinds of information such as reports on guerrilla violence in Colombia. But the papers refused on the ground that such a commitment would be unethical.

Censorship of the newspaper Patria in Manizales was lifted completely several weeks ago. Last week, three opposition newspapers in Medellin—El Colombiano, El Correo and El Diario—were told that all they had to do was to submit what might be questionable articles to the secretary of the Governor of Antioquia Province.

Assembly Speeches Printed

Most other newspapers in Colombia have been free of direct censorship all along. But as they are either completely pro-Government or at least carefully neutral, they seldom printed anything the regime could find objectionable.

At present all newspapers are permitted to publish almost all speeches in the Constituent Assembly, even those that are anti-Government or contain personal attacks on General Rojas. Opposition dailies are allowed to criticize the regime's policies, though it has to be done in guarded language.

Opposition editors also report that the harassment of their newspapers that for long was the practice of the Rojas regime has virtually ceased.

Censorship over foreign correspondence has also been eased in most instances.

This correspondent, who on a visit here in August was subjected to every form of harassment, has now received considerate helpful treatment from the authorities. Included was the granting of an interview with General Rojas, something that had not been done in at least a year.

There are fears here, however, that the new press freedom may be only temporary. Some think it will end when the Constituent Assembly completes the sessions in which the President is seeking approval of programs that would greatly strengthen his personal role.

The argument also is advanced that the month-long freedom of the press was ordered solely with an eye on the Inter-American Press Association, which is meeting in Havana this week. The regime is extremely sensitive to foreign press criticism, and many think the relaxation of censorship is designed to forestall condemnation of the Rojas regime by the association.

New Press Law Sought

But General Rojas told this correspondent that he intended to maintain the present state of affairs. So far there has been no evidence to the contrary.

The President expressed hope that the Assembly would approve soon a new press statute regulating newspaper practices. He said the draft elaborated in April by a commission headed by Eduardo Zuleta Angel, former Ambassador to the United States, was incomplete on the ground that it failed to set forth "minimal requirements for working newspaper men."

The President's idea appears to be that newsmen should be licensed like lawyers and doctors.

"Newsmen here go to newspapers directly from jail," he said.

The Zuleta draft was essentially libel and slander legislation excluding any form of censorship.

The drastic change in press restrictions can be traced to the turning over of the National Press Directorate from civilians to the military late in August.

The office now is headed by an Army colonel schooled in the United States, Juan B. Cordoba, and Navy Capt. Oscar Herrera Rebolledo, a Korean war veteran. Both appear to feel that there should be a maximum of press freedom while certain controls must remain.

* * *

February 1, 1958

CUBA SEIZES MAGAZINE

Confiscates 25,000 Copies of Bohemia Featuring Castro

Special to The New York Times

HAVANA, Jan. 31—Military authorities of Oriente Province confiscated about 25,000 copies of the Havana weekly magazine Bohemia that went on sale in the province today. Armando Arrue, agent of Bohemia in Santiago de Cuba, capital of the province, was arrested and held for four hours.

On the streets of Santiago de Cuba soldiers snatched copies of Bohemia, which contained photographs and stories about Fidel Castro and his insurgents, from persons who had purchased the magazine, according to the report.

Copies of the Havana weekly magazine Zig Zag, which carried reprints of photographs of Señor Castro and his rebel army printed recently in the United States by Look Magazine, also were seized and destroyed.

* * *

October 6, 1958

AMERICAS' PRESS KEEPING A DATE

Group Is Fulfilling Promise to Meet in Argentina Without Peron

By JUAN de ONIS
Special to The New York Times

BUENOS AIRES, Oct. 4—The Inter-American Press Association keeps a joyful date here next week with the free Argentine press.

When the Peronist régime confiscated La Prensa in 1951, the Inter-American Press Association said that one day it would meet again in an Argentina without Juan D. Perón and with freedom of the press. This has now come about.

The 300 delegates to the association's fourteenth assembly, which begins tomorrow and ends next Sunday on Pan-American Day, will find the Argentine press enjoying complete freedom. This was re-established three years ago by the revolutionary Government that overthrew Señor Perón, and it has been extended by the elected President, Dr. Arturo Frondizi, by the elimination of restrictions on Peronist propaganda.

A Buenos Aires newspaper stand is a gaudy spectacle. There are ten daily newspapers, six full nine-column publications that include the traditional La Prensa and La Nacion, and four tabloids, led by the multicolor Clarin. The major afternoon newspapers, La Razon and Critica, publish two editions and use banner headlines and pictures.

Many Political Weeklies

A weekly political press flourishes. Twenty-five or more papers are sold in Buenos Aires, expressing every shade of political opinion in the turbulent political life this country now is passing through. Black headlines demanding that President Frondizi resign, full-page photographs of Señor Perón and publications in color of the achievements of the Soviet Union are a common sight.

Fat family magazines, such as Vea y Lea or El Hogar, share space on the stands with foreign periodicals from all over the world. For the large foreign communities there are daily newspapers in English, Italian, German, Yiddish and Japanese, and weeklies in half a dozen other languages.

The official chain of newspapers forged by Señor Perón has been broken up. The publications have either been returned to their former owners, as in the cases of La Prensa or La Razon, or sold at auction to private publishers or employee cooperatives. This was begun by the preceding provisional Government of Gen. Pedro E. Aramburu and continued under the new Administration.

Since La Prensa was returned to Dr. Alberto Gainza Paz, publisher and director, in February, 1956, this national morning newspaper has made a strong comeback. Circulation is now averaging 320,000 daily and 380,000 on Sunday. The size of La Prensa, as well as of all the other major metropolitan dailies, is limited to an average of twenty-four pages by the newsprint shortage.

Reporting on Administration and political activities is enterprising and detailed, but objective in the major dailies. La Prensa and La Nacion are more outspoken editorially than they were under the revolutionary government. Dr. Frondizi governs under the scrutiny of a vigilant and sometimes sharply critical press, with Peronist abuses fresh in its memory.

The Administration has found it expedient to encourage the appearance of a new morning newspaper, El Nacional, which frequently expresses the views of Dr. Frondizi's collaborators, particularly of Rogelio Frigerio, a leading economic and labor adviser. El Pueblo, a morning newspaper identified with Roman Catholic policy, has recently been purchased by a financial group also linked to the Administration.

There has been criticism of continued Government control of radio stations and the only Argentine television channel. Sr. Frondizi suspended auctions of radio stations started by his predecessor, so all the major networks remain in the hands of a Federal administrator. The Government also runs the television station. This is a situation created by Señor Perón's nationalization of radio stations, many of which were bought at forced prices from owners who are now seeking recovery of their property.

Sr. Frondizi has promised that the Government will return radio stations to private hands. Congress failed to act on this issue during this year's session, however. The Administration has also said it will award new television channels.

There are at least five groups applying for channels, including the newspaper "Clarin," three groups of television set manufacturers and the Colegio del Salvador, a Jesuit institution. There are an estimated total of 120,000 television sets in Greater Buenos Aires.

Newspapers still remain the basic medium of information and advertising. A newspaper is one of cheapest articles in Argentina's inflation-ridden price structure. All sell for only 1 peso, or less than 2 cents on the free market.

Advertising rates are among the lowest in the world, according to comparative studies made by advertising agencies. A column-inch of display advertising costs about 250 pesos. Classified ads cost about 25 pesos a line.

This situation does not contribute to the economic strength of the Argentine press, which is actually subsidized by a highly favorable exchange rate for importing newsprint and for paying wire services and other foreign costs. The central bank permits the importation of 130,000 tons of newsprint at a rate of exchange computed at 75 per cent at the official rate of 18 to $1, and 25 per cent at the free rate, which has risen steadily to record levels of more than 58 pesos to $1 under the new Administration.

* * *

August 24, 1959

CASTRO METHODS HURT CUBA PRESS

It Is Kept in Dark on Official Events—
Readership and Revenues Are Declining

By R. HART PHILLIPS
Special to The New York Times

HAVANA, Aug. 23—Premier Fidel Castro's government by television has left the press in the dark. Newspaper readership is said to have declined sharply.

Newspapers are given little or no official information during periods of crisis. No official statements were issued during the recent upheaval over an alleged conspiracy against the regime. Official sources said, "Wait until Dr. Castro appears on television and radio to tell the people what has happened."

At the same time, the press is severely criticized by Premier Castro and his Government for picking up information wherever it can be found.

The foreign press has been a target of continuous attack since Dr. Castro came to power last Jan. 1. According to Cuban officials, the foreign press, particularly that of the United States, is carrying on a "campaign of lies" instigated by the "vested interests of the United States in Cuba and abroad."

Favorable Articles Ignored

On the other hand, none of the favorable articles that have appeared in the United States press since the revolution have been an object of comment here.

Newsmen here, both foreign and Cuban, complain of the extraordinary facilities being granted to Prensa Latina, a recently organized news agency.

Exclusive interviews and reports are being given to the agency, which is said to be the realization of a dream of various Latin-American countries to present their viewpoint to the world. Latin Americans have complained for many years that favorable reports about them have never been carried by world-wide news agencies.

The domestic press is in a precarious position. During all past administrations the majority of publications received subsidies and most newsmen, who received low wages, held sinecures in various Government departments that gave them substantial livings.

When the revolutionary Government assumed power one of its first steps was to cancel the subsidies and to remove all newsmen from governmental payrolls. Dr. Castro castigated the members of the press as "grafters and sycophants."

Confusion Prevails

The result has been a state of confusion. Dr. Castro talks of trying to help the publications and members of the press, but he has said that there are too many newspapers and magazines and too many reporters.

A proposed law to force newspapers and magazines to pay a living wage has never been approved, since the publications have said that a majority would have to close.

Meanwhile there is little criticism of the regime's policies. When any criticism is voiced Dr. Castro denounces the critics during his radio-TV appearances, which are said to reach 95 per cent of Cubans.

In view of the tremendous drop in advertising suffered by newspapers since the beginning of the year, it is predicted that many will close within a few months.

The only newspapers that are flourishing are Revolucion, official organ of Dr. Castro's 26th of July Movement; Diario Nacional, taken over recently by a group of 26th of July members, and several smaller publications that are regarded as "voices" of the Government.

Only through Revolucion did the public and press learn of Dr. Castro's temporary resignation as Premier several weeks ago.

* * *

October 21, 1962

CUBA IS ASSAILED AT PRESS PARLEY

Hemisphere Meeting Told of Falsification of Dispatches

By EDWARD C. BURKS
Special to The New York Times

SANTIAGO, Chile, Oct. 20—Cuba was accused of persecuting newsmen and falsifying their dispatches as a watchdog committee of the Inter-American Press Association convened here today.

To a lesser extent, supression of freedom of the press in such countries as Haiti, Paraguay and Bolivia was also condemned.

In addition, the committees heard reports on Government repressive measures directed this year against certain newspapers in Argentina, British Guiana and Peru.

Some areas, including Central America and the Dominican Republic, which have traditionally had censorship or governmental interference with the press, reported better conditions. However, danger signs were reported in the Dominican Republic and Nicaragua.

The Freedom of the Press Committee of the Inter-American Press Association is holding a two-day session here as a prelude to a meeting of the full association all next week. About 300 publishers and newspaper representatives from the United States, Canada the West Indies and Latin America are expected to attend.

None Defend Castro

No disputes developed today over charges against Cuba. No delegation rose to defend the regime of Premier Fidel Castro or its press policies.

Jules Dubois of The Chicago Tribune, chairman of the Freedom of the Press Committee, devoted most of his opening speech to castigating the Castro Government as a Communist regime that wants to undermine press freedom throughout the Americas.

He noted recent arrests in Cuba of foreign correspondents, who were held incommunicado for several days before their release. He declared that the few foreign correspondents still in Cuba were subject to rigid traveling restrictions, and that their dispatches were either censored or rewritten without their knowledge by Cuban officials.

The report on Cuba said thousands of Cuban newsmen had been thrown out of work by the Castro regime's closing of newspapers.

Mr. Dubois described Haiti as intimidating its press through censorship exercised by threat of "machete, bullet or jail."

John H. Perry, publisher of a chain of Florida newspapers delivered the report on the United States. There is freedom of the press in the United States, he said, but a major worry has been "Government secrecy."

He added that there had been breakthroughs against unwarranted Government secrecy but that "it is still a serious problem." There has been improvement at the top level, he declared, but newsmen still run into trouble "down through the ranks" of Government offices.

Mr. Perry's report also asserted that there was a growing tendency by Government agencies to violate the First Amendment by placing copyright restrictions on the contents of Government publications and documents that are legally the public's business. In addition, the report said that five states—Texas, North Carolina, Georgia, Kentucky and Alabama—had sales taxes on the sale of newspapers and that such levies tended to restrict the dissemination of news.

A report by a Brazilian representative said that Gov. Leonel Brizola of the State of Rio Grande do Sul had curtailed electric power to opposition papers and even threatened them with violence during the recent election campaign.

Agustin Edwards, publisher of El Mercurio of Santiago and president of the host committee, made the shortest report. He said: "In Chile there is absolute freedom of the press."

German Ornes, publisher of El Caribe of Santo Domingo, said there was press freedom in the Dominican Republic but that it was endangered.

He declared that after thirty years of dictatorship, which ended with the assassination last year of Generalissimo Rafael Leonidas Trujillo Molina, political parties in the Dominican Republic had no conception of the meaning of freedom of the press. Mr. Ornes accused even so-called democratic parties of trying to smash the press when it failed to serve as their mouthpiece.

Mr. Ornes' newspaper has been closed by labor troubles, for which he blamed a union he described as Communist influenced.

The report on Nicaragua said there was press freedom there but that the Government had issued veiled threats to newsmen about the forthcoming elections, indicating that the opposition press could be accused of inciting violence.

* * *

October 4, 1964

CENSORSHIP TIGHT IN LA PAZ AS BOLIVIAN UNREST PERSISTS

Special to The New York Times

LA PAZ, Bolivia, Oct. 3—Newspapers here report a tightened domestic censorship, even to interference with commercial advertising. Dispatches sent abroad are not censored.

According to La Paz editors, the censors delete anything referring to the Socialist Phalange rebellion, a rightist guerrilla action that has flared in outlying parts of the country for several weeks. Also forbidden is the publishing of "any material contributing to subversion."

* * *

October 8, 1964

CASTRO EASING CURBS ON FLOW OF NEWS FROM CUBA

By JUAN de ONIS

Special to The New York Times

HAVANA, Oct. 7—Premier Fidel Castro has accepted an invitation to dine this month with foreign newsmen in Cuba.

Cuban information policy has been moving toward relaxation of restrictions on foreign newsmen, particularly from the West.

Working facilities for correspondents accredited at the Ministry of Foreign Affairs have improved significantly. Telephone and cable communications to New York, still the major channels for Western newspapermen, are now rapid, under normal circumstances. This is on express instructions from Premier Castro.

Until a few months ago there were unexplained delays up to several days in putting through telephone calls and occasionally cable dispatches were not sent at all.

Of course communications can still be shut down unexpectedly for security reasons. Two Cuban military guards shot each other to death before the Algerian Embassy two weeks ago. It was declared later that the shootings resulted from a personal quarrel, but for 12 hours there was no communication with New York.

There is also greater official cooperation now on the question of correspondents' travel around Cuba. If a newsman requests it, the Ministry of Foreign Affairs will issue a letter to the coordinator of the United Party of the Cuban Socialist Revolution in the province the correspondent wants to visit. The reporter is then free to travel there. His identity card is normally valid only for the capital.

Premier Castro had assigned Ramiro del Rio as Director of Information in the ministry with instructions to iron out problems encountered by foreign newsmen. Mr. del Rio, a frank and amiable man, was active in the underground revolutionary movement against President Fulgencio Batista, and he helped put out the clandestine pro-Castro newspaper Revolución.

The Premier's personal contact with foreign newsmen has developed through informal news conferences at diplomatic receptions, which the Premier attends fairly often. The correspondents are usually tipped in advance if Dr. Castro will be present and he makes a point of receiving them. Sometimes the question-and-answer, session goes on for two hours.

It is still difficult for a Western newspaperman to get interviews, with other high officials. The normal process is to make application through the Foreign Affairs Ministry's Information Section—and then wait. Minor officials when encountered in unannounced visits are usually cooperative, but they have limited information.

About 40 correspondents are now accredited. They include resident correspondents of the two major United States news agencies, The Associated Press and United Press

International; of Reuters, Agence France Presse, and the Middle East News Agency of the United Arab Republic; of Tass, the Soviet agency; P.A.P., the Polish agency; Ceteka, the Czechoslovak agency, and Hsinhua, the Communist Chinese agency, as well as other Communist organizations.

For this year's 26th of July celebration of the Castro revolution, the Premier experimented by inviting about 40 United States newspapermen to visit Cuba. Those who came represented a cross-section of the daily and weekly press.

After examining the published results, Cuban officials said Premier Castro was satisfied that the reports were generally favorable. They said the doors would remain open to further visits by United States newsmen.

The Cuban leaders believe that the press remains the only regular channel of communications open between Cuba and the United States, and that even reports that are critical, or what the Cuban officials consider biased, are better than a curtain of silence.

The authorities would also like to open a cultural exchange, including expositions of Cuban art in the United States, and visits by United States sports and artistic groups.

* * *

October 25, 1964

4 LATIN COUNTRIES SCORED ON PRESS

Meeting in Mexico Hears of Government Restraints

By PAUL P. KENNEDY
Special to the New York Times

MEXICO CITY, Oct. 23—Four countries in the Western Hemisphere have no freedom of the press whatsoever and the pretensions to a free press by some other countries are doubtful, a press gathering was told here this week.

The charges were raised by the Freedom of the Press Committee of the Inter-American Press Association, which concluded its 20th annual assembly here Thursday. The organization's committee said that there was no press freedom in Haiti, Bolivia, Honduras or Paraguay.

The committee charged that news was being managed in the United States and in Latin America. It reiterated its stand against monopolies of any nature that might affect the freedom of the press.

Particular criticism was leveled at alleged inequities in newsprint supply, equipment, freight rates and, especially, legislation dealing with or taxing advertising.

Concern Expressed

The committee gave its approval to Mexico, the host country, as having freedom of the press. It expressed its concern, however, over a system by which a quasigovernmental organization, Productora Importadora de Papel Sa, had a monopoly on newsprint. The organization distributes newsprint to virtually all Mexican papers at advantageous rates.

The newspaper situation in Ecuador was termed "fluid." The committee explained that all reports indicated there had been attacks on newspapers in Guayaquil and that some newspapermen there had been imprisoned.

A heated debate arose in the committee and later in the General Assembly over the status of press freedom in Guatemala.

Roberto Carpio, editor of El Grafico, and Roberto Alejos, a Guatemalan political exile representing La Hora, maintained there were glaring infringements on freedom of the press in the Guatemalan capital.

Censorship Lifted

John R. Reitemeyer, outgoing president of the organization, said that he had communicated with Guatemala's chief executive. Col. Enrique Peralta Azurdia, and that subsequently censorship had been lifted in Guatemala.

Mr. Alejos retorted that a bomb had been placed in La Hora, allegedly by Government employes, and the editor, Clemente Marroquin Rojas, had been threatened with exile.

A compromise report was issued stating that the Guatemalans had insisted there was no freedom of the press but that members of the committee had noted the lifting of censorship in Guatemala.

The committee dealt extensively with the Government's participation in news distribution in the United States, particularly with a market report being distributed by the Department of Agriculture. It noted that a recently enacted law directed the Secretary of Agriculture to see to it that a leased-wire system be limited strictly to agricultural market reporting.

Efforts to Control News

In further reference to the United States's position in the Western Hemisphere press, the committee report said that "the struggle to control the channels of communication is never-ending, in efforts to impose discriminatory taxes, restrictive and regulatory licenses and, in a more subtle way, bureaucratic withholding of nonsecurity information."

It was noted that in recent court rulings, two suits in Birmingham, Ala., against The New York Times and libel suits against the Benton Harbor, Mich., News-Palladium and the Jacksonville, Fla., Times-Union, had been dismissed.

In Southern states alone, it was reported, at least 17 libel actions had been brought by public officials against newspapers and magazines seeking total damages exceeding $288 million.

Pedro G. Beltran, editor and publisher of La Prensa, Buenos Aires, was installed as president for the coming year. Other officers named were:

Jack R. Howard of Scripps-Howard newspapers, New York, and Julio de Mesquita of O Estado of São Paulo Brazil, vice presidents; Alfredo Silva Carvallo of La Union, Valparaiso, Chile, secretary; and John A. Brogan Jr., of the Hearst newspapers, New York, re-elected treasurer.

* * *

Africa and Asia

October 1, 1945

NO PALESTINE CENSORSHIP

Only Material in Local Press Remains Under Supervision

By wireless to The New York Times

JERUSALEM, Sept. 30—All forms of censorship in Palestine end tonight with the exception of the supervision of material for publication in the local press, which will continue indefinitely. Palestine censorship began in 1936 when disorders started.

Notwithstanding the removal of censorship, a provision exists under Palestine's emergency defense regulations providing for the restrictive scrutiny of outgoing press message, should any general emergency situation arise.

As far as the local press is concerned, the overriding consideration for censors—who work under the direct orders of the chief secretary to the Palestine administration—is eliminating the publication of any articles or material likely to fan radical friction or create alarm and despondency by printing premature, non-official or speculative announcements about Britain's political intentions, or generally indulging in subversive comment. The effect of such broad directives in recent years has been to foster an active underground press, especially among the Jewish population.

* * *

September 7, 1946

RED KOREAN PAPERS RAIDED AND BANNED

Hodge's Military Police Arrest Heads, Writer of 3 Organs for 'Endangering' U. S.

By RICHARD J. H. JOHNSTON
Special to The New York Times

SEOUL, Korea, Sept. 6—Under the direction of the Army's Counter-Intelligence Corps, 175 heavily armed United States military police raided early today the offices of three extreme leftist newspapers and arrested their publishers, editors and writers to an undisclosed number.

In an official explanation of the crackdown on the Red publications, Lieut. Gen. John R. Hodge, United States commander in Korea, later announced that, "for endangering the security of the United States Army forces in Korea, certain persons have been taken into custody by the Army authorities."

"The publications, Chosun Inmin Po (organ of the South Korea Communist party), Hyun Dai Ilbo and Choon Ang Sin Moon, have been suspended pending further investigation of their activities," the announcement said.

General Hodge's headquarters indicated that the prosecutions will take place in American military courts, as the raids and arrests were made on charges of "violations of proclamation No. 2, General Headquarters, United States Army Forces in the Pacific, dated Sept. 7, 1945."

Headquarters then quoted the proclamation, addressed by General Douglas MacArthur to the people of Korea at the beginning of the occupation, which made actions hostile to our forces subject to the death penalty.

The three suspended papers, Chosun Inmin Po, official mouthpiece of the Communists, and the other two, which follow its policy, have a combined circulation of 75,000.

They have been charging the Americans with suppression of liberties, atrocities and attempts to enslave the Korean people and colonize the country. All three papers espoused the cause of the seventeen defendants in the current counterfeiting ring trial, and have accused the United States authorities of framing the case to discredit the Communist party.

The three newspapers editorially have been urging their readers to refuse to cooperate with the Military Government and have, according to the United States authorities, incited to riot and made vicious attacks on the United States.

A recent attack printed in Chosun Inmin Po was to the effect that, on Aug. 15, the first anniversary of Korea's liberation, United States troops bayoneted innocent laborers in the southern province of Cholla Namdo during a demonstration.

In addition to daily fulminations of the Communist line here Chosun Inmin Po has been echoing anti-United States propaganda emanating from the Soviet-occupation zone of North Korea and warring against the American efforts to collect grain, maintain order, restore Korea's economy and foster political unity.

* * *

April 23, 1947

TURKEY SUSPENDS TWO MORE PAPERS

Opposition Organs Published Deputy's Speech Calling Assembly Illegal

By RAYMOND DANIELL
Special to The New York Times

ISTANBUL, Turkey, April 22—Freedom of the press here received another setback today when the Government indefinitely suspended two important opposition newspapers for publishing a speech by a Deputy criticizing the administration. The Government acted under the martial law still in force in six provinces around Istanbul—theoretically, at least, because of the danger of foreign aggression.

The two new suppressions bring the total of banned publications, daily and weekly, to eleven. The latest victims were Democrasi and Tasvir, both important organs and both critical of the Government. The action closely followed a riot in Smyrna last Saturday when students demonstrating against communism attacked the offices of Zincirli Hurriyet [Freedom in Chains].

The titular owner of Democrasi is Gen. Saldik Aldogan, an opposition Deputy. The chief editorial writer for Tasvir is Cihad Baban, Independent Deputy who has been highly critical of the Government and the dominant People's party.

On April 19 both papers published reports of a speech by Adnan Menderes, one of four founders of the opposition Democratic party, declaring that "democracy cannot be established by force, trickery and deceit." He charged that Celal Bavar, Democratic leader, was followed on his campaign tours by members of the secret police.

The Government's announcement of the suspension said: "Tasvir and Democrasi of April 19, 1947, which, despite an announcement issued by the state of siege command on July 24, 1946, to the effect that writings arousing doubt and suspicion should not be published and that the state of siege command would take action against provocation, printed a provocative report quoting a Deputy as saying the Grand National Assembly was illegal, are suspended and their printing offices are closed for an indefinite period."

Witnesses to Saturday's riot said the outbreak did not appear to be spontaneous and the police made no effort to intervene. The mob destroyed copies of papers, threatened the staff with violence and did some damage to the plant.

The editor is Mehmit Ali Aybar, whose wife is the American-educated director of physical education at the American College for Girls. The paper has been regarded as Leftist, pro-Russian and opposed to the American loan.

The necessity for martial law here was questioned by Kenan Oner, an influential Democrat, who charged that "internal political questions" were the real reason for the maintenance of the state of siege adopted seven years ago. He said that the latest newspaper suspension was "nothing else but another in the series of steps taken by the Government to crush the opposition."

* * *

April 28, 1947

COCHIN CHINA BARS 13 ANNAMESE PAPERS

Special to The New York Times

PARIS, April 27—President Dr. Le Van Hoach has suspended publication of thirteen Annamese-language newspapers whose policy is friendly toward Ho Chi Minh, President of the Viet Nam Republic, according to advices from Saigon today.

The action was taken after an ambush in Mytho, in which two members of the Cabinet of French Indo-China were killed. The grounds given were that this attack had been instigated by an article published in Annamese-language newspapers.

Only one newspaper of the Unionist party, which has been moderate in tone, was permitted to continue publication.

The suppression of the papers does not affect foreign correspondents or French correspondents in Saigon.

* * *

April 14, 1949

11 SYRIAN PAPERS BANNED BY ZAYIM

Damascus Chief's Act Stresses Press Plight in Arab World as Democracy Ebbs

By ALBION ROSS

Special to The New York Times

BEIRUT, Lebanon, April 13—The plight of the free press in the Arab Orient was described today in the most literate city of the Middle East as desperate following Gen. Husni Zayim's abrupt decree suppressing permanently eleven out of nineteen Damascus newspapers.

The Syrian decree, editors and journalists stated, is the heaviest single blow to press freedom in the Middle East since Arab states became self-governing, but it was described as only part of an increasingly serious press crisis that apparently is part of the general crisis of democracy in the Middle East.

The opinion of experienced editors and publishers is that the wholesale slaughter of newspapers in Damascus would be acquiesced in because of the hopeless state into which the Syrian and much of the rest of the press of the Arab nations has fallen. The press as a whole, it is stated, has found it almost impossible to defend the principle of press freedom because a large number of papers practice deliberate blackmail, sell themselves to the highest bidder, and neglect news reporting for violent, highly personal editorial writing, including the distortion of facts.

General Zayim, it is stated, has taken a stand on safe ground, attributing his wholesale suppression to the necessity of doing away with the great number of weak and therefore often corrupt papers to make way for a healthier because financially sounder press.

Editors and publishers emphasized, however, that in the process of "purifying" the press General Zayim also has, in effect, crushed press opposition. Leading papers that opposed him and were associated with the regime of the former President, Shukri al-Kuwatly, have been swept away, it is explained, while the two Damascus pro-Kuwatly papers that remain have shown since the coup d'etat that they are prepared to support the new regime devotedly.

The once strongly pro-Kuwatly paper, Kabbas, for example, argued in its editorials that General Zayim should not be in any hurry to have new elections because the country did not want the old system repeated but needed a period, perhaps more than a year, of the present type of government. This amounted to an appeal to General Zayim to exercise his present absolute legislative and executive powers for a much longer period than he himself proposed.

In Lebanon, which has been as a whole the freest country in the Middle East, the press is fighting against a law passed last September that permits the Public Prosecutor to go to court to have a paper suppressed for a maximum period of one year. Lebanese editors say that the law does not delimit charges that the Prosecutor can bring and that a paper can be suppressed on a vague charge of a threat to public security.

Increasing restrictions placed on the press throughout the Arab world, editors and publishers say, is part of a steady drift toward increasingly authoritarian forms of government, including control of public opinion favored by the dishonesty and inadequacy of a large part of the Arab press.

* * *

May 5, 1949

KOREA SHUTS NEWSPAPER

Action Is Laid to Its Backing of Northern Pro-Soviet State

Special to The New York Times

SEOUL, Korea, May 4—The largest newspaper in South Korea, Seoul Shin Mun, was temporarily closed today on the order of D. S. Kim, Director of Public Information.

Mr. Kim said the newspaper "has printed stories clearly reflecting a support of the unlawful and totalitarian police state imposed upon our brethren in Northern Korea through the force of Russian arms."

A majority of the paper's stock is held by the Korean Government. However, Mr. Kim declared that the publishers and editors have been under the influence of North Korean Communists. He added that Seoul Shin Mun published noticeably fewer official Government news releases than any other newspaper and that it failed to print more than a few lines concerning President Syngman Rhee's recent inspection tour of South Korea, although other newspapers gave generous space to the same subject.

Ha Kyung Duk, publisher of Seoul Shin Mun, denied the charges today and declared the newspaper was not influenced by Communists.

* * *

July 24, 1950

PRESS CENSORSHIP ON RISE IN MIDEAST

Lebanon, Most Liberal of Arab Countries, Now Suppresses Embarrassing Dispatches

By ALBION ROSS

Special to The New York Times

DAMASCUS, Syria, July 23—Freedom of the press has suddenly become an issue of major importance in the three northern Arab countries, Lebanon, Iraq and Syria.

Lebanon, which had long been the most liberal of the Arab countries as regards the press, is now imposing on foreign correspondents an oppressive censorship frankly based on the principle that, irrespective of the truth, only news favorable to Lebanon can be sent to foreign publications.

News of recent events in that country that, while not dangerous or sensational, was rather embarrassing to the Government, has been deliberately suppressed by the director of the Press Bureau, who acts without specific regulations, selecting on his own authority the news that the foreign public shall be permitted to receive.

The general feeling of those most directly affected by this outbreak of censorship is that it is concerned primarily with protecting the reputations of certain prominent political men, rather than with anything that could legitimately be considered as affecting the security of the state. The only concrete explanation given for this suppression is that certain news would hurt the country's reputation among Lebanese emigrants.

A Major Source of Income

The number of Lebanese who have emigrated is roughly equivalent to half the present population. These emigrants are a major source of income to the state through their remittances to relatives and the Government hopes that they will also invest considerable sums toward further development of the country. Although there is mail censorship in Lebanon, investigation indicates that these emigrants are kept adequately informed of the rather discouraging political conditions in the country through letters, as the volume of mail is too great to permit airtight censorship.

In Iraq, meanwhile, a draft law has been introduced providing for what seem like blanket Government powers to halt criticism in the press. The law stirred up a hornet's nest in Parliament and brought on a strike of nearly all the Baghdad newspapers.

The Syrian Parliament also has before it a draft law providing punishment for attacks on Ministers and the Constituent Assembly that are calculated to damage the prestige of members of the Government or the Assembly.

The news suppression in Lebanon stemmed from an incident arising out of the practice of arresting editors or proprietors of newspapers and bringing them before a special Press Court. The incident resulted in a political struggle that went on for a month. This was discussed in full detail in the Lebanese press after an initial ban on discussion of the affair had been lifted.

Dispatch Is Suppressed

The New York Times correspondent was informed yesterday that an account of this political struggle, although it had been fully discussed within Lebanon and the facts were all familiar, was not to be read abroad. A dispatch containing an account of the affair was accordingly suppressed by the censorship on instructions of the Director of the Press.

The not very sensational facts were that Said Frayha, editor of the newspaper Cayad and a strong supporter of the present Premier, Riad es-Solh, had been summoned for investigation more than a month ago by the Director of Police, Nasser Said.

This was done without informing Riad es-Solh in his capacity as Minister of Interior.

The Director of Police was suspended for one month, ending yesterday. Said Frayha was later charged before the Press Court with defaming the President of the Republic, found guilty and sentenced to three months' imprisonment, while his paper was suspended for six months. He was pardoned by President Bechara el-Khoury.

Meanwhile Selim el-Khoury, the politically influential brother of the President, demanded that the Director of Police, who is his friend, be reinstated immediately. Partisans of Premier es-Solh in the Basta district of Beirut staged political demonstrations and fired a great deal of ammunition into the air. Inevitably, some persons were wounded and there were said to have been some deaths, though it is impossible to verify these reports.

One day the entrances to the city from the mountains were closed by a security cordon because partisans of Selim el-Khoury, filled with equal fervor for their cause were coming into town to demonstrate their enthusiasm in similar fashion.

Naturally, there is a general feeling that this sort of thing is a disgrace for the country with the highest standard of literacy in the Middle East.

In the end, the Director of Police served out his full month of suspension, returned to his office and the crisis was over.

During these events, however, Ghassan Tueni, a strong journalistic opponent of Premier es-Solh's Government who had been calling for the resignation of the Cabinet, was arrested. He went into hiding, having spent last summer in prison, was sentenced by the Press Court in absentia to two months in prison, and his paper was ordered suspended for twenty days.

* * *

July 4, 1952

LEBANON FACES ISSUE ON FREEDOM OF PRESS

Special to The New York Times

BEIRUT, Lebanon, July 3—The Republic of Lebanon, which enjoys the greatest degree of freedom of opinion of any of the Arab states and has no censorship, is going through a freedom of the press crisis that has caused within a fortnight a one-day strike of possibly half the business establishments in this city and two official newspaper strikes authorized by the press syndicate.

Ten newspapers, including several of Beirut's leading papers, have been suspended for periods ranging from one to nine months for carrying an article accusing President Hashim Bey al-Atassi of having come to power through foreigners and being an instrument of foreign influences. This was regarded in the context in which it appeared as a seditious attack on the head of the state. Two editors received jail sentences.

Communist newspapers and other papers have been suspended on other grounds.

The reaction of a considerable part of the public and solidarity of the newspapers in the protest strike was taken as evidence that the principle of freedom of the press was apparently taken seriously here.

* * *

February 14, 1953

MOSSADEGH TAKES POWER OVER PRESS

Designed as Curb on Leftists, Iran's New Decree Is One of Most Severe in World

By CLIFTON DANIEL
Special to The New York Times

TEHERAN, Iran, Feb. 13—With scarcely a peep of protest from the press, one of the most stringent newspaper control laws in the world has come into effect in Iran. It was promulgated by Premier Mohammed Mossadegh under his plenary powers without reference to Parliament and became operative last Saturday.

Under the law the Iranian Government has the authority to grant or withhold licenses for publication of newspapers and magazines, prescribe regulations for the journalistic profession, determine the qualifications and salaries of newspaper men and suppress publications that it considers a menace to public order and welfare. The newspaper licenses are renewable every six months.

The law is one of a series that Dr. Mossadegh has taken since he first received full powers six months ago to buttress his position, reinforce public security and restrain any opposition.

While such a law would be assailed by every newspaper in the United States as the gravest menace to freedom of the press, its advent in Iran has scarcely been remarked upon. Control of the press has been exercised in some degree or other by every Government since the beginning of newspapers in this country and it is taken as a matter of course.

Majority Accept Need of Law

In the Government's view, the new law replacing a statute of 1907 was necessary to check excesses of the Teheran press, particularly organs of the Left, and to minimize incitements to violence, disorder and revolt. At least tacitly that view has been supported by the majority opinion in Teheran.

Before the law was enacted newspapers protested against some sections, which were amended to meet their objections.

Since the law has taken effect the only strong protests have come from the newspapers at which the law particularly was aimed. Among those newspapers are some of the most scurrilous and irresponsible in the world.

Despite the new law, examples of vituperative comment still were appearing in the press this week. Bessouye Ayandeh and Shahbaz, generally known as the voices of the underground Tudeh [Communist] party, have said in recent issues that Dr. Mossadegh has been trampling on the Constitution and leading the country to fascism and dictatorship and that the chief of the national police was a criminal guilty of atrocities and torture who should be hanged.

Under the new law, the police chief or any other citizen who considers himself wrongly attacked in a newspaper has the right to make a reply and have it published with the same prominence as the original charge.

Heavy fines are provided for publishing an illegal unlicensed newspaper. A paper once suppressed cannot be revived under another name and no one may have more than one newspaper license. These provisions are designed to prevent owners of banned papers from issuing them immediately under new names as has been the practice here in the past.

Backing Must Be Revealed

Newspapers are required to keep business accounts, have them certified by the public prosecutor and publish them annually. This requirement is intended to disclose the financial backing of newspapers, which often are subsidized by political or private interests.

Imprisonment and fines are provided for journalists who incite the people to sabotage, arson, murder and plunder or incite the armed forces to desertion and indiscipline, publish military secrets, encourage public disorder, insult foreign diplomats, publish material detrimental to public morals, insult official personages, print scandalous remarks about the private lives of citizens or insult religious and racial minorities. Those accused under the law are guaranteed trial by jury.

The public prosecutor, with the consent of a criminal court and without a jury trial, can suppress any newspaper that publishes articles detrimental to the Islam state religion of Iran, discloses military secrets, incites disorder or resistance to the armed forces or commits lèse majesté—that is, disrespect toward the royal family.

* * *

February 17, 1954

TURKEY PLANNING NEW PRESS CURBS

Regime's Moves to Punish 'Insults' Greeted Skeptically by Opposition Forces

Special to The New York Times

ANKARA, Turkey, Feb. 16—Turkey is expected to adopt a stringent new law imposing up to nine years imprisonment on newspaper men who "insult the honor" or "invade the privacy" of public officials.

The bill, made public today, has already been approved by the Parliamentary group of the ruling Democratic party, whose majority in the Grand National Assembly is sufficient to assure its enactment. Simultaneously the Government presented amendments to Turkey's penal code providing heavy prison terms and fines for persons disseminating "false, exaggerated or tendentious news."

Premier Adnan Menderes has assured Istanbul newspaper publishers the Government will use the new legal authority only to prevent such vilification, not as a means to suppress legitimate criticism of its policies.

Opposition Skeptical

The People's Republican party, the strongest opposition group, and a large segment of the independent press are openly skeptical of the Government's intentions. The Republicans assert the new law would be employed by the Government to muzzle opposition newspapers during the political campaign now in progress.

The draft press law prescribes imprisonment up to three years and a fine of 10,000 liras ($3,570) for anyone who through the medium of press or radio "insults another's honor, dignity or probity" or "invades another's private life or family affairs" or "threatens to commit either of these offenses."

If the offense is committed "against a person with an official position by reason of such position" the penalties are increased by one-third to one-half. If the offense is committed more than once the penalties are doubled.

Publisher Would Face Fine

Besides setting punishment for newspaper reporters or others immediately responsible for such crimes, the law authorizes the court to fine the responsible newspaper publisher up to 50,000 liras ($17,850).

Persons who publish anything "that can harm the political honor or national reputation of the state or that can create alarm and anxiety in public opinion" are punishable by up to three years in prison and a 10,000 lira ($3,570) fine. These penalties also are doubled if the offense is repeated.

In the proposed amendments to the penal code the Government would impose a two-year prison sentence and a 5,000 lira ($1,785) fine to anyone "who carries on activity harmful to the national interest in peacetime." In wartime the minimum sentence is five years imprisonment or a life term if the activity is conducted in concert with the enemy.

"Activity harmful to the national interest" is specifically defined to include "dissemination of false, exaggerated or tendentious news or anything that would arouse public alarm or anxiety."

* * *

June 3, 1954

NEWS MEN SEIZED IN KARACHI RAIDS

5 Among 11 Taken in Drive on 'Reds and Subversives'— 73 Arrested in East

By JOHN P. CALLAHAN
Special to The New York Times

KARACHI, Pakistan, June 1—Eleven Pakistanis were arrested in a round-up early today of "Communists and other subversive elements" in Karachi.

Simultaneously, police and military intelligence officers in East Pakistan arrested seventy-three others for "activities prejudicial to public safety."

Since May 18, 303 Communists and left-wing associates have been jailed for a minimum of one year under the Pakistani Security Act.

Among those arrested in Karachi were two editors of Dawn, M. A. Shakoor and Ahmad Hasan; M. Akhtar a sports reporter for the Times of Karachi; Anis Hashmi, advertising manager of the Times of Karachi, and Eric Rahin, the Karachi correspondent of the left-wing Pakistan Times published in Lahore.

Editor Is 'Distressed'

Altar Husain, editor of Dawn, said that "in the absence of facts" he was "distressed" at the arrests of Messrs. Shakoor and Hasan, although he acknowledged he had an "idea" Mr. Shakoor had been active in a left-wing cultural association.

Z. A. Suleri, editor of the Times of Karachi said he had no suspicion that Messrs. Akhtar on Hashmi were members or associates of Communists.

Police records show that a brother of Mr. Akhtar was among six persons arrested here May 18. Mr. Hashmi served six months' imprisonment in 1952 for "political activities inimical to the interests of Pakistan."

Mr. Shakoor was president last year of The Karachi Union of Journalists. Mr. Hasar is a member of its executive committee and Mr. Akhtar is assistant secretary. Tonight the union voted a resolution demanding that offenses charged to the arrested journalists "be proved in open court of law or else release them unconditionally."

Mr. Suleri will say in a lead editorial in The Times of Karachi tomorrow that the Government should clarify its policy on the Communist party or declare it to be unlawful, otherwise those who are not Communists may fall prey to the prejudices and misinformation of the Administration. As it is, there is a large margin for abuse of power which must be eliminated."

* * *

August 8, 1954

VIETNAM CENSORS ANNOY REPORTERS

News Dispatches Must Pass Two Military Hurdles and One Political

By HENRY R. LIEBERMAN
Special to The New York Times

SAIGON, Vietnam, Aug. 2—A thoughtful young Frenchman who lives at the press camp in Hanoi came to Saigon today for a short leave and was good enough to bring down the mail. It included a July 30 notice addressed to this correspondent by the Vietnamese Controller of Telegraph in Hanoi.

The notice read: "I have the honor to inform you that your telegrams No. 636 Armistice Four and No. 637 Armistice Five of July 27, 1954, addressed to Press Nyktimes Paris are stopped in Saigon. Reason: Forwarding not authorized."

The blocked telegrams were sections four and five of a dispatch dealing with the July 27 cease-fire in North Vietnam.

A total of 395 words in these telegrams, including a nineteen-word message were "killed" by censors in Saigon after the entire dispatch had cleared French military censorship in Hanoi.

Three days elapsed before the Vietnamese telegraph office served notice that the two telegrams had been blocked. Were it not for the Vietnamese Government's new policy of bringing their former invisible censorship out into the open, this correspondent would probably never have learned that the telegrams had been "killed."

Numbers at Issue

Various press messages sent by other foreign correspondents from Hanoi also have been blocked by Vietnamese here after clearing on-the-spot French military censorship in the North Vietnam capital. The French correspondent for Le Monde of Paris said today he had had six dispatches "killed" by censors here.

In Saigon, correspondents are now involved in daily wrangling with Vietnamese authorities on censorship. Wrangling is over such matters as Vietnamese troop desertions and whether or not 1,000, 2,000, 3,000 or more persons took part in a Vietminh-sponsored "peace" demonstration here.

The two blocked dispatches to The New York Times of July 27 dealt with Vietminh propaganda efforts to subvert Vietnamese Nationalist troops and with comments of Gen.

René Cogny, commander of French Union ground forces in North Vietnam, on Vietnamese troop desertions. General Cogny had emphasized the importance of maintaining morale among Vietnamese soldiers in the north.

In blocking the telegrams, the Vietnamese were censoring not only this correspondent but also the commander of their troops in North Vietnam. But this type of thing is not unheard of here. Toward the close of June, the French military censor in Hanoi censored a statement by Nguyen Huu Tri, late Governor of North Vietnam, to the effect that French Union troops had started to withdraw from the lower Red River delta.

The reason given for censoring this statement was "military security." This was at a time when the French Union command was moving all of its heavy military equipment out of the lower delta, when warehouses were being emptied, and sector headquarters being stripped of all furnishings and when thousands of civilian refugees were fleeing north.

The domestic press as well as international news copy is subject to censorship here.

There are three kinds of censorship for foreign dispatches: French military censorship, Vietnamese military censorship and Vietnamese political censorship. Until recently Vietnamese political censorship was handled invisibly in the Saigon post office by what came to be known as the "black cabinet."

The "black cabinet" started censoring foreign dispatches behind the scenes before the present Government of Premier Ngo Dinh Diem assumed office.

The new Government actually seems to be trying to improve this censorship system. Although it has eliminated invisible censorship, it is still applying political censorship.

On July 30 foreign correspondents here were informed by Vietnamese authorities that they would henceforth be notified if there were any delay or censorship of their dispatches. After a group of news men had voiced their objections to political censorship, visible or invisible, they were told a new system would be tried for one week to see how it worked.

Four Copies Required

When a correspondent "files" a dispatch here he is required to submit four copies, two being retained by the French military censor and two going to the Vietnamese post office. Inasmuch as Saigon is the only direct transmission center for news dispatches sent abroad, dispatches written in Hanoi or elsewhere in Indochina must be routed through here.

News copy submitted at the press camp in Hanoi is sent to the telegraph office there after clearing through an on-the-spot French military censor. Usually French military authorities uphold the principle of single French censorship, but there have been cases in which dispatches cleared by the French military censor in Hanoi have been recensored by French military censors in Saigon.

This practice has now been officially terminated.

No specific rules have been made available to correspondents, either by French or Vietnamese authorities, on what is censurable and what is not. On the basis of past experience, correspondents are also not absolutely sure that once a censor's stamp is on a dispatch the dispatch will go through intact.

French military censorship is erratic, operating by fits and starts. For a long period of time it is as lenient as can be expected. And then suddenly there is a sudden clampdown. Sometimes the reasons given for censoring dispatches are difficult to fathom.

* * *

September 21, 1955

MILITARY CLOSES 5 TURKISH PAPERS

Ankara and Istanbul Organs Accused of Breaking Rules of Military Censorship

Special to The New York Times

ANKARA, Turkey, Sept. 20—Martial law authorities in Ankara and Istanbul tonight ordered closed five major newspapers, including the organ of the opposition party. The papers were accused of having violated censorship regulations imposed since the destructive riots of Sept. 6 and 7 in Ankara, Istanbul and Izmir (Smyrna).

The riots were directed largely at Greek residents. They followed a report, later proved to be false, that a bomb had damaged the house in Salonika, Greece, where Kemal Ataturk founder of the modern Turkish state, was born.

Ulus, newspaper of the opposition Republican People's party, was suspended indefinitely by Maj. Gen. Ihsan Bingol, military governor of Ankara after it had attacked the Government's handling of the disturbances.

Four major Istanbul papers were ordered shut for two weeks. They were Hurriyet, largest Turkish newspaper with a circulation of more than 300,000; Milliyet, third largest paper with a 60,000 circulation; Tercuman, a new paper with 50,000 circulation, and Hergun, afternoon paper with 20,000 circulation.

Hergun was banned by Lieut. Gen. Nurettin Aknoz, Istanbul military governor, after it had published a message from Secretary of State Dulles to the Greek and Turkish Premiers asking them to heal the breach between the two countries for the sake of the unity of the North Atlantic Treaty Organization.

Hurriyet, Tercuman and Milliyet were said to have been suspended because they had published extracts from a Ulus editorial criticizing the Government. The editorial signed by former President Ismet Inonu, opposition leader, demanded that the Government summon a special session of Parliament in order to give a full explanation of the riots.

One Izmir opposition paper, Sabah Postasi, was suspended several days ago for criticizing the conduct of the local governor during the disorders.

* * *

November 29, 1955

NEW EGYPTIAN LAW HITS AT 'FALSE NEWS'

Special to The New York Times

CAIRO, Nov. 28—Newspaper men working in Egypt are subject to prison sentences and fines for publishing "false news" contrary to the "public interest," according to an amendment to the penal code, approved last Wednesday and published today in the official gazette.

The amendment says: "Any person who publishes, through any of the means specified in the penal code, false news, fictitious or forged documents or reports falsely attributed to others, shall be liable to a term of imprisonment up to twelve months and/or a fine of £20 to £100 Egyptian [An Egyptian pound is equal to $2.89] if such news or documents are connected with the security or the public interest unless the accused proves his or her goodwill."

If such a publication entails "a disturbance of the public security or harm to the public interest," a heavier penalty is prescribed.

According to an official of the information administration, the amendment applies to both foreign correspondents and local reporters.

* * *

July 14, 1956

MENDERES DECLARES NEW CURBS IN TURKEY ARE AN INTERNAL ISSUE

Premier Says That Criticisms Abroad of Restrictions on Press Offend Nation

By SAM POPE BREWER
Special to The New York Times

ANKARA, Turkey, July 12—Premier Adnan Menderes said today that Turkey's stringent new press law and the law on public assembly were matters to be settled among the Turks. He declined to make a statement on them for publication.

Talking of these laws in an interview, Premier Menderes said he could not say anything to be attributed to him "because this is basically an internal question which might oblige me to criticize some groups of my fellow citizens."

"It is repugnant to me to bring such discussions and criticism into the international field," he added. "These are things to be settled among us Turks."

The Menderes Government has been severely criticized here and abroad for the new press law and the severe limitations of political meetings.

The press law prevents any very outspoken criticism by newspapers. Many Turks who are supporters of the Menderes Government feel the news law is unduly harsh.

Law Covers Foreign Press

The press law provides punishment for writing or publishing virtually anything that displeases the government. Foreign correspondents are included by the provision that it is an offense to "publish or cause to be published abroad" any of the matters banned under the law including criticism of the government and reports of economic shortages, or anything that may diminish the prestige of the Turkish Government.

The law on assembly restricts public political meetings to a period of forty-five days immediately preceding elections. Premier Menderes denies that there is any intention of limiting the constitutional rights of citizens.

Opposition sources contend that the new laws are completely unconstitutional in their limits on freedom. They do not share Premier Menderes view that this question should be aired only among Turks, and they would like to present their case before the world.

The Government's thesis is that press freedom and political speaking were abused. It says the country was in a state of "anarchy" and that disciplinary measures were necessary to insure order and restraint.

The Government is preparing a book of selections from the press during the last six years that it says will prove its case as far as the language of the press is concerned.

As for the law on assembly it maintains that forty-five days is sufficient time to prepare a campaign. Government spokesmen add that additional forty-five-day campaign periods are permitted for municipal or other elections, as well as for the national elections that are held every four years.

The Government maintains that an excessive number of political meetings, which it estimates at thirty to forty a week throughout the nation, was keeping the country stirred up and interfering with the administration.

One official source appeared incredulous when, in answer to a question, he was told that Americans could hold as many political rallies as they wished.

The opposition newspaper Ulus published an announcement today that it had been warned by the public prosecutor not to print a report of yesterday's proceedings in Parliament. Opposition deputies had protested against the Government's repeated postponement of by-elections.

A newspaper editor said today that "that is the only thing it would appear safe to publish under the new press law, and now they are warning editors not to do even that."

* * *

September 13, 1956

SOME PRESS CURBS ON TAIWAN LIFTED

Editorial Criticism of Chiang Regime Causes Remedial Efforts by Officials

By GREG MacGREGOR
Special to The New York Times

TAIPEI, Taiwan, Sept. 9—Most of the eleven newspapers here are planning to publish reports of the Chinese Communists' eighth conference in Peiping Saturday, for readers in Taiwan (Formosa), the publishers disclosed today.

These plans indicated a radical departure from the press policies of previous years and a marked change from the Nationalist Government dictates of recent months.

Only last spring, The China Post, a leading English-language newspaper in Taipei, was threatened by Taiwan's "Peace Preservation Command" for having printed an invitation from Premier Chou En-lai in Peiping for Nationalist leaders to meet with him to settle differences.

Independent newspaper publishers of Taiwan said today that the Nationalist Government's attitude toward a free press had changed considerably in recent months. Top publishers view the change as a healthy sign and a strong indication of growing confidence.

Six years ago, they said, little more than Nationalist propaganda would have been allowed. They said, however, the Government's attitude in 1950 might have been justified by the perilous position of Taiwan.

Evidence of the gradual policy change toward the press has appeared repeatedly in recent news reports here. Not only has the press attacked the Government repeatedly, but the Government also has taken steps to remedy its faults in response.

One good example of the beginnings of a completely free press appeared last March when The China News, a lively English-language publication, stated:

"The National House Commission of the Executive Yuan might as well be dead. Its usefulness in relieving the housing shortage of civilians is becoming a national farce."

The publication went on to say that "figures showed the commission had done practically nothing for the bulk of the homeless." The Government commission was also accused of having extended preferential treatment to legislators and influential groups.

Instead of censorship and retaliation, the Government dismissed some of the commission members, investigated and changed the sales program, and built 200 new houses on the outskirts of Taipei for the most needy.

* * *

September 14, 1957

INDONESIA CLOSES PAPERS IN CAPITAL

2 News Agencies Also Shut for Their Reporting of National Unity Talks

By BERNARD KALB
Special to The New York Times

JAKARTA, Indonesia, Saturday, Sept. 14—The military commander of the Jakarta area ordered early today the closing of nearly all leading newspapers and two national news agencies here.

The P. I. A. agency quoted the office of the commander, Lieut. Col. Endang Dachjar, as having said the action stemmed from the publications' "reporting" of the current conference on national unity. The shutdown is for an "indefinite" period, it was added.

The conference which began Tuesday, has brought together top leaders of the central Government and of the defiant outer regions in a major effort to reunite the sharply divided country.

A critical stage in the conference was reached yesterday when a special effort was made to restore the working relationship of President Sukarno and Dr. Mohammed Hatta, who resigned as Vice President last December. The outcome is not yet known.

Only a few days ago Colonel Dachjar's office issued a statement calling on the press to refrain from publishing reports or opinions that might "trouble" the atmosphere during the conference. He warned that action would be taken against violators under the state of war and siege now prevailing throughout the country.

A spokesman for P. I. A. said the agency itself was directed to cease operations as of last night. Among the thirteen news organs also affected are such major papers as Indonesia Raya, Pedoman and Kengpo the Communist paper Harian Rakjot and the leftist Bintang Timur, the spokesman reported.

At the unity conference yesterday, a special committee was assigned to confer separately with President Sukarno and Dr. Hatta.

The former Vice President, a Sumatra-born anti-Communist, is regarded by the outer regions as a kind of guardian of their interests. These regions have been pressing for increased economic and administrative autonomy.

Since his resignation last December, Dr. Hatta has been highly critical of the controversial steps taken by President Sukarno toward a "guided democracy."

Success or failure of the effort to reunite President Sukarno and Dr. Hatta will be the major factor in determining the success or failure of the conference, according to Indonesian observers.

The leftist newspaper Bintang Timur published a report that purported to give something of the inside story of what had occurred at the meeting between President Sukarno and Dr. Hatta Wednesday. The newspaper said the President was prepared to ask Dr. Hatta to resume the post of Vice President or to take another position in the Government.

* * *

October 5, 1957

SAIGON SETS TRIAL OF 8 PUBLISHERS

Charges They Solicited Aid for Vietnam-Born Chinese Who Rejected Citizenship

By GREG MacGREGOR
Special to The New York Times

SAIGON, Vietnam, Oct. 4—Eight Chinese-language newspaper publishers here have been accused of printing articles and participating in acts opposed to the best interests of the Government.

The trials of the eight accused have been set for next week, according to the Saigon Prefecture Mayor.

The principal charge against the publishers is centered on the "illegal" collection of funds to aid Vietnamese-born Chinese who have refused Vietnamese citizenship. A secondary charge accuses the publishers of having printed articles of criticism against Chinese born here who had accepted Vietnamese citizenship, as dictated by a national law.

The charges against the publishers are the latest development in the campaign of President Ngo Dinh Diem to force all residents of Chinese ancestry born in Vietnam to pledge full allegiance to Vietnam or leave the country. Chinese in this category had traditionally claimed dual citizenship.

Earlier this year, the President set the month of August as the deadline for decision and named eleven categories of employment principally engaged in by Chinese to be denied to any residents other than Vietnamese nationals. These included jobs, such as those of butcher, grocer, pawn broker, agent and so on.

1,200 Comply with Law

Out of the Government's estimate of 60,000 Chinese born here, only about 1,200 complied with the law by the August deadline. About 500 more left for Taiwan [Formosa] and 1,000 others hold exit permits to depart soon. The remainder have been eluding the police and defying the Government, according to the authorities.

Many in this group remained illegally in their businesses and trades by transfering titles to their wives, relatives or friends who held Vietnamese citizenship. The majority, however, were forced to leave their employment or abide by the law.

It was for this substantial group of unemployed that the newspapers solicited the public for emergency funds to support defiance of the law, the Government charges stated.

In defense of this unemployed Vietnamese-born Chinese group, however, the Nationalist Chinese legation has explained that screening, evacuation, transport and resettlement for any large part of so sizable a group would be a major undertaking for a nation confined within the limits of Taiwan and asked for leniency on the time limit.

Undesirables in Group

Other well-informed sources believe that Vietnam is as eager to deport certain undesirable elements, such as narcotics peddlers, gangsters and known trouble-makers, as Taiwan is reluctant to accept them.

Despite the latest flare-up over the nationality issue, most observers agreed that much less tension was evident than earlier this year, and particularly last summer just before the Government deadline was reached.

When a suspect was found who did not produce proper identity papers as a Vietnamese national he was deprived of his former credentials and new papers identifying him as a citizen were issued, a police source explained. He said that under existing law all Chinese born in Vietnam became citizens automatically last August when the deadline passed, but had no rights until proper papers were issued.

* * *

August 5, 1958

CENSORSHIP CONFUSES LEBANESE NEWS

Special to The New York Times

BEIRUT, Lebanon, July 31—Rigid and often irrational censorship has confused the reporting of the crisis in Lebanon.

It has been based more on political than security considerations. The local press has been much more severely affected than foreign correspondents. However, outgoing dispatches suffered severely during the long political crisis because the censorship would not allow the name of the outstanding candidate, Gen. Fouad Chehab, to be mentioned.

Until three days before the general's election as President today, he could be referred to only as a "leading non-political figure." The general had given strict orders that his name was not to appear.

The New York Times

Pages from Beirut newspapers bear many blanks as a result of censorship. In many cases it takes little imagination to guess what has been deleted. At left, photos have been dropped from reports of arrival of U.S. Marines.

The capricious character of censorship has been as exasperating as any other feature. What was passed in one dispatch would be arbitrarily stopped in another.

United States spokesmen here have emphasized in their news conferences the close liaison between American forces here and the Lebanese forces. On most occasions, censors have refused to permit a discussion of this in dispatches.

When rebel leaders make accusations against President Camille Chamoun, the censors delete them from the local press and usually from cablegrams. Uncomplimentary remarks about the President are not allowed in dispatches.

In a recent cablegram the censor firmly struck out the fact that General Chehab had attended a staff briefing with Admiral James L. Holloway Jr., commanding the United States forces in Lebanon. Yet this fact was published in the local press.

Other topics that have been taboo are the heavy weapons brought ashore by the United States Marines and soldiers, the capture of weapons by the rebels from Lebanese forces and, above all, the Lebanese Army itself.

In all but the most general connections, the army must be referred to only as "the security forces." Mention of the army's movements is forbidden, even when it could not possibly be of danger to its security.

On one occasion, a correspondent said that the movement of army forces into the Bekaa Valley had restored peace and order. The censor stopped that, but eventually agreed to permit the statement that "the presence of army forces" had restored peace and order.

The object seems not so much security as suppression of any idea that the Lebanese Army is involved in the fighting here. In fact, it has been involved in very little of it.

Political items have been less severely censored, but in general, correspondents cannot discuss the political position freely and frankly. They are often stopped from reporting objections raised to Mr. Chamoun and to the landing of United States forces.

In fairness to the Lebanese, it should be said that even this censorship is far more logical and less severe than those in Jordan, Syria or Iraq, not to mention Saudi Arabia, which outdoes them all.

In the local press, anything that is censored is blanked out, the context frequently makes the meaning clear.

The newspaper An Nahar has suggested running a contest in which free subscriptions would be awarded to readers filling in all blanks correctly.

One day before the election, L'Orient, a French-language newspaper, published a lengthy article on possible candidates. Throughout the story, wherever the names were listed, General Chehab's name was replaced by a blank, although his identity was clear.

Even the headline was affected. It said: "Presidential election: Three principal candidates, former Presidents Alfred Naccache and Bechara el-Khoury," followed by a blank space that just fitted "General Chehab."

On July 19 L'Orient appeared with the single word "censored" at the top, where an eight-column banner headline on United States military activities had been suppressed. The two right-hand columns were largely blank, with the word "censored" here and there.

* * *

May 2, 1959

OPPOSITION PAPER CLOSED IN KOREA

News Falsification Charged—Shutdown Protested by U. S. Embassy

Special to The New York Times

SEOUL, Korea, May 1—A leading Opposition daily newspaper, Kyunghyang Shinmun, was closed by the Government Information Office last night on the ground that it had printed editorials and news articles of a false nature.

Dr. Chun Sung Chun, the Director of Information, issued a statement listing five reasons for the ban on the publication, including propaganda and instigation in support of a revolt in a column written by an editorial writer last February. The writer, Chu Yo Han, who also is a member of the National Assembly, has been indicted and has resigned from his post on the paper.

The closing of the paper was criticized today by Walter C. Dowling, the United States Ambassador, who said in a statement that American public opinion had long held that "suppression of the press is not a remedy for press errors." The United States Embassy made an oral protest against the closing to the South Korean Foreign Ministry.

Political Curb Charged

Vice President John M. Chang, leader of the Opposition Democratic party, charged that the Government had closed the paper "to curb the Opposition's political activities through the press in next year's Presidential elections." Dr. Chang is a political foe of President Syngman Rhee.

The statement by the information director accused the Kyunghyang Shinmun, among other things, of having printed a fabricated story about a news conference held by President Rhee. The article reported that the President opposed amendment of the controversial National Security Law.

Another charge against the paper was that it intended to disturb the Korean political situation by an editorial last January dealing with a false report that an unpleasant conversation had taken place between Lee Ki Poong, Speaker of the House, and Dr. Frank W. Schofield, his Canadian friend who gave aid to Korea's 1919 independence movement against the Japanese.

Kyunghyang Shinmun printed a clarification in each case.

Dr. Chun's statement also said the paper printed an untrue article last February on misappropriation of gasoline by a Korean Army division commander. The director of information added that the paper also had obstructed effective operation of the intelligence police by prematurely reporting last month the seizure of a North Korean spy.

Eo Im Yung, a reporter for the paper, was indicted this week on a charge of violating the security law by having reported the arrest of the spy.

In closing the paper the Government invoked Ordinance 88 of the former United States Military Government of South Korea. The ordinance was proclaimed in May, 1946.

Ambassador Dowling said that "the intent of the American Military Government in promulgating Ordinance 88 in 1946 was clearly to curb Communist subversive propaganda which threatened Korean internal security at that time."

Kyunghyang Shinmun had Roman Catholic support and was a backer of Vice President Chang. Its circulation of more than 150,000 was second only to the 200,000 circulation of Tong-a Il Bo, another Opposition paper.

Kyunghyang Shinmun is expected to file an administrative suit against the Government.

* * *

December 20, 1959

RABAT ENDS PRESS CURB

Moroccan King Acts to Spur Wider Expression of Views

Special to The New York Times

RABAT, Morocco, Dec. 9—King Mohamed V repealed a decree curbing the press today in a move to encourage a wider representation of opinions prior to Morocco's first nation-wide elections.

The decree signed in September authorized the Interior Minister to take legal action against any publication attacking a Government official or a member of the army or the police forces.

In protest the conservative Istiqlal (Independence) party suspended all five of its publications. The only Arabic daily that continued to publish in this Arab country of 10,000,000 inhabitants was the Leftist Al Tahrir.

* * *

August 27, 1960

RABAT BANS 3 PAPERS

Foreign Journals Are Scored for Criticism of Morocco

Special to The New York Times

RABAT, Morocco, Aug. 26—The Moroccan Ministry of Information said tonight that three foreign newspapers published in Morocco would be closed down Sunday.

A British weekly, The Tangier Gazette, was banned for "taking a position on internal Moroccan affairs and criticizing national policy."

The Gazette irked the Government when it carried a bitter campaign denouncing the integration of the former free city of Tangier into the Moroccan kingdom.

The other newspapers no longer authorized to appear are the country's only daily financial paper, Stocks et Marches, published at Casablanca, and the only French daily published in Tangier, La Dépêche Marocaine.

* * *

September 26, 1960

SUKARNO DECREE CLOSES 8 PAPERS

Indonesia Seizes Printing Plants of Anti-Red and Anti-Regime Press

By BERNARD KALB
Special to The New York Times

JAKARTA, Indonesia, Sept. 25—President Sukarno confiscated six printing plants this week-end, halting publication of the majority of Indonesia's most important Opposition and anti-Communist newspapers.

Among the newspapers affected was Pedoman, Jakarta's largest daily, with a circulation of 55,000 and a wide following among Indonesian intellectuals.

The seizure, carried out last night and disclosed today, was taken on the ground that some of these plants had been used or would be used to disrupt law and order and the implementation of state policy.

The takeover of the plants, five on Java and one on South Celebes, was ordered in a decree signed by Mr. Sukarno in his capacity as Supreme War Administrator.

Government Bought Plants

The seized plants were purchased by Indonesia several years ago to promote the development of the Indonesian press. The plants were made available to various newspapers, which were still making payments on an installment basis.

The only major newspaper with pronounced anti-Communist views that will appear in Jakarta tomorrow is Nusantara, with a circulation of 33,000. It is published on privately owned presses.

The decree did not name any newspapers. But the confiscation of the six plants had the practical effect of silencing, for the present at least, about eight newspapers published by them. The Communists have frequently demanded that some of the affected papers be banned.

Whether the dailies can make new arrangements to continue publication was said to be doubtful, both because printing plants are scarce and because of the publishers' fear of antagonizing the Government through the issuance of critical newspapers.

Linked to Sukarno Aims

The action was considered a part of Government plans that appear to be aimed at regimenting the national press in behalf of the Government's "Left progressive" ideology, as outlined in Mr. Sukarno's political manifesto.

The seizure, coming on the eve of Mr. Sukarno's departure for the United Nations tomorrow, was seen as a move to preclude the possibility of the newspapers' stirring anti-Communist and anti-Sukarno sentiments while he was out of the country.

Mr. Sukarno has been championing unity among Nationalists, Moslems and Communists. He has been criticized by most of the eight newspapers affected. Several of the dailies have been temporarily suspended in the past.

Seized Papers Listed

Among the newspapers whose printing plants were seized are:

Pedoman, reflecting the views of the anti-Communist Socialist party, which dissolved itself this month in compliance with a Sukarno order.

Abadi, published in Jakarta, circulation about 20,000. It is the organ of the anti-Communist Moslem Masjumi, also dissolved at Mr. Sukarno's order.

Suara Rakjat, published in Surabaya, circulation 14,000.

The other newspapers affected include Pikiran Rakjat, published at Bandung; Pedoman Rakjat, published at Macassar, South Celebes, a daily in Semarang, one in Surabaya and one in Macassar. These newspapers range from non-Communist to anti-Communist. They often support the Government.

* * *

December 14, 1960

TURKISH PAPERS SEIZED

Issues of Four Confiscated and Two Are Suspended

Special to The New York Times

ANKARA, Turkey, Dec. 13—Today's issue of two Ankara newspapers, Oncu and Yenigun, and two Istanbul papers, Dunya and Tercuman, were confiscated for carrying reports of leaflets attacking Gen. Cemal Gursel, head of the military government.

Oncu and Yenigun have also been suspended for an indefinite period by the Ankara military commander.

The warrant ordering the suspension said that the papers had violated the ban on political activity and broken the law prohibiting the causing of undue public excitement and panic by reporting the contents of leaflets distributed in Ankara last night by the National Salvation Committee. Three journalists were detained by the police as a result of the reports on the leaflets.

This is the first time the military coup of May 27, which ended the rule of Premier Adnas Menderes' Democratic party, that journalists have been arrested and papers suspended in Turkey.

* * *

May 29, 1961

KOREA CHARGES ABUSES IN PRESS

Junta Bans 834 Periodicals and News Agencies

By BERNARD KALB
Special to The New York Times

SEOUL, Korea, May 28—The South Korean military junta outlawed 834 newspapers and news agencies today and arrested twenty-five business men, former military officers and Government officials.

The publications and news agencies were outlawed on the ground that they were not genuine news organs or that they had violated registration regulations. The arrested men were accused of illicit accumulation of wealth.

The junta's latest moves were expected to meet popular favor. Many Koreans were disgusted with the irresponsibility of many recently founded news organs and with the ineffective way that the ousted Government of Dr. John M. Chang had dealt with the widespread problem of corruption.

Main Media Unaffected

Most of the press units banned today have been described by sources close to the new military regime as "pseudo news organs."

The junta, which took power in a May 16 coup d'état, permitted a total of eighty-two daily newspapers, news agencies and weeklies, including all the country's prominent news media, to continue operating. Collectively, these eighty-two news organs are said to reach more Koreans than the banned 834 did.

The ban reduced the number of daily newspapers in Seoul, a city of about 2,000,000, from forty-nine to fifteen and the number of "news agencies" here from 241 to eleven.

A proliferation of press enterprises followed the student revolution of April, 1960, which ended twelve years of authoritarian rule by Dr. Syngman Rhee. As an atmosphere of free inquiry developed, hundreds of newspapers, news agencies and weeklies—some with nothing more than one reporter and a calling card—came into being throughout the country.

Many of these newcomers used their power chiefly to force officials to grant favors, or even for blackmail. Corruption became widespread.

The press censorship imposed immediately after the coup was replaced yesterday with what amounts to self-censorship, putting the burden on editors to decide what to print. But the ban on articles, cartoons or photographs "detrimental to the national security" was continued and editors here took this to mean that criticism of the military regime would be risky.

The second decree by the junta today ordered the arrest of twelve prominent business men, five retired officers of high rank and twelve former Government officials. They were charged with having illicitly accummulated wealth between 1953 and the May 16 coup.

The accused were ordered to return all illegally accumulated funds to the Government within three months.

Among the accused were Paik Too Chin, Premier in 1953–54; Sing In Sang, Finance Minister under Dr. Rhee; Kim Young Seun, Finance Minister under Dr. Chang; Im Heung Soon, former Mayor of Seoul, and Vice Admiral Lee Yong Woon, former Chief of Naval Operations.

* * *

July 8, 1962

PRESS IN KOREA FEARS NEW CURB

Seoul Regime Sets Policy to Discipline Papers

Special to The New York Times

SEOUL, Korea, July 1—Leading Seoul newspapers have expressed fear that the South Korean press might eventually be placed under tight control of the government when the recently announced press reform policy becomes effective.

A detailed "press policy" was announced Thursday by the military junta under Gen. Chung Hee Park. The announcement called for sweeping changes by the press both in operation and in management. The date for the changes to be effective was set at Aug. 15.

The "policy" is not a law, but the junta said that it would put into effect by means of "strong recommendation." One Seoul paper remarked that a "policy" under the military government would be "just as influential as a law."

The junta "recommended" the voluntary closing or merging of "incompetent" newspapers and press agencies that did not meet Government-set requirements. As a result perhaps twenty-five of the thirty-eight South Korean daily papers might be closed, and the number of the press agencies would decrease to "one or two."

It recommended that the newspapers publish only one edition a day, instead of the present two or more daily editions

Ministry Supplying Data

Also, newspapers were advised to expand the number of pages from the present four to eight or twelve pages, so as to "provide more educational material for the public." Much of the material would be supplied by the Ministry of Public Information.

The reform policy further stipulated that the "qualifications" of newspaper publishers would be regulated by the Government. The Government would also set increased pay scales for reporters and other newspaper employees "to prevent the recurrence of corruption in the press."

The junta applied press censorship immediately after the military coup in May, 1961. This was lifted after eleven days with the warning that the newspapers refrain from publishing articles "detrimental to the performance of the military revolution."

Reporters were then required to register and be cleared by the head military officers in the Government agencies. This brought down the number of the so-called reporters in South Korea from 100,000 to several thousand.

The junta also banned seventy-six purported newspapers that had no printing facilities and 305 "news agencies," many of which were alleged to be fronts for blackmail. Under the junta's orders, the police arrested hundreds of alleged bogus reporters for intimidation and blackmail.

Threat of a Purge List

The junta has urged the press to conduct its own clean-up and dismiss all journalists who were corrupt in the past. It has warned repeatedly that the Government would decree a "press purification" law, and make public a purge list of corrupt publishers and reporters, if the press did not comply with the request.

General Park recently ordered the release of ten newspaper reporters under detention for allegedly stealing Government documents or misreporting.

When the new policy press is in effect next month, the junta stated, the Government will make loans available to the newspapers and put taxes on newspaper enterprises and import duties on newsprint and wood pulp.

* * *

September 10, 1963

PRESS LAW BRINGS STRIKE IN PAKISTAN

Special to The New York Times

KABACHI, Pakistan, Sept. 9—More than 1,000 newspaper reporters, editors and printers went on a nationwide strike in Pakistan today to protest a new law regulating the press. No papers went to press.

The law, promulgated last week, forbids publication of anything but certified accounts of proceedings in the National Assembly, provincial legislatures or the courts. It also requires that newspapers publish Government press releases textually without cutting or editing.

Editors charge that the law seeks to muzzle criticism of the Government by blocking publication of opposition charges made in legislative assemblies. Widely published criticism was voiced at the last session of National Assembly regarding a large company in which the son of President Mohammad Ayub Khan is interested.

Twenty-four hours after the law was promulgated, one of the oldest newspapers on the Indian subcontinent, the Civil and Military Gazette of Lahore, halted publication. The Civil and Military Gazette was in its 94th year. Rudyard Kipling was one of its copy editors when he wrote "Plain Tales from the Hills," and Winston Churchill was its correspondent in the South African War from 1899 to 1902.

* * *

December 12, 1963

SAIGON REGIME SUSPENDS 3 DAILY NEWSPAPERS

Slander or Army Laid to Two—Neutralist Editorial Cited in Closing of Third

By HEDRICK SMITH
Special to The New York Times

SAIGON, South Vietnam, Dec. 11—The provisional Government indefinitely suspended publication of three Saigon daily newspapers today. Two of them, by innuendo, had criticized Premier Nguyen Ngoc Tho.

One high-ranking government source said a third daily was closed for having printed neutralist editorials.

In a table-thumping, three-hour news conference yesterday, the Premier lashed back at press critics. He hinted that one editor smoked opium and that another had Communist connections.

Within 24 hours Brig. Gen. Tran Tu Oai, Minister of Information, issued a decree shutting down three Vietnamese-language dailies—Dan Ta, Dan Den and Tan Van—"until further notice."

Press freedom has been one of most loudly proclaimed rights pledged by the new regime, and United States officials here have been closely watching the new Government's handling of the newspapers. The regime of President Ngo Dinh Diem, which was overthrown last month, rigidly controlled the press.

Although Western diplomats had been disturbed by some excesses in the Saigon press recently, they had hoped the new regime would refrain from heavy-handed retaliation. The suspensions caused concern to some of these diplomats.

The Government charged in a communiqué that the three newspapers had "cynically slandered the army and thus damaged the morale of the soldiers." General Oai said he acted at the request of Maj. Gen. Tran Van Don, Minister of Defense and second-ranking member of the military junta.

Other Vietnamese officials said, however, that it wasn't criticism of the army but political criticism of Premier Tho by two of the newspapers and neutralist editorials in the third that had provoked the Government action. The army has been considered above criticism since it overthrew President Diem.

All three newspapers had been publishing for less than a week. They were among the 40 or so dailies granted publishing permits by the new Government since the coup of Nov. 1–2.

On Nov. 21 the junta suspended two publications for having printed photographs that were said to show Mrs. Ngo Dinh Nhu in a bathing suit with an Indian diplomat. The Government closed the newspapers for seven days on grounds that the woman in the picture was not Mrs. Nhu and that the photos embarrassed a foreign dignitary.

Mrs. Nhu is the widow of the man who was President Diem's closest adviser. Both men were killed in the coup that overthrew the Diem regime.

Tan Van, the newspaper accused of having printed neutralist editorials printed a front-page article yesterday proclaiming a popular desire for peace and the end of the war against the Communist guerrillas.

* * *

January 10, 1964

REGIME'S CENSORSHIP DISTORTS PICTURE OF GHANA

By LLOYD GARRISON
Special to The New York Times

LAGOS, Nigeria, Jan. 9—There are two images of Ghana today: the real one and the one projected by the Government-controlled press and radio.

A visitor to that country was recently approached by a member of the Ghana National Students Association, which had just adopted a number of resolutions. Two of them, the student said, were omitted from the account transmitted by the Government-owned Ghana News Agency.

One resolution decried racial prejudice in Communist countries against Africans studying there. The second was critical of President Kwame Nkrumah for dismissing Ghana's Chief Justice, Sir Arku Korsah, following his acquittal of three ranking officials charged with treason.

"The people of Ghana will never know what we feel," said the student. "But can't you tell the rest of the world?"

All foreign correspondents are subject to censorship.

One recent item that failed to pass censorship was an account of how police took Sir Arku Korsah from his home Saturday and questioned him throughout the night. The 69-year-old former Chief Justice was released the next morning. Unconfirmed reports say he is now under house arrest.

News coming into the country is also censored. The official Ghana News Agency maintains only a few correspondents abroad. It obtains most of its foreign coverage from the Reuters news service, and any reports reflecting criticism of Ghana or its President are deleted when the Ghana News Agency forwards the material to Ghanaian newspapers and radio stations.

In keeping with the Government position that racism is nonexistent in the Socialist camp, reports of the recent African student demonstrations in Moscow following the death of one student there never appeared in the Ghanaian press.

The Government's policy is made clear to newspaper and radio news editors who assemble every morning in Flagstaff House, President Nkrumah's official residence.

There is little question that what appears in the press usually reflects the Government's viewpoint. This is especially true of several anonymous columnists who write under such bylines as "Mr. Rabbit."

The identity of these columnists is not known, but they certainly write with authority.

For example, after an attack this Tuesday by "Rambler" on Ghana's police commissioner, F. R. T. Madjitey, and his deputy superintendent, S. D. Amaning, there was no doubt that their careers were finished.

Solely on the basis of "Rambler's" comments, many foreign embassies immediately sent dispatches reporting that the long-awaited purge of the police was about to begin.

The next day Commissioner, Madjitey and nine other senior officers were dismissed and Mr. Amaning and another superintendent were arrested.

Now and then "Mr. Owl," "Mr. Rabbit," and "Rambler" overstep their bounds. But they are quickly put in their place.

Several weeks ago the first few copies of The Evening Times appeared on the streets with "Rambler" condemning discrimination against Ghanaian students in Russia. But this indiscretion was soon spotted and remaining issues of the first edition were promptly burned.

* * *

July 19, 1964

LAST FRENCH-RUN ALGERIA PAPER PROTESTS SEIZING OF PARIS DAILIES

Special to The New York Times

ALGIERS, July 18—Algeria's only remaining French' operated newspaper, the weekly Cooperation, protested today against the Socialist regime's repeated seizures of incoming Paris newspapers.

Without discussing President Ahmed Ben Bella's right to cut off his fellow Algerians from all but the Communist French press, the weekly's editor, R. A. Soyer, wrote that these measures "in effect constitute a serious blow to freedom of opinion of Frenchmen working in Algeria."

The Government seizures of the French newspapers—with the exception of the Communist party organ L'Humanité, and the extreme-left newspaper Liberation—are a part of the life in Algiers. On occasion, authorities in Paris have retaliated by seizing Algerian periodicals.

Seizures of English-language journals by the Ben Bella regime have been rare. Most literate Algerians read Arabic and French but not English.

However, to a far greater extent than in neighboring Tunisia and Morocco, the 22-month-old Ben Bella regime has reacted publicly to criticism, distortions or embarrassing information appearing in the Western press.

Seven Western journalists, including an American and a British woman, have been expelled or barred from re-entry.

Even sympathetic Paris newspapers have been seized on arrival for periods up to 10 days, a sure sign to irritated readers that all is not running smoothly somewhere. Mr. Ben Bella or his Cabinet ministers attack the "reactionary Western press" or "a certain press" almost weekly. On occasion, Mr. Ben Bella has publicly upbraided French journalists.

One reason for the regime's sensitivity, according to Government officials, is the "paternalistic tone" of even friendly French news coverage. Another is that many educated Moslem Algerians, including Government officials, look to the liberal French press to tell them what is really happening here and abroad.

Even Government spokesmen concede that information in the party-controlled local daily press, which has a circulation of about 130,000, is skimpy and "domesticated."

Le Monde, the liberal Paris daily, is perhaps the most influential paper sold here. It devotes at least a column a day to Algerian affairs, unlike its competitors, which are losing interest. According to French sources, its newsstand sales alone average 8,000 daily.

Another Paris newspaper, France-Soir, a "popular," feature-laden daily, is reported to sell more than 10,000 copies a day.

A week ago, condemning free entry of foreign newspapers and Western notions of "freedom of the press," Hocine Zahouane, press chief of the Political Bureau, told Algerian journalists:

"We are perpetually confronted by a foreign press whose professional and technical superiority is incontestable. This foreign press finds an echo among many Algerians because it gets support from old habits and because it is easier to read. Can one allow, in the name of 'liberty,' a competition unequal from the start?"

* * *

December 15, 1964

PAKISTANI EDITORS DEFY REGIME; REFUSE TO JOIN PRESS TRIBUNAL

By JACQUES NEVARD

Special to The New York Times

KARACHI, Pakistan, Dec. 14—The Government of President Mohammad Ayub Khan, facing an election in less than three weeks, has encountered defiance and criticism from the nation's leading newspaper editors and lawyers.

In a surprise move, the Council of Pakistan Newspaper Editors made public its defiance of a repressive press law drafted by the Ayub regime.

The editors' council announced that it would not nominate a member to serve on a proposed tribunal that would rule on appeals of actions taken under the Pakistan Press and Publications Ordinance of 1963. Instead, it demanded repeal of the ordinance.

The decision was made at an emergency meeting of the council's standing committee last night. The committee declared the amendments to the ordinance made last month did not liberalize the press law, as Government spokesmen contended, but would "make it more stringent."

Bar Group Assails Ayub

The editors acted a day after the Karachi Bar Association, the most influential lawyers' group in Pakistan, voted overwhelmingly for a resolution expressing "its deep sense of resentment against the derogatory remarks made by President

Mohammad Ayub Khan regarding the members of the bar in general."

By a vote of 286 to 27 the organization called upon Field Marshal Ayub's ruling Moslem League to rid itself of the "notion that wisdom, righteousness and patriotism are the monopoly of their yes men and that everybody who differs from them is misguided, a mischief monger and an enemy of the country."

The lawyers also voted by a 10-to-1 margin to condemn the formation of the rival Pakistan Lawyers Association, which is sponsored by Government officials. The group emerged following votes of support by bar associations throughout Pakistan for Field Marshal Ayub's chief rival for the presidency, Miss Fatima Jinnah. She is the sister of Mohammed Ali Jinnah, who is revered as the founder of Pakistan.

In its action, the editors' council said recent amendments to the press law made it subject to even greater misinterpretation and abuse.

It noted that the amendments raised from 10,000 rupees ($2,100) to 30,000 rupees ($6,300) the maximum deposit the Government could demand as security from publications deemed guilty of violations of the press law. The council also criticized provision for forfeiture of the printing presses in certain violations.

Largest Papers Represented

The editors of the English-language Dawn and the Urdu-language Jan, the two most widely circulated newspapers in the country, were present when the council adopted its stand.

Public expressions of defiance and criticism by the editors and the lawyers were a major topic among Karachi politicians.

It heightened a belief that the Ayub Government was not doing as well as it had expected in the election campaign. Although Field Marshal Ayub was still heavily favored to win reelection in the Jan. 2 voting, the new boldness of lawyers and editors was viewed as a sign that politically aware Pakistans felt that his grip over national and provincial legislatures would be considerably weakened.

PART VI

THE VIETNAM WAR ERA, 1965–1974

DEVELOPMENTS IN THE UNITED STATES AND VIETNAM

July 1, 1965

VIETNAMESE PRESS IS SUSPENDED BY KY

Special to The New York Times

SAIGON, South Vietnam, June 30—Premier Nguyen Cao Ky has suspended all Vietnamese-language daily newspapers despite earlier assurances to the publishers that he was rescinding the suspension order.

The suspension, effective tomorrow, is expected to be brief, far less than the one-month period the Government had announced at first.

Sources close to Air Vice Marshal Ky said he had decided to proceed with the order because he was worried that he would appear indecisive if he allowed himself to be swayed by the publishers.

He had promised them that he would produce a code of ethics, involving a reduction in the romantic stories and horoscopes that all Vietnamese papers carry, and would close only the papers that did not comply with the code.

The journalists sent telegrams appealing for support to several press federations, including the International Press Institute in Zurich, Switzerland.

A delegation of journalists is scheduled to meet with Marshal Ky tomorrow.

The press suspension does not affect the Chinese-language papers and the two French and two English daily newspapers published in Saigon.

* * *

June 4, 1967

KY STILL CENSORS THE SAIGON PRESS

Political Items Often Cut Despite the Constitution

By R. W. APPLE Jr.

Special to The New York Times

SAIGON, South Vietnam, June 3–On April 1, the ruling generals promulgated a national Constitution, to take effect immediately. Article 12, Paragraph 2 said: "Censorship is abolished except for motion pictures and plays."

On May 16, speaking to a group of Vietnamese journalist at Longxuyen in the Mekong Delta, Premier Nguyen Cao Ky took a completely different stand.

"From now until election day, any newspaper article that might create dissension among the people will be censored," he said. "The aim of the election is to march toward the unity of the people, not to create dissension or to divide unity."

Furthermore, the Premier said, any newspaper that tries to print articles about frictions between refugees from North Vietnam and native-born South Vietnamese will be closed down. Such frictions are a fact of South Vietnamese political life and are expected to be an important issue in the presidential election campaign this fall.

Premier Ky, a Northerner, is disliked by many Southerners. His two chief civilian rivals for the presidency—Tran Van Huon and Phan Khae Suu—were born in the delta.

The Constitution notwithstanding, the censors are hard at work. Blank spaces on the front pages of Saigon newspapers have become more frequent in recent weeks, and political news in particular seems to get extremely close scrutiny.

When Lieut. Gen. Nguyen Van Thieu, the chief of state, announced that he intended to oppose Marshall Ky for the presidency, the censors permitted the English-language Saigon Post to print only one sentence about General Thieu's plans.

Premier Ky, the commander of the air force, has installed young air force officers in the censor's office to oversee the work done there by a military and civilian staff.

But the most important figure in the Government's relations with the press is Maj. Mai Van Dai, the Deputy Information Minister. He is a brother-in-law of Brig, Gen. Nguyen Ngoc Loan, the widely feared chief of the civil and military police, who is regarded as the Premier's most autocratic associate.

The "continued lack of press freedom," one prominent civilian politician said this week, "suggests that we aren't going to have a very free election after all. Who ever heard of a free election when one candidate controls the press?"

According to the Constitution, the constituent assembly, now functioning as an interim legislature, must draft a press freedom law before the September election. But editors here view the prospect skeptically.

"We have lost interest," one editor remarked. "If the Constitution is promulgated and censorship becomes tighter, who needs another law of promises? No matter what Ky says about this. It's utterly useless."

The Government responds to its press critics by reminding them that "Vietnam is at war."

Of South Vietnam's 30 newspapers—27 printed in Vietnamese, seven in Chinese, three in English and two in

French—a number have been suspended during the last year for "offenses against the public welfare."

Dat To ("The Fatherland"), the Buddhist-sponsored daily, was closed last summer following the suppression of the anti-Government movement led by the Buddhist. Its proprietors were told that they would never be permitted to resume publication.

Daily Attempts to Reopen

Than Chung (Golden Bell), a Southern-oriented paper with a circulation of 45,000, which is large for Saigon, was suspended for a month, beginning May 9, for "pro-Communist views." The newspaper's editorials had advocated peace talks.

The Vietnam Guardian, an English-language daily, was suspended on Dec. 12 and has not been permitted to reopen. Although its circulation was not large, it was widely read in the foreign community and by Vietnamese officials, and its suspension has become a kind of test case for press freedom.

Ton That Tien, the paper's managing editor, said in an interview today that The Guardian had sent three letters to the Information Ministry asking whether it could resume publication. He said that no replies had been received.

Six weeks ago, Premier Ky told Mike Wallace, a correspondent for the Columbia Broadcasting System, that the paper would be permitted to reopen within a few days.

A spokesman for the Premier said today that "we are busy with a lot of things more important than The Guardian."

The paper which was started last June by Mr. Tien and Nguyen Van Tuoi, a Saigon advertising executive, had built its circulation to 8,000 a day in six months. Mr. Tien said he considered its editorial page "independent and critical, but not oppositionist."

* * *

August 13, 1967

SAIGON'S EDITORS CENSORING THEMSELVES NOW

Despite Lifting of Controls, Papers Remain Cautious—No Candidates Endorsed

By PETER BRAESTRUP
Special to The New York Times

SAIGON, South Vietnam, Aug. 12—"The government lifted censorship," a Saigon editor observed recently. "Now we have to censor ourselves. Everybody is still pretty cautious."

After considerable urging by American diplomats and newsmen, the Government suspended censorship of South Vietnam's 39 daily newspapers on July 20. The move came two weeks before the official start of the presidential election campaign.

The order came from Lieut. Gen. Nguyen Van Thieu, the chief of state, and Premier Nguyen Cao Ky. The two men are, respectively, the candidates for President and Vice President on the military ticket that faces opposition from 10 civilian tickets.

There have been few complaints of a "one-party press" from civilian candidates since censorship was lifted.

Balanced Reports Asked

A spokesman for Premier Ky said that the Government-run press agency, Vietnam Press, and the Government radio had been told to give the election campaign balanced coverage. So far, according to Vietnamese editors and anti-Ky politicians, balance has been maintained by the Government-run media.

For their part, Saigon's editors have shunned polemics. Indeed, according to one survey, no candidate has received open endorsement from a Saigon newspaper. Even the pro-Government Saigon Post, an English-language paper, has yet to endorse the Thieu-Ky ticket. Instead, in an editorial Saturday, The Post commented on the candidates televised statements as follows:

"None of the candidates is endowed with the intellectual integrity and eloquence at a level approaching that of Winston Churchill. Suffering is no novelty for 15 million South Vietnamese. Mutual trust between the rulers and the governed is."

Before July 20, a Post staff member said, such an editorial would not have passed the censors.

Some Parts Toned Down

In general, anti-Ky, editors have contended themselves with reporting what anti-Ky candidates have said about the military. The candidates' more inflammatory remarks were usually toned down or deleted.

One event provided a test of the new freedom. Sunday a travel mix-up in Quangtri Province resulted in the temporary refusal of 10 civilian presidential candidates to continue a 22-city campaign tour. Some candidates angrily accused the Ky regime of "sabotage."

Although The Saigon Post reported the story Monday morning, 10 Vietnamese-language dailies in Saigon waited another day to follow suit. "They were not sure how the Government would react," said an editor. As the controversy has continued, coverage has improved.

Premier Ky, at a news conference yesterday, voiced irritation at the civilian candidates' public polemics over the "Quangtri affair." But he has not sought to black out the incident in the local press.

Saigon's newspapers—27 Vietnamese, 7 Chinese, 2 English and 2 French—have a combined circulation estimated at 867,000. Few are prosperous.

According to informed sources, their publishers were warned last month to be "responsible" or face possible suspension, seizure of their day's output or cuts in allocations of imported newsprint.

Under the Ky Government's policy under censorship, the press was obligated to "develop the anti-Communist spirit among the people," "promote the higher standards of the people," "inform and comment accurately and constructively" and "provide healthy entertainment."

The Government's censors, mostly army officers, took no chances. They ordered editors to kill any articles that verged on "controversy"—occasionally including accounts of impromptu speeches by the outspoken Premier. Every night Saigon's publishers sent galley proofs to the Government press center and the next day, patches of white space appeared where articles had been rejected.

There have been no white spaces since July 20. But each day newspapers must send over their first copies. Presumably if a newspaper offends, the Government can then seize all the copies.

However, so far, according to a spokesman for Premier Ky, "we are satisfied with the situation."

* * *

May 26, 1968

SAIGON CENSORSHIP BATTLE GROWS, AND NEWSPAPER GAPS ABOUND

By DOUGLAS ROBINSON
Special to The New York Times

SAIGON, South Vietnam, May 25—The newspapers of Saigon are increasingly sprinkled with blank spaces these days as a battle between censors and editors rages with neither side willing to concede a column inch.

Judging from appearances, the censors currently have the upper hand, but the editors, who fume and rant about Government control, are determined not to be blue-penciled into submission.

The two English-language newspapers—The Saigon Daily News and The Saigon Post—have recently borne the brunt of the censors' "noes for news," as one editor put it.

"The censors take out anything that appears to criticize the Government," said Tran Nha, editor of The Saigon Post in a recent interview. "We also have a good deal of trouble because the censors don't really understand English."

Mistake of Censors

Mr. Nha said that a recent headline had read, "Pacification Hardly Touched by Second Red Offensive."

"The censors took out 'hardly touched' because they felt the words meant 'hard hit,' " Mr. Nha said mournfully.

The preliminary peace talks in Paris and the resignation of Premier Nguyen Van Loc and his Cabinet have caused headaches for Saigon's harassed editors, since the word "peace" was not allowed in headlines and speculation on Government actions is forbidden.

After tortuous circumlocutions during the initial days of the Paris negotiations, the newspapers were finally permitted to use "peace" in headlines. Speculation on the future Cabinet, however, continued to be excised with the resulting gaping holes on page 1.

Prohibitions Listed

The censors, who are part of the Ministry of Information, work in a crowded room on the second floor of the National Press Center in downtown Saigon. The room, which has no air-conditioning, has a blackboard on which are listed the prohibited subjects for the day.

Each day, the editors of Saigon's 36 newspapers must submit their final page proofs to the censors for examination. These proofs are brought in three hours before press time, since the editors have learned that the process may be excruciatingly slow.

In addition to the two English-language daily newspapers, the city has 25 Vietnamese, seven Chinese and two French newspapers.

Before last year's election campaign, there were no censors as such. The Government simply suspended publications when they overstepped the bounds of what officials decided was poor taste or inaccurate reporting.

Then, during the campaign, censorship was abolished to permit candidates to air their views. Pro-Communist or "neutralist" writings were not permitted, but since there were virtually no candidates of either persuasion, there were few problems.

During the enemy's Lunar New Year offensive in February, when South Vietnam was placed under martial law, the present form of censorship was established and it has not been relaxed.

A ray of hope for the editors was seen today when it was announced that Ton That Thien had been appointed Information Minister. Mr. Thien was once the chief editorial writer for The Saigon Guardian, a newspaper that was suspended by the Government last year.

Newsmen hope that Mr. Thien's appointment will mean that measures now pending before the legislature that would strengthen the censorship laws will be abandoned or toned down. Of particular concern is a proposal for the death penalty for anyone writing what could be considered Communist or neutralist stories.

Not all editors, however, are up in arms against censorship. Nguyen Lau, publisher of The Saigon Daily News and a columnist of considerable reputation, is relaxed about the whole matter.

"I write what I see and feel and the censors take it out," he said. "But at least I can go home with a clear conscience and not worry about going to jail."

* * *

March 24, 1969

SOUTH VIETNAMESE REVISING OUTMODED PRESS LAWS

By JOSEPH B. TREASTER

Special to The New York Times

SAIGON, South Vietnam, March 23—For months, Khieu Thien Ke, chairman of the House of Representatives Committee on the Press and Information, has been perplexed.

He and a handful of other legislators have been trying to establish a new set of regulations that would provide for a truly free press in South Vietnam.

But they have made little progress, and in the meantime the Government has continued to shut newspapers that failed to operate within the confines of a jumble of outdated codes and the whims of officialdom.

In the last nine months, since press censorship was officially eliminated, 24 newspapers and two magazines have been suspended—sometimes for as short a time as three days, sometimes permanently.

"We have a serious problem," Mr. Ke said recently. "It is a problem shared in common with all those who attempt to establish democratic institutions in time of war.

Advantage to Enemy Noted

"How do we have real freedom and democracy without letting the enemy take advantage of these principles?" he asked. "It is hard to get the press law out at this time."

According to the Constitution adopted two years ago, a set of press regulations must become law by next November. Three drafts, now are being studied and modified. Whatever adaptation is written into the Constitution in the fall will probably provide for much less freedom than its framers or the newsmen of South Vietnam would like.

But as the military and political situation in the country changes, the law can be amended, and at least there will be on paper in one place a set of guidelines for the Government and the press.

Once the law is in effect, whimsical or arbitrary decisions by the Government should be less frequent and the uncertainties faced by South Vietnamese editors should be eased.

The existing press regulations are French in origin and date back more than a century and it is doubtful whether anyone has read all of them, let alone tried to adhere to them.

"The Information Ministry has never tried to enforce the existing press laws strictly," said Nguyen Van Noan, director of the National Press Center. "Otherwise there would have been many more newspapers suspended.

"If all the articles were enforced to the letter, there would be no newspapers in Saigon at all," he added with a smile.

Confusion and Frustration

For editors and publishers, this kind of situation means confusion and frustration. "We don't know where we stand," said Nguyen Lau, publisher of the English-language Saigon Daily News. "One day the Vietcong are banned, the next day they are to be 'recognized as a reality, but not an entity.'" That phrase was used by Vice President Nguyen Cao Ky last December.

Mr. Lau said that while it was possible to print more news now, there were fewer pressures on a newspaperman in the time of the late President Ngo Dinh Diem, so long as the newsmen did not fight the system.

"Diem said bluntly that he was not going to tolerate freedom of the press," Mr. Lau recalled. "There were no illusions then.

"We are living a lie now," he went on. "People say they are giving you freedom, and someone without experience in journalism may be innocent enough to believe that this is a paradise. Now you may be carried away by your illusions and land in trouble."

Mr. Lau's newspaper has been suspended at least once a year since November, 1963, when the Diem Government fell. The most recent suspension was ordered for three weeks last fall after the paper had given more prominence to a critical statement by Clark M. Clifford, then the United States Secretary of Defense, than to a rebuttal by the South Vietnamese Minister of Information. Mr. Clifford had charged that the South Vietnamese were delaying the Paris peace talks.

2 Papers Suspended

Just a few days ago two Vietnamese-language newspapers were suspended for 30 days each.

Chanh Dao [True Religion], a Buddhist paper, was penalized for having hinted that the trial of Thich Tien Min, a militant Buddhist leader who was sentenced to 10 years at hard labor for harboring rebels and illegal possession of weapons, was unfair. A Government spokesman said that the newspaper had attributed the harsh sentence to "religious reasons."

Tin Sang [Morning News] was closed because it hinted that Premier Tran Van Huong had made recent changes in his Cabinet "under pressure that might lead the people to feel that there is wrangling among national leaders."

The Government said that, despite warnings, the newspaper had also used offensive terms concerning national leaders—terms that could harm their prestige.

Although the former Information Minister, Ton That Thien, announced the formal abolition of press censorship last summer, the work of several men serving under Mr. Noan at the National Press Center has not changed.

Every day, these men read the 32 daily newspapers that are printed in Saigon, a few hours before they appear on the streets. These readers are isolated from interviewers by a wall of red tape, but Mr. Noan described their work.

Basically, he said, they look for material that might be harmful to the national cause—the anti-Communist cause—or to national security.

Notes Sent to Editors

When they find something "harmful," they either send a note or telephone the newspaper office. One editor said he sometimes gets two or three notes a day concerning news developments even before he submits his page proofs.

Mr. Noan said that editors, after having been notified of objectionable material, may either modify it or stand firm on their original decision. Sometimes a decision to stand firm results in suspension, sometimes it does not. At any rate a game of chance begins when an editor decides to reject the Press Center's advice.

To complicate matters further, there have been cases in which the press center staff has somehow failed to see the "harmful nature of an article until it has been published and read by a high-ranking Government official. In such cases, suspension has come without warning.

Suspension is expensive and for a newspaper on a tight budget it can be fatal. Mr. Lau said that The Saigon Daily News lost about $20,000 during the 21 days that it was closed most recently. "It would have been better if they had shut us down completely," he said. "This way we had to keep paying rent and salaries and nothing was coming in."

Yet with all these difficulties, the Ministry of Information currently has on file more than 250 applications for permission to publish daily newspapers. It has nearly 500 applications for permission to publish weekly, monthly and bimonthly magazines.

The explanation is simple: newspaper publishing is one of the few businesses in Saigon where big profits are legally possible and a man can get started for about $20,000.

For all but the three English-language dailies, the secret to profit is in low production costs and high circulation—a phenomenon similar to the penny press of New York at the turn of the century. Labor costs here are still relatively low.

Like most of today's American newspapers, the English-language papers in Saigon depend heavily on advertising revenue for their income. The publishers of those newspapers are interested in increasing their circulation mainly because it will enable them to charge a higher space rate for advertising directed largely at free-spending non-Vietnamese readers.

The popularity of newspapers in Saigon fluctuates greatly and no one seems to have figured out exactly what makes for sales appeal.

"The newspaper business here is like a lottery," Mr. Lau, the publisher, said. "You can get started with small capital and if you win the lottery you can make a fortune in two years."

* * *

October 1, 1970

4 ARE ARRESTED IN FILM SEIZURE

Judge Rules 'Censorship in Denmark' to Be Obscene

By ARNOLD H. LUBASCH

A film distributor and three theater managers were arrested yesterday after a criminal court judge here authorized the seizure of the film "Censorship in Denmark: A New Approach."

The ruling by Judge Jack Rosenberg prevents further showings of the film in New York County pending a trial of the distributor and the managers on charges of promoting and distributing obscene material.

"This court finds for the purposes of the issuance of a warrant of seizure that 'Censorship in Denmark,' taken as a whole, has as its dominant theme appeals to a prurient interest in sex," the judge ruled.

"It is patently offensive to most Americans because it affronts contemporary community standards relating to the description or representation of sexual matters," he added, "and even the effort to present it as a documentary study of pornography fails to give it any redeeming social value."

Judge Rosenberg set Oct. 9 for a hearing in the case of the distributor Saul Shiffrin of Livingston, N. J., and the managers, Thomas DeGraffenreid of the Evergreen Theater at 55 East 11th Street, Henry Young of the Lido East at 211 East 59th Street and Chung Louis of the 55th Street Playhouse at 154 West 55th Street.

The film, which opened at the three theaters in June, was still playing only at the 55th Street Playhouse when Judge Rosenberg authorized its seizure.

Assistant District Attorney Richard Beckler said that he started action in July to prevent the showing of "Censorship in Denmark" after some viewers had complained to the police that the film was obscene.

Under recent Federal court decisions, he explained, the police cannot seize a film without an adversary hearing in court to allow the defendants to argue against the seizure.

Documentary on a Boom

Mr. Beckler said the adversary hearing that was subsequently held before Judge Rosenberg on "Censorship in Denmark" was the first one conducted here in accordance with the recent court rulings.

The accused distributor and theater managers could face maximum sentences of one year in prison and $1,000 in fines if convicted.

In his review when the film opened here, Vincent Canby of The New York Times, said: "The movie, produced and directed by a San Franciscan named Alex deRenzy, is a documentary on the boom that followed the Danish Government's abolition, one year ago, of all restrictions against the manufacture and sale of pornographic material (by and to adults only)."

The reviewer called it "a new approach to the distribution of hard-core pornographic films in the United States."

* * *

July 1, 1971

SUPREME COURT, 6-3, UPHOLDS NEWSPAPERS ON PUBLICATION OF THE PENTAGON REPORT; TIMES RESUMES ITS SERIES, HALTED 15 DAYS

BURGER DISSENTS

First Amendment Rule Held to Block Most Prior Restraints

By FRED P. GRAHAM
Special to The New York Times

WASHINGTON, June 30—The Supreme Court freed The New York Times and The Washington Post today to resume immediate publication of articles based on the secret Pentagon papers on the origins of the Vietnam war.

By a vote of 6 to 3 the Court held that any attempt by the Government to block news articles prior to publication bears "a heavy burden of presumption against its constitutionality."

In a historic test of that principle—the first effort by the Government to enjoin publication on the ground of national security—the Court declared that "the Government has not met that burden."

The brief judgment was read to a hushed courtroom by Chief Justice Warren E. Burger at 2:30 P.M. at a special session called three hours before.

Old Tradition Observed

The Chief Justice was one of the dissenters, along with Associate Justices Harry A. Blackmun and John M. Harlan, but because the decision was rendered in an unsigned opinion, the Chief Justice read it in court in accordance with long-standing custom.

In New York Arthur Ochs Sulzberger, president and publisher of The Times, said at a news conference that he had "never really doubted that this day would come and that we'd win." His reaction, he said, was "complete joy and delight."

The case had been expected to product a landmark ruling on the circumstances under which prior restraint could be imposed upon the press, but because no opinion by a single Justice commanded the support of a majority, only the unsigned decision will serve as precedent.

Uncertainty Over Outcome

Because it came on the 15th day after The Times had been restrained from publishing further articles in its series mined from the 7,000 pages of material—the first such restraint in the mane of "national security" in the history of the United States—there was some uncertainty whether the press had scored a strong victory or whether a precedent for some degree of restraint had been set.

Alexander M. Bickel, the Yale law professor who had argued for The Times in the case, said in a telephone interview that the ruling placed the press in a "stronger position." He maintained that no Federal District Judge would henceforth temporarily restrain a newspaper on the Justice Department's complaint that "this is what they have printed and we don't like it" and that a direct threat of irreparable harm would have to be alleged.

However, the United States Solicitor General, Erwin N. Griswold, turned to another lawyer shortly after the Justices filed from the courtroom and remarked: "Maybe the newspapers will show a little restraint in the future." All nine Justices wrote opinions in a judicial outpouring that was described by Supreme Court scholars as without precedent. They divided roughly into groups of three each.

The first group, composed of Hugo L. Black, William O. Douglas and Thurgood Marshall, took what is known as the absolutist view that the courts lack the power to suppress any press publication, no matter how grave a threat to security it might pose.

Justices Black and Douglas restated their long-held belief that the First Amendment's guarantee of a free press forbids any judicial restraint. Justice Marshall insisted that because Congress had twice considered and rejected such power for the courts, the Supreme Court would be "enacting" law if it imposed restraint.

The second group, which included William J. Brennan Jr., Potter Stewart and Byron R. White, said that the press could not be muzzled except to prevent direct, immediate and irreparable damage to the nation. They agreed that this material did not pose such a threat.

The Dissenters' Views

The third bloc, composed of the three dissenters, declared that the courts should not refuse to enforce the executive branch's conclusion that material should be kept confidential—so long as a Cabinet-level officer had decided that it should—on a matter affecting foreign relations.

They felt that the "frenzied train of events" in the cases before them had not given the courts enough time to determine those questions, so they concluded that the restraints upon publication should have been retained while both cases were sent back to the trial judges for more hearings.

The New York Times's series drawn from the secret Pentagon study was accompanied by supporting documents. Articles were published on June 13, 14 and 15 before they were halted by court order. A similar restraining order was imposed on June 19 against The Washington Post after it began to print articles based on the study.

Justice Black's opinion stated that just such publications as those were intended to be protected by the First Amendment's declaration that "Congress shall make no law . . . abridging the freedom of the press."

Paramount among the responsibilities of a free press, he said, "is the duty to prevent any part of the Government from deceiving the people and sending them off to distant lands to die of foreign fevers and foreign shot and shell.

"In my view, far from deserving condemnation for their courageous reporting, The New York Times, The Washington Post and other newspapers should be commended for serving the purpose that the Founding Fathers saw so clearly," he said. "In revealing the workings of government that led to the Vietnam war, the newspapers nobly did precisely that which the founders hoped and trusted they would do."

Justice Douglas joined the opinion by Justice Black and was joined by him in another opinion. The First Amendment's purpose, Justice Douglas argued, is to prohibit "governmental suppression of embarrassing information." He asserted that the temporary restraints in these cases "constitute a flouting of the principles of the First Amendment."

Justice Marshall's position was based primarily upon the separation-of-powers argument that Congress had never authorized prior restraints and that it refused to do so when bills were introduced in 1917 and 1957.

He concluded that the courts were without power to restrain publications. Justices Brennan, Stewart and White, who also based their conclusions on the separation-of-powers principle, assumed that under extreme circumstances the courts would act without such powers.

Justice Brennan focused on the temporary restraints, which had been issued to freeze the situation so that the material would not be made public before the courts could decide if it should be enjoined. He continued that no restraints should have been imposed because the Government alleged only in general terms that security breaches might occur.

Justices Stewart and White, who also joined each other's opinions, said that though they had read the documents they felt that publication would not be in the national interest.

But Justice Stewart, a former chairman of The Yale Daily News, insisted that "it is the duty of the executive" to protect state secrets through its own security measures and not the duty of the courts to do it by banning news articles.

He implied that if publication of the material would cause "direct, immediate, and irreparable damage to our nation or its people," he would uphold prior restraint, but because that situation was not present here, he said that the papers must be free to publish.

Justice White added that Congress had enacted criminal laws, including the espionage laws, that might apply to these papers. "The newspapers are presumably now on full notice," he said, that the Justice Department may bring prosecutions if the publications violate those laws. He added that he "would have no difficulty sustaining convictions" under the laws, even if the breaches of security were not sufficient to justify prior restraint.

The Chief Justice and Justices Stewart and Blackmun echoed this caveat in their opinions—meaning that one less than a majority had lent their weight to the warning.

Chief Justice Burger blamed The Times "in large part" for the "frenetic haste" with which the case was handled. He said that The Times had studied the Pentagon archives for three or four months before beginning its series, yet it had breached "the duty of an honorable press" by not asking the Government if any security violations were involved before it began publication.

He said he found it "hardly believable' that The Times would do this, and he concluded that it would not be harmed if the case were sent back for more testimony.

Justice Blackmun, also focusing his criticism on The Times, said there had been inadequate time to determine if the publications could result in "the death of soldiers, the destruction of alliances, the greatly increased difficulty of negotiation with our enemies, the inability of our diplomats to negotiate." He concluded that if the war was prolonged and a delay in the return of United States prisoners result from publication, "then the nation's people will know where the responsibility for these sad consequences rests."

In his own dissenting opinion, Justice Harlan said: "The judiciary must review the initial executive determination to the point of satisfying itself that the subject matter of the dispute does lie within the proper compass of the President's foreign policy relations power.

"The judiciary," he went on, "may properly insist that the determination that disclosure of that subject matter would irreparably impair the national security be made by the head of the executive department concerned—here the Secretary of State or the Secretary of Defense—after actual personal consideration.

"But in my judgment, the judiciary may not properly go beyond these two inquiries and redetermine for itself the probable impact of disclosure on the national security."

The Justice Department initially sought an injunction against The Times on June 15 from Federal District Judge Murray I. Gurfein in New York.

Judge Gurfein, who had issued the original temporary restraining order that was stayed until today, ruled that the material was basically historical matter that might be embarrassing to the Government but did not pose a threat to national security. Federal District Judge Gerhard A. Gesell of the District of Columbia came to the same conclusion in the Government's suit against The Washington Post.

The United States Court of Appeals for the Second Circuit, voting 5 to 3, ordered more secret hearings before Judge Gurfein and The Times appealed. The United States Court of Appeals for the District of Columbia upheld Judge Gesell, 7 to 2, holding that no injunction should be imposed. Today the Supreme Court affirmed the Appeals Court here and reversed the Second Circuit.

The supreme court also issued a brief order disposing of a few other cases and adjourned until Oct. 4, as it had been scheduled to do Monday.

* * *

July 1, 1971

MOST CONGRESSIONAL LEADERS APPLAUD COURT DECISION; THE WHITE HOUSE IS SILENT

DROP IS EXPECTED IN 'SECRET' MEMOS

Fulbright Says That Ruling Will Have 'Psychological Effect' on Government

By MARJORIE HUNTER
Special to The New York Times

Washington, June 30—Congressional leaders today generally applauded the Supreme Court decision on publication of material from Pentagon papers.

The ruling was greeted with almost total silence by the White House and officials of the Nixon Administration.

Asked if the White House had any reaction, Ronald L. Ziegler, press secretary to the President, replied, "I have no comment on the Supreme Court decision today."

Asked what the President thought of the decision, Mr. Ziegler said: "The President is aware of the Supreme Court decision. He has been in a National Security Council meeting this afternoon."

And asked if the President supported freedom of the press, Mr. Ziegler replied: "There is no need for me to comment on that. The President's stand on the First Amendment and freedom of the press is well known."

Mitchell: No Comment

A Justice Department spokesman said that Attorney General John N. Mitchell would have no comment on the Court's ruling.

But at the State Department and on Capitol Hill, the court decision was generally viewed as certain to speed up the process of declassifying many documents, some of them dating back many years, now stamped "secret" and "top secret."

State Department officials said that the Court decision was certain to discourage many officials from writing too many "secret" memos, but they said they did not think that this would seriously affect the foreign policy process.

Senator J. W. Fulbright, Democrat of Arkansas, chairman of the Foreign Relations Committee, said that the decision was certain to have "a tremendous psychological effect" on secrecy in government and "indiscriminate" classification of documents.

"I could not be more pleased if I were editor of The New York Times," he said. "The Times has justified the First Amendment."

'Great Day for Freedom'

The Senate democratic leader, Mike Mansfield of Montana, reacted more cautiously to the decision but said that, barring curity, "this will be a good move in the freedom of information area for the American people and, many I say, for the United State Congress as well."

Senator Hubert H. Humphrey, Democrat of Minnesota, said in a floor speech: "The Court has performed its most valuable service for many a year . . . . This is a great day for freedom in the land."

While reaction to the Court's decision was generally favorable, several Senators were openly critical of the New York Times for printing the documents and of Dr. Daniel Ellsberg, a former Defense Department official who has said that he gave the press the 47-volume Pentagon study on United States involvement in Vietnam.

Senator Barry Goldwater, Republican of Arizona, said that he felt that the New York Times and Dr. Ellsberg should be charged under the Espionage Act.

Dr. Ellsberg was indicted this week on a charge of unauthorized possession of "documents and writings related to the national defense"—it carries a penalty of up to 10 years in prison, a $10,000 fine or both—and was released on $50,000 bail. No criminal charges have been filed against The Times or other newspapers.

Newspapers Criticized

Senator Gordon Allott, Republican of Colorado, said that he felt that The New York Times and other papers had set themselves above the law. "This cannot be permitted," he added.

The main issue, Senator Allott said, is whether people in government with the responsibility of classifying documents "are going to be allowed to make those decisions, or whether the press is going to make the decisions for them."

Several Government panels are now looking into the question of classification and declassification of documents.

State Department officials disclosed today that Secretary William P. Rogers had quietly ordered the creation of such a panel shortly after articles on the Pentagon study began appearing in The Times and other newspapers.

Department officials said that the group would study how best to make available to Congress or to the press information that was now classified.

Another governmental panel, headed by Assistant Attorney General William H. Rehnquist, is reviewing the Government's system of classification and declassification.

Mr. Rehnquist told a House government operation subcommittee today that too many Government documents are classified. David O. Cooke, a Deputy Assistant Secretary of Defense, told the subcommittee yesterday that at least 20 million Government documents are now classified, a number that he said he felt was excessive.

Meanwhile, a Defense Department official said tonight that consideration was being given to printing copies of the Pentagon papers for members of Congress. However, he said that no final decision had been made.

Senator Edmund S. Muskie, Democrat of Main, said today that he would introduce a bill to create an independent board to declassify appropriate documents "and provide Congress and the public the information they must have to play their proper roles in our democratic system."

Senator Muskie said that the Court decision "is a victory for the American people's right to know."

Symington 'Gratified'

Senator Jacob K. Javits, Republican of New York, termed the Court ruling a "historic reaffirmation of freedom of the press" and a reaffirmation of "the good judgment and high patriotic sense of The New York Times and The Washington Post."

Senator Stuart Symington, Democrat of Missouri, said that he was "gratified by the decision."

"What the press is really doing here," he said, "is a job the legislature should have done for itself." He added that he did not think The Times should be criminally prosecuted for publishing the documents.

Senator George S. McGovern of South Dakota, the only announced candidate for the Democratic Presidential nomination, said that he "never doubted the First Amendment meant what it said."

Senator McGovern said he also never doubted that the court would "stand with the men who wrote the Constitution rather than those in this Administration who think that freedom of the press is just another political catchphrase."

The Senate Republican leader, Hugh Scott of Pennsylvania, said that he was "pleased that the Supreme Court has ruled in favor of a free press."

But Senator Robert A. Taft Jr., Republican of Ohio, while praising the Court for upholding freedom of the press, said that the ruling presented "some serious problems for Congress" on protecting truly sensitive documents.

Representative William S. Moorhead, Democrat of Pennsylvania, chairman of a House government operations subcommittee investigating government secrecy, said that he was "gratified" at the court ruling.

The ranking Republican on the Moorhead subcommittee, Ogden R. Reid of Westchester, a former editor of The New York Herald Tribune, said that "freedom of the press is more secure tonight because the supreme court has recognized that a press subject to prior restraint cannot be free."

But Representative Samuel A. Stratton, Democrat of upstate New York, said that he felt the Court had made "a very serious mistake."

* * *

October 21, 1971

SAIGON WARNS PAPERS ON 'DETRIMENTAL' MATERIAL

Special to The New York Times

SAIGON, South Vietnam, Oct. 20—The Government's Office of Information has issued a new directive to the press to avoid material "detrimental to national security and public order."

In its statement, made public yesterday, the agency listed three "proposals" to be followed by the 44 daily newspapers of South Vietnam to preclude seizures and Government prosecution. These urged the press:

Not to publish any leaflets or proclamations issued by illegal organizations or by militant factions that might "sow confusion among the broad masses," or "foment troubles harmful to the national security and public order."

Not to use "inciting headlines related to irresponsible statements or law-breaking actions."

"To avoid playing up or dramatizing facts or spreading inaccurate news."

"In the recent past," the statement said, "some Saigon dailies have usually printed irresponsible statements, anti-government leaflets or proclamations issued by illegal political groups with a view to attract readers."

The proposals are being looked upon here by many South Vietnamese editors and reporters as increased pressure to restrict the coverage of any groups who are critical in any way of any Government policy.

"I'm just worried it's the beginning of a bad time for the Vietnamese press," said Le Hien, the publisher of the daily, But Thep.

The most frequently used article in the three-year-old Vietnamese press code cited as ground for confiscation is Article 28. It states that papers will be seized for "disseminating false arguments, and distortions detrimental to the national security or public order or to the national economy and finance."

Later today, the Government announced that 14 dailies, many of which carried articles on the new censorship recommendations, were seized yesterday.

* * *

December 31, 1971

THREAT IS SEEN TO THE WILL OF JOURNALISTS TO SPEAK OUT

By THOMAS J. HAMILTON
Special to The New York Times

GENEVA, Dec. 30—The International Press Institute reported today that in the democratic world "the will of the journalist to say what he thinks is being slowly and imperceptibly weakened."

The institute, in its survey of press developments in 1971, said that this "potentially fatal malady" was more dangerous than outright censorship or self-censorship.

The report was written by Ernest Meyer, a Frenchman who is director of the institute. A private agency, with headquarters in Zurich, it was founded in 1952 to promote freedom of the press and the improvement of journalistic practices. It now has 1,700 members from 62 countries.

"Since governments and pressure groups have tasted the power of slanted information and good public relations, the press, short of the resources to pursue individual reporting, is depending more and more on official statements," the report said.

It added that independent journalists were being threatened with the loss of their jobs and with subpoenas if they refused to reveal their sources of information.

The fact that newspapers have been closed, taken over by force, or hampered in obtaining newsprint shows "how fragile is this freedom of the press which has been taken for granted in a modern society," the report said.

Turning to radio and television stations, the report said that they had developed "a conditioned reflex compelling them to press the button of caution" because they were owned or controlled by governments or felt it necessary to seek government approval and the goodwill of sponsors to obtain renewal of their licenses.

The report said that the media in Britain remained "as free as any in the world—and freer than most." It added that some British politicians were attempting to censor radio and television coverage of the disturbances in Northern Ireland.

Elsewhere in Europe, the report noted disputes in France between journalists and the police but no cases affecting freedom of the press in West Germany or Austria. Economic difficulties are affecting independent coverage in the Netherlands and Italy, it said.

Among the totalitarian countries in the area, the report said that "it is in Turkey that the picture of press freedom has darkened the most."

The report said that, despite "justified" differences of opinion, the publication of the Pentagon papers by The New York Times was "very courageous" and the "decision of responsible newsmen acting in the very best traditions of responsible journalism."

It added that the Supreme Court decision authorizing publication "showed that the First Amendment to the Constitution is not just a pious declaration but a legal reality."

The report cautioned, however, that freedom of the press was still under attack by some branches of the Nixon Administration that were demanding that journalists disclose confidential news sources and hand over unused notes, film and photographs.

The Columbia Broadcasting System, it said, held out against this pressure in the case of the documentary film "The Selling of the Pentagon."

Its action was described as "parallel" to the publication of the Pentagon papers. The report said that the final outcome of court actions against a number of journalists was still uncertain.

* * *

January 1, 1973

PRESS INSTITUTE IS CRITICAL OF U.S.

It Charges Courts Are Used to Chip Away at Freedom

Special to The New York Times

GENEVA, Dec. 31—The International Press Institute asserted today that the Nixon Administration was "attempting to chip away at press freedom through the courts and by the threats of court action."

In its annual world review of press freedom, the institute said that the Nixon Administration apparently intended to make the "journalist timid in research for the facts and the public nervous when confronted by a reporter asking for them."

Nevertheless, the study by the institute's French director, Ernest Meyer, found that in the United States the "foundation stone of freedom of speech and the press edifice that has been built on it remains almost unscathed."

The institute, a nongovernmental organization with headquarters in Zurich, is supported by 1,700 editors and publishers in 62 countries.

More Curbs Seen

Reviewing press developments over the last year, the institute said that the trend to restrict press freedom was stronger than in 1971. Barely one-fifth of the 132 members of the United Nations "enjoy what can genuinely be called freedom of information," it reported.

The survey also cited what it termed the "continuing efforts of governments to erode freedom of expression through intimidation of journalists and manipulation of mass media."

The aim, it said, is to "give the impression that the interests of the country are necessarily identical with those of the government in power."

But the "true danger," the review continued, "lies in the fact that a growing number of governments, parliamentary representatives, citizens and even some members of the press begin to accept that attacks on freedom of expression are legitimate and justifiable."

Marcos Assailed

The most serious attack on this freedom in the last year, according to the institute, was the "silencing of the most courageous and frank press in Asia, that of the Philippines."

Actions by President Ferdinand E. Marcos, following the establishment of quasi-martial rule in the Philippines, amounted to a "deliberate dismantling of the free mass media in his country," the survey said.

The review listed what it called the "notorious decision" of the United States Supreme Court in the case of Earl Caldwel, a New York Times reporter, among last year's "threats to the freedom of the press."

In the case the Supreme Court ruled that reporters did not have the right to withhold from Federal grand juries the sources of information given in confidence or to refuse to testify about criminal acts they had been told about under a pledge of secrecy.

The institute noted an increase in press complaints of government secrecy and evasion by Government officials in the United States. But it said that there was also a growing number of Government "secrets" being given to the press by anonymous official sources.

* * *

March 11, 1973

PORNOGRAPHIC SHOWS SPREAD IN MIDWEST

By SETH S. KING
Special to The New York Times

MINNEAPOLIS, March 10—"Our main hang-up in dealing with commercial sex and pornography in Minneapolis is that so many people these days just don't think it's a serious problem," said Sgt. Jon Prentice.

As head of the Police Department's nine-man morals squad, Sergeant-Prentice was lamenting the city's inability to halt a neighborhood theater showing of "Deep Throat," by now the most celebrated hard-core pornographic film of the decade.

New York City, still regarded by many here as the nation's Sodom and Gomorrah, may have succeeded in snuffing out the movie last week, with a Criminal Court ruling that it was "indisputably and irredeemably" obscene.

But in such bastions of mid-America as Milwaukee, Indianapolis and Chicago, "Deep Throat" was still playing this week, with few serious problems from the law. In Chicago, Mayor Richard J. Daley ordered it closed on March 2, only to have a Federal District judge promptly order it opened the next day.

This week the state's attorney went into another local court and the judge, after viewing it, ruled that "Deep Throat" was obscene and should be confiscated. But a Federal Court order kept the theater open, and yesterday it was running large ads in the newspapers proclaiming that Souzie was better than Linda Lovelace ("Deep Throat's" heroine) and offering two new hard-core films, "Souzie's House" and "Lucky's Friends."

In the last year the spread of commercial sex from the wicked coasts of New York and California to the interior has been rapid and wide.

Flourishing in Iowa

In Des Moines, a half-dozen hard-core pornography theaters are operating. Others are doing nicely in other Iowa cities like Davenport, Ames and Cedar Rapids—and in Eddyville (population (945) and Diagonal (327).

In Indianapolis the police now count 19 massage parlors within the city and half a dozen in its environs, and "not more than one of them is a bona fide massage establishment," said Lieut. Reed L. Moistner, head of the vice branch.

The New York Times/Gary Saffle

A movie house in Minneapolis's lively section of striptease bars and small burlesque houses. Commercial sex and pornography are becoming more evident in many U.S. cities.

In Nashville there are six massage parlors in the city-county area and six downtown movie houses offering explicit sex films.

Hard-core pornographic movies, as well as adult book stores and peep shows, flourish in Kansas City.

And in the wake of all this—the flood tide of explicit peep shows and films, the nude waitresses, the massage parlors that do much more than massage—the enforcers of public morals in many communities have been left frustrated and resentful over their inability to achieve any effective action against these attractions.

Every Legal Move

In such cities as Cleveland, Dallas and Denver, local prosecutors have tried every legal move they could think of to try to shutter up the X-rated movies and pornographic book stores.

"We've moved against 29 pornographic movies, including 'Deep Throat,' in the last three years," Sergeant Prentice said sadly in Minneapolis. "All the city has gotten are two convictions and a hung jury, and both guilty verdicts are still under appeal. In most instances it took so long to get a judgment that everybody who wanted to had already seen the movies."

Before "Deep Throat" became the in thing in New York and Criminal Court Judge Joel Tyler condemned it, the movie suffered a largely unnoticed run in Des Moines.

"It really didn't catch on too well," said a local connoisseur of pornographic films. "But now that it's had all that publicity, I hope it comes back. I'd like to see it again."

It may well do that. Des Moines has come a long way in commercial sex since the days when the only thing in town close to public sin was at Ruthie's, a beer place whose owner, a spectacularly equipped young woman, gathered nightly crowds to watch her fill beer glasses that she placed on her cantilevered (though largely clad) bosom.

Ads For Massages

Since the beginning of the year, seven massage parlors have taken newspaper ads to describe the charms of their masseuses, and a "studio" advertises the availability of four nude models for painting or photographing.

A few of the massage parlors, Des Moines policemen say, provide little else but a shower and a rub-down. But in most of them a customer can get just about anything he asks for.

Lieut. Lawrence Carpe, head of the vice bureau, said there was little the police could do because they had trouble building a case.

"Few masseuses actually solicit for prostitution," he said. "They let the customer make the suggestion for 'added services' and so technically they aren't soliciting."

In Wichita, Kan., four massage parlors are now operating and a fifth is under construction. All are situated just over the city line in Sedgewick County, outside the jurisdiction of the city's strict massage control laws.

A team of reporters from The Wichita Eagle and Beacon recently did a study of these "health clubs," as the massage parlors are called. This included one female reporter training as a masseuse and another "joining" a club with facilities for women and getting the $15 massage.

Wichita's massage parlor operators have been careful to limit extras to hand stimulation of the genitals, known in the trade there as "a local." There is nothing in the state's prostitution law that prohibits this, and the district attorney has told the sheriff that there are no grounds for prosecution.

In Minneapolis, whose large Scandinavian population has long used the sauna bath, the sauna and massage have been turned to new use. This week's newspapers carried ads for 28 sauna and massage parlors in this city and adjoining St. Paul. Two of the ads were for a service called "Dial-A-Masseuse." By calling the number listed, a customer can have a masseuse come to his home or office.

Survey By Reporter

The extra services at most saunas was confirmed by Minnesota University's Daily, which recently sent a reporter to visit seven local saunas. He found that for fees ranging from $10 to $25 above the basic sauna and massage price, he could have manual stimulation, fellatio or sexual intercourse.

St Paul's City Council is preparing legislation to regulate sauna and massage parlors.

Lieutenant Moistner in Indianapolis termed massage parlors "the new hub of prostitution."

"We've forced them off the streets and out of the taverns, and now they're into this," he said. "But it's even harder to arrest here."

The Indianapolis police have made six arrests in massage parlors this year and have gone into court to try for convictions under a seldom used charge of conspiracy to engage in prostitution.

But the Indianapolis prosecutors are not overly optimistic after their experience in trying to prosecute some operators of pornographic bookstores and peep shows.

A projectionist at one explicit-film house in Nashville said that couples were attending in increasing numbers. His theater gets its liveliest couples business on Sundays, he said, and some come dressed as though they had just been to church.

The Nashville-Davidson County police believe the massage parlors are fronts for prostitution, Capt. Charles L. Stoner, head of the vice squad, said. Captain Stoner said the city-county legal department was preparing legislation that would prohibit massage parlor attendants from serving a customer of the opposite sex.

Kansas City's City Council enacted a tough obscenity law two years ago and the police began arresting operators of adult book stores and movie houses. The operators promptly appealed their convictions and their cases are still pending before the Missouri Supreme Court.

Their stores and theaters are still open. The police still make periodic arrests, and to get some sort of penalty against the owners, they are charging them with operating disorderly houses. They usually get off with a small fine.

But across the Missouri River in neighboring Kansas City, Kan., the watchers of morals are struggling to control prostitution in nearly a dozen massage parlors as well as trying to regulate strip teasers and nude waitresses in the score of "private" clubs that flourish there.

The Kansas Legislature has bills before it that would put clothes back on the bar girls. And the City Council has enacted a stringent massage parlor control ordinance it believes will at least drive the prostitutes out.

The Minneapolis antipornography law considers something obscene when, to the average person applying contemporary community standards, the dominant theme in the material appeals only to prurient interests.

"That's a very broad definition indeed," said Robert J. Milavetz, a Minneapolis lawyer.

Since 1970, Mr. Milavetz says, he has appeared for the defense in more than 200 obscenity cases. Only four of these have gone to jury trials. No defendant has pleaded guilty. One was found not guilty, one got a hung jury, and two were convicted but are still on appeal.

"You won't ever close out pornography as long as the majority of people are not really stirred up about it," Mr. Milavetz said. "Or as long as they are willing to pay for it."

* * *

September 9, 1974

SAIGON ASSAILED FOR PRESS CURBS

Newsmen Drop Timidity and Join in Accusing Regime of Terrorizing Them

By JAMES M. MARKHAM
Special to The New York Times

SAIGON, South Vietnam, Sept. 8—A newly formed committee of publishers, journalists and Opposition politicians denounced the Government today for "oppressing and terrorizing the press, newspapermen, writers and artists."

The formation of the group, which includes the chairmen of both the publishers and the working journalists associations, marks a sharp change in attitude. Fearful of official retaliation, Saigon journalists have been timid about organizing into groups to attack the Government.

"The cup is too full," said Tran Van Tuyen, an Opposition Deputy who is a member of the group. "In any case, the Government has condemned the press to death."

He was referring—perhaps with a touch of exaggeration—to recent actions against several Saigon papers that have never been conspicuously anti-Government in their political posture.

Anticorruption Drive Backed

But all were advancing in one way or another an anti-corruption campaign that formally began June 18th with the publication of a harshly worded petition signed by 301 Roman Catholic priests.

Catholics have generally been pillars of the anti-Communist regime of President Nguyen Van Thieu. The defection of the priests has made the Government edgy. Though the police prevented the dissident Catholics from holding a news conference June 18, their petition has been circulated in parishes throughout the country.

On Aug. 31, Hoa Binh, a centrist daily, suspended publication after its editions had been repeatedly confiscated by the police, causing it financial difficulties. The paper, which is edited by a priest, had been outspoken in its support for the Catholic anticorruption campaign and had called for the implementation of the Paris peace agreements on Vietnam, which were signed in January, 1973.

The official reasons given for the confiscation of Hoa Binh were often trivial—stories on "what women think of Frenchmen" purportedly "infringed on traditional morality."

Three Are Arrested

Five weeks ago, a reporter for Chinh Luan, a highly respected conservative newspaper, was arrested after writing an article pinpointing an allegedly corrupt official in the Premier's office. The official, who had allegedly been facilitating the illegal export of brass castings, was also arrested—as was the source of the story.

The paper's managing editor, Nguyen Thai Lan was repeatedly summoned to the police and held for one day.

"It looks like persecution," observed Dang Van Sung, the paper's publisher. "It gives a bad image to South Vietnam abroad. It's a pity that things like this happen—it only gives the other side an opportunity to attack the regime."

In addition to these moves, the government prosecuted the publisher of Song Than, an independent daily, for an article that implied that the office of Vice President Tran Van Huong had shielded a colonel accused of murdering an elderly peasant who was conducting a lonely campaign against corruption.

Plans a Seminar

According to Deputy Tuyen the new press group—which calls itself the Committee struggling for the Right to Freedom of the Press and of Publication—plans to hold a seminar this week to air its complaints.

Additionally, representatives of the Association of Vietnamese Newspaper Publishers are scheduled to meet Tuesday with Information Minister Hoan Duc Nha. Mr. Nha, who is a cousin of President Thieu, personally orders the confiscation and censorship of South Vietnamese newspapers.

The committee states in its "resolution" that the Government has "stripped the people of almost all basic rights, especially the right to freedom of the press and of publication."

It vows to "actively struggle" for freedom of the press and the repeal of South Vietnam's severe press laws.

* * *

November 18, 1974

THIEU CENSORSHIP BACKED IN A TEST

Power to Confiscate Issues of Papers Is Continued in Altered Press Law

By DAVID K. SHIPLER
Special to The New York Times

SAIGON, South Vietnam, Nov. 14—The lower house of the National Assembly thwarted an opposition drive for press freedom today by approving a slight relaxation of the press law that leaves President Nguyen Van Thieu with his most effective tool of censorship: the power to confiscate issues of newspapers.

The survival of this provision casts into relief the extent of the impact of anti-Government protests upon Mr. Thieu's political influence. While Mr. Thieu has been forced into accepting a certain modification in the law, politicians are not yet ready to abandon him.

Two days ago Mr. Thieu invited 76 of his supporters in the heavily pro-Government House to Independence Palace, where he examined the proposed press amendments, gave his approval and warned against further liberalization. He reportedly talked about sending tanks to the National Assembly if necessary.

The deputies who voted today for the amendments bearing Mr. Thieu's imprimatur numbered 76. Swift approval by the Senate and a signature by Mr. Thieu are virtually assured.

Press censorship has become one of the two main issues fueling the recent wave of street demonstrations and protests aimed at ousting President Thieu from office. The other is governmental corruption, corruption, considered a more politically potent issue in the context of deteriorating economic conditions.

The two are inextricably linked, however. The press issue gained prominence after stern Government action against papers that had publicized charges of corruption.

"We should clearly put down on paper that the press can denounce corruption," one opposition deputy, Nguyen Van Kim, declared during today's debate. "The people have the right to be informed of the good or bad performance, the honesty or dishonesty of those who hold public office."

Confiscation has become extremely costly for papers that operate on thin profits, and the threat of Government seizure is usually enough to prompt self-censorship. Most papers check questionable articles with the Ministry of Information before publication.

Opponents sought an amendment shifting the authority to confiscate from the executive to the courts, but it was clear from the outset that this was unacceptable to Mr. Thieu and his majority in the House.

"We are in a country at war," said pro-Government Deputy Duong Vy Long. "We still have to face Communist armed aggression. Confiscation of papers is an emergency measure to help us check any effort to abuse the press for attempts against national security and order. We can't afford to wait for a court order each time a paper should be confiscated."

Among the amendments passed, perhaps the most significant was the one abolishing the requirement that newspaper publishers deposit 20 million piasters—about $30,000—with the Government. When the regulation was put into effect in 1972 about a dozen papers folded. A proliferation of new dailies is now expected, though some of them may not prove to be economically viable.

The other approved amendments are as follows:

The Ministry of the Interior will no longer have the power to suspend a newspaper's publication after two days issues are confiscated, only a court may do so.

During confiscation, the day's painting plates may not be seized.

Violations of the press law will no longer be tried by military courts, but by civilian courts.

Certain penalities are lightened. Publishing articles deemed detrimental to the national security and public order, for example, would subject the publishers and editors to jail terms of six months to two years, down from one to three years, and a fine of 300,000 to three million piasters down from one to five million.

* * *

AMERICAN ALLIES

August 15, 1965

SPAIN'S PRESS CENSORSHIP CURB VIEWED AS ESTABLISHING PATTERN

By TAD SZULC
Special to The New York Times

LA CORUNA, Spain, Aug. 14—Spain has taken a step that observers believe may turn out to be the first major move on the long road back to the political freedoms virtually suspended since the Civil War of the nineteen-thirties.

The step was the approval by Generalissimo Francisco Franco and his Cabinet yesterday of a bill to eliminate direct censorship of the Spanish press. The Government is to submit the bill to the Cortes, or Parliament, this fall. Yesterday's action in practice is tantamount to approval, although amendments acceptable to the Government may be written into the bill. Spanish editors will probably have an opportunity to test the flexibility of the new legislation early next year.

Formal censorship now operates only in Madrid and Barcelona, but it is just as effective elsewhere through indirect methods.

Discussion Is Indirect

While editors of the independent newspapers may take their time in catching up on heretofore forbidden matters—and thus risk possible reprisals—there are persons close to the regime who think that before long the press will gradually start discussing Spain's central political question, which is the succession to General Franco who is 73 years old.

Thus far public discussion of this issue has been highly indirect and often subtly disguised in articles on other subjects for the benefit of readers adept at reading between lines.

The press law draft, the text of which has not yet been published, eliminates direct censorship but sets up a mechanism under which the Government may sue editors of newspapers considered by the public prosecutor to have violated such statutes as that covering the security of the state.

Private citizens may also sue editors for libel or slander.

Traditionally, direct censorship may be reimposed in time of national emergency or other "exceptional situations."

It is understood that the press law will not define specifically the offenses under which editors may be held legally responsible for what they publish.

The new law is to apply to Spain's 104 dailies and 9,000 magazines and periodicals, as well as to book publishers.

Intentions Face Test

It is widely believed that the regime's intentions will best be tested by the manner in which the Government goes about implementing the new legislation.

Minister of Information and Tourism Manuel Fraga Irribarne, a 42-year-old "new generation" member of the Cabinet who for three years has championed the press law, said that he believed the decision represented "an important new step in Spain's political life."

The older generation of high Spanish officials, who seem to lack General Franco's new flexibility, are expected to apply pressure against establishing real press freedom.

But it is argued in some Government circles that yesterday's step may well open many new political doors that it may become difficult to close without embarrassing the regime in the eyes of its own nascent public opinion and of the international opinion that Spain now takes with growing seriousness.

In that sense, many informed Spaniards believe, the decision on the press law is a part of a process of political transition.

* * *

October 31, 1965

MADRID EXPLAINS NEW PRESS BILL

Editors Wary Despite Plan to End Direct Censorship

By TAD SZULC
Special to The New York Times

MADRID, Oct. 30—Manuel Fraga Iribarne, Minister of Information and Tourism and chief sponsor of Spain's proposed new press law, said at a news conference this week that the administration's bill represented an "intermediary law."

Mr. Fraga stressed that while the long-awaited bill removed the direct censorship that has formally existed in Spain since 1938, it did not imply the Government's self-removal from the field of press and information.

Today the weekly Roman Catholic Church magazine Ecclesia, which under Spain's concordat with the Vatican is not subject to censorship, sharply criticized in its lead editorial some of the key provisions of the proposed new law.

It said the bill presented "notable breaches of internal logic," inasmuch as it proclaimed the abolition of censorship while requiring, at the same time, that newspapers submit a copy of each issue to the Information Ministry one hour before publication.

Improvement Held Barred

Ecclesia stressed that the bill's prohibition of questioning the "existing constitutional order" in Spain closed the door to any "improvement" of it.

Mr. Fraga said in his presentation that the state would remain "active" in press matters because it was its duty to do so.

While the Information Minister described the proposed legislation, three years in preparation, as an important advance, many independent-minded Spanish editors felt that it substantially changed little in the practice of press control and, in fact, might subtly tie their hands even more than before.

The bill's Article 2 sets forth the "limitations" of the right of free expression.

It lists them as "the respect for morality and truth; the observance of the existing constitutional order; the requirements of national defense, of the security of the state and of the maintenance of internal public order and external peace; the discretion surrounding actions of the Government; the independence of the courts in the application of laws and the preservation of individual honor and privacy."

Prosecution Is Provided

Under the bill the violation of these principles, which the editors believe to be too vaguely defined to serve as a realistic guide, would lead to criminal prosecution of publishers, editors or writers before the courts.

Furthermore, so-called administrative penalties, ranging from fines to the suspension of newsmen and publications for varying periods, may be imposed for the violation of such regulations as the publication of official decisions or documents prior to their public release or the failure to publish the Government's announcements.

Spanish editors, who were shown the text of the new bill six days ago, believe that the system of limitations and punishments built into the legislation would greatly discourage freedom of the press and lead to considerable self-censorship.

'Voluntary Consultations'

To assist with such self-censorship, the bill specifies that the Ministry of Information and its agencies will be available for "voluntary consultations." It provides that an "approving answer" or "silence" would exempt a publication or writer from any subsequent administrative responsibility.

Discussing this point, Mr. Fraga acknowledged that he expected wide usage of the mechanism of "voluntary consultation" in the first months of the new law's operations.

While the law is expected to be approved in Parliament late this year, possibly with some amendments, Mr. Fraga has excluded its discussion in newspapers prior to its passage.

There should be no public debate parallel with the debate in Parliament, he said. A special commission is working on the bill in executive sessions.

With all the reservations among editors over the new legislation—and Mr. Fraga acknowledged that they existed—it still loomed in the relative terms of Spanish political realities as at least a theoretical improvement over the 1938 law, passed at the height of the civil war.

The old law proclaimed the institution of censorship and the right of the state to intervene in the naming of editors and offered virtually no appeal against governmental decisions.

The new law offers a wide range of possibilities of appeal and it does no more than define the limitations on the choice of editors.

But in the last analysis, most editors agreed, the real extent of press freedom here will be regulated more by the implementation of the law by the regime than by its actual wording.

* * *

January 16, 1966

CENSORSHIP AS THE GERMANS DO IT

By THOMAS J. HAMILTON
Special to the New York Times

BONN, Jan. 15—It is almost impossible for Americans to conceive of a really free government without a free press, one that calls the shots as it sees them, regardless of government approval or disapproval.

Although the Federal Republic's Constitution, or "basic law," forbids censorship, the West German press, radio and television do not enjoy such freedom—or if they do they do not exercise it fully.

Since political in-fighting here is highly developed, and leaders of the same party attack each other more openly than in the United States or in most democracies, at first glance one would think that the news media were giving the news with no holds barred.

On closer examination, however it becomes apparent that most West German editors are highly selective, and either play down or omit news stories that they consider detrimental to the nation's interests.

The many cross-currents involved in this issue came to the surface last Monday, when the programming council of the North German Television Network in Hamburg modified its ban on a particularly free-wheeling edition of "Hello Neighbor." This is a political satire—modeled on the British Broadcasting Corporation's "That Was the Week That Was"—which has been appearing on a national network about once every six weeks.

Survival

In view of the present-day German dislike for satire the surprising thing is that a program that ridicules leading politicians and shibboleths of national policy has been on the air as long as it has.

The banned edition, for example, satirized Bonn's uncertainties about how to exploit the suicide of Dr. Erich Apel, an East German official who shot himself last month as a protest against a new trade agreement with the Soviet Union which gave the Russians much the better part of the bargain.

However, there were widespread protests over the ban, and the network decided that "Hello Neighbor" could continue, subject to the right of network officials to approve future editions.

Hereafter, the network ruled, "facts, not fiction," must be presented, and public figures must not be portrayed as doing things "which they had not actually done." Since this was the whole basis of the "Hello Neighbor" format, the principal writer of the show said he would have to think it over before deciding whether to continue.

Treason laws and staff regulations which are used to safeguard official secrets are the reasons why news media in general are less independent in West Germany than in the United States. The treason laws provide the Government with a powerful weapon against the publication of military information or other information detrimental to the state.

The most notorious example of its use against journalistic initiative came in 1962, when Franz-Josef Strauss, then Minister of Defense, ordered the prosecution of editors of Der Spiegel for publishing the contents of a classified report listing deficiencies in the West German Army.

Although Mr. Strauss was eventually forced out of office, the charges against the magazine were not dropped until last year, and this precedent has not encouraged the publication of exclusive stories of any kind.

Penalties

Staff regulations in the various ministries impose severe penalties for the disclosure of information and constitute censorship at the source. A Foreign Office official who gives such information, even to a member of the Bundestag, is dismissed.

One recent bizarre example—also satirized by "Hello Neighbor"—came with the summary dismissal of Count Huyn, a young pro-Gaullist Foreign Office official, for tipping off pro-Gaullist deputies to the fact that Dr. Gerhard Schröder, the Foreign Minister, was making secret plans to turn to London for support in his disputes with Paris.

Government public relations officers, like their counterparts in Washington, industriously bring in correspondents, editors and publishers for off-the-record briefings aimed at obtaining their support. Cooperative correspondents are given preference when the time comes to leak a story.

Management of news is facilitated also by the unchanging German respect for officials of all kinds and grades, the "Beamten" whose authority is seldom challenged by private citizens, including the press.

There are exceptions, notably Der Spiegel, the Frankfurter Allgemeine, the Frankfurter Rundschau, and Die Zeit, a Hamburg weekly, but by and large West German editorial writers and reporters bow to the voice of authority.

Book publishing seems to be as free as in any Western country, as witness the success of such writers as Gunther Grass, whose novels recall a Nazi past most West Germans prefer to forget. The same applies to the theater, where hard-hitting political satires continue to win favor, especially among West Berliners.

As part of a general reform of the criminal code, the Bundestag started debating Government amendments to the treason laws last Thursday. The amendments are intended to "put the interest of the public first" as regards the publication of news. But it is not clear how real a change will result.

What is clear is that West Germany still has a long way to go before it develops a completely free press.

* * *

February 6, 1966

SPAIN ABOUT TO CONFIRM A PRESS-FREEDOM BILL IN PREPARATION FOUR YEARS

By TAD SZULC
Special to The New York Times

MADRID, Feb. 5—For 18 days the majestic old palace of the Spanish Parliament has echoed to a public debate on freedom, not heard in Spain since the civil war broke out 30 years ago.

When the debate ended Thursday night, the 57 members of the Information Commission of the Cortes (Parliament) had approved the text of a law abolishing direct censorship and opening the way to relative freedom of the press in Spain—if the regime chooses to exercise with moderation the control powers it retains.

The commission's passage of the law, achieved after the delivery of 848 long and short speeches and the consideration of 119 amendments offered to the Government's original bill, is tantamount to its approval by the Cortes.

A plenary session of the Cortes, expected to be held later this month, is to confirm the text as it now stands and the new press law will become operative immediately.

The legislation, is preparation since 1962, is intended as the first of the major "liberalizing" laws that the regime of Generalissimo Francisco Franco hopes to enact in the near future as a part of Spain's quickening political transition.

Yet, because this transition is gradual and Spanish politics are conducted in highly relative terms, the press law will in the final analysis be only as liberal as the Franco regime wishes it to be.

Thus, while the law proclaims the principle of freedom of expression through the printed word and specifically abolishes censorship except in wartime and in special situations, it simultaneously sets forth a series of vague limitations.

These limitations are defined as the respect for truth and morality; obedience to the principles of the National Movement, which is the Franco regime's political organization, and other fundamental laws; the requirements of national defense and state security, and the maintenance of internal public order and external peace; due respect for institutions and individuals in criticisms of political and administrative acts; the independence of the courts, and the safe-guarding of person and family privacy and honor.

Under the law, publishing companies, editors and writers may be held responsible for violating these ill-defined strictures, and subjected to penalties ranging from temporary suspension of publication and suspensions in journalistic employment to relatively high monetary fines.

In the often heated debates in the Cortes commission, the deputies succeeded in lessening the penalties from the levels originally proposed by the Government. Where the regime had asked for the suspension of an editor or a writer for three to six months, the commission made it one to six months.

Where the regime's bill proposed fines for publishing companies as high as $16,000, the commission made it $8,000. Likewise, the commission ruled that editors and writers can be suspended or fined, but not both as the regime demanded.

The Government, which can also seize newspapers and magazines before turning the matter of an offense to the courts, has the authority to define a violation and ask the courts to prosecute.

The law is to be administered by Information and Tourism Minister Manuel Fraga Iribarne, who sponsored the legislation. His office will make available a system of voluntary consultation for editors not willing to risk a touchy decision. "Administrative silence" by the Ministry in response to such consultation is to be taken as approval.

One delicate point left unresolved in the law concerns church publications which, under the terms of Spain's concordate with the Vatican, have always been free of censorship and had often been embarrassingly outspoken.

To deal with this, the commission wrote in a provision ordering the Government and church authorities to work out pertinent agreements.

* * *

April 24, 1966

SPAIN TRIES A LITTLE LIBERTY

By TAD SZULC
Special to The New York Times

MADRID, April 23—Spring has ushered in a new political era for Spain this year, the 30th anniversary of the eruption of the bloody Spanish civil war.

The new era represents essentially the formal beginnings of the country's transition from what has been in recent years a more or less benign dictatorship, to what most Spaniards hope before too long will be a constitutional state with all the normal political freedoms.

The immediate and inevitable question facing Spain in this new period, however, is how quickly the liberalizing and democratizing process can reach full fruition.

The tendency on the part of Generalissimo Francisco Franco and the regime's "old guard"—his fellow veterans of the civil war—is to administer the liberalization slowly and gradually; there are powerful men here who would just as soon see things remain as they are now, even after the 73-year-old "Caudillo" leaves the scene.

But while General Franco is a past master of noncommital delays in politics, his Government is no longer the monolith of the old days. The very dynamics of Spain's new generation and of the whole situation may prevent the maintenance of the carefully controlled policy of gradualism.

United Press International

NEW GENERATION: Spain's younger generation is among those "clamoring for more liberties."

Having deliberately opened the new political era here with this month's press law and the timid beginnings of free debate in his rubber-stamp Parliament, the Generalissimo may have also opened a Pandora's box of pressures that he may find difficult, if not impossible, to keep in check.

The emerging political forces, ranging from monarchists to Socialists, are determined to create a climate that would accelerate the liberalizing process in defiance of the regime's wishes.

The opening of the current process of transition was formalized with the press law, which went into effect on April 9, although the process had been under way for some time in many segments of society.

For the last two weeks, Spaniards have been finding out through their newspapers that, yes, there are major university disturbances in Barcelona, that there are labor strikes here and there, that people are sentenced to prison for conspiracies, and that both the young generation of the Roman Catholic Church and the nation's leading intellectuals and artists are clamoring for more liberties.

They suddenly have been exposed to public political dialogue on Spain's future and to incipient criticism of the administration, though both are still couched in cautious and almost over-elegant terms.

Controls Remain

Still the Franco regime remains authoritative and it retains enough legal controls to silence anew the press if it chooses to do so.

But, as Information Minister Manuel Fraga Iribarne put it this week:

"In this Spain, there is and there will be more liberties every time . . . the liberties that range from the expression of our differences to a responsible criticism of the public administration. . . . through the interplay of ideas and interests as in every civilized society."

The Spanish society seems to have fully recovered from the long illness of the post-civil war period. This dynamic new society nowadays wishes to stand, walk and run on its own feet. Thus it poses the great challenge to the regime whose facade is already being increasingly cracked by deep fissures.

Organized labor, long the exclusive domain of the "National Movement"—the Falange-based political instrument of the regime—is breaking away from the fold.

Spain's leading intellectuals and artists, commanding respect here, have become fully involved in political struggles by college students.

The question is how long and how effectively the Franco regime may maintain its policy of carefully measured dosages of freedom.

* * *

April 5, 1967

NEW SPANISH PENAL CODE RESTRICTS THE PRESS

Editors Who 'Insult' Regime Subject to Six-Year Terms—Students Also Curbed

By TAD SZULC
Special to The New York Times

MADRID, April 4—The Cortes (Parliament) voted today without discussion to revise three articles of the Penal Code to provide severe prison sentences for editors and writers who violate the legal limitations on freedom of the press or who "insult" the Government.

The revision of a fourth article established prison penalties for students involved in political agitation in university departments in which they are not enrolled.

Ten or eleven legislators, including at least two Spanish newspaper editors, voted against the measures. About 150 supported the revisions.

Newsmen's Appeal Fails

In the Cortes, where until recently Government bills were usually passed unanimously, votes are not tallied and not announced. Observers in the chamber believed, however, that the Penal Code revisions had been approved by a vote of 150 against 10 or 11. The full membership of the Cortes is 594.

The Cortes ignored an appeal, signed by 170 Madrid newsmen and published in this morning's papers, for withdrawal of the press measures. The appeal, sent to Antonio

Iturmendi, president of the Cortes, described the legislation as a grave threat to freedom of the press.

It also accused the Government of retreating, in effect, from the Press Law adopted almost a year ago.

The Press Law was hailed as the first major opening toward the political liberalization of Spain after 30 years under Generalissimo Francisco Franco.

Since the adoption of the law, an increasingly open political dialogue has developed in the Spanish press, with agitation in the labor unions, the universities and the Roman Catholic Church in favor of still greater liberties.

Regime Seems Nervous

Spaniards not identified with the Government suggest that this breakthrough led conservatives in the Government to reconsider the new policies.

Nervousness in the Government was again indicated tonight when hundreds of policemen filled a square mile area in uptown Madrid after reports that young members of a leftist labor movement planned a demonstration there.

The Labor Ministry, reported to be the target of the planned demonstration is in the ultramodern complex of the "new ministries" on Generalissimo Avenue, a main thoroughfare. The police sealed off the block.

The foremost question tonight was whether the passage of the restrictive legislation, drafted by the Cortes Justice Commission, would immediately stifle growing press criticism of plans for additional laws.

These draft bills grant the National Movement—the Franco Government's loose political organization—a continued monopoly over Spanish political life, doing away with hopes for a freer interplay of ideas and groups.

Many newspapers have outspokenly criticized these plans, but the revision of the Penal Code could put an end to such comments.

Publication of "dangerous information" may now bring prison terms up to six years. The Press Law carried no criminal penalties for violations, and newsmen could be punished only by fines or expulsion from their profession.

With the Government acting as the arbiter of suspected violations, an editor or newsman may be found guilty of such offenses as "lack of respect for truth and morality" or endangering public peace.

* * *

July 21, 1967

MUNICH CONFISCATES PAPER LIKENING DAYAN TO HITLER

Special to The New York Times

BONN, July 20—The Civil Court of Munich today ordered the confiscation of this week's edition of the right-wing newspaper Deutsche National und Soldaten Zeitung because it compared Israel's Defense Minister, Maj. Gen. Moshe Dayan, to Hitler.

Associated Press Cablephoto

Munich policemen confiscated several hundred copies of the paper in the publishing house and more at various distributing agencies.

The July 21 edition of the paper, generally called the Soldaten Zeitung, carried pictures of General Dayan and Hitler side by side on the front page. The headline read: "Israel's Auschwitz in the Desert—The Mass Murder of the Arabs—Dayan in Hitler's Tracks."

An official of the court said the legal basis for its confiscation order lay in the presentation of Hitler's photograph on the front page. The Bavarian press law forbids publication of Nazi symbols.

Dr. Gerhard Frey, the paper's editor, said it was the first time in 17 years of publication that it had faced court action. He said the seizure had been brought about by the headline which he defended, saying, "It presents Hitler as a negative personality and condemns Nazi crimes as much as Israeli ones."

The West German authorities have been waiting to pounce on the paper for a long time. Last May 18 Gustav Heinemann, the federal Minister of Justice, said that he and the Minister of the Interior, Paul Lücke, were studying means to bar it.

Today a spokesman said that the Interior Ministry "hailed" the Munich court's action as being "in the interest of democracy."

* * *

July 30, 1967

GREECE WILL END PRESS CENSORSHIP

But Regime Plans Punitive Laws to Deter Criticism

Special to The New York Times

ATHENS, July 29—The Government has decided to abolish press censorship, but plans to decree punitive laws as a deterrent to criticism of the regime.

Publishers were informed officially that the action, expected next week, would end the preventive censorship under which the Greek press was at the mercy of censors who ruled not only on the content of newspapers but also on their typography and display of news.

Under the legislation being drafted, publishers will face court-martial if they publish any reference to banned or inactive Greek political parties. Two Greek parties—the Communist party and the pro-Communist United Democratic Left—are banished by law. All other parties became inactive after the April 21 army takeover.

The publishers will also face court-martial if they reprint objectionable articles or comments from the foreign press.

Six Newspapers Close

The regime's decision followed strong representations from the International Federation of Journalists, the International Press Institute and the foreign press. Since the coup 6 of 14 Athens dailies have closed.

Pressure has also come from Mrs. Helen Vlachos, publisher of the conservative Athens dailies Kathimerini and Messimevrini and the weekly Eikones. Mrs. Vlachos has refused to publish until the Government restores Article 14 of the Greek Constitution—one of 11 suspended by the coup leaders—which safeguards freedom of the press.

Under Article 14 "Everyone may publish his opinion by speech, by writing or by printing, observing the laws of the state." The new law will qualify this freedom.

The proposed measures were viewed as an inducement to Mrs. Vlachos to resume publication. Last May she dismissed her 385 employes, pleading causes beyond her control that led to the closing of her papers.

Columnist Given Official Job

One of her dismissed employes, Theophylaktos Papaconstantinou, a columnist, was nominated Monday as Press Under Secretary in the military-civilian Government.

Mr. Papaconstantinou, who had turned down an earlier offer for the post, is understood to have accepted on condition that a free press be restored soon.

Immediately after his appointment this week, he stated: "I am happy to announce to the press and the Greek people that press freedom, temporarily suspended, will be restored shortly."

Mr. Papaconstantinou's appointment and the plan to abolish preventive censorship were also viewed as moves to placate Greek journalists who were upset by the Government decision last week to abolish the "journalists' lottery."

Earnings from this lottery, a privilege held by the Union of Greek Journalists for 33 years, went to finance the union's health and pension funds.

George Rallis, a former conservative minister, was arrested last night and charged for defying a martial-law ban on unauthorized indoor meetings of more than five people. He was released today.

* * *

January 1, 1968

BRITAIN TIGHTENS PRESS RESTRAINTS

Law, in Effect Today, Limits Reports of Crime Hearings

By ANTHONY LEWIS
Special to The New York Times

LONDON, Dec. 31—Starting tomorrow, newspapers will ordinarily be forbidden to report on the preliminary hearings that have long been a source of sensational crime news in Britain.

This new restraint is part of a general reform of criminal procedure. A package of changes was included in a comprehensive Criminal Justice Act passed by Parliament earlier this year. Some provisions were to take effect in 1968.

One change allows judges to suspend sentences, for the first time in England. Judges are also encouraged to release defendants on bail before trial. Restrictions are put on the use of alibis by defendants.

The limitation on press reporting has provoked strong criticism from the newspapers and some other commentators.

Britain already has heavy restraints. Before trial, for example, the press must not publish anything that might prejudice a jury against a criminal defendant unless it has been officially disclosed in court. References to a confession or a previous criminal record are thus strictly forbidden.

Sentences Imposed

Violation of those standards is contempt of court, punishable by heavy fines and even jail sentences for editors.

In light of the strict rules against publication that might prejudice a defendant, the right to cover preliminary criminal proceedings freely has seemed anomalous and illogical to observers.

The hearings are held to determine whether the prosecution has enough of a case to require the accused person to stand trial—something like an American grand-jury proceeding.

Often, a notorious defendant has, in effect, two public trials. After full newspaper coverage of the prosecution's case at the preliminary hearing, the jurors drawn for the trial might be prejudiced.

Reduction in Hearings

The new Criminal Justice Act aims to eliminate not only the press coverage but most of the preliminary hearing itself.

From now on, the magistrates who decide whether to make an arrested person stand trial may get written statements of the prosecution's evidence instead of hearing witnesses.

The way is then left open for the defense to offer no evidence and, in effect, waive any objection to being held for trial. That course is expected to be taken in most cases.

If there is no defense objection, the magistrates may commit the accused for trial without considering the evidence at all.

The press will ordinarily be admitted to preliminary hearings. But newspapers will not be allowed to publish anything about the hearings except such basic facts as the name of the accused, the charge against him and whether he has been ordered to stand trial.

If the magistrates find no case for trial and dismiss the prosecution, then the restraints on reporting will be lifted at once. Otherwise, reports of the preliminary hearing may be published only after the formal trial.

Some critics have argued that persons who know something about a crime, but have not been questioned, may come forward after reading about it. To meet this point, the new statute allows any defendant or his lawyers to demand the right of free publication of the preliminary proceedings.

The rule requires defendants to give notice before trial of any alibi defense they intend to make, with particulars and names of witnesses to support the alibi.

* * *

January 1, 1968

CENSORSHIP IN GREECE IS SCORED BY PRESS INSTITUTE

Survey Finds Situation Has Worsened Since Failure of Constantine's Move

Special to The New York Times

GENEVA, Dec. 31—The International Press Institute has termed the "overnight abolition" of a free press by the military junta in Greece the "most dramatic suppression" of press freedom in the last 15 years.

The situation of the Greek press has even worsened since the failure of King Constantine's attempt earlier this month to overthrow the military regime, the institute said yesterday in its annual survey of press freedom.

Five more Greek newspapermen, the survey found, have been reported arrested. Among them is said to be Leon B. Carapanayotis, a member of the institute, which represents about 1,600 newspaper editors and executives of more than 50 countries.

Written by Per Monsen, a Norwegian who is director of the Zurich-based institute, the survey described the disappearance of a free press in Greece as a "body blow" to believers in freedom of the press.

This was because it took place just when a "strong ferment was working in authoritarian countries in East Europe and in Spain and Portugal in favor of greater freedom of information and expression."

"Today" the survey continued, "more than half the people of Europe live without press freedom. In 12 European countries with a population of over 350 million, the government controls all channels of information on subjects the press to surveillance and censorship."

The 12 countries are not listed, but it is clear from the survey itself that they are the Soviet Union, East Germany, Bulgaria, Poland, Czechoslovakia, Rumania, Hungary, Yugoslavia, Albania, Greece, Spain and Portugal.

A "significant advance" for the press was seen in the United States Supreme Court rulings that "removed from the realm of libel statements made in good faith about people in the public eye."

As a result, the survey said, the American press is "now in a stronger position to publish in the public interest."

The institute described the press and television coverage of the war in Vietnam as "unequaled in any war in history" because of the information policy followed by the United States.

It conceded that this policy "may have helped the growth of world opinion against the American conduct of the war." But the institute added that it has "also served as a useful example to those many governments who mistrust the press."

Even before the brief war last June between Israel and her Arab neighbors, the press in those countries had become "mere instruments of war propaganda," the institute said.

"In Africa, it continued "there was nothing during the year to show that the battle for press freedom there would not be long and hard."

The survey found that increased stability in Central and Latin America has improved the position of the press, but that remaining "black spots" include Cuba and Haiti.

* * *

February 11, 1968

ONE ATHENS PAPER TAKES A BOLD TACK

By RICHARD EDER

Special to The New York Times

ATHENS, Feb. 10—With one exception, the Greek press has taken only the most cautious advantage of the experimental and limited relaxation of censorship announced by the Government 10 days ago.

The exception is Eleftheros Kosmos, the country's largest newspaper and the one that until recently was regarded as enjoying the greatest favor with the junta. In the last week, to the surprise of almost everyone and to the junta's ostensible annoyance, Eleftheros Kosmos has made strong attacks on two Cabinet Ministers.

In front-page articles, one of them extending over eight columns, the newspaper's publisher, Savas Constandopoulos, angrily criticized Adamantios Androutsopoulos, the Finance Minister, and Theophylactos Papagoistantinou, the Education Minister, all but calling for the latter's resignation.

Two Explanations Seen

The Finance Minister was accused of trying to harass the taxpayer and deny him his rights. The newspaper charged that the Education Minister had refused to receive the rector of the University of Salonika and had finally forced him to deliver his message to the doorman at the Ministry.

There are two schools of thought as to the reasons for the Eleftheros Kosmos campaign, which reverts to the old blistering Greek editorial style that has not been seen here since the military coup last April.

One is that Mr. Constandopoulos, who has been close to Premier George Papadopoulos but is known to be critical of some of the junta's tactics, has in fact decided to register his opposition.

Version of Junta Backers

This version is circulated by junta sources who say they are angry at the attacks and who hint that the conservative Mr. Constandopoulos is distressed by evidence that the junta may be swinging to a mildly leftist social policy.

Other sources, not connected with the junta, think that Eleftheros Kosmo's attacks are a put-up job. Citing reports that some of the colonels who favor a hard line but who now hold secondary jobs in the ministries are to move into the Cabinet these sources suspect that Premier Papadopoulos may be preparing the ground to justify a Cabinet shake-up.

Their suspicions are bolstered by the fact that even under the new rules all articles must be approved by the censor. The suggestion by some Government sources that in this case the censor made a mistake is not widely accepted.

The doubts that surround the new editorial line of Eleftheros Kosmos make it something of a special case. The reaction of other newspapers to the slight relaxation of censorship is more cautious, though unmistakable.

The new rules allow editors to decide on their own makeup, write their own headlines and engage in what is called "constructive criticism."

One provision, which shows how tight the censorship has been, allows newspapers to print items appearing in the Official Gazette, something that had been forbidden.

The reason for this odd situation was that government actions are official only when they have been printed in the gazette. The junta, highly legalistic in some respects, was anxious for this legal formality to be given to some actions that it did not necessarily want widely known.

Experienced observers here point to small liberties now taken in the press that would have been impossible two weeks ago. One newspaper put an exclamation point after a headline announcing that a bank manager had been jailed for having allowed his employes to work overtime. The implication was that the punishment was overly harsh.

* * *

November 2, 1968

PORTUGAL TASTES FREEDOM OF PRESS

Newspapers Use Restraint in New Liberalization

By MARVINE HOWE
Special to The New York Times

LISBON, Nov. 1—The Portuguese are taking to the current liberalization of the press eagerly but warily as to a heady new wine.

One month after the end of the authoritarian regime of Premier António de Oliveira Salazar, who suffered a stroke, the most important change wrought by the new Premier, Marcelo Caetano is the relaxation of government controls on the press.

For the last four decades, censors virtually stifled all forms of dialogue except during brief electoral periods. The press was governed by a 1928 decree that provided for censorship of all periodicals and banned criticism of members of the government as well as foreign policy.

Now the Portuguese press is publishing discreet criticism of the Administration and public debate on subjects of national interest and is even lifting certain taboos.

"Some favorable prospects of liberty of expression and thought are now opening before us, but there is still a long way to go," A Capital, an influential Lisbon newspaper noted this week. "And every thing indicates it is too early to proclaim victory."

Intoxication Is Feared

A Capital likened the new press freedom to new wine and warned that it must be consumed "prudently and in small doses" or it could lead to intoxication.

Thus far, the press has reacted to the easing of restrictions with restraint. Lisbon's main afternoon newspapers have taken the lead in pushing liberalization: A Capital, reflecting liberal business and intellectual circles: Diário de Lisboa, traditionally democratic and intellectual, and Diário Popular, independent with the largest circulation in the country.

But there are even signs of the new times in the conservative morning newspaper Diário de Noticias.

The leading editors and publishers are urging the Government to establish the rules of the game by passing a press law.

"We must have a press law otherwise we are at the mercy of the whim of the censors," Francisco Balsemão, dynamic young administrator of Diário Popular said. "Without a press law, we have no insurance, no appeal against arbitrary decisions."

Mario Neves, associate editor of A Capital said:

"We need a press law, even a severe one like the Spanish law; any law is better than no law. We are conscious of our responsibilities.

Press Law Prepared

Premier Caetano is putting the finishing touches on a press law that will give the press "greater right and greater responsibilities," according to high official sources. The Premier is expected to introduce the new law at the next session of the National Assembly, which opens at the end of November.

From the start, Mr. Caetano has shown interest in improving the Government's relations with the press. At his first Cabinet meeting, the Premier promoted the Department of Information and Tourism to ministerial rank. Shortly after taking office, he called newspaper publishers for a meeting and promised them a "more enlightened" censorship and greater cooperation from the Administration.

There are still a good number of things left unsaid. Censors are sensitive over local labor problems, opposition petitions, and above all the wars in Portuguese Africa.

The changes in the press are hardly perceptible to the outside observer. But for the Portuguese public, and above all for local journalists, Mr. Caetano has accomplished a minor revolution.

"There's a new spirit in Portugal," a prominent newsman said, "for the first time, the Government appears concerned about justifying its acts before the public."

Debate on Education

First of all, the press has been authorized to hold an open debate on a vital national problem: the crisis in the university. Prominent educators, some of them known for opposition views, have publicly criticized the lack of qualified professors, low salaries, inadequate school buildings and deficiencies in the education system as a whole.

Under Dr. Salazar's strict censorship, such problems could be discussed only behind closed doors. But now, even Diário da Manhã, organ of Dr. Salazar's National Union, has swung behind this movement, by defending the right to public debate if it remains on a high level.

The press is also appearing with polite but unusual criticism of the Administration. Censors let Diário de Lisboa publish an attack against the institution of censorship itself. The newspaper reported a declaration by Lyon de Castro, book publisher, accusing the censors of "dominating and restricting" creative thought in Portugal.

"Many of us, publishers and artists have lost the habit of thinking freely," Mr. de Castro said, expressing the hope that censorship would soon be ended.

* * *

June 6, 1969

6 FILMS WITHDRAWN FROM SYDNEY FETE

Special to The New York Times

SYDNEY, Australia, June 5—Difficulties with censors have caused the withdrawal of six productions from the Sydney Film Festival, which opened last night, leading to accusations that artistic expression is being stifled by "wowserism." Wowser is the Australian word for "puritan" or "square."

The film controversy followed closely upon the fining of an actor in Brisbane for using an obscene word on stage, the banning of records of the American musical "Hair" in Queensland State and the seizure of 15 erotic posters by the 19th-century British artist Aubrey Beardsley in a Brisbane bookstore.

An Australian production of "Hair" was to open in Sydney tonight. Authorities have indicated indifference to the celebrated nude sequence although complete nudity on stage will be new to the Sydney theatrical scene.

The Sydney film festival's troubles began when the Australian censorship board in charge of motion pictures ruled that the official Swedish entry, Stig Bjorkman's production of "I Love, You Love," was unfit for showing on moral grounds.

The ensuing controversy went as far as a debate in the Australian Senate before Mr. Bjorkman, here for the screening, decided to withdraw the picture from the festival.

Five Australian producers thereupon withdrew their own entries from the festival in a protest against the banning of the Swedish film.

* * *

August 15, 1969

NONPERSONS LIST IS LONG IN GREECE

Censored Press Also Must Deal With Nonevents

By ALVIN SHUSTER
Special to The New York Times

ATHENS, Aug. 14—A new circular made the rounds of newspaper offices the other day, telling how to treat crime news: Play it down and condemn violence.

A newspaper was told not to publish any pictures of tanks in Prague to accompany dispatches about the first anniversary of the Soviet-led invasion Aug. 21.

Only after two Germans were accused of murdering six Greeks during a five-week period did the Greek public learn about the crimes.

When Vanessa Redgrave won an international film award, she was referred to in newspapers only as the "leading actress of the film 'Isadora.' "

In the censored Greek press, many events never happen and many people do not exist. Greek-American relations have never been better. Army officers never have auto accidents. The economy has no problems.

Military Coup in 1967

Today, 28 months after the army seized power and installed press censorship, newspaper editors know the general limits. The Government, to be more specific, is preparing a new press law to detail the responsibilities of newspapermen and to say what should and should not be published.

The new law—two years in the making—will allow what the Government calls a trial period without censorship. Editors are not letting their hopes rise. It has been made clear that journalists will still not be allowed to criticize the

Government, and those who violate the new rules can be punished under existing martial law.

"I have not seen the law yet," an editor said. "But I think we'll be free—free to support the Government."

Editors hope that the new law will at least be an improvement over the present system, which they consider unimaginative, rigid and often mysterious in detail at best. The censors, for example, have a list of several hundred people who, for a variety of reasons, are considered to be foes of the Government and who may not be mentioned.

Besides Miss Redgrave the list is said to include Arthur Miller, Melina Mercouri, Arnold Toynbee and Senators J. W. Fulbright and George S. McGovern. Recently it was said to have been extended to the 50 members of Congress who sent a letter to the State Department suggesting a tougher line toward Greece.

Not even editors who have served all through the days of this Government can remember all the forbidden names. But the censors—most of them either army or security officers—have the files at hand. . . . The press, for example, may not go into the details of the battle now being waged between Aristotle S. Onassis and Stavros S. Niarchos over a Government contract for a new oil refinery and other investment projects.

The Athens newspapers, many of them free-swinging and noisy before the coup, still occasionally manage to get a point across. The comments on Anatoly Kuznetsov, the Soviet writer who defected to the West two weeks ago, are examples. One paper said that he did the right thing to leave the country where he could not report the truth. Another said that he should have remained because a writer should try to work in a totalitarian state "even if he is thrown into prison or sent into exile."

In both cases, the message was not lost on many in Athens.

Since the coup Athens has lost six newspapers, including the two published by Mrs. Helen Vlachos, who had said she would never publish under censorship and later escaped to London while under house arrest.

* * *

October 4, 1969

ATHENS EASES ITS MARTIAL-LAW RULE

Special to The New York Times

ATHENS, Oct. 3—Greece's Army-backed regime today modified three martial-law rules—on press censorship, arbitrary arrest and trial by military courts—but the new measures contained a number of qualifications, assuring that control would continue. Greek newspaper editors were told today that the press was free. But they were handed a two-page list of banned topics and were told that although they no longer needed to submit galley proofs to the censors, a copy of each paper must still be submitted for approval before it goes to the newsstands. At the same time, summary arrests and imprisonment were barred "except in cases involving crimes against public order and security" and the jurisdiction of special military courts was narrowed. The new measures were announced by Primer George Papadopoulos at a news conference in the marble-walled Senate chamber in downtown Athens.

The timing of the measures puzzled foreign diplomats in Athens.

Some noted that they came 24 hours after George Tsistopoulos, an Under Secretary in the Foreign Office, returned from the United States, where he had talks with Secretary of State William P. Rogers, and passed on to the Greek leaders the strength of feeling in Washington in favor of substantial liberalization in Greece.

It is also possible that the announcement was intended to counteract a statement in Paris Tuesday by former Premier Constantine Caramanlis, who said that the regime was making no progress toward democracy and intended to perpetuate its oppressive rule.

It came a day too late to prevent the approval of a resolution by the Consultative Assembly of the Council of Europe in Strasbourg condemning the regime.

The list of taboo newspaper topics included these.

All news and comments "directed against public order, security and national integrity," such as "slogans or statements of outlawed parties or organizations aiming at the violent overthrow of the prevailing lawful order."

Topics of a subversive nature, including incitement to citizens or the armed forces to violate orders and laws, or instigating demonstrations, mass meetings or strikes.

Publications directed against the national economy, including rumors likely to provoke anxiety on the progress of the economy or the stability of the currency or divulging state economic secrets.

Reports likely to revive political passions and feuds.

The 50 year-old Premier said the new measures were justified by a substantial improvement of the domestic situation since the coup of 29 months ago and by the support his regime enjoyed from the Greek people.

"The patient is no longer in the plaster cast," he said, using his favorite analogy in which Greece is the patient and he the surgeon. "The patient is now in small splints. Let's hope he won't break his limbs again."

Mr. Papadopoulos told reporters he had issued orders, effective at once, abolishing press controls as well as banning arbitrary arrests and trials of civilians by special military courts. These controls had been authorized under the martial law in force since the coup.

'Freedom Is Inviolable'

"Personal freedom is inviolable," the Premier declared. All arrests and imprisonments from now on will be carried out in accordance with the Constitution—"except in cases involving crimes against public order and security," he said.

The jurisdiction of special military courts, set up by the regime to punish security offenses, will now try only cases of treason, espionage and sedition, including charges of disturb-

United Press International

Premier George Papadopoulos announcing new measures.

ing the peace, spreading false information and arousing discord, he said.

Most of the cases tried by special military tribunals since the coup have involved charges of sedition.

Mr. Papadopoulos said the regime was negotiating with the International Red Cross for investigating allegations of torture of Greek political prisoners. He said, "This should put an end to the infuriating campaign of lies about tortures in Greece."

Mr. Papadopoulos, asked to comment on the statement by Mr. Caramanlis, said he was not prepared to discuss the future of Greece with "anyone except the Greek people."

Mr. Caramanlis, a rightist whose attack on the regime drew wide support from most Greek political groups warned the Athens rulers to make way for democracy or face violent overthrow.

Asked if, in view of the fact that he had announced the freedom of the press, he would now allow the Greek papers to publish Mr Caramanlis's statement, Mr. Papadopoulos replied: "I will not."

* * *

November 2, 1969

COPIES OF PAPER SEIZED IN GREECE

Government Cracks Down as Defiance Mounts

Special to The New York Times

ATHENS, Nov. 1—The military-backed Government cracked down on Athens newspapers today to discourage mounting press defiance following the abolition of press censorship four weeks ago.

The police seized copies of the Apogevmatini, which has the largest circulation in the country, from Athens newsstands today. The action followed a selective ban on the circulation of four Athens dailies in several provincial cities.

No official source was willing to confirm that the Government had issued orders to hamper the sale of these newspapers, but news venders today confirmed that their copies of Apogevmatini had been confiscated by plainclothes policemen.

Newspaper publishers also confirmed that unopened bundles of newspapers were being returned from several provincial districts, although they could not pinpoint the source of the ban.

Trouble started soon after Oct. 3 when Premier George Papadopoalos announced that he was restoring "press freedom" by abolishing preventive censorship, which had been in force since the military takeover on April 21, 1967.

While editors were given a list of topics that were banned—particularly those likely to impair public order, the national economy, or revive old political passions—journalists made use of foreign reports, headlines and even cartoons to indicate hostility to the regime.

One Athens daily carried this week a 3-inch-high headline saying "More Democracy." It added in smaller print, "—Brandt Promises."

One cartoonist ridiculing the Portuguese elections showed one woman voter at a polling station being told by the guard: "What do you want a screen for. You want to undress?"

Irritated by this attitude which it describes as an "abuse of press freedom," the Government warned Athens publishers this week that unless they stopped provocative reports and headlines, stern action would be taken.

* * *

November 6, 1970

IN PORTUGAL, CURBS ARE SLOWLY BEING EASED

By MARVINE HOWE

Special to The New York Times

LISBON, Nov. 5—Lunch is late at the Grand Hotel of Portugal but the scholarly chef serenely stirs his ingredients and counsels waiters to give impatient clients warm smiles until the meal is ready.

This clear mockery of Premier Marcello Caetano's slow-moving reforms is the most applauded sketch in the new revista, or review, "Pepper on the Tongue," which contains the sharpest political satire anyone can remember here.

The revista has acquired new perspectives, vigor, breath and color, according to Lisbon's leading conservative daily, Diário de Notícias, which emphasizes that until now, political and social satire was "suffocated in an avalanche of silk, velvet, feathers and sequins."

In recent months, the authorities have shown new tolerance not only toward revistas but also toward films and plays that were frequently banned or cut in the days of former Premier António de Oliveira Salazar, who died on July 27, after a long illness.

Moscow Circus Hailed

The Moscow Circus has come to town for the first time and received triumphal first page coverage. Such an event was unthinkable in Dr. Salazar's time.

Portuguese playwrights, formerly considered somewhat subversive, have had their works presented on stage for the first time. Luis Sttau Monteiro's "The Hands of Abraham Zacut," a fierce picture of life in a Nazi concentration camp, opened here last year and will be performed again this season.

Similarly, "The Forge," a social critique by the late Alves Redol, has also been staged after long years of prohibition. Even Bernardo Santareno's "The Sin of João Agonia," a sympathetic treatment of homosexuality, passed the censors.

This week, Kafka's "Trial," which had long been on the official blacklist, opened in Lisbon and received favorable notices, even from the conservative Diário de Notícias.

Films censors are currently reviewing a list of 132 films that were banned under Dr. Salazar. They have passed 49 of the 70 films re-examined so far, including: "La Dolce Vita," "The Comedians," "Who's Afraid of Virginia Woolf?" and "For Whom the Bell Tolls."

Some See a Prelude

This easing in the domain of entertainment has been interpreted by some as a prelude to a more general liberalization of Portuguese life. For others, it is merely the opening of a safety valve in a society that remains basically closed. The revistas characterize the situation eloquently: Caetano is Salazar with a smile.

In effect, in two years of government, Premier Caetano has brought about a decided relaxation of the regime without making any basic changes in the authoritarian structure. The Premier is still the prime source of power, although he has given greater voice to the National Assembly.

This is still a one-party state, although the name of the ruling movement has been changed from the National Union to National Popular Action.

The political police force remains a major force even though it, too, has had a change of name, from the International Police and Defense of the State to the General Bureau of Security. There is still no freedom of press, trade unions, political parties, meeting or association.

Mr. Caetano is an "evolutionist," according to his close associates. "He would like to go further faster but he has very little possibility for maneuver," a Government source said.

Seeks Own Power Base

Although Mr. Caetano appears to be in full control of the situation, his partisans picture him as a kind of prisoner, caught between the past and the future. He came to power with the support of Dr. Salazars followers, the army high finance and the conservative Catholic Church hierarchy. Ever since, he has tried to form his own power base among young liberal technocrats.

The Premier's program was defined as "continuity and reform," but until now the accent has been on the former, an indication that the forces of the past still exercise preponderant weight. However, in recent months there have been various signs that Mr. Caetano is ready to initiate reforms.

Press Bill Is Planned

The first test of Mr. Caetano's liberalizing intentions will come this winter when the Government will present to the National Assembly the long awaited draft press law. The terms of this law have not been made public but sources close to the Government say that it will lift censorship, except for matters dealing with the military situation in Portuguese Africa. It is also expected to contain a wide array of legal checks and controls.

Another press bill will be presented by the leaders of the liberal wing of the National Assembly, a lawyer, Francisco Sa Carneiro, and a newspaper administrator, Francisco Balsemão. This bill has little chance of passing but some of its provisions could be incorporated into the Government's law.

"Any press law is better than censorship," Mr. Balsemão says. The Portuguese press has been governed by censorship legislation which has stunted thought and information in this country for 42 years.

The National Assembly, which resumes its work on Nov. 25, has a heavy agenda. In addition to the usual discussion of the budget and the press bill, the Assembly will be called on to pronounce on bills for religious liberty, a new industrial policy, defense of competition, and to make any necessary revisions of the constitution.

In Dr. Salazar's days, the National Assembly offered little interest and no surprises, loyally approving the dictator's every gesture. "Salazar had such a strong personality that institutions like the National Assembly fell asleep," a Government official said, adding that Mr. Caetano wanted to restore a sense of responsibility to the legislative body.

The 130 deputies elected to the National Assembly last fall are still something of an unknown quantity, since many of them are new politically and did not have an opportunity to reveal their views in the last short session. There is no actual opposition, but the deputies represent the wide span of views among the supporters of the regime.

* * *

March 1, 1973

GREECE'S PRESS, AFTER RELATIVE FREEDOM, IS COMING UNDER GROWING PRESSURE

By ALVIN SHUSTER
Special to The New York Times

ATHENS, Feb. 28—After a period of relative freedom, the Greek press is coming under increasing pressure from the army-backed Government to maintain silence on sensitive issues in a campaign that has left publishers and journalists confused and angry.

As part of the effort, the Government's Press and Information Department also called in six foreign journalists to protest what it thinks are false reports on Greece. Such reprimands have been infrequent for Athens-based foreign correspondents in recent years.

The main targets, however, have been the Greek newspapers, which had become surprisingly lively in the last 18 months as they tested the limits of the 1970 press law. Criticism of Government policies, satirical cartoons and comments, and descriptive and varied reporting—all within limits—had provided Greeks with a marked change from the newspaper diet they received in the early days of the Government, which seized power in 1967.

Word 'Student' Disappears

Obviously concerned that the recent student agitation could inspire more, the Government has now made it clear that it wants that issue virtually to disappear. Last Thursday, the papers were full of stories and pictures of demonstrating students. Since then, the word "student" is hard to find.

Asked why the newspapers are no longer writing about students, Byron Stamatopoulos, the chief Government spokesman, said: "The Greek newspapers are free to write, in accordance with their opinion, what they like. What is forbidden is to write false reports."

The key reason for the shift stems from a session Thursday night when Deputy Premier Stylianos Patakos called in editors and publishers for an "exchange of views" on the handling of reports on the student unrest. The message was clear and the stories disappeared.

About 100 reporters are now circulating a petition asking the Athens Union of Journalists to explain to readers why all news of student unrest has suddenly vanished. They feel that their professional prestige and reputations are at stake.

'This System Is Chaos'

"The present system is worse in many ways than when we had censors in our office," one publisher said. "At least then we knew what we could say and what we couldn't. This system is chaos. And the pressure is never in the form of a frontal attack. They try to get at you in subtle ways, down narrow back lanes."

The case of George Athanassiadis, the publisher of Vradyni, a right-wing Athens afternoon newspaper, illustrates the point. He is now reluctantly the symbol of press freedom.

Sitting in his first floor office on Piraeus Street, the 61-year-old publisher told what happened after he decided to print more details of the student troubles than the Government desired.

On Saturday, he said, a team of 20 tax officers entered his offices and made a detailed search of desks and files of all members of the staff, including copy boys. A group also went to his home where, among other items, they confiscated some love letters he wrote to his wife during World War II, he said.

"When the revolution started six years ago," he said, "I thought it would do some good, that the colonels were honest and well-meaning. Then it grew on me that they were not in power provisionally but for personal advantages."

"I thought I would try to guide them toward an evolution toward democracy," he continued. "I am writing, I am shouting, but nothing happens. This, after all, is a right-wing paper and it was being read by people in the army. I began to criticize the Government and they began to attack me."

Loss of Advertising

The 1970 press code, which brought press offenses under the jurisdiction of civil courts, allowed some leeway in the news. But newspapers that criticized the Government found they were not receiving the lucrative advertising placed by Government agencies.

"My paper is regarded now as the most critical," Mr. Athanassiadis said. "But I am not a hero and don't want to be one. I feel I am doing my duty as a journalist.

"The fact is that this is a financial sacrifice. It is not only the Government advertising we are losing. But many big companies refuse to give us their business for fear of making the regime unhappy. These are all subtle pressures, but effective. If I have done something wrong, then bring me to court man to man."

The fullest coverage in town on the student agitation now appears in The Athens News, which is published in English and is not usually viewed with concern by the Government. English-speaking Greeks say they are translating its articles for their fellow workers. But its owner, John Horn, is being prosecuted for publishing a "misleading" headline.

* * *

November 21, 1973

RADIO AND TV NEWS IN SPAIN ACCENTS POSITIVE AT HOME BUT NEGATIVE ABROAD

By HENRY GINIGER
Special to The New York Times

MADRID, Nov. 20—Spain is a haven of peace and contentment in a world of conflict and unrest.

This, at least, is the conclusion that Spanish listeners can draw from the first morning major news program produced by the state-owned and managed radio network. The impression is confirmed throughout the day in other newscasts. The evening news show on the television network, also state-controlled, does nothing to change it.

Dissatisfaction that occasionally reaches exasperation is evident throughout the Spanish press, radio and television corps about the way it is able to inform the public. For some time, the Government has been promising greater participation by the Spanish people in public affairs and a new electoral law is in the offing. But incompatibility is seen between this participation and the limits placed on information.

The dissatisfaction is accompanied by envy at the freedom enjoyed in other countries. The envy occasionally finds its way into print with articles praising the role of the American press in the Watergate controversy.

Only newspapers and periodicals, which have had greater latitude since 1966, print what radio and television never divulge.

No Word of Conflict

In the Spain depicted on radio and television, conflict of any kind—a strike, a demonstration, an opposing opinion—almost never casts its shadow over the nation's political or social scene. If a misfortune is reported, such as a flood, a forest fire or a road accident, it is always something beyond the power of control of those who lead the nation.

On the other hand, there are detailed accounts of troubles in other nations by the networks' own correspondents, who receive guidance from the home office on what to say and what to leave out. Some of the frustrations involved in such control, when some independent judgment is attempted, were recently disclosed by one correspondent, who reported that 40 per cent of the material he sent to Madrid was never used, another 40 per cent was heavily cut and only 20 per cent survived more or less intact.

Although there is no privately owned and managed television, there are private radio stations, but they are not allowed to produce news programs of their own except for carefully controlled reports of purely local events. They are, in fact, obliged to carry the national radio chain's major news programs.

The private stations periodically receive from the Ministry of Information and Tourism lists of records that cannot be put on the air. Why the records are banned is not explained, but presumably they are unacceptable on political or moral grounds. From time to time stations also get lists of records that were considered objectionable but are no longer. Here, too, mystery surrounds the change of opinion.

Debates on radio or television are unknown, as is any critical opinion. The director of a private station in Barcelona discovered a few years ago the dangers inherent even in seemingly innocuous programs. The routine broadcast of a Sunday morning Roman Catholic mass brought about his dismissal after the priest, whose sermon had not been checked beforehand, spoke of political prisoners in Spain.

Greater Press Latitude

"Spain at 8 o'Clock," the morning program, confines its news of the country to a reading of the principal Government measures announced in the day's official bulletin, followed by a series of regional reports from local correspondents of fiestas, conventions, official visits and inaugurations of public works. The accent is exclusively on the positive in contrast to the exhaustive discussion that follows concerning political trouble in Washington, strikes in Rome, demonstrations in Paris, bombs in London and scandal in Bonn.

In the newspapers and periodicals the public gets some relief from this bland diet. Thus readers but not listeners can learn that there has been a major strike in Pamplona, 113 opponents of Generalissimo Francisco Franco have been arrested in Barcelona, an extreme nationalistic group has staged a commando raid in the Basque country, prices are going up all the time and Manuel Fraga, a former Information Minister who became a critic of the Government before being named Ambassador to London, has proposed a popular referendum on whether Spain ought to join the European Common Market.

Manuel Fraga, former Information Minister, got a law passed in 1966 abolishing prior censorship of the press in Spain.

Mr. Fraga pushed through a new press law in 1966 that abolished prior censorship and theoretically established freedom of expression in the press. There has subsequently been a notable increase in critical discussion in the press of the country's problems, but those who run the newspapers and periodicals or write for them still report strong limitations on their ability to communicate.

Article 2 of the law imposes some specific requirements: respect for truth and morality, respect for the nation's fundamental laws and its political system, and respect for institutions and persons in the criticism of political and administrative acts, the requirements of national defense and the maintenance of public order.

National Security Terms

An Official Secrets Act passed in 1968 further hemmed in freedom of expression by giving officials the right to prevent the publication of news that might prejudice the national interest or security. According to those who have suffered official rigor, the Government has considerable latitude to clamp down on the press.

Editors complain that the frontier between what is officially admissible and what is not is fuzzy, with no set policy for determining what is out of bounds. Since the press law was passed publications have been hit frequently with confiscations and fines.

Editors also report frequent telephone calls from officials forbidding publication of a news item, ordering papers to take a certain stand or prescribing how they should present news. Because such orders are extralegal acts, they are always given orally. Papers were recently forbidden, in telephone calls, to print death notices on President Salvador Allende Gossens of Chile because the notices had a political character not congenial to the Government.

In Barcelona last week, the local press was forbidden to mention, immediately after it happened, the arrest of 113 well-known opponents of the Government who had been attending a clandestine meeting in a local church. Other papers in Spain did report the event the next day, and 80 exasperated Barcelona newsmen delivered a strong protest against their lack of freedom to report what was happening in their own city.

* * *

July 12, 1974

REVOLUTION BRINGS ART TO LISBON

By HENRY GINIGER
Special to The New York Times

LISBON—One of this city's biggest art shows in years has opened as one of the most striking examples of how the revolution in April has brought cultural opportunities to Portugal that she has not had for almost 50 years.

The São Mamed Gallery, one of Lisbon's largest, is showing 186 works by 87 artists that have never been shown publicly because either the work or the artist was objectionable to a regime that attempted to dictate all aspects of Portuguese life.

According to the gallery director, Francisco Pereira Coutinho, and a sponsoring committee of writers and artists, the show is a way of celebrating a military coup that abolished censorship over all means of expression. Since the April 25 coup, however, there has been a retreat. Censorship has not been restored but some severe rules, applied by a military commission, have been established for the news media and there has been considerable grumbling among journalists in particular about the clampdown.

Denounces the Church

Artists are faring better. In the São Mamed show, most all the works are figurative or semifigurative and have a strong political bias. They include denunciations of the political and social system and the kind of capitalism that was allied with the dictatorship, as well as the Roman Catholic Church, also considered an ally, and of the war fought in the African colonies. Other paintings, drawings and engravings would, on the face of it, be unobjectionable under any regime, but the artists were under a cloud for their political ideas and had difficulty showing their works. Some spent time in prison and a few lived in exile. There are also some works with a strong erotic content.

One of the best-known names, from a political viewpoint, is Cunhal. Alvaro Cunhal, an artist and designer, is secretary general of the Communist party and a minister without portfolio in the provisional Government. He is not displaying, but his father, Avelino, a brother, Antonio, and a cousin, Miguel, are all represented. Another well-known artist-politician in the show is Arlindo Vicente, who was a presidential candidate for the democratic opposition in 1958.

Ballet lovers will get a chance to see a troupe from Moscow's Bolshoi Theater next week as one of the first fruits of the recent establishment of diplomatic relations between Portugal and the Soviet Union. Filmgoers are having a field day with pictures they had not seen before or with scenes restored that had been cut by the censors in the old days. Thus, the battleship Potemkin is drawing big crowds and Charles Chaplin's speech in favor of democracy at the end of "The Great Dictator" gets nightly applause.

Erotic Scenes Restored

The newspapers are carrying advertisements for pictures that emphasize they are being shown either for the first time or for the first time completely. "The Music Lovers," the film about Tchaikovsky, was shown before the coup, then brought back with the erotic scenes restored. The British picture "Don't Look Now" is giving the Portuguese public its first taste of frontal nudity on the screen and there is considerable giggling in the packed house.

On the street, only a few doors away from the Ministry of Information, a display of erotic books draws a continuous crowd most of the day. Foreign magazines and newspapers are entering the country without restraints on either political or moral grounds. A book fair on Lisbon's main thoroughfare, the Avenida da Liberdade, is doing a brisk business in Marxist texts and erotic literature, previously hard to find.

Some of the literature now freely available here was circulated clandestinely in the old days or had only a limited edition and distribution, the old regime being more tolerant about books than about newspapers and periodicals. Publishers now have expanded their lists, including translations of foreign works.

The Democratic Movement of Plastic Arts marked the shift in the regime recently by covering over with a black cloth the statue of Antonio Salazar, founder of the dictatorship, which stands in the inner courtyard of the Ministry of Information. The joke going about is that he was covered over after being caught spying on Portugal's new Government.

* * *

July 30, 1974

NEW FREEDOM IS CHANGING GREEK LIFE

By STEVEN V. ROBERTS
Special to The New York Times

ATHENS, July 29—The lively music of Mikis Theodorakis is playing again on the radio and in the nightclubs of Greece.

An outspoken leftist, his works had been banned by the military men who governed for more than seven years. But the ban has been lifted since the military Government handed over power last week to a civilian administration.

"Every day many, many people have come in asking for his records," said a clerk in a record shop here. "We could sell a hundred a day if we had them, but we haven't been able to get them yet."

That is only one small way in which life has changed during the first week of Greece's emergence from what one newspaper termed "2,285 days of medieval darkness." There have been many other changes: prisoners released, newspapers freed from censorship, elections promised.

Probably the biggest change is in the ordinary Greek—in his view of the world. "The Greeks can now look with some hope for the future," a Government official commented. "They don't have the fear of doing something, of saying something, that might not please those in power. That's what it all boils down to."

Newspaper Revived

Even the shadow of war with Turkey cannot obscure all the real changes of the last week. Three daily newspapers closed by the military have resumed publication, and three others are scheduled to reopen soon. The six existing papers have been rejuvenated, and even Eleftheros Cosmos, long known as the spokesman of the military, has denounced the former government as a dictatorship.

Athinaiki, a leftist journal, has called for exemplary punishment of the military leaders, but most papers have followed the lead of the new Government and not urged retribution.

For years the papers were so barren of news that many people stopped reading them. Now news venders are everywhere, and most seem to be doing a brisk business. Many Greeks had also abandoned radio news, but at important moments in the last week one could walk down a street and hear a radio going in every house.

Another significant change has been the order limiting the military police to military matters. Under Brig. Gen. Demetrios Ioannides, the military police had been transformed into a virtual Gestapo and everyone lived in fear of a knock on the door.

"There is no big brother watching me now," said Michael Pantelides, the owner of a bookstore. "I'm not afraid of having my rights violated."

With the formation of the civilian cabinet under Premier Constantine Caramanlis, changes in fortune have been sharp.

Only a short time ago Evangelos Averoff-Tossizza was a shuffling, almost sad figure as he gossiped in the coffee houses and issued occasional futile statements to foreign newsmen. A former Foreign Minister and a distinguished diplomat, he also spent time in prison. Now he is Defense Minister. His baggy brown suit has been replaced by a well-cut black one, he rides in a chauffered limousine and he walks with a purposeful stride, to the sound of clicking heels.

At still another level thc Press Ministry here used to be like a tomb—empty of information and of reporters. Now there are briefings, news conferences, statements, transcripts.

"To tell you the truth, I didn't expect the change so soon," said the bookseller, Mr. Pantelides, as he greeted a customer with a hearty "Welcome to the free world!"

* * *

COMMUNIST COUNTRIES

March 16, 1968

PRAGUE CENSORS SAY THEY WANT TO QUIT

Special to The New York Times

PRAGUE, March 15—The censors, who for 20 years have ruled sternly on what could be printed in Czechoslovakia, asked today to be allowed to stop.

"We have reached the conclusion that preventive political censorship should be abolished at the present state of development," the Communist party unit at the Central Publications Administration declared after a membership meeting.

The resolution, which is to be published in tomorrow's newspapers, lifted the veil from a number of facts well known but never publicly acknowledged.

The first was the very existence of a censorship body. No one in this highly literate country had been in any doubt that there was more news in the world than ever appeared in the Czechoslovak press and that someone was instructing newspapers and magazines what not to publish.

The resolution called for an end to the secrecy.

"We said that the citizens and organizations have a right to know that in Czechoslovakia there exists such a state body that carries out such control," the resolution said.

The Communist members of the body, who may be assumed to include all above the lowest clerical level, also suggested that the standards for censorship be specified and the possibility of appeal against the decision be investigated.

Also acknowledged for the first time was that the internal security apparatus controlled the press. The resolution charged that, soon after its creation in the nineteen-fifties, the head of the censorship organization, as well as its deputy, were high police officers.

They ruled the organization on the principle that nothing could be published that they considered against the public interest, the censors said. Their methods were harsh and enforced by party and administrative punishments.

For example, the resolution said that when President Antonin Novotny, who was deposed as Communist party chief two months ago, criticized a book in a speech, those responsible for failing to censor it were fined and given party punishment.

Published Untrue Data

Not only did the censors have to delete information, they complained, but "they were forced to publish information that we knew was not true."

The censors bitterly criticized their chief, Interior Minister Josef Kudrna, for failing to be responsive to criticisms made immediately after Mr. Novotny's overthrow. Mr. Kudrna was removed from his post today for laggardness in rehabilitating victims of the Stalinist purges.

Since Mr. Novotny was removed from his party post, censorship of the press has virtually disappeared. But editors remain prudent in matters affecting Czechoslovakia's foreign relations and no public criticism of the new party leader, Alexander Dubcek has appeared.

In another indication of the new freedom, a soap corporation announced this morning that it would show on television a series of old documentaries on the bourgeois past of Czechoslovakia. Without delay, it released for showing this evening a film on Thomas G. Masaryk, the founder of modern Czechoslovakia, whose name had gone almost unmentioned here until recently.

* * *

July 27, 1968

FREE PRESS IS KEY IN CZECH REFORMS

Leaders Feel Soviet Seeks to Halt Wider Changes

By DANA ADAMS SCHMIDT
Special to The New York Times

PRAGUE, July 23—The key reform of the regime of Alexander Dubcek, which is both its strength and, in the eyes of Soviet officials, its most serious offense, has been the lifting of censorship.

This action in January set in motion a process that will culminate in the extraordinary party congress in September. Before that action, it could always be said there were no guarantees that the hard-line Communist leaders might not stage a comeback at any time.

In September the machinery will be established to anchor the new liberalism and to make any reactionary resurgence more difficult. There will be a new electoral law, a new National Assembly, a new constitution and wide-ranging legislation.

As some of the top liberal Communist leaders in this country understand the situation, it is to head all this off that the Russians have been, in effect, threatening military intervention, allowing their troops to linger following the Warsaw Pact maneuvers, proposing permanent garrisoning of the Czechoslovak-West German border by Warsaw Pact forces, arranging—it is widely believed—for a cache of American weapons to be found near that German border.

Critical Phase Believed Over

While the Soviet Union could still take over at any time, Czechoslovak leaders feel that last Friday and Saturday, when Soviet military units were moving in Bohemia near Prague, was critical. The phlegmatic attitudes of the Czechoslovak public notwithstanding, some top officials had their families ready to flee that weekend.

As part of its overwhelming strength, the Soviet Army had radio-jamming equipment ready to silence Czechoslovak radio stations. It knew that most of the Czechoslovak Army's highest officers would be unwilling to fight against the Soviet Army and that the new liberal leadership, in any case, had no intention of engaging in a test of physical strength.

The reasons that the Soviet Union, nonetheless, has not intervened, these Czechoslovak leaders emphasize, are entirely political and moral, underwritten by public opinion and the new freedom of the press.

They believe, also, that the Russians have been unable to find in Czechoslovakia a man of sufficient standing to take over domestic political power if the Russians took over militarily. Former President Antonin Novotny, they feel, is too discredited, and none of the other conservatives is of sufficient stature.

In order not to give the Soviet any pretext for intervening and to gain time until the September meeting can take place, the Czechoslovak press has been exercising restraint. While leaving no doubt as to their freedom newspapers and magazines have refrained from the harsh tone commonly heard in conversation as the Soviet army stayed on.

The press has also been refraining from some of the political philosophizing that has upset the Soviet Union and others in the Eastern bloc since January.

Most basic of the philosophical questions that are upsetting to Moscow is, How can the Communist party maintain a right to leadership, much less to rule, and at the same time talk about democracy and humanism? Such a right implies a kind of faith in the revealed truth of Marxism, it reduces non-Communist parties in a so-called national front to captives.

Privately the Czechoslovak Communist liberals say that they are willing to compete with other parties on a basis of equality and to accept the possibility that, some day, they might lose an election.

But that is not practical politics in the Communist world now. Apart from the problem of not shocking the Russians, the Czechoslovak leadership must consider that even after the September congress of the party and the election of a new party Central Committee they must reconvene the old

National Assembly, which contains many conservatives, to vote a new and more democratic electoral law.

* * *

August 26, 1968

FREE, CLANDESTINE RADIO AND TV UNITY THE RESISTANCE MOVEMENT

Special to The New York Times

PRAGUE, Aug. 25—Signs have been changed and detours put up on roads all over Czechoslovakia.

In the Teschen area on the Polish border, Polish troops, part of the five-nation army occupying this country, found themselves back at the border after traveling 60 kilometers.

Czechoslovakia's clandestine radio stations, which urged such sign changes, were responsible for the Poles' discomfiture.

The free radio and its adjunct, free television, are a thorn in the side of the occupation armies and the chief unifying force for the passive resistance movement.

Both operate with surprisingly high quality. The television program tonight, for instance, was a highly professional satirical sketch on the occupation.

To the background of popular big-beat music, the viewer was taken for a ride as a tourist through downtown Prague with the announcer pointing out such landmarks as Russian tanks, howitzers in the opera square and antiaircraft gun positions near Charles Bridge.

In addition, there was a calm round-table discussion of the occupation and a burlesque of a Russian lesson.

The radio does far more than simply advise Czechoslovaks on the best ways of resisting the invasion armies without getting shot.

For 18 hours and sometimes round the clock it broadcasts a steady stream of fairly objective news about the occupation. Most of the news generally turns out to be true, and when it is not, the radio itself frequently issues a correction.

The Russians have snatched transistor radios from the hands of Prague citizens but as yet have found no way to home in on the transmission points.

The radio operates from about 15 points throughout the country. Each area broadcasts, both on medium and short-wave bands, for about 15 minutes. The shifts from station to station used to mean radio silence for about five minutes. Now the breaks are as smooth as station changes by American broadcasting companies.

Local and National News

Each point broadcasts local as well as national news about the occupation. In addition, they broadcast coded warning messages to each other such as "George, call Geronimo."

The free radio came on the air within a half hour after the Russians closed down the operations of the Prague radio last Tuesday. Many of those who used to work for the Prague radio now work for the secret radio.

The head of the operation is believed to be Jiri Pelikan, the former director of Czechoslovak television. He is a youthful-looking flamboyant man with great popularity in the country.

Also encouraging the resistance movement are the underground newspapers printed on flat-bed presses in cellars in many parts of Prague.

The newspapers bear the names of those closed down during the occupation. Articles are written by many of the same writers.

The papers are brought secretly to factories that serve as the main distribution centers. Workers share the circulation chores, each man taking small bundles and putting them in car trunks and handing them out free in the city center.

The operation has become more dangerous because of spot checks by the Russians of cars in the city.

* * *

September 5, 1968

CZECH AIDES ARE RELAXED IN IMPLEMENTING NEW CENSORSHIP

By TAD SZULC

Special to The New York Times

PRAGUE, Sept. 4—The new press censorship rules in Czechoslovakia forbid discussion of the recent Soviet-Czechoslovak agreement and the use of the word "occupation" in referring to the presence of 600,000 Soviet, Polish, Hungarian and Bulgarian troops.

These are among five prohibitions, according to a spokesman of the Culture Ministry's new Press Control Office, which is headed by 45-year-old Josef Vohnaut, a liberal. The three other banned subjects were not disclosed.

Censorship was re-introduced under the terms of the Soviet-Czechoslovak agreement, concluded Aug. 26, as one of the conditions for the eventual and gradual withdrawal of the Warsaw Pact occupation forces.

But implementation is relaxed and without direct enforcement. Instead of maintaining censors at the newspaper offices, as was done for 20 years before the liberalization program was launched here last January, the Czechoslovak Government has established an 18-member control office, where meetings with editors are to be held twice a week.

Troops Hold Some Offices

Meanwhile, Soviet troops still occupied the editorial offices of at least three daily newspapers and of a number of weekly magazines.

Tonight, an armored car, a jeep and 12 Soviet soldiers stood guard at the building of the Socialist party newspaper Svobodne Slovo, preventing it from publishing. Also occupied were the offices of the People's party newspaper Lidova Demokracie and the youth newspaper Mlada Fronta.

As a result of day-long negotiations between editors and the Czechoslovak Central Committee, which, in turn, has been negotiating with the Government and with the Soviet occupation commander, troops were removed from the trade union newspaper Prace, which is scheduled to publish tomorrow.

The only daily newspapers published in the last two days were Rude Pravo, the Communist party's official organ, the evening newspaper Vecerni Praha and the sports newspaper, all printed in the Rude Pravo plant.

The party newspaper, which now has a new, liberal editor, Jiri Sekera, replacing Oldrich Svestka, a conservative, was evacuated by Soviet troops two days ago.

Official TV Resumes

Czechoslovak television went on the air tonight, broadcasting from its own studios for the first time since the invasion Aug. 20. Operated by the resistance movement, the television network transmitted from a secret location for some 10 days after the Prague studios were occupied by the Soviet troops.

Despite damage to equipment, the Prague station returned to the air with a perfect signal. It resumed broadcasting at 7 P.M. with a news program read by a woman announcer and followed by a short film showing the Czechoslovak soccer team practicing for the Olympic games. A quick shot showed helmeted and armed Soviet soldiers watching from the bleachers.

The contents of Rude Pravo and the television programming suggested that there were subtle ways of making points despite the censorship.

Rude Pravo published the text of a message from the Italian Communist party to the Czechoslovak party extending greetings to "those comrades who, after the Moscow meeting, under difficult conditions defended the line of socialist renaissance and solidarity approved by your party, and who returned to their leading functions in the party and state."

This was a clear allusion to the internment and then the release by the Soviet authorities of the party's First Secretary, Alexander Dubcek, Premier Oldrich Cernik and Josef Smrkovsky, President of the National Assembly.

Rude Pravo also reported that the journalists' union had expelled Miroslav Sulek, the former director general of the C.T.K. press agency, for actions "against the legal organs of the party and government."

Dismissed Last Week

Mr. Sulek, who was dismissed last week from his agency post, was believed to have been one of the Czechoslovak officials with advance knowledge of the Soviet led invasion.

The Interior Ministry made public a statement denying reports, notably from international P.E.N. clubs (organizations of Poets, Essayists and Novelists) that intellectuals and writers had been arrested since the invasion.

The ministry said the "appropriate Czechoslovak authorities have taken no measures to limit the personal freedom of these cultural workers . . . They work normally and participate actively in our public life."

While many intellectuals have left the country there is no evidence available to contradict the ministry's statement concerning those who remained.

Meanwhile, the Slovak National Council, a regional administrative body, met in Bratislava to study the future federal relations with the Czechs in this bilingual nation.

The council was addressed by Gustav Husak, the new First Secretary of the Slovak party and a newly elected member of the national party's Presidium.

Mr. Husak is the architect of the blueprint for the creation of a federated Czech-Slovak state, which is one of the highlights of the action program of the Dubcek reformers.

The Slovak and Czech national councils are expected to meet together next week.

There was no confirmation here of foreign reports that Mr. Dubcek is preparing to fly to Moscow again in preparation for an expected Warsaw Pact meeting in Dresden, East Germany, later this month.

As part of the Czechoslovak fulfillment of Soviet demands, non-Communist political organizations began disbanding.

The West Bohemia regional chapter of the 231 club, made up of former political prisoners, announced that it was dismantling its organization "to help the Government."

Soviet troops continued to withdraw gradually from Prague in preparation for total removal of the occupation forces from Czechoslovak cities and towns to the countryside.

Truckloads of Soviet infantry were taken to Ruzyne international airport, the headquarters of the Soviet supreme commander in Czechoslovakia, Gen. Ivan G. Pavlovsky.

* * *

LATIN AMERICA

October 15, 1965

URUGUAY INVOKES NEWS CENSORSHIP

Seizes an Edition as Paper Calls for Wider Strike

By HENRY RAYMONT
Special to The New York Times

MONTEVIDEO, Uruguay, Oct. 14—The Government took the first major steps today to enforce censorship of the press and radio since it suspended constitutional guarantees last Thursday to smother a threat of labor violence.

Reacting with unusual firmness, the police confiscated this morning's edition of the pro-Cuban newspaper La Epoca, which has continued to incite workers to strike in violation of the emergency decrees.

The Communist-dominated newspaper guild and printers' union immediately protested the move, calling it a threat to civil liberties. They announced they would begin tonight a strike that could last until the newspaper is again allowed to publish freely.

The Interior Ministry sent a circular letter to all radio stations, warning that it would not tolerate any further criticism of the security measures. Previous communications advised the owners of the stations that reports about disturbances and police actions other than those mentioned in Government announcements would bring fines and other penalties.

Country Remains Calm

Two photographers of the opposition Colorado newspaper, Acción, were arested this afternoon as they photographed employes of the Bank of the Republic being dispersed by the police. The men were released an hour later after their films had been seized.

The country remained calm during the otherwise uneventful second day of a 72-hour strike by about 100,000 civil servants, who are demanding wage increases.

The action against the newspaper sharpened the anger of the three Colorado members of the nine-man National Council, who have opposed the emergency powers.

The Government has been highly sensitive to reports on the Uruguayan economic crisis published by newspapers in Argentina and Brazil. Officials tend to blame foreign press agencies for what they call "alarmist" reporting.

The pro-Government newspapers El Pais and El Plata discontinued the use of The Associated Press in their news columns, after Council members complained about the agency's reporting.

The Government announced that since the security measures went into effect 323 persons had been arrested, but that some had been released.

Eleven students were seized last night when the police raided the university's social services school. Police officials said the students were printing leaflets in support of the strike.

To protest the arrests, the student federation has called for a special assembly to consider an indefinite strike to begin tomorrow.

* * *

July 24, 1966

ARGENTINA CLOSES SATIRICAL MAGAZINE THAT ATTACKED THE MILITARY REGIME

By H. J. MAIDENBERG
Special to The New York Times

BUENOS AIRES, July 23—The new military regime closed Argentina's only satirical political magazine today.

Lieut. Gen. Juan Carlos Ongania, whose supporters ousted the elected Government of President Arturo U. Illia June 28, ordered the closing of Tia Vicenta because its editors had refused to abide by the Government's "gentlemen's agreement with the press" about attacking the new regime.

Tia Vicenta is carried as a Sunday supplement in the newspaper El Mundo, which has a circulation of 350,000. Yesterday the managing editor of El Mundo, Carlos Infante, was asked by the paper to "take an indefinite leave of absence."

Mr. Infante was replaced by Juan Carlos Forteza, a former diplomat and a relative of the new Minister of the Interior, Enrique Martinez Paz.

"I have had my magazine closed before," Juan Carlos Colombres, the editor of Tia Vicenta said last night, "but even Perón used more finesse."

Mr. Colombres's magazines were banned by the late President, Ramón S. Castillo, in 1942 and during the regime of Juan D. Perón, the former dictator, who was overthrown in 1955. Mr. Colombres is better known to Argentines as the cartoonist Landru.

Since the military takeover, Tia Vicenta has been the only periodical that has continued attacking Government figures.

In recent issues, for example, the military leaders have been referred to as walruses because of their ample mustaches. Last Sunday's issue carried the headline "Era of the Walrus" under its masthead and suggested that the military boot replace the clasped hand as Argentina's national emblem.

A devout Roman Catholic, Mr. Colombres recalled that his magazine had not spared any Argentine leader since it reappeared.

Maj. Gen. Pedro E. Aramburu, Provisional President from 1955 to 1958, was often drawn as a cow. Arturo Frondizi, President from 1958 to 1962, was referred to as a black ant. Dr. José Maria Guido (1962–63) was portrayed as being sealed in a liquor bottle. President Illia usually appeared as a dozing old man in an oversized chair.

Asked about his plans, the editor replied, "Our staff has to live, so we are planning to produce a popular women's weekly and wait."

Most newspaper editors have refrained from open criticism of the new regime. They say they were told to do so after being called to Government House a day after the coup d'état.

Many Argentines who appeared indifferent to the fate of the Illia Government are becoming concerned about the military Government's preoccupation with reforming their way of life. Traffic tickets are being handed out in huge numbers for violations that were previously ignored.

The Government is demanding that motorists give ambulances and fire trucks the right of way. Drivers must observe traffic lanes and one-way streets and those who can find no curbside parking space are forbidden to leave their cars in the middle of the road. This has enraged drivers, who often ignored the relatively few traffic lights, and several traffic policemen have been beaten in the last two weeks.

Today many Porteños, as the citizens of this capital are referred to, were surprised at the appointment of Luis Margaride as head of the General Inspection Board of the Municipality. He was removed from a post a few years ago after many victims of his stringent antivice campaigns brought a flood of lawsuits.

Mr. Margaride was appointed by the Buenos Aires police chief, Enrique Green, a retired navy captain and a brother-in-law of President Ongania.

In a brief speech to the press, Captain Green introduced Mr. Margaride as "the head of a new campaign to eradicate a very contagious disease — immorality."

"The root of the trouble is liberal atheism, which we will fight," he said. "Liberal atheism is out to destroy the pillars of Argentine society and has eroded the respect for religious and moral principles and historic tradition."

Because of his past associations with anti-semitic and extreme right-wing groups, Captain Green took pains to say that "I respect all other religious doctrines as long as they in turn respect our religious, social and political system."

* * *

November 29, 1967

ARGENTINE POLICE BLOCK MAGAZINE

Order Type Melted in Raid After Court Backs Editor

Special to The New York Times

BUENOS AIRES, Nov. 28—Officers from the political department of the federal police confiscated 250 copies of a weekly magazine and ordered the type to be melted down, it became known today. The raid on a printing shop ended the third attempt by the editor Jorge Vago, to get around a presidential decree that has been used to ban all his publications.

Last Thursday Mr. Vago won a verdict from the Federal Court of Appeal upholding his right to publish the weekly magazine Prensa Confidencial and declaring a Government ban unconstitutional.

Dailies Stress Decision

He sent telegrams to the Minister of the Interior, Dr. Guillermo Borda, and the police chief, Gen. Mario Fonseca, announcing that he planned to go ahead and publish Prensa Confidencial Monday. He cited the appeal court's decision in his favor, which reversed the decision in a lower court in favor of the Government.

But Saturday night, when Mr. Vago was seeing his magazine off the press, officers from the political department of the federal police stopped the run, confiscated the copies that had been printed and saw that the printing forms were destroyed.

On Sunday the newspaper La Prensa published an editorial declaring that the appeals court decision upheld the guarantee of press freedom included in the Argentine Constitution.

The newspaper La Nacion went further today in stressing that the decision was of the highest importance for the Argentine press and the country's international prestige.

The press, said La Nacion, "wants to live with a system of clear norms and not under the sway of administrative interpretations that could have very serious consequences."

The appeals court's decision has been particularly welcomed by newspapers here because the de facto government of President Juan Carlos Ongania has announced its good intentions toward the press but has not endorsed Constitutional guarantees.

Prensa Confidencial and two successive magazines launched by Mr. Vago were all banned on the ground that the Constitution is overruled by the Statute of the Revolution declared after the military-coup of June 28, 1966.

The appeals court's decision will now go to the Supreme Court.

* * *

May 4, 1968

CURB ON MAGAZINES UPSET IN ARGENTINA

Special to The New York Times

BUENOS AIRES, May 3—Argentina's Supreme Court last night ordered the reinstatement of three publications that had been forced by the Government to close.

The three publications include Zazuly Blanco, an ultraright-wing magazine that frequently had attacked the United States and had charged that Juan Carlos Ongania's regime was too liberal.

The other two periodicals, Prensa Confidencial and Prensa Libre, were owned and edited . . . campaign for freedom of expression under the Ongania Government has been marked by a challenge to a duel and three months in prison.

The decision was a clear embarrassment to Interior Minister Guillermo Borda. He had issued the orders to the police that closed the periodicals.

* * *

December 21, 1968

MILITARY REGIME IN BRAZIL EASES ITS CENSORSHIP

By PAUL MONTGOMERY
Special to The New York Times

RIO DE JANEIRO, Dec. 20—The military regime of President Arthur da Costa e Silva eased today the complete censorship it imposed on Brazil a week ago.

Army censors who had manned cable offices handling international press telegrams since the President suspended the National Congress last Friday and assumed virtual one-man rule, were removed this afternoon.

The military censors, who had screened many of last week's developments from the public, also left broadcasting stations and some newspapers.

It was understood, however, that press and broadcasting offices left without censors had agreed to submit to self-censorship by following the regime's guidelines.

Under the guidelines, the mention of any of the following subjects is prohibited: political arrests made by the military following the suspension of Congress, dissension or differences of opinion within the armed forces, criticism of the regime's acts or the existence of censorship itself.

Censorship is under the control of the commander of each army district. In Rio de Janeiro, controlled by the First Army headed by Gen. Siseno Sarmento, it has been strict. In São Paulo, under another commander, mention of arrests has been allowed but censorship and armed forces affairs are still forbidden subjects.

General Sarmento is regarded as a leader of the hard-line, nationalistic forces in the military, while President Costa e Silva has tended toward moderation. The general has had several meetings with the President this week. Today he saw Mayor Faria Lima of São Paulo, a retired air force general.

President Costa e Silva, who has been here since assuming rule by decree, has made no public appearances but has attended armed forces functions.

The President continued to issue decrees regulating the political and economic life of the country. The principal one today dealt with the conditions under which the political rights of citizens could be removed.

Under the decree, ministers may petition for the removal of rights of public employes under their charge. The Minister of Justice is assigned the task of presenting cases against elected officials. The removal of political rights means that the persons affected may not run for office or make political statements in public for 10 years. The action is subject to review by the National Security Council—a military group.

Since suspending Congress a week ago, more than 200 politicians, journalists and others have been arrested. They include former President Juscelino Kubitschek, whose political rights were removed by the military coup of 1964, and a former Governor Carlos Lacerda, one of Mr. Costa e Silva's most outspoken critics. A dozen opposition members of Congress also are in jail.

* * *

January 6, 1969

MEXICO SHUTS 'HAIR' AND EXPELS ITS CAST AFTER ONE SHOWING

Special to The New York Times

MEXICO CITY, Jan. 5—The America musical "Hair" has been closed after one performance in Acapulco, the Pacific coast resort, and 17 foreign members of the cast have been expelled from Mexico.

The effort to bring the off-beat show, now running on Broadway, to a city never noted for its staid morals ran into strong opposition from municipal authorities, who were backed by the Ministry of the Interior in Mexico City.

Members of the Mexican and international jet set who have made Acapulco one of their major capitals appeared to enjoy the show at its premiere on Friday night. A large part of the audience, which included the show's authors, Jerome Ragni and James Rado, had made a special trip to be present at the opening.

Sponsored by a local cabaret owner, Alfredo Elias Calles, a grandson of the late President Plutarco Elias Calles, the show features some nudity, and it is believed that it was this that the Mexican authorities found objectionable. There has also been a strong official prejudice in Mexico against hippies, many of whom have been expelled on various occasions from the country.

Mr. Calles said he was planning to protest to the Ministry of the Interior against what he termed a violation of freedom of expression.

On Saturday morning seals were placed on the theater doors without warning. Early this morning agents of the Ministry of the Interior knocked on the doors of the foreign cast members, took them to a detention center and told them they had 24 hours to leave Mexico.

The unexpected end of the theatrical venture found the foreign cast members with no ready way of obeying the expulsion order, because air traffic out of Acapulco after the holiday season was heavy. The cast was said to be planning to travel first by bus to Mexico City.

* * *

January 6, 1970

BRAZILIANS CURB NEWS MAGAZINE

Article Cut Despite Stand of No Official Censorship

By JOSEPH NOVITSKI
Special to The New York Times

RIO DE JANEIRO, Jan. 5—While officially there is no Government censorship of the Brazilian press, this week's edition of the weekly news-magazine Veja was reviewed by two army commands and the Brazilian Federal Police before it was allowed onto newsstands across the country today.

The magazine, patterned after Newsweek and Time and known for its hard-hitting political reporting among a generally cautious press, lost a little more than 450 words of text. The deleted material dealt with the Brazilian Army's role in politics.

The cuts were ordered by two men, who identified themselves as an army colonel and an agent of the Federal Police Department. They spent more than two hours in the managing editor's office, reading the magazine's political section.

Editors of Veja said that the same two men, Col. Americo Ribeiro and Lis Monteiro, the federal agent, had conducted such activity at the magazine for four weeks. During that time, the Brazilian Foreign Minister, Mario Gibson Barbosa, said at a luncheon of foreign correspondents here that, as far as he knew, there was no government censorship of the Brazilian press.

Tortures Alleged

After President Emílio Garrastazu Médici took office last Oct. 30, Brazilian newspapers and magazines became noticeably freer in their political reporting. Censorship had been practiced since December, 1968, under the former President, the late Gen. Artur da Costa e Silva.

Last month, Veja began reporting alleged cases of torture of political prisoners. On Dec. 5, newspapers and television and radio stations in Rio de Janeiro, Sâo Paulo and Porto Alegre received orders from local army commanders not to publish such articles.

Three days later, Veja published accounts of two alleged instances of police torture. It is believed by some that because of that, the magazine is the only publication in Brazil that is being censored before publication. Other newspapers and magazines exercise self-censorship.

Last Saturday night a skeleton writing and production staff in Veja's main offices in Sâo Paulo made the latest changes ordered by the two censors.

A copy of the magazine was delivered to Col. Carlos Pinto, of the First Army Region in Rio de Janeiro. He authorized its circulation after reading the issue.

* * *

January 11, 1970

PRESS CURBS GROW IN SOUTH AMERICA

Latin Newsmen Protest Acts of Government Censorship

By MALCOLM W. BROWNE
Special to The New York Times

BUENOS AIRES, Jan. 10—The last year has been a bad one for South American newspapermen, even in the region's nominal democracies.

Prospects are that the coming year will be even worse, as far as both direct and indirect governmental pressures on independent news reporting are concerned.

The Inter-American Press Association declared recently that press freedom in Latin-America had declined alarmingly. The association has sent a steady stream of protests to various governments, usually to no avail.

The struggle between governmental control and independent newspapers is currently most intense in Peru, but newsmen throughout the continent view the Peruvian problem as having profound implications for the entire area. The Peruvian press problem has become front page news in Argentina, Bolivia, Chile and most other nations.

Ownership Restricted

On New Year's eve, Peru's military Government decreed a *"Law of Freedom of the Press"* which provides fines and prison sentences for newspaper executives and writers deemed to have insulted the Government. The law includes many other restrictions.

One part of the law requires Peruvian newspaper owners living abroad to divest themselves of their news outlets in Peru. This provision is clearly aimed at Manuel Ullóa who was Finance Minister in the cabinet of former President Fernando Belaúnde Terry. President Belaúnde was deposed by a bloodless military coup on Oct. 3, 1968.

Mr. Ullóa was forced to go into exile, living part of the time in Argentina. But he has remained the owner and active manager of two of Lima's most important newspapers, Expreso and Extra, and a television station. Editorials in the two newspapers have been critical of the new military Government, which is headed by Gen. Juan Velasco Alvarado.

Earlier, the Velasco Government had exiled Enrique Zileri Gibson, director of the biweekly news magazine Caritas. It had been the only influential non-leftist news magazine in Peru.

Peru has also banned the magazine Visión, a Spanish-language magazine published formerly in the United States and now printed in Mexico.

Peruvian journalists conducted a protest demonstration and a strike against the Government last year. The Government then granted a few concessions.

There are several other nations where newsmen are also having serious problems.

In Argentina, since the military coup in 1966, pressures on the press have become increasingly intense.

Publication Halted

During the last year, the Government permanently closed Argentina's leading news weekly, Primera Plana, and several other periodicals. Some prominent journalists were jailed.

In Paraguay, the dictatorship has never tolerated major criticism by the press. But this year, the Government of Gen. Alfredo Stroessner became even more restrictive. The Government closed Comunidad, the only magazine in the country that strongly opposed the regime.

In Brazil, since Dec. 13, 1968, Brazil's military Government has progressively eliminated press freedom, exercising close, direct censorship of all publishing and broadcasting enterprises, and imprisoning opponents and critics of the regime. At the same time the regime declares that the only censorship of its press is self-exercised by the press itself.

Even Uruguay and Chile, whose Governments take pride in being among the most democratic in the hemisphere, have exercised repressive controls of the press during the last year.

In Uruguay, a law decreed last year forbids newspapers to report news about planned strikes or demonstrations. They also are resricted on discussions of the armed forces, certain forms of political strife or general criticism of the Government.

A total strike by journalists of all newspapers last year, resulting in a news blackout lasting several weeks, had little effect on the Uruguayan Government's policy.

In Chile, where the press traditionally has been granted great freedom to comment and criticize, a series of moves were made last year against magazines and newspapers. Difficulties generally resulted from published accounts of dissatisfaction in the armed forces with the Government of President Eduardo Frei Montalva.

* * *

May 31, 1970

PRESS IN ARGENTINA LEADS A RISKY LIFE

By MALCOM W. BROWNE

BUENOS AIRES—Inexplicably, the French movie "Z," an attack on military totalitarianism, got by Argentina's censors. Crowds of Buenos Aires residents packed the street waiting to see the film and cheered the downfall of the movie's main villain, a general who bears a striking physical similarity to Argentina's Interior Minister.

Cheering in movies seems to be one of the few remaining forms of free expression in Argentina, and even that is threatened. A tear gas bomb was thrown two weeks ago into the theater where "Z" is showing. Totalitarian government seems to fit Argentina like an old shoe, and periods of political freedom during the past four decades or so have broken through the clouds of authoritarianism only fitfully.

Harsh Reaction

In recent years, press freedom has deteriorated alarmingly throughout Latin America, and the trend has been particularly notable in Argentina. Always touchy about its power base, the regime of Lieut. Gen. Juan Carlos Ongania invariably reacts harshly when news organizations suggest possible disunity in the armed forces. Other pet peeves include information tending to encourage student or labor opposition to the Government, criticism of the draft, leftist ideas and naked girls.

Since seizing power in 1966, the Government has been cautious in deploying its arsenal of weapons against the press. Extensive criticism of the Government has been tolerated in certain forms, and the respected, conservative daily La Prensa frequently takes the government to task. Other publications have been less fortunate.

At first, it seemed that the government censors would generally limit their attention to radio and television.

Later, the political police under the control of the Interior Ministry began acting against magazines and provincial newspapers. Magazines such as Prensa Confidential and Azuly Blanco were closed and their editors jailed.

Three main instruments were used against too independent provincial newspapers. The first was the threat to cut off government advertising—a major source of income. The second was to block bank credit to offending publications. Third, and perhaps most effective, an editor, publisher or reporter could be charged with the crime of "desacato"—disrespect for authority. The legal definition of this crime is so broad that it can be made to fit almost any form of press commentary involving government operations.

Then, despite criticism from the press, including La Prensa, last year, the Ongania Government began moving against national magazines, books, plays and every other form of expression. The main victim was the weekly news magazine, Primera Plana, in both circulation and prestige, Argentina's leading news weekly.

Last Monday, police, acting on orders from their military commanders, closed down Cronica, the largest newspaper in Argentina. A tabloid with three daily editions, Cronica has a circulation of 720,000.

The ensuing storm of protest, abroad as well as in Argentina, surprised even Argentine newspapermen. To the extent that professional pressure can be brought to bear on a government like that of Argentina, it was applied to the maximum.

Another factor in Cronica's favor was its close ties with the working class and the illegal but politically powerful remnants of the dictatorship of Juan Domingo Peron. The Peronistas were suspected in Friday's kidnapping of one of their arch-enemies, former President Pedro Eugenio Aramburu who "disappeared" from his home when summoned by two men dressed as army officers.

But the Government's latest displeasure with Cronica resulted from a report saying that a student had been killed during a clash between demonstrators and police in Cordoba. The Government charged that Cronica was promoting riots and unrest by publishing false news. Political police moved into and closed the editorial offices.

But by Tuesday night, the Government apparently was smarting from criticism, while at the same time it was certain that it had made its point. A communiqué signed by President Ongania himself announced that since "the causes which motivated the closure of the newspaper Cronica have disappeared," the ban was to be lifted.

No Argentine newspaperman was under the illusion that the Government had grown suddenly liberal. The news magazine Periscopio appeared last week with one page torn out by the publisher. The page had carried graphic reports of police action in Cordoba, including several bloody photographs.

The threats of closure, personal prosecution, financial sanctions and many other measures have generally intimidated the Argentine press.

Book stores are extremely careful about stocking potentially dangerous volumes. There is a proscribed list of books, but no outsider is entirely sure what is on the list. Book dealers have gone to jail during the past year for guessing wrong.

In January, John O'Rourke, retired former editor of The Washington Daily News, visited President Ongania on behalf of the Inter American Press Association. Mr. O'Rourke's mission was to persuade the President to relax his ban on Primera Plana and other publications. The American newspaperman wrote later that his interview had been "Kafkaesque" and that President Ongania had told him: "If a free press would make it possible for Communists to take over Argentina, then I would be proud to say that there is no free press in Argentina."

* * *

November 29, 1970

ARGENTINA EASES CONTROL OF PRESS

But Neighboring Uruguay Has Stern Censorship

By MALCOLM W. BROWNE
Special to The New York Times

BUENOS AIRES, Nov. 28—Although a military Government controls Argentina and an elective democracy prevails in neighboring Uruguay, the press in Argentina has become relatively free in recent months while the Uruguayan press is rigidly controlled.

Censorship in Uruguay has become so severe, in fact, that major Argentine newspaper publishers have announced that they would no longer seek to distribute across the river in Uruguay.

Uruguay has close traditional ties with Argentina, of which she was once an eastern province. The country's official name still is the Eastern Republic of Uruguay.

Uruguayans and Argentines are of the same mixture of Spanish and Italian and speak Spanish with the same accent. Traditionally, Argentine tourists spend their summers on the Uruguayan beaches and buy Argentine newspapers from home.

Politically the two countries evolved very differently. Through most of her history, Argentina has been a military or civilian dictatorship. Uruguay has been an elective democracy with a moderately socialist economy, and her traditions of press freedom are often cited by Latin-American liberals as a desirable model.

Curbs Under Onganía

An interval of elective government in Argentina was ended in 1966 when the military overthrew President Arturo U. Ilifa, installing Lieut. Gen. Juan Carlos Onganía in power.

General Onganía's stern government involved restrictive checks on the press, and a number of magazines were closed down. The mass-circulation newspaper Crónica was briefly closed and the censorship of books and movies was strict.

Last June 8, another military coup overthrew General Onganía, who was replaced by Brig. Gen. Roberto Marcelo Levingston.

President Levingston promptly lifted the restrictions on magazines and declared that there would be absolute freedom of expression. However, books and movies are still censored.

The trend has been such that two months ago the Argentine Association of Newspaper Publishers declared that press freedom had been re-established.

In Uruguay, meanwhile, the simmering war between the Government of President Jorge Pacheco Areco and the Marxist guerrillas called Tupamaros became intense.

President Pacheco has repeatedly broadened the terms of the limited state of siege, including increasing restrictions on the press.

A Word Is Forbidden

First, the Government prohibited the word "Tupamaro," insisting on such substitutes as "terrorist," "criminal," "seditionist" or "unmentionable."

Then the press and broadcasting industry were forbidden to report strikes or political demonstrations and economic or political difficulties of the Government.

At first Montevideo newspapers found ways around the rule. One was the printing of congressional speeches, a right upheld by the Constitution. Some legislators, including Communists frequently gave long speeches, mainly for the purpose of getting them in the press. In recent months the Government has been curbing even that practice.

Journalists, foreigners among them, are regularly arrested. A typical case was that of Julio Camarero, a Spaniard, who was detained for four days after having reportedly obtained an interview with a Tupamaro.

Newspapers and broadcasting stations are penalized by suspension or shut down so often that journalism has become a highly uncertain profession. Protest strikes and denunciations in Congress have had no apparent effect.

Flyers and Leaflets

The Uruguayans have taken to informing themselves clandestinely, principally with flyers and leaflets. If a strike is planned, for instance, a car may speed along the main avenues of Montevideo throwing thousands of flyers into the street. The method risks long prison terms, but drivers are rarely caught.

Last year the renounced Buenos Aires newspaper La Prensa ceased distribution in Uruguay because many issues had been confiscated. This month La Nación, Clarín and La Razon also ended distribution.

In Argentina censorship of books and movies is still in effect. A magazine editor can be removed at the suggestion of the Government.

A newspaper editor, especially one working in the provinces, still can be sent to jail for the crime of desacato, or disrespect for authority, and the threat of prosecution blunts commentary.

Nevertheless, Uruguayan journalists find the atmosphere good. "I never thought I would find myself saying that it's nice to breathe free air by coming to Argentina," one said.

* * *

March 25, 1974

BRAZILIAN PRESS FACES NEW CURBS

Editor Calls the Censorship Grotesque After Ban on Articles on Streaking

By MARVINE HOWE
Special to The New York Times

SAO PAULO, Brazil, March 24—Despite assurances from Brazil's new Government that censorship would be eased, official censors last week issued a ban on press mention of devils, angels and streaking.

"Press censorship has become grotesque, humiliating," Mino Carta, managing editor of Brazil's leading weekly news magazine, Veja, declared.

Mr. Carta was one of several prominent newspapermen to receive assurances from aides of the new President, Gen. Ernesto Geisel, that censorship would be eased after the new Government took office on March 15.

The new Minister of Justice, Armando Falcao, told him two weeks ago that he would recommend an end to censorship and the establishment of general self-censorship.

Similar pledges are said to have been given to Julio de Mesquita Neto, publisher of the influential daily newspaper O Estado de São Paulo, which has led the struggle for press freedom here.

Some New Restrictions

But last week the censors maintained all the old taboos on reports of terrorism, torture, subversion and the like and added a few new ones.

The ruling against articles on streaking is in line with an earlier ban on subjects considered erotic or obscene and with the puritanism of the military-led Government.

But the prohibition of devils and angels was less comprehensible.

The ruling was actually aimed at Veja, which in symbolic protest has lately filled spaces intended for articles that were censored with images of devils from exorcism rites and with angels.

"Nothing has changed," said Raimundo Rodrigues Pereira, editor of the main opposition weekly Opinao, adding that censors cut half of the cover story of General Ceisel's inauguration.

Several editors at O Estado de São Paulo agreed. "Whatever their good intentions, the new Government will soon see that a free press is incompatible with their type of authoritarian rule."

"I still have some hope of a slight relaxation in press curbs or at least clearer, more coherent rules," 40-year-old Mr. Carta declared after recounting Veja's problems with censors over the last five years.

The censors showed up as usual last week in the newsrooms of Veja and the Mesquita family's two newspapers, O Estado de São Paulo and Jornal da Tarde.

Most other newspapers, magazines and television stations have agreed to exert guided self-censorship. This is done by telephone, with the officials showing extreme reluctance to give any kind of written order. Every week or so, the censors telephone their latest orders on forbidden subjects to the newsrooms.

Many newsmen report a hardening of the situation lately and point to the case of Carlos Garcia.

Mr. Garcia, the 40-year-old bureau chief of O Estado de São Paulo in the northeastern city of Recife, was arrested and held incommunicado for 28 hours earlier this month for reporting the arrest of a local municipal councilman.

After Mr. Garcia was released on pressure from the newspaper, he charged the police had subjected him to various kinds of torture, including beatings and electric shock.

Colleagues feel that the police action against Mr. Garcia, who has a high reputation for journalistic integrity, was intended as a warning to other newsmen not to become overzealous with prospects of liberalization.

Critics Encouraged

Despite the continued tight press controls, critics of the system have been encouraged recently by signs of a relaxation by the Government.

At São Paulo University, for example, the social sciences department has held a series of lectures by well-known liberal figures without interference and most of some 40 Roman Catholic lay workers arrested last February have recently been released without charges.

The main test of liberalization, however, is generally felt to lie in the lifting of press controls.

Paulo Evaristo Cardinal Arns, Archbishop of São Paulo, declared in a recent interview that the licensing of the archidiocese's Ninth of July radio station was a precondition for "satisfactory relations" with the new Government. The former Government refused to renew the license of the station last Oct. 30.

Editors here, however, generally feel that now that the new men are in power, they are beginning to have second thoughts about the lifting of press censorship.

One of President Geisel's close aides, who earlier had suggested that press censorship should be lifted immediately, told an editor last week, "After all, you can't expect us to do everything overnight.

* * *

September 6, 1974

PERU'S SEIZED PRESS SHOWS NEW FREEDOM

By MARVINE HOWE
Special to The New York Times

LIMA, Peru, Sept. 5—"They've taken the press away from the dominant class to give it to the people and that's good, but what's bad is that there will be no more criticism of the Government," says a 37-year-old mineworker who moved to a Lima slum to find a better job.

His comment reflects the mixed feelings of many Peruvians about the partial take-over of the press a few weeks ago and the course of the Armed Forces Revolution, now in its sixth year.

The new press law is a major step in the military Government's effort to transfer the power of the old ruling élite to a new, more representative society. Many people approve of the principle of the law, which decrees that the country's main daily newspapers, owned by families or special-interest groups, will be turned over to organizations of workers, professional people and peasants.

But there is widespread uneasiness here over the heavy-handed manner in which the newspapers were seized by police squads on July 27, over the arrests of more than 500 people who demonstrated against the action and over the naming of pro-Government committees to run the papers until they are handed to the new organizations.

Wide Press Uncertainty

There is wide uncertainty in the newly expropriated newspapers as to how they will be turned over to the representative organizations. There is even more uncertainty in the newsrooms of the independent publications that were not expropriated, where employes feel they are working on borrowed time.

"The question now is whether the revolutionary leaders can create their new social order without resorting to totalitarian methods and stifling all opposition," said a newspaperman on an independent publication who is sympathetic to the Government.

President Juan Velasco Alvarado has guaranteed freedom of expression, and to prove it his Government has allowed widespread criticism since the take-over.

Never before in recent times has the Peruvian press appeared so free, publishing political debates, sharp attacks on the Government's press policy and even a campaign charging police torture.

Late last month Caretas, the country's leading independent magazine, reappeared, vigorously denouncing the press takeover and political repression. It had been closed down for two months for calling members of the Government "paranoiac." Enrique Zileri Gibson, the editor of Caretas, was allowed to resume publication of the magazine, and a deportation order against him was rescinded.

Circulation Has Grown

The magazine's circulation has now increased to 50,000 from the 40,000 it had before the seizure, and the price has risen by a third to nearly $1.

"Caretas has now become a symbol of resistance," Mr. Zileri says. But he praised President Velasco for having the courage to allow the magazine to publish again without conditions.

Francisco Igartua, a Socialist whose weekly magazine, Oiga, has generally supported the military revolution, said two weeks ago that he disagreed with the press law in general and the Government's policy on freedom of expression. The people, he said, are not sufficiently organized to take over the press in a really representative fashion.

On the other hand, Carlos Delgado, chief civilian theoretician of the Government and a leader of its Agency for Social Mobilization, says that "the expropriation of the big press was essential to the revolution because we are against the monopoly of power of all kinds and want to build up a society of participation."

Mr. Delgado explained in an interview that the Government was using the same approach with the press as it had used with agrarian reform, taking over large properties in the hands of a few families and interest groups, providing compensation, setting up transitional committees and, within a year, turning them over to freely elected, autonomous organiztions.

Acknowledges Dangers

"This has worked with agrarian reform, and there's no reason to think that it's not going to succeed with the press," Mr. Delgado said.

He acknowledged there were "many dangers" in this move to create "a new journalism" and stressed that much depended on the behavior of the newspapermen, the attitude of the Government and the character of the representative organizations.

Before the take-over, the major papers were in the hands of a few families and special-interest groups, and they generally opposed the socialist policies of the Government.

"They tried to break us because we are anti-Communist," says Luis Miró Quesada, 93-year-old patriarch of the family that owned and ran El Comercio, Lima's oldest newspaper, founded in 1839.

Mr. Miró Quesada was put under house arrest a few hours before the expropriation of the newspapers. It is said that the authorities had feared that he would occupy the premises of El Comercio and cause an embarrassing clash.

Alajandre Miró Quesada Garland, co-publisher of El Comercio, insists that the newspaper was independent and points out that it supported the Government in its nationalization in 1968 of the International Petroleum Company, owned by Standard Oil of New Jersey.

"But the state is taking everything and does not want independent newspapers," Mr. Miró Quesada said, adding that the Government had begun to put pressure on the paper as early as 1970.

Labor Agitation Alleged

He accused the Government of having stirred up labor troubles at El Comercio, reducing its supply of newsprint by 40 per cent and forcing it to pay the highest salaries in the industry. He said that although the Government tried "to strangle" the newspaper financially, it had reached a record circulation of 150,000 and record advertising three months ago. He said he would take the issue to the Organization of American States.

General Velasco disdainfully rejects the younger Mr. Miró Quesada's demands for what the publisher calls a free press.

"There has never been true freedom of the press here," the President told the nation recently, "only freedom for companies and spokesmen for families or interest groups, never the people or the nation."

On July 27, the Government expropriated Lima's six leading newspapers that circulate nationally and said that they should be considered a "social service." Magazines and newspapers with a circulation under 20,000 were allowed to remain under private ownership.

Supporters of the Government were named as interim directors of the expropriated newspapers, which are to be turned over to "the organized sectors of the population" within a year. As compensation, the former owners are to receive cash payments for 10 per cent of the value of the property now and the remainder in 10 annual payments with 6 per cent interest.

Against Its Own Interests

"La Prensa never published articles or letters against its own interests as we do now," Walter Peñaloza Ramella, the newspaper's new director, said recently. La Prensa had been owned by the Beltrán family and reflected the interests of landowners and sugar-cane exporters.

Mr. Peñaloza, who was Ambassador to West Germany and a leader of the Government's educational reform, insists that the Government has given him "complete independence" to run the newspaper.

La Prensa used to have a circulation of 120,000 but, Mr. Peñaloza said, was down to 90,000 when it was expropriated. He added that he had increased circulation to 100,000 and that there had been a slight shift in readers, with returns of unpurchased papers coming from the upper-middle-class neighborhood of Miraflores, where the demonstrations against the press take-over occurred. The Government has increased its advertising in the paper and private companies have maintained their advertising at the former level.

Mr. Peñaloza said 10 to 12 journalists had resigned since the expropriation of La Prensa—"people completely committed to past policies." He said that he had dismissed only three employes.

Foreign Agencies Unaffected

Most newsmen appeared to be accommodating themselves to the press changes, basically because it is not easy to find jobs elsewhere. There is a certain disappointment in some newsrooms, where journalists expected the newspapers to be turned over to them.

Foreign news agencies here say that they have encountered no censorship or threats of censorship, only the usual difficulties of getting payment in foreign currency.

The Peruvian Times, an independent English-language business weekly, has not been affected by the new press law and is pursuing a careful, objective course.

La Crónica, which was a sensational tabloid belonging to the Prado family and representing banking and insurance interests, was taken over by the state five years ago. Now it is a modern, attractive paper and a serious competitor to the staid El Comercio and La Prensa.

La Crónica will remain under Government ownership and be "the voice of the revolution," says the new director, Guillermo Thorndike. He hopes to convert more of the middle class to the revolution by defending their interests through the paper.

* * *

AFRICA AND ASIA

January 26, 1965

TSHOMBE CLOSES OPPOSITION PAPER

Leopoldville Weekly Banned 6 Months as Public Danger

By J. ANTHONY LUKAS
Special to The New York Times

LEOPOLDVILLE, the Congo, Jan. 25—Premier Moise Tshombe has banned a Leopoldville newspaper that opposed his Government.

The weekly, L'Action, was ordered to cease publication because it published "articles endangering order and public tranquility."

According to the decree signed by Mr. Tshombe, the ban will last six months. However, observers here doubted that the newspaper would reappear, at least under its present direction.

The paper's two top officials, Sam. B. Kassanda, its administrator-director, and Paul Kalambay, its editor, were jailed last week. Yesterday they were reported to have been released. However, efforts to locate them today proved unsuccessful.

Offices Locked

The newspaper's offices on a dusty street in one of Leopoldville's shantytown communes were locked and guarded by six Congolese policemen. When asked where Mr. Kassanda or Mr. Kalambay could be found a policeman said:

"That's what we want to know. We're looking for them too. I think they've fled."

Last week officials of the security police searched the two rooms occupied by L'Action. They seized all copies of its last issue, published Jan. 16, as well as a number of files, books and periodicals.

The banning of L'Action removes virtually the only independent voice in the Congolese press. Leopoldville's three daily newspapers and three weeklies, Elisabethville's three dailies and two weeklies and papers in Bukavu and Stanleyville all follow the Government line.

Syndicate Owns 4 Papers

Four of the country's most important papers—Le Progress in Leopoldsville, La Dépeche in Elisabethville, La Presse Africaine in Bukavu and Le Gazette in Stanleyville—are owned by a syndicate controlled by the so-called "Binza Group," which includes Victor Nendaka, chief of the security police, and Gen. Joseph Mobutu the army commander. These papers, which once supported former Premier Cyrile Adoula, now back Mr. Tshombe.

L'Action, which first appeared last November, was published by a company that also distributes The New African Agency, a daily news bulletin that has also been sharply critical of Mr. Tshombe. It was not clear today whether the ban on L'Action included the bulletin.

There has been much speculation here as to who provided the financial backing for the two publications. It is generally believed that money was given by the Algerian and United Arab Republic Embassies before they were closed by Mr. Tshombe last October. Since then, the Ghanaian Embassy is believed to have provided most of the funds.

Observers believe that Mr. Adoula may have given L'Action some funds. In recent weeks the paper has supported his proposals for a political solution of the Congolese problem, particularly his demand for negotiation with the rebels.

* * *

July 2, 1965

SOUTH AFRICA RAIDS PAPER OVER PRISON ARTICLES

Detectives Seize Copy and Notes From Offices of Rand Daily Mail

By JOSEPH LELYVELD
Special to The New York Times

JOHANNESBURG, South Africa, July 1—The police raided the newsroom of the Rand Daily Mail today and seized the notes and drafts for a series of articles on conditions in South African prisons.

The Mail, generally considered the Government's most outspoken newspaper critic had published two of the three articles. Tonight it went ahead and printed the third, which had been set in type before the raid.

The paper now faces prosecution under the Prisons Act, a law that makes it a crime to publish information about a prisoner or ex-prisoner or about the administration of any prison. The law allows only one defense: proof in court that the published information was entirely accurate.

As described in the articles in The Mail, prisoners in South African jails are subjected to systematic humiliation, beatings and repulsively unsanitary surroundings.

Author Is Ex-Prisoner

The author of the series is Harold Strachan, a former political prisoner who was released in May after having served three years for conspiracy to use explosions.

His last installment begins, "I want to talk about assaults." It describes beatings with sticks and straps that Mr. Strachan says he witnessed.

"The worst assaults I saw anywhere in jail," he writes, "were those on Africans at the hospitals."

Regularly, he goes on, scores of black prisoners were forced to stand naked outdoors in the cold prison yard while awaiting medical examination. The wait usually began at 6:15 A.M., the article says, although the doctor never arrived until 9 o'clock.

The stripping of prisoners, according to the articles, was an ordinary prelude for any punishment.

Deprivation of Showers

The worst treatment, Mr. Strachan says, was often reserved for political offenders. They were allowed to shower only outdoors, even in the winter. Ordinary criminals could have at least two hot showers a week.

In one of the prisons where he was held, Mr. Strachan writes, prisoners had to draw water for bathing from the toilet bowl.

He spent 11 months, he says, in one isolation section, where he was allowed to do nothing all day except sit on his bunk.

"I used to wake up at half past five in the morning when the gong rang," he says, "and just sit and hope and wait and shiver and pray for half past four in the afternoon" when he could get under the covers.

For stretching out too soon, he says, a prisoner could be deprived of food for 38 hours.

Limitation on Letters

The worst section was called segregation. Prisoners there could receive only one 500-word letter and one half-hour visit every six months.

"Men used to go off their heads in jail," he says, "and go rushing at the walls and doors of their cells, screaming and weeping, banging with their fists and kicking. Some also mutilated themselves."

Laurence Gandar, the editor of The Mail, said tonight that the paper was convinced of the accuracy of Mr. Strachan's articles and was prepared to offer supporting evidence to the courts.

If convicted of an offense under the Prisons Act, Mr. Strachan, Mr. Gandar and the reporter who compiled the articles, Benjamin Pogrund, could each be sentenced to one year in prison.

Since the Prisons Act was revised in 1959, conditions in the country's jails have not been discussed in most newspapers.

* * *

November 20, 1965

NIGERIA'S REGIME SEIZES 2 EDITORS

Accuses Them of Sedition Over Election Coverage

Special to The New York Times

LAGOS, Nigeria, Nov. 19—Intimidation of newspaper readers, the arrest of editors and crippling circulation boycotts have plunged the free press here into serious political and financial straits.

The arrests took place today when Nigeria's Federal Government charged the editors of The Daily Telegraph and The West African Pilot with sedition.

The trouble began with conflicting press coverage of last month's turbulent Parliamentary elections in Nigeria's Western Region.

The ruling Government party won over the favored Opposition, but there was evidence of widespread vote-rigging. Both The Telegraph and The Pilot reported that the Opposition had actually won despite an official Government announcement proclaiming its party the victor.

Because of this, Stephen N. Iweanya, of The Pilot and Smart O. Ebbi of The Telegraph were accused of sedition under the year-old Newspaper Amendment Act.

The law holds editors responsible for reporting any false news or rumors likely to cause public disturbance. An editor found guilty may be jailed up to three years.

Ordinances Ban Some Papers

Many Western Nigerians seeking revenge for what they believed was an electoral fraud, embarked on a wave of violence. Thus far, it has taken more than 80 lives.

More than 200 people have been wounded, and at least 30 homes owned by Government figures have been burned.

In the populous Eastern Region, whose political powers are aligned with the Opposition Action Group in the West, key city councils adopted ordinances banning papers that stayed neutral or actively backed the Western Government's return to power.

This group included the Federal Government's Morning Post, the Western Government's Daily Sketch and the independent Daily Express and the Daily Times, Nigeria's most widely read paper.

The net effect of the ordinances has been to block the entrance of these papers into the Eastern Region by either air or road.

In retaliation, city councils in the West have made it a crime not only to read the pro-Opposition Pilot, Telegraph and Daily Tribune but also to tune in the Eastern Region radio. If caught, errant newspaper readers and radio listeners are subject to a year's imprisonment.

The East has imposed no such penalties. But purple-uniformed political thugs have set up roadblocks, searched cars for the "wrong" papers and beaten the occupants who possessed them.

* * *

December 6, 1965

INDONESIA TO CURB MORE NEWSPAPERS

Special to The New York Times

JAKARTA, Indonesia, Dec. 5—A total of 46 of 163 newspapers in Indonesia has now been banned on charges of Communist affiliation or for failure to comply with country's new press laws.

In disclosing this, Colonel Harsono, chief of press and public relations in the Ministry of Information, said further reduction in the number of papers was expected until about 65 remained. He has control of licensing of newspapers as well as of supplies of newsprint.

The principal reason for a further reduction in the number of newspapers is a ruling that there may be only one daily for each of the eight remaining political parties and one each for several organizations and Government establishments.

"What we are trying to do is to create a responsible press that is loyal, nationalistic and free from foreign influence, or at least foreign influence that is bad," a senior armed forces official explained.

Antara, the official Indonesian press agency, is a government agency and the sole source of foreign news for the country's newspapers.

* * *

February 9, 1966

RHODESIA WIDENS CENSORSHIP CURBS

Bans Mention of Them and Prohibits White Spaces

By LAWRENCE FELLOWS
Special to The New York Times

SALISBURY, Rhodesia, Feb. 8—The Rhodesian Government has assumed sweeping new powers of censorship, prohibiting newspapers and magazines even from suggesting whether they or the censor are responsible for the material they print.

The regulations, announced in Parliament today by the Deputy Minister for Information, P. K. van der Byl, gave the censors the power to alter articles and headlines, and to dictate the page on which they should appear.

It is now an offense to state or even to imply that publications are subject to censorship.

Since Rhodesia seized independence from Britain last Nov. 11 and censorship was imposed, all the newspapers have carried notices on their front pages that they were subject to censorship.

White Space Must Be Filled

Not only has this been made unlawful, but editors will now have to close up the white spaces by which they have shown their readers where and to what extent the censor made his excisions.

The white spaces have been perhaps the hardest for the Government to bear. Some of the staunchest supporters of independence have registered disappointment at not being trusted by the authorities to read criticism from home or abroad.

In many cases the reader need not be especially discerning to figure out what has been removed from his paper.

If he reads something about Sir Humphrey Gibbs with a blank space where the preceding words have been deleted, he can deduce that the words "the Governor" have been taken out, simply because the Government no longer recognizes that Sir Humphrey holds this office. In fact, it has been attempting without success to get Sir Humphrey to move out of the Governor's official residence.

A 'Do It Yourself Issue'

The most recent issue of The Central African Examiner, a liberal monthly magazine, was so full of white space that it was advertised as a "do it yourself" issue: Small prizes were offered to the readers who could most accurately fill the blanks.

The Examiner challenged censorship last month in Rhodesia's High Court. The case was thrown out without the legality of Rhodesia's new Constitution ever coming to the test, but the paper announced today that it would appeal against the decision.

Frequently the editorial columns of the daily newspapers have been nothing but white space. Even parliamentary reports have contained white spaces.

Mr. van der Byl was asked in Parliament for assurance that censorship would not now be used to cover up the Government's failings. Constructive criticism will not be censored, he replied, but destructive criticism designed to cast doubts about the validity of the Government will not be permitted.

* * *

February 10, 1966

STRICT CENSORSHIP DEFIED IN RHODESIA

Special to The New York Times

SALISBURY, Rhodesia, Thursday, Feb. 10—Rhodesia's two daily newspapers defied the Government's sweeping new powers of censorship today.

The Rhodesia Herald appeared on the streets in Salisbury and The Chronicle in Bulawayo, both with white spaces showing where the censor had done his work.

The white spaces and any other indication that the publications are subject to censorship are offenses under the new regulations, announced in Parliament two days ago by the Deputy Minister for Information, P. K. Van der Byl.

Offenders are liable to two years' imprisonment and a fine of £500.

Uniformed policemen picked up copies of The Chronicle early this morning when the papers were first brought from the presses to the street.

The white spaces in the papers have nettled the Government since it declared its independence from Britain last November and censorship was imposed.

The public was baffled by yesterday's editions. The lead stories told about the new, stricter censorship, but the white spaces still appeared in both papers, along with boxes on the front pages stating that the papers had been subjected to censorship.

* * *

March 2, 1967

GHANA'S PRESS EXERCISES FREEDOM WITH RESTRAINT

Once Muzzled by Nkrumah, It Remains Wary of New Government's Decrees

By LLOYD GARRISON

Special to The New York Times

ACCRA, Ghana, Feb. 28—One year after Kwame Nkrumah's overthrow, Ghana's once tightly muzzled press is exercising its new freedom with restraint.

In the first few weeks after the coup d'état, the press was docile. It seemed to be operating by automatic reflex. Never question, always praise.

This was the state of journalism under President Nkrumah, who either banned or bought out all privately owned newspapers. Editors of the Government-run journals were told every Monday morning what the line was to be for the week to come. Deviation was punished by dismissal, and in some cases erring newsmen were placed in preventive detention.

Several months after last February's take-over by the army and the police. Col. A. A. Afrifa, a member of the eight-man National Liberation Council, chided the press for its skittishness and invited constructive criticism.

The new editors gradually began to open up with mildly critical editorials.

But today editors of new privately owned publications are wary of "going too far" in the face of new antisubversion decrees that could be used to curb freedom of expression as well. Some editors say they would like to hit out harder at some Government policies, but fear the Government might hit back.

The National Liberation Council continues to voice its faith in a "responsible" free press. Its new decree makes it a crime to air any statement, even if true, that might cause "disaffection" against the Council, the police or the armed forces.

The Council justifies this decree as a necessary deterrent to mounting acts of subversion by pro-Nkrumah infiltrators plotting the return of the deposed President from exile in Guinea.

Government sources insist that the decree is aimed not really at the press but at preventing defamatory pamphlets from being published and circulated clandestinely. For the time being at least the press appears to accept the Government's sincerity.

So far the decree has been applied only once. The defendant, a former district organizer for Mr. Nkrumah's Young Pioneers, was sentenced to three years for having prepared a pro-Nkrumah tract highly critical of the present regime.

The Government has also armed itself with the power to hold a suspect for 28 days without recourse to the courts and has decided to try subversion cases before military tribunals. Army personnel from the rank of sergeant up have been given the power of arrest.

Both press and public opinion are divided over these developments. Many who feel that the National Liberation Council has been far too soft toward Mr. Nkrumah's most militant followers have welcomed these "get-tough" measures. Others caution that they could be used to prolong the Government in power.

Even among the Government's strongest newspaper critics there is no suggestion that Mr. Nkrumah would be preferable. This is due neither to reticence nor to fear but reflects what most seasoned observers here believe is a widespread popular confidence in the new regime's ultimate intentions.

* * *

June 3, 1967

PRESS RESTRICTED IN MIDDLE EAST

Israel Censors Articles — Egypt Curbs Travel

By JAMES FERON
Special to The New York Times

JERUSALEM (Israel), June 2—The composing room of The Jerusalem Post sounded like a stonemason's studio for a while one evening last week as a printer chipped away at a page that was already in type.

With a hammer and a screwdriver, the man was mutilating the paper's main headline. When he finished all that remained was . . . "changes in Top Posts."

The words that had been removed were "Cabinet Meets," but the Israeli censor had been told, at a fairly late hour, to ban references to the emergency Cabinet session.

The next day correspondents were permitted to write of the midnight Cabinet session. That night the same restriction was imposed, when the Cabinet met again, only to be lifted in turn the next day.

More than 100 newsmen and broadcasters have come to Tel Aviv and Jerusalem in the last two weeks. Many are learning for the first time of Israel's censorship.

Every dispatch transmitted from the country is scrutinized by censors in the Government press offices in Tel Aviv and Jerusalem. Local newspapers are under similar restrictions.

Censorship is intended to protect national security and is administered by young men, some in civilian clothing and some in uniform, who work under an army officer.

Censorship is applied under an emergency regulation imposed by the British authorities during the latter days of the Palestine Mandate which terminated in 1948. Ironically, it was aimed originally at Jewish terrorists.

The censors vary in their application. Foreign correspondents are able to argue their case, but usually to no avail. Sometimes the ban involves something specific so the correspondent is able to change his phrasing and thus not lose the meaning.

British and American newsmen especially have been puzzled by the changing nature of Israeli censorship. Items that are prohibited one day are permitted the next day and then banned again later.

At first it was forbidden to refer to panic-buying in Israeli stores. The phrase was changed to overbuying. When the two-day panic dissipated, the entire incident could be reported without restriction.

Military References Watched

Journalists have been taken on tours of military zones and shown a lot more than they are permitted to transmit. References to locations of military units are watched carefully by the censors.

Any suggestions that military leaders have had any influence on political decisions is swiftly deleted in news articles.

Dispatches dealing with the morale of soldiers are generally censored, even if the references are to high morale. Reporting of the attitudes of soldiers to political events is banned.

The censors do not allow any references to political opinions of military leaders. It was permissible to say that Foreign Minister Abba Eban urged Premier Levi Eshkol to voice a plea for peace in a speech on May 22, but it was only permitted to say that "other circles" were concerned that such emphasis might be mistaken for signs of weakness.

Cairo Limits Reporters

By ERIC PACE
Special to The New York Times

CAIRO, June 2—Officials of the United Arab Republic's Information Department said today that military censorship would be imposed on the dispatches of foreign correspondents if war broke out with Israel. It said, however, that there was no censorship now.

In the more than two weeks since the Middle East crisis began there has been no evidence of deletions by Government authorities in outgoing press cables, but the scope of reporting by the more than 250 foreign correspondents now in Cairo has been restricted in another way: they have been for the most part forbidden to travel to the areas near the Israeli border where Arab forces are massed.

As far as is known the only exception to this prohibition was a Government-organized trip by 24 television and news agency journalists to the Sinai Peninsula and the Gaza Strip last Sunday.

Repeated assurances by the Information Department that other trips would be organized have not been fulfilled.

Apparently for reasons of military security, foreign correspondents have been forbidden to drive from Cairo to Suez, Ismailia and Port Said, but the Government permitted them to travel to Port Said and Ismailia one day this week to watch the passage through the Suez Canal of the United States carrier Intrepid.

Access to the Sinai Peninsula and to the Gaza Strip has been specifically forbidden to foreign reporters.

Civilian officials have said that the prohibition on travel by reporters was at the Egyptian army's behest. Military authorities have not given an explanation.

The United States Embassy also restricted activity of reporters, within its precincts briefly this week. On Tuesday and Wednesday, Embassy officials declined to make statements for publication and no appointments were made for reporters to meet the political and economic experts on the Embassy staff. This policy was rescinded yesterday.

* * *

November 22, 1968

SIHANOUK STOKES FEUD WITH THE PRESS

By TERENCE SMITH
Special to The New York Times

PNOMPENH, Cambodia, Nov. 18—It was in the midst of a reception he was giving for visiting Western newsmen early this month that Prince Norodom Sihanouk announced his new policy on the admission of foreign journalists.

"I have a bit of news for you," the Chief of State said cheerfully, as white-jacketed waiters circulated with trays of champagne, caviar and pâté de foie gras. "Instead of letting you come into Cambodia once a year, we have decided that we would be clever if we only let you in once every five years."

"You have been with us this year for the 15th anniversary of our independence," he continued. "You may come again for our 20th and 25th, and so on—every five years, but not more often. That way we will have four years of tranquillity between your visits."

The combination of caviar and bad news was a perfect example of the unpredictable policy Prince Sihanouk has applied toward the representatives of the Western press, radio and television.

And Then, a Perfect Host

Since he severed diplomatic relations with the United States in 1965, the Cambodian leader has barred all but one Western newsman from his country for all but two weeks of the year. During the two weeks he has admitted other Westerners he has been the perfect host, providing every possible convenience and courtesy. The purpose of his policy has been to keep as tight a rein as possible on what is published and broadcast abroad.

The only Western news organ represented here at all times is Agence France-Presse, which benefits from Cambodia's long and close relationship with France, the colonial ruler of Indochina until 1954, when Vietnam and Laos as well as Cambodia were established as separate entities.

Also excepted from the restrictive policy have been the press representatives of the Communist countries, including both the Soviet Union and Communist China. They are customarily granted full visas and many are here permanently.

For reasons he has not made clear Prince Sihanouk has apparently decided to shield his country from Western scrutiny even more than before.

Luxuriates in Publicity

"This is a sovereign state that wants to be isolated," he told the visiting reporters. "We have nothing to hide, but we prefer not to become involved with the external affairs and policies of other countries. I want Cambodia to live alone, like the Lord Buddha, who went into the forest and stayed there alone."

Norodom Sihanouk has had his difficulties with the press over the years. He was deeply embarrassed a year ago when three American newsmen discovered evidence of Vietcong use of Cambodian territory—something he had strenuously insisted was not going on. Since then, he has acknowledged the Vietcong presence.

Many observers here, including several senior Western diplomats, doubt that Prince Sihanouk will adhere to his decision to bar the Western press for five-year intervals. They note that he has frequently made use of the annual visits to divulge some new emphasis or change in foreign policy and that he is a man who luxuriates in the limelight.

A compulsive reader of newspapers and magazines, the 46-year-old Prince keeps an elaborate clipping file of every article published about Cambodia. Those he likes he frequently reprints, those he objects to he denounces.

He also categorizes reporters into three broad groups and assigns their names to lists. Those whose articles have been favorable go on the white list, while the others go on either the gray or the black list. A man on the black list is unlikely to get a visa.

Although there is no formal censorship, all articles written here are read before they are transmitted.

Prince Sihanouk also maintains tight control over the local press. A year ago, during a dispute with Communist China, he closed down all independent newspapers on the ground that they had been proselytizing. Since then, five have opened again, but none has a circulation of more than a few thousand in a country of six million.

* * *

November 17, 1969

ZULUS CAN'T SEE 'ZULU' IN SOUTH AFRICA

Special to The New York Times

JOHANNESBURG, South Africa, Nov. 16—Five hundred Zulus waving property-room assagais—or spears—helped make a movie called "Zulu" on location in South Africa a few years ago. It dealt with the battle of Rorkesdrift where about 80 British soldiers held out against an overwhelming force of Zulu impis, or battle divisions, on Jan. 22–23, 1879.

But not one of the 500 extras nor any of South Africa's 15 million blacks has seen the movie although it has made the circuit of local theaters twice.

South Africa's Publications Control Board, an autonomous body, decided that the movie was not fit for black African consumption. Presumably the censors felt it might give the now docile Zulus the idea of taking up their assagais again.

In South Africa apartheid policies are as strict on movie-going as they are on living areas, jobs and the use of public transport.

Movies Are Limited

Movies banned to nonwhites have included "The Incident," "Sweet Charity," "The Detective," "Prudence and the Pill," "The Boston Strangler," "Rosemary's Baby," "West Side Story," "Africa Addio" "The Mercenaries," "Valley of the Dolls," and "Che!"

Black Africans, but not coloreds or Indians, have been forbidden to see "Tom Jones," "The Dirty Dozen," "Darling," "The Magnificent Seven," "From Russia with Love," "Spartacus," "A Farewell to Arms," and "One Hundred Rifles," which starred a Negro actor, Jim Brown.

A black African recently complained in a letter to a nonwhite weekly newspaper that black Africans are allowed to see only "second rate secret-service films and rather low-type Westerns."

Recent titles at Johannesburg theaters for black Africans included "Booted Baby," "Busted Boss," "Glory Guys," "Track of Thunder," "Long Ride from Hell," "Stage Struck," "Kiss the Girls and Make Them Die," and "Tarzan and the Huntress."

Film makers here estimate that only 7 per cent of the black African population has ever seen a movie. This is due in part to a shortage of theaters. Soweto, a sprawling African township outside Johannesburg with a population of 600,000, has just opened its second movie theater. Curfews, township crime and inadequate transport limit movie-going.

There are a few multiracial movie theaters in the larger towns and cities.

Demand Increasing

"Not for Bantu. No children 4–12" is the notice frequently displayed outside box offices.

As black Africans become more urbanized and better educated and as their importance as consumers grows, the demand for better movies increases.

Mrs. D. Mabiletsa, director of a welfare center in Alexandra Township—a shanty town outside Johannesburg—says: "Cinema-going is an aspect of our new township culture. Standards and aspirations are rising. More and more Africans have radios and they are asking: 'If you can hear why not also see?' "

Johannesburg's Urban Bantu Council recently attacked the Publications Control Board's restrictions. "The judgment of a particular group is being imposed on the freedom of choice of the whole African community," it said.

Censorship has become harsher as the attitudes of international film-makers have changed. The freer use of sex, the appearance of Negroes in dignified and leading roles and the growing emphasis on civil rights make movies increasingly unacceptable to the South African censors.

One certificate issued by the censors said: "No Bantu. No persons 4–12. Excisions: eliminate shot of white man kissing colored girl. Eliminate whole of bed scene."

Local Movies Planned

It is estimated that eight times as many films are banned to Africans as to whites.

South Africa's small movie industry is planning to cash in on this movie starvation. Encouraged by a recent Government decision to increase subsidies for films in Afrikaans—the language of most of South Africa's whites—two groups have announced plans to make films specifically for African consumption.

Thirty-year-old Andre Pieterse, who built up a massive chain of drive-in movies, has set up a new organization called Film Trust. "South Africa has a responsibility toward its Bantu people," he says. "My plan is to develop a Bantu film industry with an estimated annual turnover of 25 million rand (about $35-million)."

"The choice of imported films is becoming increasingly difficult since liberal and permissive thinking seems to predominate in most overseas films," he says. "I intend to make South Africa the Hollywood of Africa. It is we, the people of South Africa, who understand the Bantu. We are better able to produce films to their liking than Hollywood, Moscow or Peking."

Mr. Pieterse is starting with a James Bond-type series of films. Another local moviemaker, Anthony Handley, has already begun filming "Knockout," the first of a projected series of movies. The theme is boxing instead of espionage.

* * *

October 17, 1972

MARCOS APPROVES NEW NEWSPAPER

Daily Will Print 'Positive News,' Official Says

By HENRY KAMM
Special to The New York Times

MANILA, Oct. 16—The martial-law Government of President Ferdinand E. Marcos today authorized the publication of a new daily newspaper, The Times-Journal.

Lorenzo J. Cruz, Assistant Secretary of Public Information, said that the staff of the new paper, The Times Journal, had been found to be "respectable" journalists not involved in corruption or subversion.

"They've agreed to write positive news," he said.

For the time being, The Times-Journal, which hopes to begin publishing Saturday, will not be allowed to comment on the news.

A Tone of Approval

The Daily Express, the only newspaper now publishing, prints no editorials or analyses either, but throughout its articles there runs a tone of fervent approval of what President Marcos has termed the "New Society."

In a related move, Francisco S. Tatad, head of the newly-created Department of Public Information, said that censorship of dispatches by foreign correspondents would soon be ended.

But Mr. Marcos has made it clear that the ban on Philippine newspapers, radio and television, which he decreed with the proclamation of martial law on Sept. 23, is far more than a temporary suspension.

What the Government is in fact doing is to consider which newspapers it will kill and which it will eventually allow to resume publication under stringent self-censorship. Meanwhile, some 16 Manila editors, reporters and columnists remain detained without charges in military stockades.

In ordering seizure of the press, Mr. Marcos declared without further specification that newspapers, magazines and broadcasting stations had participated in the alleged conspiracy to take over the Government by force.

While the Government is giving "serious consideration" to allowing two established newspapers to resume publication soon, Mr. Cruz said, two or three papers might be permanently suppressed. In journalistic circles, speculation is that these will include The Manila Times, considered the country's leading newspaper, and The Manila Chronicle.

Publisher Detained

The publisher of The Times, Joaquín Roces, is among those detained. The Chronicle is owned by the family of Vice President Fernando Lopez, whom Mr. Marcos castigates as an oligarch. The Chronicle's editor, Armando Doronila, is under arrest.

When a newspaper's right to resume publication is considered, the loyalty to the Government of its staff is examined by military intelligence.

"We don't want them to destroy what we are trying to build," Mr. Cruz said.

But even a newspaper that President Marcos declared had not participated in the reported conspiracy, the conservative Philippines Herald, has had its authorization to publish held up after the President issued it on Sept. 26.

No reason for the continued ban has been given.

* * *

December 18, 1972

CAIRO PRESS ASKS CENSORSHIP'S END

Journalistic Code of Ethics to Be Offered to Sadat

By HENRY TANNER
Special to The New York Times

CAIRO, Dec. 17—The Egyptian press syndicate appealed to the government today for the immediate lifting of censorship on newspapers except in military matters involving national security.

The syndicate, an association whose members range from apprentice reporters to editors in chief, recalled in a statement that President Anwar el-Sadat had promised to lift censorship as soon as the newsmen adopted a code of ethics. The code has been adopted unanimously by the Syndicate's general assembly.

The President made his promise in a closed-door talk with editors and reporters last February, the authoritative and semi-official daily Al Ahram, which, with other newspapers, urged in its issue today that censorship be lifted.

Leading journalists expressed the belief that Mr. Sadat would respond favorably and approve the code by decree, since he wants to preserve his reputation as a liberal ruler who is steadily permitting more freedom of expression than obtained under his predecessor, Gamel Abdel Nasser.

Egyptian officials have been stung by suggestions from abroad that recent events, including the unprecedented free debate in the National Assembly last week, betrayed a weakness in the Government and an erosion of political power.

May Be Limited to Papers

However, even if censorship of Egyptian newspapers is lifted except in matters of military security, it is likely that foreign correspondents here will remain subject to a form of censorship.

Censorship of outgoing news dispatches has been largely limited to passages referring to the army. But opponents of all censorship have been pointing out that that specific censorship takes in a large area, since the Egyptian Army has been the most important single factor in the country since the revolution of 1952, in which military leaders ousted King Farouk.

Egyptian newspapers have resident censors to whom all copy is submitted before the papers appear. The censors are civilian officials responsible to the Ministry of Information and Culture.

In past years Government officials have often stated that censorship is confined to military matters. The resolution adopted by the press syndicate indicates that this has not been the case.

During the debate in the Assembly several speakers complained that their remarks had been kept out of the newspapers by censors and submitted a list of such deletions to the Assembly secretariat.

Al Ahram, authoritative sources said today was prevented for two days from reporting the departure for Moscow last month of a military delegation led by Gen. Hosni Mobarak, The mission had been announced weeks earlier by Premier Aziz Sidky. The delegation left on a Thursday and Al Ahram was not allowed to report the departure until Sunday.

In another example, a responsible Egyptian diplomat told newsmen that the Government had prevented a press attack on President Gaafar el-Nimeiry of the Sudan.

Structures and Practices

Egypt's newspapers were nationalized 15 years ago and belong by law to the Arab Socialist Union, the nation's only political party. In practice, each paper has administrative and financial independence.

Al Ahram and Al Akhbar, each of which has a circulation of 300,000, are prosperous. Al Ahram, directed by Mohammed Hassanein Heykal, appeals to the educated élite, while Al Akhbar, headed by Ihsan Abdel Kuddous, has a more brisk, and more popular style.

Al Gomhouriya, another Cairo daily has a much smaller circulation and depends on Government subsidies.

Both Mr. Heykal and Mr. Kuddous write weekly editorials that, according to informed sources, are not submitted to the censor before publication. They are believed to be the only writers with that privilege.

Mr. Heykal was a close confidant of the late President Nasser, but Mr. Kuddous was not. Mr. Kuddous, however, has long been a close friend of Mr. Sadat's.

Under the syndicate's code, the relationship between the papers and the Arab Socialist Union would be more clearly defined; officials would be prevented from interfering with the operation of the papers; officials would be obliged to give facts and information to newsmen on request, and writers would have the right to express their views regardless of approach.

Editors and reporters would be bound to obtain information by "legitimate means only," to preserve professional secrets and resist pressure to divulge them, and respect the privacy and reputation of citizens. They would be pledged to "objectivity, particularly in criticizing public personalities," and they would be committed to the principle of socialism.

* * *

January 7, 1973

ISRAELI INTELLECTUALS DEMAND ABOLITION OF CENSORSHIP OF THEATER

Special to The New York Times

JERUSALEM, Jan. 6—A campaign to abolish governmental censorship of the theater has been started by 145 of Israel's leading writers and intellectuals. Their drive came in the wake of the banning of a controversial play that satirizes the Israeli Establishment.

The campaign picked up an influential ally last month when Yigal Allon, the Deputy Premier and Minister of Education and Culture, came out publicly against theater censorship and formally proposed its abolition.

After losing an initial round in a Cabinet subcommittee last week, Mr. Allon has taken the issue to the full Cabinet, which is scheduled to debate it soon.

A scene from "Jesus, As Seen by His Friends." Play was closed after seven performances in Tel Aviv.

The play that initiated the controversy is a satirical review entitled, "Jesus, As Seen by His Friends," by Amos Kenan, a well-known actor, playwright and newspaper columnist.

It was closed after seven performances in a small, experimental theater in Tel Aviv by the Government's Board of Film and Theater Censorship, which must approve all the films and plays produced in Israel.

A British Legacy

The 19-member board is a legacy from the British, who first introduced censorship of plays in Palestine in 1927. Its members are bureaucrats, academics and professionals who serve without pay.

In its decision, the board voted unanimously to stop the Kenan play on the ground that it was "insulting and degrading to religious beliefs in general and the Christian community in particular."

It also found the play offensive to the feelings of the parents of slain Israeli soldiers and contended that its obscene language and gestures violated accepted moral standards.

Protesting that his play was merely a commentary on modern Israel, Mr. Kenan appealed to the Supreme Court. After lengthy consideration, the court upheld the board.

The decision stunned the intellectual community here since it was only the second time in the history of the state that a play had been banned in its entirety. The first was a British drama that was closed in 1971 on the ground that it depicted excessive violence.

Jesja Weinberg, the director of Tel Aviv's respected Cameri Theater who is one of the leaders of the abolishment campaign, said that the new ban "reminded a lot of people who had almost forgotten that we still have excessive censorship in Israel."

Critics and columnists denounced the decision as hypocritical, contending that the board members' real objections had been to the play's political and social commentary, not the religious allusions.

Despite the title and the central figure—a man on a cross—the target of Mr. Kenan's frequently savage satire is obviously Israeli society. It mocks the widespread admiration here of the military and ridicules the Government's policies in the occupied Arab territories.

In one of the play's sketches, an Israeli housewife praises the efficiency of the army:

"We have a lot to learn from the army. Yesterday, I noticed that my maid doesn't dust the table properly. So I called in the army. It's a real delight to see how they rub.

"My husband turned out to be inefficient, too. So I called in the army. Everything is more efficient since the army has taken control. The synagogues are more efficient. The Dead Sea is more efficient. The Wailing Wall is more efficient.

"What pleases me the most is that the army has become a god. Now God is more efficient, too."

In another scene, entitled "Our Secret Weapon—Jacob the Robot," Mr. Kenan turns his needle to the military solution he believes many Israelis seek automatically to every problem.

On the stage, Jacob answers every question that is posed to him (How much are two and two? What do you think of our foreign policy?) with a burst of machine-gun fire, finally gunning himself down in the process.

In one of the most controversial sketches, two Israeli mothers argue over whose son died a more horrible death in the war.

"Mine was blown away like a piece of dust," one says smugly.

"Mine walked for thousands of miles; they had to give him a new pair of legs," the other counters.

Mr. Kenan readily admits that such scenes will be painful for many Israelis, but he contends that he is trying to shock them into recognizing the changes that are taking place within their society.

"Many people have begun idolizing the army without realizing it," he says. "It will take something drastic to open their eyes."

'Village, Demented Mind'

Judging by letters to editors that the play has provoked the Israeli press, not everyone is willing to take their lessons from Mr. Kenan. "What we don't need," wrote one outraged man after he had seen the play, "is instruction from a vulgar, demented mind."

To circumvent the censor's ban, Mr. Kenan is rewriting the play and deleting all references to Jesus, the cross and Mary. The title will be changed to "Spartacus, As Seen by His Friends."

"Jesus is not central to my play," Mr. Kenan said in an interview. "I used him and the cross as a symbol of persecution."

* * *

October 17, 1973

ISRAELI PRESS CURB ILLUSTRATES PROBLEMS IN COVERAGE OF WAR

By TERENCE SMITH
Special to The New York Times

BEERSHEBA, Israel, Oct. 16—Israeli military authorities today barred newsmen from the Sinai Peninsula, where a major battle of the war remains to be fought.

The action was one illustration of why certain aspects of the Israeli-Arab war are reported in detail, and others not at all.

A group of journalists including this reporter was turned back early this morning when it reached this Negev town, which serves as the headquarters for the southern command. The newsmen had departed for the canal front from Tel Aviv two hours earlier with an escort officer and full authorization to visit the Israeli lines in Sinai.

An Israeli source said later that the newsmen had been barred because of intensified shelling and fighting in the central sector of the front.

Problem for Newsmen

The curb was an example of the problems the still-growing army of foreign journalists is encountering in attempting to report Israel's fourth war with the Arabs.

The international press corps that gathered in Israel—this week is one of the largest ever assembled anywhere. More than 600 newspaper and magazine reporters, photographers and television personnel from more than 30 countries have been accredited since the war began 11 days ago.

The basic Israeli policy is not to permit newsmen to accompany forces at the front. The policy seems to stem not so much from a desire for secrecy as a concern over congestion at the front and the safety of the newsmen.

As a result, no newsmen were permitted to visit either front until last Wednesday, the fifth day of the war. By then, the Israelis had broken the back of the Syrian offensive in the Golan heights and had retaken all but small pockets of the area west of the former cease-fire line.

Since then, reporters have had considerable freedom of movement on the Golan heights.

Because of the area's rolling, almost treeless terrain and because the forces there are relatively concentrated, it is possible to see the fighting on the Syrian front and to follow its course in at least a limited area.

In Sinai, however, it has been another story. The area is vast, the front is three times as long as that on the Golan heights and the Israeli forces have been mostly on the defensive.

Until the area was closed today, newsmen were able to drive to bases 15 to 20 miles back from the canal. But they saw little real action.

In the absence of personal observation, newsmen have only the official military communiqués issued several times a day and a nightly briefing provided in Tel Aviv by a reserve colonel from the army spokesman's office.

Data Often Conflict

Frequently the information and battle-damage figures conflict with the descriptions emanating from the Arab countries, leaving the newsmen little alternative but to take account of both.

One factor influencing the reporting from the Israeli side is the military censorship of all news articles and film transmitted from here. All articles, including this one, must be submitted in advance of transmission to military censors who scrutinize them line by line for information they regard as useful to the enemy. Israeli censorship is in effect even in peacetime, but is far more rigorously applied in wartime.

In most cases, the deletions ordered by the censors are arguable on the grounds of legitimate security interests of a nation at war. In some instances, however, the objective is clearly to sustain the public morale and protect the Israeli image.

* * *

June 2, 1974

THAILAND'S PRESS PLAYS WIDER ROLE

Papers Enjoy New Freedom Under Civilian Regime, but Responsibility Is Urged

By JAMES M. MARKHAM
Special to The New York Times

BANGKOK, Thailand, May 30—Thailand's press, which has long been one of the freest in Asia, is trying to come to grips with the almost limitless freedom bestowed on it by the new civilian administration.

Even under the military government of Field Marshal Thanom Kittikachorn, the Thai press was free of formal censorship, though telephone calls to newspaper offices and threats to revoke publishing licenses were common.

But, almost symbolically, shortly after the collapse of the Thanom regime last October, the new civilian Premier, Sanya Dharmasakti, called leading editors to meet with him to tell him, as one put it, "what the people wanted."

Since then, in the absence of a popularly elected legislature, the press has become the de factor voice of that great abstraction, the people.

Mr. Sanya, a distinguished jurist and former university rector whose frequent chats with reporters resemble Socratic dialogues, declared early in his tenure that he would resign if the press wanted him to.

Cabinet Widely Criticized

And last week he did resign, following criticism of his Cabinet not only in the press but by university organizations, the interim National Assembly and other groups.

This week Mr. Sanya, who accepted a parliamentary appeal to return to office, was in the process of heeding another long-standing demand of the press: reshuffling his Cabinet.

The press's new-found powers have given some thoughtful Thai journalists pause. For Thai newspapers, as Thai journalists freely concede, are not without their shortcomings.

"Freedom of the press does not automatically improve the media because it does not bring with it an instant awareness of responsibility," said Suthichai Yoon, editor of The Nation, an English-language daily.

Rumors are sometimes published as fact ("Sanya to Use Computer to Select Cabinet," one paper said this week); facts are not always checked; headlines are often misleading ("Kukrit Commits Suicide," said a banner headline in one paper over a report about the Assembly Speaker, Kukrit Pramoj, who had "committed political suicide" by holding a birthday party in a time of austerity); photographs are doctored.

'The Hired Gun'

Certain small newspapers, such as one known among journalists as "the hired gun," have been known to blackmail businessmen with the threat of unfavorable publicity. Some gossip columnists, whose offerings are avidly read, reportedly accept payoffs. Crime reporters, whose articles regularly begin with long lists of policemen's names, are said to be too cozy with their sources of information.

"Journalists believe about 60 per cent of what they read in other newspapers," said Pongsak Payakvichien, who edits the weekly Pracha Chart and writes a column of news about the press for it. "But they believe their own newspapers a little more," he said.

Mr. Pongsak was half-joking, but Thai newsmen do worry about the credibility of their profession.

"Sometimes there's too much freedom," said Sanit Ekkachai, chief editor of the mass circulation Daily News. "I want to keep the freedom but have someone control the irresponsible papers so they will not misuse the new freedom."

Mr. Sanit, who was jailed in 1958 by the military government for a year, is concerned that remnants from the "old regime" are using small newspapers to make what he considers groundless partisan sallies against the new civilian order.

Favors Press Council

Though he believes that the bulk of the Thai press is responsible, Mr. Sanit, like some other editors, favors the establishment of a press council to establish certain standards of ethics. He also would like to see Thailand's nominal libel law strengthened.

As is the case in other countries, there are editors here who oppose the idea.

"We will not be a member," said Narong Ketudat, the 31-year-old editor and publisher of Prachathipatai, a highly respected daily. "We will be responsible, but by ourselves," he declared.

Prachathipatai, which has a conservative layout and sober tone that set it off from most Thai papers, emerged in 1972 under Mr. Narong's management and provided a striking example of a new generation of journalists' coming of age.

Since last October, more than 400 applications for newspaper licenses have been filed with the Government and about 300 have been accepted, a guarantee that as Thailand moves toward a full democratic system, the press will be heard from.

PART VII

THE DECLINE AND FALL OF COMMUNIST REGIMES, 1975–1999

THE UNITED STATES AND WESTERN EUROPE

February 1, 1976

MADRID LIFTS FILM CURB AS CULTURAL REINS EASE

Special to The New York Times

MADRID, Jan. 31—Abolition of censorship for film scripts has just been announced and it appears to be part of the effort to make Spain less different from the rest of Western Europe in culture as well as in politics.

But just as there is resistance to political change by conservatives who used to proclaim that "Spain is different," the liberalization—noted in movies, the theater and the press, especially in the treatment of sexual matters—is not making everyone happy here. The Roman Catholic Church has been particularly critical.

The movies and the theater have been the last fields where prior censorship has been exercised. It was abolished for the press eight years ago and it is applied to books only in a very limited way. The decision to lift the requirement that a film script be submitted to official review before shooting could start was greeted with great satisfaction in the industry. Now the Government is under stronger pressure than ever to take the same step for plays. It is expected to yield soon.

But like opposition groups that have daily grown more aggressive in testing and seeking to widen the limits of political freedom in Spain, the theater, the movies and the press have for several months been taking matters into their own hands. As far as moral and political standards are concerned, they have found the greatest official tolerance in 40 years.

Two plays on homosexual themes, one of them Matthew Crowley's "The Boys in the Band," are playing to packed houses, Bertolt Brecht's "The Resistible Rise of Arturo Ui" on the theme of Nazism and dictatorship, is one of Madrid's biggest hits despite some threats from extreme-right groups.

A number of films that would not have been shown here a year ago, like "Midnight Cowboy" and "A Clockwork Orange," have been allowed in, receiving favorable reception by critics and public. Movies and plays are showing more uncovered flesh than ever before.

So are magazines, a number of which have experienced a spectacular rise in sales. Wary of official disapproval and the still relatively rigid moral climate here, most of the magazines adopt the Playboy style, but without removing all the clothes. When one does carry a nude, the issue is usually sold out or else seized on the ground of being "offensive to good customs."

The question of "destape," uncovering of the body, has become a major issue. The church's Commission for the Doctrine of the Faith recently warned against "moral deterioration" in the movies, the theater and the press. It attacked Government tolerance of certain movies that had "clearly pornographic bedroom scenes."

The Ministry of Information, where censorship is centered, indicated how much official thinking had changed by answering that "public opinion should no longer confuse nudity with pornography, nor pornography with eroticism." The ministry said: "Pornography is absolutely forbidden by censorship norms now in force which authorize nudity only when it is not pornographic."

The norm as far as movies and plays are concerned is that nudity is permissible when it is essential to the story and is not displayed for its own sake. The Government's statement said that movies ought not to be harmful to children, adolescents and youths "since only those older than 18 are authorized to witness films in which there are themes and scenes of a problematical nature.

"Even in these cases," the statement added, "attendance in movie houses is a voluntary act by each spectator who is the one ultimately responsible for his conduct."

But the Government has indicated that the new permissiveness will have its limits. A new law on pornography is reported to be in preparation and officials of the Ministry of Information said foreign publications featuring nudity would continue to be kept out of Spain. An occasional nude in a review of general circulation will be acceptable "as long as it is not obscene or pornographic."

* * *

April 27, 1976

SPANIARDS, IN POLL, REJECT MOVIE CURBS

By HENRY GINIGER

Special to The New York Times

MADRID, April 26—After almost 40 years of film censorship, most Spaniards reject the notion that the state should watch over public morals, according to a poll just taken.

The poll was commissioned by the Government and, in accordance with the freer climate here, it has served as a basis for loosening state controls. Censorship of movie scripts was abolished recently and greater tolerance toward Spanish and foreign pictures is now seen in the variety of films being shown here compared with last year.

The results of the poll were cited by the Minister of Information. Adolfo Martin-Gamero, at the opening of a film festival in Valladolid yesterday. "The state has the duty," he said. "to see that the process of communication represented by movies be carried out freely and smoothly."

Mr. Martin-Gamero promised that the Government, through a new cinema law, would seek diversification—"a cinema that is pluralistic, since Spanish society also is pluralistic."

2,000 People Questioned

The poll was taken among 2,000 people over the age of 15 described as representative. Those most favorable to the liberalization of films, tended to be younger than the rest, and the best educated and lived in urban areas with a relatively high attendance at movies.

Some 62 percent of those questioned said that the state should not be the guardian of a person's morals. Only 52 percent, however, were in favor of allowing adults to see all films without cuts and 78 percent said that if censorship was abolished controls should be imposed to protect minors.

According to 62 percent, any danger within a film does not depend on whether someone appears nude in it but rather on the story it tells. Some 46 percent thought freedom of films to express ideas on political, social and cultural problems was good for people's education while 19 percent thought it made no difference one way or another.

While films are now benefiting from the freer atmosphere, the state-run television network continues to be a controversial subject because of several recent cases of censorship of programs that were considered objectionable on political or moral grounds. A series of programs by the Spanish playwright Antonio Gala, who has also run afoul of censors in the theater, was canceled, as was a popular program of irreverent comment by a Spanish journalist named Alfredo Amestoy.

Books Are Seized

Habits of the past also continue in book publishing, although it has traditionally been the freest from official control of any means of expression. Last week, the police seized copies of a book by two Spanish journalists on events in Vitoria last month where five persons died in labor riots. The book was critical of police action.

Another book containing letters and drawings by children from 6 to 11-years of age and addressed to "Dear Mr. King" was also seized without explanation. The publisher said, he could not understand the seizure since the book attacked neither King Juan Carlos nor the monarchy.

However, a letter from another Juan Carlos, aged 9, said: "In Vitoria, there were three dead and the police said they fired in the air. On the walls in front of my school they have written 'Elda—a worker assassinated.' And also 'Elda—no to the murderous monarchy.' " Elda is a town near Alicante where a worker was shot by the Civil Guard.

* * *

March 27, 1979

CENSORSHIP OF TEXTBOOKS IS FOUND ON RISE IN SCHOOLS AROUND NATION

Focus Is on Language Viewed as Obscene, but Ideas, Attitudes and Philosophy Are Challenged as Well

By WAYNE KING

Parent and community groups across the country appear to have stepped up efforts to censor reading materials and course content in the public schools.

The censors, in part reacting to the permissive attitudes that disturbed traditionalists in the late 1960's and early '70's, seem mainly concerned with language they consider obscene or profane, and somewhat less so with sexual or erotic material.

But there is censorship of ideas, attitudes and philosophy as well, as in the case of the Island Trees school district in Nassau, County, where the school board removed 11 books from library shelves on the ground that they were "anti-American, anti-Christian, anti-Semitic and just plain filthy." Two of the books had won the Pulitzer Prize.

In other districts, material has been removed from student access because it was deemed unsupportive of free enterprise or other similar political values.

Significant Increase Found

The Committee Against Censorship of the National Council of Teachers of English found in a recent survey of secondary school teachers that censorship of books and other curriculum material, as well as of school newspapers, had increased significantly since a similar survey in 1966.

A check of school districts in a dozen states and localities across the country by The New York Times found none free of some censorship or controversy; although concerns over the suitability of reading matter varied widely. Censorship ranged from library review committees in most districts to the public burning of a high school English text in Warsaw, Ind.

At Arcadia High School in Scottsdale, Ariz, a course called Paperback Power was renamed Directed Reading and Literature and stripped of graduation credit after parents complained about some of the 6,000 books, which were purchased with student donations rather than school funds and made available in a reading room designed to encourage random reading.

The school board ordered 20 of the books removed, including "Once Is Not Enough" by Jacqueline Susann, all books by Rosemary Rogers and most books by Harold Robbins.

Mature but Easy to Read

"I used them because they were easy to read, but mature," said Robert A. Larabell, the instructor in the course, adding that he was no longer permitted to select the books.

Counselors now suggest that the course no longer exists, Mr. Larabell said, and participation has declined so much that the number of sections of the class has been reduced from seven to two.

In Thatcher, Ariz., the town librarian returned from summer vacation last year to find all periodicals except Arizona Highways and The National Geographic removed from the shelves. The librarian, Emalee Philpott, was instructed, on the ground of limited space, to keep a list of each periodical she stocked and who read it. Earlier, an issue of Sports Illustrated was removed because of an article featuring women's swimsuits, and an issue of Time magazine was removed because of an illustrated article on fashion models.

In Louisiana, state legislators concerned by a rising teen-age pregnancy rate sought unsuccessfully to overturn the state's eight-year-old law forbidding "any courses specifically designated 'sex education' or a course by any other name in which instruction is given to the pupil at any grade level, primarily dealing with the human reproductive system as it pertains specifically to the act of sexual intercourse."

Most Louisiana teachers avoid entirely using the words "sexual intercourse" because of an opinion by the State Attorney General that such use would violate the law, and a standard biology text, "Action Biology," has been banned because it dealt explicitly with the topic.

A study by Tulane University found that 30 percent of people from middle-class homes and 53 percent from lower-class homes had no knowledge of reproductive physiology. Louisiana has the fourth highest teen-age pregnancy rate in the country.

In the 33,000-student Union High School District in Anaheim, Calif., the largest west of the Mississippi, the school board has established a list of 270 books that can be used in English class, and no others are permitted.

James Bonnell, president of the Anaheim school board, said: "The only effort to restrict comes from the content of basic grammar classes. If they teach grammar properly, they will have no need for further books. Nor will they have time for them."

Sharon Scott of the Anaheim Secondary Teachers Association said the district owned more than 200 titles that could no longer be used because they were not on the approved list. Efforts to have other books listed have been rebuffed, she said.

A Course on Capitalism

Seniors are required to take a course called "Free Enterprise," which Miss Scott said contained such questions as "True or false: The Government spends too much money on the environment." The correct answer is "true," she added.

In the Island Trees district, the American Civil Liberties Union is representing parents and students in a lawsuit against the school board for removing 11 books from classrooms and library shelves in early 1976. The suit is pending in Federal District Court. Richard Emery of the A.C.L.U. said the case "brings more clearly to focus a new issue, that is, can books be banned for political, religious and cultural reasons?"

Early in 1976, the school board removed 11 books from classrooms and libraries in the district to review language and attitudes in them.

The books removed were: "Go Ask Alice," author anonymous; "A Reader for Writers," by Jerome W. Archer and A. Schwartz: "A Hero Ain't Nothing but a Sandwich," by Alice Childress; "Soul on Ice," by Eldridge Cleaver; "Best Short Stories by Negro Writers," edited by Langston Hughes; "The Fixer," by Bernard Malamud: "The Naked Ape," by Desmond Morris; "Laughing Boy," by Oliver La Farge; "Black Boy," by Richard Wright; "Down the Mean Streets," by Piri Thomas, and "Slaughterhouse-Five," by Kurt Vonnegut Jr.

Two Won Pulitzer Prizes

"Laughing Boy," which was later returned to the shelves, won the Pulitzer Prize for fiction in 1930, and "The Fixer" won the Pulitzer for fiction in 1967.

Of the 630 high school English teachers who responded to the Committee Against Censorship's survey, 30 percent reported pressure for book censorship, compared with 20 percent in the 1966 survey.

The teachers reported that parents raised 78 percent of the objections, while 19 percent were from some member of the school staff—a dramatic shift from 1966, when 48 percent came from parents and 42 percent from the school staff.

"In a given year," said Lee A. Burress Jr., a member of the committee, one out of five teachers hears objections to books. The result is that in approximately one-third of the cases, books are removed from libraries and recommended reading lists. Thus, one-third of the time censorship efforts are effective in getting books out of use."

* * *

May 3, 1981

FILM ON REVELRY OF CHURCH TREK BANNED IN SPAIN

By JAMES M. MARKHAM

Special to the New York Times

MADRID, May 2—Freedom of artistic expression in post-Franco Spain is a matter of two steps forward, one backward. In the highest tradition of this dialectic, a judge in Seville has banned the showing of a documentary film about a popular Andalusian festival after a right-wing politician said it "gravely insults and ridicules the Catholic religion."

The film, entitled "Rocio," portrays the annual *romeria,* or religious pilgrimage, in the southern Andalusian town of Almonte, which draws tens of thousands of people. Centered on the veneration of a carved wooden image of the Virgin Mary, the festival, like many in the south of Spain, is a wild mixture of unchecked religious passion and drunken revelry.

"At various moments," wrote a film critic, Fernando Lara, "one has to rub one's eyes to believe the passages of violence and fanaticism which we see really happening in a country that calls itself 'civilized' in the final stretch of the 20th century."

One scene depicts several thousand frenzied men trying to seize the chariot bearing the fragile statue.

Set in Civil War Context

The documentary, directed by Fernando Ruiz, recounts the revival of the romeria in the 1930's and maintains that the upper classes used it to steer popular enthusiasm away from the rising leftist tide of the Second Republic.

From the mouths of survivors, the script also recounts right-wing killings of leftists that broke out in Almonte when the civil war began in 1936. By naming names, "Rocio"—the word means "dewdrop" but popularly refers to the Almonte romeria—touched sensitive nerves.

In February, when the documentary had its premiere in Madrid after winning a film festival prize in Seville, movie houses in Andalusia quietly refused to show it.

Last month, when the village of Pilas agreed to allow a showing of "Rocio" in Andalusia, Jose Maria Reales Cala, a right-wing political figure from Almonte, lodged a legal complaint against it.

'The Reaction of the Bosses'

"This is the reaction of the bosses who are still powerful in lower Andalusia," fumed Jose Suarez, the Socialist Mayor of Pilas. "We, who are free men, have to make freedom something that is more than just written on paper. In this country, we have bishops. If the film really offended the church, the bishops could have protested against it."

Mr. Reales Cala, who was the appointed mayor of Almonte for four years until he was replaced by a Socialist in the 1979 elections and who is a member of the brotherhood that organizes the Almonte procession, said he was reluctant to discuss his legal action since the case was before the court.

Initially, the judge, Jose Juan Cabeza, ordered the seizure of all copies of the film in Spain. After seeing the film, however, he ruled that "Rocio" could not be shown in the Andalusian provinces of Huelva, Seville and Cadiz, where the tradition of the romeria is strongest—as is interest in the movie.

Judge Cabeza rejected the argument that "Rocio" insulted the church, but he found that, by suggesting that Mr. Reales Cala's father had instigated the killings of leftists in Almonte in 1936, the documentary might insult the family's honor.

The judge said that the film could be construed as presenting the Reales Cala family as "sons of a leader of a gang of murderers."

Memory of War Still Strong

"The memory of the Civil War is so strong," he wrote, "that one cannot consider its events as belonging to history." Until the case is decided on appeal, Mr. Ruiz, the director, and the film's script writer, Ana Vila, must present themselves twice a month at the Seville court, and they have been obliged to put up a bond equivalent to $57,000.

Mr. Reales Cala's legal quarrel has delayed the distribution of "Rocio" and, some filmmakers fear, may have given ideas to others who, leaning on Spain's antiquated penal code, might want to hamper future productions. But at the same time, the former mayor of Almonte has given the film free publicity that it would never have enjoyed as just another documentary. The betting in legal circles in Seville is that the film will eventually be shown.

"Rocio" is not the first film to stir the ire of the right wing. In 1978, a film entitled "The Marvelous Life of Father Vicente" mocked the life of Vicente Ferrer, the patron saint of Valencia and one of the founding fathers of the Inquisition. The theater that held the premiere of the film was bombed, and "Father Vicente" was later boycotted in much of the region.

Another Film Is Cleared

If the action against "Rocio" was one step backward, then freedom of artistic expression took two steps forward last month when another controversial movie, "The Crime of Cuenca," was finally declared by a state prosecutor to be fit for showing. Without explanation, but under clear pressure from the military, the Government had ordered the film seized in December 1979. It later passed to military jurisdiction.

The film, which depicts a miscarriage of justice that occurred in 1913, has several gruesome passages in which Civil Guards torture two innocent men into confessing to a crime that never happened.

"This has been like a liberation," declared Pilar Miro, the director of "The Crime of Cuenca." Jokingly she added: "Now I'm thinking about a movie about a coup d'etat that attempts to topple a democratic system."

* * *

December 20, 1981

BOOK BANNING IN AMERICA

By COLIN CAMPBELL

A censorial spirit is at work in the United States, and for the past year or so it has focused more and more on books. Efforts to remove certain titles from school and public libraries, from paperback racks and bookstores, from the eyes of the adults as well as children, have increased measurably.

Two months ago, the Supreme Court agreed to review a case stemming from the decision in 1976 by the school board of Island Trees, Long Island, to remove nine books from its libraries and curriculum: Bernard Malamud's "The Fixer"; Kurt Vonnegut's "Slaughterhouse-Five"; "Go Ask Alice," the anonymous diary of a young girl who died of a drug overdose; Eldridge Cleaver's "Soul on Ice"; "A Reader for Writers," an anthology edited by Jerome Archer; "Down These Mean Streets," Piri Thomas's realistic novel of Puerto Rican street life in New York City; "A Hero Ain't Nothin' But a

Sandwich" by Alice Childress; "The Naked Ape" by Desmond Morris; and "Best Short Stories by Negro Writers," edited by Langston Hughes. According to one of the board's press releases, the books were "anti-American, anti-Christian, anti-Semitic [sic] and just plain filthy."

A Federal Court of Appeals declared last year that it was "permissible and appropriate" for local school boards "to make decisions based upon their personal, social, political and moral views." The court thereby upheld a 1977 ban by the school board in Warsaw, Ind., against five books, including Sylvia Plath's novel "The Bell Jar." The case became notorious after a local senior citizens' organization supported the board's ban on another book—"Values Clarification," which discusses marijuana, divorce and other controversial topics—by collecting 40 copies from school authorities and setting them on fire.

In Abingdon, Va., the public library has been fending off attacks on "Goodbye, Columbus" by Phillip Roth, "The Lonely Lady" by Harold Robbins, "Bloodline" by Sidney Sheldon and other novels that the Rev. Tom Williams of Emmanuel Baptist Church calls "pornography." Pastor Williams is supported by a slim minority of county supervisors who keep threatening to cut off library funds. In a recent county election, which threw out one anti-library candidate, a supporter of the banning was nonetheless re-elected, and one supervisor who had supported the library declined to run.

Last summer in Atlanta, Ga., a recently passed state law against displaying "lewd" and "lascivious" books and pictures wherever minors might see them caused the chief book buyer for a chain of department stores, Rich's, to postpone ordering any new books. The law, which a Federal judge overturned in October, would have outlawed the "showing" of "any book. . . which contains descriptions or depictions of illicit sex or sexual immorality." Faith Brunson, the Rich's buyer, said recently that the law would have required her to change the department store's purchasing policies "totally." Similar "harmful-to-minors" laws have been enacted, and are still on the books, in Florida, Pennsylvania, Maryland and Colorado.

Such cases are on the increase nationally, according to the American Library Association's Office for Intellectual Freedom in Chicago. Over the past six months, more than 100 titles have been either removed or threatened with removal from both school and public libraries in more than 30 states. During the early 1970's, the office received approximately 100 complaints a year that library books had been removed or threatened with removal. The complaints shot up to 300 a year in the late 70's, and are nearing 1,000 a year this year. (That does not mean 1,000 titles; objections are being registered to many of the same books.) And, although three years ago just 10 percent of the complaints concerned public libraries, now 20 to 30 percent concern them—a rise from a couple of dozen in 1979 to more than 200 this year. There have been more and more demands as well that certain books in public libraries not merely be restricted to adult readers but that they actually be removed from the premises.

The reason that censors and would-be censors give most often is that a book is unsuitable for minors because of its vulgarity or its descriptions of sexual behavior. But the censors also condemn the depiction of unorthodox family arrangements, sexual explicitness even in a biological context, speculation about Christ, unflattering portraits of American authority, criticisms of business and corporate practices, and radical political ideas.

Significantly, there are no clear Federal laws that specify what rights school boards or local governments have to decide what books will be available in school or public libraries. That is one reason why the Supreme Court has agreed to review the Island Trees case, as a way of sorting out the conflicting rights of local authorities and readers.

In Island Trees, five high school students first took the local school board to court in 1976 to challenge its right to remove books from its school libraries. The plaintiffs argued that the board had denied them their First Amendment rights of free expression and had introduced "a pall of orthodoxy" into the school community. The board has replied that parents and elected school boards are empowered by state law and long-established custom to decide what will be taught and read in local public schools. The board has also argued that the students' rights of free speech were not denied by the removal of the libraries' books and that the First Amendment rights of minors are in any case circumscribed by law and common sense. The case could become a landmark and is being carefully watched.

Recent attempts to remove books from school libraries are better documented from public libraries and bookstores. According to a national survey sponsored by the Association of American Publishers, the American Library Association and the Association for Supervision and Curriculum Development, the following books are among those that have either been removed from school libraries or been allowed to remain only after being altered or restricted.

The fiction titles include "Jaws" by Peter Benchley; many books by Judy Blume, a best-selling author of sexually explicit books for children and young adults; "The Pill Versus the Springhill Mine Disaster" and other novels by Richard Brautigan; "Manchild in the Promised Land" by Claude Brown; "Kramer vs Kramer" by Avery Corman; "Catch-22" by Joseph Heller; "Sons" by Evan Hunter; "Valley Forge" by MacKinlay Kantor; "The Thorn Birds" by Colleen McCullough; "The Godfather" by Mario Puzo; "Portnoy's Complaint" by Philip Roth; "One Day in the Life of Ivan Denisovich" by Aleksandr Solzhenitsyn.

And among nonfiction: The American Heritage Dictionary; The Dictionary of American Slang; "Trial of the Catonsville Nine" by Daniel Berrigan; "Our Bodies, Ourselves" by the Boston Women's Health Book Collective; "The Art of Loving" by Erich Fromm; "Boss: Richard J. Daley of Chicago" by Mike Royko; "The Electric Kool-Aid Acid Test" by Tom Wolfe.

Also: "A Farewell to Arms," "1984," "Brave New World," "The Merchant of Venice," and "Stuart Little."

The survey names scores of other titles. Yet only 15 percent of such incidents are ever mentioned in local newspapers, according to the survey's finding. Even fewer get national attention.

In the vanguard of this nationwide campaign to take some books out of general circulation are dozens of religious and political organizations whose names aren't necessarily familiar in the context of books. They include the Heritage Foundation, a Washington brain trust known for its conservative position papers; The Moral Majority; the Gabler family in Longview, Tex., which analyzes textbooks and distributes a newsletter to more than 10,000 Americans; Phyllis Schlafly's Eagle Forum; the Pro-Family Forum; state groups like Parents of Minnesota; and countless local outfits like Western Pennsylvania Citizens Against Pornography in Butler County or Citizens for True Freedom in Ogden, Utah.

The fundamentalists and far-rightists among those groups have received support, at least for their ideas on school libraries, from large numbers of more traditional conservatives; from more liberal-minded people who have recoiled from the full effects of the recent, extraordinarily uncensored social environment; and, most significantly, from the courts.

The censors have also found support, and in some cases, precedents, among feminists who decry pornography, blacks opposed to the way blacks are depicted in films and history books, homosexuals organized against unpleasant images of homosexuality, Jews who believe that young people should be protected from "The Merchant of Venice," and textbook publishers who have responded to shifting educational fashions by jerkily revising the facts and tone of American history.

Most local groups zero in on titles they learn about from the newsletters and direct mailings of right-wing and special-interest groups. Some organizations also provide useful ideological contexts for their efforts—such as the Moral Majority's contention that a "religion of secular humanism" values lead to promiscuity, divorce and crime.

"We're not censors," more than one school-library critic has said; the issue, rather, is how one raises children according to society's values. Ivan B. Gluckman, general counsel to the 33,000-member National Association of Secondary School Principals, says that if school board meetings have become battlegrounds where even an author like Malamud may get shot down, well, "There' s a remedy for such bad decisions—vote 'm out of office." rule. On the contrary, they want to protect certain other principles that majority opinion may endanger: The American Booksellers Association, the American Library Association, The Media Coalition, the Coalition Against Censorship, The Association of American Publishers—whose president, Townsend Hoopes, recently testified against Georgia's "minors-access" books from censors. So do those who have offered friend-of-the-court briefs and other legal aids during the litigation over Island Trees, including: The American Civil Liberties Union, the American Jewish Congress, the Writers Guild of America, the National Council of Teachers of English, the Unitarian Universalist Association, the Anti-Defamation League of B'nai B'rith, the American Jewish Committee, PEN American Center and the National Education Association.

Some of these groups, like the American Library Association's Office for Intellectual Freedom, publish newsletters that carry information about cases of book banning. All, despite disagreements, worry that books may become less available. "You just can't start taking books off the library shelves by majority vote," said Leanne Katz of the National Coalition Against Censorship.

The political passions now let loose are intense. Defenders of books have called the banners "New Yorker magazine wondered out loud if school board members bent on banning books realized what trouble they might face in court: "Would you feel comfortable having to elaborate on why you find the material objectionable?. . . Do you like publicity? Notoriety?" This one board member told me that if I had any personal property I should get it out of my name. If the district wins, he said, they're going to sue me, personally.

Mr. Pico, who was Student Council president when he first became a plaintiff in the Island Trees case, has now graduated from college. Unlike many of his supporters, he has some sympathy for what his community and its school board want to do. "They're trying to protect their children," Mr. Pico's lawyers say the banning was a political purge rather than an exercise of the community's normal authority to educate the young. Two board members entered the high school library at night with a checklist of titles and authors they had acquired at a conservative political meeting. The school board subsequently ordered that nine books be removed from the library on the basis of selected quotations from them. Only later did the board give the books a full reading. The decision to ban the books remained firm.

"The facts are awful," says Gwendolyn Gregory, a lawyer for the National Association of School Boards in Washington. She was using "facts" in the legal sense, and was suggesting why some organizations like hers—which would normally bend over backwards to defend a school board's authority—had decided not to join the Island Trees board in its legal fight.

Although the board's lawyers have argued that "bad taste" and "vulgar language" made the books intolerable, early attacks on them by board members seemed to make as much of the books' political and religious views as of their language. One banned book, "A Reader for Writers," infuriated three board members originally because a selection in it had compared Malcolm X favorable with the Foundation Fathers; one of the board's objections to Vonnegut's "Slaughterhouse Five" was that it has a character who insults the name of Jesus Christ. In an affidavit the school board's president explained his position this way: "I feel that it is my duty to apply my conservative principles to the decision-making process in which I am involved as a board member, and I have done so with regard to fiscal matters, student discipline, teacher performance, union negotiations, curriculum formation and other educational matters," margins. In the meantime, while lamenting efforts to "sanitize the library," First Amendment was not at issue. Judge Pratt's 1979 ruling also endorsed the reasoning of the Federal Court of Appeals in a 1972 case over "Down These Mean Streets." The court had said than that books do not acquire "tenure" by sitting on a shelf, and that the school board is as free to remove books as it is to acquire them.

These were not the last words, however. Later in 1979 the case went to a three-man panel of the Federal Court of Appeals for the Second Circuit. With one judge dissenting, the panel last year reversed Judge Pratt's decision. It said that the First Amendment might be at stake, and that a trial was needed to decide the matter. Last spring the whole Court of Appeals met and disagreed 5-5 over whether to overturn the panel's ruling. The case was still headed for trial when the Supreme Court granted the school board's request that it intervene with an opinion of its own.

The board's latest brief was sent to Washington a few weeks ago. It repeats the argument that school boards have the right to protect juveniles from "indecent expression." But it also observes that "all school systems carry on some form of political indoctrination in the better sense of the word" and that a public school is "an instrument of political socialization.

This puts the issue in plain terms. And although the board's asserts that, in its own case, "the record" happens not to disclose any "political motivation," it nonetheless asks the Court to comment on whether "political" thinking may be inevitable and proper in such decisions.

Lawyers for both camps in Pico v. Island Trees have come to agree: The law itself is less than clear.

The Supreme Court has said, in a 1969 decision concerning students'right to protest, that neither teachers nor students "shed their constitutional rights to freedom of speech or expression at the schoolhouse gate." Yet the Court has also said, in Epperson v. Arkansas (1968), that courts "school systems and which do not directly and sharply implicate basic constitutional values." for example, preceded a court ruling that upheld the right of school authorities to remove the volumes. Other opinions, in sharp contrast, have been more concerned with protecting the rights of readers and students. One Federal Court of Appeals held in 1976 that, once the state of Ohio and an Ohio school district had created a high school library, "neither body could place conditions on the use of the library which were related solely to the social or political tastes of school board members." Two rulings from district courts later added that a library's decisions must not be based on content, but must deal only with such "neutral" matters as shelf space.

These cases have raised other questions. Is the freedom to speak and write linked inextricably to a "right to read," as some court decisions have suggested in limited contests? If so, does such a principle apply even to a public school, which the Island Tree board and many others argue is a " unique social structure?"

A few battlers on each side would be content to see the Supreme Court uphold their own most extreme personal views—such as that school boards should be allowed to require instruction in religion and patriotism, or that students should be allowed to test in court any number of school decisions. Yet the more widespread desire is simply for guidance. As Gwendolyn Gregory, the lawyer for the National Association of School Boards, says: "I hope they go to the heart of the matter"—of rights in conflict. One often mentioned route to compromise would be to protect school libraries from excessive community pressures by providing clearer definition of what constitutes acceptable library procedure for acquiring, removing and circulating books. The Court, for instance, might authorize librarians to reconcile local values and pedagogic values when they are in conflict. Some defenders of books, however, fear that procedural compromises might only legitimize book banning along administratively "correct" lines.

As for removing books from bookstores and public libraries, the law is also less than clear.

Lawyers who have been fighting state "minor-access" laws consider them extremely dangerous. According to Maxwell J. Lillienstein, the lawyer for the American Booksellers Association, the legal removal of books from retail shelves because they are "harmful to minors," though not legally obscene, could strip the bookracks in supermarkets, drugstores, airports and other places—besides bookstores—where adults buy best sellers and classics. Michael Bamberger, the lawyer for the Media Coalition of publishers and distributors who persuaded a Federal judge to strike down Georgia's law, wonders if similar statues might be worded subtly enough not to offend other judges.

The law is far less clear about public libraries, since few cases for removal or restriction have gone to court. Librarians do have certain rights of due process; a Federal judge not long ago ordered that a librarian in Utah be rehired after she was fired for refusing to take a book of the shelves. But this and a few state-level precedents don't weigh much.

One might assume that adults have the right to borrow whatever library books are available. But what about the "rights" of library boards and city councils to censor the shelves, as several have attempted to do? What about a local government's power to install librarians who suit its tastes in acquisitions? Most library boards across the country are either appointed by elected officials or are directly elected—like school boards.

According to a lawyer for the American Library Association, it is hard to know how such questions might be answered in court if challenges to public library books sharpen.

What defenders of books and their free circulation hope is that certain principles will remain firmly established. Among them:

The literary marketplace for adults must not be legally restricted in such a way that it reduces "the adult population to reading what is only fit for children." So the Supreme Court said in Butler v. Michigan (1957). The Supreme Court has also stated, in Erzoznick v. Jacksonville (1975): "Minors are entitled to a significant measure of First Amendment protection, and only relatively narrow and well-defined circumstances may government bar public dissemination of protected materials to them." Moreover, Judge Jon O. Newman pointed out last year that even a 1972 Court of Appeals decision which acknowledged that indoctrination is "a principle function of all elementary and secondary education" nevertheless condemned " 'indoctrination' in the sense of endeavoring to insist that one set of values must be accepted by the students." partially political could easily be seen as "an official message" to the community "considered."

What many want to see preserved, whether through law or some deeper cultural and political consensus, is a spirit of tolerance toward the written word.

There are signs that such views will indeed weather the recent challenges. After all, Georgia's "minor-access" law was struck down. Some censorial school boards have been voted out of office; so have some local officials willing to pull books from public libraries. In Oak Lawn, Ill., for instance, a furious campaign to remove the picture book "Show Me!" who borrow "questionable" volumes have been foiled by the passage of laws that keep this information secret.

Faith Brunson, the Atlanta book buyer, was asked what she thought the future held for censors. "Supreme Court will agree and, beyond that, whether the conflicting rights, as they are now being argued, can be easily reconciled in practice whatever the Court decides.

* * *

April 5, 1982

THE FAMED WILL GATHER TO READ THE FORBIDDEN

By MICHIKO KAKUTANI

"Censorship ends in logical completeness," George Bernard Shaw once wrote, "when nobody is allowed to read any books except the books nobody can read."

Shaw's own plays, ironically enough, were once withdrawn from New York City library shelves, just as many other classic works of literature have, from time to time, been banned, expurgated or restricted in this country. Indeed, the list of books currently being challenged in public schools and libraries across the nation includes such disparate works as Ernest Hemingway's "A Farewell to Arms," John Steinbeck's "Grapes of Wrath," J.D. Salinger's "Catcher in the Rye," P.L. Travers's "Mary Poppins" and L. Frank Baum's "The Wizard of Oz."

This evening at 8 o'clock, a group of prominent writers and actors will assemble at the Public Theater to read from some of these "Forbidden Books," as the program is called. Among others, John Irving will read from Hawthorne's "The Scarlet Letter," Erica Jong from Kurt Vonnegut's "Slaughterhouse-5," E.L. Doctorow from F. Scott Fitzgerald's "The Great Gatsby" and Toni Morrison from Ralph Ellison's "Invisible Man."

Organized by the writer's group P.E.N., the evening marks the start of that organization's "American Right to Read" program, which will send writers to communities across the country to speak about books and First Amendment rights.

Calling Attention to Banning

Dedicated by its charter to defend freedom of expression, P.E.N. has frequently worked on behalf of imprisoned writers and censored writing abroad. Its president, Richard Gilman, says if "you defend writers in one place, you have to defend them in another—we need to call attention to the fact that books, books the literary community considers important, are being banned in this country today."

"Any attempt to censor, control or modulate the creative act is a sign people aren't being as responsive to freedom of expression as they should be," said Edward Albee, who will read from Aleksandr Solzhenitsyn's "One Day in the Life of Ivan Denisovich."

"If you want to use the metaphor, minimal censorship is a signal our democracy is in danger—it certainly shows cracks," Mr. Albee added, speaking of the growing number of national attempts to restrict certain books.

The American Library Association reports that in the early 1970's it received about 100 complaints a year concerning the removal or threatened removal of books from library shelves. This rose to an average of 300 complaints a year during the late 70's, and since mid-1980 has increased to nearly 1,000 a year. All in all, 148 titles have been challenged in 34 states—a figure that the association emphasizes represents only reported cases of censorship.

"I think we're sort of in a bad national mood insofar as the Bill of Rights is concerned," said Arthur M. Schlesinger Jr., who is scheduled to read from Aldous Huxley's "Brave New World."

Ultimate Victory Predicted

"I think the Moral Majority and other groups are taking advantage of local situations to deny access to people in local high schools and people who depend on public libraries," Mr. Schlesinger said. "But we've been through things like this in the past and we'll get out of it this time, too—by objecting."

Conservative political and religious groups such as the Moral Majority and Phyllis Schlafly's Eagle Forum have figured prominently in recent attempts to remove books from libraries and schools.

Judith Krug, director of the library association's office of intellectual freedom, said, however, "Over a given period of time, the number of complaints will level out over the political spectrum—there will be as many left-of-center complaints as right-of-center complaints."

During the late 1960's and early 70's, she said, objections centered on material—from "Little Black Sambo" to "The Merchant of Venice"—that was considered racist, sexist or discriminatory. Today, charges tend to focus on titles regarded by the right of center as anti-American, antifamily or obscene.

For some writers, this trend—like the efforts of right-wing groups to eliminate sex-education courses in the schools and to censor textbooks—reflects the growing conservatism of the country galvanized by the election of President Reagan. Others see it as less a strictly political matter than a social one—a kind of reaction to the confusions of the 60's.

Frustration and Fear Cited

Studs Terkel, for instance, whose book "Working" was recently the subject of controversy in Girard, Pa., regards the new censorial mood as the result, in part, of certain frustrations and fears. Feeling incapable of protecting their children, he says, some parents have reacted to threatening ideas and language by trying to dispose of the books that contain them. "They're looking for something they can control," he said, "so they go after something easy—something they can get rid of like the dirty word."

For Gay Talese, though, who will read from "A Farewell to Arms," the recent wave of book bannings is not a new phenomenon at all. It is simply the latest manifestation of a moralizing spirit that has infected American communities since the days of the Puritans. "In the interests of virtue and the betterment of society," said the author of "Thy Neighbor's Wife," "we've always had elements trying to control what can be read or distributed, whether it's film, pictures or the written word. We've always had moral vigilantes who want to tell us what's good for us."

What's "good for us" apparently differs greatly from community to community. P.E.N. reports, for instance, that parents in Sumner, Wash., tried unsuccessfully to ban "Brave New World" from the local school curriculum, arguing that the novel promoted drug abuse, sexual promiscuity, anti-Christianity and secular humanism. The American Heritage Dictionary was removed from school libraries and classrooms in Eldon, Mo., because of objectionable definitions it offered for such words as "bed," "tail," and "nut." And the Detroit Public Library System has banned "The Wizard of Oz" since 1957, for reasons of "negativism" and being generally "of no value."

Long Island Ruling Awaited

One of the most controversial and most important of recent cases concerns the 1976 decision by the school board of Island Trees, L.I., to remove nine titles—including Bernard Malamud's "The Fixer," Kurt Vonnegut's "Slaughterhouse-5," Eldridge Cleaver's "Soul on Ice," and Desmond Morris's "The Naked Ape"—from its curriculum and its libraries on the grounds that the books are anti-American, anti-Christian, anti-Semitic "and just plain filthy."

It is a complicated case involving the question of whether education is a local or Federal responsibility, and the Supreme Court, which heard arguments last month, is expected to decide the case before the current term ends. Charles Rembar, the lawyer who worked on obscenity cases involving "Lady Chatterley's Lover," "Tropic of Cancer" and "Fanny Hill," says that whatever the Court's decision, he is essentially optimistic. "If there are setbacks, I think they'll be small and temporary," he said. "The overall graph of history in this country is an ascending line of freedom of expression."

To insure that curve of history, P.E.N. members say they will continue to fight censorship attempts of any kind. Some plan to testify in court cases—P.E.N. has filed a friend-of-the-court brief in the Island Trees case—and others will travel around the country to speak to students and their teachers.

"From our perspective," said Frances FitzGerald, who recently returned from testifying in a book-banning case in Baileyville, Me., "writers don't have to deal with questions of what the authority of school boards should be. If you write something you believe is true and says something about society, and someone censors it in any way, it seems a violation. It's not a question of writers' rights, but of a standard of truth in the community."

* * *

July 3, 1982

BRITISH REPORTERS TELL NEW SIDE OF FALKLAND STORY

By JAMES FERON
Special to the New York Times

LONDON, July 2—British journalists returning from the Falkland Islands, no longer constrained by censorship, have been writing critical accounts of apparently inadequate British intelligence and military bungling there.

The news stories, unfolding each day for the past week, provide a background for the forthcoming parliamentary inquiry into the South Atlantic war. Many of them recall the reporting of the war in Vietnam.

Many reporters and editors believe that it was the Vietnam experience that influenced the British Ministry of Defense in its handling of the press during the Falkland fighting. John Nicholson, a correspondent for Independent Television News, said "it was a question of 'Look what you people did in Vietnam, turning a nation against the war.' "

The written testimony is being submitted to a bipartisan panel of the Parliamentary Defense Committee, which will begin hearings July 21 into the Government's handling of public and press information.

Non-British Journalists Excluded

Parliament's inquiry into information procedures will be followed by an investigation of intelligence matters by the Foreign Affairs Committee and then a committee of the House of Commons into the entire background of the invasion by Argentina.

The difficulties over coverage of the Falkland war began with a dispute over the selection of correspondents and grew worse as major difficulties developed over censorship and related matters. It has extended to non-British journalists, still unable to visit the islands.

They might find, as did John Witherow of The Times of London, that "the initial mood of delight" among Falkland Islanders that Argentine troops were gone had changed to a realization "that they are still an occupied people, albeit this time occupied by their own forces." He described bitter words between soldiers, who lost friends in the fighting, and locals seeking to get on with their lives.

Fred Emery, executive editor for news at The Times, said the comparison with Vietnam, where he served twice as a correspondent, was "stunning." The American policy, he said, is to "let it all hang out—the press could go anywhere and see anything, and it did.

"We got free helicopter rides all over the country and were just told not to take pictures out of an aircraft, a rule that was generally violated, and not to report operations until they began, which was followed because it was for everyone's safety, including our own."

'An Amazing System'

"That's an amazing system for a British reporter," he said, "because the view of our people is, 'If you are not with us, you're against us.' " The Defense Ministry, he said, "was out to provide facilities under fairly close supervision and it expected people to be part of the team."

A spokesman for the Defense Ministry took exception to a reference to censorship, saying it was the job of ministry officers aboard the task force "to be of assistance to reporters." He declined to describe the terms of reference of the inquiry and said he would not respomd to allegations of what ministry officials "did or did not do" aboard the task force.

Peter Archer of the Press Association, Britain's domestic news agency, was aboard the aircraft carrier Hermes, the flagship of the task force. He said it was "a problem of too many censors, or press officers, on board the ship who did not know what was being done in London."

According to Mr. Witherow, who was on the Invincible, the other aircraft carrier in the task force, news reports went through at least three hands—"the Defense Ministry officer on board the ship, the ship's captain and then the Defense Ministry in London."

"The real problem was being told we could not write about the Sheffield being hit, the Belgrano being sunk or two Sea Harriers colliding at sea, only to turn on the BBC World Service and hear it being announced in London."

Press Blamed for Cod War Defeat

The censorship at sea was "not bad," however, "and on a few occasions they let out stories reluctantly." Editors in London would collect the accounts from the Defense Ministry, sometimes with phrases bracketed indicating that Defense officials hoped they would not be printed.

He said the reporters were briefed fully each day aboard the Invincible by its captain, Jeremy Black, "who told us at one point that he felt Britain lost the cod war with Iceland," a dispute in the early 1970's over fishing rights, "because of a bad press, and he was trying to rectify it."

But another high-ranking officer in the task force drew another conclusion from the Vietnam parallel, a reporter said. "He referred to 'America's traumatic experience,' saying immediate coverage of soldiers being wounded and civilians being killed as turning the public against the war."

In any event, life changed in the war zone. The disputes between reporters and military officials revolved not over restrictions on security matters, which the press accepted, but over delays in transmission, discrepancies in policy with London and the seemingly arbitrary deletion of adjectives, phrases and sometimes entire accounts.

Film Was Not Transmitted

"I know of some copy that never got through," said Mr. Witherow. "A reporter was alongside Sir Galahad when it was hit, killing 50 men. It was the worst single incident of the war for Britain, and the account never arrived."

Brian Hanrahan of the BBC said "the censor on one occasion had a piece of paper on his desk saying no messages are to be transmitted to London."

He added: "We asked him to ring London and request that the restriction be lifted, but he said no messages were to be sent. Finally somebody did ask, and London lifted the restriction."

Mr. Nicholson and Mr. Hanrahan were aboard the Hermes, working as a team with a television crew, but film was never transmitted from the ship. It came later, after the landings, and is still arriving from the Falklands.

Some press officials believe the navy never intended there to be television coverage. Others have said that the width of the transmitting band was insufficient for television, a circumstance known only after the television teams were aboard.

But Mr. Nicholson said "there's no doubt that the signal from Hermes to Scott," a military satellite, "could have worked—black and white and poor quality, perhaps—but we never had the chance. We had a senior technical manager who said all we needed was a test, but it was never granted."

Security Called Main Concern

Military officials, perhaps represented by the Defense Minister, John Nott, are expected to testify that the press agreed to certain restrictions and that security was the main concern. The transmission equipment was to be turned over to television when its was not needed for operational traffic, but that moment never came.

But Mr. Hanrahan, describing what he said was a generally frustrating experience, said "there is a balance to be struck between the military need to keep things secret, to keep their communications locked up, and to provide information in an acceptable form to the country which is supporting, financing and running the operation."

Reporters said they saw the need for censorship, offering as one example the disclosure that many Argentine bombs failed to explode. If that was reported, one journalist said, "it would have prompted the Argies to look quickly to improving their fusing and timing, and we understood that."

* * *

June 26, 1982

HIGH COURT LIMITS BANNING OF BOOKS

By LINDA GREENHOUSE
Special to the New York Times

WASHINGTON, June 25—The Supreme Court ruled today that the First Amendment's guarantee of freedom of speech limits the discretion of public school officials to remove books they consider offensive from school libraries.

In a fragmented ruling on a Long Island case that did not produce a majority opinion, the Court did not define the precise limits of the constitutional right it recognized.

The ruling was nevertheless hailed as an important constitutional victory by book publishers and civil liberties lawyers. In it, five Justices did agree that school officials who are sued by students for taking particular books off the shelves may be required to defend their motives in Federal court.

'Access to Ideas'

The case involved a suit brought by students against the school board of Island Trees Union Free School District in Nassau County, which six years ago removed from the high school library nine books that a politically conservative parents' organization had objected to.

Four of the five Justices, in a plurality opinion for the Court, said the student plaintiffs could win such a suit by proving that the school officials intended to deny them "access to ideas' with which the officials disagreed, "Our Constitution does not permit the official suppression of ideas," Associate Justice William J. Brennan Jr. said in an opinion that was joined by Associate Justices Thurgood Marshall, John Paul Stevens and Harry A. Blackmun.

Tentative as the riding was, it kept the student lawsuit alive. The case now goes back to the Federal District Court for a trial. As it worked its way to the Supreme Court, the Island Trees case became a symbol of a growing national debate over whether school officials who respond to community pressure by removing books from library shelves act appropriately as educators or improperly as censors. There have been dozens of similar incidents around the country.

While the ruling today did not place the Supreme Court firmly on either side of the debate, an opposite ruling would have removed the debate entirely from the realm of constitutional law. With Associate Justice Byron R. White providing the fifth vote, in a cryptic opinion that said little more than that the Island Trees students are entitled to prove their case at trial, the Court essentially held today that the First Amendment applies to such cases.

In a dissenting opinion, Chief Justice Warren E. Burger said that subjecting school board actions of this sort to Federal court review would bring the Supreme Court "perilously close to becoming a 'super censor' of school board library decisions."

Associate Justices Lewis F. Powell, William H. Rehnquist and Sandra Day O'Connor joined the Chief Justices dissent, and all filed dissenting opinions of their own.

'The Fixer' and 'Soul on Ice'

The nine books involved in the case were: "Slaughterhouse-Five," by Kurt Vonnegut; "The Fixer," by Bernard Malamud; "The Naked Ape," by Desmond Morris; "Down These Mean Streets," by Piri Thomas, "Best Short Stories of Negro Writers," edited by Langston Hughes;

"A Hero Ain't Nothin' but a Sandwich," by Alice Childress; "Soul on Ice," by Eldridge Cleaver; "A Reader for Writers," edited by Jerome Archer; and "Go Ask Alice," by an anonymous author.

The Island Trees school board ordered the books removed from the shelves after finding them on a list of "objectionable" books distributed by in organization called Parents of New York United. A school board press release at the time called the books "anti-American, anti-Christian, anti-Semitic and just plain filthy" and said the board had a duty to protect schoolchildren from "this moral danger."

Five high school students, represented by the New York Civil Liberties Union, sued the school board on the ground that the action violated the students' rights under the First Amendment. The Federal District Court ruled without a trial in favor of the school board, a procedure known as summary judgment.

Question of Summary Judgment

Under Federal court procedure, summary judgment is appropriate when the issue is purely one of law, with no significant facts in dispute. The Federal District Court said that no facts were in dispute and that as a matter of law the school board had not infringed upon the students' First Amendment rights.

The United States Court of Appeals for the Second Circuit reversed that ruling. Summary judgment was inappropriate, the appeals court said, because the school boards motives might have been impermissible under the First Amendment and the students were entitled to a trial to determine, as a question of fact, what those motives were.

The school board appealed to the Supreme Court, arguing that it was entitled to summary judgment because the First Amendment was inapplicable to decisions about the contents of school libraries.

Since there has never been a trial, the case, Board of Education v. Pico, No. 80-2043,

presented the Supreme Court with an abstract question: Was there a First Amendment tight at stake at all, or was the school board's action one of unreviewable discretion?

Because Justice White, who cast the fifth vote for that result did not join the plurality opinion, the Federal District Court will not be bound to weigh the evidence under any particular standard when it considers the case.

Reasoning of the Justices

The four Justices in the plurality indicated that the First Amendment would not be violated if the school board "had decided to remove the books at issue because those books were pervasively vulgar" or if "it were demonstrated that the removal decision was based solely upon the 'educational suitability' of the books."

School boards, Justice Brennan said, "rightly possess significant discretion to determine the content of their school libraries." He added "But that discretion may not be exercised in a narrowly partisan or political manner." The test, he said, was whether the board members "intended by their removal decision to deny" the students "access to ideas" with which the board members disagreed.

Justice Brennan delineated the constitutional basis for his views in another section of the opinion in which only Justices Marshall and Stevens joined.

He said the First Amendment protected the students' "right to receive information and ideas," especially in a library. School board members, he said, "might well defend their claim of absolute discretion in matters of curriculum" by the need to "transmit community values." But, Justice Brennan concluded, they cannot "extend their claim of absolute discretion beyond the compulsory environment of the classroom, into the school library and the regime of voluntary inquiry that there holds sway."

In his dissenting opinion, Chief Justice Burger said that the plurality opinion "demeans our function of constitutional adjudication."

Justice Powell Dismayed

While the Chief Justice's tone was angry, Justice Powell, who once served as president of the school board in Richmond, Va., described his own reaction in a dissenting opinion as "genuine

dismay." Whatever the outcome of the suit, Justice Powel said, "the resolution of educational policy decisions through litigation, and the exposure of school board members to liability for such decisions, can be expected to corrode the school board's authority and effectiveness."

Justice Powell's opinion included seven pages of excerpts from the books. Ira Glasser, executive director of the American Civil Liberties Union, said today that the ruling was "a major victory that comes against the backdrop of a national epidemic of school book censorship."

Bruce Rich, general counsel to the Freedom to Read Committee of the Association of American Publishers, called the ruling "marvelous" and said it "sends a very important message to school boards—Act carefully."

* * *

October 3, 1983

BATTLE INTENSIFYING OVER EXPLICIT SEX ON CABLE TV

By SALLY BEDELL SMITH

A nationwide battle is taking shape over sexually explicit programs on cable television.

In a growing number of communities, politicians and citizens' groups are trying to curb such programs, primarily by enacting laws setting new standards for what constitutes indecency on cable television.

At the same time, cable operators are fighting back in court, contending that these restraints amount to censorship. In several cities, most recently Miami, Federal judges have struck down these new laws as unconstitutional, and further legal confrontations are looming.

The efforts to limit what some regard as indecency on cable have increased with the proliferation of programs that offer far more nudity, simulated sex, and profanity than have ever been seen on television.

Unlike conventional commercial television, which is restrained by broadcasting standards in its depiction of sexual content, or movie theaters, which through a ratings system theoretically can exclude minors from seeing sexually explicit films, cable television, once subscribed to, can bring such programs into the home virtually unchecked.

While subscribing to a cable television service is a voluntary act, now that cable is reaching nearly 40 percent of the nation's 83.8 million television households, the prospect of having children view this kind of programming has provoked special concern among some groups. As a result, legislators in more than a dozen states have drafted legislation to restrain cable television with the protection of children in mind.

The cable television programs with explicit sexual content appear on the home screen in several forms. A major source is subscription movie services—channels that offer programming for which viewers pay monthly fees in addition to their basic charge for cable.

These services have been offering an increasing number of sexually explicit films. Among the more daring is "Young Lady Chatterly," which appeared last month on Cinemax, a service with 2.5 million subscribers that is operated by Home Box Office, and "Carry On Emmannuelle," which was shown last month on Showtime, with 4.2 million subscribers.

Subscription services are also featuring original programs, such as "A New Day in Eden," a soap opera with nudity, on Showtime, and nightclub comedy acts laced with off-color jokes, on Home Box Office, which reaches 12.5 million subscribers. And they are offering programs devoted to sexual topics, such as "Eros America," to be introduced this year on Cinemax.

These services also feature other forms of entertainment, including children's shows and sports. But it is the appeal of recent movies—mostly made in Hollywood and screened uncut, uncensored and without commercials—that is credited with establishing the cable television market. And many television executives say that competition posed by such films results in network television presenting programs with increasingly bold sexual content.

In addition to the cable movie services, viewers can subscribe to national cable services that offer nothing but sexually explicit programming; these now can be seen in nearly 2 million homes across the country.

The largest and fastest growing of these ventures is the Playboy Channel. The channel, a joint venture of Playboy Enterprises, was founded by Hugh Hefner of Playboy and several cable system owners: Cablevision of Woodbury, L.I., Daniels and Associates of Denver, and Cox Cable Communications of Atlanta.

Topless Dancing and Fantasies

The Playboy Channel has 500,000 cable subscribers in 275 cable systems around the country, including a scattering of communities in the New York metropolitan area. Among its offerings are such films as "Love and the Sensuous French Woman," topless dancing, dramatizations of sexual fantasies and reports on such items as the making of a pornographic film and the manufacturing of sexual aids.

Another way that cable viewers can see sexually explicit programming is on local cable channels that are received by viewers as part of the basic cable subscription cost. Most of these programs are shown in Manhattan, where there are 250,000 cable subscribers. Among them are "Midnight Blue," which frequently offers clips from heterosexual pornographic movies, and "Men and Films," which screens explicit selections from homosexual pornographic movies.

Such programs can be shown, in part, because cable television does not use the public airwaves and thus is not subject to the Federal Communications Commission regulations on obscenity, indecency and profanity that govern broadcast television.

In the last year, legislation has been introduced or approved in more than a dozen states to subject cable television to similar standards. These laws have been challenged by cable operators and civil liberties organizations, and several have been struck down as unconstitutional. Many legal experts believe, however, that the United States Supreme Court will eventually rule on the issue.

A related development is legislation that has been wending its way through a number of state legislatures, including those in New York and California, that would require cable operators to offer consumers, without charge or for small fees, special devices that can be attached to a television set to block out certain channels.

The devices have been sought by, among others, those who want cable service but do not want to watch, or to permit their children to watch, the specific channels that provide sexually explicit material.

The legal battle precipitated by these legislative actions has turned on the question of whether the attempt to limit the sexual content of cable systems is censorship or legitimate regulation.

Frame from "Dueling for Playmates" on Playboy Channel.

Cable operators maintain that because they do not use public airwaves, the First Amendment to the Constitution gives them the right to present programs according to their own editorial discretion. The industry also contends that viewers have the right to decide what they want to watch in their own homes.

On the other side, government officials, religious groups and parents concerned about the spread of pornography argue that the government should have the authority to apply standards on obscenity and indecency to cable programs.

Need for New Laws

The Federal Communications Act of 1934 first spelled out such standards for broadcasting, and now the advocates of regulation contend that new laws are necessary to limit the advance of sexually explicit material from bookstores and movie theaters to the living-room television set.

"The decibel count is high when people discuss this because on both sides of the debate people are relying on moral precepts in addition to legal ones," said Floyd Abrams, a New York lawyer who specializes in First Amendment cases.

There is evidence that some people refuse to buy cable television because of what they regard as obscene programming on some of its channels. In a study last spring by Benton & Bowles, the advertising agency, 33 percent of the 4,000 viewers across the nation who were questioned about their attitudes toward cable television said they did not subscribe to such services because they did not want their children exposed to some of its programming.

In a similar study two years ago, 25 percent raised that objection.

But millions of people subscribe to cable precisely because they can receive uncut films. Michael Fuchs, president of the entertainment division at Home Box Office, said about 40 percent of the Home Box Office film schedule is R-rated and these are among the most popular films shown.

'Let Us Know Very Clearly'

"We have more viewers wanting more R-rated movies than wanting less," Mr. Fuchs said. "Viewers let us know very clearly that they want the opportunity to see these movies."

R-rated (Restricted) films on Home Box Office do better in the viewer ratings than the more tame PG (Parental Guidance Suggested) or G-rated (Recommended for General Audience) films, Mr. Fuchs said. For example, "Tarzan" an R-rated film starring Bo Derek that received unfavorable reviews from many critics, was one of the most popular films on Home Box Office this year.

According to the film classification system administered by the Motion Picture Association of America, films with an R rating usually contain nudity and profanity and can be seen in a movie theater by children under 17 years of age only if they are accompanied by an adult. For films with a PG rating, parental guidance is advised for children under 17, and G-rated films are considered appropriate for all audiences.

Films given an X rating generally show sexual intercourse; theaters showing X-rated films are prohibited from admitting anyone under 17. Only about a half-dozen of nearly 4,600 cable systems show X-rated films, according to the National Cable Television Association, the principal cable industry trade organization.

The battles over sexually explicit programs have been fought principally in communities that want to stave off such material before it appears on the home screen.

Mayor Maurice A. Ferre of Miami, for example, was spurred into action last year after he saw a group of six naked men and women engaged in erotic discussion and activities on a local cable channel in New York City.

"It was certainly not the kind of thing I wanted to see on television in Miami," Mr. Ferre recalled.

On his return to Florida, Mr. Ferre proposed an ordinance to bar programming on Miami's new cable television system judged to be obscene or indecent. The ordinance was endorsed in a referendum and was passed unanimously by the City Commission. Although the legislation was later struck down by a Federal judge as being unconstitutional, the city is pressing an appeal.

About 100 groups are working around the country to ban or curb what they consider indecent or obscene programming from cable television, according to Bruce A. Taylor, general counsel of Citizens for Decency Through Law, a 25-year-old nonprofit group that advocates the use of obscenity laws. Many of these groups have religious affiliations.

Argument for Regulation

Such advocates have argued in the courts, for the most part unsuccessfully, that cable television should be subjected to the Federal law prohibiting obscenity, profanity and indecency that governs radio and television—Section 1464 of the United States Criminal Code.

"The state has legitimate business in the protection of children," said David L. Wilkinson, the Attorney General of Utah. "When you are talking about the home, there are certain things the state can attempt to regulate."

Although cable television does not use the public airwaves, the opponents of sexually explicit programming say that cable should be regarded as the equivalent of broadcasting.

"Why should you have to stand still for indecency just because you ask for the great new invention of cable?" said Paul J. McGeady, general counsel of Morality in Media, a nonprofit interfaith organization that has advocated using obscenity laws since 1962. "You can't logically make a distinction just because it comes in on a wire as opposed to over the air."

The cable television industry has persuaded several Federal courts, however, that it is entitled to the same First Amendment rights as publishers. It contends that cable is different from network television because it requires a series of choices: a consumer must first purchase the cable service and then pay an additional fee to subscribe to a channel offering R-rated films or X-rated programming.

Availability of Lockout Devices

"The significant thing is the consumer is putting money up front for his purchase and has the right to make the decision whether to continue," said Thomas E. Wheeler, president of the National Cable Television Association.

Cable industry officials also say that with the availability of lockout devices, subscribers can shield their children from objectionable shows—a capability absent from broadcast television.

These mechanisms come in varying degrees of sophistication and they range in price from $15 to $25.

The simplest is a "trap," a small metal box with a key that can be attached to the cable wire that feeds into the television set and blocks out a specific channel. A more complicated system involves a remote-control device that uses a computer chip. The consumer punches in a code specifying the channel and the amount of time it is to be blocked out.

Most cable systems do not publicize lockout boxes but have them available on request, said Ed Dooley of the National Cable Television Association. But, according to cable officials, few subscribers actually make use of them. At Gill Cable in San Jose, Calif., for example, 300 families out of 96,000 subscribers—10,000 of whom take a special adult subscription service called Rendez-vous—have obtained the "parental key," or lockout device, that is offered free.

New York Law Enacted

Among those systems that do not supply free lockout boxes are Manhattan Cable and Group W Cable in Manhattan.

Donald H. Mitzner, president of Group W Cable, said his company had obtained boxes for about eight customers who requested them and had charged them about $20 each.

John F. Gault, president of Manhattan Cable, a subsidiary of Time Inc., said that the system had had only a handful of requests for lockout boxes and that he was opposed to supplying them in the absence of great demand.

In New York, Governor Cuomo signed into law last July a measure that requires not only that boxes be offered to all customers at 15 percent over the manufacturing cost but also that cable companies prominently advertise the availability of the devices. The law, which was supported by the New York State Cable Association, goes into effect on Jan. 1.

Opponents of sexually explicit programs are trying to stem the supply of such programs before they become a lock-out-box issue. One of the methods they have employed is to try to influence the requirements of the franchising agreements that permit cable stations to operate. In a recent agreement in Houston, for instance, cable companies agreed not to show obscene or indecent programming.

A cable deregulation bill passed by the United States Senate last June would give cities the right to prohibit certain cable services if they were shown to be obscene or if they depicted child pornography. It is uncertain, however, whether that provision will be part of a similar bill that is expected to be introduced soon in the House of Representatives.

Quarrel Over Local Access

New York State prohibits cable companies from showing obscene programming. But because cable operators, under both a state law and the New York City cable franchising agreement, are prohibited from controlling what appears on local "leased access" channels, they must allow programs such as "Midnight Blue," which contains sexually explicit material.

As a result, critics of such shows are seeking laws that will set standards for indecency as well as obscenity. For the most part, the new cable laws in Utah and Miami have defined indecency as representations of human sexual or excretory organs that could be found patently offensive by an average person applying community standards.

Another approach is an increased scrutiny of adult cable services for violations of existing obscenity laws. "We have urged cities to go after the worst abuses, the most graphic shows, to see if that will change the character of the boldest programmers," said Mr. Taylor of Citizens for Decency Through Law.

Perhaps the first of these cable obscenity actions came in Cincinnati last June, when a grand jury indicted Warner Amex Cable Communications on four obscenity counts for the showing of two sexually explicit films on the Playboy Channel. As the holder of the Cincinnati cable franchise, Warner Amex was held responsible by local authorities for the content of its channels.

The city later withdrew the charges after securing a formal agreement from Warner Amex not to carry any X-rated films or unrated films that would qualify for X rating. Warner said Playboy did not show this category of film anyway, but Arthur M. Ney Jr., the prosecutor, took credit for keeping the two films off television.

Challenges in Court

The Playboy Channel was taken out of service in Cincinnati for "technical problems" before the indictment, according to Richard Berman, a Warner Amex Cable general counsel. He said that the channel's removal had no bearing on the agreement with the city and that it would be brought back when it could be made technically secure.

Many of the legislative efforts by cable opponents are being challenged in the courts. In Cincinnati, the local chapter of the American Civil Liberties Union has filed a suit that contends that subscribers have a right to X-rated programs if they want them.

Of the handful of laws concerning indecency or obscenity that have been passed so far, three—two in Utah and the one in Miami—have been struck down by Federal judges as unconstitutional. In some cases the definition of indecency was judged to be too broad, and in all the cases it was found that cable was, in fact, different from broadcasting.

Some legal experts predict that the issue of sexually explicit programming on cable television will ultimately be decided by the Supreme Court. The Miami case has already been appealed to a higher court, and a new law passed last spring in Utah is being challenged in Federal court.

"The resolution of whether cable is to be more like broadcasting or more like newspapers," Mr. Abrams, the New York lawyer, said, "will determine a good deal of the future of what our country is likely to be watching in years to come."

* * *

March 4, 1984

PORTUGUESE PRESS OPPOSES NEW LAW

By JOHN DARNTON

LISBON—Portuguese journalists have expressed strong opposition to a proposed new press law, calling it "the most violent attack on the freedom of the press" since the 1974 revolution.

The Union of Journalists said a draft text of the law would impose severe restrictions on what can be printed and provide prison sentences for violators.

Parts of the bill, a union statement said, were even worse than the "former fascist laws" under the 48-year-long Salazar-Caetano dictatorship, a declaration that seemed a bit exaggerated since the regimes of Antonio de Oliveira Salazar and Marcello Caetano enforced strict censorship.

The bill, which is still in a formative stage, was drawn up and circulated to journalists by Antonio de Almeida Santos, the Minister of State and top adviser to Prime Minister Mario Soares. He said he might be willing to make some changes here and there but basically defends it as a document that enhances the rights of journalists.

Opposition Called 'Sentimental'

"This opposition from journalists is more sentimental than anything else," he said. "When I talk to them they will see that they didn't consider the whole law—in 80 or 90 percent of it there should be no objections."

"It's unbelievable that anyone should think that people like me or Mario Soares are against press freedom," Mr. Almeida Santos said. "We fought for it for 35 years, and some of the journalists opposing us now weren't there alongside us then."

But the journalists are not likely to be convinced. "I don't know of a single reporter or politician—left, right or center—in favor of this bill," said Manuel Beca Murias, editor of the weekly O Jornal. "It's nothing but trouble."

Some objections center on a series of provisions that, in theory at least, are intended to define under what circumstances journalists are entitled to keep their sources secret. One clause says that "journalists are not obliged to reveal their sources of information and their silence cannot be directly or indirectly punished."

Exceptions Listed

But this is followed by another clause that says that the right of secrecy does not apply for "information necessary to investigate and punish public crimes."

Mr. Almeida Santos said the exception is justified as a provision for the good of the public welfare in investigating crimes of overriding importance such as terrorism.

But the journalists assert that the language is so sweeping that it can take in virtually anything, including governmental malfeasance. The Watergate scandal in the United States, they contend, could never have been uncovered with such a law in effect.

Other sections of the draft set limits on access to certain kinds of information. They include secret legal proceedings, classified state or military documents, and "facts or documents" that are qualified as confidential by the legislature. These include information that concerns "the intimate or private lives of citizens," that "seriously affect the competitive position" of companies, or that are supposed to be kept private under commercial regulations.

Prison Terms Specified

Punishment for a reporter who gets such material, even indirectly, is a prison sentence ranging from one month to one year, along with a fine.

Still another section prohibits publication of a wide range of information, including material about legal proceedings not explicitly authorized, identification of victims of sexual crimes or suicides, the workings or findings of any parliamentary committees of inquiry, and documents or decisions from various councils of magistrates and public prosecutors beyond what may be contained in an official communique.

The journalists' union asserts that all this adds up to "a drastic limitation of the rights and guarantees indispensable to the production of free news." In some cases, the reporters say, they could be open to prosecution just for having the information even if it goes unpublished.

Journalists in Portugal appear to wield unusual influence and the line between journalism and politics sometimes seems to disappear. There are a large number of newspapers—10 dailies in Lisbon and 4 in the northern city of Oporto—but the total circulation of all of them does not exceed 500,000.

Newspapers Attack the Bill

Virtually all the newspapers have attacked the bill, ranging from the right-wing weekly Tempo to the state-owned Diario de Noticias to the pro-Communist daily O Diario.

Mr. Almeida Santos appears to be mystified by the storm of criticism he has raised. "People just haven't read the law," he said. "This big point about limiting press freedom—the current law is more dangerous to journalists. It allows the penal code to be used and talks of defending the public interest and the public order. That's a basket you can put anything into.

"My law explicitly says that the only limits to the freedom of the press are those contained in this law itself. And what formulation did I use? The European Convention on Human Rights."

The literacy rate in Portugal is about 70 percent, and most Portuguese get their news from the state-owned television or the three nationwide radio networks, of which two are state-owned. Before the revolution, a number of major newspapers were owned by the banks. When the state nationalized the banks, they also took over the newspapers. Six are now state-owned.

* * *

May 13, 1984

OPENING THE BOOKS ON CENSORSHIP

By RICHARD BERNSTEIN

"When I read Orwell, my hair stood on end at mere words running across the page in front of me, at a mere idea."

So, in the forward to a clandestine copy of "1984," did the Czechoslovak dissident writer Milan Simecka express the astonishment, the thrill of discovery, the "torment of self-flagellation of the mind," that can come from reading a forbidden book. Then he went on to strike a note of bittersweet irony as he claimed a unique, if unwanted, intensity in the life of the mind for those who live under dictatorships.

There are certain countries, Mr. Simecka wrote for his underground Czechoslovak audience, "where you can read newspapers which print unofficial views, or go to a public library and borrow just any book you want, or make fun of the country's leaders . . . or even bring a stool to a certain park and spout whatever you please to a bunch of people who have enough patience to stand there and listen to you." In those countries, he went on, independent thought can hardly be described as an adventure: "This is thought without jeopardy." But if you want "adventure by reading," he wrote, you have to be born "in the right place, at the right time, in the appropriate historical conditions"—a dictatorship like Czechoslovakia, for example.

In American society, self-critical, demanding, always scrutinizing itself for moral or political defects, Mr. Simecka's ironic recollection—published in the British bimonthly Index on Censorship—serves as a reminder of the need to make some elementary distinctions. Particularly since the enormous surge of self-doubt spurred by the Vietnam experience, it has become strangely out of fashion among many Americans to utter praise of themselves, or to acknowledge that, however flawed and beset by problems of their own, they remain far more fortunate than that huge global mass that dwells in places where reading Orwell, and many other authors, is an act of defiance and courage.

These thoughts come to mind on the eve of a major and ambitious exhibition at the New York Public Library that deals directly with the issues of freedom, of the silencing of opinion, and of the persistent effort by some to control the minds of others. In the end, the exhibition, scheduled to open June 1, can be taken as something of an occasion for self-congratulation. It shows that, after centuries of struggle in this part of the world, free expression has triumphed, even as, in many other parts, the struggle is as intense and as difficult as ever.

Called "Censorship: 500 Years of Conflict," the exhibition is the inaugural event of what is being called the "new" New York Public Library. The refurbished grand old monument on Fifth Avenue and 42d Street has completed the first stage of an ambitious $45 million renovation project designed to reverse the decline it has suffered since New York's fiscal crisis. Officials at the library say that the censorship exhibition will be the first in a series of events that will display the extraordinary treasures of the collection, much of which has rarely, if ever, been seen in recent times.

Intended to trace the history of the struggle for free expression in the West since the invention of the printing press in the middle of the 15th century, the exhibition will display books, drawings and other documents illustrating the effort to suppress or control ideas and opinions. The nearly 300 objects on display will include a banned copy of Luther's German Bible and George Washington's personal copy of Voltaire's letters, which, banned in France, were read by the father of our country during the terrible winter at Valley Forge. There will be original copies of the Papal Index of proscribed books and lists of the works destroyed for political reasons in Nazi Germany—from the stories of Thomas Mann to Albert Einstein's general theory of relativity. The show will be set in the D. Samuel and Jeane H. Gottesman Exhibition Hall, opened for the first time to the public since World War II.

The library exhibition comes at a time when fears and doubts are being raised about the validity and durability of the Western system of self-expression. Controversies and battles continue over pornography, over sexually explicit images on cable television, over books and films in the schools. Some months ago, a kind of prior censorship was imposed by the Government when journalists were refused permission to accompany the troops landing in Grenada. Also in recent months, President Reagan attempted, apparently without success, to impose lifetime secrecy on those who have served in key Government positions. And in spite of the Supreme Court ruling last month in the Consumers Union case, supporting strict judicial standards for libel judgments, there are worries that the courts are making it easier for individuals to win judgments against writers and newspapers and thus, perhaps, weaken the nation's commitment to uninhibited and robust debate.

Vartan Gregorian, the New York Public Library's president, sits among some books that will be part of the exhibition on censorship that he helped put together.

The exhibition, coming in this year of 1984, also seems likely to stir up deep, brooding fears raised by George Orwell's masterpiece. In the exhibition catalogue, Joan Hoff-Wilson, professor of American history at Indiana University, warns that advanced technology may make possible deadlier and more effective forms of mind control. Winston Smith, the hero of Orwell's anti-utopian novel, is under constant surveillance by a television monitor in his living room; "thoughtpolice" in helicopters peer into the homes of citizens in pursuit of "thoughtcrimes."

Orwell, in fact, was writing a satire on Soviet totalitarianism; he does not seem to have been projecting some dark fantasy about the evils that lurk in the democratic West. Yet the machinery of modern society—the computers, the information banks, the credit cards, the listening devices and spy gadgetry, the capacity to collect, sort and recall vast amounts of data on individual citizens—has induced fears of a mind control that was impossible when censorship was a matter of proscribed books and straightforward persecution.

"Assassination," George Bernard Shaw once said, "is the extreme form of censorship," and, indeed, the exhibition in the library reminds us that over the centuries many have been subjected to that extreme, or they have been jailed, silenced, tortured or disgraced. In a flier sent out by the library announcing the censorship exhibition, the warning takes this form: "Censorship has stifled the attempt to communicate in every century, under dictatorships and democracies alike—and if the past is any indication, may do so again."

Surely it is always useful to be reminded that liberty requires struggle and vigilance, but the library's flier tends to put democracy and dictatorship into the same category. And indeed, many have complained that, though generally less brutal, the West has its own machinery of censorship. The English poet Stephen Spender, in an essay written for the exhibition catalogue, tells of overhearing a conversation between two poets, the American Robert Lowell and the Russian Andrei Voznesensky, during which Lowell expressed a kind of rueful envy of the Russian. It must, Lowell said, be good to live in a society where the Government takes poets seriously enough to put them in prison and ban their poems. The West is better, of course, Lowell seems to say, but at the same time, poetry suffers from a crass indifference that is in itself a form of censorship.

In fact, the history of censorship in the West shows not even an incidental similarity between the two worlds. The items on display at the library exhibition indicate that, in the West, it was for only brief periods during the long age of monarchial or religious autocracy that those in power managed to create the kind of totalistic, airtight structures of repression that effectively seal people from ideas.

Indeed, reading the history of censorship since Gutenberg set up the first printing press around 1450, one is struck not only by the intensity of the struggle for freedom, but also by the tenacity of ideas, their tendency to slip through virtually any kind of repressive network and, in many cases, eventually be incorporated into the received wisdom of Western political culture. Ralph Waldo Emerson's claim seems warranted: "Every suppressed or expunged word reverberates through the earth." Not to put too fine a point on it, the censorship show demonstrates that today, whatever battles may remain to be fought in this corner of the globe, we have never been freer to express ourselves; our marketplace of ideas and cultural products has never been so crowded.

The same, however, cannot be said of other major portions of the political universe, the totalitarian societies and many of the third-world countries, where organization and technology have been used not to spread ideas or to diversify culture, but to control them and to impose homogeneity. As Mr. Spender writes in his essay for the exhibition catalogue, "The difference between censorship in the West and in the Communist countries is so great that it amounts, not to a difference of degree, but of kind." He goes on: "Censorship in totalitarian societies is more than a matter of the persecution of individual writers and other artists. It is a matter of the dictatorship monopolizing all the media of communication with the people, who are told only what the Government wants them to know."

Mr. Spender might have added that it is a matter of labor camps, of imprisonment in psychiatric hospitals, of the worship of the larger- than-life leader inculcated by a vast propaganda network of newspapers, radio and television programs, theatrical extravaganzas, songs, dances, mass meetings and political lectures as well as books, magazines and photographs, all aimed at justifying for the sake of the "revolution" or the "people" an absolute monopoly on political power.

The president of the New York Public Library, Vartan Gregorian, who has achieved a kind of celebrity status in New York as the energizing force behind the rejuvenated public library, likes to talk of the institution's role as the preserver of the whole of culture, of the good and the bad, the memorable and the forgettable, the immortal and the transient. In the three years since he arrived from the University of Pennsylvania, where he was provost, Mr. Gregorian has introduced the smart New York set to the task of preservation and scholarship. He has brought the captains of industry and the arbiters of high society into an effort to raise money for an institution that, while blessed with marble corridors and rococo ceilings, grand chiaroscuro reading rooms and gleaming oak tables, was suffering from financial shortages, curtailment of service and dilapidation.

Using the arts of publicity and glittering social occasions—last December there were 95 fund-raising dinners on a single night, each hosted by a different writer or socialite—Mr. Gregorian has more than just added to the library's coffers; he has made the library fashionable in much the same way that Thomas Hoving made the Metropolitan Museum of Art a center of both social and cultural life a decade ago.

In a sense, what Mr. Gregorian has been trying to do is remind this city of the extraordinary treasures that the library contains, its status as a repository of knowledge. Comparable in size to the Library of Congress and the French Bibliotheque Nationale, it contains some six million books and pamphlets, 2,500 newspapers in 62 languages, 500,000 musical recordings and videotapes. There are 175,000 original prints and drawings, 350,000 sheet maps and such rare books as six first folios of Shakespearean plays, the first Gutenberg Bible brought to the New World and a draft in the hand of Thomas Jefferson of the Declaration of Independence. Each year, 1.5 million people use the 42d Street library and three other research libraries, not to mention the 82 branches scattered around New York.

During the planning for the censorship exhibition, which will run through Oct. 15, a list was drawn up of the items needed for display. It turned out, Mr. Gregorian said in a recent interview, that all but 1 percent were already in the library's collection. According to Mr. Gregorian, the library has 28 percent of all the books on the Americas and Europe printed in the world between 1450 and 1660.

For much of the history of New York City, moreover, this richness has served an essentially democratic purpose. The library, the use of which has always been free, has made the power that is knowledge available to all. Mr. Gregorian likes to point out that even in the darkest days of the Great Depression, the 42d Street library was open for 87 hours a week, compared to 67 hours today. "The library was the last thing to be affected by an economic turndown," he said.

Censorship in our age may appear, at first, to have lost its elements of controversy. It would probably be difficult to find respectable figures from any part of the political spectrum proclaiming support for censorship—except in the single area of pornography, which many in this country believe goes beyond the boundaries of what should be legally permissible. One sign of the times is simply that, by contrast with earlier eras, it takes no courage these days to advocate totally free expression. It has become part of the Western political culture.

Arthur Schlesinger Jr., writing for the exhibition catalogue, contends that the period covered by the show "witnessed the great shift in the moral balance between expression and authority." The history of modern times, Mr. Schlesinger goes on, is one in which censorship gave way to the concept of liberty as a practical necessity. "Individuals and groups," he writes, "were prepared to concede liberty of expression to others in order to assure it for themselves; and censorship, except at the margins, began to lose legitimacy."

There is even something retrospectively comic about some of the efforts to keep offending works away from the public eye. Those efforts shown in the exhibition have an anachronistic feel about them, an air of silliness and of futility, somewhat akin to pressing confidently the claim that the world is flat. In banning "The Adventures of Huckleberry Finn" from the shelves of the Concord Public Library, one trustee, quoted by Mr. Schlesinger, accused the book of "a very low grade of morality" and "a systematic use of bad grammar." Mark Twain's reply is instructive of the entire effort to suppress. He said that the banning of the book would assure sales of 25,000 copies.

The displays in Gottesman Hall demonstrate that throughout Western history, ideas have survived; they have always leaked through even the most systematic and concerted efforts to suppress them. When Martin Luther publicly burned the papal bull Contra Errores, his act of defiance was spread through Europe—as Ann Alter, a guest curator at the library, writes in the catalogue—"by merchants, journeymen, humanists and soldiers, who passed pamphlets, vernacular Bibles and Protestant and humanist tracts to friends and comrades-in-arms." Even at the height of absolute monarchy in Europe, there existed what Ann Alter has called an anti-censorship network, stretching through London, Cracow, Copenhagen and Rome.

In 1564, the papacy promulgated the first Index of Prohibited Books, which included the names of authors whose entire work was banned, lists of individual banned titles and instructions for expurgating portions of other books whose contents were in the main acceptable. Yet, the curator points out, "book smuggling was so widespread that it might more accurately be termed the 'clandestine trade' that supplemented the open commerce."

The clandestine trade continued for virtually as long as there was censorship. In 18th-century France, many of the great English works that influenced les philosophes like Voltaire and Diderot—the works, for example, of Locke and Hobbes—were French translations published in Amsterdam and distributed in Switzerland. To control the press, as the catalogue points out, meant controlling all of Europe.

In 1579, a French Huguenot pamphlet entitled Vindiciae Contra Tyrannos (A Vindication Against Tyranny) was published in Scotland. It gave a justification for revolt against the French monarchy. A century later, the pamphlet appeared in English translation and was used by Puritan rebels in England to justify the eventual execution of Charles I. Daniel Bell, the Harvard sociologist, pointed out in an interview that many of the great thinkers of Western civilization—Hobbes, Hegel, Kant among them—wrote under systems of censorship, developing methods of couching heterodox ideas in subtle, indirect terms. "There was a kind of subterranean tradition for those who knew how to interpret certain texts," Dr. Bell said.

In 1832, the caricaturist Honore Daumier, whose satirical drawings are to be seen in the exhibition, was jailed by King Louis Philippe for—as the catalogue puts it—"exciting hatred" for the king. A generation later, Flaubert, after writing "Madame Bovary," was put on trial in France for lasciviousness and immorality. He was acquitted, and "Madame Bovary," which might well have otherwise found only a small audience, became a best seller. Nonetheless, between 1876 and 1906, there were an average of 55 obscenity cases a year in France, most of them ending in conviction. In England and the United States, Thomas Bowdler's "Family Shakespeare," which excised whatever could not "with propriety be read aloud in a family," gained great popularity. It exemplified the spread of Victorian prudery, amounting to a new kind of censorship, the censorship of inhibition.

In the United States, works by Whitman, Stephen Crane and Theodore Dreiser were banned for years in some places, as were Havelock Ellis's studies of homosexuality. Private pressure groups proliferated after the Civil War and waged relentless war on what were perceived as obscene publications. The notorious Comstock Laws, named for the secretary of the New York Society for the Suppression of Vice, led to the prosecutions of Edward Bliss Foote and Margaret Sanger for advocating birth control and to the exclusion of works by Rabelais, Boccaccio and Voltaire. It was only after the American courts ruled against a ban on D. H. Lawrence's "Lady Chatterley's Lover" in 1960 that moral censorship essentially came to an end in the United States.

The victory of free expression in the West provides a stark contrast to the truly Orwellian outcomes in the totalitarian worlds—Nazi Germany, the Soviet Union, the Guinea of Ahmed Sekou Toure or latter-day Iran—where unprecedentedly powerful networks of repression were being created even as the more fragile networks in the West were crumbling. Anthony Comstock was not in the same league with Lenin, Hitler, Toure or the Ayatollah Khomeini. Their first acts upon coming to power—often legally or, at least, with enthusiastic public support—included gaining control over the press, creating extralegal secret police forces and manufacturing a self-contained world of propaganda to justify the new dictatorship.

Ideas do get through, however; there are radio broadcasts, travelers from abroad, even clandestine copies of "1984." Yet the arguments are strong that contemporary censorship enforced by an apparatus of control is harsher and more thoroughgoing than that of earlier eras in the West.

At the root of the impulse toward modern-day control of ideas is the pseudoscientific notion that all of history points to a single end and that nothing which diverges from that end has any worth. In that sense, there is a corollary to the suppression of dissident ideas. It is the inculcation of the approved ones, the revolutionary classics learned in school, the "scientific truths" of Marxism-Leninism, the heroic deeds and brilliant thoughts of the leader.

At the same time, censorship in today's dictatorships has a hypocritical aspect that makes it very different from censorship in the past. In earlier centuries, the control of ideas was undisguised; it was viewed as a moral necessity. Today's totalitarian societies control ideas despite formal guarantees of such freedoms as speech and of the press. In China, where this is the case, free expression must adhere to what are officially called "fundamental principles," including advocacy of "the socialist road" and the "leadership of the Communist Party." In the Soviet Union and Eastern Europe, the law allows prosecutions for "incitement against the state" or "anti-Soviet slander," which usually means any sharp criticism of the system.

In an interview published last year, the Czechoslovak playwright Vaclav Havel, who spent 1979 to 1983 in prison, recalled reading in the official newspaper, Rude Pravo, a comment by the then Minister of the Interior Jaromir Obzina, that crime in a Communist state was the result of "insufficient social homogeneity of the population." The nature of life itself is heterogeneity, Mr. Havel said; it is a mixing of diversity. Indeed, he added, "once we become exactly like one another there will be no more need for courts of law and prisons."

Writes Stephen Spender: "Censorship is the absolutely indispensable preliminary to dictatorship." He adds: "It involves censoring the whole people, dividing the world into the free and un-free." Mr. Spender argues that one practical effect of this is nothing less than the threat of war. By suppressing the advocacy of disarmament in his own country, Hitler, in effect, turned pacifists in England into "his assistants in rearming Germany." The same thing might be said about the Communist states today. The suppression of fledgling, private peace groups in the Soviet Union, East Germany and Hungary, and the encouragement of such groups in the West represent a form of censorship with far more than literary consequences. It could well have consequences for the survival of the planet.

The situation in the West, with its profusion of opinions and its floods of disclosures, is different. When, for example, the Government of the United States tried to prevent The New York Times from publishing the Pentagon Papers 13 years ago, the paper went to court and prevailed. In many other countries, the Government would have sent in the police and censorship would have prevailed. Even the most recent effort of the American Government to control information, by denying the press its normal right to cover the first few days of the invasion of Grenada, was a limited operation that itself brought such a storm of censure and protest that the Pentagon was forced to apologize and vow not to repeat the mistake.

Still, there are deep concerns in our part of the world both about the residues of traditional forms of censorship and what are alleged to be new varieties of it. In one instance, there are fears that government power endangers the fullness of self-expression.

Joan Hoff-Wilson of Indiana University, in her essay for the exhibition catalogue, warns not only of the danger that government bureaucracies may gain greater control over the freedoms and rights of citizens because of new technology; she also believes that the swing toward the right by the American electorate in the last few years has already produced an "avalanche of reaction" blocking further progress on behalf of "civil-liberties issues such as busing, abortion, the ERA, affirmative action, obscenity and gay rights." She contends that since the mid-1970's there has been an "epidemic of attempts to censor books and films in the schools," a contention supported by others. The Washington-based citizens' group, People for the American Way, which supports First Amendment rights, claims that last year there were attempts to remove, alter or restrict textbooks, library books or teaching materials and courses in 48 states.

Joan Hoff-Wilson, in particular, seems less dismayed that censorship is on the rise—though that is part of her concern—than that certain Government policies are misdirected. Not everyone would agree, for example, that busing, abortion and obscenity are civil liberties; they are policies or phenomena that one is free to support or oppose.

Of more profound concern is what has been called "repressive tolerance," a notion developed by the radical social critic Herbert Marcuse. It suggests that disturbing ideas are simply ignored in this country; they are tolerated but overwhelmed and obscured as the mass of citizens are manipulated by ever-more-skillful image makers. An ironic result of the triumph of permissiveness might, some writers have complained, be a sort of censorship in reverse.

"We live in a society in which the main consensus seems to be that the artist's duty is to entertain and divert, nothing more," said the Canadian writer Margaret Atwood at a conference in Toronto three years ago. She added, "We control through the marketplace and through critical opinion. We are also controlled by the economics of culture." The French novelist Michel Tournier, at the same conference, spoke of the ultimate censorship of the Gulag Archipelago, but he added that Western society also contained poisons which, "though they may be milder, are nonetheless equally effective in taming the untamed writer." They are, Mr. Tournier said, "the literary prizes, the academies, the official posts, and more significantly, the confidence and loyalty of a particular public of readers."

Clearly, censorship is a subtle and complex matter these days. It involves less the heavy hand of political repression and far more the pressures and constraints of normal social life. Mr. Tournier may justly grieve that artists and writers are made less honest, less faithful in their efforts to hold up a mirror to the world than they would be if there were no prizes, no rewards. But the censorship exhibition suggests that in the past, at least, the problem was a good deal less benign than today. We have progressed that far at least.

There is, in fact, yet another school of thought, one that sees the danger to free expression coming not from overt political repression or from social or economic suasion or even from inertia in the face of the power of received opinion. Censorship can also be privately motivated; it can come as a kind of self-restraint, as a failure to tell the truth, perhaps out of fear or, what may be less forgivable, from a sense of political commitment.

Jean-Francois Revel, for example, in "The New Censorship," published in France in 1978, charged that intellectuals have persistently refused to tell what they know to be the truth about Communism largely because they are unwilling to provide ammunition to their perceived enemies on the right. Mr. Revel and others have charged that a confusion of political values, a failure to realize our own self-worth, has led to a fashion of self-criticism and a willful self-delusion about the denial of liberty elsewhere.

In "The Book of Laughter and Forgetting," the Czechoslovak writer Milan Kundera tells of the festive air of acceptance in the West that followed the Soviet-inspired Communist coup in his country in 1948. Two years later, he says, there was dancing in the streets in the wake of the execution of Zavis Kalandra, a friend of the French poets Andre Breton and Paul Eluard. Mr. Kundera, who lives in Paris now, his books banned in Czechoslovakia, recounts that Eluard refused to join Breton in dismissing the "absurd accusation" of treason against Kalandra. Eluard, Mr. Kundera writes bitterly, was "too busy reciting his beautiful poems about joy and brotherhood" to "stand up for a man who had betrayed the people."

Many besides Eluard have, in their desire for revolutionary change, looked the other way at revolutionary atrocities. This habit of mind does not appear among the exhibits soon to be on view at the New York Public Library. Yet it is, in its way, as insidious a form of censorship as any.

Richard Bernstein is the chief of The Times' United Nations bureau.

* * *

May 29, 1985

REPORT SAYS U.S. MUST ALLOW PRESS IN WAR ZONE

By ALEX S. JONES

The presence of journalists in war zones where American forces are fighting is essential—"not a luxury, but a necessity"—according to a report issued yesterday on the relationship between the military and news organizations.

The responsibility for making policy decisions on press access and censorship in military actions should rest with the President and his civilian advisers, not with the military, asserted the report, issued by a nonpartisan research organization.

The report, "Battle Lines: Report of the Twentieth Century Fund Task Force on the Military and the Media," also described a "culture gap" that threatens to turn the adversary relationship between journalists and the military into hostility that would be damaging to both.

Young journalists and young military officers, with little sympathy or in-depth knowledge of the other's calling, view each other with increasing suspicion, the report concluded, and such a trend could be dangerous for the nation.

A 13-Member Task Force

No representatives of Secretary of Defense Caspar W. Weinberger have seen the report yet, according to Edward N. Costikyan, a lawyer based in New York and chairman of the 13-member task force.

The task force consisted of former military and Government officials, scholars and journalists, and heard presentations from military officials, journalists and others. The Twentieth Century Fund, a nonprofit and nonpartisan research foundation in New York, has done similar reports on other public policy issues.

The creation of the task force was prompted by the exclusion of news organizations from covering the early stages of the United States invasion of Grenada in October 1983, according to Mr. Costikyan.

The decision to exclude news organizations was made by military authorities after they had been given authority over press access by Mr. Weinberger. Military officials said they based their decision on security concerns.

From before World War II until the Grenada invasion, setting information policy in a war zone had been considered a civilian decision, rather than a military one, according to the report.

'Tacit Agreement' Until Grenada

"There was tacit agreement between the military and the media that the President, in his role as Commander in Chief, and his civilian subordinates assumed responsibility for media policy," the report stated.

The report called on "the President and his civilian deputies" to assume responsibility for policy decisions on press access and censorship, a responsibility that the report found had not been clearly re-established since the Grenada invasion. Should the President and his deputies fail to do so, the report said, Congress should "exert its influence to guarantee a speedy restoration of the historic understanding between the military and the media."

"The Secretary of Defense has taken the welcome step of assembling his own advisory group of veteran journalists," the report said, "but he has yet to give unequivocal support to the notion that information policy is a civilian responsibility and not one that can be delegated, as it was during the Grenada invasion, to military commanders."

Fullest Possible Access

The report noted that the panel on press-military relations known as the Sidle commission after its chairman, Winant Sidle, a retired major general of the Army, was instituted by the military, not the Secretary of Defense.

The Sidle panel, whose findings were commended by the report issued yesterday, was formed after an outpouring of press complaints following the Grenada invasion. It recommended that the press be given the fullest possible access to military operations.

The recommendation was endorsed by Mr. Weinberger when the report was made public last August, but Mr. Weinberger said military security would remain the paramount consideration in guidelines for news coverage.

The Twentieth Century Fund report said that "no valid security reason existed for excluding all reporters" from the Grenada invasion, and it recommended a policy of voluntary guidelines for reporting military actions, with "procedural details to be left to commanders in the field."

The report said the presence of journalists in war zones had resulted in few security violations in World War II, the Korean War or the Vietnam War.

A Post-Vietnam 'Culture Gap'

But the legacy of Vietnam has helped to create a dangerous "culture gap" between journalists and military officials, the report found. The gap is most pronounced, it said, among younger journalists and officers who increasingly view each other with hostility born of a lack of understanding and experience.

The task force concluded that while an adversary relationship between the press and the military was healthy, an antagonistic one was not.

The report noted that unlike previous generations of journalists, many younger journalists today have no military experience. Many came of age in the 1960's and early 70's when the military was unpopular on campuses.

While most military officers view the press with some antagonism, the report asserted, many older officers have had personal experiences with individual journalists in the field that have tempered their suspicion with understanding. Younger officers have often had no such personal experience with journalists, the report added, and have been influenced by "powerful myths" that news organizations were responsible for military defeat in Vietnam.

A copy of the report may be obtained for $10 from the Twentieth Century Fund, 41 East 70th Street, New York, N.Y. 10021.

The members of the task force were: Edward N. Costikyan, chairman, partner in law firm of Paul, Weiss, Rifkind, Wharton & Garrison and author of "Behind Closed Doors: Politics in the Public Interest."

Peter Braestrup, editor of The Wilson Quarterly.

Charles Cordry, defense correspondent for The Baltimore Sun.

Shelby Foote, author of "The Civil War: A Narrative."

Edward M. Fouhy, executive producer for NBC News.

Jerry W. Friedheim, executive vice president of the American Newspaper Publishers' Association.

Roswell L. Gilpatric, lawyer with Cravath, Swaine & Moore and Deputy Secretary of Defense from 1961 to 1964.

Charlayne Hunter-Gault, national correspondent for "The MacNeil-Lehrer Newshour."

Samuel P. Huntington, Eaton Professor of the Science of Government and director of the Center for International Affairs at Harvard University.

Robert J. Murray, director of national security programs at the John F. Kennedy School of Government at Harvard University and former Under Secretary of the Navy.

Col. Harry G. Summers Jr., holder of the Gen. Douglas MacArthur Chair of Military Research at the Army War College.

Craig R. Whitney, assistant managing editor of The New York Times.

Adm. Elmo R. Zumwalt Jr., president of Admiral Zumwalt and Associates Inc., a consulting firm, and Chief of Naval Operations and member of the Joint Chiefs of Staff from 1970 to 1974.

* * *

May 21, 1986

U.S. AIDES SAID TO HAVE DISCUSSED PROSECUTING NEWS ORGANIZATIONS

By STEPHEN ENGELBERG
Special to the New York Times

WASHINGTON, May 20—In the past 25 years, Government officials have discussed numerous times whether to prosecute news organizations for disclosing highly sensitive material, according to former officials.

But they have always been dissuaded by various political pressures or by fears that a court case would confirm the accuracy of a report and bring to light even more damaging information, the officials say.

With his remarks in recent weeks, William J. Casey, the Director of Central Intelligence, has begun publicly pushing for a new, more confrontational approach to the publication of classified Government information.

Mr. Casey has cited the mounting attacks against Americans by terrorists as a justification for bringing prosecutions under a 1950 law that bars publication of classified communications intelligence. No news organization has ever been prosecuted under this statute.

Prosecution of NBC Sought

On Monday, Mr. Casey announced that he had asked the Justice Department to consider prosecuting the National Broadcasting Company for its report on a secret intelligence gathering operation by the National Security Agency. The report on the "Today" show Monday described Ivy Bells, a program the Government contends was compromised by Ronald W. Pelton, a former employee of the National Security Agency who is now on trial on espionage charges. The network said the effort involved eavesdropping by American submarines in Soviet harbors.

Mr. Casey has also warned The Washington Post that it would be prosecuted if it published its report on the National Security Agency project.

The Post published an article about the Pelton case in its Wednesday issue, but gave none of the technical details of the N.S.A. project and did not mention its code name. The article said Benjamin C. Bradlee, the executive editor of The Post, continued to believe that the paper's original, more detailed article "would have revealed nothing that was already known to the Soviet Union."

But, the article added, "because The Post has been unable fully to judge the validity of the national security objections of senior officials, and because of Post lawyers' concerns, the paper has decided to print this article without a description of the technology Pelton allegedly betrayed."

The article reported that on May 10, "at Casey's request, President Reagan telephoned Katharine Graham, chairman of the board of the Washngton Post Co., to urge that The Post not publish the article."

It said, "Earlier, Vice Adm. John M. Poindexter, Reagan's national security affairs adviser, Lt. Gen. William E. Odom, director of the National Security Agency, and other officials told The Post that publication of the article could endanger national security."

Description of Process

Howard Simons, the curator of the Nieman Foundation for journalists at Harvard, said that newspapers' decisions about whether to publish national security articles were generally made after private consultations with Government officials. Mr. Simons was managing editor of The Washington Post from 1971 to 1984.

"It was all done very quietly," said Mr. Simons. "They would call you over to the C.I.A. or the White House. They wouldn't ask you not to publish. They would outline what damage would be caused by a story. Then you went back and made your own decision."

There have been a number of incidents in which publications have published information viewed as highly sensitive by the Government. These included reports in the 1970's of an effort by the United States to raise a sunken Soviet submarine from the ocean floor as well as disclosures about a host of intelligence gathering activities.

In 1975, for instance, The New York Times printed an article about a Navy program code-named Holystone in which specially equipped submarines eavesdropped on the Soviet Union.

The Times article described several mishaps involving the submarines, including two collisions with Soviet submarines, and it detailed some of the intelligence successes in the program.

'Different Climate'

Former Government officials said that there was serious consideration given to prosecuting Seymour M. Hersh, the Times reporter who wrote the article, but they said the idea was eventually dropped.

"It was an altogether different climate at the time in which the idea of prosecuting a reporter was just impossible," recalled James R. Schlesinger, who served as the Director of Central Intelligence from 1973 to 1975 and was later Secretary of Defense. "You had the C.I.A.'s alleged involvement in Watergate. The C.I.A.'s reputation on Capitol Hill was mixed and the people in the White House just didn't want to get President Ford involved in prosecution of a reporter."

In 1971, the Nixon Administration sought to prevent The New York Times and The Washington Post from publishing excerpts from secret documents on the origins of United States involvement in the Vietnam War. The Supreme Court ruled 6 to 3 that the Government had failed to meet its "heavy burden" needed to justify prior restraint.

Under President Carter, the Justice Department was successful in winning prior restraint of an article prepared for The Progressive magazine that gave technical details on how a hydrogen bomb operates. Prosecutors secured a temporary restraining order barring publication under the Atomic Energy Act but the United States Court of Appeals for the Seventh Circut lifted it six months later, shortly after a local newspaper in Wisconsin published a letter to the editor that contained much of the disputed information.

Philip Heymann, the head of the Justice Department's criminal division under President Carter, said he recalls no instance in which officials suggested prosecution of a news organization. He said there were recommendations for investigating and prosecuting Government officials who disclosed sensitive information, but that these failed.

* * *

October 16, 1986

PORNOGRAPHIC MATERIAL: SHOULD IT BE OUTLAWED?

By EDWIN McDOWELL

In 1970, a Presidential commission found that pornography did not contribute to crime, delinquency or sexual deviancy. This year, the Attorney General's Commission on Pornography, established at the request of President Reagan, found a "causal relationship" between certain kinds of pornography and acts of sexual violence.

In the 16 years between the two reports, public perceptions and attitudes have undergone significant changes. Moreover, Ronald Reagan was elected in 1980 with the support of social conservatives and religious fundamentalists who disputed the findings of the 1970 commission, and they have helped to revive the national debate over pornography—a debate that many people thought had been settled by several Supreme Court rulings in 1973 (notably Miller v. California) that obscene materials should be judged by contemporary standards in each community.

But pornography is not the exclusive concern of the social and religious right. Politicians in both major parties are preaching the virtues of traditional morality and family values, with which pornography seems to be strongly at odds, and a growing number of religious leaders are speaking out against it. Many feminists insist that pornography encourages sexual violence by portraying women as willing objects of male degradation and abuse. Even some liberals have become disillusioned by the sexual permissiveness of the 1960's and 70's.

"The debate on pornography now has been mainstreamed—it is no longer the concern of just the extremists in this country," said the Rev. Bruce Ritter, the founder of Covenant House, an agency that aids homeless and abused children. Mr. Ritter was also a member of the Attorney General's Commission, familiarly known as the Meese commission, after Attorney General Edwin Meese 3d.

Mr. Meese said the two-volume, 1,960-page report would not be used as a basis for censorship. Other supporters of the report say none of its 92 recommendations—ranging from more vigorous enforcement of existing laws to citizens' boycotts of pornography merchants—are designed to encourage book burners.

The Background

While the Meese commission focused largely on X-rated films, videotapes and adult magazines, censorship of materials deemed to be pornographic or obscene has historically been directed at the written word. James Joyce's "Ulysses" was banned from the United States as obscene, under the 19th-century Comstock Act, until Judge John M. Woolsey declared in 1934 that it was "a sincere and serious attempt to devise a new literary method for the observation and description of mankind." Today the book is regarded as one of the finest novels ever written.

Similarly, the unexpurgated "Lady Chatterley's Lover" by D. H. Lawrence was banned as obscene until 1959, yet it is now regarded as a major work by a major author.

The national debate about pornography revolves primarily around material that is, to quote the commission's definition of pornography, "sexually explicit and intended primarily for the purpose of sexual arousal." The Supreme Court has ruled that obscene material—sexually explicit material that lacks artistic or literary merit—is unprotected by the First Amendment, and that judges can apply "contemporary community standards."

For Censorship

Supporters of legislation to outlaw pornography insist that they are not vigilantes. But they argue that the pornography industry is increasingly offering films and publications depicting acts of violence, bestiality, bondage and pornography involving children.

Opposition to exploitation of children in pornographic films has galvanized a large group of activists, including the National Organization for Women, which also warned against using revulsion over pornography "as an excuse to spread bigotry and hatred against lesbians and gay men."

Supporters also say laws against pornography are no more restrictive of freedom of the press than libel laws or laws against plagiarism, and they insist it is possible to prohibit smut without affecting books and magazines that are not pornographic.

Against Censorship

Opponents of anti-pornography legislation say such laws necessarily violate the First Amendment. They assert that those pushing for such legislation, like those who prevented Americans from having access to "Ulysses" and "Lady Chatterley's Lover," fail to distinguish between pornography and that which is merely erotic. Since no one is compelled to buy pornographic films, videotapes or magazines, they say, the popularity of such material proves there is a demand for it among adults, who should be permitted to view or read what they want.

Moreover, most foes contend there is no scientific evidence to support the Meese commission's finding of a causal relationship between pornography and sexual violence. "It tries to deceive Americans into believing that there is a sound scientific and legal basis for suppressing sexually oriented materials," said Barry Lynn, legislative counsel for the American Civil Liberties Union.

The Outlook

Pressure from Washington has already helped to prompt more than 17,000 stores, apparently including the 4,500-store 7-Eleven chain, to stop carrying sex magazines, most of whose circulations had been falling even before this year. But Mr. Meese himself has said that such issues should be left primarily to local governments. At the same time the sex industry is said to be suffering from falling sales and revenues, dozens of cities and states have passed anti-pornography laws or are debating doing so.

In June, by a margin of more than 2 to 1, voters in Maine rejected a proposal that would have made it crime to sell or promote obscene material, and there is little Congressional enthusiasm for any sweeping anti-pornography legislation. Even Americans who would support laws curtailing the worst aspects of pornography are not likely to give governments broad authority to regulate what they or their neighbors can read or watch in their homes.

* * *

August 3, 1987

BRITISH PRESS DOES/DOESN'T OBEY BOOK BAN

By FRANCIS X. CLINES
Special to the New York Times

LONDON, Aug. 2—The British press, banned by the nation's highest court from reporting the memoirs of a retired intelligence agent, resorted to mockery and traditional Fleet Street opportunism today.

As the anomalies of the ban are working out, people in northern England and Wales were able to "overhear" less expurgated news accounts of the memoirs, "Spycatcher," broadcast from Scotland and Northern Ireland, which have separate laws.

Only one newspaper directly violated the ban: The News on Sunday printed excerpts from the memoirs under a big headline, "A Law Made to Be Broken."

Government Called Tyrannical

"We refuse to be silenced by Thatcher's obsessive and increasingly tyrannical Government," the paper declared. The paper printed part of a chapter describing the charges by the author, Peter Wright, a retired secret service deputy director, that right-wing colleagues had bugged foreign embassies and plotted more than a decade ago to use the M.I.5 counterintelligence agency against a Labor Government they considered sympathetic to Communism.

The Thatcher Government has not yet cracked down here under the ban, which was affirmed 3 to 2 by the House of Lords' law committee Thursday. But Downing Street's continuing vigilance was clear as it reached out to Hong Kong for an injunction to stop The South China Sunday Morning Post from continuing its serialization of the book.

Although many Sunday newspaper articles and editorials implied defiance, the nation's major large-circulation newspapers, with large fines a possibility, declined to cross the Rubicon of printer's ink laid down by the House of Lords and publish direct excerpts from the book. Rather, the papers expressed their outrage by publishing paraphrasings of past debates in the House of Commons, whose proceedings are not covered by the ban.

"This news report is published under British Government restrictions," The Observer declared in an small-type preface to its front-page article, a device obviously intended to echo the cautions regularly carried on dispatches censored by the South African Government. The Observer further made its point by printing a page from the book and opting for self-censorship in inking out lengthy passages and words to dramatize the effect of the ban.

The book itself continued to sell at marked-up prices on the streets, arriving by mail order from the American publisher and even being read aloud in Hyde Park in a censorship protest that was a quandary for broadcasters faced with taping the event for newscasts. Hyde Park was the site of an 1855 riot that civil libertarians thought had established an unfettered British press "into perpetuity."

Nothing from the park that would violate the ban was broadcast initially, but radio listeners hearing Alistair Cooke's weekly "Letter From America" were told how the British ban had made a "skyrocketing" best seller of the book in the United States, even though Mr. Wright's tale may seem arcane in the colonies. "I imagine thousands of Americans are going to be deeply disappointed, not to say baffled," Mr. Cooke said of the book, which some reviewers have noted is long on melodramatic cliché and short on corroborating evidence.

The first front in Prime Minister Margaret Thatcher's campaign to silence Mr. Wright—the leaking of official secrets—appeared lost with the book's publication last month in New York by Viking Penguin Inc. But the press ban and a related court fight in Australia, where Mr. Wright lives, are still directed against the second front—his profiting from the exploitation of his Government service.

Farcical, Press Says

In its outcry at the lack of an explicit constitutional guarantee of press freedom, the press has called the "Spycatcher" situation farcical, Byzantine and reactionary, noting that most of the world but Britain can read all about it.

The BBC's venerable World Service, still the hallmark for objective radio newscasting, chose to discontinue extensive coverage of the Government's court action in Australia aimed at banning the book. The BBC has long been under intense scrutiny from Thatcherite critics, and the House of Lords' ruling restricted the British press from using Australia as a forum to publicize Mr. Wright's charges. Scottish and Northern Ireland journalists, however, have decided they are entitled to present full court reports.

In declining to sail into the teeth of the ban and print direct excerpts from the memoirs, The Sunday Times contended that "enough information can be culled from existing published sources to tell the substance of the story." Instead, it resorted to a standard device for thorny issues and polled the public, finding that 56 percent feel the Government's handling of the affair had gone "badly."

However, any campaign for stronger press guarantees was not supported in the poll, with voters diffused roughly evenly at about 25 percent among options on whether the existing official secrets laws are restrictive, lax or about right. On this, the British public presented its strongest feeling, 27 percent, in registering "no opinion."

* * *

December 6, 1987

CRIES OF CENSOR AS BRITAIN BARS ANOTHER BROADCAST

By FRANCIS X. CLINES
Special to the New York Times

LONDON, Dec. 5—The British Government has stepped up its court actions against news organizations, stirring charges of authoritarian censorship as it blocked a BBC radio series on the inner workings of the intelligence agencies.

The BBC denounced the injunction against Friday's program as a draconian extension of the Government's resolute campaign against the publicizing of intelligence-related activities by Government employees.

The corporation complained the court writ obtained Thursday night stops it from even naming the author in the "Spycatcher" controversy, the now more than well-known Peter Wright, and from fully covering court hearings into the Government ban on publicizing his memoir and its charges of misdeeds by government agents.

The injunction bars the BBC from broadcasting any program containing interviews with present or former members of the security and intelligence services.

As the Government defended its actions as proper to protect state secrets, it obtained a separate and apparently unrelated court injunction against a television broadcast about the Irish troubles. Scheduled for Thursday night on Channel 4, an independent station, the program was to have presented a dramatic recreation of the literal record of a public court hearing into the murder convictions of six Irishmen in the 1973 bombing of two pubs in Birmingham that killed 21 people.

In that injunction, the Government, which has been rebutting charges of police abuse, successfully convinced the judges hearing the Birmingham appeal that the drama was "likely to undermine public confidence" in the court's ultimate ruling.

The effect of the double action heightened complaints from news executives that the Thatcher Government was trying to stifle open presentation of information in a democracy. Critics in Parliament raised cries of "tin-pot dictatorship" and a "dangerous slide into authoritarianism."

Sir Patrick Mayhew, the Attorney General, rose in response to declare that no Government censorship had occurred, only the enforcement of "the duty of the Government to protect the confidentiality that is owed to it" by officials in the intelligence services. Prime Minister Margaret Thatcher has spiritedly pursued the principle that agents must not be allowed to profiteer from confidences.

Critics complain that with the "Spycatcher" book widely brought in from America, the campaign has made a worldwide joke of Britain's preoccupation with its "officials secrets." "Spycatcher," banned here but a best seller in the United States, spawned the initial confrontation in which the Government previously blocked three newspapers from reporting Mr. Wright's charges that, before retiring from the intelligence service, he was privy to purported misdeeds by rogue groups of Government agents. These charges, which critics say had earlier been aired in publications never challenged by the Government, included purported bugging of foreign embassies by agents and attempts to destabilize the Labor Government of Prime Minister Harold Wilson.

In the latest dispute, the Government first sought a transcript in advance of the three-part BBC inquiry into intelligence activities, entitled "My Country Right or Wrong." When the network insisted the series breached no secrets and declined to cooperate, the Government won an order in the High Court stopping the broadcast.

The three-part report includes interviews with eight former or present intelligence officials and, in focusing on them, the Government successfully argued before the court its responsibility to insure that such officials maintain lifelong confidentiality.

John Birt, the BBC deputy director general, said the series was "a responsible examination of the role and accountability of the secret service."

The program moderator, Paul Barker, said the Government had taken a "quite ridiculous" action against a program that aimed not at breaching secrets but at presenting "very level-headed programs which would have added to public knowledge in the right sort of way."

* * *

January 14, 1988

COURT, 5–3, WIDENS POWER OF SCHOOLS TO ACT AS CENSORS

By STUART TAYLOR Jr.,
Special to the New York Times

WASHINGTON, Jan. 13—The Supreme Court ruled 5 to 3 today that public school officials have broad power to censor school newspapers, plays and other "school-sponsored expressive activities."

The Court held that in activities that are 'part of the school curriculum' and might seem to carry the school's imprimatur, officials may bar dissemination of student statements about drugs, sexual activity, pregnancy, disputed political issues and other matters when doing so would serve "any valid educational purpose,"

The case began in May 1983 when a high school principal in Hazelwood, Mo., deleted two pages from the school newspaper, published as part of the journalism curriculum, because he considered two articles about divorce and student pregnancy inappropriate.

Narrower View of Rights

Justice Byron R. White's majority opinion upheld the deletion saying, "no violation of First Amendment rights occurred."

The ruling, reversing a Federal appellate decision, continued a recent trend in which the Court has taken a narrower view of the constitutional rights of public school students than that suggested by its earlier rulings.

The decision did not overrule any Supreme Court precedent.

But Justice William J. Brennan Jr., who wrote the dissenting opinion, assailed the majority for "deviating from precedent" to approve censorship and "thought control in the high school."

'A Civics Lesson'?

He added: "The young men and women of Hazelwood East expected a civics lesson but not the one the Court teaches them today." Justices Thurgood Marshall and Harry A. Blackmun joined in the dissent.

Chief Justice William H. Rehnquist and Justices John Paul Stevens, Sandra Day O'Connor and Antonin Scalia joined in the majority opinion. The decision ended a suit by three former students of HazelWood East High School who were staff members of the newspaper Spectrum. The ruling was denounced by many press groups and civil rights and civil liberties organizations but was praised by some educators and others. The Court did not say whether its ruling would apply to state universities as well as schools. But in other contexts, the Court has suggested there is broader protection of constitutional rights in universities.

The two deleted pages of the paper contained six articles, two of which were considered inappropriate by the principal, Robert F. Reynolds. One article included interviews with three unnamed but possibly identifiable students about their pregnancies and experiences with sex and birth control, The other discussed divorce and included a student's complaints about her father. Neither contained graphic accounts of sexual activity.

Student staff members of the paper had challenged the censorship as a violation of their First Amendment right of free speech. The First Amendment bars government officials, including public but not private school officials, from violating those rights.

The Court's Reasoning

The Court ruled there had been no First Amendment violation. Citing the familiar rationale that public school officials may restrict student speech in school more than government many restrict the speech of citizens generally, it added that schools have especially wide latitude to censor student speech in newspapers and other activities that are sponsored and financed by the schools.

Some lower courts have held that student speech in school newspapers, plays and other activities enjoy far broader constitutional protection than they apparently will enjoy after today.

Justice White's opinion extended the Court's previous reasoning that a school need not tolerate student speech inconsistent with its "basic educational mission" even though "the government could not censor similar speech outside the school."

The case was the Court's third decision in the past two years limiting students' constitutional rights in public schools. Two years ago, it approved "reasonable' searches, without a warrant, of students and their lockers.

Justice White's opinion limited a rule that the Court laid down in a major 1969 decision, Tinker v. Des Moines School District, protecting students' right of free speech.

Distinction of Curriculum

In that case the Court upheld the right of students to wear black armbands to protest the Vietnam War, and cast doubt on school censorship of student speech that does not "materially disrupt classwork or involve substantial disorder or invasion of the rights of others."

Today, Justice While reaffirmed the Tinker decision's statement that students in public schools do not "shed their constitutional rights to freedom of expression at the schoolhouse gate."

But he said the Tinker rules limit only "educators' ability to silence a student's personal expression that happens to occur on the school premises," and not speech that occurs within the school curriculum.

Protecting Anonymity

Mr. Reynolds, the principal, had based the decision to censor the newspaper on relatively narrow grounds: protecting the anonymity of the three unnamed students whose pregnancies were discussed in one article, and the rights of a father who had not been given a chance to respond to his daughter's sharply critical comments about him in the other. He also believed references to sexual activity and birth control were inappropriate for younger students.

But Justice White's opinion suggested the Court would approve any official censorship of school newspapers that could be related to "legitimate pedagogical concerns," even in the absence of such specific concerns.

He wrote: "A school must be able to take into account the emotional maturity of the intended audience in determining whether to disseminate student speech on potentially sensitive topics, which might range from the existence of Santa Claus in an elementary school setting to the particulars of teen-age sexual activity in a high school setting.

"A school must also retain the authority to refuse to sponsor student speech that might reasonably be perceived to advocate drug or alcohol abuse, irresponsible sex or conduct otherwise inconsistent with 'the shared values of a civilized social order.' "

Justice White added that schools could censor speech that might "associate the school with any position other than neutrality on matters of political controversy."

Newspaper as a Forum

One key aspect of the Court's decision was Justice White's rejection of the appellate court's ruling that the school newspaper was a "public forum" intended to be "a conduit for student viewpoint." Under the Court's precedents, government officials have very little latitude to limit expression in a "public forum."

Justice White emphasized that students writing for the Hazelwood East newspaper received academic credit and were edited and graded for their work. "The evidence that school officials never intended to designate Spectrum as a public forum is overwhelming," he wrote.

In his 15-page dissent in the case, Hazelwood School District v. Kuhlmeier, No. 86-836, Justice Brennan said the Hazelwood principal and the majority in today's decision "violated the First Amendment's prohibitions against censorship of any student expression that neither disrupts classwork nor invades the rights of others."

He said the decision "denudes high school students of much of the First Amendment protection that Tinker itself prescribed," instead of teaching youths "to respect the diversity of ideas that is fundamental to the American system."

Although the principal had said his chief concern was the privacy of the people mentioned, the former students, Cathy Kuhlmeier, Leslie Smart and Lee Ann Tippett-West, the real reason for the deletions was that the articles offended the "Personal sensibilities" of the principal and other officials.

Leslie D. Edwards, a St. Louis lawyer who represented the students who filed the suit, said she had not charged her clients a fee. Ms. Edwards said that if she had prevailed in the Supreme Court, she could have recovered the reasonable value of her services, which she estimated to be $150,000, from the school district and various school officials.

* * *

January 17, 1988

HIGH COURT GIVES A CIVICS LESSON

By FRED M. HECHINGER

In 1969, the Supreme Court ruled that students "do not shed their constitutional rights to freedom of speech or expression at the schoolhouse gate."

Last week, in a 5 to 3 ruling, the court put some limits on this broad view of the Bill of Rights when it decided that a student newspaper was part of a high school's curriculum and subject to censorship of any content that conflicted with a "valid educational purpose."

The case, Hazelwood School District v. Kuhlmeier, grew out of a long-standing conflict between two theories of education. The court sided with the traditionalists, who see the school as a molder of values for the immature. In the words of Justice Byron R. White, who wrote the majority opinion, schools must set "standards that may be higher than those demanded by some newspaper publishers or theatrical producers in the 'real' world."

On the other side of the controversy is a view of schools set forth by Horace Mann, the 19th-century patron saint of universal public education, and, more recently, by John Dewey, the philosopher of progressive education. These men, though not rejecting limits on students' rights, held that schools are not enclaves apart from the "real world." Dewey described them instead as "embryonic" versions of society in which students learn to act as citizens in a democracy.

In a dissent that was solidly in the tradition of Dewey, Justice William J. Brennan Jr. wrote that the mere claim by school officials that student expression is incompatible "with the school's pedagogical message" does not justify suppression.

Otherwise, he wrote, school officials could convert public schools into "enclaves of totalitarianism."

Instilling Morality

Justice Brennan conceded that educators have an "undeniable, and undeniably vital, mandate to inculcate moral and political values" but that this is "not a general warrant to act as thought police."

"The young men and women of Hazelwood East," he wrote, "expected a civics lesson, but not the one the Court teaches them today."

The case began in 1983 when Robert Eugene Reynolds, the principal of Hazelwood East High School in a suburb of St. Louis, barred the school newspaper, Spectrum, from publishing articles about teen-age pregnancy, birth control and the impact of divorce on children. Cathy Kuhlmeier and two other student editors charged unsuccessfully in Federal District Court that their First Amendment rights had been violated. The ruling against them was reversed by the Court of Appeals for the Eighth Circuit. Invoking Tinker v. Des Moines Independent Community School District, a 1969 ruling that upheld the right of students to wear black arm bands to protest the Vietnam war, the appeals court agreed that constitutional freedoms had been abridged.

In the Supreme Court's reversal of the appellate court, Justice White upheld the school authorities' right to censor speech that is "ungrammatical, poorly written, inadequately researched, biased or prejudiced, vulgar or profane, or unsuitable for immature audiences," none of which (with the possible exception of the last point) was at issue in the Hazelwood case.

Students' rights, Justice White wrote, are not automatically those of adults. He referred to an earlier ruling, Bethel School District No. 403 v. Fraser, which upheld a principal's right to discipline a student for delivering a speech in a school auditorium that, though not legally obscene, was "sexually explicit."

The Court did not charge the Hazelwood students with obscenity or violation of good taste. It merely held that interviews with students about their pregnancies violated their privacy, even though their real names had been withheld, and that another, also anonymous student's comments on her father's behavior prior to his divorce had not given the parents a chance to respond.

The Hazelwood ruling is not likely to put an end to the controversy. There is much agreement, shared by the dissenting Justices and spelled out in the Tinker decision on antiwar arm bands, that limits exist to student rights, in particular those of the student press. But there is no consensus about how far school administrators can go in imposing their own views, or those of the political mainstream.

On this point the disagreement is clear-cut: Justice White believes that principals may reject any student expression that could "associate the school with any position other than neutrality on matters of political controversy." Justice Brennan emphasizes the importance of "teaching children to respect the diversity of ideas that is fundamental to the American system."

For decades the student press has taken a zig-zag course between docile publications that attract little attention and the more enterprising or provocative ones that are read and debated. During the campus upheavals of the late 1960's, students came to equate supervision with suppression, and rebelled by creating an underground press that eluded adult influence altogether. This same spirit of rebellion led to the Tinker case and the limits it placed on the authority of school administrators. With last week's ruling, the principals have regained lost ground, but they will be under an even greater burden to draw the difficult distinction between instilling values and repressing developing minds.

* * *

March 6, 1988

GLIMMERINGS OF IRISH HERO FOR THE BRITISH

By FRANCIS X. CLINES
Special to the New York Times

BRISTOL, England, Feb. 28—A tiny part of the British public claimed a blow for free expression as they gathered here to view some forbidden glimmerings of Michael Collins, the Irishman who led the rebel war against Britain almost seven decades ago.

A dramatic presentation of the life of Collins, barred from British television 15 years ago as politically inflammatory, fluttered across screens in a conference room here filled by about 100 people.

The event was presented at a two-day regional meeting of the Campaign for Press and Broadcast Freedom, both as a fresh dare to the authorities and a celebration of incremental progress by English and Irish critics of censorship over news coverage of the sectarian troubles in Ireland.

"I can't understand how they got a hold of it," said Lord Grade, the private-sector television executive who chose to keep the show, "Hang Up Your Brightest Colors," off the air. "I thought all copies were destroyed."

There are no plans now for broadcast in Britain of the program, which was discovered in the National Film Archives in London.

Called Civil Rights Problem

Lord Grade still feels it is too one-sided and unfairly anti-British to merit screening. But participants at the weekend conference, which attracted several hundred people, were acknowledging its bias even as they argued that the larger issue was a civil rights problem with the variety of ways in which the free flow of information about Ireland can be crimped.

In particular, critics cited the "reference upward system" used by the British Broadcasting Corporation to double-check with superiors whether anti-terrorist regulations permit various journalistic endeavors on the Irish story that underlings might be anxious about. The system has been defended by broadcasting authorities as necessary and reasonably used but denounced by critics as a pro-Government form of self-censorship.

Conference participants also cited the British Government's use of laws to bar from England some of the more articulate non-paramilitary spokesmen of the continuing nationalist campaign in Northern Ireland. Government officials have defended these travel limitations as justified, citing the at times incendiary level of tensions punctuated by pub bombings in England.

Critics also cited the Irish Republic's moves to take its own anti-terrorist laws a step further and ban from the airwaves the views of any spokesmen for Sinn Fein, the political arm of the outlawed Irish Republican Army. One resultant anomaly is that listeners in the southern republic, who can vote for Sinn Fein candidates, might occasionally hear a Sinn Fein voice over British airwaves, but not on their own.

Measures Defended

Over the years, both Governments have defended the measures as warranted in the face of the emergency presented in this modern era of renewed violence. But critics like Liz Curtis, a specialist on journalism and Ireland, contended here that any limitation on the broadcasting of information and sectarian viewpoints only compounded the problem of ever finding a solution.

Conference participants attended showings of some of the four score television programs about Northern Ireland that Miss Curtis has documented as banned, censored or delayed in the last three decades. The list begins with a "See It Now" excerpt in 1959 when British authorities intervened to prevent BBC transmission of an interview by Edward R. Murrow with Siobhan McKenna, the Irish actress who attracted attention by referring to rebel internees in the Irish republic as "young idealists."

The conference here provided a reminder that publications and television constitute one of the many battlefronts in the centuries-old British-Irish struggle. And the Collins film was the source of a heated skirmish back in 1973, with its impassioned evocation of the ghost of Collins through a polemical series of dramatic monologues that tended to blister the British history.

A Critic's Viewpoint

One film critic in the audience, Susan Boyd-Bowman of the University of Bristol, concluded that the intense dramatization was clearly short on historical balance and "a hagiography of one lone hero-martyr."

But she and other conference participants emphasized that at least it engaged them in an issue riddled with ignorance and shadows.

"Even a film with factual errors, but which makes the conflict resonate, deserves a place alongside the sober TV histories of the troubles and the lyrical celebrations of Irish culture," Miss Boyd-Bowman said.

* * *

November 6, 1988

CENSORING CAMPUS NEWS

By DIRK JOHNSON

When the student newspaper at Northern Illinois University in DeKalb uncovered a scandal that was costing the school thousands of dollars, the paper, The Northern Star, was widely praised.

But not everyone was pleased. The muck being raked involved the university president, Clyde Wingfield. Remodeling work being done at his home, The Northern Star had learned, far exceeded what the school had budgeted. Mr. Wingfield condemned The Star for "negative" reporting, and later removed the newspaper's adviser, Jerry Thompson, from his post.

"When I received the memo kicking me out of the building," Mr. Thompson said, "I had never even seen Wingfield," on that subject or any other.

Ultimately, it was the college president who was kicked out of the building. When the smoke cleared, Mr. Wingfield had been dismissed from his post as president, and Mr. Thompson was eventually returned to the newspaper.

For proponents of a free press on the college campus, the story had a happy ending. But collegiate press watchers express concern that censorship on campus—most such cases, they say, are not publicized—might be on the rise. The Supreme Court in January gave its blessing to high schools that wish to censor the student press. And advocates of the college press worry that the decision will embolden administrators in higher education to crack the whip too.

In the Supreme Court case, a majority held that administrators at Hazelwood High School, in Hazelwood, Mo., were entitled to prevent students from writing about specific cases of pregnancy and divorce at the school, even though no names were used. Justice Byron R. White, writing for the majority, declared that "A school need not tolerate student speech that is inconsistent with its basic educational mission, even though the government could not censor similar speech outside the school."

And in a footnote that has raised concern among collegiate journalists, the Court left unclear whether it might sanction censorship of college papers: "We need not now decide whether the same degree of deference is appropriate with respect to school-sponsored activities at the college and university level."

Even before the Court decision, at least one study pointed to widespread censorship of college papers. Ivan Holmes, a professor at the University of Arkansas, visited 18 colleges to gauge the extent of press censorship, an investigation financed by a grant from the Gannett Foundation, in Rochester, N.Y., affiliated with the Gannett newspaper chain. "The censorship dragon," Mr. Holmes said, "is alive and well on university campuses throughout the United States."

Some college administrators, however, contend that if the university finances a school paper, it has not only the right but the responsibility to guide that paper's editorial policy. "As long as you take the king's shilling, you can't avoid doing some of the king's bidding," said Dr. John R. Silber, president of Boston University. On the other hand, Dr. Silber believes that campus newspapers should remain financially independent of the university, and thus free to pursue an independent editorial direction.

According to Mr. Holmes, the most practiced censor is the college administrator. But he found that student governments, faculty advisers and even student journalists themselves had been responsible for stifling free expression. Newspapers at some universities, he found, functioned largely as appendages of the public relations department. In one case, the newspaper adviser also served as the college public relations spokesman.

Mr. Holmes, a former adviser to the newspaper at Northeastern Oklahoma State University in Tahlequah, was himself no stranger to administrative attempts to control press coverage. After the paper, The Northeastern, published an account of an uproar over the dismissal of a football coach, university officials made it plain that such "negative" news was not the appropriate mission of a college publication. The university eventually tried to bring The Northeastern under the wing of the public relations director.

In his report, "Censorship of the Campus Press: A Study of 18 University Newspapers," Mr. Holmes found censorship in each case study. "A final conclusion," he said, "was that even though heavy-handed control and censorship of the campus press is widespread, no one really seems to care. In the cases at hand, not only did journalism organizations fail to help student editors in the censorship battle, but professional media in the area offered little or no assistance."

Many professional journalists, however, have voiced outrage over attempts to muzzle their student colleagues and expressed concern that in too many cases, collegiate reporters are being cheated of the chance to hone their news gathering skills. For students considering careers in journalism, these stifling conditions can sour them on the field. In the words of Paul McMasters, the deputy editorial director of USA Today, the administrators will have "won their public relations battle, but lost the academic war."

Mr. McMasters, who serves as freedom of information chairman for the Society of Professional Journalists, mocked the Hazelwood decision for "discovering a subspecies of citizens—those who can study the Constitution but are not extended the same rights as others."

He said, though, that he thought the vast majority of administrators respected the rights of a free college press. And he said those who sought to ban "negative" news were overreacting. "No university walls are going to tumble down as result of an article, editorial or cartoon," he said, "but there is the possibility of a lot of great journalists rising out of a free college press environment."

Since most cases of censorship, blatant or subtle, go undetected, it is difficult to gauge the effect on young journalists just beginning to test their limits and the system. In the DeKalb case, the university president's undisguised attempt to curb the newspaper's reporting not only failed, ultimately, to block the news about his actions; it also strengthened the resolve of the student paper's staff, which learned a lesson about press freedom that no textbook could have done as effectively.

Phil Luciano, who was The Star's city editor during the investigation, said the story, and its results, helped make up his mind about choosing a career. "I saw how a newspaper story could have an affect on people—how it could make a difference," said Mr. Luciano, 24, who now works the night police beat for The Peoria Journal Star. "There's always someone who tries to suppress the truth. But in journalism, there's a chance that the good guys will win."

But the "good guys," when it comes to battles over press censorship, don't always win. With a courageous newspaper adviser leading the way, Mr. Luciano and others forged ahead in the face of the college president's opprobrium. But it takes a supremely confident student to stand up to the authorities.

The Washington-based Student Press Law Center, which provides legal counsel to high school and college newspapers, said complaints of censorship had been rising in recent years. So far this year, the group has received more than 350 calls from student journalists complaining about censorship. And since the Supreme Court decision, the center said many student journalists now believed they had little recourse against censorship.

"It's not as if the problem is new, but we are seeing an increase in cases of censorship," said Mark Goodman, executive director of the center. "The emphasis given to free expression is definitely on the wane. Fifteen or twenty years ago, there was a greater tolerance on campus for individuals offering viewpoints that differed from those of administrators or a majority of students."

In part, Mr. Goodman contended, the changed atmosphere for the student press results from a new attitude among college administrators. "School administrators today seem to have much more training in the corporate-management point of view," he said. "To them, running a school is like running a business. These administrators might be very good at things like the bottom line, maintaining the quality of the physical plant and so forth. But they tend not to view free expression as quite as relevant as we think it should be in an educational environment."

In addition, many of the faculty members now advising college newspapers do not come from news backgrounds. Rather, according to observers, they are trained as advertising or public relations experts—fields perhaps less used to flexing the muscle of the First Amendment.

As has historically been the case with free-expression battles, many censorship issues today have been triggered by unpopular views. A growing percentage of the censorship cases, Mr. Goodman said, involve "racial sensitivity." In most of these cases, he said, a student journalist has expressed a view that has offended members of a minority group.

Last year, many students and faculty members at the University of California at Los Angeles became enraged when the daily "U.C. Rooster" cartoon in the student newspaper, The Daily Bruin, one day showed the rooster being asked how he was admitted to U.C.L.A. "Affirmative Action," he responds.

The cartoon led to the suspension from The Bruin of two editors by the Associated Students Communications Board, which oversees student publications, on grounds that the cartoon was racially insensitive. The board revoked the suspensions the next day. But the cartoon continued to cause outrage—and sparked another issue of press freedom—at another California college.

At the California State University in Northridge, a student editor of The Daily Sundial, James Taranto, was angered by what he considered a violation of press freedom in the U.C.L.A. case. Mr. Taranto, the news editor, wrote and published an article contending that the cartoon addressed a political issue—affirmative action—and not race per se.

"A university exists to promote the search for truth," Mr. Taranto wrote, "and censorship is always detrimental to that search." With the editorial, the paper published the controversial cartoon. As a result, Mr. Taranto was suspended from his post for two weeks.

The suspension was invoked by the newspaper's publisher, Cynthia Z. Rawitch, a journalism professor, who said Mr. Taranto had violated a policy that requires editors to consult with the publisher when dealing with controversial matters that could affect the legal standing or reputation of the paper. The newspaper's editors took the side of Ms. Rawitch, editorializing that The Sundial had learned "a valuable lesson in common sense."

"It is ironic that statements on race are being censored, just as they were 20 years ago," said Mr. Goodman. "Then, those who promoted racial desegregation were accused of 'inappropriate or offensive' views. Where would we be today if we had let those justifications . . . prevail?"

While the Supreme Court opinion in the Hazelwood case has raised some alarm about the college press, courts have traditionally backed collegiate journalists against efforts at censorship. Louis E. Ingelhart, professor emeritus at Ball State University in Muncie, Ind., and author of the book "Freedom of the College Student Press," said courts had ruled explicitly that university censorship amounted to state censorship, which is forbidden. "It doesn't matter if the paper is official, underground, funded by the university or not," said Mr. Ingelhart. "University administrators cannot legally censor student newspapers. But they try."

Mr. Holmes, in his study, contended that repressive conditions on campus were responsible for a recent decrease in students enrolling in the news-editorial sequence in the study of journalism. Other journalism professors believe that a tight job market and low starting wages have discouraged more potential journalists than have repressive administrations.

But clearly, many students are unwilling to incur the time, expense or wrath of faculty and administration by publishing controversial matters. Instead, they decide winning a battle is not worth losing a personal war. These quiet incidents, which rarely get reported, are perhaps most troubling, collegiate journalists said. In the Holmes study, for example, one newspaper editor said he bowed to pressure not to publish an article about a lawsuit filed by a film student against a professor. And the film student, who contended that the professor had plagiarized her work, dropped the lawsuit after being told she would not otherwise graduate, the editor said.

University officials commonly justify censorship on grounds of legal liability. But ironically, it is just such an effort to control newspaper content that can make the university legally responsible, Mr. Ingelhart said. "The universities that try to control editorial content get themselves into hot water on two counts," he said. "They are violating the First Amendment. And they are making themselves responsible for the content."

When the university allows the student paper to publish unfettered, it is the student journalists, not the university, who have legal responsibility, he said. That precedent, legal experts say, was set in a case involving the student newspaper at the University of Minnesota, The Minnesota Daily, which in 1979 published a parody that included a mock interview with Jesus that offended many on the Twin Cities campus. The following year, the university offered to allow students to take back the portion of their student-activities fee budgeted for the newspaper. The newspaper sued, charging censorship, and won a decision in 1983 from the U.S. Court of Appeals for the Eighth District.

Mr. Holmes has called for the creation of a national foundation to fight censorship of student newspapers, which would offer legal representation when necessary. The Student Law Press Center, which was established in 1974 by the Washington-based Robert F. Kennedy Memorial, set up by journalists, is largely limited to giving advice, he said. Moreover, he said, the foundation should compile and publish a list of those student newspapers that function as "public relations tools" for university officials.

Censorship on campus has become so pervasive, Mr. Holmes contends, that it could ultimately lead to a more docile professional journalistic work force. But he added, "There are still a number of bright, dedicated, free-press-minded journalism students on university newspapers doing their jobs, and doing them well, under some very trying circumstances."

Dirk Johnson is The Times's Denver bureau chief.

* * *

March 5, 1989

THATCHER PUTS A LID ON CENSORSHIP IN BRITAIN

By JAMES ATLAS

Charter 88 arrived on the newsstands of Britain with the rhetorical force of a Tom Paine tract.

"We are losing our liberties—because they do not belong to us as citizens," read the text in colorful bold print on the cover of the New Statesman & Society last December.

Inside was a two-page manifesto: The untrammeled mandate of Margaret Thatcher, the most powerful Prime Minister in England since the end of World War II, had enabled her "to menace the independence of broadcasting; to threaten academic freedom in the universities and schools; to tolerate abuses committed in the name of national security." What was urgently needed, the charter's authors declared, was a bill of rights, a written constitution that would guarantee the basic liberties on which democracy is founded: "The time has come to demand political, civil and human rights in the United Kingdom."

Among the supporters of this fiery proclamation were the novelists Martin Amis and Julian Barnes, the philosopher Sir Alfred Ayer, the playwright Michael Frayn and 250 other highly recognizable names—a significant proportion of the English intelligentsia, in fact.

But Charter 88 was more than a left-wing magazine's isolated protest. To hear people talk, England in 1988 was Prague in 1977. There was the 20th of June Group, founded last summer by a cadre of disaffected writers who convened for dinner at the home of the playwright Harold Pinter to form what the eminent barrister and novelist John Mortimer described as "a strong and sensible Opposition." There was a special issue of Index on Censorship, featuring contributions from Stephen Spender, Richard Hoggart and other distinguished commentators on the cultural scene, dedicated to the proposition that freedom was being "diminished" in the United Kingdom. There was Samizdat, a newsletter established to "challenge the divisiveness of the Government and the fear of the new of so many of its opponents."

The people may not have been ready to storm Parliament and exile Thatcher to France, as they did James II. Freedom of the press is an issue that excites the press and intellectuals more than anyone else. Yet it wasn't only the "chattering classes" (as disdainful Tory columnists refer to the Charter 88 constituency) who were up in arms. Even the glossy Illustrated London News published an article by the novelist Ludovic Kennedy in its December issue chronicling the Government's authoritarian drift: the British Broadcasting Corporation, long the showcase of British culture, was being brought to heel by attempts to censor programs hostile to Thatcher's policies; a ban on live radio or television interviews with terrorists was in effect, and Parliament was considering a revision of the Official Secrets Act that would essentially do away with the "harm," or public interest, making the disclosure of Government information a crime—no matter what kind or whether disclosing it would pose a danger.

The remarkable thing about Kennedy's enumeration of grievances was the ideological diversity of the politicians he enlisted on their behalf: Roy Hattersley, deputy leader of the Labor Party; Richard Shepherd, a Conservative Member of Parliament; even J. Enoch Powell, a former Member of Parliament not known for his liberal sentiments.

None of Kennedy's deponents was prepared to say that totalitarianism loomed on the horizon, but clearly something had gone wrong. "Liberty is ill in Britain," warned the American legal philosopher Ronald Dworkin, a professor of jurisprudence at Oxford, writing in Index. "The very concept of liberty—the universal, seamless idea at stake in all these separate and diverse controversies—is being challenged and corroded by the Thatcher Government."

Certainly "the intensification of authoritarian rule" that the authors of Charter 88 detected in contemporary Britain was more than a reflexive protest against the growing political power of Thatcher's "regime"—as her long tenure in office is often and without irony described, even by the Prime Minister herself. In the last few months, newspapers of every political persuasion have been obsessed with the new measures her Government has put forth, especially the Official

Secrets Act reform and the protection of privacy bill now before Parliament, an attempt to crack down on the excesses of England's gossip-mongering tabloid press.

The biggest furor was over "Death on the Rock," a Thames Television documentary about three Irish terrorists who were gunned down by the Special Air Services regiment in Gibraltar in 1988. In Parliament, Thatcher denounced the program as "trial by television," and tried to have it suppressed, even threatening to suspend the network's license. After an independent inquiry largely vindicated the program's findings this winter, Thatcher rejected the report as biased and inaccurate. By the end of January, even the normally conservative Sunday Times of London was warning that "the defense of personal freedom has now slid alarmingly low in the priorities of Mrs. Thatcher's Government."

The press wasn't the only constituency under assault. Civil libertarians could point to the Public Order Act, designed to restrict the public's right to engage in political demonstrations; and, perhaps most sinister of all, a change in legal procedure that would limit a defendant's right to not testify. The purpose of this proposed amendment was to make it easier to convict terrorists unwilling to testify on their own behalf—but Home Secretary Douglas Hurd would like to see it become law throughout England, and in the end it probably will.

To an American, accustomed to the defense of individual rights afforded by the Constitution and the Bill of Rights, the power concentrated in the hands of the British Government is extraordinary. Thatcher has often expressed her belief in the rule of law; but it's Parliament that makes the laws. The right to freedom of speech can be found in England's Bill of Rights of 1689—parliamentary free speech. One axiom I heard a lot when I was over there in December: "We're subjects. You're citizens." This difference is fundamental, inscribed in the two nations' divergent histories. The opposition to censorship affirmed by John Milton and John Stuart Mill, those classic defenders of liberty, is "sewn into Britain's banner," notes Oxford's Ronald Dworkin. But so is official tyranny. Milton's "Areopagitica" was written as a protest against a 1643 Order of Parliament requiring a license to publish. "There is, in fact, no recognized principle by which the propriety or impropriety of Government interference is customarily tested," Mill observed two centuries later.

And so it still is in England. Freedom of the press, freedom of speech—what Dworkin calls "the culture of liberty"—is just that: a culture, not a legal code. There is nothing like our First Amendment, nor does Thatcher feel the need for one. In her view, measures such as the Official Secrets Act and the protection of privacy bill are essential to the maintenance of an orderly society. "The Prime Minister does not believe that people have a right to know," contends Kevin Boyle, director of Article 19, an international organization devoted to monitoring censorship.

"The White Paper on the Government's proposed reform of the Official Secrets Act is talking about information on any subject," objected Richard Shepherd, writing in The Times of London. "E.E.C. proposals on taxation, consumer

Associated Press

Peter Wright wrote the long-suppressed "Spycatcher," about his days as a spy.

affairs, acid rain or the allocation of airline routes would be caught." In other words, only the Government can determine what constitutes a threat to it.

But what makes Thatcher so powerful has less to do with any legislation she has put forward than with the sheer force of her personality and her determination to implement her beliefs—"conviction politics," she calls them. England must become competitive; socialism must be "killed" (Thatcher's word); the Irish Republican Army must be stopped.

Indeed, it's the doings of the I.R.A., I suspect, that have impelled the Prime Minister to strengthen her hand. Governments have always been obsessed with national security: Witness the Reagan Administration's persistent attempts to subvert the Freedom of Information Act. What is happening in England now is a response to an actual enemy within. There's a war on. When Amnesty International announced its intention to monitor the I.R.A. shootings in Gibraltar, Thatcher told the House of Commons, "I hope Amnesty has some concern for the more than 2,000 people murdered by the I.R.A. since 1969." And when "Death on the Rock" was shown, she was asked by a foreign journalist if she was furious; her response, she said, went "deeper than that." The I.R.A. bombed a Brighton hotel during a Tory conference in 1984, and several Government officials were killed; Thatcher herself nearly died in the attack. England, to her way of thinking, is under siege.

Why has resistance to Thatcher's repressive policies suddenly erupted with such vehemence? After all, they're nothing new. In 1983, a Government clerk who leaked to The Guardian a memorandum from the Minister of Defense that United States cruise missiles were about to be installed in England was sentenced to six months in jail. A year later, there was the notorious trial, and subsequent acquittal, of Clive Ponting, a Ministry of Defense official who gave Parliament details of a Government memo that raised questions about the sinking of an Argentinean battleship during the Falklands War.

But these were misdemeanors compared with "Spycatcher"—a synecdoche for the disastrous effort to suppress Peter Wright's best-selling memoir of his life as a spy in the British Security Service. The Crown sued to prevent publication on the ground that the book contained state secrets. The court vindicated Wright, but the Government obtained an injunction enjoining newspapers in England from any mention of the case. Last October, after years of litigation, the Law Lords—England's Supreme Court—found against the Government. The book had already been widely read all over the world, they reasoned. Thanks to this bit of legalistic casuistry, "Spycatcher" could finally be published in England.

What was it about Wright's memoir that provoked such stringent measures? To be sure, it does contain some embarrassing revelations, among them an account of the campaign (since substantiated by David Leigh in "The Wilson Plot") to discredit Prime Minister Harold Wilson as a Soviet agent and drive him from office. But, in the end, as Wright's collaborator, Paul Greengrass, says in his introduction, "Spycatcher" is "just a book," war stories "told by the fire, a drink in hand."

The Government saw it otherwise. To publish state secrets—or what were perceived as such—violated an ancient unwritten code of ethics. From the Privy Counsellor's Oath of Confidentiality, drafted in 1250 and still sworn by Cabinet ministers on bended knees before the Queen, to the Official Secrets Act of 1911, Government has required blind fealty of those in its service. The notion that a public official could be answerable to some higher authority, either moral or religious, is simply—in the English phrase—not on.

Government employees aren't the only ones who've been singled out for prosecution. Duncan Campbell, one of the most zealous investigative journalists in England, was virtually put under house arrest after he did an episode for the BBC television series "Secret Society" about an $800 million spy satellite that the Thatcher Government had developed without informing Parliament. The Government seized film from BBC offices in Glasgow and raided Campbell's North London home.

Donald Trelford, editor of The London Observer, has also run afoul of the Government. "We're a bit beleaguered," said Trelford when I spoke with him in The Observer's offices. Dapper in a well-tailored dark suit, Trelford scarcely seems the beleaguered sort, but he has been dragged into court on a number of occasions.

"Knowledge is an offense now," Trelford lamented. "Information is Government property." It's not unusual, he says, for the Treasury Solicitor to demand that he promise not to publish certain information, otherwise he'll be served with an injunction. It has made for a contentious atmosphere: "When the Government threatens, I say, 'Well, sod them, we'll publish.' "

If newspaper editors feel a chill in the air, television is braced for a storm. In November, the Government issued still another White Paper, on "Broadcasting in the 90's," which put forth a series of proposals that could utterly transform the "culture of television."

No one is more aware of television's potential influence than Thatcher, who has called it "the most powerful form of communication known on this planet." But until now, control of this ubiquitous medium has eluded her grasp, especially the BBC, which Roy Jenkins, the Chancellor of Oxford, includes among the nation's "four great institutions"—the others being the Church of England, the House of Lords and "the ancient universities, Oxford and Cambridge."

Even though it is subsidized by the Government, the BBC is supposed to be an independent entity, with its own editorial policy and its own board of governors. Virtually since she took office, Thatcher has struggled to subdue the network to her purposes. A decade ago she was scolding the BBC for giving publicity to Irish terrorists; when the Falklands War broke out, she objected to certain broadcasters who didn't know it was "their duty to stand up for our boys."

What exasperates Thatcher about the BBC isn't just its independence. The way it's financed, by a licensing fee in the form of a tax on television sets, contradicts her "pay-your-own way" philosophy. In 1988, she summoned the nation's leading broadcasters to Downing Street and unveiled an innovative plan. Her vision, as The Times of London described it, was "new channels, more competition, and more efficiency." Deregulation, or "privatization"—a system of private financing—would make for "a more open and competitive broadcasting market," contended the Government's White Paper on Broadcasting.

John Birt, who took over as deputy director general of the BBC last year with a mandate to overhaul the system, was at first widely viewed as the Government's man, a television apparatchik. Despite his corporate demeanor, Birt is no company man. A few weeks earlier, he had published a stern article in The Independent opposing the ban on televised interviews with terrorists. To deny journalists the right to cover events as they saw fit, Birt argued, would undermine "some of the most cherished elements of a democratic society."

During a visit to Broadcasting House, I noted my surprise that he had come out with such a strong denunciation of the Home Office. It was "a departure," Birt conceded, but not the only instance. He reminded me that he had also resisted a Government injunction against another controversial program, "Spy in the Sky," about Zircon, the Government's controversial spy satellite. The BBC, he made it clear, would continue to be "very vigorous in wanting to assert its independence"

Whether it would be allowed to do so is another matter. As described in the recent White Paper on Broadcasting, the role of advertising would be greatly expanded. There will be open bidding for commercial television franchises, and the "eventual" replacement of the BBC licensing fee with some form of self-generated subsidy.

The networks reacted vehemently, predicting an era of game shows and soap operas. For Stuart Prebble of the

Campaign for Quality Television, the White Paper was "a detailed epitaph for the television which has been the envy of the world."

But in a way, it was too late to do much more than mourn. Satellites had already been launched that would soon give viewers access to as many as 25 channels, compared with the four they receive today. For England, like it or not, the age of cable has begun. It promises to be a commercial free-for-all, but with an Independent Television Commission to oversee the "liberalized commercial television sector," and a Broadcasting Standards Council to "reinforce standards of taste and decency." Deregulation, in other words, will mean more regulation for the independents.

"It is happening," Harold Pinter, a founding member of the 20th of June Group, said with quiet emphasis. We were talking in the comfortable, book-lined study of his Holland Park house. Pinter was troubled with ominous premonitions. "The country is in a much more extreme situation than is commonly realized. The power of the police to do whatever they like is extraordinary." England today, he maintained, has "a McCarthy period feel to it. The people are bewildered, fearful, undermined. Lost."

"Mountain Language," Pinter's new play, is a terse political allegory. The title refers to the dialect of the peasant women in the play, who have been forbidden by the authorities to speak their own language. It's a play, Pinter acknowledged, that says a good deal about what is happening in his own country.

But wasn't he himself allowed to write and say whatever he pleased? Well, yes, but there was a kind of unconscious self-censorship at work, he explained. One felt the Government there . . . lurking: "Phones are bugged. I know people who are under surveillance."

No doubt, there is an official vindictiveness emanating from Whitehall. But is it "the death knell of a democratic society," as Pinter contends, or merely a squabble between factions of the ruling class? To find out, I called on Lord Rees-Mogg, chairman of the Broadcasting Standards Council and former editor of The Times of London, at his antiquarian bookstore, Pickering & Chatto on Pall Mall. Lord Rees-Mogg, who is empowered to preview and prevent the showing of programs that he finds offensive, professed not to find the political climate "so very sinister. I can't remember when it wasn't so."

Indeed, what did all these dissenting writers have to complain about? They were making lots of money, Tory columnists were quick to note. They wrote whatever they pleased. Perhaps; but events of recent weeks have given renewed urgency to their cause and made it distinctly more real. Acting in response to the Ayatollah Ruhollah Khomeini's death edict against Salman Rushdie, the author of "The Satanic Verses," members of Article 19, Charter 88 and other writers' organizations convened to form an international committee for the defense of Rushdie. If there had ever been an instance of intolerable censorship, this was it.

For once, a conflict was unambiguous. When it came to the media-Thatcher feud, which side you were on seemed to

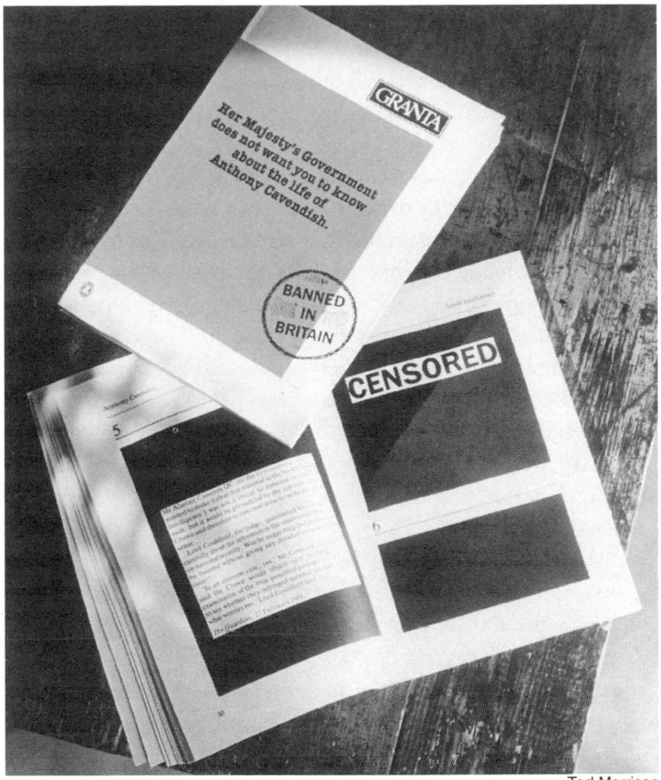

Ted Morrison

The censored issue of Granta, featuring Anthony Cavendish's "Inside Intelligence," from a banned book about his M16 days.

matter less than whether you had a visible byline. Paul Bailey had at John Mortimer, who had at The Spectator's Paul Johnson, who had at the whole British press. Writing in The Observer, Donald Trelford ended a vigorous editorial deploring the Official Secrets Act reform with a little anecdote: "Over the strawberries at Wimbledon last week, Lord Armstrong"—the Attorney General who tried the Government's case against "Spycatcher"—"said to me: 'The test of a new act is whether it is better than what went before.' Over the strawberries at Wimbledon . . .

I think there'll be massive public indifference and ridicule to the whole thing," predicted a Thatcher spokesman, responding to a question about Charter 88. The press simply doesn't have the power in England that it does in the United States; it doesn't go about its business with the same investigative zeal. The practice of leaking information from Government sources is virtually unknown. Without a mandate to challenge the information it receives, the press has become a courier between the Government and the public. The Telegraph itself, in a recent editorial, noted that journalists were "probably the most unpopular section of the community." So why bother about their problems? "Thatcher is an extremely shrewd judge of what the public cares about and what it doesn't," says Max Hastings, editor of the right-wing Daily Telegraph. "These are issues it doesn't care about."

I wondered if he wasn't right. One night, I attended a rally sponsored by the Campaign for Freedom of Information at the Friends Meeting House on Euston Road. I arrived early, expecting a noisy, passionate crowd. The auditorium was half-empty. The oratory was firm but polite. Paddy Ashdown, leader of the Social and Liberal Democrats, declared: "We have a Government that believes in 'need to know' and never in 'the right to know.' "

"Hear, hear," muttered the audience.

Listening to speech after speech in the drafty hall, I remembered something the American columnist Anthony Lewis had told me before I left: "The issues that make us rise in passion don't move the English." Which doesn't make them any less important, I thought. The essence of a democratic society, Mill argued in "On Liberty," is the right of its citizens to express unpopular beliefs, unfettered by "the moral coercion of public opinion." And freedom of the press is the means by which that right is guaranteed. Whether or not a majority of the people care about it is beside the point.

On my last night in England, I had a drink with Bill Buford, the editor of the literary magazine Granta. We met in the Groucho Club on Dean Street, a chic-seedy bar and restaurant straight out of an Anthony Powell novel. Black-stockinged waitresses circulated among the novelists and book reviewers lounging on sofas and plush chairs. Buford, a bearded, intense American who has made Granta a significant force on the Anglo-American literary scene, recounted how it came to pass that the summer 1988 issue carried on its cover the terse headline: "Her Majesty's Government Does Not Want You to Know About the Life of Anthony Cavendish."

Cavendish was a former agent in MI6, Britain's Secret Intelligence Service (if MI5 is Britain's Federal Bureau of Investigation, MI6 is its Central Intelligence Agency). He had written a memoir about his clandestine life and submitted it to MI6, only to be threatened with a fine—perhaps even a prison sentence—if he went ahead with publication. After a long court battle, his publisher, Cassell, gave up on the project, discouraged by mounting legal fees.

A year later, Cavendish self-published 500 copies of his book as a "Christmas card" to friends and associates. The Times of London acquired a copy and reported on the contents, upon which the Government obtained an injunction against any further printing of the book in any form.

It was hard to understand what all the fuss was about. Cavendish was the prototype of the British spy, at once upper-class and faintly decadent. The story of his exploits in Germany and the Middle East was fascinating and vividly written, but largely innocuous.

The Crown was adamant. The book couldn't appear. "I testified before a Q.C. Queen's Counsel," Buford said, "and he completely panicked. He'd been attending the 'Spycatcher' hearings, and he was afraid the Government would sue Viking Penguin for illegal profits on 'Spycatcher.' Basically, what he said was: 'They will go for you. They will kill you.' "

In the end, Buford went ahead and published excerpts in Granta.

As I was leaving, he gave me a copy of the Cavendish issue, and I read it on the bus out to Heathrow. Or tried to read it. Phrases, paragraphs, whole pages were blacked out. On others was a single word: CENSORED.

James Atlas is an editor of The New York Times.

* * *

July 9, 1989

ART ON THE FIRING LINE

By GRACE GLUECK

When, at the prospect of Congressional disfavor, the Corcoran Gallery of Art in Washington canceled a touring show of photographs by the late Robert Mapplethorpe, financed in part by the National Endowment for the Arts, the action raised issues about artistic freedom and censorship that bear directly on public support for the arts in this country.

Should such support include the right to sanitize art? Should a museum be subject to political pressures, or should its role as a protector of art entitle it to immunity from them? Should the public be kept from seeing a show it has helped pay for? What does a museum owe an artist to whose work it has committed itself? And who should decide how taxpayers' dollars are used—legislators, panels of esthetic experts or the "public," whoever that constitutes?

The Mapplethorpe show is a retrospective of the artist's work that contains images depicting homosexual and heterosexual erotic acts and explicit sadomasochistic practices in which black and white, naked or leather-clad men and women assume erotic poses. Along with these photographs are fashionable portraits of the rich and trendy, elegant floral arrangements and naked children—images that might not necessarily be considered indecent if viewed singly but that in this context seem provocative. (Signs accompanying the show on its tour suggested that it might be unsuitable for children.) Opposition to the exhibition by members of Congress, among them, Senator Jesse Helms, Republican of North Carolina, Senator Alfonse M. D'Amato, Republican of New York, and Representative Dick Armey, Republican of

The New York Times/Michael Geissinger

Protesters outside the Corcoran Gallery of Art on June 30—Was the cancellation Censorship or prudence?

"Self Portrait (With Gun and Star)," a 1982 Mapplethorpe work—Was the Corcoran the right setting?

Texas, has focused on the question of whether Government money should be used to support art that can be considered by some to be blasphemous or pornographic.

"I clearly know offensive art when I see it," said Representative Armey in a recent statement. "And there ought to be a way for the endowment to establish procedures where they can clearly deny funding for art like that. The arts do serve a role of probing the frontiers, but I would say let that be funded from the private sector."

In the simplest terms, the Mapplethorpe case could be called a tug of war between two hallowed elements the First Amendment guarantee of free speech and the community perception of what is pornographic or indecent. Yet to put it that way ignores the symbolic role of artists and museums in our culture. Artists are important to us, among other reasons, because of their ability to express what is deep or hidden in our consciousness, what we cannot or will not express ourselves. And museums are traditionally the neutral sanctuaries—entered voluntarily by the public—for this expression. What we see there may not always be esthetic, uplifting, or even civil, but that is the necessary license we grant to art.

A New Furor and a New Initiative

Cancellation of the Mapplethorpe show last month—coming after recent incidents involving artists criticized by elected officials and citizens' groups for works in which a flag was provocatively spread on a floor and a crucifix was submerged in urine—has not only created a new furor but has now prompted a specific legislative initiative that would make the National Endowment for the Arts more accountable for the nature of what it finances.

Recently, Representative Sidney R. Yates, the Illinois Democrat who heads the House subcommittee that authorizes the annual budget for the arts endowment, has proposed that the endowment itself be in charge of all of its grants, with subcontracting organizations no longer allowed to make grants in their own right. But Representative Yates remains a firm believer that the endowment, not legislators, should be the judge of its grantees.

To some people, the Corcoran's cancellation of the show was censorship, despite the protestations of Dr. Christina Orr-Cahall, the museum's director. "After all," she said in an interview last week, "the institution has a right to make a choice, too, right up until the exhibition goes on the wall. Canceling it is certainly preferable to the censorship of taking things out."

In the Corcoran case, the public was prevented from seeing a scheduled exhibition because the museum anticipated that certain Congressmen would judge its content as unsuitable and, in Dr. Orr-Cahall's opinion, penalize the National Endowment.

"The very notion that Government pressure has resulted in the inability of people to see an art exhibition is distressing and threatening," said Floyd Abrams, a lawyer specializing in First Amendment cases.

The Corcoran's action is not the first time a museum has canceled a controversial show. In 1982, for example, the Metropolitan Museum of Art in New York bowed to anticipated Arab pressure and canceled a scheduled exhibit of biblical artifacts. Some of these were from a museum in East Jerusalem, an area whose control by Israel is disputed by the Arabs. The Met finally presented the show in 1986, after protests from Jewish leaders and the securing of indemnification from the State Department against prospective lawsuits.

In the opinion of Dr. Jacob Neusner, University Professor at Brown University and a Reagan—appointed member of the National Council on the Arts—an advisory body to the endowment—the Corcoran's decision "set a dangerous precedent in canceling an artist's show because it was controversial."

"It was pusillanimous and dishonest in the extreme," Dr. Neusner continued. "There was absolutely no pressure on them from the endowment, and to say they were defending us is ridiculous. It is our job to take the heat, and our process knows how to deal with controversy. But they betrayed the process by acting as censors. In doing so, they raised the stakes. Had they not, the whole thing would've gone away. A Congressman or two might have visited the show and complained, and that would have been the end of it. Now it will never go away."

A Background Of Dismay

The decision to cancel, Dr. Orr-Cahall said, occurred against a background of Congressional dismay over National Endowment financing for an earlier exhibition in North Carolina. The show included a photograph by Andres Serrano, an artist, of a plastic crucifix submerged in his urine. The decision to cancel was also influenced by newspaper stories reporting that the endowment planned to review its grant processes, presumably because of the Serrano and Mapplethorpe issues.

"We were just in the wrong place at the wrong time," Dr. Orr-Cahall said. The Mapplethorpe show "was scheduled for July 1, to run during a month when the endowment's budget would be under consideration at various levels of Congress. We had the institutional responsibility to decide if this was the right environment in which to present the show.

"There would have been a lot of folderol about it, with attention directed away from substantive issues, such as the effort in Congress to emasculate the endowment. It would be a three-ring circus in which Mapplethorpe's work would never be looked at in its own right. We knew that certain Congressmen were just waiting for us to open the show, and we felt we shouldn't bow to that pressure. It was a no-win situation. We decided we wouldn't be anyone's political platform."

In planning for the show last March, Dr. Orr-Cahall wrote a letter to one of the museum's board members, Betsy Frampton, asking for a grant to cover the $25,000 that the Institute of Contemporary Art—which organized the show—charged each participating museum. The letter made a point of the show's importance to the Washington community, and said among other things that the Corcoran also intended to contact members of Congress and enlist their help in enlightening the public about the impact of AIDS. Dr. Orr-Cahall said the fact that Mapplethorpe died of AIDS last March, on the day the letter arrived, played a part in Ms. Frampton's decision to give the money.

"We never questioned the importance of the show," Dr. Orr-Cahall said. "Our decision wasn't about the esthetics of the work, but about the circumstances in which it was to be shown. It was a matter of time and place." She also confirmed reports that the Corcoran's lawyers had raised the issue of child pornography in connection with the show, pointing out that some of the images might be in violation of local laws. "But we certainly didn't use that as an excuse not to mount it," she said.

In the wake of the Corcoran's decision, the Washington Project for the Arts, an artists' group that also receives Federal financing, has undertaken to bring the Mapplethorpe show to Washington from July 21 through Aug. 13.

On Reflection After the Vote

But although a majority of the Corcoran's board voted to support the decision, there was a feeling among some board members that it was wrong for the museum to disavow the artistic judgment it exercised—under a previous director, to be sure—in committing itself to the show in the first place, that it would have been more exemplary to go ahead with it and let the chips fall where they may.

"I'm disappointed that external pressures, political or otherwise, have caused the Corcoran to second-guess its artistic judgment and in the process relinquish our responsibility to be, as is carved in stone over the entrance, 'Dedicated to Art,' " said Robert Lehrman, a Corcoran board member who has also served on the board of the Washington Project for the Arts.

"I'm deeply concerned," he said, "that this signals a willingness to be bullied and pressured by outside factions whose interests are not those of the Corcoran."

According to Tom Armstrong, director of the Whitney Museum of American Art, "When an art museum reverses a decision based on professional judgment because of outside pressures, the integrity of the museum is severely impaired." The Whitney mounted a separate Mapplethorpe exhibition of photographs last summer. However, it contained fewer of the most provocative Mapplethorpe images than the show scheduled for the Corcoran.

Except for a few letters, no public or legislative protest attended the Mapplethorpe show at two prior stops on its scheduled six-museum tour, the Institute of Contemporary Art in Philadelphia and the Museum of Contemporary Art in Chicago. Both institutions receive financing from their state arts councils. The Mapplethorpe show organized by the Whitney came and went also without incident.

Homosexuality is a subject that has deep emotional resonance for many people. For some, the show was certainly distasteful. The fact that it was photography rather than painting, with identifiable subjects, made the erotic confrontations more uncomfortable. Yet would anyone argue that the hideous, even depraved imagery of Goya's "black" paintings—the most famous of which shows an act of cannibalism—not be exhibited in a museum? Or that the public should be "saved" from viewing Picasso's late paintings and etchings with their graphic, highly charged erotic themes (heterosexual, to be sure)?

Whatever one thinks of Mapplethorpe as an artist—and there are critics on both sides—his images are intended as art, presented as such and are judged to be art by those qualified in such matters. They have been chosen for exhibition by well-established art institutions (the next stops after Washington for the show are the Wadsworth Atheneum in Hartford, the Art Museum at the University of California at Berkeley, the Contemporary Art Center in Cincinnati and the Institute of Contemporary Art in Boston).

The Public Role and Tax Dollars

To pre-empt the public's chance to make its own judgments—ironically the very public whose tax dollars helped finance the show is, in the opinion of Jock Reynolds, an artist and director of the Washington Project for the Arts, "an insult to that public's intelligence."

If the Corcoran acted in bad faith toward the public, it did so toward the artist as well, according to Mr. Reynolds. "The Corcoran made a commitment to Mapplethorpe," Mr. Reynolds said. "When an institution says it wants to work with an artist, it creates a bond both with the artist and with the larger artists' community. By breaking the bond in the Mapplethorpe case they broke their commitment to the artistic community as a whole. Their action would give other artists real pause as to how they might deal with others kinds of work."

At the height of the controversy last month, J. Carter Brown, director of the National Gallery of Art in Washington, was asked at a National Press Club luncheon to comment on the question of artistic expression versus community standards raised by the Mapplethorpe matter.

"There's a principle involved here, which is at the heart of what it means to be an American, and that is freedom," Mr. Brown said. "All of us in this country emigrated here, and a great number for a reason, which was to achieve the kind of freedom denied under other systems. And as we watch the other systems and historically look at them in the degenerate art show that Hitler had, or what the Soviets did to suppress their artists, and what is happening in capitals in the Far East, we have to recognize how fragile our freedoms are and how important it is to defend the process and to keep a sense of our First Amendment."

Although some Congressmen have argued that taxpayers' money should not be used to support exhibitions containing material that many might find offensive, what some consider offensive is not regarded as such by all. Taxpayers include arts professionals and many others who would favor the freedom of cultural expression that would allow a Mapplethorpe show.

The money given to the arts by the Federal Government through the endowment—about $170 million in 1988 and not substantially increased for many years—is certainly a token sum compared with government arts expenditures in other countries and, say, the vastness of Federal subsidies to such applicants as, for example, the savings and loan industry.

Yet it is highly important money, not merely because it confers prestige but because it provides support for unpopular or controversial projects that other fiscal sources shun. Most of the grants given by the endowment, except for individual fellowships, have to be matched locally, and thus such projects have the additional weight of community support.

The review processes of the endowment are carried out by professional peer panels in which esthetic judgments are made by those with expertise in their fields. They may not be perfect. The essential question raised by the Mapplethorpe and Serrano disputes, however, is whether that approach will endure and whether the endowment, which in its nearly 25 years of existence has remained remarkably free from political interference, will continue to be so.

* * *

June 9, 1990

RECORDING RULED OBSCENE BRINGS ARREST

By JAMES LeMOYNE
Special to The New York Times

MIAMI, June 8—Armed with a Federal judge's finding that the lyrics of a best-selling rap music record are obscene, the authorities today arrested a record store owner who had continued to sell the album.

The Broward County sheriff, Nick Navarro, said he had ordered the arrest of the store owner, Charles Freeman, because Mr. Freeman had defied the judge's finding in selling the record, "As Nasty as They Wanna Be," by the Miami-based rap group 2 Live Crew.

For months, while a series of hearings on the album moved through the courts in South Florida, Mr. Freeman had spoken out against the efforts to suppress the recording. In newspaper and television interviews after the ruling on Wednesday by the Federal district judge, Jose Gonzalez, Mr. Freeman declared that he would not obey any court ruling regarding the record. He said restrictions would be a violation of freedom of speech and also a racially biased ruling aimed at suppressing the music of a black group.

Mr. Freeman, who is black, was released on bond this evening after being booked on a state misdemeanor charge of selling obscene materials. The charge carries a penalty of up to one year in jail. Mr. Freeman could not be reached immediately for comment.

Part of Larger Battle

The arguments over the rap album form part of a larger battle over lyrics in popular music that has been fought across the nation, with some parents' groups demanding an end to sexually explicit and violent language in records that are popular among minors.

Further, the issue of song lyrics and videos echoes a broader national debate over the distinction between art and pornography. That debate has focused on government's right to impose such a definition, either by law or by withdrawal of public financing, on arts as diverse as photography, painting, theater and now, rap music.

In Cincinnati, the law-enforcement authorities are prosecuting a museum that exhibited photographs, some of them sexually explicit, by the late Robert Mapplethorpe.

The rap album by 2 Live Crew, released in 1989, is a national bestseller, with more than 1.7 million copies sold.

Its hard-driving rap tunes are filled with explicit depictions of male and female genitalia, as well as with anatomical descriptions of copulation in a variety of physical positions. One of the milder songs is titled, "Me So Horny."

It Carries Warning Label

From the time "As Nasty as They Wanna Be" was first released, the group's record label, Skyywalker Records, has voluntarily placed the words "Warning: Explicit Language Contained" on the packaging of the recording.

The music of 2 Live Crew has provoked legal trouble before. Most recently, on March 15, a record-store clerk in Sarasota, Fla., was arrested for selling a copy of "As Nasty as They Wanna Be" to an 11-year-old girl. He was charged with selling material harmful to minors, a felony, that carries a maximum term of five years in prison and a $5,000 fine. Charges in the case were later dropped.

But the case against Mr. Freeman is different because it has behind it the force of a Federal judge's ruling that the record is obscene and that the county may try to prosecute any sales of it.

Officials of Dade County, which includes Miami, said today that they would also arrest anyone selling the album. Faced with that legal threat, no major record chain appeared to be selling the album in South Florida and few, if any, radio stations are playing any of the album's songs.

He Ordered More Records

To demonstrate the depth of his feelings, Mr. Freeman ordered a new shipment of the album this week and began selling them this morning in defiance of the Federal judge's obscenity ruling, according to one of Mr. Freeman's employees.

The employees at Mr. Freeman's shop, the E. C. Record Store, on the outskirts Fort Lauderdale, said an undercover police detective purchased the record and then immediately arrested Mr. Freeman. The employees said the owner was taken away in handcuffs.

"They put handcuffs on him—I mean, you know, handcuffs for a misdemeanor," said Edward G. Robinson, the assistant manager who watched the arrest. "For us this is a free speech issue. Sheriff Navarro is from Cuba and he's acting like a Communist. This is a totalitarian thing to do."

Sheriff Navarro denied he was either a totalitarian or a racist.

'A Country of Laws'

"To try to cloud the issue with racism is beside the point," he said in an interview. "This is a country of laws, not men. I simply applied the law. A judge found that this record is obscene."

The arrest of the record store owner intensified an already raging debate in Florida over the state and Federal courts' right to ban the sale of the album.

A local lawyer, Jack Thompson, initially began a statewide campaign to ban sales of the rap record. As part of that effort he mailed the lyrics of several songs to a number of state officials. In February Gov. Bob Martinez denounced the album as obscene.

In March a Florida State Circuit Court found "probable cause" that the record was obscene. After that ruling, a number of Florida municipalities warned record shops that they risked legal action if they sold the album.

That state ruling was stiffened when Judge Gonzalez ruled in a civil proceeding that the album definitely was obscene. His finding of obscenity was based on a three part judicial standard. Judge Gonzalez found the rap album to be patently offensive, found that it lacked serious artistic, political or scientific value, and found that an average person in the community would find that the album appeals to prurient interests.

Extensive Legal Test

The leading defense lawyer for the band, Bruce Rogow, a law professor at Nova University in Fort Lauderdale, said he was appealing the ruling. The American Civil Liberties Union also has said it may appeal the finding of obscenity as an unwarranted restriction of speech and artistic freedom.

Mr. Rogow said the arrest of Mr. Freeman sets the stage for a more extensive legal test, since it will present a criminal proceeding in which the state will be forced to show "beyond a reasonable doubt" that the rap album is obscene.

That is a stiffer standard of proof than was required in the civil judicial proceedings regarding the album. In the civil proceedings in which the state sought to have the record found obscene, Mr. Rogow said, the state only had to show by a "preponderance of the evidence" that it was obscene, a less taxing burden of proof.

Singer Denounces Arrest

Luther Campbell, the lead singer for the rap group, denounced the arrest of Mr. Freeman and the court's obscenity ruling in a news conference here today. He said he believed he was a victim both of an undue limitation of his freedom of speech and of racism. He called the banning of his record a "black-white issue."

The rap group is giving a live concert late Saturday night in Hollywood, in Broward County. Sheriff Navarro said today that if the group sings any of the lyrics found to be obscene by the Federal judge, he would consider arresting the four-member group.

"If the judge says the lyrics are obscene, they are obscene whether they are on a record or if they are sung live," Mr. Navarro said. "If they sing them, they are putting themselves at risk of arrest."

* * *

July 23, 1990

PHOTOS OF NUDE CHILDREN SPARK OBSCENITY DEBATE

By KATHERINE BISHOP
Special to The New York Times

SAN FRANCISCO, July 22—In a city known for being broad-minded about nearly every form of expression, the taking and exhibiting of photographs of nude children is seen as neither startling nor necessarily a cause for alarm.

So in May when agents of the Federal Bureau of Investigation raided the photography studio of Jock Sturges, who is known for his black-and-white portraits of families in the nude, and confiscated his work in an investigation of child pornography, it set off a storm of charges of Government censorship.

People involved in the arts, newspapers and the city's Board of Supervisors have rallied to his support. Without having seen the pictures, which are in the custody of the F.B.I., the supervisors in a 9-to-2 vote passed a resolution on July 9 urging the United States Attorney here to drop the investigation.

The resolution cited "a dangerous state of hysteria and repression over freedom of expression of artists" and said the First Amendment is under a "national assault." Mayor Art Agnos signed it on July 17. The Federal prosecutor has made no response to the nonbinding action.

Substantially Different Pictures

But the issue is complicated by the fact that law-enforcement officials and others involved in the investigation who have seen the photos say they are substantially different from Mr. Sturges's other work. The pictures raise concerns that laws aimed at protecting children from exploitation may have been violated, these people say.

Unlike the recent disputes over the Robert Mapplethorpe photographs depicting homosexual scenes or the rap music of 2 Live Crew that was deemed obscene by a Federal judge in Miami, the Sturges photographs are not available for public scrutiny. People who have seen them describe them as 35-millimeter color slides of nude girls 12 years old and younger.

Still, sponsors of the supervisors' resolution said in interviews that they were unwilling to accept the characterization of the photos by Federal officials as being "extremely different" from Mr. Sturges's exhibited work.

Supervisor Terence Hallinan, the chief sponsor, said the investigation is "part of a nationwide attempt through restriction of culture to bring about a more conservative state."

The vote came after hours of testimony the previous week, including a statement by Mr. Sturges that his work "could not be considered by any healthy mind, by any stretch of the imagination, to be pornographic."

Cincinnati Official Testifies

The supervisors also heard testimony from Dennis Barrie, the director of the Contemporary Arts Center in Cincinnati, who is to go on trial in September on obscenity charges for the museum's display of two photographs of naked children that were part of the Mapplethorpe exhibition. He characterized the San Francisco case as, like his, an assault on the First Amendment right of free expression.

Criticism of the investigation and the Government's motives has been so heated that the United States Attorney here, William T. McGivern Jr., went on the radio to respond to an editorial by the station. The editorial questioned whether Mr. McGivern's office believed "that the human body itself is obscene" and urged that the investigation be dropped.

Mr. McGivern pointed out that "many people have voiced opinions on this matter without even having seen the evidence," and added, "While it is not our intent to chill First Amendment rights or to regulate morality standards, we will prosecute those who sexually exploit children."

Mr. Sturges, who left for a brief teaching job in France soon after his appearance before the board, has not been arrested or charged with a crime, although thousands of his photographs and his personal correspondence and records were seized more than two months ago.

"I'm more than pleased by the Board of Supervisors' taking a strong stand for preservation of our constitutional rights," said Michael H. Metzger, the lawyer representing Mr. Sturges. "If you look at Jock's work as a whole and at the intent of the photographer, it is not obscene or even suggestive of obscenity."

Nude Portraits of Families

Mr. Sturges's published work includes photos of fashion models and ballet dancers, all clothed. His work also includes pictures of adults and their children posed in the nude. These black-and-white photos were commissioned as family portraits by "naturists" and were made at beaches where nudity is allowed, Mr. Metzger said.

Examples of these pictures, printed with newspaper articles about the case, show parents sitting or lying in the sand with their children. All are clearly naked but posed in ways that avoid showing frontal nudity.

But an F.B.I. spokesman said such photos were not the subject of the investigation. "Nudity is not obscenity," said the bureau spokesman, Duke Diedrich. He said applicable Federal law defines child pornography as the "lascivious display of genitalia" of any person under 18 years of age and forbids interstate transportation of such material.

While it is ultimately up to a jury to decide whether any of the pictures are obscene, Mr. Diedrich said it was the bureau's policy to investigate when it seemed "the focus of the photos is directed toward the genitalia."

State law in California defines as obscene the developing or duplication of a photograph that shows "the genitals, pubic or rectal areas" of a person under 14 years of age "for the purpose of sexual stimulation of the viewer."

Pictures Planned as Gifts

The investigation began when Mr. Sturges hired Joseph Semien, a film processor, to make negatives from color slides he had taken of some of the children he had photographed in black-and-white portraits. The negatives were to be used to make color prints that he intended to give as gifts to the families, his lawyer said.

Mr. Metzger, who has seen the photographs, said they were all made with the permission of the children's parents.

The police were notified by the San Francisco branch of Newell Colour, a photo processing laboratory based in London that has 32 outlets around the world. Mr. Semien had taken the negatives there to be printed. State law requires such commercial processing laboratories to report photographs that may violate child pornography statutes. Failing to do so, they risk losing their business licenses.

Mr. Semien was arrested under the state law on two felony and 10 misdemeanor charges of possession of obscene material depicting minors, and his arrest led to the raid of Mr. Sturges's studio. The charges against Mr. Semien were recently suspended, and he was allowed to enter a program under which his record can be cleared in six months if he has no further incidents.

Chris Lopin, the general manager for Newell Colour, said the San Francisco branch had been open for 14 years and had developed more than one million images a year. The Sturges photos were the first ones that the laboratory's workers ever thought should be reported to the authorities, he said, adding that six people viewed them and had no trouble agreeing on that course.

Mr. Lopin said that F.B.I. officials had asked him not to discuss the contents of the Sturges pictures, but that they were "a different focus from his normal shots."

"I wish that everybody would withhold judgment until they see the photos for themselves," Mr. Lopin said. "Society should wait until they see what the content is before they jump to conclusions."

* * *

October 25, 1990

SENATE PASSES COMPROMISE ON ARTS ENDOWMENT

By MARTIN TOLCHIN

Special to The New York Times

WASHINGTON, Oct. 24—After an emotional debate about the Government's role in the arts, the Senate today adopted a bipartisan compromise that would leave judgments about obscenity and pornography to the courts.

The vote of 73 to 24 followed a session in which some Senators deplored Federally subsidized "slime and sleaze" and others assailed Government "censorship" as they debated restricting Federal grants for works deemed "obscene" and "pornographic."

The measure that passed is similar to one approved by the House of Representatives last week. Both bills would require recipients of grants from the National Endowment for the Arts to return the money if they are convicted of obscenity.

White House officials have suggested that the Administration would go along with the compromise. Arts groups preferred the compromise to current law and other alternatives, said Liz Robbins, a lobbyist for several arts groups.

'Restriction Is the Real Issue'

Two conservative Republicans were the major antagonists in the Senate debate. Senator Orrin Hatch, a Utah Republican who is the chief sponsor of the compromise, told the Senate that "Congress cannot effectively micro-manage matters that are inherently subjective."

"Content restriction is the real issue," Mr. Hatch continued. "I think everyone in this body does not want to see patently offensive art in any form, but when you try to describe what that means, you have difficulty."

But Senator Jesse Helms, a North Carolina Republican who is the chief Congressional critic of the endowment, told his colleagues that "we can't duck our responsibilities" and permit the Government to subsidize "slime and sleaze." He lamented "the assault on the nation's basic values by these self- proclaimed artists who insist on mocking the American people."

Mr. Helms won one victory. On a voice vote, the Senate agreed to prohibit grants for works that "denigrate the objects or beliefs of the adherents of a particular religion."

Differences with the House

The debate on one of the most contentious issues confronting Congress came on a bill to provide $170 million for the endowment and extend its life for one year. The House bill would provide $180 million and extend the endowment for three years. These and other differences in the bills will be resolved in a House-Senate conference.

The Senate action followed two recent court victories for opponents of government restrictions, involving jury acquittals of obscenity charges against the rap group 2 Live Crew and the Contemporary Arts Center in Cincinnati, which exhibited photographs by Robert Mapplethorpe.

Under the Senate bill, any recipients of endowment grants who are convicted of obscenity by a trial court would have to repay the money at the time of conviction, rather than upon a final decision by an appeals court as provided in the House bill. Under the Senate measure, the artists could get the money back if an appeals court reversed the conviction.

Under the Senate version, an artist convicted of obscenity would be ineligible for additional grants for three years. The House bill has no such provision.

Current law prohibits grants for works depicting sadomasochism, homoeroticism and other activities, if, in the opinion of the endowment, those works lack "literary, artistic, political or scientific value."

A Helms Proposal Is Defeated

Mr. Helms, who is in a tough re-election campaign, did not filibuster the arts bill, as he has in the past, but made a veiled threat to do so in the future. He said, "Assuming that I am in the Senate next year, which is up to the good Lord and the people of North Carolina, you ain't seen nothin' yet."

The Senator was defeated in his attempts to broaden restrictions against grants for works considered "obscene" and "pornographic." By a vote of 70 to 29, the Senate rejected Mr. Helms's proposal to bar Government grants for materials "that depict or describe, in a patently offensive way, sexual or excretory activities or organs."

The Senate defeated, by voice vote, Mr. Helms's proposal to deny endowment grants to artists whose family income exceeded 1,500 percent of the poverty level, which is $12,675 for a family of four, or $190,125. The senator argued that money should be earmarked for struggling artists, not those who were "financially secure."

Mr. Helms said the endowment has subsidized artists who disdained "the moral and religious sensibilities of the majority of the American people." He told the Senate that endowment grants had subsidized a woman whose performance consisted of urinating on the stage and inviting members of the audience to give her a "gynecological" examination. Another nude performer covered herself with chocolate, Mr. Helms said.

The Senator noted that his position on the arts had been sharply criticized by the media, but he said that no newspaper had published objectionable works, including Mr. Mapplethorpe's photograph of "a naked man with a bullwhip protruding from his posterior."

Subjective Judgments

But Sen. Orrin Hatch, Republican of Utah, said that judgments on obscenity and pornography were inherently subjective. "I know some people in this country who might be offended by Michelangelo's work," Mr. Hatch said.

"The Supreme Court has spent decades trying to define obscenity and pornography, and they're as far away today as when they began," he added.

Mr. Hatch said that the endowment was to be congratulated because out of 85,000 grants it had made, only 20 had been questionable.

The restrictions on arts grants are strongly opposed by arts organizations, which consider them censorship and say they stifle creativity. But Mr. Helms and other supporters of restrictions say censorship is not the issue. They say they would not ban obscene works but would prohibit spending taxpayers' money to finance them.

"There's all the difference in the world between censorship and sponsorship," Mr. Helms said. "I'm not talking about banning these works. I'm talking about subsidizing them."

The Senate compromise would require that the panels that recommend arts grants have "a wide geographic, esthetic, ethnic and minority representation," including people who are not artists. The panels would be required to "change substantially from year to year," with a three-year limit on a member's service on the panel.

The compromise includes conflict-of-interest provisions to insure that someone who has a pending application for a grant, or who works for or is an agent of anyone with a pending application, does not serve as a panel member. There have been charges that applicants and panelists have feathered one another's nests.

* * *

May 6, 1991

KEEPING THE NEWS IN STEP: ARE THE PENTAGON'S GULF WAR RULES HERE TO STAY?

By JASON DePARLE
Special to The New York Times

WASHINGTON, May 5—Midway through the air war against Iraq, two words began to reappear in the press, spooking White House aides with ghosts from conflicts past: "credibility gap."

Reporters who had spent months complaining about strict new press restrictions were taking their concerns public, asking what the Government was trying to hide. The aides, determined to quell comparisons with the Vietnam war, began to talk of easing the restraints on what reporters could see or say.

Then reassurance for the Administration came from an unlikely quarter—"Saturday Night Live." The NBC show, known for lampooning President Bush, began its Feb. 9 broadcast with a skit depicting reporters in a briefing room as comically self-absorbed, with little understanding of national security and even less concern.

After coming in Monday morning, John H. Sununu, the White House chief of staff, picked up on the talk of the office and quickly ordered a tape. By the afternoon, aides had hurried a copy to President Bush, offering it as evidence that the public was on their side.

Sole Moment of Doubt

"It was not a trivial component," said a senior White House official, referring to the skit. He said the program "gave us an indication that things weren't being handled too badly."

That closed the book on what Government officials have called their only moment of doubt in placing dramatic new restrictions on the way the nation's press covers military operations.

According to interviews and documents examined by The New York Times in a six-week review of the press policy, President Bush and his inner circle had vowed from the start of the deployment to the Persian Gulf in mid-August to manage the information flow in a way that supported their political goals. They punctuated that determination on the war's eve with a Pentagon rule limiting all press coverage of combat to officially escorted pools.

When the air bombardment began on Jan. 17, officials turned their attention from formulating the restrictions to putting them into effect, surprising even themselves with the control the system provided.

A Divisive Argument

The details of how that system worked during the six weeks of actual combat, and how officials moved to capitalize on it, have formed the starting point of a divisive argument between the Pentagon and the press over the policy's merits.

"I look at it as a model of how the Department ought to function," said Defense Secretary Dick Cheney, the primary architect of the policy, who has said the system provided "better coverage" than "any other war in history."

But representatives of 15 major news organizations complained in a letter to Mr. Cheney last week that "the flow of information to the public was blocked, impeded, or diminished" by the policy.

The signers of the letter, who included representatives of The New York Times, The Washington Post, The Associated Press and the four major television networks, requested a meeting and told Mr. Cheney, "We are intent on not experiencing again the Desert Storm kind of pool system."

Changes and Delays

As the war began, reporters found that censors changed and delayed their dispatches, while escorts kept them far from the action and the military police arrested those trying to operate independently. Access to real action was so limited that even when public affairs officials tried to get reporters airborne in B-52's, to curry favorable publicity for the fearsome machines, they were thwarted by suspicious commanders.

With few opportunities to gain firsthand reports, the press responded by giving increased prominence to the official statements and Government-issued videotapes being promulgated in briefing rooms in Riyadh and Washington.

Administration officials said that even they had failed to anticipate the power the briefings would take on in shaping public opinion. But they were quick to capitalize on that power, staging elaborate rehearsals for key Pentagon briefers, like Lieut. Gen. Thomas W. Kelly. General Kelly recalls that one day's preparation was so complete that he turned to an aide and asked in jest "if they'd passed out the questions in advance" to the journalists, who seemed to be dutifully reading them back to him.

The choreographing of public opinion was in mind even when commanders chose names for the operation's two phases, as Gen. H. Norman Schwarzkopf, the mission's commander, and Gen. Colin L. Powell, Chairman of the Joint Chiefs of Staff, huddled with aides and swapped suggestions by telephone. "Desert Sword," "Desert Thunder" and "Desert Strike" all hit the discard list before the commanders settled on "Desert Storm."

" 'Storm' was appropriate to the type of operation we were planning," said General Powell. "And it kind of had a cute angle to it with 'Stormin Norman,' " General Schwarzkopf's nickname.

The Rules Control Exercised Through Pools

The decision to restrict all combat coverage to official pools brought a fundamental tilt in the balance of power, taking the most basic journalistic decisions out of the hands of correspondents and giving them to commanders.

One set of complaints focused on the review of news dispatches for security violations—a reversal of the Vietnam practice of trusting journalists to comply and expelling those who broke the rules. While Pentagon guidelines stated that escorts would not suppress material "for its potential to express criticism or cause embarrassment," reporters sometimes found otherwise. When The Associated Press reported that Navy pilots were watching pornographic films before leaving on missions, an escort deleted it.

A second problem, acknowledged by the military, concerns delays in the military's transmission of reporters' copy. Some dispatches did not arrive until after the war's end.

But the journalists say the most important power the military exercised was the decision over where to send the pools. As Deborah Amos, a correspondent for National Public Radio, put it, this turned officers into assignment editors, determining story lines by dictating what reporters could see.

Circumventing the System

Six days into the air war, for instance, Judd Rose, a correspondent for ABC News, was part of a pool pressing for interviews with pilots. Instead, the reporters were shuttled to the military motor pool, whose commander complained that his "unsung heroes" had not been receiving the publicity they deserved.

As the war progressed, an increasing number of reporters tried to circumvent the pool system, despite some detentions by the military, and their efforts produced some of the war's most memorable reporting. After linking up with the Saudis, Forrest Sawyer, a correspondent for ABC News, became the only reporter of the war to accompany a pilot on a bombing mission.

Mr. Sawyer faults reporters for not resisting the rules sooner and in greater numbers. "I think we were too docile for too long—all of us," he said.

THE BRIEFINGS
Key to Success: Preparation

The military briefings spoofed by "Saturday Night Live" were so popular with the public that some critics have wondered whether they were part of a preconceived strategy. But Marlin Fitzwater, the White House press secretary, said, "We had no idea how that was going to work."

The cameras seemed to spotlight the reporters' weaknesses, since many had little previous experience with the military. At the same time, the sheer length and frequency of the briefings made the military seem candid, even when the long lists of innocuous statistics, like number of missions flown, added little real knowledge. As one admiring White House official put it, the briefings made the Pentagon seem to be making public "much more information than it was."

Among those staying tuned on a daily basis was the President himself. "There weren't many where he didn't see at least a piece of it," said Mr. Fitzwater. And when the Riyadh briefings got off to a shaky start, with junior officers who seemed to lack confidence and candor, the White House was quick to complain to Pete Williams, Mr. Cheney's chief aide for public affairs. "I did mention that to Pete, and he got higher-ranking guys in there," Mr. Fitzwater said.

Praise for the Performance

In tapping General Kelly for the duty at the Pentagon, General Powell was turning to an officer whose performance as a briefer during the American strike against the Panamanian Government had already won White House praise.

By 8 each morning, General Kelly's staff would start to assemble lists of questions that they expected journalists to ask. They were aided by the journalists themselves, who were walking the Pentagon halls and asking such questions all day. Public affairs aides began quietly appending the inquiries to their lists, which they used at the 2 P.M. rehearsal. "I never let on to any of them," said one aide.

With the briefing room's power now clear, other officials also prepared carefully. While rehearsing his important Jan. 23 briefing, General Powell had a nagging concern.

In a few hours he would step in front of television cameras and deliver one of the most confident predictions in American military history. Of the Iraqi Army, he promised, "First we're going to cut it off and then we're going to kill it."

But first he tested the line on an aide, asking, "What do you think?"

"He was concerned it would seem too harsh, too severe," the assistant said.

THE WAR IMAGES
The Bombs Never Missed

Perhaps the most enduring image of the war is the remarkable gun-camera footage of precision bombs, produced not by journalists but by the military. While 90 percent of the bombs dropped on Iraq were the highly inaccurate "dumb bombs," only the precision weapons produced videos, and the American Government, unlike the British, never showed one that missed.

"Those videos had an enormous impact on the American public," said David Gergen, who as an aide in the Reagan White House helped pioneer the use of images to form public opinion. Mr. Gergen, now editor at large of U.S. News and World Report, said the military set a benchmark for disseminating "a kind of video press release."

Mr. Cheney said he did not think of the tapes as a press release, but added, "I will admit we did clean it up," by removing the audio portions that disclosed the raw sounds of "guys in combat."

Faced with requests for footage of errant bombs, American spokesmen used the same reasonable tone that worked to their advantage throughout the conflict, avoiding a flat No. Mr. Williams, for instance, told journalists on Jan. 21, "I will look into giving you some of that footage."

In recent interviews, officials adopted a tone of innocent forgetfulness.

Mr. Cheney said such tapes would have been "pretty dull, boring stuff."

Mr. Williams said, "That's one that fell through the cracks."

Capt. Ron Wildermuth of the Navy, General Schwarzkopf's chief public affairs aide, said the item "was not high on my priorities."

Copter Video Barred

The military also refused to make public vivid videotape of Apache helicopter attacks on Iraqi positions, although when several reporters arrived at a forward unit without their escorts they got an unauthorized viewing from a commander proud of the machines' performance.

John Balzar, of The Los Angeles Times, said the tape showed Iraqi soldiers "as big as football players on the T.V. screen." He added: "A guy was hit and you could see him drop and he struggled up. They fired again and the body next to him exploded."

But after his article about the tape appeared, Mr. Balzar said, he was never again allowed near an Apache unit. And top commanders refused repeated requests by other reporters to see the tape.

Capt. Mike Sherman of the Navy, who ran the military's Joint Information Bureau in Dharhan, Saudi Arabia, until December, said there was no deliberate attempt to sanitize the war, but agreed that battle footage was scarce. "I didn't see the images I thought I was going to see," he said. "I haven't seen a tank battle yet, have you? Why there weren't any video teams there is beyond me."

Cheney's Rare Blunder

Beyond the briefing room, several official policies also helped keep disturbing images from the television screens, including one that banned cameras from Dover Air Force Base as military coffins arrived.

Another Pentagon policy forbade any spokesman from appearing on television programs beside any of the 16 plaintiffs from a lawsuit challenging the pool system.

One of the few blunders in briefing performances acknowledged by Administration officials occurred on Feb. 23, the night the ground war began. With what struck his colleagues as excessive zeal, Mr. Cheney sternly announced a 48-hour information blackout.

Mr. Fitzwater said he immediately thought it was a mistake. "I watched him on camera, and I said, 'My friends in the press are going to find that a little eager.' "

So did General Schwarzkopf, who called the next day and said, "I've got to brief."

By most accounts, Mr. Fitzwater weighed in heavily and got Mr. Cheney's decision reversed. He declined to confirm that directly, but added, "If there are things you can't say, you just go out and say you can't say them. But it's not proper for Government to run and hide."

To some in the press corps and some senior officials, however, the memory of that night lingered as a moment when Mr. Cheney's true attitude toward journalists seemed to pop through his habitual Western reserve.

"I think it was uncharacteristic," Mr. Fitzwater said. "I'm glad it didn't last."

What Next?

Second Thoughts On Restrictions

Some analysts, like Bill Kovach, curator of the Nieman Foundation at Harvard, have called the policy a watershed that will change the flow of official information not only in the military but throughout the Government, increasing officials' power to bend public opinion to their will.

Mr. Kovach argues that such power has been growing for a decade. He cites as other examples Mr. Gergen's work in the Reagan White House, and the use by Mr. Bush's media consultant, Roger Ailes, of negative campaigning during the 1988 presidential campaign.

The gulf war policy, Mr. Kovach said, "worked so clearly, so well, and the public accepted it so fully, I think it has established a new standard in terms of the amount of information the Government is willing to give its people."

But others see the Government's success as a product of particular circumstances unlikely to be repeated. Reporters were unusually constricted in getting to the action, they say, since most of the fighting being done in the air and most of the dying occurred behind enemy lines. After just four days of ground fighting, they say, the pool system was on the verge of collapse. Pool reporters, angered by how long it took the military to review and transmit articles, started filing them directly to their home offices, and reporters not in pools raced into Kuwait and hooked up with American forces on their own.

News Executives Wary

"The way this war was made up made this policy possible," said Representative Les Aspin, chairman of the House Armed Services Committee, who worked in the Pentagon in the early days of the Vietnam War. "This thing would have blown up in their face if the war had dragged out or you had a lot of casualties."

Since the war's end, the Administration's public relations professionals—Mr. Williams and Mr. Fitzwater—have said that they now find some of the gulf rules overly restrictive.

Mr. Fitzwater said he was uncomfortable with having officers review articles before publication. "I blame myself" for allowing such provisions to take effect, he said.

"There's something wrong with that," he said. "I don't like the idea of anybody in the Government ever reading a piece of copy by a reporter."

Mr. Williams, who also now professes some discomfort about reporters' dispatches being read by escorts, said, "I think the presumption in the future should be against pools." He said they inevitably produced complaints from reporters and headaches for the Government.

But some news executives, who are meeting to forge a counterproposal to the Pentagon press policy, view such talk with suspicion.

"They believe that by saying some nice things about freedom of the press, the whole thing will just sort of blow over," said George Watson, Washington bureau chief of ABC News.

Appearing at a recent meeting of the American Society of Newspaper editors, Brig. Gen. Richard Neal of the Marine Corps, a main briefer in Saudi Arabia, said bluntly, "I can tell you: the pool system is here to stay."

And Mr. Cheney said, "If we had to do it tomorrow, I would start with what we've just done," adding, "We'd be willing to listen to recommendations on how to improve it."

But he went on: "Bottom line is you've got to accomplish your mission. You've got to do it at the lowest possible cost in terms of American lives. And that takes precedence over how you deal with the press."

* * *

July 3, 1991

17 NEWS EXECUTIVES CRITICIZE U.S. FOR 'CENSORSHIP' OF GULF COVERAGE

By JASON DePARLE

Special to The New York Times

WASHINGTON, July 2—Military restrictions on news gathering during the Persian Gulf war amounted to "real censorship" and confirmed "the worst fears of reporters in a democracy," a report by 17 of the country's news executives says.

The report, addressed to Defense Secretary Dick Cheney, was delivered last week along with a statement of 10 principles that the journalists say should govern future war coverage.

But the news executives, who want to meet with Mr. Cheney, said nothing about what they would do if the Government refused to alter the rules. Since the war's end, President Bush and other top officials have called the system a model for the future.

"We're hoping that we will find a reasonable hearing of what we have to say," said Louis D. Boccardi, president of The Associated Press, who is coordinating the group's efforts. "It wouldn't make any sense for me to speculate on what we'll do after that."

News executives have bitterly complained that the restrictions placed on reporters by the Pentagon were intended to promote a sanitized view of the war. The Administration says the rules were needed to preserve military security and served the public well.

Pete Williams, the chief Pentagon spokesman, said Mr. Cheney would meet with the journalists. But no date has been scheduled, and Mr. Williams declined to say what changes the Pentagon envisioned, if any.

At the center of the disagreement is the Pentagon's use of news pools—small groups of reporters who are escorted by military officials.

Military Control Cited

The Persian Gulf war was the first American conflict this century to restrict all official coverage to pools. "By controlling what journalists saw and when they saw it, the military exercised great power to shape and manage the news," the report said.

It cited the battle of Khafji, saying military officials waited 18 hours before sending in a news pool and then kept it far from the action. Several reporters operating independently, in violation of official rules, entered the Saudi town and provided the most vivid accounts of the battle. Those independent accounts directly contradicted the statements of military officials in Riyadh, who implied that Americans played little role in the fighting.

While pools may be useful in getting journalists to the scene of fast-breaking and remote action, the report said, the system should generally be abandoned within 36 hours. Thereafter, it said, reporters should be on their own.

The report was especially critical of military escorts. While several escorts risked their lives to help reporters, the report accused the majority of keeping reporters away from negative news.

The report heaped criticism on what it called unwarranted delays by the military in transmitting copy. It called for abolishing the practice of reviewing reporters' copy for security reasons.

The executives' report calls for a system in which reporters are allowed in all major military units. It calls on the military to assist with transportation and to help reporters transmit articles. It says officers should not review copy or interfere with interviews.

In seeking a meeting with Mr. Cheney, the journalists are in effect resuming the same unsuccessful strategy that they pursued before the war. For months last fall, journalists met with Mr. Williams, stating their objections to the use of pools in the Persian Gulf, but the rules were not changed.

Some news executives have contemplated a boycott if the Pentagon insists on future pool coverage. But there is virtually no precedent for such coordinated action in the competitive news business. Even the signing of a letter of principle is considered rare.

The report was signed by ABC News, NBC News, CBS News and CNN, and by The New York Times, The Washington Post, The Associated Press, United Press International, Knight-Ridder, The Los Angeles Times, The Wall Street Journal, The Dallas Morning News, Time-Warner, USA Today, Newsweek, Cox Newspapers and The Star-Ledger in Newark.

* * *

January 10, 1992

WHEN THE LAW AND MUSIC CLASH, UPROAR FOLLOWS

By STEVEN LEE MYERS

Special to The New York Times

GUILDERLAND, N.Y., Jan. 9—A uniformed police officer walked into the Records 'N Such store here two days ago and, delivering a letter signed by the Police Chief, told Donna M. Smith that a number of the records she sold might get her into trouble with the law.

The letter, also sent to two other record stores here, warned against the "illegal selling" of recordings marked with "Parental Advisory: Explicit Lyrics" labels, citing New York's laws on obscenity.

The police chief, James R. Murley, defended the warning as a measured response to the complaint of a woman whose daughter bought a rap music tape she described as shockingly obscene. Others here, however, called it a shocking violation of First Amendment rights.

Using Obscenity Laws

Either way, the letter and the storm of publicity around it have forced people in this woody suburb of 30,000 people just west of Albany to draw a line between free speech and obscenity and to ask whether music today has crossed it.

"I was stunned," Ms. Smith, the store's general manager, said today as a trickle of customers browsed through some of the recordings that could be affected by the ruling. "I thought this was over. It seems almost absurd that in 1992 this is going to happen again."

In recent years, the police in communities in several states have taken actions against people who sold records deemed objectionable, including the highly publicized prosecution of a record store owner for selling an album by the rap group 2 Live Crew in Broward County, Fla., in 1990. But this is the first time law-enforcement officials in New York have raised the possibility of prosecuting record sellers under the state's obscenity laws, which were written in 1967.

"We're certainly not looking to violate the First Amendment," Chief Murley said today in an interview in his office in Town Hall, where he has been besieged for two days by telephone calls from reporters and citizens. "But we have to interpret the penal code to some degree, whether it's robbery or obscenity. We thought this was a reasonable way to handle it."

Chief Murley, the police chief here since 1974, said that arrests are unlikely and that his intent was never to force the town's record stores to pull potentially offensive recordings from the shelves, but for Ms. Smith, that is effectively the result. Until the matter is settled, she said she would simply not stock the recordings rather than subject herself or her employees to arrest.

"They're basically saying this is obscene and this is obscene without even hearing it," she said. "That's what scares me."

The controversy began when Suzanne Shafer, 37 years old, a hairdresser from nearby Voorheesville, took her 14-year-old daughter Shannon shopping at the Crossgates Mall on Dec. 26. As Mrs. Shafer shopped in another store, her daughter bought two cassette tapes in Record Town, one of two shops in the mall owned by the Trans World Music Corporation, a 600-store chain based in Albany.

One of them was "EFIL4ZAGGIN," the latest release by the California rap group N.W.A., known for its "gangster style" of music. The recording is infused with racial epithets, vulgarities and descriptions of sexual acts.

"I had never paid much attention to what records she bought," Mrs. Shafer said. "But when I heard this record, I couldn't believe they sold such stuff in records stores, much less to children."

A Call to the Police

Like many other rap and heavy metal albums, N.W.A.'s carry a label warning parents about the content of the songs. The recording industry adopted warning labels in 1985 under pressure from parents' groups and state lawmakers. In 1990, they agreed on a standard, black-and-white label that reads "Parental Advisory: Explicit Lyrics."

Mrs. Shafer said that labels are one thing, but obscenity is another, and she called Guilderland's Police Department to complain.

Warning Sign for Minors

After reviewing the recording with the Albany County District Attorney's Office, Chief Murley drafted the letter. Citing the advisory labels and Section 235 of the State Penal Law, he warned the stores that it is a "misdemeanor to sell, or possess with the intent to sell, any obscene material" and a felony "to sell this material to a minor less than 17 years of age."

The question, industry executives and civil rights lawyers said, is what is obscene? Arthur N. Eisenberg, legal director of the New York Civil Liberties Union, said that only a court can decide what is obscene, applying community standards as laid down by the United States Supreme Court.

"Those industry labels are not the equivalent of a judicial determination of obscenity," he said.

Michael W. Cover, an executive of the Recording Industry Association of America in Washington, said the industry "certainly did not adopt the labels as a method for law-enforcement officials to prohibit the sale of material to minors."

For now, that has been the effect. A sign at the Tape World in the sprawling Crossgates Mall here explained that only shoppers over 17 would be allowed to buy recordings with the labels.

At the mall yesterday, Scott Van Valkenburgh said that trying to prohibit the sale of records with the warning labels would simply enhance their popularity. "It really doesn't prevent people from listening to it," the 19-year-old said. "They'll just dub it."

Anyway, he said, "there are a lot more problems with drugs and crime than with people buying records."

Chief Murley acknowledged that the wording of his letter was inexact in implying that arrests were imminent or that stores should remove tapes with parental advisories. "Maybe the letter should have been more explicit," he said.

His intent, he said, was not to determine what was obscene but rather to alert the stores to the fact that under the law they could face criminal charges. He emphasized that if an outraged parent were to press charges, he would have to pass them on to the office of District Attorney Sol Greenberg.

The Town Supervisor, Anne T. Rose, has expressed support for the chief's efforts, saying that perhaps music, as well as film and literature, have gone too far.

"We're not trying to stop anyone from selling anything," Ms. Rose said. "We're asking record store owners to exercise some judgment so that very young children don't buy it. When we're talking about children we have to draw the line."

* * *

January 19, 1992

STUDENT GROUPS CENSOR STUDENTS ON 3 CAMPUSES

NEW BRUNSWICK, N.J.—Cries of censorship at colleges and universities are usually directed at administration officials, but recent incidents of students censoring students have set off debate at Rutgers University here.

Student governing associations at three of Rutgers's campuses in New Brunswick have been accused of violating First Amendment rights by stifling free speech in recent months.

At Livingston College, a newspaper was forced to halt publication when the student association temporarily froze the paper's financing after it printed an article the association declared "racially offensive." At Douglass College, a resolution was passed recommending that three magazines the association considered pornographic not be sold at the campus co-op store. And at Rutgers College, a student was told to stop using a campaign slogan that relied on the words "sex," "condoms" and "beer."

Humor That Angers

"It's been an incredible education on the delicacy of speech and the hypersensitivity of the college campus," said Richard Haelig, a senior English major from Bridgewater, N.J., who is the editor in chief of The Medium. The weekly paper, which is underwritten by the Livingston Governing Association, was denied $16,500 in student fees after printing a Page 1 humor article that infuriated some Asian students at the university.

The American Civil Liberties Union of New Jersey threatened legal action against the association if financing for The Medium was not reinstated immediately. It was.

Edward Martone, the executive director of the A.C.L.U.'s Newark office, said in an interview that student governments at state universities like Rutgers must abide by state law, "including guaranteeing protection of free speech under the Constitution."

Mr. Martone, who also teaches a class called "Journalism Ethics and the Law" as a part-time instructor at Rutgers Law School in Newark, said the incident was in keeping with a national trend, with many groups challenging expressions of opinion they disagree with. "Once you allow someone to draw boundaries, though," he said, "you also give them the license to slap back whoever steps over the line."

Magazines Attacked

Members of the Douglass College Governing Association recommended that, in addition to the magazines Playboy, Playgirl and Penthouse, the co-op should stop selling a greeting card listing 10 reasons why beer is better than women.

Margaret Monte, the president of the governing association and a senior in political science from Bridgewater, said sales of the three magazines contradict the college's traditions by "promoting sexual subordination."

But Victoria Ackerman, a senior in political science from Marlboro, N.J., who is the chairwoman of the 15-member co-op board, disagreed. "I don't feel we're advocating sexism," she said. "Pornography is part of our culture; we are not changing the issue by removing the magazines."

Sales of the three magazines have doubled since the uproar began, she said, and the greeting cards have sold out.

The co-op placed an advertisement in The Daily Targum, which is distributed on all the New Brunswick campuses, asking co-op shareholders to let the co-op know their opinions of the association's recommendation. The results will not be known until after school resumes Jan. 21.

Campaign Issue

"Obnoxious speech becomes more titillating" when it is forbidden, Annamay Sheppard, a constitutional law professor at Rutgers Law School, said of the widespread debate over a student's campaign slogan that was rejected by the Rutgers College Elections Committee for "distasteful language." Scott White, a political science major from East Brunswick, N.J., running for vice president of the freshman class, had signed an agreement to abide by the committee's guidelines for the campaign. Then he came up with his slogan: "SEX for a pleasurable freshman year. CONDOMS for a safer freshman year. BEER for a blasted freshman year." The committee told him the slogan promoted an image that did not fit the guidelines and should not be used.

When Mr. White ignored the order and began distributing fliers carrying the slogan, the committee informed him it was going to start a procedure to force him to withdraw the slogan or quit the campaign. Mr. White contacted the A.C.L.U., which called Anne Milgram, the committee president, a senior from East Brunswick majoring in English and political science, and told her that the proposed action was illegal.

As it turned out, Mr. White lost the election.

* * *

February 27, 1993

WHEN THE ARTS WERE IN NAZI HANDS

By HERBERT MITGANG

One historic photograph in a provocative new exhibition at the New York Public Library says it all. It shows four smug-looking Nazi storm troopers in gleaming jackboots, their arms loaded with books they are carrying away to be torched. The place is Hamburg, the time May 15, 1933. Libraries and bookstores are being purged of so-called racially impure books written by Jewish, pacifist, socialist and foreign authors. In the Nazis' Campaign Against the Un-German Spirit, tens of thousands of books were burned in cities and university towns all over the Third Reich.

The photograph is one of the items in "Assault on the Arts: Culture and Politics in Nazi Germany," which opens today in the Gottseman Exhibition Hall in the library, at Fifth Avenue and 42d Street, and runs until May 28.

Even 60 years after the book burnings, the documents in the exhibition are chilling. In a video documentary, Josef

Bildarchiv Preussischer Kulturbesitz

Nazi storm troopers carrying books to be burned in a 1933 photograph that is in the exhibition at the New York Public Library.

Goebbels, Reich Minister for Popular Enlightenment and Propaganda, proclaims at the Berlin book-burning on May 10, 1933, that "excessive Jewish intellectualism" has finally ended.

More than 200 books, photographs, posters, prints and periodicals are on display to trace the National Socialist Party's rise to power. There are election posters from the period, 1919–1932, and political drawings by George Grosz from 1921 satirizing the Weimar Republic. One exceptional item is a stereoscopic viewer with three-dimensional images of Hitler and Mussolini, reviewing classical sculptures in an Italian museum.

A Family Business

An original police blacklist, from Leipzig in 1938, cites banned authors and their works. The books included works by all the writers in the Mann family: Thomas, the Nobel laureate in literature; Heinrich, his older brother, also a novelist, and two of Thomas's children, Erika and Klaus, who were active in liberal causes. The Mann family later emigrated to the United States and both of Thomas's sons, Klaus and Golo, served in the American Army.

Authors and philosophers who at one time championed Nazi Germany's ideals are represented by the writings of Ernst Junger, Gottfried Benn and Martin Heidegger.

Paintings and sculptures were also condemned and confiscated by the Third Reich, as shown by original catalogues, postcards and posters. "The Great German Art Exhibition" in 1937 displayed officially approved works. In the same year, more than 16,000 works were collected that were judged "racially impure" because the artists were called "mentally deranged."

The day after the official German art exhibition opened, 600 items in another exhibition, labeled "Degenerate Art," were displayed in Munich. Works by "degenerate" artists in the public library exhibit include prints by Max Beckmann, Otto Dix, George Grosz, Paul Klee and Emil Nolde. There's a 1922 color lithograph, "Composition," by Wassily Kandinsky from a portfolio of Bauhaus prints.

Two Kinds of Opera

Film and music are also covered in the exhibition of degenerate works attributed to Jews and "Bolshevist elements." There are original photographs and a 1929 program for "Threepenny Opera" by Kurt Weill and Bertolt Brecht, whose works were banned during the Nazi era. There's a listening booth: press one button and you hear approved music, like a Wagner opera; push another and it's the forbidden "Threepenny Opera."

The exhibition was inspired by "Degenerate Art: The Fate of the Avant-Garde in Nazi Germany," originally presented by the Los Angeles County Museum of Art in early 1991 and later moved to the Chicago Art Institute and the Smithsonian Institution in Washington. When Robert Menschel, a member of the board of the New York Public Library, saw "Degenerate Art" in Los Angeles, he suggested to Susan Saidenberg, the library's manager of exhibitions, that New Yorkers should get a chance to see it, too. Ms. Saidenberg and library officials agreed but emphasized the library's own material.

It was found that the library's collections, including items in the Lincoln Center branch, contained enough material to mount a version that emphasized the literary, cultural and performing arts rather the fine arts featured in the Los Angeles show. Only four items, a newspaper clipping and three catalogues of degenerate art and music, were borrowed from Los Angeles for the New York exhibition. So the result is largely a new show.

Some items on display were borrowed from other institutions and private collections. The co-curators of "Assault on the Arts" are Anson Rabinbach, professor of European history at Cooper Union, and Dr. Gail Staviitsky, an art historian, who were not involved in the Los Angeles show.

* * *

December 10, 1993

MURDER TRIAL IN CANADA STIRS PRESS FREEDOM FIGHT

By CLYDE H. FARNSWORTH
Special to The New York Times

TORONTO, Dec. 9—An Ontario judge's order banning news reports about a trial concerning a particularly grisly murder has stirred a debate here about press freedom and set the stage for a constitutional challenge that might reduce the power of judges to issue similar gag orders.

The issue is one faced often in the United States: the balancing of a free press with a defendant's right to a fair trial. Because of different history and traditions, trial judges in Canada have come down harder against press freedom than their counterparts across the border.

In the United States, publication bans are virtually nonexistent. Other procedures are used to try to guarantee a fair trial, including changes of venue, orders forbidding people close to a case to discuss it, and permitting extensive challenges of jurors.

The Ontario case has demonstrated to many Canadians that in an age of instant global communications, it is impossible to maintain a complete information blackout. What the Canadian media is barred from publishing or broadcasting has been flooding in from the United States, where the judge's order cannot be enforced.

"Bans of this type," said Lou Clancy, managing editor of The Toronto Stair, "are holding our court system up to ridicule."

News Groups to Argue Appeal

The Star, The Toronto Sun, The Globe and Mail, the Canadian Broadcasting Corporation and other news organizations begin three days of arguments on Jan. 31 before the Ontario Court of Appeal to try to get the judge's order quashed.

Justice Francis Kovacs of the Ontario Court's General Division ordered the ban in July when Karla Homolka, 23, of St. Catharines, was sentenced to 12 years in prison for her role in the sex slayings of Kristin French, 15, also of St. Catharines, and Leslie Mahaffy, 14, of Burlington, about 30 miles to the east. Both towns are just across the border from Niagara Falls, N.Y.

Ms. Homolka, who worked after high school as a veterinarian's assistant, was convicted of two counts of manslaughter. She now is expected to testify against her estranged husband, Paul Teale, 29.

Mr. Teale, a former accountant, faces two charges of first degree murder in the deaths of the two teen-age girls. In addition, he has been accused of 50 sex-related offenses, allegedly committed when he was living in Scarborough, a suburb of Toronto. He is scheduled to appear in court in April for a preliminary hearing. his trial has been tentatively scheduled for July.

Attempt to Insure Fair Trial

Justice Kovacs, citing the need to insure that Mr. Teale gets a fair trial, forbade publication of the "circumstances of the deaths of any person" disclosed at the Homolka trial.

A long statement of facts agreed to by the defense, and other evidence presented in court, cannot be legally published or broadcast here. The press was limited to reporting Ms. Homolka's conviction, her sentence and the contents of the indictment against her.

Included in the banned information is the defense's reported admission at the trial that both young victims were sexually assaulted for days before they were killed. To keep them from escaping, according to some accounts, the couple used veterinary surgical instruments to sever tendons in their legs. The girls were eventually strangled.

Sister Among Victims

Ms. Homolka reportedly also acknowledged at the trial that her 14-year-old sister Tammy was another victim. Ms. Homolka and W. Teale reportedly drugged and sexually assaulted Tammy, who died of asphyxiation in December 1990. A local coroner ruled the death accidental. After the Homolka trial, the body was exhumed for further investigation.

In fact, lawyers for Mr. Teale did not agree with Justice Kovacs that public knowledge of the Homolka trial would prevent him from being fairly tried. They contend that full disclosure would have helped their client.

The Homolka-Teale case has riveted the nation because of its luridness. The news blackout has further heightened interest by creating what is in effect a national guessing game in trying to determine just what the facts are. Some lawyers argue that rumors could be doing more damage to the future trial process than the publication of the actual evidence.

U.S. Papers Keep Game Alive

Newspapers in Buffalo, Detroit, Washington, New York and even Britain, together with border radio and television stations, have kept the game alive by reporting details gleaned from sources at Ms. Homolka's trial. The Fox Television show "A Current Affair" has aired two programs on the crimes. Information and rumors have also spread across myriad electronic networks available to anyone with a computer and a modem in Canada.

So great is demand for information that Canadians were bootlegging copies of The Buffalo Evening News, which carried banned material in one recent edition, across the border, prompting orders to Niagara regional police to arrest all those with more than one copy at the border. Extra copies were confiscated. Copies of other newspapers, including The New York Times, were either turned back at the border or were not accepted by distributors in Ontario.

The Ontario Attorney General, Marion Boyd, insists that the ban is working. "I don't believe almost everybody knows," she told reporters, referring to the details of the crime. "There may be many people who know. Whether there is a general enough knowledge to disrupt the court process or not—I do not believe that is the case."

Ms. Boyd said the media are engaged in a "feeding frenzy" motivated by commercial interests, "an effort to sell newspapers and profit out of this horrible situation."

Bruce Durno, president of the Criminal Lawyers Association of Ontario and another defender of the ban, said Justice Kovacs expected that American publications and broadcast outlets "would not try to breach the Canadian court order."

Canada's Charter of Rights and Freedoms, adopted in 1982, upholds "freedom of thought, belief, opinion and expression, including freedom of the press." But in Canada the authorities have more discretion than in the United States to muzzle the press when it comes in potential conflict with an individual's right to a fair trial.

TV Play is Banned

The protection of an individual's right to a fair trial has also been invoked in curtailing other forms of expression. "The Boys of St. Vincent," a television play about the sexual abuse of young boys, set in a fictitious Roman Catholic orphanage in Newfoundland, was kept off the air last year by a judge hearing a case against a group of former Ontario Christian Brothers who were about to go on trial for offenses similar to those depicted in the drama.

The program was broadcast last Sunday and Monday, but only after another judge rejected an application to ban its airing by lawyers for another group of former Christian Brothers.

Although judges have used gag orders for years, their authority to do so has never been tested in the higher courts. The challenge to the gag order in the Homolka-Teale case before the Court of Appeal offers the opportunity.

"The trial judge has the power to insure the integrity of the trial process," said Alan Brudner, a law professor at the University of Toronto. "But it's time for the broader question of the extent of that power to be finally looked at by the Supreme Court."

* * *

December 15, 1993

GERMANS ASK IF FILM HURTS OR AIDS NAZIS

By STEPHEN KINZER

Special to The New York Times

BERLIN, Dec. 14—Is it right for a state-subsidized German film to show an attractive young neo-Nazi spouting lies and propaganda? Does government have the right, or even the duty, to ban such a film?

Germany is wrestling with these questions as it confronts an 83-minute documentary called "Profession: Neo-Nazi." The debate spilled past German borders this week when organizers of an Amsterdam film festival announced plans to show it on Wednesday, even though it has been pulled from distribution in Germany.

"Profession: Neo-Nazi" centers on the life of Bela Ewald Althans. Backers of the 27-year-old Munich agitator hope he can help them in their campaign to impose a "new order" on Germany and the world. His big assets are good looks, stage presence and the ability to project a hateful ideology with a winning smile.

Mr. Althans supports Nazi ideology with disarming frankness. In the scene that has set off the most protest, he is shown visiting the site of the Nazi death camp at Auschwitz-Birkenau. There he launches into a monologue asserting that accounts of mass gassings there are untrue. A young American challenges him, but although he is momentarily thrown off balance by the youth's demand that he remove his sunglasses, he defends himself with well-prepared arguments.

Bankrolled by 4 States

Not only does the ventilation system show that gassings at Auschwitz were technically impossible, Mr. Althans asserts, but Jews who were imprisoned in Nazi camps survived and are now living off German Government subsidies.

"The film is a horror," said Ignatz Bubis, the head of Germany's principal Jewish organization. "It's pure Nazi propaganda."

Like many German films, "Profession: Neo-Nazi" was made with the help of financial grants from several state governments. The grants, from four states, amounted to $220,000.

After protests, officials of the four sponsoring states reviewed the film. Hamburg and Mecidenburg-West Pomerania declined to take any action against it. Brandenburg urged that a commentary be added, and Hesse, in the harshest reaction thus far, not only demanded its subsidy money back but also banned the film.

A Storm of Pros and Cons

A spokesman for prosecutors in Hesse said the film sought, without rebuttal, "to lie and to discredit as propaganda the historical fact of the systematic murder of Jewish people in the gas chamber at Auschwitz."

"The film without additional explanation is unsuitable," the spokesman said. "The neo-Nazi is left with the last word."

The ban could be enforced in other German states, and distributors of the film decided to withdraw it "for a short time" while they decide how to proceed.

In Berlin, prosecutors are considering indicting both Mr. Althans and the film makers and distributors on charges of incitement to racism and displaying symbols of forbidden organizations.

The film's director, Winfried Bonengel, and his associates are committed and reputable anti-Nazis who have no sympathy for the views expressed in the film. They are anxious to defend their right to free expression but highly uncomfortable at being portrayed as accomplices to racist propaganda.

"I took the hard way by intentionally not including any commentary," Mr. Bonengel said in an interview. "Everyone knows what really happened at Auschwitz. Moralizing commentary would only turn off the young people I'm trying to reach."

Is It Too Subtle?

Among officials who opposed a ban was Torsten Teichert of the state agency that distributes film subsidies in Hamburg. Mr. Teichert called the protests excessive.

The manager of a movie theater in Kreuzberg, a Berlin neighborhood where many leftists and foreigners live, said most patrons responded positively to the film in the week it played there.

"It's remarkable that the film is now being taken as dangerous even though it's aimed at making people aware of the danger of right-wing extremism," the theater's manager said.

Others have argued, however, that although the film may have meant to condemn neo-Nazi ideas, it does so too subtly for some viewers. For example, when Mr. Althans is shown addressing a cheering audience in Cottbus, dressed in jeans, white T-shirt and open yellow jacket, he is shot from below, lighted from behind, and takes on the romantic aura of a bad-boy rock star. He and his supporters are reportedly distributing copies of the film abroad.

Michael Sontheimer, editor of Berlin's leftist daily newspaper Tageszeitung, said opinion on his staff is mixed. "The people in the culture department are all against the ban, but the people who cover politics are for it," he said.

* * *

January 7, 1994

CANADIAN TEST CASE: 'PORNOGRAPHY' VS. IMAGINATION

By CLYDE H. FARNSWORTH
Special to The New York Times

TORONTO, Jan. 6—A painter in Toronto has become the first artist to be charged under a new child-pornography law because his renderings are about sexuality and children.

Civil libertarians say the case is likely to test the new legislation, which was enacted in the closing months of the last Conservative Government, on the ground that it is too sweeping.

The artist, Eli Langer, "is not the sort of person that this law was designed against," said Brian Blugerman, a lawyer who specializes in the media and communications. "The motive for the law was to reduce child abuse, not to curb the activity of legitimate galleries and serious artists."

Mr. Langer's lawyer, Frank Addario, said, "The only thing obscene in this case is the obscene rush for votes to get the law enacted last summer, just before elections." The bill, the Child Pornography and Corrupting Morals Amendment, was passed in June. Four months later, the Conservatives were defeated by the Liberals.

Facing 10 Years in Prison

The new law makes it a crime to own, make, exhibit or sell anything that depicts a sexual act by anyone under 18. If convicted, defendants face up to 10 years in prison and fines.

Exemptions exist for works with artistic merit or an educational, scientific or medical purpose. But the law puts the burden of proof on the accused.

Passage of the law and the seizure of Mr. Langer's works on Dec. 16 by the Police Morality Squad reflect a greater willingness by the authorities to intrude on freedom of expression than is generally the case in the United States, where the First Amendment stretches far to safeguard such values.

Canada's Charter guarantees freedom of thought, belief, opinion and expression but allows imposition of "reasonable limits" to guarantee other rights. In this delicate balance, freedom of expression is often restricted.

Judges routinely ban press coverage of murder trials to keep prospective jurors from being swayed. Since a Supreme Court decision in 1992 that expanded the definition of obscenity, Customs officials routinely seize serious literary books as well as pornography.

"People feel there are linkages between violent crime and pornography," said Michelle Fuerst, chairwoman for national criminal justice at the Canadian Bar Association.

Mr. Langer's works—5 paintings and 35 drawings—were seized at the Mercer Union, one of Toronto's most respected artist-run galleries. They portray children and adults in sexual behavior, including sodomy, fellatio and masturbation. Mr. Langer says his works were made not from models but from his imagination.

Review Tips Off Police

In announcing the show, the gallery said the artist's "images are largely informed by intuitive personal and social drives, exploring the phenomenon of intimacy where it exists without the compensation of social and cultural consent."

After a review by Kate Taylor, art critic for The Globe and Mail, who called the works "horrible" but said Mr. Langer "can paint marvelously well," Detective John Ferguson seized the canvases and pressed charges. "It's our feeling that the exhibit is simply not art and falls under the category of child pornography," he said.

"I believe it is the Mercer Union's right and responsibility to show art, Eli Langer's to make it and mine to write about it—without any of us being stifled by the police," she said. Few other critics reviewed the show.

The United States Congress passed the Protection of Children From Sexual Exploitation Act in 1982, but First Amendment lawyers say that law could not be used to prevent a showing similar to Mr. Langer's.

"I think the courts correctly would hold that the law doesn't apply to an artist's rendering," said Barry A. Fisher of Los Angeles, vice chairman of the First Amendment Rights Committee of the American Bar Association. "Real harm needs to be dealt with, not someone's imagination."

Court Date Set

Mr. Langer, 26, is to appear in court on Jan. 17. His lawyer, Mr. Addario, said he would try both to show the artistic merit of the works and to prove that the new law is an unconstitutional abridgment of free expression. "This is a poorly worded law that has ensnared whole groups of people who ought not be ensnared," he said.

At a recent news conference, Mr. Langer defended his work. "I am not a pornographer," he said. "I am an artist. I deeply resent having to justify my work. Even so, I feel obliged to say that my art is the product of my imagination. I did not use models."

Acknowledging that the issues are "complicated and emotional," he said: "I did nothing more than accept my responsibility as an artist to provoke a dialogue. In the intimate relationship between artists and society, there is a mutual vulnerability. I feel particularly vulnerable now."

* * *

May 1, 1994

STUDENT PRESS IS HAMSTRUNG, REPORT SAYS

By WILLIAM GLABERSON
Special to The New York Times

SAN FRANCISCO, April 27—High school newspapers around the country have lost financial support while school administrators increasingly censor their contents, according to a report presented here at the annual convention of the nation's newspaper publishers.

The report, by the Freedom Forum, an international journalism foundation, found that financial and editorial restrictions on high school newspapers have tightened since a similar study 20 years ago. Even that study found widespread censorship and blandness.

The report, the product of two years of work, is based in part on information gathered by forum researchers in hundreds of interviews at scores of high schools nationwide, and on a statistical study of the state of high school journalism at 234 schools. The report also cited the results of studies by academics and others who have investigated high-school journalism.

Improving Student Press

Freedom Forum officials said they had presented their findings to the Newspaper Association of America meeting here to encourage journalists to help improve the student press.

"High school newspapers are dying a slow death," Judith D. Hines, who helped organize the report, said in an interview. Youngsters are discouraged from becoming journalists, Ms. Hines said, and they are discouraged from becoming newspaper readers because of skepticism they learn firsthand in high school about the independence of newspapers.

Citing several surveys, the Freedom Forum report concluded that high school journalism was mainly flourishing in the nation's wealthier suburbs, and that even in those communities a majority of student journalists were relatively wealthy and white. The issues that high school newspapers cover, the report said, are seldom important to minority students in their schools.

The forum report indicated that in the environment of shrinking school budgets, high school journalism had suffered most in city schools. One study cited in the report found that of 149 inner-city schools surveyed, 19 had stopped publishing newspapers in the last 10 years.

Ms. Hines said such statistics might drastically understate the problem, because many more schools had cut back on the number of times they published a newspaper or had reduced the resources available.

Threat of Censorship

John Seigenthaler, former publisher of The Tennessean in Nashville and chairman of the Freedom Forum First Amendment Center at Vanderbilt University, said growing censorship might be the greatest threat to school newspapers.

In 1988, the United States Supreme Court said that school officials could control the content of school newspapers as long as their actions were reasonably related to educational concerns.

First Amendment lawyers say the Court may not have intended to encourage widespread censorship. But school administrators, the report found, have interpreted the 1988 ruling as supporting them in sharply limiting the freedoms of high school journalists.

In a study of 270 high school newspaper advisers, 37 percent said school principals had rejected newspaper articles or required changes.

The report, "Death by Cheeseburger," takes its title from a 1971 censorship incident at Vance Senior High School in Henderson, N.C. The high school newspaper was closed, the adviser was let go and a novice was hired to teach English and journalism because of three articles: among them, a satirical tale of the death of the writer after eating a high school cafeteria cheeseburger.

* * *

March 26, 1995

DESPITE A NEW PLAN FOR COOLING IT OFF, CYBERSEX STAYS HOT

By PETER H. LEWIS

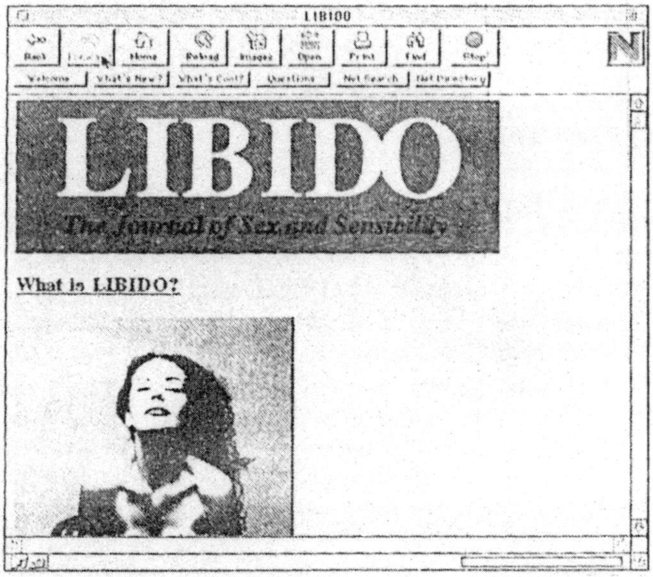

The New York Times

Libido, an electronic journal published on the Internet's World Wide Web, features nude photographic studies and eroticism but not the sort of explicit fare generally classified as "hard core" pornography.

Amateur Action, a computer bulletin board service that advertises itself as "the nastiest place on earth!," was still open for business yesterday despite the conviction of its owners last year on charges of transmitting obscene material over computer networks. The only change appears to be a warning that greets all callers:

"Amateur Action B.B.S. is for the private use of the citizens of the United States! Use by law enforcement agents, postal inspectors and informants is prohibited!"

Business appears to be good: a reporter was told he was "caller No. 1,083,677" just before he was offered a menu of choices that included "Oral Sex," "Bestiality," "Nude Celebrities" and "Lolita Schoolgirls."

Sexually explicit fiction and digitized photographs of naked people are common on the nation's rapidly growing computer networks, as are forums for discussing sexual fantasies. And computer experts and lawyers who specialize in cyberspace issues say a proposal in the Senate to bar such material from the nation's information networks is impractical, unenforceable and perhaps unconstitutional.

"My major concern is to make the new Internet and information superhighway as safe as possible for kids to travel," said Senator Jim Exon, Democrat of Nebraska and author of the proposed Communications Decency Act of 1995, in a telephone interview yesterday.

The proposal, which cleared the Senate Commerce Committee on Thursday without dissent, would impose fines of as much as $100,000 and two-year prison terms on anyone who knowingly transmits any "obscene, lewd, lascivious, filthy or indecent" communications on the nation's telecommunications networks. The law would apply to telephone systems, cable and broadcast television systems, and public and private computer networks, including the global Internet.

Similar laws have been proposed in several states, reflecting a growing national concern over use of a new communications medium that now reaches millions of homes in the United States.

"The potential danger here is that material that most rational and reasonable people would interpret as pornography and smut is falling into the hands of minors," Mr. Exon said. "The information superhighway is in my opinion a revolution that in years to come will transcend newspapers, radio and television as an information source. Therefore, I think this is the time to put some restrictions or guidelines on it."

The proposals for restrictions have been met with incredulity and outrage by Internet users, legal experts and civil libertarians, who contend that efforts to halt the flow of information in cyberspace—where, in effect, every computer is both a bookstore and a printing press—are futile on both technical and legal grounds.

There are more than 70,000 private computer bulletin board systems in the United States, and even more private business networks. Private commercial computer networks, including America Online, Prodigy Services and Compuserve, have nearly six million subscribers. Many of them are connected to the Internet, the biggest network of all.

The Internet is a vast collection of mainly private computer networks, connecting millions of users in an estimated 150 countries. More than half the users are outside the United States. But because of the interconnected nature of the Internet, transmissions from one foreign user to another frequently pass through computer systems in the United States. And because of the lightning speed of computer-based communications, a computer user in New York can retrieve information from a computer in Denmark, say, as easily as from a computer across town.

The overwhelming majority of material on computer networks is not sexual, and the fastest-growing segments of Internet traffic are related to the transmission of business information and computer software.

So trying to filter out sex-related material from the torrent of digital bits passing through tens of thousands of computer networks "is like shooting an ICBM at a gnat," said David Banisar, a lawyer for the Electronic Privacy Information Center, a lobbying group in Washington. "It can't be done without the absolutely most Draconian methods being used."

Dan L. Burk, visiting assistant professor of law at George Mason University in Fairfax, Va., noted that courts had repeatedly rejected attempts to restrict telephone sex services because lawmakers did not use the "least restrictive means" to accomplish their goals. The courts finally allowed restrictions, including a requirement that users present credit card numbers, that would presumably block access by children without restricting access by adults.

A comprehensive ban on such material on computer networks, he said, could restrict information that courts have ruled legal to disseminate to adults.

"If the burden becomes too high for protected adult speech, then the statute clearly is not going to pass muster" in the Federal courts, Mr. Burk said.

Most of the sexual material found on computer networks appears to consist of photographs scanned from adult magazines in violation of copyright law. A 44-year-old writer in Illinois who uses the pen name Billy Wildhack said on Friday: "In 98 percent of the adult boards I visited, the graphic images were nothing beyond what you might find in an adult video rental store. But I did find some strange things on some boards, including graphic images of women who are lactating and some bestiality."

Internet experts note that while information flows freely over the Internet, the medium differs significantly from broadcast media like television or radio. With few exceptions, users have to actively seek sex-related material, which can be difficult to find among the vast resources of the global network. In the case of some photo files, in particular, the user typically must use more than casual technical skills to assemble the images for viewing.

Because of the international nature of the Internet, creators of sexually explicit material can quickly set up operations overseas or transfer their material to foreign computer networks. Americans participating in sex-related discussions on their computers can just as easily route their messages through so-called anonymous remailers who hide their identities.

Given the likelihood that sex-related materials will continue to proliferate in cyberspace, there is a growing interest in finding a way to filter objectionable material from the torrent of information. But computer programmers say there is no way to determine easily whether a stream of data stored as 1's and 0's will eventually coalesce into a photo of a wildflower or a wild sex act, a copy of the First Amendment or a treatise on pedophilia.

"Anybody who knows anything technical about the Internet would understand that this is ridiculous," said Ron Newman, a computer programmer in Somerville, Mass., who until recently worked at the Media Labs at the Massachusetts Institute of Technology.

Echoing sentiments that have become common in cyberspace discussion forums in recent days, he said of the Exon proposal: "I suspect it will be laughed at collectively by the Internet users of this country and ignored, and as for the rest of the world's Internet community, it will make the United States a laughingstock."

Still, some schools and companies are taking initial steps to restrict access to portions of the Internet where sexual content is common, especially the global network known as Usenet.

Typically reached through the Internet, Usenet consists of more than 10,000 discussion groups. Of the 20 most popular Usenet forums, half are on sex-related topics.

Some universities, including Carnegie-Mellon in Pittsburgh, have filtered out access to sex-related Usenet groups, ostensibly to preserve scarce computing resources for more academic topics. As more elementary schools and high schools connect to the Internet, however, the trend toward filtering at lower grade levels is growing.

Siecom Inc., an Internet service provider in Grand Rapids, Mich., supplies 20 elementary and secondary schools with restricted, one-way access to Usenet discussion groups. The company eliminates some discussion groups from its service, then gives schools the option of eliminating more. The schools may scan all incoming and outgoing student electronic mail for objectionable words. A school can designate the words it will not allow.

"We really had no idea that the level of interest in our service would be so high," said Rob Oates, the president and general manager of Siecom.

Commercial on-line services that connect to the Internet, including Prodigy and America Online, already include simple software tools that can be used by parents or teachers to restrict access to some of the dicier areas of the network.

"We do not believe our role should be as surrogate parents for anybody," said Brian R. Ek, a spokesman for Prodigy, a service based in White Plains that has an estimated two million users. "We tell you about the good, the bad and the ugly on the other side of the curtain and let you make the choice."

Prodigy's software requires a household's main account holder, who must have presented a valid credit card number and thus is presumed to be an adult, to activate access to individual Usenet, chat and bulletin board areas for other members of the household. Without such action, the areas are blocked.

"We also have a software program through which every bulletin board note passes, and it looks for obscenities and slurs in a straight keyword search," Mr. Ek said.

America Online, the country's fastest-growing commercial service, simply hides the names of sex-related news groups from a menu of Usenet options. To gain access to a sex-related board, the user must type the exact name of the news group.

Many Internet users have suggested that controls by parents or teachers are preferable to controls by the Government.

"Governmental control sufficient to shield children from any chance of exposure to indecent material would have to limit it to the point that adults couldn't access it either," said Mr. Burk, the law professor, "reducing adult speech, as the Supreme Court says, to the level appropriate to a child."

* * *

June 23, 1996

LESSONS FROM THE PENTAGON PAPERS

By R. W. APPLE Jr.

WASHINGTON—Twenty-five years ago this month, The New York Times began publishing the Pentagon Papers, a documentary history tracing the ultimately doomed involvement of the United States in a grinding war in the jungles and rice paddies of Southeast Asia.

They demonstrated, among other things, that the Johnson Administration had systematically lied, not only to the public but also to Congress, about a subject of transcendent national interest and significance.

The Government sought and won a court order restraining further publication after three articles had appeared. Other newspapers then began publishing. They, too, were restrained, until finally, on June 30, 1971, the United States Supreme Court ruled, by a vote of 9 to 0, that publication could resume.

Pivotal Moment

Then as now, the fight over the top-secret papers, whose compilation had been ordered by Robert S. McNamara when he was Defense Secretary, stood as a pivotal moment in the ages-old struggle between the Government and the press. But few would have guessed how much it would change the news media, how much it would change the public view of the news media and the Government and how little it would change the way the Government conducts its business.

Opponents of the Vietnam war, including Daniel Ellsberg, the onetime hawk turned dove who played a key role in making the papers public, hoped that doing so might persuade President Richard M. Nixon to change his policy on Vietnam. It did not. Less than a year after publication, Haiphong Harbor was mined, and the war dragged on.

The Pentagon Papers prompted the first attempt ever made by the Federal Government to impose a prior restraint on the press in the name of national security. In his new book, "The Day the Presses Stopped" (University of California Press), David Rudenstine argues that some of the papers (though not the ones printed) could indeed have compromised national security.

Few if any of the main players in the drama share that view. But even if it is correct, that only makes the precedent stronger; the Constitution, in the Court's view, makes prior restraint impermissible even if there is some danger to national security.

Victory emboldened the news media, and the contents of the Pentagon Papers themselves guaranteed, at least for the generation of journalists directly involved, that every Government utterance would be subject to skeptical (and too often cynical) scrutiny. The Nixon Administration responded by creating the Plumbers unit (so called because they were to deal with leaks like that of the papers). That step in turn led to the Watergate scandal and ultimately to Nixon's resignation.

For both the news media and the public, revelations about the Watergate burglary, the ensuing cover-up and the associated horrors, as they came to be known, compounded the doubts they harbored about the Federal Government.

But as reporters, editors and commentators challenged top officials they had once treated deferentially, and as they probed their characters and personal lives as well as their public actions, many Americans came to resent the press. Journalists' standing in opinion polls sank along with the politicians'.

Governments, meantime, have continued to conceal and, on occasion, to prevaricate. The Iran-contra affair, almost certainly illegal, was conceived and carried out by the Reagan Administration in total secrecy, and no one involved blew the whistle—any more than anyone had done so during the months and years as the nation stumbled ever deeper into the Vietnam quagmire.

While pretending otherwise, the Bush Administration allowed Iraq to build its strength by buying foreign arms. In the Persian Gulf war, the Pentagon sought to limit journalists' access, having decided that in Vietnam reporters knew too much, not that they had been too often lied to.

Many familiar with the situation in the Balkans as the United States and its allies seek to maintain a shaky peace wonder how far, in an election year, the White House will go in trying to make that peace seem more solid than it really is.

Though the Pentagon Papers dealt with a foreign war, they taught a lesson applicable to domestic politics as well: It is almost always better, once trouble breaks, to get out all the damaging evidence at once, rather than stonewalling and allowing it to trickle into the public domain, thus creating the impression of an ever-mounting crisis. It is a lesson mostly unlearned.

Why? Partly the natural impulse for self-protection, partly the deep-seated governmental belief that the public should not be allowed to watch the sloppy business of policy-making because it would not understand and partly the conviction that the policy makers know best and mean well.

In the Whitewater affair, one new Administration version of events has succeeded another. Having seen the consequences of the Watergate cover-up, David Gergen tried during his brief tenure as an adviser in the Clinton White House to avoid incremental revelations, but he has told friends since that he failed.

The Birth of Spin

A more-or-less permanent tension between reporters and officeholders has developed—not an altogether unhealthy state of affairs, perhaps, so long as it does not degenerate into deep-seated animosity and distrust. For reporters, the official version of events is "spin," not fact. Government officials tend to believe that reporters judge and interpret before they bother to report.

Mr. Ellsberg thinks there is probably no avoiding the tension. "That's the lesson of the Pentagon papers," he said in an interview last week. "No matter how smart people are in the White House and the Pentagon, no matter how well intentioned, they can get into crazy and illegal activities. And once they're in, and these schemes begin to fail, you cannot count on them to have the moral courage to admit a mistake, to cut their losses, to throw in the towel, to get out."

Stop the Presses

The following telegram was sent to The New York Times on June 14, 1971. Before it was received by The Times, an F.B.I. operator in Washington mistakenly transmitted the message to a fish company in Brooklyn.

Arthur Ochs Sulzberger
President and Publisher
The New York Times
New York New York
I have been advised by the Secretary of Defense that the material published in The New York Times on June 13, 14, 1971 captioned "Key Texts From Pentagon's Vietnam Study" contains information relating to the national defense of the United States and bears a top secret classification.
As such, publication of this information is directly prohibited by the provisions of the Espionage law, Title 18, United States Code, Section 793.
Moreover further publication of information of this character will cause irreparable injury to the defense interests of the United States.
Accordingly, I respectfully request that you publish no further information of this character and advise me that you have made arrangements for the return of these documents to the Department of Defense.
John W. Mitchell Attorney General

Correction:

An article last Sunday on the 25th anniversary of the Pentagon Papers court case misstated the Supreme Court's vote to let publication resume. It was 6 to 3, not 9 to 0.

* * *

August 30, 1996

THE MAYOR, SEEING RED, PURGES THE READING LIST

By CRAIG R. WHITNEY

ORANGE, France—Until recently, this Provencal town of 28,000 people was better known for its sunny Mediterranean ways and the rustic charm of its local accent than for being a center of the kind of right-wing ideological militancy that could make even a John Bircher blanch.

But that was before Jacques Bompard, a bespectacled dentist with a mordant sense of humor, took over in June 1995. Now he sits in the Mayor's office, just around the corner from Orange's greatest tourist attraction, a magnificent Roman theater whose summer festival is popular with the Parisian vacation set, clogging the one route through town the other day on their way back to the capital at holiday's end.

His pet project, and the one that has turned Orange into an intellectual cause celebre, is a campaign to censor the public library.

In an interview, Mr. Bompard, a founding member of the far-right National Front, made no bones about what he has done in the library, whatever anybody in Paris thinks about it. Indeed, he made censorship sound like a battle for freedom of speech for the local people who elected him.

"All French libraries are controlled by the left and the extreme left," he said. "I want all political currents to be represented, unless a book is immoral or outlawed."

What kind of currents is clear from the list of 56 that the Mayor's office has suggested so far that the librarians should put on the shelves.

Some they should have had anyway, arguably, like the "History of France" by Jacques Bainville, a respected popular historian who was active in the monarchist movement in the early part of this century. Others, such as Emmanuel Ratier's "Mysteries and Secrets of B'nai B'rith," an attack on the "Judeo-Masonic plots" that were a favorite target of French fascist movements in the 1930's, were more troubling.

The interference became too much for the librarian, Catherine Canazzi, who has left the city payroll.

"It was impossible to work under those conditions," she said. "They insisted on reviewing the lists of books that were to be acquired and saying yes or no to each one, something no other city administration had ever done before."

Andre-Yves Beck, the head of the Mayor's communications office, began visiting the library frequently to go over lists of proposed acquisitions, even for the children's shelves.

Outraged, the Mayor's opponents persuaded the Minister of Culture in Paris to send a senior library inspector to see what was going on. His report, published in July, said: "Questioning the Mayor on his refusal to approve acquisition of the series 'Regional Tales From All Countries,' it was apparent that we did not speak the same language. For a librarian, tales are one of the principal genres of children's literature. Their interest comes from their brevity, their closeness to oral tradition, and from the symbolic memory and

Guillaume Atger/Editing

Mayor Jacques Bompard's drive to censor the library in Orange, France, site of a Roman theater, has become a cause célèbre, with an inspector sent from Paris charging "ethnocentrism" by the Mayor's office.

universal wisdom they transmit. Mr. Bompard wants to put the accent instead on national or regional roots, and rejects cosmopolitanism and globalism."

The inspector's report criticized the "ethnocentrism" revealed in the selections of the Mayor's office and recalled that sound library principles included diversity and encouragement of cultural dialogue.

The acting librarian, Roselyne Blanc, said she was forbidden to talk with a reporter. But people familiar with the Orange library say that Mr. Beck has rejected the purchase of children's books about North African culture.

"Even just a book cover with a black face on it gets rejected," one said.

The presence of many Muslim immigrants from the Maghreb region of North Africa in southern France is a sore point with many supporters of the National Front, which appeals to popular sentiment for sending millions of foreign immigrants back where they came from to make jobs available for the 12.5 percent of the workers in France who do not have any.

Mr. Bompard estimates that 15 to 20 percent of the people living in Orange today are of North African origin. He recently denied permission for a local mosque to expand its premises to build a Koranic school, he said.

"I consider that for the Maghrebians who live here and want to become French, it's better to go to secular public schools than to a religious school in a mosque," he said.

Bernard Vaton, a leftist politician who lost his post as a deputy mayor when the National Front came in first in last year's municipal elections with 37.5 percent of the vote, said that the number of North Africans here was probably between 7 and 8 percent; French law forbids ethnic or religious census questions.

"Provence is an area in the throes of economic transition," he said. "The old economy of small business and farms is disappearing and being replaced by tourism and service industries, and the indigenous population is declining as wealthy people from other places all over Europe come here to spend their retirement."

"North Africans come in via Marseilles and get work harvesting peaches and grapes, and they start small businesses," Mr. Vaton went on. "The Parisians parachute in with their summer music and theater festivals. And the natives, the people who used to work the farms, speak Provencal and sing the local troubadour songs, feel as if they are slowly being dispossessed."

With Government parties and those on the left locally divided last year, the National Front filled the vacuum. Mr. Vaton and many others here hope things will change by the time of the next national parliamentary elections, in 1998.

* * *

June 27, 1997

COURT, 9–0, UPHOLDS STATE LAWS PROHIBITING ASSISTED SUICIDE; PROTECTS SPEECH ON INTERNET

By LINDA GREENHOUSE

WASHINGTON, June 26—In a sweeping endorsement of free speech on the Internet, the Supreme Court today declared unconstitutional a Federal law making it a crime to send or display indecent material on line in a way available to minors.

The decision, unanimous in most respects, marked the Court's first effort to extend the principles of the First Amendment into cyberspace and to confront the nature of a new, and—to most of the Justices—an unfamiliar medium.

The result left the coalition of Internet users, computer industry groups and civil liberties organizations that had challenged the Communications Decency Act exultant. The forceful opinion for the Court by Justice John Paul Stevens held that speech on the Internet is entitled to the highest level of First Amendment protection, similar to the protection the Court gives to books and newspapers. That stands in contrast to the more limited First Amendment rights accorded to speech on broadcast and cable television, where the court has tolerated a wide array of Government regulation. "Content on the Internet is as diverse as human thought," Justice Stevens said in a quotation from a special three-judge Federal District Court in Philadelphia, which struck down the Communications Decency Act a year ago in a decision the Supreme Court affirmed today.

The Internet is a rapidly expanding global computer network, which allows as many as 60 million people to communicate on line and connect with information and entertainment sources around the world. A large majority of its users live in the United States.

The decision makes it unlikely that any Government-imposed restriction on Internet content would be upheld as long as the material has some intrinsic constitutional value. Obscenity, which is outside the protection of the First Amendment, is also covered by the Communications Decency Act, and the Court left that provision intact today without even analyzing it.

The indecent material at issue today was not precisely defined by the 1996 law—one of its serious vulnerabilities, as the Court saw it—but was referred to in one section of the statute as "patently offensive" descriptions or images of "sexual or excretory activities."

Justice Stevens said that the Court regarded the law's goal of protecting children from indecent material as legitimate and important, but concluded that the "wholly unprecedented" breadth of the law threatened to suppress far too much speech among adults and even between parents and children. "The interest in encouraging freedom of expression in a democratic society outweighs any theoretical but unproven benefit of censorship," Justice Stevens wrote.

He noted that people could not "confidently assume" that discussions of birth control, homosexuality, or prison rape, or even the transmission of "the card catalogue of the Carnegie Library," would not violate the law and place computer network users at risk of severe criminal penalties. Violations of the Communications Decency Act, which never went into effect because of a stay issued by the lower court, carried penalties of two years in prison and a $250,000 fine. "The severity of criminal sanctions may well cause speakers to remain silent rather than communicate even arguably unlawful words, ideas, and images," Justice Stevens said.

The law made it a crime to use a computer to transmit indecent material to someone under 18 years old or to display such material "in a manner available" to a person under 18. Justice Stevens said that given the nature of the Internet, there was no way someone transmitting indecent material could be sure that a minor would not see it. He noted that most uses of the Internet, like chat rooms, newsgroups, and the World Wide Web, "are open to all comers."

Nor, Justice Stevens said, could people rely on a defense provided by the law for those who take "good faith, reasonable, effective and appropriate actions" to restrict access by minors. No current technology satisfied those demands, he said.

The opinion, Reno v. American Civil Liberties Union, No. 96–511, was signed by Justices Antonin Scalia, Anthony M. Kennedy, David H. Souter, Clarence Thomas, Ruth Bader Ginsburg, and Stephen G. Breyer.

In a separate opinion by Justice Sandra Day O'Connor, she and Chief Justice William H. Rehnquist, who signed her opinion, subscribed to much of the Court's approach. They said the law could be constitutionally applied, but only in the very limited circumstance of deliberate transmission of indecent material "where the party initiating the communication knows that all of the recipients are minors." If an adult might be among the recipients, the speech cannot constitutionally be suppressed, Justice O'Connor said.

Justice O'Connor said that on the surface, the Communications Decency Act was analogous to a zoning regulation, similar to the "adult zones" for bookstores and X-rated movie theaters the Court has upheld in a series of decisions. But the analogy was inexact, she said, because there is no way in cyberspace to make sure that minors can be screened out while still allowing adults to have access to the regulated speech.

Justice O'Connor said the law was clearly unconstitutional because it was "akin to a law that makes it a crime for a bookstore owner to sell pornographic magazines to anyone once a minor enters his store."

The Communications Decency Act was a last-minute Senate amendment to another bill, the Telecommunications Act of 1996. It was adopted without hearings and amid substantial doubts about its constitutionality. For that reason, its sponsors agreed to add a provision guaranteeing quick Supreme Court review after a hearing by a single three-judge court, a shortcut through the normal appellate process.

President Clinton signed the bill and Administration lawyers defended the law vigorously. At the same time, White House officials worked on a substitute Internet policy in the event the law was overturned, as some in the Administration hoped it would be.

The law was challenged by two main coalitions of plaintiffs, representing a wide spectrum of the Internet community. The United States Chamber of Commerce entered the case at the Supreme Court stage to argue that the law presented a threat to the country's ability to compete globally in an age of new communications, an argument that very likely got the attention of the free-market conservatives, including Justices Thomas and Scalia, who joined Justice Stevens's opinion.

The trial before the court in Philadelphia produced opinions by the three judges, Dolores K. Sloviter, Ronald L. Buckwalter and Stewart Dalzell, totaling 147 pages with 123 separate factual findings. The Court today relied heavily on these findings, including Justice Stevens's observation that the Internet was not as "pervasive" a medium as television or radio—where the Court has permitted greater Government regulation—because computer users have to actively search for indecent material and "seldom encounter such content accidentally."

Christopher A. Hansen, a lawyer for the American Civil Liberties Union, which organized one of the plaintiff groups, said today that in establishing the highest level of First Amendment protection, the Court's decision "was more about speech than about technology." That made the decision important for all future Internet cases even as the technology may change, Mr. Hansen said.

In his opinion, Justice Stevens was critical of several aspects of the Government's defense of the law, but singled out one in particular. That was the argument that unless the law was upheld, development of the Internet would be stifled by parents' fears about having on-line access if they could not shield their children from indecent material.

"We find this argument singularly unpersuasive," Justice Stevens said, adding that "the dramatic expansion of this new marketplace of ideas contradicts the factual basis of this contention" given the "phenomenal" growth of the Internet. "As a matter of constitutional tradition," he said, "in the absence of evidence to the contrary, we presume that governmental regulation of the content of speech is more likely to interfere with the free exchange of ideas than to encourage it."

* * *

September 7, 1997

STUDENTS CENSORED, BUT ISSUE LIVES ON

By The New York Times

CHICAGO, Sept. 6—When student reporters for the Naperville Central Times, a suburban high school newspaper, learned that district administrators spent taxpayers' money on travel at the time of a budget crisis, they did what any responsible journalist might do. They investigated.

Using public records, they uncovered the expense vouchers of three principals and one administrator, who spent an average of $1,400 each to attend professional conferences in New York, New Orleans, San Francisco and Phoenix.

But the information never made it into the paper. Tom Paulsen, the principal of Naperville Central High School, directed the students to remove the administrators' names before publication. His action, three years ago, thrust Naperville Central, a school of 2,700 in an affluent bedroom community west of Chicago, into rekindling a longstanding journalistic debate: do high school newspapers have the same constitutional rights as the rest of the press?

Lawmakers in Illinois broadly answered yes. By a wide margin they passed a bill restricting administrators' powers of prior review.

But last month, the Illinois Governor, Jim Edgar, vetoed the bill.

"The legislation creates a situation in which the entity ultimately responsible for the newspaper—the school board—cannot exercise full control over the paper's content," Mr. Edgar said in his Aug. 10 veto message. He said he feared the bill would make school boards vulnerable to lawsuits.

The Governor's surprise veto has angered many civil liberties groups and brought lawyers from around the country to the aid of the Naperville students.

The issue of freedom of the press for high school newspapers was taken as far as the Supreme Court nine years ago, when it ruled that a high school principal in Missouri could censor the school newspaper because an article interfered with the school's "basic educational mission."

The Court's language in that case, which has become known as the Hazelwood decision, has led to confusion, however, with varying interpretations of who determines "educational mission" and how it is defined.

That confusion has prompted a number of states to establish guidelines of their own.

Arkansas, California, Colorado, Iowa, Kansas and Massachusetts have decided that student journalists should be protected, establishing laws that permit administrators to intervene only when a publication uses obscenity or libelous material or invades privacy. The Illinois Legislature had passed a similar measure.

Mark Goodman, executive director of the Student Press Law Center in Arlington, Va., said Governor Edgar's concern was unfounded.

"Schools are sued hundreds of more times for events that take place on the athletic fields," Mr. Goodman said, "yet no one is suggesting that the principal should be calling plays in the huddle."

Proponents of the Illinois measure are weighing whether to accept the veto, push for a legislative override or introduce a new bill.

At Naperville, Mr. Paulsen said recently that he supported the Governor's veto.

"Administrators have the responsibility to allow the students as much freedom as possible," he said, "but many times we have the experience and the perspective that the students or adviser may not have to recognize when a situation may be harmful."

Mr. Paulsen said the article on spending was the only one he had ever censored.

"My concern," he said, "was that there may have been an appearance that these administrators did something wrong and that would affect their ability to lead."

All four administrators' vouchers raised questions about their expenses. The administrator visiting San Francisco, for example, was reimbursed for five nights in a hotel even though his conference was two days. But none of the administrators was found to have misspent any money.

For their part, the Naperville student reporters, who are now in college, say Mr. Paulsen's actions worked to their advantage.

"It really backfired for him," said Sal Shaw, now at the University of Illinois. "This wouldn't have received nearly the attention that it did if he would have let us print the names."

The article appeared with an editor's note explaining that the students had been censored, but it listed the voucher numbers they had uncovered, making it easier for others to look up the names.

The students also gave the names to professional reporters in Chicago, and they published them.

Mr. Shaw said he felt that the students had made their point.

"Administrators don't trust that we can act responsibly," he said. "This is about giving students their voice back."

* * *

January 28, 1998

COLORADO BOARD LIMITS FILMS IN CLASSROOMS TO PG AND PG-13, AND DISCONTENT ARISES

By MINDY SINK

CASTLE ROCK, Colo., Jan. 27—High school history teachers here are no longer permitted to show the Academy Award-winning film "Schindler's List" to illustrate a lesson on the Holocaust or Oliver Stone's "Platoon" for a discussion of the Vietnam War.

R-rated and NC-17 rated films like those or excerpts of them cannot be shown in any Douglas County school under a policy unanimously adopted by the school board earlier this month. The previous policy permitted their use with parental consent. The school district, in one of the nation's fastest-growing counties, has about 27,000 students in 44 schools, including 5 high schools.

"I learned about the Holocaust without watching a movie about it," said Jody Bennett, 41, who has two children in the local schools. "The kids can learn about history without having to see the gore of it all through Hollywood."

The policy also requires that teachers ask the principal before showing films rated PG and PG-13 if they think any aspect of the work could be considered controversial, so English teachers may have to get permission before showing a film version of a Shakespearean text.

Teachers who used "Platoon" and "Schindler's List" are unhappy about the change.

"It's archaic to believe that the only way we can teach is with a textbook," said Susan Noll, a social studies teacher at Douglas County High who has shown "Platoon." "Students remember what they feel, and you can have a tremendous impact with a hook like a film."

The most recent catalyst for controversies over movies in the classroom is "Schindler's List," an R-rated movie by Steven Spielberg, which became available on video with a 64-page study guide for instructors three years ago.

"It is plainly within a parent's right to choose what their kid does or doesn't see," said Matthew Freeman, senior vice president of People for the American Way, which tracks book banning in schools. "It is when a parent says they don't want anybody else's kid to see it either that problems arise and it becomes public policy."

The issue arose in Douglas County when Mrs. Noll heard that a fellow teacher had not been permitted to show "Schindler's List." She went to the principal to find out if she was still allowed to show "Platoon," also rated R for violence and language, in a history class called "America Since '45." She said she always sent a parental consent form home before showing it to her classes, based on the school's nearly 20-year-old policy.

"Our old policy only allowed certain films that were rated PG as a last resort if no other materials were available and if parental consent was in hand," said Pat Grippe, assistant superintendent for Douglas County Schools. Mr. Grippe's interpretation of that policy was that there always was a ban on R-rated films.

According to the Motion Picture Association of America, children under the age of 17 must be escorted by an adult to any R-rated film, and no one under 17 is admitted to an NC-17-rated film.

The board's new policy leaves no room for differing interpretations; only PG and PG-13 films may be shown. It asks that teachers take into consideration the "varied interests, abilities, intellectual development and maturity levels of the pupils and the standards of the community" as well as the possible offensiveness of "any violence, nudity and language" in the material.

"Well, holy cow, under this policy, what isn't controversy?" said Fran Henry, an English teacher at Douglas County High.

Ms. Henry has shown her students PG-13-rated film versions of "Hamlet" and "Henry V" but now says "it's not worth the trouble."

"Shakespeare was meant to be acted and seen, not just read," she said. "These kids are visual learners, and we are supposed to teach them to be critical viewers."

The new policy does allow teachers to assign films—even those rated R and NC-17—as homework, with parental approval.

But Kennard Z. King, a history teacher at Douglas County High, asked: "Where would there be 100 copies of 'Schindler's List'? It's absurd, and it defeats the idea of discussing the film."

Mr. King took students to a public movie theater for a special screening of that film last month, and defends the use of film in his classes.

"A lot of history is R-rated," he said. "There is a lot of violence in history, and it can be offensive."

But one of Mr. King's students, who chose not to go with her class for the screening, disagrees. "We don't need to see the blood coming out of somebody," said Katie Wilson, 16, a junior at Douglas County High. "If we read somebody was shot, then we know what happened."

The Douglas County School Board also approved a policy this week that defines "controversial learning resources," a topic that includes things like texts or guest speakers. The policy states that when a teacher is selecting a resource material, he should consider "whether the resource is representative of the many religious, ethnic and cultural groups and their contribution to our American heritage," among other things.

There will be a second and final reading of the policy next month.

"You can't hold a shade over students' eyes," said Danielle Brenneis, 16, a junior at Douglas County High. "The school board may be doing this to protect themselves, but not the students, and that is what should come first."

Miss Brenneis was one of many students and faculty members who spoke out against the new policies at a meeting last week.

"At the heart of a good education should be controversy," said Yvonne Tricarico, a counselor with the Douglas County Schools for 26 years.

A similar case in a neighboring school district is being fought out in the Colorado Supreme Court. A high school English teacher, Alfred E. Wilder, was suspended in 1995 for showing Bernardo Bertolucci's "1900," which is rated R for violence, nudity and language. Although Mr. Wilder has won his case in the courts, the school district dismissed him in 1996. It also continues to appeal the court decisions and not allow him to return to work.

"Regardless of what you think of the Douglas County policy, at least it's a clear ban telling teachers what they can and can't do," said Sharyn Dreyer, a lawyer with the Colorado Education Association. "That was not the case with Mr. Wilder."

Ms. Dreyer said Mr. Wilder, who has been staying with family on the East Coast for many months and could not be reached for comment, wanted to return to his job and be awarded all back pay.

* * *

February 13, 1998

MAGAZINES FOUND TOO ADULT FOR SCHOOL

By JOHN T. McQUISTON

HAUPPAUGE, N.Y., Feb. 12—Three of the most popular magazines for teen-age girls—Seventeen, Teen and YM—have been pulled from the library of a Long Island middle school by the district's Superintendent following complaints by a group of parents and a priest over the sexually oriented material in the magazines.

The Superintendent, Dr. Paul A. Lochner, ordered the magazines removed from the Hauppauge Middle School even after an advisory committee of teachers, administrators and a parent voted to keep the publications.

"Based upon the age of the students in the middle school and sound pedagogical principles, it was determined by me that the materials are not age appropriate," he said in a brief statement.

One of the opponents was Msgr. E. Raymond Walden of the St. Thomas More Roman Catholic Church in Hauppauge, who urged his parishioners in a church bulletin to file a formal complaint with the Hauppauge School Board.

"We're talking about 10- , 11- , 12- and 13-year-olds reading about how to perform sex when they have no basis on which to make such decisions," Monsignor Walden said.

Critics of the magazines specifically objected to letters from readers seeking advice and articles on topics like having sex, using at-home pregnancy tests, taking the birth-control pill, vaginal discomfort, using a condom, masturbation, tampons, stretch marks and worries about various body fluids and H.I.V.

When the formal complaint was filed with the school district last month—and after about 200 of Monsignor Walden's parishioners appeared at a school board meeting—Dr. Lochner ordered the three magazines removed pending further investigation.

The Board of Education, following policy guidelines, appointed a seven-member advisory Curriculum Complaint Committee that included the middle school librarian, Joyce Sullivan, two teachers, three administrators and one parent. The panel voted, 4 to 3, to return the magazines to the library shelves.

Dr. Lochner, however, overrode the advisory panel and today defended his decision to cancel the library's subscriptions to the three magazines. On Feb. 10, he said, the Board of Education "by unanimous resolution approved and reaffirmed my actions in this matter."

Ms. Sullivan, who voted with the panel's majority, said she was disappointed by the Superintendent's decision. "It makes me wonder why we had a committee in the first place," she said.

She said she believed that there were many worthwhile articles in the magazines that addressed concerns like peer pressure, conformity and divorce. As director of the library, Ms. Sullivan chooses a wide variety of magazines and newspapers for the 825 students in grades six through eight.

Some students said today that they would miss the magazines. One 13-year-old seventh grader who stopped in the hall outside the Superintendent's office as he was answering reporters' questions about the ban said she read all three magazines. "They should keep them here in school," she said. "Some of the subjects are good and have information you need."

Another student, also 13, said that banning the magazines was "not the right thing to do, because people are going to read them anyway."

Judith James, a former president of the Long Island School Media Association, an organization of professional librarians, said the decision in Hauppauge would have a chilling effect elsewhere.

"The issue is intellectual freedom," said Mrs. James, who is the library director of Friends Academy in Locust Valley, N.Y.

She said the magazine ban brought to mind a case involving the banning of several books from the Island Trees School District on Long Island 20 years ago. "Catcher in the Rye," "Huckleberry Finn," "Of Mice and Men" and "The Diary of Anne Frank" were among the books removed from school library shelves.

Arthur N. Eisenberg, legal director of the New York Civil Liberties Union who as co-counsel argued the Island Trees case before the Supreme Court and won, said today that the action in Hauppauge involved the same overriding issue.

"Politicians and school board members and even superintendents should not intrude on the decision of a trained librarian concerning educational material," he said. "That's a matter that must be left to educators."

Meredith Berlin, the editor in chief of Seventeen, which has 2.5 million readers age 12 and over, called the decision by Dr. Lochner and the Hauppauge Board of Education an "unfortunate mistake."

"It's not my place to tell them what to do, but when you start banning things, it's always a mistake," she said. She said that Seventeen's philosophy toward sex had always been, "When in doubt, wait."

She added, "But there are many teen-agers out there who don't wait, and when they ask us questions, we take their questions very seriously and respond factually, without being judgmental."

Lesley Seymour, editor in chief of YM, which has 2.1 million readers age 12 and over, said, "Teen-agers are bombarded by terrifyingly inaccurate information about health and sexuality, and if we don't address these matters openly, nobody does, and they are left with gossip and inaccuracies."

Roxanne Camron, editor in chief of Teen magazine, which has 1.7 million readers between age 12 and over, said: "Teen is extremely responsible when it comes to subject matters of a sexual nature, and we never encourage readers to become sexually involved. In fact, we advocate for thinking carefully, and perhaps delaying, sexual involvement."

The Hauppauge teachers' union, meanwhile, is considering taking the matter to court. "We feel this is a censorship issue and we are investigating ways we can take legal action," said Catherine D. Killian, a spokeswoman for 285-member Hauppauge Teachers Association.

* * *

July 8, 1999

IN NORWAY, A NANNY STANDARD FOR MOVIES

By WALTER GIBBS

Johnny Syversen for The New York Times

Ingeborg Moraeus Hanssen decides what films may be shown in Oslo.

OSLO, July 7—A country where violent films and videos are banned, pornographic cinemas are nonexistent, and advertisers are forbidden to focus on children was probably not what President Clinton had in mind this summer when he challenged Hollywood to tone down its act.

But for Norway, censoring entertainment is as natural as sweeping the streets. The streets are well swept indeed. By almost any standard this Scandinavian capital might be considered a bastion of wholesomeness. The police are unarmed, the children frolic in public fountains, and the most divisive political issue in Parliament this year is kindergarten policy.

No one manning the cultural ramparts, however, takes Norway's platonic order for granted, least of all a vigilant woman named Ingeborg Moraeus Hanssen.

A political celebrity with swirling capes and robes, Ms. Moraeus Hanssen leads the Oslo Municipal Cinema Company, a branch of city government that owns all 31 movie screens in the city. She must approve every commercial film before it is shown. At stake, in her view, is the mental health of Norwegian young people.

"I care much more about my public than I do about the movies," she said recently in her office overlooking Karl Johans Gate, the cultural hub of Oslo. "This industry can be very, very gruesome. You live just once on this earth, and I don't want people wasting their time watching stupid movies filled with violence and raw sex." As she spoke, she rapped her knuckles on her large wooden desk. Spread before her were the day's newspapers, which had not yet reported her latest thumbs-down ruling. The American action thriller "Universal Soldier: The Return," featuring computerized warriors, will not be shown in Oslo because Ms. Moraeus Hanssen considers its violence "speculative" and of no artistic value. (The film is scheduled for release in the United States on Aug. 20.)

Last year the French director Jan Kounen called Ms. Moraeus Hanssen "the lady of darkness" for rejecting his gangster film "Dobermann" on the same basis.

"This could maybe happen in Iraq or China," Mr. Kounen thundered to Norwegian reporters, "but in a democratic society, such censorship is scandalous." He threatened to get even by setting his sequel, "Dobermann II," in Oslo.

Because Norway's population of 4.4 million is smaller than that of many cities, its restrictive policies are no more than an irritant to the film industry, which regards Norway as a throwback. In 1980 the national authorities banned the Monty Python comedy "Life of Brian" because of content deemed blasphemous. In neighboring Sweden, gleeful cinema owners ran advertisements under the headline "Too funny to be shown in Norway!"

Since the Monty Python experience, Norwegian officials describe their position on films as progressive rather than backward. They hope that American lawmakers, shaken by a string of high school shootings, will take steps to dam the global flow of disturbing images in film and other media.

Trond Waage, the Cabinet-level Commissioner for Children in Norway, said young people not weaned on American media lacked the detachment and irony necessary to deal with harsh or manipulative messages.

"Children are the holiest and best thing about our world, and we can see they are under attack," he said, calling on the United Nations to develop international media standards. He insisted that the "mental pollution" emanating from entertainment capitals was a matter of public health, not just morality.

"I'm not moral," he said. "I'm furious."

Norwegian agencies that shield children from the media admit they are fighting a rear-guard battle. When a 5-year-old Norwegian girl was killed roughhousing with playmates in 1994, the action-packed American children's television series "Mighty Morphin Power Rangers" got the blame and was pulled off the air. But satellite television signals and the Internet continue to provide forbidden fruits ranging from advertisements for children's cereal to escapist violence and pornography.

Norwegian officials planning for the long term say schools must give youngsters the psychological means to make healthy choices. In the meantime the authorities joust away at perceived threats. No private organization exists to defend artistic expression, and few people seem to think one is needed.

"We have always been a control-seeking country with faith in the authorities," says Tom Loeland, director general of the Norwegian Board of Film Classification. "Regulation is a very well integrated part of our democracy."

Since 1997 Mr. Loeland's board has banned three dozens films that distributors wanted to import for the home-rental market. But it is the municipal ownership of theaters, a framework unique to Norway, that occasionally causes fireworks.

Every town with a movie house has a public official responsible for programming, but none have the clout of Ms. Moraeus Hanssen. When she shuns a foreign movie it is hardly worth importing because Oslo accounts for a third of the filmgoers in Norway. Filmmakers around the world know of her prickliness.

"When I refused the movie 'Crash,' David Cronenberg called me up angry and shouting," she recalled, referring to the film's director, a Canadian. "But I am used to it. Directors always tell me their film is a masterpiece. They say the violence is necessary. Sometimes they even say it is funny. I love that one. Finally they just say, 'How dare you!' Well, I dare." (In the United States "Crash" was rated NC-17: no one under 17 admitted.)

She knows that a relationship between violent films and violent behavior is hard to prove, she said, and she knows that youngsters are savvy about film technology. But she also believes that they need help to identify the good, the true and the beautiful.

"I am against censorship," she insisted. "What I am is an editor."

One of her decisions that came under scrutiny regarded Oliver Stone's "Natural Born Killers." The film board called it a social commentary and allowed it to enter the country with an "18" rating limiting its audience. Ms. Moraeus Hanssen refused to schedule it, but the outcry against censoring a potentially historic work was so great that she gave in. She assigned the movie to a little-known art-film house and told people not to go.

"That film is devil's work," she said. "Oliver Stone is a genius in many ways, but even a genius can sometimes be in the hands of the Devil."

Saul Zaentz, the American producer of "One Flew Over the Cuckoo's Nest," "Amadeus" and "The English Patient," has never crossed the imperious Oslo cinema director. He said her methods would never work in the United States, but were well suited for Norway.

"I have known Ingeborg for many years and have always admired her," he said. "She loves what she is doing, she knows what she is doing and she has a lot of courage. She deserves her freedom of speech."

* * *

November 2, 1999

GIULIANI ORDERED TO RESTORE FUNDS FOR ART MUSEUM

By DAVID BARSTOW

A Federal judge ruled yesterday that Mayor Rudolph W. Giuliani violated the First Amendment when he cut city financing and began eviction proceedings against the Brooklyn Museum of Art for mounting an exhibition that the mayor deemed offensive and sacrilegious.

Judge Nina Gershon of United States District Court in Brooklyn ordered the mayor to restore the city's monthly payments to the museum and end his campaign to evict it and remove its board of trustees over an exhibition that includes a painting of the Virgin Mary on a canvas adorned with elephant dung.

"There is no federal constitutional issue more grave," the judge wrote in her 38-page decision, "than the effort by government officials to censor works of expression and to threaten the vitality of a major cultural institution as punishment for failing to abide by governmental demands for orthodoxy."

Dith Pran/ The New York Times

Robert S. Rubin, left, chairman of the Brooklyn Museum of Art, with the museum's director, Arnold L. Lehman, and its lawyer, Floyd Abrams, called the judge's ruling "a victory for the citizens of New York."

Mr. Giuliani called Judge Gershon's decision "the usual knee-jerk reaction of some judges" and said the city would appeal.

Museum officials immediately hailed the decision.

"This is a victory for the citizens of New York and for freedom of expression across the nation," Robert S. Rubin, chairman of the museum board, said at an afternoon news conference. "We believe that the people of New York and the nation are intelligent, independent-minded and, as guaranteed under the First Amendment, able to decide for themselves what exhibitions to see, books to read and opinions to express.

"We cannot allow censorship or politics to undermine our most important rights as citizens of the United States of America."

Mr. Giuliani described the ruling as "precipitous" in light of an article in The New York Times on Sunday that described how museum officials raised money for the exhibition by soliciting hundreds of thousands of dollars from companies and individuals with a commercial interest in the display.

Mr. Giuliani ordered lawyers for the city yesterday to seek permission from Judge Gershon to "follow the money trail" by taking sworn statements from museum officials and others involved in the exhibition, "Sensation," which includes works by some of Britain's leading artists.

Judge Gershon's ruling came in the form of a temporary injunction against the city. The museum will now seek a permanent injunction.

It was clear yesterday that both sides regarded Judge Gershon's ruling as merely the next milestone in a case that has transfixed the city with its implications for cultural institutions, the First Amendment and the political future of a mayor who is considering a campaign for the United States Senate.

Lawyers for the museum said that they might try to depose the mayor and other top city officials as they prepare their request for a permanent injunction.

In a letter to Judge Gershon yesterday morning, the city corporation counsel, Michael D. Hess, asked her to hold off on her ruling until the city had time to investigate the exhibition's financing. Judge Gershon rejected the request and issued her decision, but city officials vowed to pursue the issue.

"This is all about dollar signs," Mr. Giuliani said yesterday. "It isn't about free speech. It's actually a desecration of the First Amendment, as much as it is a desecration of religion, to use the First Amendment as a shield in order to take money out of the taxpayers' pockets in order to put that money into the pockets of multimillionaires."

But Floyd Abrams, the museum's First Amendment lawyer, charged that Mr. Giuliani was simply seizing on the financial issue to shift attention from his own "lawless behavior" and "to avoid First Amendment talk."

"It is always gratifying to receive a ruling that vindicates the First Amendment," Mr. Abrams said yesterday, "but it is a little sad to even be here today. The events that led to this lawsuit should never have happened. The behavior of the mayor that led to it should never have occurred. The pretexts offered to the courts should never have been uttered. And the contempt for the First Amendment reflected in the entirety of the events of the last month are intolerable."

Mr. Hess, in his letter to Judge Gershon, accused the museum's director, Arnold L. Lehman, of showing "lack of candor" when he was questioned by city lawyers about the exhibition's finances. He also criticized Mr. Lehman for approving "willful lies to members of the press regarding the financial involvement of Charles Saatchi," the British advertising entrepreneur who owns the "Sensation" art collection.

Mr. Saatchi, who has made millions of dollars buying and selling contemporary art, has pledged up to $160,000 toward the costs of staging "Sensation."

An internal museum memorandum that was described in court papers shows that Mr. Lehman endorsed a decision by a high-ranking museum official to conceal that fact in an interview with a reporter from The New York Observer. Mr. Rubin strongly defended Mr. Lehman's actions in putting together "Sensation."

"The museum, the director, the staff acted responsibly and appropriately in this matter," Mr. Rubin said during the news conference as Mr. Lehman looked on, at times fighting back tears. "I personally and the trustees stand by Arnold and the staff, and they have had, do have and will have our continued support."

Asked about the issue of soliciting donations from those who stand to gain financially from an exhibition, Mr. Rubin replied, "I will not respond to that directly, because I do not think that this is the appropriate forum for a discussion of museum exhibition funding practices, and I am not prepared to answer any question on that matter."

The city, which provides about a third of the museum's annual $24 million operating budget, began withholding the museum's monthly subsidy in October. The November subsidy, for nearly $500,00, was due yesterday. But city officials did not send either payment, saying they did not want the museum to spend city funds while they were pursuing an appeal.

"We are going to ask the judge if we can put the money in an escrow account, because this whole thing has not unraveled," Mr. Hess said.

Yesterday's ruling did not break much new legal ground. Judge Gershon cited a long line of legal precedents that forbid public officials to use their control of government funds to punish unpopular or offensive speech. And in word and deed, Mr. Giuliani made it abundantly clear that he was acting against the museum because he disapproved of the art in "Sensation," particularly a portrait of the Virgin Mary by Chris Ofili.

Mr. Ofili, a Roman Catholic of Nigerian descent, decorated the painting with elephant dung and cutouts from pornographic magazines.

Mr. Giuliani and several Catholic leaders took great offense at the painting, but Judge Gershon said their outrage was no basis for trying to "coerce the museum into relinquishing its First Amendment rights." She quoted a 1952 United States Supreme Court decision overturning a New York statute that authorized the state to deny licenses to motion pictures thought to be sacrilegious.

"It is not the business of government in our nation," the Supreme Court ruled, "to suppress real or imagined attacks upon a particular religious doctrine, whether they appear in publications, speeches or motion pictures."

Judge Gershon noted that among the museum's collection of 1.5 million artworks are many reverential depictions of the Madonna.

"No objective observer," she wrote, "could conclude that the museum's showing of the work of an individual artist which is viewed by some as sacrilegious constitutes endorsement of antireligious views by the city or the mayor, or for that matter, by the museum, any more than that the museum's showing of religiously reverential works constitutes an endorsement by them of religion."

* * *

November 23, 1999

ANOTHER ART BATTLE, AS DETROIT MUSEUM CLOSES AN EXHIBIT EARLY

By ROBYN MEREDITH

DETROIT, Nov. 22—Visitors to the Detroit Institute of Arts, the grande dame of museums here, could visit a room in the modern gallery to see a toy Jesus wearing a condom, a pile of human excrement and a brazil nut labeled with a racial epithet. For two days.

But the one-room exhibition, containing 15 provocative pieces, was shuttered on Friday after its brief run because of concerns that it would offend the community, and the local artist whose work now stands behind closed doors has accused the museum of censorship.

The museum's director disagrees. "The museum is always selecting works of art, and selection is not censorship," said Graham W. J. Beal, who joined the museum two months ago. "Asking an artist to exclude one work in favor of another is not censorship."

The artist saw it differently. "It would be like if I painted a picture of a nude and they said, 'It might offend some people; why don't you paint a dress on it,' " said Jef J. Bourgeau, who runs a nonprofit museum in nearby Pontiac, Mich. "It is push-your-button art, it is aggressive art, but it is art."

But Mr. Beal saw it more as a question of choosing his battles.

"We have to be the ones comfortable with the position we are taking, and not just say, well, the artist demands it so we are going to put it in the show," said Mr. Beal, who likened the situation to that of an exhibition at the Brooklyn Museum of Art, "Sensation," that Mayor Rudolph W. Giuliani recently tried unsuccessfully to shut down. "The museum and art become a political and moral football kicked around by all sorts of people," Mr. Beal said.

The American Civil Liberties Union has criticized the decision to close the exhibition, called "Van Gogh's Ear," which opened Wednesday and was to have run through Sunday.

"The essence of modern art in general is to allow people to make up their own mind about art," said Kary L. Moss, executive director of the Michigan branch of the A.C.L.U.

Mr. Bourgeau's exhibition was commissioned two years ago, and he had worked with a museum curator in planning it. But the new museum director had not been aware of what the exhibition would contain before it opened, said a museum spokeswoman, Annmarie Erickson.

It was meant to explore how artists are intertwined with the art they create, particularly in the context of artists who had gained notoriety in the 1990's, Mr. Bourgeau said.

One item on display is a jar of urine, labeled as that used in Andres Serrano's photograph of a submerged cross. "It was supposed to be the actual urine used, but it wasn't," Mr. Bourgeau said.

Similarly, there is a video that purports to be the work of British artist Tracey Emin, showing her taking a shower while menstruating. But another naked woman is on the screen. And the Jesus with a condom is attributed to Chris Ofili, the artist whose "Holy Virgin Mary" painting is adorned with elephant dung at the Brooklyn museum. Despite the label, it is meant to be taken as the pretend response of Mr. Ofili to the controversy created by his work.

"Some people understand and some people don't," Mr. Bourgeau said. And so in a post-modern spectacle of its own, art pretending to be that of controversial artists of the past has become controversial itself.

Mr. Beal, who said he turned down the "Sensation" exhibit while director of the Los Angeles County Museum of Art, said that it was sometimes appropriate for museums to show art likely to offend, but that it was not warranted in this case.

Photographs by Associated Press

Jef J. Bourgeau, left, waited yesterday to retrieve his art, after Graham W. J. Beal, the museum director, right, closed the exhibit.

"They were afraid somebody might be offended—nobody had been yet," said Mr. Bourgeau, who said few people had seen the exhibit. "We've got this huge controversy over work no one's ever seen."

THE SOVIET UNION AND EASTERN EUROPE

October 20, 1975

DIGGING OUT THE NEWS IN SOVIET BLOC IS NOT ANY EASIER UNDER DETENTE

By MALCOLM W. BROWNE
Special to The New York Times

BELGRADE, Yugoslavia, Oct. 19—Despite the smooth treatment Western newsmen have generally been accorded in Eastern Europe since détente became a diplomatic, catchword, correspondents are finding direct coverage of the workings of Communist power almost as difficult as in cold war days.

The Western correspondents no longer work in constant fear of arrest and even long imprisonment. Direct censorship has disappeared. Provocations, blackmail and extortion directed against newsmen have largely ended.

Western European and American correspondents are sometimes ostentatiously followed by police plainclothes men in the Soviet Union and its bloc, seemingly more to intimidate them than for other reasons.

Correspondents have had experiences proving that their telephones are at least occasionally monitored, that their offices and apartments contain hidden listening devices and that in some cases their cars have been bugged.

Leaving Communist countries, Western journalists are sometimes carefully searched, and their papers and interview notes photographed by the secret police.

Expulsion Threat Remains

Despite the recent European summit conference at Helsinki, which dealt in part with freedom for news correspondents to carry out their work, they still live under the threat of expulsion or exclusion.

On the other hand, the tendency these days is to avoid direct confrontations with foreign correspondents and to adopt many of the tactics of Western press-agentry.

Most Western correspondents arrive in European Communist capitals interested, among other things, in talking with dissidents, looking for cracks in the Communist party apparatus and examining the political, social and economic life of the country as if it were an open society.

The Communist authorities, when possible, block or obscure such investigations. They seek to involve the correspondents in their own favorite themes—national industrial growth, supposedly rising standards of living, bright prospects for increased trade with the West, cultural matters and so forth.

In all the Communist countries special government institutions have been established, ostensibly to help foreign correspondents in their work but actually to try to channel reporting away from certain subjects.

Soviet Agency Sets an Example

Most of these agencies copy the style and techniques of the Soviet agency Novosti, through which foreign correspondents must arrange interviews with government and party officials, travel around the country and accreditation for special events.

Novosti, like Interpress of Poland, charges the correspondents for its services. The Czechoslovak press and information center for foreign journalists charges a $15 licensing fee for each visit.

All these agencies have a major voice in deciding whether a foreign newsman will be allowed into the country. All maintain extensive files of Western publications and have experts who read and appraise what visiting correspondents have written.

These agencies are usually dependencies of foreign ministries and they are all linked to the interior ministries—that is, the secret police.

This correspondent once received a telephone tip in an Eastern European capital that an attempt had been made on the life of the visiting Soviet Communist party leader, Leonid I. Brezhnev. The only authoritative light that could be shed on the report would have had to come from the local police, who were supposed to have arrested the assassin as he was smuggling a grenade into Mr. Brezhnev's presence.

A query was lodged with the local government news assistance agency—the only possible channel through which the police could be approached.

'No Comment or Reply'

Two days later, an official of the agency reported back: "I am sorry but I can get you no comment or reply. I must warn you of something. It is lucky you asked me and not some other worker in our agency, because I must tell you that some of them actually work for the secret police."

"You must realize," he continued, that police all over the world are rather hard and sometimes not very intelligent or understanding about the needs of newsmen. I ask you not to pursue the subject about which you asked if you ever hope to return to this country. Even if you do not, things here could be made extremely unpleasant for you."

Probably the most popular Communist technique with visiting correspondents is to fill their schedules with so many interviews, meetings, social functions and trips, all of marginal news interest, that little time remains for other things.

Among the biggest time-killer the Communist agencies use is the ritual visit to the collective farm—preferably two or three collective farms, all models of their kind—with lengthy interviews, inspections and meals.

'What Do You Expect?'

Efforts to evade collective farms and long lunches are turned aside with professions of injury and distress. Scores of key workers and officials have had to leave their jobs all day in preparation for the visit or lunch, the correspondent is told, and the authorities in the capital will almost certainly take it amiss if the hospitality is spurned.

The newsman tries, often without success, to meet people on his own. In some countries, Bulgaria and Rumania, for example, people who talk with foreign correspondents without the intercession of the authorities can find themselves in grave trouble.

"What do you expect?" an East European journalist asked a Western colleague recently, adding:

"Strip away their veneer of détente and our two countries are still at least potential enemies. That makes you at least a potential spy, probably an agent provocateur and certainly a writer of damaging reports.

"Remember also that our system of government is still the dictatorship of the proletariat, which will never tolerate the West's kind of journalism. What amazes me is that they let you in at all, even if it's only to look at the shadows on our walls."

* * *

January 2, 1978

POLES TALK OF HUMAN RIGHTS—WHAT IS AND ISN'T ALLOWED

By DAVID A. ANDELMAN
Special to The New York Times

WARSAW, Jan. 1—President Carter's 35-hour visit to Poland that ended yesterday has focused renewed attention on an issue hotly though quietly debated throughout this East European nation—the nature and quality of Poland's commitment to human rights.

It is a commitment that the President equated with that of his own Administration in this sensitive area, telling a news conference later carried in its entirety by Polish radio and television, "Our concept of human rights is preserved in Poland."

"The words are the same," said the editor of a leading intellectual monthly magazine that is allowed to appear, heavily censored, in a small issue each month. "But the words mean different things in the United States and Poland."

Compared with much of Eastern Europe—the Soviet Union, Czechoslovakia, Rumania and East Germany—Poland is a paragon of respect for human and civil rights, of free speech and a free media. Films of extraordinary political frankness are produced and shown regularly. Strikes and economic protests produce as much response from a sensitive Government as they do repression. Nearly 30 million Roman Catholics freely practice a religion that is an integral part of their daily lives.

The Limits of Dissent

But the Polish Government still regards with a degree of suspicion certain freedoms—such as freedom of the press, the right to challenge openly the tenets of the regime, even in many instances the right to travel freely abroad.

These limits are influenced as much by the international realities of Poland's integral role in the Soviet-led Warsaw Pact as they are by economic and political realities inside Poland.

"It is as embarrassing to the Poles to have it pointed out that their system is substantially freer and more egalitarian than that of the Soviet Union as it is to have it pointed out, for example, that secret police dragged hunger strikers from a church," said one West European diplomat who follows closely the progress in this area.

Dissent has always been part of the Polish system. But to challenge and control it an extensive network has grown up, responsible ultimately to the inner circles of the powerful Central Committee of the Polish United Workers Party.

Nothing is published in Poland without the imprimatur of this organization. No licensed printing plant is allowed to produce anything without the small round black stamp that bears the Polish words for "permit of state committee on printing." Even visiting cards and party invitations must be submitted for approval, according to editors and publishers of several publications.

Earlier this year, a member of a provincial censorship bureau defected to Sweden and took with him the 700-page book that lists in extraordinary detail every concept, every name, indeed, every word that is forbidden to appear in print in Poland. The book is to be translated and published in London next year. Copies have already made their way back to human-rights groups in Poland who promised to circulate them clandestinely.

Forbidden, according to this list, is every major Polish writer who has defected to the West in the past 30 years. Likewise banned are any export-import trade figures, even the fact that Czech rivers flowing into Poland bring industrial waste.

But there are some curious exceptions and lapses, too. Some writers, for instance, can write for some media but not for others. The Polish novelist Mark Nowakowski, for instance, is understood to be able to write for Catholic literary magazines but not for general-circulation publications, although he is said not even to be a practicing Catholic. There are cases where poems have been published without the authors' names. The poems are fine, but the authors are on the censorship list.

Some Avoid Sensitive Subjects

Gradually, over the years, editors learn to avoid sensitive subjects, gradually mutating the character of their publication until often it bears little resemblence to the journal as it was established.

"Our magazine started out as a journal of political and social commentary on the major issues of the day that face Poland," said the editor of one such publication. "Now we discuss history, theology and literature—not literature of Poland today, but Proust, for example."

Clearly, there are those who flout the norms. Opinia is perhaps the best known of the samizdat, or self-published, journals that are produced on typewriters with many carbon copies.

It was the editor of Opinia, Adam Wojciechowski, to whom President Carter referred at the opening of his news conference Friday when he said, "There are a few who wanted to attend who were not permitted to come. There questions will be answered by me in writing."

Friends of Mr. Wojciechowski said he had been seized by the police in front of his house yesterday morning after President Carter's departure. He was released four hours later.

It is this question of police interference in the free functioning of the social order that is perhaps the most sensitive issue confronted by the Polish Government.

Western diplomats who follow civil rights in Poland were hard pressed to name a single political prisoner known to be presently under detention. "There are undoubtedly a few," said one. "But it is by no means the pattern at all."

Riots and worker protests over sudden price increases in June 1976 resulted in a number of arrests and in the formation of two human-rights groups to press for the rights of Polish workers. Those arrested then have long since been freed. But the groups, apart from some of their peripheral activities, such as publications like "Opinia," have little widespread and continuing impact.

But they continue their activities. Yesterday morning, two hours after President Carter's departure from Warsaw, five of them ended a 24-hour hunger strike to protest the detention on petty theft charges of two sons of a leader of the committee on political and human rights, Kazimierz Switon. During the night, police had entered the sacristy of the Holy Cross Church, the scene of the hunger strike, and seized Mr. Switon's daughter when she left the chapel to go to the toilet. Her mother rushed to her side and the two were taken by the police to a nearby stationhouse, then bundled onto a train for their home town, Katowice.

Mr. Switon said later that he planned to continue his work, which consists of operating a "walk-in center" in Katowice where workers can present grievances and complaints about "human-rights violations." He said about four or five persons a week show up there, some indication of the following that such groups still maintain.

But the problems the workers discuss—the inability to protest or strike over unequal pay, illegally long working hours, substandard working conditions, bad food and shortages of meat and other staples—still are widespread and are often quite openly debated.

Earlier this year, three controversial films dealt explicitly with just such subjects and ran for weeks to packed houses throughout Poland. The best known, "Man of Marble" by the noted director Andrzej Wajda, told of the attempts by a modern filmmaker to produce a movie about the tragedy of a bricklayer and a friend who becomes a victim of heavy-handed police tactics. The complex plot ends with the filmmaker being told she will not be allowed to produce her movie, but with her father enjoining her to continue "finding out the truth."

A Pattern Emerges

Throughout this crazy-quilt pattern of control and permissiveness in Poland, many foreign diplomats and Polish intellectuals see a pattern emerging.

As the economic situation tightens, it would appear, written censorship that can describe such ills in detail also tightens. In February, for instance, orders quietly went out that publication of economic statistics would be even more tightly regulated than in the past.

But at the same time, cultural censorship of films, paintings and television that provide a soothing opiate and escape loosens.

"It's been a constantly shifting cycle since Edward Gierek took over the Communist Party here," said one western diplomat. "But Gierek continues to have good intentions, I think. The problem is the constant tug-of-war within the party and the bureaucracy, the apparat, that operates often on its own. This is what he must control and set in the right direction. That's where the uncertainty always comes in."

* * *

June 8, 1978

CZECH WRITERS FEAR ANOTHER CRACKDOWN

20, Citing Arrest of Novelist, Say Regime Rejects Tacit Accord on Underground Works

By DAVID A. ANDELMAN
Special to The New York Times

PRAGUE, June 7—Twenty of Czechoslovakia's leading writers, poets and dramatists said in a letter today that the Czechoslovak Government had repudiated a tacit understanding that had long allowed the underground reproduction of literary works that do not challenge the Communist system.

The letter, addressed to a number of fellow writers and playwrights in the West and released to Western correspondents here today, said that the repudiation came last week when the novelist and poet, Jiri Grusa, was arrested and charged with "incitement" because of the reproduction of his novel "The Questionnaire" by the underground operation known here as the "padlock press."

In the last several years this operation has brought out more than 120 volumes by some 50 authors, all in typewritten form but neatly bound and often elaborately illustrated. They have been circulating in widening circles as the quantity and quality of officially published works have deteriorated.

The Grusa novel is due to be published this fall in Lucerne, Switzerland by the Reich Publishing Company and in Paris by the large publishing house of Gallimard.

Overstepping the Line

The letter signed by the 20 Czechoslovaks charged that, with the arrest of the novelist-poet, "the authorities thus overstepped not only the law, but the thus far quietly respected dividing line between civil and political activities such as a number of writers have been involved in and literary activities such as people like Grusa are engaged in."

Most of the principal Czech authors known in the West, including Ludvik Vaculik, Pavel Kohout, Vaclav Havel and Ivan Klima, signed the letter. Many have also been involved in anti-Government political activity, particularly the Charter 77 movement that has publicized Czech violations of human rights. Such activity has resulted in arrests and a range of police intimidations.

But these authors and others are concerned that this latest arrest and a number of other interrogations that have occurred over the last several weeks may signal a new crackdown aimed directly at purely literary activities and designed to dismantle the underground press operation, which up to now has been allowed to continue with only minor harassment.

In March, to celebrate the "Month of the Book." Nove Knihy, the weekly magazine of the book wholesalers in Prague and Bratislava, published an extensive list of books officially available. Only two original Czech titles are listed in the literature section and two Slovak works—a novel and a poetry anthology celebrating the 30th anniversary of the 1948 Communist takeover. Most of the other titles are translations.

Socialism Is Given Priority

"All works must contribute to the building of socialism," explained an official of the Czechoslovak Writers Union, in explaining why none of the works published by the underground press had been accepted by any of the Government book houses though a number have been published by major Western publishers.

Censorship is as severe here as anywhere in Eastern Europe—largely a reaction to the brief attempt at liberalization by Prague in 1968 when literary license led almost directly to the Soviet invasion of Czechoslovakia. Yet the operations of the underground publishing network in recent years has been as free here as anywhere in Eastern Europe.

"It would seem that its limited circulation and the outcry from the West if they were to close it down made them feel the disadvantages of taking action against one of the top editors of the underground press in an interview on the street outside his apartment. But—recent—events have spread fear in this small literary community that more difficult times may lie ahead.

The underground press has acted in effect as a literary safety valve for the highly creative Czech people. Most of the new and most talented writers in Czechoslovakia have not been admitted into the writers union and are therefore not eligible to be published officially.

* * *

January 8, 1979

POLITICAL CABARET, EVEN CENSORED, IS A PLACE WHERE POLES CAN LAUGH

By DAVID A. ANDELMAN
Special to The New York Times

CRACOW, Poland—"The dollar is going down, down, down everywhere," the master of ceremonies shouted in the packed cabaret. He paused for effect, then added, "because in Poland its value is going up."

"Oh, oh, oh, what a story," the four-voice chorus burst out as the piano pounded out the melody, and the master of ceremonies squinted again at the newspaper he held, "Yes," he said, holding up one finger for emphasis, "we will succeed in getting rid of, uh, prosperity." He choked on the last word as he realized his mistake, at the same moment his audience burst into laughter and applause.

For the first time in six months the cabaret, Michalka's Den in downtown Cracow, was open. "The Devil's Due" was the title of its show, a broad takeoff on the Faust story of the man who sold his soul to the Devil. And it took little sophistication to realize the man here was Poland and the Devil was the bureaucracy that seems to be strangling the country.

Cabarets, particularly those with a message, have long been one of the great joys in this somewhat joyless country. There people relax, escape, exchange risqué jokes and see just how far they can go before the Communist Party clamps down. The result is that most cabarets have a rather short life span these days.

"If there's one thing the Communist Party doesn't have," smiled one member of the audience, "it's a sense of humor, especially about itself and its failings."

Cracow has a long history of political cabarets. In the grim days of Nazi occupation during World War II, Karol Wojtyla, the man who was later to become Cardinal of Cracow, then Pope John Paul II, won fame here for organizing and acting in the underground Rhapsody Theater, the theme of which was anti-Nazi. Even earlier, the precursor of Michalka's Den, the Green Balloon, opened in 1901.

This performance of "The Devil's Due," which took place recently, was the second. The first was private, because it was given for the city's censors. Even at the first performance before a live audience, the censors were in attendance.

"They're watching to see what everyone laughs at hardest," said one young university professor. "Then they order that cut, just in case they didn't understand it." Using that criterion, there were a couple of skits that seemed likely candidates for the scissors.

"I remember trains that ran on time, or even got there," the female lead began. "Machines that worked, sausage with real meat in them, clean streets. TV that told the truth. Or even, being able to, uh, do our own thing. And if I remember these, well, perhaps I should wait till my children are 40, and they'll be singing how beautiful things were in our time."

Then, to a marching tune, there was "Walls, Long Live the Walls."

"We are building walls, paper walls. We have walls that have bumps, walls with no square corners and walls where you can see through to a neighbor's walls." The song was an allusion both to the shoddy quality of Poland's new housing construction and, metaphorically, to the walls the Government has built between itself and the people.

There was also the newspaper skit, with its reference to the black market—the worthless zloty and the value of the dollar, which has become virtually a second currency.

One cabaret in Warsaw recently coined a joke that is now widespread here: "What do America and Poland have in common? You can't buy anything with the zloty in either place."

The jokes are all topical, very local and very carefully honed, each word chosen for its maximum effect on the audience and minimum effect on the censor.

At the first public performance, the audience loved every moment. It was late starting—nearly 11 P.M.—because the entire cast of five had appeared in the above-ground Cracow Dramatic Theater earlier in the evening. But the audience never wavered. The place was packed, with 10 extra tables crammed onto the floor. Only those very much in the know would have heard about it by word of mouth well enough in advance to have bought a ticket.

Other forms of entertainment more easily controlled and regulated have largely replaced the once-omnipresent cabaret—films, television, or jazz clubs with music and no lyrics.

* * *

September 4, 1980

POLISH PRESS FEELING FREER, IN THEORY

By JOHN DARNTON
Special to The New York Times

WARSAW, Sept. 3—Two days after the signing of the accord between the Polish Government and the strikers in Gdansk—which, among other things, included a curb on censorship—the editor of a major newspaper here asked for a photograph of the signing ceremony from the state-controlled press-photograph agency, C.A.F. His request was denied. The reason: The photograph had not been passed by the censor.

Technically, the censor was within his rights, since presumably the old regulations are to remain in force for three months while a law to narrow the scope of censorship is drafted and put to Parliament.

But it was also clear that the censor was either being obstinate, overcautious or vindictive, since the full text of the agreement had been published in newspapers all over the country and the signing ceremony was broadcast first on live television and then over and over again on videotape.

Censor's Habits Die Hard

The story illustrates problems that may be encountered if the Government follows through on its pledge to restrain the apparatus that, for three decades, has assiduously controlled what information Poles may and may not have access to. In the bureaucracy of the censor's office, old habits die hard, even assuming there is a willingness to kill them.

For the moment there is confusion and a vacuum. Some liberal intellectuals feel that the newspapers should rush in to fill it and test the perimeters of what is permissible. By doing so, they argue, the papers will establish their own dominion and influence the legislation to come.

But the press has been cautious. It is still under Government control, and most of the major editors are Communist Party members and pillars of the establishment. But some journalists, especially the younger ones, are anxious to try more accurate and unfettered reporting. A group of 25 signed a petition in the Lenin Shipyards last week, complaining that their dispatches about the strike were being unreasonably censored.

One editor at Polityka, the country's major theoretical party weekly, said he felt that the newspapers must follow a moderate, responsible course because the forces against liberalization were still quite strong.

'We Need a Moderate Course'

"No restraint at all could have the same effect as total restraint—it could encourage the authorities to take back control," he said. "We need a moderate course to gradually enlarge the areas of freedom from the censor. We can't push too hard. That will provoke a counterreaction."

"We all have in mind the Czechoslovak experience," he said, referring to the liberal regime of Alexander Dubcek that brought a Warsaw Pact invasion in 1968. "We know that whoever wants too much may lose everything."

The editor acknowledged that there existed what he called "a crisis of public belief in Poland," and he said that the journalists were much to blame.

"Journalists here have been and are now the tools of the establishment," he said. "They have been rightfully identified with insincerity and manipulation." He expressed doubt about fully overcoming the Communist axiom that holds that the press is only a handmaiden of the governing party.

A New 'Line' Emerging

"We have an expression in Poland, 'The new comes back as old,' " he said. "Already it's beginning. The problem isn't the threat of the Soviet Union. It's in the everyday running of the country. People aren't used to running factories with a free trade union and they're not used to a press that isn't censored"

Already, he said, there was a new "line" emerging. "We must emphasize consensus, the agreement, the conditions under which it was struck, rather than the past errors of the party," he said. "The first point is that the party will never admit its failure. The party itself decided to have new independent trade unions—that's the new line.

"There is a crisis of public belief in Poland. More and more often, I meet people who don't believe the weather forecasts, the train schedules, what their own doctors tell them. They see a trick in everything."

Even though the media has been moderate and restrained, in the past two weeks the public has read and seen things that were inconceivable before.

Regular Broadcasts of Masses

There was, for example, a televised, 40-minute sermon by the Roman Catholic Primate of Poland, Stefan Cardinal Wyszynski. Although his address appeared to serve the aims of the Government, since it counseled moderation and patience, never before had the powerful Roman Catholic Church been granted such a block of air time. In the future, masses are to be broadcast over radio.

There is a general news hunger now. Poles, accustomed to lining up for meat and other staples, are now lining up at news kiosks. People actually watch the nightly television news and keep it on until the very end.

"I'm furious," joked one former Government official a few days ago. "Today I had to spend an hour reading Zycie Warszawy. There was actually news in it. I used to get through it in five minutes."

He said that he had been visited earlier in the day by a courier, who furtively produced a typewritten paper that listed the strikers' demands. "Thanks a lot, "he said he told him, chuckling. "But I've just read them all in the newspaper."

* * *

November 30, 1980

FOR MOSCOW'S INTELLECTUALS, THE NIGHT IS LONG AND COLD

By ANTHONY AUSTIN

MOSCOW—You can tell present-day Moscow intellectuals by their libraries. However modest the apartment, there will be shelves of books placing them in the "intelligentsia," that cultural elite whose catalytic role in Russian history distinguishes it from the merely educated.

Among the poets on these shelves will be the martyrs of the Lenin and Stalin years, Anna Akhmatova, Marina Tsvetayeva, Osip Mandelshtarn. Also Boris Pasternak, whose persecution came later. Among the purged novelists of the 1920's and 1930's, Mikhail ("The Master and Margarita!") Bulgakov is de rigueur; the Russian classics, of course; such outstanding contemporaries as Yuri Trofimov, Andrei Bitov, Valentin Rasputin; prerevolutionary Russian philosophers like Nikolai Berdyayev and the mystic Vladimir Solovyov.

But no Maxim Gorky. No Vladimir Mayakovsky, no Mikhail Sholokhov, unless they are relegated to some obscure comer. Disdain for the exalted laureates of Marxism-Leninism is as much a mark of today's Russian intellectuals as the rediscovery of oppressed writers of the 20's and 30's whose sin was un-Soviet independence of spirit. Their bookshelves attest to a general loss of interest and belief in official ideology by the Russian thinking class.

Sovfoto

Producer Yuri Lyubimov (center) with performers at Moscow's Taganka Theater.

Yet if the reading matter and the conversation within the walls of these Moscow apartments seem curiously removed from the Communist doctrine by which the country supposedly lives, the polemics in Madrid—Western delegates denouncing Soviet repression of human rights at the European security conference—seem equally remote.

The creative minority in the Soviet arts and sciences does not, on the whole, identify with dissidents who have stepped out of line to challenge the authorities directly. It's not that the poets and novelists, the playwrights and the directors, the scholars in the humanities who themselves try to push against the limits of the permissible do not credit the courage of the frontal attack. But they regard it as a hopeless undertaking.

Restoring Tradition Against All Odds

The virtual destruction of the dissident movement by the K.G.B. has confirmed for them that the system is not going to be changed by several hundred protesters in Moscow and a few other centers of intellectual life. The wave of arrests and political trials since the banning of Andrei Sakharov to the city of Gorky in January has persuaded them that, whatever the restraining influence of unfavorable publicity in the West, that effect has been drastically reduced by the foundering of detente. In their view, change for the better, if it is to come, can only come gradually and in response to pressure, not from dissidents or from the White House, but from within the system, in short, from people like themselves.

Top party bureaucrats, though coming in the main from industrial backgrounds unburdened by cultural concerns, are not unaware that intellectuals have abandoned the Gorkys and the Mayakovskys, the tribunes of the Leninist order, in favor of the Akhmatovas and the Mandelshtams, the order's victims. The party's reaction was to yield: Let the dishonored dead be rehabilitated. Better that they be "ours" than that they belong to our critics.

Hence the reappearance in recent years of long out-of-print work, though in limited and expurgated editions. The recent inclusion of four poems from "Doctor Zhivago" in a major anthology seems to complete the rehabilitation of Mr. Pasternak as poet and translator. Even the novel that won him the Nobel Prize and provoked official Soviet wrath seems to have been removed informally from the index of the damned. Many intellectuals who have read the Russian edition published in the West profess to wonder why it caused such a fuss 20 years ago.

The reason seems clear. As the first novel since the pre-Stalin period to take an independent view of life in revolutionary and civil war years, it seemed shockingly un-Soviet. However, with the passage of time, the party and public have become more accustomed to writing free of ideological cant. This they owe to a handful—at most a score—of new poets and novelists, mostly in their 40's, who have, against all odds, restored the tradition of candor, sensitivity and free thought in Russian literature, though their work does not vie with Mr. Pastemak's in depth. There has been progress in other cultural fields as well.

The well-made play, examining the shortcomings of the society or the disintegration of an individual under harmful social pressures, has won a place on the Soviet stage. Occasionally the theater will produce something unusual that takes everyone's breath away. That was the case with "The House on the Embankment," the play adapted by Yuri Lyubimov, director of the avant-garde Taganka Theater, from a novella by Mr. Trofimov.

In the original, the force of the tale of personal betrayal under Stalinist terror was conveyed indirectly, by hint and allusion. The demands of the stage stripped the story to its core. "That March of 1953" became, explicitly, the month of Stalin's death. The character in the novel who might have been a wheel in the N.K.V.D. appeared ominously in N.K.V.D. uniform. There is something about the Soviet theater—perhaps the Russian genius for dramatic art—that permits more truth to be acted out on the stage than to be set down on the printed page.

In music, too, latitude has been greater. Hitherto banned chorales and other sacred music and interesting modem compositions, both Western and Soviet, now augment the concert programs. A few small rock ballet groups provide an outlet for choreographic talent that classical companies seem not to welcome. Jazz and rock ensembles in Moscow, Leningrad and the Baltic republics have millions of young fans.

It's worth going to the movies again. In the last few years, a whole crop of films—many of Georgian origin—have shown thematic and artistic quality. Nonconformist artists, whose outdoor exhibition was leveled by bulldozers in 1974, now may exhibit in an authorized hall of their own.

Paradoxically, the creators of these works and those who form their principal audience are not optimistic. The openings for the fresh and original have been widening, but not nearly fast enough to keep up with growing expectations. The general feeling, therefore, is one of arrested progress, of things bogging down.

This is particularly true of literature. The best of the establishment writers must contend constantly with hydraheaded censorship. Those who will not yield to emasculation of their prose are forced either to emigrate, like Vasily Aksyonov, or, like Georgy Vladirnov and Vladiink Voinovich, to confine their hopes to publication abroad. Those who cannot face these hard choices are mostly reduced, after one notable work, to the lot of official hacks.

The strain is most acute for the younger generation of writers in their 20's and 30's, who regard themselves as the successors to the older favorites. Their complaints are depressingly similar: An iconoclastic first novel that other writers are sure would make a splash has been turned down by every publisher in Moscow. A play that has excited private gatherings in friends' apartments is deemed "too daring" for public performance. Poetry is unpublishable, not because it is anti-Soviet but because of its lack of ritual obeisance to the social virtues or simply because the language is too "different" from the hackneyed norm. One result is a dearth of interesting writers under 40 years old.

This month, seven frustrated younger writers appealed to the Moscow City Council to authorize an "experimental" writers' workshop that would be independent of the official Soviet Writers' Union, the citadel of hidebound esthetics and ideological conformity. The seven asked that the new club be allowed to publish a periodical of no more than 300 or 500 copies containing the members' uncensored writings.

Perhaps because of official alarm over Poland and determination to prevent any "independent" group from following the example of the new Polish trade unions, the writers' project was promptly squashed. Would-be sponsors were taken to police stations for questioning, their apartments were searched and their manuscripts confiscated. Repression seemed even more automatic than the rejection, 18 months ago, of plans by more established writers to put out an uncensored collection entitled "Metropol."

The new episode has contributed to the cheerless mood. Some intellectuals with a proven feel for cultural trends argue that even spectacular breakthroughs of the past year or so were atypical. "The House on the Embankment," they contend, was permitted only because Mr. Lyubimov had threatened to resign as Taganka's director, staking everything on one card and winning because his resignation would have been a blow to Soviet prestige.

The real liberalization has been internal. It is said that the intelligentsia got over the cult of Stalin in the 1960's and the cult of Lenin in the 1970's. The idea that Lenin's "good" beginnings were spoiled by the "bad" Stalin finds few takers among intellectuals today, particularly among those under 40 years old. The more common view is that Leninism was fatally flawed from the start by totalitarianism. Compared with 10 years ago, many more intellectuals seem open to notions of a freer, more pluralistic society. Today, within the intelligentsia, to be politically orthodox is to be in bad taste.

Yet this readiness for basic reform goes hand in hand with profound pessimism. Intellectuals are a small minority and the Russian mood is generally conservative. Political leaders are clearly not prepared to budge. Many intellectuals say they could be reconciled to the system if only things would ease up a little—if only life could be a little livelier, if mediocrity could be less overwhelmingly the rule, if they could see Western movies and could have freer access to more books; if only, in short, there were a little more air. Yet perhaps because of this sense of aimlessness, because, as one young intellectual put it, "our culture is occupied territory, occupied by bureaucrats and second-raters," there is also widespread and keenly felt longing for anything new, talented, good.

When Viktor Yerofeyev, a young writer expelled from the Writers' Union for his part in the Metropol affair, read his story from that collection at a literary evening in a public theater, he was greeted first by stunned silence and then by outraged protests and stormy applause.

" 'My God,' I thought," recounts Mr. Yerofeyev, " 'what power of the written word.' There is a great hunger in Russia for anything fresh, more so, I think, than in any other country. That is why, as a writer, I would not want to live anywhere else."

* * *

January 18, 1981

TIPTOEING AROUND THE CENSOR IN POLAND

By NINA DARNTON

WARSAW—For years Polish playwrights have dreaded the special preview, just before opening night, when they stage a command performance for an audience of one—the censor.

The censor has to approve the script before any play can even start rehearsals, but he comes to a last-minute preview to be sure he hasn't missed anything. By now, Polish playwrights have evolved some dodges to deal with this vital performance. Some tell the actors to play at half power and mumble their best lines. One frantic author, worried about a scene to be played on stage, knocked over an ashtray to create a diversion while the director coughed loudly. Another playwright who heard that the censor was making return visit to his play to gauge audience reaction, stacked the audience with his family and friends. He gave them strict instructions not to laugh at the funny lines. The play opened uncut.

The question in Warsaw theater circles these days is whether these devices to skirt censorship will become relics of the past. According to the agreement reached with the Baltic Coast strikers in August, censorship in certain areas would be relaxed under a bill to be introduced in Parliament this month.

At this writing, preparation of the bill was already a month and a half behind schedule and the Polish press is again under heavy censorship pressure from the Communist Party—which is no doubt reacting to the menace of Soviet troops on the Polish border. The new bill, which is by no means certain of passage, would exclude from censorship many specialized publications and would make life easier for independent writers, journalists and film makers. No one knows whether its benefits would extend to Polish playwrights.

Up to now the power of the authorities to block objectionable material has been exerted in a number of ways. First, a play has to be approved by the local city council, which sometimes rejects it outright as politically unsuitable. If it passes this hurdle, it goes to the censor, who may strike out certain words, whole passages, or turn down the entire production. In big cities such as Warsaw, where the censor tends to be an anonymous bureaucrat, censorship is more strict. In smaller towns where the censors may be known, the rules are often more relaxed. In both cases there is haggling and some room for discussion, but there is no appeal.

It's unclear what the new bill will mean for the Polish theater or how far it will go, but already some signs of change are in the air. In Cracow a production of a play entitled "The Brother of Our Lord" is now in performance. The music is by Krzysztof Penderecki, the world-famous composer. The play's author is Karol Wojtyla—Pope John Paul II—and it is being produced in Poland for the first time. Another first, according to sources close to the production, is that the play went into rehearsal without being approved by the censor.

But many people here point out that the problems created by censorship cannot be eliminated so quickly by simply relaxing the censor's power. They run deeper, and it may take several years for the situation to improve.

"In the last ten years," said Konstanty Puzyna, editor in chief of Dialogue, Poland's most prestigious theater magazine, "there have not been too many good plays—a few, by Mrozek, Rozewicz or Glowacki, but not too many. Why? Because it was impossible to write about reality, about everyday life. After 1956 censorship relaxed a bit, but in the 70's it became harsher again. There was this propaganda of success that affected everything. There is also a problem here between playwrights and directors—it is like a conversation between two people interested in two different things. The directors are interested in spectacles, in changing the play to their own ideas. They prefer to stage classics and through the classics to comment on Poland today, rather than take on modern plays."

Zygmunt Hubner, artistic director of the Teatr Powszechny, one of the best theaters in Warsaw, also worries about the caliber of Polish playwriting. "You can't have a Stoppard, or a Williams or an Albee in this society because the playwrights simply don't make enough money to write only plays," he said. "If they write plays, they do it because they want to speak to the people from the stage, to say something to them." Naturally, censorship interferes with this. Slawomir Mrozek, Poland's best living playwright, lives in Paris.

Janusz Glowacki, one of the few popular Polish playwrights who attempts to deal with social reality, is the author of "Cinderella," one of the season's top hits. The play, which takes place in a rehabilitation home for delinquent girls, explores the social mechanisms that manipulate people's lives. When asked how reduced censorship would affect his work, Mr. Glowacki leaned back in his chair and spoke slowly. "There is a problem of self-censorship," he said. "Now we are in transition. We don't know how much of our work and thinking is determined by censorship. This is more really than just self-censorship, because it enters the realm of the origin of the thought and the creative idea itself. We just don't know. I wrote 'Match' and 'Cinderella' and both use metaphor to make a larger point about my own society. Would I have chosen to write in that metaphor if there was no censorship and no metaphor was needed? It is not clear, even to me."

"As far as getting audiences for productions in Poland, we have no problem. That is our problem," said one Polish director. "We have lost the knack of knowing whether or not we have a success or how to make a success," he said half-jokingly, "because at least 85 percent of our seats are sold no matter what we do."

Up until now the government-dominated trade unions designated cultural representatives whose job it was to provide workers with theater tickets. The union representatives bought large blocks of tickets at greatly reduced rates, and busloads of workers were brought to the theater. This system of sales resulted in most Warsaw productions playing to practically full houses. In the provinces, where there is not as large a theater-going population, it kept many theaters in business. Mr. Hubner worries that one of the side effects of the new independent trade unions, which are no longer subsidized by government funds, will be an end to factory theater excursions, and thus an end to many small theaters in provincial towns.

In addition to the factory-guaranteed audiences, the state subsidizes about 80 percent of the expenses of each Polish theater. Since there are 58 theaters with 89 stages in Poland, as well as 41 music theaters and 9 operas, the amount of money laid out by the state each year is sizable—about 100 million zlotys or over $3 million. The average price of a theater ticket in Warsaw is about $1. The government subsidizes each seat by about $5.

It is difficult to get a ticket for a popular play without pull, and the tickets even have an exchange value on the black market. One playwright gave two tickets to his garage mechanic to get a new carburetor. "In Poland," said Mr. Hubner, "it is not the critics who determine the success of a new play, it is word of mouth. When Glowacki's 'Cinderella' opened, we knew we had a success the second day because there was a two-hour queue in front of the box office."

"Actually," said Mr. Glowacki with a wry smile, "reviews in the newspapers here are like everything else in the newspapers; no one believes them. Sometimes a bad review can help."

The Poles are great theatergoers and each season a lively, varied repertory is available to them. Polish theater excels in spectacle—imaginative design elements, intricate sets, elaborate costumes. Its actors, whose salaries range from about $100 a month for beginners to about $700 for top stars, are well trained and highly professional.

There are about 400 new openings a year. Of these, about 120 are modern Polish plays, 110 modern foreign plays, 100 Polish classics and 70 foreign classics. The Poles often say proudly that they are culturally smack in the middle between East and West, and a look at the number of foreign plays taken from each camp bears this out. In 1979, 60 of the modern foreign plays that opened were written by playwrights from socialist countries, and 50 from western countries.

"Often I want to do a modern American play and I can't because of the profanity," said Mr. Hubner. "This is not because of censorship, but because of the taste of the Polish audience." Mr. Hubner, whose Teatr Powszechny is the only theater in Warsaw to show a growth of audience in the last three years, says that if his box office drops below 90 percent, he closes the play. "In Poland we have a different view of theater than you do in the West," he said. "We do not think of it as mainly entertainment, but as a kind of social education. During the partition, the only place you could hear beautiful Polish spoken was on the stage. During the time of Stalin, when we had no freedom at all in our press, literature or theater, we could at least perform a Polish classic and people could hold their heads up. So the theater has became sort of the church of the Polish language. People use profanity on their way to and from the theater, but they don't want to hear it on the stage."

Many people agree that the success of the Teatr Powszechny is due largely to its attempt to produce plays that deal with current reality—disguised as it sometimes must be. One of the plays currently in its repertory is "Cesarz," adapted from a book by a foreign correspondent, Ryszard Kapuscinski. The play concerns Haile Selassie, the former emperor of Ethiopia, and is one of Warsaw's most popular plays.

The play is in two acts. A handful of courtiers around the emperor discuss the life at court. There is no plot, no action and no conflict. The audience listens to two hours of often witty discussion, supposedly about Ethiopia but transparently about all forms of totalitarian government. There are many barbs that strike home, judging from the enthusiastic response and laughter of the audience. In talking about the emperor one of the courtiers says, "He didn't fight corruption. He just required loyalty from the people he dealt with in court." Or later, "The first knowledge important to gain in the court was negative—what not to do, what not to write." Or again, "He tells the foreign press everything is fine here, they can just read our newspapers and see. But our press is loyal to the emperor. It is run by men whose job is supposed to be to inform people, but whose real job is to hide everything."

The actors wear blackface to look like Ethiopians, but it is unevenly and inexpertly applied. The costumes are bizarre, generally exotic but not scrupulously authentic, including muslin robes, gold embossed velvet, and western shoes. All this suggests an attempt to make the setting exotic enough to get by the censor and unauthentic enough to leave no doubt what is really being criticized. "You must understand," said one young playwright, "we have no newspapers. Sometimes our theater has to fulfill the role of your newspapers."

If most Americans know anything at all about Polish theater, they know one man, Jerzy Grotowski. In the 1960's, his avant-garde workshop in Wroclaw became a kind of shrine for actors and directors from Europe and the United States. But as far as Polish audiences go, Mr. Grotowski's productions might as well be marked "for export only." The company rarely comes to Warsaw and spends most of its time abroad. "It is easier to see Grotowski in Paris or New York than in Warsaw," complained one avid theatergoer.

"It is interesting," Mr. Puzyna said, "that although Grotowski has greatly influenced the course of the modern theater in the West, he has had virtually no influence on any theater here in Poland." Mr. Grotowski has actually left active participation in the theater now. His group is more interested in philosophy and pedagogy, although it occasionally performs old works. It has introduced no new productions in the past ten years.

Two other significant experimental groups are still active in Poland: the Studio Theater of Jozef Szajna, based in Warsaw, and Tadeusz Kantor's Cricot Theater, based in Cracow. Mr. Szajna began his career as a painter and calls his work "visual narration." His productions make elaborate use of sets, props and design elements in a series of frozen moments, sometimes dramatic, often grotesque. "It is a kind of static theater," Mr. Puzyna said. "It moves from one portrait to another."

Mr. Szajna, who was imprisoned in Auschwitz during World War II, says his work opposes fascism and passivity. "Our theater speaks against terror, against threats to man's humanity, against the loss of individualism and independence," he said. "The fascists dressed people in the same clothes and made numbers of them. If our civilization shows one model as suitable for everyone, it too can be totalitarian."

Mr. Szajna says that his work is not usually censored. Perhaps it is because he deals with abstract or recognized evils—dehumanization, fascism—that his plays are not censored as strictly as playwrights attempting to deal with more quotidien themes. "These experimental theaters can speak as much to the overindustrialized Western countries as to the more totalitarian Eastern countries," said one theater critic. "All are suffering from a kind of dehumanization."

The man most theater people in Poland have their eye on these days is Tadeusz Kantor. Mr. Kantor also travels widely and it is difficult to see his company perform in Poland, but the central theme of his work comes directly from his homeland. "It is a preoccupation with the culture that has disappeared," said Mr. Puzyna, "the milieu of the Jewish communities in Poland which existed before the war and exist no more—the small Jewish towns of his childhood." Mr. Kantor is recognized by critics and directors alike as one of the most important avant-garde visual artists in Poland.

Many people, including the artists themselves, view the state subsidy as indispensable to the growth of experimental theater in Poland. Grotowski and his company, they point out, needed time to experiment without the necessity of performances and box-office pressures. "If he had started in the West," said Mr. Puzyna, "he might not be Grotowski today, or at least he may not have gotten there so fast."

"In the West, the institutions that subsidize experimental theater want box-office results too fast," said Mr. Szajna. "One year is not enough time to develop an art. If you demand results too soon you get kitsch, not art." Mr. Szajna said that there is an unwritten understanding in Poland that a new group has about three years to prove itself worthy of a continuing subsidy.

Mr. Szajna's plays frequently have nudity in them. Although nudity is not common in Polish theater, it does occur, not only in experimental theaters but on the main stage of the Warsaw Opera House. A year ago the Stuttgart Opera Company performed Penderecki's "Paradise Lost" in the National Opera House. Adam and Eve appeared throughout in transparent body stockings. The Tomaszewski Mime Company, based in Wroclaw, performed at the Opera House last Christmas and featured several scenes in which men and women performed completely in the nude.

Mr. Szajna said the only trouble he ever had with a censor was an objection to a scene in "Cervantes" in which the main character appears nude. "The censor objected because it was a man," Mr. Szajna said. "He said a naked woman was all right, but a naked man was pornographic. I said it was for artistic reasons, and wouldn't it be worse to have him in just his underpants?" The censor agreed to leave the scene unchanged.

One actress in his company said that Mr. Szajna's theater is usually the first stop for Russian and Bulgarian tourists. "They can't see any public nudity in their own countries," the actress said, "so they suddenly develop a taste for experimental theater and rush to see Szajna's group when they get to Warsaw." The price of a theater ticket is a lot cheaper than the price of a ticket to a striptease show, which also exists in Warsaw.

Nina Darnton is a freelance writer who lives in Warsaw.

* * *

February 7, 1981

WARSAW PRINTERS' UNION IS A THORN IN CENSOR'S SIDE

By JOHN DARNTON
Special to the New York Times

WARSAW, Feb. 5—The Communist authorities here are coming to realize an uncomfortable fact: control of the press may be exerted through censors, compliant editors and fainthearted journalists, but there are others who have a hand in the final product and they get the last crack at it—the printers.

Angered by what they regard as a devious return to heavy-handed censorship, the printers have organized under the banner of the independent labor union, Solidarity, and are demanding a loosening of censorship by Tuesday. Otherwise, they say, Friday the 13th will be a day of no newspapers for Poland.

They are in a position to make good on the threat, because about 50,000 of the country's 60,000 printers are members of Solidarity. They have won hefty raises and are among the union's most dedicated, militant and idealistic members.

"All we want is to print the truth," said Witold Slezak, head of the printers' union in Warsaw. "We feel that we have a moral responsibility for the information that we provide to society through our work."

This position has led, inevitably, to a clash with the censors, whose heavy red-pencil markings on page proofs have long galled the printers, who were in a position to read the information that was denied to the rest of Poland.

Their ultimatum on censorship was delivered after weeks of tangled negotiations. The talks involved the Communist Party Central Committee's press department, the journalists' union and the Solidarity printers. At various points, each group opposed the others. The fracas is one more proof that the thrust for greater democracy here is being spearheaded by workers, not by intellectuals. The printers became concerned in December, when they noticed that the proofs contained more and more of the censor's deletions. By January they decided to render this information public by printing blank spaces to denote omitted material—a practice, they learned, that their forefathers had employed, with great effect, under the czarist and Austrian occupations of the last century.

The journalists, learning of the protest, persuaded the printers to postpone the action until Feb. 10 and to negotiate until then. But the issue was forced on Jan. 20, when three particularly egregious censor's cuts in copy prepared for Zycie Warszawy, the major Warsaw daily, moved the printers to rebel. The paper would be printed with blank spaces, they said, or not at all.

The censor's office, apprised of this unsettling turn of events, countered by threatening to revoke the paper's distribution permit so that the embarrassing issue would never reach the streets.

Four hurried negotiating sessions were held between the Government and the printers, with the journalists mediating. A compromise was reached. Instead of blank spaces, the paper would contain three tiny dots set inside brackets to mark each place the censor had intervened.

But when the newspaper appeared, the printers were dissatisfied. The message was lost on the general public, they felt, and three little dots did not convey the breadth of the material that had been cut.

Two days later, the editor-in-chief of Zycie Warszawy refused to include an article outlining Solidarity's reasons for calling a strike. Without it, the printers refused to set type, and the paper did not appear. At this point, the journalists' union became concerned that the printers were too militant, but the printers insisted that they would not work on articles that were critical of Solidarity.

Meanwhile, the talks between the printers and the Government, represented by Josef Klasa, the Central Committee's chief of press and propaganda, were not fruitful. The printers brought along texts printed under the Austrian occupation with the telltale blank spaces. They also brought along Adam Michnik, Poland's foremost dissident. Mr. Klasa not only refused to negotiate with him, he refused to sit in the same room, so the two sides communicated by messenger.

Withdrawal to Neutral Territory

Stefan Bratkowski, the new chairman of the journalists' union, was called in to settle the problem. He arranged for the "outside experts" on both sides to withdraw to the neutral territory of the lobby.

"We were totally against their position," Jacek Kalabinski, a leader in the journalists' union, said of the printers, "that they should have a say in what is and is not published. They simply didn't want to print anything that they regarded as slanderous to Solidarity. This amounts to a double censorship, one from above and one from below."

Fruitless talks were held between the printers and the Government, and between the Government and the journalists. Only the talks between the journalists and the printers brought a partial agreement: the printers would set into type any articles they considered unfair to Solidarity, but in return they would have the right of full reply in the next issue of the same publication.

The talks between the Government and the printers produced only misunderstanding. "We began," said Jerzy Halas, deputy chairman of the printers' union, "by explaining that the party now stands on a platform of wide consultation with society and demanding to know how this could be achieved with the censor in the way." He said Mr. Klasa called this stance "printer adventurism" and "wanted to know who had put us up to it."

No further talks have been scheduled, and the journalists, angered by the censor's latest turn of the pen, are no longer willing to act as mediators. They drew up an impassioned "open letter to society" that warned that Poland's "democratic renewal" was being threatened largely by the authorities. The letter was censored—in its entirety.

Aside from "newspaperless Friday," the printers have other weapons at their command. This was seen in a recent issue of Trybuna Ludu, the Communist Party's own organ. It carried a cartoon opposing the five-day workweek that showed workers frantically bailing out a sinking boat while a Solidarity member stood with his arms folded and said: "Gentlemen, we don't work on Saturdays."

On top of the broken mast there presumably should have been a Polish flag. But when the cartoon appeared in print, the Polish banner was neatly airbrushed out, and in its place was a Soviet flag. It was the work, no doubt, of a printer's devil.

* * *

January 18, 1982

CZECH CULTURE AIDE DEFENDS CONDITIONS FOR ARTISTS

By HENRY KAMM

Special to the New York Times

PRAGUE—"The conditions for creative freedom," a high official of the Czechoslovak Culture Ministry said, "are guaranteed to all artists who want to contribute to the development of culture."

He excluded from that category many authors and playwrights who enjoy high international reputations, but he said they were on no list of forbidden writers since such a list did not exist. Their works are not published, he noted, but said the decision not to issue them was based on strictly commercial considerations.

These statements were made during a 90-minute interview by Miloslav Kaizer, who a s the ministry's Director of the Arts holds a key position in deciding what books can be published and what plays can be performed in Czechoslovakia.

Writers still in Czechoslovakia who attained international fame before the Soviet-led invasion by Warsaw Pact forces in

1968 are either in prison, like the playwright Vaclav Havel, or know that their works have no chance of being published or staged.

Mr. Kaizer, however, said that "nobody is interested" in their works. "Our writers don't have to serve the regime," he said. "But those people have expressed hatred of the Czechoslovak state and didn't serve it. Nobody is interested in this kind of work."

Publishers Called Censors

A senior Foreign Ministry official, Zdenek Kamis, asserted in a separate interview that it was in Western countries where censorship was achieved by publishers who he said refuse to print the works of opponents of the Government because they know nobody would buy them.

Mr. Kaizer, who was interviewed in his office, said he was "sorry that there is a small group of people in our society who try to create political pressures on our Government by saying that they have no freedom."

He went on to describe culture in Czechoslovakia as flourishing as never before and cited statistics on the large number of books published, foreign works translated, theatrical performances and concerts.

"Every day confirms that our cultural life is very fruitful and varied," Mr. Kaizer said, "and all is subsidized by the state."

Asked about restrictions imposed on cultural life since the liberalization period of 1968 known as the "Prague spring" was ended by the Soviet-led invasion, he said he was confused by the question.

He said the number of works presented to the public was the same as it was in 1968. He listed a number of new cultural ensembles and pointed out that each ticket to a cultural performance that was sold was matched by a far higher state contribution to the arts.

"No theater was closed in 1981," he added, "and no prohibition to publish an author was issued last year." The works of such writers as Milan Kundera, who lives in France, Pavel Kohout, now in Austria, and Ludvik Vaculik, who remains in Prague, circulate clandestinely in typewritten copies in Czechoslovakia. All are published only in foreign countries, in translations from the Czechoslovak originals.

Writers' Works Assailed

Discussing Czechoslovakia's internationally famous novelists and playwrights, none of whose past or present works are officially available here, Mr. Kaizer declared that Mr. Kundera's recent novels had been "a disappointment" to him; Mr. Vaculik was "not a meaningful personality in Czechoslovak literature and against the interests of our society," and Mr. Kohout was "not a writer of original works."

Of Mr. Havel, who is serving a four-and-a-half-year prison term on subversion charges in connection with his role as spokesman for the Charter 1977 dissident group, Mr. Kaizer said:

"The plays of Havel were critical but only from the point of view that sprang from his political views. The literature he writes is against his own nation. It doesn't represent the view of the whole nation. When we speak of creative freedom, we speak of that which helps progress. His work has nothing in common with Czechoslovak culture."

'People Can Live Without Them'

Asked why even some books and plays that were published before the "Prague spring" were no longer available, Mr. Kaizer said: "Our people can live without them. They don't need these adventurers. The majority of the creative front has come to the conclusion that they support our Government's policy."

Mr. Kaizer reiterated that "no command was given not to publish these authors." He expressed surprise when informed that their works had also disappeared from libraries but expressed doubt that librarians had withdrawn them from their shelves as a result of a centrally issued order.

"I want to answer you," he said. "But I have worked here only since 1974. Maybe an order was issued right after 1968, but we didn't order it."

* * *

October 26, 1982

HOW FILM WAS REPRESSED IN POLAND

By EDWARD ROTHSTEIN

A transcript of a film-censorship proceeding, sent secretly from Poland to the West, offers an unusual glimpse into the cultural policies of the regime in Warsaw.

The transcript, which first circulated among members of the outlawed Solidarity union, provides details of a censorship meeting that took place April 23 at the Ministry of Arts and Culture in Warsaw, four months after the imposition of martial law in Poland. The meeting was called to advise the Government whether to release a film dealing with the repressions of the Stalin era in Poland. Out of fear that the subject would be inflammatory, the film was withheld from circulation.

At the meeting, which was surreptitiously recorded, the Stalinist period, the contemporary regime and the film were discussed by a deputy minister, professors, film makers and writers. The transcript, which has been published in the October issue of The New Criterion, a new journal of the arts, has been called a "remarkable document" by emigres from Communist countries because it provides a graphic example of cultural debate under totalitarian conditions.

Difficult to Authenticate

Some weeks after the meeting, copies of a 15-page single-spaced Polish typescript made their way, reportedly through Paris, to the Committee in Support of Solidarity in New York. The document was translated into English by Jerzy Warman, a Polish emigre, member of the committee and graduate student of political science at Columbia University.

While such documents from underground sources in Communist countries are difficult to authenticate, inquiries by The

New York Times here and abroad show that the salient aspects of the transcript are genuine. It has been confirmed that the Polish director Andrzej Wajda, who is working in Paris, in fact sent a letter supporting the film. The text of the letter accurately appears in the transcript.

The film's director, Ryszard Bugajski, has also confirmed that the meeting took place, that he was present and that arguments were presented by participants matching those in the document.

Transcripts of similar Government debates have been published in the Polish underground press and in the journal Index of Censorship, but this is the only such document known to exist since the imposition of martial law Dec. 13.

Moreover, the film, "The Interrogation," deals with a sensitive historical issue—the arrests and tortures of the Stalin era. Its graphic scenes of torture touched so sensitive a nerve in the Government that after the hearing, the decision was made not to release the film.

Every New Film Is Discussed

Mr. Bugajski, who works in the studio X led by Mr. Wajda, has said that he thinks it unlikely the film will be released in the foreseeable future. The only print is kept in the Central Cinematographic Administration in Warsaw.

The central participants in the meeting made up a purely advisory board that is convened to discuss every new film in Poland. All speakers are aware that they are not making actual decisions. The debate, in fact, has the quality of a staged drama. Mr. Warman, in his introduction to the transcript, points out the remarkable qualities of the transcript's arguments and language.

The discussion follows certain unwritten rules; there are no criticisms of the regime, no mention of Solidarity and no explicit discussion of Stalinist practices. Words are chosen with caution. Everyone seems to know that there is a very important ear listening at the keyhole. But everyone also pretends it is not there.

The Deputy Minister of Arts and Culture in charge of the film industry, Stanislaw Stefanski hopes that "nobody will lack the courage to express his opinion, here as well as outside." A professor of philosophy, Henryk Jankowski, stresses that the commission would be effective only "if we do not allow ourselves to be frightened."

'2 Bad Alternatives'

Yet the arguments and language are rarely straightforward. Kazimierz Kozniewski, a writer supportive of martial law, argued that the film was "greatly moving," with its story of "degenerate things," but perhaps should not be seen in the contemporary "political situation."

"We are," he said, "choosing—well, maybe not us, because we are only advisers, but perhaps we, too, have the duty to say it—between two bad alternatives. A film of such passion will evoke great passions in return. Still, to pass over those things in silence . . . But one could say: Silence?—There is no silence on the subject." He concludes, "So I admit that I feel helpless" "one thing is certain: the decision should not be taken lightly."

Even the minister is cautious, not quite getting the party line correct on Stalinism. It is generally referred to as that "painful period." The minister becomes alarmed and confused after making too literal a reference to the "years of terror."

The result is a dialogue, as Mr. Warman pointed out in an interview, in which "all the speakers are quite adept at concealing what they are saying while alluding to it."

Surreal Verbal Worlds Recalled

The rhetoric becomes knotty and contradictory. "I do not want to employ circumlocutions," the minister says before proceeding to do so.

"I do not wish to enter into polemics," announces an opponent of the film before beginning his argument. Like art works in totalitarian conditions, every expression also takes on double meanings for safety. The transcript recalls the surreal verbal worlds of Eastern European literature.

Joseph Brodsky, the Russian emigre poet, commented on the discussion style: "This is accepted locution in Socialist countries. You can't call things by name because then you would have to take the next step."

More Than Abstractions at Stake

Stanislaw Baranczak, a Polish emigre and associate professor of Slavic literatures at Harvard University, pointed out that the minister's style was even an "official language in Poland." He "tries to be cautious and not offend anybody, because he is not sure what future developments will be." There is an awareness in all speakers that more than abstractions are at stake.

Everyone present is aware that the film does have a political meaning. During 1981, when it was made, the cultural thaw under the influence of Solidarity went along with interest in the Stalin period. The film originally included a contemporary subplot concerning Solidarity. One actress, Agnieszka Holland, is a member of Solidarity. Another is Krystyna Janda, who was featured in Mr. Wajda's films, including "Man of Marble"—which, coincidentally, concerned a film maker's difficulties in attempting to make a documentary about the Stalin years.

But the film's advocates cannot acknowledge that criticism of the regime is implied, so, as Mr. Warman points out in his introduction, they argue that the film is not political, but purely "historical."

Art or History?

Another group of speakers, "the moderates," make a distinction between the film's "high" esthetic quality and difficulties in releasing it. Passions would be raised and the audience would be unable to make the necessary distinctions between the past and the present, between, as one professor put it, "Stalinist non-Socialism and the Socialism of the state of war." This group, playing on both sides of the fence, uses the most convoluted and most theoretical arguments.

But it is the opponents of the film who have the most strength and have least to fear. Mr. Baranczak pointed out that they use the fewest euphemisms. They attack the work as both art and as history. They call it "one-sided to the point of offending artistic dignity," "loathsome" "disgusting," "simplified" and "tendentious."

The key opponent is Bohdan Poreba, a film maker whose father was imprisoned in the Stalin era. He leads the Grunwald Patriotic Association, an anti-Semitic nationalist group opposed to Solidarity. He objects to the omissions of background information from the film, alluding to Jewish influence in the Stalinist regime. He says:

"Really, dear friends, there must be a standard of truth in art's generalizations." Such arguments do not explicitly defend Stalinism, but they do attack the film's version of it, asking that it give background reasons for the Stalinist excesses; this tactic implies a defense for the regime as well.

Exercise of Power

These positions, their argumentative strategies and their contorted style, are not atypical in totalitarian countries. Mr. Brodsky recalled similar discussions on editorial boards in the Soviet Union. Despite the discussion's "terminological maze," Mr. Brodsky said the "level of discussion is slightly higher than that in the Soviet Union."

He also felt that public knowledge of such a transcript might actually be to the Government's benefit; it "demoralizes the opponent," revealing the limits being imposed. It is clear from the transcript, from the fate of the film and from recent events in Poland that the film's most virulent critics are representative of those holding cultural power.

Yet Mr. Baranczak noted a difference from earlier published examples of such hearings: "Everybody here was very concerned with the present situation. Everybody knows how the audience would react to this film. That is a new factor in these discussions."

That concern acknowledges that large portions of the Polish public are opposed to Government policy. This might be a sign of a precarious position. Even permitting such a hearing is a pretense of democratic propriety; it serves to let off critical steam.

The transcript's lesson for the West, according to Hilton Kramer, editor of The New Criterion, is less ambiguous. "It presents us with a salutary warning of what can happen when the state is in a position to control art and thought." He calls it a "stunning glimpse into the fate suffered by both artistic integrity and historical truth under Communist dictatorship."

* * *

January 20, 1983

MEDVEDEV, A DISSIDENT HISTORIAN, IS GIVEN FORMAL WARNING IN SOVIET

By JOHN F. BURNS
Special to the New York Times

MOSCOW, Jan. 19—Roy A. Medvedev, the dissident Marxist historian whose writings on Stalin, Khrushchev and other Soviet subjects have been published in the West, has been formally warned to halt his "political lampooning" or face criminal charges.

Mr. Medvedev said he was summoned Tuesday to a meeting with a Deputy Prosecutor General of the Soviet Union. During the 40-minute session he was shown a document declaring that if he wished to remain out of jail he must cease all writings hostile to the Soviet system and turn to "socially useful activities."

The 57-year-old historian, perhaps best known in the West for his chronicle of the Stalin period, "Let History Judge," said he regarded the warning as part of a crackdown on dissidents, shirkers and others who flout the Soviet system, initiated by Yuri V. Andropov, the new Soviet leader. Mr. Medvedev said the action would in no way effect his activities, including his contacts with Western reporters.

A Top Law-Enforcement Official

"I told him, 'If I have been breaking the law for 20 years, you ought to put handcuffs on me right away and take me off to jail,' " Mr. Medvedev said, recounting his exchange with the prosecutor, Oleg V. Soroka, who is one of the top national law-enforcement officials.

Chatting with Western reporters in the cramped, book-lined study of his Moscow apartment today, Mr. Medvedev said that he took the warning against him, and against other dissident intellectuals who he said have been under pressure in recent weeks, as a symbol of what could be expected from Mr. Andropov, whose path to the Soviet leadership lay through 15 years as head of the K.G.B., the internal security agency.

"At first, when people asked me what sort of leadership we could expect after Brezhnev, I said it would be strict, but intelligently so," Mr. Medvedev said. "Now that we have seen the new leadership at work, we can say without question that it is going to be strict, but still not intelligent."

Although Mr. Medvedev was warned by a lower prosecutor eight years ago, he has generally escaped the kind of harassment meted out to lesser dissidents.

His contacts with foreigners, including discussions on such sensitive issues as the power alignment in the Kremlin and articles he has written for Western newspapers, have also pressed on the frontiers of what is normally allowed.

Various theories have been advanced for the Soviet leadership's inaction until now. One was that, as a former party member, expelled in 1969, Mr. Medvedev retained high-level friends who were able to protect him. Another was that he owed his position to his standing among the Western European Marxists, whose loyalties the Soviet Union has been eager to regain. Mr. Medvedev himself surmised that the authorities recognized that his writings are mainly historical, not polemical tracts.

His session at the Prosecutor General's Office was attended by two other officials, one of them a man who identified himself as being from the K.G.B., Mr. Medvedev said.

According to his account, Mr. Soroka said he had been "assigned by the leadership" to warn Mr. Medvedev to cease "anti-Government activities" that had caused harm to the country.

"Either you stop writing such articles and books," Mr. Medvedev quoted Mr. Soroka as having said, "or we will put you in jail. The fact that we have not called you in for 20 years is a reflection of our great patience. But that patience is coming to an end. We have very little patience left, and it may run out in 1983."

Mr. Medvedev said he had refused to sign a statement referring to his writings as lampoons and repeating the warning of criminal charges. Instead, he delivered a statement of his own today, defending his writings as those of "a citizen struggling to see his country live at peace with the world, flourishing in democracy and socialism."

Abuse of Power Is Charged

"Unfortunately," the statement continued, "it is difficult to be a historian and chronicler in a country where a vast number of political and felonious crimes in recent years have been committed by the people in power, and where corruption and abuse of power have penetrated deeply into many areas of party and state activity, not excluding the judicial system, the procuracy and the K.G.B.

"It is difficult to be a political writer in a country where the Constitution requires all citizens to work toward strengthening the authority of the state, but where many of those in the highest positions of state leadership care little, abusing their power for personal gain or for the removal of rivals and critics. The interests of the state, of socialist society and of the people are of far less concern to these people than their personal interests and privileges.

"In a country such as the Soviet Union, an honest historian often has to step forward not only as a researcher but also as an investigator and judge, and to express moral and political opinions, regardless of whether these are in accord with the views of the existing government. I am little troubled as to the value attached to my work by the prosecutor or the K.G.B. Any honest and independent historian should be concerned with only one thing—the search for truth."

* * *

February 9, 1984

AS TABOOS FALL, PRESS IN YUGOSLAVIA TURNS BOLD

By DAVID BINDER

BELGRADE, Yugoslavia—For years it was an axiom of Western foreign correspondents that their Yugoslav colleagues were likely to be among the best informed reporters, especially in other Communist capitals.

During China's Cultural Revolution in the 1960's, the Central Intelligence Agency itself counted on the dispatches of Branko Bogunovic of the Tanyug press agency for news from Peking.

Now this foreign expertise has been complemented by an incisive and bold style in the domestic coverage by the Yugoslav press—sometimes too bold for senior Communist Party officials.

Last fall in Ljubljana a reporter for the Slovenian daily Delo learned that the price of gasoline was soon to be increased—as it was a week later, to the equivalent of $2.50 a gallon—and Delo published the news.

"The Government and other newspapers and the television screamed that Delo had caused a run on the pumps," a journalist recalled. "It was a big stink."

A View of Yugoslav Press

"From my point of view, the entire Yugoslav press is an opposition press," said Mitko Calovski, the Secretary for Information, in a mildly sarcastic tone during an interview. As an example of his problems he recounted with a pained smile the consequence of a false report in a Belgrade tabloid about pending changes in the law regulating foreign currency. It caused a brief run on the banks.

There has been no official prepublication censorship of the press for many years in Yugoslavia, although varying degrees of self-censorship have been practiced by individual newspapers and radio and television stations.

However, journalists often come into sharp conflict with Communist party officials. Such was the case last spring of Politika, Yugoslavia's oldest daily newspaper. The chief editor, Dragoljub Trailovic, felt compelled to resign because, he explained, he had "lost the confidence of the political leadership of the Federated Republic of Serbia for reasons which have not been conveyed to me."

Most professional journalists are also party members and therefore subject to the party's rules and reprimands. For the most part, however, the bolder journalists have functioned under the protection of the worker councils of the enterprises, which enjoy a measure of autonomy.

The audacity of the press in this Communist country has been evident not only in disclosing hot news items, but also in investigating sensitive disputes among Yugoslavia's diverse ethnic groups, in uncovering waste and fraud in the economy, and in discussing political infighting.

Few Taboos Are Left

"It has been a revolutionary change," said Zivko Milic, editor of a new Croatian news magazine called Danas.

The New York Times/David Binder Associated Press

Vladimir Dedijer, left, biographer of Tito, who says he still combats censorship at home. Branko Bogunovic, right, Yugoslav journalist noted for reporting from China.

"There are very few taboos. I don't think there are any taboos. The press is open to opinions not identical to the party line. It more realistically reflects all dreams and thoughts, excluding anti-Communist, nationalist ideas. We have the feeling we are in a great debate. The problem is, not getting lost in a jungle of open questions."

The perils of this openness have also been brought home to editors. Mr. Milic's predecessor had to resign when charges leveled by Danas against party officials in Karlovac were found to be lacking in substance. The editor was held responsible for libel.

And last autumn the Slovenian journalistic establishment was roiled by disputes over the contents of the satirical magazine Pavliha, in which accusations were leveled against party "pastors who stifle the freedom of journalism" and against a "ministry of truth" operated by Jak Koprivc, who is head of the Delo publishing house and at the same time a member of the Presidium of the Slovenian Central Committee.

A Mirror of Society

In Zagreb, Mladen Plesa, the vigorous editor of Start, one of Yugoslavia's most successful magazines, says he can trace elements of the social evolution in the transformation of his periodical.

"We started 15 years ago focused on Yugoslav tourists, writing mostly about actresses and singers," he said. "Now we carry a lot more about politics, because our readers have changed. They are mostly urban and have a fairly high level of education."

Start still features a centerfold of unclothed young women—sometimes West European, sometimes American, sometimes Yugoslav—but in the last two years it has carried articles on such topics as the potential threat to Yugoslavia posed by Soviet Army divisions stationed in nearby Warsaw Pact countries. The striking aspect of Start's circulation of 200,000 is that more than half of the sales are outside Croatia, including Serbia, where the Cyrillic alphabet is used instead of the Latin alphabet employed by Croatians.

Belgrade Journalist Skeptical

In Belgrade, scene of the liveliest press disputes of all, a journalist spoke skeptically of the party leadership's attitude toward the press.

"These guys have been running this place for 35 or 40 years," he said. "More democracy comes and they try to push it back to the ways they knew, the only way they know how to run things. The press, it goes along for a while, and you think it's improving, and then they slap you down."

An example of the party leadership attitudes may be found in the remarks of Dimce Belovski of the Presidium of the Macedonian Central Committee. In an interview in December he said, "There are even occasions when the press is losing its basic characteristic of public information media and becomes a power above society."

Problems of publication continue to bother authors as well as journalists and were exemplified recently by Vladimir Dedijer, who left the party 30 years ago and is now negotiating the publication of the third volume of his biography of Tito.

Even though some of the events in the latest volume took place nearly 40 years ago, there are still efforts at censorship, Mr. Dedijer said. The Croatian leaders wanted to eliminate a passage suggesting that one of their own once sought Soviet recognition of an independent Croatia.

At 69, well over 6 feet tall and blind in one eye, Mr. Dedijer looks like a storm-battered Bosnian crag. On a recent stroll from Makedonska Street to Belgrade's Kalamegdan Fortress, Mr. Dedijer recalled that last summer fires were set outside his home in Istria and at the home of one of his sources for party history. Had the coastal winds blown the other way, he said, his house could have been destroyed.

Mr. Dedijer said that Tito gave him his personal papers telling him to "be critical," and saying he counted on him to "protect them from the small fry, and to 'let history judge me.'" Although out of the party for decades, Mr. Dedijer asserts: "The party is the only thing holding Yugoslavia together."

Correction:

Because of an editing error, a dispatch from Belgrade Thursday on the press in Yugoslavia misidentified a Communist Party member. Dimce Belovski is a member of the presidium of the Central Committee of the League of Yugoslavia.

* * *

March 20, 1984

IN POLAND, NEWS IS NOT ALWAYS NEWS

By JOHN KIFNER

WARSAW, March 19—There seem to be two kinds of news in Poland: what the newspapers print and what the people want to know.

Today, for example, newspapers were filled with the news of the windup of a national Communist Party conference, a matter of apparently less interest to many Poles than the latest development in the dispute over the presence of crucifixes in schools.

There was not a single word about crucifixes in the Polish press. People hunched over short-wave radios to learn about this and other issues through dispatches filed by Western resident correspondents that were then broadcast back from abroad.

In 1980 and 1981, when the independent Solidarity movement was a significant factor in Polish life, Poland had one of the most independent presses in the Soviet bloc. Today newspapers have a drab sameness, enlivened only by an occasional obscure innuendo among party factions or a critical attack on "the enemies of socialism."

Importance of Western Stations

Where people get their news instead is the Polish-language broadcasts of Western radio stations—the Voice of America, Radio Free Europe, the BBC and the French radio.

These stations, in turn, get much of their material from the dispatches of the 64 Western news agency, newspaper and television correspondents permanently accredited in Warsaw.

The controlled press and the dependence on foreign radio stations are similar in every country of the Soviet bloc, although Poles probably find it easier to listen to Western broadcasts than, say, people in the Soviet Union.

Since the dispatches of Western reporters here tend to focus on dissent, the authorities are vexed.

On a warm evening, when windows are open, one can stroll through an apartment block and hear uninterrupted Western news broadcasts. In the cramped, book-lined rooms of intellectuals are often found, despite the shortage of consumer goods, two or three of the latest Sony receivers.

Dialing the Radio for News

"I spend all evening dialing the radio from one news to the other, "said a once prominent, now unemployed Polish journalist. "It is necessary."

Perhaps the most striking example of official irritation concerns the affair of Wladyslaw Sila- Nowicki, a lawyer and one-time Solidarity adviser.

A couple of weeks ago he wrote what he called an "open letter" to Gen. Wojciech Jaruzelski, the Polish leader, charging that the authorities had corrupted the system of justice to cover up the case of a young man who died of internal injuries after being held by the police and had falsely charged a lawyer investigating the case.

Mr. Sila-Nowicki's letter was not published in Polish newspapers, although he later said he had sent a copy to P.A.P., the press agency.

But copies found their way into the hands of some correspondents, and others learned of it through clandestine news sheets circulated by the underground. They filed news reports.

Official Response to Broadcasts

Within a few days, on March 1, the major Polish newspapers carried a lengthy, identical article saying: "The latest sensation in the Western press and especially on Radio Free Europe is that some retired lawyer wrote an open letter. In a week's time, the news of the day may be that a party member's dog has bitten Walesa."

The article was signed Jerzy Nowomiejski, a byline that no one could recall seeing before. The surname may be translated as "New Urban."

The Government spokesman, whose name is Jerzy Urban, when asked about the unknown writer, said only: "He has been published before."

The Nowomiejski article gave the first official version of an incident last May 3 in which undercover policemen broke through the back door of a convent and beat members of a church committee aiding Solidarity internees.

The gist of the description, which differed from earlier accounts by witnesses and raised eyebrows among Polish journalists who have covered the police, was that plainclothesmen had been set upon by what was described as "a band of intellectuals." None were arrested in the ensuing melee, although there had been hundreds of riot policemen in the area. It was not immediately clear how the purported attackers were identified.

Police Misconduct Charged

That raid on St. Martin's Church, the death soon after of 19-year-old Grzegorz Przemyk, whose funeral turned into a silent Solidarity demonstration of 20,000 mourners, and the subsequent arrest of Maciej Bednarkiewiez, the lawyer looking into the possibility of police misconduct, are among news topics that have attracted interest abroad, but have received scant coverage in Poland.

The day the Nowomiejski article appeared, charges were brought against Mr. Sila-Nowicki for 13 slandering the Polish state.

The controversy over the removal of the crucifixes from lecture halls in an agricultural school has gone unmentioned in the Polish press, although it has galvanized public opinion in this Roman Catholic country. A statement from senior bishops calling for the crosses to be "defended" was read at all masses on Sunday.

In the town of Garwolin, center of the crucifix dispute, a protest mass is to be held on Tuesday, and it is likely to be covered by Western—but not by Polish—reporters.

Official Focus on Party Parley

The big news here, if one read the papers, was the completion of the Communist Party conference, a follow-up to the party's ninth congress of 1981.

A red banner headline in the party paper, Trybuna Ludu, said:

"The conference of the Polish United Workers Party declares: The party consistently implements the program of the ninth congress."

There was little new in the statements that filled nine of the 12 pages in the party newspaper. Parts of General Jaruzelski's two-hour keynote speech had been published before.

"They are in another country," said a Polish journalist about those responsible for the press coverage. "It is not even a real country."

* * *

May 3, 1986

IN A CRISIS, WHO TO TUNE IN? IN THE SOVIET BLOC, PROBABLY WESTERN RADIO

By ALEX S. JONES

Since Monday, with little information available from official sources about the nuclear accident in the Soviet Union, Radio Free Europe and Radio Liberty have been a source of breaking news to their Soviet bloc audience.

They have also tailored their programs to contain practical advice on survival that would normally be the function of a local radio station.

For instance, the Polish language broadcast of Radio Free Europe was two hours ahead of radio stations in Poland in reporting that high radiation levels had been detected in Scandinavia and in broadcasting the Soviet announcement that a nuclear accident had occurred, according to Jacek Kalabinski, senior program editor for the Polish service in New York.

Mr. Kalabinski said the Polish service of Radio Free Europe had repeatedly broadcast an interview with a Polish-speaking hematologist based in New York who gave advice on such things as how to wash vegetables that might be contaminated with radiation.

Source of Information

It is in emergencies like the disaster at the Chernobyl nuclear reactor in the Ukraine that Eastern Europeans are most likely to turn to Western radio for information unavailable elsewhere, according to executives of several American foreign language radio services. They said their audience in the Soviet Union and the Eastern bloc was in the millions.

"Whenever there is a crisis, there is a craving for information, and they go out of the cities and into rural areas where there is no jamming to get information," said Jane Lester, assistant secretary for Radio Free Europe and Radio Liberty, which broadcast in 21 languages to the Soviet Union, Poland, Czechoslovakia, Hungary, Rumania and Bulgaria. The service is financed by the United States.

According to Miss Lester, Radio Free Europe provides people in the Eastern bloc with information about what is going on in their nations that their domestic press organizations might not report, and Radio Liberty is broadcasts news about Soviet affairs to Soviet citizens.

Last Tuesday, Oleg A. Tumanov, a Soviet defector who became the third-ranking editor at Radio Liberty and then returned to the Soviet Union after 21 years in the West, denounced Radio Liberty and Radio Free Europe as intelligence operations. But Mr. Kalabinski said the stations were "intended to be a journalistic vehicle, but must not be contrary to the broad objectives of U.S. foreign policy."

Focus on U.S. News

Voice of America, which also broadcasts in several languages to Eastern Europe and is underwritten by the United States Government, focuses on presenting United States news to foreigners and includes a daily editorial that represents the viewpoint of Washington.

In the last week, Voice of America has been broadcasting around the clock to the Soviet Union in English and in languages like Ukrainian, according to Richard W. Carlson, acting director of the radio service, which broadcasts in 42 languages. Mr. Carlson said radio broadcasts last week were "a perfect example" of the "terribly important role" Voice of America and other Western radio stations play in providing information to those living in the Soviet bloc.

Voice of America's reporting has focused on the accident itself, leaving domestic concerns such as advice on safety precautions to Radio Free Europe and Radio Liberty.

The BBC, which has foreign broadcasts in 37 languages, has carried extensive coverage of the nuclear accident in recent days, but has been concerned with the accident and not with advising local residents.

According to several foreign-language radio executives, there was no heightened effort in Eastern European countries to block radio broadcasts from the West last week, but they said there was an enormous blocking effort at all times.

Philip Bosley, senior international press officer for the BBC, said the Soviet Union spent more than $900 million a year to block radio broadcasts from the West. According to officials, the operating budgets for Radio Free Europe, Radio Liberty and Voice of America total about $260 million a year, and the British Government provides about $160 million a year for the BBC external radio service.

* * *

February 24, 1987

SOVIET WRITERS REINSTATE PASTERNAK

By PHILIP TAUBMAN

Special to the New York Times

MOSCOW, Feb. 23—The Soviet writers' union has posthumously reinstated Boris Pasternak, completing the rehabilitation of the author of "Doctor Zhivago."

The Soviet writers' union has posthumously reinstated Boris Pasternak, completing the rehabilitation of the author of "Doctor Zhivago."

The decision, made by the secretariat, or executive committee, of the union on Feb. 19, was announced today by the English-language service of the Soviet press agency Tass. It follows the announcement two weeks ago that "Doctor Zhivago" would be published serially beginning early in 1988.

The decisions, spurred by Mikhail S. Gorbachev's drive to ease censorship and increase openness, have removed the blight from Mr. Pasternak's official reputation, 27 years after his death and 30 years after publication of "Doctor Zhivago" in the West placed him in conflict with the authorities. He was expelled from the writers' union in 1958.

An 'Historic' Step

"It is a very important step, you could say an historic one," the poet Andrei Voznesensky said today of the decision, which had been mentioned briefly in recent days in a number of newspapers.

Mr. Voznesensky is chairman of a commission that reviewed the work of Mr. Pasternak and recommended reinstatement to the union.

He said his commission—composed of 30 writers, editors, critics and scientists—had also recommended that the Pasternak country home in Peredelkino, a southwest suburb of Moscow, be turned into a museum and that annual readings of his poetry be held there. The wood house was closed two years ago and most of Mr. Pasternak's effects were removed.

The anniversary of his death on May 30 has become an occasion for scores of Russians to visit his grave at a small, hillside cemetery in Peredelkino.

Mr. Voznesensky said that, "As long as the expulsion stood, Pasternak and his works were, in effect, illegitimate."

Symbol of a New Climate

Mr. Voznesensky said that the decision by the secretariat was not unanimous but that a majority of its 25 members agreed during a special meeting that the time had come to reverse a decision made when Khrushchev was the Soviet leader.

Mr. Pasternak's rehabilitation has become perhaps the most visible symbol of the changing cultural climate under Mr. Gorbachev and a willingness by the authorities to re-examine longstanding restraints on literature and the performing arts.

Steps to restore the official standing of Mr. Pasternak, best known in the Soviet Union for his poetry, actually began six years ago when Mr. Voznesensky, who was a protege of Mr. Pasternak's, published a favorable memoir about him in the writers' union journal, Novy Mir. The memoir was followed by publication of four of the poems in "Doctor Zhivago."

Other long-suppressed works, including Anatoly Rybakov's "Children of the Arbat," an unflinching look at Stalin's oppression, are slated for publication later this year. The novels of Vladimir Nabokov, the Russian-born writer, were not published here until last year, and the poetry of Nikolai S. Gumilev, who was shot in 1921 for anti-Soviet activity, has begun to appear.

Solzhenitsyn Still Banned

At the same time, many writers and works remain forbidden to Russians, illicitly circulating in Russian-language volumes published in the West.

The works of Aleksandr I. Solzhenitsyn, Vasily P. Aksyonov, Vladimir Voinovich and other emigre writers are among the banned books, although at one time Mr. Solzhenitsyn and Mr. Aksyonov were both widely read in the Soviet Union.

Although Soviet cultural officials have reportedly invited a number of performers who have left Russia to return for tours, including the dancers Mikhail Baryshnikov and Natalia Makarova, many other Russians who went to the West still are shunned.

Although "Doctor Zhivago" continued to be banned, following the decision in 1980 to partially rehabilitate Mr. Pasternak, the writer's poetry has been increasingly published and warmly received in the Soviet Union.

"Doctor Zhivago," for which Mr. Pasternak was awarded the Nobel Prize in Literature in 1958, is a panoramic portrait of the turbulent years of the Russian revolution, with the lives of its principal characters caught up in the ambiguities of the changing tides of the civil war and the years that followed. After publication in the West, it was quickly condemned by the authorities as anti-Soviet because of the acclaim it received abroad for its negative portrayal of some aspects of the Bolshevik side.

Mr. Pasternak rejected the Nobel Prize under pressure from the authorities and to avoid being forced to emigrate from Russia if he were allowed to travel to Sweden to receive the award.

* * *

January 12, 1988

FOR SOVIET ALTERNATIVE PRESS, USED COMPUTER IS NEW TOOL

By BILL KELLER

Special to the New York Times

MOSCOW, Jan. 11—In the living room of his southwest Moscow apartment, Lev M. Timofeyev has a Toshiba 1000 personal computer and a Kodak Diconix printer.

Using this precious equipment, purchased by friends at a Moscow second-hand store, Mr. Timofeyev has turned out two issues of the latest—and most legible—Soviet unofficial opinion magazine, called Referendum. In the process he has broken yet another patch of new ground for a struggling but spreading movement to create an alternative press.

"Modern technology will spread and come into its own," Mr. Timofeyev said confidently. "The authorities already are losing control over the spread of information. Now, if we could get hold of a laser printer, well . . ."

Despite shortages of money and supplies, a Government monopoly on printing presses and occasional police harassment, a new generation of "samizdat," or self-published, journals is offering an open challenge to the official press.

The alternative press now includes dozens of magazines in Moscow and Leningrad, with others reported in the Baltic republics, the Ukraine and Armenia.

The movement has grown to the point that a Leningrad group recently began publishing a Journal of Journals, featuring samples from various samizdat publications along with demands for an end to official restrictions on the independent press.

Like the samizdat of the 1960's and 1970's, the publications are usually pecked out on typewriters in carbon copies, passed hand to hand and reprinted along the way. They reach a readership numbered only in the hundreds, although Mr. Timofeyev's example suggests that will change.

Unlike their predecessors, the samizdat publishers of the era of Mikhail S. Gorbachev include not only traditional journals of dissent, but also a wide array of self-proclaimed reformers seeking peaceful coexistence with the authorities while maintaining editorial independence.

Where the samizdat press once focused on human rights or anti-Stalinism, it now touches on issues that include the environment, foreign policy, economic change, domestic politics and rock music.

Where the independent press was once underground, it has now emerged into the open. Many publishers send copies of their works to the official press and Communist Party leaders.

With the exception of a few self-published magazines, such as Roy Medvedev's Political Diary and XX Century, which remained loyal to the Government in the 1960's and 1970's despite persecution, most older samizdat writers saw little hope of changing the system. Many new publishers say they do.

One respected independent magazine, Merkury, published in Leningrad by a coalition of artistic, environmentalist and political groups, has been cited in the Communist Party newspaper Sovetskaya Rossiya, and its articles on ecological themes appear to have influenced coverage in the central newspapers.

"Samizdat as we knew it before is dead," said Merkury's editor, Yelena Zalinskaya, referring to the aspirations of the new samizdat to play the role of loyal opposition.

Editors Allowed to Meet

In October, the authorities allowed editors of 20 independent publications to meet in Leningrad to compare notes and work out a joint declaration endorsing broader press freedom. Representatives of such official publications as Literaturnaya Gazeta and Izvestia and of the Communist Party youth organization, Komsomol, took part in the discussion.

Official newspapers have not published accounts of the meeting, but partial transcripts published in the new Journal of Journals reflected a lively debate on the limits of press freedom in a Communist society.

Correspondents from the official press accused the alternative press of being too predictable and one-sided, and they taunted it for limited circulation and influence.

The samizdat editors, in turn, called for greater freedom of the independent press, including access to printing equipment.

Reporting the Unreported

Contemporary samizdat often includes significant news that goes unreported in the official press, and not just the imprisonment of political dissidents. For instance, the independent magazines Glasnost and Svidetel were the best sources of information on demonstrations protesting the ouster in November of Boris N. Yeltsin as chief of the Moscow city party organization.

Many new magazines are associated with informal political clubs that have grown up in the last year.

The Moscow Perestroika Club, a political discussion group named for Mr. Gorbachev's policy of "restructuring," has begun a magazine called Open Area, and the Federation of Socialist Clubs, a group that styles itself "new left," published Left Turn.

Among the publications focusing on human rights, the best known are Glasnost and Ekspress-Khronika.

Glasnost, published by Sergei Grigoryants, a former political prisoner, as a test of Mr. Gorbachev's policy of greater openness, is reprinted abroad in several languages, including an English-language version published by an emigre group in New York.

Ekspress-Khronika is a weekly compilation of reports on demonstrations, arrests and public declarations, supplemented by articles on Government policy.

Aleksandr Podrabinek, an editor, said a few copies were mailed to about 40 cities around the Soviet Union, to be reprinted and circulated. Sometimes the magazines are returned by the post office.

Religious publications make up another category of samizdat that seems to be growing. Aleksandr Ogorodnikov's Bulletin of the Christian Community focuses on Russian Orthodox activists, and it takes an uncompromising position toward the authorities. Lea, for Leningrad Jewish Almanac, is a six-year-old publication that is written primarily for Jews who do not seek to emigrate to Israel.

Mr. Timofeyev, a former political prisoner and human rights campaigner, said his new biweekly journal aims to attract contributions from prominent scientists and writers. The first issue includes articles on Afghanistan and the state of the church.

Because his printer was designed to work most efficiently using the Roman alphabet, the Russian-language publication in the Cyrillic alphabet takes a long time to print. Thus, he is still a long way from mass circulation—about 70 copies is his maximum.

Issue No. 1, published in December, had 10 articles on 18 pages. Some of the articles deal with economic issues and political changes.

In addition to pioneering a new stage of technology, Mr. Timofeyev's magazine has another novel feature. It is the first to include a column on astrology.

* * *

February 23, 1988

PRAGUE JOURNALISTS TRY FOR INDEPENDENT VOICE

By JOHN TAGLIABUE

Special to the New York Times

PRAGUE, Feb. 21—Citing precedents in the Soviet Union, a group of Czechoslovak journalists is negotiating with the Government in an effort to register an independent newspaper.

The exercise, whose outcome is far from certain, is a measure of how much the Soviet Union is being looked to as a force for widening freedom in this severely restricted society.

The independent newspaper, Lidowe Nowiny or People's News, has already appeared, in two regular monthly editions since Jan. 1. Its pages have featured uncensored political, cultural, economic and foreign news, including articles on Soviet-American disarmament, reports on Afghanistan and Poland, theater and film reviews, and a calendar of events 20 years ago.

"Now we are seeking to have the newspaper registered," said Jiri Ruml, the paper's editor.

The newspaper is a product of the thinking of journalists who enjoyed freedom to work during the intellectual blossoming of the Prague Spring of 1968, but were barred after the Soviet-led invasion of that August.

Mr. Ruml was deputy editor of one of the liveliest publications of the period, the weekly news magazine Reporter. The effort is draped in ironies. When Arvo Valtona, the president of the Union of Estonian Writers in the Soviet Union, was interviewed for the first edition, the Czechoslovak police sought to block the meeting.

"He discussed with them and became angry," one contributor to the newspaper said. "He said he published in Pravda. We had to calm him."

While recent changes instituted by the Soviet leader, Mikhail S. Gorbachev, have stirred a modest process of economic change here, they have done little to open intellectual and artistic life. Moscow has permitted a degree of independent journalism, as in the newspaper Glasnost, and the Polish Government has allowed Catholic intellectuals to publish an independent monthly journal of ideas.

"We spoke about the situation in Moscow," Mr. Ruml said of the talks he is conducting for the nine-member editorial board with the Federal Office for Printing and Information.

He quoted Government lawyers as saying that a major obstacle was a legal requirement that only organizations belonging to the National Front, the Communist-dominated alliance that includes labor unions and other social organizations, may publish newspapers.

But the editorial board, citing the example of Pacem in Terris, an association of Catholic priests friendly to the Government that is not part of the National Front, proposed formation of a "society of friends of Lidowe Nowiny" to sponsor the newspaper. "They said to us, 'Try this as an experiment,' " Mr. Ruml said.

The experiment is particularly intriguing because Prague once enjoyed some of Central Europe's most brilliant journalism, in both the Czech and German languages. This, however, gave way to drab uniformity under Communist dominance.

The name Lidowe Nowiny was taken from a Prague newspaper that was banned in 1948.

Hurdles to Overcome

Mr. Ruml said the idea was to increase the frequency of publication gradually from monthly to daily, and to augment the present circulation of only several thousand copies.

That entails overcoming material and ideological hurdles, such as obtaining adequate newsprint and the right to use state-owned printing presses. It also entails schooling a new generation in how to be independent journalists.

Jiri Dienstbier, a banned journalist who spent three years in prison for publishing his anti-Government views and is one of the editorial board, said: "I am 51. We are the last people who in their 20's and 30's worked on uncensored newspapers. We are completely without a middle generation. The problem is how to teach a new generation."

Mr. Ruml, in an effort to explain why the regime of Milos Jakes, the new Communist Party leader, is willing to negotiate, said, "As I see it, Jakes is only two months into his function. So he does not want to proceed in a brutal fashion. When he has the apparatus in his hands, that could change."

* * *

September 10, 1988

IN A TIME OF OPENNESS, THINGS WORTH READING REMAIN ELUSIVE

By BILL KELLER

Special to the New York Times

MOSCOW, Sept. 9—The Soviet reader in the days of glasnost knows the frustration of Tantalus. The rich fruits of Moscow spring hang on the branches, many of them no longer forbidden but just out of reach.

The latest indignity was the announcement a few weeks ago that the Communications Ministry had placed limits on subscriptions to 42 magazines and newspapers, including the most popular purveyors of provocative thinking, sensational exposes, and literature newly freed from the censor's vault.

The official explanation is a national shortage of paper, plausible enough in a country where toilet tissue is frequently in short supply. But official explanations do not go over as smoothly as they once did.

"Putting limits on subscriptions could easily be perceived as a victory for the so-called forces of stagnation, as a means for rolling back glasnost," Andrei Nemzer, a literary critic, wrote in the innovative magazine Ogonyok.

Ogonyok, the colorful weekly that is the first to disappear from the newsstands, has howled loudest about the subscription freeze.

Its editor, Vitaly A. Korotich, said some readers slept overnight outside post offices for the opening of the subscription season on Aug. 1, only to be told that subscriptions to Ogonyok, Novy Mir, Znamya—all the most daring publications—had been frozen at 1988 levels. Hundreds of letters and telegrams have poured in pleading for exemptions.

The Communist Party newspaper Pravda, which is not on the restricted list, attributed it all to a paper industry so outmoded, neglected and wasteful that the United States produces nine times as much paper per capita as the Soviet Union.

Maybe so, wrote a literary critic, Vladimir Lakshin, in Moscow News, another publication on the restricted list. In that case, he proposed, the state should divert paper from "propaganda sheets and pseudo-scientific works that no one needs."

The subscription limit is just the latest sign of a chronic complaint in this nation of voracious readers—so much to read, so hard to get a copy.

The books in greatest demand are published in such limited numbers that the country has long had a flourishing black market in reading matter. Anything from thrillers to Bibles may be available from that furtive man with the suitcase loitering outside the bookstore.

Nowadays, the hottest items are used magazines—especially the "thick journals" like Novy Mir, Znamya and Druzhba Narodov, which serialize novels long before the archaic book-publishing industry gets them between hard covers. A dog-eared copy of the April 1985 issue of Druzhba Narodov containing Anatoly Rybakov's novel "Children of the Arbat" may sell for $50.

Stagnation Does Stagnate

By contrast, in a back room at Public Library No. 73, a shady 19th-century mansion on Sushchevskaya Street, Leonid I. Brezhnev and his contemporaries wait for the junkman.

The memoirs and speeches of the former leader, who presided over the country for the 18 years now called the period of stagnation, are being thinned from library shelves where they have sat untouched in multiple copies, to make way for the more candid and livelier literature of Mikhail S. Gorbachev's era.

"If it had been up to me, I'd have thrown them out myself long ago," said Svetlana V. Rostkovskaya, the director of the library. The Culture Ministry recently extended to librarians the discretion to give dormant reading matter the heave-ho.

A librarian from the Crimea indignantly charged early this month in a letter to the Government newspaper Izvestia that the ministry had ordered a wholesale removal of pre-Gorbachev political literature, a charge the ministry heatedly denied.

Visits to several of Moscow's 421 neighborhood libraries the week after the letter was published found little evidence of such a purge. Only duplicate copies are being sent to warehouses and paper-recycling centers.

A reader intent on savoring Mr. Brezhnev's ghostwritten account of how he stopped the Nazis in World War II, or poring over the speeches of Konstantin U. Chernenko, will still find these works on the shelves—no waiting required.

On the other hand, the reader will not find many books published since Mr. Gorbachev came to power in 1985, a shortcoming librarians said reflects the fact that book publishing has lagged behind demand.

As a result, the real action in local libraries is in the periodical reading rooms. Readers who once came in search of Dostoyevsky or of a good detective novel now come to peruse the lovingly dogeared issues of the likes of Ogonyok or Novy Mir.

Librarians note another change: the records of official party gatherings, once checked out only by local party functionaries beavering their way to the top, have become items in popular demand.

Miss Rostkovskaya said that when the press published detailed accounts of the tumultuous Communist Party conference earlier this summer, she rushed out to buy copies with her own money to satisfy readers flocking to her little sanctuary of the printed word.

A Spectator Sport?

Suppose someone manages to find that book or magazine. Then what?

A study conducted in 24 Soviet cities has discovered that 20 percent of the public will read that book or magazine on the bus or subway, 19 percent while eating or watching television, 9 percent on the job, and 7 percent while standing in line.

The Izvestia correspondent who reported all this found it to be a rich lode of information about Soviet society.

For example, he asked, what kind of jobs are these where one worker in 10 feels free to keep a book propped open on his desk? And what kind of books are those that can be read with one eye on a television variety show?

More troubling, have books in this country evolved from a treasury of cultural values into something more mundane, a relief from "the discomfort of everyday life?" It seems so, he sighed.

After all this sociology, though, it turned out that what the correspondent was really up to was a new rationale for doing something about the book shortage.

"The modern reader," he wrote, "is denied a whole range of literature—professional fiction, books for adolescents and women, popular biographies, historical and adventure books, etc.—which, psychologically speaking, are an effective way of easing tension."

* * *

December 1, 1988

SOVIET UNION ENDS YEARS OF JAMMING OF RADIO LIBERTY

By SERGE SCHMEMANN
Special to the New York Times

BONN, Nov. 30—The Soviet Union has stopped jamming Russian-language broadcasts by the American-financed Radio Liberty and two other foreign radio stations, apparently clearing Soviet airwaves of deliberate interference with foreign broadcasts for the first time since the early 1950's.

Officials of Radio Liberty in Munich said jamming of their Russian-language shortwave broadcasts stopped late Tuesday. They said listeners reported that broadcasts to the Ukraine, Byelorussia, the Baltic states, the Caucasus and Central Asia were "loud and clear" today.

The West German station Deutsche Welle and the Israeli radio, the other two stations that were still being jammed in the Soviet Union recently, also reported that the interference was lifted today.

Two in East Bloc Still Jamming

The Soviet Union had already stopped jamming two other major Western broadcasts last year—those by the British Broadcasting Corporation in January 1987 and those by the Voice of America in May 1987. Jamming had also been halted in recent years in all East European countries except Czechoslovakia and Bulgaria, where it was reported continuing today. Deutsche Welle also reported that its transmissions to Afghanistan were still being jammed.

E. Eugene Pell, president of Radio Liberty and its sister station, Radio Free Europe, said today, "The cessation of jamming represents a significant step on the part of the Soviet Government toward the free flow of information."

Called Hostile Propaganda

In New York, Malcolm S. Forbes Jr., chairman of the Board for International Broadcasting, the Federal agency that oversees the two stations, said that by making the move, Mikhail S. Gorbachev, the Soviet leader, "has sent a strong signal of his commitment to glasnost."

The Soviets have justified jamming on the ground that foreign stations were trying to undermine the Soviet system with hostile propaganda. Jamming has been particularly effective in big cities. Some Soviet citizens have regularly taken their shortwave sets outside the city limits to try to pick up broadcasts in areas where the jamming is less intense.

There was no official announcement from Moscow of the cessation of jamming, and no indication that it would not be resumed. But American officials at Radio Liberty and at human rights talks in Vienna said they had been expecting the move for months.

The officials noted that Mr. Gorbachev is to visit New York and London next week, and they said Moscow had traditionally made dramatic gestures just before such trips.

In addition, the radio jamming had been one obstacle to American and British acceptance of an international human rights conference that Moscow would like to hold as a follow-up to the Conference on Security and Cooperation in Europe now under way in Vienna.

The jamming has also been an obstacle to beginning new talks on reducing conventional arms in Europe. The United States has said such talks could not begin until the Soviet Union improved its human rights record by ending jamming and releasing political prisoners, among other steps.

In another significant development, Administration officials and members of Jewish groups said in Washington that the Soviet Union appeared to be moving to allow the emigration of some people long denied permission to leave. David Waksberg, vice president of the Union of Councils for Soviet Jews, said his organization knew of 20 people who had been informed that they no longer were deemed to be in the possession of state secrets.

The jamming, which was estimated by Radio Liberty officials to cost the Soviet Union more than $1 billion a year, had appeared to contradict Mr. Gorbachev's campaign to introduce more openness to Soviet society and his program to cut costs.

Although relatively few people in the United States own shortwave radios, many Soviet citizens do and use the radios to receive broadcasts from foreign countries and from distant parts of the Soviet Union.

The jamming of foreign broadcasts began at about the time Western nations began beaming shortwave signals into the Soviet Union in the early 1950's. With the development of radio technology, the Soviet network came to include about 200 large "skyway" jammers that bounced high-powered shortwave signals off the ionosphere to mingle with incoming broadcasts.

Forest of 'Broken Umbrellas'

In addition, tens of thousands of smaller "ground wave" transmitters were mounted in cities and towns to interfere with radio signals. The characteristic "broken umbrella" antennas are a common feature of Soviet urban skylines.

Because of those devices, Radio Liberty and Radio Free Europe, which are financed by the United States Government and have their headquarters in Munich, had continued to find their broadcasts jammed. Radio Liberty broadcasts to the Soviet Union in 12 languages, while Radio Free Europe broadcasts to East European nations.

The stations have always been held in particular contempt by the Soviets because unlike the Voice of America, which is an official outlet of the American Government, Radio Liberty and Radio Free Europe purport to be "surrogate radios" for Communist-controlled nations, presenting programs that those countries would have access to if they had an independent press and broadcasting.

Both stations were revealed long ago to have been financed secretly by the United States Central Intelligence Agency, and since then both have been publicly financed by Congress.

New Challenge Seen

For Radio Liberty, which began existence in 1952 as Radio Liberation and as the voice of Soviet emigres, the end of jamming was likely to prove as much a challenge as a boon.

For one thing, the station had designed its programs around jamming, with virtually no music or other material that would be inaudible through jamming, such as telephone interviews. For another, the policy of glasnost has opened to internal Soviet debate many topics that were previously available to Soviet citizens only through illicit foreign broadcasts.

In a telephone interview, Mr. Pell said the station had already begun studying programming changes, including the introduction of music and call-in telephone interviews.

Officials of Radio Free Europe and Radio Liberty said surveys had shown that the stations' Soviet audience had remained steady at about 16 million a week even with greater openness in the Soviet press and the lifting of jamming of the Voice of America and the BBC.

Soviet emigres at the station said they thought it would take a long time before Soviet citizens began trusting their own broadcasting enough to abandon the "Western voices."

They said many Russians, conditioned by decades in which domestic news was entirely controlled by the state, still looked to the Western broadcasts for confirmation of what their own press was carrying. In any case, they said, many themes remain taboo or little covered in the Soviet Union, such as power struggles within the Kremlin, the situation of Soviet Jews and other aspects of human rights.

The selection of those themes has been a matter of heated dispute at times at Radio Liberty. Most of its broadcasts are produced by Soviet emigres of different generations and backgrounds who often hold sharply divergent views.

While older emigres, who fled in the aftermath of the Revolution and after World War II, were accustomed to the militantly anti-Soviet tone of the cold war, newer emigrants, many of them Jewish, have pushed for more subtle programming that would recognize that modern Soviet citizens are likely to dismiss blatant anti-Soviet propaganda. The differences have led to bitter wrangling, sometimes accompanied by accusations of anti-democratic and anti-Semitic attitudes.

The infighting was one of the challenges facing a new supervisory board under Mr. Forbes and a new president, Mr. Pell, when they took charge in 1985. Since then Mr. Pell has installed new management and has created special offices to check Russian-language broadcasts before they are transmitted and to analyze all broadcasts afterward to insure that they meet Congressional guidelines laid down after the stations were taken away from C.I.A. control in 1972.

* * *

April 12, 1989

KAFKA'S HOMELAND LIFTS ITS BAN

By JOHN TAGLIABUE
Special to The New York Times

PRAGUE—Twenty years after his writings were denounced and suppressed following the brief political and artistic flowering that came to be known as the Prague Spring, Franz Kafka is to be published once again in his native land.

In the last few months, Odeon, one of the largest publishing houses in Czechoslovakia, has been preparing the publication of Kafka's principal writings, including 32 previously unpublished letters. Ivo Zelezny, an editor at Odeon, said the newly found letters, in the original German with a Czechoslovak translation, will appear this year.

Further volumes, including the short stories and the novels—"The Castle," "The Trial" and "America"—are planned for this year or next, to be followed by more letters, diaries and other writings.

The size of the edition will depend on demand from booksellers, Mr. Zelezny said, but will probably amount to about 40,000 copies. "People are not as fond of Kafka as at the end of the 1960's," he said. "There are new people, new interests. He's now one of the authors, not the author."

Some Czechoslovaks believe Kafka's re-emergence reflects the Prague regime's grudging desire to project a liberal image, at a time when it is under fire for resisting Mikhail S. Gorbachev's lead in liberalizing intellectual and artistic life in the Soviet Union. Communist Party officials here are grappling with a new outbreak of cultural pluralism.

Other Authors Still Banned

Though Kafka's works have been released for publication, dozens of other Czechoslovak authors remain banned. Indeed, the country's most prominent playwright and leading dissident author, Vaclav Havel, is currently serving an eight-month prison term, having been convicted earlier this year on charges of anti-Government incitement. The playwright was among those who took part in the commemoration of the death 20 years ago of a student who set fire to himself to protest the Soviet-led invasion.

Mr. Havel was imprisoned despite the bold initiative of more than 1,000 Czechoslovak writers, actors and artists, who signed a petition on his behalf. Though the effort was unsuccessful, it was a sign that pressure for change is building. Meanwhile, Mr. Havel's work cannot be staged in his native land. A production of his play "Temptation," a Kafkaesque vision of life in a repressive society, is now at the Public Theater in New York.

Kafka, too, has a play in New York currently, an adaptation on Broadway of perhaps his best-known story, "Metamorphosis," which stars the Soviet-born dancer Mikhail Baryshnikov.

The son of German Jewish parents, Franz Kafka was born in 1883 in Prague, a city that was then home to a sizable German-speaking minority. He lived most of his life in Prague, working for many years as a kind of insurance claims adjustor. In the last seven years of his life, however, he spent more and more time in hospitals and health resorts, finally dying of tuberculosis in a sanatorium near Vienna in 1924.

He was branded decadent and defeatist when the Communists seized power in Czechoslovakia in 1948. His rehabilitation began in 1963 at a literary conference organized by the Czechoslovak scholar and diplomat Eduard Goldstucker, and his writings remained available until the tolerant spirit of the Prague Spring was suppressed.

Communist critics were sometimes uncomfortable with Kafka. The Prague Spring celebrated him, in part at least, because the paranoia over faceless power and the atmosphere of emotional suffocation that suffused his works appeared to some to mirror conditions under Communism.

"The question was whether the alienation Kafka chronicled was valid for socialism," said Jiri Vesely, a Kafka specialist at the Czechoslovak Academy of Sciences. "Then the Prague Spring ended, the armies came. Of course, Kafka was hardly the guilty one."

'Simply Not Presentable'

"The cultural outlook of the 1950's was narrow and dogmatic," said Josef Cermak, the senior editor at Odeon. "Into such a world not only Kafka, but other writers—Joyce, Proust—could not fit. These end-figures of a bourgeois epoch produced a great oeuvre, but one that was simply not presentable."

"Now, however," he added, "with everything being reconsidered, a young generation is coming along, so Kafka returns."

In late 1987, the first statement of revived interest appeared when the literary weekly, Kmen, dedicated an issue to Kafka, including an article by Mr. Cermak relating how the 32 new letters turned up one day in 1986 in a used-book shop in Prague, and another article about Kafka's last completed novel, "The Castle."

At about the same time, a Prague theater staged a play about Kafka's anxiety-ridden life. Earlier, a novel about the writer had appeared in an official publication, after an underground paper had serialized it.

Chagrin Over Neglect

While printed praise of Kafka is rare here, a kind of embarrassment hangs over his neglect.

In a recent issue of the popular weekly Tvorba, a correspondent, Lenka Vtipilova, described a conversation with two Soviet film makers, identified simply as Sasha and Dina, during a trip to Moscow.

The Russians profess a love of Kafka. But when asked whether they would be interested in making a documentary film about him, Sasha replies, "If they invited us to Austria, why not?" "Or to Hungary," Dina adds. "Wouldn't Prague do?" Miss Vtipilova asks, continuing: "They looked without understanding, and it chilled me. I had to explain who Kafka was. And all of a sudden I didn't know whose fault it was, ours or those two young Russians'."

Still, some Czechoslovak scholars insist Kafka was never suppressed.

"He was a bit forgotten, but he never disappeared from the libraries," Mr. Vesely said. "Unhappily, a political issue was made of Kafka."

Nevertheless, commemorations of the writer's 100th birthday, in 1983, were modest. Prague's dwindling Jewish community obtained permission, after much haggling, to assemble at his stark headstone in the monumental Jewish cemetery. A thin volume of short stories was reissued.

House Marked by a Plaque

Since then, none of the works have appeared, and none of the many bookstores visited recently in Prague had any of his works or any books about him for sale, though a plaque still marks the house where he was born.

In Goldsmiths' Lane, behind the towering St. Vitus Cathedral, a crooked house where Kafka's sister Ottla once lived and where he wrote the collection of stories called "A Country Doctor" now houses a book shop. When a recent visitor asked about a book by Kafka, a clerk made him leave the store.

In these and other respects, Kafka might well feel at home in present-day Prague.

Last November, for example, when plainclothes police broke up a historical conference attended by Western human rights organizers, the participants were handed typewritten notices that read, in four languages: "I am warning you that the action called Symposium Czechoslovakia 88 is illegal, and its performance would be contrary to the interests of the Czechoslovak working people and consequently illegal."

Describing the events later, Timothy Garton Ash, a British historian and one of the participants in the conference, told how the notice, though written in the first person, was unsigned.

"Kafka," he said, "thou shouldst be living at this hour."

* * *

July 18, 1989

THE LIFE OF A SOVIET CENSOR: ANYTHING GOES? NOT JUST YET

By BILL KELLER
Special to The New York Times

MOSCOW, July 17—Suppose an inquisitive Soviet reporter were to unearth evidence that a member of the Communist Party Politburo had a mistress. Could he publish it?

Vladimir A. Boldyrev, the chief censor of the Soviet Union, ponders the question for a long time. A very long time.

"Well, I think the answer is, yes, we are now approaching the stage where personal details can be made public that it was not customary to publish before," he replied at last.

Then he added, with a nervous laugh that suggested that the verdict was not final, "I hope this is just a hypothetical question."

Mr. Boldyrev is the keeper of a shrinking but still formidable catalogue of what the press cannot write, the publishing houses cannot publish, the movies cannot show, the libraries cannot put on public display, and the post office cannot deliver.

The New York Times/Bill Keller

Vladimir A. Boldyrev, chief censor of the Soviet Union, who boasts that he has cut by half the list of what is forbidden.

Playboy Bunnies Unbanned

In his three years as chairman of Glavlit—the Administration for the Protection of State Secrets in the Press—Mr. Boldyrev boasts that he has cut the list by half, lifting the ban on such diverse secrets as the works of Aleksandr Solzhenitsyn, the bunnies of Playboy magazine, and the crime rate.

Indeed, it is difficult to extract from Mr. Boldyrev exactly what is forbidden anymore in the Soviet Union, in part because the boundary is moving so fast and in part because the idea of censorship has become so unfashionable in the day of glasnost that even the censor in chief finds the subject a bit distasteful.

"In the classical sense, it is no longer really correct to call us censors," he insisted in an interview at his office midway between the Kremlin and the K.G.B. headquarters. "Today we do not impose limits of a purely political or ideological character, which was one of our duties before."

Still, there is much room for discretion in Glavlit's current standard of what is prohibited, which Mr. Boldyrev recently elaborated to the newspaper Izvestia as follows: "The use of the press for purposes of undermining or eliminating the established socialist system in the U.S.S.R., to propagandize war, to preach racial or national exclusivity or hatred and violence on a national, religious or other basis, to damage the country's security interests or defense capability or public order, or to publish materials incompatible with the requirements of public morality and protecting the population's health."

Protecting Secrets

Mr. Boldyrev said most of the thick catalogue of forbidden themes—a document that is itself restricted to a narrow circle of editors and publishers—consists of military and industrial secrets.

Glavlit's clout is such that it has occasionally overruled the Defense Ministry on what constitutes a secret, Mr. Boldyrev said, although it has never found occasion to overrule the K.G.B., the state security police.

His agency is also responsible for preventing the dissemination of pornography, which like many arbiters of official taste he has trouble defining.

"You probably have to see it," said the censor, who is 59 years old and an economist by training. Once resolutely puritanical, Glavlit has become more permissive. Soft-core erotica is now considered acceptable in films and publications, and formerly taboo themes like homosexuality can be discussed in a positive light, although an article on that subject is almost certain to pass Boldyrev's desk before it reaches the readers.

Despite his disclaimer about politics and ideology, Glavlit is also empowered to decide that hostile literature poses a danger to the state.

'Debates Over' on Solzhenitsyn

Mr. Boldyrev said Glavlit ruled last year that the works of Mr. Solzhenitsyn, the fiercely anti-Communist Russian living in exile in Vermont, were no longer a threat. Mr. Solzhenitsyn's epic labor camp memoir, "The Gulag Archipelago," is to be excerpted next month in the magazine Novy Mir, and a publishing house has announced plans to publish seven volumes of selected Solzhenitsyn works.

"Regarding Solzhenitsyn, all debates are over," the censor said. "We released all of his works from the closed archives, and our publishing houses have the right to publish them—of course, without violating the copyright."

Mr. Boldyrev said the vast bulk of writings by emigres and exiles, once banned automatically regardless of the contents, have now been removed from the closed archives of libraries, and the rest are to be reviewed by the end of the year.

The liberated writers include some of the bitterest critics of Soviet authority, among them such emigre novelists as Vladimir N. Voinovich, Vladimir Maximov—who once damned Communism as "an evil ideology"—and Viktor Nekrasov, and the non-emigre Vasily Grossman, whose thinly fictionalized attack on Lenin, "Forever Flowing," was published last month in the magazine Oktyabr.

The books written by Trotsky before he was expelled from the country as a Bolshevik heretic are now open, but what he wrote in exile is still under review.

Also locked away are foreign works that Glavlit feels might "undermine" Soviet power or outrage public sensibilities.

'Mein Kampf' Still Banned

"Mein Kampf," the Hitler manifesto widely studied in other countries as a model of political pathology, is here banned as an offense to memories of the Great Patriotic War Against Fascism.

"I think it will eventually be published, but first we have to live through a certain period of time to absorb what is being done today," Mr. Boldyrev said of the book. "It would be wrong to overfeed the public."

The limits of contemporary writing are murkier.

"If some paper wants to publish a call to arms to overthrow the authorities, we will not allow it to be published," he said.

And what about a scathing satire of President Mikhail S. Gorbachev? Not likely, Mr. Boldyrev said.

"This affects not only the prestige of our country, but perestroika itself," he said. "If we trample on the leader of perestroika, how can we make any progress?"

Many Other Censors

He added, however, that an attack on the Soviet leader would probably be squelched long before it reached his desk. While Glavlit is the supreme court of censorship, the Soviet system has countless less formal ways of saying "nyet."

A magazine, for example, depends on the good will of the officially sanctioned organization that sponsors it, of the ideology department of the Communist Party, of the state committee that controls printing presses and newsprint, of the official writers' union, and of local authorities who sometimes block distribution of publications approved in Moscow.

Editors who rise in this system have cultivated a keen sense of protective self-censorship.

Thus while Glavlit says it has imposed no limits on writing about the recent bloody events in China, no Soviet publication has dared criticize the Chinese regime. On matters of foreign policy, editors take their cues from the party and Government leadership, which has been carefully nurturing its recently normalized relations with Beijing.

Reviewing Half of the Output

Mr. Boldyrev estimates that about half of the information dispensed for public consumption in the Soviet Union is reviewed in advance by Glavlit's agents. The rest—including reprints of literary classics, many local and regional newspapers of scant circulation, certain reference works, and publications with a demonstrated devotion to self-censorship—do not undergo prior review, but are spot-checked.

Periodicals that suddenly develop a free spirit may find themselves back under Glavlit's wing. That happened this year to 20th Century and Peace, a long-quiescent little magazine that fell into the hands of a free-thinking editor and began publishing critiques of the K.G.B.

Mr. Boldyrev explained to the disbelieving editors that the publication had been leashed because it wrote about disarmament, raising the risk that it would disclose some privileged detail of a Soviet negotiating position.

The reins on the press may be loosened further when the new legislature approves a long-awaited law on the rights and responsibilities of the press. But legislators say the new law is unlikely to curtail Glavlit's authority seriously or to permit a truly independent press. Mr. Boldyrev is not worried about job security.

"The system of protecting secrets was created by people who are not completely unreasonable," he said. "It was built up over time, and it has its rationale."

* * *

October 1, 1989

POLAND'S CENSORS BEGINNING TO FADE

By JOHN TAGLIABUE

Special to The New York Times

WARSAW, Sept. 29—Poland's censor, still officially ensconced in the Government bureaucracy, reached for his scissors 2,528 times last year, and 80 percent of his snipping was done in 20 mostly non-Communist, church-related newspapers.

But since the Solidarity-dominated Government took power, the instances of censorship have declined sharply. Last month Polish censors made 62 deletions, ranging from proscribed words to pages, compared with 198 ordered in the same period a year ago.

If the recently installed non-Communist Government fulfills its pledges to change the operation of newspapers, radio and television, the floodgates of information in Poland, already the Eastern bloc's most open society for information, will open even wider.

A measure of the new approach was apparent last week, when Prime Minister Tadeusz Mazowiecki appointed a staunchly pro-Solidarity writer and expert on Soviet literature, Andrzej Drawicz, to head the Committee for Radio and Television Affairs, long the disseminator of Communist propaganda.

Three Anchormen Removed

Despite pledges to tread cautiously, Mr. Drawicz, who spent 11 months in jail after the Communists imposed martial law in 1981 to crush Solidarity, moved quickly to remove the national networks' three news anchormen, who he said were too closely linked to the Communists.

In a further indication of where the Solidarity Government wants to go, the new 57-year-old television chief declared that one of the most urgent problems facing him was to resolve the status of thousands of radio and television reporters who were purged under martial law.

The numbers on censorship were released on Thursday by the Government's new spokesman, Malgorzata Niezabitowska, at her first news conference, called to lay down the outlines of information policy.

The appointment of Miss Niezabitowska is another reflection of the dramatic turnaround in information policies. Miss Niezabitowska, who was a journalist for Solidarity publications, is sitting in the same chair that since martial law had been occupied by Jerzy Urban, the spokesman for the old Government. His Solidarity-baiting on television once won him the highest rating on a government survey of the most abhorred public figures.

With her husband, Tomasz Tomaszewski, a photographer, Miss Niezabitowska has written a book, "Remnants," about the lives of the few thousand Jews who still live in Poland.

The book was published in the United States, where Miss Niezabitowska studied as a Nieman fellow at Harvard University three years ago.

When martial law shut down the Solidarity weekly for which she worked, she found professional sanctuary writing for Catholic publications, including Tygodnik Powszechny, a liberal Cracow weekly, and Wiez, whose editor, Mr. Mazowiecki, is now the Prime Minister.

In her news conference, Miss Niezabitowska listed these objectives of the new Government:

- The gradual elimination of censorship, first in books, later in monthly magazines and newspapers.
- Concessions for private radio and television stations.
- The liquidation of privileges for press concerns, like the Communist-controlled press giant RSW Prasa, which obtains more than half of the country's perennially short paper supplies and contributes a percentage of profits to the Communist Party treasury.
- The accreditation of journalists working for Western radio stations, including the American-financed Radio Free Europe, that broadcast Polish programs back to Poland from abroad.

Vows to Avoid Polemics

Miss Niezabitowska, trying to set her style off from Mr. Urban's, pledged to shun polemics and avoid seeking to respond personally to all queries. "We want to ease access to the sources," she said.

Since the signing of the round-table accords by the Communists and Solidarity in April, the shape of Poland's press, radio and television, has changed dramatically.

Solidarity's daily newspaper, Gazeta Wyborcza, with a paid circulation of 460,000, is now the nation's largest paper, outstripping the party daily Trybuna Ludu, with 300,000. Gazeta's business manager, Grzegorz Lindenberg, said 700,000 or 800,000 copies could easily be sold if the press distribution monopoly succeeded in delivering the paper everywhere in the country on the day of printing.

* * *

May 12, 1990

EVOLUTION IN EUROPE; SEX MAGAZINES AND MASSAGE PARLORS TEST HUNGARY'S NEW LIMITS

By CELESTINE BOHLEN
Special to The New York Times

BUDAPEST, May 5—Pornography, long banned by the Communists as the worst spawn of Western decadence, has broken into the open in Hungary, taking its place on the newsstands as another example of a newly emboldened press.

But the explosion of sexually explicit material has already produced a backlash. Parents, religious groups and feminists are recoiling from the shock of seeing photographs of nudes and graphic depictions of sexual acts on the covers of publications like Sexexpress, Popo, Sexy Lady, Lesbi Girls, Apollo and the other pornographic magazines prominently displayed at their local kiosks.

"It is no wonder after 40 years of oppression that this profit-oriented business is flourishing," said Miklos Hasznos, an official of the Christian Democratic Party. "Pornography is part of democracy, but human rights means taking the other side into consideration, too."

The Christian Democratic Party, through its newspaper, Yes, began a campaign against pornography last winter, collecting 90,000 signatures. Distributors have since been required to seal sexually explicit material in clear plastic, but now the campaign has moved on to demands that the magazines be wrapped in brown paper or be otherwise kept from plain sight.

"We are only protesting against the fact that these newsstand pictures are practically yelling out to the 13- and 14-year-olds," Mr. Hasznos said.

Feminists Are Upset

Many here expect Hungary's newly elected Parliament to seek to have the growing sex industry brought under some form of control, with the effort spurred by a coalition of center-right and Christian parties led by the Hungarian Democratic Forum.

Feminists, upset by the exploitation of women, worry that controls will be put in place for the wrong reasons. "I'm very depressed," said Judit Revesz, an English teacher active in women's groups.

She said the spread of these materials was understandable in light of the years of oppression. "But what is missing from the debate is the articulation of the view that this is offensive to women," she said. "People are mixing liberty with bad taste."

Laws regulating sexual mores are now in a state of limbo. This is one reason for the increase in sex shops, sex clubs, sex videos and sex advertisements. Practically everything that can be had in Times Square is now for sale in Hungary.

Elsewhere in Eastern Europe

In this field, Hungary is either far ahead or, depending on the point of view, far behind all the other Eastern European countries emerging from Communist rule. There is no legal pornography for sale in Romania or Czechoslovakia. In Poland the Roman Catholic Church has waged a successful struggle against the open distribution of such material.

But in Hungary, along with the graphic photographs, the magazines—those that print articles—stick to standard fare; an "objective" history of the breast appears in an issue of Sexexpress, alongside a historical essay on underwear. There are also articles on AIDS and advertisements for dieting devices.

Given this competition, many here say Playboy magazine, which began a Hungarian edition last December, has been surpassed.

In Hungary, even more than in other Eastern European countries, a strong consensus exists in support of liberalizing the puritanical code imposed by the Communists.

A poll taken last fall by the Hungarian Public Opinion Research Institute showed that 75 percent of those interviewed favored legalizing prostitution, with men and women of an equal mind on the issue. Brothels here were closed in the 1950's, and a public debate is under way on when to allow them to reopen.

King of Hungarian Pornography

Antal Laszlo Voros, the self-styled king of Hungarian pornography, is not worried about any kind of a clampdown.

"Hungarians have always been more relaxed about sex, and more aggressive about business, than others," he said, adding that a petition signed by thousands "is not enough to stop millions."

"I have talked to a lot of members of the Hungarian Democratic Forum," Mr. Voros said. "They are just like us. They like to make love; they like pretty girls."

Mr. Voros says he refuses to advertise sex with animals, with children, or between men, but otherwise the only limit he sees is what the market in Hungary will bear. "For five years, it will keep going up and then it will stagnate," he said.

Mr. Voros, 37 years old, a former journalist, photographer and part-time magician, started with a nudist travel agency and has gone on to create an empire built on pornography.

He now operates Budapest's only sex club, publishes six photos-only sex magazines, sells sex tours to Thailand, Greece and other countries, has filmed two pornographic movies and has many more plans—including brothels, a fleet of sex taxis to provide transport for call girls, two sex ships on Lake Balaton in Hungary, and expectations for a pornography export business to Romania, Czechoslovakia and even the Soviet Union if markets there open up.

Boasting of His Success

Clearly enjoying his role as kingpin of Hungary's sex business, Mr. Voros likes to boast of his success, even embellish it. Since he went into the business full time a year ago—he still has a car repair and an advertising business on the side—he said he has grossed up to $15 million.

Whatever the exact amount, it is apparently enough to build himself a villa with eight rooms and two swimming pools on 10 acres overlooking Budapest, and to make him into one of Hungary's most visibly successful small entrepreneurs.

Mr. Voros said the business took off last June when it became clear to him and his contacts at the Ministry of Trade that pornography was no longer off limits. Until then, he had periodically been harassed by the police during filming of his movies, he said.

As it is, many of the regular customers of Mr. Voros's sex club—a cramped bar in a backyard in Budapest's Ninth District, decorated with sex paraphernalia and equipped with sauna and massage room in the back—are foreigners, mostly Germans who find the prices in Hungary cheap. The cost of a sex massage is $50 at the official exchange rate.

Mr. Voros says he believes that by allowing pornography last summer, the authorities, then still Communist, were making a deliberate effort to siphon off political pressure.

"If we want to be truthful, it was used to take people's attentions from problems—like rising prices," he said. "By giving people pornography, travel and free passports, this was how they tried to cover up for the bad life."

"My goal is to have bad conditions," Mr. Voros said. "Then people will spend their sorrow on women and travel."

* * *

June 13, 1990

SOVIETS APPROVE LAW TO PROVIDE PRESS FREEDOMS

By FRANCIS X. CLINES
Special to The New York Times

MOSCOW, June 12—The Soviet Parliament today approved a law on freedom of the press that is intended to end decades of Government censorship and allow individual citizens to start newspapers.

The law, hailed by its supporters as the first in the nation's history to detail guarantees for journalists, is the latest step in the policy of glasnost, or increased openness, introduced by President Mikhail S. Gorbachev.

But the new law does not deal with what journalists say is the equally basic problem of the Government's monopoly on the limited supply of printing paper.

Sweeping Statement of Principle

As a statement of principle, the law is sweeping, flatly declaring, "Censorship of mass information is not allowed."

As a practical matter, its effects will be closely followed by such proponents as Anatoly Yezhelev, a member of Parliament and leader of the Leningrad Union of Journalists, who said tonight that free-press advocates had beaten back all "changes for the worse" and even established the right for any individual 18 years or older to begin a newspaper.

Critics of the new law had sought to keep newspaper publishing a prerogative of the nation's institutional and collective enterprises, a device that helped cement the Communist Party's long monopoly and still considerable residual powers over the nation's mass communications.

Newspaper and magazine workers have been complaining lately about the chronic shortage of newsprint and the Government's power to allocate it to preferred organs and diminish the voice of critics. But Mr. Yezhelev said the new law was shaped to address the basic principles needed for a free press.

He said the advent of a freer economy, which is being promised in the next five years by the Gorbachev Government, should make paper adequately and fairly available. In the meantime, he said, independent publishers can contract with job printers. But that process still relies ultimately on Government control and distribution of paper.

Party's Traditional Power

The press has been in a great state of flux, with public attention beginning to offset the party's traditional power in cases like that of Vladislav A. Starkov, editor of the nation's most popular newspaper, the weekly Argumenty i Fakty. He was targeted for removal by President Gorbachev but has held on to his job by simply refusing the Kremlin's demand that he leave.

At the same time, the Kremlin is accused of using publishing's economic factors as a lever. Sergei Zalygin, editor of Novy Mir, long the nation's most respected literary journal, has repeatedly complained that the Government has exploited the paper shortage to punish the more critical publications.

The press law was approved after months of revision and debate, with considerable attention paid to international human rights standards, which the Gorbachev Government has pledged to uphold in its campaign to gain full world standing and the economic benefits that might entail.

The new law does not satisfy all free-press advocates. Some are suspicious of a new requirement that newspapers be registered with central or local government executive councils. The penalty for publishing without official registration would be up to 200 rubles—about three weeks' salary for the average worker—plus possible confiscation of the newspaper and its plant.

Requirement Called Technical

But Mr. Yezhelev said that the registration requirement was not intended as a device for limiting the number of newspapers and that the law allowed "very few" grounds for rejecting potential publishers. He said the grounds were only technical ones like the concern that newspaper titles not be duplicated.

"All the main democratic articles we fought for were left in," Mr. Yezhelev said.

The articles in the law include a statement of journalists' rights, including the right to withhold bylines from "material distorted during editing" and to refuse assignments that run counter to personal convictions.

Newspapers will also have the right to try suing Government agencies that refuse to supply information. The risks of disclosing stories based on secret Government information are to rest with the sources, not with the newspaper that publishes the stories.

Soviet news outlets have changed considerably in Mr. Gorbachev's five years of power, principally in inviting and tolerating a greater degree of criticism of the Government. But the current political changes, in which insurgent political forces are scoring initial victories, have demonstrated the continuing power of the Communist Party in owning and physically controlling most printing presses and television stations.

Insurgent City Governments

Battles are being waged here and in Leningrad between new city governments controlled by insurgents and traditional party machines for communications power, with the party thus far maintaining its dominant edge and facing no threat of action in the traditionally weak Soviet court system.

The new law bars political interference in broadcasting and the press. It also bars newspapers from printing pornography, calls to violent overthrow of the Government or appeals to religious and racial intolerance.

The law also attempts to allow press enterprises to be more profit-motivated and independent of traditional bureaucracies, with the right to run their own finances and to open bank accounts. This is a right already extended theoretically in some other spheres, where critics say the bureaucrats still reign arbitrarily.

* * *

November 13, 1990

EAST EUROPE'S CULTURAL LIFE, ONCE A REFUGE, NOW ECLIPSED

By CELESTINE BOHLEN

Special to The New York Times

BUCHAREST, Romania—In Prague, theaters reported a sharp drop in attendance. In Budapest, no new feature films went into production for the first half of this year. Here in the Romanian capital, fewer books were published this year than in any year of the Communist dictatorship of Nicolae Ceausescu.

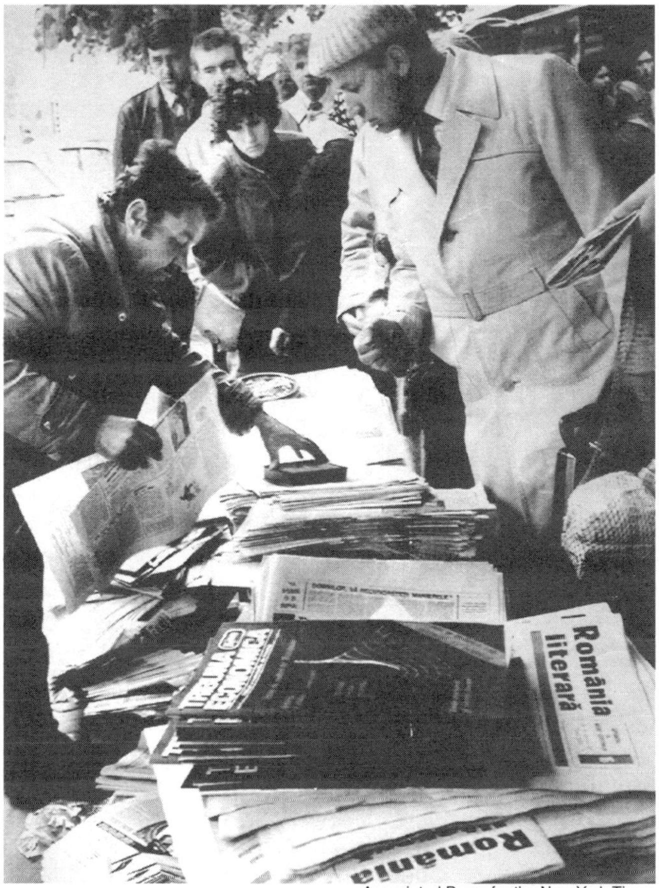

Associated Press for the New York Times

Romanian newspapers and journals, like those at a newsstand in Bucharest, have quadrupled in number to more than 1,200 since last December. They now consume most of the country's scarce supply of newsprint at the expense of book publishing.

As Eastern Europe assesses its first year in freedom, the verdict is that culture, once a refuge from Communist reality, became an unintended victim of its demise, as it lagged behind the real-life drama that was unfolding daily before people's eyes.

"Under totalitarianism, culture was a way of breathing normally," said Andre Plesu, a respected man of letters and Romania's Minister of Culture. "Now reality has become so absorbing that the streets, the television and the journals have confiscated the public interest, and people are no longer so thirsty for culture on a higher level."

Bewildering Swiftness of Change

For those who direct and produce, who write and read, the swiftness of the changes in Eastern Europe has been bewildering. Janos Zsombolyai, a Hungarian film maker, said he has still not figured out how to capture the moment on film, or how to draw the attention of a distracted audience.

"It is hard to find culture that would be in competition with this kind of fast craziness," he said. "What I think today could change tomorrow. Everything has become so strange. A year ago, the Communists ran the country. Today you can't find a Communist anywhere.

"Last December, I was shooting a film about the Hungarian uprising in 1956, and I came home, switched on the television and watched the revolution in Romania. I thought, what am I doing? We are sitting in the middle of a region where history is happening now. Maybe the best thing is just to take a camera and go out in the streets."

Now Bereft of Guides

Forced to match history's relentless pace, the societies of Eastern Europe this year were left strangely bereft of guides. With the cultural world paralyzed, the job of both witnessing and explaining events fell to the press and broadcasting, which many feel have proved inadequate to the challenge.

In virtually every country, the press was the first to benefit from the new conditions of freedom. Censorship was lifted almost overnight, information came flooding out of once-secret sources, and travel and foreign news became easily available. New newspapers opened, old ones changed their names, and people stood in line in cities and towns all over the region to buy publications offering everything from political analysis to pornography and scandal-mongering.

In Warsaw, the old clandestinely produced Solidarity newspaper quickly became the city's most popular paper when it gained legal status. At the same time, Trybuna Ludu, no longer powerful as the organ of the Communist Party, began calling itself the country's "leading opposition paper."

Since last December, the number of Romanian newspapers and journals has quadrupled to more than 1,200, and they now consume the bulk of the country's scarce supply of newsprint at the expense of book publishing.

"Before in Romania, no one read the newspapers and everybody read books," said Darie Novoceanu, a poet, critic and translator of Spanish literature who became editor of the Romanian newspaper Adevarul in December. "Now it is the reverse."

Has the Press Failed To Do Its Job?

Yet many feel the press in much of Eastern Europe has failed at its chief responsibility, to provide people with the information they needed to make the choices they suddenly faced. Instead, with some notable exceptions, readers often got either a powerful dose of polemics or prose so dense that they still had to read between the lines to find out what was going on.

"Neither the press nor the people had had freedom before, and both understand it badly," Mr. Novoceanu said. "The press has managed to set people against each other. Instead of making a society of 23 million Romanian citizens, it has created 23 million individuals, who have little love for each other."

In both Hungary and Romania, the newly elected Governments complain loudly and frequently that the main newspapers are overly critical and biased toward the opposition, while the opposition continues to lobby against state control of the most crucial medium of all, television.

Recently in Hungary, the two views clashed over coverage of the Oct. 26–28 taxi strike that opposed a 65 percent increase in gasoline prices and that ground the country to a halt. A spokesman for the governing Hungarian Democratic Forum argued that the strike might have been averted had the Government had a "loyal" broadcasting channel to report the reasons for the gasoline increase, while journalists published long critiques of the pro-Government bias of television's coverage of events.

In Poland, where a presidential election campaign is under way, the staff of Lech Walesa, the Solidarity chairman and front-running candidate, has repeatedly complained that the state-run television is presenting the election unfairly, favoring Mr. Walesa's major opponent, Prime Minister Tadeusz Mazowiecki. The Prime Minister leveled similar charges against some of the regional affiliates of Polish television, charging that they have allowed news presenters to slant their accounts in ways that benefited Mr. Walesa.

These kinds of skirmishes often reveal a deep confusion over the role of a free press. Some people talk about "too much" criticism of government as a dangerous luxury in societies where democratic institutions have shallow roots. Many newspaper editors see objective reporting as an abdication of their right to act as political players.

"We cannot refuse our duty to give the reader a political education," said Anton Uncu, editor of Romania Libera, the main opposition newspaper in Bucharest. "We are trying to decrease the ratio of opinion to information, but until the political situation settles down in Romania, the political commentary will have to continue. Besides, keeping an equal distance from all political points of view is in itself a political point of view."

Nationalism, an increasing force in politics in the region, puts additional pressures on the press. In Yugoslavia, newspapers in the rival republics of Croatia and Serbia provide shamelessly one-sided coverage of ethnic disputes. Defending the rights of a free press in one breath, the editor of a Romanian nationalist newspaper in the next asserted that anyone who challenges the Romanian view of history is an "enemy."

The Hungarian Foreign Minister, Geza Jeszenszky, got involved in a similar debate this fall when he publicly lobbied against the sale of a major Budapest daily to a Swedish newspaper, which, he said in an open letter, was "hostile or simply indifferent to the Hungarian nation."

Czechoslovakia, which has the strongest democratic traditions in Eastern Europe, has produced the most objective press, although some argue that it has been too slow to challenge President Vaclav Havel. It also has its blind spots, in particular the ongoing national debate over relations between Czechs and Slovaks.

Slovaks, who historically have felt slighted by what they see as Czech arrogance, complain that Prague newspapers fail to pay adequate attention to Bratislava, the capital of the Slovak Republic. Czech newspaper editors respond by saying they have difficulty sending good correspondents to live and report in the provinces.

In Romania, the press has been plagued by the same kind of free-wheeling distrust that has kept the country in a continuing state of instability. "In the beginning, there was a kind of euphoria," said Adrian Sirbu, the former Media Minister. "Everyone thought they were free. Afterward began the witch hunt, when anytime someone hated someone else they accused them of being Communists, or neo-Communists."

In some countries—particualarly the Balkan nations of Romania, Bulgaria and Yugoslavia—freedom of the press has already proved to be a fragile notion. When bands of miners descended on Bucharest in June to clean the capital of anti-Government demonstrators, one of their first targets was Romania Liberia. Led by a man later identified as a former member of Mr. Ceausescu's secret police, a group of miners used threats of violence to shut the paper down for three days.

"Yes, there is freedom of the press," Mr. Uncu said. "But what good is it when the journalist is afraid to print the truth because of death threats or miners are ready to stop the presses? This paper has proved to be uncomfortable for somebody."

As in much of Western Europe, people have to buy several newspapers to get a range of political opinion. The difference is that Eastern Europeans have less experience of sorting them out.

Revolution Shakes Journalism Too

The changes that shook the region last year stunned journalists too. Editors say they still have to fight off a tendency by their reporters to climb on a soapbox, or to use verbal formulas that have no meaning.

The transitions for Romanian journalists was particularly rough given the extent to which the press had been compromised by the Ceausescu regime. "Freedom came like a typhoon," Mr. Uncu said. "The journalists were not ready. We had to recoup our moral sense and even the Romanian language itself, which had been strangled by propaganda."

How much of a change actually took place in the Romanian press is still a matter of debate. "The press that appeared in January was totally different from the one that existed on Dec. 22, but it was put out by the same people," Mr. Novoceanu of Adevarul said. "What that proved was that the same people are capable of putting out two different kinds of newspapers."

Many Eastern European countries are only now grappling with laws dealing with press ownership—how to privatize the press, how much foreign investment to allow and how to monitor state involvement. These issues have typically been most volatile in Romania, where the editors of Romania Libera recently declared the newspapers independence by simply assuming ownership of what had been a Government-owned operation. In another showdown, the Government threatened to cut off all subsidies to state-run television.

Many of the new newspapers and journals that sprang up in the early months of democracy are expected to fail under the weight of market forces. In Hungary, foreign press magnates have already bought up shares in several major dailies, but there is some uncertainty about how many Hungarian newspapers will survive the coming competition over readers and advertisers.

Most of Eastern Europe's new governments are committed to continuing state support for the arts, but again, the debate over how aid is to be distributed has only begun. One issue, for instance, involves who should take responsibility for supporting provincial theater, the central Government or local jurisdictions. Movie and theater prices have gone up, but many fear that if they go up much higher, attendance will fall off even more sharply, as people turn to the wide selection of entertainment now available from videos and cable television.

Public Prefers Foreign Films

After the first rush to print once-forbidden books by dissidents and leading cultural figures, book publishers are also finding it difficult to keep up with the demand for mass-market foreign books. An added problem in many countries is that writers, like President Havel of Czechoslovakia, are now so deeply involved in politics that they have no time to write.

Eastern European film studios are also up against stiff foreign competition, as Hollywood box office hits open in cities like Budapest within weeks of their release in the United States. Having recently won freedom from censorship, no one wants to now step in with a new set of controls. Still, many worry how their national cultures will survive the trend to commercialization.

"We are a small country, and a small language area," said Mr. Zsombolyai, the Hungarian film maker. "The wrong way would be to have some kind of control. The right way is to help our Hungarian films. We have no other choice."

But Hungarian films, which until now have been heavily protected against market forces, tend not to draw big audiences. This year, for instance, Hungarian films have focused almost exclusively on a re-examination of 1956, the year of the Budapest uprising and its suppression by the Soviets. The three feature films and dozens of film and television documentaries devoted to the subject have been released.

"We all fear losing our public," Mr. Zsombolyai said. "The question is what kind of movies would be best to win back the Hungarian audience."

With pressure of inflation and economic hard times mounting, some see the fight to preserve Eastern Europe's unique and rich cultures as a doomed one. Not long ago, Mr. Novoceanu was incensed to learn that Bucharest's best book store, once a haven for the city's intelligentsia, was being closed and a French-owned electronics store moving in to take its place.

"We tried to save it, but it was no use," he said. "Culture is now being thrown from the center into the margins."

* * *

December 11, 1991

FREED FROM CENSORSHIP, CULTURE IN HUNGARY NOW SUFFERS LACK OF SECURITY

By HENRY KAMM

Special to The New York Times

BUDAPEST—Censored and pampered, troubled and self-satisfied in the Communist decades, the creators of Hungary's always vigorous cultural life are seeking their bearings two years after the coming of democracy and a market economy.

No firm principles and practices have yet taken the place of the contradictions and compromises that governed literature, theater and films under Communist rule.

The former rulers treated artists in varied ways—privileged if they echoed the prevailing line, people to be bought off for keeping divergent views out of their works, or opponents to be suppressed. But few artists were permanently either friends or foes, and much creative energy of writers, composers, choreographers and performers was spent making arrangements with the guardians of culture.

With the Paper, Money

But however uncertain were the chances of publication or performance, material security was assured through membership in the official unions, which guaranteed a steady salary and a steady job.

"There were several great advantages in totalitarian culture," said Laszlo Rajk, an artist and theatrical and film designer. "If you got the paper that you're an artist, you got your money."

Now, artistic expression is unhampered, but the security based on full state subsidy has vanished. With it has gone the sheer quantity of performances, which assured that even in country towns, almost any evening a Hungarian could go to a play, opera, ballet or concert.

"Now," said Laszlo Rigo, director of the Vigado, a leading concert hall in Budapest, "I can tell a musician that I'm sorry, but he should not be a soloist but play in an orchestra."

The price for a higher standard of performance in his hall, he said, is a drastic reduction in the number of concerts. Instead of the 150 performances a year, Mr. Rigo said there would be 30 this year.

All orchestras are maintained by the Government, with the railroad system and the post office sponsoring leading ensembles. "All are in danger now," said Ildiko Gedenyi, director of an artist management agency.

Budapest's city administration has issued an international appeal for donations to buy instruments for the Budapest Festival Orchestra, giving it the chance to become the city's permanent ensemble.

With the removal of ideological barriers, cultural life has been fully opened to foreign artists. So far, many cultural figures interviewed said, the results have been catastrophic for Hungarians.

This has been particularly true in movies, said Janos Zsombolyai, a director and president of a new production company, who added that American movies are killing the Hungarian industry.

Flood of American Films

The first result of the coming of capitalism, the director said, was the forming of American-Hungarian distribution companies, which have flooded the market with American films. No Hungarian film of the last two years has stood the box-office test against Hollywood competition, Mr. Zsombolyai said.

"That's our biggest problem," he said. "We can't compete."

Mr. Zsombolyai said that film makers, assured of subsidies, concentrated more on artistic achievement and slipping political points past censors than on drawing crowds to movie houses.

"Films were a safety valve for the system," the director said. "We were happy; we felt we were doing something. But what can we do now?"

Quite a different view came from Andras Kereszty, managing editor and former Washington correspondent of the newspaper Nepszabadsag. "They were boring, useless movies," Mr. Kereszty said. "I hated these films."

Nepszabadsag, the former Communist Party daily, has come under control of the Bertelsmann publishing conglomerate from Germany and is anti-Communist Hungary's most popular newspaper.

The Government continues an annual subsidy to the movie industry of about $10 million, to be distributed by a board of artists and public figures. But 30 percent inflation has drained its purchasing power and reduced the number of films produced to half the former 20 to 25 a year—this even though film making in Hungary is cheap by American standards. Here, a feature film can still be made for around $1 million.

Writers and publishers are strained, too. The market for serious books has "collapsed," said Miklos Vasarhelyi, who as director of a foundation created by George Soros, a Hungarian-born New York financier, has been a major force since the late Communist period in supporting independent cultural ventures.

"Violence and tear-jerkers, sex and pornography, have flooded the market and make it hard to get anything serious published," he said.

Books Are Harder to Sell

Gyorgy Konrad, novelist and president of International PEN, the writers' organization, said that as Communist authority waned in 1989, his books, for many years published only abroad, had been issued in editions of up to 70,000. Now, he said, the entire book market is down, whether serious or popular work. His books come out in editions of 10,000.

He faulted the distribution system, in which inefficient state-owned outlets continue and private stores have not taken root. "Socialism doesn't work any more," he said, "and capitalism hasn't begun to work yet."

Theater subsidies have been maintained, but are also shrunk by inflation. Gabor Zsambeki, director of the Katona Jozsef Theater, said the cuts in subsidies were pushing the stage toward some commercialization.

"I'm not against that," he said. "It's the duty of the state to support theater, but not all theater." He cited operetta and cabaret as forms that he felt should be self-sustaining. "The art theater is the real question," the director said. "The real danger is the same in all branches of culture—that real values will not be supported any more."

"Rubbish is spreading," Mr. Zsambeki said. "The repertory is much lighter. Before, in the biggest theaters in Budapest, you could see Shakespeare. Now you see the complete works of Andrew Lloyd Webber."

Danger in the Provinces

Mr. Zsambeki said theater outside Budapest faced great danger. "They had their own orchestras, own ballet," he said. "Perhaps they will have to send them away."

At the State Opera, considered the jewel in Hungary's cultural crown, Sandor Venczel, the financial director, said that ensemble pride was suffering as singers discovered that they could earn more in one performance at a German opera house than in months of work at the Hungarian State Opera.

The average singer here earns about $400 a month, an orchestra player $300 and a stagehand $200.

But Mr. Venczel said the State Opera was benefiting from an opportunity presented by the even less favorable conditions that liberalization had brought to the Soviet Union. He said the company was employing four or five first-rate Soviet singers, for whom coming here means about the same as going to the West does for Hungarian artists.

* * *

March 6, 1992

AT MOSCOW BOOK PARTY, MEMORIES OF A TIME OF REPRESSION FLOW FREELY

By SERGE SCHMEMANN
Special to The New York Times

MOSCOW, March 5—Several of the writers and intellectuals who gathered today to celebrate the publication of the Literary Almanac Metropol pointed with some satisfaction to the fact that they were meeting in the former Soviet Ministry of Culture on the anniversary of Stalin's death in 1953.

These were the very forces that had delayed the publication of the almanac in Moscow for some 13 years. Back in those now-distant days known as the "period of stagnation," the collection by 23 writers, many well known and quite "official," provoked so strong a response from the jealous state that Metropol became something of a benchmark for literary repression.

Now, gathered among admiring friends, many of them successful and respected as scarred veterans of the brutal struggle for freedom of expression, they gathered to celebrate and, like veterans everywhere, to tell a few war stories and to reminisce about times that were a lot tougher, but perhaps a lot simpler.

"I remember how naïvely we planned a champagne buffet back then to launch the almanac," recalled Yevgeny Rein, a poet and film writer "We discussed what kind of herring to order, whether to invite this prima donna or that one, since everybody knew they would not attend the same party.

But I see there's some champagne waiting here. Maybe now we can finally drink it—Veuve Cliquot, I believe, of a 13-year vintage."

Police Arrive, Uninvited

The champagne was neither French nor vintage, but no matter. Thirteen years back, the planned party at the Cafe Rhythm, a popular music club, was blocked by the police, who declared that the cafe was infested by cockroaches and threw a huge cordon around it.

The writers were hauled before the Union of Writers, which organized a smear campaign in the press and ousted two young organizers of the project, Viktor Yerofeyev and Yevgeny Popov. In every way possible, the culture watchdogs let it be known that they would never surrender any of their iron ideological grip on the arts.

What made the incident especially notable was that the writers were not "dissidents," in the sense of the word at the time. They were all recognized or rising artists—stars of the 1960's like the poets Bella Akhmadulina and Andrei Voznesensky or the writers Fazil Iskander, Andrei Bitov and Vasily Aksyonov, honored veterans like Semyon Lipkin, a poet and translator, and his wife, Inna Lisnyanskaya, a poet too, or national heroes like the bard Vladimir Vysotsky.

There were also underground stars like Yuz Aleshkovsky, whose ironic song "Comrade Stalin, You're a Great Scholar," was known across the land, and Genrikh Sapgir, who had begun writing illicit works in the late 1940's.

All were joined by the hope that attempting an uncensored collection of writings might gain for literature the same small measure of independence that painters had achieved after the celebrated bulldozing of an unsanctioned outdoor exhibition in 1977. But the time was not ripe: driven underground at home, Metropol was published in the United States and France.

The coming of freedom found the writers far afield.

Some had flourished—Mr. Yerofeyev was in Italy promoting his best-selling novel, "Russian Beauty," Mr. Popov had just returned from a fellowship in Bavaria. Mark Rozovsky had his own theater, "Theater at the Nikitsky Gates." Many others were being published voluminously.

Some had gone abroad—Mr. Aksyonov to the United States, Yuri Karabchiyevsky, a writer, to Israel, Fridrikh Gorenshtein, a scriptwriter, to Germany. One, Yuri Kublanovsky, a poet, had "re-immigrated" and was fighting to be restored to citizenship. Mr. Vysotsky, the legendary bard, died in 1980.

But like veterans of any war, those who survived and those who gathered today seemed to cherish the memories of the common struggle and to recall with a twinge of longing the days when the sides were still clearly drawn.

"They were years of humiliation and hardship, but they were our happiest years," Mr. Popov said. "We worked well together, we respected and appreciated each other, we were friends."

Others recalled how the compilers worked to glue the pages together by hand. They paid tribute to Tanya Pavlova, the sole typist, who later committed suicide, and to Carl Proffer, the late American publisher of Ardis books who published Metropol and many another repressed writer.

Semyon Lipkin, at 81 the gentle and universally respected elder of the group, read a recent poem of his called "Soldier's Memory" in which he invoked the front of long ago:

How freely I breathed then
How difficult it is to breathe now

"Of course it was all simpler then," he said. "The division of forces was exactly as at the front—we were right, and they were scoundrels. Now it's difficult to believe in anybody's words, words don't match deeds, nobody knows what will become of our Russia. I want to believe Russia will live, but I'm not certain I'll live to see it."

The Joy of Reunion

But there was also the joy of a triumphant reunion. And that they were triumphant, there was no question—the hall in which they met was in the old Soviet Ministry of Culture, whose spacious headquarters was turned over to the Actors' Union after the Soviet Union was disbanded.

There were plenty of jokes along those lines. "Please wait for the camera," somebody said, and after a pause everybody broke out laughing—"camera" in Russian is also a prison isolation ward.

"What we need to do now is something as bold in today's circumstances as 'Metropol' was then," said Mr. Popov, a richly bearded Siberian with a keen eye for the ironies of his world. "I know, let's raise 23 pigs!"

* * *

December 25, 1994

IN BOSNIA, THE WAR THAT CAN'T BE SEEN

By ROGER COHEN

ZAGREB, Croatia—The Bosnian war is increasingly invisible. Its most recent crises, at Bihac in western Bosnia and Gorazde in the east, have had enormous repercussions around the world, but the two small towns themselves have remained lost in the fog of second-hand reporting. Western journalists, almost without exception, have been unable to get there.

The result is troubling, and the reports sometimes baffling. Serbian forces advance and advance and advance across towns you can drive through in five minutes. Villages are taken, then retaken by the same army a few days later. Casualty figures swing wildly, reported by local witnesses who may be hunkered down in their basements or distant from the scene.

The precise locality of photographs is often vague. Television crews plead for "bang-bang pictures" from commanders not above a touch of stage management.

The bizarre situation thus created in Bosnia is that journalists' access to information stands in inverse proportion to the volume of sophisticated gear they carry around to communicate what they know. The very possibility of instantaneous and worldwide transmission, it seems, has made the facts that much more politically explosive and so that much more necessary to conceal.

The Usual Reasons

Of course, there have been attempts to limit or censor reporting in most wars. The Pentagon set strict standards for the gulf war that provoked the ire of many editors. But concern over divulging military information has usually been the main consideration behind the constraints.

In Bosnia, where attempts to manage and manipulate the press are now accorded as much importance by Muslims and Serbs as maneuvers on the battlefield, the concern is much wider: that any graphic image or report could shift public opinion and so public policy. Thus does information become suspect and the journalist dangerous.

It took a while to learn this in Bosnia. The war was chaotic in the early months and more treacherous. But there were few restrictions. In August, 1992, I crossed the Bosnian border from Serbia in a bus full of Serbian volunteers armed to the teeth, and I followed them to the hills overlooking Sarajevo: telling images—too telling for today's bureaucratic and intensely media-conscious managers of the war in the Serbian stronghold of Pale and in Sarajevo.

The responsibility for the war's increasing disappearance from view lies with both sides, but particularly the Serbs, and with the United Nations, for its apparent complicity in this exercise.

Acutely aware that a strong press report can affect U.N. sanctions or NATO's role, the Serbs have taken to sealing off areas under their control. The United Nations has allowed them to do so. The Muslim-led Bosnian Government has also become more restrictive, limiting access to advances in central Bosnia, perhaps out of concern that its image as victim could be affected.

When was a reporter last in Srebrenica, the seething and Serbian-encircled Muslim enclave in eastern Bosnia? Or in Gorazde? When another shell hits the Bihac hospital, what does that really look like? As for Zepa, another eastern enclave, no western reporter has managed to get there since it was surrounded by the Serbs.

At the end of the Gorazde crisis last April, Lieut. Gen. Sir Michael Rose took to berating the Sarajevo press for inflating Muslim casualties and so, he claimed, almost precipitating World War III. Why, then, I asked him, would he not put a handful of reporters into one of the U.N. helicopters then going to the town? Oh no, he replied, that would irritate the Serbs and cut off U.N. access to Gorazde. When I suggested he was kowtowing to the Serbs, he got angry.

But that, in essence, is the United Nations' policy toward the press. There is scant evidence that General Rose, or anybody else, has pressed the Serbs to allow journalists into Muslim enclaves, and on no occasion has the United Nations taken the initiative in deciding that information was more important than the Serbs' objections.

Announcing last week that journalists would henceforth be allowed on United Nations flights in Bosnia, Kofi A. Annan, the United Nations under-secretary for peace operations, said: "Peacekeeing operations in particular depend for their support on widespread public awareness of the conflicts, and we are committed to doing everything we can to facilitate the work of the media." Up to now, however, this has not been the case.

In the Line of Duty

Of course, it is not the United Nations' business to do journalists' work for them. It is always possible to try to circumvent restrictions, by walking over a mountain and across a front line, for example. But in this conflict, where such courage has not generally been lacking, 46 journalists have been killed—far more than in Vietnam.

Journalists have been directly targeted, particularly by the Serbs, who think they are biased against them. Last month, Luc Delahaye of the Magnum photo agency and a colleague were picked up by the Serbs just north of the Bihac pocket. They were held for two days, kicked, punched, doused in cold water in freezing rooms, threatened with death, made to lean against walls with their entire body weight on their heads until they collapsed, kicked again and repeatedly interrogated. "Every time I would deny that I was a spy for the Muslims and say I worked for Magnum, I braced myself for the next blow," Mr. Delahaye said. "You say the word—Magnum—and you know what it will trigger."

For "Magnum," the word "journalist" could easily be substituted. The Muslim-led government and the Serbs, not used to any open flow of information after five decades of Communist rule, have come increasingly to see international reporters as either tools or enemies.

It is not just in Bosnia that information is under attack. In another bitter conflict, in Algeria, 24 journalists have been killed in the last two years. The most recent, Said Mekbel, the editor of Le Matin of Algiers, was assassinated by Islamic fundamentalists on December 3. In his last, prophetic article, he wrote:

"This thief who, at night, hugs the walls as he walks home, is him. This father who recommends to his children never to mention his profession is him. This vagabond who does not know where to spend the night is him. This man who swears he will not die with his throat cut is him. He is all these things, and he is only a journalist."

* * *

June 8, 1995

WITH OLD TRICKS, ROMANIA'S OLD REDS CURB PRESS

By JANE PERLEZ

BUCHAREST, Romania—On the top floor of a Communist-era apartment block, Neculai Munteanu dons headphones and readies himself before the microphone of a jerry-built hi-tech radio studio for his show, "News for the Trash Can."

His breakfast-time barbs are delivered in a crackling style: How is President Ion Iliescu, a foe of the deposed Romanian monarchy, going to treat the visiting Duchess of York? Why is his rendition of the Romanian flute so weak compared with Bill Clinton's lusty sax?

Mr. Munteanu, a reporter for Radio Free Europe whom Romanians used to tune into secretly, is back home poking fun at the Government. His presence shows that freedom of the press has made a start in a country where such an idea would have been laughed at six years ago.

But Mr. Munteanu acknowledges that it still has a long way to go.

"There is freedom of the press and opinion; it's the most important acquisition of the revolution," Mr. Munteanu, 53, said. "But our greatest problem is the average Romanian does not understand this, does not understand the issues and still lives in terrible misery. There's no such thing as a civil society here. But God himself needed seven days to create the world."

Since the overthrow and execution of Nicolae Ceausescu in 1989, the coalition Government of former Communists and nationalists manipulates the levers of the mass media in ways learned under one of Communism's most successful propaganda machines.

The Government controls the only nationwide television channel and has taken recent steps to prevent competition. At 8 every night, about 80 percent of the television audience watches the Government's stodgy newscast dominated by President Iliescu and his aides.

The 14 newspapers that Mr. Munteanu tucks under his arm on the way to work give a deceptive impression. The papers, many of them filled with sex and fantasy that pass as news, have plunged in circulation, in part because of the Government's control of newsprint production and distribution.

Private FM radio stations like Mr. Munteanu's reach only small audiences. Private television stations have opened in Bucharest and in the countryside but are restricted by regulation to local penetration.

Similar problems trouble television and the press in the region. Even in Hungary and Poland, the Governments, composed of former Communists, remain uneasy with press freedom. But in Romania old habits seem harder to shed.

In the heady days of 1990, opposition newspapers opened. Romania Libra, an avowedly opposition newspaper, sold 1.5 million copies at its peak in 1992. But its circulation has dropped to 140,000 today, because, says Petre Bacanu, editor in chief, of the Government's control of newsprint production.

Only one newsprint plant exists in Romania, at an antiquated site more than 120 miles northeast of Bucharest. To make sure that he gets his ration, Mr. Bacanu says, he sends out a car to follow the newsprint truck along the route to Bucharest to insure that the driver does not stop and get drunk or that if the truck breaks down it is fixed. "If we didn't do that, the newsprint wouldn't arrive," he said.

With a national election scheduled next year and widespread irritation among Romanians at their dismal standard of living, the Iliescu Government appears determined to maintain its television monopoly.

Thus, the governing coalition postponed indefinitely a tender it opened last year for a national commercial television station. It had received bids from three private Bucharest channels, including one owned by the former tennis star Ion Tiriac.

The Government has also blocked the establishment of a 13-member board intended to guarantee the independence of the national television station, a move that was supposed to satisfy fairness criteria established by the Council of Europe.

Dumitru Iuga, the leader of the trade union at the station, went on a monthlong hunger strike in March to protest the Government's refusal to accept the two board members elected by the television workers.

"From a political point of view it would be better for the Government to show they're having a dialogue and to be able to say, 'Look, we have these people from the opposition on the board,'" said Mr. Munteanu, who was one of the two people chosen by the employees. "But in my opinion the Government believes, 'Those who are not with us are against us.' "

Mihai Tatulici, one of Romania's most prominent television journalists, who worked for the Government channel but who left last year to join one of Bucharest's private stations, said it was proving difficult for private television to compete.

The other day security guards at Channel 7, where Mr. Tatulici works, forbade him from entering the studio, because, he said, his show was called "The Presence of Extremists in the Government," a topic selected after the coalition chose two new ministers from its nationalist party partner. Mr. Tatulici said the station's owners apparently did not want to offend their friends in power.

But in a society that was trained to be silent in the Ceausescu era, the recent flowering of radio talk shows has been surprising.

Radio Total's show "Watchdog" recently featured two newspaper reporters with documents about corruption in the Customs Department. To the reporters' astonishment, one caller was a customs official who wanted advice on how to remain conscientious in the face of temptation.

* * *

July 23, 1995

IRON FIST MEETS RUBBER FACE

By ALESSANDRA STANLEY

MOSCOW—Russians have always loved a political joke, mostly because the punchline has always been illicit. Before 1917, people could be put in jail for publicly mocking the Czar. In Communist times, the slightest crack about party leaders landed people in Siberia. (Aleksandr Solzhenitsyn, not usually known for his sense of humor, was sent to the Gulag for irreverently describing Stalin as "the mustached one," in a letter to a friend.)

Under Mikhail Gorbachev's perestroika, the rules slackened a bit, and high-minded satire began slipping onto radio and television, but never anything as low-down and biting as the average Reagan skit on "Saturday Night Live."

Most Russians therefore were not entirely shocked last week when the Government moved against the popular satirical puppet show "Kukly," a weekly program modeled on Britain's "Spitting Image" and France's "Les Guignols de Lenfo." Unlike France or Britain, Russia does not have a tradition of indulging political satire.

But even in Russia there was something comical about the state cracking down on inanimate rubber enemies.

The prosecutor general opened a criminal case against the creators of the show, which is aired on NTV, Russia's only nationwide independent station. The charge was that "the highest officials in the Government were portrayed in an insulting manner." It was the first time since Boris N. Yeltsin became president that a law prohibiting insults of high officials was invoked against a television show.

"Kukly" (the word means "puppets") first aired a year ago, and it mercilessly tweaks the authorities on such issues as privatization and the fall of the ruble. The life-size puppets are modeled on various political figures, including President Yeltsin and Prime Minister Viktor S. Chernomyrdin.

The show often falls back on Russian classics to make a contemporary point. An episode about the Chechen war, which ran in January when the Russian invasion of Chechnya was at its most brutal, featured puppets dressed as 19th century characters from Lermontov's novel "Hero of Our Time," which describes Russia's efforts to conquer the fierce warriors of the Caucasus. The writers used Lermontov's text for dialogue about the current war in Chechnya.

On "Kukly," the digs are rarely personal—there are no send-ups of the private lives or family foibles of the nation's leaders. But just the sight of puppet caricatures of Mr. Yeltsin or his unpopular Minister of Defense, Pavel Grachev, bobbing, weaving, and talking in vulgar street slang, is titillating enough for many viewers.

The show that caught the attention of the prosecutor general aired on July 8th, and used Maxim Gorky's play "The Lower Depths" as the background for a skit on the new minimum wage of $10.00 a month. It portrayed Mr. Yeltsin and Mr. Chernomyrdin and others as flophouse bums, drunkenly rummaging through garbage and singing old Soviet patriotic songs that, for Russians, recall Stalinist times.

Otto Pohi for The New York Times

Last week, the Yeltsin puppet from "Kukly" learned the limits of his power.

The whiff of alcohol alone may have offended official viewers. Mr. Yeltsin's drinking, which has gotten sufficiently out of hand on numerous public occasions to generate news stories abroad, is handled quite gingerly in the mainstream Russian press. Columnists deplore the President's rowdy "behavior" without directly mentioning the root cause.

Warning: Election Ahead

But few in Russia really believed that the prosecutor general acted solely out of concern for Mr. Yeltsin's sensibilities. Igor Malashenko, the president of NTV, insisted the case was a ploy to punish the station for its aggressive coverage of the war in Chechnya. He and others claimed that the action was a warning that was linked to the upcoming election campaign. Mr. Malashenko said he did not expect the case to ever get to court, and said the producers planned to run another episode of "Kukly," a rerun, to test the waters.

Action and Reaction

Officials of the state-controlled television network, ORT, agree that the Government wants to rein in the airwaves as the election campaign approaches. "Definitely, with the election campaign in the offing, television has been subject to more attention from the authorities," said Aleksei Pushkov, director of public affairs at ORT.

"The real question is whether the authorities plan to use a velvet glove or an iron fist," he added. Mr. Pushkov said he found the July 8th "Kukly" show offensive, but noted that the Government's reaction to it was equally deplorable. "The 'Kukly' case—this was an iron fist."

* * *

October 9, 1996

CROATIA CHIEF SEEKS TO MUZZLE A RADIO THAT AIDED HIS RISE

By CHRIS HEDGES

ZAGREB, Croatia, Oct. 8—A retired Croatian general, critical of President Franjo Tudjman's drive to turn this small country into a military power in the Balkans, took to the airwaves today to spell out what he said was the folly of such a course.

"We don't have the human, material or economic resources to be a regional military power," said the general, Antun Tus. "Our future should be in alliances, not in exhausting ourselves to build up our armed forces."

The broadcast was made over Radio 101, the last independent radio station in Croatia. It highlighted the fight by the dwindling number of news organizations in the Balkans to broadcast views contrary to those of the ruling parties that govern the six republics in the former Yugoslavia.

But Radio 101, which often gave air time to Mr. Tudjman when he was a dissident challenging the Communist authorities, may soon be silenced by the man who used its studios as a platform to build his political career. And its demise, many contend, would effectively end any hope for independent news media.

"There is very little diversity now in the Croatian press," said Marvin L. Stone, a former editor in chief of U.S. News and World Report and a visiting fellow at Zagreb University. "The Government has either tamed, taken over or closed nearly all independent media. As far as Eastern Europe goes, only Serbia is in the same league as Croatia. President Tudjman is always parading, talking or smiling on the state-run television. There is no room for the opposition."

New restrictive press laws, including a decision by officials at the Interior Ministry to limit the visas of foreign correspondents to three months, have been passed recently despite requests by Croatia's European and American allies to end a Government crackdown on the press. A new press law promulgated this month, intended to bolster Croatia's bid to join the Council of Europe, gives the Government the power to force newspapers to run corrections or clarifications and sets the qualifications for chief editors.

There are troubling signs that Radio 101, which for 13 years braved the intolerance of Communist and nationalist politicians alike, will be turned over to Tudjman supporters when its license expires in November. The Government commission that is deciding who will be awarded the frequency now used by the radio station has been busy the last few weeks handing out radio frequencies to party loyalists.

The station, with a 32 percent share of the Zagreb audience, according to independent telephone surveys, dwarfs that of any other radio station in the city. It can be heard by nearly a quarter of Croatia's 4.7 million people. And its listeners say that losing the station would recall the days of a dictatorship many hoped had ended when Croatia declared its independence five years ago.

"The radio is a symbol," said Nenad Vukadinovic, a lawyer. "It has given a voice, and hope, to those of us who yearn to see this country become a European democracy."

The governing political party, the Croatian Democratic Union, controls all television and radio, along with three of the four national newspapers. The three independent newspapers are all currently fighting several Government-backed lawsuits, any one of which, if successful, would throw them into bankruptcy. The suits were filed shortly after a new law was passed this year making it illegal to criticize the President or other top Government officials. Government tax inspectors have also been searching newsrooms and combing the newspapers' record books looking for irregularities.

The radio station, which broadcasts out of a cramped two-story building in downtown Zagreb, pumps out round-the-clock programming that includes popular call-in shows and rock music, although the 800-watt transmitter strains to reach the outskirts of the city. Reporters, editors and announcers often get their pay two or three months late.

Natasha Babic, a 30-year-old producer, stood recently in the door of a small studio, equipped with antiquated reel-to-reel tape players and old sound-mixers and turntables.

"The tactics used by the Communists to try to silence us are about the same used by Tudjman's Government," she said. "And this is because, in many cases, we are still dealing with the same people."

* * *

October 15, 1998

SERBIA SHUTS 2 MORE PAPERS, SAYING THEY CREATED PANIC

By JANE PERLEZ

BELGRADE, Serbia, Oct. 14—Less than 24 hours after the American special envoy Richard C. Holbrooke swept out of here with a peace plan for Kosovo province, the man he negotiated with for nine days shut down two newspapers and renewed a decree against the freedom of the press.

The actions today against what remains of the independent news media in Yugoslavia by the Government of President Slobodan Milosevic were a continuation of the censorship and shutdowns that started nearly two weeks ago. Those actions came when NATO threatened air strikes because of the crackdown on ethnic Albanians in Kosovo.

The Minister of Information, Aleksandar Vucic, accused the two newspapers, Danas and Dnevni Telegraf, of "fomenting defeatism, panic and fear."

A third newspaper, Nasa Borba, received a similar letter from Mr. Vucic later today and there were expectations that its offices would also be sealed by plainclothes policemen.

Slavko Curuvija, the editor in chief of Dnevni Telegraf, a newspaper with reliable sources inside the Government, said the Information Ministry had taken exception to a headline that said, "NATO authorizes attacks, Milosevic signs plan."

In a statement today, the Ministry of Information said: "We urge the media to place their editorial policies in the function of preserving the territorial integrity, sovereignty and independence of Serbia and Yugoslavia."

The crackdown on the news media—which includes the closure of two independent radio stations last week and the banning of Serbian-language broadcasts relayed from the BBC, the Voice of America and Radio Free Europe—appeared to be part of a well-organized campaign by Mr. Milosevic to consolidate his power in the wake of his concessions over Kosovo.

In targeting the outlets in Serbia that print or broadcast news that differs from the official point of view, reporters and editors said Mr. Milosevic was yet again using his technique of stirring up xenophobic feelings to justify strict censorship.

"The number of newspapers and radio stations is decreasing every day," said Veran Matic, the founder of B-92, a Belgrade radio station that has expanded to incorporate a network of stations with 1.6 million listeners around Serbia and Montenegro, the two republics that make up what remains of Yugoslavia.

From the top of a mountain of papers and books on his desk, Mr. Matic picked up a fax from the Ministry of Information. It was a notice saying that the decree issued last week insisting that the news media only print or air material in the national interest would be continued indefinitely.

Mr. Matic, 37—with little capital, some small subscriber donations and grants from the American Government and Western foundations—has built the Association of Independent Electronic Media over the last nine years. The 34 local radio and 18 television stations that belong to the group are considered counterculture here because they disseminate Western liberal views in contrast to the Serbian propaganda that dominates the state-run television and radio.

The member stations receive programming such as entertainment tapes as well as Serbian-language news broadcasts from abroad. Two member stations were closed last week—Radio Index in Belgrade and Radio Senta, a Hungarian-language station in northern Serbia—and Mr. Matic is deeply worried that B-92, the heart of the association, will be among the next targets.

For Mr. Matic, who met with Hillary Rodham Clinton last month and with Vice President Al Gore last year, one of the biggest disappointments of the last week has been the virtual silence about the press crackdown from the American Government.

The United States Agency for International Development is one of the major financial backers of B-92.

"They have abandoned us here," Mr. Matic said of the Administration. "That means the whole story about supporting democracy here is not altogether honest. This time there hasn't been any pressure from governments, only from groups like the Committee to Protect Journalists, Human Rights Watch and Article 19," he said, listing nongovernmental organizations.

The Committee to Protect Journalists issued a statement expressing alarm over the threats against the independent news media here. Kati Marton, the wife of Mr. Holbrooke, is a member of the board of directors of the committee and a former chairman.

"The core of the problem is that Milosevic was allowed to destroy the democratic opposition and in the same way he will be allowed to destroy the independent media," Mr. Matic said, referring to the lukewarm support Washington gave the Belgrade street demonstrations against Mr. Milosevic two years ago.

Like many opponents of the Milosevic regime—journalists, academics, students—Mr. Matic is puzzled by the seemingly singular devotion to Mr. Milosevic by senior American officials who come here.

"I've never met Mr. Holbrooke or Ambassador Christopher Hill," he said. Mr. Hill, who visits Belgrade fairly often on the Kosovo issue, worked alongside Mr. Holbrooke in the latest negotiations.

LATIN AMERICA

July 9, 1975

BRAZIL EASING SOME CURBS, BUT ARTS STAY UNDER A STERN CENSOR

By MARVINE HOWE
Special to The New York Times

RIO DE JANEIRO, July 6—Brazil has fiery debates in Congress on human rights, newspaper denunciations of political corruption and even incipient student strikes, but a political song or a racy play is still taboo.

The authoritarian military Government is beginning to relax controls over the press, politics and the universities, but there has been no perceptible Jetup in the arts.

Protests against the recent ban on a play by a popular playwright have swollen into a national campaign against censorship of the arts.

For a time the authorities had appeared receptive, and there have been persistent reports about some new agency that would not do away with government controls but would at least bring some rationale to procedures that are arbitrary, erratic and often senseless. Now that the whole liberalization process, seems to be stalled any relaxation is viewed as doubtful.

Easier Mood for a Time

President Ernesto Geisel, an austere general, came to power in March, 1974, with a pledge to return slowly to the democratic system after a decade of military rule based on law and order and development. The military established censorship, as soon as it came to power, there were periods of easing, but controls were tightened with the unrest of 1968–69 and the harsh repression that followed.

In his first year President Geisel brought an easier atmosphere, widely referred to as "decompression." There were free congressional elections, with the democratic opposition winning large minorities. Congress, meeting in Brasilia, is no longer just a tourist attraction but a place of important debate, although it still does not have real power.

Censorship was lifted from the two leading independent daily newspapers, O Estado de São Paulo and Jornal da Tarde (the other main daily papers observe government guidelines and exercise self-censorship). Allegations of police torture of political prisoners were published for the first time, and greater freedom of discussion was allowed in universities and other intellectual groups.

Now the trend seems to have waned, and leading political analysts have reported that the slow road to democratization has reached a block.

Various factors have contributed to the mood of political stagnation, particularly the opposition's strong election showing and the campaign for civil liberties. These are said to have alarmed military sectors in favor of keeping the status quo and to have brought serious pressures on the Geisel Government.

One of the most serious blows to liberalization has been the illness of a principal artisan, Gen. Golbery do Couto e Silva, chief of President Geisel's civil household and his closest adviser.

Further Easing Pledged

There is still a good deal of talk about what decompression means and what it doesn't and official voices have insisted that it has not ended with General Couto e Silva's departure, which, it is widely hoped, will be temporary.

The Minister of Justice, Armando Falcão, has announced that the slow liberalization will continue and that a committee of representatives of the Ministries of Justice and Education is working on a project to remove censorship from all news organs still under control.

However, press circles viewed the announcement with skepticism, particularly after the news that censorship would be extended to two more newspapers—the São Paulo political monthly Ex and a new weekly, Movimentio, which has not even appeared.

Meanwhile, the campaign against the censorship of the arts has gathered momentum.

Two weeks ago the Brazilian Democratic Movement, the only legal opposition party, opened an emotional debate in the Senate. An opposition Senator, Marcos Freire, denounced the "intolerant, abusive, aggressive, insulting, discriminatory censorship" in music, the theater, literature, the cinema and painting as well as in the press and university life.

A Series of Debates

"The debility of Brazilian cultural life in this last quarter of the 20th century is not a lack of talent or aspirations," said Tristao de Athayde, a widely respected columnist, writing in Jornal do Brasil on "a decade of censorship of thought and expression." "It is a crisis caused by political authoritarianism and censorship."

The first series of so-called debates on contemporary culture was held in April and May in the Casa Grande Theater here before packed audiences, mostly students. Censorship was the main theme, with a diversity of artists and others agreeing that it was the principal obstacle to the development of Brazilian culture.

The protest movement achieved national dimensions in May when the Government, arguing that a play about prostitution called "Lilac Lampshade," was "offensive to good morals," rejected an appeal by its author, Plinio Marcos, for its release. All the theaters of São Paulo, Brazil's cultural as well as industrial capital, shut down for a day in protest.

To justify the ban the Justice Ministry distributed copies of the play to the press, excluding women journalists out of propriety. This only increased the hostility.

Citing "Lilac Lampshade," Flavio Rangel, a leading director, said in an interview in São Paulo that there had been no relaxation of controls on the cultural scene despite the decompression in other areas.

'Dead End in Brazil'

"They think art is subversive because it is always against something," Mr. Rangel said, adding, "Our generation has reached a dead end in Brazil because we cannot express ourselves."

Visão, an influential fortnightly magazine, did a cover story on the theater and censorship, including a frank roundtable discussion.

"Censorship is serious, but for me what is worse is that many artists are adjusted to it, putting out mediocre texts and blaming censorship," the author of "Lilac Lampshade" said in Visão, adding that the censorship was increasing the penetration of foreign works.

In cinema the situation is much the same. Films with social themes are prohibited and crotic comedies encouraged. The best-known movie director, Glauber Rocha, has gone to Europe. Quality foreign films are frequently barred, but the public is inundated with third rate American Western and crime films.

Popular Music Hindered

Brazil's vigorous and talented school of popular music is also showing the wean of censorship. The best composers write between the lines, and even then their works are often banned. The most popular singer-composer, Chico Buarque de Holanda, has seen scores of his songs prohibited, the latest being a nostalgic work sympathizing with Portugal's revolution. When he took a pseudonym none of his songs were banned for some time.

Early this year the censors excluded the record "The Rights of Man at the Beggars' Banquet," taken from the tape of a show presented in Rio in December, 1973. The show, which went on without trouble, contains excerpts from the Universal Declaration of the Rights of Man, but the censors declared that the recording "contained political connotations unfavorable to the Government."

Book censorship is less rigorous, some say, because many Brazilians cannot read or afford books. Nevertheless, not only historians and social scientists but even novelists and poets refrain from writing anything that could be considered critical of the military regime.

Though press censorship has eased considerably, the leading weekly newsmagazine, Veia, has censors in its printing room, as does the sensationalist Rio newspaper Tribuna da Imprensa and the Roman Catholic Church's weekly, O São Paulo.

* * *

November 9, 1978

POLITICAL JOKES MAKE A COMEBACK IN BRAZIL

By DAVID VIDAL

Special to The New York Times

RIO DE JANEIRO, Nov. 6—The comic is dressed as a cook and tells television viewers of a recipe for a democracy cake that he says is tasty but not swallowed by many.

"First, get some mass and work it over well because the secret of democracy is the mass," he says. "Avoid beating. Take two parties but pour only one in. Then take a knife and make a slight opening, take it to a warm chamber, let it cook in simmering water, remove after 14 years and serve amid general expressions of relief."

Fourteen years of rapid industrialization and unequal but fairly continuous growth under military rule have brought many changes to Brazil, but few have been as influential as those introduced by the rapid spread of television. Today, some 12 million households across this continent-sized nation own television sets. Close to half the total population of 115 million is reached by its message.

Because of this enormous power, whatever appears on television is closely watched by the military Government. Authorities censor newscasts and shows, and during the campaign for congressional elections scheduled for Nov. 15 only monotonous recitations of the qualifications, identification numbers and parties of candidates have been permitted under a law intended to undercut the appeal of the opposition. Moreover, only still photographs of candidates are shown and their voices are kept off the air. Viewers have responded by turning off half the television sets in Rio during these mandatory five-minute spots.

Yet this evidence of Government control of television has not kept a telling development from taking place in recent months. After an absence of at least 10 years, the political joke has been tacitly rehabilitated in Brazil.

Abruptly, major national comedy programs have moved from slapstick to political satire and the country is laughing at the likes of Baptista. Baptista, an obvious namesake of President-elect Joao Baptista Figueiredo, is the lay assistant to a parish priest who is always telling him to shut up.

He appears on what is perhaps the most popular of these programs, "The Planet of Mankind," which is shown Monday evenings on TV Globo, the largest Brazilian network. Other characters include an intelligent ape named Socrates—who ends his probing questions to humans by saying, "You don't have to explain, I just wanted to understand"—and a chubby and evidently paranoid citizen whose answer to every question—"I deny it, I d-e-n-y it"—has been absorbed into the urban jargon as a result of the show.

"We always tried that type of humor but the censors always cut it," said Max Nunes, a scriptwriter. "Now things are improving."

Few Officials Recognized

"The difficult thing," he added, "is that Brazilians recognize few public officials and there is a scarcity of personalities to write about."

The dominant personality now is undoubtedly General Figueiredo. He became President-elect on Oct. 15 by predictably winning an election held by a Government-dominated electoral college. But he had campaigned across the nation as if an election for president was going to be decided by the voters, making intemperate remarks that earned him a certain notoriety.

Humorists have made much of these remarks, as they have of the extreme fondness of this 60-year-old former cavalry officer for horses, printing mock interviews with his horse and frequently picturing the general himself in cowboy gear.

The return of political satire comes in response to a general easing of censorship that has accompanied the process of liberalization sponsored by the administration of President Ernesto Geisel, who is to step down in March. Newspapers have printed previously forbidden articles dealing with guerrilla activities in the Amazon jungles five years ago, allegations of corruption against Cabinet ministers, and reports of missing and tortured persons.

Few Read the Newspapers

But newspaper readership is low. Television has the biggest role in reaching citizens and some events appearing in newspapers are banned from television. An example is a street demonstration recently in Rio in which students chanting anti-Government slogans clashed with troops and trained dogs. Whole pages of newspapers were given over to this clash, considered the worst in Rio in many years, but not one scene appeared on the censored evening news shows.

Thus, political satire is used with the awareness that it may not last long and that certain topics are still taboo.

"The censorship order against talking about Brazilian politics still exists," Mr. Nunes said in a recent interview. "The opening goes by alphabetical order and will only really be good when we reach the letter 'G' for Geisel."

* * *

July 3, 1981

ARGENTINA PUTTING PRESSURE ON PRESS

By EDWARD SCHUMACHER
Special to the New York Times

BUENOS AIRES, July 2—When Manfred Shonfeld, a newspaper columnist, stepped from a taxi last week and was greeted by someone wearing brass knuckles, he learned the limits of press freedom in Argentina.

Mr. Shonfeld lost five teeth, but, undeterred, he was back at his typewriter several days later. "They failed again," wrote the widely read columnist, who has become boldly critical of the military Government in recent months. "The man is writing again. And he will continue to do so—God willing, beginning next week—in the same manner, about the same themes, with similar focus and identical tone as before."

The assailants were unidentified, and the Government condemned the attack. It was only the latest in a series of incidents directed against Mr. Shonfeld's paper, La Prensa, one of the most anti-Government newspapers in the country.

Government Removed Its Ads

Two weeks ago, the Government removed from the paper almost all of its notices and advertisements for state enterprises. Last week, several men barged into the newsroom, identified themselves as policemen and said they would return shortly to censor the next issue.

They did not, but a group calling itself the New Argentina Command claimed responsibility for the intrusion and for the attack on Mr. Shonfeld. The wide assessment here is that it is one of many small, right-wing extremist groups with links to the police or military.

The military does not impose prior censorship on the press. But under the state of siege it maintains, it has arrested editors for printing articles on subversive activity and has banned the sale of issues of magazines carrying articles deemed morally threatening to the family or supporting Communism.

More than 60 journalists have disappeared since the military took power in a coup five years ago. Such disappearances have stopped since last year, but the other actions against the press have been enough to produce an effective self-censorship. Some editors check with military authorities before publishing questionable articles.

Little Reporting on Disappearances

With the exception of The Buenos Aires Herald, a small but influential English-language paper, all Argentine papers have steered away from reporting on disappearance and allegations of torture, usually consigning occasional small articles on habeas corpus suits to the back pages.

In the last year, however, many newspapers have become increasingly critical of the Government's economic policies and are beginning to question the military itself. None is bolder than La Prensa, which has seen its circulation rise from its normal 85,000 to about 100,000 in recent weeks.

The paper's tone and philosophy is set by Maximo Gainza, the fourth publisher in a family line that started the newspaper 113 years ago. La Prensa staunchly defends civil and individual rights and the capitalist economy and has little love for military dictatorships.

"It was an absurd measure," Mr. Gainza said of the Government's removal of its advertising. "It's been tried so many times before, and it does not work with this newspaper."

The campaign against La Prensa began when Mayor Osvaldo Cacciatore, an Air Force general, was angered by the paper's charges that he had been imperious in pushing through highway and other projects. He began withholding some city notices, and his complaints to his military colleagues found sympathy.

Called Officers Cowards

La Prensa had begun to break with others papers 18 months ago when it published a list of more than 4,000 people who had disappeared. Its reporting stays with bare facts, but its columnists in recent months have repeatedly criticized the military. One column by Mr. Shonfeld all but called military officers cowards for not acknowledging responsibility for those who have disappeared.

When the advertisements stopped, Mr. Gainza sent a reporter to interview Gen. Alberto Ortiz, the Public Information Secretary, and his comments were printed on page one the next day. "As there is freedom of the press, there is freedom to choose recipients of publicity," he was reported to have said.

A few Government ads have crept back into the paper, and General Ortiz now denies he ever ordered them cut. In the meantime, public response has been overwhelming. The Publishers' Association called the removal of advertising a "brutish reaction" and "an attack that clashes painfully with the democratic sensibilities of our country." Readers have placed paid notices in the paper to express support.

* * *

August 6, 1982

PANAMA PAPER SAYS CRACKDOWN WAS AIMED AT IT

By ALAN RIDING
Special to the New York Times

PANAMA, Aug. 5—The national guard's closing of the country's newspapers last week appears to be an effort aimed mainly at silencing the country's main opposition daily, the newspaper's publisher said today.

The action came in the wake of the national guard's decision to topple President Aristides Royo and replace him with Vice President Ricardo de la Espriella. The order, issued by the national guard commander, Brig. Gen. Ruben Dario Paredes, said the papers were being closed to "moralize" the press and put an end to "insults and verbal violence."

But Roberto Eisenmann, the publisher of the main opposition paper, La Prensa, said: "The suspension of all the press last week was simply to disguise the closure of La Prensa. Paredes threatened to close us and did."

The fate of La Prensa in coming weeks will be an important indicator of Panama's likely political direction. The paper's survival will be evidence that, despite last week's shake-up, the country is continuing its gradual return to democracy, but its permanent closure—or the introduction of direct censorship—would badly bruise hope for free elections scheduled for 1984.

Troops Raid Newspaper

While other newspapers were simply informed of the suspension, heavily armed troops and policemen burst into La Prensa last Friday afternoon. Striking some secretaries with rubber hoses, they drove reporters and other employees out of the building.

When soldiers finally withdrew from the daily Wednesday afternoon, editors found that corrosive acid had been poured into computers, electronic composers and even the printing presses. Drawers and cupboards had been forced open, files had been removed and some money had been stolen. Damage was estimated at about $150,000.

Although much of the newspaper's equipment was made at least temporarily useless, editors and reporters worked throughout the day in the hope of producing a small eight-page issue Friday.

"The important thing is that we come out with something," Mr. Eisenmann said. "Our readers need to know that we haven't been intimidated."

Compensation Is Offered

Significantly, President de la Espriella linked the credibility of his new civilian administration to the early re-opening of La Prensa, which he was eventually able to negotiate with the national guard. And after La Prensa's installations were found to have been damaged, the Government offered to pay compensation to the newspaper.

The foundation of La Prensa in August 1980 was itself evidence that, after dominating the country for 12 years, the national guard was willing to relax its control of news organizations and opposition parties. But the guard—and former President Royo—proved highly sensitive to criticism.

La Prensa was conceived by a group of liberal businessmen and lawyers as an opposition organ, but ownership is shared by over 500 stockholders who represent a broad spectrum of democratic opinion and numerous different political parties. "Our editorial line is simply to be democratic in an autocratic situation," Mr. Eisenmann said.

In exposes, cartoons and a widely read satirical column, La Prensa constantly challenged the Royo Government and the national guard. And the daily's readers—its circulation stands at around 14,000—frequently responded by providing reporters with secret information about corruption within the regime and the guard.

Scandals Brought to Light

Over the last two years, La Prensa has brought to light numerous scandals deeply embarrassing to the regime, including a major fraud in the Social Security Institute. It recently reported that the brother of a senior guard officer had, inexplicably, more than $4 million in his personal bank account and that bank officers were said to be involved in drug trafficking and arms smuggling.

Officials frequently responded furiously. President Royo brought four criminal libel suits, one of which resulted in the daily's editor, Carlos Gonzalez de la Lastra, being sentenced to five months' imprisonment, a case still under appeal. Last fall, an armed band linked to the official Democratic Revolutionary Party entered the newspaper, firing shots and beating up employees.

More recently, three newspapers owned by the Government began campaigns of personal insults against key figures of La Prensa, suggesting that Mr. Eisenmann was a contrabandist and that other editors were sexually depraved. After one report that linked the national guard to a trading company supposedly involved in dubious business practices, Mr. Eisenmann said, he was summoned by General Paredes and warned that the paper could be closed.

When Panama's Supreme Court accepted La Prensa's request for an injunction ordering General Paredes to lift the suspension, however, the national guard chief said he had not issued the order but had merely "suggested" the closing to Mr. de la Espriella. As a result, the President was able Wednesday to order that La Prensa be returned to its owners.

Papers Resume Publication

Three other newspapers, La Estrella, the English-language Star and Ya, have resumed publication after accepting that censors be placed in their offices. On Wednesday, though, Justice Minister Justo Fidel Palacios said there would be no prior censorship and that the three Government-owned newspapers would be on the streets again Monday.

"De la Espriella was very anxious not to start his Government with the stigma of censorship," a close friend of the President said. "Ironically, he needs a free press as much as the opposition if he's going to gather any power of his own."

Today, General Paredes said he would send a commission to La Prensa to establish whether the damage to installations was "selfsabotage." But if the national guard's responsibility is established, he said, it would pay compensation.

* * *

October 23, 1983

CURBS ON FILMS AND BOOKS EASED A BIT IN CHILE

By STEPHEN KINZER

SANTIAGO, Chile, Oct. 22—For the first time in a decade, spring has brought fresh cultural ferment to Chile.

Ten-year-old restrictions on the sale of books have been lifted, and films are no longer censored so heavily as they had been since the 1973 military takeover. Artists and producers, however, say that limits on cultural expression remain.

Anti-Government protests have shaken Chile in recent months, and the Government has eased its control of artistic expression as a concession. Artists and writers, including some who have only recently been allowed to return to Chile, have taken prominent roles in protest rallies. They complain that television stations, which are under Government control, do not reflect the country's cultural diversity and that motion pictures, which also reach a mass audience, are still closely regulated.

Managers of movie theaters said they were limited in which films they could present and that some had to be cut by Government censors before they could be shown. They said Chileans had become accustomed to applying contemporary interpretations to films or plays that ostensibly have nothing to do with modern-day Chile.

One of the surprise successes of this year's film season, for example, was "Giordano Bruno," made by the Italian director Giuliano Montaldo. Although it is set in the 16th century, an employee of the theater where it is being shown said many Chileans saw its story of a free-thinking intellectual who is arrested, tortured and executed as an allegory for modern Latin America.

The publication and importation of books was strictly controlled until this summer, when the Government lifted a regulation that required official approval of any book sold in Chile.

Two Examples of Relaxation

Among books on sale in Santiago that booksellers said would probably not have been permitted last year are a volume by Andres Zaldivar, a Christian Democratic politician, about his years in forced exile, and "Lonquen," which reports in detail about the discovery of decomposed bodies, apparently victims of torture squads, in a mine shaft outside Santiago.

"If it had not been for the discovery of these remains and the publication of the story," Patricio Aylwin, an opposition politician, said, "many ingenuous Chileans would probably still believe the official propaganda that missing persons had simply gone underground or were living happily abroad."

Among the thousands of Chileans who were sent into exile or fled the country after the 1973 military coup in which the Marxist Chilean leader, Salvador Allende Gossens, was killed, were many young writers, poets, dramatists and film makers.

They have continued to work abroad, especially in Mexico City and Paris, but little of their work has been allowed to reach their countrymen.

Jorge Edwards, a prominent Chilean intellectual and former diplomat, said: "For years, Chile was very sensitive to what was happening in the cultural world. Chileans bought more books per capita than any other country on the continent, and we were the first country to become interested in writers like Faulkner, Hemingway, Thomas Mann, Sartre and Camus. But we have lived through a decade of isolation. I have no idea what young Chileans think about politics or what is their outlook on life. This is unfortunate, because in order to consolidate democracy you need people who can think analytically and make intelligent choices."

* * *

December 22, 1984

ANTI-SANDINISTA EDITOR DECIDES ON EXILE

By STEPHEN KINZER

MANAGUA, Nicaragua, Dec. 21—The editor of the opposition daily newspaper, La Prensa, said today that he had gone into exile and would make his home in neighboring Costa Rica until press censorship was lifted in Nicaragua.

"If the censorship ends, I'll go back," the editor, Pedro Joaquin Chamorro Barrios, said in a telephone interview from the Costa Rican capital, San Jose. "That could be one day, two days or 20 years."

"I was no longer fulfilled fighting with censors," Mr. Chamorro Barrios said. "My passion wore out. I didn't want to stay there and work just to fill up files at the censorship office."

Mr. Chamorro Barrios said he would work against the Sandinistas by traveling and writing.

"Many people know about La Prensa and censorship in Nicaragua, but I want to dramatize the situation by not going back there," he said.

"I don't like the word permanent," he said of his self-exile. "You could use the word indefinite. I don't think the Sandinistas are a permanent Government."

Uncle Replaces Him

The Chamorro family, which owns La Prensa, voted at a meeting Thursday to replace the departed editor, who is 33 years old, with his uncle, Jaime Chamorro Cardenal. In an interview today, Mr. Chamorro Cardenal said La Prensa would continue to publish.

"It is vital that we keep La Prensa alive," the new editor said. "Even if the paper cannot say much now, the moment will come when it will play an important role again."

In a related development, the Chamorro family this week filed a legal complaint asserting that press censorship violated Nicaraguan laws and international human rights agreements to which Nicaragua is a party. The 24-page brief cited 180 articles, photos, cartoons and headlines that it said had been cut or banned by censors in the first 12 days of December.

During the recent national election campaign, the Sandinista Government substantially loosened controls on La Prensa. During August, September and October, the paper was full of denunciations of the Government, many of them contained in reports of speeches made by opposition candidates. Shortly before the Nov. 4 election, Interior Minister Tomas Borge told reporters that La Prensa had abused its relative freedom by engaging in sensationalism.

More Censorship Now

Since the election, censorship has tightened considerably, and La Prensa's editors say it is now heavier than before. On Wednesday and Thursday, 28 articles were banned by censors. They included stories about shortages of Christmas toys, wire service reports of military activity and excerpts from the newspaper's legal brief charging that press censorship was illegal.

Mr. Chamorro Barrios left Managua on Nov. 15 for a trip to Japan and Spain. He was initially denied permission to leave Nicaragua but was allowed to leave after the Japanese Embassy intervened with Mr. Borge, whose ministry controls the airport and border posts.

More than two dozen other Nicaraguan opposition leaders were unable to leave the country after the election, but the restrictions, which were never officially acknowledged, appeared to have been lifted recently.

After visiting Japan, Mr. Chamorro Barrios went to Costa Rica rather than returning home to Nicaragua. His wife and children have been living in San Jose since early this year.

"Pedro was very frustrated by the situation here," said Mr. Chamorro Cardenal. "He felt he couldn't express himself. He was really unhappy."

Some Sandinistas have speculated privately that he would become an ally of Alfonso Robelo Callejas and Eden Pastora Gomez, anti-Sandinista insurgent leaders who are based in San Jose.

But Mr. Chamorro Barrios said today that he would not support armed anti-Sandinista groups. Asked about his relationship with Mr. Robelo and Mr. Pastora, he replied, "We are only friends, there is no political alliance."

* * *

October 24, 1985

IN NICARAGUA, RIGHTS CURBS BRING UNCERTAINTY AND MORE CENSORSHIP

By STEPHEN KINZER

Special to the New York Times

MANAGUA, Nicaragua, Oct. 23—La Prensa, the acerbic and partisan daily newspaper that has irritated every Nicaraguan Government over the last half-century, was to have carried six articles on its front page on Monday.

Only one, an account of injuries during an exhibition bullfight in Managua, survived the censor's pencil. The others, all covering aspects of Nicaragua's domestic or international situation, were banned.

Since the Government issued a decree suspending many civil liberties last week, politicians, business leaders, Roman Catholic clerics and other critics of the Government have continued to act almost as if nothing had happened. But at La Prensa, the decree is being felt as nowhere else.

"Over the last year, between 20 and 40 percent of our material has been cut by censorship," said Carlos Ramirez, the editor who has supervised production in the days since the decree was issued. "Now it's up to 80 percent and more. This week, we are a paper that says nothing about Nicaragua."

A review of material censored since the decree was issued Oct. 15 suggests that La Prensa is able to publish only a small number of articles that touch on politics or government. Some news developments, such as President Daniel Ortega Saavedra's declaration that he would seek to meet with President Reagan in New York this week, were covered in the pro-Sandinista press, but La Prensa was not allowed to mention them.

A list of the legal provisions suspended under the decree was also banned. Sandinista leaders, including President Ortega, have said the decree was aimed at preventing the emergence of an "internal front" that would support anti-Government insurgents.

For most Nicaraguans, life is no different than before the emergency decree was issued. The decree suspended the rights to free expression and assembly, the right to strike and most guarantees for defendants. But during the week the decree has been in force, these provisions have not been invoked systematically.

On Sunday, Miguel Cardinal Obando y Bravo of Managua, the Roman Catholic Archbishop of Managua and a hero of the opposition, was cheered by thousands of admirers when, after celebrating mass, he greeted crowds outside a church in the northern town of Esteli. Sandinista policemen nearby made no move to interfere, although the right of assembly had been suspended.

Interior Minister Tomas Borge called Cardinal Obando to a private meeting afterward, according to diplomats, and warned him he should seek official permission before addressing large public gatherings. The diplomats said Cardinal Obando gave no indication he would do so and is expected to celebrate mass Sunday in his home town, La Libertad.

Also over the weekend, three leaders of the Democratic Coordinator, a coalition of opposition groups, were summoned for a lecture by one of Mr. Borge's principal deputies, Lenin Cerna, the State Security Chief. He told them to stop fomenting unrest. Two days later, they held a news conference to accuse the Government of repressing human rights.

"We have not yet been able to determine how far these measures go," said one opposition activist, Andres Zuniga, president of the National Confederation of Professionals. "They want to create that psychological fear in people."

Opponents Vow to Continue

Mr. Zuniga said the opposition would continue to act as vigorousiy as possible.

Several diplomats said that Sandinista leaders, principally Mr. Borge, fear that the insurgents could take advantage of discontent stirred up by the internal opposition to launch a campaign of urban terror. Thus far, there have been no significant urban actions attributable to the rebels.

On Monday, six days after the decree limiting public freedoms was issued, Vice President Sergio Ramirez Mercado called a news conference and sought to minimize its importance.

Mr. Ramirez said that people were still free to move about as they pleased, and that citizens accused of crimes that were not political would still be guaranteed all the rights they had held. He said the decree only affects "those who are involved in conspiratorial activities against the revolution and the country's internal order."

He said that "meetings of a social, political, festive or religious nature" would require prior approval by the authorities, and that "organizations with a political, economic or social character" could be formed only with official permission.

* * *

December 14, 1985

IN ARGENTINA, A CULTURAL RENAISSANCE

By LYDIA CHAVEZ

Special to the New York Times

BUENOS AIRES, Dec. 13—The Italian director Lina Wertmuller talked about film in one room while Argentine novelists discussed literature in the next. On the same evening, a new political play had a premiere.

Since censorship was lifted more than two years ago as Argentina returned to democracy, exiled artists, directors, painters and actors have returned to produce several award-winning works. In the last year, Argentines won awards at the Cannes and Venice film festivals and the Moscow International Ballet Competition.

In short, Argentina is enjoying a cultural renaissance. And after seven years of military rule in which hundreds of artists fled for artistic or political reasons, a lack of funds has not spoiled the country's enthusiasm for culture.

"Culture is the consciousness of a society," said Mario O'Donnell, director of culture for Buenos Aires. "It is a country's self-image, and the difference in a democracy is enormous."

The man who sat in Mr. O'Donnell's chair as cultural director during the military regime banned works and drew up blacklists. Mr. O'Donnell said his own aim was to "take culture to the people."

In a demonstration of the country's new openness, Miss Wertmuller and 33 other foreign artists, many of whom shunned the country during the military's rule, are here to celebrate Argentina's new cultural identity. The visitors and Argentine artists are taking part in seminars on such topics as women in the theater, the Argentine novel and the future of film. Large audiences have turned out.

Neighborhood Groups Blossom

The most striking difference between the country's new cultural life, according to many artists, is the variety of new productions in the theater, dance, movies and fine arts. Neighborhood arts groups have blossomed in the last year, they say.

Among the Argentines who have returned from political exile is the actress Norma Aleandro, who is the star of the film "The Official Story."

The young couple portrayed in the movie adopt a child who they later discover was kidnapped during the military's counterinsurgency campaign. Miss Aleandro shared the best actress award at the Cannes Film Festival with Cher. Her return, and the movie, would not have been possible under the military regime.

Norman Briski, who worked with Joseph Papp in New York during his political exile, recently appeared in the play "Twenty Years is Nothing," a tragicomic look at recent Argentine history. Mr. Briski and his play would also not have appeared here under military rule.

Not all of the Argentine works honored recently had political themes. Julio Bocca, who recently won a gold medal at the Moscow International Ballet Competition, chose the tango for his presentation. The film that won a special jury prize in the Venice Film Festival, "Tangos, the Exile of Gardel," was also apolitical.

Democracy and Culture

Carlos Gorostiza, the Argentine Culture Minister and a playwright, said it was impossible to draw a direct line between the recent set of arts awards and democracy. Nevertheless, he said, "a rich cultural life is more possible under a democracy, and more authentic." because artists are championed on the basis of artistic accomplishment rather than political beliefs.

Despite a lack of equipment and limited opportunities, many Argentine artists say they prefer to work here. Exiled artists whose personal or professional commitments have prevented a permanent return nonetheless visit Argentina for special projects.

"It is important to work here," Mr. Briski said. "It is my life, my theater, my country." But he will continue to work in New York as well, he said.

A lack of money has influenced some artists' work and work habits. Argentine painters, for example, work in group studios to save money. Drawing with pencils is more popular than working with oils, which are expensive. Painters have been helped by a new interest in Latin American art, according to a gallery owner.

'You Have to Travel'

Most actors and actresses say that to support their families, they must work abroad at least part of the year. "You have to travel to be able to do the kind of work you want to," Miss Aleandro said. Argentine movies must also depend on foreign sales to turn a profit, she said. "The Official Story," for example, did well in Argentina, but it failed to make a profit until it was released abroad, Miss Aleandro said.

Mr. Bocca, the dancer, said he must also perform abroad to supplement his $400-a-month earnings as a dancer for the Colon Theater. The professional opportunities abroad are also an attraction, he said.

"My dream has always been to be able to dance all over the world," he said in an interview in one of the theater's basements. His goal is to study or dance with American Ballet Theater. But Argentina, he insisted, will always be his base.

As for the public, few people seem to mind the problems that can occur when events are staged on a low budget.

Such patience was evident one recent evening when Miss Wertmuller took part in a roundtable discussion. When the moderator asked her a question in Spanish, she smiled and said she did not understand a word he was saying. A woman in the audience who spoke Italian jumped up, but someone else had already moved to Miss Wertmuller's side to translate the question.

When the interpreter failed to translate the answer into Spanish, many of the 300 people in the audience sat patiently but were perplexed.

"We understand enough," said Pedro Urtaga, a 65-year-old retired seaman attending the seminar. "They didn't do anything like this under censorship. You know, there was a genocide here then."

* * *

June 27, 1986

MAIN NICARAGUA OPPOSITION PAPER INDEFINITELY CLOSED BY SANDINISTAS

By STEPHEN KINZER
Special to the New York Times

MANAGUA, Nicaragua, June 26—La Prensa, the combative opposition newspaper that for 60 years has been a principal source of news for Nicaraguans, was ordered shut today by the Sandinista Government.

The action was announced in a two-sentence letter from Capt. Nelba Cecilia Blandon, head of the press censorship office.

"In accordance with instructions from above, I notify you that from this moment the newspaper La Prensa is closed for an indefinite time," Captain Blandon wrote. "With nothing more to add, I send my considerations."

U.S. Vote to Aid Rebels

The indefinite closing came less than 24 hours after the United States House of Representatives voted in favor of President Reagan's proposal to provide $110 million to anti-Government rebels.

President Daniel Ortega Saavedra, accompanied by other senior Sandinista leaders, said this evening that in the wake of the House vote, the Nicaraguan Government would begin to enforce the existing state-of-emergency decree "strictly and severely."

The state of emergency decree was issued last Oct. 15, but there were few visible effects. Under provisions of the emergency decree, many civil liberties are suspended, and the Government is given broad powers to act against those it considers enemies.

Carlos Hollmann, an editor of La Prensa, said in an interview that he did not know why the Government had shut the paper. He said he expected more information Friday.

"Closing La Prensa means that the country's situation is getting worse," Mr. Hollmann said. He said he would appeal the order "to the highest authorities."

Previous Closings of Paper

Guards in front of La Prensa's offices said this evening that the letter was received late in the afternoon by Carlos Ramirez, who was acting as editor today. The guards said no Government troops had occupied the premises, but said they had been told soldiers might arrive Friday morning.

In the past, the Government has ordered several brief closings of La Prensa as punishment for specific infractions of press laws, and on more than 20 occasions over the last two years the paper's editors have refused to publish an issue after large amounts of copy were cut by Government censors. But tonight's action marked the first time the Government has ordered the paper closed indefinitely.

Editors of La Prensa had circulated copies of articles censored by Captain Blandon to a limited number of diplomats and others in Managua, but they were ordered to stop doing so several months ago.

In April, a senior editor of La Prensa, Jaime Chamorro Cardenal, said he had been approached and asked if he would be willing to sell the newspaper. He said he believed the offer originated with Government officials seeking to silence La Prensa, and turned it down.

Opposition Leader's Comment

A leading opposition figure, Virgilio Godoy Reyes of the Independent Liberal Party, said in an interview following the closing of La Prensa that the Government was "moving to silence the only press outlet that was independent of the Government."

"Now we are left only with the official press and a few radio news programs that are subject to self-censorship," Mr. Godoy said. "It's a serious blow to the internal struggle here. We are now disconnected from the only newspaper able to transmit any of the truth."

La Prensa has been the principal anti-Sandinista organ in Nicaragua during recent years. It had been subject to censorship, but was still able to publish some material critical of the Government.

Pedro Joaquin Chamorro Cardenal, who was a fierce opponent of the deposed Somoza dictatorship, used the pages of La Prensa to castigate the Somoza Government. He was assassinated in January 1978, and it is widely believed that his killing, which was blamed on allies of President Anastasio Somoza Debayle, was a key spark to the anti-Somoza uprising that led to the Sandinista takeover in July 1979.

Member of Original Junta

Mr. Chamorro's widow, Violeta Barrios de Chamorro, was a member of the original Sandinista junta. She later quit the junta because of her political disagreements with the Government.

In a recent speech, Mrs. Chamorro said she considered La Prensa's situation more difficult now than at any time during the Somoza regime.

This evening, Mr. Ortega read a communique in which he vowed that the Government would punish "criminal unpatriotic acts." He made no direct reference to La Prensa.

He said the Government was taking steps that had been agreed upon earlier and that were to be taken if the American Congress approved the proposal to aid the rebels.

'The New Threat We Face'

He said new steps, which he did not specify, would provide "better conditions to confront the new threat we face." He said political opponents of the Sandinistas inside Nicaragua were giving "civilian cover to counterrevolutionary plans."

He said the House vote "requires the revision of some policies." He said Sandinista leaders would hold a series of meetings beginning Monday to determine what steps to take.

Mr. Ortega said Nicaragua would present its complaints against the United States to a variety of international bodies, including the United Nations security council.

In comments Wednesday night immediately following the vote in Washington, Mr. Ortega indicated the Government would move against "those who betray their country."

Several opposition leaders said they took those comments to mean that a crackdown might be imminent.

La Prensa is not the first news outlet to be ordered closed by the Sandinistas. Soon after assuming power, they closed more than a dozen radio news programs. Last October, they ordered the closing of the radio station operated by the Roman Catholic Church.

* * *

April 20, 1987

IN NICARAGUA, THE CYNICISM OF CENSORSHIP

By STEPHEN KINZER

Special to the New York Times

MANAGUA, Nicaragua, April 19—The newsstand at the busy Lewites Market in Managua offers a limited selection of periodicals, and even the proprietor, Ramon Ramirez, says he cannot find much that he wants to read.

On display are a few local magazines produced by pro-Government groups, an issue of Reader's Digest that one of Mr. Ramirez's friends brought from Costa Rica, some Soviet sports journals and copies of a Trotskyite weekly.

"The full information about what's happening, they don't give it," Mr. Ramirez said, looking up from his copy of a morning newspaper, Nuevo Diario. "In this country, people no longer believe what we read. We only believe rumors."

'Certain Points of View'

Many Nicaraguans share Mr. Ramirez's cynicism about the press. With the Sandinistas at war against United States-backed rebels, the Government maintains control over what can be published or broadcast.

"Everything is politicized," said a construction worker, Ramon Sanchez. "Only certain points of view are presented."

Nicaraguan journalists and editors, in interviews this month, agreed that Nicaraguans yearned for wider news coverage. But there was a wide difference of opinion over whether Government censorship is justified.

All printed matter must be approved by the Interior Ministry before it can be published. The ministry maintains a team of censors who review every article written for the two morning newspapers, as well as magazine articles and other material.

The Sandinista Government appears to welcome and even solicit criticism that does not challenge its legitimacy, but it draws the line there.

It is acceptable, for example, to say there are food shortages because the distribution system is flawed. But asserting in print that Marxist agricultural policies caused the shortages would probably not be permitted.

Independent radio news programs are more spontaneous than newspapers and magazines but operate under self-censorship, and the Interior Ministry monitors all radio broadcasts. The two television stations are owned and operated by the Government.

A limited selection of foreign newspapers and magazines is available to those who can pay in dollars, including hotel guests. Foreign television broadcasts are received in the

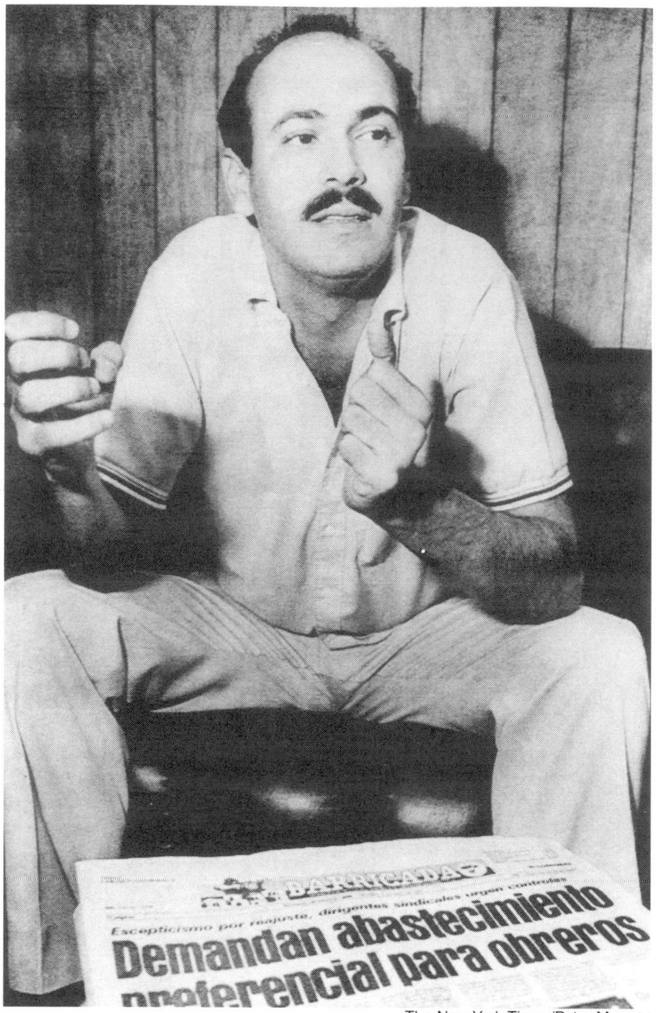

The New York Times/Peter Morgan

Carlos Fernando Chamorro Barrios, the editor of the official Sandinista newspaper Barricada, in his office in Managua.

offices of senior Sandinista leaders but are available to the public only at one Managua hotel.

During the rule of the Somoza family, which held power in Nicaragua for more than 40 years until it was overthrown in 1979, clashes between the Government and news organizations were common. There was no prior censorship, but the Government's will was harshly imposed at times.

The editor of La Prensa, the opposition newspaper, was assassinated in January 1978 as his anti-Somoza campaign stepped up, and the newspaper's plant was later blown up by army tanks.

After Somoza: A Voice Is Silenced

After the Somoza regime fell, La Prensa at first supported the new Sandinista Government. But it later turned against the Sandinistas, and last June the authorities finally shut it down, asserting that its editors supported United States policy on Nicaragua.

The two remaining daily papers are Barricada, the official organ of the ruling Sandinista Front, and Nuevo Diario, which was founded seven years ago by a breakaway group of employees of La Prensa sympathetic to the Sandinista cause.

In the months since La Prensa was closed, both remaining newspapers have sought to capture its former readers. Nuevo Diario in particular appears to have taken a more critical approach to reporting the news.

"Nuevo Diario is in search of its profile," said the paper's editor, Xavier Chamorro Cardenal. "We are going through an evolution, a transformation. We are not going to assume a role of opposing and confronting the revolution, but we have come to the conclusion that within limits we should try to fill the vacuum left by the suspension of La Prensa."

Mr. Chamorro Cardenal said Nuevo Diario, which is nominally independent, had in the past been too quick to defend all aspects of Sandinista rule.

"La Prensa was very polarized, and as a reaction we also became polarized," he said. "We know we have to give more information than we did before. We are opening the paper a bit to opinions that are not necessarily revolutionary."

Prior Censorship: A Fact of War?

Nuevo Diario recently printed an interview with a labor organizer who declared that labor-union freedom was "seriously limited" in Nicaragua. It also ran a story saying the Housing Ministry was operating with a mentality of "bureaucratic feudalism."

Mr. Chamorro Cardenal said an average of three articles a week were cut from Nuevo Diario by Government censors. "We protest every time," he said.

Nonetheless, he does not advocate abolition of prior censorship. "We live in a situation of war and aggression," he said. "While that continues, I don't see how we can end censorship."

Across town, Mr. Chamorro Cardenal's nephew, Carlos Fernando Chamorro Barrios, edits the official Sandinista newspaper Barricada. He also heads the Department of Agitation and Propaganda, making him one of the shapers of Government press policy.

Mr. Chamorro Barrios said that before La Prensa was closed many people bought it not because they sympathized with its anti-Sandinista stance, but rather because it printed more news than the other two papers. He said Barricada was trying to appeal to those readers by offering better coverage of culture, world news and sports.

"We speak for the Sandinista Front and reflect Sandinista policies," he said, "but we don't want to be a house organ or a bulletin for party members."

Another Outlook: Small Journals Survive

Barricada regularly prints extensive interviews with Government officials and full-page excerpts from speeches by top leaders.

Although both newspapers draw attention to inefficiency and other problems in the bureaucracy, criticisms published in Nuevo Diario are often sharper than those in Barricada.

Coverage of Sandinista labor unions, peasant groups and other "mass organizations" is heavy in Barricada.

With the disappearance of La Prensa, there is no anti-Sandinista press in Nicaragua. But there are some small journals that try to provide news not covered in the two daily papers.

One is Avance, the weekly newsletter of the Nicaraguan Communist Party. Although Avance's circulation is only 15,000, compared with more than 100,000 for each of the two daily papers, it is read in many political circles.

Neither Barricada nor Nuevo Diario reported the contents of a nine-point peace proposal made in January by the Nicaraguan Communists and other non-Sandinista parties. The proposal included a general amnesty for prisoners and the formation of a commission to negotiate a cease-fire with the contra rebels, suggestions the Government has rejected in the past. Avance, however, published the proposal in full.

The editor of Avance, Rene Blandon, said much material was censored from each issue. The paper was shut down for three months in early 1985 after it tried to publish articles suggesting that the presidential election in 1984 might have been tainted by fraud.

Censorship Policy: Of Two Minds

Government policy is to censor any unofficial news relating to the war and any material that could cause economic problems. But editors say many other kinds of articles are also cut.

A recent issue of Avance was to carry a report about peasants said to have been pushed from their land in Matagalpa Province because they refused to join Sandinista organizations, along with an editorial accusing the Government of using "corrupt and perverse maneuvers" to intimidate members of the National Assembly. Both articles were cut by censors. But the censors allowed publication of an article charging that two road workers were being dismissed from their Government jobs because they were trying to organize an independent labor union.

"Barricada and Nuevo Diario are two sides of the same coin," Mr. Blandon said. "Our newspaper does not directly oppose the Sandinista thesis, but we do not support it."

The freest discourse takes place every morning on "Contact 620," a radio call-in program that may have more listeners than any other radio show in Nicaragua. For four hours, callers report on inefficiency and frustrations with the bureaucracy.

One recent morning, a woman called to say she had witnessed the dumping of several hundred spoiled chickens by a roadside and demanded to know who was responsible. Another caller said several car accidents had been caused by a malfunctioning street light on her corner.

A Call-In Show: Radio Gets Results

"This program is the terror of the slow-moving bureaucrat," said a teacher who called to say his paycheck and those of 400 colleagues were being held up by a computer malfunction.

In several Government agencies, someone is assigned to monitor "Contact 620" all morning and investigate complaints that affect that agency.

The program's host, Noel Fuentes, often telephones officials who are the targets of complaints and asks them to defend themselves on the air. In an interview, he said callers were free to say what they pleased.

"Our orientation is to let people speak," Mr. Fuentes said. "But 'Contact 620' is not a forum for discussions of universal political questions. It is a program that tries to resolve problems and make Nicaragua better within the framework of the revolution."

Although editors and censors review all written copy before it is published, some embarrassing slips occur.

Readers of Barricada were startled recently by a front-page report of a speech that President Daniel Ortega Saavedra made to a group of Protestant clergymen. The report concluded with a remarkable observation, "Everyone present said they didn't want to see Ortega, because he doesn't go down well with them."

The next day Barricada published a retraction for the "grave error." The managing editor, Xavier Reyes, was dismissed soon afterward.

"Apparently the President can't take a joke," a Nicaraguan journalist said.

But Mr. Chamorro Barrios, Barricada's editor, defended the dismissal. "That was no joke," he said.

* * *

August 4, 1987

PANAMA PRESS

By STEPHEN KINZER

Special to the New York Times

PANAMA, Aug. 3—In its campaign to break the momentum built up by eight weeks of protest rallies and demonstrations, the Government has found press censorship one of its most potent weapons.

Last week, the country's three opposition newspapers were ordered closed for an unspecified period while charges of sedition against them were investigated. It was the second time they had been silenced in as many months.

All anti-Government radio programs have also been halted. Television news remains under indirect Government control.

Because of these restrictions on news reporting, Panamanians must rely on each other to keep abreast of developments, often falling prey to rumormongers. Opposition leaders circulate mimeographed instructions to their followers and communicate through telephone networks.

The military leader, Gen. Manuel Antonio Noriega, has indicated that he is angry not only at the local press, but also at reporters from abroad, whom he described as "a plague."

"Respect Panama," the general advised foreign correspondents who sought unsuccessfully to question him about political matters following a public ceremony Friday. "Respect Panamanian laws."

The threats are not idle. A veteran Reuters correspondent, Tom Brown, was expelled from Panama last week, and the government accused other news agencies of taking part in a "disinformation campaign" aimed at undermining the Noriega-backed regime.

Anti-Government sentiment appears to cut across the lines of race and class, and it often erupts at unexpected moments.

On Friday night, several thousand raucous boxing fans filled an arena in the capital to watch one of their countrymen, Francisco (Rocky) Fernandez, try to win the junior lightweight championship from a South African fighter, Brian Mitchell. Suddenly, before the fight began, a handful of fans in the cheaper seats stood up and began waving white handkerchiefs, which have become a protest symbol.

Within seconds, the entire arena was a sea of white and people began to chant "Justice! Justice!" That is the slogan adopted by those pressing for an impartial investigation into the 1985 murder of anti-military activist Dr. Hugo Spadafora.

Policemen watched quietly, and the chanting faded at the opening of the fight, which the local hero lost.

Mourners filled a church in the Santa Maria section of the capital Thursday for a funeral mass for the only protester known to have been killed by the police during the eight weeks of upheaval that have shaken Panama. The victim, Eduardo Enrique Carrera, was killed by a pistol shot in the abdomen during a nighttime confrontation with police at El Valle de Ancon, 80 miles west of the capital.

The official account of the killing reported that Mr. Carrera and other protesters attacked the police, but relatives of the victims said the shooting occurred after one member of the group yelled "Down with the Pineapple!" General Noriega's enemies call him "pineapple" because of his heavily pock-marked face.

Mr. Carrera, 24 years old, was a university student who worked at a shoe store while studying business administration. After he was killed, the authorities ordered the university campus shut, apparently to prevent protests. It reopened today after being shut for a week.

"Eduardo was a young idealist, but he wasn't part of any political group," said his sister Patricia. "He had been arrested once for protesting. Like the rest of us, he just wasn't in agreement with this kind of Government."

Human rights campaigners in Panama find their work deeply frustrating because they are able only to collect information about abuses, not to act on it.

"There is no justice system here at all," said Otilia de Koster, coordinator of the year-old Human Rights and Legal Aid Investigation Center. "From the Supreme Court to the lowest tribunal, everything is controlled by the armed forces. You can have all the lawyers in the world, but it doesn't matter because in political cases, there are no rules."

The most prominent human rights advocate in Panama is Osvaldo Velasquez, a graying ophthalmologist who, in addition to his work in Panama, is a leading member of International Physicians for the Prevention of Nuclear War, the group which won the Nobel Peace Prize in 1985. In an interview this week, Dr. Velasquez said that military control over the executive, legislative and judicial branches of government "is what makes all the other human rights violations possible."

Agence France-Presse

Tom Brown, a correspondent for the Reuters news agency, leaving Panama Sunday after he was expelled by the Government.

"Lately I have been giving talks at the university, and I am distressed to find the students talking about violence as a way to get rid of the regime," Dr. Velasquez said. "I do my best to steer them away from that, but they say rebellion is the only way out because all other avenues are closed to them. I fear that Panama is getting to where El Salvador was five years ago."

Many Panamanian human rights advocates believe that the United States is largely to blame for allowing military rule in Panama to continue for 19 years. "The role of past American ambassadors in propping up this regime and covering up its abuses is absolutely shameful," Dr. Velasquez said.

* * *

September 22, 1987

MANAGUA'S BID TO CENSOR IS REPORTED

By STEPHEN KINZER
Special to the New York Times

MANAGUA, Nicaragua, Sept. 21—The Sandinista authorities agreed to allow the opposition newspaper La Prensa to reopen without censorship only after the paper's publisher rejected a suggestion that it accept censorship, the publisher said today.

"They wanted censorship," said the publisher, Violeta Barrios de Chamorro. "I told them no."

A Government order late Saturday lifted all restrictions on La Prensa, which has been closed since June 1986. Before that, the newspaper had been subject to Government censorship for four years.

On Saturday morning, at the initiative of the visiting Costa Rican Foreign Minister, Rodrigo Madrigal Nieto, a longtime friend of the Chamorro family, Mrs. Chamorro met with President Daniel Ortega Saavedra in her home. She said that as they discussed the reopening of La Prensa, Mr. Ortega brought up the possibility of Government censorship.

Censorship Again Is Mentioned

"I told Daniel that if we were talking about censorship, there was nothing to talk about," Mrs. Chamorro said. "I also told him: 'I don't want to hear the word C.I.A., because this idea you've gotten into your head, I just can't listen to it anymore.' "

Mr. Ortega and other Sandinista leaders have accused La Prensa of being a tool of the United States and specifically of the Central Intelligence Agency.

Later Saturday, Mrs. Chamorro said, she was visited by another senior Sandinista leader, Jaime Wheelock Roman, the Agrarian Reform Minister, who also brought up the possibility of censorship.

"I told him what I already told Daniel: 'There is complete press freedom or there is nothing,' " Mrs. Chamorro said.

Plans to Resume Publishing

Mrs. Chamorro said today that La Prensa would probably begin to circulate early next month. She said it might publish more pages than before because of heightened public interest in current events here.

Under terms of the Central American peace accord, signed by five presidents in the region last month in Guatemala, Nicaragua must allow full press and political freedom by Nov. 7, in exchange for an end to outside aid for anti-Sandinista guerrillas, known as contras. The Sandinista press today described the decision to reopen La Prensa as "advance compliance" with the accord.

Some of the 230 people who worked at La Prensa before it was closed 15 months ago have left Nicaragua and now publicly support the contras. Among the editors and contributors who remain are some of the most outspoken anti-Sandinista ideologues in Nicaragua. If they write in the forceful terms which they have been using privately over the last year, they are liable to provoke the regime more seriously than it has ever been provoked inside Nicaragua.

Mrs. Chamorro said today she did not know how Mr. Ortega would react to attacks on his Government published in La Prensa. "If one day it comes out and he doesn't like it, that's up to him," she said.

Restrictions a Fact of Life

Press censorship has been an important fact of Nicaraguan life since it was imposed in 1982. The Sandinistas said censorship was required by the escalating civil conflict, in which

Reuters

Workers oiling the presses at La Prensa, Nicaragua's main opposition newspaper, in preparation for resumption of publication. The newspaper has been shut since June 1986.

Government forces are fighting rebels supported by American aid. But opposition leaders say it was used to protect the Government from criticism.

Before La Prensa was closed, it was read by many Nicaraguans seeking an alternative to official information.

The memory of its late editor, Pedro Joaquin Chamorro Cardenal, who was assassinated in 1978, is widely revered. Under his leadership, the paper vigorously opposed the Somoza family dictatorship.

His widow, Mrs. Chamorro, became a member of the first post-Somoza ruling junta in July 1979, but she and other owners of La Prensa became disillusioned with the new Sandinista regime.

Delicate Topics

The paper became a bulwark of the anti-Sandinista cause, and it refused to condemn United States aid to the contras.

Nicaragua's two other daily newspapers support Sandinista rule.

In recent days, as the Government seemed to be preparing to lift its ban on La Prensa, Nicaragua journalists, editors and opposition leaders had wondered how the Government would react if La Prensa chose to press certain delicate topics.

Among those mentioned as potentially provocative are conditions in Nicaraguan jails and the stories of prison inmates, abuses committed by Sandinista soldiers, the country's foreign debt, which has increased nearly tenfold since 1979, and the personal lifestyles of Sandinista leaders.

The Government has not yet indicated whether it will act on applications from opposition leaders to open non-Sandinista television stations here. Since 1979, television broadcasting has been a Sandinista monopoly.

Neither has the Government acted to lift restrictions on radio broadcasting, which also is covered by the freedoms required under terms of the peace accord. More than 20 radio news programs were ordered off the air in the first years of Sandinista rule, and directors of several of the programs have already petitioned the Government to allow them to reopen.

* * *

February 14, 1988

PANAMANIANS USE TECHNOLOGY TO BALK CENSOR

Special to the New York Times

WASHINGTON, Feb. 13—With the help of modern-day technology, a small band of exiles is piercing the censorship in Panama.

"The telefax and computers, they are death to dictators, because what can they do to stop transmission?" said Carlos Ernesto Gonzalez de l'Astra, one of six political exiles who make up the staff of the Panamanian News Center here in Washington.

Press freedom in Panama is shaky at best. Four newspapers were closed in 1987. Three later reopened but one strayed too far and was quickly shut again. Two radio stations were closed by the Government in the first week of February. Such repression makes it "more difficult to get the news into Panama," said Jose Pretto Rosanio, director of the operation, known in Spanish as Centro Panameno de Noticias and by the initials C.P.N. "But the whole point is to take a position that will force the Government to take off a mask of democracy and let the rest of the world see its true face, Noriega's face."

A Clipping Service

To fill the void, Mr. Pretto's center translates and transmits dozens of articles each day that ran in prominent United States publications. It is thus something of a clipping service.

Six staff members, who were businessmen and lawyers before fleeing Panama, work in an office that is cramped, noisy and off the beaten path. So does a corps of other exiles and student volunteers.

Reports by Facsimile

They send their reports by facsimile to 6 to 10 points in Panama—law firms, small shops and other businesses that belong to the Civic Crusade, an umbrella organization that wants to oust the nation's leader, Gen. Manuel Antonio Noriega. The news then ripples out through a much larger facsimile transmission network. Churches, schools, banks and labor groups help copy and disseminate the information.

The material also goes to newspapers and radio stations willing to risk using it. Radio stations in Colombia and Costa Rica make use of Panamanian news sent by the service.

50,000 Panamanians Covered

The office estimates that 20,000 to 50,000 Panamanians see the articles it picks up from publications that include The New York Times, The Washington Post, The Christian Science Monitor and Time magazine. The service gives credit to the original publications and gets no commercial benefit since it does not charge for translations and transmissions. The operation, which costs $25,000 a month, is financed by Gabriel Lewis Galindo, a former Ambassador to the United States who owns a string of businesses in Panama.

Mr. Pretto said: "We only translate the news. We are not saying it is our news. We are not selling it."

He added that there had been no complaints so far from any of the publications.

Several Panamanian journalists living in the United States contribute their work, such as the columnist Guillermo Sanchez Borbon. Each day, he sends his column of satirical political gossip, "En Pocas Palabras" or "In a Few Words," from Miami to Washington, where it is then sent to Panama.

When the service began operations, its fliers were openly distributed on street corners and gathering places, but that has changed. The police have begun arresting people who hold any material that might be construed as anti-Government, C.P.N. says.

Newspapers have also been harassed. The bureau began life after the Government closed four opposition papers in 1987. Three later reopened under a limited amnesty.

One newspaper, El Siglo, was closed again after it reprinted material from C.P.N. Its editor flew to Washington and assembled a makeshift newspaper on one of the service's two small computers. The pages were sent to Panama and photocopied for distribution.

"C.P.N. is a free press, a truly free press," Mr. Lewis said. "I don't agree necessarily with everything we fax, but unlike Noriega, I don't stop it from being transmitted because that is what true freedom of the press is."

* * *

June 21, 1988

THE EDITOR: OUTSPOKEN BY DAY, MUZZLED BY NIGHT

By SHIRLEY CHRISTIAN

Special to the New York Times

SANTIAGO, Chile, June 20—When Juan Pablo Cardenas, a magazine editor, checked in recently for his usual night in jail under a sentence for offending the military, he was arrested on another charge and taken to jail in another town.

Although in Chile's pre-election climate the press appears to be publishing anything it might want to, Mr. Cardenas's problems reflect the fact that the Government of President Augusto Pinochet still has the power arbitrarily to punish those who do.

Mr. Cardenas, the editor of Analisis, a weekly newsmagazine, is the most celebrated of 28 journalists who have been charged with crimes or who are serving sentences for what they have published. Most, like Mr. Cardenas, must face military courts on charges of offenses against the armed

The New York Times/Santiago Llanquin

Juan Pablo Cardenas, the editor of the Chilean weekly newsmagazine Analisis.

forces. The majority are free on bail while they fight their cases, with only Mr. Cardenas serving a sentence as the result of a conviction.

Closing In on One Year

On July 8, Mr. Cardenas will complete one year of his 541-night sentence for an editorial two years ago calling the Chilean Army "the army of occupation of Pinochet" and asserting, among other things, that the Pinochet Government was repressive and lacked civilian support.

Throughout his sentence, which he serves by staying in jail from 10 P.M. to 7 A.M. each night, he has continued to go to his office daily to edit the magazine. In mid-April, the magazine carried an article about the armed forces' purchases of helicopters and other military equipment from France, South Africa and Israel.

In response, the naval prosecutor in Valparaiso, the port city that is the home of the Chilean Navy, had Mr. Cardenas arrested on May 25 when the editor showed up for his night at the jail in Santiago.

Some Added Detention

He spent the next five days detained in Valparaiso, along with the author of the article, Ivan Badilla, until the court learned that Mr. Cardenas had been ailing and out of the office when that issue of the magazine was prepared. Mr. Cardenas was freed and the assistant editor, Fernando Paulsen, was arrested. Mr. Badilla and Mr. Paulsen are seeking release on bail.

Mr. Cardenas, who puts the readership of his magazine at 25,000 to 40,000, identifies himself freely as an opponent of General Pinochet. He said that the objective of Analisis was "to collaborate in the establishment of a democratic regime" and that he considered the magazine's most important role to be that of publicizing human rights abuses in Chile.

During nearly 15 years of military Government, Chile has experienced brief periods of prior censorship, but the Government has a wide range of other controls at its command.

Under the Constitution's so-called transitory laws, which govern the country during what is seen as a period of transition to democracy, the Government has the right to approve new publications and it can order journalists not to publish information on the grounds of national security.

An Aggressive Military

In addition, military prosecutors have been much more aggressive in charging journalists with offenses against the armed forces than was the case under civilian governments.

In 1983, the Government began to ease the rules, and opposition magazines like Analisis proliferated. In early 1987, two daily newspapers linked to the political opposition began to publish. Several of the most listened-to radio news programs are independent of the Government, and television, although largely Government-controlled, has begun to open itself to opposition views.

With Chileans expected to vote later this year on whether to extend General Pinochet's tenure for eight more years, print and broadcast news outlets are filled with the declarations, accusations and debate of almost two dozen political parties. The cacophony is joined by General Pinochet and his advisers and by myriad campaign organizations.

The Government contends that the Chilean press is operating freely and that the public is getting all the information that it needs or wants.

'To Inform but Not to Injure'

Foreign Minister Ricardo Garcia said during a recent conversation with foreign journalists that the Chilean press had "all the rights to inform but not to injure."

He said the fact that 28 journalists were in some form of legal entanglement had nothing to do with the electoral campaign and did not interfere with the coverage of it. The charges against the journalists, he said, could have been made at any time.

Other civilians in the Government, who asked not to be identified, said inquiries were made within the Government about reducing Mr. Cardenas's sentence, but that legal experts rejected the idea because the editor had already been sentenced.

Another prominent editor identified with the opposition, Emilio Filippi, recently won a four-year-old case brought against him by a military prosecutor. A charge of offenses against the armed forces was overturned by the Supreme Court in a case in which the news magazine Hoy distributed chapters of a book by a former political prisoner.

Mr. Cardenas, 38 years old, has attracted international attention with his nightly sojourns in jail. Many nights, he checks in surrounded by colleagues, other sympathizers, television crews and photographers.

Arthur Miller and Rose Styron

Earlier this month, the American playwright Arthur Miller and the poet Rose Styron left a dinner at the home of the novelist Jorge Edwards to accompany Mr. Cardenas to jail. Visitors are not allowed inside the jail, and so they left him at the door. The night of Mr. Cardenas's second detention, on the charges from Valparaiso, a British television crew happened to be on hand to film the scene.

Mr. Cardenas said one benefit of his fame was that the other prisoners, mostly convicted thieves and swindlers, have become so impressed by his apparent importance that they have stopped stealing his money and personal items while he sleeps.

* * *

October 19, 1993

ONE MORE SHORTAGE IN HAITI: NEWS

By GARRY PIERRE-PIERRE
Special to The New York Times

PORT-AU-PRINCE, Haiti, Oct. 18—Minutes after a United States warship was spotted a few miles offshore on Sunday, the quiet streets of this capital city suddenly came alive as people scurried to get some news.

Radio stations did not interrupt their musical programs to give a special report. Newspapers did not run any special editions the next day. The only radio station broadcasting news on Sunday, Radio Tropic, simply told its listeners that two United States ships were visible at sea.

To learn more, Haitians had to rely on foreign broadcasts like the Voice of America and CNN, which explained that the vessel was one of six dispatched here to enforce an international oil and arms embargo placed on Haiti to force the country's military leaders to accept the return of President Jean-Bertrand Aristide, who was ousted in a bloody coup in September 1991.

That people here had to rely on foreign newscasts underscores the danger that Haitian journalists face and how the military Government has managed to keep most Haitians in the dark about critical events.

Practicing Self-Censorship

"It means that the Haitian press does not have access to the authorities to find objective information," said Nelson Jean-Louis, a resident of Bel Air, a working-class slum. "When something happens in Haiti, people in the United States know about it before we do."

It is not so much that the news organizations in Haiti do not have access. Rather, they practice self-censorship and often will wait to attribute a story to a foreign news organization to avoid the wrath of the military.

For instance, today, the front page of Haiti's largest and oldest daily newspaper, Le Nouvelliste, had no bylined articles. Another daily, Le Matin, ran a French wire service story on the local reaction to the assassination of Justice Minister Guy Malary last week.

"You take a risk because you have to work," said Guy Jean, owner of Radio Tropic, one of a few stations still broadcasting local news. "If you're not careful, you can't function. They are waiting for you to slip so they can get you. We are not against anyone, we're not for anyone."

Broadcasts Bring Threats

Mr. Jean, who spent about 15 years living in Brooklyn, opened his radio station shortly after the election of Father Aristide two years ago. He said his format is similar to stations in the United States.

The station broadcasts a three-minute news update every half hour, and threats after broadcasts are common, he said.

"I take them seriously," Mr. Jean said. "I have written to the chief of police about them. But he told me to get my own security force."

One of the station's reporters, Colson Dorme, was abducted shortly after filing a live report from the airport when Dante Caputo, the special United Nations envoy, arrived here in February to begin mediating the return of Father Aristide.

Mr. Caputo was met by raucous protesters, and Mr. Dorme said on the air that the mob was unruly and that armed soldiers took no action to control the mob. Before he could put away his microphone, he said, he felt a sharp blow on the back of his head. He fell down and was taken away in a Jeep, blindfolded and kept in a dark room for four days until national and international pressures brought his release.

"I am more careful now," said Mr. Dorme, sitting in the spacious newsroom of Radio Tropic. "But I am not afraid. The work can't be done if I am afraid."

While Mr. Dorme is determined to stay and practice his trade, many journalists have left the country; others stopped working altogether.

Some Haitian reporters are indeed not objective; many are staunch supporters of Father Aristide. "Unfortunately they all get painted with the same brush," said a Western diplomat. "Not all of them are like that."

Today the director of the United States Information Services here, Stanley Schrager, began briefing Haitian journalists on developments. The daily briefings are to last seven weeks and may continue longer.

For two minutes he answered questions ranging from the naval blockade to whether Father Aristide will be back in Haiti on Oct. 30.

"It's a good thing," said Yolette Mengual, information director of Radio Arc-en-Ciel. "We need to keep our listeners better informed."

* * *

February 19, 1995

PRESS PROTESTS 'GAG' BILLS IN ARGENTINA

By CALVIN SIMS
Special to The New York Times

BUENOS AIRES, Feb. 18—The administration of President Carlos Sal Menem sent three bills to Congress last month that could muzzle the press in this an election year if they are approved, advocates of free speech say.

The bills, which have a good chance of passing the Menem-controlled legislature, would greatly increase the penalties for libel and slander, make it a crime to offend the memory of the dead, and force news outlets to take out costly libel insurance.

A campaign to oppose the bills has been begun by outraged newspaper publishers, broadcasters, press associations and opposition parties. They say the measures are intended to intimidate the press and quash investigations into Government corruption that could be damaging to Mr. Menem's re-election campaign.

Justice Minister Rodolfo Barra, who is leading the administration's effort to pass the bills, said there was strong support for them in Congress, which is dominated by Mr. Menem's Peronist party. He said the legislation was necessary to protect individuals against defamation and insult.

"One of the most important precepts in our society is to protect the honor of an individual, because a person without honor is a person without liberty," Mr. Barra said in an interview. He denied assertions that the proposed laws were intended to restrict press freedom or to influence the elections, saying that they would not go into effect until after the balloting on May 13.

But Danilo Arbilla, the chairman of the Freedom of the Press Committee of the Inter-American Press Association, disagreed. The Government, he said, is trying to silence the press, which in recent years has aggressively reported on white-collar crime and corruption in the federal Government, often involving Mr. Menem's relatives and advisers.

Chacho Alvarez, the opposition Frente Grande candidate for President, called the new press law "a gag aimed at encouraging self-censorship."

"Menem pursues an authoritarian image," Mr. Alvarez said. "Instead of taking on corruption in his own ranks, he has decided to gag the press."

Under the proposed legislation, reporters and editors would face a maximum sentence of three years in jail and a $100,000 fine if found guilty of defamation and a six-year maximum sentence and $200,000 fine for libel. Suspects would not be released on bail.

The legislation also introduces the crime of offending the memory of the dead, the proposed punishment for which was not disclosed.

Furthermore, the legislation requires all publications to obtain $500,000 worth of insurance to protect against libel suits.

Claudio Escribano, executive editor of La Nacion, a respected daily here, expressed concern that the insurance requirement would cripple small newspapers and magazines and cause them to shy away from controversial issues that might lead to lawsuits.

Horacio Verbitsky, a leading investigative journalist here, said the press was the only institution that was not controlled by the Menem Government.

"There is a good amount of respect for the press in Argentina today, much more than for politicians, and this makes Mr. Menem very, very concerned," Mr. Verbitsky said.

Two years ago, when Mr. Verbitsky's newspaper, Pagina 12, uncovered corruption scandals involving friends and relatives of Mr. Menem, the President asserted that the publication was financed with drug profits and called Mr. Verbitsky a "criminal journalist."

Mr. Menem's advisers said that their efforts to pass the libel laws were strengthened last month after the arrest of a team of journalists and models for the Noticias weekly magazine, who the police said tried to stage a mock attack on a Jewish sports club. The police said the magazine was preparing a cover story to show how unprepared the police were for terrorist attacks.

Mr. Menem said the news magazine's behavior was "grotesque and an affront to serious, responsible and informative journalism."

* * *

August 15, 1996

MEXICO'S NEW PRESS BOLDNESS STOPS AT LEADER'S DESK

By SAM DILLON

MEXICO CITY, Aug. 14—President Ernesto Zedillo was seated on a wooden throne in the National Palace recently, taping an interview with Jacobo Zabludovsky, Mexico's No. 1 television anchor, when he suddenly interrupted his questioner.

"Pardon me, I don't want to go into all those details," Mr. Zedillo snapped. "What's more, the question you asked before didn't work either."

"Ah, fine," Mr. Zabludovsky responded meekly, offering to cut the preceding question from the video.

"No, the other one also," Mr. Zedillo insisted. And when millions of Mexicans watched the nightly news minutes later, the irritating questions were gone.

Americans might find it difficult to imagine President Clinton ordering Larry King or Dan Rather to cut an unwelcome question from an interview. Even in Mexico, Mr. Zedillo's blunt editing instructions—which were not trimmed from an official transcript distributed to journalists—came as a surprise, given the President's frequent endorsements of an independent press and declarations of a new era in Government-media relations.

For more than a century, the Mexican Government has kept a tight grip on the press and broadcasters. Today, many reporters are exercising an outspoken new brand of journalism, often investigative and frequently irreverent.

Several vigorous and nonpartisan newspapers are flourishing, and competition among television broadcasters is growing.

Mexican journalism is responding to the increasing demands for reliable information from a once insular society that has been opening to the world, especially in the 20 months since the North American Free Trade Agreement took effect. Government press controls have been loosening, with the encouragement, or at least acquiescence, of Mr. Zedillo. But old habits die hard, and the Mexican presidency can still wield a heavy hand at times to influence news coverage.

"It's still an authoritarian system," said Sergio Aguayo, a political scientist who studies Mexican journalism, "though the media are establishing their autonomy."

Carlos Almada, the presidential spokesman, said Mr. Zedillo had worked hard to foster news media independence. In more than 20 interviews this year before Mr. Zabludovsky's, the President "has never eluded a single question," Mr. Almada said.

The President may have felt comfortable interrupting this time, he said, because the anchor had broken off the taping minutes earlier to correct a fumbled question.

"This incident should be interpreted as absolutely exceptional," Mr. Almada said.

The interview, on July 25, followed the President's signing of a pact on national election reform. Mr. Zedillo interrupted the questioning when Mr. Zabludovsky began to examine how the pact would affect the President's power to appoint municipal officials in Mexico City.

Mr. Zabludovsky, in a phone conversation later, portrayed the interruption as a result of a mutual decision to steer the questioning back to national issues.

"Since this was to be broadcast to the entire country," Mr. Zabludovsky said, "we thought those questions were only of local interest, so we decided to redo them."

The anchor said his network, Televisa, which until three years ago enjoyed a virtual monopoly over Mexico's television airwaves and wielded it with a stark pro-Government bias, was now trying to offer not only Government but also opposition points of view on the air.

"The country has changed, and we have to change as well," Mr. Zabludovsky said.

For decades, Presidents irritated by news coverage unabashedly exercised their power to retaliate. In 1972, President Luis Echeverria sent agents to destroy the entire press run of a newspaper that included an article by Mr. Aguayo describing the new millionaires then emerging inside the governing Institutional Revolutionary Party.

In 1989, President Carlos Salinas de Gortari's agents coerced a publisher with whom the President was displeased into selling his paper to the Government for $1 million and forced him into exile.

But clumsy repression has rarely been needed, because until recently pro-Government attitudes prevailed among broadcasters and newspaper owners, many of whom have profited from Government advertising.

Newsroom bribery was such an accepted part of journalism that each payment earned a name: the chayote, or squash, was paid by a Government ministry to a reporter in exchange for cooperative coverage, while the cebollazo, or big onion, bought a flattering profile of an individual politician. The sablazo, or saber slash, rewarded a journalist for a hatchet job written to injure an official's rival.

Whether these payments continue today is in dispute. Government officials say Mr. Zedillo has ended them. Raymundo Riva Palacio, a prize-winning editor at Reforma, a Mexico City newspaper, which has forbidden its reporters to accept the payments, said colleagues at other publications and people on Mr. Zedillo's staff had told him that the payments continued. "The structure hasn't changed," Mr. Riva Palacio said.

Nonetheless, journalists are exercising greater liberties, and Reforma is one obvious example. Established in 1993, Reforma has shown its autonomy in its evenhanded treatment of the political parties as well as in its modern business reporting.

Its quarterly reports by a full-time polling unit on Mr. Zedillo's approval ratings are an unusual feature of Mexican politics. In June, Reforma reported that 57 percent of Mexicans disapproved Mr. Zedillo's performance, while 35 percent approved.

At least half a dozen other outspoken newspapers have emerged across Mexico, and like Reforma they have achieved financial independence from the Government by catering to a middle class clamoring for reliable information.

"Before, credibility was worthless in Mexican journalism," said Bruno Lopez, Mexico correspondent for Univision, the Miami-based broadcaster. "Now it's become a valuable commodity."

Change has come fastest to newspapers, but even television is evolving, said Sergio Sarmiento, a vice president of Television Azteca, since 1993 a competitor to Televisa.

"The Government used to give commands," Mr. Sarmiento said. "Now they offer suggestions."

But one rule appears to continue: neither Azteca nor Televisa directly criticizes President Zedillo.

* * *

February 3, 1997

NEW TV LAW IN COLOMBIA PROVOKES COMPLAINTS OF CENSORSHIP

By DIANA JEAN SCHEMO

BOGOTA, Colombia, Feb. 1—The Colombian Congress has granted a regulatory commission broad authority to take television news programs off the air on the basis of their content. Many journalists see the move as an attempt to punish programs that have investigated suspected ties between drug traffickers and prominent politicians, including President Ernesto Samper.

The measure, part of a new broadcast law canceling television news concessions that were to have run until 2003, was signed by Mr. Samper in December.

Six months earlier, Congress exonerated the President in a scandal stemming from charges that his 1994 election campaign had knowingly accepted contributions from major drug dealers.

"It's a very direct measure against news shows that have been critical of Samper over the last two years," said Enrique Santos Calderon, a columnist for the daily El Tiempo and part-owner of QAP, a television news production company.

Daniel Coronell, an investigative journalist and news director of New Colombian Television, agreed. "It assures the President that he won't be criticized for the rest of his term," he said.

The new law creates regional stations and two private networks in addition to the two public stations currently on the air and grants Congress its own channel. Its most controversial provision allows the two-year-old National Television Commission to review the contents of television programs every six months to determine whether they comply with the Constitution, which promises Colombians the right to their "honor" and demands that the news be "truthful and impartial."

Although news organizations have filed suits challenging the new law, the Constitutional Court is not expected to rule on it for several months.

But the television commission, four of whose five members are appointed by the Government and Congress, will begin reviewing the contents of news programs this month. Programs can be taken off the air before the court has a chance to issue its findings.

In its annual human rights review, released on Thursday, the State Department in Washington criticized the broadcast law, which it called "an obvious effort by the Samper administration to eliminate troubling television news coverage of a scandal-ridden administration and to reward its powerful backers for remaining loyal."

Supporters of the law argue that it is not intended to censor news shows, but to open the airwaves to a wider range of sympathies. They dismiss the criticism from the United States as part of a campaign in Washington to undermine Mr. Samper.

Complaining that reporters were overwhelmingly hostile to the President during the inquiry into suspicions that he had drug connections, one of the bill's sponsors, Congressman Carlos Alonso Lucio, called it a way to broaden access to the airwaves. "Undoubtedly, during this last crisis in Colombia the news shows went beyond the mission of informing people to assume a defined political position," Mr. Alonso said. "Anybody who was a friend of the Government was a crook, and whoever was against the President became the great ethical saints of the country."

Mr. Alonso, a former member of the M-19 guerrilla organization who reportedly has made frequent visits to imprisoned leaders of the Cali drug cartel, Miguel and Gilberto Rodriguez Orejuela, co-sponsored the section of the new law requiring twice-yearly reviews of news programs with another lawmaker, Martha Catalina Daniels. The reviews mean that news programs—with their employees, leases and millions of dollars in studios and equipment—are threatened every six months with being shut down and barred from broadcasting for five years.

Mr. Lucio and Mrs. Daniels have been strong supporters of President Samper, and have been highly critical of news coverage of the investigation of possible connections between drug dealers and politicians.

Mrs. Daniels is herself being investigated for corruption by the Supreme Court, and her husband, Hernando Rodriguez, is being sought by the authorities on charges that he stole $13 million from a longshoremen's pension fund.

Mrs. Daniels said the owners of the news programs, who she estimated earned $35,000 for every half-hour broadcast, were defending not so much freedom of the press as "their own economic interests."

Monica de Grieff, the chairwoman of the National Television Commission, said the commission was studying other countries "that have no connotation of censorship" to figure out how to measure program content.

Last year, Mrs. de Grieff broke off a transmission from Congress when then-Senator Maria Izquierdo took the microphone to confess that she had accepted money from drug dealers to help Mr. Samper's election campaign.

Mrs. de Grieff said the commission did not like the mandatory reviews, "but we have to do it, and that's why we're trying to do it as carefully as possible."

Maria Isabel Rueda, news director of QAP, said the production company was already feeling the effects of the new law. Defense Minister Guillermo Alberto Gonzalez, who is reputed to have ties with a drug trafficker named Pastor Perafan, has complained to the commission that QAP was persecuting him and his family when a reporter questioned him about the allegations. More disquieting, she said, was that her news program stood alone.

"My competition never asked him about the charges at all," she said.

In the face of criticism, most recently from the Inter-American Press Association, President Samper said recently that he did not agree with the twice-yearly reviews, but signed the law because of its overall content. He said that if the Constitutional Court upheld the television law, he would propose a bill to modify it. But a minister in his Government has said publicly that the law is precisely the one the Administration hoped for.

* * *

July 22, 1997

CRUSADING TV STATION IS THE CITY'S DAYTIME DRAMA

By CALVIN SIMS

LIMA, Peru, July 21—When leftist guerrillas bombed Frecuencia Latina TV here five years ago, killing three employees, the television station's owner, Baruch Ivcher, enclosed the station with a concrete wall 20 feet high and persuaded the Government to post soldiers and tanks outside.

Today, the soldiers who once guarded the television station, which the guerrillas accused of being pro-Government, may soon be told to storm it, as part of what many Peruvians say is a Government crackdown on news organizations that broadcast reports critical of President Alberto K. Fujimori's administration.

But to take control of the station, troops would first have to break through the scores of journalists and thousands of supporters who have held a vigil there, sleeping on mattresses and cots, because of rumors that the military is planning a raid.

"We will defend this station with our very lives if we have to," said Ivan M. Garcia, the station's news director. "The only way they'll get in here is by using tanks to blast through the door or helicopters to come through the roof."

Inside the state-of-the-art station, which was rebuilt in 1992 after the attack, it was business as usual, but with a new sense of mission. Reporters and producers, working double and triple shifts, scurried through the hallways racing to get the latest news of their plight on the air.

"When you're job is to report the news, it's a bit uncomfortable when all the sudden you become the news," said Fernando V. Viana, the station's editor in chief. "But we are now forced to defend everything we stand for."

Technicians have positioned cameras on the station's roof to monitor any suspicious activities or, in the event of a military raid, to broadcast an incursion live.

The station became the focal point of Peru's worst political crisis in recent memory after the Government stripped Mr. Ivcher of his citizenship last week, apparently in retaliation for investigative reports that exposed torture and corruption in the military and illegal wiretapping by the national intelligence agency.

Because Peruvian law requires owners of television stations to be Peruvian citizens, Mr. Ivcher could lose his controlling interest in Frecuencia Latina.

But the Fujimori Government's decision to revoke Mr. Ivcher's citizenship has been criticized here and abroad. Thousands of Peruvians, wearing blue ribbons to show their solidarity with Mr. Ivcher, have gathered daily outside the television station to express their support for Frecuencia Latina, which in recent years has gained a reputation for exposing corruption and providing public service.

Outside the station's towering concrete wall, supporters have posted colorful signs, including those reading: "The Military Is Not Welcome Here," "Ivcher Is Peru," "Without the Press We Are Not Free," and "19 Percent and Dropping," referring to Mr. Fujimori's declining approval rating in opinion polls.

Carmen de Soto, a nurse, said that when her brother was falsely accused last year of being a terrorist, she called producers at Frecuencia Latina, who intervened on his behalf and convinced the police that he was innocent.

"Fujimori controls everything in this country—the judges, Congress, business—everything except the press," Mrs. de Soto said. "If we allow him to take our right to be informed, what will we have left?"

In a telephone interview from Miami, where he fled last month after receiving death threats, Mr. Ivcher, who was born in Israel and became a Peruvian citizen in 1984, said that if the Government succeeded in taking over Frecuencia Latina, no media organization in Peru would be free.

"I am just an easy target that the Government is using to send a message to all other television channels and publications in Peru that it will not tolerate free, independent, honest reporting," Mr. Ivcher said. "This demonstrates that there are no rights left in Peru and that the only way Fujimori knows how to run his Government is with tanks and soldiers."

The Government has said it canceled Mr. Ivcher's citizenship because of omissions in the application forms and lack of proof that he had given up his Israeli nationality. But his naturalization documents were signed and approved in 1984 by Fernando Belaunde Terry, then the President, who said last week that there had been no irregularities in the procedure.

Mr. Ivcher said that by revoking his citizenship, the Government was trying to place the station under the control of his partners, Mendel and Samuel Winter, who own a minority stake.

The Winter brothers, who did not return phone calls to their offices, are widely considered to be pro-Government, and local newspapers have reported that they have petitioned the court to take administrative control of the station to protect their investment.

Mr. Ivcher, who is married to a Peruvian and has four daughters who were born here, said that until a few years ago he had good relations with the Government, until he brought a new team of journalists to the station who were more aggressive in ferreting out corruption.

Mr. Ivcher said that he wanted to return to his home in Peru but that he would continue to run the station by telephone from Miami until a Peruvian court decided whether the Government was justified in revoking his citizenship.

In his absence, his daughters—Dafna, 26, Miki, 24, and twins Tal and Hadas, 18—have returned to Peru and have been sleeping at the station to support the journalists.

"My father loves Peru and works 12 to 15 hours a day at this station for the good of our country," Tal said. "This is very unjust what they've done to him."

The Middle East

January 4, 1977

LEBANON BEGINS PRESS CENSORSHIP

Special to The New York Times

BEIRUT, Lebanon, Jan. 3—Syrian troops of the Arab League peacekeeping force today ended their occupation of the offices of six daily newspapers and one weekly magazine as strict censorship of the press by the Lebanese Government went into effect.

Several of the suspended publications are expected to resume operation this week under the new regulations.

A decree introducing censorship was adopted by the Cabinet of Prime Minister Selim al-Hoss Saturday under the emergency powers that it had received from Parliament for a six-month period.

An order issued by Interior Minister Salah Salman put the decree into effect today. All material for publication must now be submitted to the police department before it can be published. Under the decree, violations are punishable not only by suspension of the publication involved but also by imprisonment of those responsible, for terms of one to three years, plus a fine of $2,000 to $5,000.

The Interior Minister's order also subjected to censorship all press dispatches destined for foreign countries, as well as outgoing television films and radio news and commentaries.

Editors Urged to Cooperate

This is the first time such a measure has been applied in Lebanon since 1973, when martial law was in effect for two weeks.

The press association, consisting of owners of about 100 newspapers and other periodicals, urged editors to cooperate with the Government in the interest of the country "during these crucial times."

Riyad Taha, president of the association, inspected offices of the suspended newspapers after the troops left them. The newspapers were seized last month for printing material that was regarded as detrimental to the Arab League's "deterrent force." The force was sent here in November as part of a peace plan laid down by Arab heads of state for ending the Lebanese crisis.

Press censorship is one of the measures through which the Government of President Elias Sarkis is gradually reasserting its authority after the disintegration brought on by 19 months of factional fighting.

A police communiqué today urged Lebanese to obtain new passports and to seek reconfirmation of their identity cards.

* * *

March 19, 1978

INVASION FOCUSES ATTENTION ON CENSORSHIP IN ISRAEL

By DEIRDRE CARMODY

The Associated Press received a dispatch from its Tel Aviv bureau Friday describing the military action in Lebanon and saying that a guerrilla rocket had smashed into a residential section across the Israeli border.

A short while later a second message came from the Tel Aviv bureau saying that the Israeli censor had asked that the description be changed from "smashed into a residential section" to "smashed into a house."

It was a reminder that in Israel all news organizations are under military censorship. The foreign press there must submit all articles, news dispatches, television scripts, photo captions, photographs and film to the Office of Military Censor, where they are scrutinized for sensitive military information.

Telephone lines in news offices are monitored by the censors.

The Israeli press is also subject to censorship laws, which have been in effect since the days of British rule. There is a list of subjects that might affect national security and if journalists write on any of these subjects, the articles must be submitted to the censor. An editor who wants to contest the censor's decision can do so and a special committee is quickly called in to rule on the matter.

Israeli officials are sensitive to the charge that they exercise censorship at all and say quickly that military censorship exists only for reasons of security and that there is no political censorship. However, editors point out that there are times when the line between the military and political can be somewhat obscure.

The censorship example from The Associated Press yesterday is not typical because censors usually catch items before they have been transmitted. An assistant foreign editor of the Associated Press, Edward Butler, commented that he did not know whether the correction had been made because the censor had second thoughts or because more specific information had been received about the rocket attack after the dispatch had been transmitted.

Face of Soldier Blacked Out

The Associated Press was also involved in a censorship matter Wednesday, when censors blacked out in a photograph the face of an Israeli soldier holding two prisoners captured in Lebanon. United Press International sent out an almost identical picture some time later in which the soldier's face was left untouched.

"We protested to the censor," said Hal Buell, executive news photo editor of The Associated Press. "It appears that we were early and then orders changed on the matter."

Television, too, is subject to scrutiny on military matters. The night before Israeli troops crossed into Lebanon a CBS crew shot film of armored vehicles moving north and of troops massing. The crew members were told to hold the film until after the invasion had begun and had been announced.

"We've had a lot of fights with the Israeli censors," said Sidney Feders, foreign editor of CBS News. "Sometimes the telephone will go dead and the censor will cut in on the telex."

Foreign correspondents view aspects of this as somewhat of a game. The night before the invasion of Lebanon, a correspondent in Jerusalem was talking with his editor in New York. Suddenly the phone went dead in New York as the censor in Jerusalem cut in and reminded the correspondent about what could and could not be transmitted.

The correspondent argued with the censor, meanwhile dialing another phone. As soon as he had reached New York, he hung up on the censor and continued the conversation with his editor on the other phone.

One of the dodges used by correspondents—and presumably recognized by the censors—is to attribute information that might not otherwise pass the censors to "published reports."

For instance, while the censor will not allow the correspondent to write about the size of the invading force, a sentence saying "foreign press reports placed the combined Israeli forces as high as 20,000" tends to get through.

* * *

January 20, 1980

WESTERN PRESS A CONVENIENT SCAPEGOAT FOR TROUBLED IRAN

By CHRISTOPHER S. WREN

TEHERAN—American journalists generally consider it poor form to run in packs, but last week some of them were given no choice. More than 100 representatives of American newspapers, news agencies television and radio networks and news magazines were ordered to leave Iran.

The ruling Revolutionary Council's justification was that the Americans were guilty of biased reporting, having focused more on the plight of the American diplomatic hostages, and other less attractive aspects of the Islamic revolution, than on Iranian complaints about the deposed Shah. British and West German journalists were put on notice that they might be turned out next if their coverage did not become more sympathetic.

Some Iranian officials tried to put the best face on the expulsion, contending that it might facilitate the release of the hostages by depriving their captors of publicity. Certainly the militants who seized the United States Embassy on Nov. 4 have played upon the Western media to convey their radical opinions: on virtually every subject. Yet as a diplomat from a Third World nation observed, by this logic "they should have thrown out everyone."

A veteran British reporter, who asked not to be named because he is remaining in Teheran, said "I think that the Iranian Government wanted a scapegoat for the failure of the world at large to show any sympathy for its position. They chose to pin the blame on what they called the Zionist press barons in America."

Different Notions of a Free Press

The basic divergence, however, was more cultural than ideological. "What they seemed to find lacking in us was a restraint or self-censorship. That the press would have a mind of its own is very alien to them," said Arden Ostrander, a CBS-TV producer who had been in Iran since the first week of the embassy takeover.

"On the basis of what we read or see in the press, there is a large gap between our concept of press freedom and that of Western nations," acknowledged Abolghassem Sadegh, the Deputy Minister of National Guidance responsible for the foreign press. "Unfortunately, Western mass-media-reports certain matters that may be factual as far as the occurrence is concerned, but they do not induce to the reader the truth of the matter as it should be."

Iran has known only a brief taste of press freedom, in the interregnum between the Shah's departure and Ayatòllah Ruhollah Khomeini's return. The Shah kept the domestic press under his thumb and tried to bribe or intimidate foreign reporters. Under the Ayatollah, the Iranian press has regressed to become what Mohammed Abdoli, an Iranian college teacher of journalism, called a "public relations bureau for broadcasting and printing the communications and news releases of top clergymen and other key Government officials."

Yet, as the Minister of National Guidance, Nasser Minachi, observed, foreign journalists were allowed a surprising amount of freedom for a new revolutionary state, despite individual expulsions of some American reporters last summer. A formal oath binding visiting journalists to tell the truth was shelved as was a rule requiring a ministry official's presence at all interviews.

Western reporters were admitted en masse after the embassy seizure because the Government saw an opportunity to expose them to the corruption and cruelty that had prevailed under the Shah. Sightseeing tours were organized to the most damning remnants of his regime—its palaces and prisons. The abuses were reported, but many Americans annoyed the Iranians by not devoting more attention to what one newsman dismissed as "a year-old story."

The speed with which most American reporters are accustomed to working made them unwitting participants in the hostage drama. "The nature of our job is to play both ends against the middle," explained a wire service reporter. He noted that whenever Foreign Minister Sadegh Ghotbzadeh floated some conciliatory suggestion, reporters immediately sought a telephone reaction from Ayatollah Khomeini or the militants, who invariably dismissed it.

Rebounding Reports

Some American news organizations, notably the television networks, were accused of becoming part of the scene around the embassy. While the crowd chanted and waved their fists to the cameras—in one instance switching into French to accommodate a Canadian television crew from Quebec—the rest of the Iranian capital went calmly about the mundane business of living. One Teheran official fretted that Iranians living in the United States were getting a warped picture of their own country. Ayatollah Mohammed Beheshti, the Secretary General of the Revolutionary Council, said that some. "clever" American reports were even finding their way back into the Teheran press.

The final straw was probably not the preoccupation with the embassy but the extensive coverage of ethnic clashes between Azerbaijani followers of Ayatollah Kazem Shariat-Madari and Khomeini loyalists backed by revolutionary militiamen. After a firing squad executed 11 Azerbaijanis earlier this month, prompting new unrest, the militiamen steered all the reporters they could find on a flight back to Teheran and the provincial governor banned foreign journalists from landing at Tabriz airport.

By last Monday evening, the Revolutionary Council concluded that the Americans had become more a liability than an asset. But curiously, the parting lacked any real animosity on either side. Mr. Sadegh, for one, hinted that the Americans, who were given a leisurely four days to leave the country, eventually would be allowed back one by one. The departing reporters were thoroughly searched at the airport, but when customs officers began confiscating carpets that some of them had bought in the Teheran bazaar, the protests got a hearing in the Ministry of National Guidance. A deputy minister sent down instructions that the banished press be allowed to depart bearing its Persian rugs along with the cameras and typewriters.

* * *

February 21, 1980

SADAT'S PLAN FOR A LAW TO PUNISH CRITICS STIRS CONCERN

By CHRISTOPHE S. WREN

Special to The New York Times

CAIRO, Feb. 20—The Government of President Anwar el-Sadat, casting about for a device to muzzle annoying critics abroad, has managed instead to offend jurists, writers and politicians at home.

The controversy developed over a "law of shame" that Mr. Sadat proposed late last month to punish people who disparaged Egypt and its political system.

In urging Parliament to adopt legislation on ethics, Mr. Sadat indicated that he had in mind several dozen Egyptians, mostly Nasserites and leftists, who have criticized his policies through publications and radio stations supported by Arab countries opposed to Egypt's peace treaty with Israel.

Mr. Sadat had suggested such a law earlier. The project is widely regarded as the idea of Sufi Abu Taleb. Speaker of the People's Assembly, in which Mr. Sadat's National Democratic Party holds most of the seats. This time, the call was followed by publication of a draft in the newspaper Al Ahram. Lawyers called the draft law unconstitutional, writers considered it menacing and opposition parties asserted it was undemocratic.

Political Quandary for Sadat

Several Egyptian intellectuals suggest that the law was proposed because Mr. Sadat's policies have put him in a quandary. With Egypt fighting an Arab boycott, Mr. Sadat needs to persuade other Arabs that his peace policies have unanimous backing from the Egyptian people.

At the same time, Mr. Sadat wants to show the West, particularly the United States, which is providing over $1 billion a year in aid, that he has replaced the dictatorship of the late Gamal Abdel Nasser with a pluralistic democracy where personal freedom is encouraged.

Mr. Sadat unwittingly touched upon the contradictions earlier this week when he told a group of prominent Egyptian journalists that the secret of Egypt's stability "lies in its sound democratic system of Government." Mr. Sadat reiterated his familiar boast that no other Arab regime had the courage to try such democracy for even two hours because "their people would kick out the rulers at once."

Draft Causes Uneasiness

When the draft of the projected law was published several weeks ago, unease spread among educated Egyptians that the Government was seeking sweeping authority to suppress free thought.

Among its other provisions, the draft envisioned setting up a court of ethics to try and punish Egyptians who preached any antireligious philosophy, incited opposition to the state's economic, political and social system and disseminated "false" or "extremist" statements that hurt the prestige of the state, irritated public opinion and threatened national unity and social peace.

Bribery, drug peddling tax evasion and treason were other offenses that would fall within the competence of a court of ethics, which would function outside the present judicial system.

According to the draft, a tribunal of four members of Parliament and three judicial consultants would handle most defendants, meting out punishments that included imprisonment, fires, house arrest, job dismissal and bans on travel abroad.

Opponents of the new law did not take long to unite around the issue. The weekly Al Shaab of the Socialist Labor Party, the largest minority in Parliament, devoted a full issue under the banner headline "No to the Law of Shame," with critical reactions from prominent writers such as Tewfik al-Hakim, Naguib Mahfouz and Youssef Idris. An independent member of Parliament, Montaz Nassar, was quoted as having said: "It closes all the windows of freedom."

The biggest outcry came from lawyers, who objected that the new law would regulate ethical behavior and set up a parallel judicial system in which legislators rather than judges would have the majority decision.

Last Friday, several thousand lawyers gathered at their syndicate, or bar association, in Cairo to discuss the proposal. According to several lawyers who were present, Mr. Sadat's National Democratic Party packed the room with supporters who repeatedly heckled Mustafa Marei, one of Egypt's most distinguished retired jurists, when he spoke against the measure.

Hecklers Disrupted Speech

Mr. Marei, who during his years on the bench clashed with both King Farouk and President Nasser over civil liberties, charged that the proposed law was meant to insulate the Government from criticism. He could not finish his address because of heckling, according to the lawyers present.

Meanwhile, the syndicate of judges has also put out a long brief against the proposed "law of shame," viewing it as an attack on the independence of the judiciary. At least one Cabinet member was reported opposed to the measure.

Opposition became so vehement that Vice President Hosni Mubarak tried to remind everyone that no draft law has actually been prepared for Parliament's consideration.

The expectation is that the embarrassed Government may quietly back down, though it has not yet done so.

* * *

March 30, 1982

ISRAEL TIGHTENS CONTROL OVER ARAB NEWSPAPERS

By DAVID K. SHIPLER
Special to the New York Times

JERUSALEM, March 29—In an effort to dampen the unrest in the West Bank and to play down the political strength of the Palestine Liberation Organization, the Israeli military authorities have tightened their censorship of Jerusalem's Arab newspapers and have prevented most of them from circulating outside the city.

During the last four days, taxicabs and trucks carrying copies of the papers for distribution on the West Bank have been intercepted before dawn at army checkpoints, and all copies have been confiscated. On Friday, all three Arabic dailies, plus an Englishlanguage weekly, were seized; the three dailies were confiscated again Saturday and Sunday, an army spokesman said, and today two of the three—the pro-P.L.O. Al Fajr and Al Shaab—were barred from the West Bank, while only the more moderate Al Quds was allowed to pass.

As a result, the 800,000 Arabs in the West Bank, where widespread rioting has occurred during the last 10 days, have had to depend mostly on Israeli radio and television broadcasts in English and Arabic, and on overseas broadcasts by Jordan, Syria and the P.L.O., for news of events in their own territory.

West Bank Reporting Deleted

Editors complain, and Israeli officials acknowledge, that the military censor has excised all reporting on the West Bank disorders by the Arab papers' own staffs, forcing them to publish only material that had already appeared in the Hebrew-language Israeli press. Even a good deal of that information has been cut out of the Arabic-language papers, editors say.

"This is the worst for the last 15 years," said Mahmoud abu-Zalaf, the editor in chief of Al Quds. "Last week we appeared for two days without a single line of news on the West Bank. And if we appear with only five percent of the news, they confiscate the paper. They won't even allow us to print the news covered by the Israeli radio and television—not even news printed from the Israeli papers."

The confiscations have also inflicted a financial cost on the papers. "It is almost worse than closing us," said the editor of Al Fajr, Hanna Siniora. "Ninety percent of our issue is stopped from being distributed, after we spend money on paper and ink, electricity, printing. We have to repeat the advertisements. The paper has been constantly losing money during this period."

'Adding Oil to the Fire'

The official Israeli reasoning is that while tensions are high, it is very easy for Arab newspapers, with inflammatory descriptions of Arab-Israeli clashes, to start chain reactions that could lead to further bloodshed. "It was only adding oil to the fire," one official said of the papers' reporting. "Try to find a single word pleading for the mob to be silent. They are not papers in the Western meaning. They are political organs. They publish only items which go in the line of their ideology."

Israeli military censorship, based on the 1945 emergency regulations of the British mandate in Palestine, is always stricter with the Arab press than with the Israeli or foreign press, officials explain. Arabic papers must submit all material to the censor, including obituaries, lest they contain political statements, while Israeli news items and dispatches by foreign correspondents based here are examined by the censor only if they relate to military security matters and certain other narrow topics, such as the fate of Jewish populations in Arab countries.

Support for P.L.O. Is Barred

In addition, West Bank Palestinians may say things in the Israeli press that are cut by the censors from the Arabic press—expressions of support for the P.L.O., for example, are barred from Arab papers. Recently, when Mayor Elias Freij of Bethlehem wrote an article in The Washington Post calling on the P.L.O. to recognize Israel, the weekly English-language edition of Al Fajr was barred from including Mr. Freij's statement of support for the P.L.O., which was obviously designed to shield him from political or physical attack for his moderate views.

Mr. Freij had written: "It is up to the P.L.O. to make the decision because the P.L.O. is the official spokesman and representative of all Palestinian Arabs wherever they live, and I fully accept this." The censor ordered the sentence deleted from Al Fajr, although it had appeared in The Washington Post; consequently, Mr. Freij pulled the whole article from Al

Fajr, according to Daoud Kuttab, a member of the editorial board, feeling that the deletion would distort his argument. Al Fajr was therefore unable to report his conciliatory position.

'Commandos' and 'Terrorists'

"We have to play the P.L.O. role down as much as possible," explained an Israeli official who contended that this had always been the censor's policy. It has taken on enhanced importance in the context of a recent political campaign by Menachem Milson, Israel's administrator of the occupied West Bank, to limit the P.L.O.'s influence.

Proofs marked by the censor show numerous deletions and changes involving articles on the P.L.O. In one story, the description of the P.L.O. as a "national liberation movement" was stricken. In a report on a call by an Israeli committee for "the death penalty against Palestinian commandos," the censor changed "commandos" to "terrorists." In an article about "Palestinian graduates inside Palestine," the censor changed "Palestine" to "Israel" and the phrase "outside Palestine" to "abroad."

Many of the banned articles are highly editorial. One, entitled "Two Thousand Years Ago," likened Palestinian youths who throw stones at Israeli vehicles to David who felled Goliath. The censor struck it entirely. A brief story portraying a violent demonstrator sympathetically as he argued with his more conservative parents was ordered deleted.

21 of 37 Articles Banned

Open letters of protest from residents of the Golan Heights opposing Israel's annexation of the territory were mostly censored, including one to Secretary of State Alexander M. Haig Jr. Factual reports on arrests, restrictions to hometowns or prison sentences have also been banned with frequency.

Mr. Kuttab said that three of the English Al Fajr's last six editorials were killed by the censor, one was at least half censored and only two were allowed to run. Of 37 articles submitted last week, 21 were banned in their entirety, 2 were rendered meaningless by deletions, 6 were partially censored but published and 8 were passed unchanged.

A complicating problem for editors is that the law prohibits blank spaces or any other indication in the papers that material has been censored, which means that on deadline, editors must race to fill their pages with acceptable items. They usually prepare at least two or three times as much type as they have room for, assuming that most of it will be killed.

"There is self-censorship, too," said Mr. Kuttab. "One has to be somewhat pragmatic, and sometimes consciously, sometimes subconsciously, one starts thinking of censorship more and more. One waters down a story or takes out gory parts—any descriptions of soldiers we water down. We start to avoid things we are pretty sure will never make it. Knowing very well that all this work and all this expense will not be used, one thinks twice."

* * *

October 28, 1982

SATIRICAL ISRAELI REVUE DEFIES CENSORS' BAN, CAUSING AN UPROAR

By WILLIAM E. FARRELL
Special to the New York Times

JERUSALEM, Oct. 27—A stinging satirical revue that was banned as seriously harmful "to the basic values of the nation, the state and Judaism" has caused an uproar in Israel and reopened the question of whether Israeli films and theater should be censored at all.

The ban, ordered on Monday by the Film and Theater Censorship Board, might have gone relatively unnoticed if it had not been defied in Tel Aviv. The revue, called "The Patriot" and written by Hanoch Levin, one of Israel's most acerbic writers, opened at Tel Aviv's Neve Zedek Theater Monday night and became an instant hit.

It is almost impossible to obtain tickets for the revue, which depicts much of Israeli society as corrupt and cruel and strikes at such issues as the war in Lebanon by picturing the death of a hero on military service in "Israeli-occupied Albania." The police have made no move to enforce the ban while the furor over it has continued.

Today "The Patriot" was the subject of two motions in Parliament to abolish the Censorship Board, which dates from 1929, when the area that is now Israel was under British control. Another motion, however, was presented to increase the board's powers.

Censorship Loses on First Vote

At the same time, a group from the National Religious Party, part of the ruling coalition of Prime Minister Menachem Begin, petitioned the High Court of Justice to close the revue. The head of the Religious Party, Minister of the Interior Yosef Burg, called on the Attorney General to see if it was possible to close it immediately.

Tonight the 120-member Parliament indicated, through a 44-to-33 vote on a preliminary reading of one abolition bill, that the censorship law should be repealed. But the vote was only a first step in the battle.

Israel's censorship is normally limited to reports on military matters that might have a security impact. In addition, Arab newspapers and some books have been banned in occupied areas.

Seldom does the Censorship Board interfere with a theater performance in Hebrew. But it decided to ban "The Patriot," a revue that combines dialogues, monologues and songs to strike at current issues—the occupation of the West Bank, Israel's relations with Arabs, which are depicted as fiercely anti-Arab, and tensions between Orthodox and secular Jews. The revue also includes a skit on how to get a visa to the United States and get away from it all.

The board voted 11 to 7 on Monday to ban "The Patriot." Among the features considered objectionable by the majority was a scene in which a Jewish settler shoots a Palestinian.

On Friday, actors and entertainers are expected to demonstrate in Tel Aviv on Dizengoff Street, one of the main thoroughfares, against restrictions on theaters and films. Mr. Levin is writing a skit on censorship to be performed at the rally.

An earlier work by Mr. Levin, "The Queen of the Bathtub," also caused a stir but not one equal to the furor touched off by "The Patriot."

Among the views presented by members of Parliament was a statement by Rabbi Haim Druckman that he wanted another play, called "The Jewish Soul," banned as well on the ground that it mocks religious values. The play is by Yehoshua Sobol.

"It laughs at Jewish prayers," the rabbi said. "I'm sure if such a play would have been put on somewhere else in the world everybody would have yelled 'anti-Semitism,' and here in the state of Israel you can do anything."

Public to Have Right to Decide

Shulamit Aloni, a member of the political opposition who wants the censorship law abolished, said: "If we are democrats we have to accept that every person with a normal I.Q. knows what's good for him and knows how to enjoy his life. He has the right to decide if he wants to see something or not."

But the issue is not a partisan one. Several members of Mr. Begin's coalition Government want the censorship statute abolished. Haaretz, Israel's respected independent newspaper, said in an editorial today that the play "may indeed" do harm to the nation's basic values. That, the newspaper said, was not the point for an enlightened country to take.

"An enlightened country doesn't need censorship to set public taste," it said. Hatzofeh, the publication of the National Religious Party, said, "Creative freedom and the chance to knock the Government are apparently preferred over respect for the law."

* * *

February 2, 1984

UPSET BY 'SADAT,' EGYPT BARS COLUMBIA FILMS

By JUDITH MILLER
Special to the New York Times

CAIRO, Feb. 1—Egypt has banned all films produced or distributed by Columbia Pictures because of its objections to "Sadat," a Columbia film about the life of Egypt's assassinated leader that appeared on American television.

Abdel Hamid Radwan, the Minister of Culture of Egypt, announced the decision last Thursday after he reviewed the film, which starred Louis Gossett Jr. as President Anwar el-Sadat. Mr. Radwan concluded that the 1983 film contained "historical errors that distort the accomplishments of the Egyptian people," according to the Egyptian press accounts of his decision.

Martin Blau, the vice president for advertising and publicity of Columbia Pictures International, said in a telephone interview today from New York that "in the non-Arab world, I would imagine this threat will have no effect."

Objections to the film are complex. They range from resentment in some circles over the selection of a black to play Mr. Sadat, to often-cited objections concerning "distortions" of Egyptian leaders and life, to complaints of historical inaccuracies.

Throughout his presidency, Mr. Sadat appeared particularly sensitive about his dark complexion, which prompted jokes and ridicule. The portrayal of Mr. Sadat by a black has revived the issue of race in Egypt, where it is usually deeply submerged.

The producers said they intended the film to be a tribute to Mr. Sadat's life and his courageous decision to make peace with Israel. Indeed, a small group of Westerners and Egyptians who viewed the three-and-a-half-hour film in an illegal showing at an office Tuesday found the portrait of Mr. Sadat glorified and at times almost obsequious.

While the ban in Egypt is not likely to have a significant effect on Columbia globally, film industry observers said it demonstrated the dangers that American film companies face when attempting to market overseas an American view of foreign leaders or heroes. Foreign sales of movies and television programs are an important source of income to American film companies. Countries such as Egypt have strict censorship rules and populations that are unaccustomed to seeing anything other than the government view of their leaders or heroes.

Egypt routinely refuses to let many foreign and domestic films be shown in theaters and on its state-run television. Before 1979, when Egypt signed a peace treaty with Israel, foreign actors, actresses and film companies that were prominent in their support of Israel were frequently banned in Egypt. Since the peace treaty, there has been no such blanket censorship that anyone here can recall.

Spokesmen for the Ministry of Culture have declined to explain the decision to ban all films produced or distributed by Columbia. One Western diplomat called the step "a gross overreaction."

It was considered unlikely that other Arab governments would be interested in the film since it portrays Mr. Sadat in such a favorable light. Most Arab countries consider him a villain for having made peace with Israel.

A spokesman for the United States Embassy said that the dispute was "between Columbia and the Egyptian Government," and that the embassy had not been involved.

The Israeli press, which has been following the "Sadat" controversy closely, views the Egyptian ban with alarm because Israel's relations with Egypt have been under considerable strain recently.

The film is a biography of Mr. Sadat that attempts to explain how and why he made peace with Israel, a decision that many believe cost him his life. The film covers about 40 years, charting Mr. Sadat's rise to power from relatively humble origins as a hot-headed young army officer and ending with his assassination in Cairo in 1981 after his historic trip to Jerusalem and the signing of the Camp David peace accords with Israel.

Seen on Cassettes

Although the film has not been shown in public, many Egyptians already have seen it on pirated video cassettes. Whether they detest or idolize Mr. Sadat, the reactions of those commenting about it are unusually hostile.

Egyptian commentators in the semi-official press have denounced the film, which was broadcast in two parts in the United States last October and November. Its American reviews were mixed. For example, in a review in The New York Times, John J. O'Connor described it as "a thoroughly admiring portrait of Egypt's Anwar el-Sadat" and as "history as viewed by Sadat supporters." He added that Mr. Gossett, who won an Academy Award for his performance in "An Officer and a Gentleman," "commands unflagging attention" and emerges from the film as "an unqualified star," although "some of the characterizations, most notably those of Nasser and of Leonid Brezhnev, border on caricature."

Mussa Sabri, the editor in chief of Al Akhbar, a major Arabic-language daily newspaper, praised a decision by Egypt's Cinema Syndicate, a labor organization of film industry representatives, to try to file suit against Columbia for slander against the Egyptian people. The Cinema Syndicate was the group that pressured the Egyptian Government to take action against the film. The syndicate said it felt that the Egyptian people were being slandered because of the false representation of the nation's leaders and heroes.

The film "Sadat," Mr. Sabri wrote in an editorial, was a plot by "evil Zionist powers."

Anis Monsour, the highly respected editor of the Arabic weekly magazine October and a close friend of President Sadat, called the film "a cheap insult" that made Egyptians appear "ridiculous."

At the same time, he blamed the Egyptian Government for the perceived distortions because it had turned away the film's original sponsor when he came to Cairo seeking help.

Daniel H. Blatt, who produced the film for Columbia, said in a telephone interview Tuesday from Los Angeles that the Egyptians disliked the film and banned it because "the mood has changed in Egypt."

"They no longer like Sadat and the peace that he made," he said. "It's all political."

Egyptians Express Outrage

At the private showing of the film on Tuesday that was attended by a small group of Egyptians and foreigners, reactions were divided by nationality. The foreigners said they found the film poorly made and distorted in parts, but they were more deeply distressed by the ban. The Egyptians present, none of whom wished to be identified because of the ban, expressed outrage about the film and support for the censorship.

"The film not only distorts Sadat's motives for making peace, it also ridicules King Farouk, Gamal Abdel Nasser, and others whom Egyptians still consider heroes," said a young professional.

"It's trash," said a Cairo office manager.

Far more troublesome, the Egyptians said, was the film's unfavorable portrayal of President Nasser, who still retains considerable respect and some devotion.

Egyptian viewers at the private showing took strong exception to what they said was the film's implication that President Sadat made peace with Israel primarily because he had been personally saddened by the death of his brother and because Menachem Begin, the former Prime Minister of Israel, had warned Mr. Sadat of an assassination plot. They said they felt that these segments trivialized an important national decision made by Mr. Sadat.

They also expressed discomfort with the portrayal of the close relationship between President Sadat and his wife, Jihan. Scenes that showed passionate embraces at their wedding and in other public places were hooted and ridiculed. A young Egyptian woman groaned when the film showed Colonel Nasser kissing Jihan on the cheek during a visit.

"These appear to be small items to you," she said. "But they indicate that the producers never bothered to learn anything about Egyptian life, culture and social traditions. No Egyptian man would ever demonstrate that kind of affection in public."

Some Events Omitted

American viewers observed the same inaccuracies, but with greater dispassion. Several who lived in Egypt during the post-Camp David era noted that the film did not show Mr. Sadat's sweeping crackdown on dissidents. The foreigners also said the film did not mention the widespread corruption tolerated by his regime that turned so many of his countrymen against him, despite their support for the peace accords.

The film also did not discuss the controversy that surrounded Jihan Sadat, who was far more visible and prominent than any other woman in modern Egyptian history. Many Egyptians felt she should have been less visible in the country's political and public life.

Mr. Blatt, the film's producer, discounted such criticism.

"We did a lot of research," he said. "We studied every detail, down to his clothes and his cane. The alleged inaccuracies are not the reason Egyptians don't like my film."

Mr. Blatt said that he had never been to Egypt and that he decided not to make the $6 million film there because "I feared for my safety and the crew's."

He also said that accepting Egyptian help would have meant permitting Egyptian censorship, since all movies filmed on location in Egypt have censors attached to the productions.

Sandy Frank, a New York-based producer who still has the rights to Mr. Sadat's autobiography and who was initially involved in the project, said that the film was shot in Mexico, not Egypt, primarily for budgetary reasons. He said he dropped out of the project because he saw the script and was "appalled."

But Mr. Frank added that he came to Cairo in May 1982, seeking Egyptian help on the film, and got no response.

Hoda Sief-e-Din, an Egyptian and general manager of the Arab-American Film Company, said Tuesday in a telephone interview from her Los Angeles office that she had raised $20 million to make a "genuine" film about President Sadat's life that the Egyptian Government and Mrs. Sadat would like.

* * *

April 30, 1984

ISRAELI COURT BACKS CLOSING OF PRINTER

By DAVID K. SHIPLER

JERUSALEM, April 29—Israel's Supreme Court ruled today that the military censor had the right to close an Israeli newspaper's printing plant for four days after the editors published information without prior submission to censorship.

The case arose amid efforts by the Government of Prime Minister Yitzhak Shamir to suppress news about the unexplained deaths of two of four Arabs who hijacked an Israeli bus with 35 passengers aboard on April 12.

The newspaper, Hadashot, published a brief article Friday reporting that a commission of inquiry into the deaths had been established by Defense Minister Moshe Arens.

Mr. Arens acted after evidence, gathered principally by Hadashot, was made public indicating that at least one of the hijackers had been captured alive and killed later after Israeli troops stormed the bus. During the assault, an Israeli woman was killed and seven other passengers were wounded. Two hijackers were also killed on the spot, but the circumstances surrounding the deaths of the other two are unclear.

Publication of Photo Barred

The key piece of evidence is a photo taken by a Hadashot photographer of a man being led away by two security agents after the assault. The censor barred publication of the picture, but one of the newspaper's reporters took it to the Gaza Strip, where relatives and neighbors easily identified the man as Majdi Abu-Jumaa, who had been named by the army as one of the hijackers. His body was seen by his uncle and a neighbor when all four hijackers were buried.

Hadashot is an afternoon tabloid that began publication two months ago and has a circulation of about 50,000. It is owned by the Schocken family, which also owns Haaretz, a lively morning paper that takes a sharply critical line on the Shamir Government.

The editors of Hadashot have observed the censor's ban on publishing the photograph. But because of the paper's aggressiveness in pursuing the story and in sharing its information with foreign news organizations, the impression prevails that the Government is now bent on driving it into oblivion.

Yossi Klein, the paper's editor, said he had been told about the establishment of the inquiry commission by Nachman Shai, the spokesman for Defense Minister Arens. Mr. Shai asked him to delay publication, he said, arguing that the commission's findings would be made public soon. A similar request was made by Mr. Arens of other Israeli editors at a meeting last week.

Censor's Jurisdiction Questioned

Mr. Klein said he did not feel the item fell under the censor's jurisdiction and he published it without prior submission.

As a result, the same authorities that provided the information then punished the paper for printing it. The censor, an army general, is subordinate to the Defense Minister; after consulting with Mr. Arens the censor ordered the paper's printing plant closed for four days.

The paper won a restraining order from the Supreme Court Saturday night and was published today. But in a hearing this morning, a three-judge panel ruled in favor of the censor.

The judges issued a restraining order, however, against another decision by Mr. Arens, to ban distribution of the paper among soldiers and other Defense Ministry personnel. The Defense Minister was also enjoined from carrying out an order to cut off all relations between the military establishment and the paper, which would have meant that the army could not deal with the paper's reporters or photographers. This would be a crippling blow to a newspaper in a society where the military is so important an institution.

In addition, the censor asked the police to investigate the paper's editors to see whether criminal action could be taken against them.

Editor Sees 'Severe Damage'

Mr. Klein said the four-day closing would hurt the paper's finances and popularity. "It's severe damage," he said, "because it's a matter of ads which people ordered."

In addition, he explained, "The whole situation is not very popular here in the streets. It will seem that we are fighting against the Government, so it's not a very popular stand that we took. But still we believe it is good for the state that it is known that justice can be done."

Although some Israelis have deplored the possibility that one or two of the hijackers were killed after capture, many others have expressed satisfaction, arguing that terrorists who take hostages should be killed, preferably after being tortured. Such comments can be heard on buses and in supermarkets.

In affirming the censor's right to close the paper, the Supreme Court did not give a reasoned decision, but it is expected to do so within a week or so.

The commission investigating the deaths of the hijackers is to be headed by a former army general, Meir Zorea, who was on the commission that investigated Israel's unpreparedness for the 1973 Middle East war. It is to comprise an unspecified number of officials with military and intelligence backgrounds.

However, Mr. Shai said in an interview that no decision had been made yet on whether its findings would be made public.

* * *

May 20, 1985

EGYPT BANS COPIES OF '1,001 NIGHTS'

By JUDITH MILLER
Special to the New York Times

CAIRO, May 19—An Egyptian judge approved the confiscation today of 3,000 copies of an unexpurgated edition of "A Thousand and One Nights," on the ground that the centuries-old Arabic classic contained obscene passages that posed a threat to the country's moral fabric.

Judge Ahmed el-Hossainy, whose court handles misdemeanors, also fined a publisher and two booksellers 500 pounds each, about $600, for violating Egypt's pornography laws by printing, importing or distributing the new editions of the book.

The judge said his decision was not a precedent banning all copies of the book and affected only the 3,000 copies seized earlier this month by the Ministry of Interior. But writers and other prominent intellectuals said the confiscation set a dangerous precedent.

"If we continue to censor and eliminate obscene words from our literature, it will not stop there," said Anis Mansour, former editor of October, a prominent Arabic journal.

Islamic Forces Blamed

The uncensored version of the book, which is a collection of such stories as Ali Baba and the 40 Thieves, Aladdin and his Magic Lamp, and Sinbad the Sailor, was ruled obscene because of sections among the more than 100 stories containing explicit descriptions of sexual acts.

Several critics of the decision said the ruling reflected growing Islamic fundamentalist sentiment here. Conservative Islamic forces have been demanding a crackdown on what they see as pornography and other "un-Islamic" influences on Egypt's culture. They have also sought even tighter censorship than already exists on books, television and films.

"This is but one of several signs that the religious trend is gaining momentum here," said Mohammed Sid Ahmed, a writer for the left-wing Arabic weekly Al Ahali.

A few weeks ago the Egyptian Supreme Court struck down as unconstitutional a 1979 law opposed by fundamentalist groups that enhanced the right of women to sue for divorce and to gain custody of their children. The court ruled that the law, promulgated by President Anwar el-Sadat, had not been properly enacted.

The Egyptian Parliament also recently voted to "scientifically and systematically" review Egypt's laws to eliminate those inconsistent with Islamic law, the 1,300-year-old legal code favored by fundamentalists.

Moslem Holy Month Begins

The Parliament is also expected to consider soon a law that would fine any Egyptian 50 pounds for eating or smoking in public during Ramadan, the worldwide Moslem holy month of prayer and dawn-to-dusk fasting that begins early this week. The proposal is vehemently opposed by Egypt's Coptic Christians, who total six million of Egypt's 48 million people.

Today's court ruling was in sharp contrast to the less restrictive and liberal environment for the press that has been encouraged by President Hosni Mubarak's Government. Mr. Mubarak has permitted previously banned opposition and religious newspapers to publish again. Only once since he became President after the assassination of Mr. Sadat in October 1981 has a newspaper been confiscated, and that edition was ordered released the following day.

The three main defendants in the book case—Hussein Sobaih, the publisher, and Hussein Lebib el-Zeiny and Mohammed Rashad, the booksellers—may appeal the ruling within 10 days. They declined to say today whether they would do so.

Under Egyptian law, they could have been sentenced up to 2 years in prison.

Tales of Scheherazade

The book, a Middle Eastern classic of stories that scholars say are Persian, Indian and Arab in origin, is a collection of tales that legend holds were told by Queen Scheherazade to prevent her husband, King Shehrayar of Samarkand, from killing her.

Scholars say the folktales are perhaps the best known and most widely read book of Arabic authorship apart from the Koran, Islam's holy book.

Brig. Adly el-Kosheiry, head of the morals department of the Interior Ministry, which prosecuted the case, told reporters before the ruling today that the new edition of the book, which was printed in Beirut, posed a threat to the morals of Egypt's youth.

"The book is not part of our heritage," Brigadier Kosheiry said. "But even if it were, any part of our heritage which includes dirty words should be locked up in a museum and an expurgated version should be made available to youth."

Says Publishers Added to Book

He said the book had "no known author" and asserted that "over the years, each publisher has added what he wants to the stories to sell more copies and attract more readers."

Unlike newspapers here, where self-censorship has replaced Government controls, television, films and imported books are strictly censored by the Government and religious representatives from Al-Azhar, the Islamic world's oldest institution of higher learning.

Ahmed Baha'al-Din, a prominent Egyptian columnist, said today that he was encouraged that the judge did not ban the book generally or order other editions confiscated.

"The book is our heritage and it cannot be obliterated from our libraries and schools," Mr. Baha'al-Din said. "But passages are definitely obscene. The new edition would have enabled any youngster to buy a popular version of the book cheaply on any street corner," he said. "The court ruling will not affect the ability of our scholars and serious students to find and read it, so it's not all that terrible a decision."

* * *

August 23, 1987

ISRAEL DEBATES THE ROLE OF ITS ARTS CENSORS

By RONI C. RABIN

JERUSALEM—Israeli society, accustomed to a free and outspoken press and public, has in recent months become embroiled in a fierce debate over a Government censorship board's screening of all movies and theater productions.

The controversy was sparked last December when, just two days before the opening of "The Last Secular Jew," a musical satire portraying Israel as a Jewish theocracy, the Film and Theater Censorship Board banned the show.

Artists, writers and theater enthusiasts reacted with an outcry that forced the board to retreat and allow "The Last Secular Jew" to go on, with only minor revisions.

The debate was rekindled last month when the board prohibited people under 18 from seeing the play "Yellow Time," a work based on a journalist's expose of Israel's military occupation of the West Bank and the Gaza Strip. The board felt that the sensitive and complex issues the drama addressed should be limited to a more mature audience. Although the article's original text had already been published in a magazine and in book form, a board official said the play required "the viewer's mature and responsible discretion."

The board rescinded its decision a week later, but only after provoking widespread criticism. David Grossman, author of the magazine article that inspired the play, called the age limit "ridiculous," especially in light of the fact that young men and women in Israel are drafted into the army at 18.

The uproar over such incidents has left in its wake a much sharper awareness of the contradictions between Israel's democratic traditions and the censors' desires to reduce tensions among the country's heterogenous, but volatile population. The controversy also renewed the legislative effort to outlaw the censorship statutes, which derived from regulations imposed during the British mandate.

"There is no reason in the world to justify censorship of theater," said Mordechai Virshubski, a member of the Israeli Parliament, who sponsored the legislation, which has already passed a preliminary vote.

But Yehoshua Justman, chairman of the censorship board, says his group performs a "moderating function" in a society wracked by tensions—ethnic and political, religious and sec-

Micha Bar-Am

A scene from "The Last Secular Jew," a musical satire that ran afoul of Israel's censorship board.

ular—from within and without. Furthermore, he said, the board is extremely liberal in its views.

During the past three years, he said, only 12 "excessively violent" movies have been banned of the more than 700 mostly American-made films submitted for approval. Six plays, of 419 submitted during the past seven years, have been banned, he said.

But the board does not keep figures on the number of times it requires modifications and deletions before licensing a show. Such alteration took place last year, with both "The Last Secular Jew" and the Broadway show "Oh! Calcutta!," which faced a ban until the producers agreed to alter six scenes.

According to Mr. Justman, the board's areas of concern seem to fall into three main categories. The first, excessive violence, is the primary reason for either imposing age restrictions, banning or occasionally even cutting scenes out of films. The second category applies to films or plays considered to be either "political speeches" or "incitement against the state"; these were the reasons given for excluding one film and four Arabic plays in recent years. (A separate system of military censorship oversees all news reports issued from Israel dealing with military and security-related matters, as well as written material distributed in the Israeli-occupied territories.) Most disturbing, however, to the majority of Israelis is a third category that encompasses what the board calls plays involving "assaults on basic Jewish values."

"It's a question of where freedom of expression stops, and assault and injury to others begin," Mr. Justman said.

The board's policy is to avoid political censorship—thus, Mr. Justman said, it gives the green light to plays such as Yehoshua Sobol's work "The Palestinian," a sophisticated look at what happens when a young Israeli man falls in love with a Palestinian woman. On the other hand, modern Israeli playwrights grappling with difficult, relevant material, often touch a raw nerve with the censors.

In "The Last Secular Jew," for example, censors insisted on deleting what the playwright called a crucial scene, when the last secular Jew in Israel—the only one left who has not abandoned his allegiance to the state in exchange for riches and obedience to an ultra-Orthodox Jewish life style—is forced to make fun of the national anthem.

"That was the heart of the play, the turning point, the scene that gave the play its entire meaning," said Shmuel Hasfari, the playwright, who removed his name from the playbill in protest and refuses to accept royalty payments from the show. "That scene was crucial in order to jolt the viewers, to confront them with what is happening. Now the play is just a series of satiric sketches, and that is not what I intended."

An outright ban was imposed in 1982 on Hanoch Levin's work, "The Patriot," a political satire about an Israeli willing to pay any moral price to get a visa for the United States and escape Israel's wars and inflation. The censorship board branded the play "gravely offensive to the fundamental values of the state and Jewish tradition," and banned it entirely.

More recently, the board barred "Ephraim Returns to the Army," a play about the corrupting effects the Israeli military occupation of the West Bank and Gaza Strip have on one Israeli army officer. The objection, Mr. Justman says, is to a scene in which an officer, originally from Eastern Europe, tells young soldiers entering an Arab town not to harass a little Palestinian boy who is carrying a suspicious-looking school bag. "Stop him, check his school bag, he has jewelry, give it back to him," the officer says.

A younger soldier asks him how he knew.

"That's how I transferred my family's jewelry," the older officer says, "when the Germans came."

Israel's Supreme Court recently overturned the board's ban on the play, but Mr. Justman said he would resign from his post if the play is ever performed in Israel. The theater originally planning to produce the play dropped the work and there are currently no plans for production.

"I cannot allow the comparison of Israeli soldiers to Nazis," he said. "It is too sensitive to too many people in this country. There are limits, even to freedom of expression."

Within the artistic community itself, there is a pervasive fear that, without the formal censorship board, theaters will exercise self-censorship in their selection of scripts, due to fear of libel suits and of losing funds from official and semi-official bodies.

Ironically, "The Last Secular Jew" became a box-office hit, running through last month, as crowds flocked to the theater, despite poor reviews, simply to see what the fuss was all about. Mr. Hasfari said that, despite the changes in the script, the ban succeeded in driving home the play's message.

* * *

June 5, 1988

ISRAELI CENSORSHIP TAKES ON TWO MEANINGS

By JOEL BRINKLEY

JERUSALEM—The Israeli Army raised no objections recently when several Israeli newspapers printed an evocative photograph of a soldier confronting an angry crowd of Arabs. But military officials shut down a Palestinian newspaper for a month after it published the same photo a few days later.

This was not an isolated case. Several times in recent months Prime Minister Yitzhak Shamir and other Israeli officials have reaffirmed Israel's commitment to freedom of the press, but for Arab journalists in the occupied territories these words ring hollow.

Thirty Arab journalists have been imprisoned since the Palestinian uprising began in December. Most of the dozen or so newspapers, magazines and news services in the West Bank and Gaza Strip have been closed down for at least a few days and often for much longer. Even when they are allowed to publish, the publications—whether widely read mainstream daily newspapers or polemical pamphlets—complain that censorship is heavy.

Black Star/Christopher Morris for The New York Times

Reading the Palestinian newspaper, Al Quds, in East Jerusalem.

"Even things already published outside are censored," said Maher Abu Khater, managing editor of the English-language version of Al Fajr, a weekly paper published in Arab East Jerusalem.

For that, the Army censor offers no apologies. "Our considerations are not public relations," said Lieut. Col. Avi Gur-Ari, the censor for Jerusalem. "We have to follow the law."

One extreme left-wing Israeli newspaper, Derech Hanitzotz, was closed in February and its Jewish editors imprisoned, but not because of what they wrote, Israeli officials insist. The Government has formally charged them with treason, in essence, saying that they had become agents of Democratic Front for the Liberation of Palestine, a hardline Palestine Liberation Organization group. The case is unusual. Unlike the Arab press, Israeli papers seldom get in serious trouble. Israeli law says the Army can apply wholly different standards to Arab and Israeli journalists, and this is just one part of a broader paradox: While Israelis live in an open, vibrant democracy, they extend freedoms to their occupied terrorities only when those freedoms do not seem threatening.

Arab papers are censored more heavily because "the target population of these papers is different than the ones in Israel," Colonel Gur-Ari said. "Our job is not to evaluate the truth of an item. If the message is likely to incite or motivate violence from its audience, then I censor all or part of it, and it doesn't matter where the information came from."

No Charges Filed

What sense does this make, Arab journalists ask, when Palestinians can see the very same stories in Israeli papers anyway? But Colonel Gur-Ari said his information convinces him that most Palestinians do not see Israeli newspapers. That is why, he said, the Palestinian newspaper, Al Quds (the Arabic word for Jerusalem), "was punished" for printing the already-published photo of the soldier confronting the Arab crowd. The 30 Arab journalists under arrest have been placed in administrative detention, meaning they are held in jail for up to six months, even though no charges have been filed or hearings held. Palestinians assert that many of the 30 were picked up because the Israelis did not like what they had been writing. But a senior Israeli official said: "That's a lie. No one was arrested for what he wrote, intended to write or said he was going to publish." Most of these people, he said, are terrorists who, after they were released from prison, took newspaper jobs as a cover for work on behalf of the P.L.O. Palestinians vehemently dispute this view. There are cracks in the wall of Israeli Government intolerance. Several Arab journalists had complained that they had been arrested while taking articles in for review by the censor. Informed of the problem, the journalists said, the censor's office gave them special passes so they would not be arrested. Then, "as a show of good will," one Arab journalist, Radwan Abu Ayyash, the chairman of the Arab Press Association, was released from prison. At home a few days after his release, Mr. Ayyash, managing editor of the Arabic weekly magazine Al Awdah, was not bubbling with gratitude. He had been in prison 25 weeks, he said, "and I was due to be released in eight days anyway."

Then, to make matters worse, when he got home he found that he was unemployed. The Israeli Government had closed his magazine.

* * *

August 10, 1989

ISRAELI THEATER GETS A CENSOR-FREE RUN

Special to The New York Times

JERUSALEM, Aug. 9—Israel's theater censorship board will be abolished this month on a two-year trial basis, giving Israeli playwrights free rein for the first time in the country's history.

The legislative move came largely in response to a Supreme Court decision that went against the censorship board.

"The mere existence of such a power shouldn't exist in a modern democratic state," said Mordechai Vershuvski, a member of Parliament from the left-wing Citizens Rights Party, who championed the bill eliminating the theater censorship.

After two years, the legislation will be re-evaluated, a provision regarded as mostly a gesture to win the support of the religious parties. But few believe theater censorship will be renewed.

A holdover from the British Mandate period, censorship has been retained despite Israelis' pride in their country's democratic freedoms. There is also a separate military censor who oversees all press reports and other written material like books and magazines.

Over the years, the Israeli Theater and Movie Censorship Board has censored a handful of plays and dozens of films, citing security considerations, excessive violence or offense to religious beliefs—a particularly sensitive subject here.

Films Still Face Censorship

The censored plays—usually productions the board describes as extremely leftist—have included "Friends Talk About Jesus," by Amos Kenan, "The Patriot," by Hanoch Levine, and "Ephraim Returns to the Army," by Yitzhak Laor.

Even with the change in theater censorship, movie censorship remains in place. Of approximately 300 films screened each year, the board censors half a dozen or so, usually because of excessive violence, said Joshua Justman, the board's chairman for the last 10 years.

But the movie censorship board also suffered a setback recently. In June, the Israeli Supreme Court overturned the censor's ban on the American-produced "Last Temptation of Christ." The 23-member censorship board banned the film in Israel last October on the ground that it "was offensive to the Christian community," Mr. Justman said. The court ruled unanimously that the film's scenes didn't warrant limiting freedom of expression.

Many Government officials see a clear distinction between censoring movies and censoring plays.

"I didn't see any benefit in retaining the theater censorship," said Interior Minister Aryeh Deri, a young politician from the religious right who advocated abolishing the theater censorship board, which falls under the jurisdiction of his agency.

But Mr. Deri favors retaining the board's censorship of movies. "Films are very different from plays," he maintained, because they attract a much wider, younger audience who are influenced much more easily.

Envisions a Ratings System

Mr. Virshuvsky is now working on another law that would virtually eliminate the censorship of movies, too. He wants to create a ratings system similar to the one used in the United States, under which entry to a film can be limited based on age.

Even though the theater censors did not invoke their authority frequently, they left their stamp on the types of plays produced here.

"The minute there's a censor, it creates a self-censorship," said Nissim Tzion, the director of Tzavta, an experimental theater club in Tel Aviv. "People thought twice before doing something because they were afraid that the censor would ban it."

In 1982, for example, the censor cut a few scenes from "The Patriot," by Mr. Levine. One of those scenes alluded to the Nazis while depicting an Israeli settler shooting and killing an Arab child.

To evade the censor, the Neve Tzedek theater group decided to stop the play at the disputed sections, switch on the lights and then have someone read the censored lines from the audience. The censor decided to take the theater group and others to court, where it lost an initial decision but won on appeal.

Special Security Situation Cited

"To a large extent, the Israeli Supreme Court has accepted the precedents of the United States Supreme Court and adopted the test that freedom of speech can be limited only by the principle of 'a clear and present danger' to the society," said Yoram Elroy, a lawyer in the Neve Tzedek case. "But a play that wouldn't be considered threatening in the U.S. could still be considered so in Israel because of Israel's special security situation."

In another play, Mr. Kenan's "Friends Talk About Jesus," the courts upheld the censor's ban on the ground that the play "offended the sensibilities of the Christian community here."

Now, though, if someone feels offended or libeled by a particular play, a case will have to be filed in court.

"Ephraim Returns to the Army," a mirror of the moral questions Israeli soldiers face today as they battle the Palestinian uprising, served as the test case that finally lowered the curtain on theater censorship.

In 1985, the play was censored because, the censor said then, it took a negative attitude toward the army and was pro-Palestinian. Shortly thereafter, Mr. Laor, the playwright, appealed the decision to the Israeli Supreme Court.

"I don't know if people who weren't censored can understand what it feels like," Mr. Laor said. "It feels like someone put plaster in my mouth and tied up my hands. All I wanted was to say something about the occupation."

Censor Reversed by Court

In 1987, the Supreme Court reversed the censor's decision and severely limited its power, thus laying the foundation for the new law adopted in April abolishing censorship of theatrical productions.

On April 14, "Ephraim Returns to the Army" opened at Tzavta, and it has been playing occasionally in Israeli theaters to critical acclaim.

At one point in the play, the main character, Major Ephraim, carries on a monologue about his role as military coordinator in an Arab village.

"What kind of a military coordinator am I anyway?" he asks. "The street will be filled with mothers hurrying before the curfew is reimposed to buy milk for their children. I'll be happy when they drink—thousands of mouths. And me? I can only permit in order to forbid . . . I've become the loudspeaker of a curfew."

Despite the lifting of censorship, most playwrights and theater directors said they did not think the new freedom would have much effect on the type of plays produced—at least, not immediately.

Arabs Not Enthusiastic

Many expect legislators, during the two-year probationary period, to monitor the theater world closely. In addition, some playwrights said that theaters would still not stage controversial plays because they would be risking state subsidies and heavy court costs.

In addition, Arab playwrights were not enthusiastic about the measure, although they welcomed the abolishment of the censor.

"If the censor is abolished," said Riad Masarway, an Arab playwright from Nazareth whose play "The Ninth Wave" was recently banned, "it doesn't mean our problems are over."

His play, "The Ninth Wave," is about the killing of a Palestinian groom by an Israeli soldier in the occupied West Bank and Palestinian memories of Israeli excesses. It is to be staged next month.

Mr. Masarway may not be censored now, but he said he expected the police to charge him with incitement against the state.

* * *

March 3, 1990

ISRAEL TO CENSOR NEWS ON EMIGRES

By JOEL BRINKLEY
Special to The New York Times

JERUSALEM, March 2—The Israeli military authorities issued a highly unusual order today requiring news organizations to submit all reports on Soviet Jewish immigration to military censors.

The order, approved by Prime Minister Yitzhak Shamir, comes as the issue of settling Soviet immigrants in the occupied West Bank and Gaza Strip continues to plague Mr. Shamir, who said in January that a "big Israel" was needed to accommodate the emigres.

Normally only news reports dealing with certain military and security matters are subject to censorship, and even then the censorship is seldom imposed on material published abroad. It is left to the journalists themselves to decide whether to show their reports to censors, and most never do.

Request From Immigration

An official in the Prime Minister's office explained that the new order was issued at the request of the immigration authorities because of Arab opposition to the wave of new immigrants and because of the possibility that some Soviet immigrants might be attacked on their way here.

But the order was not limited to information about how the Soviet Jews arrive. It was sweeping. The army communique, issued to everyone in the domestic and foreign press, read, "The army censor announces that all material pertaining to the immigration of Soviet Jews must be submitted to the censor prior to publication."

The Association of Foreign Correspondents in Israel issued a protest today. And recognizing that the order was likely to cause criticism and debate, the official in the Prime Minister's office said the question of whether the censorship requirement would be kept in place will be put before the Cabinet, which is to meet on Sunday.

It was Mr. Shamir himself who drew Arab attention to Soviet Jewish immigration and the possibility that some of the immigrants might move to the West Bank and the Gaza Strip.

"Shamir's talk of a big Israel can't be forgiven," said the Labor Party leader, Shimon Peres. "It caused damage that can't be fixed."

Mr. Shamir's "big Israel" speech, as it has come to be known, has set off almost two months of extraordinary and continuous complaint from all quarters, and especially from the Arab world. Last month, the Soviet Union retracted a commercial agreement to begin direct flights between Israel and the Soviet Union for Soviet immigrants because of Arab protests over Mr. Shamir's remark.

Now most immigrants fly to Budapest or Bucharest, Romania, where they transfer to El Al charter flights—a cumbersome and not always reliable process that cannot accommodate the numbers of Soviet Jews who want to leave.

Direct flights were badly needed, and Mr. Shamir's political opponents blame him for the Soviet refusal.

But Avi Pazner, a close aide to the Prime Minister, said it was unfair to attribute all that to Mr. Shamir.

"That's a mistake," he said. "The Arabs were already worried by the big numbers" and would have protested to Moscow even without Mr. Shamir.

Still, no one in the Arab world or anywhere else had openly complained about the huge wave of Soviet immigration before Mr. Shamir's speech—despite at least six months of intense press coverage of the matter.

About 10,300 Soviet Jews moved to Israel in the first two months of 1990, almost as many as arrived in all of 1989. The numbers grow larger every month, causing Israel to constantly enlarge its estimates.

Last fall, when the state budget was drafted, officials were expecting 40,000 Soviet Jews to arrive in 1990. Money was allocated for settling that many. But by the time the budget was put into place at the start of the year, the estimate had risen to 100,000. Then last week, an immigration official said the latest estimate was that 230,000 Soviet immigrants would move here next year.

Israel is requesting more than $1 billion in loans, gifts and donations from American Jews and from the United States Government to help pay for resettling the Soviet Jews. And paradoxically, Government officials have openly and repeatedly solicited American reporters to write articles on the size and scope of the immigration wave, in the hope that the news coverage would encourage donations.

Reacting to the criticism this evening, a senior Government official noted that the subject of immigration is included on the Government's long list of possibly censorable topics, along with most everything else that could be the subject of news articles here. But most items on the long list are never actually subjected to censorship.

The only recent time when censorship has been imposed on immigration articles was in 1985, when Israel was secretly airlifting thousands of Jews from Ethiopia. As the official noted, when someone broke the censorship and published an article about the airlift, the Ethiopians canceled it.

U.S. Group Declines To Comment

The American Jewish organization that most closely monitors Jewish emigration from the Soviet Union said yesterday that it preferred "not to comment at the moment" on the Israeli Government's decision to censor news reports from there on the immigration of Soviet Jews into Israel.

The remark, by Martin A. Wenick, executive director of the National Conference on Soviet Jewry, was relayed to a reporter by Debra Strober, a spokeswoman for the organization.

Ms. Strober said the Ministry of Absorption in Israel "provides figures" on immigration to the conference "on a monthly basis and we've had no indication that this will cease."

* * *

January 20, 1992

TUNISIA CRACKS DOWN HARDER ON MUSLIM MILITANTS

By CHRIS HEDGES
Special to The New York Times

TUNIS, Jan. 19—The Tunisian Government, in an effort to eradicate the outlawed Islamic fundamentalist movement from the political landscape, has stepped up measures including censorship, frequent detention of suspected movement members and harassment of those who have beards or wear veils.

The moves have crippled the Islamic movement, which has seen its leaders and hundreds of followers flee into exile, land in prison or go into hiding. It has swelled the confidence of the Tunisian authorities, who once tried a policy of reluctant accommodation of the fundamentalists. It has brought a collective sigh of relief among Egyptian, Moroccan and Algerian officials, who are struggling to contain their own Islamic movements.

"We are in full serenity," said Noureddine Mejdoub, the second-ranking official in the Foreign Ministry. "Things are under control."

But the crackdown has created consternation among Western diplomats, opposition leaders and campaigners for human rights. They argue that the repression has halted Tunisia's tentative steps away from a one-party state, weakening the democratic movement and bolstering the credentials of fundamentalists.

"The Government is at an impasse," said Mustapha Benjaafar, the secretary general of the opposition Movement of Social Democrats. "It has the fundamentalists under control, but if it keeps these security measures in place over the long term, it will destroy our efforts to create a democratic society. It will leave us with a discredited party clinging to power by any means and radical extremists who appear to be the only alternative."

A Strong Position

Tunisia, tucked in a small corner of North Africa between Algeria and Libya, has avoided the recent upheavals endured by its two neighbors. Its seven million people have a low birth rate, an economy that is opening up to the free market, a solid work ethic and despite its refusal to support allied war efforts in the Persian Gulf, strong ties to the West. The Government spends 50 percent of its budget on education, health and social services. Even the slums around Tunis lack the squalor and overcrowding of those in Cairo or Algiers.

But Tunisia remains a dictatorship, governed for over 30 years by the party now known as the Democratic Constitutional Union, and its officials show no sign that they are ready to hand over power. The democratic reforms promised by President Zine al-Abidine Ben Ali when he took power in 1987 remain unfulfilled.

The press is not permitted to publish communiques from the Islamic movement or reports by the Tunisian League for Human Rights. Twelve opposition publications, including the

Islamic newspaper The Dawn and the main independent weekly, The Magreb, have been shut down or suspended. The editor of The Magreb, Omar Shabou, remains in prison.

The five opposition parties also charge the Government, which controls all 141 seats in Parliament, with fraud in the last parliamentary elections, in April 1989. Many here contend that the fundamentalists won 20 or 30 percent of the vote.

Officials of human rights groups say the security forces, which set up nightly roadblocks throughout the country to search for Muslim militants, have beaten and tortured suspects in detention, a charge the Government denies.

"We have had over 100 complaints of torture in the last year, most of them from people suspected of belonging to the fundamentalist movement," said Moncef Marzouai, the president of the Tunisian Human Rights League.

Benefits of Persecution

But fundamentalist leaders say the fervor of their followers will only be fueled by persecution.

"You can lock us up for 20 years," said Abdelfatah Mouro, one of the founders of the Tunisian fundamentalist movement, who has been allowed to remain at liberty because of his repudiation of violence, "but the day we get out of prison, we go right back to working for an Islamic state."

Government officials said they are trying to expand social service programs to blunt discontent, especially among the 15 percent of the work force they list as unemployed.

They are also working to meet the demands of women, who already have professional and social opportunities denied in most of the Arab world.

"We constitute half of the population," said Neziha Mezhoud, a member of the governing party's central committee and the vice president of Parliament, "and we have the most to lose if an Islamic state comes into being. The Government is working closely with us to institute a series of reforms, such as the removal of the legal control a husband has over his children and wife, even after a divorce."

Involvement From Abroad

While the Tunisian authorities contend that they have managed to check the fundamentalists internally, they say there is little they can do to block the activities of militants abroad. Tunisian officials rail against the Governments of the Sudan and Iran, which they say aid the fundamentalists. Libyan officials, who have cut off oil supplies to the Sudan because of its increasing ties to Iran, have publicly threatened to back the fundamentalist movements in Arab countries that support the proposed United Nations sanctions against Libya.

"The fundamentalists across North Africa have built an intertwined network that allows them to work in tandem," said Interior Minister Abdullah Kallal, "and they clearly get money from outside sources to carry out their activities."

The head of the movement, who until a few weeks ago traveled with a Sudanese diplomatic passport he says he has now returned, is Rachid Ghannouchi. Mr. Ghannouchi, along with one of his two wives, is now in Manchester, England, meeting with local Islamic leaders, Tunisian officials said. He travels with an Iranian diplomatic passport under the alias Mohammed Jamali Aouidh, these officials said.

Tunisian officials contend that Mr. Ghannouchi, with active support from the Iranians, the Sudanese and the Islamic Salvation Front in Algeria, where he has spent much of the last year, tried to organize two armed uprisings and assassinate the President and five Cabinet ministers. The plan, these officials assert, was thwarted by security officials last fall.

"The last few months have been crucial in our efforts to stop the fundamentalists," Mr. Kallal said.

Sympathy for Fundamentalists

But the current crackdown, however successful, has generated sympathy for the fundamentalists, who appear, especially to many young people, to be the only force standing up to the Government.

"About half of the students sympathize with the fundamentalists," said Adel Benlagha, a 23-year-old student at the University of Tunis. "The more these fundamentalists suffer, the more support they have."

Secular critics of the governing party say they fear that its resistance to democratic reform will only harden, fed by the fear of the fundamentalists and the desire to retain power, creating a political vacuum that the fundamentalists will one day step in to fill.

"I am very pessimistic," Mr. Marzouki said, "because both the ruling party and the fundamentalists have no interest in promoting democracy or human rights. People look to the fundamentalists just because they are against the Government and because the democratic opposition has been ineffectual."

* * *

March 4, 1992

TV IS BEAMED AT ARABS. THE ARABS BEAM BACK.

By YOUSSEF M. IBRAHIM
Special to The New York Times

RIYADH, Saudi Arabia, March 3—At 9 every night, from Dhahran on the Persian Gulf to Riyadh in the middle of the Saudi desert, thousands of television viewers blithely ignore the nightly news program on Saudi television to tune into a television channel that is barred from the Government-controlled airwaves.

Elsewhere in the Arab world more and more people are doing likewise, spurning the boring, censored, Government-produced programs that in most Arab countries have been the only television fare since the medium was introduced to the region in the 1950's.

The object of their attention is the Middle East Broadcasting Center, known to its viewers as MBC. By all accounts, the satellite channel, owned by Saudi investors and beaming its fast-paced programs to all Arab countries from its studios in London, is gaining big audiences.

With its thoroughly Westernized look and intensive news coverage, MBC aspires to become an Arab version of the major American networks. The prize for MBC and its advertisers is a lucrative market of 300 million Arab viewers from Morocco to Oman.

A Bureau in Jerusalem

MBC offers a full range of entertainment shows, but its biggest attraction is its news programs, which have pushed the limits of Arab press freedom. Among other things, it has become the first Arab television company to open a Jerusalem bureau. The owners of MBC say that its Palestinian correspondents in Israel receive favorable treatment from the Israelis and that viewer interest in their reports is high.

"Israel is there and we have to deal with it," said Walid al-Ibrahim, one of MBC's principal owners. Mr. Ibrahim, whose sister is married to King Fahd, was interviewed in the Riyadh office of ARA International Productions, which produces a vast number of programs for Saudi and other Arab television stations and is a holding company for MBC.

He said he began to dream of an independent network while watching American television in his days as a business administration student at Portland State University in Oregon.

"Our belief is that the Arab citizen has the right to know the situation fully," he said. "Being based in London makes it easy for us to resist any attempt by any state to use us."

MBC employs about 200 people, most of whom are reporters, editors, cameramen and others involved in the news operation. Abdallah al-Masry, the London-based executive director of MBC, said in an interview that in addition to Jerusalem it maintained bureaus in Washington, London and the main Arab countries where its programs are seen or which are big news centers, including Cairo, Riyadh, Damascus, Algiers, Amman, Casablanca, Bahrain, Abu Dhabi and Kuwait City.

MBC stands apart from the Government-owned stations for a number of reasons, not the least of which is that it broadcasts to countries that are not shy about imposing censorship and filling the Government-controlled airwaves with propaganda and distorted news reports.

When it began beaming its signals to Saudi Arabia in September, MBC was permitted to use a regular Saudi Government channel. But that privilege was withdrawn after a month. Some conservatives in the religious and Government establishment in Saudi Arabia objected to its unveiled anchorwomen, its Egyptian-made romance movies, and above all its uncensored news reports.

Coming in on a Dish

But wealthy Saudis can pick up the station with their satellite dishes, and their poorer compatriots who live close to Bahrain or Kuwait can tune in to broadcasts from those countries, where MBC is carried on the Government channels.

For now, Morocco is the only other country where MBC is allowed to make conventional broadcasts. But Mr. Ibrahim says the channel expects to be authorized soon by Jordan, Tunisia and Lebanon, which would increase its potential audience to at least 100 million.

Jonathan Player for The New York Times

Thousands of television viewers in the Arab world have abandoned their state-run news programs in favor of MBC, a satellite channel owned by Saudi investors that beams its programs to all Arab countries. Nicole Tannouri and Nidal Kablan made a recent broadcast from the station's London studio.

Mr. Ibrahim says he is prepared to invest $300 million over the next five years before he would expect to turn a profit.

There is agreement here that the project will continue to thrive in Saudi Arabia because of the tacit support of King Fahd. The King, who favors the slow but steady modernization of Saudi Arabia's deeply conservative society, has publicly praised the station, pointing out in a recent interview on MBC that he watched with great interest its coverage of the opening round of the Middle East peace talks in October.

The interview was also broadcast on the official Saudi television network, suggesting that even though the King yielded to conservatives on the restriction on MBC, his support for it was undiminished.

"It's absolutely great," said a senior Government official, who described MBC as the "best friend of Saudi liberals."

MBC applies a far broader standard to its news selection than the Government-owned stations. Its intensive reporting of the Jan. 11 coup that overthrew the Algerian Government was the only real coverage available to many Arab television viewers. MBC also includes news analyses and round-table discussions that venture into areas of politics that few Arab Government-owned stations would dare contemplate.

Although Mr. Ibrahim says it is too early to estimate MBC's audience size, a survey of 1,000 television viewers in Kuwait showed that the station had 77.2 percent of the audience during the news hour.

The survey, carried out in January by the Kuwaiti daily Al Anbaa, indicated that 12.2 percent of the Kuwaiti viewers were watching Egypt's satellite channel, which is beamed throughout the Arab world and which MBC hopes to dethrone as the No. 1 pan-Arab television station.

Coming in last, with only 6.6 percent of the Kuwaiti audience surveyed, was the Government's channel.

* * *

July 19, 1992

MOVIES OF IRAN STRUGGLE FOR ACCEPTANCE

By JUDITH MILLER

TEHERAN, Iran—There are no nude scenes. In fact, men and women rarely ever touch. There are no "Lost Weekends," featuring Iranian Ray Millands, no alcoholics—no alcohol—no "Saturday Night Fevers," bars or discos. There is, in short, nothing remotely resembling sex, drugs or rock-and-roll.

But despite the daunting limitations imposed by the Koran, or the Islamic Republic's literal-minded interpretation of Islam's holy book, Iranian film is flourishing. Some 13 years after the revolution that toppled the Shah and his Western-oriented regime, Iran is turning out a growing number of impressive, small-budget, quintessentially Iranian movies. They explore with candor that often borders on bitterness the searing social, economic and personal problems of ordinary Iranians in post-revolutionary Iran. Overcoming the obstacles of censorship at home and suspicion abroad, these films have increasingly been winning critical acclaim and prizes at international film festivals.

"In 1990 alone, we had 330 entries in international film festivals, and we won 11 first prizes," said Sayed Mohammed Beheshti, the director of the Farabi Cinema Foundation, the Government-sponsored but quasi-independent group whose mission is to increase the quantity and quality of Iranian films.

Richard Pena, the program director of the Film Society of Lincoln Center in New York, called contemporary, or post-revolutionary, Iranian film "one of the most exciting in the world today." In November, the Film Society will present a series of 15 to 20 contemporary Iranian films, a first for the society.

Much is still taboo in Iranian cinema—women with uncovered hair, women singing on screen or dancing. And Government censors still ban films that they conclude openly challenge the legitimacy of the Islamic republic, of rule by Moslem clerics and of the country's numerous religious martyrs—first and foremost among them, the revolution's leader, the late Ayatollah Ruhollah Khomeini, whose stern, unsmiling visage continues to adorn all Government offices and many a private home. But as the revolution has evolved, many of the most fundamentalist and dogmatic film censors have been replaced by younger, better educated men and women, who at least by comparison with their predecessors, are more tolerant.

If post-revolutionary Iranian film is slowly winning international recognition, its success is attributable to the fierce determination of a handful of talented Iranian film makers who have courageously tested and stretched the cultural restrictions of this dour regime. It is also due in part to Mr. Beheshti and his foundation's dogged, politically savvy efforts to promote movies that are original, nonpropagandistic and, in Iranian terms, daring.

Today, about 30 percent of Iranian films are Government-made, work with which Mr. Beheshti has no involvement and for which he has even less regard. But his foundation provided assistance—such as long-term, low-interest loans, subsidized film and studio facilities—to about 35 percent of the 70 Iranian movies made by the private sector in 1991.

"Given Iran's image abroad, we've had a hard time overcoming the shock generated by our requests to participate in festivals," said Mr. Beheshti, a 40-year-old, German-speaking film buff who, unlike most Iranian officials, does not sport a beard. "We had four years of correspondence with the Germans before they let us participate in the Berlin festival. It was the same with the Italians. We finally got a booth at the Milan festival in 1986. But few people were willing even to watch our films then. Most just ate a few pistachios and left. So it has been tough persuading people that our films are not just about people praying."

In some ways, the evolution of the Iranian film industry mirrors that of the society itself. For one thing, there has always been censorship in Iran; what has changed is who the censors are and what they censor for.

The first modern Iranian film was produced in 1964, Mr. Beheshti says. After that, the industry grew rapidly, though always under the watchful eye of the Shah's so-called exhibition board. The Shah's regime preferred syrupy melodramas and action films, as did the Iranians, who flocked to the movies, then and now among the cheapest forms of entertainment. But artistic film makers, those who strived to make movies that highlighted the plight of the poor or contained a whiff of criticism of the regime, suffered under the Shah. Their films were often banned. A few had to choose between not making movies and exile.

In the first years after the 1979 revolution, just a few movies were made. Film makers and intellectuals in general were hampered not only by the post-revolutionary chaos and the bloody power struggle that followed the fall of the Shah but also by the Iraqi invasion of Iran only a year after the Ayatollah Ruhollah Khomeini had come to power.

Despite the chaos and the war, the Farabi Foundation was established in 1983, and the number of films being made increased immediately. That year, 23 movies were produced. In 1984, the number rose to 57; in 1991, when Iran produced 70 films, the total almost equaled its pre-revolutionary record of 90 films in 1972.

But what delights Mr. Beheshti, he says, has been the improvement in quality and the expansion of subjects now being critically addressed. Today film makers are exploring such politically sensitive topics as the Iran-Iraq war. For example, "Flight Into the Night," made in 1985, is about a group of Iranian soldiers who were either severely wounded or killed after being surrounded by their Iraqi counterparts. "There is no glory or victory for these men," Mr. Beheshti said. "There is no triumph at all in this movie."

Photographs by Frabi Cinema Foundation

"Marriage of the blessed"—A savage portrait of the effects of war.

Photographs by Frabi Cinema Foundation

"Bachu, the Little Stranger"—Censors disagreed with the critics.

Photographs by Frabi Cinema Foundation

"Maybe Some Other time"—Afterward, its star went into exile.

Over the objections of the Supreme Defense Council office that was responsible for rallying public support for the war, the film was shown, in Iran and abroad. So was "Marriage of the Blessed," Mohsen Makhmalbaf's savage portrait of the effects of the war, made in 1989. Haji, the film's hero, is a combat photographer who keeps having flashbacks. When he tries to document for his newspaper the misery of the poor in the slums of south Teheran, the only photo the paper publishes is one of a sunflower.

At the office, Haji encounters Youssef, a friend who served at the front with him. Youssef's face has been partially blasted away in battle. "Haji," the mutilated veteran importunes the shocked photographer, who instinctively shrinks away. "Don't you recognize me?"

Haji's marriage to the daughter of a wealthy war profiteer also begins traumatically when the groom, repelled by the lavishness of his own marriage feast, starts ranting about his father-in-law's corruption. "He will defeat the revolution from within!" Haji screams at his host and his stunned bride. "The oppressors are coming back." Haji's subsequent confinement in an isolated, eerie hospital ward filled with other shellshock victims forced audiences to face the unseen victims of the war that the Ayatollah Khomeini chose to continue years after Iraq sued for peace.

"I wouldn't say that Makhmalbaf's films question the revolution itself," said Mr. Beheshti, when asked about the savage attacks in the Iranian press on the director. "I think he's questioning parts of it," he added diplomatically.

But even highly respected directors like Mr. Makhmalbaf, who comes from a devoutly religious family, have run afoul of the censorship system, which under the clerics censors first the scripts and then the final product. The fate of a recent Makhmalbaf film, "The Time to Be in Love," illustrates the often deadening effect and erratic results of persistent clashes between pragmatists and radicals on Iranian culture, and on movie making in particular.

The film, which focuses on a love affair between a married woman and a stranger, was screened and highly praised last year at the Fajr film festival, Iran's own annual festival of Iranian and foreign films. But after radicals savagely attacked the Ministry of Islamic Guidance for approving a movie about the mortal sin of adultery (even though it shows no sex), the Ministry suppressed the work.

One of Iran's best films in recent years and one of the few to be shown commercially in the United States, "Bashu, the Little Stranger," was withheld for three years before its release in 1990, according to its director, Bahram Beizai.

"Bashu" is the story of a 10-year-old stowaway who is adopted by a woman in another part of Iran after his parents are killed and their village destroyed by Iraqi bombs. It was called "small, simple and quietly effective" by Janet Maslin in The New York Times and "pure joy" in The Los Angeles Times.

But Iranian censors did not initially share the enthusiasm, despite the fact that the 54-year-old Mr. Beizai is among the country's most admired directors. "Ershad, the Ministry of Islamic Guidance, objected to the film not only because it was perceived as being antiwar but also because the central character was a woman," he said in an interview at his home in a Teheran suburb. "To this day, publicity posters for the film show Bashu, and not Susan Taslimi, who plays Nai, the main character," he complained.

A few years later, Miss Taslimi decided to go into exile in Sweden. Mr. Beizai says the move reflects the hardships that actors and film makers face in the Islamic republic. Miss Taslimi, whom Mr. Beizai calls one of Iran's finest actresses, came under pressure soon after the revolution to play characters who were Islamically correct. Specifically, revolutionary actors and actresses were expected to take parts in plays that often portrayed various other nations as animals—mice, cats, dogs. But Miss Taslimi refused, protesting in a letter to the director of the National Theater that this was demeaning for performers. She was fired, Mr. Beizai said, although he continued to use her.

In 1981 Mr. Beizai made "The Death of Yazdgerd," about the death of the last Persian king before the Arabs came to Iran in the seventh century. It has still not been released. "The film really had three strikes against it," said Mr. Beizai, who sports a gray, neatly trimmed mustache. "The censors did not feel that the film's position on Islam was clear. Second, they objected to the fact that the film was made shortly before all women were required to have their hair covered in public. And three, the film's central character was a woman, and that woman was Susan."

When Mr. Beizai made his next movie, "Maybe Some Other Time," the Ministry said it would authorize the script, provided he did not cast Miss Taslimi in the lead role. Mr. Beizai refused. "She was so nervous making it that she broke out in hives," he recalled. "But she was committed to the project and we persevered. However, she left Iran soon after that."

In March, the film was shown on Iranian television, to wide acclaim.

Students of Iranian cinema say that in some ways, the Islamic revolution has not dramatically affected art films. "Before the revolution, there were only four or five directors making intelligent, artistically valuable films," said one film devotee. "Today it is those same people—Makhmalbaf, Beizai, Darioush Mehrjui and Abbas Kiarostami—who are still making those films."

Both Mr. Beizai and Mr. Beheshti say they are most encouraged by the new young directors who are finding creative ways of circumventing some of the more unwieldy thematic restrictions and requirements. "Iran is now turning out some 15 first-time directors each year," said Mr. Beheshti.

Mohammad Atebbai, of the Farabi Foundation, agreed. "Many of them deal quite candidly with social and political problems, despite the limitations," he said.

Those limitations are not merely political or religious. They are also financial. "We couldn't make 'Star Wars' or 'Terminator 2,'" said Mr. Beheshti. "They are too technologically sophisticated and expensive for us to produce. The average Iranian film costs $130,000."

But Iranians do see virtually every American movie. While videocassette recorders are illegal in Iran, they are omnipresent in middle-class households. Each week, networks of young free-marketeers deliver door to door the latest, usually pirated, videocassettes, tucked furtively under newspapers.

"Iranians, like most people, prefer American films," said one Iranian journalist. "We're pleased that our films win prizes, but what we really want to see is 'Basic Instinct.'"

No one expects an Iranian director to produce a film criticizing the revered Ayatollah Khomeini or any of the senior clerics who continue to rule. Nor do they expect to see women singing or dancing or without "hejab" or head scarves.

Mr. Atebbai said restrictions had led Iranian directors to be, as he put it, "creative." When a script recently featured a role for a Western woman, one director filmed her with a towel wrapped around her head, as if she had just emerged from a shower.

But what about epic films, such as, say, a movie about the Romans? Mr. Atebbai initially demurred and then allowed himself a tiny smile through his thick black beard. "We don't make films about the Romans," he replied.

* * *

August 20, 1992

CRACKDOWN SEEMS TO HEAD ALGERIA INTO CHAOS

By YOUSSEF M. IBRAHIM
Special to The New York Times

TUNIS, Aug. 14—The Algerian Government plans "drastic measures" to prevent political activity in mosques.

The action, announced Aug. 13, was the latest indication that the seven-month campaign of repression, press censorship, mass arrests of Islamic fundamentalists and stiff jail sentences has failed to stem a rising wave of public discontent.

Diplomats and officials in Tunisia and in Morocco say the evident loss of control by the Algerian Government is giving rise to fears that the nation of 26 million people is moving steadily toward a total collapse of law and order.

"If Algeria sinks into chaos, the only credible political force in that country that can take over is that of the Islamic fundamentalists, and that's bad news for Tunisia and Morocco, which have a serious fundamentalist problem of their own," a Western diplomat said.

In recent weeks signs of disintegration have multiplied as the economy ground to a halt, armed clashes between fundamentalists and Government forces erupted in every town and the Government banned newspapers and restricted political freedoms.

A commission appointed to investigate the killing last month of the Algerian President, Mohammed Boudiaf, has come close to publicly accusing the army's military security organization, the most powerful instrument of the Government repression, of hindering the investigation.

Every week, Algeria's Government-owned factories reduce production further because a shortage of hard currency makes it impossible to import spare parts and cash is short to pay the workers. Strikes are called daily.

The Algerian journalists' association has accused the Government of suppressing the press as its only answer to the accumulating problems. Early this month, the Government shut down three daily independent newspapers, Le Matin, La

Nation and Al Djezair al Joum, accusing them of "endangering the nation's interest."

President Ali Kafi, who took over after the still-unsolved assassination of President Boudiaf, has vowed to reinstitute the "authority of the state." But it is not evident that he is succeeding.

Increasingly bold fundamentalists stage hit-and-run raids daily on army officers and police officials. Large stocks of weapons and ammunition have been stolen from barracks and police stations.

Since February well over 130 state officials have been killed in these assaults, as were many of the fundamentalist attackers.

Earlier this month, fundamentalists took responsibility for an attempted assassination for the first time. The target of the attempt was the Security Minister, Mohammed Tolba.

The admission came in an pamphlet signed by the Islamic Salvation Front, the country's largest political party, which was deprived of an electoral victory in January and then banned by the military-led Government.

It was the boldest attack yet on a senior official, and the admission of responsibility suggested that the Islamic Front feels enough popular support to proclaim openly that it is at war with the Government.

With 7,000 fundamentalists being held in five prison camps, the increase in attacks and sabotage underlines the fact that a new, harder generation of has emerged to carry on the challenge to the Government.

* * *

December 2, 1992

ISRAEL REPRIMANDS FOREIGN REPORTERS

Special to The New York Times

JERUSALEM, Dec. 1—The Israeli Government indefinitely suspended the press credentials of two foreign correspondents and reprimanded four others today, charging them with having violated censorship laws in their reporting on a fatal army training accident last month.

A Government statement accused the reporters, two Americans and four Britons, of having created "a threat to the security of the state of Israel," a charge the journalists denied.

The sanctions seemed likely to intensify a public debate on official censorship here, one that was already under way in Israeli newspapers, which had complained of being shackled in their coverage of the training accident.

The Six Journalists

The correspondents whose credentials were suspended, for "an unspecified period," were Carol Rosenberg of The Miami Herald and Ian Black of The Guardian of Britain. The four who were told to appear before the military censor for an official reprimand were Clyde Haberman of The New York Times and three British journalists: Richard Beeston of The Times of London, Sarah Helm of The Independent and Anton La Guardia of The Daily Telegraph.

All the reporters may continue to work here, but the two who lost their credentials may be denied access to Government officials and functions.

Articles by the six journalists over the last 10 days contained details about an elite army unit in which five young soldiers were killed on Nov. 5 by a missile that was mistakenly fired during an exercise at the Tseelim training grounds, in the Negev.

The Army Officers

An army inquiry board charged several officers with negligence, including the commander of the exercise, Maj. Gen. Amiram Levine. Its findings touched off a political storm over the army's safety procedures and the military censor's behavior. The censor ordered that certain details not be published, including the fact that the Chief of Staff, Lieut. Gen. Ehud Barak, and other top commanders had seen the soldiers die.

In the ensuing debate, questions were raised about whether censorship had been invoked to protect national security or the reputation of senior officers.

Before receiving Government accreditation, foreign journalists in Israel must sign a statement saying they have "read and understood" the censorship regulations. These rules say that "all written material, photographs and recordings intended for transmission abroad must be presented to the censor's office."

In practice, it is usually left to the reporters to decide what should be submitted.

* * *

July 4, 1993

BELOVED INFIDEL

By CHRIS HEDGES

TEHERAN, Iran—When the Ayatollah Ruhollah Khomeini returned to Iran in triumph after the 1979 overthrow of the Shah's monarchy, Googoosh, the country's most popular vocalist, promised to sing him the song that had become an anthem of the Islamic revolutionary movement.

But the Ayatollah announced that he did not want to hear Googoosh sing "My Dear, Lovable Sir." In fact, he promptly ordered all female singers to be silenced, condemning them as temptresses. Records, cassettes, movies and posters featuring Googoosh, and every other female artist, were rounded up by Islamic militants and destroyed. The clubs and cabarets where they sang were closed.

Googoosh, in a swift and furious descent, found herself banned, publicly condemned and forced to sign a statement promising that she would never sing again.

But if the ruling clerics thought that was the end of the story, they were wrong.

Fourteen years after making her last recording, Googoosh, whose full name is Googoosh Faegheh Atashin, has emerged as one of the most popular symbols of opposition to the stern Islamic rule.

Her cassettes, and compact disks of pre-revolutionary material smuggled in from recording studios in California, are some of the most coveted recordings in Iran. Her lyrical songs that speak of lost love, despair and loneliness and her more upbeat works, which sometimes project an overt sensuality, are embraced by today's teen-agers, who were toddlers when she last broadcast on the nation's airwaves.

"Look at my long, thick curls and melt, you stone-hearted men," goes one song. "I will have you for my own. I have no competition."

The endurance of Googoosh, despite the best efforts of the Government to stamp her out, is more than a love affair between Iranians and a singer.

The Iranian revolution was, first and foremost, a cultural revolution designed to eradicate the decadence of the past and instill in Iranians a new Islamic way of looking at the world. Googoosh's staying power is a potent reminder of how badly the clerics have failed.

"How can you even ask me about this woman?" one leading Iranian parliamentarian, Said Rajai Khorassani, said angrily. "Most people, after the revolution, did not want to hear anything about her. She was silly and tasteless."

Googoosh has also emerged as a central figure in the struggle by Iranians to build bridges with the neighboring Farsi-speaking republic of Tajikistan, where she has another wide following. When an Iranian delegation recently visited the republic, the clerics were forced to sit and listen as Tajiki officials, apparently believing they were honoring the Iranians, played one of Googoosh's songs. In another visit by Iranian ministers, Tajiki officials publicly asked the Iranians to bring the singer with them on the next visit.

Tajiki television, after months of haggling, obtained permission from Iranian officials not long ago to film the star reading a cultural magazine, but the Iranians did not allow Googoosh to speak on camera. And after the silent film clip was flashed across Tajiki television, Googoosh was called in by the Iranian police for questioning.

"She paid a high price for those few seconds on television," said a family member who, like all the singer's friends and relatives interviewed, insisted on remaining anonymous. "Many of the clerics were furious. It was a good lesson in how much control they still want to exert over her and how much they fear her."

Googoosh, called "G.G." by some friends, is now 42 and lives alone in Teheran. She is not allowed to give interviews. The singer began her career at the age of 3 when her father, descended from Russian immigrants, took her to perform with his Azeri dance troupe.

"Her father used to throw her up in the air and dance with her," said a family member. "By the time she was 4 she was singing in the show."

Googoosh sang regularly on a national radio show for children at the age of 6, made her first movie, called "The Fear of Hope," when she was 8 and began recording when she was 15. She married a cabaret owner when she was 17 and had her only child, a son to whom she dedicated "Lala-i," a haunting lullaby that most Iranians know by heart. Her son now lives in exile in the United States.

"Wake not from your dreams to the sadness of life," the lullaby goes. "Sleep, my darling. Mother is awake. The wolf lurks behind the door.

"Your kite has lost its tail, and will never reach the clouds. But sleep, my darling. Mother will never leave you."

Googoosh went on to marry and divorce two more times. Before the revolution, her private life was followed in detail by the Iranian press. When she lopped off her long hair for a short pixie cut, many Iranian women followed suit. The cut is still known as a Googooshi.

"Perhaps the saddest thing about Googoosh is that she has been manipulated and used by so many people," said one Iranian man, a psychiatrist. "From her father, who turned her into a child star, to her husbands, who built their careers around her, to these clerics."

Friends who spend time with the singer say she is often depressed and remote.

"We sit at the piano and sing old songs," said a musician and close friend. "This regime cut off her career when it was at its height, and she knows she can never have it back."

Late one evening, four young factory workers sat in a barren two-room apartment outside Teheran. After a long day, the men were squat-legged on the floor with a bottle of homemade arak in front of them. They carefully poured out tiny portions of the outlawed liquor into a mismatched collection of glasses. The drinks, which they all sipped slowly, seemed more symbolic than effective.

The television set in the room showed a bearded cleric, seated at a desk, speaking about Islam. But the men had turned off the volume and took little notice.

"They have nothing to do but talk," one said as he placed a cassette into an old black recorder and turned on a scratchy tape, pirated from a recording that was probably not an original.

The throaty, full voice leapt up out of the machine. On one song, the worker turned up the volume.

"Goodbye friends," Googoosh sang. "I leave to discover my destiny. I do not know what will happen to me. Before me lies only sadness, but still I hope. Don't ask me where I am going. I pray that the devil cannot hear me. I pray that I will come back. Do not forget me."

* * *

July 30, 1994

PALESTINIAN AUTHORITY BLOCKS PRO-JORDANIAN PUBLICATIONS

By JOEL GREENBERG

Special to The New York Times

JERUSALEM, July 29—In a sign of rising tensions between the P.L.O. and Jordan, Palestinian officials blocked the distribution of a pro-Jordanian newspaper and a weekly magazine in the Gaza Strip and West Bank, forcing them to cease publication today.

A statement by the Palestinian self-rule authority in Gaza and Jericho accused the newspaper, An Nahar, of advocating "a line that contradicts the national interests of the Palestinian people."

Palestinian critics called the measure a flagrant violation of freedom of expression that contradicted promises by officials of the Palestine Liberation Organization to uphold democratic freedoms in the areas of Palestinian self-rule.

The ban, the critics said, was reminiscent of similar Israeli measures in the occupied territories that Palestinians had protested for years.

"This is very serious," said Hanan Ashrawi, head of the Palestinian Independent Commission for Citizens' Rights, a monitoring group. "It is a clear violation of freedom of the press and freedom of speech. I hope it is an isolated incident, and not indicative of an emerging pattern."

Mustafa Sawaf, Gaza correspondent for An Nahar, said: "The Palestinian Authority wants to hear only its own voice. This is a one-man democracy."

The ban on the pro-Jordan publications was apparently ordered by the P.L.O. chairman, Yasir Arafat. It followed a Jordanian-Israeli declaration in Washington this week in which Israel promised to give "high priority" in future negotiations to Jordan's role as custodian of Muslim holy places in Jerusalem. The statement reportedly unsettled Mr. Arafat, who claims Jerusalem as the capital of a future Palestinian state and asserts that the holy sites should be under Palestinian jurisdiction.

In an apparent effort to soothe Palestinian feelings, Jordan said today that it supported the P.L.O.'s campaign to gain political sovereignty over Jerusalem, adding that this did not clash with Jordan's religious custody of Muslim sites there.

First Official Comment

"There is no contradiction between restoring political sovereignty over Arab Jerusalem through Palestinian-Israeli negotiations and Jordan continuing to play its role in exercising its religious jurisdiction over the Islamic sites," said the official statement, translated by Reuters.

"Jordan's firm position is support of the Palestine Liberation Organization's efforts to gain political and geographic sovereignty over all Arab Palestinian lands, including Holy Jerusalem," said the statement, Jordan's first comment since the declaration aroused Palestinian fears.

The reference in the accord to Jerusalem was only an admission by Israel of the traditional role of Jordan's royal Hashemite family in "custodianship of the Islamic holy sites to achieve Arab Islamic rights, including Palestinian," it added.

It was unclear whether the Jordanian declaration came in response to the ban on the pro-Jordanian publications. An Nahar's editorial policy has consistently supported Jordan, and Palestinians say it has occasionally published news items that have angered P.L.O. officials.

The magazine, Akhbar al Balad, is published by Nasser al Din Nashashibi, a veteran journalist and former diplomat who is an associate of King Hussein of Jordan and an opponent of the P.L.O.-Israeli accord on self-rule.

Both publications are printed in East Jerusalem.

Copies of An Nahar were confiscated on Thursday morning by Palestinian security men at the entrance to the Gaza Strip, and employees at the paper said they were later warned not to distribute it in the West Bank and East Jerusalem. The warnings were reportedly backed by threats that papers found on newsstands would be burned.

Hussein al Sheikh, a senior P.L.O. official in the West Bank, said the publisher of An Nahar, Othman Hallaq, was ordered to stop printing the newspaper. Mr. Hallaq refused comment, but confirmed that publication had been suspended.

Jibril Rajub, the chief of internal security in Jericho, defended the ban, saying that it was unreasonable for "a state to provide a media platform for another state." He added, "We believe in democracy and pluralism, but democracy has its limits."

The official reason for the ban on An Nahar was that it had not renewed its circulation permit. The Palestinian Authority said the paper had not received the required P.L.O. approval for publication.

Mr. Nashashibi said that though he had not received any official notification of measures against his magazine, news of the restrictions had led him to stop publishing.

"This is intellectual terrorism," he said.

* * *

November 1, 1994

IRANIAN WRITERS ASK FOR AN END TO CENSORSHIP

Special to The New York Times

TEHERAN, Iran, Oct. 31—A group of dissident Iranian writers has called for the abolition of censorship in Iran in an open letter sent to news organizations, saying, "Writers must be free to create their work and express themselves."

The letter was signed by 134 novelists, publishers and translators, who said again today that they would continue their campaign against censorship in any form. The letter was sent last week to foreign news organizations and the state-run press.

"We are writers," the letter said. "That means we write and publish our sentiments, imagination and thought. It is our natural social and civil right that our books reach readers freely and without any impediment."

Books, magazines and newspapers are subject to censorship in Iran. Novelists say many manuscripts have been held up for a long as five years.

In April, 150 writers published an open letter protesting the arrest of Saidi Sirjani, a 63-year-old author and former professor of Iranian literature, on charges of espionage and drug abuse. Mr. Sirjani's criticism of the country's clerical leadership in scores of literary essays was widely believed to have led to his imprisonment.

Iranians say the writers' letter was significant in its timing, because the Islamic Government has been facing an increasing number of public demonstrations, urban rioting and strikes over the economy.

"The Government is very vulnerable now," said an Iranian writer who insisted on anonymity. "The climate is right for such protest letters."

Nevertheless, the state-run English-language Teheran Times denounced the signers of the letter as Communists, demanding legal action against them.

But some of the authors who signed the letter insisted that the Government reaction was mild compared with two years ago, when a demand for greater freedom of expression led to the bombing of bookstores and death threats.

* * *

December 28, 1994

AS TOLL RISES IN ALGERIA'S WAR, A DEARTH OF NEWS

By YOUSSEF M. IBRAHIM
Special to The New York Times

PARIS, Dec. 27—The world's press has been largely shut out of the Algerian civil war, which has claimed 600 to 1,000 victims each month since this summer.

Islamic militants fighting for more than two years to establish a Muslim theocracy in the Iranian mold have declared Algerian and foreign journalists to be prime targets

According to Reporters Without Frontiers, which is based in France, 26 Algerian journalists and a French reporter have been killed in Algeria this year alone in a campaign embraced by the Islamic Salvation Front, the major opposition party. The slayings were carried out by the party's armed branches, which are battling Algerian authorities from one end of the country to the other.

Widening the war with equal brutality, the Army has moved in the last year to muzzle the local press and keep the international press from reporting or witnessing warfare that includes widespread use of napalm and executions.

The policy is part of what senior commanders of the Algerian army have called a "total eradication strategy" against Muslim opposition.

Over the past year the Algerian Government has severely limited the ability of the local news media to cover the civil conflict beyond authorized news bulletins. Few visas are granted for foreign reporters.

As a result of intimidation by both sides, international news organizations have pulled out correspondents and hesitate to press journalists to go, even on occasional visits.

"The first reason is fear," Robert Menard, director of Reporters Without Frontiers, said tonight. "It would be a colossal risk for any editor to send a reporter to Algeria. For working journalists, Algerians and foreigners alike, the place is 100 times more dangerous than Bosnia or Rwanda. Going there is like playing Russian roulette with a journalist's life. Most editors are reluctant to make this decision."

Alan Thomas, chief of the Reuters Mideast bureau in Nicosia, Cyprus, said the agency decided to pull its correspondents out of Algeria a year ago. "The advantage of having a dateline out of there is outweighed by the security situation, the danger to the lives of the reporters," he said.

The blackout, as many editors call it, has eclipsed the profile of a war that is victimizing an increasing number of civilians.

After announcing that the number of dead was 3,000, the Algerian Government conceded earlier this year that the actual number was closer to 10,000. Independent French and Algerian estimates put the number of dead since the conflict began in 1992 at a minimum of 30,000.

Muslim fundamentalists are also taking aim at other foreigners. This year they have killed scores of French expatriates and at least 70 other foreigners, including four Roman Catholic priests today—three Frenchmen and a Belgian.

The Algerian war has been particularly frustrating for the French press, which has retained a historical and emotional commitment to covering Algeria in view of its 130-year occupation.

President Charles de Gaulle granted Algeria its freedom in 1962 after a war of independence. The French refer to the war raging now as the "Second Algerian War."

"I think there are large zones of shadows over what happens in Algeria today," said Alain Frachon, foreign editor of Le Monde, the French newspaper, whose correspondent covering Algeria now visits only occasionally for brief periods when she is satisfied she can enter and leave safely.

"Because of these restrictions imposed on most of the international press, and, more important, those imposed by the Algerian Government over our largest source of information, the Algerian press itself, there is much we don't know," Mr. Frachon said.

Jose Garcon, one of the French media's top experts on Algeria for the daily Liberation, said that the Algerian war had become a "story without images, because no one is there to record them."

Indeed, the only televised report to have come out of Algeria in the past two years was a BBC documentary broadcast a few months ago that showed armed groups of Islamic fundamentalists operating freely in the Algerian mountains.

* * *

October 10, 1995

IN A SMUTTY WAR, EGYPT SAYS, ISRAEL EXPORTS SEX

By DOUGLAS JEHL

CAIRO, Oct. 9—The last shooting war between Israel and Egypt ended 22 years ago this week. But in the Egyptian cap-

The New York Times

In Egypt, all records and videotapes are scrutinized by Government censors. At the Ministry of Culture, Sam Fahmi, Khadiga Saad and Thuraya al-Ghindi, the chief music censor, listen to a tape by Cranberries.

ital, there is anxious talk this fall about a subtler invasion from the neighbor to the north.

Israel's new weapon is sex, Egyptian conservatives say. They cite pornographic videotapes, explicit pop music cassettes and even Arabic-language advertising for a phone-sex line that newspaper commentators and other critics say have made their way from Tel Aviv to Cairo.

In a society in which a knee-length skirt is considered daring, there is scant sign of such foreign corruption, outside of a few urban entertainment districts. But mistrust of Israel here remains so pervasive that reports of the seaminess smuggled over the border have rekindled something of a cultural clash.

Even Rosa el Youssef, the Egyptian magazine that is banned in parts of the Arab world for its frequent pictures of bikini-clad women, condemned the phone-sex ads as an Israeli ploy to corrupt Egyptian sons and daughters. Opposition newspapers, which regularly refer to Israel as the Zionist enemy, have warned that the influx amounts to "sexual war."

And in Alexandria and other cities, the authorities have been trying to halt distribution of a banned tape by Saida Sultan, an Israeli singer whose breathy delivery and provocative lyrics have come to be seen as embodying the threat to Islamic culture.

That Egypt was first within the Arab world to make its peace with Israel is a source of pride to the Government here. But the ties forged by the two countries since the signing of the Camp David accords remain constrained by what many Egyptians see as powerful differences.

Though even now, only one in 2,000 Egyptians visits Israel each year, what Egyptians have seen and heard of Israeli films, songs and topless beaches has created an image of it as a modern-day Gomorrah.

In Egypt, no videotape or record album may be legally sold until it is scrutinized by a government censor, a process that often leads to mandatory editing to insure that the work meets what a senior Ministry of Culture official, Thuraya al-Ghindi, described as the country's "specific moral standards."

"Censorship is the conscience of society," said Mrs. al-Ghindi, the country's chief music censor. "Our job is to sift through what could be damaging for society and for young people."

Of the hundreds of films and videotapes from the West submitted to Egyptian authorities last year, 4 in 10 were ordered cut to eliminate nudity and sexual suggestiveness before they could be distributed. Among the 10 pieces of music rejected last week alone by Mrs. al-Ghindi was a song by a British pop group, 2 Unlimited, that a handwritten dossier showed had been judged objectionable for sexual meanings.

By Western standards, the lyrics to the song "Eternally Yours" that raise the hackles of the Egyptian censor and her all-female staff are almost innocuous.

But in Egypt, such censorship goes unchallenged. Under assault by Islamic militants, who have in the past attacked video stores in their fight against Western influences, the authorities may now be carrying out their work with extra diligence.

In practice, it means that the lyrics of Arabic-language songs must be approved even before they are recorded. It also means that whatever music does find its way around the censors carries extra shock value.

Among those whose cassettes have been smuggled into Egypt from across the Israeli border, Ms. Sultan and her tape "Sousou Ya Sousou" have become by far the most notorious, in part because she sings in Arabic as well as in Hebrew and English.

With a vocabulary shocking to those familiar only with the chaste Arabic-language songs that can win official approval, Ms. Sultan won a following among trendy young Egyptians. Some even played the banned music out loud on trains, reveling in its heavy-breathing suggestiveness: "Come all men look at me. I am passionate. I am desirous. Help me."

When the tape could be found in seedy marketplaces like Cairo's el Attaba square, demand this summer had pushed its price to as much as $15, nearly 10 times the standard rate. But with the authorities now more aggressive in policing the trade, even Ms. Sultan has fallen victim to the anti-Israeli backlash.

A new book prominently displayed in bookstores here describes the singer as an example of an Israeli effort to co-opt the musical heritage of the Arab world and claim it as Israeli. Al Hayat, the influential Arabic-language newspaper that is published in London, last week devoted a front-page article to what it portrayed as Egypt's efforts to combat an Israeli "sexual invasion."

Rosa el Youssef was among the first into the fray. In a cover story in August, it reprinted an Arabic-language advertisement for a phone-sex line that had appeared in a rival weekly, and noted that the long-distance telephone number for the service began with Israel's telltale 972 code.

The article announced that Rosa el Youssef itself had refused a lucrative offer to publish the advertisement, and it suggested that the Israeli intelligence services might be behind the scheme.

In an interview, Adel Hammouda, the deputy editor in chief, said the magazine had called attention to Israel's role as a corrupting influence in order to "exaggerate things with bad consequences before they actually get bigger."

* * *

January 23, 1996

SAUDIS FEAST FREELY FROM TV DISHES

By DOUGLAS JEHL

JIDDA, Saudi Arabia—Whether the satellite dishes that crown nearly every roof here are, well, entirely legal is not entirely clear.

But in a country in which censors still black out magazine photographs that display too much cleavage, no one in this seaside city seems to be standing in the way of the latest onslaught from abroad.

This remains a thoroughly Islamic society, where enforcement of morality includes patrols by the religious police. But while women dare not stray in public uncovered by a black veil, the dishes now freely pluck American B-television programs like "Models Inc." from the airwaves for viewing behind private walls. "Satellite television is here," a senior Saudi official said, "and the Government is looking the other way."

With its wide roads, gleaming office buildings and fancy boutiques, Saudi Arabia has long paired modern trappings with the strict tenets of the dominant Wahabi Muslim sect. But there may now be no sharper juxtaposition than the pervasive presence of the satellite dishes in a country in which even movie theaters are banned.

The technology, almost unknown here before the Persian Gulf war, is seen by many among Saudi Arabia's religious establishment as an outrage, a vehicle for Western films, music videos and television broadcasts they regard as devilish.

Some of those views are shared by ordinary Saudis, who in the words of Ahmed Tweijri, a lawyer, believe that "what is good in what is broadcast is far outweighed by what is bad."

Other Islamic countries like Iran have simply outlawed the dishes, mounting raids to confiscate black-market equipment. But while the sale and import of the dishes are technically prohibited here as well, Saudi Arabia appears to have decided for now not to try to stand between its citizens and the sky.

"They close their eyes," the manager of a strip-mall satellite outlet said of the Saudi authorities, who now enforce only a prohibition that prevents the satellite broadcasts from being demonstrated in public shops.

The manager, who said he sold as many as 75 satellite dishes a day, refused to give his name. Even his shop on the outskirts of Jidda carried no sign of its own, and was identifiable only by stickers on the door.

"In our tradition and our heritage, we don't like seeing kissing and we don't like seeing a man and a woman in bed," said Abdullah al-Ghamdi, a British-educated electronic engineer who was examining the latest model of compact satellite dish. "That is bad for the children, and it is bad for Islam."

But Mr. Ghamdi, who said he and his family already owned two satellite dishes, said he was thinking seriously about buying the new model, a three-foot-diameter version marketed by Orbit, a Rome-based service that became available here 18 months ago and whose products include the British Broadcasting Corporation's Arabic service and 18 other channels.

"I'd keep it in the master bedroom," Mr. Ghamdi declared, adding that his only question now was whether the $1,500 initial price was a bit too steep.

By Western standards, the fare on offer here even via satellite is rather tame, with none of the pornography that is common elsewhere in the world. But in Saudi Arabia, the uncut offerings can seem arresting, particularly when compared with heavily censored rental videos.

Among the favorite offerings, young people say, are music videos broadcast on often-raunchy equivalents of MTV, which display a world very different from their Saudi surroundings, where unmarried men and women may not mix in public.

While Saudi officials say they cannot estimate how many among the country's population of 18 million now tune into satellite television, the merest glance across roofs here and in Riyadh makes clear that it has made great inroads. And with as many as 80 channels available to those who are willing to pay, other Saudis regard the phenomenon as portending an important shift.

Businessmen who before the gulf war had no choice but to rely on Government television and Government-controlled newspapers now tend to describe the nightly BBC broadcast or CNN International as a main source of news.

And Saudi teen-agers have begun to demonstrate a new affection for Western dress, with young men beginning to venture outside the house in baseball caps instead of the traditional Arab headdress.

For parents like Dr. Talal Eshky, a businessman who complained that some of the satellite offerings amounted to "indecent exposure," it is a troubling trend. "We are losing our identity," Dr. Eshky said. "Where are we going from here?"

With Saudi Arabia planning to introduce its own Government-controlled cable television system soon, some here believe the authorities may yet try to rein in the satellite-borne products and their un-Islamic excesses.

But in a Saudi society that has maintained its conservative ways even through years of close ties with the West, others say they see little threat in the technology that is being beamed past the censors.

"In the old days, all people knew was Riyadh and Jidda and Mecca," a Saudi official said. "Now they know about New York and the snow in Washington, but that doesn't mean our culture is at risk."

* * *

October 8, 1996

WITH MIXED FEELINGS, IRAN TIPTOES TO THE INTERNET

By NEIL MacFARQUHAR

TEHERAN, Iran—In a special office where Iranian computer experts are devising just how much access their compatriots should have to the Internet, English words scrawled in felt pen fill a large white bulletin board across one wall.

A dense green line running down the middle of the board is marked "Firewall," and the first entry on the banished side of the barricade reads "Playboy.com."

The Islamic Republic is in a quandary over just how extensive its electronic links with the outside world should be. It is eager to propagate its theocracy and become a source for questions of Islamic law. But the Government fears that everyone from die-hard supporters of the deposed Shah to Western pornographers will storm in via cyberspace.

"There is stuff on the Internet that people have access to that is as offensive as 'The Satanic Verses' and it is updated every day," Deputy Foreign Minister M. Javad Zarif said, referring to the novel that prompted the Iranian Government in 1989 to call for the killing of its author, Salman Rushdie. "We believe a certain level of decency must be provided."

The Government's response to the spread of a similar phenomenon—satellite television—was to ban satellite dishes outright last year. Sobh, the monthly newspaper of the most puritanical clergy, has called for a parallel ban on the Internet.

But Parliament has yet to take up the issue, and the combination of scientists and clerics seeking access, plus upgraded telephone lines, means that those eager to be on line are likely to get there soon.

Anticipating that day, the Government is trying to centralize all access through the Ministry of Posts and Telecommunications. Having screened thousands of sites on the World Wide Web and at least started blocking those deemed unhealthy, the ministry is expanding subscriptions.

Government officials said the number of banned sites was not available, but they include those with information distributed by opposition groups like the Mujahedeen Khalq, based in Iraq, or by faiths that Iran abhors like the Bahai, as well as pornography and any information seen as Western propaganda.

"The brains of the young are very impressionable, so the Mujahedeen Khalq might be able to brainwash people to join them, or they might be able to influence an election," said a senior Government official familiar with the Internet project.

Price remains a hurdle for most people. On-line Iranians said the Government treats internet use like long-distance phone calls, with three or four hours a week billed at $50 to $130. One nightly user said he ended up with a three-month telephone bill for $70,000, which he bargained down to $20,000. And there are large initiation fees.

Outside the Government, a few services have established Internet links. For two years much of the Iranian university system has depended on a trunk line established by the Institute for the Study of Mathematics and Science to a sister institution in Austria. But with an estimated 30,000 people having accounts and the line limited to six people at once, getting through requires patience.

Users also said that the international telephone lines have sometimes been severed because of a continuing feud with the Government over whether the universities will retain their independent access once the Telecommunications Ministry system is fully operational. Irnet, the only private operator, has set up a domestic bulletin board service but has yet to get the international access it seeks.

Teheran's energetic Mayor, Gholam Hussein Karbaschi, also set up a municipal bulletin board and an E-mail system that forwards messages internationally, but exchanges are always delayed at least 24 hours.

Iranian students and professors are convinced that the degree of Government control means Big Brother is somehow out there watching.

Mr. Karbaschi denied that any messages were vetted, blaming the huge backlog for lost exchanges.

"Maybe in the future we will have to open the curtain surrounding Iran," the Government Internet official said. "Ultimately we know we can't control it mechanically—that we will have to control it spiritually."

The spiritual is one of the reasons Iran is so eager to get connected to the Internet. It wants the world to start referring to resources like the Center for Islamic Jurisprudence in Qum. Researchers have computerized 2,000 texts of both Shiite and Sunni law and hope eventually to expand it to 5,000.

The library now fields questions through the regular mail and wants E-mail to increase the scope of users.

"We hope the information banks of Qum become available throughout the world," said Ali Kourani, the clergyman running the center. "I've heard Mr. Clinton complain about the values of the young in America. This kind of criticism alone won't do any good. The young have to have access to the sources of good morals."

One recent foray onto the Internet indicated that Iranian students will peruse anything they can. A researcher unexpectedly given unrestricted access to the Internet to demonstrate the system to a visitor found a Web site marked Israel within minutes.

"I wonder what is on this," he said, passing the arrow back and forth across the screen in momentary indecision before clicking hard twice to whisk the information on screen. "What's the worst they can do, execute me?"

* * *

May 26, 1997

LESE ARAFAT'S MAJESTE

By ANTHONY LEWIS

Imagine an American President having the head of C-Span thrown in jail because he broadcast sessions of Congress in which the President was criticized. That is a rough translation of what has just happened in Yasir Arafat's Palestine.

The victim of Mr. Arafat's displeasure is Daoud Kuttab, a leading Palestinian journalist. He is being held incommunicado in a prison in Ramallah, in the West Bank.

I have known Mr. Kuttab for years, and like other foreign reporters and diplomats I respect him for his courage and honesty. The first concern has to be for his safety. Others imprisoned by the Palestinian Authority have been brutalized, and killed.

But the broader issue is the nature of the Palestinian polity. As President of the Authority, Mr. Arafat is intolerant of criticism and intemperate in his disregard for basic standards of freedom. His performance is blighting Palestinian hopes, and the Kuttab case is a telling example.

Mr. Kuttab has written unflinchingly about abuses of power by Israeli occupation authorities and by the new Palestinian regime. He was a columnist for Al Quds, an Arabic paper in Jerusalem, until the publisher gave in to an Arafat demand in 1994 and fired him. Last year the Committee to Protect Journalists gave him its International Press Freedom Award for his bravery.

He has been running a project very much like C-Span at an independent broadcasting station, Al Quds Educational Television. It carries live, uncut broadcasts of the Palestinian Legislative Council. The U.S. Agency for International Development provided a $25,000 pilot grant, and it has European support.

The Legislative Council, in its short life, has been remarkably independent of Mr. Arafat. Its members frequently criticize corruption in the Authority and abuses of human rights.

The Palestinian on the street could not read about that criticism because Palestinian newspapers were afraid to anger Mr. Arafat by printing it. When the verbatim broadcasts started, they attracted a wide audience. People watched through four hours of often prolix sessions.

Soon a curious thing happened. When Al Quds television broadcast a council session where Mr. Arafat was criticized, another signal covered the screen with a black rectangle.

The jamming came from thc Authority's official Palestinian Broadcasting Company. So Mr. Kuttab found when he was invited to check in the PBC control room. He was warned not to say anything.

Last Tuesday, May 21, The Washington Post carried a story about the jamming. That night Mr. Kuttab was telephoned by the Ramallah police chief, Col. Firas Ameleh, and asked to come in. He lives in Jerusalem, outside the control of the Authority, but he went anyway—and was arrested.

The next day Mr. Kuttab's family tried to find out where he was. So did U.S. consular officers, who inquired because Mr. Kuttab is an American citizen. Colonel Ameleh and other Palestinian officials denied for hours that he was under arrest. Finally they admitted he was.

Mr. Kuttab's lawyer and the U.S. Consul General, Edward Abington, were able to visit him on Wednesday. But the next day his wife and three children were turned away. Colonel Ameleh said he had orders from President Arafat's office to let no one visit him. Mr. Kuttab started a hunger strike in protest.

On what charge was he held? After two days of silence, officials said he would be charged with violating the "journalism law." No one is sure what that means.

The whole affair, with its arbitrariness and mendacity, reeks of the view that it is lese majeste to challenge Yasir Arafat. Palestinians deserve better than that. They want democracy. The Legislative Council's spirited criticism of corruption shows that, and so does the public response to Mr. Kuttab's legislative broadcasts.

But more is at stake. Such action costs Mr. Arafat dearly in the respect he needs to negotiate a viable Palestinian homeland—respect in the world, and in Israel. It is essential for him, as for Palestinian hopes, to release Daoud Kuttab.

* * *

July 28, 1997

AT PALESTINIAN PAPERS, MONEY IS AS ELUSIVE AS FREEDOM

By JUDITH MILLER

RAMALLAH, West Bank—Just as Palestinians are struggling to establish a state of their own, an independent Palestinian press is fighting to be born. So far, neither effort has been easy.

For Arabic-language Palestinian newspapers in Jerusalem, the neighboring West Bank and the Gaza Strip, political turmoil, censorship and intimidation have combined with soaring paper and printing costs and a severe recession to make publishing an extremely risky venture. Moreover, competition is fierce among the three leading dailies—for market share, the skimpy number of advertisers, and readers.

Israel continues to censor the Jerusalem-based Arabic press, but things are not that different on the Palestinian side of the military checkpoints. While the Palestinian Authority, Yasir Arafat's government, does not formally censor newspapers, its corruption and heavy-handed crackdown on Islamic and secular dissent, among other things, have made it increasingly unpopular. Rather than censor, it is inclined to intimidate papers on the rare occasions they report on official abuses.

The Palestinian press law enacted in 1995 ostensibly guarantees a free press—as do most Arab states, at least in theory—and the "absolute right" of every Palestinian "to express his opinion in a free manner either orally, in writing, photography, or drawing." But self-censorship, editors agree, is often more insidious than official control. "You can't have genuine freedom of the press without real democracy," said Khaled Amayreh, an American-educated columnist who writes for non-Palestinian Arabic-language newspapers and for several English-language journals. The Palestinian Authority, he added, "is a police state without a state."

But editors of major papers agree that their toughest challenges are economic. "You can't have an independent press without a strong economy," said Marwan Abu Zalaf, the editor of Al Quds—Jerusalem in Arabic—the oldest and largest Palestinian Arabic-language paper.

Al Quds, top, is among the diverse fare offered to Palestinian readers.

So far, Mr. Arafat's Palestinian Authority offers Palestinians neither prosperity nor enough democracy, critics say. According to the World Bank, the Palestinian gross domestic product has plunged 38 percent since the Palestinian Authority began ruling Gaza and the West Bank three years ago. This is mostly because of the loss of Palestinian jobs in Israel and repeated Israeli border closings.

Officially, unemployment stands at more than 22 percent, with underemployment at 28 percent. Palestinian trade between Gaza, an isolated strip between Israel and Egypt that is home to more than 900,000 people, and the West Bank, which borders Jordan with about 1.1 million people, have also declined sharply. Unemployment would be far higher if Mr. Arafat had not more than doubled the authority's civil service rolls.

Though Palestinian newspapers are relatively cheap, selling for between one and 1.5 Israeli shekels—28 to 42 cents—they are expensive for Palestinians, whose annual per-capita income is now less than $1,000.

Hanna Siniora, who publishes The Jerusalem Times, an English-language weekly, and the monthly Palestine Business Report, said that his surveys showed that each newspaper sold had eight readers, on average.

While there are some 400 Palestinian journalists at newspapers, radio and television stations, Mr. Amayreh estimated that no more than 20 were truly independent. So, many Palestinians read about the authority's abuses first in the Israeli press.

Most Palestinian reporters, he said, cannot afford to be bold, at least not in Arabic. "I get away with it because I write mainly in English," Mr. Amayreh said. Low pay reinforces the political pressure. "The average journalist earns between $400 and $500 a month," he said. Such wages make bribes hard to resist.

Mr. Siniora complains about soaring costs. Paper prices have more than doubled in the last decade, he said, to $750 a ton from $300. New printing presses cost more than $5 million, up from about $500,000. His two English-language publications have a combined circulation of 4,200 and little advertising. "We're losing about $10,000 a month," said Mr. Siniora, who covers the deficit himself and with contributions from Palestinian businessmen.

Al Quds, the largest daily, is a 24-page color broadsheet whose circulation is officially 50,000, more than double that of the two competing papers published in this West Bank town—Al Ayam, which calls itself independent, and Al Hayat al Jadida, a semiofficial paper with ties to the Palestinian Authority.

Because his newspaper is based in East Jerusalem, which Israel has annexed, Mr. Abu Zalaf of Al Quds must still send articles that affect security to Israeli censors. But, he said, censorship became more relaxed when Yitzhak Rabin came to power in 1992; the Likud Government has not reversed this policy.

Since Al Quds is also sold in the West Bank and Gaza, Mr. Abu Zalaf also needs a license from the authority, with which he has already had several confrontations. In July 1994, it blocked the paper's distribution in Gaza for five days after he refused to print a low estimate of the number of participants at an opposition rally as Mr. Arafat's government had demanded. And its night editor was detained for five days in 1995 by the authority's security service after he failed to run an article about the Greek Patriarch's Christmas message to Mr. Arafat on the front page.

"Journalists should not be spoon-fed," said Mr. Abu Zalaf, who is British-educated.

In many ways, he has the sensibilities of an editor in a small American city. Al Quds features several pages of death notices and notices of weddings and graduations. And about a year ago, it began devoting a full page to economic news—publishing, among other things, the weekly performance of the fledgling Palestinian stock exchange.

A litmus test of the Palestinian press's ability to handle controversy came in May, with the Palestinian Authority's arrest of Daoud Kuttab, an independent journalist whose TV broadcasts of legislative debates had irked Mr. Arafat.

Neither Al Hayat nor Al Quds covered the arrest, though Mr. Abu Zalaf says that Al Quds mentioned Mr. Kuttab's release. But Al Ayam, which is sympathetic to Mr. Arafat, did cover the arrest, despite its political affinities. So did Al Resaleh, a weekly that prints 7,000 copies in Gaza and is affiliated with Hamas, the militant Islamic faction.

Al Ayam, which published its first issue in December 1995, now prints 10,000 copies of a 20-page daily at spacious new offices in Ramallah, which house a new color press that cost more than $3 million and was partly subsidized by France. Senior editors hope that it will turn a profit within five years.

"It's a good newspaper that has been deft in reporting on corruption, even though its editor, Akram Haniye, is Arafat's adviser," said Danny Rubinstein, who writes about Palestinian affairs for the Israeli daily Haaretz. Al Ayam's editors say that Mr. Arafat has no financial stake in the paper, which they say is backed by 15 Palestinian companies and businessmen. Last year, Al Ayam began home delivery in Ramallah, where 90 percent of Palestinian papers are sold on the street. Another innovation: a full page devoted to the Palestinian economy.

To earn extra revenue, the paper prints textbooks for the Palestinian Authority, which Mr. Kuttab says is an indirect government subsidy that reinforces the paper's desire to maintain cordial relations with Mr. Arafat's team. "But perhaps because of the close ties between Haniye and Arafat, the paper is often bolder than others in what it feels it can cover," Mr. Rubinstein said.

The daily with the closest ties to Mr. Arafat, however, is Al Hayat al Jadida, whose $60,000-a-month deficit is said to be covered by the authority, several Palestinian journalists, who asked not to be identified, said.

But of the three biggest papers—Al Ayam and Al Hayat on the West Bank and Al Quds in Jerusalem—only Al Quds is profitable. It made about $100,000 last year, Mr. Abu Zalaf said—40 percent from circulation and 60 percent from advertising.

* * *

September 18, 1998

IRAN SHUTS POPULAR NEWSPAPER THAT QUESTIONED HARD LINE ON TALIBAN AND ARRESTS TOP EDITORS

By DOUGLAS JEHL

TEHERAN, Iran, Sept. 17—In a new setback for political moderates, Iran has closed a leading daily newspaper and arrested its top editors for publishing articles deemed detrimental "to the country's national interests and security."

The action, announced on Wednesday by the Islamic Revolution Court, came hours after the country's supreme leader, Ayatollah Ali Khamenei, issued an ultimatum against the "creeping excesses" of an increasingly free-wheeling Iranian press.

With its wholehearted embrace of President Mohammad Khatami's calls for greater openness in Iranian society, the newspaper, Tous, has regularly infuriated Iranian conservatives by challenging accepted policy. It had questioned the wisdom of Iran's hard-line stand against the Taliban movement in Afghanistan, and the authorities apparently cited that as the reason for halting its presses on Tuesday night.

Founded early this year, the highly popular newspaper has escaped two previous court-ordered closings, once by changing its name. But several Iranian political experts said the handling of the current case suggested that the shutdown could well be permanent and—at a time of tensions over Afghanistan—could presage wider curbs on public expression in the name of public security.

The arm of Mr. Khatami's Government that is supposed to regulate the press responded with a thinly veiled complaint against the action, carried out by public prosecutors closely aligned with Ayatollah Khamenei.

"Any press crime should be tried in a public and open court and with the presence of a jury," the Ministry of Culture and Islamic Guidance said in a statement today. The Islamic Revolution Court operates behind closed doors.

Among those arrested were the newspaper's editor, Mahmoud Shamsvolazein, and the director of its publishing company, Hamid Reza Jalaipur, according to the official Iranian news agency.

There has been no obvious sign of a schism between Mr. Khatami and Ayatollah Khamenei over Afghanistan, the target of a mounting Iranian military buildup and vociferous threats over the killing there of a number of Iranian diplomats.

But many of Mr. Khatami's supporters have expressed private concern that the crisis with Afghanistan might draw attention from his declared quest to ease the restrictive atmosphere of Iranian society. And some have seen in Ayatollah's Khamenei's recent harsh words toward Afghanistan and his direct call for a crackdown on "enemies of the revolution in the press" a possible sign that conservatives hope to use the crisis to regain the spotlight.

In the last six months the rivalry between supporters of Mr. Khatami, a relative moderate, and conservatives aligned with Ayatollah Khamenei has claimed several victims.

One was the Mayor of Teheran, Gholamhossen Karabaschi, an ally of the President who was sentenced in July to five years in prison after being convicted of corruption charges that his supporters say were politically motivated. Another, the former Interior Minister, Abdollah Nouri, was forced from office by the conservative-dominated Parliament in June, in part because of his outspoken support for Mr. Karabaschi. Two weeks ago Mr. Nouri and another Khatami lieutenant, Ataollah Mohajerani, the Minister of Culture and Islamic Guidance, were beaten by thugs after attending a Friday prayer service.

* * *

July 4, 1999

ARAB TV GETS A NEW SLANT: NEWSCASTS WITHOUT CENSORSHIP

By JOHN F. BURNS

DOHA, Qatar—In millions of homes and offices across the Arab world, television sets are regularly tuned these days to Al Jazeera, a hard-hitting Arabic-language news channel that explores issues long suppressed by the region's rulers, including the lack of democracy, the persecution of political dissidents and the repression of women.

From studios in this tiny emirate in the Persian Gulf, Al Jazeera offers round-the-clock programming based on a principle revolutionary by the traditional standards of Middle

East broadcasting, that all coverage should be free of censorship or bias. In another innovation for the Arab world, ordinary Arabs can air their views on an array of freewheeling phone-in shows.

The result has been a sensation in the 22 Arab countries where Al Jazeera's broadcasts can be seen. In Algiers's Casbah, in Cairo's slums, in the suburbs of Damascus, even in the desert tents of Bedouins with satellite dishes, the channel has become a way of life. In its 30 months on air, it has drawn viewers in droves from the mind-numbing fare offered by the region's state-run networks, whose news coverage often amounts to little more than a reverential chronicle of government affairs.

Even where Al Jazeera cannot be seen live, in countries like Iraq that ban satellite dishes, videos of its shows are traded eagerly in bazaars. Sometimes, viewer interest has been piqued by scoops like the lengthy interview the channel broadcast three weeks ago with Osama bin Laden, the Islamic militant who has been indicted as the alleged mastermind of the bombings of American embassies in East Africa last year that killed 224 people, including 12 Americans.

The interview gave Arab audiences their first opportunity to hear Mr. Bin Laden speak uncensored, and in their own language. Ironically, for an enterprise often accused of acting as a mouthpiece for American ideas, Al Jazeera's management faced pressure not to broadcast the interview from American diplomats who expressed fears that Mr. Bin Laden's calls for new attacks could heighten risks for Americans in the Middle East.

The Qatar channel has been watched with growing interest by Middle East scholars, many of whom see it as emblematic of deep stirrings across the Arab world.

Some specialists see its popularity as evidence that Islamic conservatism, long seen as the rising force in the Arab world, faces a challenge from a new generation yearning for societies that are more, not less, tolerant and democratic.

"What Al Jazeera shows is that people across the Arab world want open discussion of the issues that affect their lives, and that new communications technologies make it impossible for governments to stop them," said Dale Eickelman, a Dartmouth College professor who recently visited Al Jazeera's studios in Doha. He added: "The days have gone when Arab governments can control what their people know, and what they think."

The region's rulers, unable or unwilling to take the drastic steps that would be necessary to deny their people access to the channel, such as confiscating satellite dishes, have struck back in other ways. In Saudi Arabia, Government spokesmen have dubbed it "the suspicious channel," and described its programming as "poisonous." In Algeria, an Al Jazeera program exploring the darker corners of that country's civil war suddenly went off the air when the Government cut electrical power in several major cities.

But among ordinary Arabs, the channel is credited with breathing much-needed fresh air into the stifling climate in which Arabs have traditionally debated political, social and

The New York Times

Bold news from Doha reaches millions throughout the Arab world.

religious issues. Programs have dealt with previously unmentionable topics like the prevalence of torture in Arab jails, the killing and "disappearing" of political opponents in countries like Algeria, and even the modern relevance of ancient Islamic codes, such as the right of Muslim men to marry up to four wives.

Little has been glossed over in the channel's readiness to challenge old taboos, even when the subject touches on the most sensitive issue of all, the teachings of the Muslim prophet Mohammed, as embodied in the Koran. Discussion programs have pitted conservative Muslim clerics against reformist scholars, and feminists against traditionalists, in exchanges that have explored the bitter differences over Islamic doctrine within the Arab world.

Confirming what visitors to Arab palaces already knew—that the channel is widely watched by the powerful, as well as the powerless—one phone-in program was called last year by Col. Muammar el-Qaddafi, the Libyan ruler, offering his views on Arab nationalism. Other callers, usually from sanctuaries outside their own countries, have condemned leaders like President Saddam Hussein of Iraq, and urged their overthrow.

For some of the Arab world's most powerful leaders, Al Jazeera's feistiness is all the more galling for the fact that it is broadcast from Qatar, a nation of 600,000 people, the smallest in the Arab world. Eighteen months before the first broadcast in November 1996, power passed in a bloodless palace coup from one of the most conservative Arab rulers to his son, Sheik Hamad bin Khalifa al-Thani, a graduate of Britain's Sandhurst military academy.

The new Emir of Qatar, who is 47 years old, has proven to be one of the Arab world's most reform-minded leaders. Shortly after taking power, he abolished the country's Information Ministry, and with it a system of censorship that kept tight control on the country's newspapers and broadcasting. A few months later, while pondering the possibility of establishing what some Qataris call "an Arab CNN," a fortuitous turn of events in London suddenly made the step more practicable.

In 1995, the BBC, long famed in the Middle East for the Arabic-language broadcasts of its World Service radio network, expanded into television in a deal with a Saudi-backed company, Orbit Communications, which operates several satellite channels of its own. With an annual payment of about $35 million from the Saudis, the BBC provided regular Arabic-language newscasts to be carried on Orbit's main Middle East channel.

After 20 months, the deal foundered when the BBC's insistence on editorial independence ran headlong into Saudi refusal to tolerate BBC reporting on issues seen as impugning Saudi Arabia's ruling family, including executions in the desert kingdom and the activities of a prominent Saudi dissident in Britain. When Orbit pulled the plug on the BBC deal, Qatar hired 20 of the BBC's editors, reporters and technicians, all with Arab backgrounds, as the nucleus of Al Jazeera's team.

The Qatar Government pledged $140 million to finance the channel for five years, but bound Al Jazeera's managers to make the enterprise self-sustaining after that with advertising revenues. Nearly three years later, despite its popular success, the channel has been largely shunned by the big multinational companies that are the major advertisers on the Middle East's tamer satellite channels, almost certainly because the companies fear a backlash from powerful countries like Saudi Arabia.

Despite the reaction of Arab governments, Sheik Hamad, the Qatar ruler, says he intends to stick by Al Jazeera. "What a headache," he said, chuckling, when asked about the satellite channel during an interview at his sumptuous palace in Doha. "It's caused no end of problems, but all the same I think of it as a kind of oxygen, invigorating our thinking. I tell my children, if you want to know the issues of real importance in the Arab world, watch Al Jazeera."

Sheik Hamad has taken other steps to liberalize life in Qatar. Earlier this year, Qataris, including women, had their first election, for a municipal council. The next step will be an elected Parliament, with powers yet to be defined.

Although most Qataris applaud the changes, many say the Emir's motives in setting up Al Jazeera and carrying out his reforms have a logic beyond enthusiasm for democracy: the Qatar leader, they say, seized the satellite channel as an effective way to strengthen Qatar's fragile sovereignty and identity, and particularly to give his small gulf nation an image distinct from Saudi Arabia, Qatar's powerful and often hostile neighbor, where the ruling family has shown little appetite for reforms.

"It's been a very intelligent way of telling the world that Qatar exists," said Dima Khatib, a 28-year-old reporter at the channel. "It's put Qatar on the map."

But the new renown has come at a price, and not only in relations with Saudi Arabia. Last November, Jordan closed Al Jazeera's news bureau in Amman after a Syrian commentator on Al Jazeera, fulminating against Jordan's peace treaty with Israel, described Jordan as "an artificial entity" populated by "a bunch of Bedouins living in an arid desert."

After apologies from Qatar the order was rescinded. But last month, Kuwait took a leaf from Jordan's book and ordered Al Jazeera's bureau in Kuwait closed after an Islamic militant calling an Al Jazeera phone-in program from Europe suggested that Kuwait's ruler, Sheik Jaber al-Jaber al-Sabah, should be ousted for agreeing to extend the vote in Kuwaiti elections to women. That dispute remains unresolved.

But these spats have paled beside the controversies stirred by Al Jazeera's handling of some of the Muslim world's hottest social and religious issues. On programs with names bursting with irreverent intent—like "The Opposite Direction," "More Than One Opinion" and "Without Boundaries"—the channel has used its studios to foment debates of a candor unimaginable in a public forum in the Arab world before Al Jazeera's arrival.

The most popular show, "The Opposite Direction," uses a format similar to CNN's "Crossfire," with two studio guests chosen for their opposing views confronting each other in the Doha studio, or by live video link. The program has made a star of its presenter, Faisal al-Kasim, a 37-year-old Syrian whose bespectacled appearance and scholarly background—he holds a doctorate in English literature—belies a Rottweiler-like snappiness that helps give the show its nervy edge.

One of Mr. Kasim's most talked-about shows featured two women debating polygamy among Muslim men. One participant, a leftist member of the Jordanian Parliament, set the tone for a furious exchange by saying that a practice authorized by the Prophet Mohammed in the seventh century, when many Arab women had been widowed in war, had outlived its validity. "Why should we put up with this rubbish now?" she asked.

Her adversary for the show, an Egyptian woman with strongly conservative views on matters of Islamic doctrine, stood up, tore off her microphone and headed for the exit. When a startled Mr. Kasim attempted to dissuade her, noting that the program was "on air" across the Arab world, she shot back: "I don't care if we're on the planet Mars, I'm not going to tolerate this blasphemy." With that, she slammed the door behind her, and departed for Cairo.

* * *

November 25, 1999

ISRAEL EASES SECRECY OVER NUCLEAR WHISTLE-BLOWER'S TRIAL

By DEBORAH SONTAG

JERUSALEM, Nov. 24—The Israeli government today allowed a newspaper to publish censored excerpts from the classified transcript of a treason trial of 12 years ago. They provided the first glimpse ever into the courtroom where Mordechai Vanunu was convicted for blowing the whistle on Israel's secret nuclear program.

The excerpts, published by the newspaper Yediot Ahronot, contained no earth-shattering revelations about an infamous case with a spy novel plot. But their release signaled the government's increasing awareness that it can no longer maintain absolute silence on whether it has nuclear weapons.

The state attorney, avoiding a court challenge, pre-emptively released more than 1,200 pages of censored testi-

Reuters

Israel made public yesterday parts of the trial of Mordechai Vanunu.

mony to the newspaper, which had been fighting to obtain the documents.

"Things have changed since the trial and it was decided by defense officials that anything that will not harm the security of the country will now be published," said Devora Hen, a lawyer for the state attorney.

Officially, Israel refuses to confirm or deny reports on its nuclear weapons program, maintaining a long-held policy of what it calls "deliberate ambiguity" about its offensive capacity.

The Bulletin of Atomic Scientists, citing what it said was a classified United States Department of Energy study, said this fall that Israel has the sixth-largest nuclear arsenal in the world.

"I think that there is an evolving understanding that a long-term policy of complete secrecy is untenable and creates whistle-blowers like Vanunu," said Avner Cohen, an Israeli scholar whose book, "Israel and the Bomb," was published last year in New York. "There is stuff that really should be classified, but not the fact of the nuclear policy itself."

Though Mr. Cohen's study was initially banned in Israel, it was recently approved for publication in Hebrew in Israel, another sign of a relaxation of the government's strict secrecy.

Yediot Ahronot devoted almost 10 pages of its newspaper today to the case, and it dominated the airwaves.

The documents showed that Mr. Vanunu, a former nuclear technician, testified in his closed-door trial that he had exposed Israel's nuclear warchest in an effort to force the government to acknowledge its existence and accept international supervision of the program.

"I wanted to confirm what everyone knows," he said about the information he sold to the Sunday Times of London in 1986. "I wanted to put the matter under proper supervision."

Mr. Vanunu further testified that as a result of his revelations, Shimon Peres, who was prime minister at the time the article was published, could not "keep lying to Reagan and telling him that we do not have nuclear weapons."

In the fall of 1986, the Sunday Times published Mr. Vanunu's claim that Israel had stockpiled roughly 100 nuclear weapons. Mr. Vanunu, a Moroccan-born Jew who grew up in a religious home, had worked at the Dimona nuclear reactor for nine years before emigrating to Australia and converting to Christianity. The newspaper paid him to fly to London and collaborate on the story about Israel's nuclear capacity.

"It was clear to me that Vanunu was in danger," Peter Hunam, an English journalist for the Sunday Times, testified, according to the transcripts.

"I wanted him to move to another hotel, but I realized he was exceedingly nervous and was talking about leaving London or the country."

After his interviews with the newspaper, but before the story was published, Mr. Vanunu was lured from London to Rome by a blond female Mossad agent called "Cindy." There he was kidnapped and flown to Israel to stand trial as a spy and a traitor.

"I didn't know if they were going to shoot me or kill me," he said about his abduction during the trial.

The documents show that the prosecution believed that it had the authority to sentence Mr. Vanunu to death but refrained from requesting this. In 1988, he was sentenced to 18 years in prison, where he has served 13 years, mostly in solitary confinement. Only recently has the government allowed even a photograph of him in jail to be published.

Mr. Peres, who is credited with organizing Israel's nuclear program as a young aide to David Ben-Gurion, today denounced the release of the transcripts for bringing to the surface a subject that is best left suppressed.

"The public knows that there are certain things it does not want to know," he said in an interview with Israeli television.

Earlier in the day, on Israel radio, Mr. Peres said, "The whole Vanunu affair makes my blood boil. One day a man gets up in the morning and he decides what is good for the country. Does he carry the responsibility?"

During the trial, Yediot Ahronot reported, Mr. Peres said that he believed that the revelations in the Sunday Times had injured Israel, increasing "beyond what is desirable, suspicions and reservations about Israel."

Mr. Vanunu's detailed allegations about the scope and sophistication of Israel's nuclear weapons program have never been challenged by Israeli officials or by knowledgeable Israeli civilian defense experts. Independent assessments by international arms-monitoring organizations have also concluded that Israel's nuclear stockpile is exceeded only by those of the United States, Russia, China, France and the United Kingdom.

Mr. Cohen said the Israelis have long maintained that Mr. Vanunu's revelations accelerated Arab nuclear projects. "I do not believe this," he said, "even though in my opinion Vanunu had a serious effect on the Arab press and attention to the subject."

"It was not Mordechai Vanunu who caused the Iraqi nuclear program to move fast," Mr. Cohen continued. "It was an Iraqi decision following Israel's bombing of its nuclear reactor in 1981."

In 1981, Moshe Dayan, then the defense minister, said publicly that Israel had no active "atomic bombs" but had the capacity to assemble weapons for attack in short order.

Africa

April 7, 1979

PRETORIA IS PREPARING NEW RESTRAINTS ON THE PRESS

Special to The New York Times

JOHANNESBURG, April 5—Ever since confrontations between riot policemen and black demonstrators threw South Africa into turmoil three years ago newspapers here have been bracing themselves for an assault on their tenuous freedoms.

Now what they consider as that assault is under way by a Government that believes that many of its problems are created—or at least compounded—by a hostile press. The papers conclude that they may never again be able to offer objective accounts of events such as the Soweto riots in 1976 or the scandal a year later over the death in detention of the black leader Stephen Biko. The Government, for its part, is insisting that all it seeks is responsibility from "bad elements" in the press.

The assault foreseen by the newspapers has taken the form of three bills, two before Parliament and a third due for enactment before this session ends. When put into law, the measures will take their place alongside dozens of press restraints that occupy more than 300 pages in a legal handbook considered an indispensable aid by most South African journalists.

Checking With the Authorities

One bill, already approved by the lower house of Parliament, will make it an offense to publish "any untrue matter" about the police "without having reasonable grounds for believing the statement is true." The burden of proof will rest with the newspapers, whose editors and reporters will be liable for a maximum penalty of five years in jail and a fine of $11,800.

In practice, Justice Minister James T. Kruger has indicated, newspapers will be expected to check their reports, whether on police action in a riot, the death of a political detainee or even routine matters, with a police liaison unit. A precedent exists for reports on matters involving prisons and the armed forces, which must be checked with the authorities before publication.

A second bill will make it an offense to "prejudice, influence or anticipate the proceedings or findings" of an inquest, again with stiff penalties. In Parliament, Opposition legal experts have warned that the measure could be interpreted as prohibiting reporting on the cause of death—of a rioter, for example, or a detainee—after the police launch an investigation, which can be immediate.

Through the commission appointed to investigate the Biko scandal, which has exonerated all present ministers, the Government has also attempted to obtain court—orders forbidding independent scrutiny. After an initial success in which the editor of The Rand Daily Mail was fined, the commission has failed to obtain gag orders, but its efforts have contributed to a general atmosphere of caution.

One problem for the papers is the large legal cost involved in fighting the Government in the courts. A decade ago The Rand Daily Mail paid nearly $350,000 in a losing defense against charges of publishing untruths about the prison system. This year the paper and its sister publication, The Sunday Express, have several times been represented by Sydney W. Kentridge, the country's foremost advocate.

Protecting the Police

Defending the new police bill, the Justice Minister has said that his only purpose is to protect the police against lies and biased accounts of the kind that, in his opinion, characterized the press coverage of the Soweto riots and Mr. Biko's death. "The work of the South African police is too important to let any Tom, Dick or Harry write what he likes about police action," Mr. Kruger told Parliament, adding the assurance that the police welcomed "fair criticism."

Critics have seen more sinister motives. Kelsey Stuart, the legal expert whose book "A Newspaperman's Guide to the Law" is the standard work on the subject, said that the measure was likely to have an effect similar to that of the law forbidding publication of untruths about prisons. As a result of that statute, he said, no newspaper has dared for 10 years to publish articles about prisons "except such reports that place the Prisons Department in a favorable light."

* * *

December 4, 1980

CENSORS IN SOUTH AFRICA RELAX SOME GROUNDS RULES

By JOSEPH LELYVELD

Special to the New York Times

PRETORIA, South Africa—The Publications Appeals Board, a part of the censorship apparatus that has been operating increasingly in reverse gear to unban books, gave long consideration the other day to a novel that has as its climax a chilling and clinical description of the murder in detention of a black nationalist by a South African security policeman.

A few years ago, no one would have imagined for a moment that such a book could have been published here.

Now, in the light of its recent decisions, there seems to be a reasonable chance that the appeals board will cancel the banning order on "Store Up the Anger," the novel by Wessel Ebersohn whose plot is bound to remind readers of the death in detention three years ago of Steve Biko, the young black leader.

The case has added piquancy because of a coincidence of names. In the novel, which is to be published in the United States by Doubleday, the policeman who gives in to a sadistic impulse to demonstrate how "you can scramble a man's brains without leaving a single mark" happens to be named van Rooyen. The chairman of the appeals board, who will write the decision on "Store Up the Anger," also happens to be a van Rooyen.

Professor Jacobus van Rooyen of the law faculty of the University of Pretoria does not pretend to be a liberal. But he does believe it is possible to apply standards of judicial reasonableness to the enterprise of censoring.

15,000 Books Banned

Over the years, South Africa has forbidden the publication or sale of more than 15,000 books and the Government Gazette regularly lists new titles.

But under Professor van Rooyen's influence, the appeals board has been trying to come up with consistent definitions of terms like "offensive" and to establish clear precedents that publishers and writers would then be able to cite. In the past, an offensive book was, basically, a book that offended some censor.

However they are finally defined, blasphemy and pornography will continue to be treated severely. But in politics and literature, Professor van Rooyen says he hopes to establish the idea that no theme or subject is automatically forbidden, that the presumption is in favor of publication unless it can be shown that the book is likely to incite behavior that could endanger the state.

This effort to strike an attitude that is neither arbitrary nor permissive is recognized in literary circles as a marginal improvement on the past conduct of the censors, but it is not applauded. Both Ravan Press, an English-language publishing house that brings out much of the work by black writers that gets printed as well as risky books like "Store Up the Anger," and an avantgarde Afrikaans publishing house called Taurus refuse to appeal when censorship decisions go against them.

Strikingly, in their attitude to the censors the younger Afrikaans writers appear to be virtually indistinguishable from black writers who reject the legitimacy of the laws under which the censors operate. "We don't talk to them at all," said Ampie Coetzee, an Afrikaans literary critic who helped to found Taurus. "We don't accept their existence. Our view is you can't change this system from inside. These guys are too strong. If you join them, you join them."

Author Refuses to Appeal

Some students of the latest trends in censorship here believe that the new attitude was prompted more by the local reaction to the banning of works by such prominent Afrikaans writers as Andre Brink and Etienne LeRoux than by the international outcry against the banning last year of "Burger's Daughter," Nadine Gordimer's latest novel.

The New York Times/Stephen Hone

Wessel Ebersohn, the author of "Store Up the Anger," a novel that has been banned by the South African appeals board.

Miss Gordimer refused to appeal, so the Director of Publications, the official charged with overseeing the censorship machinery, appealed himself against the decision of one of the censorship committees he had appointed. The book was then unbanned. A few weeks later the same procedure was followed to secure the release of "A Dry White Season," a novel by Mr. Brink.

At the time Miss Gordimer predicted that "such special treatment" would not be given to black writers and that the process of reversing notorious censorship decisions against white writers had "sinister implications." But this year the Director of Publications started appearing on behalf of blacks. An anthology of black writings called "Forced Landing" was banned and unbanned and the last issue of Staffrider, a black literary magazine with a tone that whites tend to call militant, became the object of an appeal by the director within 48 hours of its banning.

In the case of "Store Up the Anger," the appeal was sponsored by the novel's British publisher, Victor Gollancz, since Ravan Press held to its stand of refusing to acknowledge the board's legitimacy with an appeal. Mr. Ebersohn, whose previous works had been mystery thrillers, sat tensely with his wife at what amounted to the defense table as John Dugard, an internationally respected legal scholar at Witwatersrand University, sought to persuade Professor van Rooyen and the four other whites on the board that the novel was a work of literature rather than propaganda.

An Understated Manner

After the work had been banned by the censorship committee and before it got to the appeals board, a third kind of panel, known as a "committee of experts," had decreed that it could not be literature because it referred to real events and characters. So did "War and Peace," "Armies of the Night," "Animal Farm," and "The Decline and Fall of the Roman Empire," reported Professor Dugard, whose manner, through nearly three hours of argument, was understated, precise and devoid of rhetorical flourish.

"Burger's Daughter" also referred to real events, he said, bringing the argument home. Members of the panel fastened on a passage in which the imprisoned black leader contemplates the policemen who are tormenting him and ruminates: "I hate you more than ever before because you'll always be blind to what you do not want to see and you'll only understand as far as your fear allows you. You'll go on brutalizing and killing until we stop you. And we will stop you. We will come for the Browns and the van Rooyens and the Fouries."

Did this and similar passages, not to mention the novel's title, they add, tend to incite feelings of hatred and revenge against the security police?

Skillfully offering the panel a range of reasons for releasing the book, Professor Dugard replied that police brutality was a problem in many societies; that abuse of authority was a hallowed literary theme; that the novel encourages reform rather than revenge; that it was not incitement to consider the idea that there would be a day of reckoning by blacks; and that, in any case, "A Dry White Season" went further in its condemnation of the police.

'I'm a Reformist'

Later Mr. Dugard explained that he has been handling censorship cases because he sees a chance to enlarge the area of free expression in South Africa. "I'm a reformist," he said. "I believe in using the available machinery. And I see reform. I see more reform coming from the appeals board than I do from the courts on other issues."

In previous decisions releasing books, the appeals board has sometimes found it useful to belittle their literary merit in order to argue that the likely reader would find them hard to understand or unpersuasive and that they were, therefore, harmless. Sometimes it almost seems to be saying that the books it allows through would have had to be banned if they had been better.

Miss Gordimer complained that "Burger's Daughter" had been "mauled over at public expense" but at the end of the long hearing, Mr. Ebersohn said he mainly felt numb. "It's all dealt with in such an unemotional manner, it seems so dispassionate, that I don't seem to be closely related to the whole thing," he said.

* * *

October 16, 1981

TWILIGHT WORLD OF ZIMBABWE'S PRESS

By JOSEPH LELYVELD
Special to the New York Times

SALISBURY, Zimbabwe—Only a few voices were raised to warn of encroachments on press freedom when the Government engineered the creation of a semi-independent trust early this year to buy out the South African interests that had controlled nearly all the newspapers in the former Rhodesia.

The press that was being taken over, it was recognized, had been tamed, if not broken, by the white minority regime of Ian D. Smith, so there was not much independence left to be compromised. The Government, which had used the unusual device of a trust to avoid a direct takeover of the press, said it wanted the newspapers to be "constructive," not subservient.

"Positivity is news; negativity is not news," declared the Director of Information, Justin Nyoka, setting a standard for what was supposed to be a "new order" in journalism.

Eight months later, Zimbabwe's newspapers are still operating without any official controls or explicit political guidelines—either from the Government or the new Mass Media Trust—but they have also done little to test the freedom that has supposedly been preserved for them.

Little Space for Criticism

Speeches of Cabinet ministers tend to dominate the front pages and criticisms of the Government tend to be ignored, especially when they come from black opposition figures such as Bishop Abel T. Muzorewa, the former Prime Minister who has had some moderately well-attended political rallies recently that went unreported .

Similarly, Edgar Z. Tekere, who was eased out of the Cabinet and then his post as secretary general of Prime Minister Robert Mugabe's Zimbabwe African National Union after his involvement in a murder case, gets no coverage at all when he makes a political statement. Recently, however, when he ignored a speeding ticket, it was news.

Willie Musarurwa, editor of The Sunday Mail, said he would not print reports that tend to undermine stability and unity in the country.

"We can't pretend our political situation is normal and stabilized," he remarked. "If someone makes statements to create political tensions, I'm not going to allow my paper to be used as a vehicle to create confusion."

A 'Balance' Was Expected

The secretary of Mass Media Trust, Mtungadzimwe Marere, said the Government wanted the papers "to retain some independence, but not total independence." The newspapers were expected to strike a balance between support of national objectives as defined by the Government and outright partisanship, he said.

In practice, no editor has yet found occasion to criticize Mr. Mugabe directly for any reason, big or small, but now and then one of his Cabinet colleagues attracts a little fire. Mr. Musarurwa, for instance, has written a couple of editorials assailing Health Minister Herbert Ushewokunze, a volatile figure who is widely seen as Mr. Tekere's heir as the promoter of an ostensibly radical line in the Cabinet. The nub of the criticism was that he was a force for disunity.

(Mr. Mugabe evidently agreed. Immediately upon his return from a Commonwealth conference in Australia, he dismissed Dr. Ushewokunze.) The Information Minister, Nathan Shamuyarira, appointed the first three members of Mass Media Trust; from then on it was supposed to be self-perpetuating. Two of the three he appointed were whites, a businessman who is president of the Confederation of Industries, and Grace Todd, the wife of former Prime Minister Garfield Todd.

News Agency Is Also Bought

Using a grant from the Nigerian Government, the trust then bought up the dominant 45 percent interest that the Argus Company of South Africa had owned in a holding company called Zimbabwe Newspapers that runs daily and Sunday English-language papers in Salisbury and Bulawayo, plus a weekly in Umtali. The trust also bought the country's only news agency, the Zimbabwe Inter-Africa News Agency, which had been owned and managed by the South African Press Association.

The Government said it was unthinkable that foreign interests—especially South African—could be allowed to control the press of a newly independent black country.

In the event, it was the small Umtali Post that provoked the first instance in which the Government was plainly seen to be putting pressure on the trust. The weekly, which has something of the small town, gossipy flavor of a rural New England paper, was the first in the country to report the arrival of a North Korean military mission to train one of five army brigades. In an accompanying editorial, headlined "Sinister Trend," it then asked why the army needed help, "least of all from foreigners from East Asia."

Two days later the paper's editor and the reporter who wrote the article, both whites, were driven to Salisbury by officers from the Central Intelligence Organization, the state security apparatus, and escorted into the presence of the Prime Minister and Mr. Shamuyarira. According to Stan Higgins, the reporter, Mr. Mugabe started by saying he had no quarrel with the news report but only with the editorial's tone.

'Racist' Thinking Charged

Shortly after the meeting, the editor, Jean Maitland-Stuart, was told by Zimbabwe Newspapers that she was about to be replaced. Mr. Shamuyarira then acknowledged in Parliament that the Government had made its displeasure known to the trust over the "racist" and "South African thinking" reflected in the editorial. The Umtali Post, he noted, had never complained about the presence of South African troops in the country when the Smith regime was still in power.

Whites and blacks generally reacted differently to the editor's dismissal, with whites bemoaning the incursion on press freedom and blacks saying the newspapers could not be run by people who were plainly unreconciled to the new Zimbabwean order.

Editorial writers in South Africa found a somber omen in what has happened to the press under black rule in Zimbabwe. The Citizen, a right-wing daily in Johannesburg that was started with Government funds, asked rhetorically what the reaction would have been in the West to a similar "press grab" in South Africa.

"The International Press Institute would have yelled blue murder," it declared. "The New York Times would have jumped on South Africa from a dizzy height." Nothing was said about Zimbabwe, The Citizen said, because the world has "one set of values for black Africa and another, completely different for South Africa."

* * *

June 13, 1982

IN CHAD, MOVES TO CURB FOREIGN PRESS

By ALAN COWELL

Special to the New York Times

KOUSSERI, Cameroon, June 12—The new authorities in Chad today introduced regulations designed to let them censor reports by foreign journalists.

Moumine Hamadi, an aide to the country's new ruler, Hissen Habre, said reporters who wanted to transmit articles from Ndjamena would have to submit their dispatches in advance to a Chadian official who would read them in the presence of the journalists.

"You have the right to send your stories," Mr. Hamadi told a Western correspondent. "We have the right to see them to make sure they are correct."

Asked what would happen if the articles did not match the official line, Mr. Hamadi, a pistol at his hip, said that it would not be "a serious problem" and that the censor would help the reporters "get their facts right."

Mr. Habre's guerrillas captured Ndjamena last Monday and forced President Goukouni Oueddei to flee to neighboring Cameroon.

Sensitivity to Image Abroad

The introduction of press restrictions is the first indication that Mr. Habre may be sensitive to the image abroad of his fledgling Government. Mr. Hamadi did not explain why the measures had been introduced. The previous Government did not have such regulations.

The measures are not totally enforceable because reporters are permitted to cross the Shari River into Cameroon to use the telephone in the riverside settlement of Kousseri, a short boat ride away from Ndjamena.

Mr. Habre is consolidating his administrative hold on the war-battered capital of Ndjamena, where a dusk-to-dawn curfew is still in force. His 8,000 guerrillas, the Armed Forces of the North, are unchallenged militarily.

The new leader, who everybody now calls "the President," does not seem to have many administrators and technical experts in his largely military entourage.

A Feeling of Languorous Chaos

There is a feeling of languorous chaos in the desert heat of the city. Foreign diplomats and representatives of international organizations say they are experiencing difficulties in finding anybody to talk to in the new Government. The Chadian people seem unsure of the authorities.

During a ride through Ndjamena today in a minibus, one of Mr. Habre's heavily armed guerrillas clambered aboard to the evident bewilderment of the civilian passengers. The guerrilla took the front seat and the civilians halted their conversations, nervous about how the armed man would react to them and how they should behave toward him.

With a shortage of personnel and an apparent unfamiliarity with the ways of the city after months in the desert, there is much about Mr. Habre's administration that seems uncertain and confused.

Mr. Habre has already scolded those who seek to discover the precise, legal position of his administration or ask other technical questions.

'Western Formalism' Rejected

Such concerns, he said at a news conference, reflect "Western formalism"—a style that has been eschewed by his desert warriors, long used to a hand-to-mouth existence.

A more critical issue is the future of the Organization of African Unity's peacekeeping force that was sent here last November to replace Libyan troops. The Libyans intervened in December 1980 to halt a civil war by backing Mr. Goukouni. Mr. Habre sought sanctuary at the time in the Sudan.

The chairman of the Organization of African Unity, President Daniel arap Moi of Kenya, announced Friday that the 3,000-man force, made up of units from Senegal, Zaire and Nigeria, would begin withdrawing immediately.

Mr. Habre protested the decision, arguing that the force is needed to deter intervention by Mr. Goukouni's foreign supporters—notably Algeria and Libya—and to help end continued hostilities in the south of the country.

Western diplomats elsewhere in Africa have indicated that the United States, which is reactivating its embassy here after evacuating the staff a week ago, favors a continued presence by the African force in Chad.

A Western diplomat in Ndjamena indicated today that negotiations had begun on drawing up a new mandate for the O.A.S. unit to stay on as a stabilizing force while Mr. Habre consolidates his Government.

* * *

December 5, 1982

SOUTH AFRICA BANS SCRIPT OF A BROADWAY PLAY

Special to the New York Times

JOHANNESBURG, Dec. 4—South Africa's censors have decreed that it is a criminal offense to import or distribute copies of "Master Harold . . . and the Boys," a play by the South African dramatist Athol Fugard that is starting its eighth month on Broadway.

The order from the Directorate of Publications, which came on its weekly list of bannings, applies only to printed copies of the play. But lawyers familiar with the country's censorship law said it was doubtful that the play could be staged in South Africa until the order was reversed.

Reached by telephone in New York, the playwright said that he and his South African producers would lodge an appeal next week against the banning order.

The play, which had its first performance at the Yale Repertory Theater in New Haven this year before moving to Broadway, is scheduled to have its South African opening in Johannesburg in March.

Mr. Fugard and others in theater circles here were baffled as much as shocked by the banning, the first ever of a Fugard play.

Love and Betrayal

"Master Harold" is a partly autobiographical work that deals with the relationship between a bookish white adolescent and two black men who work as waiters in a tea shop run by the youth's parents.

The drama turns on the themes of love and betrayal, and the South African racial context is essential to it. But the play deals less explicitly with sensitive political scenes than such recent plays by Mr. Fugard as "Statement After an Arrest Under the Immorality Act," "The Island" and "A Lesson From Aloes," all of which have been performed in South Africa.

For this reason there was speculation that an appeal against the banning was likely to succeed. It even seemed possible that the Publications Appeals Board might consider the case on its own initiative, as it has done on at least two occasions in order to minimize embarrassment and press comment, here and abroad, after the bannings of works by well-known authors.

Bannings of both "Burger's Daughter," by the South African novelist Nadine Gordimer, and "The Covenant," by James Michener, were reversed in this way. The board has been systematically easing censorship of writings that strike it as falling short of revolutionary incitement.

Ban on 'Lolita' Is Lifted

The same announcement that listed the banning of Mr. Fugard's play lifted the banning of Vladimir Nabokov's "Lolita" and a Harold Robbins novel called "The Spellbinder."

The banning of "Master Harold" coincided with the return home after 11 years of the expatriate South African actor

Zakes Mokae, who won a Tony Award this year for his performance in the play on Broadway.

Mr. Mokae flew back to South Africa in the hope of supporting the appeal of a younger brother who has been sentenced to death for his role as an accomplice in a burglary in a white residential neighborhood that resulted in two murders.

On his arrival here Thursday evening, the actor was told that his brother's appeal had failed and that he was now due to be hanged in Pretoria on Wednesday.

* * *

May 8, 1983

SOUTH AFRICA JAILS BLACK OVER A BANNED BOOK

By JOSEPH LELYVELD
Special to the New York Times

JOHANNESBURG, May 7—A prominent black journalist recently drew an unusually heavy prison sentence of two and a half years for possession of a single banned book. The sentence was a result of plea bargaining that suddenly cut short the trial of nine people charged with being underground activists of the outlawed Pan Africanist Congress.

The journalist, Joe Thloloe, a former reporter whose newspaper career had been suspended by a Government "banning" order that made it a crime for him to write for publication, had originally faced far more serious charges of conspiracy to commit terrorism and furthering the aims of an illegal organization.

Of the eight people charged with him, seven had reportedly given the police statements after being held without charge for interrogation. One, a former exile, had pleaded guilty to being sent back into the country by the Pan Africanist Congress to help lay the groundwork for acts of sabotage.

The trial was regarded as having unusual significance, for it was the first in several years involving the activities of the Pan Africanist Congress, a rival as a movement of resistance to white rule of the more prominent African National Congress. The Pan Africanist Congress had almost slipped from view in South Africa during a period in which its exile organization was reportedly plagued by dissension.

The 40-year-old Mr. Thloloe, who was honored for his reporting by Harvard University's Nieman Foundation two years ago, had ties with the movement before its banning in 1960. In that year, as a youth of only 17, he was arrested and charged with the Pan Africanist Congress's founder and leader, the late Robert Sobukwe, in a protest march against the law the requires blacks to carry special passes, or "reference books," when they are in supposedly "white" areas.

The terrorism charges, which he denied, said a small machine gun had been found hidden in the roof of his home in the black township of Soweto at the time of his arrest last June.

But the elaborate machinery of prosecution stalled when the first witness, Sipho Ntshingane, indicated he was prepared to testify that he had been tortured by the security police until he agreed to put his name to a false statement.

In a highly unusual verdict scarcely two weeks before Mr. Ntshingane indicated his readiness to defy the police, a magistrate in a suburb called Kempton Park acquitted four blacks on terrorism charges on the ground that state witnesses had been assaulted or otherwise intimidated to give evidence against them.

In an effort to avoid further embarrassment to the police in the Thloloe case, the prosecution agreed to drop charges against five of the accused, including Harrison Nogqekele, the man who had originally pleaded guilty, if the remaining four would plead guilty to the lesser charge of possessing banned books. Normally that charge is considered relatively minor and results in either a suspended sentence or fine, but on April 20 Magistrate Theo Kleinhans gave Mr. Thloloe the two-and-a-half-year sentence for possession of a single Pan Africanist Congress publication, "The New Road."

Two others, Sipho Mzolo and Nhlanganiso Sibanda, got three years because they had more than one publication; a fourth man, Sipho Ngcobo, also got two and a half years.

* * *

September 14, 1983

ZIMBABWE KEEPING BAN ON NEWSMEN

By MICHAEL T. KAUFMAN

HARARE, Zimbabwe, Sept. 13—As the Government here continues to bar entry to foreign correspondents based in South Africa, other southern African nations that supported such exclusions in principle are shying away from them in practice.

Of the six countries that issued a joint statement in July declaring their intention to ban international journalists accredited to South Africa, only Zimbabwe and Angola have adhered to the policy categorically.

And since Angola has since 1975 effectively kept out virtually all Western journalists based anywhere in Africa, the ban essentially relates to the coverage of news in this country, where events have been actively reported for years by a resident press corps as well as by correspondents based in Johannesburg and Nairobi.

Botswana, one of the signers of the so-called Kadoma Declaration, said it had not made a final decision on the issue. President Kenneth D. Kaunda of Zambia said four days ago in reference to the declaration, signed in the Zimbabwean town of Kadoma, "Although it was a collective decision, it was described as a position, in principle, and it is up to particular countries to effect the front-line decision."

Two Nations Disregard Ban

In fact Zambia and Mozambique, another signer, have issued visas to Johannesburg-based correspondents since the issuance of the declaration. The sixth country joining in the declaration, Tanzania, has hardly ever been visited by South

African-based journalists and is usually covered by correspondents from Nairobi.

In contrast to such loose observance elsewhere, Information Ministry officials here have imposed the ban strictly on all journalists based in South Africa. They have steadfastly defended the policy in the language of the Kadoma Declaration, which contends that with South Africa used as the main information center in the region "credibility is given to Pretoria's biased view of reality in southern Africa."

In private conversations, information officials here have argued that South Africa has been able to co-opt journalists in South Africa subtly by effectively exempting them from taxes. "If a newsmen spends most of his time in South Africa he can be seduced to Pretoria's point of view," said Justin Nyoka, deputy secretary of Zimbabwe's Department of Information.

Black Nations Urged as Bases

When Mr. Nyoka was asked whether the new policy would prevent Johannesburg-based reporters from having their views tempered and their consciousnesses stirred by visits to black African states, he said the ideal would be to have them establish themselves in the black-governed countries and make occasional trips to South Africa.

He cited the example of The Washington Post, which keeps a staff correspondent here in Harare while covering South Africa with a part-time, locally hired correspondent.

So far, the response of the Western press has been measured. The major news agencies, The Associated Press, United Press International, Reuters and Agence France-Presse, have all had bureaus here and all of them file their dispatches directly to their central offices. Some British papers such as The Telegraph, which covered Zimbabwe, and before that Rhodesia, through its Johannesburg bureau, have now sent reporters here from London on temporary assignments.

Reports of 'Terrorism' Barred

Six days after the six-nation declaration was approved, the Zimbabwean Government issued a regulation making it a criminal offense punishable by up to two years in prison for any journalist to report "any act of terrorism or sabotage or any action by security forces to combat terrorism in any area designated by the Government."

The Government decree was issued under the 18-year-old Emergency Powers Act that was invoked in the last years of the Rhodesian Government of Ian D. Smith to require journalists to submit their dispatches to censors before sending them abroad.

In the 14 years that Rhodesia existed as an internationally outlawed nation, its Department of Information carefully culled news accounts and maintained a list of journalists to be barred at the airport because of reports the authorities considered offensive. There were at least 27 such journalists. In addition, there were scores more who had been notified by telephone that they would not be welcome.

* * *

April 30, 1984

NIGERIAN MILITARY REGIME IS REINING IN ONE OF THE FREEST PRESSES IN AFRICA

By CLIFFORD D. MAY

LAGOS, Nigeria, April 27—The military regime that seized power here on New Year's Eve has taken strong measures against the Nigerian press, jailing five journalists and, in the view of some, intimidating many others.

On April 17 the military Government issued a decree granting itself the power to close down newspapers and radio and television stations that are deemed to be acting in a manner detrimental to the interest of the Government. It also assumed the power to imprison journalists for inaccurate reporting or for writing articles that bring Government officials into ridicule or disrepute. The decree was reminiscent of a decree signed into law in 1976 by the head of state, Lieut. Gen. Olusegun Obasanjo.

The April 17 decree was made retroactive so journalists would be liable for what they wrote or broadcast before the decree was issued as well as after.

No charges have been made public against the five journalists in detention. And in most cases, the articles that appear to have led to their arrests do not seem to have been either erring or mocking.

'The First Time'

"This is the first time in Nigeria's independent history that a concerted attempt has been made to restrain the freedom of the press," said Ray Ekpu, chairman of the editorial board of the independent Concord newspapers. "They are demanding press sycophancy at gunpoint. No other regime, military or civilian, has ever done that here."

The Nigerian press has long been considered exceptional in Africa. Several newspapers are sensationalist, and many are unabashedly partisan. But they offer a diversity of information and opinions.

Until civilian rule ended on the last day of 1983, both the newspapers owned or controlled by the opposition parties and Nigeria's independent papers harshly criticized President Shehu Shagari's handling of the economy, the corruption in his administration and the conduct of elections last summer.

When the military took over, the press overwhelmingly applauded the move, and coverage of the new regime's actions and statements has been largely favorable.

"Nothing the press has done in the past four months warrants this overkill," Mr. Ekpu said. "On the contrary, the press has stood behind this administration in the hope it would be better."

Cartoon Shows the Disenchantment

A cartoon in The National Concord appears to express the disenchantment of many journalists in recent days. It shows a man, labeled "press," being led away in handcuffs by a soldier. The man is pleading, "But, but, we won the battle together."

A senior Western diplomat in Lagos noted that although the ousted civilian Government was often irked by the press, it relied on the country's newspapers to report on the public mood. "By curbing the press, the military guys are going to cut themselves off from the country," the diplomat said. "Governments here have always given the press free rein so that they would know where problems were arising."

Nigerian journalists argue that the current restrictions will also discourage reporting on corruption, something the new regime has pledged to wipe out.

'Decree Is Self-Defeating'

"If it's illegal to bring an official into disrepute, you run a real risk by writing a story about his questionable financial dealings," said Eddie Iroh, managing editor of The Guardian, an independent newspaper. "So if the Government means what it says about corruption, this new decree is self-defeating."

Other journalists say the most troubling aspect of the crackdown is that no clear guidelines have been set down.

For example, Tunde Thompson, diplomatic correspondent for The Guardian, was detained on April 11 after publication of a story outlining the Government's plans to overhaul the Foreign Service. Several of the changes Mr. Thompson reported on have since come to pass.

The National Security Organization, which is roughly the equivalent of the Federal Bureau of Investigation, has indicated that Mr. Thompson would be released when he revealed his sources for the article. Mr. Thompson has refused, saying that to do so would violate professional ethics.

2 Reporters and Editor Ousted

In another example, two reporters for The Statesman, a newspaper in Imo state, wrote an article questioning the Government's reasons for imprisoning former Vice President Alex Ekwueme, while former President Shagari has been allowed to remain under house arrest. The article suggested that tribal discrimination may play a role.

Charged with not identifying with the goals and the aspirations of the new Government, The Stateman was ordered closed for two months and the editor and the two reporters were dismissed.

The other journalists who have been detained are Niyi Onigoro, publisher of a newspaper in Oyo state; Haroun Adamu, editorial consultant to The Punch newspaper in Lagos; Idowu Odeyemi, editor of a newspaper in Ibadan, and Nduka Irabor, assistant news editor of The Guardian.

Several other journalists have been detained and later released. Many have been dismissed, particularly those who worked for Government-owned papers or radio and television stations.

Trial by Tribunal

Those journalists charged with violating the new press decree, or Decree No. 4, face trial by a special tribunal under the chairmanship of a High Court judge sitting with three senior military officers. The onus of proof is on the accused, who can be jailed for up to two years. News organizations brought to trial will face a minimum fine of $13,000 or be shut down for 12 months. No appeal will be allowed against decisions of the tribunal.

Many journalists say they think the Government campaign has already had an impact. Several reporters and editors will now speak candidly only with the understanding that they not be quoted by name.

"If you were to do a content analysis of Nigeria's newspapers over the last two to three weeks," Mr. Ekpu of the Concord newspapers said, "you'd see that a noticeable timidity had taken hold, a toning down. This is exactly the effect the Government wanted to achieve."

Some Are Fighting Back

At the same time, Mr. Ekpu said, some Nigerian reporters have started to fight back. The Nigeria Union of Journalists has filed suit in Lagos High Court seeking a declaration that the Government's press decree is unconstitutional. Some university professors, students' groups and lawyers' associations have also issued statements protesting the Government's press restrictions.

"We're not all going to just throw up our hands and say we're helpless," Mr. Ekpu said.

But many journalists appear less than confident about their chances for success.

"If things continue as they have been, I'll leave the country," said Mr. Iroh of The Guardian, who was a strong critic of the Shagari Government. "I'm a journalist. If I'm not allowed to work as a journalist, what's the point in my staying here?"

* * *

May 5, 1985

SOUTH AFRICAN PRESS HAS A TOUGH BEAT

By ALAN COWELL

JOHANNESBURG—In South Africa, more than 100 laws restrict the way the press reports the nation to itself. Sometimes, said Percy Qoboza, a black newspaper editor, he and his colleagues spend more time with their lawyers deciding what they may publish than they do at home with their spouses.

Other journalists, though, say that while the statutes are restrictive some editors do not publish to the limits of what the law allows. Characteristically, too, for a splintered people, there are categories and divisions among black, English-speaking and Afrikaans-language newspapers, each with separate notions and self-images.

The authorities, for their part, like to say their press is the freest in Africa. But however it is defined, press freedom seemed diminished last week by the demise of The Rand Daily Mail, South Africa's leading daily newspaper. The Mail was closed by its management, like The Sunday Express before it, because of financial losses. That left the morning market in South Africa's most populous area to pro-Government newspapers, and bereft of rebellious crusaders.

Over the years, the press has scored its victories. English-language newspapers, The Rand Daily Mail and The Sunday Express prominent among them, have exposed major scandals that severely embarrassed the authorities. Black-readership newspapers, despite bannings and harassment, have survived; The Sowetan and The City Press continue to needle the Government, albeit in a township arena remote from most whites' field of vision.

The Afrikaans press, instrumental in the rise of Afrikaner political dominance, has changed, too. Once a virtual mouthpiece, and supportive still of fundamental Afrikaner interests, it seems readier now to prod the authorities and to pursue notions of limited change and initiatives such as dialogue with representatives of the outlawed and exiled African National Congress.

But these developments have been matched by an almost visceral desire to control the press. Over the years, laws have been tightened and Government pressure has been such that newspapers have agreed to self-restraints through a Media Council, to head off new laws curbing them.

Some analysts last week viewed as an irony the role of the Anglo American Corporation, which has a controlling interest in the English-language press. Anglo-American avows support for political change but did not save The Rand Daily Mail or The Sunday Express. Yet it was willing to countenance a loss equivalent to $12.5 million—more than The Mail lost last year—as the cost of the work stoppage when it dismissed thousands of restive black miners at the world's biggest gold mine to punish them for wildcat strikes and disruptions.

In recent months, coinciding with widespread unrest in the black townships, South Africa's newspapers have generally reported fully on the violence, flavoring their interpretation with their views of the causes of unrest. The Government's South African Broadcasting Corp. has also shown film of tear gas smoke and confrontation, choosing words such as "the police were forced to use tear gas" and omitting the information that, on occasions, it was the police presence itself that black nationalists blamed for the violence.

In many black localities, the television station is not popular. South African cameramen have reportedly asked American colleagues to lend them United States network decals for their cameras, to avoid the wrath of black crowds.

Still, visitors familiar with overt press controls of some black-ruled African nations say they are surprised by the relative freedom here.

And yet radical analysts in South Africa say that the very appearance of freedom is a cloak that lends legitimacy to a society reviled elsewhere because of its racial policies.

Moreover, some studies have suggested that the liberty of the South African press comprises freedom to comment, but not freedom of access to information or the freedom to demand it as a right.

Over the years, laws have been enacted to severely limit reporting about the military, the police, prisons, the oil industry, nuclear research, official corruption, terrorism or matters deemed to promote racial hostility. It is an offense, too, to quote "banned" persons, such as Winnie Mandela, wife of Nelson Mandela, the jailed leader of the African National Congress. Reports can be published in the newspapers about claims of guerrilla activity by the Congress, but its exiled leader, Oliver Tambo, may be quoted only with ministerial permission.

Editors such as Mr. Qoboza say the main restriction on press freedom lies in "the minefield of legislation." But Ken Owen, former editor of The Sunday Express and now editor of a new financial daily, Business Day, offers another point of view, which he terms "maverick."

"Everybody knows that we have restrictive laws that in some cases amount to censorship," Mr. Owen said. "Everybody knows that we are under fluctuating pressure."

But, he added, recalling disclosures reported in his former newspaper, "I don't think that we frequently publish up to the limits of the law. The main fault lies in the newspapers' not using the liberty that newspapers are still allowed."

* * *

June 14, 1986

KEY ELEMENT OF EMERGENCY DECREE: TOUGH NEW CURBS AGAINST THE PRESS

Special to the New York Times

JOHANNESBURG, June 13—South Africa's newest emergency decree, covering the entire country, offers the authorities far greater powers of censorship than ever before, lawyers said today, making it an offense to publish a wide range of utterances deemed "subversive."

The decree also forbids television, radio and photographic coverage of violent protest or official measures to curb it.

The authorities seem determined today to underscore their readiness to act against foreign journalists perceived as hostile. Wim de Vos, a Dutch national working for CBS News as a cameraman, was ordered expelled from the country for an unspecified offense before the emergency decree, while the authorities seized copies of two anti-Government newspapers, The Sowetan and The Weekly Mail.

Mr. de Vos was given leave to appeal his expulsion. The cameraman, along with two other CBS journalists, was ordered out of South Africa on a previous occasion in March, but the authorities later withdrew their expulsion.

New Propaganda Arm

"We are not kidding, we will not hesitate to take action," David Stewart, director of the Bureau for Information, the Government's newly created propaganda arm, said at a news conference in Pretoria, at which he suggested reporters hire lawyers to interpret the emergency decree declared Thursday.

Two United States television crews, filming interviews with members of the public on the streets of Johannesburg, were detained briefly today, and Mr. Stewart warned that the Ministry of Law and Order was investigating further purported breaches of the decree's harsh censorship.

In an often-repeated criticism of foreign reporting of South Africa, he warned reporters not to call the Government a "white minority regime" since it included two nonwhite ministers, neither of whom have a portfolio.

"Journalists who use this factually incorrect approach will place their position in South Africa in jeopardy," Mr. Stewart said. He said reporters would not be given the identities of people detained under the emergency decree and that all news about the emergency would be channeled through the Bureau for Information, headed by Louis Nel.

Lawyers for Journalists

Neither, Mr. Stewart said, would the authorities assist journalists in interpreting the latest censorship and suggested they hire lawyers. "I think the legal profession is in for a lot of business, and the longer they mull over it, the more money they will make," he said.

Under the nation's previous, partial emergency decree, which lasted from July 1985 until last March, television cameras were not at first barred from those segregated black townships within the emergency areas. Neither was there a prohibition on newspaper reporting of political statements by the Government's adversaries.

The decree was lifted after President P. W. Botha said he believed violence had eased. But, since then, violent protest has continued. The newest decree was imposed Thursday to avert what Mr. Botha depicted as the likelihood of major protest Monday, the 10th anniversary of the start of the Soweto uprisings.

But under the latest emergency decree, it became an offense for news organizations to film, record or photograph "any public disturbance, disorder, riot, public violence, strike or boycott, or any damaging of any property, or any assault on or killing of a person."

Rules on Filming

The prohibition extends to filming, photographing or recording "any conduct of a force or any member of a force with regard to the maintenance of the safety of the public or the public order or for the termination of the state of emergency."

The new decree seems to outlaw, for instance, the kind of television coverage that Americans saw from the Crossroads squatter camp last week.

A further clause in the emergency regulations empowers Government officials to seize copies of any publication deemed to include a subversive statement "or any other information which is or may be detrimental to the safety of the public, the maintenance of public order or the termination of the state of emergency."

For newspaper reporters, the regulations seemed designed to inhibit, or suppress, a wide range of coverage.

Under the Previous Decree

Under the previous emergency decree, enforced in magisterial districts around Johannesburg, Cape Town and Port Elizabeth, reporters were permitted to be present in segregated black townships at times of violent protest, provided they reported to police officers when unrest broke out.

There was no prohibition on coverage of political statements by the Government's foes.

Under the new decree, however, reporters, and anybody else, can be ordered away from any area by security force personnel, who are empowered to use whatever force they deem necessary if their orders are not obeyed. From a literal interpretation of the decree, that means people could be shot for failing to obey the orders of policemen, soldiers or security personnel.

Whole areas, moreover, can be declared, under the decree, off-limits to nonresidents, a prohibition that applied under the previous emergency decree.

This time, however, the regulations set out an array of what are called subversive statements, whose possession or dissemination is an offense.

Statements That Are Barred

The list of such statements includes any statement that might promote the interests of outlawed political groups, or incite people to take part in unlawful strikes, boycott actions, unlawful demonstrations, acts of civil disobedience or in campaigns against compulsory service.

Moreover, it is deemed subversive to oppose the Government's enforcement of the decree, to incite hostilities among South Africa's population, to weaken or undermine the "confidence of the public or any section of the public in the termination of the state of emergency" or to promote disinvestment, sanctions or "foreign action" against South Africa.

The decree says that no one may write, disseminate or distribute any "subversive statement" to any other person.

Whereas reporters a few months ago were able to report Bishop Desmond M. Tutu as calling for sanctions against South Africa, that could now be deemed an offense. Even an appeal by the Bishop for Christians to attend church services on Monday, the Soweto anniversary, could now be said to be subversive, because all such commemorations have been declared illegal under a previous Government order.

The authorities have added a further hindrance to reporting of the nation's violence by suspending the twice-daily police reports that gave at least the official version of the extent of violence. The reports stipulated which townships had been affected and how many people had died.

"Unrest reports" are now to be issued by the Bureau for Information, and its first report today did not specify where unrest had occurred, only that seven people had died since the state of emergency was imposed, one shot by the authorities and the six others victims of what was called "black-on-black violence."

* * *

August 29, 1986

SOUTH AFRICA COURT EASES PRESS CURBS

Special to the New York Times

JOHANNESBURG, Aug. 28—Two key restrictions on reporters seeking to cover unrest under South Africa's emergency decree have been relaxed in recent days because of court challenges to their legality.

The rulings affect both reporters for South African news organizations and foreign correspondents.

Theoretically, reporters may now witness protest and write about it. In Soweto, Johannesburg's huge black satellite, reporters could write this week about the actions and deployments of the police and army without fear of official reprisals under the newest emergency decree, imposed on June 12.

Before the Aug. 20 withdrawal of the two orders, reporters would have courted the possibility of reprisals by, say, quoting Soweto residents as saying the police seemed to be firing indiscriminately on protesters opposed to the eviction of tenants who had joined a mass boycott of rents.

Two Orders Ruled Invalid

A court action brought by leading English-language newspaper groups last week challenged the authorities' right under the emergency decree to bar reporters from segregated black townships, and state attorneys conceded that two orders issued by the Police Commissioner, Johann Coetzee, were invalid.

The reason was that General Coetzee had issued the orders in a telexed message to the South African Press Association news agency. The emergency decree stipulates that such orders should be promulgated either in the Government Gazette or in other ways, but not in the manner the police chief used.

The orders barred reporters from unauthorized reporting of the actions of security forces and prohibited their presence "for the purpose of reporting" in segregated black residential areas or in an area seized with unrest.

Since the orders were ruled unlawful because General Coetzee did not observe emergency procedures in promulgating them, they could be reimposed, lawyers said.

Contraints Still in Force

Despite the easing of restrictions, constraints remain.

Photographs or videotapes of violence and protest are still unlawful under the emergency decree, presenting television networks and photographers with a great problem in depicting events such as the fighting in Soweto this week.

Moreover, newspaper reporters and other journalists face catch-all regulations that permit any member of the security forces—the police, army, prison service or the railway police—to order any person out of any area, and to use whatever measures are deemed necessary to enforce their departure.

Under the emergency regulations, reporters may not publish anything which may be interpreted as subversive, lawyers said. While a court ruling has narrowed the definition of "subversive," it nonetheless remains an offense to publish statements urging civil disobedience, boycotts or strikes.

The regulations also forbid reports that might endanger public safety or promote a loss of faith in the termination of the state of emergency.

Lawyers acting for the country's English-language newspapers, many of them controlled by the Anglo American Corporation, the country's biggest multinational mining conglomerate, are challenging other aspects of the emergency decree in court.

* * *

January 30, 1987

PRETORIA GIVES POLICE WIDE POWER TO BAR PUBLISHING ON 'ANY MATTER'

By The Associated Press

JOHANNESBURG, Friday, Jan. 30—The Government imposed new press restrictions Thursday under the state of emergency, allowing the Police Commissioner to ban publication of "any matter" he chooses.

The action was taken hours after a judge nullified one of the Commissioner's restrictions on publication.

A lawyer who represents the press, Paul Jenkins, said the Police Commissioner, Johan Coetzee, had been "elevated to the country's chief censor."

Ban on Advertisements

The Commissioner used his new authority within two hours, issuing an order at 1 A.M. today prohibiting publication of advertisements "which defended, praised or endeavored to justify unlawful organizations' campaigns, projects, programs or actions."

The judge, H. Daniel of the Rand Supreme Court in Johannesburg, had invalidated an order Commissioner Coetzee issued Jan. 8, the day after 22 newspapers published advertisements urging legalization of the African National Congress, the main group fighting to overthrow white rule.

Although Commissioner Coetzee's order this morning referred only to advertisements, the one struck down by the judge also had prohibited news reports and comment that explained, defended, supported or might enhance the public image of any banned organization, such as the Congress.

New Rules on Publications

Under the new rules, according to a Government gazette, "The Commissioner may, for the purpose of the safety of the public, the maintenance of public order or the termination of the state of emergency, and without prior notice to any person and without hearing any person, issue any order not inconsistent with a provision of these regulations prohibiting any publication, television recording, film recording or sound recording containing any news, comment or advertisement on or in connection with any matter specified in the order, to be published."

The rules are encompassed in a strict press code President P. W. Botha promulgated Dec. 11 under the state of emergency imposed last June 12.

Those rules severely restricted or banned reporting on unrest, security force actions, treatment of detainees, most forms of peaceful protest and a broad range of statements the Government considers subversive. They are being challenged in the Supreme Court of Natal Province in Pietermaritzburg.

Commissioner Coetzee now appears to have the power to decide what matters are subject to the existing regulation on "publication control," which covers both print and broadcast reports.

According to the South African Press Association, the new regulations also appear to broaden the definition of subversive statements to include taking part in or supporting the "campaigns, projects, programs or actions of violence or resistance against the authority of the state" by an unlawful organization.

Reports on Tambo-Shultz Talks

South African newspapers reported Thursday on a meeting in Washington between Oliver Tambo, head of the African National Congress, and Secretary of State George P. Shultz, noting that Mr. Tambo had made statements but reminding readers that he could not be quoted. Quoting most A.N.C. leaders has long been banned in South Africa.

In the main report on the Government television's evening news, however, the reporter read two quotations from Mr. Tambo that appeared in American newspapers. One said: "The killing of white civilians would have a beneficial effect."

The reporter said Mr. Vlok had given permission for "certain astounding" quotations by Mr. Tambo to be published in South Africa.

* * *

May 3, 1987

COURT ACTIONS ARE BLUNTING BOTHA'S TOOLS OF REPRESSION

By JOHN D. BATTERSBY

JOHANNESBURG—The South African courts provided the cutting edge last week for renewed anti-apartheid resistance, overshadowing the final campaigning for the election of the controlling white branch of Parliament this Wednesday. The state has responded with tear gas and bullets to a strong challenge by black labor unions.

But the anti-apartheid groups were scoring victories in the courts, which have shown a growing willingness to rule against the Government in recent years.

Important aspects of the Government's emergency decrees on censorship and restricting criticism of apartheid were overturned in the Natal Province branch of the Supreme Court, which has repeatedly ruled against the Government since the early 1980's. The independence of the courts is guaranteed in the nation's Constitution, but judges are appointed from a group of senior Supreme Court lawyers. All but one are white and most belong to the Afrikaans-speaking ruling elite. However, as was clear last week, not all accept the Government's legal arguments.

Experts such as Prof. John Dugard of the University of Witwatersrand attribute the changing mood among some judges to increasing concerns about a growing lack of confidence in the courts, particularly among blacks, and criticism from the International Commission of Jurists, which said the judiciary was helping to legitimize the system. "During the 1960's and 1970's lawyers wanting to challenge the system all but gave up because the courts did not rule against the executive," Professor Dugard said. "Today there are more lawyers concerned with human rights and they have become more imaginative as a result of the change in mood amongst some judges."

Because of the Natal court ruling, photographs and reports of actions by the security forces returned to the front pages of newspapers and world television screens and the national campaign of defiance threatened to reduce to a sideshow the election of the dominant white chamber of the segregated tricameral Parliament. The chambers for Indians and mixed-race people have only limited powers; the country's black majority is excluded altogether.

Although the Government is assured of an overwhelming victory Wednesday, and apparently is safe from any direct military or internal security challenge, its credibility and legitimacy seem increasingly vulnerable, some analysts said. Lawyers said court rulings had eroded the legal basis of harsh Government rule to the point where laws underpinning the state of emergency could no longer cope with the climate of resistance.

"Mr. Botha's options have been considerably narrowed again," said an attorney for press and broadcasting interests. He added, "Unless the Appeal Court lets him off the hook, he has two options: suspend the courts and resort to martial law, or enter into negotiations with authentic black leaders."

In other court actions last week, the Natal Supreme Court overturned a controversial decree that had empowered the Police Commissioner, Gen. Johan Coetzee, to outlaw organized campaigning for the release of 4,500 people detained under the emergency.

The campaign of defiance was expected to increase Tuesday and Wednesday, when anti-apartheid groups have called for "peaceful protest" against the election and against the repression of black workers. It is illegal under emergency regulations to call for a work boycott, but the police said they had made "contingency plans" for such an action.

The surge of black defiance is being coordinated by the 600,000-member Congress of South African Trade Unions, or Cosatu, which is closely aligned with the United Democratic Front, a broad anti-apartheid coalition. "We cannot allow whites to go to the polls pretending that nothing is wrong in the country," a front spokesman said. At Cosatu House, the union headquarters, where the police recently stormed in and wrecked offices, the courts were also playing an important role. Responding to union motions in Rand Supreme Court, the authorities agreed to make no further

Magnum/Odeon Mendel

Striking transport workers meeting inside Cosatu House, the union offices that were stormed by the police.

Reuters

Riot police firing tear gas at students holding demonstration at University of Witwatersrand in Johannesburg last week.

assaults on Cosatu House. When it was raided again last week, witnesses said, the police produced a search warrant and negotiated with union officials and lawyers before systematically searching 400 workers. Black informers, their identities shielded by hoods, identified 11 suspects in the gruesome burning to death of five blacks who, the police said, were transport workers suspected of being strikebreakers. The unions have condemned the killings and denied any responsibility for them.

A federation affiliate, the South African Railway and Harbour Workers Union, also filed court papers in Johannesburg preparing a challenge to the legality of the dismissal April 22 of 16,000 black transport workers after a six-week dispute that disrupted bus and rail lines.

For its part, the state-run transport board also went to court. In Rand Supreme Court, it accused the unions of "intimidating, assaulting or murdering" workers and extracted a union promise to refrain from intimidation and assault.

The mood of black defiance was reflected at the sentencing of nine black members of the African National Congress, also in the Natal Supreme Court last week. The defendants, who were sentenced to jail terms of 10 years or more, jumped onto their benches, faced the public gallery and exchanged clenched-fist salutes while chanting liberation slogans and saluting jailed and exiled leaders of the African National Congress such as Nelson Mandela, its founder.

Opposition white politicians said efforts by the United Democratic Front to diminish the white election were beginning to have an effect, particularly among young whites such as the anti-Government activists who clashed with the police last week on the campuses of English-speaking universities.

Looking ahead to the virtually certain outcome of Wednesday's election, a Western diplomat said wryly, "The reason the National Party will score another overwhelming victory is that it reflects all the confusion and ambivalence of the white electorate."

* * *

September 6, 1987

IN CAMEROON, PRESS FINDS CAUTION PAYS

By JAMES BROOKE
Special to the New York Times

DOUALA, Cameroon—Of sub-Saharan Africa's 44 countries, only Botswana, Gambia and Mauritius have a "generally free" press, according to a report by Freedom House, a New York-based group that tracks civil liberties throughout the world.

While radio news reports across this continent told Africans the other day that South Africa planned to tighten censorship of its anti-Government newspapers, the broadcasters undoubtedly neglected to mention that few black-ruled countries had such newspapers.

"Sub-Saharan Africa and the Middle East are the worst in the non-Communist world," Raymond D. Gastil, who conducts the press survey, said in a telephone interview from New York.

Dr. Gastil classifies the press in 11 African nations as "partly free." The press in 30 African nations ranks as "generally not free."

For example, the press in Cameroon, a prosperous nation of 10 million people on the west coast of Africa, is on the "generally not free" list.

Role of Press at Issue

As recently as four years ago Cameroonian protesters carried placards proclaiming "Down with Press Censorship" and

"Free Speech at Last." The continuing tension here highlights the clash between those in Africa who believe the press should mobilize for development and those who believe the press should play an independent oversight role.

Abodel Karimou, who has a typewriter but no telephone in his cramped newspaper office here, is an energetic member of the oversight camp. Mr. Karimou edits La Gazette, one of Cameroon's privately owned weeklies. The existence of a private press in Cameroon is a rarity on a continent where most newspapers are written and published by government employees.

When a visitor commented that an issue of La Gazette seemed a bit bland, Mr. Karimou grimaced and then patiently explained the mechanics of censorship.

When an edition is ready for press, a photocopy of each page is sent to the Ministry of Territorial Administration in Yaounde, the nation's capital, three hours north of here.

There, the newspaper pages work their way through the bureaucracy—from the Reading Bureau, to the Director for Public Freedoms, to the Deputy Director for Political Affairs. Each official makes notes on the articles, which are presented in resume form to the minister.

Censorship Called Necessary

"The censorship which I exert leaves me at ease because I know it is an action necessary for our democracy," Eric Sousse, Deputy Director for Political Affairs, said at a seminar last year. "In the great democracies whose example we follow we know very well that censorship exists under many forms."

At the ministry, each approved page must be stamped and signed by an official, usually Mr. Sousse. Printers are not allowed to print material without the censor's stamp. From the printers, 10 copies are carried back to the ministry for final approval and a second stamp. Newspaper distributors are not allowed to distribute any publications without the censor's stamp.

In recent weeks, censors have deemed unfit for public consumption an article critical of Israel's military links with South Africa, an article criticizing the French national anthem as "violent" and an article advocating a reduction in the number of government ministries to cope with Cameroon's financial crisis.

Until last June, editors could alert readers to the inroads of censorship by not replacing cut articles. Now the white spaces must be filled. "More and more the private press is throwing itself into sports and crime coverage," Mr. Karimou said resignedly.

Two Are Sent to Jail

A different philosophy reigns in the newsroom of Cameroon's official newspaper, The Cameroon Tribune, which recently published such banner headlines as "The Golden Age of Cooperatives," "The Benefits of the Reforms" and "To the Fields!"

"You can't say the President is great day in, day out—people get tired of it," said Paul C. Ndembiyembe, the newspaper's new managing editor. "You have to explain, to enlighten."

"I'm in favor of censorship, not for the sake of censoring, but to make journalists responsible, to make them work for the common interest of the country," he said.

Working under a self-censorship system, civil servants of the Information Ministry publish The Cameroon Tribune, which is Cameroon's dominant daily with a press run of about 65,000. Occasionally, editors misread the Government's signals.

Earlier this year, Mr. Ndembiyembe's predecessor and another Cameroon Tribune editor spent nearly a month in jail for publishing a presidential decree that apparently was to remain secret.

Last year, a Government attempt to buy favorable coverage backfired. A French journalist, Jacques Tiller, acknowledged that the Cameroon Government had regularly paid him about $30,000 every three months since 1985 to write favorable articles on Cameroon.

Indeed, maintenance of appearances seems to be a driving force behind much of African censorship.

Last June, shortly before the Israeli Prime Minster, Yitzhak Shamir, visited here, Cameroonian officials met with local reporters who were to attend a news conference he was to give. The purpose was to assign individual reporters to ask questions prepared in advance by the Government.

* * *

January 7, 1988

5 ANTI-APARTHEID JOURNALS ARE WARNED BY PRETORIA

By JOHN F. BURNS
Special to the New York Times

CAPE TOWN, Jan. 6—Four months after adopting emergency powers enabling it to censor or close publications it deems subversive, the South African Government has warned that it may use the powers against five of the country's most forthright anti-apartheid journals.

The publications include a daily newspaper, The Sowetan; three weeklies, The New Nation, The Weekly Mail and South, and a monthly journal with a strong left-wing bent, Work in Progress. A warning has also been issued to Die Stem, an extreme right-wing newspaper published in Afrikaans, the language of the dominant group among the country's 4.5 million whites.

The warnings were issued in the last month by the home affairs minister, J. Christoffel Botha. In letters to the anti-apartheid publications, Mr. Botha said that they were "promoting a revolutionary climate" by, among other things, conveying a positive image of the outlawed African National Congress and its leaders. In particular, the warnings cited stories covering the release from prison in November of Govan Mbeki, former chairman of the A.N.C., which has been a main force of opposition to white rule here since 1912.

Specific Passages Cited

In his warning to The Weekly Mail, Mr. Botha complained that the newspaper had promoted the image of the Congress with articles that described Mr. Mbeki as a widely accepted leader among black people.

In a letter to The New Nation, the minister accused the publication of fomenting "hatred or hostility" for Government security forces by, among other things, referring to actions taken by the forces as "raids." In addition, he said that the newspaper had fostered "the breaking down of public order" by supporting a clemency campaign on behalf of 32 men condemned to death by South African courts for their involvement in politically motivated killings.

The warnings were issued under a decree adopted by the Government in August that empowers the Home Affairs Minister, after determining that a publication is subversive, to require its editors to give reason within two weeks why he should not proceed against it. After that, he must publish a formal finding against the publication in The Government Gazette before he can invoke powers of pre-publication censorship or closure.

Press Controls Rarely Used

Over the 40 years that the ruling National Party has been in power it has acquired wide controls over the press. But since the 1960's it has only rarely used them to close publications, and then under conditions that have made it answerable, at least to some degree, in the courts. Under the new powers, recourse to the courts has been sharply reduced, largely to the issue of whether the minister adhered to the procedures laid down in the decree.

One theory among Government opponents is that Mr. Botha issued the warnings to inhibit the publications, without any immediate plan to act. At the publications involved, the hope is that the Government will be deterred by the storm of protest against the minister's actions. Typical of the reaction was that of The Star, a leading Johannesburg newspaper, which published a front-page editorial two weeks ago under the headline "The Lights Go Out."

The editorial classed the warnings to the publications with the continued detention of as many as 2,000 people under the state-of-emergency decree that has been in force, with a three-month lapse, since July 1985. Like the new press powers, also declared under the emergency, the detentions are largely beyond redress through the courts. Calling on South Africans to protest, The Star said: "Our country is not yet a police state. Yet our differences from totalitarianism are rapidly dwindling."

One of the newspapers, The Sowetan, has a circulation of 120,000, second largest, after The Star, of any South African daily. Successor to two other newspapers for blacks that were banned in the past decade, The World and The Post, it circulates mainly in Soweto, the black satellite city outside Johannesburg. Of the other newspapers warned, New Nation, published by the Roman Catholic Church, has a circulation of about 60,000; The Weekly Mail and South, the latter sold mainly among Cape Town's mixed-race community, sell about 25,000 copies each.

'Alternative Press'

The small newspapers are among those commonly referred to here as the "alternative press." The Weekly Mail, in particular, is valued among its readers for its sharp-penned analysis of apartheid, much of it by writers who previously worked for The Rand Daily Mail, once the country's leading anti-apartheid newspaper, which closed amid heavy losses in 1984. Originally not much more than a news sheet financed out of severance payments to Rand Daily Mail staff members, it has grown to a 30-page publication that attracts advertising from some of the country's largest corporations.

In its latest issue, the newspaper went further than any other publication in its coverage of the arrest of three white soldiers in Cape Town, saying that the men had uncovered information about a "dirty tricks" plan to discredit an anti-conscription movement. Other articles used words like "repression" to describe Government policies, gave up-to-date details on the number of detainees that are rarely available in other papers, and poked fun at the President, P. W. Botha.

An Englishwoman, Sally Hutchins, was deported last year only hours after tossing two tomatoes at the President, and missing. The Weekly Mail, alluding to the incident, offered a series of tongue in cheek accolades that it called the Tamatie Awards, using the Afrikaans word for tomato; the recipients were mostly pro-Government figures, one of them a senior cabinet minister.

With Parliament in recess, Mr. Botha has not been exposed to opposition questioning on his warnings, but he set out his thinking on the need for Government controls on the press in an interview in the current issue of Leadership, a glossy periodical.

Lawyer for Newspaper Group

At one point in the interview, he referred to himself as a "media man," a reference to his service for many years as a lawyer for Afrikaanse Pers, a powerful group of pro-Government, Afrikaans-language newspapers.

Referring to his new powers, the minister said, "As a lawyer I do not like it, as a media man I do not like it."

However, he told the periodical that the country was "in a revolutionary state" that necessitated the Government equipping itself with powers over the press that circumvented the "laborious" procedures previously required. "I am not referring to normal criticism, even severe criticism, by anyone who disagrees with the Government," he said. "I am referring to propaganda promoting the violent overthrow of the existing order."

* * *

May 10, 1988

ANTI-APARTHEID PAPER FIGHTS GOVERNMENT FOR ITS RIGHT TO FIGHT

By JOHN D. BATTERSBY
Special to the New York Times

JOHANNESBURG, May 9—A liberal weekly newspaper that has consistently challenged the white-run South African Government is fighting for its life.

"We will pull out all the stops," said Anton Harber, co-editor of the newspaper, The Weekly Mail, in an interview. "That means public campaigns, private lobbying, legal action and any other means we can think of."

The Government has accused the paper of fanning revolution by publishing reports that portray guerrillas of the outlawed African National Congress in a favorable light while undermining the image of the security forces. The newspaper is facing suspension for three months under arbitrary emergency censorship laws intended to dissipate protests.

With hardly a ripple of dissent, the Government closed on March 22 the biggest anti-apartheid journal, New Nation, a national weekly tabloid with a press run of 60,000. South, a weekly tabloid based in Cape Town, was ordered closed for four weeks today.

No Court Review

The censorship laws, enacted eight months ago, enable Home Affairs Minister J. Christoffel Botha to censor or close for three months any newspaper he deems to be subversive. His opinion as to whether a publication constitutes "a threat to public safety and the maintenance of public order" is final and cannot be scrutinized by the courts.

"The new system insures that any public outcry will fade to a whimper long before the climax of the whole tediously boring, excruciatingly drawn-out process of death by a thousand pin-pricks," said The Weekly Mail's co-editor, Irwin Manoim. "But suspension will indeed mean death—commercial death. And the Minister will be free to protest: 'My hands are clean. I didn't close them.'"

An Alternative Press

The Weekly Mail is prominent in South Africa's alternative press of low-budget anti-apartheid weeklies that sprang up to fill the gap left by the closing of the anti-apartheid Rand Daily Mail in 1985, as well as to cover areas ignored by the mainstream press.

The alternative press includes left-wing analytical journals, like Work in Progress, working-class news sheets such as Saamstaan (Stand Together) and Grassroots, and the weekly and monthly anti-apartheid tabloids.

Unlike the other weekly tabloids, which are more openly aligned to anti-apartheid organizations, The Weekly Mail has maintained a critical distance in its objective reports on human rights. In doing so it has often exposed the timidity of the mainstream English-language press.

The New York/Anna Zieminski

Under threat of suspension by the Government, staff members of The Weekly Mail in Johnnesburg worked to get an edition of the anti-apartheid newspaper to press. Musa Zondi was at a word processor; Irwin Manoim, a co-editor of the paper, was on the telephone.

"It would be unfair to say that the mainstream newspapers ignore events in the black townships and rural areas," Mr. Manoim said. "They are conscious of injustice and have spoken out strongly often enough in the past. But they tend to cover the townships as if they were foreign lands: exotic, remote, of sporadic interest."

Ken F. Owen, the editor of Business Day and one of the more outspoken editors in the mainstream press, described The Weekly Mail as "radical chic" rather than revolutionary.

"Its political coverage is stylish, sophisticated, frequently clever, and aimed at an elite market," he said in an editorial critical of the Government's threat to close The Weekly Mail. "It is probably inconsequential."

A List of Readers

The Government has devised more than 100 statutes curbing the press besides the censorship imposed under the current state of emergency. But it has stopped short of taking control of the press because South African officials know the symbolic power of a free press in the United States and Europe.

The Weekly Mail has responded to the official threat of closure by seeking support among business executives, diplomats, editors and trade unionists. It has also responded by portraying Mr. Botha as a subject of ridicule.

In an advertisement in The Johannesburg Star, South Africa's largest daily newspaper, The Weekly Mail poked fun at Mr. Botha's claim that it was promoting revolution and constituted a threat to public safety. The advertisement said: "Just how wide-eyed a revolutionary should a Weekly Mail reader be? Ask some of our distinguished subscribers."

The advertisement then listed 14 key Government departments that subscribe to the newspaper. A personal subscription for Mr. Botha headed the list. This impish sense of humor is one of the qualities that has endeared the gutsy tabloid to its 60,000 readers, an estimated 40 percent of whom are black and set it apart from other alternative newspapers.

The Weekly Mail has exposed excesses by the security forces, kept alive the voice of exiled black guerrilla groups and made the plight of blacks under apartheid real to its increasingly influential readership.

An Outside Defender

A leading South African businessman, Robert S. Tucker, spoke out on The Weekly Mail's behalf in a speech March 30 at Witwatersrand University. Mr. Tucker, managing director of the South African Permanent Building Society, said that the press, like the business community, had been co-opted by reactionary forces and he favorably compared The Weekly Mail's news coverage with that of The Sunday Times, the most profitable mainstream newspaper in the country with a circulation of 520,000.

From a news sheet with a circulation of 8,000, The Weekly Mail has grown to a 32-page tabloid that carries advertisements from major private corporations and sells 21,000 copies a week.

The newspaper is written and produced by a dedicated multi-racial staff of about 20 who work long hours for low salaries in modest offices in downtown Johannesburg.

It does not normally carry editorials because it would be difficult to find a political consensus among the divergent political views shared by its staff.

"It is a newspaper which raises questions rather than provides answers," said Mr. Manoim, the co-editor.

Charge Denied

But late last month, The Weekly Mail ran its first-ever editorial denying the Government's contention "that our wailing threatens public safety."

The front-page editorial concluded: "We deny the charge. Our newspaper kicks at consciences and tears down barriers. It does not throw bombs. Don't let us go quietly. Carry on reading us. Carry on subscribing. Make a fuss. Wail, dammit."

* * *

August 19, 1988

MAGAZINE EDITOR JAILED BY KENYA

By JANE PERLEZ
Special to the New York Times

NAIROBI, Kenya, Aug. 18—The editor of a church magazine that has been critical of the Government's election practices has been sentenced to nine months in jail.

The surprisingly harsh sentence was handed down on Wednesday, two weeks after changes in the nation's Constitution gave President Daniel arap Moi unrestricted power to dismiss judges and gave the police enhanced powers of detention.

The sentencing of the editor appeared to increase the already high tension between the National Council of Churches of Kenya and the Moi Government.

"We were shocked by the decision because we understood the offense to be really that of a technical oversight," said Sam Kobia, the General Secretary of the National Council of Churches of Kenya, the publishers of the magazine, Beyond. "As far as we know, it is an offense for which the sentence is usually a fine."

The editor, Bedan Mbugua, was charged for failing to file annual returns of sales and accounts of the monthly magazine with the Registrar of Books and Newspapers. He pleaded not guilty, arguing that it was not his responsibility to submit the returns but that of the publishers.

Reported Election Irregularities

Mr. Mbugua was arrested in March after that month's issue of Beyond and all previous issues of the three-year-old publication were banned. In the March issue, Mr. Mbugua had written a sharp editorial condemning what he said were irregularities in the selection of candidates for parliamentary elections later that month. In those elections, by secret ballot, President Moi was elected to a third five-year term.

The editorial castigated the Government for introducing "queue voting," whereby members of the sole legal party, the Kenya African National Union, voted for candidates on Feb. 22 by lining up behind the photograph of the candidate of their choice.

Mr. Mbugua called the public system of voting for the nominating election "a mockery of justice" and accused the Government of terrorizing citizens.

Law Society Also Criticized

The sentencing of Mr. Mbugua, which is being appealed, came on the same day that the newspapers here devoted front-page articles to harsh criticism of the Kenya Law Society by President Moi.

Mr. Moi said the society, which had attacked the constitutional changes, was serving foreign interests who did not have the interests of Kenyans at heart. The society, he said, was "respecting thoughts of foreigners which militate against the interests and aspirations of Kenyans."

The constitutional changes, which give the police authority to hold people suspected of capital offenses for as long as 14 days without charges, were described by the Law Society of Kenya as "revolutionary change." It said the passage of the amendments "strikes at the very soul of the ability of a judge to perform his functions independently."

* * *

October 6, 1989

IN A LAND OF THE CENSOR, A BOLD MAGAZINE ENDURES

By JANE PERLEZ
Special to The New York Times

NAIROBI, Kenya, Oct. 5—After the second issue of Gitobu Imanyara's monthly magazine appeared on the newsstands, with a bold title about human rights and a chilling graphic of barbed wire splashed across the cover, some friends in the security forces got in touch with the editor. Not a good idea, they warned. Dangerous copy, they said.

"I said I would try and find out what was dangerous in the magazine," Mr. Imanyara recalled, only slightly facetiously. "But no one quite knew." In the meantime, the security people ferreted out the printer, who happened to be Asian, and told him he would be expelled from Kenya if he handled any more issues.

Fourteen issues and some sharp covers later, The Nairobi Law Monthly survives, an outspoken magazine in a political milieu where the press has become increasingly restricted. Mr. Imanyara, a lawyer turned journalist, manages to tell his readers—not only lawyers, diplomats and businessmen but ordinary Kenyans curious about their society—what others can't, or won't.

In a nation that once boasted the most unfettered press in Africa, the retinue of press closings and restrictions has been long lately.

Church Magazine Banned

The magazine of the National Council of Churches in Kenya, was banned last year. More than five months ago, a lively weekly, The Financial Review, was shut down when its coverage of the economy and political issues irritated the Government. A rather innocuous magazine, Development Agenda, was prohibited in August after two issues, apparently because of its political connections.

Perhaps most ominous of all, The Nation, the largest selling and most comprehensive daily newspaper, established 28 years ago by the Aga Khan, was stopped in June by Parliament from covering Parliament. Legislators complained about "subversive elements" at the paper and how its training program with The St. Petersburg Times, in Florida, was tainting the paper.

Editors at The Nation used to resist calls from the office of President Daniel arap Moi requesting that articles be suppressed.

Since the banishment from the press gallery, the editors acquiesce, fearful that a consequence of publishing displeasing articles will mean a shutdown.

A free press is a rare species in most of Africa. In the neighboring Sudan, for example, a flourishing press—about a dozen dailies—was shut down after the military coup in June. The broadest points of view on Africa can often be found in magazines and newsletters printed in Europe, out of the way of the censors. But the recent crackdown in Kenya has disappointed people here because the country regards itself as a democracy.

A Pocket-Sized Office

Mr. Imanyara, a lithe, mild-mannered 36-year-old graduate of Nairobi University's law school, who puts out his magazine from a pocket-sized office with the help of only three others, has experienced his own problems.

The third issue of The Monthly featured a cover article on the release of a jailed human rights lawyer, Gibson Kamau

The New York Times/Raymond Bonner

The Nairobi Law Monthly has become an outspoken magazine in a country where the press has become increasingly restricted. Gitobu Imanyara, right, the editor, is shown with Njenga N'Ganga, general manager.

Kuria (winner of the Robert F. Kennedy human rights award), and a prominent letter to the editor suggesting the Commissioner of Police should resign because of reported deaths of people in police custody.

"I was arrested and then released," Mr. Imanyara said. "They said the magazine was spreading 'alarm and despondency among the wananchi' and giving a lot of prominence to dissidents and their sympathizers. I wrote a statement saying I was a lawyer and wouldn't accept being told what to print." Wananchi is Swahili for "the people."

Before turning to journalism, Mr. Imanyara attracted attention as a lawyer. He defended the employee accused of killing the conservationist Joy Adamson. He lost the case, but as he puts it now, won "a lot of exposure." Several years later, he defended 120 members of the air force charged with treason in connection with a failed coup of 1982. Not surprisingly, he lost that case, too.

Jailed for 5 Years

By that time, his political activities, viewed as courageous by some but threatening by others, had earned him the ire of the Attorney General. He charged Mr. Imanyara on the basis of a complaint that a client of the lawyer's had filed with the Law Society but the society had dismissed as groundless.

Mr. Imanyara was jailed for five years—he spent two years in solitary after which he was released—in what was widely seen as a vendetta for having dared to defend the air force officers. In jail he laid plans for starting his law magazine.

While he has many criticisms of what he sees as abuses by and of the Kenyan judicial system, he also believes in its strengths. Each month he goes out of his way to point these out.

"Our bias is covering civil rights and human rights, but by selecting cases for publication we are able to educate people so they know there are judges who've acted favorably," he said, as he took a break from writing an assessment of the new Chief Justice for the next issue.

On Western Foundations

Mr. Imanyara's magazine, with its push for human rights, is just the kind of effort that Western foundations and agencies line up to endow. The calling cards of potential donors lie on top of his desk.

"I would not accept money from a U.S. foundation," he said. "It would encourage us to be dependent. A lot of Kenyans leave too much to outsiders. I'd rather have 50,000 subscribers in the United States than $50,000 that might help us only in the short term."

A case against Mr. Imanyara dealing with his second arrest over an issue of the magazine is still pending. In the meantime Mr. Imanyara's eye-catching, sell-out publication—3,000 to 5,000 issues depending on the print run—has not been shuttered.

"They still haven't closed it and they can't," he said. "They want to show the world we have a judiciary that functions."

There is another reason, too, Mr. Imanyara said. He is well aware of the possibility that the Government may find the magazine useful. "The Government can say: 'How can you say we have no freedom of the press when you are reading this magazine?' It's a contradiction, of course, to say we have freedom of the press, because we don't."

* * *

July 23, 1990

SOUTH AFRICA EASING UP ON ITS POLITICAL CENSORSHIP OF BOOKS

By CHRISTOPHER S. WREN
Special to The New York Times

CAPE TOWN—In a basement room of the South African Library there rest hundreds of books, political tracts and magazines that the Government thinks South Africans, for their own good, should not read.

Over the years the collection has included not just pornography or incitements to revolution, but critically praised novels by Andre Brink and Nadine Gordimer or poems by Breyten Breytenbach.

But now, the basement stacks are being winnowed of their illicit contents. A flurry of white slips marks spaces where about 500 forbidden books have been removed for re-evaluation by the censors.

"We have definitely noticed an easing-up," said Peter Coates, the chief librarian at the South African Library.

More Is Permissible Now

The more liberal political climate introduced by President F. W. de Klerk has extended to censorship. What was once forbidden has now become merely undesirable or, increasingly, even permissible.

"Ten, 15 years ago, maybe the word Marxism affected a book to be found undesirable," said Pierre Cronje, the deputy director of the Directorate of Publications. "It's no longer true."

At the directorate, Mr. Cronje and four other full-time employees toil away "interpreting the mores of the people of South Africa," as he described the job.

Johan Louw, a retired South African Navy captain who serves on the directorate, said he wanted to correct the misconception that books are banned in South Africa.

"People are banned, but books—either the distribution or the possession—are prohibited," Captain Louw said.

The works still prohibited include "The Satanic Verses" by Salman Rushdie, which was declared offensive to the feelings of Muslims in South Africa.

Mandela but Not Playboy

But political writings by Nelson Mandela and other critics of apartheid are now legal. The criteria have become more sexual than political. Playboy and Penthouse magazines remain prohibited; Marx and Lenin now are not.

"We're less tolerant as regards explicit sex, less tolerant as regards profanities and crude language," Mr. Cronje said. His colleague Stephanus du Toit said the censors were guided in part by what he called "the Christian view of life."

Last year, 70 new publications and objects were prohibited, Home Affairs Minister Gene Louw reported in Parliament. A total of 372 other publications and objects and 132 films were declared undesirable, meaning that they could be privately owned but not distributed. Undesirable objects include battery-powered vibrators, a sexually explicit key chain and a record with obscene lyrics.

In reviewing printed matter, the directorate, which is based in Cape Town, responds to complaints from the public across South Africa. Years ago, a copy of Fair Lady, a women's magazine, was seized after someone objected to a photograph of Queen Victoria's bloomers. Among publications confiscated in recent years were a yachting magazine with a cover model wind-surfing bare-breasted and a pharmaceutical journal with an advertisement showing two brightly painted nudes sitting inside a bottle.

Not Entirely Deprived

If South Africans are legally deprived of pornography, they do have access to sexually suggestive material. The Sunday Times, the country's largest selling newspaper, devotes an entire back page to pin-up girls alongside articles about people described as "saucy," "naughty" or simply "topless," under boldface headlines like "I Was Pop Star's Sex Slave." Mr. Cronje said The Sunday Times, and its back page, fell under the scope of the Media Council and not his directorate.

Unlike a book or magazine, a film must be examined before release. "It can be rejected," said Marie van der Westhuizen, who supervises the screening of films and videos. "It can be allowed with a high age restriction."

Nudity and profanity are excised, she said, but political controversy is increasingly permitted.

In 1987, the film "Cry Freedom," which dramatized the killing of the black-consciousness proponent Steve Biko, who died in police custody, was approved by a screening committee with only an age restriction. Then the police seized the film on ground that it threatened public order. Under President de Klerk, "Cry Freedom" was released this year without incident in commercial theaters.

The screening committee initially withheld approval for another film denouncing apartheid, "A Dry White Season," based on the novel by Mr. Brink. It ruled that "this film can only have a negative effect which poses a clear and present danger." The ban was overturned on appeal, and "A Dry White Season," with graphic scenes of a white policeman torturing a black prisoner, was approved for adult audiences in theaters with fewer than 200 seats.

Eugene Louw, the Minister of Home Affairs, has assured Parliament that censorship curbs would not disappear, despite their declining popularity.

"We dare not risk no control over morals, pornography and such," Mr. Louw said.

In the meantime, those who feel radical, prurient or just curious can walk into the South African Library and ask to read something forbidden. The law requires such readers to sign a register. But, Mr. Coates said, "in all the years of the system, nobody has ever consulted the records."

* * *

December 8, 1991

POLITICAL PRISONER'S NOVEL REACHES KENYA'S SHELVES

By JANE PERLEZ
Special to The New York Times

NAIROBI, Kenya, Dec. 7—Five years ago, Wahome Mutahi was writing his Sunday column in the newsroom of The Nation newspaper when the secret police stopped him in midsentence and hauled him around to the local precinct. Mr. Mutahi, whose easygoing, common man touch had long made him Kenya's most popular newspaper columnist, spent 30 days in prison without being charged before being forced to plead guilty to subversion.

A fictional account of life as a political prisoner, written by Mr. Mutahi before his arrest and revised afterward, appeared in the bookshops here two months ago. "Three Days on the Cross" became an instant best seller. It is unusual for a Kenyan book to sell 4,000 copies in a year; Mr. Mutahi's book sold that number in six weeks. The publisher, Heinemann Kenya, is now rushing out a second printing.

To the surprise of many Kenyans, Mr. Mutahi's novel has not been banned. This might give the impression that freedom of expression is unfettered in Kenya. This is not quite so. Rather, the publication of "Three Days on the Cross," a politically sensitive novel by a well-known writer, helps illustrate the arbitrary nature of censorship in this East African nation that is being pushed both by internal ferment and international pressure toward greater democracy.

In the past 18 months, the Government has banned six plays, including a Kenyan adaptation of George Orwell's "Animal Farm" and a play by Kenya's most celebrated novelist, Ngugi Wa Thiong'o, who lives in Britain.

For a long time, Kenyan newspapers shied away from reporting on subjects that might earn them a disapproving call from the office of President Daniel arap Moi. In recent months, however, the papers have become noticeably bolder: reporting at length on a judicial inquiry into the 1990 slaying of Foreign Minister Robert Ouko, and running allegations of corruption by senior Cabinet officials on the front pages, though the papers have been careful not to place the President in a negative light.

Visit by PEN

A delegation from PEN, the international organization of writers and editors, visited Kenya this summer in an effort to start a chapter here. And the Kenya Writers Association, moribund for eight years after being co-opted by the Government, is being revived.

Even so, writing in Kenya remains a delicate business. Both the publisher of "Three Days on the Cross" and the author adopted some special techniques to try to insure the survival of the novel on the bookstands.

"In due course, the Government will take action," said Henry Chakava, the managing director of Heinemann Kenya. "The thing to do is to print them very quickly so by the time the Government catches up you have a lot of books out. We're into our second printing of 5,000. This will go faster than the first printing. Word spreads. We're receiving letters from the rural areas for copies of the book."

When Mr. Mutahi was interviewed on television, both the writer and his interviewer skirted the novel's subject matter. "We talked about publishing in general but not the content of the book," the 37-year-old Mr. Mutahi said. "But that the television channel managed to get the book mentioned was a victory in itself." A monthly magazine ran a cover line "Will This Book Survive?" and inside, without saying anything about its content, said Mr. Mutahi had just published a novel. It was enough of a notice to entice readers who admire Mr. Mutahi's newspaper columns but not enough to catch the attention of the authorities.

Mr. Mutahi insists that the novel is not entirely autobiographical. He said it is intended as a parable of any African country ruled by a despot. Its plot rings true for many Kenyans: a bank employee and a newspaper reporter are arrested to help fill the quota of arrests the security police must make during a crackdown on dissidents ordered by a president known as the "Illustrious One."

Book Completed Before Arrest

He finished writing the book and sent the manuscript to the publishers before he was arrested. There had been enough political arrests at the time that Mr. Mutahi said he had no problem creating the story line. Mr. Mutahi said he was not arrested for anything he had written for the newspaper but for allegedly knowing about subversive literature and not reporting it to the authorities. He was innocent, he said.

After his month in prison, Mr. Mutahi took back the manuscript for some revisions. Mr. Mutahi added such convincing descriptions of torture that the reader can only conclude that the author has experienced such pain. "I was in the basement in Nyayo House and very close to a lot of things," he said, a little enigmatically when asked what he went through.

Nyayo House is a showcase Government building in Nairobi with more than 20 floors of offices, and underneath are Kenya's most feared prison cells where prisoners have told of torture by beatings and cells flooded with cold water.

Mr. Mutahi is such a hot newspaper property that he has switched employers three times, each time for a higher salary. He is using his prison experience for another book, this time a humorous one tentatively titled "The Prison Bugs."

And since his work in progress is light-hearted, he doesn't mind acknowledging that it is derived solely from his month behind bars. "I don't believe any writer can write only from imagination," he said.

* * *

August 1, 1993

THE URGE TO SUPPRESS PERSISTS IN SOUTH AFRICA

By BILL KELLER

JOHANNESBURG—It is more than three years since the words of Nelson Mandela were unbanned in South Africa, and 10 years since the censors legalized "Tropic of Capricorn" and "Portnoy's Complaint." At talks on building democracy, all the major parties have included free speech in their proposals for a new bill of rights. Freedom is so much in fashion that even the former state censor now presents himself as a born-again champion of artistic and political liberty.

But two events in recent days have aroused debate about whether the temptation to suppress is really dead or merely dormant, waiting to be called up in service of different sensibilities.

One was the forced cancellation of the showing of a Nazi-era German film, "Sweet Jew" ("Jud Suss"), to a conference exploring the limits of free expression.

The other was a proposal to ban public appearances or press statements by political figures deemed to be advocates of violence.

In each case the censorial voice was not that of the South African Government but of a public organization that regards itself as democratically inclined and politically progressive. The stated purpose was not to defend the state against the threat of change but to defend the country's uncompleted changes against the threat of violence.

South Africans have grown up under the censor's paternalism, in a world of whited-out newspapers, happy-talk TV, sex-free cinema and laundered literature. Since 1980 the old rules have been enforced less and less, until today's censors mainly worry about prurience and blasphemy: whether to snip Sharon Stone's lesbian scene from "Basic Instinct" (no) or to permit bookstores to sell Salman Rushdie's "The Satanic Verses" (no).

Reuters

South Africans are debating whether violent acts, like the attack last week on a church near Cape Town that left 12 dead, are encouraged by too much freedom of expression.

Familiarity with the censor has bred contempt for the state, but not necessarily a tolerance of dissenting views.

Blacks, in particular, who have been most thoroughly denied the luxury of free expression, are most likely to view it with suspicion. One recent poll found, for example, that a majority of blacks do not believe white parties have a right to conduct election campaigns in black townships. Journalists are often harassed in townships, and some have been killed there.

"Black people have never owned presses here, so they have never had a reason to place great store in press freedom," said Pat Sidley, who campaigns against censorship and is a columnist for The Weekly Mail, which sponsored last week's film festival on the theme of censorship. "As a consequence, press freedom here has been the preserve of a few white liberals."

Albie Sachs, a human rights lawyer who helped draft a proposed bill of rights for the African National Congress, said the habit of state control is strong among whites, too. Afrikaners, for example, have long defended the conservative bias of state television as necessary to offset what they saw as a more liberal English domination of the newspapers.

"The argument here has always been that the state has to balance out the imbalances," Mr. Sachs said.

Even South Africans who say they abhor censorship tend to be wary of the kind of freedom embodied in the United States Constitution's First Amendment; they argue that too much license can be dangerous in a divided and changing society.

When The Weekly Mail chose to include "Sweet Jew," a famous work of anti-Semitic propaganda, in its censorship festival, a leading Jewish organization lobbied the German copyright holder to withdraw permission. Ironically, said The Weekly Mail's Stephen Laufer, the sponsors had selected the film because it is so skillfully insidious that "it makes a strong case for some kind of restrictions."

The opponents, who had not seen the film, argued that its imagery was reputed to be so powerful that even liberal intellectuals watching it as part of an educational program might emerge filled with anti-Jewish emotions.

"This is a time of tremendous political and economic upheaval," said Joycelyn Hellig, a professor of religious studies and a member of the Jewish Board of Deputies, the organization that blocked the film. "It's not an ideal time to be exploring in a leisurely way whether a particular group should be targeted for hatred."

The conviction that words can kill also underlies a proposal being considered by the National Peace Committee, a multiparty forum that is supposed to help curb the country's daily slaughter. The proposal, aimed at giving the often feckless committee some teeth, is to set up a tribunal with power to ban public speech by anyone caught inciting violence.

A Familiar Idea

"It's not a gag on the press," said Antonie Gildenhuys, the committee official who broached the idea. "It's a gag on a particular individual who has been found guilty of war talk or another offense. He may then not appear on a public platform or issue statements to the press. If he ignores the order he could be charged in the criminal courts."

Mr. Sachs of the African National Congress, who was banned for much of his life because of his anti-apartheid views, said he found the idea chillingly familiar. And he said he would probably have allowed the anti-Semitic film to be shown, at least as part of an educational conference.

But the African National Congress, like most other parties here, does favor laws against promoting race hatred. Mr. Sachs said the congress would ban speech with a "direct potential" to incite violence.

When apartheid was at its most censorious, the playwright Pieter-Dirk Uys outwitted the official spoilsports by dressing in drag and impersonating them on stage. There was a barb in the joke last week when he ended a panel discussion with a promise that he would "see you all at the next anti-censorship conference in 10 years' time."

"I don't think we'll ever get something as entertaining or absurd as we had in the past," he said later, wistfully. "But we could get a situation where people are too scared to have opinions, or to express them. I think everybody's being extremely sensitive about our freedoms at the moment because it's the thing to do. But when power is in one's hands, the fist will close."

* * *

October 9, 1994

KENYA'S PRESS IS RESISTING THE CENSORS

By DONATELLA LORCH
Special to The New York Times

NAIROBI, Kenya, Oct. 8—In his first two weeks in prison, David Makali was in solitary confinement and had to break stones for five and a half hours every day. Conditions for him eventually eased, but the 26-year-old journalist, who was serving a four-month term in a maximum security prison for contempt of court, was badly beaten, he said, and suffered from dysentery.

Mr. Makali's crime? As a writer for the weekly newspaper The People he had written an article critical of a Kenyan court ruling, indicating that the court was subject to interference from President Daniel arap Moi and his Government. He refused to sign an apology drafted by the court or pay a $5,000 fine. The editor-in-chief of The People, Bedan Mbugua, was jailed for five months.

Their cases, closely monitored by diplomats and human rights officials, underscore the fact that two years after the advent of multiparty democracy in Kenya, criticism of the Government can still bear a heavy cost. But they also draw attention to the growing strength of the Kenyan press and its expanded freedoms. Since his release on Sept. 2, Mr. Makali has openly spoken about his detention and remained defiant. A few years ago, he would have been immediately re-arrested.

"The objective of the Government is to bully us into self-censorship," Mr. Makali said. "As long as you avoid touching on the presidency and the core of people around it, then your freedom of speech is not curtailed.

"I think the press will get bolder with time. Prison has only enhanced my courage. For us it will get better. The more we look like we are going to stand up for what we believe in, the less the Government will bully us."

In the last two years, under pressure from countries and organizations that give it aid, the Kenyan Government has made improvements in the economy but has set no clear policy toward the news media, alternating between repression and freedom.

A Government task force on the media is expected to present a report to Parliament by the end of next year on new press laws that would cover issues like access and dissemination of information as well as professional ethics and standards. In the last few years, newspapers and magazines have become much more critical of the Government, publishing reports on crime and corruption.

"The Government has made a longstanding practice of using the criminal justice system to penalize critics," Human Rights Watch wrote in its July report on Kenya. "Charges such as sedition and contempt of court have been regularly used to harass critics and the courts have been reluctant to oppose the Government by standing up for individual rights."

Since January, 18 Kenyan journalists have been fined, arrested or jailed for contempt of court or violation of libel laws. Intimidation and harassment have also been directed at the foreign press, which uses Nairobi as a base for covering sub-Saharan Africa.

Last month, angered by an article on crime in Nairobi with a headline that said the Kenyan capital was becoming as insecure as Mogadishu, the Government threatened to evict an American correspondent for the The Daily Telegraph of London on the ground that his work papers were not in order.

The Ministry of Information withdrew the accreditation of the reporter, Scott Peterson, and accused him of "filing inaccurate and misleading stories about Kenya which from a professional point of view is unacceptable." Under international pressure, the Kenyan Government accredited Mr. Peterson.

The increase in the rate of violent crime in Nairobi is a very sensitive topic in a country that relies on foreign tourism as its main foreign exchange earner. The principal immigration officer, F. J. M. Kwinga, said Mr. Peterson's articles were "offensive."

"I am going to be more firm with any journalist that reports what he thinks," warned Mr. Kwinga. "More strict—if you report an untrue story."

Mr. Makali's ankles are still swollen from the beating he received. His hands are still calloused from breaking stones. He talks about the intense humiliation of prison, where prisoners were stripped naked every day during searches and arbitrarily clubbed by the guards. But by refusing to apologize and instead going to jail, he says he has won a victory. He believes that the Government has understood they cannot force him or his paper into self-censorship.

"The presidency is so sensitive about anything that might portray this country as unmanageable or insecure," Mr. Makali said. "He wants an image that all is well in Kenya and that this is the land of peace."

* * *

January 14, 1996

PRESS FACES REPRESSION IN AFRICA

By HOWARD W. FRENCH

ABIDJAN, Ivory Coast, Jan. 13—When this country opened the way for an independent press at the turn of the decade, the blossoming of newspapers of nearly every political persuasion was widely hailed as a critical stepping stone toward true multiparty democracy.

But here, as elsewhere in Africa, rather than marking a clean break with an authoritarian past, the era of multiparty politics has been a time of increased hardship and repression for journalists who dare criticize powerful incumbents.

Since Henri Konan Bedie became President in 1993, the Government has repeatedly jailed journalists and fined publications that are judged too critical under press laws that international human rights experts say give the authorities unusually free rein to crack down on enemies.

In one example, a leading opposition newspaper, La Voie, recently published a headline saying Mr. Bedie's presence at a continent-wide soccer championship brought bad luck to the Ivory Coast side, which lost the match. The Government imposed two-year prison sentences on the editor and two reporters and suspended the newspaper for "offense to the head of state."

"Since Bedie came to power, journalists sleep with one eye shut," said Diegou Bailly, president of the Ivory Coast Journalists Union, and editor of the independent paper Le Jour. "Arrests, beatings, insults and scorn have become the daily lot of the press. This does nothing to honor the Government, which ought to think about changing its strategy."

Beyond the outcry among local journalists, the move against La Voie and another critical paper, Le Republicain, provoked swift condemnation from diplomats and international press groups.

"Among diplomatic observers, patience is definitely beginning to fray, and informed sources will be looking with interest at the forthcoming human rights reports to be issued on Ivory Coast," one Western diplomat said. "In the beginning, there was a very big benefit of the doubt here waiting to see the democrat buried deep down inside this man. We haven't seen it yet."

In an exchange of New Year's greetings with the diplomatic corps, Mr. Bedie urged foreign diplomats to invite "your journalists" to witness the workings of an opposition press that he said had confused "their mission with the organizing of public disturbances."

Journalists in the pro-Government press here have defended Mr. Bedie's stance toward the press, using an argument that has long served as a justification for some of Africa's most ruinous dictatorships.

"Our small nations are still fragile and require a lot of serenity to develop," said Venance Konan, editor of Ivoire Soir, a pro-Government tabloid. "Liberty of the press, as seen by a Westerner, is different from what we see as Africans. We still have ethnic problems that can explode at any moment, for example, and when a journalist incites tribal hatred, it is better to put him in jail."

International press watchdogs say the crackdown here reflects a much broader trend in Africa, where multiparty systems are still typically headed by leaders who cut their political teeth during long years of one-party rule, and have never reconciled themselves to being called to account by a critical press.

In Ethiopia and Zambia, which have been widely praised for democratic and economic reforms after years of corrupt and repressive government, press experts say critical journalists have nonetheless been the target of frequent and sometimes violent witch-hunts.

In Kenya, which is preparing to hold multiparty elections, the authorities recently announced that they were contemplating new rules governing press behavior, including that of foreign journalists.

In Nigeria, which long had what was arguably the most vibrant press in Africa, the military authorities have recently arrested dozens of journalists, ransacked their offices and closed their publications.

"In one country after another we have seen the press lose many of its top editors, as papers have been closed down, reporters jailed and people forced into exile," said Kakuna Kerina, the Africa coordinator of the Committee to Protect Journalists, a New York-based press group.

"Under the one-party dictatorships, people at least knew where they stood. Nowadays, when we have these supposed rights, every time a journalist takes a step toward claiming them, they are yanked two or three steps backwards."

* * *

April 15, 1998

NIGERIA'S PERSECUTED PRESS FIGHTS BACK UNDERGROUND

By HOWARD W. FRENCH

LAGOS, Nigeria—Every week without fail since Gen. Sani Abacha seized power in 1993, Kola Ilori has somehow managed to put out Tell, Nigeria's most influential and combative news magazine.

For some issues this has meant scrambling to secretly reprint the magazine after an entire press run has been seized by the country's military authorities, who routinely smash up printing shops and arrest their owners to block publications like his. Other times it has required desperate last-minute efforts to patch together an issue after seeing the bulk of the staff carted away in police sweeps. Once, Mr. Ilori said, he eluded capture by State Security agents only by posing as a lowly truck loader during a police raid.

Tell is officially published in Lagos, but Mr. Ilori uses printers all over the country.

Until late last year, Mr. Ilori was mostly responsible for production matters at the magazine. But the abduction of one of the magazine's top editors and the forced exile of another has left him virtually alone at the head of the enterprise.

For many of its 38 years of independence from Britain, Nigeria had the freest and most diverse press in Africa. But for the last several years, independent journalists have been arrested, beaten, forced into exile, and even assassinated. Nigeria has experienced "the most extreme deterioration of conditions for the press in Africa," according to the Committee to Protect Journalists, a United States-based advocacy group.

To keep the police off balance, Mr. Ilori changes sleeping places regularly, sees little of his family, rarely uses the same printing press for more than two weeks in a row, and meets secretly with other reporters and editors to hash out story ideas only under the cover of religious services in churches and mosques.

Despite its hit-and-run existence, Tell consistently manages to beat the competition, revealing details of coup plots, tensions inside the armed forces and corruption scandals that make it a must read for the masses, the Nigerian intelligentsia and foreign diplomats alike.

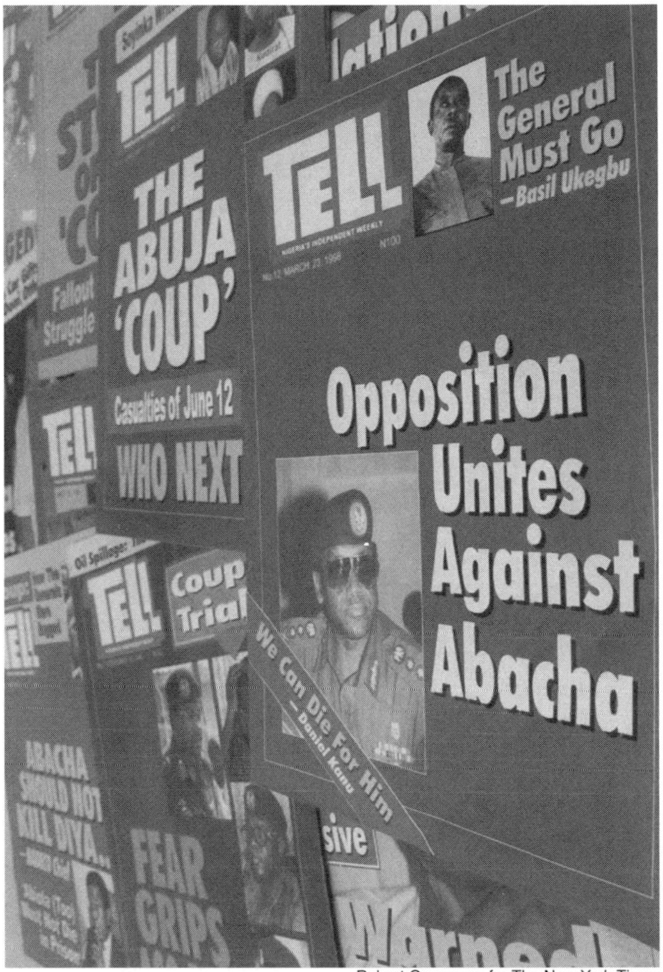

Robert Grossman for The New York Times

Tell, Nigeria's most influential news weekly, faces a campaign of harassment and intimidation by the Government of Gen. Sani Abacha.

"That we come out every week is the result of sheer ingenuity," said Mr. Ilori, 48, who spoke in long and impassioned sentences at a carefully arranged meeting place. "We have had to perfect a fleet-footed art of mobile production. It taxes your brain, it taxes your blood, it taxes your body, but it is the only way to survive."

Each week Tell publishes a photograph of its last managing editor, Onome Osifo-Whiskey, under the stark headline, "Where is Onimo Osifo-Whiskey?" He was abducted at his Lagos home last November as he dressed to go to church, and has not been heard from since.

Having already spent six months in prison, Tell's editor-in-chief, Nosa Igiebor, fled the country for Britain in November when State Security agents raided his home after the publication of an article that discussed rumors of a serious illness afflicting General Abacha.

One well-known journalist, Christine Anyanwu, has been imprisoned since 1995 and is serving a 15-year sentence as an "accessory to treason" for publishing a story debunking official accounts of a coup plot. Ms. Anyanwu, 46, is reported by human rights groups to be going blind for lack of medical care.

Another reporter, Oni Egbunine, was beaten into a coma by the police last July in punishment for an article that reported corruption by state Government officials in the provincial capital of Owerri.

As widespread as press repression has become in Nigeria, the harshest focus remains on Tell, and a small number of competitors, among them The News and Tempo—all known for their credibility.

Dapo Olorunyomi, Mr. Ilori's counterpart at The News, was forced to flee to the United States in 1996 after repeated attempts to arrest him. Once he had left, security agents simply began focusing on his wife.

During the next year, Ladi Olorunyomi, a mother of two and staff member of Lagos' Independent Journalism Center, a press training organization, was arrested twice and held for over three months without charge. Never asked about her own work, Mrs. Olorunyomi was repeatedly interrogated about her husband's activities and whereabouts.

"If you walk through newsrooms in Nigeria they are mostly empty, because to stay at your desk is to face arrest," said Mrs. Olorunyomi, who fled to the United States last November. "Even the clean-up men get arrested. That is what is happening to the press under Abacha."

Of the 17 journalists now known to be under arrest in Nigeria, 10 are from the staff of The News.

Many of the founders and top editors of Tell and The News cut their teeth at another pioneering weekly, Newswatch, which was founded in 1985 under the previous military regime of Gen. Ibrahim B. Babangida.

Newswatch set new standards in Africa both for production values patterned after Newsweek and Time, and for a no-holds-barred treatment of issues like Government corruption and human rights abuses.

The Babangida Government, of which General Abacha was deputy head of state, set new standards in the brutality it was willing to use to enforce the limits on criticism.

In October 1986, less than two years after its founding, Newswatch's editor, Dele Giwa, was killed in a bomb blast that has gone unclaimed and unpunished.

After the assassination, Newswatch dramatically softened its tone, and many of its top editors, including Mr. Ilori, left in disenchantment.

"The regime has grown even harder since then, but we can no longer be stopped so easily" Mr. Ilori said. "They can seize all of our copies at six in the morning and by evening we are back on the street again because we know that this is the last lap in a deadly race between our military rulers and the people of Nigeria.

"One or two of us may disappear, but we are prepared for survival. We cannot afford to fail."

ASIA AND AUSTRALIA

March 9, 1975

A TOP SEOUL PAPER DROPS 18 NEWSMEN

Dismissals in Fight Over Press Freedom Reach 31—Sit-In Strike Goes On

Special to The New York Times

SEOUL, South Korea, March 8—Gloom pervaded South Korea's press community today as more newsmen fighting for press freedom were dismissed from their jobs.

Dong-A Ilbo, the country's largest national daily, abruptly dismissed 18 of its editors and reporters tonight in what it said was a move for economy.

The action raised to 31 the number of South Korean journalists ousted by newspaper managements in the last three months. Many of them had played leading roles in fighting against the Government's press restrictions as well as their own publishers' self-censorship.

Yesterday, five reporters on the staff of Chosun Ilbo, the country's oldest daily, were arbitrarily retired for opposing what the reporters said was the management's "soft" attitude toward the Government of President Park Chung Hee. About 70 of their colleagues continued a sit-in strike for the third night, demanding reinstatement of the dismissed men and the right of the editors to publish news critical of the Government.

In a concurrent move, a third major daily, Joongang Ilbo, abruptly dismissed six editorial writers. Together, these three privately owned publications reach two-thirds of South Korea's total newspaper readership.

None of the publishers have offered any comments on the dismissals. All three newspapers have recently been trying to cope with internal revolts by younger reporters who regard their publishers as vulnerable to Government interference because of their other business interests.

The Chosun Ilbo publisher, Bang Wu Young, owns a large tourist hotel built with foreign loans guaranteed by the Government, Lee Byung Chul, the wealthy publisher of Joongang Ilbo, represents a large business conglomerate called Samsung. The businesses of both men can easily be affected by administrative authority of the Government.

In statements and resolutions, the Chosun Ilbo reporters charged that articles reporting on anti-Government moves had been suppressed by their editors and the publisher in fear of official reprisals. Their statement asserted that, at the order of outside sources, the paper had refrained from reporting on charges of torture made by university students recently released from prison by the Government.

One striking newsman quoted Mr. Bang as having said: "You want to defend press freedom but I want to defend my paper." However, a spokesman for the publisher denied that the strike was over press freedom. "The younger reporters are breaching our company discipline," he said.

It was not known whether the wave of ousters represented a coordinated move by the nation's publishers, but there was speculation that the current campaign by journalists for a more outspoken press would be severely set back as a result of their new toughness.

The striking reporters have won widespread support from religious and civic groups. The National Association of Christian Women issued a statement today saying that it would boycott Chosun Ilbo if its reportorial function remained hamstrung and if the owners did not take back the dismissed employes.

The civic and religious groups, which have played a leading role in the present anti-Government protests, have been active in supporting Dong-A Ilbo from collapsing under what is understood to be pressure from the Government against its advertisers. The paper, which has consistently reported on anti-Government activities, had all its commerical advertisements canceled without explanation several months ago.

The mood of conflict between conservative publishers and liberal reporters was illustrated graphically this afternoon when Chosun Ilbo's management, beleaguered by the newsroom revolt, had a barricade erected in front of its offices to stop outside sympathizers from pouring in.

In the newsroom itself, the striking reporters chanted slogans and made speeches. Amid the confusion editors and news executives, who do not share the views of the strikers, worked to produce tomorrow's issue of the paper.

* * *

June 28, 1975

NEW CENSORSHIP INDIA'S STRICTEST

Curbs Tougher Than During Wars—Threat to Stability and Security Are Cited

By JAMES M. MARKHAM
Special to The New York Times

NEW, DELHI, June 27—Citing danger to India's "security and stability" during the current political crisis, Prime Minister Indira Gandhi's Government has imposed the toughest press censorship in the 28 years since independence. It exceeds the measure taken during the three wars India has fought in that time.

In New Delhi, electricity was cut off in the offices of major English-language dailies, halting publication. Tonight a Government spokesman said the electricity had been restored.

In the past, dispatches of foreign journalists faced little governmental security. But now an elaborate censorship network has been established for the fast-growing corps of correspondents.

According to the rules, dispatches based on the two daily Government briefings may be sent without official inspection. But other dispatches must be stamped by censors before being telephoned or telegraphed. As a result, some foreign journalists here are trimming their sails.

The few newspapers appearing here—a handful of pro-Government dailies—have adopted a cautious tone. The same was true in the provinces, though some publications in the state of Tamil Nadu reportedly violated guidelines.

Since Mrs. Gandhi ordered a wave of arrests of her political opponents, many Indian journalists are wondering whether they may be next. Privately, the local press corps seems saddened and angered by the silencing of what was once the freest press in Asia.

"I hope it is not the end," said one prominent editor, in his dim, sweltering office. "It is a very sad blow." The editor, once known for his outspokenness, asked not to be quoted by name.

Editor Arrested

As far as can be established, only one journalist has been arrested—K. R. Malkani, the editor of Motherland, the English-language organ of the rightist Jan Sangh party. Today there were reports that the editor's wife had filed a petition of habeus corpus with the Supreme Court to free him.

The censorship mechanism swung into action yesterday before noon following the declaration of a state of emergency.

A set of press "guidelines" was distributed, requiring editors to suppress any "plainly dangerous" news themselves. Though editors do not have to give the Government censor copies of stories in advance of publication, they have a clear picture of what is acceptable and what is not: the guidelines instruct editors to refer questionable material to the Government's chief press adviser. The guidelines contained such injunctions as:

No publication of rumors.

No reproduction of objectionable matter already published in any Indian or foreign newspaper.

No publication of anything likely to bring into hatred or contempt or to excite disaffection toward the Government.

Long-time Indian journalists recalled that in 1962, when India and China fought a brief war in the Himalayas, and in 1965 and 1971, when India and Pakistan went to war, the Government imposed certain press curbs to guard against the disclosure of military secrets.

While Mrs Gandhi has hinted that her opponents' "subversive" political activities might encourage India's foreign enemies, in the opinion of most dispassionate observers the country now faces no comparable threat.

Twice daily, the Indian and foreign press is briefed on the state of the nation by Dr. A. R. Baji, an amiable, donnish information official who gently parties with his questioners. Asked today about a series of rumors, particularly about arrests. Dr Baji said: "I'm just denying whatever the rumors are, are denied."

* * *

July 3, 1975

CENSORSHIP IN INDIA: GRIM EDITORS, LIFELESS PAPERS

By ERIC PACE

Special to The New York Times

NEW DELHI, July 2—An Indian newspaper executive with tired eyes gestured furtively toward the turbaned policeman guarding the entrance of The Motherland, an opposition newspaper that has been closed down.

"What shall we do now?" he murmured. "We are all under such a gloom."

Depression and despair have spread across the newspaper industry, once one of India's main democratic institutions, the first week of the Government's new censorship policy.

The censorship, the roughest in the 28 years of India's independence, is a principal ingredient of Prime Minister Indira Gandhi's far-reaching crackdown on her political opponents, which she says is to forestall threats to India's "security and stability."

Five Papers Silenced

Since censorship began, last Thursday, it has led to the silencing of five newspapers here in the capital area. It has persuaded editors to use Indian news agency dispatches because they are conveniently precensored. And it has had many other effects, ranging from a dearth of signed columns to an upsurge of articles on such noncontroversial subjects as fertilizer.

India now has more than 12,000 newspapers. Hindi is the language most widely used, in 3,300 papers. English is the second most prevalent, with 2,400 papers.

In recent years, many of the papers, notably influential English language ones here in the capital, were critical of Mrs. Gandhi and her Government, charging that it was authoritarian.

The Indian press, one of the freest in the world was subject to some Government pressures, but it was governed principally by the will of its editors.

Accordingly, the press expressed widely differing views. Last Wednesday, for instance, The National Herald in New Delhi, called for Mrs. Gandhi to remain in office, saying in an editorial, "Whatever the discomfort and inconvenience, she has to continue, not only for the sake of the country but for the sake of the rest of the world, to which she will remain the representative Indian."

That same day, The Motherland, published here by the right-wing Jan Sangh party, described Mrs. Gandhi at a rally this way: "The prima donna stood there on a makeshift dias, keeping the evening sun away by clutching an umbrella. She was the master of all she surveyed—the debris of the moral and political core of her regime."

That was the last full issue of The Motherland. A power failure, presumably arranged by the Government, prevented most papers from publishing the next morning, although The Motherland rushed out a broadsheet reporting the crackdown, which has also entailed hundreds of arrests.

Since then most newspapers in the capital have resumed publishing, but not the Motherland, which has been shut by the Government because it refused to abide by the censorship and press guidelines that the Government rushed out hours after the crackdown began, barring publication of rumors, reproduction of objectionable matter, and publication of anything likely to excite disaffection toward the Government.

Accordingly The Motherland's management put its 200 employees on half pay, hoping the situation would change. But police guards have been preventing more than a handful of employees from entering at any time.

The Organizer, a weekly published by the Jan Sangh, has also been closed down.

Another publication notable for its strong criticism of Mrs. Gandhi, the weekly Everyman, voluntarily suspended publication, journalists report, because it preferred not to meet the Government guidelines. Everyman was the organ of the opposition movement led by Jaya Prakash Narayan, a revered nationalist who has been arrested.

The editors of two other opposition newspapers in the capital area, Prajaniti, which is in Hindi, and Mulq-O-Milet, in Urdu, have suspended publication rather than submit to censorship and the guidelines.

Journalists critical of Mrs. Gandhi assert that the 50 other papers in the area are back because most of their owners are big businessmen who depend in one way or another on the Government's favor and do not wish to incur Mrs. Gandhi's wrath.

Circulation of the papers ranges from a few thousand to 450,000 for the powerful Indian Express. Some journalists are predicting, however that circulation will fall off now that the content of the big daily papers is largely the same.

Editors are using more of the dispatches provided by the two private Indian news agencies—the Press Trust of India, and United News of India—because censors sit in the office of those organizations, and approve dispatches before they appear. Otherwise, newspapers would have to send their articles to the Press and Information Bureau, where officials censor them firmly.

Many editors say they are not submitting their editorials to censorship. But they are observing the guidelines, and they are showing a marked preference for editorials on harmless subjects.

Gone are the barbed political cartoons that used to delight readers. And many respected Communists, and writers such as Dilip Mukerjee, political analyst for The Times of India, have stopped writing altogether.

By and large, the provincial press has been affected in the same way as the press in the capital. But a rounded picture of the national situation is not obtainable here because of censorship.

* * *

July, 28, 1975

MANY NATIONS TRY TO REGULATE NEWS GOING ABROAD

By MARTIN ARNOLD

India's sudden and dramatic effort to control reporting by foreign correspondents there is only one illustration of the ways many governments try to regulate the flow of news abroad.

Few countries have official censorship. In one that does, Israel, regulations call for dispatches to be approved officially before being transmitted abroad.

Actually, however, foreign reporters in Israel seldom submit their dispatches for censorship before transmission. The reporters generally have a loose and informal working relationship with the censors.

Many reporters there have Telex machines in their offices or homes and transmit directly on them. If a reporter feels, however, that some of the information he wants to send might affect military security, he will usually discuss it in advance with a censor.

In India last month, when the Government imposed a state of internal emergency, rigid censorship was ordered. Under it, the Indian press has been tightly muzzled. Publications in India have been printing only news approved by Government censors.

At first, foreign correspondents were told by Indian authorities to sign pledges of self-censorship, in which they would promise, under threat of expulsion from the country, to comply with the Government's censorship rules.

One such rule prohibited a correspondent from even telling his readers that a news dispatch had been censored.

After many foreign journalists refused to sign the pledge, it was modified considerably. Now the correspondent is asked to sign a statement only that he has received the Indian censorship rules and takes "full responsibility" for his news reports in regard to them.

Four Were Expelled

In the last month, before the official position was modified, India expelled two British and two American correspondents.

Even most totalitarian countries do not have official censorship. Instead, a reporter in those countries often must contend with other problems, such as various forms of harassment, which can make his work extremely difficult and sometimes induce him to censor himself.

Sometimes foreign correspondents, although not subject to censorship themselves, are hampered because of official restrictions on the local press, often a prime source of news tips and background information.

In many countries foreign reporters face possible expulsion if they report news that the government does not want reported. This can dampen their efforts.

Sometimes foreign journalists are denied entrance visas or are granted them for only a short time.

China, for example, does not have official censorship of foreign reporting, but she has not permitted any American newsmen to be stationed there. Occasionally the Peking Government grants visas for limited periods to American reporters and then carefully controls their travel in China and their access to Chinese citizens.

Foreign correspondents in the Soviet Union are not allowed to travel more than 25 miles from the Kremlin without special permission from the Foreign Ministry, which often is difficult to obtain. Nor are they allowed to interview officials or to seek interviews with ordinary citizens without special permission.

When a correspondent is stopped by Soviet security agents while he is talking with a citizen, the reporter is usually not hampered if he says that he does not plan to use the citizen's name. Under Soviet regulations, the conversation would not be considered an interview, and it would be acceptable to quote the citizen anonymously.

Sometimes, however, foreign reporters conduct attributable interviews when they are sought out by Soviet citizens, such as political dissidents.

Reporters who displease the Soviet authorities are often summoned to the Foreign Ministry for reprimands. Foreign reporters are sometimes denounced by name in the Soviet press.

Foreign newsmen who have worked in the Soviet-bloc countries of Eastern Europe report various forms of harassment, though no formal censorship.

Denials of visas are common. Reporters in those countries are also sometimes faced with sudden and unexplained losses of power on their telephones or Telex machines.

Albania Bars Americans

East Germany has a detailed decree defining and controlling the activities of foreign newsmen. Albania, a pro-Chinese Communist country not in the Soviet bloc, has for years barred American reporters.

There is no formal censorship of outgoing news from South Africa, but resident permits for foreign journalists are carefully controlled. In recent years, however, the Government has granted more visas for visits by reporters—even those representing publications whose editorials may be critical of the country's racial policies.

The Associated Press, America's largest news-gathering agency, said recently that news from its correspondents in Saigon, South Vietnam, as received in New York, showed no evidence that words or particular sentences or paragraphs were being deleted, but that sometimes entire pages of articles ordered by New York failed to reach here.

Only One American Left

Since then, however, all American correspondents of The Associated Press have left South Vietnam. United Press International is the only American agency that is still represented there by an American—Alan Dawson.

In May, a delegation representing 120 correspondents from 13 countries complained to the new Communist authorities in Saigon that they were having trouble gathering and transmitting news, photographs and television film. They also complained that they had been stopped from taking pictures on the streets and that reporters had difficulty in meeting with the press officers of the Communist Government.

Egypt, like most Arab countries, does not have official censorship. Reporters working there, however, often find it difficult to reach potential news sources.

* * *

January 18, 1976

INDIAN PRESS CONTROLS, DESIGNED TO HALT RUMORS, SEEM TO FOSTER MORE RUMORS

By WILLIAM BORDERS
Special to The New York Times

NEW DELHI, Jan. 15—A midnight telephone caller passes along news of a protest march, a rumor that turns out to be false.

A chance comment at a diplomatic reception, another rumor, leads to the disclosure that a former cabinet minister has in fact been arrested.

Rumors. In today's India, with all the regular information media now controlled by the Government, the rumor has become a conversational staple, especially in this gossipy capital city.

Prime Minister Indira Gandhi says that one of the reasons for the censorship that her Government imposed last June was to end the spread of "vicious rumors."

"The papers were printing all manner of falsehoods and hearsay," the Prime Minister has said repeatedly.

But some Indians think that rumors have an even more central role now than they had before the strict new political order was imposed.

There are rumors about the Government, several different plans are circulating that purport to describe how the Indian Constitution will soon be amended to give Prime Minister Gandhi greater power.

And there are rumors about the opposition—about demonstrations, protest strikes and underground meetings.

"Nobody knows anything; it's all rumor and hearsay," complained M. C. Chagla, a former cabinet minister and ambassador who is now in the opposition. Describing the case of a New Delhi man who was held for seven weeks under the emergency, Mr. Chagla said.

"Nobody knows that he was ever arrested, nobody knows that he was released, and nobody knows what judgment was delivered. If you want to read the judgment, you will have to go to the London Times."

But The Times of London, like Time Newsweek and the other foreign publications still circulating here, is likely to be blocked at the airport if it contains any unfavorable news about events in India.

Indians accustomed to follow public affairs closely now share the complaint of a Bombay housewife who asked sadly, "How are we supposed to have any idea what is really happening?"

A traveler will be questioned closely about what he has seen and heard in other parts of India; and even a government official will often begin a conversation with an outsider—a newspaper reporter, for example, or a diplomat—by seeking-verification of this rumor or that or simply asking, "What have you heard?"

With India's newspapers and government radio disseminating only approved news, a number of mimeographed news sheets have emerged, circulating covertly, with roundups that focus on opposition activities.

* * *

December 5, 1976

IN YEAR AND A HALF, INDIA'S PRESS MOVES FROM ACCEPTING CENSORSHIP TO ACTIVELY PROMOTING REGIME'S VIEWS

By WILLIAM BORDERS
Special to The New York Times

NEW DELHI, Dec. 4—Of the 30 issues that The Hindustan Times published during November, 21 had front-page pictures of Prime Minister Indira Gandhi, her son Sanjay, or both.

With the pictures, the newspaper, one of India's leading dailies, carried articles with such headlines as "Prime Minister: No one will be allowed to weaken nation," "Sanjay surveys flood damage in Madras" and "Prime Minister spends birthday among tribals."

The deferential and submissive tone of The Hindustan Times, which is typical of nearly all newspapers in India these days, reflects a change that has come gradually since the imposition of strict censorship in June 1975. One of New Delhi's dispirited editors described it this way: "Not only do we not print anything the Government wants to suppress, we've now gotten so that we will also print whatever they do want. It is an affirmative kind of censorship, which is even worse."

In the months after the censorship was imposed, first as part of what Mrs. Gandhi called a national emergency and subsequently as permanent law, many editors salved their badly wounded pride by boasting in private that even if prevented from attacking the Government, they would never be forced to support it in print. Those days, and that boast, are largely past.

In place of articles about the activities of opposition politicians, the papers now give almost exclusive display to the Government's point of view—to the often-repeated contention, for example, that the suspension of civil liberties must be continued because the threat of disruption of public order continues.

All the papers routinely describe as rousing or enthusiastic the public reception that Mrs. Gandhi and her son get on their travels around the country. Most of them print one government statement after another that the national economy is "poised for takeoff," with scarcely a mention of any negative economic indicators, such as recent increases in the cost of living.

A couple of months ago The Indian Express, the largest paper in the country, published an editorial sharply critical of S. S. Ray, Chief Minister of West Bengal, who has fallen into disfavor with some elements in the central Government. Although the editorial was signed "from a correspondent," it was reported to have originated in circles close to the Government.

In the Government's view, what has happened to the newspapers is that they have become more responsible during the 19 months of the new political order since they no longer devote their columns to the views of dissidents who, as the Prime Minister says repeatedly, "had no popular following."

Information Minister V. C. Shukla, asked recently about what used to be a conflict between government and press, replied: "Now there is full understanding between the two." Mr. Shukla, who is thought to be in Mrs. Gandhi's inner circle, also said that "our Government and our party are fully wedded to true freedom of the press" and described the state of press freedom as one of the best in the world.

A Bombay lawyer who describes himself as essentially apolitical has found in his own reaction to the transformation of the press, a lesson in its power. "I find that reading these statements month after month about how wonderful everything is, I begin to believe it," he explained. "And in the absence of articles about criticizing what is going on, I tend to forget that the opposition exists at all.

* * *

May 11, 1977

INDIA'S PRESS GAINS VERVE, BUT THERE ARE SOME QUALMS

By WILLIAM BORDERS
Special to The New York Times

NEW DELHI, May 10—West Bengal is in the grip of a severe drought, Indian newspaper readers learned the other day, and there was a violent transit strike in Madras.

Both of these were routine news reports, to be sure. But under the good-news-only rules of press censorship here during the country's 19-month emergency period, neither would have been allowed, and their publication now is, as much as the strident new columns of political commentary, a reflection of how dramatically the newspapers have changed.

Of all the institutions affected by Indira Gandhi's abrupt turn to authoritarianism two years ago, none was altered more radically than the press, which generally became slavishly pro-Government. Now, as the new Government under Prime Minister Morarji R. Desai sets about rebuilding those institutions, the newspapers have once again undergone a radical transformation, and some of the leading figures hope that the result will be an even stronger and more valuable press than India used to have.

High Priority for Press Freedom

"Having gone through all that hell and fire, perhaps the institution of the press has been burnished and forged to a new strength, imbued with a greater sense of responsibility," said one of the country's best-known political columnists, musing, as many Indian journalists are these days, on what Mrs. Gandhi's Government did to them, and what will happen to them under the new one.

Prime Minister Desai has attached the highest priority to restoring press freedom in India, and as that freedom has returned during his first two months in office, there have been these other developments on India's journalistic scene:

- The Government not only has removed all censorship but also has moved to reduce its own indirect influence on the press, promising, for example, not to base its newspaper advertising on political considerations, as Mrs. Gandhi's Government did, or to use the Information Ministry for personal propaganda.
- Newspapers are now trying to outdo one another with articles deploring the excesses of Mrs. Gandhi's Government, especially with articles criticizing the activities and business dealings of her 30-year-old son, Sanjay, whom they used to mention only in tones of the greatest praise.
- A mood of bitter recrimination has developed in some quarters, with antipathy between journalists who feel that they behaved courageously during the emergency period and others accused of having yielded cravenly at the first sign of Government pressure.

"Let no one be fooled by the brave words now pouring forth from the pens of editors and columnists," declared K. R. Sundar Rajan, a Bombay journalist whom the Gandhi Government jailed because of the hostility of his columns. "Many of them did not even observe the virtue of silence," he said. "They gleefully jumped on the emergency bandwagon, boosting Mrs. Gandhi as infallible, projecting Sanjay Gandhi as 'the man who gets things done.'"

L. K. Advani, the new Information Minister, who was himself in jail as a political prisoner until the day last January when Mrs. Gandhi called the general election, chided the journalists this way: "When you were merely asked to bend, you chose to crawl."

In the first five days of the new Parliament, Mr. Advani steered into law a bill repealing the censorship imposed by the old Government, and he also issued a number of executive decrees to back up what he called "a policy of not discriminating against anyone on political grounds."

For example, less than two weeks after taking office, Mr. Advani formally canceled a ban on Government advertising in newspapers whose reporting the old Government had considered hostile. His predecessor, V. C. Shukla, had drawn up a list of nearly 100 "unfriendly" publications and circulated it among the officials who place advertising.

Since some publicly held corporations do a good deal of consumer advertising the ban had a crippling effect on some newspapers during the closing months of Mrs. Gandhi's Government.

Mr. Advani has also restored a rule prohibiting personal attacks on political leaders over the government radio network. He said this had been canceled by Mr. Shukla during the emergency so that the radio could be used regularly for attacks on leaders of the opposition.

A Symbol of Authoritarianism

Mr. Shukla, whom Mrs. Gandhi named as Information Minister two days after she declared the emergency in June 1975, became, as much as anyone, a symbol of authoritarianism. Supporters of the new Government castigate him bitterly, and even the defeated Congress Party formally rebuked him a few days ago for "misuse of power" when he headed the Information Ministry.

It was Mr. Shukla who subjected the newspapers to what many of their editors regard as the gravest indignities, and now that the press is on top again, he is the target of some of its most vindictive articles, including speculation about charges of Shukla family corruption in the state of Madhya Pradesh.

Similarly, Sanjay Gandhi, who often became personally involved in the subjugation of the newspapers, appointing his own men to take over the newsrooms, is now vilified constantly in their columns. The papers are full of such headlines as "How Government Officials Had to Kowtow to Sanjay" and "Sanjay Trips Financed From Public Coffers."

During the emergency period, Prime Minister Gandhi and her leading advisers were candid about how heavily the success of the new order depended upon vigorous news censorship. "When there are no papers, there is no agitation," Mrs. Gandhi told Parliament shortly after clamping down on the press. "That is why we imposed censorship. We found how right we were. Newspapers were spreading rumors, allegations and inciting people into agitations."

Now that the newspapers are free again, a number of Indian journalists are privately expressing deep concern at the way they were subjected to control and pointing out that censorship came to an end only because Mrs. Gandhi voluntarily lifted it, as she voluntarily took the country to the polls.

There is exultation in the newsrooms and press clubs around India these days, and pride that this country once again has a press as independent as any in the world. But there is also an overlay of guilt, and concern centering on the question whether or not it could all happen again.

Sundar Rajan, who was an editor at The Times of India, expressed it this way: "The challenge before journalists today is to salvage their credibility. The man in the street knows that we were among the first to betray the cause of freedom."

* * *

October 7, 1977

BURMESE THEATER: OUTLET FOR DISSENT

But Popular Troupes Must Tread Lightly, Expressing Criticism in Ambiguous References

By HENRY KAMM
Special To The New York Times

NYAUNGU, Burma—All public expression in Burma is censored, and the press is uniform in its praise of President Ne Win's 15-year-old "Burmese way to socialism." But recently, press censorship has tightened to the point of not only prescribing to editors what they must not print but also what they must print. The range of optional items has become narrower than ever.

Rangoon's three newspaper editors, their deputies and their chief editorial writers must now meet daily and read for each other's benefit the editorials that each has prepared for the following morning. Together with Information Ministry officials, they subject them to criticism and agree on a mutually suitable wording. Earlier this month orders were issued for journalists not to meet with visiting foreign colleagues.

But in a country of limited literacy and no television, the popular theater takes an important place in cultural life, and Burma's popular troupes continue to enjoy a jester's freedom that dates to precolonial days. It flourished in the days of British colonialism because the ruler did not understand the language of the ruled.

"It's like walking on a roof," said Kyay Mhon, principal comic of a traveling troupe called People's Storm. "If you step carelessly, you fall off."

Stepping carefully, the 29-year-old actor-dancer explained, meant keeping remarks ambiguous enough so that when the police call on him after a performance he can offer a plausible explanation of his material that differs from the obvious political point that was made and understood.

The actor and some of his colleagues in the 74-member company said that criticism about the painful inefficiencies of Burma's almost totally nationalized economy and the flourishing black market was allowed. No criticism of socialism or even implicit criticism of General Ne Win is allowable.

In fact, an author explained that in a comic historical sketch that he wrote about a Burmese king who enjoyed absolute power and a reputation for womanizing he could not fully expend his wit on those two qualities because, whether he intended it or not, audiences would read into it a caricature of Burma's present ruler.

The comedians evoked the strongest audience participation during the show in this small town in central Burma. The show began around 8 P.M. and ended at 5:30 the following morning, as is the custom. The comic interludes, which sometimes got mixed with the dancing and serious drama, were impromptu and topical and featured many pratfalls and much swordplay. Kyay Mhon showed his cut and scarred hands to prove that the swords were real.

Typical Routine

The actor performed throughout the night, as stars are expected to do. In addition to the frequent comic routines, he played in a comic historical sketch, a modern play of romantic love, danced in classical Ramayana tales, played a king in a historical drama and a prince in a drama about one of the incarnations of Buddha. The program was typical of the work the People's Storm and perhaps 100 similar troupes are expected to offer.

The People's Storm played three nights in a large, dirt-floor hall, always before packed houses. About half the audience seemed to consist of children. It is assumed that most people from Nyaungu and the surrounding villages saw all three performances. Two more shows had been scheduled but had to be canceled because the Government pre-empted the hall for a political meeting.

The spectators paid the equivalent of 70 cents for a rattan mat seating a family of five. The local elite sat on chairs—for 29 cents each.

The actors' pay is correspondingly low. Kyay Mhon, as top banana, earns about $8 a night. Above him is the author and star of the modern play and other pieces in the repertory, who earns $14.

The star dancer of the People's Storm earns $20. But the dancer, 29-year-old Tin Tin Myint, defended herself against possible accusations of excessive earnings, explaining that she had to supply her own costumes and props, as do all stars, and that her pay was the principal income for 13 persons, including her 5 children, her parents and various other relatives.

Minor actors, dancers, musicians and stagehands earn about 70 cents a night. The People's Storm performs 20 to 25 nights a month while on tour, which it is for about half the year. The rest of the time it plays in and around Rangoon.

On the road, the 74 members live communally, sleeping either in the three trucks that they hire to transport them or in the hall in which they play. They eat in a communal mess. The author writes out the plays and sketches in longhand and each actor then copies out his part.

The low pay forces some of the players to earn a little money on the side during their free afternoons. A leading actor, for instance, blows up dozens of oddly shaped balloons when he rises, hangs them on a huge rack and sells them to children in front of the theater.

"It is a hard life," said Tin Tin Myint, "but once I stand on the stage I forget that."

* * *

July 20, 1982

SINGAPORE, CITING UNITY, AGAIN REINS IN THE PRESS

By COLIN CAMPBELL

Special to the New York Times

SINGAPORE—For the second time in 11 years, the Government of Prime Minister Lee Kuan Yew has sought to advance its campaign for a national consensus by cracking down on the press.

Since January, the Government has harshly criticized several editors and persuaded them to stop news coverage of the tiny political opposition, which has had one member in Parliament since last October.

The Government has also named a former director of national intelligence to oversee a leading English-language daily in Singapore, The Straits Times, and has ordered the Straits Times Group to give up its afternoon paper, The New Nation, for a nominal fee and turn it over to a company that had planned for two years to start a rival morning paper.

Little Public Dissent

These developments have met with almost no public protest. The Government is said to be acting under the authority of the Newspaper and Printing Presses Act of 1964, which gives it the power to license newspaper editors and directors and lets it distribute managing shares in newspaper companies to people approved by the Minister of Culture.

In other recent newspaper-related actions, the Government has arranged a merger of two rival Chinese-language dailies, placed The New Nation under this new managerial umbrella and appointed senior Government officials to the management of the new company.

The Government has also begun articulating some long-cherished concepts about the role of the press in this city-state. Suppiah Dhanabalan, Minister for Foreign Affairs and Culture, said in an interview published May 18 in The Straits Times:

"A servile press does not serve the purpose that the press should serve in society. But it doesn't mean, therefore, that the press should feel that it has to adopt an anti-establishment attitude, that only then it is credible, which is the problem with many in the Western liberal press."

The minister said also that "the national interest is paramount" and added, "Once the Government officers have the confidence that you share the framework, then there can be a lot of give and take within the framework."

A Crackdown in 1971

The Government crackdown has been less severe than in 1971, when Prime Minister Lee was widely criticized in the West for closing down three newspapers and arresting several journalists.

He halted publication of Nanyang Siang Pau, a Chinese daily, asserting that it was spreading what he described as

Chinese ethnic chauvinism. Four executives of the paper were detained.

And he closed two English-language newspapers—Eastern Star, saying that it was backed by Communists in Hong Kong, and The Singapore Herald, charging that it had subverted Singapore's will by opposing national military service, the Internal Security Act and the Government's strict rules on public behavior.

There have been no public charges this year that the country's newspapers have been subversive. Instead, statements from the Prime Minister's office, Mr. Dhanabalan and other officials have accused the press of inaccurate coverage and of being staffed with untrained reporters.

The statements have also said that there is a need to avoid relying on foreign editors at English-language papers. The Government says that it wants to upgrade the quality of journalism, especially in the growing English-language market, and to insure that Chinese journalists do not lose their jobs as the study of Chinese continues to decline.

Warnings of Factionalism

In striving for a national consensus, Prime Minister Lee has warned that his generation of experienced leaders will soon be gone and that factionalism—political, linguistic, religious and economic—could tear Singapore apart. He has stressed the dangers of Communism and the Vietnamese.

In addition, the Prime Minister has expressed growing concern that Singapore might be lured to its destruction by calls for a relaxation of social discipline, more welfare programs than the country can afford, a less carefully administered and more political public life and a press that is less attuned to the country's elected Government.

The editor of the Straits Times Group, Peter Lim, said in a recent interview that he thought he understood why the Government had intervened in press affairs. He said that his group's English language newspapers had expanded too fast, hiring too many journalists who could be described as amateurs. He said he thought some Government charges of inaccurate reporting were justified.

He also said, however, that he had decided, after becoming chief editor in 1978, to pay more attention to Mr. Lee's critics. He himself, Mr. Lim said, supported the governing People's Action Party.

Last fall, The Straits Times, which has a daily circulation of 225,000 and slightly more on Sundays, devoted considerable space to Joshua Benjamin Jeyaretnam, the candidate of the Workers' Party, and his successful campaign for Parliament in the October elections. He was the first opposition politician to win a seat in 16 years, and Mr. Lim said the Government held the press partly responsible for this development.

Apparently supporting that assessment was a statement made in February by the Second Deputy Prime Minister, Sinnathamby Rajaratnam, who said that "the role of an opposition is to insure bad government."

'The Letters Column'

Mr. Lim said that even after the arrival in mid-February of his Government supervisor, S.R. Nathan, who is regarded by foreign diplomats as a capable administrator, there was still room for discussion—"if only in the letters column," he added, smiling.

Before the crackdown on the press, the Government had been perceived by many here to be giving Singapore's newspapers greater leeway.

The impression had grown that the governing party and the Prime Minister, 58 years old, who has been in office since 1959, were sufficiently popular, entrenched and accomplished that they had no rational grounds to fear freer examination. The Government had also recently allowed the Straits Times Group to hire more English speaking expatriates as editors. But these impressions are now being re-examined.

On May 21, 24 journalists and 2 other employees were dismissed by The Straits Times management. Although the criteria for the layoffs were not clear, some such move had been expected since Mr. Nathan's arrival.

The editorial future of Singapore's two major Chinese papers is obscure. The papers have announced that they will continue to publish separate editions despite the corporate and managerial merger. These would be the conservative, and now pro-Government, Nanyang Siang Pau and Sin Chew Jit Poh. The Prime Minister's office has hinted, however, that the two papers will become one.

As for The Straits Times, whose owners reported record pretax profits of $14 million for the last half of 1981 largely from English-language publications, the Government has announced that the company will be allowed to start a Chinese newspaper. It has also been told that it will have a morning monopoly, in English, for three years.

To date, Singapore's newspapers appear to have changed little since last fall, with the notable exception that coverage of opposition politicians has disappeared.

* * *

August 19, 1982

NEW PRESS LAW STIRS CONCERN IN INDIA

By WILLIAM K. STEVENS

Special to the New York Times

NEW DELHI, Aug. 18—In what is viewed by its opponents as a serious threat to India's free press, the government of Bihar, the nation's second most populous state, has passed a law making it a criminal offense to publish, sell or possess any printed matter whose content is "grossly indecent" or "scurrilous."

Government officials, contending that it is within their right under the Indian Constitution to place "reasonable restrictions" on free expression, say that the law is intended to curb the irresponsibility of "yellow" journalists. These journalists, it is charged, engage in character assassination, foster social discord through untruth and damage the morale of government officials.

But opponents of the measure, including members of the press and opposition politicians, say that the government of Bihar, whose leaders belong to the Congress Party of Prime Minister Indira Gandhi, is merely trying to protect itself against exposure of corruption and mismanagement.

Suspension of Rights Recalled

The opponents say further that the law is a Draconian measure reminiscent of the suspension of constitutional rights that took place here under Mrs. Gandhi from 1975 to 1977, particularly since it would apparently allow minor governmental administrators, agents of the executive branch, to act as judges. Conviction on a first offense would carry a prison term of up to two years; on a second offense, of six months to five years.

The issue is now in the lap of the central Government, where its prospects are considered uncertain. Before the law can go into effect, it must be approved by President Zail Singh. Mr. Singh is expected to take no action counter to the advice of the Cabinet, and particularly of Mrs. Gandhi.

The decision, when it comes, will almost surely be interpreted as a sign of the Gandhi Government's present-day attitude toward press freedom and press responsibility. It will come at a time when criticism of her party's stewardship at the state and local level is widespread. The next national elections are scheduled in 1985.

Pressure against what has become known as the Bihar press bill has been intensifying since it was approved on July 31, with the national press solidly in opposition and with demonstrations taking place in a number of cities. In Bihar itself, journalists vowed Tuesday that they would print nothing about government activities there and they turned in their accreditation cards en masse.

Similar Laws in 2 Other States

Although the Bihar legislation will apply to only one state if approved, opponents point out that two other states, Tamil Nadu and Orissa, enacted virtually identical laws in 1960 and 1962, respectively. Both are now in force, and not long ago two journalists were arrested in Madras under the Tamil Nadu law. Opponents of the Bihar bill fear that Indian press freedom will be eroded piecemeal through such state laws.

The laws, said The Times of India, "are indicative of an alarming trend toward greater executive abridgement of press freedom through creeping legislation, first in one part of the country, then another, until the press is muzzled everywhere."

The issue arises at a time when there have been reports of physical intimidation of journalists in several parts of the country, and when the press as a whole has grown more aggressive in publishing reports alleging official misconduct.

Dr. Jagannath Mishra, the Chief Minister of Bihar, who sponsored the press bill, maintained in arguing for it that while he supported a free press as necessary and vital to a democracy, it must be controlled if one section of it acts irresponsibly. Citing instances of "character assassination" in the press that would damage the Government's credibility, he said that he expected commitment to national goals and aspirations from journalists.

Government Still Undecided

Contending that freedom of expression is not absolute under the Indian Constitution, Ramaswamy Venkataraman, the Minister of Home Affairs, said in Parliament that "wherever the necessity arises," such freedom "will have to be regulated." He said, however, that the Government had not yet determined whether the Bihar bill was necessary or valid.

For most of India's 35 years of independence, except for the two years when Mrs. Gandhi clamped a variety of authoritarian controls on the national life, the country's press has been considered generally free and unfettered. The tradition of a free press goes back to the days of British India, when newspapers were frequently critical of the colonial administration.

The press today displays little timidity, as the forceful editorial outcry against the Bihar bill has demonstrated. Some segments of the press in recent years have aggressively tried to uncover corruption that some critics say has become endemic to Indian Government. One crusader, Arun Shourie, editor of The Express, won a highly prized Ramon Magsaysay Award for service to Asia this month.

Defenders of press freedom do not deny that some journals and journalists act irresponsibly, and Dr. Mishra exempted much of the press from his category of "yellow journalism," remarking that "a large section of the press in the state is sober and responsible."

India has libel laws, but progress in libel suits can reportedly take 12 to 15 years. "It is rarely that a person files a defamation case against a newspaper and pursues it to the end," Dr. Mishra said.

Debate on Bill Was Uproarious

The Bihar bill was passed, during an uproarious shouting match, as the last item of business before the Bihar legislature adjourned its summer session. It prohibits the publication, sale, possession and advertising of any printed or written document that is "grossly indecent, or is scurrilous or intended for blackmail."

The bill defines "scurrilous" as including "any matter which is likely to be injurious to morality or is calculated to injure any person." It says, however, that "it is not scurrilous to express in good faith anything whatsoever" respecting the conduct of a public official in the discharge of his public function, or his character as it bears on his public conduct. It similarly accepts good-faith comment on "any person touching any public question."

Under the terms of the bill, a person can be charged with an offense, with the approval of the state government, by "any magistrate."

* * *

January 2, 1983

TURNING UP THE PRESSURE ON INDIA'S FREE PRESS

By WILLIAM K. STEVENS

NEW DELHI—A serious browser picking up a book in an Indian book shop may be taken aback to discover that passages have been deleted. In Bombay, a volume of essays and pictures about that city bears ink smears blurring what someone considered an unflattering portrayal of an ethnic group. In New Delhi, whole paragraphs about the politically sensitive state of Kashmir in a popular travel guide have been blacked out.

The censoring, whether official or not, says something about the climate of expression in India—along with the newspapers, magazines and books of great variety, also on display, that have not been tampered with. Free and open publication is the rule and except during the 1975-77 emergency, when Prime Minister Indira Gandhi's Government suspended civil liberties, the country has enjoyed a free and vigorous press.

But the People's Union for Civil Liberties warned earlier this year against ignoring "the fact that the traditions of democratic polity and essential freedoms have not had very long innings in India" and that "intolerance of inconvenient speech or writing therefore comes easily to many people." Thus, it is perhaps not surprising that when an Indian politician feels put upon by the newspapers, he may try to silence them. That happened in Bombay in 1981, when the Chief Minister of Maharashtra state, Abdul Rahman Antulay, was stung by a corruption expose in The Indian Express. For a time, the paper closed its Bombay edition, blaming political pressure and related labor troubles. But The Express survived in Bombay and Mr. Antulay was eventually dismissed.

Then last year, in the eastern state of Bihar, another Chief Minister, Jagannath Mishra, responded to repeated charges of corruption by newspapers by proposing legislation that would have put editors, publishers, advertisers and even newspaper vendors in jail, without bail, on the say-so of a policeman. A bitter struggle over press freedom ensued in this often-turbulent society, which still remembers Mrs. Gandhi's heavy hand during the emergency. The issue acquired even more urgency because the printed word is almost the sole bulwark of free public expression. Television, radio and movies are Government-controlled or censored.

Dr. Mishra rushed a bill through his legislature that would make it a criminal offense to publish, sell or possess printed matter that is "grossly indecent" or "scurrilous." Offenders could be arrested without a warrant, held without bail and tried by an executive magistrate, an agent of the state executive. Upon conviction, they could be imprisoned for up to two years, five for a second offense. Dr. Mishra contended the bill was necessary to curb "yellow" journalists and "character assassination." Opponents said he was trying to suppress corruption charges. Its critics said the bill in Bihar could set a precedent that in time would hobble the entire national press. During five months of strikes and sometimes violent demonstrations, central Government officials and journalists have negotiated over the Bihar situation while millions of words kept the issue before the public. The very fact of this unfettered and spirited debate is considered by some to be a measure of the basic state of press liberty.

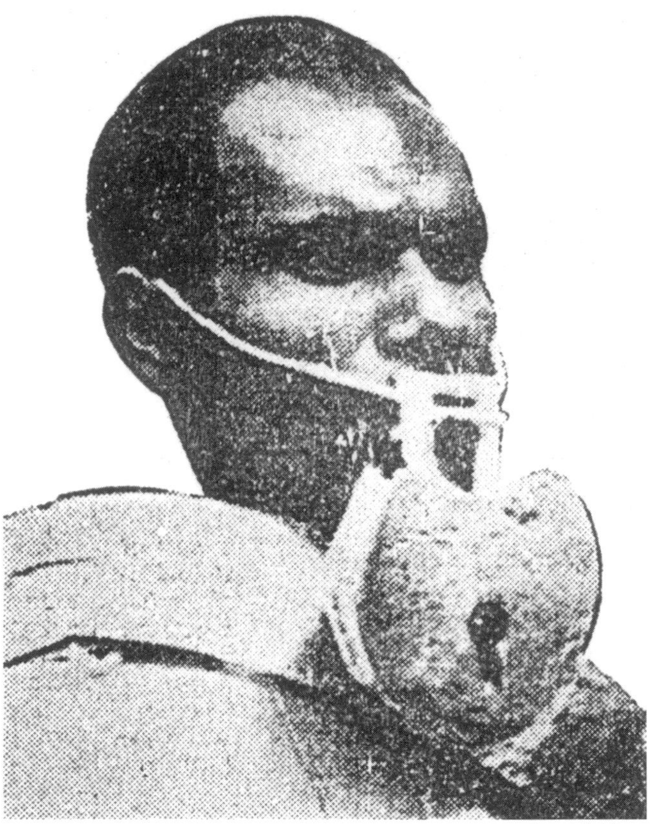

Associated Press

Journalist protesting Bihar state's proposed press law.

The depth, breadth and persistence of the protest, which reportedly startled the Government, is being interpreted as a sign of democratic health.

Last month, the central Government, which must assent to the bill before it can become law, returned it for reconsideration. New Delhi recommended amendments to define "scurrilous;" to limit coverage to printers, publishers, writers and editors; to grant bail to offenders; to require an independent judicial magistrate's warrant for arrest, and to require trial before such a magistrate. Some opponents say this would omit the bill's most objectionable features. Others point out that essential features would remain. The generally pro-Gandhi Times of India called the changes "cosmetic" and urged the state to forget the bill. But Dr. Mishra said that he would seek to have it amended and passed.

Mrs. Gandhi's role is unclear. Like many heads of democratic states, she has displayed no particular affection for the press. It is widely assumed that she called the tune in deciding the official stance on the bill, but an official close to the decision point insisted she was not directly involved.

In the end, the question is likely to be settled in court. The Supreme Court of India is reviewing a similar law from the southern state of Tamil Nadu. If it kills that law, the Bihar bill would likely die as well. India's courts have a tradition of independence. But the Constitution, unlike America's, does not prohibit legislative interference with the press. Rather, the right of free expression is qualified by "reasonable restrictions" in the interest of "the security of the state, friendly relations with foreign states, public order, decency or morality, or in relation to contempt of court, defamation or incitement to an offense." This provision has been invoked as authority for the Bihar bill.

There have been calls for a constitutional amendment guaranteeing absolute freedom for the media, but no groundswell of support is apparent. A move is afoot to create a national code of conduct, promulgated by a national press council composed mostly of journalists but also of members of Parliament. This has found favor among some journalists as a means of curbing excesses. But A.S. Abraham, senior assistant editor of the Times of India, insists that "Press freedom defined is press freedom abridged, and press freedom abridged is well on the way to press freedom being denied."

* * *

May 3, 1984

INDONESIA, UNDER SUHARTO, ALLOWS FEW DISSENTING VOICES TO BE HEARD

By ROBERT TRUMBULL

JAKARTA, Indonesia—A sales clerk chatting with a customer complained about Indonesia's press censorship and other authoritarian measures of the Government of President Suharto, who has ruled for 17 years.

Later she followed the departing customer to the sidewalk and asked that she not be quoted by name. "I could lose my job," she said.

"People don't dare to speak out," said a lawyer, who also requested anonymity.

Such reticence on the part of most Indonesians encountered by a foreign visitor is in contrast with the relative freedom of expression in the nearby Philippines, where opposition to the similar governing style of President Ferdinand E. Marcos is openly fierce these days.

The lawyer said he did not think "there is any opposition here." He said that the Government controlled the bureaucracy and labor unions and that the once-feisty students had been tamed by the threat of expulsion for participation in anti-Government activity.

Outspokenness Can Be Costly

The price of speaking out can be high. Several years ago 50 retired senior military officers sent President Suharto a joint letter suggesting that the time had come to liberalize Indonesia's tightly controlled political system. The letter was ignored, one signer said, but members of the group, now disbanded, who had gone into business found that banks would no longer extend credit to their companies.

A United States State Department report on human rights in Indonesia, submitted to Congress last February under a law requiring such information on countries receiving American aid, quoted accounts of official harassment of critics of the Government ranging from cutting off telephone and electricity service to pressure put on companies through refusal to accept their bids on Government contracts.

Politically aware Indonesians chafe at the shadowy role allowed the electorate in choosing the 360-member Parliament, which is dominated overwhelmingly by Mr. Suharto's Golkar Party. One hundred members are appointed by the President. Critics charge that the candidates of the two small opposition parties are also picked by the Government.

Like President Marcos of the Philippines, Mr. Suharto, a former general, uses the armed forces for law enforcement and places military officers in key administrative posts of the Government.

Leeway Given to a Few

A few distinguished Indonesians like Adam Malik, the longtime diplomat and former Vice President, are allowed to air critical views without fear of official reprisal. Harsh measures taken against them would attract international attention and could be expected to diminish the Government's reputation in the dozen or so Western countries, including the United States, that contribute to an annual economic aid pool that now stands at $2.2 billion. The sometimes biting comments by Dr. Malik and others in interviews and articles published abroad are never permitted to reach the eyes of ordinary Indonesians. The censors, who carefully scan all incoming foreign publications before they reach newsstands or subscribers, blot out offending material with a thick layer of gummy black ink, affixing a flap of paper over the damp blotch to prevent it from blemishing the inoffensive print on the facing page.

Outgoing dispatches by foreign correspondents are not censored, but correspondents whose reporting displeases the Government may find that their visas will not be renewed.

Editors Get Guidance

One outspoken Indonesian who is allowed latitude for his comments was told by a friendly editor of a telephone call from the Information Ministry directing that nothing the critic said should be published. An editor said he had a list of people whose statements were banned.

Editors are also told when the Government does not want a news development reported. Such an event occurred in April when troops forcibly evacuated 54 retired military officers, some of them veterans of the war of independence against the Dutch, and their families from a housing project marked for commercial development.

The old soldiers protested that the compensation offered by the Government, a fraction of what their property was worth, was insufficient for the purchase of new homes elsewhere. Troops then drove them out, but some veterans defiantly set up a tent camp. This took place across a busy street from one of Jakarta's main hotels and was witnessed by thousands of tourists and residents, but not a word about it appeared in the newspapers.

Press Gives False Impression

A tourist might get the impression that Indonesia has a lively, unfettered press, judging by the accounts of official corruption that regularly appear on the front pages. Well-informed journalists say these stories concern petty graft the Government wants routed out, while the big offenders are never mentioned.

Editors say they know from experience how far they can go without incurring official anger. One editor said that ignoring an order by the Information Ministry might bring only a warning the first time, but that a second offense could result in suspension or closing of the newspaper. The result of the strictures, he said, is self-censorship to the point of overcautiousness.

* * *

May 20, 1984

PAKISTAN TIGHTENS CURBS ON DISSENT

By WILLIAM K. STEVENS

LAHORE, Pakistan, May 16—Pakistan's military Government appears to be clamping the lid ever more tightly on dissent and free expression in an attempt to prepare the ground and set the terms for the elections that President Mohammed Zia ul-Haq has promised to hold by next spring.

Last week the Zia Government, which has been in power for nearly seven years, forbade the nation's press, on pain of being closed and of imprisonment, to publish any information about the country's political parties, most of which oppose General Zia.

Two weeks earlier the Government made it a crime for members of the Ahmadi religious sect to preach or propagate their religion. The action was seen as a concession by the authorities to demands by the Moslem clergy, whose support is vital to General Zia. The Ahmadis are considered heretics by the Moslem mullahs.

And a few weeks before that, the Government banned all student organizations. Diplomats and politicians saw this as an attempt to put in its place the youth wing of the Jamiat-I-Islami Party, a group that has provided pro-Zia shock troops for street demonstrations in the past but that is now seen as having grown too strong for the regime's comfort.

Elections Called a Facade

Opposition politicians say they are sure that the promised elections, which may come as early as October, will provide nothing more than a facade for continued rule by the army rather than a real return to democratic government and a restoration of human rights.

The election plan presented by General Zia "does not merit any consideration as it is only a prescription for the perpetuation of military rule," the leadership of the opposition Movement for the Restoration of Democracy said in a statement here last week.

The movement, which led an unsuccessful revolt against the Government in the province of Sind last year, is an alliance of banned political parties. Its membership has recently increased from eight to 11 parties.

The Lahore meeting of the Movement for the Restoration of Democracy took place during a temporary relaxation of restrictions on political activity and press freedom. This included the release from jail of several leaders of the movement who were imprisoned during the 1983 rebellion.

Press Must Heed 'Advices'

But after the meeting, the Government imposed its new ban on the press, which was already required to conform to "advices" given it daily by the Government on what to print, and how prominently.

Under General Zia's announced plan, elections are to take place on a nonparty basis. Candidates and voters are to be screened. The Constitution is to be amended to incorporate certain Islamic principles and to provide for direct election of the President, who ultimately would be able to dismiss Parliament and the Prime Minister.

General Zia has consistently denied he is seeking to become the first President under the new arrangement. But it is widely believed that the election machinery will produce a solidly pro-Zia Parliament that will draft him by acclamation.

Some diplomats and politicians speculate that if this happens, General Zia might serve one term and use that period to try to bring about a gradual transformation to real democracy.

Many Dubious About Elections

Many Pakistanis doubt General Zia will allow voting to take place at all. "He has no intention of holding any election," said a well-to-do Punjabi landowner. "Only another coup will get him out."

General Zia deposed Prime Minister Zulfikar Ali Bhutto in a bloodless coup in 1977. Mr. Bhutto was later executed.

There were, in fact, reports of a coup plot against General Zia two months ago. Both the Cabinet and the army high command were shaken up, with apparently unassailable Zia loyalists placed in top positions.

A major question being asked among those who follow Pakistani affairs is how long the military Government can keep the lid on dissent and control people's behavior. Political expression, human rights and behavior considered un-Islamic, such as the drinking of alcoholic beverages, have been controlled, suspended or suppressed for most of a decade. The question is how long it may take for pressures to build to the point of a possible explosion.

Six Good Harvests in a Row

Most whose business it is to gauge such things believe that the Zia regime will survive in the short term. It is commonly pointed out that he has been lucky in that there have been six good monsoon seasons and therefore six good harvests in a row. Nearly two million Pakistanis are sending millions of rupees back home every year from jobs in the Persian Gulf region. These two factors are considered chiefly responsible for having enabled President Zia to maintain a robust economy during his entire tenure.

But beneath the lid, much is simmering. The banned student groups, for example, almost routinely kidnap policemen and minor public officials. Two of General Zia's predecessors, Field Marshal Mohammad Ayub Khan and Mr. Bhutto, were brought down in large measure by student unrest.

In the meantime, the Zia Government continues to contend, in effect, that it is necessary to deny democratic government and human rights in order to save them in the long run.

"The Government wants a peaceful atmosphere so it can carry out its program," a Government spokesman said in explaining the imposition of the press ban last week. "There was excessive reporting likely to create political confusion," he said. "Excessive reporting can lead to political confrontation."

* * *

May 30, 1984

NEW TIMES ON TAIWAN AS OLD GUARD EASES GRIP

By STEVE LOHR

TAIPEI, Taiwan—A foreign diplomat who was first posted to Taiwan a decade ago recently remarked on the changes he noticed when he returned last year. He was struck most of all, he said, by the easing of censorship, especially of opposition magazines, which now regularly carry spirited criticism of the ruling Kuomintang, or Nationalist Party, and its leaders.

"Years ago, those magazines would never have seen the light of day," the diplomat said. "And once the Government security forces got hold of them, the people who wrote and published these articles wouldn't be seeing much daylight either."

The jailing has stopped in recent years, though some censorship remains. Antonio Chiang, editor of The Eighties, a leading opposition journal, noted that his magazine had been banned by the Government 20 times for varying periods in the last three years.

But even Mr. Chiang says, "There is increasing freedom of the press in Taiwan, and political repression is greatly reduced."

Taiwan, whose strong economic growth has made it a model for some developing countries, appears to be undergoing a process of political modernization as well, diplomats and others here say. In recent months there have been indications that the pace of Taiwan's political evolution, which has lagged behind its economic development, is quickening.

One of Asia's 'New Japans'

The loosening of political reins and economic modernization are viewed here as interrelated. Taiwan's rapid economic ascent has given it a per-capita income of roughly $3,000 and the distinction of being labeled one of East Asia's "new Japans," along with Singapore, Hong Kong and South Korea. Taiwan is now straining to move into the ranks of the industrialized nations, moving out of cheap-labor industries and into fields such as computers and semiconductors.

The growth has expanded the ranks of the middle class, whose sphere of interest goes well beyond the acquisition of daily necessities. More and more people own cars and houses and travel abroad.

Accordingly, Taiwan's economic achievements are creating a more pluralistic society, people here say, and the political arena has to adjust to changing circumstances. "The economic progress leads to political progress and modernization," said Chin Sheng-pao, an associate professor at National Chengchi University.

More native Taiwanese, who make up 85 percent of the island's 18.5 million people, are being brought into positions of responsibility in the Government—a process known as Taiwanization—and democratic freedoms are gradually but steadily increasing. But the top echelons of the Kuomintang are still dominated by former mainlanders who, led by Chiang Kai-shek, went to Taiwan in 1949 and forcibly took over the island after the Communists took control of China.

A 'Real Taiwanese' Official

In February, President Chiang Ching-kuo named Lee Teng-hui, a native Taiwanese, as his Vice President for the six-year term that began May 20. He is considered to be the first "real Taiwanese" to attain such a high office.

"Lee is a symbol of Taiwanization," an opposition politician said.

The selection of Mr. Lee, which surprised many political experts here, takes on added significance because Mr. Chiang, the son of Chiang Kai-shek, is 74 years old and his health is failing. He has diabetes, has had two eye operations in the last three years and has trouble walking.

Thus, should Mr. Chiang be unable to complete the six-year term, Mr. Lee would be in line to succeed him. When Mr. Chiang passes from the scene, Taiwan is likely to enter a period of collective leadership, according to analysts here, with power shared by the Kuomintang, bureaucrats, the military, security forces and native Taiwanese.

Today, more than 70 percent of the Kuomintang's two million members are native Taiwanese. In elections last December, Kuomintang candidates won 62 of the 71 "supplementary" seats in the national legislature, and most of them were native Taiwanese. But a majority of the seats in the 371-member legislature are held by lifetime members elected on the mainland in 1947. They nominally claim to represent districts in China.

A report this year by Amnesty International, the human rights organization, noted that Taiwan, alone among Asian nations, had made improvements in the treatment of prisoners.

A Change in the Law

The organization observed that in 1982, Taiwan's laws were amended to allow suspects in custody to retain a defense lawyer immediately after arrest. Such a change is considered important, according to Amnesty International, because most torture occurs right after arrest. Later in 1982, the report said, a few Government officials were, for the first time, convicted of mistreating suspects.

Opposition politicians estimate the number of political prisoners at fewer than 200, and the number has been dwindling in the last few years.

The opposition contends that the liberalization of Taiwan's political life is proceeding too slowly. But with the gradual passing of the older former mainlanders, the pace will probably pick up.

On international issues, most opposition politicians and the Government share common ground. Some opposition figures, generally people living abroad, do argue that Taiwan should declare its independence, giving up the Kuomintang's longstanding claim that it will one day "regain the mainland." Yet most opposition politicians here agree that such a position would be "suicide," as one put it.

Unification Overtures

Peking has made several reunification overtures to Taiwan, all of which have been rejected. Still, the Kuomintang's stance that the separation of Taiwan and China is a temporary condition is one shared by Peking's leaders.

But any genuine independence movement in Taiwan would be something Peking would not watch idly, people here agree. "It would be an invitation for Peking's army to come across the Taiwan Strait," a foreign diplomat said. "And everyone here recognizes that."

* * *

June 13, 1984

NEWS FROM PUNJAB: HOW NEW DELHI CURBS WHAT IS REPORTED

By SANJOY HAZARIKA

NEW DELHI, June 12—Anyone listening tonight to the Government-run All India Radio's main newscast would have learned that Prime Minister Indira Gandhi was "anguished" by the developments in Punjab but that the situation there was improving. Listeners would have also learned that President Zail Singh felt that religion and politics should not be mixed.

The newscast went on to report that the Government would help newspapers overcome newsprint shortages. On the international front, it reported that there was new fighting in Beirut and that officials from Communist countries were meeting in Moscow.

But there was no word on All India Radio on the size or scope of the desertions by Sikhs in the Indian Army or that scores had been killed and wounded and more than 700 arrested in the most serious outbreak of unrest in the Indian Army since India became independent.

Every day millions of Indians listen to the radio, which is often described as All Indira Radio by critics of the Prime Minister, and watch television, which is also state-controlled and carries similar reports in its news bulletins.

Government Statements Reported

Television reports have shown the Golden Temple at Amritsar and security personnel clearing up the debris and stacking up captured arms. But there is a virtual news blackout on the situation there except on what Government officials are saying.

Only a handful of carefully selected Indian reporters, working for television, radio and the two major English-language news agencies, Press Trust of India and United News of India, have traveled to the temple on Government-organized trips with President Singh and Sports Minister Buta Singh.

Though nominally independent, the two Indian news agencies obtain most of their money from the Indian Government and state governments, which are the biggest subscribers, making the agencies, to some degree, susceptible to government pressure. Western news agency reports are not received directly by newspapers in India, but are funneled through, and edited by, the two Indian news agencies.

The television reporting on the Golden Temple, a Government official said, has been aimed at showing that the harimandir, the sanctum sanctorum of the temple, was undamaged in the shooting and to quash rumors among Sikhs that the religious center had been reduced to rubble.

Yet despite official efforts to show only the better side of things, an occasional slip does occur. For example, occasional gunfire could be heard on television when President Singh made a much-publicized visit to the temple last week. Reporters at the scene said the shots were being exchanged between troops and the last group of militants holding out in one of the buildings.

Foreign Journalists Barred

Reporters, along with everyone else, are not allowed to travel freely in Punjab because of the curfews on the highways and a ban on transport. Foreign journalists are barred from the area and can be arrested or even shot if they violate the ban. Indian Government officials have resisted requests to take groups of news reporters, especially foreigners, to Amritsar.

A reporter who traveled about 50 miles along the curfew-bound road into Punjab last Friday saw no army patrols between neighboring Haryana state and Chandigarh, the joint state capital of Punjab and Haryana.

The highway was totally deserted, and villagers looked out at passing vehicles from behind their windows. The markets were shut, and the children, among the most colorful features of the Indian countryside, were confined indoors. Five miles out of Chandigarh, on the road to Amritsar, the reporter's car was stopped by a soldier wielding a semiautomatic weapon, and he was threatened with arrest and ordered to return to Chandigarh.

"Pre-censorship" has been ordered in the Punjabi towns of Jullundur and Patiala, which between them publish about 14 Hindi-and Punjabi-language newspapers. A spokesman for the editors of 11 newspapers in Jullundur characterized the ban as discriminatory and said papers would not be published because of "practical difficulties." He did not elaborate.

Patterned After British Press

India's English-language newspapers and the vast array of Indian-language publications were inspired by the liberal and independent traditions of the British press in the 19th and 20th centuries.

News censorship was also originally a British creation, and Indian authorities have sometimes dusted off the old laws and updated and tightened them to censor the press.

Precensorship orders in parts of the Punjab are the most recent examples of restrictions on the press and are similar to the rules invoked by the Indian Government during the state of internal emergency from 1975 to 1977, when it used censorship with devastating effects. At that time, newspapers were ordered to submit almost every bit of printed matter, including editorials, news reports, cartoons and sometimes even advertisements, for scrutiny and approval by censors.

New Delhi has channeled news about Punjab through a variety of official sources. Two press briefings were held every day until last Sunday, one by an army general at Chandigarh and the other in New Delhi by senior Home Affairs Ministry officials. The Chandigarh briefing at first covered only operational news—mainly antiterrorist activity.

The Home Ministry dealt with Government policy and intelligence reports on the state of the terrorist movement. Apparently regarding the briefings as a duplication of effort, the Home Ministry canceled its sessions Monday and today. Now there are only the briefings in Chandigarh conducted by the army and a senior civilian official. Government sources also pass on news to the Indian news agencies, which are read closely by other journalists.

Journalists and official sources say these restrictions have meant that the Government is able to control all news out of Punjab, although it has not been able to do the same about the army deserters.

'I Am Just Confused'

Indian newspapers have largely taken a cautious position on reports of the army mutiny and the wave of desertions. "I am just confused," one executive said today. "I can't understand what is going on from these reports."

Some newspapers, like The Times of India, have taken a pro-Government approach, saying the desertions are not serious and have been contained.

But The Indian Express, which is fiercely independent, has reported on the scale of the unrest with reports from centers where desertions have occurred. On Monday, meanwhile, All India Radio dismissed the deserters as an "insignificant number" of misguided men.

Some newspapers and news agencies practice a form of self-censorship in what is otherwise one of the freest presses in the world. One editor said that sometimes a reporter and his editors would drop a report based on an official source if the source demanded it, especially if the report was potentially embarrassing to the Government.

'A Denial Will Only Hurt Us'

Another editor said that editors were reluctant to publish or transmit sensitive reports if official confirmation was lacking because "a denial will only hurt us."

The Government says there is no censorship in any part of India except Punjab. But a representative for The Associated Press here said today that technicians at the overseas communications service refused on June 2 to transmit two radio photographs of soldiers around the Golden Temple.

They gave no reason for their decision, and Victoria Graham, the A.P. bureau chief here, added that they had threatened to stop future news photographs about Punjab. A photographer with United Press International spoke of seven-hour delays in radiophoto transmission here.

* * *

February 4, 1985

TAIWAN MAGAZINES PLAY 'MICE' TO THE CENSOR'S 'CAT'

By STEVE LOHR

TAIPEI, Taiwan, Feb. 1—For Antonio Chiang, editor and publisher of The Eighties, advertising is not a concern. "We have never had an advertisement in our magazine," Mr. Chiang explains. "No one would dare."

Most of his writers use pseudonyms. Some are so wary of being identified with the magazine that they will not meet editors at its offices, up five flights of stairs in an apartment building here.

The Government licenses and controls the newspapers in Taiwan. So about a dozen dissident magazines like The Eighties provide "the sole window for the opposition to present its ideas to the public," one Western official said.

Attention is now being focused on this small band of defiant publications because of the case of Henry Liu, a Chinese-American dissident writer who was slain in California last October. Two weeks ago, the Taipei Government announced that two members of a Taiwan gang had confessed to the killing. More significant, though, was the disclosure that senior officials in the Defense Ministry's intelligence bureau were also implicated. One of them has been arrested.

Extensive Accounts of Case

Mr. Liu wrote for some of the opposition magazines in Taiwan, including The Eighties, and for similar Chinese-language publications in Hong Kong and the United States. The opposition magazines are printing the most extensive accounts of the Liu case available in Taiwan.

Last week, for instance, Mr. Chiang's magazine published three reports dealing with the activities of Taiwan gangs, contacts between the intelligence agencies and organized crime, and American press reports on the Liu case.

The Government banned the issue. The Taiwan Garrison Command, the internal security force, confiscated 10,000 copies of the magazine, two thirds of its circulation. The authorities never say precisely why they ban a specific issue, figuring that to do so amounts to free advertising. Mr. Chiang suspects it was because of the three Liu articles.

An outlawed issue of The Eighties is hardly novel. In fact, Mr. Chiang's main distribution problem is how to outsmart the police. Since The Eighties, the first of the dissident magazines in Taiwan, was first published in June 1979, nearly a third of its issues have been banned. The Government has also ordered the magazine to suspend publication for one-year stretches five different times.

'Cat-and-Mouse Game'

The latter circumstance explains why Mr. Chiang's magazine uses three names, the other two being Asian and Current. If the magazine is outlawed for a year in one name, he changes the name and continues publishing. "We play a constant cat-and-mouse game with the authorities," he said.

The situation is much the same for the other opposition magazines. For example, 30 of the last 93 issues of Progress, a popular weekly, have been banned. Among the magazines, a circulation of 15,000 or more is considered impressive; with Taiwan's population of 19 million, that is like a circulation of 175,000 in the United States.

The Eighties is widely regarded as the most professional and least polemical of the group. It says it has a diverse readership, mainly middle-class intellectuals, including some younger Western-educated members of the ruling Kuomintang.

"The Eighties is rather moderate," said Hu Fu, a professor of political science at National Taiwan University. "It is more rational and reasoned than the others."

Editor Given Credit

The magazine's reputation is attributed largely to its editor. "Antonio Chiang is just head and shoulders above everyone else in the opposition press," a foreign diplomat said.

Mr. Chiang, 40 years old, is the dean of the dissident editors. He says he is all too familiar with Government harassment, shoestring budgets and a work regimen that finds him sleeping on an office cot two nights a week.

"I see my family only on weekends, usually," he said. "To my two children, I am a voice over the telephone."

Unlike several of his peers, Mr. Chiang has a journalistic, not political, background, having spent 10 years as a political reporter for China Times, a newspaper with a circulation of more than a million. Mr. Chiang said he had been frustrated there because as a native Taiwanese, as are 85 percent of the island's people, he felt his opportunities for advancement were limited. The former mainlanders, who took control of Taiwan in 1949, still hold most of the top jobs in business and Government.

Besides, Mr. Chiang said, "It is almost impossible to work for press freedom within the party-controlled newspapers."

The Press as Propaganda

The publishers of the major dailies, such as China Times and the United Daily News, are typically senior members of the ruling party. Although there has been a gradual relaxation of censorship in recent years, the Government still views the press as a vehicle for its propaganda.

Government officials say the grounds for banning are fairly clear. The main ones concern positions regarded as subversive, including publicly advocating Communism or the overthrowing the Government, and "agitation," especially if it is designed to "drive a wedge between native Taiwanese and former mainlanders."

Dissident editors contend that the guidelines are vague, and often point to one banning reports that will "confuse the opinion of the public." And the list of items deemed subversive has included pictures of Chinese Olympic athletes.

Anything that might be considered embarrassing to senior members of the Kuomintang is also off-limits. The last issue of Mr. Chiang's magazine printed excerpts from the diary of President Chiang Ching-Kuo about his experiences in Russia during his youthful infatuation with Communism. Any reference to the President's early Communist-adoring days tends to bring the Garrison Command running, Mr. Chiang says.

Censorship Is Defended

The Government says its censorship powers are justified because the dissident magazines are often irresponsible. "They print things that are just completely made up," said James C. Y. Soong, director of the cultural affairs department of the Kuomintang Central Committee.

One magazine wrote that he and two other fast-rising young men in the ruling party had been invited to President Reagan's inauguration in Washington, but that the invitations were withdrawn because of the Liu death. Mr. Soong says, and American officials confirm, that the three were never invited in the first place.

Mr. Chiang and other editors point out that Taiwan does have libel laws, which is how democratic governments usually protect citizens from irresponsible journalism.

In the last several months, Government harassment of the opposition magazines has increased and a handful have folded.

Even so, the editor of The Eighties is guardedly optimistic that the Government may ease a bit after the slaying of Mr. Liu.

"The Government has to do something to improve our international image," Mr. Chiang says. "Things may loosen up now. I hope so."

* * *

September 16, 1985

INDIA BANS CRITICAL PUNJAB REPORT

By STEVEN R. WEISMAN
Special to the New York Times

NEW DELHI, Sept. 15—The Indian Government has banned a report on violence in Punjab state and arrested two people involved in putting out the report.

The report, published by a group called Citizens for Democracy, charges that the Government has been the major cause of bloodshed in the state, which has been the focus of an often violent agitation by Sikhs for greater autonomy.

Government officials said the report was banned and copies were seized and destroyed last week because of the sensitive situation in the state, where an election is to be held Sept. 25.

But leaders of the opposition to Prime Minister Rajiv Gandhi charged that the Government was trying to suppress political dissent. Chandra Shakhar, president of the Janata Party, said Mr. Gandhi was engaged in "sustained attempts to suppress the civil rights of the people."

#5 Others Accused of Sedition

The two people arrested were B. D. Pancholi, a co-author, and O. M. Prakash Gupta, an owner of the press where the 144-page report was printed. A police report charged that four other co-authors, as well as a respected judge who wrote the forward, were also guilty of sedition, but they were not arrested.

Civil liberties activists announced they would try to have the arrests overturned, but these activists were in turn criticized for their earlier role in putting out reports that had accused leading Government officials of being behind anti-Sikh violence.

Leading officials in the governing Congress Party have accused various civil liberties groups of endangering the lives of top party members by accusing them of encouraging anti-Sikh rioting in New Delhi last year.

Two top Congress leaders have been assassinated in New Delhi in the last two months, apparently by Sikh extremists. Party leaders said the extremists had apparently compiled a "hit list" of people named in the groups' reports and were seeking revenge against them.

'Inhuman Barbarities' Charged

The new report, titled "Oppression in Punjab," contains a forward by Judge V. M. Tarkunde, which accuses the Government of "inhuman barbarities" against the people of Punjab.

It asserts that "clearly innocent" people have been arrested and that the police in the state had carried out "sadistic torture, ruthless killings, fake encounters, calculated ill treatment of women and children, and corruption and graft on a large scale."

The three-year-old Punjab crisis was the subject of an accord between centrist Sikh leaders and Prime Minister Gandhi last summer. Sikh militants oppose the accord, but the centrists and the Congress Party are taking part in the election this month.

* * *

January 22, 1987

PRESS VS. PALACE: AQUINO WIELDS A SWORD

By SETH MYDANS
Special to the New York Times

MANILA, Jan. 21—The word "media," a spokesman for President Corazon C. Aquino said in the early days of her Government, is the plural for "mediocre."

Right from the start, something seemed to go wrong in relations between the palace and the local press, which was glorying in its newfound freedom, sometimes with more exuberance than accuracy.

The number of daily newspapers in Manila jumped to more than 20, and political columnists became celebrities as they stirred fact, gossip and rumor into a colorful daily mix.

"If you want unverified gossip passed on as truth, it is there," wrote one of the more careful columnists, Francisco S. Tatad. "If you want a person's private fault reported as public fact, it is there, too. If you want the most inconsequential nonsense blown up into an earthshaking event, you will find no shortage of it."

Another columnist, Sylvia Mayuga, said the press had come to deal in "political pornography," offering perverse thrills that distort realities and values.

Censorship Is Charged

Now, as the Government tightens its grip before a constitutional plebiscite, the press has put itself in the spotlight, accusing the Government of censorship.

When the Government television station refused last week to broadcast a discussion forum with an opposition figure, former Defense Minister Juan Ponce Enrile, journalists who had been jailed or dismissed during the martial law he administered rose angrily to his defense.

"Can one no longer criticize the Government?" wrote Ninez Cacho-Olivares, who was one of the most daring critics of President Ferdinand E. Marcos in the final months of his rule.

The Aquino Government, she wrote, "seems to have gone the way of Marcos and has violated the constitutional guarantee of freedom of the press."

Both the writers and the readers of such criticism are aware that the Aquino Government is far from duplicating the press censorship of the Marcos years, when all but a few "crony" newspapers were closed and hundreds of journalists were jailed.

The stridency of the criticism illustrates both the degree of freedom that is permitted today, and the flamboyance with which it is often exercised.

Dress Code for Reporters

The Government has often reacted with what its critics like to call "onion skin," only to provide new grist for Manila's hungry newspapers in their circulation war.

At one point the palace banned a photographer who had violated guidelines by photographing Mrs. Aquino in the act of eating.

At another it issued a dress code for reporters covering the President that required them not only to look presentable but to smell good.

Most delicious for her press critics was the President's own joke, received by political columnists with high dudgeon, that "perhaps it was my mistake that I restored the freedom of the press."

Mrs. Aquino had to back down a few days later, saying, "From now on I just have to keep reminding myself that now that I am President, I am not supposed to give jokes."

Press 'Is Too Free'

But genuine irritation did seem to be behind her quip.

Her former spokesman, Rene Saguisag, the man who said he found the media mediocre, seemed to reflect her views when he said last summer, "We are for a free press, but it is too free."

"Every day when I read the papers, I find out that I did or said or thought things that I did not do, say or think," he said.

Of the President, Mr. Saguisag said, "I don't think she jumps for joy" when she reads the morning papers.

Her problems with the press have come not only from the wild competition among the proliferating newspapers, most of which analysts here believe will eventually lose the war for readership and close down.

She has also lived for nearly a year with several hostile newspapers that remain in the hands of close Marcos associates, and with dozens of radio stations that broadcast strident pro-Marcos propaganda.

Now, Ms. Cacho-Olivares suggested, the Government "seems to be bent on doing away with the opposition media."

Last week, the National Press Club expressed "grave concern over the deepening involvement of the Government in the media."

Newspaper to Close

There are reports that the Government may not renew the licenses of several radio stations, and it has announced the closing at the end of this month of The Philippines Daily Express, which is owned by a close Marcos associate, Roberto Benedicto.

The Government says the newspaper, which was taken over by a commission investigating Mr. Marcos's holdings, is being closed because it is losing money, and not for political reasons.

The commission has also assumed control of two other pro-Marcos newspapers, and there are reports that the Government is supervising two independent television stations.

In addition, the President has not dismantled Mr. Marcos's propaganda apparatus as she promised to do during her campaign, but has attempted to improve and reorganize it.

The Government television station, once named for Mr. Marcos's World War II guerrilla unit and now renamed People's Television, frequently broadcasts film montages and other programs that celebrate the new Government.

Broadcast Is Canceled

Months ago, it committed itself to broadcast a weekly coffee-shop forum at which opposition figures often took part even during the later months of Mr. Marcos's presidency.

But last week it canceled its broadcast of the forum at which Mr. Enrile was the guest. Both the cancellation and the Government's explanation for it have disturbed several Philippine journalists.

"Do not confuse a Government entity with the private and commercial media," said Mr. Saguisag's successor as spokesman, Teodoro Benigno. "Freedom of the press is very much in practice in the commercial media."

If given airtime on People's Television, he said, Mr. Enrile would simply "rant, fume, rage and criticize the Government without giving the Government a chance to present its side."

* * *

August 2, 1987

CHINA WAGES WAR AGAINST ILLICIT JOURNALS

By EDWARD A. GARGAN
Special to the New York Times

BEIJING, Aug. 1—A young factory worker from Changchun, a city in northeast China, turned hooligan after reading "obscene and bawdy" books, the Chinese press reported recently.

A grade school teacher from the coastal city of Xingchang raped 16 of his pupils after being influenced by vulgar and pornographic novels in his youth, a national newspaper said the other day.

And in one unnamed province, 40 out of 100 juvenile delinquents went bad because they were victims of books "extolling themes such as murder, pornography and trends going against the Communist Party, the people and socialism," according to a survey cited by the New China News Agency.

A nationwide campaign documenting the supposedly pernicious effects of salacious, violent and politically suspect literature is sweeping China's Government-controlled press as officials try to halt the growth of illegal private publishing houses and the circulation of unauthorized books and magazines. By law, only the state may run printing and publishing concerns.

Concern of Government

So concerned is the Government about the unauthorized publishing that the State Council, China's cabinet, issued a seven-point order reiterating the state ban on private publishing and the selling of unofficial reading matter.

"At present," People's Daily said, "many books on murder, sex and superstition are spreading through society. Some middle and grade school students influenced by books and periodicals with obscene and unbelievable contents are depressed and undisciplined. They don't like to study."

"The surge of bad books and periodicals is a major reason for the new trend that criminals are becoming younger and younger and their criminal ways are becoming more and more like those of adults," the Communist Party newspaper continued.

Here in Beijing, a rogues gallery of illicit and decadent publications has been set up for only senior Government officials to view. Several Chinese, who know about the display but who have not been allowed in, said that senior officials were beating down the doors to see "Eighteen Kinds of Kungfu" and "A Toast," which are said to dwell on violence and sex.

Western Literature

The sudden focus on unhealthy literature comes in the wake of a six-month political campaign against Western political and literary ideas, which began after nationwide student demonstrations last winter.

In recent days, police raids on private book stalls, illegal publishing shops and even an office of the state airline have been reported in detail.

Of 967 booksellers investigated in Beijing, 518 were found to have pornographic or other illegal books in stock. More than 60,000 books have been confiscated in the last week, according to People's Daily, and dozens of booksellers have been fined.

At Beijing's airport, the police found 35,000 pornographic video cassettes in an office used by employees of CAAC, the state-owned airline, People's Daily reported.

'The Socialist Civilization'

"In our country, we have regulations that all publications must be by publishing houses approved by the state," said Xun Zhongchuan, a division chief of the publication department of the Beijing Cultural Bureau. "Publishing is part of constructing a socialist civilization. We have a very important task of propagating the policies of the Communist Party. We formally ban pornographic and counterrevolutionary books and periodicals."

Determining what can be published, Mr. Xun said in an interview, depends largely on political considerations. "Mainly we see if the ideological content suits reader needs," he said.

Over the last several years as contacts with the west, Japan and Hong Kong have grown and Government controls over the economy have been relaxed, foreign publications and video tapes have flooded China. Many of these books, magazines and video tapes have been reproduced at small printshops or factories, often on state-owned presses and equipment, and sold to a public thirsting for something more than sanitized literature and political tracts.

The crackdown on illegal publishing has not been confined to what the Government considers the dregs of popular tastes. Guangming Daily, a newspaper geared for China's intellectuals, has also attacked modern western literature and art.

Students Under Attack

"It is regrettable that in recent years, some writers and critics upholding 'literature and art for its own sake,' have forgotten the precise nature of and requirements for socialist literature and art as regards the issue of dealing with solitude, while being enthusiastic about adopting the concepts of literature and art of the new Western school of modernism," Li Zhun wrote in a recent issue of the paper. "The modern sense of solitude is the bitter fruit of the contradiction in the spiritual aspect of modern capitalism."

Even college students are coming under attack for what People's Daily called their "voracious but worrisome reading habit," a habit that has led, the paper said, to illicit sex and troubled thinking.

"While skimping on food and other expenses, many university students spend 20 yuan a month at bookshops," the paper said, referring to a sum equivalent to $5.40. "When a kind of stirring is felt between male and female students, the most natural means to initiate exchanges is to borrow books, present books and discuss books."

* * *

October 13, 1988

FANTASY OR BLASPHEMY? A BOOK IS A BURNING ISSUE

By BARBARA CROSSETTE
Special to the New York Times

NEW DELHI, Oct. 12—The banning by Indian officials of a book they apparently had not read, on the advice of Moslem leaders who also had not seen it, has opened a debate troubling to many here about the political limits of free expression and the shallowness of religious peace in India.

The book, "The Satanic Verses," by the Indian-born novelist Salman Rushdie, was banned on Oct. 5 on the orders of India's Minister of Home Affairs after protests from Moslems who say the book offends their religion and its Prophet, Mohammed. They argue that its circulation would lead to violence among India's 80 million or more Moslems.

Two chapters of the work, a characteristic Rushdie fantasy with elements of surrealism and hallucinatory imagery, have been the focus of Islamic ire. Both deal with a character called Mahound, assumed to be Mohammed. One, "Return to Jahilia," casts the Prophet's 12 wives as prostitutes in a brothel, the critics say—a characterization Mr. Rushdie rejects.

Since the ban was announced, an outcry has been rising not only here in India, where scholars and writers are arguing against the peremptory nature of the Government action, but also in Britain, where Mr. Rushdie now lives. The book is scheduled to be published in the United States in February by Viking.

No Hearing Held

There was no official review or hearing on the merits of the case before the Finance Ministry barred the importation or sale of the book under customs legislation.

"The idea that the Minister of Finance should decide what books should be read and not be read is not acceptable in a free country," Mr. Rushdie said in an interview by telephone from his home in London. He called on Prime Minister Rajiv Gandhi to assert his authority and reverse the ban.

"It seems to me that the Government has grown very weak in India while the power of religious extremists seems to have grown very strong," Mr. Rusdie said. "The book is not the issue. This is an attempt to manipulate the Government."

Many Indians have also characterized the action as a sign of Government weakness, noting that it follows by only a few weeks Prime Minister Gandhi's hasty withdrawal of a new defamation law that had aroused protests. The book ban is widely regarded as a move that can only end in another embarrassing reversal. Even if the ban remains in force, pirated copies of the book are expected to be circulating soon in large numbers.

Penguin India, the local affiliate of Viking, declined to publish it here, but copies have been imported.

A 'Comic Novel'

Mr. Rushdie, who was born into a Moslem family in Bombay and studied Islamic history at Cambridge University, said he was "no longer a formally religious person."

"But Islamic culture is the one in which I grew up, and I always wanted to write about it," he said. He described his book, which has been nominated for a Booker Prize, Britain's highest literary award, as a "comic novel," which nonetheless deals with serious issues of cultural and spiritual dislocation—a novel about change and metamorphosis.

"It is about Islamic culture seen against a basically Western background," he said.

New Delhi's pre-emptive action, taken as the book was beginning to arrive for sale in India, floodlights the gap between the sophisticated national image fostered by the Government of Prime Minister Gandhi and the powerful forces of religious fundamentalism that still motivate millions of Indians: Hindus, Sikhs and Moslems. To sustain itself, the Government needs votes in all those camps.

The ban also highlights a collision of cultures not uncommon in Asian nations struggling to set acceptable limits of "Westernization."

"When I look at Western civilization, to my mind it appears that the West has lost the line of distinction between the sacred and the profane," Sayed Shahabuddin, the Indian Moslem at the center of the controversy, said in an interview here. "For the evolution of human culture, you have to regard some things as sacred. Otherwise the spirit will not prosper."

"I may not share your opinion or your faith," he said. "But I don't have to treat it contemptuously or in an indecent manner."

Book 'Filthily Abusive'

It was Mr. Shahabuddin, a former Indian diplomat and now a Member of Parliament for the opposition Janata Party and editor of the magazine Muslim India, who by his own account first brought the Rushdie book to the attention of the Government, and then persisted with his case until he obtained the ban.

He acknowledges that he did not—and would not—read the book, which he calls "filthily abusive." But after receiving letters and telegrams from Moslems all over India beginning in late September, Mr. Shahbuddin said, he began to collect accounts of the book and comments made about it by Mr. Rushdie.

"By these interviews it becomes clear what the book is about, because Salman Rushdie does not make any bones about it," Mr. Shahabuddin said. "He in fact brags that he majored in Islam at university and knows all about it. As far as he is concerned, he does not believe Mohammed was the true Prophet."

Mr. Rushdie says these are falsifications of his work and its intent. Mr. Shahabuddin remains unconvinced.

"You must look at this in the context of how the Moslem regards the Prophet," Mr. Shahabuddin said. "As far as the Moslems are concerned, there is no divinity about the man. He is a man. But he is the messenger of God, and the entire Islamic faith is based on this notion: that he is the Prophet and that what you find in the Koran is the word of God."

"We also regard the Prophet's own life as the model for the rest of humanity, and for all times," he went on. "To a believing Moslem, you may jest about a lot—but you cannot jest about the person of the prophet."

'This Sorry Episode'

Editorial opinion in India, where almost every newspaper has entered the debate on the ban, has been largely careful to accept that the danger of Moslem violence is always very real in a country where even a rumor of a slight or an abuse can turn loose a mob.

But some writers have argued that the onus should be on the Moslem political leaders to defuse these tendencies, not pander to them.

"It is these very politicians who will emerge as the biggest losers in this sorry episode," The Times of India said Saturday. "For they have once again demonstrated their inability or unwillingness or both to convince their community not to be swayed by writings such as Mr. Rushdie's. The result is that prejudices against the minority can only gain in strength, even as the banned novel draws more readers to it than would have been the case otherwise."

Reflecting the opinion of many Indian writers, publishers and academics, The Times of India said "The Satanic Verses" was "an outstanding literary achievement" meriting respect "regardless of the deplorable ban and the bigotry that provoked it."

* * *

February 15, 1989

CENSOR'S SCISSORS: NO LONGER JUST OPEN AND SHUT

By SUSAN CHIRA
Special to the New York Times

SEOUL, South Korea—The play "Honeysuckles" closed recently, on schedule and not because the Government shut it down.

For 40 days, audiences sat huddled in winter coats in the unheated theater where the play was staged. They became jurors in the trial of a dissident, cheering as he confronted his torturer and jeering as the judge proclaimed a commitment to a fair trial.

But the movie "Oh, Dreamland" was shut down early. The Government said the film was not properly submitted to a screening committee. The film accuses Americans of complicity in the 1980 killings of protesters by Korean soldiers in Kwangju.

South Koreans are delving into a long-buried past, excavating passions as well as facts. Old taboos are being broken every day, and no one knows exactly what the new ones begin.

Days of Self-Exploration

It is a bewildering and exhilarating time for a society where the Government for years dictated the contents of television broadcasts, wrote its version of history into textbooks, and banned thousands of plays, books, songs and films tainted by references to Communism, or to North Korea, or to workers' or farmers' rights, or to other topics deemed leftist.

Now a flood of plays, films, books and television programs are broaching subjects in ways that would have once led to arrest.

A few days ago, the MBC television network broadcast the first documentary of the Kwangju confrontation, and it drew sharp criticism from the Government. Plays on the plight of political prisoners and of striking workers are openly performed.

Film makers are working on screenplays dramatizing the terrors under President Chun Doo Hwan's rule, from 1980 to 1988. South Korea's first televised program of political satire, "Mr. Chairman," features barbs aimed at politicians and corporate officials that grow sharper each week. Novels about American complicity in suppressing an indigenous Communist movement in the late 1940's are selling briskly.

U.S. Role Is Questioned

All these works raise questions about Korea's past and present. They discuss opportunism and collaboration through the years as Japan, the United States, North Korea and finally an authoritarian anti-Communist Government wielded power.

The works question an American role once portrayed as benevolent and now cast as oppressive. They point out gaps in income and status that continue despite South Korea's trading might. Those are all questions that South Koreans have been barred from discussing openly or have preferred not to confront.

"There have been tremendous changes," said Kim Myong Kon, director of "Honeysuckles" (the title compares the plight of dissidents to the flowers that survive the cruel winter and bloom in the spring).

"There is much less harassment from the Government," he said. "Before, there were times when they stopped a whole play. This time, there was no censorship at all."

Censorship Has Eased

The Government has eased controls since President Roh Tae Woo bowed to street demonstrations and pledged democratic initiatives. The Government has lifted its bans on works by Communist authors and on many books about North Korea, and it has stopped forcing playwrights and film makers to submit scripts to Government-appointed censors.

It is much rarer now, Mr. Kim Myong Kon said, for intelligence agents to watch a rehearsal and then suggest, in an ostensibly casual phone call, what parts should be changed.

Yet the Government does not endorse total freedom of expression. South Korea outlaws Communism, and many prominent Koreans have worried out loud that a public schooled to accept information unquestioningly will be swayed and confused by a flood of new ideas.

The Government has seized biographies and works of Kim Il Sung, the North Korean leader, as well as a novel about the North that was labeled propaganda. Choe Byung Yul, Minister of Culture and Information, scolded MBC television for airing what he said was a one-sided documentary that unfairly focused on the view of the victims of Kwangju and did not offer the military rationale. Politics or Bureacracy? The makers of "Oh, Dreamland" remain convinced that their political message brought the Government action, and not, as the Government insists, violations of the laws.

Kim Djun Kil of the Information Ministry said the producer and distributor of the film broke the laws requiring that they submit a finished film to a screening panel and tell the Government when and where they intend to show a commercial film.

The panel, long notorious among film makers and playwrights for its heavy-handed censorship, used to be controlled by the Government.

But as of last month, Mr. Kim Djun Kil said, committee members were nominated by their peers, not by the Government, and the panelists are supposed to work much as American censors do, evaluating and rating films for sex and violence. Had the film makers submitted the film, he said, it would have been passed regardless of its political message.

Silence Finally Shattered

Kang Soo Chang, one of the film's writers, is unconvinced. "We showed several other films like this, 8 or 16 millimeter, at commercial houses," he said. "No one stopped us before."

"The law does not apply to small-scale films and it was clearly because of its content." Hong Sun Ki, the film's director, was briefly questioned by the police and released.

Yet he and other artists said censorship had eased. Kim Myong Kon, director of "Honeysuckles," said nationally televised legislative hearings on political corruption, human rights abuses and the Kwangju killings shattered years of enforced silence.

For Kim Hyong Kon, political satire has grown easier. "Mr. Chairman," his popular television show, portrays life at a huge corporation. He plays a dictatorial chairman surrounded by sycophants, and he draws his plots from current events.

When he started his show during Mr. Chun's rule, his most daring episode had an employee accidentally smashing a vase, making the same sound that torturers reportedly made when they smashed the neck of a student into a tub of water, killing him and causing widespread outrage. Now, he said, he can be more direct.

A Challenging Play

"Honeysuckles" asks the audience to think about the limits of political action in a society where it has often been moral to challenge the unjust.

The audience judges a young political firebrand who forges his identity card to hide his student background in order to work in a factory, then rouses employees to demand better conditions and steals the jewelry of his boss's wife to donate to the cause.

The play includes slides of bloodied heads and bodies at Kwangju, a brutal re-enactment of the protagonist's torture, and an acid portrayal of a swaggering, womanizing intelligence agent. While most of the audience agrees that the dissidents should have broken the laws that prevented him from working in a factory and organizing employees, more than half drew the line at robbery.

For his next project, Mr. Kim wants to dramatize a book by a North Korean writer about the life of a rural woman. Many novels by North Korean writers are banned. While he thinks he will be able to stage that production, he thinks there are limits.

Instead of a dissident, could he have put, say, Mr. Roh on trial? "Chun Doo Hwan, O.K.," Mr. Kim Myong Kon said with a smile. "Not Roh Tae Woo."

* * *

May 24, 1989

BOLDLY AND SUBTLY, CHINA'S PRESS TESTS LIMITS . . .

By SHERYL WuDUNN
Special to The New York Times

BEIJING, May 23—Not many Chinese follow Italian politics, so perhaps it was a bit surprising for People's Daily to carry a small front-page article Sunday on the resignation of the Italian Government.

But in China, where subtlety is a way of journalism as of life, the message was obvious: China's Government should think about resigning as well. Such hints are still as much a part of Chinese newspapers as ink and paper, but the last few weeks has seen a minor revolution in what newspapers can publish.

As a result, the hints are getting ever bolder, and sometimes newspapers even make their point outright. In a dramatic contrast to the press coverage before the student demonstrations began more than five weeks ago, China's news organizations can now cover events that the Government would perhaps rather hush up.

Some say a semi-independent press may be the democracy movement's greatest achievement and a significant spur to further liberalization.

'More Transparency'

"The real victory of student demonstrations may be freedom of the press, and that press freedom is here to stay," said Fei Xiaodong, a journalist in Beijing at China's boldest newspaper, the Shanghai-based World Economic Herald. "Maybe there won't be as much as there was at the peak before martial law, but it will be better than before the demonstrations."

Journalists hesitate to call the change a revolution, and they caution that whatever independence they have won so far could be lost if the Chinese leaders in control want to clamp down. Much depends on developments in the power struggle now taking place at the highest levels.

But the journalists assert that the demonstrations have helped extend the boundaries of what they may publish in their papers.

"There is more transparency, and all kinds of voices are reflected in the newspapers now," said Fan Rongkang, deputy editor in chief at the official People's Daily.

Journalists Join Protests

Many Chinese regard freedom of the press as important not only for itself, but also as a key milestone on the road to democracy. They see an independent press as an institution that can supervise the Government and check its power, while at the same time disseminating ideas and information and hastening the entire democratic process.

China's press has always been tightly controlled by the Government and the Communist Party, or at least by factions within them. While the Soviet Union has gone far with glasnost, China has been much slower to liberalize its restrictions on information.

When pro-democracy demonstrations broke out in mid-April, they might as well not have happened, as far as the news organizations were concerned. Newspapers and other news organizations were ordered not to mention the protests except as an outpouring of expression for Hu Yaobang, the former Communist Party leader, who died April 15.

As reporters tired of writing articles that were never published, the journalists sent petitions to the Government and took to the streets, marching under the banners of their own newspapers. Journalists and editors from nearly all the news organizations, including the Communist Party's People's Daily and the Government-run New China News Agency, joined in the student marches for greater press freedom.

Subtle Tactics After Crackdown

The transformation began with an article or two on the movement in each paper. That multiplied into several articles and numerous pictures in each day's paper.

"It's a milestone, it's very great progress," said Li Datong, an editor at China Youth News, and one of the organizers in the journalist demonstrations. "For the time being the authorities have relaxed and loosened their control, but since it is not an institutional improvement, they can tighten their control again."

In the last five weeks, news organizations witnessed a startling transformation to what was for a Communist country a remarkably independent press. Then, on Saturday morning, came martial law, and all bets were off.

News organizations suddenly assumed a more cautious attitude, printing fewer articles that were not authorized, but it was not a full-scale retreat. Instead of openly criticizing the Government, newspapers tried more subtle tactics.

Placement of Articles

People's Daily on Monday published a front-page article about a Hungarian leader objecting to the use of army troops to solve domestic problems. That was a slap at Prime Minister Li Peng after his attempt to call army troops to the capital to suppress the democracy movement.

A journalist at the newspaper confirmed that the placement of the article was intended as a criticism of Prime Minister Li and his policies. He recalled the glee in the newsroom when the Hungarian leader's comment was found, and it was realized that it could be printed on the front page.

Television news and radio broadcasts have recently included daily reports on the student protests. In a subtle indication that army troops are dissatisfied with their mission to quell students, the television news today carried an illuminating interview with an officer in the military. The news tonight was clearly trying to embarrass Mr. Li by undermining the likelihood that his order for martial law would be carried out.

"As soldiers, it is our bounden duty to obey orders," the major told the reporter for the Central China Television news agency. "But we will never fire at the people."

Then, the television reporter asked the kind of leading question that is rarely seen, "Haven't you received an order to move away?"

The major answered, "Retreat, retreat."

* * *

June 2, 1989

BEIJING TIGHTENS PRESS RESTRICTION

By NICHOLAS D. KRISTOF
Special to The New York Times

BEIJING, June 1—The Government announced tough new restrictions on foreign reporters today that, if enforced, would in effect bar correspondents from writing any articles about the nation's democracy movement.

On their face, the rules go much further than restrictions that other governments, like those of South Africa and Israel, have placed on foreign reporters when they were faced with popular upheavals. The rules announced today involve not just censorship of some reports or restrictions on news gathering, but a virtual ban on press coverage itself.

It is not clear to what extent the authorities intend to enforce the new rules.

BBC Reporter Warned

Earlier regulations, announced on May 20 after martial law was imposed in parts of Beijing, forbade foreign journalists from conducting almost any kind of interview. But these rules were not enforced, although a few journalists have been warned in the last 10 days by the Foreign Ministry or State Security Bureau. A correspondent for the British Broadcasting Corporation was ordered today to stop violating the restrictions or "accept all the consequences."

In addition, the police slapped and detained a Japanese photographer this evening when he photographed a crowd in front of the Public Security Bureau, witnesses said. The Japanese Embassy said it was unaware of the incident, and other Japanese journalists said they did not know his name or affiliation because he is not based in China.

Hundreds of students jostled with the police outside the Public Security Bureau headquarters tonight to protest the beating of the journalist, and also of two other students who they said were also beaten.

Responding to the new press restrictions, the Foreign Correspondents Club of Beijing issued a strong protest this evening and called the rules "a deplorable case of press censorship and harassment."

"This calls into question China's policy of openness to the outside world," the statement added.

Ding Weijun, the Beijing city government spokesman who announced the new restrictions, presented them as "explanations" of the previous rules. While both sets of rules are nominally from the city government, they almost certainly would have to win approval of senior officials in the central Government.

The Government's Rules

The new restrictions include these:

"During the period when martial law is enforced in some districts of Beijing, press coverage . . . is subject to prior application to, and approval of, the office of foreign affairs of the Beijing Municipal People's Government."

Associated Press

A Chinese police officer, right, demanding to see the credentials of an ABC News cameraman during a demonstration by students Tuesday in front of police headquarters in Bejing.

Bans on "press coverage, photographing and video taping of activities prohibited by the martial law decrees at Tiananmen Square . . . or at other public places; or press coverage in a disguised form, such as making appointments with Chinese citizens to meet at the offices or residences of foreign journalists . . . or at hotels or elsewhere, for interviews on activities prohibited by the decrees." The decrees prohibit demonstrations, so any press coverage of demonstrations would violate the rules.

"Without approval . . ., foreign journalists . . . shall conduct no press coverage, photographing and videotaping of the troops enforcing martial law."

It is unclear if the rules presage a new crackdown. Other signs, as usual in Beijing these days, were contradictory.

Students Tell of Kidnapping

The most peculiar incident was the assertion by students occupying Tiananmen Square that four people tried to kidnap two student leaders from their tent at 3 A.M. today.

According to the students' account, Chai Ling, the general commander of the Tiananmen Square students, and her husband, Feng Cengde, the deputy general commander, were awaken by four people who tried to gag them with towels and carry them away.

Mr. Feng escaped and shouted for help, and other students seized and interrogated the four people. Three of them were also students, and one was a member of a Beijing citizen organization that has supported the demonstrators, but most students were convinced that the four were Government agents.

The students noted that it has been a carefully guarded secret where the student leaders will sleep on any night, and they frequently move around, so the kidnapping attempt had to have been supported by some careful investigation work. In addition, at about the same time, the students loudspeaker system and telephone were sabotaged so that they could not summon help, they said.

The Government has strongly condemned the student occupation of Tiananmen Square, and particularly the raising of a 27-foot reproduction of the Statue of Liberty, but so far the authorities have not intervened.

The Government's next moves may depend on the meetings now under way each day in the Communist Party headquarters to try to resolve the political crisis that has paralyzed China for two weeks. The only indication today was an acknowledgment by the Foreign Ministry spokesman that there have been no changes in the positions of the leaders of the Communist Party, army or Government.

But the spokesman, Li Jinhua, professed not to understand a question about whether the formal positions might be unchanged but somebody might now be "acting" general secretary of the party. While rumors are flying in every direction, the consensus is that no one has yet been dismissed, but that the party General Secretary, Zhao Ziyang, has been relieved of his powers and will be dismissed from his post at the next Communist Party Central Committee meeting.

* * *

October 8, 1989

JAPAN AND THE WAR: DEBATE ON CENSORS IS RENEWED

By STEVEN R. WEISMAN
Special to The New York Times

TOKYO, Oct. 7—A court decision this week upholding the Government's right to censor history textbooks has revived the long-running debate over Japan's willingness to teach all aspects of the nation's role in World War II.

The ruling by the Tokyo District Court, upholding the right of the Education Ministry to tone down references to what was depicted as Japanese atrocities, was another setback for Saburo Ienaga, a retired history professor who has been battling against Government censorship of textbooks since the 1960's. After the decision on Tuesday, Mr. Ienaga said he would appeal, although he acknowledged that prospects for winning were not bright. But he added: "To lose without fighting would be worse than losing after a fight. I am 76 years old and exhausted, but I will continue this fight until my death."

The court decision was also criticized in South Korea, which was colonized by Japan from 1911 until the end of the war in 1945. In Seoul, a spokesman for the ruling Democratic Justice Party said the decision reflected efforts by Japanese leaders who were "trying to justify" past aggressions.

South Korean newspapers also urged Japan "to stop glossing over its history of atrocities and brutalities," as one of the newspapers put it.

Praising the decision, however, the Ministry of Education said it would make further efforts "to make sure that textbooks will be appropriate."

The court decision was not entirely negative for Mr. Ienaga, since it ruled that the Education Ministry's revision of a reference to a 19th-century volunteer army established to support the Emperor did constitute an abuse of authority. The Government was ordered to pay him about $700.

The reaction to the main ruling underscored the continuing sensitivity of an issue that was most recently brought to the attention of most Japanese when Emperor Hirohito died last Jan. 7 after a 62-year reign.

At that time, Japanese television showed footage of military actions in World War II, especially in China, exposing young people to a side of Japanese behavior that has generally been kept out of school curriculums.

Latest of 3 Law Suits

At the trial on Professor Ienaga's lawsuit, which was the latest of three he has filed since 1965, Mr. Ienaga testified that the Education Ministry had tried to change the word "invasion" to "advance" in China but eventually accepted the original word.

Mr. Ienaga, a former professor at the Tokyo University of Education, added that the Government toned down references to the killings of civilians and rape of Chinese women by Japanese soldiers in the capture of Nanjing in 1937 and sanitized other references to Japanese behavior in Asia.

Also deleted, he said, was a reference to an army unit that he said used several thousand Chinese for "human body experiments."

In his lawsuit, Mr. Ienaga charged that the censorship of his textbooks had amounted to a violation of the Japanese Constitution's guarantees of free speech. But the district court disagreed, saying it was "necessary and appropriate" for the Government to screen the textbooks.

"Probably I am very un-Japanese," Mr. Ienaga said in an interview, referring to his lawsuits. "I am a very individualistic person. Of course there are many people who eagerly support my court cases. But among the younger generations, the issue has been fading."

He said that the more that Japanese young people are not taught the true history of the war, the more risk of a "similar danger" exists for Japan.

Mr. Ienaga's first lawsuit, in 1965, sought to recover royalties lost from the rejection of a high school textbook, "New History of Japan." He also sought compensation for mental stress caused by the demands for 300 alterations before the text was approved.

A second lawsuit on different grounds, filed in 1967, was actually won at a lower level court before being thrown out on a technicality. The latest lawsuit was filed in 1984 after Mr. Ienaga said he felt alarmed by a new censorship campaign by some politicians, businessmen and scholars.

* * *

January 3, 1991

INDIA'S TOP CENSOR SAYS FILMS MUST BE CLEANER

By SANJOY HAZARIKA
Special to The New York Times

BOMBAY, India—From an apartment building that overlooks the rain-swept Arabian Sea, a former police official who has battled brigands in real life has taken on what he regards as the villains of reel life—India's movie moguls who flood their films with sex and violence.

B. P. Singhal is the Central Board of Film Certification's chairman, a Government-appointed position that translates into his being the country's top film censor. Mr. Singhal remains in the position under Prime Minister Chandra Shekhar, who ousted Vishwanath Pratap Singh, the man who appointed him. Mr. Singhal says sex scenes in films should be curbed and on-screen brutality banned, and his views coincide with a feeling by many Government officials that existing guidelines on what is permissible on the screen should be tightened.

"I believe that violence of the gruesome kind, that degradation of women or scenes that give rise to libidinous tendencies should be banished from films," said Mr. Singhal, a large, amiable man. Mr. Singhal said he has nothing against mild violence. "Fisticuffs and all that is fine," he said. "But I draw the line at gruesome brutality, of people being shown with their faces being smashed, legs broken, tortured."

Mr. Singhal said in an interview that he was considering strengthening existing guidelines on film making in India. That idea is making the film industry uneasy.

What Is Forbidden

The current standards forbid showing the modus operandi of an actual crime such as a bank robbery. Women cannot be portrayed in a manner that degrades them. Scenes portraying sectarian enmity, such as Hindu-Muslim violence, are often snipped by the censor's scissors. Yet virtually all these rules are violated in some form by skillful movie operators, and rape scenes are de rigueur in many Indian movies.

Bikram Singh, a prominent movie critic and a predecessor of Mr. Singhal as censor, described a typical scene this way: "The actress is disrobed or stripped as she is chased from room to room by the villain. Actual sex or full nudity is never shown but the audience knows what is going on, with screams from the woman and the camera focusing on torn bits of dress and leering thugs."

There are even character actors who specialize in rape, like Ranjeet, who said that in his countless films he has raped virtually every major actress in the Hindi-language film industry.

Some groups, particularly women's groups, have been speaking out against the portrayal of rape in Indian films, especially since it is not the rapist but the victim's liberated life style that is usually blamed for the attack.

Film producers say audiences demand such scenes. Some say such scenes are an outgrowth of a society in which many marriages are still arranged and unmarried men have little access to romance and sex. Sociologists say that this is changing in India, especially among the middle class and the affluent. But many film makers are clearly upset by Mr. Singhal's avowals.

Problems in the Industry

"The film makers are scared of disturbing the status quo," said Amit Khanna, a prominent movie producer. The industry, which is already being eroded by the growth of videocassette recorders in India, is worried that further restrictions on sensationalism in commercial movies will mean disaster at the box office.

Mr. Khanna, who also writes songs for Hindi movies, said that out of 700 movies made in India in 1989, 650 lost money. Mr. Khanna said only a handful made handsome profits, such as the movie "Dil" ("Heart"), which grossed about $5.2 million.

"About $10 million is the optimum level for a mega-hit," said Mr. Khanna, who said that most big movies in India cost about $1 million to make.

In addition, scores of movie theaters have closed in the last year and industry figures show a decline in the movie-going audience.

The film board, largely through its regional offices, issues certificates allowing the screening of a movie after local censors have cleared it.

India is one of the world's largest producers of movies, and industry executives count prominent politicians and government officials among their friends and exert pressure to have a censor's cuts restored. In some cases, aggrieved producers have gone to cabinet ministers in New Delhi, who in turn have overruled the board, reinstated the cut scenes and hastened the clearance of movies. Film industry people and censor board officials say that this has happened many times and that it shows the political power of the industry.

Those With Connections

Among the members of former Prime Minister Singh's Government who had connections with the movie industry were Murasoli Maran, the former Housing Minister, who has made movies and written scripts, and N. T. Rama Rao, the leader of the opposition National Front in Andra Pradesh state, is a popular actor and film maker from the South.

Mr. Singh, the former censor, said that he knew of many cases in which sex scenes that had been cut by the board were reinserted after the movie was certified.

The local police are supposed to watch for these illegal restorations, but Mr. Singh said the police give the issue a low priority.

Mr. Singhal's views have brought him into open confrontation with the movie industry. The censor, who is 58, said he was aware that his job often came under political pressure, but he said, "I am not going to succumb to any pressure, money or political."

* * *

July 29, 1991

EVEN GLOOMY T-SHIRTS FALL UNDER CENSORSHIP

By NICHOLAS D. KRISTOF
Special to The New York Times

BEIJING, July 28—A popular T-shirt in Beijing these days carries this message splashed across the chest in angry Chinese characters: "I'm fed up! Leave me alone!"

The authorities are refusing to heed the message. Instead of leaving the grumpy alone, the Government has banned the manufacture and sale of T-shirts that are spiritually "unhealthy."

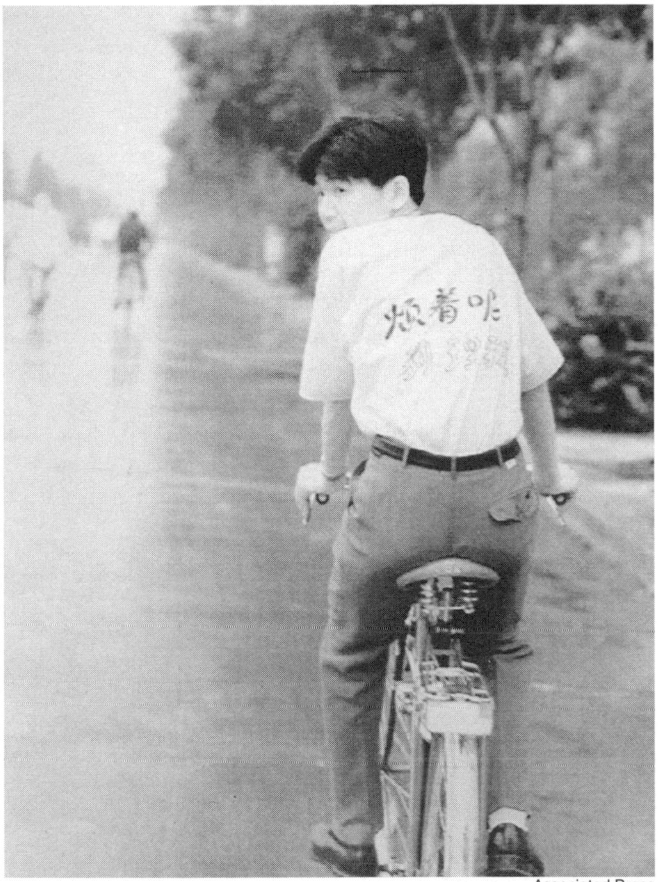

Associated Press

A cyclist in Beijing wearing a T-shirt reading, "I'm fed up! Leave me alone!" The popularity of the shirts has prompted the authorities to ban the manufacture and sale of T-shirts that are spiritually "unhealthy."

The ban, issued this month, is obviously less momentous than arrests of political dissidents or assaults on Tibetan monks. But the skirmish over T-shirts underscores two of the foremost strands in Chinese society today: a deepening sense of alienation among urban young people and the increasingly frenetic efforts by the authorities to keep a happy face glued on Chinese Communism.

The printed T-shirts, which in Chinese are called "wenhua shan," or "cultural shirts," suddenly became very popular in the free markets of Beijing in the last few months.

Withdrawn and Hopeless

The slogans are not openly critical of the Government, but they convey a sense of being withdrawn, rebellious and hopeless—instead of the gung-ho enthusiasm for Communism that young people are supposed to feel.

"Really exhausted," reads one shirt. "I don't know how to please people," reads another. Another expresses a value system that makes Communists shudder: "Getting rich is all there is."

A few make political points in subtle ways. One carries many repetitions of the slogan "Be an Honest Man," but the slogan is written in such a way that it includes the Chinese characters for "old" and "men"—both skewed as if they are collapsing. This leaves the impression that the "old men" who run China are tumbling down.

"T-shirts are the only 'private turf' people have left, where they can try to express their feelings," a middle-aged woman said.

But at the beginning of this month, the Government began a crackdown on these cultural shirts. The Beijing Legal Daily, an official newspaper, reported that new emergency regulations had formally banned the sale and production of "unhealthy" T-shirts in the capital.

1,000 T-Shirts Confiscated

The newspaper said the authorities had confiscated more than 1,000 offensive shirts, along with printing equipment for 20 designs.

"Cultural shirts transmit an ideology incompatible with our society," China Youth Daily, another official newspaper, warned its "young friends" recently. "The words—shady, negative, cynical—benefit nobody, and bear dispirited and decadent feelings."

"Cultural shirts are not a Chinese invention," the article added. "They are only a foreign trick borrowed from the West, where they have existed for decades. If we make a little study, we find that Westerners wear such shirts as an expression of decadent feelings."

To be sure, a commentary in the hard-line Beijing Daily made it clear that patriotic, pro-Communist slogans would be most appropriate on cultural shirts. Its suggestions: "Study hard and make daily progress," and "I must train myself for the construction of the motherland."

New Rules Are Secret

So far there is no indication that it is illegal for individuals to wear "unhealthy" shirts, only that they must not be manufactured or sold. The details of the new rules, and the penalties, are still secret.

A spokesman for the State Administration of Industry and Commerce, asked about the new rules, would say only, "So far, we have not received any directive on this matter."

The sense of alienation and aimlessness conveyed by the T-shirts is also an overriding theme in much of the popular culture that appeals to young urban Chinese. Rock songs by Cui Jian, books by Wang Shuo and movies by most leading young film makers depict the frustrations of characters who would probably rush out and buy unhealthy shirts if they had a chance.

"Kids feel stifled," a college teacher in his 30's explained simply.

The Government has reacted to this popular culture by trying to suppress a good deal of it. It also tries to promote its own saccharine pro-Communist songs, books and movies.

As for the cultural shirts, they are still available in the free markets of Beijing—under the table.

"We're not allowed to sell these, so we don't display them," a private vendor said as she tugged four different kinds of "unhealthy" shirts from under piles of more innocuous garments. "But we certainly have them. If you want a large order, we can even have them printed for you."

One of the shirts she pulled out read in large characters across the chest, "I can't do a thing." In smaller characters, it explained: "I'd like to be an entrepreneur, but I don't have the guts. I'd like to be an official, but I don't have the right attitude. I'd like to sell things, but I don't have a license. To hell with earning a living!"

* * *

September 24, 1991

THE REAL NEWS IN CHINA COMES OUT IN RESTRICTED PERIODICALS

By NICHOLAS D. KRISTOF

Special to The New York Times

BEIJING, Sept. 23—The Chinese sometimes complain that the one place where news is never found is in the newspapers. So perhaps it is not surprising that officials are so fond of a special breed of publications bearing the warning, "Internal Periodical—Guard Carefully."

While ordinary citizens are left to read in People's Daily how everything is great and getting better, officials enjoy one of the most important perquisites of power, real information. The Government runs a network of at least several dozen internal publications with news that is deemed too sensitive for the public.

The Communists began the publications while they were a guerrilla force, before the 1949 revolution. Today the publications range from Reference News, which virtually everyone but foreigners is allowed to read, to news bulletins distributed by fax to the offices of top leaders. Top ministers also receive a special morning news video each day, largely distilled from CNN, so that they can watch what has happened overnight.

While even the existence of most of the internal publications is supposed to be secret, informal conversations with a range of well-informed Chinese portray a system of alternative news media that is often breathtaking in scale and efficiency. Extensive excerpts from half a dozen Taiwan newspapers, for example, are republished and circulated among Beijing officials 24 hours after hitting the streets in Taipei.

'Everybody's Studying Them'

"In times like now, when there's a lot happening in the Soviet Union and elsewhere, the internal publications are especially important," an official in the central Government said. "Everybody's studying them very carefully."

Reference News, at the bottom of the pyramid, has a circulation of more than three million, more than any Chinese newspaper except People's Daily. It consists of excerpts of articles about China and other countries from the foreign press. But because virtually anyone can read it, no negative articles on the Government are included.

"Everybody used to be very interested in reading Reference News," an official in Gansu Province said. "But in the last few years it's really gone downhill, and now it's just as boring as the official press. Blah!"

Two dailies in a magazine format, Reference Materials and Reference Essential News, are circulated much more narrowly, to Government department heads.

Reference Materials, which runs about 80 pages a day of worldwide news, has become the leading source of foreign news for many senior officials. It carried 387 articles last month about every aspect of the Soviet Union, overwhelmingly translations of foreign wire-service reports.

Reference Materials does not shy from printing occasional articles carrying general criticisms of the Government, although it avoids any attack on a specific leader. One example is that a week ago it published a dispatch in which Senator Edward M. Kennedy was quoted as having said, "Congress must continue to take a strong stand against Chinese repression of democratic forces and denial of human rights."

One of the highest-level publications is Dongtai Qingyang, meaning Current Developments. It is given just to senior Government ministers and includes sensitive information about the internal situation. Information about ethnic clashes, labor strikes, economic problems or political protests often reaches leaders in this way.

Still, there are limits. No Chinese journalist would regard it as career-enhancing to tell Prime Minister Li Peng that he is unpopular.

The New China News Agency, which publishes more than 10 internal periodicals as well as fax updates, dominates the industry. Its list includes one of the most thoughtful internal publications, Selected Reference Articles, which includes essays about domestic trends and foreign developments.

In addition, many ministries have their own "Situation Reports," and major newspapers all produce confidential publications distributed to senior officials.

A former People's Daily commentator who is studying at Princeton University, Wu Guoguang, recalled in a telephone interview that in his first journalism class at Beijing University he was told that an important part of a Chinese reporter's job was to write internal articles that the public never sees. Particularly sensitive dispatches end up not on the front page, but in memos for leaders at the Politburo level, Mr. Wu said.

* * *

October 17, 1993

WHO MAKES THE RULES IN CHINESE MOVIES?

By PATRICK E. TYLER

BEIJING—Chen Kaige, the director of the acclaimed film "Farewell My Concubine," shakes his head incredulously at the most bizarre episode of Chinese censorship in recent memory.

As one of the most important of China's so-called Fifth Generation directors, he understands what it is to push the limits of state censorship under Communist Party rule. But

"Concubine," his fifth film in 10 years, has set a record of sorts. It was banned and unbanned twice as China was seeking international support to play host to the Olympic games in 2000. It was also banned in democratic Taiwan, the home of Tomson Films, its producer, and a lucrative market for any Mandarin Chinese language film. "This is not good for me," says Mr. Chen.

For those who will see the film in the United States, where it opened commercial engagements on Friday after playing in the New York Film Festival, it may seem impossible that a movie about a couple of Beijing Opera stars (played by Leslie Cheung and Zhang Fengyi) who struggle to remain true to art and to each other during five decades of war, revolution and political upheaval could make anyone so angry as to ban it. But it has been just such a year in China's tortured film industry.

For the Taiwanese, it may be that the ruling Nationalist Party did not like the undignified portrayal of its troops in the film. But for the Communist Party leaders on the mainland, "Farewell My Concubine" represents a more subtle challenge to their legitimacy. Even in censored form, this film is still a powerful statement about the excesses of the Cultural Revolution. (The version shown in the United States is about 14 minutes shorter than the uncensored version Mr. Chen exhibited at Cannes. The cuts were made by the director after discussions with its distributor, Miramax Films, to render "Concubine" more accessible to American audiences.)

The 41-year-old Chinese director, though thoroughly Chinese in his art, is deliberately cross-cultural in his outlook, owing to his stint as a student at New York University's film school and a healthy exposure to Hollywood during the last decade.

Wearing a denim shirt and jeans, sipping coffee in the atrium of the Shangri-La Hotel, Mr. Chen at times seems the Hollywood smoothie, someone who has mastered the Western rhythm of selling ideas and the public relations of commercial film promotion. He is at one moment charmed to tell you that Madonna has seen a screening of "Concubine," liked it and planned to attend one of the parties for the film in New York this month. He can move from Mandarin to English and back again effortlessly, and easily confides his best and worst fears for the chances of an Oscar.

And like any good director, he can recount a scene, as he did when he described his agony upon returning to China from the Cannes International Film Festival in June. Having won the coveted Palme d'Or award, Mr. Chen stepped off the plane and found dozens of journalists gathered to greet him, their video cameras whirring, their Nikons clicking and flashing. But he quickly discovered that while the moment was being recorded, it would not air on state television; it would not be published in the next day's press.

The Communist Party had imposed a news blackout on Mr. Chen and his award, and the film had been mysteriously banned only months after it had been cleared for release by the official censors. The journalists were there solely out of loyalty. "There is nothing we can do but shoot it and put it on the shelf," one journalist told him.

To be a film director in China today is to be a politician in the most dangerous sense, making political decisions about art and content in a vacuum. The vacuum is the one created by the Communist Party, which has taken an end-of-empire approach to censorship. The censors won't say what the rules are, and once they have banned a film, they won't even tell directors how to cut it to satisfy their objections. They simply ban films they don't like.

Their attitude toward political correctness, Communist Party style, is similar to that of former United States Supreme Court Justice Potter Stewart, who after many failed attempts by the court to define pornography, finally allowed: "I know it when I see it."

In this case, what the Communist Party is treating like pornography is realism in depicting turbulent periods in recent Chinese history that have scarred whole generations. Even though the party has officially disassociated itself from the excesses of those eras, its leaders believe that reminding the masses of what was done to them in the party's name is an assault on party "unity."

The most important and sensitive of these periods, of course, was the Cultural Revolution launched by the Communist Party Chairman Mao Zedong and lasting from 1966 to 1976. Only recently have China's Fifth Generation directors—those who emerged from film school around 1980—begun to evoke the period in their work, a process that scratches in the most personal way at their own scars and those of their leaders.

Mr. Chen's contemporaries in this effort include Zhang Yimou, who got his start as Mr. Chen's cinematographer in "The Yellow Earth" (1984), and Tian Zhuangzhuang, whose film "The Blue Kite," released this year, also addressed Cultural Revolution themes and also played in the New York Film Festival.

"Since we don't have religion," Mr. Chen said, "since we lost our belief system after the Cultural Revolution, since the Chinese people decided there is only one important thing and that is making money, we have to let people know something about the Cultural Revolution."

The person talking was Mr. Chen the firebrand, the person who is suppressed when the other Mr. Chen is dealing with the censorship bureau. One Mr. Chen can argue for hours at a time that any seeming connection to politics in his films is purely accidental, while the second Mr. Chen has hatched plots to finance and film the early life story of Jiang Qing, otherwise known as Madame Mao Zedong, who was the architect of a thousand ruthless persecutions during the Cultural Revolution.

He has also expressed an interest in making a film version of Nien Cheng's best-selling autobiography, "Life and Death in Shanghai," a wrenching piece of "scar literature" from the Cultural Revolution.

Mr. Chen cannot always suppress the rebellion in his soul. "I quite enjoy playing this game with the leaders," he said. But the other Mr. Chen quickly retreats as he admits that he has shelved both the Madame Mao project and Nien Cheng's story.

"The Cultural Revolution is too sensitive," he says, eyes downcast in resignation, "I don't think anyone can do these projects." Unapologetically, Mr. Chen admits that his next film is a retreat to the 1920's.

"Concubine" and two other films that have rumbled out of China this year represent an uncomfortable reality: film makers are forced to live in a state of self-imposed denial. The denial is that somehow their art does not represent an attack on the system that still suppresses freedom of expression in China. But, of course, it does.

Each film that holds up a mirror to the Cultural Revolution, no matter how objectively, reminds a battered Chinese population that devastating political movements have been a way of life under Communism, and there still is no system of laws, no guarantee of basic democratic or human rights, to prevent these destructive forces from being loosed again.

The end of the Cultural Revolution brought forth the first democratic stirrings in China with the Democracy Wall movement of 1978-79. It was followed by cycles of protest and repression until the Tiananmen Square pro-democracy demonstrations that ended in bloodshed in June 1989.

With the democracy movement dormant, Chinese film making may be the sole outlet in society for raising questions about the past. And Mr. Chen is not the only director who has reached back to the Cultural Revolution to provoke Chinese intellectual thought. Mr. Tian's "Blue Kite" traces the life of a small boy growing up during the political movements that culminated in the Cultural Revolution. The film, a co-production of the Longwick Film Production in Hong Kong and the Beijing Film Studio, went through script revisions before it could be shot in China and then was banned upon completion.

Its entry last month in the Tokyo International Film Festival, along with another banned Chinese film, prompted the official Chinese delegation to pack up its Communist Party-approved films and come home.

"Much literature has already been written about the Cultural Revolution, and much of it is very detailed," Mr. Tian said. "I basically don't divert historically from these references, but the present regime doesn't want any attention drawn to any of the past mistakes of the party."

What may be the Sixth Generation of Chinese film makers also showed up in Tokyo and has outraged the Chinese film police with its sense of alienation and nihilism. The 30-year-old director Zhang Yuan filmed "Beijing Bastards" completely outside Government sanction. Its portrayal of counterculture youth emerging from the Cultural Revolution proved to be too shocking for China's propagandists to tolerate.

"Concubine" set a record last winter for breezing through censorship in two days. But the movie's notoriety appears to have been its undoing, for in the days after it won the Palme d'Or, Chinese President Jiang Zemin asked for a private screening. According to some accounts, Mr. Jiang and the Communist Party Central Committee propaganda chief watched the film. Afterward the movie was denounced for its harsh depiction of the Cultural Revolution, its portrayal of homosexual love and for its climactic suicide, based on the plot of a famous Beijing opera. "Before Cannes, none of the leaders knew anything about this film," Mr. Chen said. "But then after they saw it, some of them got pretty angry."

That was the situation that greeted Mr. Chen when he returned from Cannes. But just as suddenly as the clouds had gathered, they parted a few days later when his network of friends helped arrange for Deng Xiaoping and the other members of China's first family to view "Concubine."

To Mr. Chen, that screening was a success, even though he took the advice passed along from Mr. Deng's family that some cuts had to be made in the three sensitive parts of the film to have it shown in China's movie theaters. One of Mr. Deng's daughters even suggested a world premiere in Beijing. The politician in Mr. Chen realized that he had an opportunity to pre-empt the more menacing pair of scissors that might be awaiting his film at the censorship bureau, so he cut the film himself.

Believing that his difficulties were behind him, Mr. Chen was ecstatic as Shanghai prepared to put on the largest film premiere ever in the city. All the tickets had been sold for opening night and for the next day's opening in Beijing when the phone call came.

"The ministry called and said the film would have to be changed," Mr. Chen recalled, referring to the Ministry of Television, Broadcasting and Film; the changes involved altering the suicide at the end, and if they were not made, he said, the film could not open. Whatever imprimatur had been conferred by Mr. Deng had not held.

The Shanghai Communist Party committee advised the ministry in Beijing that there could be riots in the street if the opening night was canceled. Once again a news blackout descended on the film. It played one night in Shanghai and one night in Beijing. Then it was banned, pending changes.

"I told them I would not make the changes because I did not know how to do it," Mr. Chen said. There was nothing on paper from the ministry. No guidelines, just the ultimatum about the three sensitive areas.

How could he cut the suicide scene and still call the film "Farewell My Concubine?"

But the politician in Mr. Chen knew that China, in the midst of a high-priority campaign to win the Olympic bid for the 2000 Summer Games, could not long tolerate the international uproar over censoring this film. He refused to take the knife to his work a second time.

Now that tens of thousands of Chinese in Shanghai and Beijing have seen the censored version of "Concubine," Mr. Chen seems to take little joy in its success, even though the Cultural Revolution scenes are real and harsh, even though the homosexual love is ennobled by loyalty. And the final suicide scene remains a powerful, if tragic, statement of love.

"I have not seen the film that has been changed," Mr. Chen says. "I think if I go, I will feel hurt."

* * *

March 27, 1994

IN MANILA, THE FILM MAKERS TEST THE CENSORS

Special to The New York Times

MANILA, March 26—When "Schindler's List" opened in 15 Manila theaters this month, people stood in the aisles to see it. And despite a ruling by Government censors, they saw the entire movie.

The Government's Movie and Television Regulatory and Classification Board had decided to cut portions of the film because they showed "too much breast" and a scene where Schindler has sex with his mistress. In protest, Warner Brothers, the film distributor, withdrew the movie, saying the director, Steven Spielberg, wanted it shown uncut or not at all.

The incident created a furor, and President Fidel V. Ramos intervened to keep the movie intact.

Filipino film makers say the Philippines is suffering from possibly the strictest censorship since World War II, a result of the appointment of a 35-member regulatory board of conservatives who say they are protecting the country's culture.

Speaking of "Schindler's List," the chairwoman, Henrietta Mendez, said: "The sex scene was very explicit. It is not fit for the culture of the Filipinos. The law says what is contrary to customs, good morals, should not be allowed."

The board, whose members are appointed by the President's staff, has drawn up guidelines that ban nudity "except for medical or historical reasons," and too much blood. In an odd twist, these taboos have spawned violent and sexually titillating movies that go to great lengths to avoid the censors' scissors.

"The producers always try to put in as much sex and violence in the most insidious manner," said Ricardo Lee, one of the country's leading screenwriters. "Instead of doing one sex scene, which is all that's necessary, they do four that are just within the range that censors will allow."

In President Corazon Aquino's Government, the board's rule was that one naked breast was allowed, but not two. Now both breasts have to be covered, at least partly, which is why Filipino melodramas somehow work into their plots a number of passionate kissing scenes that take place under a waterfall or on the beach, to justify the skimpy bikinis adorning the heroines.

But judging by the box office, Filipino moviegoers prefer violence to sex. The most successful Filipino films have been crime movies, shrieking versions of real-life rapes and murders that show all the brutality that the censors will pass.

Kris Aquino, daughter of the former President, has earned the nickname Massacre Queen. On the screen in the last year, the 23-year-old has been gang-raped twice, hacked to death once, and chopped to pieces and left for dead in a ravine. And the audiences love it, flocking to watch Kris Aquino in the throes of her latest celluloid horror.

"People want to see the rich go through the same hardships that they go through," Mr. Lee said. "They take some comfort in the thought that a President's daughter can be raped and murdered just like everyone else."

Scenes From Life

"Censors dictate the kind of films that producers can make," said Mel Chionglo, a director. Movies based on real crimes, he said, are intended to outwit the censors who normally object to rape and murder scenes unless producers can defend them as crucial to the plot. The best justification is always that these crimes took place in real life.

Film makers say the most creative Filipino films were produced during the corruption-ridden rule of Ferdinand Marcos, whom Corazon Aquino displaced. "One of the best things that happened during the Marcos years were good films," Mr. Lee said. "Some of them were a reaction to Marcos."

Despite censorship, film makers probed the seamy side of life under Mr. Marcos, producing disturbing and socially critical films. Weary of dictatorship, Filipinos provided an audience for these films, encouraging producers to risk their money on such movies.

"Before, producers made three formula films and one good film," said Mr. Lee. "Now they won't risk their money on something that may not earn. They only make films that make people feel good, that entertain but do not hurt, do not disturb."

* * *

July 16, 1994

FUROR OVER FEMINIST WRITER LEAVES BANGLADESH ON EDGE

By JOHN F. BURNS
Special to The New York Times

DHAKA, Bangladesh, July 15—Aziz ul-Haq, one of the most powerful Muslim leaders in Bangladesh, smiled as he pondered the case of Taslima Nasrin, the feminist writer whose bold, often startling challenges to Islamic taboos on female sexuality and the role of women have shaken this country like a cyclone blowing in from the Bay of Bengal.

"If she doesn't come back to the faith, the punishment is clear," the 75-year-old Muslim cleric said, as a crowd of bright-eyed boys pressed their noses against an iron grate in the wall separating them from their teacher's sanctuary at the Jamaya Rahmania Arabia madrassah, Dhaka's leading Muslim seminary. "She should be executed."

Since it broke away from Pakistan 22 years ago, Bangladesh has had more than its share of travails. It has been buffeted by cyclones and floods, and burdened by illiteracy and poverty that place the country's 120 million people among the most disadvantaged in the world.

It has been rocked by bloody coups, assassinations and popular uprisings against military dictatorships, although military rulers have held sway, either under martial law or through pliant parliaments, for all but seven years.

Now, once again, the country seems poised on the edge of turmoil that could engulf the government of Prime Minister

Agence France Presse

Bangladeshi women rallied last month to denounce the author Taslima Nasrin. Signs called for justice and warned Miss Nasrin to wear the veil.

Khaleda Zia, the widow of a former military ruler who was assassinated after winning election as President.

Amid the tensions swirling around Miss Nasrin, who went underground after the Government brought criminal charges against her six weeks ago for allegedly insulting the Muslim faith, Muslim militants have unleashed a battery of strikes and protest rallies in Dhaka, the capital, and in other cities.

Thousands have surged through the streets, echoing Muslim clerics' calls for the writer's head with cries of "Death, death and only death for the apostate Nasrin!"

Militant leaders have used the turmoil to promote a wide agenda of fundamentalist demands, including calls for Bangladesh to be made an Islamic republic, and for the Muslim penal code to be imposed as criminal law.

They have demanded the expulsion of privately run foreign aid organizations that administer much of the $2 billion the country receives each year in development assistance, describing the agencies' efforts to foster more jobs and education for women, among other projects, as "decadent" and "un-Islamic."

The demands have come just as international aid agencies have been saying that Bangladesh has begun to turn the corner, with striking gains in primary education for girls, in employment opportunities for women, and in lowering birth rates.

But as the social advances have gathered speed, they have met increasing resistance from the male-dominated hierarchies in the villages where 80 percent of Bangladeshis live, particularly from the Muslim clerics at the top of the rural power pyramid.

Under a stronger Government, many Bangladeshis opposed to the militants say, the militants could scarcely have hoped to turn the utterances of a writer, even one as controversial as Miss Nasrin, into a platform for creating major political unrest. Educated, urban Bangladeshis insist that the traditions of Bengali Muslims incline toward tolerance, not zealotry, in religious matters.

"The Bengali mind is basically secular," said Serajul Islam Chowdhury, an English literature professor at the University of Dhaka. "The mullahs are good men, but we have never wanted them in politics."

Instead of confronting the militants, the Zia Government has seemed eager to placate them.

The charge against Miss Nasrin was brought under a little-used statute on religious defamation dating from British colonial days. Cabinet ministers have tried to outdo one another in condemning the writer.

The Foreign Ministry's press office has been distributing translations of one of Miss Nasrin's more sexually graphic poems. "As you can see, it is more or less pornographic," a spokesman said.

The Prime Minister has maintained silence on the affair, but several of her ministers who discussed the controversy say they are merely carrying out a law designed to prevent the kind of religious violence that has racked India.

"We have gone to court to safeguard the feelings of the people, as any civilized country would," said the Foreign Minister, Mustafi Zur Rahman. "Now we leave it to the court. If she convinces them, she walks a free woman."

Senior ministers have acknowledged that they see the controversy over Miss Nasrin as a potential trigger for wider disturbances that could hasten the Government's downfall. Although initially popular in 1991, when it became the country's first truly civilian administration since 1975, the Zia Government has been weakened by a political stalemate that developed when the entire opposition walked out of Parliament five months ago, vowing not to return until the installation of a neutral "caretaker" government empowered to hold new elections.

A Political Stand-Off

The impasse has led to a competition between Prime Minister Zia and her main rival, Sheikh Hasina Wazed, leader of the Awami League, for the support of the Muslim fundamentalists.

The main fundamentalist group in Parliament, the Party of God, originally backed the Prime Minister's party, the Bangladesh Nationalist Party, allowing it to form a government after the 1991 elections, but it subsequently joined the opposition boycott. Now the Party of God, along with the Awami League, is threatening to broaden the street disturbances. The scale of the turmoil has shaken many here who had taken comfort from the apparent weakness of the Party of God.

Few can be more shaken than Miss Nasrin, who has struck an almost panic-stricken tone in messages smuggled from her hiding place. "The mullahs are everywhere," she said in a message last month. "If I stay here, they must kill me."

Messages From Hiding

The messages have been a far cry from the plucky impertinence that turned Miss Nasrin from an obscure physician in a Government clinic into the scarlet woman of Bangladesh. In newspaper columns and novels, in poems and interviews, Miss Nasrin advocated the right of women to choose their sexual partners and to have children outside of marriage. Three times married herself, she has said Muslim women should have the right to have four husbands simultaneously, just as the Koran permits men to take four wives. Her poems are ripe with sexual imagery daring even by Western standards.

Anger among Muslim militants began to boil over in 1993, after Miss Nasrin wrote a novel, "Shame," published in India as well as Bangladesh, that depicted the fictional sufferings inflicted by Muslim militants on a family of Bangladeshi Hindus.

The Zia Government banned the book after it had sold 60,000 copies here, making it a best-seller. It also revoked Miss Nasrin's passport, restoring it after protests from western Governments and writers' groups.

She lit the fuse that caused the current upheaval by giving an interview this spring to an Indian newspaper, The Statesman in Calcutta, in which she was reported as saying that the Koran should be "revised thoroughly."

As death threats cascaded from Muslim clerics in Bangladesh, Miss Nasrin issued a statement saying that she had been misquoted, a claim denied by The Statesman. Later, she added fuel to the flames with a letter to The Statesman saying that urging the Koran's revision would have been "irrelevant" since, like the Bible and other religious texts, it was "out of place and out of time."

Little Support from Peers

Always a loner, Miss Nasrin made few friends among her fellow writers and intellectuals. Many have been harshly critical, saying that by provoking fundamentalists, Miss Nasrin has endangered causes, including women's rights, that others have worked for years to achieve.

"She's been irresponsible in many ways," said Khushi Kabir, who heads a private organization, Nijera Kori, meaning "Do It Ourselves," that works for the empowerment of rural women. Miss Kabir said that she had worked for two years in a rural village, and had avoided provoking the local imams despite ignoring Muslim traditions such as the one requiring women to cover their heads.

"You learn how to handle these people," she said. "It's something Taslima has never understood."

* * *

September 11, 1994

A REPRESSED WORLD SAYS, 'BEAM ME UP'

By PHILIP SHENON

GUANGZHOU, China—Freedom is heaven-sent, or so it would seem to anyone scanning the red-tiled rooftops of this southern Chinese city. The skyline of Guangzhou, one of China's free-market boomtowns, is covered with a forest of satellite dishes that allow television viewers here to enjoy the antics of Bart Simpson and Oprah Winfrey; NFL football and Australian cricket; the scantily clad lifeguards of "Baywatch" and the unclad models of a Japanese pornography channel; CNN and the uncensored local television news from across the border in Hong Kong.

And while almost every one of those satellite dishes is illegal under an 11-month-old decree, the Government seems unwilling to force the owners to take them down. Wang Bin, a shopkeeper, said that while his 12-year-old son does not understand a word of English, "he still loves 'The Simpsons,'" the American cartoon show beamed to China by Star TV, a pan-Asian satellite service.

"Maybe the people would protest very loudly if they take away our dishes," Mr. Wang said. "Everybody loves satellite television."

Hard to Stop

In China and almost everywhere else in the world where freedom is not a given, authoritarian governments are coming to realize their worst fears about the information age. Fax machines, video recorders and cellular telephones made chinks in the censorship wall. And now it is the spread of satellite television that is threatening to bring the wall down. Governments are finding it nearly impossible to stop people from grabbing their entertainment—and more important, their news and information—from the skies.

Not that they aren't trying. In March, Saudi Arabia banned satellite dishes as "un-Islamic," ordering more than 150,000 dishes in the country to be dismantled, and neighboring Kuwait is moving toward a similar ban. Dishes for private homes have long been outlawed in Singapore and Malaysia, where foreign programs are labeled a threat to traditional Asian values. Hindu fundamentalists in India, outraged by the racy videos on the Asian version of MTV, have demanded that the Government shut out Western satellite broadcasts. An Egyptian province banned dishes last spring after the governor complained that the local furniture industry was dying because "the workers are stuck in front of the sex scenes coming off the dish."

Yet governments that try to shut down satellite technology are often finding themselves outwitted by determined viewers, a problem that will only get worse for repressive rulers as satellite dishes grow smaller, more powerful and cheaper. The dishes are already sufficiently low-tech that they can be made in kits that are easily smuggled across borders. Dishes sold in China come from several countries.

Mark L. Cong for The New York Times

Illegal television satellite dishes rise above apartment buildings in Guangzhou, China.

Bowing to what seems to be the inevitable, some repressive governments are allowing the dishes to stay. The junta that runs Myanmar, the nation formerly known as Burma, puts few restrictions on the ownership of satellite dishes—although few people in Myanmar can afford them—while the Indonesian Government has welcomed satellite technology as a means of beaming its own programs to the thousands of islands in that farflung archipelago nation.

The situation in China is instructive, if only because China has made the crackdown on satellite television such a public campaign—and because it has been such an embarrassing failure. The Government moved against satellite dishes last October, prompted by the growing popularity of Star TV, the Hong Kong-based satellite service that had been purchased only weeks before by Rupert Murdoch, the media baron. Mr. Murdoch, who paid $525 million for control of Star, made few friends in Beijing when he announced shortly after the purchase that new technology "posed an unambiguous threat to totalitarian regimes."

The Chinese decree against satellite television banned virtually all private satellite dishes, estimated to number in the hundreds of thousands. Dish owners were ordered to take them down immediately or face heavy fines. Foreigners were allowed to continue to receive satellite transmissions in their homes and offices, but the dishes were banned from all hotels with less than a two-star quality rating, the only hotels that most Chinese can afford.

Nearly a year later, little has changed. A satellite dish can still be easily, if not so openly, purchased for as little as $600. Rather than dismantling their dishes, most dish owners in Beijing have simply hidden them behind brick walls or under canvas tarpaulins. To limit the risk, neighbors have joined in communal satellite services, all of them drawing their programs from a single, well-hidden dish. In some cities of the more freewheeling south, dish owners do not bother to hide them at all.

Star TV's figures suggest that Chinese viewership may actually have increased since the crackdown. An independent audit circulated by Star among Hong Kong advertising executives last summer showed that the number of homes with television able to receive at least one Star channel in Guangzhou rose from 49 percent to 55 percent, while in Beijing it rose from 9 percent to 13 percent.

Mr. Murdoch's own relationship with the Chinese leadership doubtless improved when he decided earlier this year to drop the BBC World Service news from the Star lineup beamed to China.

"The Chinese Government has decided, and I think logically, that it really can't shut out satellite television entirely, whatever the threat," said a Western diplomat in Beijing. "We're not talking about a few dissidents here. Hundreds of thousands of Chinese have now invested their life savings in these dishes, and there would be a nasty public uproar if the Government really forced the dishes down."

In a few small, rigidly controlled countries, the crackdown on satellite TV has been reasonably successful. But even those governments are feeling pressure to open up viewing choices in ways that will almost certainly limit their ability to censor what viewers see. Kuwait and Saudi Arabia are talking about establishing sophisticated cable systems that would offer dozens of channels. Singapore has already established a government-controlled cable system that includes news bulletins from CNN and the BBC. Even as it continues to deny satellite dishes to its own citizens, Singapore has invited satellite services, including MTV and HBO Asia, to set up their regional headquarters there. Neighboring Malaysia has announced that it will partially lift the ban on satellite dishes in 1996.

Even in Iran, where the Islamic Government has long preached about the evils of Western entertainment, there is some hesitation to ban satellite dishes outright. In Teheran, an estimated 50,000 satellite dishes sprout from rooftops, and the city's most popular television show is said to be "Dynasty," courtesy of Mr. Murdoch's Star TV. Iranian state television is notoriously dull. "The cultural invasion will not be resolved by the physical removal of satellite dishes," the Teheran Times newspaper editorialized last spring. The paper suggested that the "antidote to poisonous foreign cultural invasion" was simple: improve the quality of the offerings on state television so that viewers do not bother with the satellite fare. Even some of the mullahs might buy that logic.

* * *

March 19, 1995

GET READY FOR MAO'S HEIRS; HONG KONG'S PRESS STARTS TO PULL ITS PUNCHES

By EDWARD A. GARGAN

HONG KONG—The arrival of Communist rule is still three summers away, but Hong Kong's rambunctious, free-swinging press is already beginning to pull its punches lest it offend its future rulers, many journalists here say. In the absence of official censorship, there is a growing perception of self-censorship among many editors and journalists.

"Subtle change would be the best term to describe it," said Daisy Li Yuet-wah, an editor at the independent paper Ming Pao and a leader of the Hong Kong Journalists' Association. "You see a gradual toning down of certain kinds of stories, playing down stories. Day after day this happens. Self-censorship is the greatest threat to Hong Kong journalism right now."

This is only one facet of a gestating worry about what Communist governance here will mean when the British colony passes into the mainland's hands in July 1997. Many in the civil service, in business, law, journalism and the professions have sought foreign citizenship as the ultimate protection from potential tyranny.

Yet many of this colony's 6 million residents—some 40 percent of whom fled Communism in China in the first place—are ineligible for foreign passports and have begun to prepare, in great and little ways, for the new rulers.

The preparations for what is to come are not encouraging. Already, Communist trade union leaders are trying to rally popular support for the end of colonial rule, Communist political groups are active in local elections, and Communist newspapers faithfully reprint Beijing's pronouncements. Toward Hong Kong's free press, China has adopted a mix of threats and inducements; while the Communists have not said so, many journalists are convinced that the aim is to end press freedoms.

A Warning

By far the most serious warning directed to Hong Kong's journalists, and more important, to the entrepreneurs who own the colony's television stations, magazines and newspapers, was the arrest in China in September 1993 of a Ming Pao reporter named Xi Yang. Mr. Xi had been based in China for the paper and managed to uncover the interest rate strategy of China's central bank. For such enterprising reporting, he was convicted of revealing state secrets and sentenced last year to 12 years in prison.

David Armstrong, the editor in chief of the South China Morning Post, the colony's largest English-language daily, said Xi Yang's imprisonment "worried quite a few" reporters in Hong Kong. "It worried one or two of our very good reporters to getting out of journalism."

"Whether intended by the Chinese authorities or not," said Ms. Li of the Journalists' Association, "journalists were shocked by this case. It is a warning signal that you better behave yourself."

Optimism is not entirely dead, however. This summer, a new newspaper, "Apple," is scheduled to appear on the already crowded magazine and paper stands here; according to its founder, Jimmy Lai, its name is meant to evoke Eve because "without Eve biting the apple, we wouldn't be in business—there wouldn't be any sin and there wouldn't be any newspapers." So the paper's subject will be sin and evil, and the primary core of evil, as he sees it, is to be found among the political leaders in Beijing responsible for the Tiananmen massacre in June 1989.

But the path Mr. Lai is setting for himself is an increasingly lonely one. Rupert Murdoch, who heads a sprawling, global media conglomerate, last year removed the British Broadcasting Corporation's television news from a satellite broadcasting system he owns here when the Chinese made their anger known over criticism in the BBC's China coverage. Mr. Murdoch said that to retain the BBC news would jeopardize his business opportunities in China.

Also last year, the larger of Hong Kong's two television stations, TVB, bought the rights to a highly critical BBC documentary on Mao Zedong. But it has refused to broadcast it here, and its ownership of the broadcast rights has prevented the other station, ATV, from doing so either.

Goodbye, Advertisers

Last month, one of the colony's leading China-watching magazines, Contemporary, closed down because, the owners said, advertising had evaporated. Another China-watching magazine, The Nineties, a critical journal known for its considerable range of sources within China's Communist Party, is planning to move its office abroad before 1997.

Many media owners, particularly conservative ones, are notably reticent to discuss press freedom issues. Lo Tak Shing, the chairman of Window, a pro-China English-language economic weekly, and a prominent defender of China's future role here, declined to be interviewed on his views of press freedom.

"I just think it's amazingly dismal," said Stephen Vines, the founding editor of Eastern Express, a paper that started up here last year. "It's inconceivable that if you have the regime you have in Beijing, you'll have the freedom of the press you have now. The mentality of the people who administer it will be so hostile." Mr. Vines left the Express late last year after disagreements with the management over the newspaper's editorial and business decisions.

One of the colony's most prominent columnists, Frank Ching, argues that it is very difficult to identify on a day-to-day basis the extent of self-censorship, of pulled punches in criticism of China.

"It's very difficult to come up with evidence of self-censorship unless people step forward," Mr. Ching said. "But it has been going on for years. I'm sure journalists are worried."

Mr. Lai, who has already hired 360 people to get Apple off the ground in June, is determined to run against the tide. "As we're approaching 1997 people are getting more and more uncertain about the future, more and more nervous," he said. "I think this is a good time to start a newspaper."

'Gradually They Conform'

"The media workers are being flattened by the fear of the future," Mr. Lai continued, "of being careful, of walking a fine line, of not rocking the boat. As far as the future is concerned, they know they'd better be more conservative. The second thing of course are the owners. If they have to exist in business, they have to be flexible in editorials, to make themselves acceptable to the new rulers. Gradually, gradually they conform. You can feel that. It's a very slow metamorphosis."

"Well," he said, sipping a small porcelain cup of tea, "thanks to Eve, we will do things differently. If we don't start a newspaper now, we'll never have enough political muscle or clout to tackle our political opposition. And we're going to do it."

* * *

May 29, 1995

2-EDGED SWORD: ASIAN REGIMES ON THE INTERNET

By PHILIP SHENON

HANOI, Vietnam—Tran Ba Thai sits among tangles of computer wire in his dingy Hanoi office, hoping that he can continue to connect this long-isolated nation to the distant reaches of cyberspace.

So far, the aging Communists who run Vietnam have gone along with Mr. Thai's plans for Net Nam, the first commercial service plugging Vietnam into the global web of computer networks known as the Internet. But Mr. Thai, a 44-year-old computer scientist with Vietnam's Institute of Information Technology, worries that as Vietnam's electronic postmaster, he may be walking a line as thin as a strand of computer wire.

While the Internet holds the promise of bolstering Vietnam's economy by connecting this impoverished nation to the information superhighway, it also means that Vietnam might soon be deluged with the sort of information that the Government has long sought to keep out of the public's hands: the writings of Vietnamese dissidents, reports by human rights groups, pornography.

"I'm sure the Government is concerned about this," Mr. Thai said. "But the Government knows that the advantages of this system are bigger than the disadvantages. Vietnam has been totally isolated, and the Internet is the fastest, cheapest way to reintegrate Vietnam into the world."

The cyberspace revolution may have been born in the computer labs of the West, but its impact will be felt most intensely in the authoritarian nations of Asia, the continent that is home to two-thirds of the world's population and its fastest-growing economies.

And Asian governments are vowing to do what they can to control the Internet. Last week, the iron-fisted Government of Singapore announced that it would prosecute anyone who posted defamatory or obscene material on the Internet. China is expected to restrict access by keeping the cost of local Internet service artificially high.

But it will be impossible to shut off the Internet completely, short of cutting telephone lines and confiscating computers—solutions that are not feasible in countries that are trying to build modern, technologically advanced economies. Information moves over the Internet so rapidly and uncontrollably that in many countries, censorship could be a thing of the past.

While most Asian governments have no affection for the concept of freedom of speech, their disdain for the free flow of information is tempered by the understanding that the future of the world's economy will depend on computers—and the transfer of information, including financial data and mail, over computer networks. Their economic vitality may depend on having a population that is computer literate and, more specifically, Internet literate.

And so China, Vietnam, Indonesia, Singapore and Malaysia, which strictly censor every other form of information available to the public, have been forced to open the information floodgates with the Internet, even though that means allowing everything from political dissent to pornography to go on line.

"For authoritarian governments, it's going to be a losing game to try to control this," said Anthony M. Rutkowski, executive director of the Internet Society, a nonprofit organization in Reston, Va. An estimated 200,000 computers in Asia are now connected to the Internet, a number that is expected to grow exponentially over the next several years. According to the Internet Society, there are now more than 15,000 computers hooked up to the Internet in Hong Kong, more than 8,000 in Singapore, more than 3,000 in Thailand and more than 500 in China.

Most computers are found at universities, government offices and in the offices of large corporations, although increasingly—especially in prosperous areas of Hong Kong and Singapore—computers are found at home, used for everything from word processing to computer games. But given the shortage of reliable telephone lines outside major cities, the Internet is largely an urban phenomenon in Asia.

Among Asia's authoritarian nations, only North Korea and Myanmar, formerly Burma, are sitting out the communications revolution for now, if only because they are too poor to afford computers and the telephone equipment needed to reach the network.

Internet service made its debut in China only two years ago, but there are already at least eight Internet servers there, including a commercial service available to the general public that was established in cooperation with Sprint, the American telecommunications company. The servers allow a computer hookup to the Internet through a local telephone number.

In January, Beijing announced that it would create a nationwide computer network linking more than 100 college campuses to the Internet, even though students at those same campuses were the center of political dissent before the violent 1989 crackdown in Tiananmen Square.

The Communist Government of Vietnam is allowing Internet servers to open for business, even though it has already had difficulty controlling the deluge of electronic mail from dissidents living abroad.

Some fervently anti-Communist Vietnamese dissidents in Southern California have tried to flood the personal electronic mail box of the Prime Minister of Vietnam, Vo Van Kiet, an early advocate of the Internet. That has alarmed the operators of Net Nam, which is urging its subscribers, most of them businesses and private organizations, to avoid transmitting "antisocial" information over the Internet.

No country seems to be more aware of the opportunity and the threat posed by the Internet than Singapore, the wealthy authoritarian city-state that has some of the strictest censorship laws in Asia.

In Singapore, the Government is struck by a contradictory impulse as it tries to establish Singapore as the communications and financial hub of Southeast Asia. The Government talks of making Singapore "an intelligent island," and so it not only allows the public access to the Internet, it encourages it.

The Singapore Government offers two services connecting computer users to the Internet, and a third, private service is being formed. "The choice is either we master the technology or it will master us," said George Yeo, the Minister of Information and the Arts.

But what that means is that a budding Singaporean dissident need only sit down at a computer, dial a local telephone number and type a simple instruction on the keyboard: "soc.culture.singapore," to find a plethora of mostly anonymous invective about the Government, along with some spirited defenses of it.

The free-wheeling criticism—which might well have prompted a knock on the door from the police if it had appeared in a newspaper—is now freely available to tens of thousands of computer users in Singapore—and millions around the world—through the Internet. Playboy may be banned in Singapore, but the magazine's centerfold can be viewed, in full color, on the World Wide Web, an area of the Internet devoted to individually designed collections of text, graphics and sound, ("sites" or "home pages") which are loosely linked together.

China is reportedly planning to limit access by setting high fees for Internet use. At a seminar in Hong Kong last week, a researcher for China's Ministry of Posts and Telecommunications, Jiang Lintao, said that China was looking for other ways of controlling access—"for putting a brake on certain information when the networks become popular." He did not elaborate.

Singapore is calling for self-policing of the system and has warned that it will take legal action against anyone who uses the Internet to transmit pornographic or seditious material. "We should never allow Singapore to be a source of pornographic or incendiary broadcasts," Mr. Yeo said.

Last year, the Singapore Government acknowledged it rifled through the files of users of Technet, one of the two Government-financed Internet providers, in search of pornography. The search turned up a few pornographic images, leading the Government to post a computerized warning to Technet users about "countersocial activity."

But the sweep also alarmed foreign corporations operating in Singapore that use the Internet for electronic mail. The companies feared that the Government might eventually begin snooping into confidential corporate information. The Singapore Government has since assured the companies that it has no intention of conducting more unannounced searches.

Stewart A. Baker, the former general counsel of the National Security Council who is now a Washington lawyer and a specialist in international telecommunications law, said he suspected that Singapore and other governments would crack down on the Internet through litigation against the large companies that provide access to the system—say, a defamation suit against a large multinational corporation with assets in Singapore, whose employees place rude messages about Singapore on the Internet.

"I would think there would be difficulty enforcing this against the little guys—the message senders—but they will go after the big companies that carry the messages," he said.

* * *

February 2, 1996

HANOI TAKES AIM AT WEST'S 'SOCIAL EVILS'

By TIM LARIMER

HANOI, Vietnam, Feb. 1—A copy of Paris Match hit the newsstands here recently with the model Naomi Campbell's bare breasts scratched out. Customs officials are confiscating videotapes of prime-time American television shows, and on Wednesday there was a public burning of pornographic videos and magazines.

It's all part of a reinvigorated Vietnamese Government campaign to eradicate what it calls "social evils" that have proliferated in recent years and are being blamed for everything from increases in crime to the spread of AIDS to the failure of children in school.

"This campaign is very necessary. In fact it should have taken place earlier," said Tran Binh, a concert promoter with the Ministry of Culture. "It is the right time to make pure again our cultural life."

As Vietnam has liberalized its economy and opened its doors to foreigners in recent years, the standard of living has improved. But it is clear that the Government perceives an erosion of moral values, and within it a threat to the Communist Party's control.

Beginning this week, loudspeakers hanging from utility poles in the capital have been blaring warnings about "poisonous" corruptions of Vietnamese culture.

"Don't use pornographic films! Don't use opium! Don't gamble!" reads one of the hundreds of signs—this one illustrated with a picture of a naked woman, a reel of film and hypodermic needles.

Much of the campaign has been directed at the Vietnamese sex industry, which in recent years has come out in the open, especially in Ho Chi Minh City and Hanoi.

As the proprietor of a Hanoi karaoke bar led the way down a back alley to a private room where patrons can receive personal attention from their waitresses, he passed a sign warning people about "dangers to our culture" posted nearby.

Many people say they pay little attention to the campaign.

"It's just for show," a middle-aged professor said. "We do not take these things too seriously."

But conservatives in the Government have grown alarmed by what is perceived as a growing and dangerous influence of foreign culture. State-run television and Government-owned newspapers have fed Vietnamese a steady diet of reports

Reuters

Guarding the revolution against the cultural pollution of Western films and literature filled with sex and violence, Vietnamese officials publicly burned pornographic videos and magazines in Hanoi this week.

about the impact of violent videos on young people. In one case, a teen-ager was accused of murdering an elderly woman and her grandson, supposedly because of the influence of violent films.

In recent weeks, authorities have been raiding video shops, which feature homemade copies of pirated videos, renting for the equivalent of about 10 cents. The inspectors have been confiscating any tapes that do not bear the official seal of Government censors. Vendors said the approved films are often dull and unpopular with customers.

"Video tapes with violence and sex have a bad influence on the young generation," said a 21-year-old engineering student named Dzung. "The morals of this generation might go down if this situation continues."

Do he and his friends like the "poisonous" videos—kung fu, gangster and pornography tapes?

"Of course!" shouted his friend, 21-year-old Liem.

Like many Vietnamese with access to video players, they count "Gone With the Wind" among their favorites. They saw "Forrest Gump" at a small theater that plays foreign films. They even like "Rambo," the Sylvester Stallone movie about an M.I.A.-hunter.

"Sometimes they do teach us something good," Dzung explained. Such as? "Usually all films have a happy ending," he replied. "And I like the gunfire. It is good. But I think we have watched gunfire for the last time."

* * *

April 18, 1996

THE PERILS OF THE PRESS IN INDONESIA INCLUDE JAIL

By EDWARD A. GARGAN

JAKARTA, Indonesia—The clang of a steel door slamming echoed against the concrete walls as Eko Maryadi waited for his friends, a computer disk clutched in his fingers. At the massive wooden gate of the central prison, a guard yanked on the door's iron ring, directing the visitors toward the holding cage.

"We can still write," Mr. Maryadi explained, as his visitors signed the registry. "We may be in prison, but we still write."

For the last year, Mr. Maryadi and Ahmad Taufik have been imprisoned here, charged with publishing a magazine without a permit and with spreading hatred of the Government. Danang Wardoyo, the young man who brought tea around to editors of the magazine, Independen, was also imprisoned, just for being there.

"You have to have a permit from the Ministry of Information," said Mr. Taufik as he puffed away on a sweetly scented clove cigarette, squatting on the concrete floor of the cell with his colleagues, all in their 20's. "But we didn't have a permit, because we don't agree with that. We refused."

[Jakarta's High Court recently increased the sentences on Mr. Maryadi and Mr. Taufik to three years, from 32 months, after they appealed their original sentences. In March, the Supreme Court rejected the pair's appeal.]

Edward A. Gargan/The New York Times

Indonesia's press controls remain severe, but the Government's grip is weakening and jailed journalists are able to publish over the Internet. Four journalist imprisoned in Jakarta share a cell: from left to right, Danang Wardoyo, Triagus Siswowikarjo, Eko Maryadi and Ahmad Taufik, standing.

Their imprisonment, coming on the heels of the closing of several magazines in 1994, has underscored the continuing dangers of working as a journalist in Indonesia.

Still, Indonesia has permitted Mr. Maryadi and his colleagues to continue to write on their laptop computers and has not tried to stop them from using the Internet. Their jailhouse writings now appear in a magazine put out by Indonesia's unofficial journalists' organization.

In a country of 190 million people that has been governed by an authoritarian President for three decades, controls over the press, while severe and punitive, are fraying, and technology is erasing the old boundaries of where journalism is practiced.

Indeed, even the Government has in some ways recognized that absolute control of the press is impossible because the means no longer exist and because the country is demanding a loosening of the reins.

"It's confusing to discover some of the paradoxes," explained Goenawan Mohamad, the former editor of Tempo, the country's oldest and most respected political news magazine, which was closed by the Government in 1994. "The basic thing is that there seem now to be no rules. You just test the water."

In the summer of 1994, Tempo and two other weeklies, DeTIK and Editor, aggressively investigated the purchase of former East German warships on the orders of a Government minister and the ensuing objections of the Finance Ministry over what it said was wasteful spending. Days later, President Suharto denounced the magazines for exposing the deep divisions in the Government. Twelve days later, the three publications were banned and Mr. Mohamad was out of a job.

The closings brought more than 1,500 journalists onto Jakarta's streets to protest the shutdowns. As the protests mounted in intensity, soldiers wielding rattan sticks and shields charged the journalists, ending a rare moment of public dissent.

When the Government-controlled journalists' association refused to protest the banning of the magazines, several hundred journalists organized their own association, the Alliance of Independent Journalists. Harmoko, the Information Minister, declared that the new group's "existence cannot be justified." But despite official harassment, the group survived.

"This was the first time people went to the streets to protest the banning of a publication," said Mr. Mohamad, whose careful, soft-spoken manner hardly hints at his reputation as a threat to the Government.

"Now you can't publish a newspaper or magazine without having someone the Government approves of as an investor,' he said. "You have to have a license to publish. As long as there's a license and a minister has a right to withdraw that license, there will be problems."

Immediately after Tempo was banned, Mr. Mohamad decided to challenge the Government, taking it to court seeking to overturn the shutdown order. To his amazement, and that of almost everyone in the country, he won.

"We were totally surprised," he said. "We didn't believe we would win. The idea was not to win, but to challenge the Government publicly so it had a problem to deal with."

The Government quickly appealed to a higher court. Again, Mr. Mohamad and Tempo won.

"It was extraordinary," said Mr. Mohamad, who now is the director of the Institute for Studies on the Free Flow of Information, a group of journalists that spreads news of the press and Indonesia over the Internet. Tempo's case has now been taken before Indonesia's Supreme Court, a bench that Mr. Mohamad said he frankly did not believe would be able to stand up to the Government.

Aristides Kotoppo, the former editor of Suara Pembaruan, a widely read daily here, said: "The Tempo case had a very chilling effect. That the first two courts have granted Tempo's appeal is outstanding. But the magazine is still closed. The basic problem is that the boundaries are never very clear. That is the problem editors and reporters have to cope with. Now there are cases where the court is becoming a little more assertive toward the Government."

In moments of candor, some officials express discomfort over the heavy-handed treatment of the press.

"Do not look at a static snapshot," said Adi Sosono, the chairman of the Center for Information and Development Studies, a Government research group here. "Some setbacks, like freedom of the press, the ban on Tempo Magazine—that's a part of the process that we have to go through. Tempo is just a case, but the process of liberalization is one to go through. No Government can resist the pressure of the middle class."

Still, the Government remains acutely sensitive to critical reporting and continues to lash out at journalists less established than Mr. Mohamad and Mr. Kotoppo.

When Mr. Maryadi and Mr. Taufik published an investigative article in Independent, their unregistered magazine, examining the extent of the Information Minister's involvement in ownership of newspapers, magazines and radio stations, they were immediately arrested.

"We were accused of spreading hatred," said Mr. Taufik, referring to a law remaining from Dutch colonial rule. "The court does not need to prove what kind of hatred. Actually the court couldn't prove what actually we have done. But we were convicted anyway."

At their raucous trial last September, spectators in the courtroom harangued the three judges with cries of "Show trial!" and waved banners and sang protest songs. Unmoved, the judges pronounced the journalists guilty of spreading hatred against the Government.

But while they serve their sentences, they are allowed visits in which computer disks are exchanged, news passed along and plans drawn up for activities by the independent journalists' association.

By law, all working journalists are supposed to belong to the Government journalists' organization, but younger reporters are increasingly shunning the official body in favor of the renegade association.

"The Government doesn't recognize us," said Santoso, the association's president, as he hunkered down on the cell floor with his imprisoned colleagues. "The Government doesn't even say we are illegal. There's some ambiguity."

"There are still three things that the Government won't let anybody write about," Mr. Santoso said. "One is the succession to Suharto, one is the Suharto family and its business activities and one is the role of the military in Government. But we don't care about the rule. If we think it's good to write about, we do."

Mr. Maryadi laughed and handed Mr. Santoso a floppy disk. "We don't know what will happen. It's all very unpredictable. That's Indonesia."

* * *

May 6, 1997

UNESCO AWARD TO IMPRISONED CHINESE JOURNALIST ANGERS BEIJING

By BARBARA CROSSETTE

UNITED NATIONS, May 5—Unesco, an agency attacked by Western nations little more than a decade ago for its involvement in efforts to regulate the world's news organizations, is now under threat of retaliation from China because of a press freedom award it presented on Saturday to an imprisoned Chinese journalist.

Unesco's resistance to demands from China that it dissociate itself from the award to the journalist, Gao Yu, is unusual in the United Nations system, where the Chinese, ever vigilant for potential criticism, have frequently had their way in censoring or altering events.

In 1995, during the 50th anniversary of the United Nations, China did not allow the Dalai Lama, the exiled Tibetan leader, to take any part in the celebrations, including an interfaith service at the Cathedral of St. John the Divine in New York.

This weekend Ms. Gao, 52, who was sent to jail for six years in 1994 for reporting on how Communist Party leaders controlled Government decision-making, received the first Unesco/Guillermo Cano World Press Freedom Prize intended to honor journalists whose work brought risk or punishment.

As late as last week, Chinese officials were warning Unesco's Director General, Federico Mayor of Spain, that Beijing regarded the press award as "gross interference" in Chinese affairs that would damage relations between Beijing and the organization.

Chinese diplomats say Ms. Gao is a criminal, not a journalist. Mr. Mayor rejected repeated requests from China that the award be withdrawn and went to an international conference in Bilbao, Spain, on Saturday, to make the presentation himself.

Ms. Gao was represented by the World Association of Journalists, which had nominated her. The conference was sponsored by the International Federation of Journalists.

In a statement sent to the meeting by her family, who told her of the prize during a visit with her in prison, Ms. Gao called the award a mark of recognition that should be shared with all Chinese intellectuals. She quoted from the poet Pablo Neruda, who had written: "Deny me bread, deny me light, and spring. But never your laugh, for I would surely die." Ms. Gao added, "I think I have found Neruda's laugh from this faraway international conference hall."

The Chinese are expected to raise the issue of the award to Ms. Gao at a Unesco executive board meeting beginning on May 26. Rumors are circulating in Paris, where Unesco is based, that Beijing might withdraw from the organization or cease taking part in its activities. China could also close a Unesco office in Beijing.

In Paris, a Chinese diplomat, Zhao Changxing, told journalists that the award was "illegal." Calls to the Chinese Mission in New York were not returned.

Ms. Gao, a journalist of 20 years' experience with the China News Service and then the Economics Weekly in Beijing, also published some reports abroad, including in a Hong Kong magazine, Mirror Monthly, analyzing how the Chinese Government worked.

She was arrested in October 1993, two days before she was to leave China for a year at Columbia University. She had also been detained for 14 months after the violent suppression of the protests in Beijing in 1989.

The Unesco/Guillermo Cano World Press Freedom Prize is named for a Colombian editor, Guillermo Cano Isaza, who was assassinated in Bogota in 1986 at the offices of his newspaper, El Espectador. The attack was believed to be related to the paper's campaign against drug trafficking. The recipient of the $25,000 annual award is chosen by an independent panel of journalists.

* * *

August 30, 1997

JAPAN BARS CENSORSHIP OF ATROCITIES IN TEXTS

By NICHOLAS D. KRISTOF

TOKYO, Aug. 29—In a landmark victory for Japanese who have been trying to educate young people about their country's wartime atrocities, the Supreme Court ruled today for the first time that the Government had broken the law by censoring textbooks to remove references to the slaughter of civilians.

The ruling was a remarkable triumph for an 83-year-old education professor, Saburo Ienaga, a frail and bespectacled man who has led a 32-year court battle to force the Government to allow schools to use textbooks that give children a glimpse of the brutalities committed by Japanese forces in China, Korea and elsewhere during World War II.

Mr. Ienaga's other lawsuits had ended in defeat, but today the Supreme Court sided with him and declared that the Education Ministry had gone too far in its censorship. The court ordered the ministry to curb its censorship in the future as much as possible and not to impose its own ideas on the scholarship of those who write the books.

The court ruling goes to the heart of an issue that continues to ignite soul-searching and debate in Japan and fierce acrimony between Japan and other Asian countries. The ruling was therefore not just about the past but also about the present, because a major reason for the tensions and antagonisms swirling through Asia is resentment at Japanese brutality in World War II and the perception that Japan has never confronted what it has done.

China and South Korea and North Korea, in particular, are deeply suspicious of Japan and sometimes worry that Japan's reluctance to teach children about the past suggests that it may become aggressive again.

To be sure, Mr. Ienaga's victory was only a partial one. The court declared that the Education Ministry's system of censoring textbooks is itself legal; it simply found that the ministry had abused the system by deleting references to well-documented atrocities.

"Unfortunately, we did not receive the all-out victory that we had hoped for," Mr. Ienaga said at a news conference. "But the ruling revealed that textbook screening can be illegal."

The ruling, which granted Mr. Ienaga token damages of $3,400, is likely to be important primarily for its moral force, emboldening scholars who write textbooks and making Education Ministry censors more hesitant to demand changes. Already, the censors have given up enormous ground, allowing far more straightforward treatment in the books than was imaginable a dozen years ago.

One of Mr. Ienaga's battles, for instance, was over the word "aggression" in school textbooks. The ministry ordered him in the 1980's not to characterize Japan's invasion of China as aggression, saying the term had "negative ethical connotations." It suggested that he use the expression "military advance."

Under pressure from China and South Korea, the Government later backed down, and textbooks now contain passing references to Japanese "aggression."

One point of contention in today's ruling was a mention in Mr. Ienaga's high school history textbook of the Japanese Army's Unit 731, which conducted experiments in germ warfare and tried to create plague outbreaks in China. Veterans of the unit have described dissecting prisoners-of-war while they were alive and conducting brutal experiments on Chinese mothers and children.

The ministry had ordered Mr. Ienaga to expunge all references to Unit 731 from his textbooks. But the court said the ministry had gone too far, because the atrocities of Unit 731 "had been established beyond denial." More broadly, it urged that censorship in general be curtailed as much as possible.

"It is requested that the Government refrain from intervening in educational content as much as possible," the court declared.

Japan's system of censoring schoolbooks was imposed by the American occupation authorities immediately after World War II. The American forces wanted to insure that textbooks did not encourage renewed emperor-worship and military aggression, and the system continued when the Americans left.

Until a few years ago, the public battles were between historians, often liberals who were deeply apologetic about Japanese war-time deeds, and Government bureaucrats who tended to be far less inclined to admit that atrocities had happened. But as the liberals made gains, a backlash developed.

Some scholars, led by the Sankei Shimbun newspaper and a Tokyo University professor, Nobukatsu Fujioka, have won widespread support by protesting that Japanese textbooks now teach children to take a terrible view of their own nation.

* * *

September 1, 1997

A TERROR TO JOURNALISTS, HE SNIFFS OUT TERRORISTS

By STEPHEN KINZER

ISTANBUL, Turkey, Aug. 27—In a sunlit office near the Bosporus shore, Erol Canozkan spends his days reading newspapers in search of terrorist propaganda.

Mr. Canozkan is a Government prosecutor assigned to help enforce Turkey's press laws. Many critics here and abroad say the laws limit free speech and penalize writers who speak frankly about social and political problems. But Mr. Canozkan is proud to be on the front line of what he calls a war against subversives who seek to destroy Turkey.

"We have special laws here because a war is being fought in this country," he said, referring to the 13-year-old conflict between the army and separatist Kurdish guerrillas. "As part of their strategy, the terrorists have set up all kinds of little newspapers that openly advocate the violent destruction of Turkey. The people who write for these papers are not real journalists, but spokesmen for terrorist groups."

When Mr. Canozkan finds an article that he deems an incitement to violence or that he thinks insults the security forces or the memory of Mustafa Kemal Ataturk, founder of the Turkish Republic, he puts it in a pink folder with the offending passages underlined. Then he forwards it to his superiors for possible prosecution.

"I get a very good feeling doing this work," he said. "I'm defending the Turkish nation and its unity. My only regret is that we have not been able to explain to our friends in the West why it is so urgent that we do this."

Although there is no prior censorship in Turkey, laws that restrict press freedom are considerably tighter than those in the United States and most Western countries. Foreign governments and international press organizations have condemned the laws, saying they are used to suppress not only libel of state institutions but also legitimate criticism.

It is difficult to ascertain how many Turkish journalists are currently in prison for actions that would be considered legal in most Western countries. The Publishers' Association of Turkey estimates the number at more than 100. The New York-based Committee to Protect Journalists, which sent a delegation here in July to urge loosening of press laws, said there were 78 before the release of six this month.

"We want to save Turkey from the shame of being a country where writers and intellectuals suffer in prisons," Sezer Duru, chairman of the writers' organization PEN-Turkey, said in a recent speech. "Our greatest wish is to live in a modern, civilized, democratic and peaceful environment."

The two-month-old Government of Prime Minister Mesut Yilmaz has pledged to take steps toward greater press freedom; past governments also made such promises and failed to keep them. Powerful political forces, among them the military, insist that restrictive press laws are necessary to fight subversion.

"We are not going to allow debates in which the Turkish flag is called 'a piece of cloth,' the national anthem is called 'a piece of music,' and the Turkish Republic's founder and leader, Kemal Ataturk, is exposed to humiliation," Adm. Guven Erkaya, commander of the Turkish Navy, recently told the Istanbul newspaper Milliyet. "Debates like these aim to create a vacuum which would be exploited by those who wish to replace the current regime with an outdated model."

This month, the Turkish Parliament passed an amnesty that resulted in the release of six editors who had been jailed for permitting the publication of illegal articles. Conditions of the amnesty were very narrow; the laws under which the editors had been imprisoned were not changed. The six were warned that they would be sent back to prison if they wrote or published more articles deemed illegal.

Asked a few days after his release why he thought Turkish governments had been so reluctant to allow broader press freedom, one of the editors, Ocak Isik Yurtcu, who spent

Staton R. Winter for The New York Times

Thanks to the efforts of Erol Canozkan and prosecutors like him, Ayse Nur Zarakolu, who operates a publishing house out of an Istanbul basement, has served four prison terms for subversive acts since 1982.

more than three years in prison, smiled wanly and replied: "I can't really say. Please understand that I'm on probation. You know what that means."

One of the most relentless challengers to Turkey's press laws is a publisher named Ayse Nur Zarakolu. She opened the Belge International Publishing House in 1976 and now operates it from a cluttered basement in downtown Istanbul. She describes her mission as challenging taboos, and she has done that as relentlessly as anyone in this country.

In the last few years, Ms. Zarakolu has published books that denounce the Government's war against Kurdish guerrillas, accuse the security forces of involvement with death squads and document mass killings of Armenians in the early years of the century. She has served four prison terms since 1982 and was most recently convicted for publishing a human rights report that quoted an unidentified diplomat describing some Turkish soldiers as "thugs."

Twenty-two cases are currently pending against Ms. Zarakolu, but she shows no sign of weakening. After her most recent conviction, she vowed to continue her work even if it meant more prison time.

"If we are going to have real democracy in Turkey," she said, "we have to break away from the official ideology. As long as people cannot express their identities and their views, they are not really free."

Some Turks, including Oktay Eksi, president of the Press Council, an independent group that works closely with the Government, assert that the figures on imprisoned journalists given by the Publishers' Association of Turkey and the Committee to Protect Journalists are too high.

"We have looked at every case," Mr. Eksi said in an interview, "and after eliminating journalists who were convicted of crimes like rape and fraud, and those who directly advocated terror or violence, we came up with 24 who were truly imprisoned for simply expressing peaceful beliefs. With the recent releases, we now count 18. I am not going to tell you that 18 is not a big number. One is too many. But it's important to give a true picture."

Like many Turkish journalists, Mr. Eksi was not very excited by the recent release of six jailed editors.

"Of course it's a first step," he said, "but it's not enough. It was done under pressure, and the goal was only to create some good will, not to change the situation in any serious way. We are still at the beginning stage."

* * *

October 5, 1998

50 YEARS LATER, GANDHI'S KILLER IS GAGGED IN INDIA

By CELIA W. DUGGER

BOMBAY, India—The melodrama was irresistible to the playwright Pradeep Dalvi: an eloquent, idealistic thinker who had studied the teachings of history fires three bullets into the bony chest of this century's greatest apostle of nonviolence, Mohandas K. Gandhi, then puts down his gun and shouts for the police to arrest him.

Audiences packed the Shivaji Mandir auditorium in July to see Mr. Dalvi's play about Gandhi's assassin, Nathuram Godse, 50 years after the murder of India's most beloved pacifist. Many theatergoers lustily cheered the killer's impassioned condemnations of Gandhi's philosophy.

"What kind of nonviolence is this?" the protagonist asks. "We are advised to keep quiet when Hindus are being massacred. But to allow a massacre is violence, not nonviolence."

The drama won no fans in the Hindu nationalist-led Government in New Delhi. Despite sold-out shows, "I, Nathuram Godse Speaking," was shut down after only seven performances, banned by Maharashtra State as a threat to law and order on the strong recommendation of the national Government. The play's producers say they will fight the ban in state court after they have the script translated into English from Marathi, as the court requires.

The case touches on free speech, but also on Indians' complicated attitude toward the man considered the father of their nation—and toward his assassin. Gandhi is a kind of secular saint here, but his ideals are admired more in principle than in practice.

Recently, there has been a rash of plays and books that portray Gandhi as a flawed father and husband. They have been tolerated. But Mr. Dalvi's drama, which he says does not glorify the killer, has been widely interpreted as doing so. And that has proved more than the country's leaders are willing to countenance.

If the producers lose their court battle to lift the ban, the drama's next venue may well be Dayton, Ohio. There, Harsh Trivedi, who heads a small foundation that promotes Indian culture, will put on his own English translation of the play in the spring.

"I had planned to tone down some of the provocative lines, but in view of the ban, which is quite shocking, I'll produce the play in full without changing anything," he said.

The play is largely based on court records and Mr. Godse's lengthy final speech to the court, as well as Mr. Dalvi's interviews with surviving conspirators. Mr. Godse's character, talking easily with the audience, narrates his evolution from a young militant who saw himself as a defender of Hindus to the man who committed the most dastardly crime in modern-day India. The play takes him through his trial and walk to the gallows. "People came backstage to touch the feet of the actor who played Godse," Mr. Dalvi said.

In his remarks to the court, Mr. Godse blamed Gandhi for the 1947 partition of the country into Pakistan and India, which Gandhi lobbied against behind the scenes but did not crusade against in public. Hundreds of thousands were killed in the mass migration of Hindus and Muslims after the division.

The assassin also condemned what he saw as Gandhi's favoritism toward Muslims. In his final fast, Gandhi, who believed the best way to peace between Hindus and Muslims lay in the generosity of the dominant Hindus, insisted that India pay predominantly Muslim Pakistan a financial settlement promised at partition.

Ashis Nandy, a well-known political psychologist who is a senior fellow at the Center for the Study of Developing Societies in New Delhi, makes the provocative assertion that the murder cleared the way for India to become a conventional, modern nation built on reason, science and industry. Mr. Godse advocated what Mr. Nandy calls "Kissingerian realpolitik"—that India should act in its own self-interest and strive to be a military and industrial power on the world stage.

"Godse articulated the myth of the modern nation-state in a way that the Indian middle class would like to subscribe to, but he also killed Gandhi, so they feel morally uncomfortable about agreeing with some of Godse's ideas," Mr. Nandy said. "That is why they would like to avoid confronting the issues raised by the play."

The play certainly outraged guardians of Gandhian ideals across India. Even some of those who battled censorship under the British Raj say that restrictions on expression are occasionally justified in a country where words can lead to murderous outbreaks of violence between caste and religious groups.

In 1989, the Congress Party made this argument to justify banning Salman Rushdie's novel "The Satanic Verses," which some Muslims said had blasphemed their God. And this ambivalence is written into India's Constitution, which guarantees free expression but also allows it to be restricted in the interests of public order and morality.

Critics say censorship has too often been used by elected officials who are really pandering to voting constituencies—in the case of Mr. Dalvi's play, the millions of Indians who revere Gandhi as a hallowed leader. But The Times of India, the nation's largest English-language daily, praised the decision. "Any act condoning a heinous crime offends public morality, as well," it said.

Mr. Dalvi said he got the idea for the play in the early 1980's when he met Mr. Godse's brother, Gopal, who kept the assassin's ashes in a pewter urn. "I actually saw the ashes," Mr. Dalvi said. "I touched them."

The Stage Performances Scrutiny Board in Maharashtra, a culture police that exists in all Indian states, denied permission to produce the play when Mr. Dalvi first requested it in 1984. But when he asked again this year, three years after a Hindu nationalist coalition took power here, the board gave its approval.

"We are not staunch Gandhians," said Pramod Navalkar, Maharashtra's Minister of Culture. "But we respect Gandhi and we found that there was no insult to the Mahatma."

Usha Mehta, a tiny 78-year-old woman who heads the Gandhi Memorial Trust in Bombay and who was once a soldier in Gandhi's nonviolent army, disagreed and single-handedly sparked the campaign against the play. She never saw the drama, but she was outraged when she read an article in a Marathi newspaper that quoted Mr. Dalvi as saying he hoped audiences would smash statues of Gandhi after seeing his play. Ms. Mehta immediately wrote a letter of protest to the Prime Minister, Atal Behari Vajpayee.

"We as freedom fighters know the value of freedom of expression, but we certainly do not equate freedom with license," she said.

Mr. Dalvi denies that he encouraged playgoers to smash Gandhi's statue and insists that he was only trying to explain, not justify, Mr. Godse's indefensible act.

The opposition Congress Party led the fight to ban the play on the floor of Parliament in New Delhi. Mr. Vajpayee, who heads the Hindu nationalist Bharatiya Janata Party and seeks to distance it from Mr. Godse's brand of zealotry, asked Home Minister L. K. Advani to act. Mr. Advani advised the state to ban the play.

After the play's supporters and opponents clashed outside the theater on July 17, the state—led by a coalition that includes Mr. Vajpayee's party—held an emergency Cabinet meeting and bowed to the wishes of the Government in New Delhi. The Bombay Commissioner of Police revoked the license to perform the play.

Mr. Dalvi says his motives have been misunderstood and his rights violated. In an interview, he said that Nathuram Godse himself had become "the hero of this thing" and that Mr. Godse's co-conspirator and brother, Gopal, had credited the playwright with giving the assassin a voice from the grave.

"Gopal said, 'I could not take what Nathuram wanted to say to the people for 50 years,'" Mr. Dalvi said. "'What I could not do in 50 years, Pradeep Dalvi did in eight days.'"

* * *

January 19, 1999

CHINA TIGHTENS REIN ON WRITERS AND PUBLISHERS

By ERIK ECKHOLM

BEIJING, Jan. 18—As they very publicly send the most outspoken democracy campaigners to prison, China's leaders have also quietly tightened the screws on liberal intellectuals, journalists and publications.

In the last few weeks the Communist Party's powerful Department of Propaganda has closed down an influential book publisher in Beijing and an adventurous newspaper in the southern city of Guangzhou.

It has sent stern warnings to some magazines and newspapers that strayed too far from the prescribed line, forced some editors and writers out of their jobs and halted distribution of several books that delve into political alternatives or embarrassing episodes in the history of Communist rule.

Although some writings and meetings that are relatively free by China's standards continue, the campaign reflects the leadership's concern for stability as it confronts rising unemployment and protests by workers and farmers.

Officials may also be worried about dissent related to the 10th anniversary this June of the violent smashing of pro-democracy demonstrations in Tiananmen Square and the 50th anniversary of the founding of the People's Republic of China on Oct. 1.

In the last year, liberals who want more open discussion of political alternatives have been testing the limits of public discourse. But in recent interviews, many scholars, magazine editors and journalists said they now sensed a shrinking of the boundaries.

None of those interviewed said they believed that China was in the throes of an all-out crackdown or a major shift in policy like the one in late 1989 that followed the suppression of the Tiananmen Square protests, when liberals were purged from many institutions.

Since many books, magazines and newspapers touch on sensitive topics these days, the repressive measures to date seem almost arbitrary. They have not been mentioned in the press here. But word spreads quickly, and the authorities may hope that by setting examples they will induce others to exercise new caution.

"I don't think there will be a general crackdown on liberal intellectuals," said one such scholar, Liu Junning, a political theorist with the Chinese Academy of Social Sciences and editor of a journal on political thought. "But they may tighten up on publications, making it more difficult for people to get their ideas out."

Some intellectuals interviewed said that in today's China, with burgeoning outlets for publishing, so many intellectuals chafing to explore new ideas and so many eager readers, the Government probably lacked the ability to suppress debate altogether. The Internet and electronic mail, for example, have given many Chinese new access to unauthorized writing.

Even before the recent setbacks, writers could not directly discuss multiparty politics or the possibility of ending the Communist Party's monopoly on power. Still, the last year has been a relatively loose period, with more books frankly discussing issues like corruption, crime, the effects of different economic strategies and—in a guarded, theoretical way—the nature of democracy.

Such books, in turn, have served as the basis for seminars at universities and bookstores. Only a small number of those books that the Government sees as most objectionable have been directly curbed.

Many newspapers and magazines around the country have explored similar topics and exposed local corruption and policy failures.

The publications campaign is directed by the party's Department of Propaganda, under the leadership of Ding Guangen, a onetime bridge partner of the late leader Deng Xiaoping who has become President Jiang Zemin's chief ideological enforcer.

A joke that plays on the phonetic elements of Mr. Ding's name has been circulating among intellectuals, who say he has a talent for three things: "ding," which can mean "keeping watch"; "guan," which can mean "closing down," and "gen," which can mean "rooting out."

Perhaps the most far-reaching act was the suspension in early January of operations of one of China's boldest and most influential book publishers pending "rectification" of the staff. Two top editors at the company, China Today Publishers, have been ordered to write self-criticisms—a time-honored Communist technique for forcing wayward individuals to acknowledge ideological errors—said people familiar with the situation, who spoke on condition of anonymity.

China Today Publishers, based in Beijing and operating under the authority of an information unit of the Communist Party, issued several of last year's most widely discussed books, including "China's Pitfall," a withering analysis of corruption in the dismantling of state enterprises; "Crossed Swords," a strong attack on the remaining opponents of the country's move toward a market economy and looser social control; and "Political China," a collection of essays on political change by scholars and former officials.

In the case of "Political China," which quickly sold out its first printing of 30,000 last fall, the authorities forbade a second printing. Other books from the publisher have not been quashed in this manner.

But several books recently issued by other publishers, volumes of essays on politics or memoirs of past ideological battles, have been restricted, usually by barring new printings or distribution or even book reviews.

So far, at least, the suppression of liberal writing is not universal. Mr. Liu, the political theorist, edits a journal of political thought called Res Publica that has operated on the edge.

The latest issue of the journal, which has a circulation of 10,000, contains essays exploring the difference between direct democracy, in which top levels of government are elected by the people, and the kind of indirect democracy that the leaders in Beijing say China has. Mr. Liu said he had not heard any official complaints.

A number of other small journals and magazines explore once-heretical political and economic ideas, including one called Reading Tour that has just appeared in the southern province of Guangdong.

Its maiden issue includes articles with titles like "Freedom of Thought and Democratic Politics" and "The Loneliness of the Dissident," and an essay by the late anti-Communist philosopher Isaiah Berlin.

But a highbrow Beijing journal called Way, which under its mandate for exploration of the natural and social sciences has carried venturesome articles on politics and society, is under sharp pressure from the authorities, who have told its editors to stick to more scientific subjects or close down, people who have written for the journal say.

In an interview last week, Feng Xiaozhe, the editorial director of Way, which has a monthly circulation of 20,000, would only say: "We have not received any official written complaint from the Department of Propaganda." In the absence of a formal complaint, he said, the journal will continue its efforts to promote "cross-disciplinary inquiry."

On Saturday more than 40 of the journal's editors, authors and supporters met to discuss the challenge, said one of those who took part in the meeting. While the group, including some eminent scientists, endorsed its current direction, the editors said future issues would include more articles related to science. Whether that will satisfy the authorities is unclear.

Officials have had special concern about some newspapers in Guangdong Province, which borders Hong Kong. It has a more advanced market economy and generally more free-wheeling attitude than most of China.

An adventurous weekly, Cultural Times, published under the auspices of the Guangzhou Academy of Social Sciences and distributed in major cities around China, was shut down by the authorities on Dec. 30.

In December the authorities ordered the dismissal of the chief editor and other senior leaders of another newspaper in Guangzhou, the provincial capital, called the Guangzhou-Hong Kong Information Daily.

A Communist Party circular said the paper, which concentrated on economic news, had interfered with the work of the country by reporting too critically on economic goals, among other issues, the Hong Kong newspaper Ming Pao reported.

A nationally prominent weekly in Guangzhou, Southern Weekend, which has a reputation for writing about ignored social controversies, has also felt the Government's sting. The authorities have ordered the paper to discipline some editors and writers and to dismiss a regular columnist who has written about corrupt and incompetent officials, journalists said.

But one of the affected scholars said this week, "We'll be trying in every way possible to keep writing and publishing and discussing."

"The public demand is huge" for new ideas about politics and economics, he said, "and the supply is limited."

* * *

July 19, 1999

TURKEY IS ASTIR OVER BOOK OF ARMY VETERANS' VIEWS

By STEPHEN KINZER

ISTANBUL, Turkey—A taboo fell in Turkey earlier this year when a book appeared containing interviews with 42 army veterans, many of them disillusioned by their role in fighting Kurdish insurgents.

The book, which sold about 10,000 copies, gave readers a view of the Kurdish war quite different from the official version. But although many reviewers praised it, prosecutors declared the book insulting to the military, issued an order banning it and seized unsold copies.

What many of the veterans had to say was explosive. Some said that their commanders turned a blind eye to war profiteers and drug smugglers. Others asserted that they saw soldiers mistreat Kurdish civilians. Several said they went to war poorly trained and believing the official line that their enemies were mindless terrorists, but slowly concluded that the insurgents were actually fighting for their rights and enjoyed wide popular support.

The ban on this book was one of several steps the Government has taken recently to maintain its limits on what is written about the Kurdish conflict. The arrest and conviction of the main Kurdish rebel leader, Abdullah Ocalan, has not eased the Government's pursuit of such cases. It may even have convinced the authorities that if they act vigorously now, they can wipe out Kurdish nationalism once and for all.

Those who publish dissenting views of the war being waged in southeast Turkey are often charged with abetting terrorism, a charge for which scores of Turkish writers and politicians have been jailed during the 1990's. Human rights advocates often criticize laws that restrict freedom of speech in Turkey. These laws have also been cited as one reason for Turkey's failure to be named as a candidate for membership in the European Union.

Dissatisfaction with the laws may be growing inside Turkey, though. Several months ago Parliament moved to repeal one of them, but dropped the idea after military commanders warned that a repeal would hinder their efforts to fight terrorism and religious fundamentalism.

The paperback at the center of the newest case is called "Mehmet's Book," a reference to the nickname by which army recruits are popularly known. In the country's repressive atmosphere, the book's publication was the first time that the views of ordinary war veterans had been presented to the public and it undercut the fighters' official image as committed defenders of the nation.

"What did I do?" said Nadire Mater, the journalist and human rights advocate who conducted and transcribed the interviews. "I didn't even write this book. I just put a microphone in front of these young men and let them talk." Although no case has yet been filed against her for publishing these interviews, she expects one soon.

"The people don't like the army and wish it would go away," says one veteran who, like everyone else in the book, is identified only by a first name. "With their eyes they say, 'Get out of my sight or die.'"

One veteran tells of soldiers who slice the ears off corpses to prove their kills. Another says that his commander cut off water supplies to a village for three months after a farmer complained that a soldier had shot his dog.

"I don't know what we're fighting for," said one veteran. "Who are we pointing our guns at? Those people have a reason to go to the mountains. But me—why was I in the army?"

"Mehmet's Book" shows that at least some veterans of the Kurdish war suffer symptoms of emotional stress that have also been reported by Americans who fought in Vietnam and Russians who fought in Afghanistan. "Since I've been back," says one, "every time I get angry I think about shooting someone."

Ms. Mater said: "In the 15 years we have been living with this conflict, everyone has had a chance to speak out except the young men who are doing the fighting. Now they are telling their stories. For letting them do it, I'm accused of insulting the military. It makes me very angry. I love this country, but sometimes it is very difficult to live here."

She has learned that Turkish journalists are not immune from prosecution even if the words in their books belong to others. Recently, a prominent columnist, Oral Calislar, was sentenced to 13 months in prison for publishing an interview with Mr. Ocalan, in 1993, even though Mr. Ocalan is now in a Turkish prison under sentence of death.

"It's very hard to criticize the state in sensitive areas, especially when it has to do with the Kurds," Mr. Calislar said. "Every week, 15 dead soldiers are coming back to western Turkey. In this situation, if you criticize the state you are considered a traitor. They have plenty of laws to put you in jail."

An appeals court recently upheld Mr. Calislar's sentence for "publishing written propaganda aimed at undermining Turkey's unity."

A third journalist who has recently felt the weight of Turkish law is Andrew Finkel, a British citizen who has lived in Istanbul for more than a decade and reports for The Times of London, CNN and Time magazine. Foreign correspondents here are not subject to prosecution for articles they publish abroad, but until recently Mr. Finkel also wrote columns for a Turkish newspaper. One of them has led prosecutors to file a case against him.

In a column published last year, Mr. Finkel wrote about his visit to the embattled Kurdish town of Sirnak. He said progress had been made over the years there, and that the army is now "a long way from behaving like an army of occupation."

The use of that phrase, even in what seemed to be a positive way, led prosecutors to charge Mr. Finkel with "insulting state institutions." If convicted, he could face up to six years in prison.

"The first news story I ever wrote from Turkey was in 1986, a piece for the Guardian newspaper in which I covered the appearance of Bulent Ecevit in court," he said. "He was being charged for having written an article in which, as a banned politician, he supported a political party. The year is 1999. He is now Prime Minister. I am now in court.

SUBJECT INDEX

Abacha, Sani, 501
Ackerman, Curtis, 49
Action (Congo), 304–5
Adventures of Huckleberry Finn (Twain), 335
advertisements: in Russia, 1; in South Africa, 488
Africa: press freedom in, 500–501. *See also specific countries*
African National Congress, 483, 498, 499
Aksyonov, Vasily P., 403, 419
Albania, foreign correspondents in, 505
Albee, Edward, 324
Aleandro, Norma, 431, 432
Alger, Horatio, Jr., 6
Algeria: civil war coverage in, 468; foreign correspondents in, 468; foreign news in, 261; French policy on, 193–94, 468; Islamic fundamentalists in, 464–65, 468; journalists killed in, 420, 468; newspapers in, 193–94, 196, 261, 464–65; television in, 475
Allied nations: in World War I, 29–62; in World War II, 147–70
Althans, Bela Ewald, 368–69
Amateur Action, 371
American Civil Liberties Union, Reno v., 376
American Heritage Dictionary, 321, 325
American Socialist (Chicago), 52–53
Ames, Winthrop, 20, 81
Analisis (Chile), 438–39
anarchistic publications, mail service denied to, 6–7, 54
Anastasie, censorship as, 16–17, 150–51
Andrzejewski, Jerzy, 230
Angola, foreign correspondents in, 483
Annamese-language newspapers, in China, 247
Annan, Kofi A., 420
anti-American publications, during World War I, 49–54, 57–58
anti-British publications, in Russia, 3
Aquino, Corazon C., 519–20
Arafat, Yasir, 467, 471–74
Archer, Jerome W., 319, 320–21, 322
Argentina
  books in, 301
  cultural renaissance in, 431–32
  democratization of, 431–32
  deportations in, 90
  disappearances in, 427
  films in, 300, 431
  foreign correspondents in, 92, 182, 183, 184
  libel law in, 441
  magazines in, 296–97
  Mexico City conference and, 184
  newspapers in: criticism of government in, 181–82, 300, 427; foreign news in, 183, 235; political news in, 90; regulations on, 90, 181–82; socialist, 90; suspension of, 182–83, 234, 300; United Nations on, 191–92; during World War II, 184–85
  under Onganía, 296–97, 300–301
  under Perón, 181–85, 191–92, 234, 235
  after Perón, 240, 241–42
  press law in, 181, 441
  radio in, 242
  television in, 242
  theatre in, 431–32
  Uruguay and, 301
Aristide, Jean-Bertrand, 440
Arkansas, Epperson v., 323
art(s): in Brazil, 424–26; in Canada, 369–70; in Germany, 366–67; obscenity in, 358–59; in Portugal, 291; sacrilegious, 381–83; sexual content in, 369–70; in United States, 352–55, 358–59, 381–83
Art of Loving (Fromm), 321
Asia: Internet access in, 538–39. *See also specific countries*
"Assault on the Arts: Culture and Politics in Nazi Germany" exhibition, 365–67
Associated Press: in Argentina, 235; in Eastern Europe, 206; in Israel, 445–46
Atwood, Margaret, 336
Australia: films in, 285; newspapers in, 152
Austria
  foreign correspondents in, 106, 108, 111, 128
  Nazi activity in, 112–13, 119
  newspapers in: illegal, punishment for, 119; lack of information in, 112–13; Soviet censorship of, 212–13; between world wars, 112–13, 119
  press law in, 108
  socialist activity in, 119
  underground news distribution in, 117
awards, press freedom, 542–43
Axis powers, in World War II, 170–85
Ayam (Palestine), 473–74
Ayub Khan, Mohammad, 261–62

Babangida, Ibrahim B., 502
Balkan War, First, Bulgarian press control in, 39
Bangladesh, feminism in, 533–35
banks, in Romania, 107
Barker, Granville, 21
Barricada (Nicaragua), 434–35
Barrie, J. M., 10
Baryshnikov, Mikhail, 403, 409
Bashu, the Little Stranger (film), 463
Basque publications, 187
Baum, L. Frank, 324, 325
BBC. *See* British Broadcasting Corporation
Bedie, Henri Konan, 500
Beizai, Bahram, 463–64
Belgium: radio in, 180; theatre in, 17; underground newspapers in, 180
Bell Jar (Plath), 321
Ben Bella, Ahmed, 261
Benchley, Peter, 321
Benes, Eduard, 213
Bergmeier, Fritz, 49
Berks, Theodor, 108
Berman, Jacob, 207
Berrigan, Daniel, 321
Best Short Stories by Negro Writers (Hughes), 319, 320
Bethel School District No. 403 v. Fraser, 344
Beyond (Kenya), 494
Bible, in Syria, 137
Biko, Stephen, 478, 496–97
Bin Laden, Osama, 475
Biuletyn Prasowy (Poland), 176
Black Boy (Wright), 319
Blatt, Daniel H., 451
Bloodline (Sheldon), 321
Blue Kite (film), 531, 532
Blume, Judy, 321
Bocca, Julio, 431, 432
Bogunovic, Branko, 400
Bohemia (Havana), 241
Boldyrev, Vladimir A., 410–11
Bolivia, newspapers in, 244
Bompard, Jacques, 374–75
book(s): indecency in, 138–39; obscenity in, 76–77; publishers of, 73, 76–77, 84–85; textbooks, 318, 527, 543–44. *See also under specific countries*
Book of Laughter and Forgetting (Kundera), 337
Bosnia, war coverage in, 419–20
Bosphore Egyptien, 7–8
Boss: Richard J. Daley of Chicago (Royko), 321
Botha, J. Christoffel, 491–92, 493
Botha, P. W., 487, 489, 492
Boudiaf, Mohammed, 464
Bourdet, Claude, 193

Bourgeau, Jef J., 383–84
Boys in the Band (Crowley), 317
Brautigan, Richard, 321
Brave New World (Huxley), 324, 325
Brazil
arts in, 424–26
books in, 426
under Costa e Silva, 298
cultural life in, 425
democratization of, 424–26
films in, 425
foreign correspondents in, 93
under Geisel, 302, 425, 426
magazines in, 298–99
music in, 425–26
newspapers in: liberalization of, 302, 425, 426; opposition, 239; political/military news in, 93, 298; topics banned in, 93, 298, 302
political prisoners in, 93–94, 298, 299
satire in, 426–27
television in, 426
theatre in, 424, 425
under Vargas, 93–94
Breaking Point (Garnett), 21
Brecht, Bertolt, 317
Brezhnev, Leonid I., 406
Brink, André Philippus, 479, 480
Briski, Norman, 431, 432
British Broadcasting Corporation (BBC), 341–42, 350, 475–76
Brodsky, Joseph, 397, 398
Brookfield, Charles H. E.: appointment as censor, 23–24; *Dear Old Charlie*, 25
Brooklyn Museum of Art, 381–83
Brother of Our Lord (Wojtyla), 392
Brown, Claude, 321
Brown, Tom, 435–36
Bulgaria
foreign correspondents in, 110
newspapers in: criticism of government in, 128; during First Balkan War, 39; opposition, 205; party control of, 204
Burger's Daughter (Gordimer), 479, 480
Burma: newspapers in, 508; theatre in, 508–9
Bush, George, 360
Butler v. Michigan, 323

cabarets, in Poland, 388
Cabildo (Argentina), 183
cable. *See* telegrams
Caesar, Julius, 58
Caetano, Marcelo, 284–85, 287–88
Cambodia, foreign correspondents in, 309–10
cameras, in Soviet Union, 219, 221, 231
Cameroon: newspapers in, 491; press freedom in, 490–91
Cameroon Tribune, 491
Camille (film), 82–83
Canada: art in, 369–70; newspapers in, 32, 40; pornography in, 369–70; trial coverage in, 367–68
Canby, Vincent, 267
Capital (Lisbon), 284
Cardenas, Juan Pablo, 438–40
caricatures, in Japan, 142
cartoons: in Greece, 193; in Turkey, 138
Casa Americana (United States Information Service Library), 192–93
Casey, William J., 338–39
Castro, Fidel: and foreign correspondents, 244–45; Inter-American Press Association on, 243; magazine coverage of, 241; and newspapers, 242–43
Castro, José R., 91
Catch-22 (Heller), 321
Catcher in the Rye (Salinger), 324
Catherine II (of Russia), 209
Cavendish, Anthony, 352
Censorship in Denmark: A New Approach (film), 267
"Censorship: 500 Years of Conflict" exhibition, 332–37
Central America. *See* Latin America; *and specific countries*
Central powers, in World War I, 63–69
Centro Panameno de Noticias (CPN), 438
Cesarz (Kapuscinski), 393
Chad, foreign correspondents in, 481–82
Chamorro, Violeta Barrios de, 433, 436–37
Chamorro Barrios, Carlos Fernando, 434, 435
Chamorro Barrios, Pedro Joaquin, 429–30
Chamorro Cardenal, Pedro Joaquin, 433, 437
Chamorro Cardenal, Xavier, 434
Charter 88, 348, 351
Cheney, Dick, 360, 361, 362, 363
Chen Kaige, 530–32
Chernobyl nuclear accident, 402
Chiang Ching-kuo, 515
Chicago American, 1
child pornography, 357–58, 369–70
Children of the Arbat (Rybakov), 403
Childress, Alice, 319, 320–21
Chile: books in, 429; films in, 429; journalists in, 438–40
China
books in, 520–21, 547–48
Cultural Revolution in, 531–32
democracy movement in, 524–27, 547
films in, 530–32
foreign correspondents in: alterations to dispatches of, 142, 143; on democracy movement, 525–26; interviews by, 137–38, 223, 525; objectivity of, 215; relaxation of censorship of, 143–44; treatment of, 223–24
foreign news in, 530
freedom of press in, truth vs. objectivity as, 214–15
intellectuals in, 547–48
internal publications in, 530
Internet access in, 538, 539
journalist in, award presented to, 542–43
martial law in, 525–26
newspapers in: Annamese-language, 247; criticism of government in, 139, 146; criticism of other countries by, 146; examination vs. censorship of, 139; foreign news in, 216; liberalization of, 524–25; party control of, 226; Russia's Five-Year Plan in, 140–41; students on, 143; tariff policy in, 141–42; uniformity in censorship of, 142
pornography in, 521
publications campaign in, 547–48
student protests in, 143, 524–26
telegrams in, 139–40, 141–42, 143–44
television in, 525, 535–36
T-shirts in, 528–30
China Today Publishers, 548
Chin Chung-Hua, 226
Chosun Ilbo (South Korea), 502–3
Churchill, Winston, 165–66, 204, 259
Cinderella (Glowacki), 392, 393
Cinemax channel, 328
Civil and Military Gazette (Lahore), 259
civil rights movement, 198–200
Civil War, American, 38, 59
Cleaver, Eldridge, 319, 320–21
Clemenceau, Georges, 31
Clockwork Orange (film), 317
Cobb, George H., 77–79
Coetzee, Johan, 488, 489
college newspapers, 345–48
Collins, Michael, 345
Colombia
libel law in, 238–39
newspapers in: criticism of government in, 238, 240–41; opposition, 240–41; political news in, 234, 241; suspension of, 236–37, 238–39
telegrams in, 239
television law in, 442–43
Columbia Pictures, in Egypt, 450–51
Combat (France), 180
comics, American flag in, 3
Commercial Cable Company, 30
Committee on Public Information, 46, 62
communist activities: in Cuba, 152; in Germany, 111–12; in Pakistan, 251
communist publications: in Australia, 152; in Czechoslovakia, 136; in Finland, 190; in Great Britain, 152–53; in Greece, 205; in Japan, 190; in South Korea, 246, 248
Congo, newspapers in, 304–5
Constantinowitch, Constantine, 19
Corcoran Gallery of Art, 352–55
Corman, Avery, 321
Costa e Silva, Arthur da, 298
CPN. *See* Centro Panameno de Noticias
Cracow Naprzod (Poland), 94
Crash (film), 381

Creel, George, 45–46, 62, 81
crime: in British newspapers, 282–83; in U.S. films, 40, 73, 77
Crime of Cuenca (film), 320
Croatia: newspapers in, 106–7, 423; press laws in, 423; radio in, 423
Cronica (Argentina), 300
crossword puzzles, in Hungary, 95
Crowley, Matthew, 317
Cry Freedom (film), 496–97
Cuba: Constitution of, 87; foreign correspondents in, 244–45; freedom of press in, 87, 243; Inter-American Press Association on, 243; magazines in, 241; Nazi and communist propaganda in, 152; newspapers in, 87, 242–43; Supreme Court of, 87; television in, 242–43
cultural censorship: in Germany, 98–99; in Italy, 101–2
cultural life: in Argentina, 431–32; in Brazil, 425; in Eastern Europe, 414–17; in Hungary, 417–18
Cultural Revolution, in China, 531–32
Cuomo, Mario, 330–31
Czechoslovakia
  books in, 387, 395–96, 408–9
  censorship organization in, 292–93
  collapse of communism in, 414–17
  creative freedom in, 395–96
  defamation of foreign countries in, 212
  espionage in, 217
  foreign correspondents in, 110–11, 217, 222–23
  foreign magazines in, 213
  Nazi activity in, 141
  newspapers in: communist, 136; criticism of government in, 63, 136; under Dubcek, 293–94; foreign, 213–14, 233–34; independent, 405; Nazi, 141; party control of, 205, 216; during Soviet occupation, 294–95; underground, 294; during World War I, 63
  "Prague spring" in, 396, 408–9, 409
  radio in, 216, 294
  Soviet occupation of, 294–95
  state secrets in, 222
  television in, 294, 295
  theatre in, 395–96, 408–9
  thought control in, 213
  underground literary works in, 387

Daily Worker (Great Britain), 152
Dalvi, Pradeep, 546–47
Dayan, Moshe, 281
D-Day invasion, 164
Dear Old Charlie (Brookfield), 25
Death of Yazdgerd (film), 464
Dedijer, Vladimir, 400
Deep Throat (film), 273
de Klerk, F. W., 496, 497
de la Espriella, Ricardo, 428
Democrasi (Turkey), 247
Democrito (Spain), 190
Demokratija (Yugoslavia), 204
Denmark, German occupation of, 168
Desai, Morarji R., 507
Des Moines Independent Community School District, Tinker v., 344, 347
Detroit Institute of Arts, 383–84
Deutsche National und Soldaten Zeitung (Germany), 281
Deutsche Volkszeitung (Germany), 66
Deutsche Wochenshau (Germany), 118–19
diaries, during World War II, 163
Dictionary of American Slang, 321
Dietz, Howard, 83
diseases, social, film on, 72–73
Dobermann (film), 380
Doctorow, E. L., 324
Doctor Zhivago (Pasternak), 390–91, 402–3
documentaries: on pornography, 267; on religious pilgrimage, 319–20
Dong-A Ilbo (South Korea), 502–3
Down the Mean Streets (Thomas), 319, 320–21, 323
Doyle, Arthur Conan, 139
Dry White Season (Brink), 479, 480; film of, 497
Dubcek, Alexander, 293–94
Dubois, Jules, 237–38, 243

Eastern Europe: collapse of communism in, 414–17; cultural life in, 414–17; foreign correspondents in, 200–201, 384–85; freedom of press in, vs. United States, 202–6; radio in, 206, 402. *See also specific countries*
East Germany, foreign correspondents in, 505
Ebersohn, Wessel, 478–80
Ecuador: foreign correspondents in, 93; freedom of press in, 236; newspapers in, 235–36
Egypt: books in, 453–54; films in, 450–52; foreign correspondents in, 309, 311–12, 506; Israeli exports in, 468–70; law of shame in, 447–48; music in, 469; newspapers in, 311–12; press law of, 7–8, 253
Eighties (Taiwan), 515, 517–18
Electric Kool-Aid Acid Test (Wolfe), 321
Eleftheros Kosmos (Greece), 283–84, 292
Ellison, Ralph, 324
El Salvador, newspapers in, 91–92
Emerson, Ralph Waldo, 334
England. *See* Great Britain
Ephraim Returns to the Army (Laor), 455, 457–58
Epperson v. Arkansas, 323
Erzoznick v. Jacksonville, 323–24
Espectador (Colombia), 234–35, 239
espionage law: in Czechoslovakia, 217; in Soviet Union, 136; in United States, 42–45, 48–50
Europe. *See specific countries*
exhibitions: "Assault on the Arts: Culture and Politics in Nazi Germany," 365–67; "Censorship: 500 Years of Conflict," 332–37; "Sensation," 382–83; "Van Gogh's Ear," 383–84
Exon, Jim, 371

Fahd, King of Saudi Arabia, 461
Falkland Islands War, press coverage in Britain of, 325–27
Farewell to Arms (Hemingway), 321, 324, 325
Farewell My Concubine (film), 530–32
feminism, in Bangladesh, 533–35
films. *See under specific countries; specific films*
Finland: communist newspapers in, 190; foreign correspondents in, 173; library books in, 2; in Soviet press, 170–71; in United States press, 173–74
Fischer, Ludwig, 4
Fitzgerald, F. Scott, 324
Fixer (Malamud), 319, 320–21
flag, of United States, 3
Flaubert, Gustave, 335
Flight Into the Night (film), 462–63
foreign correspondents: in Albania, 505; in Algeria, 468; in Angola, 483; in Argentina, 92, 182, 183, 184; in Austria, 106, 108, 111, 128; in Brazil, 93; in Bulgaria, 110; in Cambodia, 309–10; in Chad, 481–82; challenges facing, 109–11, 120–23, 505–6; in China, 137–38, 142, 143–44, 215, 223–24, 525–26; in Cuba, 244–45; in Czechoslovakia, 110–11, 217, 222–23; in Eastern Europe, 200–201, 384–85; in Ecuador, 93; in Egypt, 309, 311–12, 506; in Finland, 173; in France, 121–22, 168–69; in Germany, 121, 505; in Ghana, 260; in Great Britain, 148–49, 161–62, 168; in Hungary, 110; in India, 503, 505; in Iran, 446–47; in Israel, 308, 313–14, 445–46, 465; in Italy, 123; in Japan, 39; in Kenya, 500; in Lebanon, 248; in Panama, 435–36; in Poland, 201, 206; in Romania, 98, 103, 105–6, 110, 201; in Russia, 2–3; in South Africa, 486–87, 505; in South Vietnam, 505–6; in Soviet Union, 120–21, 135, 173, 211, 217–22, 226–29, 231–33, 505; in Vietnam, 251–52; during World War I, 120; between world wars, 120–23; in Yugoslavia, 108, 110, 201–2; in Zimbabwe, 483–84
Fraga, Manuel, 290
France
  Anastasie in, 150–51
  books in, 374–75
  films in, 133
  foreign correspondents in, 121–22, 168–69
  freedom of press in, 195–96
  libraries in, 374–75
  music hall shows in, 11

newspapers in: on Algeria, 193–94, 468; foreign, 37; foreign news in, 174, 175; lack of news in, 150, 175; military news in, 29, 31, 39–40, 147, 150; during Nazi occupation, 175, 178–79, 180–81; after Nazi surrender, 168–69; opposition to suppression of, 37, 195–96; propaganda in, 150; protests by, 37, 195–96; underground, 178–79, 180; during World War I, 29, 31, 37, 39; during World War II, 147, 150, 174–75, 178–79, 180–81
parodies of censorship in, 150–51
press rules in, 147
radio in, 148
theatre in, 11, 14, 18
and Vietnamese press, 251–52
France, Anatole, 11
Franco, Francisco: direct censorship ended by, 276–77, 279; underground opposition to, 187, 189–90, 195
Franco-Prussian war, 4
Fraser, Bethel School District No. 403 v., 344
Freedom Forum, on student press, 370–71
freedom of press
in Africa, 490–91, 500–501
in China, 214–15
in Cuba, 87, 243
in Eastern Europe, 202–6, 415–16
in Ecuador, 236
in France, 195–96
in Germany, 278–79
in Greece, 283
in Guatemala, 245
Inter-American Press Association on, 191, 237–38, 243–44, 245, 299–300
International Press Institute on, 271–73, 283
in Latin America, 91, 191, 237–38, 243–44, 245, 299–300
in Peru, 299, 303–4
in Soviet Union: vs. United States, 202–6, 207–8; between world wars, 134–35
in United States: Inter-American Press Association on, 243–44, 245; International Press Institute on, 283; vs. Soviet Union/Eastern Europe, 202–6, 207–8
Freij, Elias, 448–49
Fromm, Erich, 321
Fugard, Athol, 482
Fujimori, Alberto K., 444
Fulbright, J. W., 270
Fulda, Ludwig, 9
Fu Tso-yi, 146

Gandhi, Indira, 503, 504, 506, 507–8, 511
Gandhi, Mohandas K., 546–47
Gandhi, Rajiv, 522
Gandhi, Sanjay, 507, 508
Garnett, Edward, 21
Gazette (Cameroon), 491
Geisel, Ernesto, 302, 425, 426
Germany
art in, 366–67
books in, 4, 98, 365–66
cultural censorship in, 98–99
films in, 368–69
foreign correspondents in, 121, 505
freedom of press in, 278–79
Jews in, persecution of, 114–15, 119–20, 127
letters in, 172
military news in, 2, 4
minors in, 98–99
music in, 174
newspapers in: confiscation of, 281; decline in circulation of, 124–25, 133; foreign, 117, 118–19, 126, 171–72; government regulations for, 67–69; Nazi control of, 111–14, 124–28, 129–33, 171–73; suspension of, 66–67; war goals discussed in, 63–66; during World War I, 40, 63–69; during World War II, 171–72; between world wars, 111–14, 124–28, 129–33
pornography in, 99
press laws in, 127–28, 130–31
purity law in, 9
radio in, 171–73
secret police of, 117
television in, 278
theatre in, 9–10, 11–14, 17
treason laws in, 278
underground news distribution in, 116–18, 126
Ghana: foreign correspondents in, 260; newspapers in, 260–61, 307–8
Ghannouchi, Rachid, 460
Gilbert, W. S.: on censorship, 10; *Mikado*, 22
Giordano Bruno (film), 429
Giuliani, Rudolph W., 381–83
Glory (Greece), 177
Glos Polski (Poland), 177
Glowacki, Janusz, 392, 393
Go Ask Alice (anonymous), 319, 320–21
Godfather (Puzo), 321
Godse, Nathuram, 546–47
Goebbels, Paul Joseph, 125–26, 127, 129, 131, 132
Goering, Hermann Wilhelm, 114
Goethe League, 9
Golos (Russia), 5
Gomez, Laureano, 236
Gomulka, Wladyslaw, 225
Goodbye, Columbus (Roth), 321
Googoosh, 465–66
Gorbachev, Mikhail S., 403, 406, 407, 414
Gordimer, Nadine, 479, 480
Gordon, Cliff, 14
Gossett, Louis, Jr., 450, 451
Gottwald, Klement, 213–14
Granta (magazine), 352
Grapes of Wrath (Steinbeck), 324
Great Britain
books in, 138–39, 340–41, 350, 352
Falkland Islands War news in, 325–27
foreign correspondents in, 148–49, 161–62, 168
intelligence agencies of, 340–41, 350, 352
Ireland and, conflict between, 342, 345, 349
journalists in, imprisonment of, 58
legislation in: Criminal Justice Act, 282–83; Official Secrets Act, 348–49, 351; Public Order Act, 349
mail in, 35–37
music of, in Germany, 174
newspapers in: on book bans, 341; communist, 152–53; crime news in, 282–83; during World War I, 30–33, 34–35, 37, 39, 58; during World War II, 147–49, 152–53
radio in, 341–42
in Russian press, 3
telegrams in, 35–37
television in, 342, 345, 349, 350–51
theatre in, 10, 21–22, 23–24, 25–26
World War II censorship in: approach to, 161–62, 168; House of Commons on, 147–48; of newspapers, 147–49, 152–53; of opinions, 160–61; purpose of, 152
Great Gatsby (Fitzgerald), 324
Great Greece, 177
Greece
cartoons in, 193
constitution of, 282
freedom of press in, 283
martial-law rule in, 286–87
music in, 292
newspapers in: communist, 205; confiscation of, 287; criticism of government in, 281–82, 283–84; nonpersons/nonevents in, 285–86; under Papadopoulos, 281–82, 283–84, 285–87, 288–89; revival of, 292; underground, 177; during World War II, 177; between world wars, 128
press law in, 285–86, 289
student protests in, 289
Gregorian, Vartan, 333, 334
Grossman, Vasily, 411
Grotowski, Jerzy, 393
Grusa, Jiri, 387
Guatemala, freedom of press in, 245
Gumilev, Nikolai S., 403

Habre, Hissen, 481–82
Hadashot (Israel), 452
Hair (musical), 285, 298
Haiti: news shortage in, 440; radio in, 440
Hall, Radclyffe, 138
hangings, in United States, newspaper coverage of, 4
Harris Theatre (New York City), 72–73
Hasfari, Shmuel, 454, 455
Hatch, Orrin, 359
Havel, Vaclav, 336, 396, 408, 417
Hawthorne, Nathaniel, 324
Hazelwood School District v. Kuhlmeier, 342–44, 346

HBO. *See* Home Box Office
Hearst newspapers: Canadian ban on, 40; judiciary criticized in, 1
"Heed Their Rising Voices" (advertisement), 198–200
Heller, Joseph, 321
Helms, Jesse, 358–59
Hemingway, Ernest, 321, 324, 325
Herald Republican Publishing Company, 9
Heritage Foundation, 322
Hero Ain't Nothing but a Sandwich (Childress), 319, 320–21
Heyse, Paul, 12
high school newspapers, 342–44, 365, 370–71, 377
Hillquit, Morris, 55
Hitler, Adolf, 281; *Mein Kampf*, 411
Hodge, John R., 246
Holbrooke, Richard C., 423, 424
Home Box Office (HBO), sexually explicit programs on, 328, 329–30
Homme Enchainé (Man in Chains) (France), 31
Homme Libre (France), 31
Honeysuckles (play), 523, 524
Hong Kong: communist rule in, and press self-censorship, 537–38; newspapers in, 537–38; television in, 537
Hora (Ecuador), 235–36
Hosmer, Eli T., 78–79
House on the Embankment (Lyubimov), 391
Hughes, Langston, 319, 320
Humanité (Paris), 178
Humbert (Umberto I), King of Italy, 18
Hungary: books in, 418; collapse of communism in, 414–18; crossword puzzles in, 95; cultural life in, 417–18; films in, 415, 417, 418; foreign correspondents in, 110; music in, 417; newspapers in, 108, 205, 217, 416; pornography in, 412–13; press law in, 104, 108; theatre in, 418
Hun letters, 2
Hunter, Evan, 321
Hussein, Saddam, 475
Huxley, Aldous, 324, 325

I, Nathuram Godse Speaking (Dalvi), 546–47
Ibsen, Henrik, 13
Imanyara, Gitobu, 494–96
indecency: in books, 138–39; in television, 331; in theatre, 10, 20
India: bomb outrages in, 7; books in, 512, 521–23; emergency rule in, 503–4, 506–7; Explosives bill in, 7; films in, 527–28; foreign correspondents in, 503, 505; newspapers in, 503–4, 506–8, 512, 517; press law in, 7, 510–13; Punjab crisis in, 516–17, 519; radio in, 508, 516; rumors in, 506; television in, 516; theatre in, 546–47
Indonesia: conference on national unity in, 254; dissent in, 513–14; imprisonment of journalists in, 541; magazines in, 541–42; newspapers in, 254–55, 257–58, 306
Industrial Worker, 8
Inside of the White Slave Traffic (film), 27
Inter-American Press Association
meeting in Argentina, 241–42
on press freedom: in Latin America, 191, 237–38, 243–44, 245, 299–300; in United States, 243–44, 245
International Press Institute, on press freedom, 271–73, 283
Internet: in Asia, 538–39; in Iran, 471; regulation of, 371–73, 375–77; sexual content on, 371–73; in United States, 371–73, 375–77
Interrogation (film), 396–98
Invisible Man (Ellison), 324
IRA. *See* Irish Republican Army
Iran: American hostages in, 446–47; books in, 467–68; films in, 462–64; foreign correspondents in, 446–47; Internet access in, 471; music in, 465–66; newspapers in, 249–50, 474; press law in, 249–50; television in, 537; writers' opposition to censorship in, 467–68
Iraq: criticism of government in, 248; press law in, 248
Ireland: books in, 139; Britain and, conflict between, 342, 345, 349; censorship bill in, 139; newspapers in, 139
Irish Americans, in World War I, 51
Irish Republican Army (IRA), 349
Irving, John, 324
Island Trees, Pico v., 323, 325, 327–28
Israel
exports to Egypt, 468–70
films in, 454–55, 457
foreign correspondents in, 308, 313–14, 445–46, 465
newspapers in: Arab, 448–49, 455–57; military news in, 452, 476–78; PLO news in, 448–49; political news in, 308; Supreme Court on, 452
Soviet immigration to, 458–59
theatre in: Censorship Board for, 313, 449, 454–55, 457–58; debate over, 454–55; end of censorship of, 457–58; intellectuals' opposition to censorship of, 312–13; plays banned in, 312–13, 449–50, 454–55; Supreme Court on, 455, 457–58
Italy
ban on opposition in, 95–97, 100–101
cultural censorship in, 101–2
foreign correspondents in, 123
under Mussolini, 95–97, 100–103
newspapers in: foreign, 123–24, 174, 175; during World War I, 34, 35; during World War II, 174, 175; between world wars, 94–95, 101, 123–24
radio in, 175
theatre in, 18
Ivcher, Baruch, 444
Ivory Coast, newspapers in, 500
Jacksonville, Erzoznick v., 323–24
Japan
Allied occupation of, 188–89, 190
books in, 145–46, 527, 543–44
caricatures in, 142
films in, 133–34
foreign correspondents in, 39
legislation in: Peace Preservation Act, 144–45; Press and Publications Law, 146; Protective Surveillance Law, 144–46
newspapers in: during Allied occupation, 188–89, 190; during Russo-Japanese War, 38–39, 60
school textbooks in, 527, 543–44
thought surveillance in, 144–46
Jaws (Benchley), 321
Jazeera news channel, 474–76
Jefferson, Thomas, 208
Jesus, As Seen by His Friends (Kenan), 312–13
Jew(s): as journalists, in Germany, 119–20, 127; persecution of, in Germany, 114–15, 119–20, 127
Jewish Soul (Sobol), 450
Jiang Zemin, 532
John Paul II, Pope, 388, 392
Joint Committee Opposed to Political Censorship of the Theatre (New York), 80–82
Jong, Erica, 324
Joongang Ilbo (South Korea), 502–3
Jordan: PLO and, 466–67; television in, 476
journalists
deportation of, in El Salvador, 91–92
dismissal of, in South Korea, 502–3
execution of: in Algeria, 420, 468; in Russia, 5
imprisonment of: in Chile, 438–40; in China, 542–43; in Germany, 2; in Great Britain, 58; in Indonesia, 541; in Kenya, 499–500; in Nigeria, 501–2; in Palestine, 471–72; in Turkey, 544–45; in United States, 1, 9, 49, 51–52, 54
Jewish, in Germany, 119–20, 127
military officers as, 158–59
press freedom award for, in China, 542–43
as semi-state officials, in Germany, 127, 131
in war zones, U.S. policy on, 337–38
See also foreign correspondents
Joyce, James, 73, 340
Joynson-Hicks, William, 138–39
Judge (comic), 3
judiciary, criticism of, 1

Kadoma Declaration, 483–84
Kafi, Ali, 465
Kafka, Franz, 408–9
Kantor, MacKinlay, 321
Kantor, Tadeusz, 394
Kapuscinski, Ryszard, 393
Kenan, Amos, 312–13
Kennedy, Ludovic, 348

Kenya: books in, 497–98; criticism of government in, 499–500; foreign correspondents in, 500; journalists in, treatment of, 499–500; magazines in, 494–96; newspapers in, 495, 497, 499–500; theatre in, 497
Khamenei, Ali, 474
Khatami, Mohammad, 474
Khomeini, Ruhollah, 446, 465
Kipling, Rudyard, 37, 259
Kladensklobsor (Czechoslovakia), 63
Kohout, Pavel, 396
Konrad, Gyorgy, 418
Korea. *See* South Korea
Kramer vs Kramer (Corman), 321
Kuhlmeier, Hazelwood School District v., 342–44, 346
Kukly (TV program), 422–23
Kundera, Milan, 396; *Book of Laughter and Forgetting*, 337
Kuttab, Daoud, 472, 473
Kuwait, television in, 461–62, 476
Ky, Nguyen Cao, 263–65
Kyunghyang Shinmun (Korea), 256–57

Lady Chatterley's Lover (Lawrence), 335, 340
La Farge, Oliver, 319
La Follette, Robert M., 52–53
Langer, Eli, 369–70
Laor, Yitzhak, 455, 457–58
Last Secular Jew (Hasfari), 454, 455
Last Temptation of Christ (film), 457
Latin America, press freedom in: Central American conference on, 91; Inter-American Press Association on, 191, 237–38, 243–44, 245, 299–300. *See also specific countries*
Laughing Boy (La Farge), 319
law(s). *See* press law; *and under specific countries*
law enforcement officials, portrayal of in films, 78
Lawrence, D. H., 335, 340
Lebanon: emigrants in, 248; foreign correspondents in, 248; newspapers in, 248–49, 255–56, 445; press law in, 248
Lee Kuan Yew, 509–10
Lee Teng-hui, 515
Legislation. *See* press law; *and under specific countries*
Leopold II, King of Belgium, 17
letters: in Germany, during World War II, 172; in Great Britain, during World War I, 36–37. *See also* mail service
Levin, Hanoch, 449–50, 455, 457
Levingston, Roberto Marcelo, 301
libel actions, by public officials, 198–200, 245
libel law: in Argentina, 441; in Colombia, 238–39
libraries
  public: in Finland, 2; in France, 374–75; in Soviet Union, 406; in Spain, 192–93; in United States, 6, 321, 323
  school, in United States, 318–19, 320–24, 327–28, 379–80
Libre Belgique (Belgium), 180
Lidowe Nowiny (Czechoslovakia), 405
Life of Brian (film), 381
Lilac Lampshade (Marcos), 425
Lipkin, Semyon, 419
Literary Almanac Metropol, 418–19
Lolita (Nabokov), 482
Lonely Lady (Robbins), 321
Love in Marriage, or Married Love (Stopes), 76–77
Lyubimov, Yuri, 391

MacArthur, Douglas, 188
Madame Bovary (Flaubert), 335
magazines. *See under specific countries*
mail service
  in Brazil, 93
  in Great Britain, during World War I, 35–37
  U.S. publications excluded from: before World War I, 6–7; during World War I, 48–49, 52–53, 54–57, 61–62
Makarova, Natalia, 403
Makhmalbaf, Mohsen, 463
Malamud, Bernard, 319, 320–21
Manchild in the Promised Land (Brown), 321
Mandela, Nelson, 496
Maniu, Iuliu, 105, 107–8
Man of Marble (film), 386–87, 397
Mao Tzetung, 215
Mapplethorpe, Robert, 352–55, 357
Marcos, Ferdinand E., 311, 513, 533
Marcos, Plinio, 425
Margherita, Queen of Italy, 18
Marriage of the Blessed (film), 463
Marvelous Life of Father Vicente (film), 320
Mary Magdala (Heyse), 12
Mary Poppins (Travers), 324
Masarway, Riad, 458
massage parlors: in Hungary, 413; in United States, 273–74
Masses (United States), 48–49, 57–58
Master Harold . . . and the Boys (Fugard), 482
Mater, Nadire, 549
Matic, Veran, 424
Maurice, Frederick B., 59
Maximov, Vladimir, 411
Maybe Some Other Time (film), 463, 464
MBC. *See* Middle East Broadcasting Center
McCullough, Colleen, 321
Medvedev, Roy A., 398–99, 404
Mehmet's Book (Mater), 549
Mein Kampf (Hitler), 411
Menderes, Adnan, 253
Menem, Carlos Sal, 441
Merchant of Venice (Shakespeare), 321
Metropol, 418–19
Mexico: journalism in, 441–42; newspapers in, 442; television in, 441–42; theatre in, 298
Mexico City conference, 184
Michelin, André, 29
Michigan, Butler v., 323
Middle East: American military censorship in, 200–201; television in, 474–76. *See also specific countries*
Middle East Broadcasting Center (MBC), 460–62
Midnight Cowboy (film), 317
Mikado (Gilbert and Sullivan), 22
Mille, Pierre, 32
Miller, Arthur, 440
Milosevic, Slobodan, 423–24
Minneapolis Saturday Press, 87–89
Minto, Lord, 7
Misla (Russia), 5
Misuri, Alfredo, 94
Mohamed V, King of Morocco, 257
Moi, Daniel arap, 494, 499
Mokae, Zakes, 483
Monaco, theatre in, 18–19
Monde (France), 194, 196
Monty Python films, 381
Moraeus Hanssen, Ingeborg, 380–81
Moral Majority, 322, 324
Morning Post (London), 58
Morocco, newspapers in, 257
Morris, Desmond, 319, 320
Morrison, Toni, 324
Mossadegh, Mohammed, 249
Mother Earth (United States), 54
Motherland (India), 503, 504
Motion Picture Commission (New York): annual report of, 85–86; expansion of, 79; films rejected by, 78, 79; fines for violation of rules of, 83–84; on foreign films, 85–86; litigation against, 78; methodology of, 77–79; news reels censored by, 83; scenes rejected by, 78, 79–80, 85; on vice in films, 85
movies. *See under specific countries; specific movies*
Mubarak, Hosni, 453
Mundo (Cuba), 87
Mundo Obrero (Spain), 190
Munteanu, Neculai, 421
Murray, Philip, 189
museum(s): self-censorship by, 352–55, 383–84; "Sensation" exhibition in, 382–83; "Van Gogh's Ear" exhibition in, 383–84
music: in Brazil, 425–26; in Egypt, 469; in Germany, 174; in Greece, 292; in Hungary, 417; in Iran, 465–66; obscenity in, 355–57, 363–64; rap, 355–57, 363–64; sexual content in, 356; in Soviet Union, 391; in United States, 355–57, 363–64; warning labels for, 364
music hall shows, in France, 11
Mussolini, Benito, 96–97, 100–103
Mutahi, Wahome, 497–98

Nabokov, Vladimir, 403; *Lolita*, 482
Nacion (Ecuador), 235–36
Nairobi Law Monthly, 494–96
Naked Ape (Morris), 319, 320

Napoleon, 58–59
Napoleon III, 18
Nasrin, Taslima, 533–35
Nation (Kenya), 495
National Board of Censorship of Moving Pictures, 22–23, 25
National Board of Review (of films), 72
National Endowment for the Arts, 352–55, 358–59
National Security Agency (NSA), news reports on, 338–39
Natural Born Killers (film), 381
Nazi activity: in Austria, 112–13, 119; in Cuba, 152; in Czechoslovakia, 141; in Germany, 111–15, 118–20, 124–28, 129–33, 171–73
Nekrasov, Viktor, 411
Neruda, Pablo, 543
Netherlands, theatre in, 17–18
New Nation (Singapore), 509
New Nation (South Africa), 491, 493
news organizations, in United States, government prosecution of, 338–39
newspapers: impact on wars, 37–38; party control of (*See* political parties); student, 342–44, 345–48, 365, 370–71, 377; underground (*See* underground newspapers). *See also under specific countries*
news reels, 83
New York Call, 54–56
New York Public Library: "Assault on the Arts: Culture and Politics in Nazi Germany" exhibition at, 365–67; "Censorship: 500 Years of Conflict" exhibition at, 332–37
New York Times: in Italy, 123–24; libel suit against, by public officials, 198–200; mail service denied to, 61–62; Pentagon Papers in, 268–71, 373–74
Nicaragua: civil rights in, 430–31; newspapers in, 429–30, 432–35, 436–37; radio in, 433, 435; Sandinista government in, 429–30, 432–35, 436–38; television in, 433–34, 437–38
Nicholas, Prince of Romania, 107
Nigeria: elections in, 306; journalists in, treatment of, 501–2; Newspaper Amendment Act, 306; newspapers in, 306, 484–85, 501–2
Nineteen Eighty-four (Orwell), 321, 332, 333
1900 (film), 379
Ninth Wave (Masarway), 458
Nixon, Richard, 270
Nixon Administration, 270, 272, 373
Noriega, Manuel Antonio, 435, 438
Norway: films in, 380–81; radio in, 180; underground newspapers in, 180, 181
Novoceanu, Darie, 415
Novoe Vremya (Russia), 3
Novosti (Moscow), 4
Nowakowski, Mark, 386
NSA. *See* National Security Agency
nudity: in photographs of children, 357–58; in Polish theatre, 394; in Spanish magazines, 317
Nuevo Diario (Nicaragua), 434–35
N.W.A., 364

Oatis, William, 222
obscenity: in art, 358–59; in books, 76–77; on cable television, 331; in music, 355–57, 363–64; United States Supreme Court on, 339, 340
Ocalan, Abdullah, 549
Ofili, Chris, 383
Ogonyok (magazine), 406
Oh! Calcutta! (play), 455
Oh, Dreamland (film), 523–24
Once Is Not Enough (Susann), 318
One Day in the Life of Ivan Denisovich (Solzhenitsyn), 321, 324
Onganía, Juan Carlos, 296, 300–301
Opinia (Poland), 386
O'Rourke, John, 301
Ortega Saavedra, Daniel, 430, 432, 433, 435, 437
Orwell, George, 321, 332, 333
Ottoman Empire, theatre in, 18
Our Bodies, Ourselves, 321

Pacheco Areco, Jorge, 301
Pakistan: communist activity in, 251; dissent in, 514–15; elections in, 514; newspapers in, 259, 261–62; press law in, 259, 261–62
Palestine: Legislative Council of, 472; newspapers in, 246, 466–67, 472–74; press law in, 472; television in, 471–72
Palestine Liberation Organization (PLO): in Israeli press, 448–49, 456; Jordan and, 466–67
Palestinian (Sobol), 455
pamphlets, anti-Franco, 187
Pan Africanist Congress, 483
Panama: fax transmission of news to, 438; foreign correspondents in, 435–36; human rights in, 436; newspapers in, 428–29, 435–36, 438; radio in, 438
Papadopoulos, Giorgios, 284, 286–87
Paradise Lost (Penderecki), 394
Park, Chung Hee, 259
Park Theatre (New York), 27
parties, political. *See* political parties
Pasternak, Boris: *Doctor Zhivago*, 390–91, 402–3; reinstatement in Soviet Union, 402–3
Pathé Organization, 78
Patriot (Levin), 449–50, 455, 457
Patterson, John P., 199
Pelton, Ronald W., 338–39
PEN, International, 324–25, 497
Penderecki, Krzysztof, 394
Pennsylvania Board of Film Censors, 82–83
Pentagon Papers, publication of, 268–71, 373–74
Perez Soto, Vincenzio, 86
Péri, Gabriel, 178
Perón, Juan D., 240
Persian Gulf War, press coverage of, 359–63
Peru: freedom of press in, 299, 303–4; newspapers in, 303–4; press law in, 303; television in, 443–44
Philadelphia Tageblatt, 51–52, 54
Philipott, Eden, 25
Philippines: films in, 523; newspapers in, 311, 519–20; television in, 520
photography, in Soviet Union, 219, 221, 231
Pico v. Island Trees, 323, 325, 327–28
Pinero, A. W., 10
Pinochet, Augusto, 438–39
Pinter, Harold, 351
Plath, Sylvia, 321
Platoon (film), 378
play(s). *See* theatre
Playboy channel, 329, 331
Playboy magazine, 410
PLO. *See* Palestine Liberation Organization
poetry, during World War I, 37
Poland
  cabarets in, 388
  citizens' belief of news in, 233, 389
  films in, 386–87, 396–98
  foreign correspondents in, 201, 206
  human rights in, 385–87
  magazines in, 386
  martial law in, 396–97, 411
  newspapers in: confiscation of, 94; history of, 229–30; lack of news in, 401–2; party control of, 225, 389; regulations on, 97, 100; relaxation of censorship of, 388–89, 411; underground, 176–77, 179–80, during World War II, 176–77
  political freedom in, 206–7, 385–87
  printers' union protest in, 394–95
  radio in, 401
  rumors in, 233
  Solidarity in, 394–95, 396, 397, 401, 411–12, 415, 416
  television in, 411–12
  theatre in, 392–94
police officers, portrayal of in films, 78
political parties, newspapers controlled by: in Bulgaria, 204; in China, 226; in Croatia, 423; in Czechoslovakia, 205, 216; in Eastern Europe, 203–4; in Germany, 124–28, 129–33; in Poland, 225, 389
Polityka (Poland), 230, 389
Popov, Yevgeny, 419
pornography: in Canada, 369–70; child, 357–58, 369–70; in China, 521; documentary on, 267; in Germany, 99; in Hungary, 412–13; in Spain, 317; in United States, 273–74, 339–40, 365
Portnoy's Complaint (Roth), 321
Portugal: art in, 291; books in, 291; films in, 288, 291; newspapers in, 284–85, 287, 332; press law in, 284–85, 288, 331–32; theatre in, 19, 288
Possart, Hermann, 12, 14
postal service. *See* mail service

Powell, Colin L., 360, 361
Prensa (Buenos Aires), suppression of: for criticism of government, 427; end of, 242; United Nations on, 191–92; after World War II, 191–92; during World War II, 182–83
Prensa (Nicaragua): reinstatement of, 436–37; suppression of, 429–30, 432–33, 434
Prensa (Panama), 428–29
Prensa Confidencial (Argentina), 297
Prensa Latina (Cuba), 243
president(s), of United States, news during World War II on, 153–54, 165
press freedom. *See* freedom of press
press law(s): in Argentina, 181, 441; in Austria, 108; in Croatia, 423; in Egypt, 7–8, 253; in Germany, 127–28, 130–31; in Greece, 285–86, 289; in Hungary, 104; in India, 7, 510–13; in Iran, 249–50; in Iraq, 248; in Lebanon, 248; in Pakistan, 259, 261–62; in Palestine, 472; in Peru, 303; in Portugal, 284–85, 288, 331–32; in Romania, 97–98, 107–8; in South Africa, 478, 485–86, 488–89; in Soviet Union, 413–14; in Spain, 108–9, 198, 276–78, 279–81, 290–91; in Syria, 248; in Turkey, 250–51, 253, 544–45; in United States, 87–89; in Vietnam, 266–67, 271, 275–76; in Yugoslavia, 204
Price, Byron: on censorship code, 154–56, 160, 161; defense of censorship by, 166–68; on success of censorship, 156, 169–70
Primo de Rivera, Miguel, 99–100, 104–5
prior restraint, United States Supreme Court on, 268–69, 373
Profession: Neo-Nazi (film), 368–69
publishers, book: litigation by, 84–85; prosecution of, 73, 76–77
Pueblo del Pais Vasco (magazine), 187
Puzo, Mario, 321

Qaddafi, Muammar el-, 475
Qatar, television in, 474–76
Quds (Palestine), 473, 474
Questionnaire (Grusa), 387
Questiono Sociale (United States), 6–7

Radcliffe, C. J., 152
radio. *See under specific countries*
Radio Free Europe, 402, 407–8
Radio Liberty, 402, 407–8
Ramos, Fidel V., 533
Rand Daily Mail (South Africa), 305–6, 478, 485–86, 492
rap music, 355–57, 363–64
Reader for Writers (Archer and Schwartz), 319, 320–21, 322
Reagan administration, 339
Redford, George Alexander, 21–22
Redgrave, Vanessa, 285
Reference Materials (China), 530
Reference News (China), 530
Referendum (magazine), 403–5
Rein, Yevgeny, 419
Reno v. American Civil Liberties Union, 376
Resistible Rise of Arturo Ui (Brecht), 317
Rhodesia, newspapers in, 306–7
Rivera, Miguel Primo de, 99–100, 104–5
Robbins, Harold, 318; *Lonely Lady*, 321; *Spellbinder*, 482
Rocio (film), 319–20
Rogers, Rosemary, 318
Rojas Pinilla, Gustavo, 236, 237, 238–39, 240–41
Romania: church law in, 103; collapse of communism in, 414–17; foreign correspondents in, 98, 103, 105–6, 110, 201; newspapers in, 107, 205, 421; press law in, 97–98, 107–8; radio in, 421; royal family of, 107; television in, 421
Roosevelt, Franklin Delano, 153–54, 165, 174
Roosevelt, Theodore, 6–7
Roth, Philip: *Goodbye, Columbus*, 321; *Portnoy's Complaint*, 321
Royko, Mike, 321
Royo, Aristides, 428
Rozovsky, Mark, 419
Rude Pravo (Czechoslovakia), 295
Rumania. *See* Romania
Rushdie, Salman, 351, 471, 496, 521–23, 546
Russ (Russia), 4
Russia: advertisements in, 1; books in, 7, 8, 418–19; Constitutional Democratic Party of, 5–6; constitution of, 4; foreign correspondents in, 2–3; intellectuals in, 418–19; journalists in, execution of, 5; military news in, 3; newspapers in, 3, 4, 5, 31–32, 35; satire in, 422–23; television in, 422–23; theatre in, 19. *See also* Soviet Union
Russo-Japanese War, press control by Japan in, 38–39, 60
Rutgers University, 365
Rybakov, Anatoly, 403

Sabato, Ernesto, 240
sacrilegious art, 381–83
Sadat (film), 450–52
Sadat, Anwar el, 311, 447–48, 450–52
Saigon Daily News, 265, 266, 267
Saigon Post, 265
Salgado, Gabriel Arias, 196–97
Salinger, J. D., 324
Salome (Wilde), 12–13, 22
Samper, Ernesto, 442–43
Santos, Eduardo, 239
Sanya Dharmasakti, 314
Sarkis, Elias, 445
Satanic Verses (Rushdie), 351, 471, 496, 521–23, 546
Saturday Night Live, 360
Saudi Arabia, television in, 460–62, 470, 475–76
Saxe-Meiningen, Duke of, 19
Scarlet Letter (Hawthorne), 324
Schindler's List (film), 378, 533
Schlafly, Phyllis, 322, 324
Schlesinger, Arthur M., Jr., 324, 335
schools
  in Japan, textbooks in, 527, 543–44
  in United States: books in, 318–19, 320–24, 327–28; films in, 378–79; magazines in, 379–80; newspapers of, 342–44, 345–48, 365, 370–71, 377; sex education in, 319
Schuler, Eric, 81
Schwartz, A., 319
Secret Woman (Philipott), 25
"Sensation" exhibition, 382–83
Seoul Shin Mun (Korea), 248
Serbia: newspapers in, 423–24; radio in, 424
Serrano, Andres, 354
Seventeen (magazine), 379–80
sex education, 319
sexual content: in art, 369–70; in films, 267, 527–28; on Internet, 371–73; in music, 356; on television, 328–31. *See also* pornography
Shakespeare, William, plays of: in Germany, 13; *Merchant of Venice*, 321; in Russia, 19; in United States, 321
Shamir, Yitzhak, 458–59
Shaw, George Bernard, 21, 139, 324, 333
Sheldon, Sidney, 321
Shonfeld, Manfred, 427
Siglo (Colombia), 234, 236–37
Sihanouk, Norodom, King of Cambodia, 309–10
Simecka, Milan, 332
Singapore: Internet access in, 538, 539; Newspaper and Printing Presses Act, 509; newspapers in, 509–10
Singh, Zail, 511
Sinn Fein, 345
Sirjani, Saidi, 467–68
Slaughterhouse-Five (Vonnegut), 319, 320–21, 322, 324
Slovo (Russia), 4
Sobol, Yehoshua: *Jewish Soul*, 450; *Palestinian*, 455
social diseases, film on, 72–73
socialist publications
  in Argentina, 90
  in Germany, 111–12
  in Poland, 94, 97
  in United States: excerpts from, 53–54; indictment of, 57–58; mail service denied to, 48–49, 52–56
Social War (Chicago), 53–54
Society for the Suppression of Vice, litigation against, 84–85
Sodom's End (Sudermann), 9
Soldaten Zeitung (Germany), 281
Solzhenitsyn, Aleksandr: ban on, 321, 324, 403; *One Day in the Life of Ivan Denisovich*, 321, 324; reinstatement in Soviet Union, 410

Some Wild Oats (film), 72
Sons (Hunter), 321
Soul on Ice (Cleaver), 319, 320–21
South (South Africa), 491, 493
South Africa
anti-apartheid movement in, 489–90, 491–94
bill of rights in, 498
books in, 478–79, 483, 496–97
courts of, 488, 489–90
emergency decrees in, 486–88, 489
films in, 310–11, 496–97, 498–99
foreign correspondents in, 486–87, 505
freedom of expression in, and violence, 498–99
newspapers in: advertisements in, 488; anti-apartheid, 491–94; police news in, 478; prison conditions reported in, 305–6, 478; restrictions on, 478, 485–86, 488–89
police control of publications in, 488–89
press laws in, 478, 485–86, 488–89
Prisons Act, 305–6
television in, 486–87
theatre in, 482–83
unrest in, 487–89
South America. *See* Latin America; and *specific countries*
Southern Times (London), 34–35
South Korea
books in, 523, 524
films in, 523–24
newspapers in: communist, 246, 248; dismissal of journalists from, 502–3; opposition, 256–57; suspension of, 246, 248, 256–57, 258–59
press policy in, 258–59
television in, 523
theatre in, 523
South Vietnam
Constitution of, 263, 266
elections in, 263–64
foreign correspondents in, 505–6
newspapers in: opposition to censorship of, 275–76; suspension of, 260, 263–64, 266–67; during Vietnam War, 263–67, 271, 275–76
press laws in, 266–67, 271, 275–76
See also Vietnam
Soviet Union
alternative (samizdat) press in, 403–5
approach to censorship in, 135
and Austrian press, 212–13
books in: banned, 411; black market for, 406; history, 398–99; literary, 391, 402–3; reinstatement of, 402–3, 410–11; shortage of, 406–7; by young writers, 391
citizens' belief of news in, 170–71
computers in, 403–5
Czechoslovakia occupied by, 294–95
dissidents in, 398–99
espionage law in, 136
films in, 391
Five-Year Plan of, in Chinese press, 140–41
foreign correspondents in: banned topics for, 217–18, 220–21, 226–29; during Cold War, 211, 217–22, 226–29, 231–33; indirect censorship of, 231–32; interviews by, 505; isolation of, 221; shadowing of, 219–20; travel by, 218–19, 505; between world wars, 120–21, 135, 173
foreign news in, 207–8
freedom of speech/press in: after World War II, 202–6, 207–8; between world wars, 134–35
Glavlit (censorship office) of, 410–11
history of censorship in, 209–12, 228–29, 232–33
intellectuals in, 389–92
libraries in, 406
magazines in, 403–6
military news in, 210
music in, 391
newspapers in, 200, 405–6, 413–14
Novosti of, 385
opposition banned in, 134
paper shortages in, 414
photography in, 219, 221, 231
press law in, 413–14
radio in, 402, 407–8
rumors in, 222–23, 224–25
state secrets in, 136
theatre in, 391
underground news distribution in, 118
See also Russia
Sowetan (South Africa), 491–92
Spain
American library in, 192–93
books in, 108, 318
constitution of, 116
Falange in, 195
films in, 317–18, 319–20
industry strikes in, 196–97
magazines in, 187, 317
newspapers in: anti-Franco, 187, 189–90, 195; delays and omissions in, 197–98; foreign, 197; under Primo de Rivera, 99–100, 104–5; relaxation of censorship of, 276–78, 290–91; during Second Republic, 108–9, 116; "Uncle Sam" used in, 191; underground, 187, 189–90; during war in Morocco, 8; between world wars, 99–100, 104–5, 108–9, 116
nudity in, 317
Official Secrets Act, 290
pamphlets in, 187
penal code of, 280–81
pornography in, 317
press law in, 108–9, 198, 276–78, 279–81, 290–91
radio in, 196–97, 289–91
television in, 289–91, 318
theatre in, 317
Spellbinder (Robbins), 482
Spender, Stephen, 334, 336
Sports Illustrated (magazine), 319
Spycatcher (Wright), 340–42, 350
St. Paul Dispatch, 4
St. Paul News, 4
St. Paul Pioneer Press, 4
St. Paul Volkszeitung, 49, 56
stage. *See* theatre
Star (South Africa), 491–92
Start (Yugoslavia), 400
Steicher, Julius, 129, 131
Steinbeck, John, 324
Stopes, Marie C., 76–77
Store Up the Anger (Ebersohn), 478–80
Straits Times (Singapore), 509–10
Strauss, Richard, 12, 22
Stredeczky Ziondstick (Czechoslovakia), 63
Stuart Little (White), 321
student newspapers, in United States, 342–44, 345–48, 365, 370–71, 377
student protests: in China, 143, 524–26; in Greece, 289; in United States, 323
Sturges, Jock, 357–58
Styron, Rose, 440
Sudermann, Hermann, 9
Suharto, 513
Sukarno, Achmed, 257–58
Sullivan, Arthur, 22
Sullivan, L. B., 199
Sumner, John S., 84–85
Susann, Jacqueline, 318
Sweet Jew (film), 498–99
Switzerland, newspapers of, in Italy, 174
Sydney Film Festival, 285
Syria: criticism of government in, 248; newspapers in, 136–37, 247–48; press law in, 248
Szajna, Jozef, 394

Taft, William Howard, 19
Taiwan: films in, 531; gangs in, 517–18; magazines in, 515, 517–18; newspapers in, 254; prisoners in, 515–16; Taiwanization of, 515
Talese, Gay, 325
Taslimi, Susan, 463–64
Tasvir (Turkey), 247
Teen (magazine), 379–80
telegrams: in China, 139–40, 141–42, 143–44; in Colombia, 239; in Great Britain, 35–37; in Vietnam, 251–52; during World War I, 29–30, 35–37
telephone calls, by foreign correspondents, 121
television. *See under specific countries*
Tell (Nigeria), 501
Tempo (Indonesia), 541–42
Temps (Paris), 31, 32
Temptation (Havel), 409
Terkel, Studs, 325
textbooks: in Japan, 527, 543–44; in United States, 318

Thailand, newspapers in, 314–15
Thani, Hamad bin Khalifa al-, 475, 476
Thatcher government, 341, 342, 348–52
theatre: nudity in, 394; before World War I, 9–27. *See also under specific countries*
Thieu, Nguyen Van, 275–76
Thomas, Piri, 319, 320–21, 323
Thorn Birds (McCullough), 321
thought control, in Czechoslovakia, 213
thought surveillance, in Japan, 144–46
Thousand and One Nights, 453–54
Three Days on the Cross (Mutahi), 497–98
Tiananmen Square, student protests in, 526
Tian Zhuangzhuang, 531, 532
Tia Vicenta (Argentina), 296
Tiempo (Colombia), 238–39
Time (magazine), 319
Time to Be in Love (film), 463
Tinker v. Des Moines Independent Community School District, 344, 347
Tolstoy, Leo, 8
Tong, Hollington K., 143–44
Tote Löwe (*Dead Lion*), 12
Tournier, Michel, 336
Travers, P. L., 324
treason laws, in Germany, 278
Trial of the Catonsville Nine (Berrigan), 321
trial coverage, in Canadian press, 367–68
Trotsky, Leon, 134, 411
T-shirts, in China, 528–30
Tshombe, Moise, 304
Tudjman, Franjo, 423
Tuka, Voitetch, 110
Tunisia, Islamic movement in, 459–60
Tupamaros, 301
Turkey: books in, 548–49; cartoons in, 138; journalists in, imprisonment of, 544–45; Kurdish conflict in, 544, 548–49; newspapers in, 246–47, 250–51, 252, 258; political meetings in, 253; press laws in, 250–51, 253, 544–45
Tutu, Desmond M., 487
Twain, Mark, 335
2 Live Crew, 355–57

Ulysses (Joyce), 73, 340
Umberto I, King of Italy, 18
"Uncle Sam," in Spanish newspapers, 191
underground literary works, in Czechoslovakia, 387
underground news distribution: in Austria, 117; in Germany, 116–18, 126; in Soviet Union, 118
underground newspapers: in Belgium, 180; in Czechoslovakia, 294; in France, 178–79, 180; in Greece, 177; in Hungary, 217; in Norway, 180, 181; in Poland, 176–77, 179–80; in Spain, 187, 189–90; during World War II, 176–80
Unesco, 542–43
United Kingdom. *See* Great Britain; Ireland
United Nations, on suppression of *Prensa*, 191–92
United States
- art in: government funding for, 352–55, 358–59, 381–83; obscenity in, 358–59; sacrilegious, 381–83; self-censorship by museums, 352–55, 383–84
- books banned in: from bookstores, 321, 323; litigation on, 84–85; for obscenity, 76–77; PEN on, 324–25; from public libraries, 6; from public schools, 318–19, 320–24, 327–28; for sensationalism, 6
- Civil War in, 38, 59
- comics in, 3
- Congress of, 270–71
- Constitution of: First Amendment of, 198, 199, 244, 268–69, 327–28, 347, 375; Fourteenth Amendment of, 87–89
- films in: crime portrayed in, 40, 73, 77; foreign, 85–86; history of growth of, 71–72; illegal, police raids on, 24–25, 27; portrayal of law enforcement officials in, 78; legislation on, 26, 71–72, 74–76; National Board of Censorship of, 22–23, 25; National Board of Review of, 72; news reel, 83; New York Motion Picture Commission and, 77–80, 83–84, 85–86; opposition to censorship of, 26, 71–72, 74–75; Pennsylvania Board of Film Censors and, 82–83; reviews of, 33–34; sacrilegious, 383; in schools, 378–79; sexual content in, 267; on social diseases, 72–73; on television, 328–30; theatre regulations applied to, 85; before World War I, 22–23, 24–25, 26–27; during World War I, 33–34, 40; between world wars, 71–86
- flag of, 3
- freedom of press in: Inter-American Press Association on, 243–44, 245; International Press Institute on, 283; vs. Soviet Union/Eastern Europe, 202–6, 207–8
- Internet access in, 371–73, 375–77
- journalists of: imprisonment of, 1, 9, 49, 51–52, 54; in war zones, 337–38
- legislation in: Communications Decency Act, 371, 375–77; Comstock Laws, 335; Espionage Act, 42–45, 48–50; Federal Communications Act, 329; John Day Smith law, 4; Lusk-Clayton Moving Picture Censorship bill, 74–76; Sedition Act, 199; Telecommunications Act, 376
- magazines in: pornographic, 365; in schools, 379–80; during World War I, 37; during World War II, 154–56
- music in: obscenity in, 355–57, 363–64; rap, 355–57, 363–64; warning labels for, 364
- news organizations in, government prosecution of, 338–39
- newspapers in: confiscation of, 8; criticism of judiciary in, 1; details of hanging in, 4; effectiveness of censorship of, 58–61; government regulations for, 41–48, 154–56, 160, 161; impact on wars, 37–38; mail service denied to, 6–7, 48–49, 61–62; murder confession in, 9; pro-German, 49–54; student, 342–44, 345–48, 370–71, 377365; Supreme Court on, 87–89; before World War I, 1, 4, 6–7, 8, 9, 38; during World War I, 37–38, 41–62; during World War II, 154–56, 161
- Persian Gulf War coverage in, 359–63
- pornography in: on college campuses, 365; laws against, 339–40; spread of, 273–74
- radio in, 161
- schools in: books in, 318–19, 320–24, 327–28; films shown in, 378–79; magazines in, 379–80; newspapers of, 342–44, 345–48, 365, 370–71, 377; sex education in, 319
- socialist publications in, 48–49, 52–56, 57–58
- State Department of, 206
- Supreme Court of: on book banning, 320, 323–24, 327–28; on criticism of public officials, 198–200; on First Amendment, 198, 199, 268–69, 327–28, 347, 375; on Fourteenth Amendment, 87–89; on Internet regulation, 375–77; on Minnesota press gag law, 87–89; on obscenity, 339, 340; on prior restraint, 268–69, 373; on publication of Pentagon Papers, 268–69, 373; on sacrilegious films, 383; on student newspapers, 342–44, 346–47, 377; on student protests, 323
- television in, 328–31
- theatre in: difficulty of censorship of, 19–21; indecency in, 10, 20; Joint Committee Opposed to Political Censorship and, 80–82; plays banned from, 22; police regulation of, 10, 14–16; on Sundays, 14–16; voluntary jury system for, 80–81, 84
- vaudeville in, 14–16
- World War I censorship in: of anti-American publications, 49–54, 57–58; effectiveness of, 58–61; of newspapers, 37–38, 41–62
- World War II censorship in: approach to, 153–54, 160, 169–70; code of, 154–56, 160, 161; effectiveness of, 156, 169–70; of military news, 157–59, 162–63, 164; of newspapers, 154–56, 161; Office of Censorship and, 160, 161, 169; Office of War Information and, 162; officer-reporter vs. civilian-reporter and, 158–59; of presidential news, 153–54, 165; purpose of, 166–68; voluntary, 156–57, 158, 160, 169

United States Information Service Library, in Spain, 192–93
Universal Soldier: The Return (film), 380
Uriburu, José Félix, 90

Uruguay: Argentina and, 301; newspapers in, 296, 301–2; radio in, 296
Usenet discussion groups, 372
Uys, Pieter-Dirk, 499

Vaculik, Ludvik, 396
Valley Forge (Kantor), 321
Valmy (France), 178–79
"Van Gogh's Ear" exhibition, 383–84
Vanguardia (Argentina), 90
Vanunu, Mordechai, 476–78
Vargas, Getulio, 93–94
vaudeville, in United States, 14–16
Veja (Brazil), 298–99, 302
Velasco Alvarado, Juan, 303–4
Velasco Ibarra, José Maria, 235–36
Velasquez, Osvaldo, 436
Venezuela, foreign news in, 86–87
Viedomosti (Moscow), 4
Vie Ouvrière (France), 178
Vietnam: Chinese-language newspapers in, 255; films in, 541; foreign correspondents in, 251–52; foreign culture in, 540–41; French censorship in, 251–52; Internet access in, 538–39; telegrams in, 251–52. *See also* South Vietnam
Vietnam Guardian, 264
Vietnam War era, 263–315
Vlachos, Helen, 282, 286
Voice of America, 402, 407–8
Voinovich, Vladimir, 403, 411
Vonnegut, Kurt, Jr., 319, 320–21, 322, 324
Vorwarts (Berlin), 2, 63–64, 66–67
Voznesensky, Andrei, 403, 419
V Posten (Norway), 181

Washington Post, Pentagon Papers in, 268–71
Waste (Barker), 21
Watergate scandal, 373
Way (China), 548
weather reports, during World War II, 155
web sites. *See* Internet
Week (Great Britain), 152–53
Weekly Mail (South Africa), 491–94, 498–99
Weinberger, Caspar W., 337–38
Well of Loneliness (Hall), 138
Western Europe. *See specific countries*
Western Union, 29
White, E. B., 321
Wilde, Oscar, 12–13, 22
Wilhelmina, Queen of Netherlands, 17–18
William II (of Germany), 17
Willy, Collette, 11
wire. *See* telegrams
Wizard of Oz (Baum), 324, 325
Wojtyla, Karol, 388, 392
Wolfe, Tom, 321
Working (Terkel), 325
World War I: Allied nations in, 29–62; Central powers in, 63–69
World War II: Allied nations in, 147–70; Axis powers in, 170–85
Wright, Peter, 340–42, 350
Wright, Richard, 319
Wu Ching, 137–38

Yellow Time, 454
Yeltsin, Boris N., 422
Yerofeyev, Viktor, 391–92, 419
YM (magazine), 379–80
Yugoslavia: elections in, 201–2; foreign correspondents in, 108, 110, 201–2; newspapers in, 128, 204, 399–400; press law in, 204

Z (film), 300
Zayim, Husni, 247–48
Zedillo, Ernesto, 441–42
Zeitzer Volksboten (Germany), 64
Zemstvo Congress, 4
Zia, Khaleda, 534
Zia ul-Haq, Mohammed, 514–15
Zimbabwe: foreign correspondents in, 483–84; newspapers in, 480–81
Zsombolyai, Janos, 415, 417
Zulu (film), 310
Zycie Warszawy (Warsaw), 395

BYLINE INDEX

Abend, Hallett, 139–40, 143–44
Andelman, David A., 385–88
Apple, R. W., Jr., 263–64, 373–74
Archambault, G. H., 180–81
Arnold, Martin, 505–6
Atlas, James, 348–52
Austin, Anthony, 389–92

Barstow, David, 381–83
Battersby, John D., 489–90, 493–94
Bernstein, Richard, 332–37
Binder, David, 399–400
Birchall, Frederick T., 111–12
Bishop, Katherine, 357–58
Bohlen, Celestine, 412–13, 414–17
Borders, William, 506–8
Braestrup, Peter, 264–65
Brewer, Sam Pope, 189–90, 201–2, 234–35, 237–39, 253
Brinkley, Joel, 455–57, 458–59
Brooke, James, 490–91
Browne, Malcolm W., 299–302, 384–85
Burks, Edward C., 243–44
Burns, John F., 398–99, 474–76, 491–92, 533–35
Byas, Hugh, 144–46

Callahan, John P., 251
Campbell, Colin, 320–24, 509–10
Carmody, Deirdre, 445–46
Caruthers, Osgood, 231–32
Chavez, Lydia, 431–32
Chira, Susan, 523–24
Christian, Shirley, 438–40
Cianfarra, Camille M., 192–93
Clines, Francis X., 340–42, 345, 413–14
Cohen, Roger, 419–20
Cortesi, Arnaldo, 123–24, 181–82, 183–85
Cowell, Alan, 481–82, 485–86
Crane, Burton, 188–89, 190
Crossette, Barbara, 521–23, 542–43
Crouch, Henry C., 138–39

Daniel, Clifton, 249–50
Daniell, Raymond, 148–49, 246–47
Darnton, John, 331–32, 388–89
Darnton, Nina, 392–95
de Casseres, Benjamin, 82–83
DeParle, Jason, 359–63
Dillon, Sam, 441–42
Doty, Robert C., 195–96
Dugger, Celia W., 546–47
Duranty, Walter, 120–23, 134–35
Durdin, Tillman, 216

Eckholm, Erik, 547–48
Eder, Richard, 283–84
Enderis, Guido, 171–73
Engelberg, Stephen, 338–39
Ethridge, Mark, 202–6
Eyre, Lincoln, 98–99

Farnsworth, Clyde H., 367–68, 369–70
Farrell, William E., 449–50
Fellows, Lawrence, 306–7
Fernsworth, Lawrence, 116
Feron, James, 308, 325–27
French, Howard W., 500–502

Gargan, Edward A., 520–21, 537–38, 541–42
Garrison, Lloyd, 260–61, 307–8
Gedye, G. E. R., 105–6, 107–8, 109–11, 112–13, 128, 170–71
Gibbs, Walter, 380–81
Giniger, Henry, 193, 194, 289–91, 317–18
Glaberson, William, 370–71
Glueck, Grace, 352–55
Graham, Fred P., 268–69
Greenberg, Joel, 466–67
Greene, Francis Vinton, 58–61
Greenhouse, Linda, 327–28, 375–77
Gruson, Sydney, 222–23, 225, 235–36

Hamilton, Thomas J., 271–72, 278–79
Hazarika, Sanjoy, 516–17, 527–28
Hechinger, Fred M., 344
Hedges, Chris, 423, 459–60, 465–66
Hess, Gabriel L., 71–72
Hofmann, Paul, 197–98
Howe, Marvine, 284–85, 287–88, 302, 303–4, 424–26
Hunter, Marjorie, 270–71

Ibrahim, Youssef M., 460–62, 464–65, 468

James, Edwin L., 157–58, 162–63, 165–66, 173–74, 207–8
Jehl, Douglas, 468–70, 474
Johnson, Dirk, 345–48
Johnston, Richard J. H., 246
Jones, Alex S., 337–38, 402
Jorden, William J., 224–25

Kadich, R. E., 141
Kakutani, Michiko, 324–25
Kalb, Bernard, 254–55, 257–59

Kamm, Henry, 311, 395–96, 417–18, 508–9
Kaufman, Michael T., 483–84
Keller, Bill, 403–5, 405–7, 410–11, 498–99
Kennedy, Paul P., 187, 245
Kifner, John, 401–2
King, Seth S., 273–74
King, Wayne, 318–19
Kinzer, Stephen, 368–69, 429–31, 432–38, 544–45, 548–49
Kluckhohn, Frank L., 164
Kristof, Nicholas D., 525–27, 528–30, 543–44
Krock, Arthur, 153–54, 158–59

Larimer, Tim, 540–41
Lawrence, W. H., 160, 206–7
Lelyveld, Joseph, 305–6, 478–81, 483
LeMoyne, James, 355–57
Lewis, Anthony, 198–200, 282–83, 471–72
Lewis, Peter H., 371–73
Lieberman, Henry R., 214–15, 251–52
Lohr, Steve, 515–16, 517–18
Long, Tania, 177–80
Lorch, Donatella, 499–500
Lubasch, Arnold H., 267
Lubell, Samuel, 116–18
Lukas, J. Anthony, 304–5

MacFarquhar, Neil, 471
MacGregor, Greg, 223–24, 226, 254, 255
Maidenberg, H. J., 296–97
Markham, James M., 275, 314–15, 319–20, 503
May, Clifford D., 484–85
McDowell, Edwin, 339–40
McQuiston, John T., 379–80
Meredith, Robyn, 383–84
Miller, Judith, 450–52, 453–54, 462–64, 472–74
Mitgang, Herbert, 365–67
Montgomery, Paul, 298
Morrow, Edward A., 235, 240
Mydans, Seth, 519–20
Myers, Steven Lee, 363–64

Nevard, Jacques, 261–62
Novitski, Joseph, 298–99

Olsen, Arthur J., 229–30
Onis, Juan de, 241–42, 244–45

Pace, Eric, 309, 504
Parrott, Lindesay, 188
Perlez, Jane, 421, 423–24, 494–96, 497–98
Philip, P. J., 150
Phillips, R. Hart, 242–43
Pierre-Pierre, Garry, 440
Price, Byron, 166–68

Rabin, Roni C., 454–55
Ragner, Bernhard, 150–51
Raymont, Henry, 296
Reston, James B., 176–77
Riding, Alan, 428–29
Roberts, Steven V., 292
Robinson, Douglas, 265
Ross, Albion, 212, 213–14, 247–49
Rothstein, Edward, 396–98

Salisbury, Harrison E., 209–12, 218–22
Schemo, Diana Jean, 442–43
Schmemann, Serge, 407–8, 418–19
Schmidt, Dana Adams, 216–17, 293–94
Schorr, Daniel, 226–29
Schumacher, Edward, 427
Schwartz, Harry, 217–18
Shenon, Philip, 535–37, 538–39
Shipler, David K., 275–76, 448–49, 452
Shuster, Alvin, 285–86, 288–89
Sims, Calvin, 441, 443–44
Sink, Mindy, 378–79
Smith, Hedrick, 260
Smith, Sally Bedell, 328–31
Smith, Terence, 309–10, 313–14
Sontag, Deborah, 476–78
Stanley, Alessandra, 422–23
Stevens, William K., 510–13, 514–15
Sulzberger, C. L., 200–201
Szulc, Tad, 240–41, 276–81, 294–95

Tagliabue, John, 405, 408–9, 411–12
Tanner, Henry, 311–12
Taubman, Philip, 402–3
Taylor, Stuart, Jr., 342–44
Tolchin, Martin, 358–59
Tolischus, Otto D., 124–28, 129–33
Treaster, Joseph B., 266–67
Trumbull, Robert, 513–14
Tyler, Patrick E., 530–32

Underwood, Paul, 233

Vidal, David, 426–27

Weisman, Steven R., 519, 527
Welles, Benjamin, 195, 196–97
Whitney, Craig R., 374–75
Wood, Lewis, 169–70
Wren, Christopher S., 446–48, 496–97
WuDunn, Sheryl, 524–25

Ybarra, T. R., 100–103